THE SCHOTTENSTEIN EDITION

ספר

THE BOOK OF
MITZVOS

החינוך

THE JAN CZUKER FAMILY ELUCIDATION
OF THE TORAH'S COMMANDMENTS

The ArtScroll® Series

Rabbi Nosson Scherman / Rabbi Meir Zlotowitz
General Editors

ספר החינוך the BOOK OF MITZVOS

A PROJECT OF THE

Mesorah Heritage Foundation

MITZVOS

THE JAN CZUKER FAMILY ELUCIDATION
OF THE TORAH'S COMMANDMENTS

VOLUME IX
MITZVOS 491-551

The ArtScroll® Series

Published by

ArtScroll
Mesorah Publications, ltd

THE SCHOTTENSTEIN EDITION

ספר החינוך

The book of

TRANSLATED AND ANNOTATED,

WITH HALACHIC AND AGGADIC INSIGHTS

by a team of Torah Scholars
under the General Editorship of
Rabbi Eliezer Herzka
Rabbi Yosaif Asher Weiss

Originated by
Rabbi Shmuel Kirzner

Reviewed and commented on by
Rabbi Eliyahu Meir Klugman
Rabbi Nosson Klugman
Rabbi Chaim Zev Malinowitz

Newly vowelized Hebrew,
based on the
Machon Yerushalayim text

Project Coordinator
Rabbi Mordechai Sonnenschein

Designed by
Rabbi Sheah Brander

FIRST EDITION
First Impression ... December 2015

Published and Distributed by
MESORAH PUBLICATIONS, Ltd.
4401 Second Avenue
Brooklyn, New York 11232

Distributed in Europe by
LEHMANNS
Unit E, Viking Business Park
Rolling Mill Road
Jarrow, Tyne & Wear NE32 3DP
England

Distributed in Australia & New Zealand by
GOLDS WORLD OF JUDAICA
3-13 William Street
Balaclava, Melbourne 3183
Victoria Australia

Distributed in Israel by
SIFRIATI / A. GITLER — BOOKS
6 Hayarkon Street
Bnei Brak 51127, Israel

Distributed in South Africa by
KOLLEL BOOKSHOP
Northfield Centre, 17 Northfield Avenue
Glenhazel 2192, Johannesburg, South Africa

ARTSCROLL® SERIES / THE SCHOTTENSTEIN EDITION
SEFER HACHINUCH / BOOK OF MITZVOS
VOL. 9 — MITZVOS 491-551

© *Copyright 2015 by* MESORAH PUBLICATIONS, Ltd.
4401 Second Avenue / Brooklyn, N.Y. 11232 / (718) 921-9000 / FAX (718) 680-1875 / www.artscroll.com

ISBN 10: 1-4226-1681-9
ISBN 13: 978-1-4226-1681-9

Typography by CompuScribe at ArtScroll Studios, Ltd.
4401 Second Avenue / Brooklyn, N.Y. 11232 / (718) 921-9000

Printed in the United States of America by Noble Book Press
Bound by Sefercraft, Quality Bookbinders, Ltd. Brooklyn, N.Y.

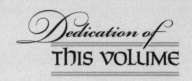

Dedication of
THIS VOLUME

This volume is dedicated to a
prince of Torah support and dissemination

Asher David Milstein

He devotes himself to spreading Torah and fostering kiruv,
and to supporting those who devote themselves to bring our
brethren close to Torah.

With incredible imagination, initiative, and generosity, he supplies
a vast array of Torah works to institutions throughout the world.
A Hebrew-English Siddur to not-yet religious students, volumes
of Tanach to people thirsting for Jewish eternity, volumes of
Yerushalmi to Torah scholars seeking entrée to a classic of Jewish
eternity – thousands of such volumes are now in countless Torah
and kiruv institutions in many countries, thanks to Asher's vision
and determination to make Torah available to Jews wherever they are.

He has dedicated ArtScroll's **Milstein Edition of the Later Prophets,**
the **Milstein Edition of Seder Nashim** in the **Schottenstein Edition
of Talmud Yerushalmi,** and the **Milstein Edition Five Megillos**
in the **Kleinman Edition of Midrash Rabbah.**

How fitting that this volume of Sefer HaChinuch/ Book of Mitzvos
is dedicated in honor of a man who is introducing so many multitudes
of our people to Torah and mitzvos.

Klal Yisrael owes Asher an enormous debt. In this merit, may Hashem
grant him many years and good health to enjoy the luxuriant fruits
of his accomplishment.

Dedication of

THE JAN CZUKER FAMILY ELUCIDATION OF THE TORAH'S COMMANDMENTS

The **Jan Czuker Family Elucidation of the Torah's Commandments** in the **Sefer HaChinuch / Book of Mitzvos** is dedicated in loving memory of our beloved father,

Jan Czuker ז"ל
ר' יוסף ב"ר מנחם מענדל ז"ל
נפ' פסח שני תש"ע

Our father survived the Holocaust, but his faith and spirit remained intact. His determination to rebuild not only his own life and family but also those of others made him a generous supporter of many Jewish institutions and individuals in the community. His good cheer and charisma drew others to him. He was a loyal friend, always ready to help. He was a blessing to all who crossed his path.

Torah education, chessed, and ahavas Yisrael were all precious to him. A devoted father and grandfather, in words and deeds he instilled Jewish values in his children and grandchildren.

And in honor of our beloved mother,

Mrs. Susanne Czuker שתחי'

She is the quintessential Eishes Chayil. Accomplished in her own right, her steady guidance and encouragement enabled our father to achieve all that he did. The love she has for her children and grandchildren lights up all of our lives. May Hashem bless her with many years of good health and the nachas of seeing that her offspring live up to her hopes and example.

Together, our parents laid the foundation for us to carry on their Torah values and ideals, and fulfill their dreams.

Edward Mendel and Elissa Czuker and Family

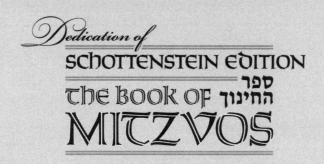

Dedication of

SCHOTTENSTEIN EDITION
THE BOOK OF MITZVOS ספר החינוך

Sefer HaChinuch / Book of Mitzvos
symbolizes the chain of learning and service
that unites generations and embraces the entire world.
It is fitting, therefore, that we dedicate it
to our children and grandchildren,

Joseph Aaron and Lindsay Brooke
Jacob Meir, Jonah Philip, and Emma Blake
Jonathan Richard, and Jeffrey Adam

We are proud that our children are forging new links in the chain that we inherited from our parents and grandparents.

We pray that they will continue to grow in their concern for others, loyalty to community, support of Torah education, and allegiance to our eternal tradition.

The Book of Mitzvos was written for the author's own son, so that he would use it as his guide in life, and we dedicate it to our family in the same spirit.

May this classic work be a beacon to them and all those who share our conviction that Torah and its commandments are the cornerstone of our existence.

Jay and Jeanie Schottenstein

With generosity, vision, and devotion to the perpetuation of Torah study, the following patrons have dedicated individual volumes of The Sefer HaChinuch

VOL. 1 **Yaakov and Chaya Willinger**
Racheli and Shmuel Yitzchak Alpert Malka Tamar Adina
dedicated to the memory of our dear parents
ישראל איסר בן מאיר ז״ל — Emerich Willinger ז״ל
נפטר כ״ו כסלו תשע״ג
דבורה יהודית בת משה יששכר ע״ה — Dorothy Willinger ע״ה
נפטרה ט׳ ניסן תשס״ח
And יבלח״ט it is dedicated in tribute to our beloved parents שיחיו
Mrs and Mrs. Binyomin and Toba (Jacobs) Jakubovic עמו״ש

VOL. 2 **David and Joan Tepper and family**
dedicated in memory of our parents
ר׳ מנחם מענדל ב״ר יעקב ז״ל — Milton Tepper ז״ל
מינדל בת ר׳ אריה ליב ע״ה — Minnie Tepper ע״ה
ר׳ ראובן ב״ר נחמיה ז״ל — Rubin Gralla ז״ל
עטיל בת ר׳ ישראל נתן נטע ע״ה — Etta Gralla ע״ה

VOL. 3 **Dedicated Anonymously**

VOL. 4 **Adam and Suri Sokol**
Dedicated in honor of our parents
Mendy and Susan Sokol Rabbi Mordechai and Edna Besser
our grandmothers Bernice Scharaga, Tzila Besser, and Zena Sales Neuhaus
and our sons Ari, Yehuda, Akiva, and Aaron

In loving memory of our grandparents and great grandparents
צבי אריה בן ר׳ יעקב מנחם ז״ל רחל בת יצחק ע״ה — Harry and Dolly Sokol ע״ה
צבי בן יצחק מאיר הכהן ז״ל — Harry Scharaga ז״ל
עקיבא בן נפתלי ז״ל — Akiva Besser ז״ל
יהודה בן אליעזר ליבר ז״ל — Leon Sales ז״ל

VOL. 5 **Dedicated Anonymously**

VOL. 6 **Mark and Barbara Silber and family**
Dedicated in honor of our mother
Rochela Scheiner תחי׳
and להבחל״ח in memory of our parents
שלמה בן אלטר יחיאל הלוי ז״ל — Shlomo Scheiner ז״ל
אברהם בן יהודה ז״ל — Abraham Silber ז״ל
שרה בת מנחם מנדל ע״ה — Sara Silber ע״ה

VOL. 7 **Rudolph Lowy and family**
Dedicated in loving memory of our wife, mother, and grandmother
אסתר רויזא בת ר׳ יצחק דוב ע״ה — Esther Rose Lowy ע״ה

VOL. 8 **Dedicated in memory of the victims of terror ע״ה,**
and in honor of their families שיחיו

VOL. 9 Dedicated to
Asher David Milstein

VOL. 10 **Avrum and D'vorah Weinfeld** (Chicago)
Flora Efriam Mordechai Ariella Faige Ita Shoshana Hinda
in memory of
הרב שלמה ברוך ב״ר אברהם קדיש ז״ל — Rabbi Shlomie Pomerantz ז״ל
נפטר י׳ שבט תשע״ב

Mitzvah Associates

A fellowship of benefactors dedicated to
the dissemination of Sefer HaChinuch

❖

Yitzchok Menachem and Gittel Raizel Haas

In Memoriam — לזכר נשמת

Dedicated by the Mitzvah Associates
to those who forged eternal links

❖

אלימלך בן יוסף ז"ל   גיטל בת אשר אנשל ע"ה
שמעון בן משה שמואל ז"ל   משה בן יעקב ז"ל

Pillars of the Book of Mitzvos

We wish to acknowledge in this volume the friendship of the following:

Robert Kent Jones

Efrem Litwin

Michael Steinberg

The Written Word is Forever

Publisher's Preface

Sefer HaChinuch has been a staple of Torah scholarship and the subject of many commentaries over the centuries.

We are proud to present this ninth volume in an unprecedented multi-volume English elucidation of a 700-year-old classic. Sefer HaChinuch has been a staple of Torah scholarship and the subject of many commentaries over the centuries. It is our privilege, therefore, to make it available to the public with all the clarity and accuracy that two generations of readers have come to expect from the exceptional team of scholars who have done so much to bring Torah to our people, through the agency of ArtScroll/Mesorah.

The Schottenstein name will go down in history as the family that brought intensive Torah study to tens of thousands of people.

We are gratified that JAY AND JEANIE SCHOTTENSTEIN and their children, JOSEPH AND LINDSAY, JONATHAN, and JEFFREY, have chosen to dedicate this historic project, and to add it to their long list of momentous contributions to Klal Yisrael. The Schottenstein name will go down in history as the family that brought intensive Torah study to tens of thousands of people in ways never before imagined.

To evaluate what the Schottenstein family has accomplished, one need only go back one generation. There was no SCHOTTENSTEIN EDITION OF THE BABYLONIAN TALMUD in English or Hebrew; no SCHOTTENSTEIN INTERLINEAR SERIES OF THE SIDDUR, MACHZOR, LITURGY, OR CHUMASH; no PEREK SHIRAH; no SCHOTTENSTEIN EDITION OF TALMUD YERUSHALMI IN ENGLISH OR HEBREW; no SCHOTTENSTEIN EDITION OF SEFER HACHINUCH/BOOK OF MITZVOS; and no SCHOTTENSTEIN EDITION OF MISHNAH ELUCIDATED. How much poorer our world would have been without them!

How much poorer our world would have been without them!

Now, their children have joined in their multiple endeavors.

It began with the foresight and generosity of the unforgettable JEROME SCHOTTENSTEIN ע״ה and has been carried on and brought to new heights by Jay and Jeanie. Now, their children have joined in their multiple endeavors, so that one of Jewry's proudest family traditions is being carried into the future by two generations. Our people is fortunate indeed, that, thanks to this family, there is a renaissance of Torah study throughout the world.

Edward Mendel and Elissa Czuker will be rewarded by the increased study and understanding of countless people.

The Elucidation of the Torah's Commandments portion of the Chinuch has been dedicated by EDWARD MENDEL AND ELISSA CZUKER of Los Angeles in momory of their beloved father Mr. Jan Czuker ז״ל. Modest people who resist honors, their generosity will be rewarded in the most meaningful way: the increased study and understanding of countless people who will benefit from their vision.

Written in the thirteenth century, Sefer HaChinuch is a compendium of the 613 commandments. It lists them, explains them, suggests

underlying purposes, or "roots," of each commandment, and provides a brief summary of the major laws. This ArtScroll treatment elucidates every phrase of the Chinuch, in the same manner that has been so universally accepted and admired in the SCHOTTENSTEIN EDITIONS OF THE TALMUD BAVLI AND YERUSHALMI, the KLEINMAN EDITION OF THE MIDRASH, and the SAPIRSTEIN EDITION OF RASHI. In addition, this treatment includes scores of beautifully presented "Insights," which present scholarly, ethical, and homiletical lessons based on the text. The sum total is truly a masterpiece that will appeal to scholar and layman alike, as they broaden the message of the text. We are confident that the Jewish public will derive great benefit from this project and that it will be a much appreciated and widely used addition to the growing ArtScroll library of Torah classics.

This ArtScroll treatment elucidates every phrase of the Chinuch, and it includes scores of beautifully presented "Insights."

Sefer HaChinuch is a remarkable work, not only for its content, but for the humility of its author. He wrote it anonymously and to this day his exact identity is unknown, although scholars have narrowed it down over the years. The author writes in his introductory letter that the reader should not be deceived into thinking that the work was written by a great scholar with encyclopedic knowledge. To the contrary, he insists he merely assembled the teachings of his great predecessors, and did so only so that his son and other youngsters could make constructive use their free time on the Sabbath. True, the Talmud teaches that although the Torah forbids falsehood, a scholar has a right to avoid praise by denying that he possesses knowledge. Nevertheless, although the author successfully concealed his identity, he fails to convince any reader that he is not a Torah authority of the highest order. His manuscript and the verdict of history prove otherwise.

Although the author of Sefer HaChinuch successfully concealed his identity, he fails to convince any reader that he is not a Torah authority of the highest order.

The concept of this elucidation was introduced to us by RABBI SHMUEL KIRZNER, at the suggestion of his father, RABBI YISROEL MEIR KIRZNER, a distinguished *talmid chacham* and Rav. R' Shmuel composed the sample draft that became the basis of the final format. He brings credit to his distinguished lineage, and, as a member of the editorial staff of this project, adds luster to the exemplary team of scholars who create the manuscript.

We are grateful to all those who have a part in bringing this project to fruition; they are named below in the Acknowledgments.

There are no adequate words to express our gratitude to Hashem for the enormous privilege of making His Torah accessible to His people for the last thirty-nine years. We pray that, with His help and the support of the friends of our work, we can continue to serve Him and Klal Yisrael for many more years.

There are no adequate words to express our gratitude to Hashem for the enormous privilege of making His Torah accessible to His people for the last thirty-nine years.

ACKNOWLEDGMENTS

We are deeply grateful to those who have been instrumental in creating this volume of the SCHOTTENSTEIN EDITION of the SEFER HACHINUCH/BOOK OF MITZVOS.

HAGAON HARAV DAVID FEINSTEIN שליט״א, the Rosh Yeshivah of Mesivtha Tifereth Jerusalem and one of the world's leading *poskim*, and a Founding Trustee of the Foundation, has been a guide and counselor from the inception of Mesorah Publications thirty-nine years ago. He recognized the importance of this project and provided invaluable guidance and counsel.

The General Editors of this project are RABBI ELIEZER HERZKA, Rav of Khal Me'or Chaim, Lakewood, N.J., who also serves as one of the Editorial Directors of the SCHOTTENSTEIN EDITION OF TALMUD YERUSHALMI; and RABBI YOSAIF ASHER WEISS, Rosh Yeshivas Ohr Hadaas, Staten Island, N.Y., who also served as the General Editor of the KLEINMAN EDITION DAILY DOSE OF TORAH – LIMUD YOMI series. Both have been instrumental in editing many ArtScroll projects, including the SCHOTTENSTEIN EDITION OF TALMUD BAVLI, the KLEINMAN EDITION OF KITZUR SHULCHAN ARUCH, and the JAFFA EDITION OF MESILLAS YESHARIM.

RABBI SHMUEL KIRZNER introduced the format of this project, and authored and edited much of this volume. The project is a credit to his vision.

RABBI MORDECHAI SONNENSCHEIN, a primary editor of the KLEINMAN EDITION OF KITZUR SHULCHAN ARUCH and JAFFA EDITION OF MESILLAS YESHARIM, undertook the difficult task of coordinating the various elements of this project and simultaneously serving as an author and editor, with his hallmark intelligence, competence, and unassuming manner.

RABBI DOVID ARYEH KAUFMAN, a primary editor of the SCHOTTENSTEIN EDITIONS OF TALMUD BAVLI and YERUSHALMI, as well as the KLEINMAN EDITION OF KITZUR SHULCHAN ARUCH, served with distinction as a primary editor of this volume. RABBI AVRAHAM Y. MORGENSTERN, a primary editor of the JAFFA EDITION OF MESILLAS YESHARIM, contributed superlatively as a primary editor of this volume. RABBI URIEL HINBERG, a primary author of the JAFFA EDITION OF MESILLAS YESHARIM, distinguished himself as an author and editor of this volume.

We are grateful to RABBI GIDON MOSKOVITZ, Rav of Meyerland Minyan, Houston, Texas, for his exceptional contribution as an author of this volume; and to RABBIS DORON BECKERMAN, DOVID HOLLANDER, NOAM LEVI, and GERSHON MEISELS, outstanding Torah scholars who authored much of the manuscript.

We are fortunate to have had the assistance of three distinguished Torah scholars to review this volume: RABBI ELIYAHU MEIR KLUGMAN is a Rosh Yeshivah of Yeshiva Neveh Zion and Rav of Beis Midrash L'Torah u'Tefillah,

Ramat Eshkol, Jerusalem. RABBI NOSSON KLUGMAN is a noted *talmid chacham* with wide-ranging Torah knowledge and the gift of painstaking thoroughness. RABBI CHAIM MALINOWITZ is one of the primary editors of the SCHOTTENSTEIN EDITIONS OF TALMUD BAVLI and YERUSHALMI, and a Rav in Beit Shemesh. His mastery of Talmud and Halachah is astounding; his knowledge and constant availability enhances the quality of virtually all of our projects. They each reviewed and commented upon the manuscript, improving the final product immeasurably with their efforts.

We are very grateful to RABBI MOSHE BUXBAUM of Machon Yerushalayim for graciously permitting us to use their text of Sefer HaChinuch.

We thank RABBI MOSHE ROSENBLUM for reviewing and correcting the *nikud* of this volume.

MRS. AHUVA WEISS read the entire volume and provided skilled literary editing, as well as many insightful comments; MRS. CHUMIE LIPSCHITZ paginated the volume with her customary typographic expertise; MRS. MINDY STERN read the manuscript for accuracy with exceptional dedication and made many important suggestions; MRS. JUDI DICK contributed significantly with many valuable editorial comments; MRS. ESTIE DICKER, MRS. ESTHER FEIERSTEIN, MRS. TOBY GOLDZWEIG, and MRS. RACHEL GROSSMAN provided typographic and editorial assistance.

Our dear friend and colleague RABBI SHEAH BRANDER has set the standard for graphics beauty for over thirty years. The clarity of the page design for this work is further testimony to his expertise and vision. ELI KROEN designed the sculpted embossed cover with his customary imagination and good taste.

RABBI GEDALIAH ZLOTOWITZ, a key member of the Artscroll administration, encouraged this project from the start.

The stellar staff members mentioned above, as well as the publishers, are grateful to the people who coordinate the production of, and facilitate the communication between, staff members on two continents. SHMUEL BLITZ, director of our Jerusalem office, is an indispensable colleague who, as per the popular saying, uncomplicates problems; RABBI AVROHOM BIDERMAN and MENDY HERZBERG oversee the often complex task of keeping the workflow smooth and efficient.

We are profoundly grateful to all the staff members who enable Artscroll/Mesorah to carry out its mission of maintaining the highest possible standard of quality in bringing Torah classics to the English-speaking public with clarity and accuracy.

We express our special appreciation to the Trustees and Governors of the MESORAH HERITAGE FOUNDATION. They are all accomplished, busy men who contribute time and expertise to the cause of Torah literacy.

Finally, we thank Hashem Yisbarach for the indescribable privilege of bringing His word to His people. May He bless all those who take part in this work with good health, and the ability to continue to serve Him.

Rabbi Nosson Scherman / Rabbi Meir Zlotowitz

Teves, 5776 / December, 2015

Table of Contents

Sefer HaChinuch / The Book of Mitzvos General Introduction

Rambam opens his Introduction to *Mishneh Torah,* his classic halachic Code that encompasses the requirements of all the Torah's commandments, by citing the verse (*Psalms* 119:6): אָז לֹא אֵבוֹשׁ בְּהַבִּיטִי אֶל כָּל מִצְוֹתֶיךָ, *Then, I will not be ashamed, when I gaze at all Your commandments.* The implication is clear: It is important for a Jew to be knowledgeable in *all* the commandments that Hashem has given us, not only those that apply to him in his daily life, but even those that he might never have the opportunity to fulfill. Why is this knowledge crucial? One reason is that studying Torah is a mitzvah unto itself (Mitzvah 419), and that mitzvah obligates us to learn and master the Torah in its entirety, both the Written Torah and the Oral Torah, as every detail in each of its commandments is the Word of God (*Smag,* Introduction). But there is another reason.

I. Studying the 613 Mitzvos

The Sages of the Talmud teach that God dictated 613 commandments to Moses at Sinai, of which 365 are Prohibitions, corresponding to the days of the solar year, and 248 are Obligations, corresponding to the number of parts in the human body (*Makkos* 23b). The commentators explain that each mitzvah is related to a different day of the year or to another one of a person's limbs. When a mitzvah is observed, the corresponding day or limb is spiritually elevated, such that observance of all the 613 mitzvos sanctifies man's entire corporeal existence and every moment of his time (see the Overview for elaboration of this theme).

A review of the 613 mitzvos, however, reveals that no single Jew can possibly fulfill all of them. Some pertain only to Kohanim and others only to non-Kohanim; some specifically to a king and others specifically to commoners. How, then, does any one individual attain the full range of sanctity inherent in the performance of *all* the mitzvos?

Early commentators explain that there are two methods. One way is to encourage and assist others in the performance of the obligations that apply to them, and likewise, to help others overcome any temptation to transgress the prohibitions that apply to them. In this manner, one becomes a partner in the observance of those mitzvos and shares in the credit for their fulfillment. Since each Jew is responsible for his brethren's observance of the Torah (*Sotah* 37b), by facilitating the observance of the mitzvos that he himself cannot physically observe, he becomes, in a very real sense, a participant in the fulfillment of all 613 mitzvos.

This approach, however, does not fully solve the problem. A large number of the 613 mitzvos are applicable only when the *Beis HaMikdash* – the Holy Temple – is standing, but not nowadays. How is one to attain the benefit of comprehensive observance of the Torah's commandments in our times? For this, the second method is necessary: If one studies the Torah and delves into its teachings, and is thereby inspired to accept upon himself to fulfill every mitzvah that he possibly can, then even if he is prevented from performing some of them by circumstances beyond his control, he is considered as though he has actually fulfilled them. As our Sages teach (*Menachos* 109a), based on Scripture, *Anyone who delves into the laws of a chatas* (sin) *offering is considered as though he has brought a chatas offering.* The Talmud goes on to say that the same holds true for the other offerings. Thus, in any situation where one is unable to perform a specific mitzvah, the in-depth study of its laws is comparable to actual performance of that mitzvah. In this manner, one is able to infuse *all* 248 parts of his body and 365 days of the year with the sanctity inherent in the full body of 613 mitzvos contained in the Torah (*Kiryas Sefer,* Introduction, Ch. 7; see also *Smak,* Introduction).

II. Is the Number 613 Exclusive?

The Vilna Gaon addresses a fundamental question: According to the Sages' teaching that the Torah contains 613 mitzvos, it emerges that many of its passages do not contain any mitzvos. Indeed, the entire Book of *Genesis* contains only three of the 613 mitzvos. Can it be that the remaining passages are merely a collection of historical facts? [Why, the very name "Torah" means *"to teach,"* for תּוֹרָה is from the same root as הוֹרָאָה, *teaching,* and מוֹרֶה, *teacher.*] How can it possibly contain passages that do not include lessons of life? Rather, says the Vilna Gaon, each and every verse in the Torah is a "mitzvah" in that it teaches some moral or halachic lesson, and it behooves us to observe every one of those teachings, for they are all the Word of God. When the Sages state that there are 613 Mitzvos, they mean that this is the number of *categories* into which the laws of the Torah are divided. In reality, each of these categories contains a myriad of details, and the observance of every single detail is a mitzvah unto itself (Vilna Gaon, cited at the beginning of *Sefer Maalos HaTorah*).[1]

To cite but one example, Chinuch counts as Mitzvah 58: The Obligation Upon *Beis Din* to Adjudge Cases of Civil Litigation. In his discussion of this mitzvah, Chinuch lists more than sixty laws, but actually, the guidelines of this mitzvah comprise nearly all of the *Choshen Mishpat* section of *Shulchan Aruch,* encompassing many thousands of individual rulings. Similarly, each of the other mitzvos has many laws, and we are commanded to observe all of them. Thus, the Vilna Gaon explains, an astute and learned person can, if he sets his mind to it, fulfill a mitzvah with his every action and every word, each moment of his life. No number can be assigned to these virtuous deeds and expressions, but they were given to us in distinct categories, and those are the 613 Mitzvos.

III. Early Works on the 613 Mitzvos

The early authorities of the post-Talmudic era invested considerable effort in identifying which Biblical passages and verses are reckoned as the 613 commandments and which laws are subsumed in those primary categories.[2] From the times of the Geonim, great authorities such

NOTES

1. Chinuch expresses a similar thought in his Author's Introduction (see note 114 there).

2. This question is not only a matter of accurate reckoning; the identification of a law as one of the 613 mitzvos

as *Halachos Gedolos, R' Saadiah Gaon,* and *R' Eliyahu HaZaken,* followed by *R' Shlomo ibn Gabirol,* composed lists of the 613 Mitzvos, sometimes in the form of liturgical poems known as *Azharos* (directives).[3]

Rambam was the first to publish an entire tome on the subject, which he titled *Sefer HaMitzvos* (Book of the Mitzvos), and which he prefaced with a discussion of fourteen *shorashim* (principles) by which he determines whether a law of the Torah is to be counted among the 613 Mitzvos or not. In this work, *Rambam* disputes the positions of many of the earlier authorities on this subject. In time, the *Sefer HaMitzvos* became accepted as the most authoritative enumeration of the mitzvos. Nearly a century later, *Ramban* wrote Glosses (*Hasagos*) to the *Sefer HaMitzvos,* in which he challenges both the *shorashim* of *Rambam* and his count of the mitzvos, and defends the position of earlier authorities such as *Halachos Gedolos.*[4]

Other Rishonim who authored works on the Mitzvos are the Tosafists, R' Eliezer of Metz (*Sefer Yerei'im*), R' Moshe of Coucy (*Sefer Mitzvos Gadol,* or *Smag*), and R' Yitzchak of Corbeil (*Sefer Mitzvos Katan,* or *Smak*).

IV. The Sefer HaChinuch

The Sefer HaChinuch was authored some time after *Ramban* published his glosses to *Sefer HaMitzvos,* and is actually based on *Rambam's Sefer HaMitzvos* together with *Ramban's* glosses. [See Section VII below regarding the authorship of Sefer HaChinuch.] At the beginning of his Order and Count of the Mitzvos (below), Chinuch states that he based this work on *Rambam's* reckoning of the 613 Mitzvos. This is not to say that Chinuch always agrees with *Rambam's* count. In his opening Missive to this work, Chinuch notes that he relied also on *Ramban's* glosses to *Sefer HaMitzvos,* which Chinuch does not refer to as "glosses" but as "a highly esteemed book." In cases where *Ramban* disagrees with *Rambam* regarding the listing of a particular mitzvah, Chinuch almost invariably cites *Ramban's* view as well in the course of explaining the mitzvah, often quoting *Ramban* at length. Moreover, there are several instances in which he states explicitly that he prefers *Ramban's* opinion over that of *Rambam* (see, for example, Mitzvos 138 and 153). Nevertheless, as he states in Mitzvah 138, in this work he did not veer from the reckoning of the mitzvos established by *Rambam,* because "he is truly our impetus for this labor, and it is through him that we merited engaging in it."

The Sefer HaChinuch has been, for many centuries since its publication, perhaps the most popular composition on the 613 Mitzvos. While not written primarily as a halachic work, Chinuch's opinion is often cited authoritatively by great halachic authorities who followed him.[5] Moreover, many prominent Acharonim wrote commentaries on Chinuch. Luminaries such as *Mishneh LaMelech* and *R' Yeshayah Pik* wrote Glosses, and in later times, a large number

---

NOTES

has practical ramifications as well. For discussion of these ramifications, see below, Mitzvah 7 with notes 17-19; Introduction to *R' Y. F. Perla's* Commentary to *Sefer HaMitzvos* of *R' Saadiah Gaon*; and Introduction to *Mitzvas HaMelech* Vols. I and III.

3. The *Azharos* are often cited by Rishonim (see *Rashi, Exodus* 24:12; *Tosafos, Yoma* 8a ד״ה דכולי and *Makkos* 3b ד״ה איכא), and numerous commentaries have been written on them. In many communities, it is customary

to study some of these *Azharos* on Shavuos or to recite them during the day's *Mussaf* service; some versions of them are therefore included in the *Machzor* for Shavuos.

4. This, in turn, induced a number of later scholars to compose responses in defense of *Rambam's* views. The most well-known of these, and other works on the 613 Mitzvos, are listed below, at the end of this General Introduction.

5. For example, see *Shach, Yoreh Deah* 25:2,70:33.

of full-length commentaries were authored.[6] Among the most famous works composed on Chinuch is the *Minchas Chinuch,* by R' Yosef Babad of Tarnipol (Lemberg 5629/1869), which is renowned for its thorough halachic analyses.

Chinuch's popularity derives primarily from two features unique among the early works on the mitzvos. The first is that whereas other Rishonim arranged the mitzvos topically, Chinuch arranges them according to the *Parashiyos* (weekly readings) of the Torah, and within each *Parashah,* in the order that the Torah records them.[7] As he states in his Introduction, this was done for the express purpose that the mitzvos be studied in conjunction with the *Parashah* of the week.

The second innovative feature is that, for each mitzvah, Chinuch offers a שׁוֹרֶשׁ, *underlying purpose* (literally, *root*). This is a moral lesson contained in the mitzvah, that may be internalized through observance of the mitzvah. Chinuch declares in his Introduction that these are mere "glimpses," and that he puts them forward only as his own suggestions. Moreover, he stresses that what he writes is in each case only one of *many* purposes of the mitzvah, for no mortal can claim to have fathomed the full purpose of any of God's commandments. In his discussion of Mitzvah 117, Chinuch adds that the underlying purposes he provided are very basic thoughts, intended to give the uneducated "youngsters" for whom he composed this work an appreciation of some of the benefits of mitzvah observance.[8] Nevertheless, the lessons that Chinuch teaches have become the basis of subsequent discussion of the mitzvos and their purposes. The scope, depth, and eloquence of this work belie the author's repeated protestations of inadequacy, and history has given Chinuch a position of prominence among the great works of the Rishonim.

V. The Format of Sefer HaChinuch

Chinuch's presentation of each mitzvah is generally divided into four or five parts.

1. *Description of the Mitzvah.* Chinuch begins each mitzvah by presenting its Scriptural source, as well as a brief description of what it entails.
2. *Underlying Purpose of the Mitzvah.* As explained above, this is a moral lesson we are supposed to glean from the mitzvah.
3. *Laws of the Mitzvah.* In this section, Chinuch gives the reader a general sense of the main laws of the mitzvah, both Biblical and Rabbinic, including a description of how the mitzvah is fulfilled.[9] Chinuch typically closes this section with a reference to where the mitzvah is discussed in the Talmud.

NOTES

6. The most prominent among these are listed below, at the end of this General Introduction.

7. The author arranged the Obligations and Prohibitions separately within each *Parashah,* first presenting all the Obligations and then all the Prohibitions. This arrangement was preserved in the earliest printed editions of Chinuch. In the 18th century, however, the format was changed, and since then the Chinuch has been printed with the Obligations and Prohibitions intermingled, in the order of their verses in the Torah. Our edition conforms to this format, which by now has become the standard one. For this reason, in instances where Chinuch refers to another mitzvah in his work, his own numbering differs from that of contemporary editions, including ours. In all such instances, we have preserved Chinuch's wording but have added the references appropriate for contemporary editions.

8. See Mitzvah 545, where Chinuch discusses at length the concept of providing logical "reasons" for God's commandments. See also note 119 to the Author's Introduction for further discussion regarding this matter.

9. It should be noted that when citing laws, Chinuch does not focus exclusively on the specific mitzvah he is discussing. Often, he includes laws that are only marginally related to that mitzvah, but actually fall under the province of other, related mitzvos. For example,

4. *Applicability of the Mitzvah.* In this section Chinuch sets forth: (a) at which times the mitzvah applies; (b) in which locations it applies; (c) to which people the mitzvah applies; and (d) what penalty (if any) its violation carries. In order to fully understand this typically terse section of the mitzvah, it is important to clarify some of the background regarding these four factors in the applicability of the mitzvah. This is provided in the following section of this Introduction.
5. *Dispute Regarding the Mitzvah.* In the instances where *Ramban* disagrees with *Rambam* as to whether something should be counted as one of the 613 Mitzvos, Chinuch addresses the dispute, sometimes analyzing each view at length.

VI. Applicability of the Mitzvos

Mitzvos vary widely in their applicability with respect to time, location, and people, and with respect to the penalties for transgression. The following are some, but not all, of the distinctions:

Time Many mitzvos can be performed at any time, but some apply only in the daytime and others only at night. There are mitzvos that are limited to special occasions, such as the Sabbath or Festivals. Additionally, some mitzvos apply constantly, while others become applicable only in specific circumstances (see Author's Introduction with notes 103-106).

Aside from the above, there are some mitzvos that apply only when the *Beis HaMikdash* is standing, and many that apply even nowadays when it is not. With regard to those mitzvos that are not limited to the Temple period, Chinuch writes simply: נוֹהֶגֶת בְּכָל זְמַן, *it applies in all times.*

Location Most mitzvos apply everywhere, but many are relevant only in Eretz Yisrael or only in the *Beis HaMikdash*. Among the mitzvos that are specific to Eretz Yisrael, some pertain only when the majority of the Jewish people reside there (see notes 99-100 to the Author's Introduction). When Chinuch describes the mitzvos that apply even outside Eretz Yisrael, he writes simply: נוֹהֶגֶת בְּכָל מָקוֹם, *it applies in every location.*

People As Chinuch explains in his Introduction, not all the mitzvos are equally applicable to all people.

(a) Kohanim, Leviim, and Yisraelim: Some mitzvos are incumbent only upon Kohanim, some only upon Leviim, and some only upon Yisraelim (see notes 94-102 ibid.).

(b) Men and Women: Men and women are equally subject to the requirement of observing the Torah's Prohibitions [מִצְוֹת לֹא תַעֲשֶׂה], except for a few that are relevant to only one of the genders.[10] With respect to the Obligations [מִצְוֹת עֲשֵׂה], however, there is a distinction. Men are required to fulfill all the Obligations, while women are generally required to fulfill those Obligations that are not time-specific (e.g., affixing a mezuzah to one's doorpost; Mitzvah 423). For the most part, women are exempt from Obligations that must be fulfilled at specific times [מִצְוֹת עֲשֵׂה שֶׁהַזְּמַן גְּרָמָא], though there are

NOTES

in Mitzvah 26, which is the first of numerous Prohibitions and Obligations in the Torah pertaining to idolatry, Chinuch lists laws that, strictly speaking, fall under some of those other mitzvos (see note 11 there).

In our elucidation of the Chinuch, we generally present the background for the laws cited by Chinuch and refer the reader to where they are discussed by the halachic authorities. While every effort was made to ensure that all citations are accurate, the reader is cautioned that this elucidation was not written for halachic purposes and should not be relied upon for any halachic application.

10. See, for example, Mitzvos 251-252.

some notable exceptions (e.g., reciting *Kiddush* on the Sabbath [Mitzvah 31], and eating matzah on the first night of Pesach [Mitzvah 10]).[11] Nevertheless, a woman may commit herself to performing time-specific mitzvos, and she is rewarded for fulfilling them.[12]

(c) Individuals: There are mitzvos that are incumbent only upon specific individuals, such as a monarch or the Kohen Gadol (see note 97 to the Author's Introduction).

(d) Community: Some mitzvos apply only to the community as a whole, rather than to each person on his own (see note 98 ibid.).

(e) Noahides: Although most of the mitzvos are limited to Jews, several of the most fundamental commandments are incumbent upon Noahides as well. Chinuch generally points these out (see note 44 ibid.).

Penalties The Torah sets various penalties for those who intentionally violate its laws. As Chinuch writes (Mitzvah 594), the Jewish people are God's children, and, in order that they repent and merit the World to Come, He decreed that they be punished for their violations in this world.

For failure to observe an Obligation, the Torah does not specify any particular punishment.[13] For the transgression of a Prohibition, a punishment is usually imposed.

The standard penalty imposed by *beis din* in earlier times for violation of a Prohibition was *malkus* (lashes). This punishment is discussed in Mitzvah 594.[14]

In certain cases involving severe transgressions, the Torah imposes the death penalty. There are four methods of execution and, in each case of a capital offense, *beis din* is commanded to execute the offender, should he be found guilty, with a specific form of execution. These forms are described in Mitzvos 47, 50, 261 and 555.

In order for a *beis din* to impose either *malkus* or capital punishment, it must be composed of judges who have received *semichah* (ordination) according to the procedure Chinuch sets forth in Mitzvah 491. Nowadays, when we lack judges who have been ordained in this manner, no *beis din* can impose these penalties.

Chinuch explains in Mitzvah 82 that neither *malkus* nor capital punishment may be imposed except on the basis of direct eyewitness testimony of two valid witnesses; circumstantial evidence does not suffice. In Mitzvah 32, he explains further that there must be absolute certainty

---

NOTES

11. Rishonim explain that the Torah releases women from having to fulfill most of the time-specific Obligations, because their time is often curtailed by the obligations of tending to their families. [This does not, however, provide license to disregard any of the Obligations that the Torah did impose on women] (see *Abudraham, Seder Tefillos Shel Chol,* p. 25 in Jerusalem, 1963 ed.; *Kol Bo* §73).

12. According to many authorities, a woman may even recite the appropriate blessings for the time-specific mitzvos, including the text אֲשֶׁר קִדְּשָׁנוּ בְּמִצְוֹתָיו וְצִוָּנוּ, *Who has sanctified us with His commandments and has commanded us ...* For discussion of this matter, see *Rama, Orach Chaim* 17:2, with *Mishnah Berurah* §2, and *Shulchan Aruch, Orach Chaim* 589:6 with *Rama*.

13. The exceptions to this rule are the Obligation of circumcision (Mitzvah 2) and the Obligation to bring the *pesach* offering (Mitzvah 5), for whose willful neglect the Torah prescribes the penalty of *kares* (see note 17).

14. There are numerous exceptions to the rule of *malkus*. Some of the categories excluded from *malkus* are:

(1) לָאו שֶׁאֵין בּוֹ מַעֲשֶׂה, *A prohibition that does not involve action,* such as keeping *chametz* in one's possession over Pesach (Mitzvos 11 and 20).

(2) לָאו הַנִּיתָּק לַעֲשֵׂה, *A prohibition that can be remedied through [fulfillment of] an obligation,* meaning that the Torah has prescribed an act that rectifies the sin. For example, one who violated the prohibition of taking a mother bird together with its eggs or fledglings (Mitzvah 544) does not incur *malkus*, because he can rectify the sin by fulfilling the mitzvah of sending the mother bird away (Mitzvah 545).

(3) לָאו הַנִּיתָּן לְתַשְׁלוּמִין, *A prohibition that is subject to repayment,* such as the prohibition of stealing (Mitzvah 229), which can be rectified by return of the stolen property (Mitzvah 130).

that the violator sinned deliberately. Thus, in order for *beis din* to punish him, the witnesses must warn him before he commits the crime that what he is about to do is forbidden, they must specify the punishment that it carries, and he must acknowledge the warning and commit the crime nonetheless (see note 38 there).[15]

An additional punishment that was sometimes imposed is the Rabbinic penalty known as מַכַּת מַרְדּוּת, *makkas mardus,* i.e., lashes of discipline.[16] This was a less severe form of punishment than the Biblical lashes of *malkus,* either because less lashes were meted out (*R' Saadiah Gaon,* cited in *Otzar HaGeonim, Nazir* 23a), or because the strap used was less painful (*Ran* to *Kesubos,* fol. 16b in *Rif*). [For another view, see Mitzvah 496 note 69.]

In some instances, the Torah declares that a transgressor is liable to the Heavenly punishments of מִיתָה בִּידֵי שָׁמַיִם, *death at the hands of Heaven,* or כָּרֵת, *kares* (excision).[17]

The preceding pertains to intentional sinners. There also are instances in which an unintentional transgressor must bring an offering for atonement, when the *Beis HaMikdash* is standing.

Chinuch explains regarding each mitzvah which, if any, of these consequences it has.

VII. Authorship of the Sefer HaChinuch

The authorship of the Sefer HaChinuch is unknown. Wishing to remain anonymous, the author, toward the end of his Introduction (see note 116 there), identifies himself simply as "a Jewish man from the House of Levi of Barcelona." However, a remark in the body of the work itself, near the beginning of Mitzvah 95, was understood by many as alluding that the author's name was Aharon, giving rise to the suggestion that the author was *R' Aharon HaLevi* (*Re'ah*), a disciple of *Ramban.* This suggestion was accepted by major Acharonim, including *Shach* (see *Yoreh Deah* 25:2, 70:33), *Pri Megadim* (Introduction to *Mishbetzos Zahav*), *R' Akiva Eiger* (*Teshuvos,* §129, 169), and *Yad Malachi* (*Kelalei Shaar HaMechaberim VeHamefarshim* §23), among others. However, *Chida,* in his work *Shem HaGedolim* (ע' רבינו אהרן הלוי), points out a number of difficulties with this identification, including numerous contradictions between Chinuch and writings of *Re'ah.*[18] For thorough discussion of this matter, see the essays of R' C. D. Chavel (*Sefer HaChinuch,* Mossad HaRav Kook ed., pp. 797-806), R' M. Leiter (Introduction to *Sefer HaHashlamah* on *Minchas Chinuch*), and R' D. Metzger (Introduction to Machon Yerushalayim ed. of *Minchas Chinuch*). In the final analysis, the author succeeded in concealing his identity, as it remains a mystery until this day.

NOTES

15. In capital cases, additional precautions are put in place to prevent the execution of an innocent person. The *beis din* must consist of no fewer than twenty-three judges, who thoroughly cross-examine the witnesses on every detail. The judges are required to make every endeavor to acquit the violator, either by disqualifying the testimony of the witnesses or by otherwise calling his culpability into question. This is discussed in Mitzvah 409. See further, introduction to Mitzvah 47.

As a result of these measures, execution was an extremely rare occurrence. The Mishnah (*Makkos* 7a) states that if a *beis din* imposed the death sentence more than once in seven years (or, according to some Sages, once in seventy years), it was called a "barbaric court."

16. This translation follows *Rav Hai Gaon,* cited in *Otzar HaGeonim, Nazir* 23a, and is based on *Targum Onkelos, Leviticus* 26:18. See also Rashi to *Shabbos* 40b ד״ה מרדות, and *Chullin* 141b ד״ה מכת מרדות, who relates the word מַרְדּוּת to רִדּוּי, *dominance*. *Aruch* v. מרד, however, understands the term מַרְדּוּת as *rebelliousness*, related to מֶרֶד, *rebellion.* These lashes are given as a punishment for the person's rebellion against the law of the Sages. [In certain instances, they are given as punishment for violation of a Biblical law (*Rambam, Hil. Sanhedrin* 18:5).]

17. "Death at the hands of Heaven" means that the sinner dies prematurely. *Kares* may entail premature death as well as the loss of future generations (see *Rashi* to *Genesis* 17:14 et al.; see, however, *Tosafos* to *Shabbos* 25a ד״ה כרת, *Ramban* to *Leviticus* 18:29 and in *Shaar HaGemul* ד״ה והכרת). In some instances of *kares,* the soul of the sinner is cut off from the next world, should he fail to repent (*Ramban* ibid.; see, however, *Rambam, Hil. Teshuvah* 8:1, and *Tiferes Yisrael, Sanhedrin* Ch. 9 §53).

18. See, for example, below, Mitzvah 73 note 34.

At the beginning of this Introduction, it was mentioned that one who learns diligently about a particular mitzvah is considered as though he has fulfilled it. The study of the 248 positive obligations sanctifies each of the corresponding 248 parts of the body, and the study of the 365 prohibitions sanctifies each of the corresponding 365 days of the solar year. It is our hope that through reading, reviewing, and studying this work, we will accrue the merits of all the 613 mitzvos, thus elevating our entire corporeal existence and every moment of our time. In this merit, may we witness the arrival of Mashiach, when the *Beis HaMikdash* will be rebuilt and the Jewish people will return to Eretz Yisrael, making it possible for our people to again observe all the 613 mitzvos in practice.

⧼ Works on the 613 Mitzvos ⧽

Aside from Chinuch, a great number of works have been written on the mitzvos, from the days of the Geonim until our time. The following is a list of some of the best-known of these *sefarim*. It includes works written directly on the mitzvos, as well as those written as commentaries to earlier *sefarim*. This list includes numerous works that are cited regularly in the notes or Insights of this edition of Chinuch.

Halachos Gedolos. The list of 613 mitzvos presented as an introduction to this work is the earliest known compilation on mitzvos. While it is known that *Halachos Gedolos* was composed in the Geonic era, its precise authorship is a matter of question. *Rambam (Sefer HaMitzvos, Shoresh* 10) attributes authorship to *R' Shimon Kaira*, who lived in the 8th century. *Tosafos (Succah* 38b ד"ה שמע et al.), however, attribute it to *R' Yehudai Gaon*, of the same era. The author is generally referred to as *Baal Halachos* (author of the *Halachos*), and sometimes by the acronym בה"ג, *Bahag*, i.e., *Baal Halachos Gedolos*.

Sefer HaMitzvos, R' Saadiah Gaon (4642-4702/882-942). Born in Egypt, *R' Saadiah* was eventually appointed to head the great Academy of Sura in Babylon. He defended the validity of the Oral Torah from those who challenged it, and, in the words of *Rambam (Iggeres Teiman)*, "the law of God would almost have become lost without him." He authored his list of the Mitzvos in the form of a poem. He also authored a poem that shows how all the 613 mitzvos are contained in the Ten Commandments.

Azharos R' Eliyahu HaZakein. The author, who was a brother-in-law of *R' Hai Gaon*, lived during the latter portion of the 10th century. Little else is known about him, but his *Azharos* were widely incorporated into the Shavuos liturgy and appear in most current *machzorim*, in the *chazzan's* repetition of the *Mussaf* prayer.

Azharos R' Shlomo ibn Gabirol (4782-4819/1021-1058). The author of this compilation of the mitzvos lived in the first half of the 11th century. In his work, he adhered to the count of the *Halachos Gedolos*. He composed his work in the form of a poem, and in many communities it was customary to include it in the prayers of the Shavuos festival.

Sefer Yerei'im, R' Eliezer of Metz (Re'eim) (circa 4874-4957/1114-1197). Cited by *Tosafos* numerous times, *Sefer Yerei'im* follows the reckoning of *Halachos Gedolos* in his arrangement of the mitzvos. He divided the mitzvos into seven categories, which are further divided into *simanim,* with each *siman* often including more than one mitzvah. Although portions of this *sefer* were published in the 16th century, the *sefer* was not published in its entirety until 5652/1892, when it appeared in print with the commentary **Toafos Re'eim** by *R' Abba Schiff*.

Sefer HaMitzvos, Rambam (R' Moshe ben Maimon) (4898-4964/1138-1204). *Rambam* wrote this work in Arabic, as an introductory work to his *Mishneh Torah*. The actual enumeration of the mitzvos is preceded by fourteen *shorashim* (principles; sing. *shoresh*), which, *Rambam* asserts, are to be used to determine whether a law of the Torah should be counted among the 613 mitzvos. Based on these *shorashim,* he challenges the count of the earlier authorities, and establishes his own reckoning of the mitzvos of the Torah. This work has become accepted as the most authoritative enumeration of the mitzvos. The *Sefer HaMitzvos* was translated into Hebrew by *R' Moshe ibn Tibbon*, and was first published in 1510. In recent times it was republished with a more precise version of *ibn Tibbon's* translation by *R' Chaim Heller*, who published his latest version in 1946.

Many commentaries have been wrtten to *Rambam's Sefer HaMitzvos.* The most famous of these, which are generally included in contemporary editions of *Sefer HaMitzvos,* are: **Megillas Esther** (*R' Yitzchak Leon*; pub. 1592); **Lev Same'ach** (*R' Avraham Alegri*; pub. 1652); **Kinas Soferim** (*R' Chananyah Kazis*; pub. 1680); **Margenisa Tava** (*R' Aryeh Leib Horowitz*; pub. 1756).

Hasagos HaRamban — Glosses of Ramban (R' Moshe ben Nachman) (4954-5030/1194-1270).

Ramban wrote Glosses to *Rambam's Sefer HaMitzvos,* in which he challenged both the *shorashim* and *Rambam's* actual count of the mitzvos. In this way, *Ramban* defended the earlier authorities (primarily *Halachos Gedolos*), whose count *Rambam* had rejected. Although composed in the form of Glosses, *Ramban's* comments are encyclopedic, and Chinuch, in his opening Missive, refers to these Glosses as "a highly esteemed book."

[The Commentary to *Song of Songs* that is attributed to *Ramban* also contains an enumeration of the mitzvos; however, because this enumeration is largely inconsistent with *Ramban's* positions in his Glosses, *Shem HaGedolim* concludes that the attribution to *Ramban* is erroneous.]

Sefer Mitzvos Gadol (Smag), R' Moshe of Coucy (circa 4960-5020/1200-1260). This work does not merely enumerate the mitzvos, but also cites the halachic conclusions of the Talmud regarding many laws of the mitzvos. Hence, it was widely accepted as a halachic text. For this reason, *Ein Mishpat* (printed in the margin of *Talmud Bavli*), which provides references throughout the Talmud to *Rambam* and *Tur*, also provides references to *Smag*.

A number of commentaries were written to *Smag*. These include, among others: **Beur of R' Eizik Stein** (d. 5256/1496); **Dina D'Chayei** (*R' Chaim Benveniste,* author of *Knesses HaGedolah*, 5360-5434/1600-1674); **Megillas Sefer** (*R' Binyamin Kazis,* pub. 5500/1740). In addition, Glosses were written by early authorities including *R' Eliyahu Mizrachi* (5210-5286/1450-1526), *R' Shlomo Luria* (*Maharshal*, 5270-5333/1519-1573), and others.

Sefer Mitzvos Katan (Smak), R' Yitzchak of Corbeil (circa 4970-5030/1210-1270). This work discusses only mitzvos that apply in our time, and was composed for use by laymen. *Smak* divided the mitzvos into seven categories corresponding to the days of the week, and urged that his work be reviewed on a weekly basis. Although *Smak* includes only limited discussion of the laws of the mitzvos, such that the author advises those seeking a more comprehensive treatment to study *Smag*, the rulings contained in *Smak* are cited frequently by later halachic authorities.

A disciple of the author, *R' Peretz of Corbeil* (author of *Tosefos R' Peretz* to the Talmud), composed a brief commentary to his teacher's work. These Glosses, known as **Hagahos Smak,** are quoted extensively in later halachic literature.

Zohar HaRakia, R' Shimon ben Tzemach Duran (Tashbatz) (5121-5204/1361-1444). This work is a commentary on the *Azharos* of *R' Shlomo ibn Gabirol*. In it, *Tashbatz* clarifies some of the disagreements between *Rambam* and *Ramban* in their counting of the mitzvos, often defending *Rambam* from *Ramban's* challenges.

Metzudas David, R' David ben Zimra (Radvaz) (5240-5333/1479-1573). In this work, *Radvaz* follows *Rambam's* enumeration, and suggests both simple and Kabbalistic reasons for the mitzvos.

Sefer Chareidim, R' Elazar Azkari (5293-5360/1533-1600). This work discusses only the mitzvos that apply in our time. It is arranged in chapters listing the mitzvos done with different parts of the body. *R' Avraham Danzig* (author of the *Chayei Adam*) published a condensed version of this work, known as **Kitzur Sefer Chareidim.** *Mishnah Berurah* (156:4) urges the study of works on the mitzvos, and mentions especially *Sefer Chareidim.*

Sh'nei Luchos HaBris (Sh'lah), R' Yeshaya HaLevi Horowitz (5325-5390/1565-1630). *Sh'lah* sets forth some of the Kabbalistic aspects of the mitzvos, and explains how man's character becomes refined through mitzvah observance.

Poel Tzedek, R' Shabsai Kohen (Shach) (5381-5422/1621-1662). This is a concise list of the mitzvos, consisting of the verses from which each mitzvah is derived. *Shach* urged that his work be reviewed on a daily or weekly basis so that the mitzvos not be forgotten.

Derech Mitzvosecha, R' Yehudah Rozanis (Mishneh LaMelech) (5417-5487/1657-1727). This work discusses the discrepancies between the counts of the various earlier authorities, as well as some differences in their interpretations of the mitzvos. The final section of this *sefer* contains Glosses on the Sefer HaChinuch, which are cited often in the notes in this edition.

Maayan HaChachmah, R' Noach Chaim Zvi Berlin (5494-5562/1734-1802). In this fascinating work, the author sets forth the mitzvos in the form of a poem, which is comprised almost entirely of Scriptural verses, and is arranged according to the letters of the *aleph-beis.* Alongside the poem, he discusses the Talmudic background of the mitzvos at length. This work is quoted in many of the later *sefarim* on the mitzvos.

Minchas Chinuch, R' Yosef Babad (5561-5634/1801-1874). While based on the Chinuch, this work quickly acquired independent recognition. It contains stimulating analyses of a broad array of aspects of the laws of the mitzvos, and, since its publication, has become very popular and has evoked widespread study.

Maharam Schik, R' Moshe Schik (5567-5639/1807-1879). The manuscript of this *sefer* was prepared many years prior to its publication. Upon publication of *Minchas Chinuch,* the author recognized that his work would seem redundant if published as it was; he thus subjected it to a thorough review, removing much of the material it originally contained. The final version was published posthumously.

Commentary to Sefer HaMitzvos of R' Saadiah Gaon, R' Yerucham Fishel Perla (5606-5694/1846-1934). This extensive work interprets and develops the concise words of *R' Saadiah Gaon,* and articulates his position regarding which Torah obligations are counted as mitzvos. R' Perla's discussion of each mitzvah has remarkable scope, and testifies to the author's encyclopedic knowledge of the Talmud and its commentaries.

Me'il HaEphod, R' Dovid Pipano (5611-5685/1851-1925). This work, published in Jerusalem in 5758, nearly seventy-five years after its author's passing, is based on the Sefer HaChinuch, and contains discussion regarding the Scriptural sources of the mitzvos and their laws.

Minchas Yitzchak, R' Yizchak Aronovski (Vilna, 1908). This work is written as a commentary to the Sefer HaChinuch and is a valuable aid in studying the Chinuch. It explains difficult passages, provides sources for many of the laws cited by Chinuch, and suggests resolutions for difficulties with Chinuch's positions.

Imrei David, R' Dovid Schlissel (5624-5699/1864-1939). This work consists of two sections: *Imrei David* and *Keser Torah*. *Imrei David* contains analytical discussion of the mitzvos; *Keser Torah* focuses on various practical questions regarding the laws of the mitzvos, and refers the reader to earlier sources related to these discussions.

Yad Halevi, R' Yitzchak Simcha Hurewitz (5629/1868-5696/1935). A commentary on *Sefer HaMitzvos* of *Rambam*. Another section, entitled *Shai LaMoreh,* consists of a commentary on the section of the reasons for the mitzvos in *Rambam's Moreh Nevuchim.* Published in Jerusalem in 5687/1926 and 5691/1931.

Minchah Chadashah, R' Yosef Papersz (pub. 5694/1934 and 5698/1938). The author of this work was a grandson of *R' Yosef Babad,* author of the *Minchas Chinuch*, and often discusses topics included in that classic work. The *sefer* addresses mitzvos 1-114.

Minchas Soless, R' Dovid Zvi Zehman (pub. 5694-5699/1934-1939). This analytical work on the laws of the mitzvos and their sources covers the mitzvos from Parashas *Bereishis* until Parashas *Kedoshim* (1-261). It consists of three volumes; the first and second volumes were published by the author, in 5694/1934 and 5697/1937, respectively, and the third volume was printed from manuscript approximately half a century later, by a grandson of the author.

Mitzvas HaMelech, *R' Ezriel Cziment* (pub. 5752-5775/1992-2015); a work in progress containing commentary and discussion on *Rambam's Sefer HaMitzvos.*

In addition to the above works, Glosses were written to the Chinuch by great Torah scholars, and these are often cited in the notes to the current edition. They include:

R' Yehudah Rozanis in *Derech Mitzvosecha*; see above.

R' Yeshaya Pik (5479-5559/1719-1799). Known for his Glosses to the Talmud, *R' Pik* also wrote Glosses to the Chinuch, first published in the Vienna, 5587/1827, edition of the Chinuch.

Tzava Rav, R' Zvi Hersh Berlin (5481-5560/1721-1800). These Glosses first appeared in part in the Torah journal *Megged Yerachim* (Lemberg, 5617-1857). They were later published in their entirety from a manuscript, in the Machon Yerushalayim edition of *Minchas Chinuch* (Jerusalem, 5748/1988).

פרשת שפטים

Parashas Shoftim

שֹׁפְטִים יֵשׁ בָּהּ אַרְבַּע עֶשְׂרֵה מִצְווֹת עֲשֵׂה
וְעֶשְׂרִים וְשֶׁבַע מִצְווֹת לֹא תַעֲשֶׂה

***Parashas Shoftim* contains fourteen Mitzvah-Obligations and twenty-seven Mitzvah-Prohibitions**

CONTAINS FORTY-ONE MITZVOS:
MITZVOS 491-531

506. מִצְוַת מַתְּנוֹת זְרוֹעַ לְחָיַיִם וְקֵבָה לַכֹּהֵן – The Obligation to Give the Foreleg, the Jaw, and the Stomach [of an Animal] to a Kohen
507. מִצְוַת הַפְרָשַׁת תְּרוּמָה גְּדוֹלָה – The Obligation to Separate Terumah Gedolah
508. מִצְוַת רֵאשִׁית הַגֵּז שֶׁיִּנָּתֵן לַכֹּהֵן – The Obligation to Give the Kohen the First of the Fleece
509. לִהְיוֹת הַכֹּהֲנִים עוֹבְדִים בַּמִּקְדָּשׁ מִשְׁמָרוֹת מִשְׁמָרוֹת וּבַמּוֹעֲדִים עוֹבְדִים כְּאֶחָד – The Obligation Upon Kohanim and Leviim to Establish Mishmaros in the Beis HaMikdash and to Serve Together on the Festivals
510. שֶׁלֹּא לִקְסֹם – The Prohibition to Practice Divination
511. שֶׁלֹּא לְכַשֵּׁף – The Prohibition to Practice Sorcery
512. שֶׁלֹּא לַחֲבֹר חֶבֶר – The Prohibition to Cast Spells
513. שֶׁלֹּא לִשְׁאֹל בְּאוֹב – The Prohibition to Consult an Ov-Sorcerer
514. שֶׁלֹּא לִשְׁאֹל בְּיִדְּעוֹנִי – The Prohibition to Consult a Yidoni-Socerer
515. שֶׁלֹּא לִדְרֹשׁ אֶל הַמֵּתִים – The Prohibition to Inquire of the Dead
516. לִשְׁמֹעַ מִכָּל נָבִיא וְנָבִיא שֶׁיִּהְיֶה בְּכָל דּוֹר וָדוֹר אִם לֹא יוֹסִיף וְלֹא יִגְרַע בְּמִצְוֹת הַתּוֹרָה – The Obligation to Obey Each Prophet in Any Generation Provided That He Does Not Add to or Detract From the Torah's Commandments
517. שֶׁלֹּא לְהִתְנַבֵּאת בְּשֶׁקֶר – The Prohibition to Prophesy Falsely
518. שֶׁלֹּא לְהִתְנַבְּאוֹת בְּשֵׁם עֲבוֹדָה זָרָה – The Prohibition to Prophesy in the Name of Avodah Zarah
519. שֶׁלֹּא נִמָּנַע מֵהֲרִיגַת נְבִיא שֶׁקֶר וְלֹא נָגוּר מִמֶּנּוּ – The Prohibition to Be Afraid to Execute a False Prophet
520. לְהָכִין שֵׁשׁ עָרֵי מִקְלָט – The Obligation to Prepare Six Cities of Refuge
521. שֶׁלֹּא לְרַחֵם עַל הַמַּזִּיק בְּדִינֵי קְנָסוֹת – The Prohibition to Have Compassion on an Assailant in Punitive Judgments
522. שֶׁלֹּא לְהַשִּׂיג גְּבוּל – The Prohibition to Change a [Property] Boundary
523. שֶׁלֹּא לַחְתֹּךְ הַדִּין עַל פִּי עֵד אֶחָד – The Prohibition to Render Judgment Based Upon the Testimony of a Single Witness
524. לַעֲשׂוֹת לְעֵדִים זוֹמְמִים כְּמוֹ שֶׁדִּמּוּ לַעֲשׂוֹת – The Obligation to Do to Zomemin Witnesses Exactly What They Sought to Do [to the Defendant]
525. שֶׁלֹּא לַעֲרֹץ מִפְּנֵי הָאוֹיֵב בַּמִּלְחָמָה – The Prohibition to Be Afraid of the Enemy During War
526. לִמְשֹׁחַ כֹּהֵן לְמִלְחָמָה – The Obligation to Anoint a Kohen for Battle
527. לַעֲשׂוֹת בְּמִלְחֶמֶת הָרְשׁוּת כְּמִשְׁפַּט הַכָּתוּב – The Obligation to Follow the Torah's Instructions for Conducting a Discretionary War
528. שֶׁלֹּא לְהַחֲיוֹת אֶחָד מִכָּל שִׁבְעָה עֲמָמִין – The Prohibition to Let Any of the Seven Canaanite Nations Survive
529. שֶׁלֹּא לְהַשְׁחִית אִילָנֵי מַאֲכָל בְּמָצוֹר וְכֵן כָּל הַשְׁחָתָה בִּכְלַל הַלָּאו – The Prohibition to Destroy Fruit Trees During a Siege or to Do Any Other Wasteful Destruction
530. מִצְוַת עֲרִיפַת הָעֶגְלָה בְּנַחַל – The Obligation to Perform the Eglah Arufah (Decapitated Calf) Procedure by a Stream
531. שֶׁלֹּא לַעֲבֹד וְלִזְרֹעַ בְּנַחַל אֵיתָן – The Prohibition to Perform Work or to Sow in a Nachal Eisan (the Place Where an Eglah Arufah Was Decapitated)

מִצְוָה תצא

מִצְוַת מִנּוּי שׁוֹפְטִים וְשׁוֹטְרִים בְּכָל קָהָל וְקָהָל מִיִּשְׂרָאֵל

לְמַנּוֹת שׁוֹפְטִים וְשׁוֹטְרִים שֶׁיַּכְרִיחוּ לַעֲשׂוֹת מִצְווֹת הַתּוֹרָה[1] וְיַחֲזִירוּ הַנּוֹטִים מִדֶּרֶךְ הָאֱמֶת אֵלֶיהָ בְּעַל כָּרְחָם, וִיצַוּוּ בָּרָאוּי לַעֲשׂוֹת[2] וְיִמְנְעוּ הַדְּבָרִים הַמְגֻנִּים[3], וִיקַיְּמוּ הַגְּדֵרִים עַל הָעוֹבֵר[4] עַד שֶׁלֹּא יִהְיוּ מִצְווֹת הַתּוֹרָה וּמְנִיעוֹתֶיהָ צְרִיכוֹת לֶאֱמוּנַת כָּל אִישׁ וְאִישׁ[5].

Mitzvah 491

The Obligation to Appoint Judges and Officers in Every Jewish Community

שֹׁפְטִים וְשֹׁטְרִים תִּתֶּן לְךָ בְּכָל שְׁעָרֶיךָ אֲשֶׁר ה׳ אֱלֹהֶיךָ נֹתֵן לְךָ לִשְׁבָטֶיךָ וְשָׁפְטוּ אֶת הָעָם מִשְׁפַּט צֶדֶק

Judges and officers shall you appoint for yourselves in all your cities — which HASHEM*, your God, gives you — for your tribes; and they shall judge the people with righteous judgment* (*Deuteronomy* 16:18).

לְמַנּוֹת שׁוֹפְטִים וְשׁוֹטְרִים שֶׁיַּכְרִיחוּ לַעֲשׂוֹת מִצְווֹת הַתּוֹרָה — We are commanded **to appoint judges and officers who will** (1) **compel [people] to perform the mitzvos of the Torah;**[1] **וְיַחֲזִירוּ הַנּוֹטִים מִדֶּרֶךְ הָאֱמֶת אֵלֶיהָ בְּעַל כָּרְחָם** — (2) **compulsorily return those who have strayed from the true path to [that path];** **וִיצַוּוּ בָּרָאוּי לַעֲשׂוֹת** — (3) **instruct** the people **about that which is proper to do;**[2] **וְיִמְנְעוּ הַדְּבָרִים הַמְגֻנִּים** — (4) **prevent unseemly incidents** from occurring;[3] **וִיקַיְּמוּ הַגְּדֵרִים עַל הָעוֹבֵר** — **and** (5) **administer the punishments** mandated by the Torah **to those who transgress** the laws of the Torah.[4] **עַד שֶׁלֹּא יִהְיוּ מִצְווֹת הַתּוֹרָה וּמְנִיעוֹתֶיהָ צְרִיכוֹת לֶאֱמוּנַת כָּל אִישׁ וְאִישׁ** — They must do all this **so that** observance of **the mitzvos of the Torah** (i.e., mitzvah-obligations) **and its restrictions** (i.e., mitzvah-prohibitions) **is not dependent** solely **upon the faithfulness of each and every person** to the Torah.[5]

Chinuch discusses the various types of courts that are included in this mitzvah:

NOTES

1. If someone refuses to perform a mitzvah, *beis din* is authorized to employ various means of compulsion (depending on the circumstance) to ensure that he does so; see *Kesubos* 86a; see also Mitzvos 6, 10, and 264.

2. Aside from judging cases between individuals, one of the primary responsibilities of Jewish courts is to decide questions regarding Jewish law.

3. In certain cases, the officers were authorized by the court to punish offenders; in other situations, they brought the offenders to *beis din* to stand trial. Additionally, their mere presence prevented much wrongdoing from occurring in the first place. See below, after note 12.

4. For example, *beis din* is charged with administering *malkus* to one who intentionally transgressed a mitzvah-prohibition in front of valid witnesses after having received *hasraah* (warning).

5. Ideally, the Torah should be observed out of an abiding love of God. However, this cannot be expected of every individual at every point in his life. Therefore, an element of enforcement — which is provided by the judicial system — is necessary to ensure that the community adheres to Torah law. As Chinuch explains below (at note 25), this will help a person come to serve God willingly, as an expression of pure love.

In more general terms, this mitzvah commands the Jewish people to set up a judicial *system* to ensure the observance of Torah law. Both judges, who adjudicate cases and issue directives, and officers, who enforce the rulings of the court, are necessary for such a system to function properly (see *Tanchuma, Shoftim* §2). Therefore, as Chinuch writes, the obligations of setting up courts and appointing officers are both included in one mitzvah; see *Maharam Schik*.

וּמִתְּנָאֵי הַמִּצְוָה הַזֹּאת שֶׁיִּהְיוּ אֵלֶּה הַדַּיָּנִין מַדְרֵגָה עֶלְיוֹנָה מִמַּדְרֵגָה, וְזֶה שֶׁנַּעֲמִיד בְּכָל עִיר וָעִיר עֶשְׂרִים וּשְׁלֹשָׁה דַּיָּנִין מִקְבָּצִין כֻּלָּן בְּמָקוֹם אֶחָד מִשַּׁעֲרֵי הַמְּדִינָה הָרְאוּיָה לְזֶה הַמִּנְיָן[6], וְזֹאת הִיא סַנְהֶדְרֵי קְטַנָּה[7], וְנַעֲמִיד בִּירוּשָׁלַיִם בֵּית דִּין גָּדוֹל מִשִּׁבְעִים דַּיָּנִין, וְנַעֲמִיד אֶחָד עַל הַשִּׁבְעִים הָהֵם וְהוּא הַנִּקְרָא רֹאשׁ הַיְשִׁיבָה[8] וְהוּא אֲשֶׁר יִקְרְאוּ הַחֲכָמִים נָשִׂיא כְּמוֹ כֵן[9], וְיִהְיוּ כֻּלָּן מְקֻבָּצִין בִּמְקוֹמָן הַמְיֻחָד לָהֶם[10]. וּמָקוֹם שֶׁהוּא מוּעָט הַמִּנְיָן שֶׁאֵינוֹ רָאוּי לְסַנְהֶדְרֵי קְטַנָּה[11] יַעֲמִידוּ בוֹ שְׁלֹשָׁה, יִשְׁפְּטוּ הֵם הַדָּבָר הַקָּטָן,

---

וּמִתְּנָאֵי הַמִּצְוָה הַזֹּאת – **Among the fundamental requirements of this mitzvah-obligation** is שֶׁיִּהְיוּ אֵלֶּה הַדַּיָּנִין מַדְרֵגָה עֶלְיוֹנָה מִמַּדְרֵגָה – **that these** appointed **judges should be** part of a multi-tiered judiciary, with one **level** of courts **above another level** of courts. וְזֶה שֶׁנַּעֲמִיד בְּכָל עִיר וָעִיר עֶשְׂרִים וּשְׁלֹשָׁה דַּיָּנִין – More specifically, **this means that in each and every city, we are to establish** a court of **twenty-three judges,** מִקְבָּצִין כֻּלָּן בְּמָקוֹם אֶחָד מִשַּׁעֲרֵי הַמְּדִינָה הָרְאוּיָה לְזֶה הַמִּנְיָן – **who are to convene in a place** located **at the gates of a city that qualifies for** a court of **this number.**[6] וְזֹאת הִיא סַנְהֶדְרֵי קְטַנָּה – **This** type of court **is** known as **a minor sanhedrin.**[7] וְנַעֲמִיד בִּירוּשָׁלַיִם בֵּית דִּין גָּדוֹל מִשִּׁבְעִים דַּיָּנִין – On top of these municipal courts, **we are to establish a high court in Jerusalem, comprised of seventy** associate **judges,** וְנַעֲמִיד אֶחָד עַל הַשִּׁבְעִים הָהֵם וְהוּא הַנִּקְרָא רֹאשׁ הַיְשִׁיבָה – **and at the helm of those seventy [judges], we are to appoint a** seventy-first **judge, who is referred to as Rosh HaYeshivah** (Head of the Assembly).[8] וְהוּא אֲשֶׁר יִקְרְאוּ הַחֲכָמִים נָשִׂיא כְּמוֹ כֵן – **He is [the judge] whom the Sages refer to as *Nasi*, as well.**[9] וְיִהְיוּ כֻּלָּן מְקֻבָּצִין בִּמְקוֹמָן הַמְיֻחָד לָהֶם – **All** seventy-one of **these** judges **are to convene in the place that is designated for them,** i.e., the Chamber of Hewn Stone (*Lishkas HaGazis*) in the *Beis HaMikdash*.[10] וּמָקוֹם שֶׁהוּא מוּעָט הַמִּנְיָן שֶׁאֵינוֹ רָאוּי לְסַנְהֶדְרֵי קְטַנָּה – With regard to **a settlement with too small a population to qualify for a minor sanhedrin,**[11] יַעֲמִידוּ בוֹ שְׁלֹשָׁה – **we are to establish in it** a court of **three** judges, יִשְׁפְּטוּ הֵם הַדָּבָר הַקָּטָן – **who are to adjudicate minor matters** themselves,

---

NOTES

6. Only a city with at least 120 adult male residents requires a court of this size (see *Sanhedrin* 17b and *Rambam, Hil. Sanhedrin* 1:10 for the reason behind this requirement). Chinuch will soon explain what type of court is required for smaller villages.

The judges are to convene at a gate of the city, as it is stated (*Amos* 5:15): וְהַצִּיגוּ בַשַּׁעַר מִשְׁפָּט, *and establish justice by the gate* (*Rambam, Hil. Sanhedrin* 1:3).

7. [The word sanhedrin comes from a Greek word that denotes an assembly of wise men (*Mussaf HeAruch* ערך סנהדרין).]

A minor sanhedrin can adjudicate cases involving monetary claims, administer *malkus,* and even try most capital cases. [For capital cases, all twenty-three judges are required; for money matters and cases involving *malkus,* a panel of three suffices.] In addition to presiding over these types of cases, a minor sanhedrin also rules upon questions of Jewish law that arise for the residents of its city.

8. This court is modeled after the first high court of the Jewish people, which was comprised of seventy elders and Moses, the seventy-first judge, at their head; see *Sanhedrin* 2a and 16b.

9. The word נָשִׂיא, *Nasi,* is from the same root as נִשָּׂא, *elevated.* It is a title given to someone who is elevated above other people; see Mitzvah 71.

10. See *Mechilta,* cited by *Rashi* to *Exodus* 21:1, for the Scriptural source that the Great Sanhedrin should convene near the Altar.

The *Lishkas HaGazis* was built in the northeastern corner of the Temple Courtyard; part of it was within the Courtyard and part of it extended beyond. Thus, half of it possessed the sanctity of the Temple Courtyard, while the other half did not. The Great Sanhedrin convened in the unsanctified section (see *Yoma* 25a).

This high court, known as סַנְהֶדְרֵי גְּדוֹלָה, *the Great Sanhedrin,* or בֵּית דִּין הַגָּדוֹל, *the Great Beis Din,* has jurisdiction over capital cases that are beyond the jurisdiction of a minor sanhedrin, such as judging a false prophet (Mitzvah 517), or a subverted city (Mitzvah 464). This court also has jurisdiction over a variety of matters that affect the nation as a whole, such as the expansion of the legal boundaries of Jerusalem, and (along with the king) the decision to go to war. The Great Sanhedrin was also responsible for the appointment of judges to minor sanhedrins (see Mishnah, *Sanhedrin* 2a, with *Rashi*). Perhaps most significantly, the Great Sanhedrin is the final arbiter of questions of Torah law. If lower courts are unable to resolve a question, it is presented to the Great Sanhedrin, whose answer is binding on the entire nation (see below, after note 32, and see Mitzvah 495).

11. See above, note 6.

וְהַדָּבָר הַקָּשֶׁה יְבִיאוּן לְמִי שֶׁהוּא לְמַעְלָה מֵהֶם.[12] וּכְמוֹ כֵן יְמַנּוּ נוֹגְשִׂים בָּעָם הַסּוֹבְבִים בָּעִיר בַּשְּׁוָקִים וּבָרְחוֹבוֹת יַבִּיטוּ עִנְיְנֵי בְּנֵי אָדָם בִּסְחוֹרוֹתָם מִמְכָּרָם וּמִקְחָם עַד שֶׁלֹּא יִהְיֶה בֵּינֵיהֶם הָעָוֶל וְאַפִלּוּ בְּדָבָר מוּעָט[13]. וְהַמִּצְוָה שֶׁבָּאָה בָּזֶה הוּא אָמְרוֹ יִתְבָּרֵךְ (דברים ט״ז, י״ח) שֹׁפְטִים וְשֹׁטְרִים תִּתֶּן לְךָ בְּכָל שְׁעָרֶיךָ, וּלְשׁוֹן סִפְרִי (כאן)[14], מִנַּיִן שֶׁמְּמַנִּין בֵּית דִּין לְכָל יִשְׂרָאֵל, תַּלְמוּד לוֹמַר שֹׁפְטִים וְשֹׁטְרִים, וּמִנַּיִן שֶׁמְּמַנִּין אֶחָד עַל גַּבֵּי כֻלָּם[15], תַּלְמוּד לוֹמַר תִּתֶּן לְךָ[16], וּמִנַּיִן שֶׁמְּמַנִּין בֵּית דִּין לְכָל שֵׁבֶט וָשֵׁבֶט, תַּלְמוּד לוֹמַר בְּכָל שְׁעָרֶיךָ,[17]

וְהַדָּבָר הַקָּשֶׁה יְבִיאוּן לְמִי שֶׁהוּא לְמַעְלָה מֵהֶם — **and bring weightier matters to a higher [court].**[12]

Having described the different types of courts that comprise the judiciary, Chinuch turns to the second component of the mitzvah — the obligation to appoint enforcement officers:

וּכְמוֹ כֵן יְמַנּוּ נוֹגְשִׂים בָּעָם הַסּוֹבְבִים בָּעִיר בַּשְּׁוָקִים וּבָרְחוֹבוֹת — In addition to establishing courts, **we are also** required by this mitzvah **to appoint officers who circulate in the markets and streets of the city,** **יַבִּיטוּ עִנְיְנֵי בְּנֵי אָדָם בִּסְחוֹרוֹתָם מִמְכָּרָם וּמִקְחָם** — **observing the** business **dealings of the people,** examining **their wares and their transactions,** **עַד שֶׁלֹּא יִהְיֶה בֵּינֵיהֶם הָעָוֶל וְאַפִלּוּ בְּדָבָר מוּעָט** — so that not the slightest amount of corruption exists among them.[13] **וְהַמִּצְוָה שֶׁבָּאָה בָּזֶה הוּא אָמְרוֹ יִתְבָּרֵךְ** — **The commandment that comes to teach this** mitzvah-obligation **is that which [Hashem], blessed be He, stated** in the Torah (*Deuteronomy* 16:18): **"שֹׁפְטִים וְשֹׁטְרִים תִּתֶּן לְךָ בְּכָל שְׁעָרֶיךָ"** — *Judges and officers shall you appoint for yourselves in all your cities.*

Chinuch cites *Sifrei* to the verse:

וּלְשׁוֹן סִפְרִי — **The language of *Sifrei*** regarding this obligation is as follows:[14] **מִנַּיִן שֶׁמְּמַנִּין** **בֵּית דִּין לְכָל יִשְׂרָאֵל** — **From where** do we know **that we must establish a *beis din* for the entire Jewish People,** i.e., a Great Sanhedrin? **"תַּלְמוּד לוֹמַר "שֹׁפְטִים וְשֹׁטְרִים** — **To this end,** **[Scripture] states:** *Judges and officers* shall you appoint for yourselves, i.e., for the entire Jewish People. **וּמִנַּיִן שֶׁמְּמַנִּין אֶחָד עַל גַּבֵּי כֻלָּם** — **And from where** do we know **that we appoint one** judge **who is in charge of all the others?**[15] **תַּלְמוּד לוֹמַר "תִּתֶּן לְךָ** — **To this end,** **[Scripture] states:** *You shall appoint for yourselves.*[16] **וּמִנַּיִן שֶׁמְּמַנִּין בֵּית דִּין לְכָל שֵׁבֶט** **וָשֵׁבֶט** — **And from where** do we know **that we must establish a *beis din* for each and every tribe?** **"תַּלְמוּד לוֹמַר "בְּכָל שְׁעָרֶיךָ** — **To this end, [Scripture] states:** *in all your gates.*[17]

NOTES

12. [Stylistic paraphrase of *Exodus* 18:26.] This refers both to matters that are beyond the jurisdiction of a court of three, as well as to questions of Torah law that prove too difficult for them to resolve.

A court of three has jurisdiction over all monetary matters, and can even administer *malkus*. It cannot, however, try capital cases.

13. For example, the officers of the court ensure that merchants are not involved in price gouging and that their weights and measures are accurate (*Rambam, Hil. Sanhedrin* 1:1; see also *Hil. Mechirah* 14:1 and *Hil. Geneivah* 8:20). They were authorized by *beis din* to issue fines and impose other consequences upon violators (*Hil. Geneivah* ibid.). Officers of the court would also circulate in public areas to deter other violations of halachah, such as inappropriate mingling of the genders (see *Rambam, Hil. Yom Tov* 6:21).

14. Chinuch cites *Sifrei* as it appears in *Sefer HaMitzvos, Asei* 176. Our text of *Sifrei* differs somewhat. See also *Sanhedrin* 16b.

15. This refers to the *Nasi* (see *Tosafos* and *Chidushei HaRan* to *Sanhedrin* ibid.; cf. *Rashi* there).

16. See *Ran* ibid. and *Malbim* for explanations of this exposition.

17. In our texts of *Sifrei*, the phrase "*your gates* (i.e., cities)" teaches the obligation to establish courts in each city, while the obligation to set up a court for each tribe is derived from the phrase, "*for your tribes.*"

Ramban (to *Deuteronomy* 16:18) suggests two ways to understand the obligation to establish courts for the tribes, in light of the fact that there is already an obligation to establish courts in every city: (1) If more than one tribe lives in one city, a separate *beis din* must be set up for each tribe; or (2) each tribe had its own high court, which functioned as a supreme court for that tribe. According to this understanding, municipal courts of that tribe would turn to this court with questions they were unable to resolve, and this court had the authority to issue decrees that were binding on the entire tribe. See *Minchas Chinuch* §1.

רַבָּן שִׁמְעוֹן בֶּן גַּמְלִיאֵל אוֹמֵר לְשִׁבְטֶיךָ וְשָׁפְטוּ, מִצְוָה עַל כָּל שֵׁבֶט וְשֵׁבֶט לִהְיוֹת דָּן אֶת שִׁבְטוֹ[18], וְשָׁפְטוּ אֶת הָעָם, עַל כָּרְחָם[19]. וּכְבָר נִכְפְּלָה הַמִּצְוָה לְמַנּוֹת שִׁבְעִים זְקֵנִים[20], וְהוּא אָמְרוֹ יִתְבָּרַךְ לְמֹשֶׁה עָלָיו הַשָּׁלוֹם (במדבר י״א, ט״ז) אֶסְפָה לִי שִׁבְעִים אִישׁ[21], וְאָמְרוּ זִכְרוֹנָם לִבְרָכָה (ספרי בהעלתך פיסקא דאספה לי) כָּל מָקוֹם שֶׁנֶּאֱמַר לִי הֲרֵי הוּא קַיָּם לְעוֹלָם[22], וְכֵן (שמות כ״ח, מ״א) וְכִהֲנוּ לִי וְגוֹ׳[23], כְּלוֹמַר שֶׁהִיא מִצְוָה נִצְחִית וְאֵינָהּ לְפִי שָׁעָה, אֲבָל יִהְיֶה זֶה עוֹד כָּל יְמֵי הָאָרֶץ[24].

שֹׁרֶשׁ הַמִּצְוָה נִגְלֶה הוּא, שֶׁעִם הַדָּבָר הַזֶּה נַעֲמִיד דָּתֵנוּ בִּהְיוֹת אֵימַת

רַבָּן שִׁמְעוֹן בֶּן גַּמְלִיאֵל אוֹמֵר ״לְשִׁבְטֶיךָ וְשָׁפְטוּ״ – **Rabban Shimon ben Gamliel says:** From the juxtaposition of ***"for your tribes"*** and ***"and they shall judge,"*** מִצְוָה עַל כָּל שֵׁבֶט וְשֵׁבֶט לִהְיוֹת דָּן אֶת שִׁבְטוֹ – we learn **that it is a mitzvah for each tribe to judge its own tribe.** That is, people from one tribe should not litigate in the courts of another tribe.[18]

Chinuch continues his citation of *Sifrei*:

״וְשָׁפְטוּ אֶת הָעָם״ – The verse then states: ***and they*** (the judges in each city) ***shall judge the people.*** עַל כָּרְחָם – This teaches that the judges in each city can judge the people of that city **against their will.**[19]

Chinuch cites an additional source for the obligation to appoint a Great Sanhedrin:

וּכְבָר נִכְפְּלָה הַמִּצְוָה לְמַנּוֹת שִׁבְעִים זְקֵנִים – **The mitzvah to appoint** a Great Sanhedrin of **seventy elders**[20] **is repeated** elsewhere in the Torah, וְהוּא אָמְרוֹ יִתְבָּרַךְ לְמֹשֶׁה עָלָיו הַשָּׁלוֹם ״אֶסְפָה לִי שִׁבְעִים אִישׁ״ – **namely,** in **that which [Hashem], blessed be He, said to Moses, peace be upon him** (*Numbers* 11:16): ***Gather to Me seventy men*** *from the elders of Israel.*[21] וְאָמְרוּ זִכְרוֹנָם לִבְרָכָה – Although those words were specifically addressed to Moses, it establishes an obligation throughout the ages, as **[the Sages], of blessed memory, stated** (*Sifrei* to *Numbers* ibid.): כָּל מָקוֹם שֶׁנֶּאֱמַר ״לִי״ – **Wherever** the phrase **"*to Me*" is stated** in the Torah, הֲרֵי הוּא קַיָּם לְעוֹלָם – it indicates that **[the matter under discussion] is everlasting;**[22] therefore, the commandment of "*Gather to Me seventy men*" is everlasting. וְכֵן ״וְכִהֲנוּ לִי וְגוֹ׳״ – **Likewise,** the words of the Torah regarding the Kohanim (*Exodus* 28:41): *You shall anoint them, inaugurate them, and sanctify them,* ***and they shall minister to Me,* etc.,** are everlasting.[23] כְּלוֹמַר שֶׁהִיא מִצְוָה נִצְחִית וְאֵינָהּ לְפִי שָׁעָה – When *Sifrei* states that the commandment of *"Gather to me seventy men"* is everlasting, **this means to say that it is an eternal mitzvah, not** a **temporary** one; אֲבָל יִהְיֶה זֶה עוֹד כָּל יְמֵי הָאָרֶץ – **rather, this will continue** to apply for **all the days of the earth.**[24]

Underlying Purpose of the Mitzvah

שֹׁרֶשׁ הַמִּצְוָה נִגְלֶה הוּא – **The underlying purpose of this mitzvah is obvious:** שֶׁעִם הַדָּבָר הַזֶּה נַעֲמִיד דָּתֵנוּ – **For through** observance of **this matter, we can uphold our religion,** בִּהְיוֹת אֵימַת

NOTES

18. *Rashi, Sanhedrin* 16b ד״ה מצוה בשבט.

19. That is, they can force someone to appear in court. Even if a litigant says that he is willing to appear before the court of another city, the court of his city can force him to appear before them (*Emek HaNetziv,* based on *Sanhedrin* 31b).

20. That is, seventy associate judges with one chief judge in charge of them.

21. When Moses complained that it had become too difficult to carry the burden of the Jewish people alone, Hashem commanded him to appoint seventy elders who, along with Moses, would constitute the high court of the Jewish people.

22. The fact that something is described as being "for the sake of God" indicates that it is everlasting, just like God Himself is Eternal.

23. Once Aaron and his sons were anointed as Kohanim, that status was passed on to their descendants forever.

24. [Stylistic citation of *Genesis* 8:22.] *Sifrei* cannot mean that the Great Sanhedrin would never cease to function, for it has been many centuries since we have had the ability to have a Great Sanhedrin (see below, note 41). Rather, *Sifrei* means that there is an obligation to establish a Great Sanhedrin whenever it is technically possible to do so. Such mitzvos are referred to as mitzvos that apply throughout the generations; see Mitzvah 96, after note 3.

אַלּוּפֵינוּ וְשׁוֹפְטֵינוּ עַל פְּנֵי הֶהָמוֹן, וּמִתּוֹךְ הֶרְגֵּלָם בְּטוֹב וּבְיֹשֶׁר מֵחֲמַת יִרְאָה יְלַמְּדוּ הָעָם טִבְעָם לַעֲשׂוֹת מִשְׁפָּט וָצֶדֶק מֵאַהֲבָה בְּהַכָּרָתָם דֶּרֶךְ הָאֱמֶת[25], וּכְעִנְיָן שֶׁיֹּאמְרוּ הַחֲכָמִים שֶׁרֹב הַהֶרְגֵּל הוּא מַה שֶּׁאַחַר הַטֶּבַע, כְּלוֹמַר, כִּי כְּמוֹ שֶׁהַטֶּבַע יַכְרִיחַ הָאָדָם לְמַה שֶּׁהוּא מְבַקֵּשׁ, כֵּן הַהֶרְגֵּל הַגָּדוֹל חוֹזֵר בּוֹ כְּעֵין טֶבַע קַיָּם וְיַכְרִיחֶנּוּ לָלֶכֶת בְּדֶרֶךְ הַהֶרְגֵּל לְעוֹלָם, וּבְלֶכֶת הָעָם בְּדַרְכֵי הַיֹּשֶׁר וְהָאֱמוּנָה וּבוֹחֲרִים בַּטּוֹב, תִּדְבַּק בָּהֶם הַטּוֹב וְיִשְׂמַח ה׳ בְּמַעֲשָׂיו[26].

מִדִּינֵי[27] הַמִּצְוָה מַה שֶּׁאָמְרוּ זִכְרוֹנָם לִבְרָכָה שֶׁהַגָּדוֹל שֶׁבַּשִּׁבְעִים יוֹשֵׁב לְמַטָּה מִן הַנָּשִׂיא[28] וְהוּא הַנִּקְרָא אַב בֵּית דִּין, וּשְׁאָר הַשִּׁבְעִים יוֹשְׁבִין לְפִי שְׁנֵיהֶם וּכְפִי מַעֲלָתָם קָרוֹב לַנָּשִׂיא[29],

---

אַלּוּפֵינוּ וְשׁוֹפְטֵינוּ עַל פְּנֵי הֶהָמוֹן – since it ensures that **fear of our leaders and judges will rest upon the masses,** making it less likely that they will transgress the laws of the Torah. **וּמִתּוֹךְ הֶרְגֵּלָם בְּטוֹב וּבְיֹשֶׁר מֵחֲמַת יִרְאָה – And as a result of accustoming themselves to goodness and uprightness out of fear** of punishment at the hands of the court, **יְלַמְּדוּ הָעָם טִבְעָם לַעֲשׂוֹת מִשְׁפָּט וָצֶדֶק מֵאַהֲבָה – the people will** eventually **train themselves to instinctively perform** acts of **justice and righteousness out of love** of God, **בְּהַכָּרָתָם דֶּרֶךְ הָאֱמֶת – as they** come to **recognize the true path.**[25] **וּכְעִנְיָן שֶׁיֹּאמְרוּ הַחֲכָמִים –** This idea is **similar to that which wise men say, שֶׁרֹב הַהֶרְגֵּל הוּא מַה שֶּׁאַחַר הַטֶּבַע – that habit is second to nature, כְּלוֹמַר כִּי כְּמוֹ שֶׁהַטֶּבַע יַכְרִיחַ הָאָדָם לְמַה שֶּׁהוּא מְבַקֵּשׁ – meaning, that just as natural tendencies compel a person to** do **that which [those tendencies] seek, כֵּן הַהֶרְגֵּל הַגָּדוֹל חוֹזֵר בּוֹ כְּעֵין טֶבַע קַיָּם – so too, a habit can become like an ingrained tendency [for a person], וְיַכְרִיחֶנּוּ לָלֶכֶת בְּדֶרֶךְ הַהֶרְגֵּל לְעוֹלָם – compelling him to always follow that habit's** desired **path.**

וּבְלֶכֶת הָעָם בְּדַרְכֵי הַיֹּשֶׁר וְהָאֱמוּנָה וּבוֹחֲרִים בַּטּוֹב – And when the Jewish **nation walks on the paths of uprightness and loyalty, choosing** to do **good, תִּדְבַּק בָּהֶם הַטּוֹב וְיִשְׂמַח ה׳ בְּמַעֲשָׂיו – the good** of Hashem **will cling to them, and Hashem,** who wishes to bestow His Goodness, **will rejoice in His handiwork.**[26]

Laws of the Mitzvah

As Chinuch will soon teach, the Great Sanhedrin sat in a semicircle. The *Nasi* would sit in the middle of the configuration, at its highest point.[27] Chinuch describes how the rest of the judges sat:

מִדִּינֵי הַמִּצְוָה – Among the laws of this mitzvah is **מַה שֶּׁאָמְרוּ זִכְרוֹנָם לִבְרָכָה – that which [the Sages], of blessed memory, stated** (see *Rambam, Hil. Sanhedrin* 1:3, and *Smag, Asei* 97), **שֶׁהַגָּדוֹל שֶׁבַּשִּׁבְעִים יוֹשֵׁב לְמַטָּה מִן הַנָּשִׂיא – that the greatest of the seventy** remaining judges **sits** just **below the *Nasi*,** to his right,[28] **וְהוּא הַנִּקְרָא אַב בֵּית דִּין – and he is referred to as *Av Beis Din*** ("Father of the Court"). **וּשְׁאָר הַשִּׁבְעִים יוֹשְׁבִין לְפִי שְׁנֵיהֶם וּכְפִי מַעֲלָתָם קָרוֹב לַנָּשִׂיא – The rest of the seventy** judges **would sit in proximity to the *Nasi*,** to his right and to his left,[29] **according to their age and**

NOTES

25. The ideal level of Divine service, observing the Torah out of love of God, is initially beyond the reach of most people. However, habituating oneself to observe the Torah for less commendable reasons effects a change in one's thoughts and attitudes, and he will eventually come to serve God for the most noble of reasons (see *Rambam, Hil. Teshuvah* 10:2,5). This principle, that a man's *inner* thoughts are affected by his *outer* actions, is repeated by Chinuch throughout this work; see, for example, Mitzvos 16, 40, and 95.

26. [Stylistic citation of *Psalms* 104:31.] Here, too, Chinuch reiterates an oft-repeated theme of his: Hashem desires to bestow His goodness upon mankind, but only those whose essence is good can receive it. By performing good deeds, one's essence is changed for the better, and he becomes more suited to receive Hashem's goodness.

27. See *Rambam, Hil. Sanhedrin* 1:3; *Smag, Asei* 97; and *Minchas Yitzchak* §6.

28. *Tosefta, Sanhedrin* 8:1; *Rambam, Hil. Sanhedrin* 1:3.

29. See *Tosefta* ibid. and *Smag* ibid. [We have followed the understanding of *Minchas Yitzchak* §6, who explains Chinuch in accordance with *Tosefta* and *Smag,* that the *Nasi* sat at the head of the semicircle, with the other judges to his right and left. *Rambam* (ibid.) seems to follow a dissenting opinion in *Tosefta,* which holds that only the *Av Beis Din* sat to the right of the

כְּלוֹמַר שֶׁכָּל הַגָּדוֹל מֵחֲבֵרוֹ בְּחָכְמָה סָמוּךְ לוֹ יוֹתֵר, וְהַשָּׁוִין בְּחָכְמָה הוֹלְכִין בָּהֶן אַחַר רֹב שָׁנִים[30], וְכֻלָּן יוֹשְׁבִין בְּעִגּוּל עָשׂוּי כְּמוֹ חֲצִי גֹרֶן[31] כְּדֵי שֶׁיְּהוּ רוֹאִין כֻּלָּן אֵלּוּ אֶת אֵלּוּ[32]. וְעוֹד מַעֲמִידִין לִפְנֵיהֶם שְׁנֵי בָּתֵּי דִינִין שֶׁל עֶשְׂרִים וּשְׁלֹשָׁה וְעֶשְׂרִים וּשְׁלֹשָׁה, כַּת אַחַת מֵהֶן עַל פֶּתַח הָעֲזָרָה וְכַת אַחֶרֶת עַל פֶּתַח הַר הַבַּיִת[33], וְהַגָּדוֹל שֶׁבְּכָל כַּת וְכַת רֹאשׁ לַכַּת שֶׁלּוֹ.

וְאֵין מַעֲמִידִין בְּסַנְהֶדְרִין בֵּין גְּדוֹלָה בֵּין קְטַנָּה אֶלָּא אֲנָשִׁים חֲכָמִים וּנְבוֹנִים בְּחָכְמַת

---

their level of scholarship. כְּלוֹמַר שֶׁכָּל הַגָּדוֹל מֵחֲבֵרוֹ בְּחָכְמָה סָמוּךְ לוֹ יוֹתֵר – **This means that whoever possessed greater** Torah **wisdom than his fellow would be** seated **closer to the [*Nasi*],** וְהַשָּׁוִין בְּחָכְמָה הוֹלְכִין בָּהֶן אַחַר רֹב שָׁנִים – **and with regard to those of equal** Torah **scholarship,** proximity to the *Nasi* **was determined based on age.**[30]

וְכֻלָּן יוֹשְׁבִין בְּעִגּוּל עָשׂוּי כְּמוֹ חֲצִי גֹרֶן – **[The judges] would all sit in a circular configuration, which was shaped like half of a threshing floor**, i.e. a semicircle,[31] כְּדֵי שֶׁיְּהוּ רוֹאִין כֻּלָּן אֵלּוּ אֶת אֵלּוּ – **so that they could all see one another.**[32]

One of the main functions of the Great Sanhedrin was to act as the final arbiter of questions of Torah law. When lower courts could not answer a question, the question was brought to Jerusalem for resolution. The question was first posed to a *beis din* of twenty-three that convened in Jerusalem. If that *beis din* could not answer the question, it was presented to a second, higher, *beis din* of twenty-three that convened in Jerusalem. If that *beis din* was also unable to answer the question, it was presented to the Great Sanhedrin (see Mishnah, *Sanhedrin* 86b). Chinuch discusses the exact location of these two courts of twenty-three:

וְעוֹד מַעֲמִידִין לִפְנֵיהֶם שְׁנֵי בָּתֵּי דִינִין שֶׁל עֶשְׂרִים וּשְׁלֹשָׁה וְעֶשְׂרִים וּשְׁלֹשָׁה – In addition to the Great Sanhedrin, which convened in the Chamber of Hewn Stone in the *Beis HaMikdash* Courtyard, **two courts, each** comprised **of twenty-three judges, were also set up in the area approaching** the location of **[the Great Sanhedrin].** כַּת אַחַת מֵהֶן עַל פֶּתַח הָעֲזָרָה – **One of these groups** of judges convened in a chamber located **at the entrance to the Temple Courtyard** (i.e., by the gate leading into the Women's Courtyard), וְכַת אַחֶרֶת עַל פֶּתַח הַר הַבַּיִת – **and the other group** of judges convened in a chamber located **at the entrance to the Temple Mount** (i.e., by the gate leading into the Temple Mount).[33] וְהַגָּדוֹל שֶׁבְּכָל כַּת וְכַת רֹאשׁ לַכַּת שֶׁלּוֹ – **The greatest** sage **in each group** of judges **was** appointed as **the head of his group.**

Chinuch discusses several of the qualifications to be appointed to a sanhedrin:

וְאֵין מַעֲמִידִין בְּסַנְהֶדְרִין בֵּין גְּדוֹלָה בֵּין קְטַנָּה – **We do not appoint to any sanhedrin, whether** to **the Great [Sanhedrin]** of seventy-one **or** to **a minor sanhedrin** of twenty-three, אֶלָּא אֲנָשִׁים חֲכָמִים וּנְבוֹנִים בְּחָכְמַת הַתּוֹרָה – anyone **other than men who are** extremely **knowledgeable and**

NOTES

Nasi, while the remaining judges sat to his left. Accordingly, the *Nasi* did not sit in the middle of the formation (see *Kesef Mishneh* ad loc.). Some, however, understand *Rambam* as agreeing that the *Nasi* sat in the middle of the formation (*Aruch HaShulchan, Choshen Mishpat* 1:15).]

30. *Rambam* (ibid., according to Chinuch's version of the text; cf. Frankel ed.) writes simply that the remaining judges were seated according to their age and stature, but does not explain how these two criteria are weighted. Chinuch explains that level of Torah scholarship is the primary consideration, and age is used only to distinguish between scholars who are on the same level of scholarship. For other understandings of *Rambam,* see *Kesef Mishneh* and *Kiryas Melech.*

31. Threshing floors were often circular.

32. [See *Sanhedrin* 37a for a Scriptural source for this configuration.] This would foster debate and discussion among the judges, which, in turn, increased the likelihood that a proper decision would be reached (see *Rashi, Chullin* 5a ד״ה שיהו רואין). Sitting in a full circle is not a viable option, because the litigants and witnesses have to face the judges, so that the judges can pay close attention to their words (*Rashi, Sanhedrin* 36b ד״ה כחצי גורן; cf. *Rashi* to *Chullin* ibid.).

Minor sanhedrins would also sit in a semicircle (*Rambam, Hil. Sanhedrin* 1:3).

33. *Chasdei David, Sanhedrin* 7:1; *Tiferes Yisrael, Sanhedrin* 11:2; *Shaarei Toras Bavel, Sanhedrin* 86b. Cf. *Rashi* to *Sanhedrin* ibid.

הַתּוֹרָה[34], וְיוֹדְעִין גַּם כֵּן קְצָת מִשְּׁאָר הַחָכְמוֹת כְּגוֹן רְפוּאוֹת וְחֶשְׁבּוֹן תְּקוּפוֹת וּמַזָּלוֹת וְאִיצְטַגְנִינוּת[35] וְדַרְכֵי הַמְעוֹנְנִים וְהַקּוֹסְמִים וְהַמְכַשְּׁפִים כְּדֵי שֶׁיִּהְיוּ יוֹדְעִין לָדוּן הָעָם בְּכָל דְּרָכִים אֵלּוּ אִם יִצְטָרְכוּ לְכָךְ[36]. וְאֵין מַעֲמִידִין בַּסַּנְהֶדְרִין אֶלָּא כֹּהֲנִים לְוִיִּם וְיִשְׂרְאֵלִים מְיֻחָסִים הָרְאוּיִין לְהַשִּׂיא בְּנוֹתָן לִכְהֻנָּה[37], שֶׁנֶּאֱמַר בְּמֹשֶׁה (במדבר י״א, ט״ז) **וְהִתְיַצְּבוּ שָׁם עִמָּךְ, וְדָרְשׁוּ זִכְרוֹנָם לִבְרָכָה** (סנהדרין ל״ו ע״ב) **בְּדוֹמִין לָךְ[38].**

---

insightful in the realm of Torah wisdom,[34] וְיוֹדְעִין גַּם כֵּן קְצָת מִשְּׁאָר הַחָכְמוֹת – **and who are also knowledgeable in some other disciplines,** כְּגוֹן רְפוּאוֹת וְחֶשְׁבּוֹן תְּקוּפוֹת וּמַזָּלוֹת וְאִיצְטַגְנִינוּת **– such as, medicine, the calculations of seasons and constellations, and astronomy.**[35] וְדַרְכֵי הַמְעוֹנְנִים וְהַקּוֹסְמִים וְהַמְכַשְּׁפִים – They should **also** possess knowledge regarding **the ways of diviners** (Mitzvah 250), **sorcerers** (Mitzvah 510), **and those who practice witchcraft** (Mitzvah 511), כְּדֵי שֶׁיִּהְיוּ יוֹדְעִין לָדוּן הָעָם בְּכָל דְּרָכִים אֵלּוּ אִם יִצְטָרְכוּ לְכָךְ – **so that they will know how to judge the people regarding all of these matters, if the need arises.**[36]

וְאֵין מַעֲמִידִין בַּסַּנְהֶדְרִין אֶלָּא כֹּהֲנִים לְוִיִּם וְיִשְׂרְאֵלִים מְיֻחָסִים הָרְאוּיִין לְהַשִּׂיא בְּנוֹתָן לִכְהֻנָּה – **We do not appoint to a sanhedrin** (either the Great Sanhedrin or a lesser sanhedrin) anyone **other than Kohanim, Leviim, or Yisraelim of untainted lineage,** i.e., **those who are eligible to marry their daughters to a Kohen.**[37] שֶׁנֶּאֱמַר בְּמֹשֶׁה – These qualities are required to serve on a sanhedrin, **as it is stated with regard to Moses** (*Numbers* 11:16): "וְהִתְיַצְּבוּ שָׁם עִמָּךְ" – *Gather to Me seventy men from the elders of Israel ... **and they shall stand there with you,*** וְדָרְשׁוּ זִכְרוֹנָם לִבְרָכָה בְּדוֹמִין לָךְ – **and [the Sages], of blessed memory, expounded** (*Sanhedrin* 36b) that the phrase, *"with you"* signifies elders **who are similar to you** (Moses); i.e., just like Moses was exceptionally wise and genealogically pure, so too, any judge who serves on a sanhedrin must possess these qualities.[38]

NOTES

34. In *Rambam* (*Hil. Sanhedrin* 2:1), which is Chinuch's source, the text reads אֲנָשִׁים חֲכָמִים וּנְבוֹנִים מוּפְלָאִין בְּחָכְמַת הַתּוֹרָה, *wise and insightful men, **who are exceptional** in Torah scholarship.*

35. The term אִיצְטַגְנִינוּת often refers to astrology, the study of how the positions of celestial bodies affect people and events. Here, however, Chinuch refers simply to astronomy; see *Rambam, Hil. Kiddush HaChodesh* 10:6 and 11:7.

Knowledge of medicine can sometimes help judges render a halachic decision. For example, the halachah is that a sick person whose life is in danger may desecrate the Sabbath in seeking a remedy, but only provided that the effectiveness of the remedy has a scientific basis. It is therefore important for judges to possess medical knowledge, so that they can rule on the appropriateness of desecrating the Sabbath for a particular remedy (*Radvaz, Hil Sanhedrin* 2:1; see there for another situation where it is important for judges to possess medical knowledge). Knowledge of the remaining disciplines that Chinuch mentions, which are all forms of astronomical knowledge, allow a judge to competently participate in decisions that relate to the setting of the Jewish calendar (*Kesef Mishneh*). Cf. *Minchas Yitzchak* §8.

36. In order to judge people accused of sorcery, divining, or witchcraft, a judge has to have the ability to determine whether the action that was performed qualifies as one of these transgressions. This requires a working knowledge in these areas (see *Rabbeinu Yonah, Sanhedrin* 17a ד״ה בעלי כשפים; see also *Tosafos, Menachos* 65a ד״ה ובעלי כשפים, citing *Rav Hai Gaon*). [Under normal circumstances, it is forbidden to study these various forms of magic; see *Deuteronomy* 18:9. However, it is permitted to do so in order to be able to provide halachic guidance and to judge competently in these areas (see *Shabbos* 75a).]

37. For example, a member of a sanhedrin cannot be a *mamzer* (the offspring of certain illicit relationships, such as adultery; see Mitzvah 560) or a *chalal* (the offspring of a Kohen and a woman who is prohibited exclusively to Kohanim, such as a divorcee; Mitzvah 268), regardless of his level of Torah scholarship. [A *mamzer* cannot marry a (genealogically untainted) *non*-Kohen either. The genealogical purity required of a member of a sanhedrin is referred to as the ability to "marry off one's daughter to a Kohen" because this description encompasses other restrictions as well.]

38. [The Gemara actually rejects this source, and concludes that these requirements are derived from another verse (*Exodus* 18:22); see *Kesef Mishneh, Hil. Sanhedrin* 2:1, and *Toras Chaim, Sanhedrin* 17a.]

Not all of these qualities are required for one to be appointed to a *beis din* of three. However, even judges appointed to such a *beis din* must possess great Torah knowledge and exemplary character (see *Rambam, Hil. Sanhedrin* 2:7).

וְאֵין מַעֲמִידִין סַנְהֶדְרִין לְעוֹלָם בֵּין סַנְהֶדְרֵי גְּדוֹלָה בֵּין סַנְהֶדְרֵי קְטַנָּה אֶלָּא סְמוּכִין[39], וּמֹשֶׁה רַבֵּנוּ סָמַךְ לְתַלְמִידוֹ יְהוֹשֻׁעַ כְּמוֹ שֶׁכָּתוּב (במדבר כ״ז, כ״ג) וַיִּסְמֹךְ אֶת יָדָיו עָלָיו[40], וּכְמוֹ כֵן סָמַךְ לְשִׁבְעִים הַזְּקֵנִים שֶׁאָסַף אֵלָיו, וְאוֹתָן הַזְּקֵנִים סָמְכוּ לַאֲחֵרִים וַאֲחֵרִים לַאֲחֵרִים עַד סוֹף כָּל הַסְּמוּכִים[41]. וְאָמְנָם הַסְּמִיכָה בְּכָל הַדּוֹרוֹת לֹא הָיְתָה בַּיָּד כְּמוֹ סְמִיכָה שֶׁל מֹשֶׁה, אֶלָּא שֶׁהָיוּ בּוֹדְקִין אוֹתוֹ שֶׁהָיוּ רוֹצִין לִסְמֹךְ אִם הָיָה בָּקִי בְּחָכְמַת הַתּוֹרָה, וְאִם הָיָה שִׂכְלוֹ בָּרִיא וְשָׁלֵם וְאִם הוּא אִישׁ אוֹהֵב אֱמֶת וְשׂוֹנֵא הָעָוֶל וְכָל עִנְיָנוֹ, וְאַחַר חֲקִירָה רַבָּה בְּעִנְיָנוֹ וּבְחָכְמָתוֹ אוֹמְרִין לוֹ שְׁלֹשָׁה חֲכָמִים סְמוּכִים אוֹ אֲפִלּוּ כְּשֶׁאֶחָד מֵהֶן סָמוּךְ הֲרֵי אַתָּה סָמוּךְ[42],

---

⧼ *Semichah* – Ordination

Chinuch discusses the type of ordination required to serve on a sanhedrin:

וְאֵין מַעֲמִידִין סַנְהֶדְרִין לְעוֹלָם בֵּין סַנְהֶדְרֵי גְּדוֹלָה בֵּין סַנְהֶדְרֵי קְטַנָּה אֶלָּא סְמוּכִין – **We never appoint to any sanhedrin, whether** to **the Great Sanhedrin or** to **a lesser Sanhedrin,** anyone **other than those who have received** a special type of ordination known as ***semichah.***[39]

Chinuch discusses the history of *semichah* and how it is conferred:

וּמֹשֶׁה רַבֵּנוּ סָמַךְ לְתַלְמִידוֹ יְהוֹשֻׁעַ – **Moses, our teacher, conferred *semichah* upon his student, Joshua,** כְּמוֹ שֶׁכָּתוּב ״וַיִּסְמֹךְ אֶת יָדָיו עָלָיו״ – **as it is written** (*Numbers* 27:23): ***He leaned his hands upon him.***[40] וּכְמוֹ כֵן סָמַךְ לְשִׁבְעִים הַזְּקֵנִים שֶׁאָסַף אֵלָיו – **Likewise, [Moses] conferred *semichah* upon the seventy elders that he gathered to himself** to serve on the Sanhedrin. וְאוֹתָן הַזְּקֵנִים סָמְכוּ לַאֲחֵרִים – **Those** seventy **elders** later **conferred *semichah* upon other [sages],** וַאֲחֵרִים לַאֲחֵרִים – **and those other [sages]** in turn **conferred *semichah* upon other [sages],** עַד סוֹף כָּל הַסְּמוּכִים – and this process continued **until no one with *semichah* remained.**[41] וְאָמְנָם הַסְּמִיכָה בְּכָל הַדּוֹרוֹת לֹא הָיְתָה בַּיָּד כְּמוֹ סְמִיכָה שֶׁל מֹשֶׁה – **However, *semichah* throughout the generations was not conferred by placing one's hand** on the *semichah* candidate's head, **in the way that Moses conferred *semichah*** to Joshua. אֶלָּא שֶׁהָיוּ בּוֹדְקִין אוֹתוֹ שֶׁהָיוּ רוֹצִין לִסְמֹךְ – **Rather, [the ones who wished to confer *semichah*] would investigate the one upon whom they wished to confer *semichah,*** אִם הָיָה בָּקִי בְּחָכְמַת הַתּוֹרָה – to determine **if he was proficient in Torah wisdom,** וְאִם הָיָה שִׂכְלוֹ בָּרִיא וְשָׁלֵם – **if his intellect was sound and wholesome,** וְאִם הוּא אִישׁ אוֹהֵב אֱמֶת וְשׂוֹנֵא הָעָוֶל וְכָל עִנְיָנוֹ – **and if he was a man who loves truth, and hates crookedness and all that is associated with it.** וְאַחַר חֲקִירָה רַבָּה בְּעִנְיָנוֹ וּבְחָכְמָתוֹ – Then, **after thoroughly investigating the [candidate's] character and his wisdom,** if he was found to be qualified, אוֹמְרִין לוֹ שְׁלֹשָׁה חֲכָמִים סְמוּכִים אוֹ אֲפִלּוּ כְּשֶׁאֶחָד מֵהֶן סָמוּךְ הֲרֵי אַתָּה סָמוּךְ – **three sages who** themselves have **received *semichah* – or even [three sages] of which** only **one had received *semichah* – say to [the candidate]: "You have hereby received *semichah.*"**[42] This declaration

---

NOTES

39. The term *semichah* means "leaning." This derives from the fact that Moses leaned his hands on Joshua's head when he ordained him (see further). Subsequent ordinations are also referred to as *semichah,* even though, as Chinuch soon writes, the essence of *semichah* is simply ordination from a person who himself has received *semichah,* and it is unnecessary for the one conferring *semichah* to actually lean his hands on the head of the *semichah* candidate.

Chinuch mentions the requirement of *semichah* only for members of the Great Sanhedrin and minor sanhedrins, but *semichah* was actually required even for those appointed to the courts of three that presided in small villages (*Rambam, Hil. Sanhedrin* 4:1).

40. See *Sifrei* to the verse; see also *Seridei Eish* [Mosad HaRav Kook ed.], Vol. IV, p. 138.

41. As Chinuch writes below (at note 50), *semichah* must be conferred in Eretz Yisrael. At the end of the fourth century of the Common Era, the relentless persecution of the Jewish nation by the Roman authorities made it impossible to maintain academies of higher learning in Eretz Yisrael, and the institution of *semichah* came to an end. [Present-day Rabbinic ordination is commonly referred to as "*semichah,*" but this is merely a borrowed term; it does not entitle its holder to judge any type of case for which *semichah* is required.] *Semichah* will be reinstituted in the time of Mashiach (see Insight).

42. Since *semichah* derives its power from being part of an unbroken chain of ordination that goes back to Moses, it must be conferred by someone who himself has received *semichah.* Additionally, *semichah* must be conferred in the presence of a *beis din* of three.

וְקוֹרִין לוֹ רַבִּי מֵאוֹתָהּ שָׁעָה, וְהָיָה לוֹ רְשׁוּת לְאַחַר מִכָּאן לָדוּן אֲפִלּוּ דִּינֵי קְנָסוֹת.[43] וְדִין זָקֵן מֻפְלָג וְסָרִיס וְסוּמָא אֲפִלּוּ בְּאַחַת וּמִי שֶׁאֵין לוֹ בָּנִים שֶׁאֵינָן רְאוּיִין לִהְיוֹת סַנְהֶדְרִין,[44]

alone, without any accompanying action, confers *semichah* upon the candidate. וְקוֹרִין לוֹ רַבִּי מֵאוֹתָהּ שָׁעָה — **From then on, he would be called "Rabbi,"** a title that was reserved for those who received *semichah*, וְהָיָה לוֹ רְשׁוּת לְאַחַר מִכָּאן לָדוּן אֲפִלּוּ דִּינֵי קְנָסוֹת — **and he was authorized to judge even cases involving fines,** which only recipients of *semichah* can adjudicate.[43]

✠§ Additional Laws

Chinuch lists several additional disqualifications for serving on a sanhedrin: וְדִין זָקֵן מֻפְלָג — This mitzvah **also** includes **the law regarding a very old man,** וְסָרִיס — **a *saris*** (i.e., one who is incapable of having children), וְסוּמָא אֲפִלּוּ בְּאַחַת — **one who is blind even in** only **one [eye],** וּמִי שֶׁאֵין לוֹ בָּנִים — **and one who does not have children;** שֶׁאֵינָן רְאוּיִין לִהְיוֹת סַנְהֶדְרִין — namely, **that they are** all **ineligible to be** a member of **a sanhedrin** (the Great Sanhedrin or a lesser Sanhedrin).[44]

A Jewish king is not permitted to sit on either the Great Sanhedrin or a minor sanhedrin.[45] Chinuch

---

NOTES

Therefore, a *beis din* of three is necessary, with at least one of its members having received *semichah* himself (*Chidushei HaGriz, Hil. Sanhedrin* 4:3).

43. There are two categories of monetary payments: *compensations* and *fines*. Examples of "compensations" are the repayment of a loan or restitution for damages. "Fines" refers to cases where the Torah imposes a fixed payment regardless of the amount of the damage (e.g. the 100 *zuz* paid by the מוֹצִיא שֵׁם רָע, *man who defames* his wife; Mitzvah 553), or a payment that exceeds the amount of the damage (e.g. כֶּפֶל, *the double payment* of a thief; see Mitzvah 54).

Under Biblical law, *all* monetary cases, including those involving "compensations," must be adjudicated by judges who have received *semichah*. However, non-ordained judges are empowered as the agents of ordained judges to preside over certain types of monetary cases, such as those involving loans. [Even nowadays, non-ordained judges are considered the agents of the ordained judges of previous times.] They were never authorized to adjudicate cases involving fines; therefore, such cases always remained under the jurisdiction of those who had received *semichah* (see *Rambam, Hil. Sanhedrin* 5:8-9).

From the language of Chinuch, it appears that *semichah* is conferred by simply telling a candidate, "Behold you are ordained"; that which the candidate is subsequently called "Rabbi," and is empowered to adjudicate cases involving fines, are *effects* of the *semichah*. However, *Rambam* (*Hil. Sanhedrin* 4:2, based on *Sanhedrin* 13b) writes that *semichah* is conferred by calling the candidate "Rabbi," and telling him, "You are hereby ordained, and you have the ability to adjudicate even cases involving monetary penalties." For discussion, see *Igros Moshe, Choshen Mishpat* I §1.

44. As mentioned above, in note 7, any sanhedrin of twenty-three can try capital cases. Since the Torah

charges judges in capital cases to do whatever is legally possible to spare the accused, it is crucial that judges on a sanhedrin be men of considerable compassion. We therefore insist that members of a sanhedrin be fathers, because raising children makes a person more compassionate. A very old person and a *saris* (even one who had children and later became a *saris*) are often calloused by the hardships they have experienced and tend to be less compassionate than the average person, which disqualifies them from being appointed to a sanhedrin (*Mahari Korkos, Hil. Shegagos* 13:1; see *Rambam, Hil. Sanhedrin* 2:3; cf. *Rashi, Sanhedrin* 36b). [It is unclear how old one must be to be disqualified. In fact, *Rambam* (ibid. 2:6) writes that it is *preferable* to appoint an "elderly" person to a sanhedrin in the first place. For discussion, see *Bahd Kodesh* (Danon) to *Hil. Sandedrin* ibid., printed in the back of *Kevod Yom Tov* (Danon); *Margaliyos HaYam* and *Einayim LeMishpat* to *Sanhedrin* ibid.]

One who is blind in even one eye is disqualified to serve on a sanhedrin, because members of a sanhedrin must be free of physical blemishes, just as they must be free of genealogical blemishes, as Chinuch wrote above (*Rambam, Hil. Sanhedrin* 2:6,9; see *Yevamos* 101a).

[Chinuch's wording implies that all these people are unfit to *be* on a sanhedrin, meaning that even if someone was appointed while fit but then developed a disqualification (e.g., a judge became "very old"), he would be removed from the sanhedrin. This is in fact the opinion of *Rashba* (*Teshuvos HaRashba,* Vol. VI §191). The language of *Rambam* (*Hil. Sanhedrin* 2:3), however, indicates that these people are unfit to be *appointed* to a sanhedrin initially, but would not be removed from a sanhedrin (*Sheyarei Knesses HaGedolah,* end of *Orach Chaim,* cited in *Sefer HaLikkutim* in Frankel ed. of *Rambam*). See *Minchas Chinuch* §8.]

45. See *Sanhedrin* 18b and *Rambam, Hil. Sanhedrin* 2:4 for the reason.

וְדִין מַלְכֵי בֵּית דָּוִד שֶׁדָּנִין וְדָנִין אוֹתָן[46], אֲבָל לֹא מַלְכֵי יִשְׂרָאֵל לְפִי שֶׁאֵינָם בְּחֶזְקַת כַּשְׁרוּת כְּמוֹ הֵם[47], וְדִין עַד אֵימָתַי יוֹשְׁבִין בְּדִין סַנְהֶדְרֵי גְּדוֹלָה אוֹ קְטַנָּה וּבֵית דִּין שֶׁל שְׁלֹשָׁה[48], וְיֶתֶר פְּרָטֶיהָ מְבֹאָרִין בְּמַסֶּכֶת סַנְהֶדְרִין[49].

וְנוֹהֶגֶת מִצְוָה זוֹ, כְּלוֹמַר סַנְהֶדְרֵי גְּדוֹלָה וּקְטַנָּה וּבֵית דִּין שֶׁל שְׁלֹשָׁה, בְּאֶרֶץ יִשְׂרָאֵל שֶׁיֵּשׁ שָׁם סְמִיכָה, אֲבָל לֹא בְּחוּצָה לָאָרֶץ שֶׁאֵין סוֹמְכִין בְּחוּצָה לָאָרֶץ[50], אֲבָל מִכָּל מָקוֹם כָּל הַנִּסְמָךְ בָּאָרֶץ רָאוּי לִשְׁפֹּט אֲפִלּוּ בְּחוּצָה לָאָרֶץ, וְזֶהוּ מַה שֶּׁאָמְרוּ זִכְרוֹנָם לִבְרָכָה

---

discusses whether a king can serve as a judge in cases that do not require a sanhedrin, e.g., monetary cases:

וְדִין מַלְכֵי בֵּית דָּוִד שֶׁדָּנִין וְדָנִין אוֹתָן – There is **also the law regarding kings of the House of David** (i.e., kings who descend from King David), namely, **that they may serve as judges** in cases that do not require a Sanhedrin, **and they may** themselves **be judged.**[46] אֲבָל לֹא מַלְכֵי יִשְׂרָאֵל – **However, Israelite kings** (i.e., Jewish kings who do not descend from King David) may **not** judge and may not be judged, לְפִי שֶׁאֵינָם בְּחֶזְקַת כַּשְׁרוּת כְּמוֹ הֵם – **because they did not enjoy the presumption of righteousness that [Davidic Kings]** enjoyed, which led to concern that having them stand trial might lead to disastrous results. The Sages therefore forbade judging kings of Israel, which in turn, disqualifies them as judges, since the rule is that only those who are subject to being judged can serve as judges.[47]

Chinuch concludes his discussion of the laws of the mitzvah:

וְדִין עַד אֵימָתַי יוֹשְׁבִין בְּדִין סַנְהֶדְרֵי גְּדוֹלָה אוֹ קְטַנָּה וּבֵית דִּין שֶׁל שְׁלֹשָׁה – Finally, there are **the laws** regarding **how long the Great Sanhedrin, a minor sanhedrin, and a *beis din* of three** are required to **be in session** each day.[48]

וְיֶתֶר פְּרָטֶיהָ – These, **and the remaining details of [this mitzvah],** מְבֹאָרִין בְּמַסֶּכֶת סַנְהֶדְרִין – **are set forth in Tractate Sanhedrin**, Chapters 1, 2, and 4.[49]

Applicability of the Mitzvah

וְנוֹהֶגֶת מִצְוָה זוֹ כְּלוֹמַר סַנְהֶדְרֵי גְּדוֹלָה וּקְטַנָּה וּבֵית דִּין שֶׁל שְׁלֹשָׁה – **This mitzvah, meaning,** the obligation to appoint **a Great Sanhedrin, minor [sanhedrins], and courts of three,** בְּאֶרֶץ יִשְׂרָאֵל שֶׁיֵּשׁ שָׁם סְמִיכָה – **applies** only **in Eretz Yisrael, where *semichah* can be conferred,** אֲבָל לֹא בְּחוּצָה לָאָרֶץ שֶׁאֵין סוֹמְכִין בְּחוּצָה לָאָרֶץ – **but not outside of Eretz Yisrael, since we cannot confer *semichah* outside of Eretz Yisrael.**[50] אֲבָל מִכָּל מָקוֹם כָּל הַנִּסְמָךְ בָּאָרֶץ רָאוּי לִשְׁפֹּט אֲפִלּוּ בְּחוּצָה לָאָרֶץ – **However, anyone who received *semichah* in Eretz Yisrael is qualified to judge** anywhere, **even outside of Eretz Yisrael,** וְזֶהוּ מַה שֶּׁאָמְרוּ זִכְרוֹנָם לִבְרָכָה – **which is** the meaning

---

NOTES

46. The rule is that only those who are subject to being judged can themselves serve as judges. Therefore, if Davidic Kings could not be judged, they could not serve as judges either, even in cases that do not require a sanhedrin (see *Sanhedrin* 19a).

47. *Sanhedrin* ibid. This prohibition was enacted on account of a tragic incident that occurred when King Yannai (a Hasmonean king during the Second Temple Era) was made to stand trial; see *Sanhedrin* ibid. and Mitzvah 122 note 9. As a result of this incident, the Sages forbade having any Israelite king stand trial. For further discussion, see *Kesef Mishneh, Hil. Melachim* 3:7.

48. Minor sanhedrins and courts of three are required to be in session from immediately following the morning prayers until midday. The Great Sanhedrin sat from when the morning *tamid* offering was brought until the afternoon *tamid* offering was brought (*Rambam, Hil. Sanhedrin* 3:1), i.e., from a short while after dawn until several hours after midday (see *Rambam*, beginning of *Hil. Temidin U'Mussafin*). See *Chazon Yechezkel, Sanhedrin* 7:1, for explanation as to why the Great Sanhedrin was expected to be in session during these hours.

49. The laws are codified in *Rambam, Hil. Sanhedrin* Chs. 1-5.

50. *Sanhedrin* 14a; *Rambam, Hil. Sanhedrin* 4:6. [The Gemara does not give a source or reason for this rule. See *Toras Chaim* ad loc. for a possible explanation.]

As mentioned above, note 39, all three types of courts included in this mitzvah must be comprised of judges who have received *semichah*. Therefore, Chinuch contends, the mitzvah does not apply outside of Eretz Yisrael, where *semichah* cannot be conferred; see further.

(מכות ז׳ ע״א) סַנְהֶדְרִין נוֹהֶגֶת בָּאָרֶץ וּבְחוּצָה לָאָרֶץ[51], וְאוּלָם אֵין לָהֶם רְשׁוּת לָדוּן בְּדִינֵי נְפָשׁוֹת לֹא בָּאָרֶץ וְלֹא בְחוּצָה לָאָרֶץ אֶלָּא בִּזְמַן הַבַּיִת וּבִזְמַן שֶׁיִּהְיוּ סַנְהֶדְרִין קְבוּעָה בִּירוּשָׁלַיִם[52].

וְזֹאת אַחַת מִן הַמִּצְווֹת הַמֻּטָּלוֹת עַל הַצִּבּוּר כֻּלָּן שֶׁבְּכָל מָקוֹם וּמָקוֹם[53], וְצִבּוּר הָרָאוּי לִקְבֹּעַ בֵּינֵיהֶם בֵּית דִּין כְּמוֹ שֶׁמְּבֹאָר בְּמַסֶּכֶת סַנְהֶדְרִין (ב׳ ע״ב), וְלֹא קָבְעוּ לָהֶם בִּטְּלוּ עֲשֵׂה זֶה[54], וְעָנְשָׁן גָּדוֹל מְאֹד כִּי הַמִּצְוָה הַזֹּאת עַמּוּד חָזָק בְּקִיּוּם הַדָּת[55].

---

of **that which the Sages, of blessed memory, said** in the Mishnah (*Makkos* 7a): סַנְהֶדְרִין נוֹהֶגֶת בָּאָרֶץ וּבְחוּצָה לָאָרֶץ – The institution of **sanhedrin functions both in Eretz Yisrael and outside of Eretz Yisrael.** That is, the Mishnah teaches that a sanhedrin comprised of judges who received *semichah* in Eretz Yisrael can adjudicate all cases – including capital cases – even outside of Eretz Yisrael. There is, however, no obligation to establish sanhedrins outside of Eretz Yisrael.[51]

While on the topic, Chinuch discusses another rule pertaining to jurisdiction over capital cases: וְאוּלָם אֵין לָהֶם רְשׁוּת לָדוּן בְּדִינֵי נְפָשׁוֹת לֹא בָּאָרֶץ וְלֹא בְחוּצָה לָאָרֶץ – **However, [a sanhedrin] is not empowered to try capital cases**, whether **in Eretz Yisrael or outside of Eretz Yisrael,** אֶלָּא בִּזְמַן הַבַּיִת וּבִזְמַן שֶׁיִּהְיוּ סַנְהֶדְרִין קְבוּעָה בִּירוּשָׁלַיִם – **except when the *Beis HaMikdash* is standing and when the [Great] Sanhedrin is stationed in Jerusalem** in the Chamber of Hewn Stone.[52]

Chinuch addresses who is charged with the obligation to establish courts: וְזֹאת אַחַת מִן הַמִּצְווֹת הַמֻּטָּלוֹת עַל הַצִּבּוּר כֻּלָּן שֶׁבְּכָל מָקוֹם וּמָקוֹם – **This is one of the mitzvos that are incumbent upon the community in each and every location, as a whole.**[53] וְצִבּוּר הָרָאוּי לִקְבֹּעַ בֵּינֵיהֶם בֵּית דִּין כְּמוֹ שֶׁמְּבֹאָר בְּמַסֶּכֶת סַנְהֶדְרִין וְלֹא קָבְעוּ לָהֶם – Therefore, **any community that meets the requirements for establishing a *beis din* in their midst, as set forth in Tractate *Sanhedrin*** (Mishnah 2b), **and did not establish** one **for themselves,** בִּטְּלוּ עֲשֵׂה זֶה – **has violated this mitzvah-obligation,**[54] וְעָנְשָׁן גָּדוֹל מְאֹד כִּי הַמִּצְוָה הַזֹּאת עַמּוּד חָזָק בְּקִיּוּם הַדָּת – **and their punishment is very great, for this mitzvah is a strong pillar for** ensuring **the continued existence of our religion.**[55]

NOTES

51. The Mishnah could have been understood as teaching that the mitzvah to establish sanhedrins applies both in Eretz Yisrael and outside of Eretz Yisrael. However, Chinuch explains, that is *not* the Mishnah's intent. The Mishnah simply teaches that it is possible for a sanhedrin to function outside of Eretz Yisrael, provided that the judges were all properly ordained, i.e., they received *semichah* in Eretz Yisrael.

Although a sanhedrin can function outside of Eretz Yisrael, Chinuch (following *Rambam, Sefer HaMitzvos, Asei* 176) argues that since *semichah,* which is a prerequisite for establishing courts, cannot be conferred outside of Eretz Yisrael, there is no mitzvah-obligation to establish courts outside of Eretz Yisrael. Others contend that even in the Diaspora there *is* a mitzvah-obligation to establish courts comprised of judges who received *semichah* in Eretz Yisrael (*Ramban,* introduction to *Parashas Shoftim;* see *R' Y. F. Perla, Sefer HaMitzvos* of *Rav Saadiah Gaon, Parashah* 1 [Vol. III, p. 212ff.] for discussion).

52. [See *Avodah Zarah* 8b for the source of this rule.] That is, even when the *Beis HaMikdash* is standing, no court is empowered to try capital cases unless the Great Sanhedrin convenes in the *Lishkas HaGazis.* Indeed, forty years before the destruction of the Second Temple, the Great Sanhedrin exiled itself from the *Lishkas HaGazis*, making it impossible for anyone to try capital cases; see *Avodah Zarah* ibid. for why they did this.

53. See General Introduction, where Chinuch writes that certain mitzvos are not incumbent on any particular individual, but on the community as a whole. [Although only the Great Sanhedrin had the authority to appoint judges to minor sanhedrins (see above, note 10), each community was obligated to ensure that the Great Sanhedrin would establish a minor sanhedrin in their community.]

54. As mentioned above (note 6), the Mishnah (*Sanhedrin* 2b) states that only a city with a population of at least 120 adult males is obligated to establish a minor sanhedrin of twenty-three. A community of this size that fails to do so violates this mitvah-obligation. Above, Chinuch taught that even a smaller village is obligated to establish a *beis din* of three. A small village that fails to establish such a court is also in violation of this mitzvah-obligation.

55. As explained above, after note 24.

וְיֵשׁ לָנוּ לִלְמֹד מִזֶּה שֶׁאַף עַל פִּי שֶׁאֵין לָנוּ הַיּוֹם בַּעֲווֹנוֹתֵינוּ סְמוּכִים, שֶׁיֵּשׁ לְכָל קָהָל וְקָהָל שֶׁבְּכָל מָקוֹם לְמַנּוֹת בֵּינֵיהֶם קְצָת מִן הַטּוֹבִים שֶׁבָּהֶם שֶׁיִּהְיֶה לָהֶם כֹּחַ עַל כֻּלָּם לְהַכְרִיחָם בְּכָל מִינֵי הֶכְרֵחַ שֶׁיֵּרָאֶה בְּעֵינֵיהֶם בְּמָמוֹן אוֹ אֲפִלּוּ בַּגּוּף עַל עֲשִׂיַּת מִצְוֹת הַתּוֹרָה וְלִמְנֹעַ מִקִּרְבָּם כָּל דָּבָר מְגֻנֶּה וְכָל הַדּוֹמֶה לוֹ[56]. וְאֵלּוּ[57] הַמְמֻנִּים גַּם כֵּן רָאוּי לְיַשֵּׁר דַּרְכָּם וּלְהַכְשִׁיר מַעֲשֵׂיהֶם וְיָסִירוּ חֶרְפַּת הָעָם מֵעֲלֵיהֶם פֶּן יַעֲנוּ אוֹתָם עַל מוּסָרָם שֶׁיִּטְּלוּ קוֹרָה מִבֵּין עֵינֵיהֶם[58]. וְיִשְׁתַּדְּלוּ תָּמִיד בְּתוֹעֶלֶת חַבְרֵיהֶם הַסְּמוּכִים עֲלֵיהֶם לְלַמְּדָם דֶּרֶךְ הָאֱמֶת וְלָתֵת שָׁלוֹם בְּכָל כֹּחָם בֵּינֵיהֶם, וְיִטְּשׁוּ וְיַנִּיחוּ וְיַשְׁכִּיחוּ מִלִּבָּם כָּל תַּעֲנוּגֵיהֶם, וְעַל זֶה יָשִׁיתוּ לִבָּם וּבוֹ יִהְיֶה רֹב מַחְשְׁבוֹתָם וְעִסְקֵיהֶם[59], וְיִתְקַיֵּם בָּהֶם מִקְרָא שֶׁכָּתוּב (דניאל י״ב, ג׳)

Chinuch discusses the applicability of this mitzvah nowadays:

וְיֵשׁ לָנוּ לִלְמֹד מִזֶּה – **We can learn from this** centrality of the mitzvah to our religion, שֶׁאַף עַל פִּי שֶׁאֵין לָנוּ הַיּוֹם בַּעֲווֹנוֹתֵינוּ סְמוּכִים – **that although nowadays, on account of our sins, we do not have judges who have received** ***semichah,*** and thus the mitzvah-obligation to establish courts does not apply, שֶׁיֵּשׁ לְכָל קָהָל וְקָהָל שֶׁבְּכָל מָקוֹם – **it** still **behooves** the members of **each and every community, regardless of its location,** לְמַנּוֹת בֵּינֵיהֶם קְצָת מִן הַטּוֹבִים שֶׁבָּהֶם שֶׁיִּהְיֶה לָהֶם כֹּחַ עַל כֻּלָּם – **to appoint some of the better among them** as officials **who will have authority over all of them,** לְהַכְרִיחָם בְּכָל מִינֵי הֶכְרֵחַ שֶׁיֵּרָאֶה בְּעֵינֵיהֶם בְּמָמוֹן אוֹ אֲפִלּוּ בַּגּוּף – **to compel them by all means that they deem appropriate, with monetary [sanctions] or even with physical [force],** עַל עֲשִׂיַּת מִצְוֹת הַתּוֹרָה – **to perform the mitzvos of the Torah,** וְלִמְנֹעַ מִקִּרְבָּם כָּל דָּבָר מְגֻנֶּה וְכָל הַדּוֹמֶה לוֹ – **and to keep out of their midst all unseemliness and anything that resembles it.**[56]

Chinuch describes how these leaders should conduct themselves:

וְאֵלּוּ[57] הַמְמֻנִּים גַּם כֵּן רָאוּי לְיַשֵּׁר דַּרְכָּם וּלְהַכְשִׁיר מַעֲשֵׂיהֶם – **These appointees should also straighten their own paths and perfect their own actions,** וְיָסִירוּ חֶרְפַּת הָעָם מֵעֲלֵיהֶם – **making themselves invulnerable to the scorn of the people,** פֶּן יַעֲנוּ אוֹתָם עַל מוּסָרָם שֶׁיִּטְּלוּ קוֹרָה מִבֵּין עֵינֵיהֶם – **lest [the people] respond to their rebuke** by telling them **that** ***they*** **should "remove the beam from between** ***their*** **eyes,"** i.e., rectify their own shortcomings.[58] וְיִשְׁתַּדְּלוּ תָּמִיד בְּתוֹעֶלֶת חַבְרֵיהֶם הַסְּמוּכִים עֲלֵיהֶם – **Also, [these leaders] should constantly endeavor to further the welfare of their fellow citizens who depend upon them,** לְלַמְּדָם דֶּרֶךְ הָאֱמֶת וְלָתֵת שָׁלוֹם בְּכָל כֹּחָם בֵּינֵיהֶם – **teaching them the path of truth, and fostering peace among them with all their might.** וְיִטְּשׁוּ וְיַנִּיחוּ וְיַשְׁכִּיחוּ מִלִּבָּם כָּל תַּעֲנוּגֵיהֶם – **[These leaders] should forsake, abandon, and make their hearts forget all their** own **pleasures,** וְעַל זֶה יָשִׁיתוּ לִבָּם – **and** instead **concentrate on [seeking the welfare of others],** וּבוֹ יִהְיֶה רֹב מַחְשְׁבוֹתָם וְעִסְקֵיהֶם – **channeling most of their thoughts and activities to this.**[59] וְיִתְקַיֵּם בָּהֶם מִקְרָא שֶׁכָּתוּב – **And** if these leaders conduct themselves in this way, **in them will be fulfilled the verse that states** (*Daniel* 12:3):

NOTES

56. For discussion regarding the ability of *beis din* nowadays to compel performance of mitzvos, see *Ketzos HaChoshen* 3:1 and *Minchas Chinuch* 557:20; see also *Shulchan Aruch, Choshen Mishphat* §2 with commentaries.

Chinuch implies that appointing judges nowadays is merely the proper course of action, but there is no formal obligation to do so. *Rabbeinu Yerucham* (*Sefer Meisharim,* end of 1:4), however, writes that there is a Rabbinic obligation to establish courts nowadays; see also *Bach, Choshen Mishpat* 1:3 and *Urim VeTumim, Urim* 1:1.

57. Text follows *Minchas Yitzchak* ed.

58. The Gemara (*Arachin* 16b; see *Rashi* there ד״ה קיסם) describes the difficulty in successfully rebuking others when one's own conduct is lacking, as follows: If one says to his fellow, "Remove the splinter from between your eyes" (i.e., "Refrain from a minor transgression"), his fellow can retort, "Remove the *beam* from between *your* eyes!" (i.e., "*You* should refrain from a *major* transgression"). See also *Bava Basra* 15b.

59. When a person senses that someone is genuinely concerned for his welfare, he is much more likely to take that person's rebuke and guidance to heart. Therefore, Chinuch counsels those in positions that require them to teach and rebuke others to devote themselves to the welfare of their community, so that they can more successfully fulfill their duties.

וְהַמַּשְׂכִּלִים יַזְהִרוּ כְּזֹהַר הָרָקִיעַ וּמַצְדִּיקֵי הָרַבִּים כַּכּוֹכָבִים לְעוֹלָם וָעֶד.

"וְהַמַּשְׂכִּלִים יַזְהִרוּ כְּזֹהַר הָרָקִיעַ וּמַצְדִּיקֵי הָרַבִּים כַּכּוֹכָבִים לְעוֹלָם וָעֶד" — *The wise will shine like the radiance of the firmament, and those who teach righteousness to the multitudes [will shine] like the stars forever and ever.*

⮜§ Insight: The Semichah Controversy of 5298

As we learned in this mitzvah, many judicial functions are restricted to judges who have received *semichah*. *Semichah* is required not only to try capital cases and those involving *malkus*, but even to adjudicate certain monetary cases, such as those involving fines (see note 43). We also learned that a scholar receives *semichah* by being ordained by someone who himself has received *semichah*, and that this is how *semichah* was conferred from the time of Moses until relentless Roman persecution in the period following the destruction of the Second Temple made it impossible to continue doing so (see above, at note 41).

Although the lack of sages who have received *semichah* makes it impossible to confer *semichah* in the conventional manner, *Rambam* (*Hil. Sanhedrin* 4:11) suggests that it is nevertheless possible to renew *semichah* nowadays. He writes that it appears to him that if all the sages in Eretz Yisrael agree to appoint judges and confer *semichah* upon them, those scholars are considered to have received *semichah*, and can serve as fully-ordained judges.

In the year 5298 [1538], the Rabbis of Tzefas (Safed) attempted to renew *semichah* based on the view of *Rambam*. They conferred *semichah* upon their leader, R' Yaakov Beirav (*Mahari Beirav*), who eventually conferred *semichah* upon four other sages, including R' Yosef Karo (author of *Shulchan Aruch*) and R' Moshe of Trani (*Mabit*). Confident in the correctness of their actions, the Rabbis of Tzefas sent a messenger to simply inform the Rabbis of Jerusalem of their initiative, but to their dismay, the Chief Rabbi of Jerusalem, R' Levi ibn Habib (*Maharalbach*) strongly disagreed with them. Another great scholar in Jerusalem, R' Moshe de Castro (who, in his youth, had studied under *Mahari Beirav*) also had several reservations, which he expressed in a letter to the Rabbis of Tzefas. A fierce exchange between *Maharalbach* and *Mahari Beirav* ensued (*Maharalbach* wrote three lengthy treatises on the subject; *Mahari Beirav* wrote two), with each side claiming that the other was making a grave mistake. At some point during the controversy, the leading Rabbi in Egypt, R' David ibn Zimra (*Radvaz*), was consulted, and he wrote a responsum, siding with the Rabbis of Jerusalem. [We do not have this responsum, but *Radvaz* summarizes his arguments in his commentary to *Rambam, Hil. Sanhedrin* 4:11.] Ultimately, the view of the Rabbis of Jerusalem prevailed, and the *semichah* initiative died out. What follows is a brief synopsis of several of the objections that were raised by the opponents of the attempt to renew *semichah*. [The relevant treatises of *Mahari Beirav* and *Maharalbach* are appended to *Teshuvos Maharalbach* as Responsum 147. In 5765, they were printed as a separate volume, under the title, *Semichas Zekeinim*. R' Moshe de Castro's letter to the Rabbis of Tzefas and *Mahari Beirav's* response to that letter were included in that volume as appendices.]

One of the strongest objections raised against the renewal of *semichah* emerged from the words of *Rambam* himself. After presenting his novel idea, *Rambam* adds the words, וְהַדָּבָר צָרִיךְ הֶכְרֵעַ, *this matter requires a final decision.* Apparently, *Rambam* himself was not convinced that his method for renewing *semichah* would be effective. If *Rambam*, the only source for this idea, doubted its efficacy, what right does anyone have to actually implement it? (*Radvaz* to *Hil. Sanhedrin* 4:11; *Semichas Zekeinim*, p. 235; see also *Chazon Ish, Choshen Mishpat, Likkutim* 1:1).

Maharalbach (*Semichas Zekeinim*, pp. 31-32) argued that even if *Rambam* had maintained that his method was unquestionably effective, there was still a compelling reason to refrain from implementing it. Nowadays, we establish the beginning of months and declare leap years based on the calendar fixed by R' Hillel HaNasi in the year 4118, because we do not have judges who are qualified for these tasks (see Mitzvah 4, at notes 20-24). If, however, we had qualified judges, *beis din* would be obligated to establish the beginning of months based on the testimony of witnesses and to declare leap years based on a specific set of variables. Now, *Rambam* and *Ramban* (see *Sefer HaMitzvos, Asei* 153) disagree about the type of judges who are qualified for these duties. *Rambam*

maintains that three judges from the Great Sanhedrin are required, while *Ramban* maintains that any three judges who have received *semichah* are sufficient. *Maharalbach* points out that *Ramban* (see glosses to *Sefer HaMitzvos, Asei* 153) also disagrees with *Rambam* about the possibility of renewing *semichah* nowadays. Taking these two disputes into account, it would be irresponsible to renew *semichah* based on *Rambam's* suggestion, because doing so would create doubt as to whether we should continue relying on the fixed calendar of R' Hillel HaNasi. For if *Rambam's* method for renewing *semichah* is effective, but *Ramban* is correct about the requirements for establishing the beginning of months (i.e., any three judges with *semichah* suffice), *beis din* would be required to assume responsibility for establishing the beginning of months and declaring leap years. But if *Rambam's* method for renewing *semichah* is ineffective (like *Ramban* held) or if *Rambam* is correct about the requirements for establishing new months (i.e., three judges from the Great Sanhedrin are required), then we must continue to rely upon the fixed calendar of R' Hillel HaNasi even if we conferred *semichah* on several judges. Since such doubt would wreak havoc on the Jewish calendar, we must refrain from adopting *Rambam's* method for renewing *semichah*.

In the view of those who opposed the renewal of *semichah*, there was another reason to question the efficacy of the *semichah* conferred by the Rabbis of Tzefas, even if *Rambam* meant his suggestion as a definitive ruling. The halachah is that *semichah* can be conferred only upon a sage who is sufficiently knowledgeable to issue rulings in *all* areas of the Torah (see *Rambam, Hil. Sanhedrin* 4:8). *Radvaz* and *Maharalbach* (*Semichas Zekeinim*, pp. 30-31) both questioned whether, even in their time, any sage met this requirement. *Maharalbach* was particularly concerned about the lack of detailed knowledge concerning the laws of *kiddush hachodesh* (establishment of the new month), an area of halachah about which there is little written in the Gemara.

Procedural objections to the *semichah* of *Mahari Beirav* were also raised. As mentioned above, *Rambam* speaks of *all* the sages in Eretz Yisrael agreeing to confer *semichah*. Although we often apply the principle of רֻבּוֹ כְּכֻלּוֹ, *a majority is considered equivalent to the whole*, both *Maharalbach* (*Semichas Zekeinim*, pp. 11-12) and R' Moshe de Castro (ibid., p. 235) argued that it is quite possible that *Rambam's* language should be taken literally, and that the consensus of *all* the sages in Eretz Yisrael is necessary to renew *semichah*. [See *Maharalbach* ibid. for several reasons why this might be true.] If so, the *semichah* conferred by the Rabbis in Tzefas was invalid even though they were easily the majority, since the Rabbis of Jerusalem did not consent to it.

Moreover, the opponents argued, even if majority consent was enough, the *semichah* conferred by the Rabbis of Tzefas would still be invalid, for it is axiomatic that the majority of a judicial body prevails only when their opinion emerges from deliberation by all of the judges. If, however, a majority reaches a decision without having discussed the matter with the minority, their opinion does not prevail. Since the Rabbis of Tzefas conferred *semichah* without first consulting the Rabbis of Jerusalem, their actions should not carry the weight of the majority (*Semichas Zekeinim*, pp. 7-8, 235).

In the time of Mashiach, the institution of *semichah* will need to be reestablished, so that the judges of that time should be able to adjudicate all laws and fix the calendar. According to the view of the Rabbis of Tzefas, *semichah* can be renewed at that time by having all the sages of Eretz Yisrael agree to confer it upon someone. But according to the Rabbis of Jerusalem, how will *semichah* be reinstituted in the time of Mashiach? Those Rabbis addressed this issue and explained that, as is well known, the prophet Elijah will reappear near the time when Mashiach comes (see *Rambam, Hil. Melachim* 12:2). Elijah possesses *semichah* in an unbroken chain from Moses, for Elijah received *semichah* from his teacher, Achiyah HaShiloni, when he prophesied for the Jewish people during the First Temple Era (see *Rambam*, Introduction to *Mishneh Torah*). Thus, Elijah will be able to confer *semichah* upon those who are qualified to receive it in the time of Mashiach (*Radvaz* ibid.; *Semichas Zekeinim*, pp. 27, 67; see also *Chidushei Maran Riz HaLevi, Parashas Pinchas*). Alternatively, Mashiach himself will be authorized by Hashem to confer *semichah*, just as Moses, our Teacher, was authorized by Hashem to begin the chain of *semichah* in his time (*Semichas Zekeinim* ibid.).

מִצְוָה תצב: שֶׁלֹּא לִטַּעַת אִילָן בַּמִּקְדָּשׁ[2,1]

שֶׁלֹּא לִנְטֹעַ אִילָנוֹת בַּמִּקְדָּשׁ אוֹ אֵצֶל הַמִּזְבֵּחַ, וְעַל זֶה נֶאֱמַר (דברים ט״ז, כ״א) לֹא תִטַּע לְךָ אֲשֵׁרָה כָּל עֵץ אֵצֶל מִזְבַּח ה׳ אֱלֹהֶיךָ וְגוֹ׳[3].

בְּטַעַם אִסּוּר זֶה כָּתַב הָרַמְבַּ״ם ז״ל (סה״מ ל״ת י״ג) לְפִי שֶׁכָּךְ הָיוּ עוֹשִׂים עוֹבְדֵי עֲבוֹדָה זָרָה בְּבָתֵּי עֲבוֹדָה זָרָה שֶׁלָּהֶם שֶׁנּוֹטְעִין שָׁם אִילָנוֹת יָפִים[4], וּכְדֵי לְהַרְחִיק כָּל הַדּוֹמֶה לָהֶם מִמַּחֲשֶׁבֶת בְּנֵי אָדָם הַבָּאִים לַעֲבוֹדַת הָאֵל בָּרוּךְ הוּא בַּמָּקוֹם הַהוּא הַנִּבְחָר[5] נִמְנַעְנוּ מִלִּנְטֹעַ שָׁם כָּל אִילָן[6], וְקָרוֹב הוּא עַל צַד הַפְּשָׁט[7].

Mitzvah 492

The Prohibition to Plant a Tree in the Beis HaMikdash

לֹא תִטַּע לְךָ אֲשֵׁרָה כָּל עֵץ אֵצֶל מִזְבַּח ה׳ אֱלֹהֶיךָ אֲשֶׁר תַּעֲשֶׂה לָּךְ
You shall not plant for yourselves any asheirah tree near the Altar of HASHEM, Your God, that you shall make for yourself (*Deuteronomy* 16:21).

In ancient times, idolaters would plant a prominent tree near their altar, either to beautify the area or as a signpost to direct passersby to the location of their worship. This tree was called an *asheirah*.[1] In this mitzvah we are commanded not to plant such a tree adjacent to the Altar of Hashem.[2]

שֶׁלֹּא לִנְטֹעַ אִילָנוֹת בַּמִּקְדָּשׁ אוֹ אֵצֶל הַמִּזְבֵּחַ – We are commanded **not to plant trees in the** ***Beis HaMikdash*** **or near the Altar.** וְעַל זֶה נֶאֱמַר ״לֹא תִטַּע לְךָ אֲשֵׁרָה כָּל עֵץ אֵצֶל מִזְבַּח ה׳ אֱלֹהֶיךָ וְגוֹ׳ ״ **– Regarding this it is stated** (*Deuteronomy* 16:21): ***You shall not plant for yourselves any asheirah tree near the Altar of HASHEM, Your God,*** etc.[3]

Underlying Purpose of the Mitzvah

בְּטַעַם אִסּוּר זֶה כָּתַב הָרַמְבַּ״ם ז״ל – **In** explaining **the reason for this prohibition,** ***Rambam*****, of blessed memory, wrote** (*Sefer HaMitzvos, Lo Saaseh* 13) לְפִי שֶׁכָּךְ הָיוּ עוֹשִׂים עוֹבְדֵי עֲבוֹדָה זָרָה בְּבָתֵּי עֲבוֹדָה זָרָה שֶׁלָּהֶם – that it is **because this is what the idolaters would do** in ancient times **in their houses of idol worship,** שֶׁנּוֹטְעִין שָׁם אִילָנוֹת יָפִים – that is, **they would plant beautiful trees there.**[4] וּכְדֵי לְהַרְחִיק כָּל הַדּוֹמֶה לָהֶם – **And in order to distance anything similar to [their worship]** מִמַּחֲשֶׁבֶת בְּנֵי אָדָם הַבָּאִים לַעֲבוֹדַת הָאֵל בָּרוּךְ הוּא בַּמָּקוֹם הַהוּא הַנִּבְחָר – **from the thoughts of the people who come for the service of the Almighty, blessed is He, in that chosen place,** the *Beis HaMikdash*,[5] נִמְנַעְנוּ מִלִּנְטֹעַ שָׁם כָּל אִילָן – **we are forbidden from planting any tree there.**[6] וְקָרוֹב הוּא עַל צַד הַפְּשָׁט – **This** reason indeed **seems the probable** explanation **according to the simple approach.**[7]

NOTES

1. In other contexts, an *asheirah* refers to a tree that was actually worshiped (see *Exodus* 34:13). [For discussion regarding the root of the word, and how it is applied to the worshiped tree or the tree planted near an idolatrous altar, see *Ramban* and *HaKesav VeHaKabbalah* to verse.]

2. The above translation of the verse, and the description of the mitzvah derived from it, follows *Rambam* (*Sefer HaMitzvos, Lo Saaseh* 13 and *Hil. Avodah Zarah* 6:9-10), and *Ramban* (to the verse), whom Chinuch follows in this mitzvah. Cf. *Rashi* to the verse.

3. As Chinuch clarifies below, planting a tree anywhere in the *Beis HaMikdash*, even in the Courtyard, is referred to by this verse as "near" the Altar of Hashem.

4. In *Sefer HaMitzvos, Rambam* implies that this was done to beautify the place of idol worship. In *Hil. Avodah Zarah* (6:9), *Rambam* writes that the trees served as site-markers to show people where to gather for worship.

5. Scripture often refers to the *Beis HaMikdash* as "the chosen place"; see for example, *Deuteronomy* 17:10.

6. Since trees are a feature of idol worship, having a tree in the *Beis HaMikdash*, even if it is planted to beautify the area, could divert the attention of the worshipers from the pure service of Hashem.

7. For other approaches to the reason for this mitzvah, see *Rashbam* and *Gur Aryeh* to the verse.

מִדִּינֵי הַמִּצְוָה מַה שֶּׁאָמְרוּ זִכְרוֹנָם לִבְרָכָה (ספרי כאן) שֶׁאֵין הָאִסּוּר בְּנוֹטֵעַ אִילָן אֵצֶל הַמִּזְבֵּחַ מַמָּשׁ כִּפְשַׁט הַכָּתוּב, אֶלָּא אַף הַנּוֹטֵעַ בְּכָל הָעֲזָרָה לוֹקֶה, שֶׁבְּכָל הָעֲזָרָה נִקְרָא אֵצֶל מִזְבֵּחַ[8]. וּבֵין הַנּוֹטֵעַ אִילָן מַאֲכָל אוֹ אִילָן סְרָק, הַכֹּל בִּכְלַל הָאִסּוּר וְלוֹקֶה עֲלֵיהֶם. וְעוֹד אָמְרוּ חֲכָמִים (שם) לִגְדֹּר אִסּוּר זֶה, שֶׁאָסוּר לַעֲשׂוֹת אַכְסַדְרָאוֹת שֶׁל עֵץ בַּמִּקְדָּשׁ כְּדֶרֶךְ שֶׁעוֹשִׂין בְּנֵי אָדָם בְּחַצְרוֹתֵיהֶם וְאַף עַל פִּי שֶׁהוּא בְּבִנְיָן וְלֹא בִּנְטִיעָה, שֶׁנֶּאֱמַר כָּל עֵץ[9], אֶלָּא כָּל הַסְּבָכוֹת וְאַכְסַדְרָאוֹת הַיּוֹצְאוֹת מִן הַכְּתָלִים שֶׁהָיוּ בַּמִּקְדָּשׁ שֶׁל אֶבֶן הָיוּ[10],

Laws of the Mitzvah

מִדִּינֵי הַמִּצְוָה מַה שֶּׁאָמְרוּ זִכְרוֹנָם לִבְרָכָה – **Among the laws of the mitzvah** is **that which [the Sages], of blessed memory, have stated** (*Sifrei* to verse), שֶׁאֵין הָאִסּוּר בְּנוֹטֵעַ אִילָן אֵצֶל הַמִּזְבֵּחַ מַמָּשׁ כִּפְשַׁט הַכָּתוּב – **that the prohibition is not** limited to **planting a tree literally adjacent to the Altar, as** might be understood from **the simple reading of the verse;** אֶלָּא אַף הַנּוֹטֵעַ בְּכָל הָעֲזָרָה לוֹקֶה – **rather, even one who plants** a tree anywhere **in the entire Courtyard** of the *Beis HaMikdash* violates this prohibition and **is liable to *malkus*** for it, שֶׁבְּכָל הָעֲזָרָה נִקְרָא אֵצֶל מִזְבֵּחַ – **because the entire** area of the **Courtyard** is also **called "near the Altar."**[8] וּבֵין הַנּוֹטֵעַ אִילָן מַאֲכָל אוֹ אִילָן סְרָק – **Also, whether one plants a fruit tree or a nonfood tree,** הַכֹּל בִּכְלַל הָאִסּוּר וְלוֹקֶה עֲלֵיהֶם – **they are all included in the prohibition and one is liable to *malkus* for** planting **them** in the *Beis HaMikdash.*

וְעוֹד אָמְרוּ חֲכָמִים לִגְדֹּר אִסּוּר זֶה – **The Sages further stated** (ibid.), **as a safeguard for this prohibition,** שֶׁאָסוּר לַעֲשׂוֹת אַכְסַדְרָאוֹת שֶׁל עֵץ בַּמִּקְדָּשׁ – **that it is forbidden to construct wooden colonnades in the *Beis HaMikdash*** כְּדֶרֶךְ שֶׁעוֹשִׂין בְּנֵי אָדָם בְּחַצְרוֹתֵיהֶם – **in the manner that people make in their courtyards,** וְאַף עַל פִּי שֶׁהוּא בְּבִנְיָן וְלֹא בִּנְטִיעָה – **even though it is** wood that is **built and not** a tree that is **planted.** שֶׁנֶּאֱמַר "כָּל עֵץ" – Scriptural support is found **for** this in the verse of the mitzvah where **it is stated**: *You shall not plant for yourselves **"any"** asheirah **tree**;* this can be understood as prohibiting building any wooden structure in the *Beis HaMikdash.*[9] אֶלָּא כָּל הַסְּבָכוֹת וְאַכְסַדְרָאוֹת הַיּוֹצְאוֹת מִן הַכְּתָלִים שֶׁהָיוּ בַּמִּקְדָּשׁ – **Instead, all the pavilions and colonnades that extended from the walls in** the Courtyard of **the *Beis HaMikdash*** שֶׁל אֶבֶן הָיוּ – **were** made **of stone,** not wood.[10]

NOTES

8. The verse mentions the Altar specifically, since trees planted in places of worship are usually associated with the Altar. The prohibition, however, applies to the entire Courtyard, which, for the purpose of this mitzvah, is considered "near the Altar" (*Malbim, Leviticus* 1:16 §86; see *Minchas Chinuch* §1).

9. Scripture uses the word עֵץ for both trees and wood. The Sages found support for their decree against building wood into the structure of the *Beis HaMikdash* from the words כָּל עֵץ, which could also be translated as *any wood*. This, however, is not a Biblical law, but a Scriptural allusion to a Rabbinic prohibition (*asmachta*). The Biblical prohibition applies only to actually planting a tree, not to building structures of wood (*Minchas Chinuch* §4, *Kesef Mishneh* to *Rambam, Hil. Avodah Zarah* 6:9; cf. *Seder Mishnah,* cited in *Minchas Chinuch* ibid.). [It should be noted that this appears to be the subject of a Tannaic dispute in *Sifrei* ibid. (There are variant readings of the words of the pertinent *Sifrei*.)] *Rashi* to the verse rules that building wooden structures does in fact violate a Biblical prohibition. For further sources of Rishonim and Acharonim regarding this issue, see *Sefer HaMafte'ach* to *Rambam,* ibid. 6:9-10.

10. In the Courtyard of the *Beis HaMikdash,* there was a colonnade consisting of a series of stone columns set parallel to the Courtyard wall. These were topped by a roof that extended from the columns to the wall, creating a portico that ran around the entire interior perimeter of the Courtyard. This portico was used to shelter those standing beneath it, and to protect utensils that were stored there (*Tamid* 28a-b, with *Rosh* and *Mefareish*).

[Many Acharonim maintain that the restriction against using wood pertains only to *additions* to the main Temple structure. The structure itself, however, may contain wood. In fact, the first *Beis HaMikdash* was entirely faced with cedar wood: הַכֹּל אֶרֶז אֵין אֶבֶן נִרְאָה, *Everything was cedar wood; no stone was visible* (*I Kings* 6:18); see *Arbaah Turei Even,* cited in *Sefer HaLikkutim* in Frankel ed. of *Rambam, Hil. Avodah Zarah* ibid.; *Hagahos Yaavetz* to *Tamid* 28b, and *Lechem Shamayim* to *Middos* 3:7 and 5:4.

Furthermore, only permanent wooden structures are prohibited. Temporary structures such as platforms

וְיֶתֶר פְּרָטֶיהָ מְבֹאָרִים בְּמַסֶּכֶת תָּמִיד (כ״ח ע״ב).[11]

וְנוֹהֵג אִסּוּר זֶה בֵּין בִּזְכָרִים בֵּין בִּנְקֵבוֹת[12], וַאֲפִלּוּ בַּזְּמַן הַזֶּה הַנּוֹטֵעַ אִילָן בְּכָל הָעֲזָרָה חַיָּב מַלְקוּת[13].

וְיֶתֶר פְּרָטֶיהָ מְבֹאָרִים בְּמַסֶּכֶת תָּמִיד — These, **and the remaining details of [this mitzvah] are set out in Tractate** *Tamid* (28b).[11]

☞ Applicability of the Mitzvah ☜

וְנוֹהֵג אִסּוּר זֶה בֵּין בִּזְכָרִים בֵּין בִּנְקֵבוֹת — **This prohibition applies both to men and women.**[12] וַאֲפִלּוּ בַּזְּמַן הַזֶּה הַנּוֹטֵעַ אִילָן בְּכָל הָעֲזָרָה חַיָּב מַלְקוּת — **Even nowadays, one who plants a tree** anywhere **in the entire** area of the **Courtyard** of the *Beis HaMikdash* **is liable to** *malkus*.[13]

NOTES

built for the king to use in the *Hakheil* ceremony (Mitzvah 612) could be built of wood (*Raavad*, glosses to *Rambam* ibid.; see also *Raavad* to *Hil. Beis HaBechirah* 1:9).]

11. The laws are codified in *Rambam, Hil. Avodah Zarah* 6:9-10 and *Hil. Beis HaBechirah* 1:9.

12. This is in accordance with the general rule pertaining to mitzvah-prohibitions.

13. Chinuch follows the ruling of *Rambam* (*Hil. Beis*

HaBechirah 6:15), that the original sanctification of Jerusalem and the *Beis HaMikdash* remains in place even after its destruction (see also end of Mitzvos 184, 363, and 390). Accordingly, the prohibition to plant a tree in that area remains in effect nowadays as well. *Raavad* (to *Hil. Beis HaBechirah* 6:14), who disagrees with *Rambam* regarding the sanctification of Jerusalem and the *Beis HaMikdash*, would maintain that this prohibition no longer applies nowadays (*Minchas Chinuch* §1).

◀§ Insight: Planting Trees in Front of Synagogues

While Chinuch writes that the prohibition against planting trees in the *Beis HaMikdash* is still applicable today in the area of the *Beis HaMikdash*, it would seem that this mitzvah has little other practical application today. Many Acharonim, however, raise the question of whether it is permitted to plant trees at the entrance to any synagogue, even today.

Scripture refers to synagogues as "minor sanctuaries," implying a level of holiness to synagogues akin to the holiness of the *Beis HaMikdash* itself (*Ezekiel* 11:16, as expounded in *Megillah* 29a). This characterization has many practical ramifications. For example, just as there is an obligation to revere the *Beis HaMikdash* (Mitzvah 254), there is also an obligation to act reverently in a synagogue. [See Insight to that mitzvah for discussion of the extent of this obligation.] As pertains to this mitzvah, therefore, it is reasonable to ask: Does the prohibition against planting trees in the *Beis HaMikdash* have a parallel prohibition, whether Biblical or Rabbinic, against planting a tree inside or at the entrance to a synagogue?

Maharam Schik was presented this very question by a congregation that was considering planting trees in its synagogue courtyard to beautify the area, as well as to provide some shelter from the elements. Was this permitted? In his response (*Teshuvos, Orach Chaim* §78), *Maharam Schik* rules that it is forbidden, as an extension of the prohibition of our mitzvah. He explains that the reasons set forth to explain this mitzvah, e.g., that it was the practice of idolaters outside of their places of worship, and that we must distance ourselves from such customs in places of Divine worship (see notes 4-6, above), apply equally to planting trees at the entrance of synagogues, which are also places of Divine worship.

Similarly, R' Akiva Eiger, in his glosses to *Shulchan Aruch* (*Orach Chaim* 150:1), cites an opinion forbidding the planting of trees outside of synagogues. [See also *R' David Arma'ah,* quoted in *Sefer HaLikkutim* of Frankel edition of *Rambam, Hilchos Avodah Zarah* 6:9; *Derech Chochmah* (R' Chaim Kanievski), *Hil. Beis HaBechirah* 1:55, citing *Chazon Ish; Teshuvos Tzitz Eliezer* 14:26.] According to this opinion, this is one of the Biblical laws of the *Beis HaMikdash* that are extended to synagogues by Rabbinic decree.

[Interestingly, *Maharam Schik* notes further that even without this specific prohibition, it is

inadvisable to maintain a garden-like area adjacent to a synagogue. Based on inferences from many places in the Gemara, he writes that this should be forbidden as it can encourage people to engage in recreation when they should be praying or studying, and may lead to improper social gatherings; see there for his full discussion.]

Other Acharonim maintain, however, that the Biblical prohibition has no counterpart, even in Rabbinic law, with regard to the synagogue. They note that there is no source in the Gemara or *Shulchan Aruch* that applies this prohibition to the synagogue, and we are not in a position to decide on our own which of the prohibitions that apply to the *Beis HaMikdash* apply to a synagogue. In fact, there is evidence from some early authorities (who debate whether a synagogue orchard must be treated with holiness), that it was common to have trees as part of the synagogue property (see *Parashas HaKesef, Hil. Avodah Zarah* 6:6; *Teshuvos Meishiv Davar* II:14 ד"ה ואשר; *Teshuvos Maharsham,* I:127 and VI:5; *Teshuvos Chavatzeles HaSharon* [תנינא] §62).

In *Teshuvos Binyan Tzion* (§9), R' Yaakov Ettlinger addresses a related question: A congregation bought a property to extend the courtyard of their synagogue, and the property contained trees. One of these was a nut tree, which, if the purchase would be concluded, would be positioned at the entrance to the synagogue. Some in the congregation wished to cut down the tree to avoid the halachic question of having a tree at the entrance to a synagogue. Now, Mitzvah 529 forbids cutting down a fruit tree. But, as Chinuch notes there, when there is a valid need for the tree to be cut, it is often permitted. The question here was whether the fact that there would be a tree at the entrance of the synagogue was enough of a necessity to permit cutting down the tree.

R' Ettlinger maintains that there is insufficient proof from the Gemara or other sources to apply the prohibition of planting a tree in the *Beis HaMikdash* to planting a tree at the entrance to a synagogue, and it is certainly not enough to warrant the cutting down of a fruit tree. While it is true that the reasons for the prohibition may be applicable to the synagogue as well, this is not sufficient legal ground to extend a prohibition beyond what is stated in its verse. He argues that the Rishonim provide reasons for the mitzvos only to give people some taste of the meaning of the mitzvah; the reasons may not be used to limit or extend the reach of the mitzvah beyond that which is detailed in the Gemara.

In addition, R' Ettlinger suggests that even if it would in fact be forbidden to plant a tree in a synagogue courtyard, there would be no obligation to cut down a tree that was planted prior to the synagogue's acquisition of the land, or if the tree grew by itself. The Biblical prohibition even with regard to the *Beis HaMikdash* is only not to actually *plant* a tree; it does not demand that we cut down an existing tree.

It should be noted, however, that even without this particular prohibition, there may be another reason to forbid having a tree at the synagogue entrance. *Maharsham* and *Chavatzeles HaSharon* (ibid.) note that in a locale where the custom of idolaters is to have a tree in the front of their places of worship, it may be forbidden to keep such a tree in front of a synagogue due to Mitzvah 262, the mitzvah-prohibition against adopting the customs of idolaters.

מִצְוָה תצג: שֶׁלֹּא לְהָקִים מַצֵּבָה

שֶׁלֹּא לְהָקִים מַצֵּבָה בְּשׁוּם מָקוֹם[1], וְעַל זֶה נֶאֱמַר (דברים ט״ז, כ״ב) וְלֹא תָקִים לְךָ מַצֵּבָה אֲשֶׁר שָׂנֵא ה׳ אֱלֹהֶיךָ[2]. וְעִנְיַן הַמַּצֵּבָה שֶׁאָסְרָה תּוֹרָה כָּתַב הָרַמְבַּ״ם ז״ל (בפ״ו מעבודה זרה ה״ו) שֶׁהוּא בִּנְיָן גָּבוֹהַּ שֶׁל אֲבָנִים אוֹ שֶׁל עָפָר שֶׁהָיָה מִנְהַג הָעוֹבְדִים עֲבוֹדָה זָרָה לִבְנוֹת וּלְהִתְקַבֵּץ עָלָיו לַעֲבוֹדָתָם הָרָעָה[3]. וְלָכֵן הִרְחִיקָנוּ הַכָּתוּב שֶׁלֹּא נַעֲשֶׂה כָּמוֹהוּ אֲנַחְנוּ וַאֲפִלּוּ לַעֲבֹד עָלָיו הָאֵל בָּרוּךְ הוּא, כְּדֵי לְהַרְחִיק וּלְהַשְׁכִּיחַ כָּל עִנְיַן עֲבוֹדָה זָרָה מִבֵּין עֵינֵינוּ וּמִמַּחֲשַׁבְתֵּנוּ, כַּטַּעַם שֶׁכָּתַבְנוּ בְּסָמוּךְ בִּנְטִיעַת אִילָן בַּמִּקְדָּשׁ עַל דַּעַת הָרַמְבַּ״ם ז״ל[4].

Mitzvah 493
The Prohibition to Erect a "Matzeivah"

וְלֹא תָקִים לְךָ מַצֵּבָה אֲשֶׁר שָׂנֵא ה׳ אֱלֹהֶיךָ

You shall not erect for yourselves a matzeivah, which HASHEM, your God, detests (*Deuteronomy* 16:22).

The term "*matzievah*," literally, *structure*, in this verse refers to a structure that was, in earlier days, associated with idol worship, and is now forbidden in other contexts as well. Chinuch will further define the term below.

שֶׁלֹּא לְהָקִים מַצֵּבָה בְּשׁוּם מָקוֹם – We are commanded **not to erect a *matzeivah* in any location.**[1] וְעַל זֶה נֶאֱמַר – **Regarding this it is stated** (*Deuteronomy* 16:22): "וְלֹא תָקִים לְךָ מַצֵּבָה אֲשֶׁר שָׂנֵא ה׳ אֱלֹהֶיךָ" – ***You shall not erect for yourselves a matzeivah, which HASHEM, your God, detests.***[2]

Underlying Purpose of the Mitzvah

Chinuch defines the mitzvah and, based on the definition, provides an underlying purpose: וְעִנְיַן הַמַּצֵּבָה שֶׁאָסְרָה תּוֹרָה כָּתַב הָרַמְבַּ״ם ז״ל – **The description of the *matzeivah* that the Torah forbids** with this mitzvah is, as ***Rambam*, of blessed memory, wrote** (*Hil. Avodah Zarah* 6:6; *Sefer HaMitzvos*, *Lo Saaseh* 11), שֶׁהוּא בִּנְיָן גָּבוֹהַּ שֶׁל אֲבָנִים אוֹ שֶׁל עָפָר – **that it is a tall structure of stones or earth,** שֶׁהָיָה מִנְהַג הָעוֹבְדִים עֲבוֹדָה זָרָה לִבְנוֹת וּלְהִתְקַבֵּץ עָלָיו לַעֲבוֹדָתָם הָרָעָה – **which it was the practice of idolaters to build, and to gather near it for their evil service.**[3] וְלָכֵן הִרְחִיקָנוּ הַכָּתוּב שֶׁלֹּא נַעֲשֶׂה כָּמוֹהוּ אֲנַחְנוּ – It is **for this reason** that **Scripture distanced** us from this practice, commanding **that we ourselves should not construct** a *matzeivah* **like it** וַאֲפִלּוּ לַעֲבֹד עָלָיו הָאֵל בָּרוּךְ הוּא – **even for** the purpose of **worshiping the Almighty, blessed is He, with it,** כְּדֵי לְהַרְחִיק וּלְהַשְׁכִּיחַ כָּל עִנְיַן עֲבוֹדָה זָרָה מִבֵּין עֵינֵינוּ וּמִמַּחֲשַׁבְתֵּנוּ – **so as to distance and to eliminate anything related to idolatry from our attention and thoughts.** כַּטַּעַם שֶׁכָּתַבְנוּ בְּסָמוּךְ בִּנְטִיעַת אִילָן בַּמִּקְדָּשׁ עַל דַּעַת הָרַמְבַּ״ם ז״ל – This is **similar to the reason that we wrote just above,** in the previous mitzvah, **regarding** the prohibition against **planting a tree in the *Beis HaMikdash*, following the view of *Rambam*, of blessed memory.**[4]

NOTES

1. This is in contrast with the previous mitzvah, which forbids the planting of an *asheirah* only in the vicinity of the Altar. Below, Chinuch further defines the kind of structure that is forbidden by this mitzvah.

2. Hashem detests the use of such structures in His service because they are a feature of idolatry, as Chinuch explains immediately.

3. In *Hil. Avodah Zarah*, this structure is described as a gathering point for people to worship an idol. In *Sefer HaMitzvos*, *Rambam* mentions that the idol would actually be placed upon the structure. Either way, this *matzeivah* played a prominent role in idolatry.

4. Since the *matzeivah* was a regular feature of idolatrous practices, the Torah forbids us to use it even in the service of Hashem. This is similar to that which *Rambam* explains in the previous mitzvah regarding

וְאֵין בִּכְלַל אִסּוּר זֶה בִּנְיַן הַמִּזְבֵּחַ, כִּי עָלָיו נֶאֱמַר בְּפֵרוּשׁ (שם כ״ז, ו׳) אֲבָנִים שְׁלֵמוֹת תִּבְנֶה אֶת מִזְבַּח וְגוֹ׳, אֶלָּא שֶׁלֹּא נַעֲשֶׂה כֵּן בִּשְׁאָר מְקוֹמוֹת[5].

דִּינֵי הַמִּצְוָה קְצָרִים[6].

וְנוֹהֵג אִסּוּר זֶה בְּכָל מָקוֹם וּבְכָל זְמַן, בִּזְכָרִים וּנְקֵבוֹת[7].

וְעוֹבֵר עַל זֶה וְהֵקִים מַצֵּבָה עַל דַּעַת לַעֲבֹד עָלֶיהָ וַאֲפִלּוּ לַה׳ חַיָּב מַלְקוּת.

Having defined the *matzeivah* of this verse as any raised structure built for the purpose of worship, Chinuch explains why the Altar of the *Beis HaMikdash* and *Mishkan*, which seems to meet this criterion, is not forbidden by this mitzvah:

וְאֵין בִּכְלַל אִסּוּר זֶה בִּנְיַן הַמִּזְבֵּחַ – **The building of the Altar** in the *Beis HaMikdash* (and *Mishkan*) **is not included in this prohibition,** כִּי עָלָיו נֶאֱמַר בְּפֵרוּשׁ ״אֲבָנִים שְׁלֵמוֹת תִּבְנֶה אֶת מִזְבַּח וְגוֹ׳ ״ – **for it is stated explicitly about that** structure (ibid. 27:6): ***Of whole stones shall you build the Altar,* etc.** Thus, Scripture clearly allows, and in fact mandates, the building of the Altar, explicitly creating an exception to this prohibition. אֶלָּא שֶׁלֹּא נַעֲשֶׂה כֵּן בִּשְׁאָר מְקוֹמוֹת – This mitzvah therefore does not prohibit the Altar of the *Beis Hamikdash,* but **rather,** dictates **that we do not construct such** a structure **in other places.**[5]

Laws of the Mitzvah

דִּינֵי הַמִּצְוָה קְצָרִים – **The laws of the mitzvah are brief.**[6]

Applicability of the Mitzvah

וְנוֹהֵג אִסּוּר זֶה בְּכָל מָקוֹם וּבְכָל זְמַן – **This prohibition applies in every location and in all times,** בִּזְכָרִים וּנְקֵבוֹת – **to men and women.**[7]

וְעוֹבֵר עַל זֶה – **One who violates this** mitzvah וְהֵקִים מַצֵּבָה עַל דַּעַת לַעֲבֹד עָלֶיהָ – **and erects a *"matzeivah"* with the intention to worship upon it,** וַאֲפִלּוּ לַה׳ – **even** if the purpose is **to** worship **Hashem,** חַיָּב מַלְקוּת – **is liable to *malkus.***

NOTES

planting trees in the *Beis HaMikdash*, i.e., so that the idea of idolatry not be raised at all in the place of Hashem's service. [See Insight regarding the permissibility of structures that are not used for worship according to the opinion of *Rambam*.]

While Chinuch follows *Rambam's* view of this prohibition, other Rishonim maintain that the *matzeivah* referred to in this verse is actually another form of altar, only that a standard altar (מִזְבֵּחַ) is constructed of many stones or of earth, whereas the *matzeivah* is constructed of a single stone. According to this opinion, the Torah forbids bringing offerings upon this kind of altar since the single-stone altar is closely associated with idolatry; see *Rashi* and *Ramban* to the verse for further elaboration.

5. [It would seem to emerge from Chinuch's discussion that one may not construct a private altar (*bamah*; pl. *bamos*) anywhere. Now, while private altars were indeed forbidden throughout most of history (see Mitzvos 186, 439-440), there were short periods when offerings upon private altars were in fact permitted. *Tzafnas Pane'ach* (*Mahadura Basra,* p. 89) suggests that this mitzvah would require one who erected a *bamah* during the times that this was permitted to dismantle it after the offering had been brought; see there for further discussion.]

6. The laws are included in the basic definition of the mitzvah set out above. *Rambam* codifies the brief laws of this mitzvah in *Hil. Avodah Zarah* 6:6.

7. It applies in Eretz Yisrael and the Diaspora, and whether the *Beis HaMikdash* is standing or not. It applies to both men and women in accordance with the general rule regarding mitzvah-prohibitions.

Insight: Memorial Monuments

Throughout their exile, the Jewish people have not been strangers to communal attacks and massacres, from the carnage of the Crusades to the devastation of the Cossacks to the pogroms of Czarist Russia. Yet after such events, it was generally possible to bring the victims to Jewish burial, giving the surviving communities a place to mourn and remember their dead within the confines

of their community's cemeteries. In the unprecedented tragedy of the Holocaust, however, even this measure of comfort was denied the survivors. Whole communities were wiped out, leaving no earthly remains at which to mourn, no lasting remembrance of their lives, or their deaths.

After the War, many Jewish communities sought some way to memorialize the events of the Holocaust and its victims, and specifically to preserve the memories of their own community members. The idea arose in some communities to erect monuments that would serve as testaments to the lives and events of the past. These would consist of a simple stone structure upon which, perhaps, some inscription would be engraved. [Items constructed in a specific form are subject to the prohibition against creating images; see Mitzvah 39.] The halachic question then arose: Does erecting such a monument violate the prohibition of this mitzvah: לֹא תָקִים לְךָ מַצֵּבָה, *Do not erect for yourselves a matzeivah*? A number of halachic Responsa were written on this subject. Here we present some of the arguments discussed in these works.

First, it is important to distinguish between this monument and gravestones, which are a part of every Jewish cemetery. There is no question that it is permitted to erect a stone upon a grave. Indeed the relative of the deceased is responsible to provide for the gravestone among the other burial needs (see *Shulchan Aruch, Even HaEezer* 89:1). The essential difference is that people gather at a cemetery due to the presence of the grave that is there; the gravestone merely marks the location of the grave. The question of a *matzeivah* arises only with regard to structures that do not mark any other physical presence, but serve purely to memorialize an event or person of the past.

Now, according to some Rishonim, the *matzeivah* prohibited by this mitzvah refers only to a single-stone Altar used to bring offerings to Hashem (see note 4). According to this opinion, there is obviously no halachic issue with a stone memorial. The question is pertinent only according to *Rambam*, who defines the mitzvah as forbidding "a structure around which people would gather, even if it is for the purpose of serving Hashem" (*Hil. Avodah Zarah* 6:6; *Sefer HaMitzvos, Lo Saaseh* 11). This general definition would seem to include any structure at all, set up for any purpose, around which people may occasionally gather for some kind of reflection.

Divrei Yirmiyahu (commentary to *Rambam*, ibid.) indeed writes that according to *Rambam*, the essential characteristic of a forbidden structure is that it is constructed for no other purpose than to focus the attention of people upon an idea or event. *Rambam* explains that this kind of structure is forbidden even if it is built for the exalted purpose of serving Hashem. The prohibition therefore certainly includes any other kind of memorial monument, such as one erected to remember those fallen in war.

Many authorities, however, take a different approach. They maintain that *Rambam's* definition specifies the purpose of the structure as one involving worship. That is, the Torah prohibits us from erecting a structure to use in our service of Hashem in the same way that the idolaters used their structures as an element of their worship. It does not pertain to structures that are purely secular in nature, around which no worship or service occurs. Thus, memorial monuments for departed people or past events are permitted.

Indeed, there are examples of this kind of monument in Scripture. Avshalom, son of King David, had no sons, and he therefore erected a monument in order that "his name be remembered" (*II Samuel* 18:18). R' Avraham ben HaRambam, in speaking of this structure, notes that it was not a violation of the prohibition against erecting a *matzeivah*, since it was intended only as a memorial, without any connection to worship (*Teshuvos R' Avraham ben HaRambam* §29).

An even earlier instance of this kind of monument is described in the book of *Joshua* (Ch. 22). The tribes of Reuven, Gad, and part of the tribe of Menasheh took their portion in Eretz Yisrael in territory on the eastern side of the Jordan (Transjordan). After participating in the conquest of Eretz Yisrael, before returning to their own territory, they erected what appeared to be a large stone altar on the western banks of the river. Since having an Altar outside of the central *Mishkan* was forbidden, the Jewish people sent an emissary, Pinchas, to investigate this action. Upon inquiring, he was told that the structure was not erected to be an actual altar for worship, but merely to serve as a symbol, a sign for future generations that the two-and-a-half tribes on the eastern banks of the Jordan were still an integral part of the Jewish people. We thus find an actual instance of a stone monument that was not meant for worship but only to represent an idea, and was undisputedly permitted.

Chinuch, too, appears to endorse this definition of the prohibition when he writes at the end of

the mitzvah that one is liable for this prohibition when he erects a *matzeivah* "with the intention to worship upon (or near) it." Accordingly, a memorial monument for people or communities that have been lost would be permitted.

The preceding pertains only to the question of whether such monuments are halachically permissible in light of this mitzvah. Some authorities have pointed out, however, that even if permitted, investing in these kinds of memorials do not take priority over other forms of memorials. With the vast number of Torah scholars, students, and yeshivos that were lost in the Holocaust, the very lifeblood of our nation was severely diminished. This loss calls for eternalizing their memory primarily with Torah, such as by rebuilding Torah institutions throughout our communities (see *Mishpatei Uziel*, Vol. II, *Yoreh Deah* 22:4).

These and many other aspects of this topic can be found in *Teshuvos Minchas Yitzchak* I:29; *Maarchei Lev* [Tzirelson], *Yoreh Deah* §42; and *Mishpatei Uziel* ibid., at length. See also *Teshuvos Shemesh Marpeh* [R' S. R. Hirsch] §47, for a related discussion.

מִצְוָה תצד: שֶׁלֹּא לְהַקְרִיב קָרְבָּן בַּעַל מוּם עוֹבֵר[1]

שֶׁנִּמְנַעְנוּ שֶׁלֹּא נַקְרִיב קָרְבָּן מִבְּהֵמָה שֶׁיִּהְיֶה בָּהּ מוּם[2], וַאֲפִלּוּ הוּא מוּם עוֹבֵר, וְעַל זֶה נֶאֱמַר (דברים י״ז, א׳) לֹא תִזְבַּח לַה׳ אֱלֹהֶיךָ שׁוֹר וָשֶׂה אֲשֶׁר יִהְיֶה בוֹ מוּם וְגוֹ׳, וְנִתְבָּאֵר בְּסִפְרִי (כאן) שֶׁבְּבַעַל מוּם עוֹבֵר הַכָּתוּב מְדַבֵּר[3].

מִשָּׁרְשֵׁי הַמִּצְוָה כָּתַבְתִּי בְּסֵדֶר אֱמֹר אֶל הַכֹּהֲנִים בְּמִצְוַת עֲשֵׂה ד׳ (מצוה רפ״ו)[4] וּבְלָאו י״ב[5]

Mitzvah 494

The Prohibition to Bring an Offering That Has a Temporary Blemish

לֹא תִזְבַּח לַה׳ אֱלֹהֶיךָ שׁוֹר וָשֶׂה אֲשֶׁר יִהְיֶה בוֹ מוּם כֹּל דָּבָר רָע כִּי תוֹעֲבַת ה׳ אֱלֹהֶיךָ הוּא
You shall not slaughter for HASHEM, your God, an ox or a lamb or kid in which there will be a blemish, any bad thing, because that is an abomination of HASHEM, your God (*Deuteronomy* 17:1).

Parashas Emor featured four separate mitzvah-prohibitions against consecrating, slaughtering, throwing the blood, and burning the sacrificial parts (*emurin*) of an animal with a permanent blemish (Mitzvah 285, 289, 288, and 290, respectively). Our mitzvah applies all of these prohibitions to an animal with a temporary blemish as well.[1]

שֶׁנִּמְנַעְנוּ שֶׁלֹּא נַקְרִיב קָרְבָּן מִבְּהֵמָה שֶׁיִּהְיֶה בָּהּ מוּם – **We are prohibited to make an offering of an animal that has a blemish,**[2] וַאֲפִלּוּ הוּא מוּם עוֹבֵר – **even if it is a temporary blemish.** וְעַל זֶה נֶאֱמַר – **Regarding this it is stated** (*Deuteronomy* 17:1): ״לֹא תִזְבַּח לַה׳ אֱלֹהֶיךָ שׁוֹר וָשֶׂה אֲשֶׁר יִהְיֶה בוֹ מוּם וְגוֹ׳ ״ – ***You shall not slaughter for HASHEM, your God, an ox or a lamb or kid in which there will be a blemish,*** *any bad thing,* **etc.;** וְנִתְבָּאֵר בְּסִפְרִי שֶׁבְּבַעַל מוּם עוֹבֵר הַכָּתוּב מְדַבֵּר – **and it is set forth in *Sifrei*** (to the verse) **that the verse is speaking of [an animal] with a temporary blemish.**[3]

Underlying Purpose of the Mitzvah

מִשָּׁרְשֵׁי הַמִּצְוָה – **Some of the underlying purposes of the mitzvah** כָּתַבְתִּי בְּסֵדֶר אֱמֹר אֶל הַכֹּהֲנִים – **I have** already **written in *Parashas Emor,*** בְּמִצְוַת עֲשֵׂה ד׳ – **in Mitzvah-obligation 4** (Mitzvah 286),[4] וּבְלָאו י״ב – **and in** Mitzvah-**prohibition 12** (Mitzvah 277);[5]

NOTES

1. See *Rambam, Hil. Issurei HaMizbe'ach* 1:5, with *Radvaz* and *Kesef Mishneh*; *Minchas Chinuch* §1. [See, however, *Minchas Chinuch* 285:1, who raises doubts as to whether *Rambam* and Chinuch prohibit *consecrating* a temporarily blemished animal, if one waits until it heals to actually offer it. Cf. *Minchas Yitzchak* 285:6; *Chazon Ish, Temurah* (*Kodashim*) 31:4. See below, note 15.]

In any event, *Ramban* (glosses to *Sefer HaMitzvos, Lo Saaseh* §95) disputes *Rambam*'s (and Chinuch's) counting of this prohibition as a separate mitzvah. He maintains that our verse merely teaches that the same four prohibitions that apply to an animal with a permanent blemish apply to one with a temporary blemish as well. See *Megillas Esther* and *Lev Same'ach* ad loc.

2. As indicated in the introduction to the mitzvah, "to make an offering" here refers to consecrating the animal, slaughtering it for an offering, throwing its blood, and burning its sacrificial parts. All these actions are included in the prohibition. [At the end of the mitzvah, Chinuch will address slaughtering specifically.]

3. *Sifrei* derives this from the words ***any*** *bad thing*.

4. This is the obligation to offer only unblemished animals. [In the original order of Chinuch, the mitzvah-obligations of each *parashah* were listed before all of its mitzvah-prohibitions (see General Introduction, note 7). Mitzvah 286 is the fourth mitzvah-obligation in *Parashas Emor*.] Chinuch explains there that the offerings are meant to inspire and focus one's thoughts on Hashem, and an unblemished animal is more conducive to bringing about this inspiration.

5. This is the prohibition against a blemished person entering the Sanctuary. Chinuch there explains that

(מצוה רע״ז), וְגַם בְּלָאו י׳ (מצוה ער״ה) יֵשׁ רֶמֶז מִזֶּה[6].

מִדִּינֵי הַמִּצְוָה, כְּגוֹן הַחִלּוּקִים שֶׁאָמְרוּ זִכְרוֹנָם לִבְרָכָה (בכורות ל״ז ע״ב) שֶׁהֵן בִּבְהֵמָה בֵּין מוּם קָבוּעַ לְמוּם עוֹבֵר, שֶׁכָּל בְּהֵמָה שֶׁיֵּשׁ בָּהּ מוּם קָבוּעַ נִפְדֵּית[7] וְגַם מִצְוַת עֲשֵׂה לִפְדּוֹתָהּ כְּמוֹ שֶׁבֵּאַרְנוּ בְּסֵדֶר רְאֵה אָנֹכִי עֲשֵׂה ד׳ (מצוה תמ״א), וְאִם יֵשׁ לָהּ מוּם עוֹבֵר לֹא קְרֵבָה וְלֹא נִפְדֵּית אֶלָּא מַמְתִּינִין לָהּ עַד שֶׁתִּתְרַפֵּא אוֹ עַד שֶׁתִּסְתָּאֵב[8].

וּבְעִנְיַן מוּמִין קְבוּעִין וּמִסְפָּרָם כְּבָר כָּתַבְתִּי קְצָת מִזֶּה כְּמִנְהָגִי בְּסֵדֶר אֱמֹר אֶל הַכֹּהֲנִים עֲשֵׂה ד׳ בְּסִימָן רס״ו (מצוה רפ״ו)[9]. וְהִנֵּה אַזְכִּיר לְךָ מַהוּ מוּם עוֹבֵר, כְּגוֹן גָּרָב לַח[10]

וְגַם בְּלָאו י׳ יֵשׁ רֶמֶז מִזֶּה – **and there is also a hint of this** in our discussion of this matter **in** Mitzvah-**prohibition 10** there (Mitzvah 275).[6]

Laws of the Mitzvah

מִדִּינֵי הַמִּצְוָה – **Among the laws of the mitzvah** are, כְּגוֹן הַחִלּוּקִים שֶׁאָמְרוּ זִכְרוֹנָם לִבְרָכָה שֶׁהֵן בִּבְהֵמָה בֵּין מוּם קָבוּעַ לְמוּם עוֹבֵר – **for example, the differences that [the Sages], of blessed memory, stated** (*Bechoros* 37b) **that there are between** an animal that has **a permanent blemish and** one that has **a temporary blemish.** שֶׁכָּל בְּהֵמָה שֶׁיֵּשׁ בָּהּ מוּם קָבוּעַ נִפְדֵּית – One difference is **that any animal that has a permanent blemish may be redeemed,**[7] וְגַם מִצְוַת עֲשֵׂה לִפְדּוֹתָהּ כְּמוֹ שֶׁבֵּאַרְנוּ בְּסֵדֶר רְאֵה אָנֹכִי עֲשֵׂה ד׳ – **and it is even a mitzvah-obligation to redeem it, as we explained in *Parashas Re'eh*,** Mitzvah-**obligation 4** (Mitzvah 441); וְאִם יֵשׁ לָהּ מוּם עוֹבֵר לֹא קְרֵבָה וְלֹא נִפְדֵּית – **whereas if [an animal] has a temporary blemish, it is neither offered** (as per our mitzvah) **nor redeemed** (as stated in *Menachos* 101a); אֶלָּא מַמְתִּינִין לָהּ עַד שֶׁתִּתְרַפֵּא אוֹ עַד שֶׁתִּסְתָּאֵב – **rather, we wait for it** either **until it heals**, and then offer it, **or until it incurs a *permanent* blemish,** and then redeem it.[8]

Chinuch provides examples of temporary blemishes in animals:

וּבְעִנְיַן מוּמִין קְבוּעִין וּמִסְפָּרָם – **With regard to the description of permanent blemishes and the** total **number of [these blemishes],** כְּבָר כָּתַבְתִּי קְצָת מִזֶּה כְּמִנְהָגִי בְּסֵדֶר אֱמֹר אֶל הַכֹּהֲנִים עֲשֵׂה ד׳ בְּסִימָן רס״ו – **I have already written a little about this, as is my practice, in *Parashas Emor*,** Mitzvah-**obligation 4, in Chapter 266** (Mitzvah 286).[9] וְהִנֵּה אַזְכִּיר לְךָ מַהוּ מוּם עוֹבֵר – **I will now indicate to you what a temporary blemish is:** כְּגוֹן גָּרָב לַח – It is, **for example, a moist *garav*;**[10]

NOTES

a blemished person clashes with the aura of grandeur and majesty with which the *Beis HaMikdash* is suffused. The same would hold true for a blemished animal brought as an offering.

6. This is the prohibition against a blemished Kohen serving in the *Beis HaMikdash*. There, Chinuch explains that it is desirable that a person who brings an offering have uplifting and purifying thoughts at the time of the offering procedure, as well as feel an attachment to the service he is observing. If a blemished, odd-looking Kohen were to make his offering, a person might become disenchanted or lose his concentration on those thoughts. The same would apply to bringing a blemished animal as an offering. See also *R' S. R. Hirsch* cited in note 8 there.

7. That is, its owner transfers the sanctity of the animal onto money, and the money is used to purchase another animal to be offered in its place. The blemished animal retains no sanctity and its meat may be eaten as *chullin* (unsanctified meat). See beginning of Mitzvah 441.

8. For other distinctions between a permanent blemish and a temporary blemish in an animal, see *Chullin* 130a and *Bechoros* 14a-b; *Rambam, Hil. Issurei HaMizbe'ach* 1:11. [An additional distinction may be that it is not prohibited to *consecrate* a temporarily blemished animal; see discussion in note 1.]

9. Chinuch teaches there that there are seventy-three permanent blemishes that disqualify an animal; fifty of them apply to people as well (in terms of disqualifying them from serving in the *Beis HaMikdash*), and twenty-three are unique to animals. See *Rambam, Hil. Bi'as HaMikdash* Ch. 7, and *Hil. Issurei HaMizbe'ach* 2:2-5 for a specific listing. See also Mitzvah 275, at notes 21-30, for a general listing of the fifty blemishes that are common to humans and animals.

10. A *garav* is a type of skin eruption, or boil. Chinuch here refers to the *garav* that is mentioned in *Leviticus* 21:20, and in the Mishnah (*Bechoros* 41a), among the blemishes that disqualify a Kohen from service. It is moist both on the outside and on the inside, and is

וַחֲזָזִית שֶׁאֵינוֹ מִצְרִית[11], וְכֵן מַיִם הַיּוֹרְדִים מִן הָעַיִן וְאֵינוֹ חֹלִי קָבוּעַ[12] וְכַיּוֹצֵא בָּזֶה[13]. וְיֶתֶר דִּינֵי הַמִּצְוָה בְּעִנְיַן מוּם קָבוּעַ וּמוּם עוֹבֵר מְבֹאָרִים בְּמַסֶּכֶת בְּכוֹרוֹת (פרק ששי)[14]**.**

וְנוֹהֵג אִסּוּר זֶה בִּזְמַן הַבַּיִת, כִּי אָז בְּיָדֵינוּ לְהַקְרִיב קָרְבָּנוֹת[15]. וּבִכְלַל אִסּוּר זֶה שֶׁל זְבִיחָה בֵּין כֹּהֲנִים אוֹ יִשְׂרְאֵלִים זְכָרִים וּנְקֵבוֹת, שֶׁהַשְּׁחִיטָה בְּקָרְבָּנוֹת כְּשֵׁרָה בְּזָרִים[16], וּכְמוֹ כֵן נֹאמַר שֶׁעוֹבְרִים עָלֶיהָ אִם עֲשָׂאוּהָ שֶׁלֹּא כַדִּין[17].

וַחֲזָזִית שֶׁאֵינוֹ מִצְרִית – or a *chazazis* that is not of the **Egyptian** variety;[11] **וְכֵן מַיִם הַיּוֹרְדִים מִן הָעַיִן וְאֵינוֹ חֹלִי קָבוּעַ – or water coming out of the eye, when this is not a chronic illness;**[12] **וְכַיּוֹצֵא בָּזֶה – or** any blemish that is **similar to this.**[13]

וְיֶתֶר דִּינֵי הַמִּצְוָה בְּעִנְיַן מוּם קָבוּעַ וּמוּם עוֹבֵר – These laws **and the rest of the laws of the mitzvah regarding a permanent blemish and a temporary blemish מְבֹאָרִים בְּמַסֶּכֶת בְּכוֹרוֹת – are set forth in Tractate *Bechoros*** (Chapter 6).[14]

Applicability of the Mitzvah

וְנוֹהֵג אִסּוּר זֶה בִּזְמַן הַבַּיִת – This prohibition applies only **when the *Beis HaMikdash*** is standing, **כִּי אָז בְּיָדֵינוּ לְהַקְרִיב קָרְבָּנוֹת – for we then have the ability to make offerings.**[15] **וּבִכְלַל אִסּוּר זֶה שֶׁל זְבִיחָה בֵּין כֹּהֲנִים אוֹ יִשְׂרְאֵלִים זְכָרִים וּנְקֵבוֹת – Both Kohanim and Yisraelim, whether men or women,** are **included in this prohibition** as it pertains to **slaughtering** an animal with a temporary blemish, **שֶׁהַשְּׁחִיטָה בְּקָרְבָּנוֹת כְּשֵׁרָה בְּזָרִים – for slaughtering of offerings by non-Kohanim,** both men and women, **is valid.**[16] **וּכְמוֹ כֵן נֹאמַר שֶׁעוֹבְרִים עָלֶיהָ אִם עֲשָׂאוּהָ שֶׁלֹּא כַדִּין – As such, we say that they violate [our prohibition] if they perform [the slaughtering] unlawfully,** that is, if they slaughter an offering with a blemish.[17]

NOTES

curable (see Mitzvah 275, note 6). This is in contrast to the *garav* that appears on the Torah's list of blemishes that disqualify an animal (*Leviticus* 22:22), which is *dry* both on the outside and on the inside, and the *garav* that is mentioned in the *Tochachah* (Admonishment) in *Deuteronomy* (28:27), which is moist on the outside and dry on the inside. These latter two types of *garav* have no cure (see *Bechoros* there).

11. A *chazazis* is another type of boil. Chinuch means that the *chazazis* to which we refer here is not the same type as the one with which the Egyptians were afflicted in the sixth of the Ten Plagues [שְׁחִין, *boils*] (see *Rashi, Bechoros* 41a ד״ה חזזית המצרית). That type of *chazazis* has no cure. We refer, rather, to the standard, temporary type of *chazazis*.

12. This is a condition in which the eye constantly waters [obstructing the animal's vision] (*Rashi, Bechoros* 38b ד״ה מים; *Rav* to Mishnah, *Bechoros* 6:3). It can be either a permanent, chronic condition or a temporary one.

13. See *Rambam, Hil. Issurei HaMizbe'ach* 2:7-8.

14. The laws are codified in *Rambam, Hil. Issurei HaMizbe'ach* Chs. 1-2.

15. In note 1 above, we mentioned that *Minchas Chinuch* (285:1) raises the possibility that, according to Chinuch (and *Rambam*), the prohibition to consecrate a blemished animal does not apply to temporary blemishes. One of his proofs is from this segment in Chinuch. Chinuch writes here that this mitzvah applies only in the time of the *Beis HaMikdash*, presumably referring to all the aspects of bringing an offering that are included in this mitzvah. In Mitzvah 285, however, which is the prohibition against consecrating a *permanently* blemished animal, Chinuch writes that the mitzvah applies in all times, since one can consecrate an animal as an offering even when the *Beis HaMikdash* is not standing (though it is Rabbinically forbidden to do so; see *Avodah Zarah* 13a-b). Now, if consecration of a temporarily blemished animal is forbidden, and is thus included in our mitzvah, why does Chinuch issue this blanket statement that the mitzvah applies only if the *Beis HaMikdash* is standing? This seems to indicate, *Minchas Chinuch* argues, that Chinuch does not include consecration in our mitzvah. [See, however, *Minchas Yitzchak* and *Chazon Ish* cited in note 1.]

16. Mishnah, *Zevachim* 31b.

17. The aspect of the prohibition pertaining to consecrating an animal with a blemish — *if* this is applicable to an animal with a temporary blemish (see notes 1 and 15 above) — would apply to non-Kohanim as well. The aspect of the prohibition pertaining to throwing the blood or burning the fats of blemished offerings, however, would apply only to Kohanim, since only they are qualified to perform these services.

מִצְוָה תצה

מִצְוָה לִשְׁמֹעַ מִכָּל בֵּית דִּין הַגָּדוֹל שֶׁיַּעַמְדוּ לָהֶן לְיִשְׂרָאֵל בְּכָל זְמַן

לִשְׁמֹעַ בְּקוֹל בֵּית דִּין הַגָּדוֹל וְלַעֲשׂוֹת כָּל מַה שֶּׁיְּצַוּוּ אוֹתָנוּ בְּדַרְכֵי הַתּוֹרָה בְּאָסוּר וּמֻתָּר וְטָמֵא וְטָהוֹר וְחַיָּב וּפָטוּר וּבְכָל דָּבָר שֶׁיֵּרָאֶה לָהֶם שֶׁהוּא חִזּוּק וְתִקּוּן בְּדָתֵנוּ[1], וְעַל זֶה נֶאֱמַר (דברים י״ז, י׳) **וְעָשִׂיתָ עַל פִּי הַדָּבָר אֲשֶׁר יַגִּידוּ לְךָ, וְנִכְפַּל בְּסָמוּךְ** (שם, י״א) **לְחִזּוּק הַדָּבָר,**

Mitzvah 495

The Obligation to Heed the Directives of the Great Sanhedrin in All Times

וְעָשִׂיתָ עַל פִּי הַדָּבָר אֲשֶׁר יַגִּידוּ לְךָ מִן הַמָּקוֹם הַהוּא אֲשֶׁר יִבְחַר ה׳ וְשָׁמַרְתָּ לַעֲשׂוֹת כְּכֹל אֲשֶׁר יוֹרוּךָ. עַל פִּי הַתּוֹרָה אֲשֶׁר יוֹרוּךָ וְעַל הַמִּשְׁפָּט אֲשֶׁר יֹאמְרוּ לְךָ תַּעֲשֶׂה לֹא תָסוּר מִן הַדָּבָר אֲשֶׁר יַגִּידוּ לְךָ יָמִין וּשְׂמֹאל

You shall do in accordance with the word that they will tell you, from that place which HASHEM will choose, and you shall be careful to do in accordance with all that they teach you. In accordance with the teaching that they will teach you, and by the judgment that they will say to you, shall you do; you shall not deviate from the word that they will tell you, right or left (*Deuteronomy* 17:10-11).

As Chinuch explained in his Introduction to this work (see Vol. I, pp. 23-27), the Oral Law, which includes the interpretation of the Torah and the many particulars of the mitzvos, was received from Hashem by Moses, who transmitted it to the Sages of Israel, who in turn passed it on to the sages of subsequent generations. In earlier times, the Great Sanhedrin, which consisted of seventy-one of the greatest sages of the generation, was the authority on the Oral Law, and from that body, law and judgment emanated to all of Israel. Every Jew must therefore accept the rulings of the Sanhedrin as the foundation of his religious observance (*Rambam, Hil. Mamrim* 1:1).

Our mitzvah expresses this requirement as a mitzvah-obligation. The next mitzvah contains a corresponding mitzvah-prohibition against deviating from the words of the Sanhedrin.

לִשְׁמֹעַ בְּקוֹל בֵּית דִּין הַגָּדוֹל – We are commanded **to heed the voice of the Great Sanhedrin,** **וְלַעֲשׂוֹת כָּל מַה שֶּׁיְּצַוּוּ אוֹתָנוּ בְּדַרְכֵי הַתּוֹרָה** – **and to do whatever they instruct us, with regard to** all **Torah matters.** **בְּאָסוּר וּמֻתָּר** – That is, **with regard to** whether something is **prohibited or permitted,** **וְטָמֵא וְטָהוֹר** – whether something is ***tamei* or *tahor*,** **וְחַיָּב וּפָטוּר** – **and,** in cases involving either punishment or monetary payment, whether a person is **liable or exempt.** **וּבְכָל דָּבָר שֶׁיֵּרָאֶה לָהֶם שֶׁהוּא חִזּוּק וְתִקּוּן בְּדָתֵנוּ** – **Also,** one must heed their directive **in any matter that** they enact because it **appears to them that it would serve to strengthen or enhance our religious** observance.[1] **וְעַל זֶה נֶאֱמַר** – **With regard to** all **this, it is stated** (*Deuteronomy* 17:10): **"וְעָשִׂיתָ עַל פִּי הַדָּבָר אֲשֶׁר יַגִּידוּ לְךָ"** – ***You shall do in accordance with the word that they will tell you,*** *from that place which HASHEM will choose, and you shall be careful to do in accordance with all that they teach you.* **וְנִכְפַּל בְּסָמוּךְ לְחִזּוּק הַדָּבָר** – **This is repeated in** the **next** verse, in order

---

NOTES

1. That is, this mitzvah requires that one heed the Sanhedrin not only when they interpret Biblical laws, but also when they themselves enact a decree. Chinuch's words here are drawn from *Rambam* (*Sefer HaMitzvos, Asei* 174), who maintains that this mitzvah and the next demand of one to abide by the words of the Sanhedrin with regard to Rabbinic enactments as well. In the next mitzvah, Chinuch will cite *Ramban's* dissenting opinion. See there for a lengthy discussion of this matter.

עַל פִּי הַתּוֹרָה אֲשֶׁר יוֹרוּךָ וְעַל הַמִּשְׁפָּט אֲשֶׁר יֹאמְרוּ לְךָ תַּעֲשֶׂה. וְאֵין הֶפְרֵשׁ בָּזֶה בֵּין הַדָּבָר שֶׁיִּרְאוּהוּ הֵם מִדַּעְתָּם[2] אוֹ הַדָּבָר שֶׁיּוֹצִיאוּהוּ בְּהֶקֵּשׁ מִן הַהֶקֵּשִׁים שֶׁהַתּוֹרָה נִדְרֶשֶׁת בָּהֶן[3] אוֹ הַדָּבָר שֶׁיַּסְכִּימוּ עָלָיו שֶׁהוּא סוֹד הַתּוֹרָה אוֹ בְּכָל עִנְיָן אַחֵר שֶׁיֵּרָאֶה לָהֶן שֶׁהַדָּבָר כֵּן, עַל הַכֹּל אָנוּ חַיָּבִין לִשְׁמֹעַ לָהֶן. וְהָרְאָיָה שֶׁזֶּה מִמִּנְיַן מִצְוַת עֲשֵׂה אָמְרָם זִכְרוֹנָם לִבְרָכָה בְּסִפְרֵי (כאן) וְעַל הַמִּשְׁפָּט אֲשֶׁר יֹאמְרוּ לְךָ תַּעֲשֶׂה, זוֹ מִצְוַת עֲשֵׂה.

מִשָּׁרְשֵׁי הַמִּצְוָה כְּמוֹ שֶׁכָּתַבְתִּי בְּכֶסֶף תַּלְוֶה עֲשֵׂה ב׳ בְּסִימָן ס״ז (מצוה ע״ח)[4].

---

to strengthen the matter: ״עַל פִּי הַתּוֹרָה אֲשֶׁר יוֹרוּךָ וְעַל הַמִּשְׁפָּט אֲשֶׁר יֹאמְרוּ לְךָ תַּעֲשֶׂה״ – ***In accordance with the teaching that they will teach you, and by the judgment that they will say to you, shall you do.***

Chinuch presents a number of ways that the Sanhedrin may reach their conclusion as to the correct interpretation of the Torah, all of which are subject to the requirement set forth in this mitzvah:

וְאֵין הֶפְרֵשׁ בָּזֶה בֵּין הַדָּבָר שֶׁיִּרְאוּהוּ הֵם מִדַּעְתָּם – **With regard to this** obligation, **there is no difference whether** the matter is **something that [the members of the Sanhedrin] perceive through their own intellect**[2] to be the meaning of the verse, אוֹ הַדָּבָר שֶׁיּוֹצִיאוּהוּ בְּהֶקֵּשׁ מִן הַהֶקֵּשִׁים שֶׁהַתּוֹרָה נִדְרֶשֶׁת בָּהֶן – **or** it is **something that they derive through one of the forms of exposition through which the Torah is expounded,**[3] אוֹ הַדָּבָר שֶׁיַּסְכִּימוּ עָלָיו שֶׁהוּא סוֹד הַתּוֹרָה – **or** it is **something that they have concluded is** contained in **a mystical aspect of the Torah,** אוֹ בְּכָל עִנְיָן אַחֵר שֶׁיֵּרָאֶה לָהֶן שֶׁהַדָּבָר כֵּן – **or it is apparent to [the Sanhedrin] through any other means that the matter is so.** עַל הַכֹּל אָנוּ חַיָּבִין לִשְׁמֹעַ לָהֶן – **In all** these cases, **we are obligated to obey them.**

Chinuch shows that this mitzvah is counted as one of the 613 Mitzvos:

וְהָרְאָיָה שֶׁזֶּה מִמִּנְיַן מִצְוַת עֲשֵׂה – **The proof that this is included in the count of mitzvah-obligations** אָמְרָם זִכְרוֹנָם לִבְרָכָה בְּסִפְרֵי – **is the statement of [the Sages], of blessed memory, in** ***Sifrei*** (ad loc.): ״וְעַל הַמִּשְׁפָּט אֲשֶׁר יֹאמְרוּ לְךָ תַּעֲשֶׂה״ זוֹ מִצְוַת עֲשֵׂה – The verse, ***and by the judgment that they will say to you, shall you do,*** **constitutes a mitzvah-obligation.**

Underlying Purpose of the Mitzvah

מִשָּׁרְשֵׁי הַמִּצְוָה – **Among the underlying purposes of the mitzvah** is כְּמוֹ שֶׁכָּתַבְתִּי בְּכֶסֶף תַּלְוֶה עֲשֵׂה ב׳ בְּסִימָן ס״ז – **that which I have written in** ***Parashas Im Kesef Talveh,*** **Chapter 67** of this work (Mitzvah 78).[4]

NOTES

2. See common texts of *Rambam, Sefer HaMitzvos, Asei* 174; cf. Kafich ed.

3. The Sages received a tradition from Sinai regarding various principles through which the Torah is to be expounded. The *Baraisa of R' Yishmael,* which appears as an introduction to *Sifra* and is recited during the morning prayers, contains the most well-known list, which consists of thirteen such principles.

4. [Chinuch's numbering follows the original format of this work; see Mitzvah 494 note 4. *"Parashas Im Kesef Talveh"* is what Chinuch calls the second half of *Parashas Mishpatim,* because in his community it was customary to divide *Mishpatim* into two weekly readings, the second of which began with the verse (*Exodus* 22:24): אִם כֶּסֶף תַּלְוֶה אֶת עַמִּי, *When you lend money to My people.* See our introduction to *Parashas Im Kesef,* in Volume II, before Mitzvah 66.]

In Mitzvah 78, Chinuch explains that if we would have no clear-cut method of resolving doubts in interpreting the mitzvos, each person would follow his own understanding of what the Torah requires. Mitzvah observance would quickly lose any measure of uniformity, and it would appear as though there are many versions of the Torah. For this reason, it is necessary for the entire nation to abide by the rulings of the Great Sanhedrin, in order to ensure that a single understanding of the Torah is followed throughout the Jewish nation. In the next mitzvah, Chinuch discusses this idea at length and develops it further.

מִדִּינֵי הַמִּצְוָה כְּגוֹן מַה שֶּׁדָּרְשׁוּ זִכְרוֹנָם לִבְרָכָה עַל פִּי הַתּוֹרָה אֲשֶׁר יוֹרוּךָ, אֵלּוּ הַגְּזֵרוֹת וְהַמִּנְהָגוֹת[5], וְעַל הַמִּשְׁפָּט, אֵלּוּ הַדְּבָרִים שֶׁיִּלְמְדוּ אוֹתָם מִן הַדִּין בְּאַחַת מִן הַמִּדּוֹת שֶׁהַתּוֹרָה נִדְרֶשֶׁת בָּהֶן[6], מִכָּל[7] הַדָּבָר אֲשֶׁר יַגִּידוּ לְךָ, זֶה הַקַּבָּלָה שֶׁקִּבְּלוּ אִישׁ מִפִּי אִישׁ. וּמַה שֶּׁאָמְרוּ זִכְרוֹנָם לִבְרָכָה (סנהדרין פ״ח ע״ב) שֶׁבִּזְמַן שֶׁבֵּית דִּין הַגָּדוֹל בִּירוּשָׁלַיִם, כָּל מַחֲלֹקֶת שֶׁהָיְתָה לְכָל בֵּית דִּין בִּמְקוֹמוֹ שׁוֹאֲלִין אוֹתוֹ לְבֵית דִּין הַגָּדוֹל[8] וְעוֹשִׂין עַל פִּיהֶם.

וְעַכְשָׁו בַּעֲווֹנוֹתֵינוּ שֶׁאֵין שָׁם בֵּית דִּין כָּל מַחֲלֹקֶת שֶׁיָּבוֹא בֵּין חֲכָמֵינוּ שֶׁבְּדוֹרֵנוּ וְהַחוֹלְקִין יִהְיוּ שָׁוִים בְּחָכְמָה, אִם אֵין אָנוּ רְאוּיִין לְהַכְרִיעַ בֵּינֵיהֶן וְלֹא נֵדַע לְהֵיכָן הַדִּין נוֹטֶה,

---

Laws of the Mitzvah

מִדִּינֵי הַמִּצְוָה – **Among the laws of the mitzvah** is, כְּגוֹן מַה שֶּׁדָּרְשׁוּ זִכְרוֹנָם לִבְרָכָה – **for example, that which [the Sages], of blessed memory, expounded** based on the above verse (see *Rambam, Hil. Mamrim* 1:2): ״עַל פִּי הַתּוֹרָה אֲשֶׁר יוֹרוּךָ״ אֵלּוּ הַגְּזֵרוֹת וְהַמִּנְהָגוֹת – When the verse states, ***In accordance with the teaching that they will teach you,*** **this refers to decrees and practices** instituted by the Sanhedrin, to strengthen mitzvah observance.[5] ״וְעַל הַמִּשְׁפָּט״ אֵלּוּ הַדְּבָרִים שֶׁיִּלְמְדוּ אוֹתָם מִן הַדִּין בְּאַחַת מִן הַמִּדּוֹת שֶׁהַתּוֹרָה נִדְרֶשֶׁת בָּהֶן – When it continues, ***and by the judgment,*** **this refers to matters that [the Sanhedrin] derive through** Scriptural **exposition, using one of the principles through which the Torah is expounded.**[6] ״מִכָּל הַדָּבָר אֲשֶׁר יַגִּידוּ לְךָ״ זֶה הַקַּבָּלָה שֶׁקִּבְּלוּ אִישׁ מִפִּי אִישׁ – And when it states, *you shall not deviate* ***from all***[7] ***the word that they will tell you,*** **this refers to the Oral Law that [the Sages] received as a tradition** from Sinai, **each person from his predecessor** of the previous generation.

וּמַה שֶּׁאָמְרוּ זִכְרוֹנָם לִבְרָכָה – **Also** pertaining to this mitzvah is **that which [the Sages], of blessed memory, stated** (*Sanhedrin* 88b), שֶׁבִּזְמַן שֶׁבֵּית דִּין הַגָּדוֹל בִּירוּשָׁלַיִם – **that in the times of the Great Sanhedrin in Jerusalem,** כָּל מַחֲלֹקֶת שֶׁהָיְתָה לְכָל בֵּית דִּין בִּמְקוֹמוֹ שׁוֹאֲלִין אוֹתוֹ לְבֵית דִּין הַגָּדוֹל – **any** unresolved **dispute within a** local ***beis din,*** **wherever it might be, would be presented to the Great Sanhedrin** for resolution,[8] וְעוֹשִׂין עַל פִּיהֶם – **and [the people] would** then **act in accordance with their ruling;** thus, all uncertainties regarding Torah law would be resolved.

Chinuch sets forth the procedure for resolving halachic uncertainties in our times:

וְעַכְשָׁו בַּעֲווֹנוֹתֵינוּ שֶׁאֵין שָׁם בֵּית דִּין – **But now, when due to our sins, there is no Sanhedrin there,** in Jerusalem, כָּל מַחֲלֹקֶת שֶׁיָּבוֹא בֵּין חֲכָמֵינוּ שֶׁבְּדוֹרֵנוּ – **whenever a dispute arises among the sages of our time,** וְהַחוֹלְקִין יִהְיוּ שָׁוִים בְּחָכְמָה – **and those who are in dispute are equal in scholarship,** אִם אֵין אָנוּ רְאוּיִין לְהַכְרִיעַ בֵּינֵיהֶן – **if we are incapable of deciding between them,** וְלֹא נֵדַע לְהֵיכָן הַדִּין נוֹטֶה – **and we do not know the direction that the law should take,**

NOTES

5. The Gemara (*Yevamos* 21a) derives from the verse, *You shall safeguard My charge* (*Leviticus* 18:30), that we are required to establish safeguards to ensure that the prohibitions of the Torah will not be transgressed (see *Rambam's* Introduction to *Mishneh Torah,* and his Introduction to the Mishnah ד״ה והחלק הרביעי הם הגזרות; see also *Ramban* to *Deuteronomy* 4:2). Since it is the responsibility of the Sanhedrin to establish these safeguards, the obligation to abide by them is included in this mitzvah. [This is the view of *Rambam*, as explained in note 1.]

6. See above, note 3.

7. This is how *Rambam* quotes the verse, but it actually reads מִן הַדָּבָר, *from the word.* See *Bris Moshe* to *Smag, Lo Saaseh* 217 (see also *Horayos* 4a).

8. As explained in the Gemara, the question would first be presented before a series of lower courts, which had progressive degrees of prominence. [See Mitzvah 491, after note 5 and after note 23.] If it could not be resolved in any of the other courts, it would be brought before the Great Sanhedrin. Chinuch omits these steps, as his intent here is merely to bring out that all unresolved questions were ultimately decided by the Great Sanhedrin.

בְּשֶׁל תּוֹרָה יֵשׁ לָנוּ לֵילֵךְ אַחַר הַמַּחְמִיר וּבְשֶׁל סוֹפְרִים אַחַר הַמֵּקֵל[9]. וּמַה שֶּׁאָמְרוּ (עדויות פ״א מ״ה) שֶׁאֵין בֵּית דִּין רַשַּׁאי לְבַטֵּל מַה שֶּׁאָסַר בֵּית דִּין הַקּוֹדֵם לוֹ, וַאֲפִלּוּ אִם יִרְאֶה בְּדַעְתּוֹ שֶׁאֵין אוֹתוֹ הַדָּבָר אָסוּר מִדִּין הַהֲלָכָה[10], כָּל זְמַן שֶׁיִּרְאֶה שֶׁפָּשַׁט אוֹתוֹ אִסּוּר בְּיִשְׂרָאֵל, אֶלָּא אִם כֵּן הוּא גָּדוֹל מִן הַבֵּית דִּין שֶׁאָסַר הַדָּבָר בְּחָכְמָה וְגַם בְּמִנְיָן[11]. וּבַמֶּה דְּבָרִים אֲמוּרִים שֶׁיּוּכַל לְבַטֵּל כְּשֶׁהוּא גָּדוֹל מִמֶּנּוּ בְּחָכְמָה וּבְמִנְיָן, כְּשֶׁלֹּא אָסַר הַבֵּית דִּין הַקּוֹדֵם לוֹ אוֹתוֹ דָּבָר כְּדֵי לַעֲשׂוֹת סְיָג לָעָם בְּאִסּוּרִין, אֲבָל אִם אָסַר הַבֵּית דִּין הַקּוֹדֵם לוֹ אוֹתוֹ אִסּוּר כְּדֵי לַעֲשׂוֹת בּוֹ גָּדֵר לָעָם בְּאִסּוּרִין,

---

בְּשֶׁל תּוֹרָה יֵשׁ לָנוּ לֵילֵךְ אַחַר הַמַּחְמִיר — then, **in** questions pertaining to **Biblical [law], we must follow the stringent** opinion, וּבְשֶׁל סוֹפְרִים אַחַר הַמֵּקֵל — **and in** questions of **Rabbinic [law],** we **follow the lenient** opinion.[9]

Chinuch now discusses the circumstances in which a Sanhedrin is authorized to overturn a ruling issued by a previous Sanhedrin. A basic rule stated in the Mishnah (*Eduyos* 1:5) is that one Court may not annul the words of another Court unless it is greater in stature than the previous Court. Chinuch will explain this, and will clarify that it also depends upon several other factors:

וּמַה שֶּׁאָמְרוּ — **Also** included in the laws of the mitzvah **is that which [the Sages] stated** (see *Eduyos* 1:5 and *Rambam, Hil. Mamrim* 2:1-3), שֶׁאֵין בֵּית דִּין רַשַּׁאי לְבַטֵּל מַה שֶּׁאָסַר בֵּית דִּין הַקּוֹדֵם לוֹ — **that** one **Court** of the Sanhedrin **is not authorized to annul a prohibition instituted by an earlier Court,** וַאֲפִלּוּ אִם יִרְאֶה בְּדַעְתּוֹ שֶׁאֵין אוֹתוֹ הַדָּבָר אָסוּר מִדִּין הַהֲלָכָה — **even if it is apparent to [the second Court] that the matter is not something** that the first Court deemed to be **prohibited by** Biblical **law,** but is something that the first Court decreed on its own,[10] except in limited circumstances. כָּל זְמַן שֶׁיִּרְאֶה שֶׁפָּשַׁט אוֹתוֹ אִסּוּר בְּיִשְׂרָאֵל — Namely, **whenever [the second Court] sees that the prohibition** issued by the first Court **has gained widespread acceptance among the Jewish people,** it may not annul that prohibition, אֶלָּא אִם כֵּן הוּא גָּדוֹל מִן הַבֵּית דִּין שֶׁאָסַר הַדָּבָר בְּחָכְמָה וְגַם בְּמִנְיָן — **unless it is greater than the Court that instituted the prohibition in both wisdom and number.**[11] וּבַמֶּה דְּבָרִים אֲמוּרִים שֶׁיּוּכַל לְבַטֵּל כְּשֶׁהוּא גָּדוֹל מִמֶּנּוּ בְּחָכְמָה וּבְמִנְיָן — **However,** there is another limitation: **When do we say that [a later Court] that is greater in wisdom and in number can annul** the enactment of an earlier Court? כְּשֶׁלֹּא אָסַר הַבֵּית דִּין הַקּוֹדֵם לוֹ אוֹתוֹ דָּבָר כְּדֵי לַעֲשׂוֹת סְיָג לָעָם בְּאִסּוּרִין — Only in a case **where the earlier Court did not institute that prohibition in order to protect the people from** a Biblical **transgression.** אֲבָל אִם אָסַר הַבֵּית דִּין הַקּוֹדֵם לוֹ אוֹתוֹ אִסּוּר כְּדֵי לַעֲשׂוֹת בּוֹ גָּדֵר לָעָם בְּאִסּוּרִין — **But if the earlier Court instituted the**

NOTES

9. This reflects the well-known rule that סְפֵיקָא דְאוֹרַיְתָא לְחֻמְרָא סְפֵיקָא דְרַבָּנָן לְקֻלָּא, *an uncertainty regarding a Biblical matter is treated stringently; an uncertainty involving a Rabbinic matter is treated leniently* (see Mitzvah 496, at note 47; see there, at notes 60-61, for further details regarding this situation).

In Mitzvah 78, Chinuch writes that when a group of Torah scholars addresses a question and they are equal in wisdom, the law always accords with the majority opinion. See also Mitzvah 496, at note 8. [For additional rules pertaining to situations of uncertainty and situations of disagreement among the authorities, see *Rama, Choshen Mishpat* 25:2; *Shach,* end of *Yoreh Deah* §242; *Chazon Ish, Yoreh Deah* 150:8.]

10. Chinuch seems to imply that the authority of the second Court is *certainly* limited in a case where the first Court ruled that something is prohibited by Biblical law. *Rambam* (*Hil. Mamrim* 2:1), however, states differently. For discussion, see *Minchas Chinuch* §4.

11. "In wisdom" means that the second Court must contain greater scholars than the first Court. "In number" does not refer to the number of sages on the Court, since the Great Sanhedrin always had 71 members (see Mitzvah 491, at note 8). Rather, it means that *in addition* to the members of the Sanhedrin, more scholars of Israel must concur with the second Court than the number that concurred with the first Court (*Rambam* ibid. 2:2). Alternatively, "in number" refers to the number of years that the members of the Court spent under the tutelage of their Torah teachers (*Ritva, Avodah Zarah* 7a; see *Raavad, Eduyos* 1:5). See also Mitzvah 496 note 60.

Chinuch states that this stipulation applies whenever the prohibition issued by the first Court gained widespread acceptance among the Jewish people. If it was not accepted by the people, it can be repealed even by a lesser Court (see *Avodah Zarah* 36a).

אֵין כֹּחַ בְּבֵית דִּין הַבָּא אַחֲרָיו לְבַטֵּל תַּקָּנָתוֹ וַאֲפִלּוּ הוּא גָּדוֹל מִמֶּנּוּ בְּחָכְמָה וּבְמִנְיָן[12]. וְאַחַר שֶׁכֵּן הוּא הַדִּין יֵשׁ לְכָל בֵּית דִּין וּבֵית דִּין בְּדוֹרוֹ לְהִתְיַשֵּׁב בַּדָּבָר וְלַחֲקֹר הַרְבֵּה וְלָתֵת לֵב בְּכָל אִסּוּרִין שֶׁיִּרְאֶה שֶׁהַדּוֹר נוֹהֵג בּוֹ[13] שֶׁלֹּא לִפְרֹץ וּלְהוֹרוֹת עָלָיו לְהָקֵל, כִּי שֶׁמָּא הַקּוֹדֵם לוֹ לִגְדֹּר הָעָם אֲסָרוֹ עִם הֱיוֹתוֹ יוֹדֵעַ שֶׁהַדָּבָר מֻתָּר מִדִּין הַהֲלָכָה, וּפֹרֵץ גָּדֵר וְגוֹ'[14]. וְיֶתֶר פְּרָטֵי הַמִּצְוָה בְּסוֹף סַנְהֶדְרִין[15].

וְנוֹהֶגֶת מִצְוָה זוֹ בִּזְמַן שֶׁבֵּית דִּין הַגָּדוֹל בִּירוּשָׁלַיִם[16] בִּזְכָרִים וּנְקֵבוֹת, שֶׁהַכֹּל מְצֻוִּין

---

prohibition in order to protect the people from a Biblical **transgression,** אֵין כֹּחַ בְּבֵית דִּין הַבָּא אַחֲרָיו לְבַטֵּל תַּקָּנָתוֹ – **a later Court does not have the authority to annul its enactment,** וַאֲפִלּוּ הוּא גָּדוֹל מִמֶּנּוּ בְּחָכְמָה וּבְמִנְיָן – **even if it is greater than [its predecessor] in wisdom and in number.**[12]

וְאַחַר שֶׁכֵּן הוּא הַדִּין – **Accordingly, since this is the law,** יֵשׁ לְכָל בֵּית דִּין וּבֵית דִּין בְּדוֹרוֹ לְהִתְיַשֵּׁב בַּדָּבָר וְלַחֲקֹר הַרְבֵּה וְלָתֵת לֵב – **it is necessary for each and every Court of its generation,** when it contemplates overturning a ruling issued by an earlier Court, **to devote thought to the matter, to explore extensively, and to pay** great **attention** בְּכָל אִסּוּרִין שֶׁיִּרְאֶה שֶׁהַדּוֹר נוֹהֵג בּוֹ – **regarding any prohibition that it sees that its generation is following,**[13] שֶׁלֹּא לִפְרֹץ וּלְהוֹרוֹת עָלָיו לְהָקֵל – **so that it should not create a breach, by ruling leniently in [the matter]** when it is not authorized to do so. כִּי שֶׁמָּא הַקּוֹדֵם לוֹ לִגְדֹּר הָעָם אֲסָרוֹ – **For perhaps the earlier [Court] ruled [the matter] prohibited** by way of a decree, **in order to protect the people** from sin, עִם הֱיוֹתוֹ יוֹדֵעַ שֶׁהַדָּבָר מֻתָּר מִדִּין הַהֲלָכָה – **with the realization that the matter is,** in fact, **permitted according to the** Biblical **law;** and in such a case, the later Court is not authorized to overturn the decree even if it is greater in wisdom and in number than the earlier Court. וּפֹרֵץ גָּדֵר וְגוֹ' – Regarding such a matter, it is stated (*Ecclesiastes* 10:8): ***One who breaches a fence*** *will be bitten by a snake.*[14]

וְיֶתֶר פְּרָטֵי הַמִּצְוָה בְּסוֹף סַנְהֶדְרִין – **The additional details of this mitzvah are** set forth **at the end of** Tractate ***Sanhedrin.***[15]

Applicability of the Mitzvah

וְנוֹהֶגֶת מִצְוָה זוֹ בִּזְמַן שֶׁבֵּית דִּין הַגָּדוֹל בִּירוּשָׁלַיִם – **This mitzvah,** in its literal sense (i.e., to heed the word of the Great Sanhedrin), **applies during the time when the Great Sanhedrin is in Jerusalem;**[16] בִּזְכָרִים וּנְקֵבוֹת – it is incumbent **upon** both **men and women,** שֶׁהַכֹּל מְצֻוִּין

NOTES

12. Many of the Sages' decrees were enacted in order to safeguard Biblical law. For example, the Sages prohibited consumption of bread baked privately by idolaters, or food cooked by them, in order to discourage socializing that could lead to intermarriage, which is Biblically prohibited (see *Avodah Zarah* 36a and *Yoreh Deah* 112:1). This type of decree can never be rescinded, even by a Court of greater stature than the original one (*Avodah Zarah* ibid.). Some Rabbinic laws, however, were enacted for other reasons. For example, the Sages commanded us to read the Megillah on either 14 or 15 Adar (depending on the type of city in which we live), to commemorate the Purim miracle. Since this enactment was not designed to protect any Biblical law, if a subsequent Court was greater than the one that enacted it, that Court could theoretically change this law (*Kesef Mishneh, Hil. Mamrim* 2:2; see there for a case in which a later Court actually repealed a decree of an earlier one).

13. I.e., any prohibition that has gained widespread acceptance among the people.

14. The Gemara (*Avodah Zarah* 27b) explains that this verse is referring to one who transgresses the safeguards instituted by the Sages. Therefore, before a Court reverses a stringent ruling that its predecessor had issued, it must confirm that the stringent ruling was not intended as a safeguard to prevent transgression.

15. See *Sanhedrin* 86b-89a for the laws pertaining to one who rejects the rulings of the Sanhedrin. *Rambam* codifies the laws of this mitzvah in *Hil. Mamrim* Chs. 1-4.

16. It is unclear why Chinuch limits this aspect of the mitzvah to the time of the Great Sanhedrin, for, as he himself writes at the end of the next mitzvah (at note 79), even today, one who disregards the teachings of the Sanhedrin of old, as recorded in the Mishnah and Gemara, has transgressed this mitzvah. [The law of a

לַעֲשׂוֹת כָּל אֲשֶׁר יוֹרוּ. וּבִכְלַל הַמִּצְוָה גַּם כֵּן לִשְׁמֹעַ וְלַעֲשׂוֹת בְּכָל זְמַן וּזְמַן כְּמִצְוַת הַשּׁוֹפֵט, כְּלוֹמַר הֶחָכָם הַגָּדוֹל אֲשֶׁר יִהְיֶה בֵּינֵינוּ בִּזְמַנֵּנוּ, וּכְמוֹ שֶׁדָּרְשׁוּ זִכְרוֹנָם לִבְרָכָה (ראש השנה כ"ה ע"ב) וְאֶל הַשּׁוֹפֵט אֲשֶׁר יִהְיֶה בַּיָּמִים הָהֵם, יִפְתָּח בְּדוֹרוֹ כִּשְׁמוּאֵל בְּדוֹרוֹ, כְּלוֹמַר שֶׁמִּצְוָה עָלֵינוּ לִשְׁמֹעַ בְּקוֹל יִפְתָּח בְּדוֹרוֹ כְּמוֹ לִשְׁמוּאֵל בְּדוֹרוֹ[17].

וְעוֹבֵר עַל זֶה וְאֵינוֹ שׁוֹמֵעַ לַעֲצַת הַגְּדוֹלִים שֶׁבַּדּוֹר בְּחָכְמַת הַתּוֹרָה בְּכָל אֲשֶׁר יוֹרוּ מְבַטֵּל עֲשֵׂה זֶה[18]. וְעָנְשׁוֹ גָּדוֹל מְאֹד שֶׁזֶּהוּ הָעַמּוּד הֶחָזָק שֶׁהַתּוֹרָה נִשְׁעֶנֶת בּוֹ, יָדוּעַ הַדָּבָר לְכָל מִי שֶׁיֵּשׁ בּוֹ דַּעַת[19].

לַעֲשׂוֹת כָּל אֲשֶׁר יוֹרוּ – **as all are commanded to act** in accordance **with every ruling of [the Sanhedrin].**

Chinuch sets out an additional dimension of this mitzvah:

וּבִכְלַל הַמִּצְוָה גַּם כֵּן לִשְׁמֹעַ וְלַעֲשׂוֹת בְּכָל זְמַן וּזְמַן כְּמִצְוַת הַשּׁוֹפֵט – **This mitzvah also includes** an obligation **to heed and to act in accordance with the instructions of the judge in all times,** כְּלוֹמַר הֶחָכָם הַגָּדוֹל אֲשֶׁר יִהְיֶה בֵּינֵינוּ בִּזְמַנֵּנוּ – **meaning,** that we must follow the rulings of **the greatest sage among us, in our time,** whenever we live. וּכְמוֹ שֶׁדָּרְשׁוּ זִכְרוֹנָם לִבְרָכָה "וְאֶל הַשּׁוֹפֵט אֲשֶׁר יִהְיֶה בַּיָּמִים הָהֵם" – This is **as [the Sages], of blessed memory** (*Rosh Hashanah* 25b), **expounded** the verse (*Deuteronomy* 17:9), *You shall come ... **to the judge who will be in those days**:* יִפְתָּח בְּדוֹרוֹ כִּשְׁמוּאֵל בְּדוֹרוֹ – **Yiftach** (who was a judge of lesser stature) **in his generation is** the same **as Samuel** (a judge of high stature) **in his generation.** כְּלוֹמַר שֶׁמִּצְוָה עָלֵינוּ לִשְׁמֹעַ בְּקוֹל יִפְתָּח בְּדוֹרוֹ כְּמוֹ לִשְׁמוּאֵל בְּדוֹרוֹ – **That is to say, we are commanded to heed the words of Yiftach in his generation, just as** we are commanded **to** heed the words of **Samuel in his generation.**[17]

וְעוֹבֵר עַל זֶה – **One who transgresses this** commandment, וְאֵינוֹ שׁוֹמֵעַ לַעֲצַת הַגְּדוֹלִים שֶׁבַּדּוֹר בְּחָכְמַת הַתּוֹרָה – **and does not follow the guidance of the greatest Torah scholars of** his **generation** בְּכָל אֲשֶׁר יוֹרוּ – **in all of their rulings,** מְבַטֵּל עֲשֵׂה זֶה – **violates this mitzvah-obligation.**[18] וְעָנְשׁוֹ גָּדוֹל מְאֹד – **His punishment will be very great,** שֶׁזֶּהוּ הָעַמּוּד הֶחָזָק שֶׁהַתּוֹרָה נִשְׁעֶנֶת בּוֹ – **as this [obligation] is the mighty pillar upon which the** entire **Torah is supported;** יָדוּעַ הַדָּבָר לְכָל מִי שֶׁיֵּשׁ בּוֹ דַּעַת – **the matter is clear to anybody with intelligence.**[19]

NOTES

zakein mamrei, an elder who denies the authority of *beis din* (see next mitzvah after note 9), however, does in fact apply only to rulings issued when the Sanhedrin is seated in the *Lishkas HaGazis* (Chamber of Hewn Stone) in the *Beis HaMikdash* (see Chinuch there, at notes 17-18, and after note 78).]

[For discussion of what status the Sanhedrin had after it was exiled from Jerusalem and established in other locations (as recorded in *Rosh Hashanah* 31a-b), see *Margenisa Tava* to *Sefer HaMitzvos, Shoresh* 1 §5; *R' Elchanan Wasserman* in *Kuntres Divrei Soferim* 2:1 (printed in *Kovetz Shiurim* Vol. 2); letter of *Chazon Ish* §3 to R' Elchanan Wasserman, printed at end of *Kovetz Inyanim*; *R' Zelig Epstein* in *Yeshurun,* Vol. 11, p. 582.]

17. The Gemara (*Rosh Hashanah* 25b) asks: Why is it necessary for the Torah to state that one must come to the judge that is "in those days"? Does one have an option to appear before any other judge? The Gemara explains that the verse is coming to teach that we must defer to the judgment of the judge who is the authority in our times, even though he may not have been considered as such in previous times. Chinuch understands this to mean that the current mitzvah applies in all times and obligates us to follow the halachic rulings of the greatest sage of our own generation (*glosses of R' Y. F. Perla* to *Minchas Chinuch,* cited in Machon Yerushalayim ed., footnote 3). From *Rambam's* wording in *Hil. Mamrim* (1:1), however, it would appear that he maintains that this mitzvah applies only to the rulings of the Great Sanhedrin in Jerusalem (*Minchas Chinuch* §3; see *Sefer HaMafte'ach* to *Rambam* there, Frankel ed.).

18. See next mitzvah for the mitzvah-prohibition that one transgresses when failing to heed the words of the Sages.

19. Torah observance requires the proper interpretation and safeguards of its laws; thus, the universal obligation to obey the Sages is most fundamental.

מִצְוָה תצו
שֶׁלֹּא לְהַמְרוֹת עַל פִּי בֵּית דִּין הַגָּדוֹל שֶׁיַּעַמְדוּ לְיִשְׂרָאֵל

שֶׁנִּמְנַעְנוּ מִלַּחֲלֹק עַל בַּעֲלֵי הַקַּבָּלָה עֲלֵיהֶם הַשָּׁלוֹם[1] וּמִלְּשַׁנּוֹת אֶת דִּבְרֵיהֶם וְלָצֵאת מִמִּצְוֹתָם בְּכָל עִנְיְנֵי הַתּוֹרָה, וְעַל זֶה נֶאֱמַר (דברים י״ז, י״א) לֹא תָסוּר מִן הַדָּבָר אֲשֶׁר יַגִּידוּ לְךָ יָמִין וּשְׂמֹאל, וְאָמְרוּ זִכְרוֹנָם לִבְרָכָה בְּסִפְרִי (כאן), לֹא תָסוּר וְגוֹ׳, זוֹ מִצְוַת לֹא תַעֲשֶׂה.

מִשָּׁרְשֵׁי הַמִּצְוָה לְפִי שֶׁדֵּעוֹת בְּנֵי הָאָדָם חֲלוּקִין זֶה מִזֶּה לֹא יִשְׁתַּוּוּ לְעוֹלָם הַרְבֵּה

Mitzvah 496
The Prohibition to Defy the Directives of the Great Sanhedrin

עַל פִּי הַתּוֹרָה אֲשֶׁר יוֹרוּךָ וְעַל הַמִּשְׁפָּט אֲשֶׁר יֹאמְרוּ לְךָ תַּעֲשֶׂה לֹא תָסוּר מִן הַדָּבָר אֲשֶׁר יַגִּידוּ לְךָ יָמִין וּשְׂמֹאל. וְהָאִישׁ אֲשֶׁר יַעֲשֶׂה בְזָדוֹן לְבִלְתִּי שְׁמֹעַ אֶל הַכֹּהֵן הָעֹמֵד לְשָׁרֶת שָׁם אֶת ה׳ אֱלֹהֶיךָ אוֹ אֶל הַשֹּׁפֵט וּמֵת הָאִישׁ הַהוּא וּבִעַרְתָּ הָרָע מִיִּשְׂרָאֵל

In accordance with the teaching that they will teach you, and by the judgment that they will say to you, shall you do; you shall not deviate from the word that they will tell you, right or left. And the man who will act with willfulness, not listening to the Kohen who stands there to serve HASHEM, your God, or to the judge, that man shall die, and you shall destroy the evil from among Israel (*Deuteronomy* 17:11-12).

In the previous mitzvah, the Torah set forth a mitzvah-obligation to obey the Sanhedrin. The current mitzvah prohibits us to deviate from their rulings. In this context, the Torah also discusses the case of a sage who maintains that the Sanhedrin erred in its ruling. If he defies their ruling, either by personally acting in a manner inconsistent with it, or by ruling against it to others, he is known as a *zakein mamrei*, an "insubordinate elder," and is subject to the penalty set forth in the verse.

שֶׁנִּמְנַעְנוּ מִלַּחֲלֹק עַל בַּעֲלֵי הַקַּבָּלָה עֲלֵיהֶם הַשָּׁלוֹם – It is prohibited for us to dispute the masters of the Oral Tradition, may peace be upon them,[1] **וּמִלְּשַׁנּוֹת אֶת דִּבְרֵיהֶם וְלָצֵאת מִמִּצְוֹתָם בְּכָל עִנְיְנֵי הַתּוֹרָה – and** it is prohibited **to deviate from their words or to depart from their instructions in any Torah matter. וְעַל זֶה נֶאֱמַר – Regarding this it is stated** (*Deuteronomy* 17:11): **"לֹא תָסוּר מִן הַדָּבָר אֲשֶׁר יַגִּידוּ לְךָ יָמִין וּשְׂמֹאל" – *you shall not deviate from the word that they will tell you, right or left;* וְאָמְרוּ זִכְרוֹנָם לִבְרָכָה בְּסִפְרִי – and [the Sages], of blessed memory, stated in *Sifrei*** (ad loc.), **"לֹא תָסוּר וְגוֹ׳ " זוֹ מִצְוַת לֹא תַעֲשֶׂה – *you shall not deviate* etc. constitutes a mitzvah-prohibition.**

Underlying Purpose of the Mitzvah

מִשָּׁרְשֵׁי הַמִּצְוָה – Among the underlying purposes of the mitzvah is **לְפִי שֶׁדֵּעוֹת בְּנֵי הָאָדָם חֲלוּקִין זֶה מִזֶּה –** that **since people's thinking differs one from the other, לֹא יִשְׁתַּוּוּ לְעוֹלָם הַרְבֵּה**

NOTES

1. I.e., the Sanhedrin, who were entrusted with interpreting the Torah and transmitting the Oral Law to succeeding generations (see introduction to Mitzvah 495).

דֵעוֹת בַּדְּבָרִים, וְיוֹדֵעַ אֲדוֹן הַכֹּל בָּרוּךְ הוּא שֶׁאִלּוּ תִּהְיֶה כַּוָּנַת כְּתוּבֵי הַתּוֹרָה מְסוּרָה בְּיַד
כָּל אֶחָד וְאֶחָד מִבְּנֵי אָדָם אִישׁ כְּפִי שִׂכְלוֹ, יְפָרֵשׁ כָּל אֶחָד מֵהֶם דִּבְרֵי הַתּוֹרָה כְּפִי
סְבָרָתוֹ וְיִרְבֶּה הַמַּחֲלֹקֶת בְּיִשְׂרָאֵל בְּמַשְׁמָעוּת הַמִּצְוֹת, וְתֵעָשֶׂה הַתּוֹרָה כְּכַמָּה תוֹרוֹת,
וּכְעִנְיָן שֶׁכָּתַבְתִּי בְּמִצְוַת אַחֲרֵי רַבִּים לְהַטּוֹת בְּכֶסֶף תַּלְוֶה בְּסִימָן ס״ז (מצוה ע״ח)2, עַל כֵּן
אֱלֹהֵינוּ שֶׁהוּא אֲדוֹן כָּל הַחָכְמוֹת הִשְׁלִים תּוֹרָתֵנוּ תּוֹרַת אֱמֶת עִם הַמִּצְוָה הַזֹּאת שֶׁצִּוָּנוּ
לְהִתְנַהֵג בָּהּ עַל פִּי הַפֵּרוּשׁ הָאֲמִתִּי הַמְּקֻבָּל לַחֲכָמֵינוּ הַקַּדְמוֹנִים עֲלֵיהֶם הַשָּׁלוֹם. וּבְכָל
דּוֹר וָדוֹר גַּם כֵּן שֶׁנִּשְׁמַע אֶל הַחֲכָמִים הַנִּמְצָאִים3 שֶׁקִּבְּלוּ דִּבְרֵיהֶם וְשָׁתוּ מַיִם4 מִסִּפְרֵיהֶם
וְיָגְעוּ כַּמָּה יְגִיעוֹת בַּיָּמִים וּבַלֵּילוֹת לְהָבִין עֹמֶק מִלֵּיהֶם וּפְלִיאוֹת דֵּעוֹתֵיהֶם, וְעִם הַהַסְכָּמָה
הַזֹּאת נְכַוֵּן אֶל דֶּרֶךְ הָאֱמֶת בִּידִיעַת הַתּוֹרָה, וְזוּלַת זֶה אִם נִתְפַּתֶּה אַחַר מַחְשְׁבוֹתֵינוּ
וַעֲנִיוּת דַּעְתֵּנוּ לֹא נִצְלַח לַכֹּל5.

דֵעוֹת בַּדְּבָרִים — when **numerous** people have **opinions about something** they **will never** all be in **agreement.** וְיוֹדֵעַ אֲדוֹן הַכֹּל בָּרוּךְ הוּא — Thus, Hashem, **the Master of all, blessed is He, knows** שֶׁאִלּוּ תִּהְיֶה כַּוָּנַת כְּתוּבֵי הַתּוֹרָה מְסוּרָה בְּיַד כָּל אֶחָד וְאֶחָד מִבְּנֵי אָדָם — that if the authority **to interpret the Torah's verses would be handed over to every individual,** אִישׁ כְּפִי שִׂכְלוֹ — for **each man** to interpret **according to his intelligence,** יְפָרֵשׁ כָּל אֶחָד מֵהֶם דִּבְרֵי הַתּוֹרָה כְּפִי סְבָרָתוֹ — **every one of them would explain the words of the Torah according to his own** personal **understanding,** וְיִרְבֶּה הַמַּחֲלֹקֶת בְּיִשְׂרָאֵל בְּמַשְׁמָעוּת הַמִּצְוֹת — **and there would be much conflict among the Jewish people regarding the interpretation of the mitzvos.** וְתֵעָשֶׂה הַתּוֹרָה כְּכַמָּה תוֹרוֹת — **As a result, the Torah would become as if** it were comprised of **many** different, individual **Torahs,** since every person would practice his own set of laws, וּכְעִנְיָן שֶׁכָּתַבְתִּי בְּמִצְוַת אַחֲרֵי רַבִּים לְהַטּוֹת בְּכֶסֶף תַּלְוֶה בְּסִימָן סז — **as I wrote in the mitzvah to follow the majority, in** *Parashas Im Kesef Talveh*, **Chapter 67** of this work (Mitzvah 78).[2] עַל כֵּן אֱלֹהֵינוּ שֶׁהוּא אֲדוֹן כָּל הַחָכְמוֹת — **Therefore, our God, Who is the Master of all wisdom,** הִשְׁלִים תּוֹרָתֵנוּ תּוֹרַת אֱמֶת עִם הַמִּצְוָה הַזֹּאת — gave wholeness to our Torah, the Torah of Truth, by including in it **this mitzvah,** שֶׁצִּוָּנוּ לְהִתְנַהֵג בָּהּ עַל פִּי הַפֵּרוּשׁ הָאֲמִתִּי הַמְּקֻבָּל לַחֲכָמֵינוּ הַקַּדְמוֹנִים עֲלֵיהֶם הַשָּׁלוֹם — in **which He commanded us to conduct ourselves in** matters of [Torah law] **in accordance with the true explanation that was transmitted** from Sinai **to our earlier Sages, may peace be upon them;** וּבְכָל דּוֹר וָדוֹר גַּם כֵּן שֶׁנִּשְׁמַע אֶל הַחֲכָמִים הַנִּמְצָאִים — **and in each and every generation as well, we are to heed the sages of that time,**[3] שֶׁקִּבְּלוּ דִּבְרֵיהֶם וְשָׁתוּ מַיִם מִסִּפְרֵיהֶם — **who received the words** [of the previous sages] **and absorbed knowledge**[4] **from their writings,** וְיָגְעוּ כַּמָּה יְגִיעוֹת בַּיָּמִים וּבַלֵּילוֹת לְהָבִין עֹמֶק מִלֵּיהֶם וּפְלִיאוֹת דֵּעוֹתֵיהֶם — **and** who **toiled diligently, by day and by night, to understand the depth of their words and the profundity of their thoughts.** וְעִם הַהַסְכָּמָה הַזֹּאת נְכַוֵּן אֶל דֶּרֶךְ הָאֱמֶת בִּידִיעַת הַתּוֹרָה — **Through this commitment** to follow the rulings of the Sages, **we will discover the true path in** our **knowledge of Torah.** וְזוּלַת זֶה — **Without this** commitment, **though,** אִם נִתְפַּתֶּה אַחַר מַחְשְׁבוֹתֵינוּ וַעֲנִיוּת דַּעְתֵּנוּ — meaning, **if we will be drawn after our** own **ideas and our** own **feeble minds,** לֹא נִצְלַח לַכֹּל — **we will not succeed at all.**[5]

NOTES

2. Chinuch wrote there that this is why the Torah commands that decisions regarding Torah law should follow the majority opinion. Here, he adds that for the same reason, the Torah commands that there be a central authority, the Great Sanhedrin, whose decisions (based on the majority of the members of *that* body) are binding on the entire nation. [See Mitzvah 495 note 4 regarding the name *Im Kesef Talveh,* and regarding Chinuch's system of numbering the mitzvos.]

3. See previous mitzvah, note 17.

4. Literally, *drank water.* [This is a stylistic reference to Torah study. Water is commonly used as a metaphor for the Torah, as Chinuch explained in Mitzvah 419 (at notes 28-30).]

5. Chinuch's words include two related points: (1) that it is necessary that the Torah be entrusted to a single body, which is charged with interpreting the Torah; and (2) that only the most learned scholars of the nation can correctly determine the true meaning of the Torah.

וְעַל דֶּרֶךְ הָאֱמֶת וְהַשֶּׁבַח הַגָּדוֹל בְּזֹאת הַמִּצְוָה אָמְרוּ זִכְרוֹנָם לִבְרָכָה (ספרי כאן) לֹא תָסוּר מִמֶּנּוּ יָמִין וּשְׂמֹאל, אֲפִלּוּ יֹאמְרוּ לְךָ עַל יָמִין שֶׁהוּא שְׂמֹאל וְעַל שְׂמֹאל שֶׁהוּא יָמִין לֹא תָסוּר מִמִּצְוָתָם, כְּלוֹמַר שֶׁאֲפִלּוּ יִהְיוּ הֵם טוֹעִים בְּדָבָר אֶחָד מִן הַדְּבָרִים אֵין רָאוּי לָנוּ לַחֲלֹק עֲלֵיהֶם אֲבָל נַעֲשֶׂה כְּטָעוּתָם, וְטוֹב לִסְבֹּל טָעוּת אֶחָד וְיִהְיוּ הַכֹּל מְסוּרִים תַּחַת דַּעְתָּם הַטּוֹב תָּמִיד, וְלֹא שֶׁיַּעֲשֶׂה כָּל אֶחָד וְאֶחָד כְּפִי דַעְתּוֹ שֶׁבָּזֶה יִהְיֶה חֻרְבַּן הַדָּת וְחִלּוּק לֵב הָעָם וְהֶפְסֵד הָאֻמָּה לְגַמְרֵי[6]. וּמִפְּנֵי עִנְיָנִים אֵלֶּה נִמְסְרָה כַּוָּנַת הַתּוֹרָה אֶל חַכְמֵי יִשְׂרָאֵל, וְנִצְטַוּוּ גַּם כֵּן שֶׁיִּהְיוּ לְעוֹלָם כַּת מוּעֶטֶת מִן הַחֲכָמִים כְּפוּפָה לְכַת הַמַּרְבִּין מִן הַשֹּׁרֶשׁ הַזֶּה, וּכְמוֹ שֶׁכָּתַבְתִּי שָׁם בְּמִצְוַת לְהַטּוֹת אַחֲרֵי רַבִּים[7].

וְעַל דֶּרֶךְ עִנְיָן זֶה שֶׁעוֹרַרְתִּיךָ בְּנִי עָלָיו אֲפָרֵשׁ לְךָ אַגָּדָה אַחַת שֶׁהִיא בְּבָבָא מְצִיעָא בְּסוֹף פֶּרֶק הַזָּהָב (נ״ט ע״ב) גַּבֵּי הַהוּא מַעֲשֶׂה דְּרַבִּי אֱלִיעֶזֶר בְּתַנּוּרוֹ שֶׁל עַכְנַאי הַמַּתְמַהַת כָּל שׁוֹמְעָהּ.

Chinuch develops this idea further:

וְעַל דֶּרֶךְ הָאֱמֶת וְהַשֶּׁבַח הַגָּדוֹל בְּזֹאת הַמִּצְוָה – **In expressing the inherent truth and the great value of this mitzvah,** אָמְרוּ זִכְרוֹנָם לִבְרָכָה – **[the Sages], of blessed memory, stated** (*Sifrei* ad loc.): לֹא תָסוּר מִמֶּנּוּ יָמִין וּשְׂמֹאל – When the Torah states, **"you shall not deviate from it, right or left,"** אֲפִלּוּ יֹאמְרוּ לְךָ עַל יָמִין שֶׁהוּא שְׂמֹאל וְעַל שְׂמֹאל שֶׁהוּא יָמִין לֹא תָסוּר מִמִּצְוָתָם – it teaches that **even if [the Sanhedrin] tells you that right is left, and that left is right, you may not deviate from their instructions.** כְּלוֹמַר שֶׁאֲפִלּוּ יִהְיוּ הֵם טוֹעִים בְּדָבָר אֶחָד מִן הַדְּבָרִים – **That is to say, even if [the Sanhedrin] is in error regarding some matter,** אֵין רָאוּי לָנוּ לַחֲלֹק עֲלֵיהֶם – **we have no right to dispute them;** אֲבָל נַעֲשֶׂה כְּטָעוּתָם – **rather, we are to act in accordance with their error.** וְטוֹב לִסְבֹּל טָעוּת אֶחָד – The reason is that **it is better to bear** the burden of **a single error,** וְיִהְיוּ הַכֹּל מְסוּרִים תַּחַת דַּעְתָּם הַטּוֹב תָּמִיד – **and that all** of the nation **be always subservient to their worthy opinion,** וְלֹא שֶׁיַּעֲשֶׂה כָּל אֶחָד וְאֶחָד כְּפִי דַעְתּוֹ – **than to have every individual act in accordance with his own opinion;** שֶׁבָּזֶה יִהְיֶה חֻרְבַּן הַדָּת – **for that would result in a devastation of the observance** of the Torah, וְחִלּוּק לֵב הָעָם – **a splintering of the heart of the populace,** וְהֶפְסֵד הָאֻמָּה לְגַמְרֵי – **and the complete ruin of the** Jewish **nation.**[6] וּמִפְּנֵי עִנְיָנִים אֵלֶּה נִמְסְרָה כַּוָּנַת הַתּוֹרָה אֶל חַכְמֵי יִשְׂרָאֵל – **Thus, for these reasons,** the authority to determine **the intent of the Torah was given over** solely **to the Sages of Israel.** וְנִצְטַוּוּ גַּם כֵּן – **[The Sanhedrin] was commanded as well,** שֶׁיִּהְיוּ לְעוֹלָם כַּת מוּעֶטֶת מִן הַחֲכָמִים כְּפוּפָה לְכַת הַמַּרְבִּין – that when a dispute arises within the Sanhedrin itself, **the smaller group of sages must always defer to the larger group,** מִן הַשֹּׁרֶשׁ הַזֶּה – **for this** very **reason,** וּכְמוֹ שֶׁכָּתַבְתִּי שָׁם בְּמִצְוַת לְהַטּוֹת אַחֲרֵי רַבִּים – **as I wrote there, in the mitzvah to follow** the opinion of **the majority** (Mitzvah 78).[7]

Based on this, Chinuch digresses to explain a difficult Talmudic passage:

וְעַל דֶּרֶךְ עִנְיָן זֶה שֶׁעוֹרַרְתִּיךָ בְּנִי עָלָיו – **Following this concept to which I have enlightened you, my son,** אֲפָרֵשׁ לְךָ אַגָּדָה אַחַת שֶׁהִיא בְּבָבָא מְצִיעָא בְּסוֹף פֶּרֶק הַזָּהָב – **I will explain to you a certain Aggadic teaching that is** found **in** Tractate ***Bava Metzia*** (59b), **at the end of Chapter *Hazahav*,** גַּבֵּי הַהוּא מַעֲשֶׂה דְּרַבִּי אֱלִיעֶזֶר בְּתַנּוּרוֹ שֶׁל עַכְנַאי – **regarding the incident with R' Eliezer and "the oven of the coiled serpent,"** הַמַּתְמַהַת כָּל שׁוֹמְעָהּ – **which astounds all who hear it.**

NOTES

6. That is, while it can generally be assumed that following the rulings of the Sanhedrin ensures that one will properly follow the Divine Will, the Torah required that we abide by their rulings even when they have erred ("when they say that right is left"), in order to ensure the continued authority of the Sages and the unity of the nation in observing the mitzvos.

7. Just as it is essential for the continuity of the Jewish nation that the people be unified in their observance of the mitzvos, so, too, it is vital that the Sanhedrin itself speak with a unified voice. Thus, when there is disagreement within the Sanhedrin, all of its members must accept the majority opinion. That matter is the subject of Mitzvah 78; see there at notes 7 and 13.

אָמְרוּ שָׁם, אַשְׁכְּחֵיהּ רַבִּי נָתָן לְאֵלִיָּהוּ וְכוּ', אֲמַר לֵיהּ מָה עֲבִיד הַקָּדוֹשׁ בָּרוּךְ הוּא בְּהַהִיא שַׁעְתָּא, אֲמַר לֵיהּ חַיֵּיךְ וְאָמַר נִצְחוּנִי בָּנַי, שֶׁהָיָה שָׂמֵחַ הַקָּדוֹשׁ בָּרוּךְ הוּא עַל שֶׁהָיוּ בָּנָיו הוֹלְכִים בְּדֶרֶךְ הַתּוֹרָה וּבְמִצְוָתָהּ לְהַטּוֹת אַחֲרֵי רַבִּים. וּמַה שֶׁאָמַר נִצְחוּנִי בָּנַי, חָלִילָה לִהְיוֹת נִצָּחוֹן לְפָנָיו בָּרוּךְ הוּא, אֲבָל פֵּרוּשׁ הַדָּבָר הוּא עַל עִנְיָן זֶה, שֶׁבַּמַּחֲלֹקֶת הַזֶּה שֶׁהָיָה לְרַבִּי אֱלִיעֶזֶר עִם חֲבֵרָיו הָאֱמֶת הָיָה כְּרַבִּי אֱלִיעֶזֶר וּכְדִבְרֵי הַבַּת קוֹל שֶׁהִכְרִיעָה כְּמוֹתוֹ, וְאַף עַל פִּי שֶׁהָיָה הָאֱמֶת אִתּוֹ בָּזֶה, בְּיִתְרוֹן פִּלְפּוּלוֹ עַל חֲבֵרָיו לֹא יָרְדוּ לְסוֹף דַּעְתּוֹ, וְלֹא רָצוּ לְהוֹדוֹת לִדְבָרָיו אֲפִלּוּ אַחַר בַּת קוֹל, וְהֵבִיאוּ רְאָיָה מִן הַדִּין הַקָּבוּעַ בַּתּוֹרָה שֶׁצִּוְּתָנוּ לָלֶכֶת אַחֲרֵי הָרַבִּים לְעוֹלָם בֵּין יֹאמְרוּ אֱמֶת אוֹ אֲפִלּוּ טוֹעִים,[8]

The Gemara there records a dispute between R' Eliezer and the Sages regarding the *tumah* status of a particular type of oven. After presenting numerous arguments and even producing a display of miracles to support his opinion, R' Eliezer declared that his opinion would be confirmed by Heaven, at which point a Heavenly Voice came out and proclaimed that the law accords with R' Eliezer. Despite all this, R' Eliezer's main disputant, R' Yehoshua, overruled him, explaining that "The Torah is not in heaven" (*Deuteronomy* 30:12); that is, since the Torah was given to mankind, it is subject to man's interpretation alone. Divine intervention has no bearing on the law, and since R' Eliezer is in the minority, we are required to rule against him. Chinuch cites the continuation of the passage:

אָמְרוּ שָׁם – [The Gemara] states there: אַשְׁכְּחֵיהּ רַבִּי נָתָן לְאֵלִיָּהוּ וְכוּ' – R' Nassan met Elijah the Prophet **אֲמַר לֵיהּ מָה עֲבִיד הַקָּדוֹשׁ בָּרוּךְ הוּא בְּהַהִיא שַׁעְתָּא** – and **said to him: What did the Holy One, blessed is He, do at that moment,** when R' Yehoshua rejected the Heavenly signal? **אֲמַר לֵיהּ חַיֵּיךְ וְאָמַר נִצְחוּנִי בָּנַי – [Elijah] replied: [The Holy One] laughed, and said, "My children have prevailed over Me!"**

Elijah's response is baffling. Why did God laugh when the Heavenly Voice was ignored? And if R' Yehoshua was justified in rejecting the Heavenly Voice, why would that be described as prevailing over the Almighty? Chinuch explains:

שֶׁהָיָה שָׂמֵחַ הַקָּדוֹשׁ בָּרוּךְ הוּא – Elijah meant **that the Holy One, blessed is He,** laughed because He **was happy עַל שֶׁהָיוּ בָּנָיו הוֹלְכִים בְּדֶרֶךְ הַתּוֹרָה וּבְמִצְוָתָהּ לְהַטּוֹת אַחֲרֵי רַבִּים – that His children were following the Torah path, and** abiding by **its commandment to follow the majority opinion. וּמַה שֶׁאָמַר נִצְחוּנִי בָּנַי – As for [His] statement that "My children have prevailed over Me," חָלִילָה לִהְיוֹת נִצָּחוֹן לְפָנָיו בָּרוּךְ הוּא – Heaven forbid that** anyone else **should** actually **be victorious in His Presence, blessed is He! אֲבָל פֵּרוּשׁ הַדָּבָר הוּא עַל עִנְיָן זֶה – Rather, the explanation of this matter is as follows: שֶׁבַּמַּחֲלֹקֶת הַזֶּה שֶׁהָיָה לְרַבִּי אֱלִיעֶזֶר עִם חֲבֵרָיו – In this dispute that R' Eliezer had with his colleagues, הָאֱמֶת הָיָה כְּרַבִּי אֱלִיעֶזֶר וּכְדִבְרֵי הַבַּת קוֹל שֶׁהִכְרִיעָה כְּמוֹתוֹ – the truth** (meaning, the letter of the law with respect to the particulars of *tumah*) **accorded with R' Eliezer, as proclaimed by the Heavenly Voice that sided with him. וְאַף עַל פִּי שֶׁהָיָה הָאֱמֶת אִתּוֹ בָּזֶה – Yet, although the truth accorded with [R' Eliezer] in this matter, בְּיִתְרוֹן פִּלְפּוּלוֹ עַל חֲבֵרָיו לֹא יָרְדוּ לְסוֹף דַּעְתּוֹ – due to his superior analytical abilities over** those of **his colleagues, they did not fully grasp his reasoning; וְלֹא רָצוּ לְהוֹדוֹת לִדְבָרָיו אֲפִלּוּ אַחַר בַּת קוֹל – thus, they were unwilling to concede to his words, even after** hearing **the Heavenly Voice. וְהֵבִיאוּ רְאָיָה מִן הַדִּין הַקָּבוּעַ בַּתּוֹרָה – And, as support** for their refusal to concede, **they cited the law established in the Torah שֶׁצִּוְּתָנוּ לָלֶכֶת אַחֲרֵי הָרַבִּים לְעוֹלָם בֵּין יֹאמְרוּ אֱמֶת אוֹ אֲפִלּוּ טוֹעִים – that commands us to always follow the majority, whether** what **[the majority] says** is **the true** meaning of the Torah, **or even if [the majority] is mistaken.**[8]

---

8. Since, when Hashem gave us the Torah, He commanded us to interpret its laws according to the understanding of the majority of sages, and He further commanded that we should follow their opinion even if we know it to be wrong, the majority opinion prevails even in the face of a Heavenly signal that favors the minority. The majority of the sages may have told us, in effect, that "right is left," but the Torah itself states

וְעַל זֶה הֵשִׁיב הַבּוֹרֵא בָּרוּךְ הוּא נִצְּחוּנִי בָּנַי, כְּלוֹמַר אַחַר שֶׁהֵם נוֹטִים מִדֶּרֶךְ הָאֱמֶת שֶׁרַבִּי אֱלִיעֶזֶר הוּא הָיָה מְכַוֵּן בָּזֶה אֶת הָאֱמֶת וְלֹא הֵם, וְהֵם בָּאִים עָלָיו מִכֹּחַ מִצְוַת הַתּוֹרָה שֶׁצִּוִּיתִים לִשְׁמֹעַ אֶל הָרֹב לְעוֹלָם, אִם כֵּן עַל כָּל פָּנִים יֵשׁ לְהוֹדוֹת בַּפַּעַם הַזֹּאת כְּדִבְרֵיהֶם שֶׁתִּהְיֶה הָאֱמֶת נֶעְדֶּרֶת, וַהֲרֵי זֶה כְּאִלּוּ בַּעַל הָאֱמֶת נָצוּחַ[9].

מִדִּינֵי הַמִּצְוָה מַה שֶּׁאָמְרוּ זִכְרוֹנָם לִבְרָכָה (סנהדרין פ״ח ע״ב — פ״ז ע״א) **שֶׁאַף עַל פִּי שֶׁהָעוֹבֵר עַל מַה שֶּׁפֵּרְשׁוּ חֲכָמִים בְּדִבְרֵי הַתּוֹרָה עוֹבֵר עַל לָאו זֶה דְּלֹא תָסוּר, מִכָּל מָקוֹם אֵין לוֹ לָאָדָם דִּין זָקֵן מַמְרֵא הַיָּדוּעַ בַּגְּמָרָא בְּסוֹף סַנְהֶדְרִין** (שם) **שֶׁהוּא חַיָּב מִיתָה עַד שֶׁיְּהֵא חוֹלֵק עַל בֵּית דִּין הַגָּדוֹל[10], וְשֶׁיְּהֵא הוּא חָכָם שֶׁהִגִּיעַ לְהוֹרָאָה סָמוּךְ**

וְעַל זֶה הֵשִׁיב הַבּוֹרֵא בָּרוּךְ הוּא נִצְּחוּנִי בָּנַי – To this, the Creator, blessed is He, responded, "My children have prevailed over Me." כְּלוֹמַר אַחַר שֶׁהֵם נוֹטִים מִדֶּרֶךְ הָאֱמֶת – That is to say, being that they are deviating from the true path, שֶׁרַבִּי אֱלִיעֶזֶר הוּא הָיָה מְכַוֵּן בָּזֶה אֶת הָאֱמֶת וְלֹא הֵם – for it is R' Eliezer who arrived at the truth and not [the Sages], וְהֵם בָּאִים עָלָיו מִכֹּחַ מִצְוַת הַתּוֹרָה – yet they oppose him with the power of the Torah's commandment, שֶׁצִּוִּיתִים לִשְׁמֹעַ אֶל הָרֹב לְעוֹלָם – in which I, the Creator, **commanded them to always follow the majority; אִם כֵּן עַל כָּל פָּנִים יֵשׁ לְהוֹדוֹת בַּפַּעַם הַזֹּאת כְּדִבְרֵיהֶם – accordingly, at least in this situation, it is proper to concede to their words, שֶׁתִּהְיֶה הָאֱמֶת נֶעְדֶּרֶת –** and **that the truth be ignored,** in keeping with My own directive in the Torah. **וַהֲרֵי זֶה כְּאִלּוּ בַּעַל הָאֱמֶת נָצוּחַ – Thus,** in this sense, **it is as though the Master of Truth has been defeated.**[9]

Laws of the Mitzvah

This prohibition has a particular application to a *zakein mamrei* ("insubordinate elder"), a Torah scholar who is himself qualified to serve on the Sanhedrin. Even if he knows that the Sanhedrin erred, he may not act against the ruling of the Sanhedrin, nor rule that others should act against their ruling. Chinuch discusses that aspect of the mitzvah:

מִדִּינֵי הַמִּצְוָה – Among the laws of the mitzvah is **מַה שֶּׁאָמְרוּ זִכְרוֹנָם לִבְרָכָה – that which [the Sages], of blessed memory, stated** (*Sanhedrin* 86b-87a), **שֶׁאַף עַל פִּי שֶׁהָעוֹבֵר עַל מַה שֶּׁפֵּרְשׁוּ חֲכָמִים בְּדִבְרֵי הַתּוֹרָה עוֹבֵר עַל לָאו זֶה ד״לֹא תָסוּר״ – that although one who violates** any of **the Sages' interpretations of the Torah transgresses this prohibition of *lo sassur*** (*you shall not deviate*), **מִכָּל מָקוֹם אֵין לוֹ לָאָדָם דִּין זָקֵן מַמְרֵא – nevertheless, a person does not have the status of a *zakein mamrei,* הַיָּדוּעַ בַּגְּמָרָא בְּסוֹף סַנְהֶדְרִין שֶׁהוּא חַיָּב מִיתָה – who, as specified by the Gemara at the end of** Tractate ***Sanhedrin*** (ibid.), **is liable to the death penalty, עַד שֶׁיְּהֵא חוֹלֵק עַל בֵּית דִּין הַגָּדוֹל – unless he disputes** a ruling of **the Great Sanhedrin.**[10] **וְשֶׁיְּהֵא הוּא חָכָם שֶׁהִגִּיעַ לְהוֹרָאָה סָמוּךְ**

NOTES

that we must still abide by their ruling, for only this guarantees the continuity of Torah observance.

Now, if the majority of the sages had been able to grasp R' Eliezer's reasoning, they presumably would have conceded that he was right. But since they could not grasp it, they stood by their opinion despite the Heavenly Voice. Being that "the Torah is not in Heaven," no heavenly signal could sway them to change their opinion to something they were unable to comprehend with their own intellect. And since the majority remained opposed to R' Eliezer, the halachah was decided against him. In short, the majority refused (1) to *change their minds* on account of the Heavenly Voice; and (2) to *let the matter be decided* by the Heavenly Voice.

9. R' Yehoshua's rejection of the Heavenly Voice brought joy to God, for it was a fulfillment of His own commandment. At the same time, however, it was a suppression of the ultimate truth regarding the issue at hand. Since God's essence is Absolute Truth, He said, "My children — in following My own commandment *as they should* — have prevailed over Me."

[For another explanation of this Aggadic passage, see *Derashos HaRan* §7 and §11, and Introduction to *Ketzos HaChoshen.*]

10. When a scholar challenged the ruling of his local *beis din,* the question would be presented to progressively greater courts, and if the matter remained unresolved, it would ultimately be decided by the Great Sanhedrin (*Sanhedrin* 86b; see Mitzvah 491). The death penalty applies only to one who disobeys the Great Sanhedrin, not to one who disobeys any of the lower courts.

לְסַנְהֶדְרִין[11], וְיַחֲלֹק עֲלֵיהֶם בְּדָבָר שֶׁזְּדוֹנוֹ כָּרֵת וְשִׁגְגָתוֹ חַטָּאת[12], וּבֵין שֶׁהוּא מֵקֵל וְהֵם מַחְמִירִין אוֹ בְּהֶפֶךְ[13] וְיוֹרֶה לַעֲשׂוֹת כְּהוֹרָאָתוֹ אוֹ יַעֲשֶׂה הוּא מַעֲשֶׂה עַל פִּי הוֹרָאָתוֹ, שֶׁנֶּאֱמַר אֲשֶׁר יַעֲשֶׂה בְזָדוֹן, וְלֹא שֶׁיּוֹרֶה לְבַד[14]. אֲבָל אִם הָיָה תַּלְמִיד שֶׁלֹּא הִגִּיעַ לְהוֹרָאָה וְהוֹרָה פָּטוּר[15], שֶׁנֶּאֱמַר כִּי יִפָּלֵא מִמְּךָ דָבָר, מִי שֶׁלֹּא יִפָּלֵא מִמֶּנּוּ אֶלָּא דָּבָר מֻפְלָא[16]. וְכֵן אִם מְצָאָן חוּץ לְלִשְׁכַּת הַגָּזִית[17] וְהִמְרָה עֲלֵיהֶם פָּטוּר, שֶׁנֶּאֱמַר וְקַמְתָּ וְעָלִיתָ אֶל הַמָּקוֹם,

---

לְסַנְהֶדְרִין – **He must also be a scholar who is qualified to rule, and has received *semichah,* making him qualified to serve on the Sanhedrin,**[11] וְיַחֲלֹק עֲלֵיהֶם בְּדָבָר שֶׁזְּדוֹנוֹ כָּרֵת וְשִׁגְגָתוֹ חַטָּאת – **and must be disputing them about a matter whose intentional** transgression **bears** liability to ***kares,*** **and whose unintentional** transgression **bears a *chatas* offering;**[12] וּבֵין שֶׁהוּא מֵקֵל וְהֵם מַחְמִירִין אוֹ בְּהֶפֶךְ – this applies **whether he rules leniently and they rule stringently, or vice versa.**[13] וְיוֹרֶה לַעֲשׂוֹת כְּהוֹרָאָתוֹ – **Also,** to be liable to the death penalty, **he must** either **instruct** others **to follow his opinion** in defiance of the Sanhedrin, אוֹ יַעֲשֶׂה הוּא מַעֲשֶׂה עַל פִּי הוֹרָאָתוֹ – **or he must himself act in accordance with his position.** שֶׁנֶּאֱמַר "אֲשֶׁר יַעֲשֶׂה בְזָדוֹן" – This is as indicated by Scripture, **for** when setting forth the penalty of the *zakein mamrei,* **it is stated** (*Deuteronomy* 17:12): *And the man **who will "act" with willfulness,** not to listen ... to the judge, that man shall die.* וְלֹא שֶׁיּוֹרֶה לְבַד – The term *act* implies that the death penalty applies only to one who defies the Sanhedrin in a way that leads to action, **but not if one merely states an opinion** contrary to that of the Sanhedrin.[14] אֲבָל אִם הָיָה תַּלְמִיד שֶׁלֹּא הִגִּיעַ לְהוֹרָאָה וְהוֹרָה פָּטוּר – **However, if [the one who defied the Sanhedrin] was a student who was not yet qualified to rule, and he ruled** in defiance of the Sanhedrin, **he is absolved of penalty.**[15] שֶׁנֶּאֱמַר "כִּי יִפָּלֵא מִמְּךָ דָבָר" – This is **because,** in the context of the obligation to approach the Sanhedrin when uncertainties arise and then to heed their rulings, **it is stated** (*Deuteronomy* 17:8): ***If a matter** of judgment **is hidden from you.*** מִי שֶׁלֹּא יִפָּלֵא מִמֶּנּוּ אֶלָּא דָּבָר מֻפְלָא – The verse speaks of **one from whom nothing is hidden other than that which is** truly **a "hidden"** (obscure) **matter,** but he is well-versed in all other matters of Torah law.[16] Thus, the capital penalty set forth in this verse for one who *defies* the Sanhedrin applies only to a great scholar who is qualified to rule and sit on the Sanhedrin. וְכֵן אִם מְצָאָן חוּץ לְלִשְׁכַּת הַגָּזִית וְהִמְרָה עֲלֵיהֶם פָּטוּר – **Similarly, if he found [the Sanhedrin] outside of the Chamber of Hewn Stone** (*Lishkas HaGazis*),[17] **and defied them** by contradicting a ruling that they issued there, **he is absolved** of liability. שֶׁנֶּאֱמַר "וְקַמְתָּ וְעָלִיתָ אֶל הַמָּקוֹם" – This is **because,** in the above context, **it is stated** (ibid. vv. 8-10), ***and you shall rise up, and you shall ascend to the place** that HASHEM, your God, shall choose ... you shall do according to the word that they will tell you from that place.*

NOTES

11. See Mitzvah 491 (after note 38), where the process of *semichah* is described.

12. Chinuch defines this requirement below, after note 18. [For a possible exception to this requirement, see *Rambam* and *Raavad, Hil. Mamrim* 4:3 with commentaries.]

13. That is, the defiant ruling of the *zakein mamrei* does not have to be one that might actually *cause* a person to incur *kares* by following it. Even if he rules more stringently than the Sanhedrin, he is considered a *zakein mamrei,* as long as his ruling pertains to a prohibition that is so *severe* as to carry the *kares* penalty (see *Rambam* ibid. 4:2 and *Toras Chaim* to *Sanhedrin* 87a ד"ה לתה; but see *Lechem Mishneh* ad loc. ד"ה אם חלב ורשב"ל).

14. If a scholar simply teaches his students an opinion that is contrary to a ruling of the Sanhedrin, but he does not instruct them to act on that opinion in practice, he is not liable to death. It is only when he applies his ruling in practice, by either acting on it himself or instructing others to act on it, that he is considered a *zakein mamrei* and is liable to death (*Sanhedrin* 86b).

15. Even if he instructed others to actually follow his ruling in practice (*Rambam* ibid. 3:5).

16. As opposed to one who has not yet reached clarity in law, to whom every matter is obscure (*Kesef Mishneh, Hil. Mamrim* 3:5, citing *Rambam, Commentary to the Mishnah* [*Sanhedrin* 11:2; see Kafich ed.]).

17. The Sanhedrin generally convened in the *Lishkas HaGazis,* a room built into the wall of the main Courtyard of the *Beis HaMikdash* (see Mitzvah 491, at note 10).

מְלַמֵּד שֶׁהַמָּקוֹם גּוֹרֵם לוֹ מִיתָה[18].

וּבֵין שֶׁחָלַק עֲלֵיהֶם בְּדָבָר מַמָּשׁ שֶׁיֵּשׁ בִּזְדוֹנוֹ כָּרֵת אוֹ בְּדָבָר הַמֵּבִיא לִידֵי דָּבָר שֶׁחַיָּבִין עָלָיו כָּרֵת, חַיָּב. כֵּיצַד בְּדָבָר שֶׁיֵּשׁ בִּזְדוֹנוֹ כָּרֵת, כְּגוֹן שֶׁנֶּחְלְקוּ בְּאִשָּׁה אַחַת אִם הִיא עֶרְוָה אוֹ אֵינָהּ[19], אִם דָּם זֶה מְטַמֵּא אוֹ אֵינוֹ מְטַמֵּא[20], אִם אִשָּׁה זוֹ זָבָה אוֹ אֵינָהּ זָבָה[21], אִם חֵלֶב זֶה אָסוּר אוֹ מֻתָּר[22], וְכֵן כָּל כַּיּוֹצֵא בָּזֶה[23]. וְכֵיצַד בְּדָבָר הַמֵּבִיא לִידֵי דָּבָר שֶׁיֵּשׁ בּוֹ חִיּוּב זֶה, כְּגוֹן שֶׁנֶּחְלְקוּ בְּעִבּוּר הַשָּׁנָה שֶׁמֵּבִיא לִידֵי אֲכִילַת חָמֵץ בְּפֶסַח[24], וְכֵן אִם נֶחְלְקוּ בְּדִין מִדִּינֵי מָמוֹנוֹת שֶׁלְּדִבְרֵי הָאֶחָד כַּדִּין נָטַל זֶה מָמוֹן זֶה מֵחֲבֵרוֹ,

---

מְלַמֵּד שֶׁהַמָּקוֹם גּוֹרֵם לוֹ מִיתָה – **This teaches that** it is specifically defying a ruling of the Sanhedrin in **that location that brings him** liability to **death.**[18]

Chinuch explains his earlier statement that the law of a *zakein mamrei* pertains only to one who ruled on a matter that bears liability to *kares* (or a *chatas* offering):

וּבֵין שֶׁחָלַק עֲלֵיהֶם בְּדָבָר מַמָּשׁ שֶׁיֵּשׁ בִּזְדוֹנוֹ כָּרֵת – **Whether one disputes [the Sanhedrin] regarding a matter that actually bears** the penalty of ***kares*** **for** its **intentional** transgression, אוֹ בְּדָבָר הַמֵּבִיא לִידֵי דָּבָר שֶׁחַיָּבִין עָלָיו כָּרֵת – **or** one disputes them **regarding something that can *lead* to a matter that bears liability to *kares*,** חַיָּב – **he is liable** to capital punishment for transgressing this prohibition.

Chinuch gives examples of each of these:

כֵּיצַד בְּדָבָר שֶׁיֵּשׁ בִּזְדוֹנוֹ כָּרֵת – **What is a case of a matter whose intentional** transgression actually **bears *kares*?** כְּגוֹן שֶׁנֶּחְלְקוּ בְּאִשָּׁה אַחַת אִם הִיא עֶרְוָה אוֹ אֵינָהּ – **For example, if they had a dispute as to whether a certain woman is** prohibited to her relative as **an *ervah* or not,**[19] אִם דָּם זֶה מְטַמֵּא אוֹ אֵינוֹ מְטַמֵּא – **whether a certain** discharge of **blood causes** a woman **to be *tamei*** as a *niddah* **or does not cause** her **to be *tamei*,**[20] אִם אִשָּׁה זוֹ זָבָה אוֹ אֵינָהּ זָבָה – **whether a certain woman is a *zavah* or is not a *zavah*,**[21] אִם חֵלֶב זֶה אָסוּר אוֹ מֻתָּר – **whether a specific** section of **fat** from an animal **is prohibited** for consumption **or is permitted,**[22] וְכֵן כָּל כַּיּוֹצֵא בָּזֶה – **and anything similar to these.**[23]

וְכֵיצַד בְּדָבָר הַמֵּבִיא לִידֵי דָּבָר שֶׁיֵּשׁ בּוֹ חִיּוּב זֶה – **What is a case of** a dispute **regarding something that can *lead* to a matter bearing this liability** of *kares*? כְּגוֹן שֶׁנֶּחְלְקוּ בְּעִבּוּר הַשָּׁנָה שֶׁמֵּבִיא לִידֵי אֲכִילַת חָמֵץ בְּפֶסַח – **For example, if they had a dispute** as to whether the year is **a leap year, which can lead to eating *chametz* on Pesach.**[24] וְכֵן אִם נֶחְלְקוּ בְּדִין מִדִּינֵי מָמוֹנוֹת – **Similarly, if they had a dispute regarding any of the monetary laws** (i.e., a monetary dispute between two litigants, where the sage disputed the Sanhedrin over which position is justified), it could lead to a *kares* liability. שֶׁלְּדִבְרֵי הָאֶחָד כַּדִּין נָטַל זֶה מָמוֹן זֶה מֵחֲבֵרוֹ – **For, according to one position, the**

NOTES

18. The repeated references to "the place" teach that the law of a *zakein mamrei* stated later in the passage is contingent on his defying a ruling that the Sanhedrin issued while they were seated in their headquarters in the *Lishkas HaGazis* (see *Sanhedrin* 87a and *Sifrei* to v. 10, with *Malbim*).

19. The term *ervah* refers to any of the women that a man is prohibited to marry under pain of *kares,* as listed in *Leviticus* Ch. 18. [As a rule, any prohibition that bears *kares* for an intentional violation bears a *chatas* liability for an unintentional violation. See Mitzvah 121.]

20. Certain shades of blood-like discharges would not render a woman a *niddah* (see Mitzvah 207, at note 20). [Intentional relations with a *niddah* subject both parties to *kares.*]

21. See Mitzvah 182. [Intentional relations with a *zavah* are punishable with *kares.*]

22. That is, whether the specific fat is included in the prohibition of *cheilev,* which bears the *kares* penalty (see Mitzvah 147).

23. In all these cases, the dispute centers on whether a specific person or food is prohibited under pain of *kares.* For discussion of the precise cases where such disputes might arise, see *Sanhedrin* 87b.

24. The Jewish year can have 12 months or, in the case of a leap year, 13 months. In earlier times, the Sanhedrin would determine annually whether the year would be a leap year. A dispute regarding whether to establish a leap year could lead to a *kares* liability, as one who fails to observe Pesach at the proper time and intentionally eats *chametz* on the festival, is liable to *kares*.

וְאִם קִדֵּשׁ[25] בּוֹ הָאִשָּׁה מְקֻדֶּשֶׁת, וְהַבָּא עָלֶיהָ בְּמֵזִיד עָנוּשׁ כָּרֵת וּבְשׁוֹגֵג חַיָּב חַטָּאת, וּלְדִבְרֵי הָאַחֵר פָּטוּר, וְכֵן בְּכָל עִנְיָן שֶׁיֵּשׁ לְהוֹצִיא מָמוֹן כְּגוֹן חַיָּבֵי חֲרָמִים וַעֲרָכִים[26] אִם חַיָּבִים לִתֵּן אוֹ אֵינָם חַיָּבִים[27], שֶׁלְּדִבְרֵי הָאוֹמֵר אֵינָם חַיָּבִים, כָּל שֶׁלְּקָחוּ מֵהֶם גֶּזֶל, וְאִם קִדֵּשׁ בּוֹ הָאִשָּׁה אֵינָהּ מְקֻדֶּשֶׁת, וְכֵן כָּל כַּיּוֹצֵא בָזֶה. וַאֲפִלּוּ חָלְקוּ בְּדִינֵי מַכּוֹת חַיָּב עֲלֵיהֶם, שֶׁהֲרֵי לְדִבְרֵי הָאוֹמֵר אֵינוֹ חַיָּב מַלְקוּת בְּבֵית דִּין חַיָּבִים לְשַׁלֵּם לוֹ דְּמֵי חַבָּלוֹ וּבְדִין יִטֹּל מֵהֶם תַּשְׁלוּמָיו[28].

---

person who took money from his fellow was legally entitled to do so, וְאִם קִדֵּשׁ בּוֹ הָאִשָּׁה מְקֻדֶּשֶׁת — **and if he was to perform** *kiddushin*[25] **with a woman with [that money], she would be married** to him, וְהַבָּא עָלֶיהָ בְּמֵזִיד עָנוּשׁ כָּרֵת — **and if [another man]** subsequently **had relations with her intentionally, he** would transgress the prohibition against relations with a married woman and **would be punished with** *kares,* וּבְשׁוֹגֵג חַיָּב חַטָּאת — **and** if he would transgress **unintentionally, he would be liable to a** *chatas* **offering;** וּלְדִבְרֵי הָאַחֵר פָּטוּר — **while according to the other position,** the money did not belong to the one who performed *kiddushin,* so the marriage never took effect, and **[the other man]** who had relations with her **would be exempt** from any penalty. Thus, a dispute pertaining to monetary law can lead to a question of *kares* liability. וְכֵן בְּכָל עִנְיָן שֶׁיֵּשׁ לְהוֹצִיא מָמוֹן — **The same** applies **to** a dispute regarding **any situation that calls for extracting money** from a person who owes it; כְּגוֹן חַיָּבֵי חֲרָמִים וַעֲרָכִים אִם חַיָּבִים לִתֵּן אוֹ אֵינָם חַיָּבִים — **such as** in the case of *cherem* **and** *erech* **vows,**[26] if there arises a situation where one's liability is in question, and this sage disputes the Sanhedrin with regard to **whether [those who utter such a vow] are obligated to give** what they pledged **or not,**[27] he is considered a *zakein mamrei,* as this situation can result in a question of liability to *kares.* שֶׁלְּדִבְרֵי הָאוֹמֵר אֵינָם חַיָּבִים — **For, according to the one who maintains that [the ones who pledged] are not obligated,** כָּל שֶׁלְּקָחוּ מֵהֶם גֶּזֶל וְאִם קִדֵּשׁ בּוֹ הָאִשָּׁה אֵינָהּ מְקֻדֶּשֶׁת — **anything that is seized from them** as payment of the "pledge" **is** considered **stolen goods, and if one were to perform** *kiddushin* **with a woman with [whatever was taken as payment], she is not considered married** to him. וְכֵן כָּל כַּיּוֹצֵא בָזֶה — **And the same** is true **in all similar cases** — whether one disputes the Sanhedrin regarding a monetary law itself, or regarding a law that has monetary ramifications, the law of *zakein mamrei* applies, as the dispute can lead to *kares* or *chatas* liability. וַאֲפִלּוּ חָלְקוּ בְּדִינֵי מַכּוֹת חַיָּב עֲלֵיהֶם — **Furthermore, he is liable** to death **even if they were in dispute regarding** *malkus*-**bearing cases,** i.e., whether one who performs a certain act is liable to *malkus;* שֶׁהֲרֵי לְדִבְרֵי הָאוֹמֵר אֵינוֹ חַיָּב מַלְקוּת בְּבֵית דִּין — **for, according to the one who maintains that he is not liable to** *malkus* **in** *beis din,* חַיָּבִים לְשַׁלֵּם לוֹ דְּמֵי חַבָּלוֹ וּבְדִין יִטֹּל מֵהֶם תַּשְׁלוּמָיו — if lashes were administered, **[beis din] is obligated to compensate him monetarily for his beating, and he is legally entitled to his payment from them;** thus, the ruling could *lead* to a *kares* or *chatas* liability if he were to extract money from *beis din* and perform *kiddushin* with that money, as in the previous cases.[28]

NOTES

25. For a woman to be halachically considered a married woman, an act of *kiddushin* must be performed with her. Most commonly, this is accomplished by presenting her with an item of value. From that point on, if she has relations with another man, the relations are considered adulterous, subjecting both parties to *kares* if the act was intentional, and to a *chatas* if it was unintentional.

26. A person who takes a *cherem* or an *erech* vow upon himself is required to make a specific payment to the Temple treasury or the Kohanim (see Mitzvos 350 and 357).

27. For examples, see *Sanhedrin* 88a. See also *Lechem Mishneh, Hil. Mamrim* 4:2 ד"ה בערכין.

28. It emerges that the only rulings excluded from the law of *zakein mamrei* are those that do not at all involve *kares,* nor *malkus,* nor financial liability, and that cannot even remotely lead to a *kares* liability in any way. See *Rambam, Hil. Mamrim* 4:2, who elaborates on this matter.

וְכָתַב הָרַמְבַּ"ם ז"ל (פ"א ממםרים ה"ב) בְּעִנְיַן לָאו זֶה דְּלֹא תָסוּר, שֶׁאֶחָד דְּבָרִים שֶׁלָּמְדוּ אוֹתָם חֲכָמִים מִפִּי הַקַּבָּלָה, וְאֶחָד דְּבָרִים שֶׁלָּמְדוּ אוֹתָם מִדַּעְתָּן בְּאַחַת מִן הַמִּדּוֹת שֶׁהַתּוֹרָה נִדְרֶשֶׁת בָּהֶן[29], וְאֶחָד דְּבָרִים שֶׁנַּעֲשׂוּ סְיָג לַתּוֹרָה וְהֵם הַגְּזֵרוֹת וְהַתַּקָּנוֹת וְהַמִּנְהָגוֹת, בְּכָל אֶחָד מֵהַשְּׁלֹשָׁה דְּבָרִים אֵלּוּ מִצְוַת עֲשֵׂה לִשְׁמֹעַ לָהֶם[30], וְהָעוֹבֵר עַל כָּל אַחַת מֵהֶם עוֹבֵר בַּעֲשֵׂה וְלֹא תַעֲשֶׂה. וְהָרַמְבַּ"ן ז"ל (בהשגתו לשרש הראשון) תָּפַשׂ עָלָיו הַרְבֵּה וְאָמַר, הִנֵּה סְבוּר הָרַב שֶׁיֵּשׁ בִּכְלַל לָאו דְּלֹא תָסוּר כָּל מַה שֶּׁהוּא מִדִּבְרֵי חֲכָמִים בֵּין שֶׁהֵן מִצְוֹת כְּגוֹן מִקְרָא מְגִלָּה וְנֵר חֲנֻכָּה[31], אוֹ שֶׁהֵן מִן הַתַּקָּנוֹת כְּגוֹן עוֹף בְּשַׂר בְּחָלָב[32] וּשְׁנִיּוֹת לָעֲרָיוֹת[33],

---

Dispute Regarding the Mitzvah

Chinuch embarks on a discussion of a debate between *Rambam* and *Ramban* as to the scope of this prohibition, first citing *Rambam's* view:

וְכָתַב הָרַמְבַּ"ם ז"ל בְּעִנְיַן לָאו זֶה דְּ"לֹא תָסוּר" – **Rambam, of blessed memory, wrote** (*Hil. Mamrim* 1:2) **regarding this prohibition of** ***lo sassur,*** שֶׁאֶחָד דְּבָרִים שֶׁלָּמְדוּ אוֹתָם חֲכָמִים מִפִּי הַקַּבָּלָה – **that whether** we are dealing with **matters** of Biblical law **that the Sages received through the Oral Tradition** from Sinai, וְאֶחָד דְּבָרִים שֶׁלָּמְדוּ אוֹתָם מִדַּעְתָּן בְּאַחַת מִן הַמִּדּוֹת שֶׁהַתּוֹרָה נִדְרֶשֶׁת בָּהֶן – **or matters** of Biblical law **that they derived with their own reasoning through one of the principles for expounding the Torah,**[29] וְאֶחָד דְּבָרִים שֶׁנַּעֲשׂוּ סְיָג לַתּוֹרָה – **or matters** of Rabbinic law **that were established as safeguards for Biblical law,** וְהֵם הַגְּזֵרוֹת וְהַתַּקָּנוֹת וְהַמִּנְהָגוֹת – **which are the decrees, enactments, and practices** instituted by the Sages; בְּכָל אֶחָד מֵהַשְּׁלֹשָׁה דְּבָרִים אֵלּוּ מִצְוַת עֲשֵׂה לִשְׁמֹעַ לָהֶם – **regarding any of these three categories, it is a mitzvah-obligation to obey** the rulings of **[the Sages],**[30] וְהָעוֹבֵר עַל כָּל אַחַת מֵהֶם עוֹבֵר בַּעֲשֵׂה וְלֹא תַעֲשֶׂה – **and one who violates** their words **in any of these** categories **transgresses a mitzvah-obligation** (the previous mitzvah) **and a mitzvah-prohibition** (this mitzvah).

It is clear that the obligation to heed the Sages and the prohibition to defy them apply to their interpretations of Biblical law, i.e., the first two categories that *Rambam* mentioned. *Rambam,* however, took the position that this obligation and prohibition also apply to a third category – the decrees and practices that the Sages enacted. In other words, according to *Rambam,* every Rabbinic law is supported by a *Biblical* mitzvah-obligation and mitzvah-prohibition that require us to obey the Sages. Chinuch now proceeds with an extensive citation of *Ramban* (glosses to *Sefer HaMitzvos, Shoresh* 1), who categorically rejects *Rambam's* position:

וְהָרַמְבַּ"ן ז"ל תָּפַשׂ עָלָיו הַרְבֵּה וְאָמַר – **However,** ***Ramban,*** **of blessed memory, challenged [*Rambam*] extensively, and said:** הִנֵּה סְבוּר הָרַב שֶׁיֵּשׁ בִּכְלַל לָאו דְּ"לֹא תָסוּר" כָּל מַה שֶּׁהוּא מִדִּבְרֵי חֲכָמִים – **Behold, the master** (i.e., *Rambam*) **maintains that the prohibition of** ***lo sassur*** **includes every** law **that is of Rabbinic origin,** בֵּין שֶׁהֵן מִצְוֹת כְּגוֹן מִקְרָא מְגִלָּה וְנֵר חֲנֻכָּה – regardless of **whether [these laws] are** Rabbinic **mitzvah-obligations, such as reading the Megillah** on Purim **and** kindling **the Chanukah lights,**[31] אוֹ שֶׁהֵן מִן הַתַּקָּנוֹת כְּגוֹן בְּשַׂר עוֹף בְּחָלָב וּשְׁנִיּוֹת לָעֲרָיוֹת – **or they are enactments** of Rabbinic prohibitions, **such as** the prohibition against partaking of **poultry together with milk,**[32] **and the secondary** ***ervah*** **prohibitions;**[33]

NOTES

29. See Mitzvah 495 note 3.

30. See Mitzvah 495 at notes 5-7.

31. Although the passage of *Rambam* that Chinuch cited does not explicitly say that these Rabbinic mitzvos are included, *Ramban* demonstrates from *Rambam* elsewhere that this is indeed his position (see *Rambam's* words following his Count of Mitzvos at beginning of *Mishneh Torah* [pp. 20-21 in Frankel ed.]).

32. The Biblical prohibition against the meat-dairy combination pertains only to the meat of domestic animals. The Sages, however, prohibited partaking of meat of wild animals or poultry with dairy; see Mitzvah 113 at notes 15-20.

33. I.e., the Rabbinic *ervah* prohibitions, which the Sages instituted as safeguards for the Biblical prohibitions; see Mitzvah 190, after note 15.

בֵּין שֶׁהֵן בְּקוּם עֲשֵׂה כְּגוֹן שָׁלֹשׁ תְּפִלּוֹת בְּכָל יוֹם[34] וּמֵאָה בְּרָכוֹת[35] וְלוּלָב שִׁבְעָה בַּגְּבוּלִין[36], וּבֵין שֶׁהֵן בְּלֹא תַעֲשֶׂה כְּגוֹן כָּל שֶׁהוּא מִשּׁוּם שְׁבוּת בְּשַׁבָּת וְיוֹם טוֹב, וְכֵן יוֹם טוֹב שֵׁנִי בַּגּוֹלָה[37] וְתִשְׁעָה בְּאָב, וְדֶרֶךְ כְּלָל כָּל מַה שֶּׁיֶּאֱסֹר אוֹתוֹ הַתַּלְמוּד אוֹ יְצַוֶּה עָלָיו[38], וְהִנֵּה הָרַב בּוֹנֶה חוֹמָה בְּצוּרָה סָבִיב לְדִבְרֵי חֲכָמִים, אֲבָל הִיא כְּפֶרֶץ נֹפֵל נִבְעֶה בְּחוֹמָה נִשְׂגָּבָה אֲשֶׁר פִּתְאֹם לְפֶתַע יָבוֹא שִׁבְרָהּ[39], לְפִי שֶׁהִיא סְבָרָא נִפְסֶדֶת בְּרֹב מְקוֹמוֹת בַּתַּלְמוּד, כִּי הִנֵּה לְדַעְתּוֹ הַמִּשְׁתַּמֵּשׁ בִּמְחֻבָּר כְּגוֹן הַנִּסְמָךְ עַל הָאִילָן בְּשַׁבָּת[40] אוֹ הַמְטַלְטֵל[41] מֵחַמָּה לַצֵּל אוֹ שֶׁאָמַר לַגּוֹי וְעָשָׂה[42] אוֹ אֲפִלּוּ הַמַּפְסִיעַ פְּסִיעָה גַּסָּה בְּשַׁבָּת[43] עוֹבֵר הוּא עַל עֲשֵׂה וְלֹא תַעֲשֶׂה מִן הַתּוֹרָה

בֵּין שֶׁהֵן בְּקוּם עֲשֵׂה – and regardless of **whether they are** laws that require us **to actively do** something, כְּגוֹן שָׁלֹשׁ תְּפִלּוֹת בְּכָל יוֹם וּמֵאָה בְּרָכוֹת וְלוּלָב שִׁבְעָה בַּגְּבוּלִין – **such as** the Rabbinic requirements to recite **three prayers every day,**[34] **to recite one hundred blessings** daily,[35] **and** to take **the *lulav*** all **seven days** of Succos even **outside of the *Beis HaMikdash*;**[36] וּבֵין שֶׁהֵן בְּלֹא תַעֲשֶׂה כְּגוֹן כָּל שֶׁהוּא מִשּׁוּם שְׁבוּת בְּשַׁבָּת וְיוֹם טוֹב – **or they are** laws that require us **to refrain from action, such as all Rabbinically prohibited activities on the Sabbath and Yom Tov,** וְכֵן יוֹם טוֹב שֵׁנִי בַּגּוֹלָה – **as well as** the prohibition to engage in *melachah* on **the second Yom Tov day in the Diaspora,**[37] וְתִשְׁעָה בְּאָב – **and** the prohibitions that apply on **Tishah B'Av.** וְדֶרֶךְ כְּלָל כָּל מַה שֶּׁיֶּאֱסֹר אוֹתוֹ הַתַּלְמוּד אוֹ יְצַוֶּה עָלָיו – **In general,** *Rambam* includes in this mitzvah **everything that the Talmud prohibits or commands.**[38]

Ramban opens his challenge to *Rambam's* position by pointing out its ramifications:

וְהִנֵּה הָרַב בּוֹנֶה חוֹמָה בְּצוּרָה סָבִיב לְדִבְרֵי חֲכָמִים – **Now, the master** (*Rambam*) **built a fortified wall around the words of the Sages,** אֲבָל הִיא "כְּפֶרֶץ נֹפֵל נִבְעֶה בְּחוֹמָה נִשְׂגָּבָה אֲשֶׁר פִּתְאֹם לְפֶתַע יָבוֹא שִׁבְרָהּ" – **however, it is** actually ***like the breach of a fallen wall, like a bulge in a lofty wall, whose collapse comes with quick suddenness,***[39] לְפִי שֶׁהִיא סְבָרָא נִפְסֶדֶת בְּרֹב מְקוֹמוֹת בַּתַּלְמוּד – **as it is a position that fails** to be sustainable **in most places in the Talmud.** כִּי הִנֵּה לְדַעְתּוֹ – **For, according to [*Rambam's*] opinion,** it emerges הַמִּשְׁתַּמֵּשׁ בִּמְחֻבָּר כְּגוֹן הַנִּסְמָךְ עַל הָאִילָן בְּשַׁבָּת – that **one who makes use on the Sabbath of** vegetation that is **attached** to the ground, **such as, if he leans on a tree;**[40] אוֹ הַמְטַלְטֵל מֵחַמָּה לַצֵּל – **or who moves** a utensil that is subject to the prohibition of *"muktzeh"*[41] **from the sun to the shade** on the Sabbath; אוֹ שֶׁאָמַר לַגּוֹי וְעָשָׂה – **or who instructs a non-Jew** to perform *melachah* on the Sabbath, **and [the non-Jew] performs** it for him;[42] אוֹ אֲפִלּוּ הַמַּפְסִיעַ פְּסִיעָה גַּסָּה בְּשַׁבָּת – **or who even walks with a long stride on the Sabbath,**[43] all of which are things that the Sages prohibited, עוֹבֵר הוּא עַל עֲשֵׂה וְלֹא תַעֲשֶׂה מִן הַתּוֹרָה – **transgresses**

NOTES

34. As was explained in Mitzvah 433, the Torah does not specify how often one must pray; the obligation to pray three times each day is a Rabbinic institution. See there, after note 9.

35. See *Menachos* 43b; *Rambam, Hil. Tefillah* 7:14-16.

36. [Literally, *in the boundaries.*] Biblical law requires that the Four Species (*lulav, esrog, hadassim,* and *aravos*) be taken on the first day of Succos in all locations, and on all seven days of Succos in the *Beis HaMikdash.* After the destruction of the Second *Beis HaMikdash,* Rabban Yochanan ben Zakkai instituted that the Four Species be taken on all seven days of Succos in every location, to commemorate the way that this mitzvah was performed in the *Beis HaMikdash.* See introduction to Mitzvah 324.

37. The Sages instituted that in the Diaspora each Yom Tov is to be observed for an additional day. See Mitzvah 301.

38. See *Rambam's* Introduction to *Mishneh Torah* [p. 3 in Frankel ed.].

39. [*Isaiah* 30:13.] Under scrutiny, it is apparent that the "wall" built by *Rambam* is unstable; i.e., his position lacks any strength.

40. See *Beitzah* 36b and *Shabbos* 154b-155a; *Rambam, Hil. Shabbos* 21:6.

41. I.e., an item that may generally not be moved on the Sabbath; see *Shabbos* 123b; *Rambam, Hil. Shabbos* 25:3.

42. It is prohibited to have a non-Jew perform *melachah* on the Sabbath on one's behalf; see *Shulchan Aruch, Orach Chaim* 243-247, and 307:2-5.

43. See *Shabbos* 113b; *Rambam, Hil. Shabbos* 24:4; *Orach Chaim* 301:1 with *Rama*.

וְרָאוּי הוּא לִלְקוֹת אַרְבָּעִים, אֶלָּא שֶׁפְּטָרוֹ הָרַב שָׁם בְּסֵפֶר שׁוֹפְטִים[44] מִפְּנֵי שֶׁנִּתַּן לְאַזְהָרַת מִיתַת בֵּית דִּין שֶׁכָּל חָכָם שֶׁמַּמְרֶה עַל דִּבְרֵיהֶם מִיתָתוֹ בְּחֶנֶק[45], וְהִנֵּה לִדְבָרָיו לוֹקֶה הוּא לְדַעַת הָאוֹמֵר בַּתַּלְמוּד לָאו שֶׁנִּתַּן לְאַזְהָרַת מִיתַת בֵּית דִּין לוֹקִין עָלָיו כְּמוֹ שֶׁהֻזְכַּר בְּפֶרֶק מִי שֶׁהֶחְשִׁיךְ (קנ״ד ע״א-ע״ב)[46], וְרָאוּי לְפִי הַדַּעַת הַזֶּה לְהַחְמִיר מְאֹד בְּדִבְרֵי סוֹפְרִים שֶׁכֻּלָּם תּוֹרָה הֵם, אֵין בֵּינֵיהֶם וּבֵין הַמִּצְווֹת הַמְפֹרָשׁוֹת בַּכָּתוּב שׁוּם הֶפְרֵשׁ, וְאֵין בַּתּוֹרָה דָּבָר חָמוּר מִן הַשְּׁבוּת שֶׁהוּא מִדִּבְרֵיהֶם אֶלָּא מַה שֶּׁיֵּשׁ בָּהּ חִיּוּב כָּרֵת אוֹ מִיתַת בֵּית דִּין, אֲבָל לֹא כָּל שֶׁיֵּשׁ בָּהּ חִיּוּב עֲשֵׂה אוֹ לָאו שֶׁהֲרֵי בְּכָל דִּבְרֵיהֶם לְדַעְתּוֹ יֵשׁ חִיּוּב עֲשֵׂה וְלָאו, עֲשֵׂה דִּוְעָשִׂיתָ עַל פִּי הַדָּבָר אֲשֶׁר יַגִּידוּ לְךָ וְלָאו דְּלֹא תָסוּר,

---

a Biblical mitzvah-obligation (i.e., the previous mitzvah), **and** a **Biblical mitzvah-prohibition** (the current mitzvah)! וְרָאוּי הוּא לִלְקוֹת אַרְבָּעִים – **In fact,** in all of these cases, **he would have been deserving of *malkus*** for having violated this mitzvah-prohibition, אֶלָּא שֶׁפְּטָרוֹ הָרַב שָׁם בְּסֵפֶר שׁוֹפְטִים – **except that there, in the Book of *Shoftim,*[44] the master** (*Rambam*) **absolved him** of this penalty, מִפְּנֵי שֶׁנִּתַּן לְאַזְהָרַת מִיתַת בֵּית דִּין – **because [this prohibition] is "a prohibition that serves as a warning regarding execution by *beis din,*"** שֶׁכָּל חָכָם שֶׁמַּמְרֶה עַל דִּבְרֵיהֶם מִיתָתוֹ בְּחֶנֶק – **as any sage who defies the words of [the Sanhedrin] is subject to execution by *chenek.*[45]** וְהִנֵּה לִדְבָרָיו לוֹקֶה הוּא לְדַעַת הָאוֹמֵר בַּתַּלְמוּד לָאו שֶׁנִּתַּן לְאַזְהָרַת מִיתַת בֵּית דִּין לוֹקִין עָלָיו – **It follows, according to [*Rambam's*] position, that [one who transgresses a Rabbinic law] *would* incur *malkus*, according to the opinion in the Gemara that one does incur *malkus* for "a prohibition that serves as a warning regarding execution by *beis din,*"** כְּמוֹ שֶׁהֻזְכַּר בְּפֶרֶק מִי שֶׁהֶחְשִׁיךְ – **as recorded in Chapter *Mi Shehech'shich*** (*Shabbos* 154a-b).[46]

Ramban continues with another objection to *Rambam's* view:

וְרָאוּי לְפִי הַדַּעַת הַזֶּה לְהַחְמִיר מְאֹד בְּדִבְרֵי סוֹפְרִים – **Moreover, according to this opinion** of *Rambam*, **it would be fitting to be very stringent with regard to Rabbinic laws,** שֶׁכֻּלָּם תּוֹרָה הֵם – **as all of them are** actually **Biblical** laws, אֵין בֵּינֵיהֶם וּבֵין הַמִּצְווֹת הַמְפֹרָשׁוֹת בַּכָּתוּב שׁוּם הֶפְרֵשׁ – and **there is no** basis for any **distinction at all between [the laws enacted by the Sages] and the mitzvos that are explicit in the Torah.** וְאֵין בַּתּוֹרָה דָּבָר חָמוּר מִן הַשְּׁבוּת שֶׁהוּא מִדִּבְרֵיהֶם – **In fact,** it emerges, according to *Rambam,* that **nothing in the Torah is more serious than a Rabbinic prohibition,** אֶלָּא מַה שֶּׁיֵּשׁ בָּהּ חִיּוּב כָּרֵת אוֹ מִיתַת בֵּית דִּין – **except for those** prohibitions **that bear** the punishments of ***kares* or execution by *beis din.*** אֲבָל לֹא כָּל שֶׁיֵּשׁ בָּהּ חִיּוּב עֲשֵׂה אוֹ לָאו – **But anything that bears the liability** of only **a mitzvah-obligation or a mitzvah-prohibition is not** more stringent than a Rabbinic law, שֶׁהֲרֵי בְּכָל דִּבְרֵיהֶם לְדַעְתּוֹ יֵשׁ חִיּוּב עֲשֵׂה וְלָאו – **for, according to [*Rambam's*] opinion, every Rabbinic law bears the liability of a mitzvah-obligation and a mitzvah-prohibition;** עֲשֵׂה דְּ״וְעָשִׂיתָ עַל פִּי הַדָּבָר אֲשֶׁר יַגִּידוּ לְךָ״ – that is, **the mitzvah-obligation of *you shall do in accordance with the word that they will tell you*** (Mitzvah 495), וְלָאו דְּ״לֹא תָסוּר״ – **and the prohibition of *lo sassur,*** *you shall not deviate from the word that they will tell you* (this mitzvah). There is thus certainly no basis to treat Rabbinic laws

---

NOTES

44. *Hilchos Mamrim,* which is the source of *Rambam's* position, appears in the Book of *Shoftim,* the final book of *Rambam's Mishneh Torah.*

45. "A prohibition that serves as a warning regarding execution by *beis din*" refers to any prohibition for which a transgressor *can,* in certain instances, incur capital punishment. This type of prohibition does not bear the penalty of *malkus*, even in situations where capital punishment does not apply (see Mitzvah 32, at note 5). Here, since a *zakein mamrei* incurs the death penalty for violating this prohibition by defying a ruling of the Sanhedrin, a person who violates it in other ways is exempt from *malkus.*

46. Although the generally accepted opinion is that "a prohibition that serves as a warning regarding execution by *beis din*" does not carry *malkus*, there is another opinion in the Gemara which maintains that the *malkus* penalty applies even in such situations. According to that opinion, one who transgresses a Rabbinic law should incur *malkus,* according to *Rambam.* This position, *Ramban* argues, seems untenable.

וְהִנֵּה נִרְאֶה לְרַבּוֹתֵינוּ בְּכָל הַתַּלְמוּד אוֹמְרִים הֵפֶךְ מִזֶּה, שֶׁהֲרֵי הֵם דָּנִין כָּל דִּבְרֵי סוֹפְרִים
לְהָקֵל כְּמוֹ שֶׁיֹּאמְרוּ תָּמִיד סְפֵיקָא דְאוֹרַיְתָא לְחֻמְרָא, סְפֵיקָא דְרַבָּנָן לְקֻלָּא,⁴⁷ וְהֵקֵלּוּ בַּחֲשַׁשׁ
אִסּוּרִין שֶׁל דִּבְרֵיהֶם לוֹמַר בָּהֶן שֶׁאֲנִי אוֹמֵר,⁴⁸ וְאָמְרוּ בְּפֶרֶק רִאשׁוֹן מִפְּסָחִים (ט' ע"ב-י'
ע"א) אֵימוּר דְּאָמְרִינַן שֶׁאֲנִי אוֹמֵר בְּדְרַבָּנָן, בְּדְאוֹרַיְתָא מִי אָמְרִינַן שֶׁאֲנִי אוֹמֵר,⁴⁹ וְהֶאֱמִינוּ
הַקְּטַנִּים שֶׁאֵינָם רְאוּיִים לְהָעִיד בְּמַה שֶּׁהוּא מִדְּרַבָּנָן כְּמוֹ שֶׁאָמְרוּ שָׁם (ד' ע"ב) בְּדִיקַת חָמֵץ
דְּרַבָּנָן וְהֵימְנִינְהוּ רַבָּנַן בְּדְרַבָּנָן,⁵⁰ וְכֵן בְּעִנְיַן תְּחוּמִין⁵¹ נֶאֱמָן הַקָּטָן לוֹמַר עַד כָּאן תְּחוּם שַׁבָּת

---

any more leniently than Biblical laws. וְהִנֵּה נִרְאֶה לְרַבּוֹתֵינוּ בְּכָל הַתַּלְמוּד אוֹמְרִים הֵפֶךְ מִזֶּה – **Yet we see throughout the Talmud that our Sages state the opposite,** שֶׁהֲרֵי הֵם דָּנִין כָּל דִּבְרֵי סוֹפְרִים לְהָקֵל – **as they treat all Rabbinic laws** more **leniently** than Biblical laws!

Ramban proceeds to cite numerous leniencies that the Gemara sets out with respect to Rabbinic laws: כְּמוֹ שֶׁיֹּאמְרוּ תָּמִיד סְפֵיקָא דְאוֹרַיְתָא לְחֻמְרָא סְפֵיקָא דְרַבָּנָן לְקֻלָּא – **(1) The Sages were lenient in** situations of doubtful Rabbinic prohibitions, **as they regularly say, "An uncertainty regarding a Biblical matter is to be treated stringently, and an uncertainty regarding a Rabbinic matter is to be treated leniently."**[47] וְהֵקֵלּוּ בַּחֲשַׁשׁ אִסּוּרִין שֶׁל דִּבְרֵיהֶם לוֹמַר בָּהֶן שֶׁאֲנִי אוֹמֵר – Similarly, **where** there is **concern for a Rabbinic prohibition, [the Sages] were lenient** and allowed us **to invoke** the principle **"I may assume,"**[48] but they did not allow us to invoke this principle where there is concern for a Biblical prohibition; וְאָמְרוּ בְּפֶרֶק רִאשׁוֹן מִפְּסָחִים – as **they stated in the first chapter of *Pesachim*** (9b-10a): אֵימוּר דְּאָמְרִינַן שֶׁאֲנִי אוֹמֵר בְּדְרַבָּנָן – **When do we say** the principle of **"I may assume"? With regard to Rabbinic** prohibitions! בְּדְאוֹרַיְתָא מִי אָמְרִינַן שֶׁאֲנִי אוֹמֵר – **With regard to Biblical prohibitions, do we say "I may assume"?**[49]

וְהֶאֱמִינוּ הַקְּטַנִּים שֶׁאֵינָם רְאוּיִים לְהָעִיד בְּמַה שֶּׁהוּא מִדְּרַבָּנָן – **(2) [The Sages] gave credibility to minors** – who generally **are not eligible to testify** – **with regard to Rabbinic matters;** כְּמוֹ שֶׁאָמְרוּ שָׁם – **as they state there** (*Pesachim* 4b): בְּדִיקַת חָמֵץ דְּרַבָּנָן וְהֵימְנִינְהוּ רַבָּנַן בְּדְרַבָּנָן – The requirement to **search for *chametz* is a Rabbinic** obligation, **and the Sages believed [minors] with regard to Rabbinic** obligations.[50] וְכֵן בְּעִנְיַן תְּחוּמִין – **Likewise, with regard to the matter of *techumin*,**[51] נֶאֱמָן הַקָּטָן לוֹמַר עַד כָּאן תְּחוּם שַׁבָּת – the Gemara states that **a minor is believed**

NOTES

47. As Chinuch has often noted, typically, if one is uncertain whether something is prohibited, if the question pertains to a Biblical matter he must take the stringent position, but if it pertains to a matter of Rabbinic law, one may be lenient. [See, for example, Mitzvah 495, at note 9. See further below, at notes 54 and 61.]

48. Literally, *for I say.* See next note.

49. The Gemara is speaking of a case where there was a pair of boxes, one containing ordinary grain (*chullin*) and the other containing *terumah* — which is permitted only to a Kohen. Near those boxes was another pair of boxes, which similarly contained ordinary grain and *terumah*, and the contents of each one of the first pair of boxes fell into one of the second pair of boxes, with the entire contents of each one falling into a different box. The Gemara states that, in the case of Rabbinic *terumah* (e.g., *terumah* from produce other than grain, olive, or grapes; see Mitzvah 507), one may proceed with the assumption that the ordinary grain fell into the box containing ordinary grain, and that the *terumah* similarly fell into its own kind; thus, the box of ordinary grain remains permitted to all. If the *terumah* status would be of Biblical nature, however, we would need

to treat the matter stringently, and be concerned that the *terumah* fell into the ordinary grain, requiring that it be treated as a mixture of *terumah* and ordinary grain.

50. One who nullifies his *chametz* before the prohibition of owning *chametz* comes into effect is not subject to the mitzvah-prohibition of owning *chametz* on Pesach (Mitzvos 11 and 20). Nevertheless, even though one nullifies his *chametz,* there is a Rabbinic obligation to conduct a search for *chametz* (*bedikas chametz*) before Pesach; see Mitzvah 9 note 7 and Insight A there. The Gemara states that, although a minor's testimony is generally not accepted, if he testifies that a specific house or room was searched, he *is* believed. Since the search is a Rabbinic requirement, the Sages were lenient and accepted the minor's testimony.

51. It is permitted to travel on the Sabbath only up to 2,000 *amos* in each direction from the edge of one's residence that was established at the onset of the Sabbath and, if one resides in a city, from the edge of that city. This area is known as the *techum Shabbos* (see Mitzvah 24), and the laws pertaining to this matter are referred to as "the laws of *techumin.*"

קָסָבַר תְּחוּמִין דְּרַבָּנָן[52] וְהֵימְנִינְהוּ רַבָּנָן בִּדְרַבָּנָן כִּדְאִיתָא בְּעֵרוּבִין (נ״ח ע״ב) וּבִכְתֻבּוֹת (כ״ח ע״א־ע״ב)[53]. וְעוֹד הֵקֵלּוּ בִּדְרַבָּנָן כְּמוֹ כֵן בִּסְפֵקוֹת כְּמוֹ שֶׁאָמְרוּ זִכְרוֹנָם לִבְרָכָה (ברכות כ״א ע״א) סָפֵק הִתְפַּלֵּל סָפֵק לֹא הִתְפַּלֵּל אֵינוֹ חוֹזֵר וּמִתְפַּלֵּל, סָפֵק אָמַר אֱמֶת וְיַצִּיב סָפֵק לֹא אָמַר חוֹזֵר, וְאָמְרוּ מַאי טַעְמָא, תְּפִלָּה דְּרַבָּנָן, אֱמֶת וְיַצִּיב דְּאוֹרַיְתָא[54]. וְלֹא עוֹד אֶלָּא אֲפִלּוּ בִּדְבָרִים הַסּוֹתְרִים זֶה אֶת זֶה הֵקֵלּוּ, כְּמוֹ שֶׁאָמְרוּ בְּפֶרֶק בַּמֶּה מַדְלִיקִין (ל״ד ע״א), אָמְרוּ לוֹ שְׁנַיִם צֵא וְעָרֵב[55] עָלֵינוּ אֶחָד עֵרֵב עָלָיו מִבְּעוֹד יוֹם[56] וְכוּ׳ כְּמוֹ שֶׁבָּא לְשָׁם[57].

---

to say "the *techum* (boundary) of the Sabbath extends until here." קָסָבַר תְּחוּמִין דְּרַבָּנָן – The Gemara explains that **[this opinion] maintains that** the laws of ***techumin* are** of **Rabbinic** origin,[52] וְהֵימְנִינְהוּ רַבָּנָן בִּדְרַבָּנָן – **and** that **the Sages gave [minors] credibility with regard to Rabbinic matters,** כִּדְאִיתָא בְּעֵרוּבִין וּבִכְתֻבּוֹת – **as is** set forth **in** Tractate ***Eruvin*** (58b) **and in** Tractate ***Kesubos*** (28a-b).[53]

וְעוֹד הֵקֵלּוּ בִּדְרַבָּנָן כְּמוֹ כֵן בִּסְפֵקוֹת – (3) **Additionally, with regard to Rabbinic** *obligations,* **[the Sages] were lenient in situations of uncertainty** whether one has fulfilled his obligation, and did not require him to repeat it. כְּמוֹ שֶׁאָמְרוּ זִכְרוֹנָם לִבְרָכָה – **As [the Sages], of blessed memory, stated** (*Berachos* 21a): סָפֵק הִתְפַּלֵּל סָפֵק לֹא הִתְפַּלֵּל אֵינוֹ חוֹזֵר וּמִתְפַּלֵּל – **One who is uncertain whether or not he prayed** the *Shemoneh Esrei* prayer **is not required to go back and pray;** סָפֵק אָמַר אֱמֶת וְיַצִּיב סָפֵק לֹא אָמַר חוֹזֵר וְאָמְרוּ – **however, if he is uncertain whether he recited *Emes V'Yatziv*** (the blessing after the morning *Shema*) **he must go back and say it.** מַאי טַעְמָא – **What is the reason?** תְּפִלָּה דְּרַבָּנָן אֱמֶת וְיַצִּיב דְּאוֹרַיְתָא – It is because **prayer is** a **Rabbinic** obligation, **while** reciting ***Emes V'Yatziv*** **is** a **Biblical** obligation.[54]

וְלֹא עוֹד אֶלָּא אֲפִלּוּ בִּדְבָרִים הַסּוֹתְרִים זֶה אֶת זֶה הֵקֵלּוּ – (4) **Moreover,** in regard to Rabbinic matters, **[the Sages] allowed even leniencies that contradict each other,** כְּמוֹ שֶׁאָמְרוּ בְּפֶרֶק בַּמֶּה מַדְלִיקִין – **as they stated in Chapter *Bameh Madlikin*** (*Shabbos* 34a): אָמְרוּ לוֹ שְׁנַיִם צֵא וְעָרֵב עָלֵינוּ – **If two people told [a third person], "Go out and make an *eruv*** *chatzeiros*[55] **for us,"** אֶחָד עֵרֵב עָלָיו מִבְּעוֹד יוֹם וְכוּ׳ – **and he made an *eruv* for one** of them **while it was still** certainly **daytime,** and that *eruv* was consumed sometime during *bein hashemashos*, and he made an *eruv* for the other during *bein hashemashos,*[56] **and so forth,** כְּמוֹ שֶׁבָּא לְשָׁם – **as is set out there** in the Gemara.[57]

NOTES

52. See end of Mitzvah 24.

53. As it appears in our texts of the Gemara, a minor is not believed in this regard, and this reasoning is stated regarding other categories of people whose testimony is generally not accepted. [For discussion, see *Tosafos* to *Kesubos* ad loc.] Even so, the Gemara states, there is a certain leniency pertaining to the testimony of a minor with regard to *techumin*: although the testimony of a minor is not accepted, an adult may testify on the basis of what he recalls witnessing when he was a minor. That is, if there is uncertainty as to the extent of the *techum*, and an adult testifies that he remembers its extent from when he was a minor, his testimony is accepted.

54. As was explained in Mitzvah 433 (after note 9), the Biblical obligation of prayer can be fulfilled with any request, recited at any time during the day (see there for *Ramban's* view). Therefore, since the actual prayer (i.e., *Shemoneh Esrei*) is only of Rabbinic origin, one who is uncertain whether he prayed is not required to go back and pray. There is, however, a Biblical obligation to recite *Emes V'Yatziv,* as that blessing contains a reminder of the Exodus, which is a Biblical obligation (see below, Mitzvah 603, and Insight to Mitzvah 420). [For another example of this distinction between Biblical and Rabbinic obligations, see Mitzvah 430, at notes 55-57.]

55. On the Sabbath, it is Biblically permissible to carry throughout a properly enclosed private domain, even if it encompasses a courtyard, neighborhood, or even an entire city. A Rabbinic decree, however, prohibits carrying objects between residences and communal courtyards or from one private residence to another, even when they are properly enclosed, unless an *"eruv chatzeiros"* is implemented before the Sabbath. This is done by collecting bread from the residents of each one of the dwellings that open onto that courtyard and placing it in one of those dwellings. All of the contributing residents are thus considered to be legally residing in the dwelling in which they left the bread, and the entire courtyard is viewed as a single communal residence, allowing one to carry items throughout the area.

56. *Bein hashemashos* is the "transition period" between days — i.e., the time in the evening when there is a doubt whether it is day or night.

57. An *eruv chatzeiros* takes effect at the moment the

וְגַם נִרְאֶה בַּגְּמָרָא שֶׁעוֹקְרִין דִּבְרֵיהֶם תָּדִיר מִשּׁוּם אִסּוּר דְּאוֹרַיְתָא כְּמוֹ שֶׁאָמְרוּ בְּמַסֶּכֶת שַׁבָּת (ד׳ ע״א), הַדְּבִיק פַּת בַּתַּנּוּר הִתִּירוּ לוֹ לִרְדוֹתָהּ קֹדֶם שֶׁבָּא לִידֵי אִסּוּר סְקִילָה[58]. וְשָׁם בְּשַׁבָּת (קכ״ח ע״ב) אָמְרוּ בִּטּוּל כְּלִי מֵהֵכָנוֹ דְּרַבָּנָן וְצַעַר בַּעֲלֵי חַיִּים דְּאוֹרַיְתָא, וְאָתֵי דְּאוֹרַיְתָא וּמְבַטֵּל דְּרַבָּנָן וְכוּ׳ כְּמוֹ שֶׁבָּא לְשָׁם[59]. וְזֶה רַב מְאֹד בַּתַּלְמוּד אָתֵי עֲשֵׂה דְּאוֹרַיְתָא וְדָחֵי עֲשֵׂה דְּרַבָּנָן. וְכֵן בְּמַחֲלֹקֶת שֶׁבָּא בֵּין הַחֲכָמִים אָמְרוּ (עבודה זרה ז׳ ע״א)

וְגַם נִרְאֶה בַּגְּמָרָא שֶׁעוֹקְרִין דִּבְרֵיהֶם תָּדִיר מִשּׁוּם אִסּוּר דְּאוֹרַיְתָא – (5) **It is further apparent in the Gemara that [the Sages] regularly suspend their** own **laws for the sake of** avoiding **Biblical prohibitions,** כְּמוֹ שֶׁאָמְרוּ בְּמַסֶּכֶת שַׁבָּת – **as they stated in Tractate *Shabbos*** (4a): הַדְּבִיק פַּת בַּתַּנּוּר – **If one attached a loaf to the** wall of an **oven** on the Sabbath, הִתִּירוּ לוֹ לִרְדוֹתָהּ קֹדֶם שֶׁבָּא לִידֵי אִסּוּר סְקִילָה – **[the Sages] permitted him to detach it before** it bakes and **he comes to** a violation of **a *sekilah*-bearing transgression.**[58] וְשָׁם בְּשַׁבָּת אָמְרוּ – **Also there, in** Tractate ***Shabbos*** (128b), **[the Sages] stated:** בִּטּוּל כְּלִי מֵהֵכָנוֹ דְּרַבָּנָן וְצַעַר בַּעֲלֵי חַיִּים דְּאוֹרַיְתָא – The prohibition against **suspending the function of a utensil is Rabbinic, but** the prohibition against **inflicting pain upon animals is Biblical;** וְאָתֵי דְּאוֹרַיְתָא וּמְבַטֵּל דְּרַבָּנָן וְכוּ׳ – **thus, the Biblical** prohibition **comes and overrides the Rabbinic** prohibition, **and so forth,** כְּמוֹ שֶׁבָּא לְשָׁם – **as is set out there** in the Gemara.[59] וְזֶה רַב מְאֹד בַּתַּלְמוּד אָתֵי עֲשֵׂה דְּאוֹרַיְתָא וְדָחֵי עֲשֵׂה דְּרַבָּנָן – **Indeed, this** principle appears **a great many** times **in the Talmud: "A Biblical obligation comes and overrides a Rabbinic obligation"!**

וְכֵן בְּמַחֲלֹקֶת שֶׁבָּא בֵּין הַחֲכָמִים אָמְרוּ – (6) **Similarly, with regard to a** halachic **dispute that arises**

NOTES

Sabbath begins. Therefore, the *eruv* must be intact at the onset of the Sabbath. Once it has taken effect, it remains in effect for the entire Sabbath, even if it was consumed during the Sabbath. If the *eruv* was made during *bein hashemashos,* a time whose status is unclear, the *eruv* is valid, as per the general rule that a doubt with regard to a Rabbinic matter is dealt with leniently.

The Gemara takes this even further, in regard to a case where two people residing in different courtyards requested of a third person to make an *eruv* for each of their courtyards (i.e., he was asked to make two different *eruvin*). The Gemara rules that if one *eruv* was made before sunset but was consumed sometime during *bein hashemashos*, and the other *eruv* was not made until *bein hashemashos,* both *eruvin* are valid. The Gemara asks: How can this be? Since the first *eruv* was consumed during *bein hashemashos,* accepting its validity means that we are considering *bein hashemashos* to be nighttime. Accordingly, the second *eruv*, which was not put into place until *bein hashemashos*, should not be valid! And if the second *eruv is* valid, we must be viewing the *bein hashemashos* period as daytime; accordingly, the first *eruv*, which was consumed during *bein hashemashos*, and thus was not in existence at the onset of the Sabbath, should not be valid! The Gemara answers that, since the law of *eruv* is of Rabbinic origin, the Sages were lenient even in such a situation, and accepted the possibility that *bein hashemashos* is night regarding one *eruv,* and the possibility that it is still day regarding the other *eruv*.

[We have followed *Rabbeinu Chananel's* explanation of the Gemara, as that approach is preferred by *Ramban* himself in his commentary there (*Shabbos* 34a). This approach is also taken by *Tosafos* there. *Rashi* and *Rambam,* however, explain that the Gemara is discussing *eruv techumin* (a mechanism that extends the distance to which one may walk in a specific direction on the Sabbath by shifting his "residence" for the Sabbath; see above, note 51). See *Orach Chaim* 415:2-3 with *Beur Halachah* ד״ה ויש חולקים.]

58. In Talmudic times, bread was baked by attaching the dough to the wall of the oven. The Sages decreed that on the Sabbath one may not remove bread that has been attached to the oven (see *Rambam, Hil. Shabbos* 22:1 for an explanation of this prohibition). Nevertheless, the Sages lifted this restriction when necessary in order to prevent a Biblical transgression. Thus, if one placed dough into the oven *on* the Sabbath, such that he would be guilty of desecrating the Sabbath once it becomes baked (a transgression that bears the punishment of *sekilah* when done intentionally), he is permitted to remove it before it bakes, to avoid a Biblical transgression.

59. It is Rabbinically prohibited to "suspend the function" of a utensil, by placing it in a position where it will become unfit for further use on the Sabbath. For example, it is prohibited to place a utensil beneath oil that is dripping from a lamp, because the oil, which is *muktzeh* (prohibited to move on the Sabbath), will prohibit the utensil for further use on the Sabbath, as it too will become *muktzeh.* The Gemara, however, states that it is permitted to place cushions beneath an animal that has fallen into a pit, even though the cushions would become unusable when the animal (which is *muktzeh*) rests upon them, as the Biblical prohibition against causing distress to an animal overrides the Rabbinic prohibition against suspending a utensil's function.

אִם הָיָה אֶחָד גָּדוֹל בְּחָכְמָה וּבְמִנְיָן[60], הַלֵּךְ אַחֲרָיו, וְאִם לָאו, בְּשֶׁל תּוֹרָה הַלֵּךְ אַחַר הַמַּחְמִיר, וּבְשֶׁל סוֹפְרִים אַחַר הַמֵּקֵל[61]. וּגְדוֹלָה מִזּוֹ אָמְרוּ (ערובין ס״ז ע״ב) בְּשֶׁל סוֹפְרִים עוֹשִׂין מַעֲשֶׂה וְאַחַר כָּךְ דָּנִין[62]. וּבְפֶרֶק מִי שֶׁהֶחְשִׁיךְ (קנ״ד ע״ב) אָמְרוּ מַהוּ דְּתֵימָא לְהֶפְסֵד מוּעָט נַמֵי חָשְׁשׁוּ קָא מַשְׁמַע לַן, שֶׁהֲרֵי חִדּוּשׁ הוּא אֶצְלָם כְּשֶׁאֵינָם דּוֹחִים דִּבְרֵי סוֹפְרִים אֲפִלּוּ לְהֶפְסֵד מוּעָט[63]. וְאָמְרוּ (ברכות י״ט ע״ב) שֶׁמְּטַמְּאִים כֹּהֲנִים עַצְמָם בְּטֻמְאָה שֶׁל דִּבְרֵיהֶם[64] לִרְאוֹת מַלְכֵי אֻמּוֹת הָעוֹלָם כְּדֵי שֶׁאִם יִזְכֶּה יַבְחִין מַה בֵּין מַלְכֵי יִשְׂרָאֵל וְכוּ׳[65].

---

among sages, Rabbinic matters are treated more leniently than Biblical matters, as **[the Sages] have stated** (*Avodah Zarah* 7a): **אִם הָיָה אֶחָד גָּדוֹל בְּחָכְמָה וּבְמִנְיָן הַלֵּךְ אַחֲרָיו** – When two sages are in dispute, then **if one** of them **is greater** than the other **in wisdom or in number,**[60] **follow him; וְאִם לָאו בְּשֶׁל תּוֹרָה הַלֵּךְ אַחַר הַמַּחְמִיר וּבְשֶׁל סוֹפְרִים אַחַר הַמֵּקֵל** – **and if no** sage is greater than the other, then **in Biblical matters, follow the stringent** opinion, **and in Rabbinic matters, follow the lenient** opinion.[61] **וּגְדוֹלָה מִזּוֹ אָמְרוּ** – **Indeed, [the Sages] expressed yet** a **greater** leniency (*Eruvin* 67b), namely, **בְּשֶׁל סוֹפְרִים עוֹשִׂין מַעֲשֶׂה וְאַחַר כָּךְ דָּנִין** – **that in Rabbinic** matters **one may** first **act** in accordance with a lenient ruling **and afterward deliberate** the validity of the ruling.[62] **וּבְפֶרֶק מִי שֶׁהֶחְשִׁיךְ אָמְרוּ** – (7) Further indication of the relative leniency of Rabbinic matters is that which **they said in** the Gemara, **Chapter *Mi Shehech'shich*** (*Shabbos* 154b): **מַהוּ דְּתֵימָא לְהֶפְסֵד מוּעָט נַמֵי חָשְׁשׁוּ קָא מַשְׁמַע לַן** – **One might have supposed that [the Sages] were concerned for even a small** financial **loss; [the Baraisa]** therefore **informs us otherwise. שֶׁהֲרֵי חִדּוּשׁ הוּא אֶצְלָם כְּשֶׁאֵינָם דּוֹחִים דִּבְרֵי סוֹפְרִים אֲפִלּוּ לְהֶפְסֵד מוּעָט** – We see **that [the Sages] find it surprising that Rabbinic laws are not set aside by** the concern for **even a small loss!**[63] **וְאָמְרוּ** – **And** Rabbinic laws actually are set aside for certain other considerations, as **they stated** (*Berachos* 19b) **שֶׁמְּטַמְּאִים כֹּהֲנִים עַצְמָם בְּטֻמְאָה שֶׁל דִּבְרֵיהֶם לִרְאוֹת מַלְכֵי אֻמּוֹת הָעוֹלָם** – **that,** although **Kohanim** are forbidden to become *tamei* from a corpse (Mitzvah 263), they **may subject themselves to** corpse ***tumah*** **on the Rabbinic level**[64] **for the sake of seeing the kings of the nations, כְּדֵי שֶׁאִם יִזְכֶּה יַבְחִין מַה בֵּין מַלְכֵי יִשְׂרָאֵל וְכוּ׳** – **so that, if [the Kohen] will merit, he will see the distinction between Jewish kings** and the kings of other nations.[65]

NOTES

60. "In number" may refer to the number of disciples with whom the sage discussed this ruling and who concurred with him. Alternatively, it may refer to the number of years that the sage spent under the tutelage of his Torah teachers (*Ritva, Avodah Zarah* 7a; see Mitzvah 495 note 11).

61. For additional rules pertaining to situations of disagreement among halachic authorities, see *Rama, Choshen Mishpat* 25:2; *Shach,* end of *Yoreh Deah* 242; *Chazon Ish, Yoreh Deah* 150:8.

62. This refers to a situation where a sage was presented a halachic question and he issued a lenient ruling in the presence of his disciples, which one of the disciples felt was in error. The Gemara states that if the ruling pertains to a Biblical matter, the disciple must voice his objection immediately, so that his argument can be reviewed before the questioner acts on the basis of the ruling. This will save the questioner from committing a possible Biblical transgression. If, however, the ruling pertained to a Rabbinic matter, the disciple should withhold his objection until after the questioner acts, even though the leniency might lead to a Rabbinic transgression.

63. The Gemara cites a Baraisa that indicates that the Sages set aside the prohibition to "suspend the function" of a utensil on the Sabbath (see note 59 above) in the case of a major financial loss, but they did not do so when the loss would be minimal. The Gemara explains that the Baraisa emphasizes the latter point because one might have expected that the Sages set aside the prohibition even in a case of minimal loss; the Baraisa therefore informs us that it is not so, for the Sages set aside their prohibition only when one is facing a major loss. We see from this discussion that Rabbinic laws are treated leniently, to such an extent that one would have expected a Rabbinic prohibition to be set aside even in a case of minimal loss.

64. I.e., to come into contact with a corpse in a manner that will cause them to be *tamei* only by Rabbinic law. See Gemara there for details.

65. The Gemara encourages a person to try to see even a non-Jewish king and thus witness the honors of royalty. That way, if he will merit to see Mashiach, he will realize how much greater are the honors accorded to Mashiach (see *Rashi, Berachos* 58a ד״ה שאם יזכה). For the sake of this objective, the Sages went so far as to permit a Kohen to subject himself to Rabbinic *tumah.*

וְאַף בְּעָנְשָׁן שֶׁל דִּבְרֵי חֲכָמִים אֵין לָהֶם אֶלָּא נִדּוּי[66], כְּמוֹ שֶׁאָמְרוּ (פסחים נ״ב ע״א) מְנַדִּין עַל שְׁנֵי יָמִים טוֹבִים שֶׁל גָּלֻיּוֹת[67]. וְאָמְרוּ בְּעוֹשֶׂה מְלָאכָה בְּפוּרִים, וּלְשַׁמְתֵּיהּ מַר[68], וּבִמְקוֹמוֹת יֵשׁ לָהֶם מַכַּת מַרְדּוּת, וְהוּא לְמִי שֶׁעוֹבֵר עַל דִּבְרֵיהֶם שֶׁהֵן כְּעֵין תּוֹרָה וְהֵן כָּל הַגְּזֵרוֹת שֶׁגָּזְרוּ בָּהֶם מִדִּבְרֵיהֶם שֶׁמַּכִּין אוֹתוֹ עַד שֶׁיְּקַבֵּל אוֹתָהּ עָלָיו אוֹ עַד שֶׁתֵּצֵא נַפְשׁוֹ כְּמוֹ שֶׁמְּפֹרָשׁ בַּתּוֹסֶפְתָּא דְּסַנְהֶדְרִין[69].

וּכְלָלוֹ שֶׁל דָּבָר, שֶׁדִּבְרֵי סוֹפְרִים חֲלוּקִים הֵם בְּכָל דִּינֵיהֶם מִדִּבְרֵי תּוֹרָה

Ramban continues, noting that after the fact, the penalties for transgressing Rabbinic laws are completely different from those for transgressing Biblical laws:

וְאַף בְּעָנְשָׁן שֶׁל דִּבְרֵי חֲכָמִים – **Also, with respect to the penalties for** transgressing **Rabbinic laws,** אֵין לָהֶם אֶלָּא נִדּוּי – **they bear only** the penalty of **excommunication,** and not *malkus*;[66] כְּמוֹ שֶׁאָמְרוּ – **as [the Sages] stated** (*Pesachim* 52a): מְנַדִּין עַל שְׁנֵי יָמִים טוֹבִים שֶׁל גָּלֻיּוֹת – **We impose excommunication for** violating **the second day of Yom Tov that is** observed **in the Diaspora** by Rabbinic law.[67] וְאָמְרוּ בְּעוֹשֶׂה מְלָאכָה בְּפוּרִים – **Similarly, they said, regarding** a certain person who was **performing labor on Purim:** וּלְשַׁמְתֵּיהּ מַר – **"Let the master excommunicate him!"**[68] וּבִמְקוֹמוֹת יֵשׁ לָהֶם מַכַּת מַרְדּוּת – **And in** some **situations, [Rabbinic laws] bear *makkas mardus*** (lashes of discipline). וְהוּא לְמִי שֶׁעוֹבֵר עַל דִּבְרֵיהֶם שֶׁהֵן כְּעֵין תּוֹרָה – **This** punishment **is** meted out **to one who transgresses those [Rabbinic] prohibitions that are similar to Biblical** prohibitions, וְהֵן כָּל הַגְּזֵרוֹת שֶׁגָּזְרוּ בָּהֶם מִדִּבְרֵיהֶם – **which includes all the decrees that [the Sages] enacted to** protect against violations of **[Biblical law].** שֶׁמַּכִּין אוֹתוֹ עַד שֶׁיְּקַבֵּל אוֹתָהּ עָלָיו אוֹ עַד שֶׁתֵּצֵא נַפְשׁוֹ – In those cases, the rule is **that [*beis din*] administers lashes to him until he accepts upon himself** to follow **[the law], or until he expires,** כְּמוֹ שֶׁמְּפֹרָשׁ בַּתּוֹסֶפְתָּא דְּסַנְהֶדְרִין – **as is detailed in *Tosefta*,** Tractate ***Sanhedrin*.**[69]

Ramban concludes:

וּכְלָלוֹ שֶׁל דָּבָר שֶׁדִּבְרֵי סוֹפְרִים חֲלוּקִים הֵם בְּכָל דִּינֵיהֶם מִדִּבְרֵי תּוֹרָה – **The sum of the matter is that**

NOTES

66. *Ramban* implies that excommunication is a less severe penalty than *malkus* (see especially the fuller version of his words in the glosses to *Sefer HaMitzvos, Shoresh* 1; p. 22 in Frankel ed.). However, the Gemara (*Pesachim* 52a) states that excommunication is a *harsher* punishment than *malkus*. The Sages imposed a heavier penalty for violations of their decrees, to ensure that people not treat them lightly (see *Emes LeYaakov* to *Pesachim* 52a, and *Mishnah Berurah* 496:2; see also *Rabbeinu Yonah* in *Shaarei Teshuvah* 3:5; cf. *Taz, Choshen Mishpat* 8:5; *Knesses HaGedolah* to *Beis Yosef, Yoreh Deah* 334, end of §81). In any event, the different penalty demonstrates that Rabbinic decrees are not included in the Biblical prohibition of this mitzvah.

67. See Mitzvah 301.

68. The source of this citation is unclear. The Gemara (*Moed Katan* 4a) cites an incident like this in which a person was performing prohibited labor on Chol HaMoed (not Purim), and one sage said to another, "Let us excommunicate him." [See Mitzvah 323 (at notes 22 and 68) for discussion of whether the prohibition against *melachah* on Chol HaMoed is of Biblical or Rabbinic origin.]

A similar incident is recorded in *Megillah* 5b, where a person was performing labor on Purim in violation of the custom in that locale, and Rav cursed him that his labor should not bear fruit.

69. [In our versions of *Tosefta*, this appears in Tractate *Makkos* 3:10.] *Ramban* apparently maintains that the general penalty for violating Rabbinic laws is excommunication; however, one who violates those Rabbinic laws that were instituted as safeguards for Biblical prohibitions is subject to *makkas mardus*. Rishonim have various opinions regarding this matter. For discussion, see *Pri Chadash, Orach Chaim* 496:1.

As for the difference between Biblical *malkus* and Rabbinic *makkas mardus,* it is generally assumed that *makkas mardus* is a less severe punishment (see General Introduction, Sec. VI). *Ramban,* however, indicates that in a way *makkas mardus* was more severe, since there was no limit of 39 lashes (though it also could have been less than 39 lashes, if the sinner relented). [See, similarly, *Rambam, Hil. Chametz U'Matzah* 6:12; *Rashi, Chullin* 141b ד״ה מכת מרדות; *Aruch* ע׳ מרד; *R' Hai Gaon,* cited in *Otzar HaGeonim, Nazir* 23a.] Others maintain that *makkas mardus* always consisted of *less* than 39 lashes (*Ran, Kesubos* fol. 16b; *R' Saadiah Gaon,* cited in *Otzar HaGeonim* ibid.), except in the case of a constant offender, who was indeed beaten until he accepted upon himself to follow the law (*Ran* ibid.). For further discussion, see *Pri Chadash, Orach Chaim* 471:2.

לְהָקֵל בִּקְצָתָן וּלְהַחְמִיר בִּקְצָתָן[70,71]. אֲבָל הַדָּבָר הַבָּרוּר הַמְנֻקֶּה מִכָּל שִׁבּוּשׁ הוּא שֶׁאֵין הַלָּאו הַזֶּה דְּלֹא תָסוּר אֶלָּא בְּמַה שֶּׁאָמְרוּ זִכְרוֹנָם לִבְרָכָה בְּפֵרוּשׁ הַתּוֹרָה, כְּגוֹן הַדְּבָרִים הַנִּדְרָשִׁים בִּגְזֵרָה שָׁוָה אוֹ בְּבִנְיַן אָב וּשְׁאָר שְׁלֹשׁ עֶשְׂרֵה מִדּוֹת שֶׁהַתּוֹרָה נִדְרֶשֶׁת בָּהֶם[72], אוֹ בְּמַשְׁמָעוּת לְשׁוֹן הַכָּתוּב עַצְמוֹ, וְכֵן בְּמַה שֶּׁקִּבְּלוּ הֲלָכָה לְמֹשֶׁה מִסִּינַי, וְעַל זֶה יֹאמְרוּ זִכְרוֹנָם לִבְרָכָה שֶׁיֵּשׁ עֲשֵׂה וְלֹא תַעֲשֶׂה בַּדָּבָר, וְאִם בְּעִנְיָן הַזֶּה נֶחְלַק אֶחָד הָרָאוּי לְהוֹרָאָה בְּמַה שֶּׁיֵּשׁ עַל זְדוֹנוֹ כָּרֵת וּבִשְׁגָגָתוֹ חַטָּאת עַל בֵּית דִּין הַגָּדוֹל שֶׁנַּעֲשָׂה בָּזֶה זָקֵן מַמְרֵא בִּזְמַן שֶׁדָּנִין דִּינֵי נְפָשׁוֹת, וְזֶהוּ אָמְרָם זִכְרוֹנָם לִבְרָכָה (ספרי כאן) אֲפִלּוּ יֹאמְרוּ לְךָ עַל שְׂמֹאל שֶׁהִיא יָמִין, כְּלוֹמַר שֶׁכָּךְ הִיא הַמִּצְוָה לָנוּ מֵאֲדוֹן הַתּוֹרָה יִתְבָּרַךְ,

---

Rabbinic laws differ from Biblical laws in every respect, לְהָקֵל בִּקְצָתָן וּלְהַחְמִיר בִּקְצָתָן – **in some [matters] leniently, and in some [matters] stringently.**[70] Thus, it cannot be, as *Rambam* maintains, that every Rabbinic law is governed by the prohibition against deviating from the words of the Sages.[71]

Ramban sets forth his own position:

אֲבָל הַדָּבָר הַבָּרוּר הַמְנֻקֶּה מִכָּל שִׁבּוּשׁ הוּא – **Rather, the clear approach, which is free of any error, is** שֶׁאֵין הַלָּאו הַזֶּה דְּ״לֹא תָסוּר״ אֶלָּא בְּמַה שֶּׁאָמְרוּ זִכְרוֹנָם לִבְרָכָה בְּפֵרוּשׁ הַתּוֹרָה – **that this prohibition, *lo sassur*, applies only to that which [the Sages], of blessed memory, said in explanation of the Torah.** כְּגוֹן הַדְּבָרִים הַנִּדְרָשִׁים בִּגְזֵרָה שָׁוָה אוֹ בְּבִנְיַן אָב – **For example, matters that are expounded by means of** the principles of ***gezeirah shavah* or *binyan av,*** וּשְׁאָר שְׁלֹשׁ עֶשְׂרֵה מִדּוֹת שֶׁהַתּוֹרָה נִדְרֶשֶׁת בָּהֶם – **or** any of **the other thirteen principles through which the Torah is expounded,**[72] אוֹ בְּמַשְׁמָעוּת לְשׁוֹן הַכָּתוּב עַצְמוֹ – **or through interpretation of the actual text of Scripture.** וְכֵן בְּמַה שֶּׁקִּבְּלוּ הֲלָכָה לְמֹשֶׁה מִסִּינַי – **Similarly,** it applies **to that which [the Sages] received through the Oral Tradition** transmitted **to Moses at Sinai.** וְעַל זֶה יֹאמְרוּ זִכְרוֹנָם לִבְרָכָה שֶׁיֵּשׁ עֲשֵׂה וְלֹא תַעֲשֶׂה בַּדָּבָר – **Regarding this** (the Sages' interpretation of Biblical law), **[the Sages], of blessed memory, stated that there is a mitzvah-obligation and a mitzvah-prohibition pertaining to it.** וְאִם בְּעִנְיָן הַזֶּה – **And, if within this category** of Rabbinic teaching, נֶחְלַק אֶחָד הָרָאוּי לְהוֹרָאָה בְּמַה שֶּׁיֵּשׁ עַל זְדוֹנוֹ כָּרֵת וּבִשְׁגָגָתוֹ חַטָּאת עַל בֵּית דִּין הַגָּדוֹל **– an individual who is qualified to rule** in such matters **disputes the Great Sanhedrin,** and his dispute has ramifications **regarding a matter whose intentional transgression bears** liability to ***kares* and unintentional transgression bears** liability to **a *chatas*** offering, שֶׁנַּעֲשָׂה בָּזֶה זָקֵן מַמְרֵא בִּזְמַן שֶׁדָּנִין דִּינֵי נְפָשׁוֹת – **this makes him a *zakein mamrei*, in times when capital offenses are judged.** וְזֶהוּ אָמְרָם זִכְרוֹנָם לִבְרָכָה – **This is** the meaning of **the statement of [the Sages], of blessed memory** (*Sifrei* to verse of the mitzvah), regarding the words, *you shall not deviate from it, right or left:* אֲפִלּוּ יֹאמְרוּ לְךָ עַל שְׂמֹאל שֶׁהִיא יָמִין – **Even if [the Sanhedrin] tells you that left is right,** you may not deviate from their words. כְּלוֹמַר שֶׁכָּךְ הִיא הַמִּצְוָה לָנוּ מֵאֲדוֹן הַתּוֹרָה יִתְבָּרַךְ – They mean **to say, this is what we were commanded by the Master of the Torah,** Hashem, **blessed be He –**

NOTES

70. As has been explained, the Rabbinic laws are subject to many leniencies, but the punishment for a violation may be more severe — though that stems from the fact that people tend to view the Rabbinic laws less seriously than the Biblical ones (see note 66). [In our versions of *Ramban's* glosses to *Sefer HaMitzvos* (ibid.), the text reads: ... *Rabbinic laws differ from Biblical laws in every respect,* לְהָקֵל בְּאֵלּוּ וּלְהַחְמִיר בְּאֵלּוּ, *to be lenient with regard to these* (i.e., Biblical laws), *and to be stringent with regard to those* (i.e., Rabbinic laws). That is, Rabbinic laws are *in all respects* more lenient than Biblical ones.]

71. See Insight for resolutions to a number of these difficulties.

72. *Gezeirah shavah* and *binyan av* are two of the thirteen principles of Scriptural exposition that appear in the *Baraisa* of *R' Yishmael* (see Mitzvah 495 note 3). *Gezeirah shavah* refers to where a common term appears in the Torah in two different contexts, which indicates a commonality between the two laws. *Binyan av* refers to where a known law sets a precedent, which is applied to other topics.

שֶׁנַּאֲמִין אֶל הַגְּדוֹלִים בְּמַה שֶּׁיֹּאמְרוּ, וְלֹא יֹאמַר בַּעַל הַמַּחֲלֹקֶת הֵיאַךְ אַתִּיר לְעַצְמִי וַאֲנִי יוֹדֵעַ בְּוַדַּאי שֶׁהֵם טוֹעִים, שֶׁאֲפִלּוּ יִהְיֶה כֵּן הוּא מְצֻוֶּה לְהַאֲמִין לָהֶם, וּכְמוֹ שֶׁכָּתַבְתִּי לְמַעְלָה בְּרֹאשׁ הַמִּצְוָה[73], וּכְעִנְיָן שֶׁנָּהַג רַבָּן גַּמְלִיאֵל עִם רַבִּי יְהוֹשֻׁעַ בְּיוֹם הַכִּפּוּרִים שֶׁחָל לִהְיוֹת בְּחֶשְׁבּוֹנוֹ כְּמוֹ שֶׁמֻּזְכָּר בְּמַסֶּכֶת רֹאשׁ הַשָּׁנָה (כ״ה ע״א)[74]. וְיֵשׁ בְּעִנְיָן הַזֶּה תְּנַאי אֶחָד לְפִי מַה שֶּׁאָמְרוּ זִכְרוֹנָם לִבְרָכָה בְּמַסֶּכֶת הוֹרָיוֹת (ב׳ ע״ב), שֶׁאִם הָיָה בִּזְמַן הַסַּנְהֶדְרִין אִישׁ חָכָם וְרָאוּי לְהוֹרוֹת אוֹ שֶׁהוּא מִכְּלַל הַסַּנְהֶדְרִין, וְהוֹרוּ בֵּית דִּין הַגָּדוֹל בְּדָבָר שֶׁלֹּא כְּדַעְתּוֹ, שֶׁאֵינוֹ רַשַּׁאי לְהַתִּיר עַצְמוֹ בְּאוֹתוֹ הַדָּבָר הָאָסוּר לְדַעְתּוֹ[75] עַד שֶׁיִּשָּׂא וְיִתֵּן עִמָּהֶם עַל הַדָּבָר, וְאַחַר שֶׁיַּסְכִּימוּ כֻּלָּם אוֹ רֻבָּם בְּבִטּוּל הַדַּעַת הַהוּא וִישַׁבְּשׁוּ עָלָיו סְבָרָתוֹ וְיַעֲשׂוּ הַסְכָּמָה שֶׁהוּא טוֹעֶה אָז הוּא רַשַּׁאי לִנְהֹג לְעַצְמוֹ הֶתֵּר בְּמַה שֶּׁהָיָה דַּעְתּוֹ לֶאֱסוֹר, וְגַם מְצֻוֶּה הוּא עַל זֶה

שֶׁנַּאֲמִין אֶל הַגְּדוֹלִים בְּמַה שֶּׁיֹּאמְרוּ – **to adhere faithfully to what the great** Torah scholars **say** in their interpretations of His Torah. וְלֹא יֹאמַר בַּעַל הַמַּחֲלֹקֶת – **Thus, an individual who disagrees** with them and understands the Torah differently **may not say,** הֵיאַךְ אַתִּיר לְעַצְמִי וַאֲנִי יוֹדֵעַ בְּוַדַּאי שֶׁהֵם טוֹעִים – **"How can I permit** this matter **for myself, when I know with certainty that they are mistaken?"** שֶׁאֲפִלּוּ יִהְיֶה כֵּן הוּא מְצֻוֶּה לְהַאֲמִין לָהֶם – **For, even if it were so,** and the Sanhedrin is indeed mistaken, **he is commanded to adhere faithfully to them,** וּכְמוֹ שֶׁכָּתַבְתִּי לְמַעְלָה בְּרֹאשׁ הַמִּצְוָה – **as I wrote above, at the beginning of the mitzvah.**[73] וּכְעִנְיָן שֶׁנָּהַג רַבָּן גַּמְלִיאֵל עִם רַבִּי יְהוֹשֻׁעַ – **And** this is **the manner in which Rabban Gamliel,** the head of the Sanhedrin, **conducted himself with R' Yehoshua,** who disputed the ruling of the Sanhedrin regarding the correct day of Rosh Chodesh, בְּיוֹם הַכִּפּוּרִים שֶׁחָל לִהְיוֹת בְּחֶשְׁבּוֹנוֹ – when Rabban Gamliel demanded that R' Yehoshua come to him with his walking stick and his money bag **on** the day that **Yom Kippur fell according to his calculation,** כְּמוֹ שֶׁמֻּזְכָּר בְּמַסֶּכֶת רֹאשׁ הַשָּׁנָה – **as is recorded in Tractate *Rosh Hashanah*** (25a).[74]

Ramban qualifies the requirement for a sage to adhere to the ruling of the Sanhedrin:

וְיֵשׁ בְּעִנְיָן הַזֶּה תְּנַאי אֶחָד – **There is, however, one qualification to this matter,** לְפִי מַה שֶּׁאָמְרוּ זִכְרוֹנָם לִבְרָכָה בְּמַסֶּכֶת הוֹרָיוֹת – **as per what [the Sages], of blessed memory, stated in Tractate *Horayos*** (2b). שֶׁאִם הָיָה בִּזְמַן הַסַּנְהֶדְרִין אִישׁ חָכָם וְרָאוּי לְהוֹרוֹת – **That** is, **if there was, during the time of the Sanhedrin, a sage who was qualified to rule,** אוֹ שֶׁהוּא מִכְּלַל הַסַּנְהֶדְרִין – **or if he was a member of the Sanhedrin,** וְהוֹרוּ בֵּית דִּין הַגָּדוֹל בְּדָבָר שֶׁלֹּא כְּדַעְתּוֹ – **and the Sanhedrin ruled against his opinion in some matter,** שֶׁאֵינוֹ רַשַּׁאי לְהַתִּיר עַצְמוֹ בְּאוֹתוֹ הַדָּבָר הָאָסוּר לְדַעְתּוֹ – **he may not permit for himself that which according to his opinion is prohibited,**[75] עַד שֶׁיִּשָּׂא וְיִתֵּן עִמָּהֶם עַל הַדָּבָר – **until he debates the matter with them.** וְאַחַר שֶׁיַּסְכִּימוּ כֻּלָּם אוֹ רֻבָּם בְּבִטּוּל הַדַּעַת הַהוּא – **But once all [the members of the Sanhedrin], or the majority of them, conclude to dismiss** his **opinion,** וִישַׁבְּשׁוּ עָלָיו סְבָרָתוֹ וְיַעֲשׂוּ הַסְכָּמָה שֶׁהוּא טוֹעֶה – **and** after **they deem his reasoning flawed and reach the conclusion that he had erred,** אָז הוּא רַשַּׁאי לִנְהֹג לְעַצְמוֹ הֶתֵּר בְּמַה שֶּׁהָיָה דַּעְתּוֹ לֶאֱסוֹר – **he may then conduct himself permissibly in that which he had** originally **held to be prohibited.** וְגַם מְצֻוֶּה הוּא עַל זֶה – **Indeed, he is**

NOTES

73. At notes 5-6.

74. The Mishnah there relates that Rabban Gamliel accepted witnesses who testified that they had seen the new moon, and, as head of the Sanhedrin, he proclaimed the beginning of the month of Tishrei on that day. R' Yehoshua, however, maintained that the witnesses were invalid, and that the month of Tishrei would thus begin a day later. Rabban Gamliel insisted that R' Yehoshua appear before him on the day that was Yom Kippur according to R' Yehoshua's calculation, with his walking stick and his money bag. R' Yehoshua would thus demonstrate his acceptance of the Sanhedrin's ruling, by "desecrating" the day that would be Yom Kippur according to his own calculation. As the Mishnah relates, R' Yehoshua acquiesced and complied with Rabban Gamliel's order — even though, in R' Yehoshua's opinion, Rabban Gamliel was telling him that "right is left."

75. That is, if he maintains that something that the Sanhedrin permitted is actually prohibited by Torah law, he is *forbidden* to conduct himself in a lenient manner at this point.

לְקַבֵּל דַּעְתָּם עַל כָּל פָּנִים[76].

אֲבָל הַתַּקָּנוֹת וְהַגְּזֵרוֹת שֶׁעָשׂוּ חֲכָמִים לְמִשְׁמֶרֶת הַתּוֹרָה וְלַגָּדֵר שֶׁלָּהּ אֵין לָהֶם בְּלָאו זֶה אֶלָּא סֶמֶךְ בְּעָלְמָא וְאֵין בָּהֶם דִּין הַמַּרְאָה כְּלָל[77]. וְיֶתֶר פְּרָטֵי הַמִּצְוָה מְבֹאָרִים בְּסוֹף סַנְהֶדְרִין[78].

וְנוֹהֶגֶת מִצְוָה זוֹ לְעִנְיַן זָקֵן מַמְרֵא בִּזְמַן הַבַּיִת, וּלְעִנְיַן הַחִיּוּב עָלֵינוּ לִשְׁמֹעַ לְדִבְרֵי חֲכָמֵינוּ הַקַּדְמוֹנִים וְאֶל גְּדוֹלֵינוּ בְּחָכְמַת הַתּוֹרָה וְשׁוֹפְטֵינוּ שֶׁבְּדוֹרֵנוּ נוֹהֶגֶת בְּכָל מָקוֹם וּבְכָל זְמַן בִּזְכָרִים וּנְקֵבוֹת[79].

וְעוֹבֵר עַל זֶה וּפוֹרֵץ גָּדֵר[80] בְּדָבָר אֶחָד מִכָּל מַה שֶּׁלִּמְּדוּנוּ רַבּוֹתֵינוּ בְּפֵרוּשׁ הַתּוֹרָה כְּגוֹן בְּאַחַת מִשְּׁלֹשׁ עֶשְׂרֵה מִדּוֹת אוֹ בְּדָבָר שֶׁהוּא אָסוּר מֵהֲלָכָה לְמֹשֶׁה מִסִּינַי וּכְעִנְיָן שֶׁכָּתַבְנוּ

---

obligated by this mitzvah **in this regard,** לְקַבֵּל דַּעְתָּם עַל כָּל פָּנִים – that is, **to accept their opinion regardless.**[76]

The preceding pertains to the Sages' interpretations of Biblical law. *Ramban* now distinguishes between those teachings and laws that the Sages themselves instituted:

אֲבָל הַתַּקָּנוֹת וְהַגְּזֵרוֹת שֶׁעָשׂוּ חֲכָמִים לְמִשְׁמֶרֶת הַתּוֹרָה וְלַגָּדֵר שֶׁלָּהּ – **However, the enactments and decrees that the Sages established as safeguards and barriers for the** sake of upholding the **Torah** אֵין לָהֶם בְּלָאו זֶה אֶלָּא סֶמֶךְ בְּעָלְמָא – **have no** basis **in this prohibition, other than a mere allusion.** וְאֵין בָּהֶם דִּין הַמַּרְאָה כְּלָל – **Thus, the law of *insubordination*** (i.e., *zakein mamrei*) **does not apply to them at all.**[77]

וְיֶתֶר פְּרָטֵי הַמִּצְוָה מְבֹאָרִים בְּסוֹף סַנְהֶדְרִין – **The additional details of this mitzvah are set forth at the end of** Tractate ***Sanhedrin*.**[78]

Applicability of the Mitzvah

וְנוֹהֶגֶת מִצְוָה זוֹ לְעִנְיַן זָקֵן מַמְרֵא בִּזְמַן הַבַּיִת – **With regard to** the law of **a *zakein mamrei*,** who is subject to execution for defying the Sanhedrin, **this mitzvah applies** only **during the times of the *Beis HaMikdash*.** וּלְעִנְיַן הַחִיּוּב עָלֵינוּ לִשְׁמֹעַ לְדִבְרֵי חֲכָמֵינוּ הַקַּדְמוֹנִים וְאֶל גְּדוֹלֵינוּ בְּחָכְמַת הַתּוֹרָה וְשׁוֹפְטֵינוּ שֶׁבְּדוֹרֵנוּ – **However, with regard to our obligation to heed the words of the early Sages, as well as the Torah greats and the judges of our generation,** נוֹהֶגֶת בְּכָל מָקוֹם וּבְכָל זְמַן – **[this mitzvah] applies in every location and in all times,** בִּזְכָרִים וּנְקֵבוֹת – and is incumbent **upon** both **men and women.**[79]

וְעוֹבֵר עַל זֶה – **One who transgresses this** mitzvah, וּפוֹרֵץ גָּדֵר בְּדָבָר אֶחָד מִכָּל מַה שֶּׁלִּמְּדוּנוּ רַבּוֹתֵינוּ בְּפֵרוּשׁ הַתּוֹרָה – **and "breaches the fence,"**[80] **with regard to anything that our Sages taught us in explanation of the Torah,** כְּגוֹן בְּאַחַת מִשְּׁלֹשׁ עֶשְׂרֵה מִדּוֹת – **such as, regarding** something derived from **one of the thirteen principles** through which the Torah is expounded, אוֹ בְּדָבָר שֶׁהוּא אָסוּר מֵהֲלָכָה לְמֹשֶׁה מִסִּינַי – **or something that is prohibited by the Oral Tradition received by Moses at Sinai,** וּכְעִנְיָן שֶׁכָּתַבְנוּ בְּסָמוּךְ – **as we have just**

NOTES

76. As R' Yehoshua did in the incident just cited.

77. *Ramban* has thus explained why Rabbinic enactments are subject to different rules than Biblical laws, as he demonstrated at length above. The Rabbinic enactments are *not* included in the Biblical mitzvah-obligation to heed the Sanhedrin (the previous mitzvah) or the mitzvah-prohibition to defy them (this mitzvah). Since they are *purely Rabbinic* in nature, they are subject to many leniencies that do not apply to Biblical laws.

78. See *Sanhedrin* 86b-89a. *Rambam* codifies these laws in *Hil. Mamrim* Chs. 1-4.

79. As Chinuch pointed out above (at notes 17-18), the law of *zakein mamrei* applies only to a sage who rejects a ruling that was issued in the *Lishkas HaGazis*; thus, it applies only in the times of the *Beis HaMikdash*. However, the actual prohibition against rejecting the words of the Sages [as well as the mitzvah-obligation to abide by their rulings, which was the subject of the previous mitzvah] applies even in our times. As with other mitzvah-prohibitions, it applies to women as well as men.

80. See previous mitzvah, note 14.

בְּסָמוּךְ[81], עָבַר עַל לָאו זֶה מִלְּבַד שֶׁבִּטֵּל עֲשֵׂה שֶׁבּוֹ, אֲבָל אֵין לוֹקִין עַל לָאו זֶה לְפִי שֶׁנְּתָן לְאַזְהָרַת מִיתַת בֵּית דִּין בְּזָקֵן מַמְרֵא וּכְמוֹ שֶׁכָּתַבְנוּ[82].

---

explained,[81] עָבַר עַל לָאו זֶה — **transgresses this prohibition,** מִלְּבַד שֶׁבִּטֵּל עֲשֵׂה שֶׁבּוֹ — **aside from violating the associated mitzvah-obligation** (Mitzvah 495). אֲבָל אֵין לוֹקִין עַל לָאו זֶה — **However, one does not incur** *malkus* **for** violating **this prohibition,** לְפִי שֶׁנְּתָן לְאַזְהָרַת מִיתַת בֵּית דִּין בְּזָקֵן מַמְרֵא וּכְמוֹ שֶׁכָּתַבְנוּ — **for it "serves as a warning regarding execution by** *beis din,*" in the case of a *zakein mamrei,* **as we have written,** and such prohibitions do not carry the penalty of *malkus.*[82]

NOTES

81. According to the approach of *Ramban*.

82. See above, with note 45. [In all cases where the violator is exempt from capital punishment, the Sanhedrin punishes him, and does whatever it sees fit to prevent him from continuing his deviant teachings (*Rambam, Hil. Mamrim* 3:7).]

◈§ Insight: Rambam's Position Regarding the Rabbinic Laws

As discussed at length by Chinuch, according to *Rambam*, the current prohibition — *lo sassur* — requires one to follow all of the dictates of the Sages, not only their interpretations of Biblical law, but even the decrees and practices that they enacted. *Ramban* strongly attacks *Rambam's* position, citing many places where it is evident that Rabbinic laws are treated more leniently than Biblical ones. For example, argues *Ramban,* we find that a situation of doubt involving a possible Rabbinic prohibition is treated leniently, unlike a situation of doubt involving a possible Biblical prohibition. This clearly indicates that one who transgresses a Rabbinic law has not committed a Biblical violation.

The question of how *Rambam* explains the leniencies associated with Rabbinic law is discussed by many commentators, who offer various resolutions of *Rambam's* position. We will explore a number of those resolutions.

Some commentators explain that when the Sages instituted their laws, they allowed for certain leniencies. For example, they stipulated at the outset that their laws apply only when the prohibition is certain, not in a situation where the prohibition is in doubt. Therefore, any case involving a questionable Rabbinic prohibition is not included in the prohibition at all. The same applies to the other cases that *Ramban* cited in his challenge (see *Derashos HaRan, Derush* 7, end of ד"ה ויש כאן [p. 260, MHK ed.] and *Derush* 13 [p. 519, MHK ed.]; *Zohar HaRakia* to *Shoresh* 1 of *Sefer HaMitzvos*). *Ramban* himself actually mentions this possibility, but rejects it as being insubstantial.

Mabit (Introduction to *Kiryas Sefer,* Ch. 5; *Hil. Mamrim* Ch. 1), however, explains that our mitzvah and the previous one apply only when one *defiantly* rejects a Rabbinic law, similar to the case of the *zakein mamrei.* These Biblical mitzvos demand that one accept the authority of the Sages. Thus, if a person accepts the authority of the Sages and the validity of the law, and, for whatever reason, goes ahead and transgresses a Rabbinic law, he has not violated these mitzvos. Accordingly, it is understandable why we find leniencies with regard to Rabbinic law, for in all of the cases where we are lenient we are speaking of one who is following Rabbinic law, not rejecting it. He simply has encountered a situation where, for example, he is not sure whether something falls under the Rabbinic prohibition. It follows that in a case of doubt (and the other cases that *Ramban* cited) we may be lenient with regard to Rabbinic law, for since we are not *denying the validity* of the law, the situation is not subject to the stringencies of Biblical law.

Some commentators (see *Shaarei Yosher* 1:7 ד"ה ובהא דהקשה; *Meshech Chochmah* to the verse) have a different explanation for why we may deal leniently with a doubt regarding a Rabbinic matter. They state that there is a fundamental difference between things that the Torah itself directly prohibits (i.e., Biblically prohibited items, such as pork), and things that the Sages prohibit but are subject to the Biblical prohibition of *lo sassur.* Neither the Torah nor the Sages ever issued a specific prohibition for cases of doubt. The reason a Biblical prohibition is in force in a case of doubt is because the *actual prohibited act* is something that is unwanted and despised by Hashem, and we

need to be concerned about performing the unwanted act. For example, when the Torah prohibits pork, it does not specifically state that the prohibition applies even to something that *may* be pork. Nevertheless, since one who eats pork has performed an act that is unwanted by the Torah, we are required to refrain even from something that may be pork, since we might end up eating pork and doing something that the Torah does not want us to do.

Rabbinic laws, however, are different. Even if we accept *Rambam's* position that the Torah prohibits us to violate any Rabbinic decree, the Torah did not reject the actual *act* that the Sages banned. For example, although the Torah obligates us to abide by the Sages' prohibition against consuming fowl with milk, the Torah has not indicated that it inherently despises "mixtures of fowl with milk." What the Torah despises is "violating a law of the Sages," and one who violates their prohibition has transgressed *that* Biblical law. The act per se, however, is not considered sinful (see *Nesivos HaMishpat* 234:3). Now, when the Sages prohibited something, such as fowl with milk, they did not specifically include a doubtful situation in their prohibition. Thus, in a case of doubt (e.g., one has a dish before him that may contain a mixture of fowl and milk), even if he ends up performing the act (i.e., the dish does contain fowl mixed with milk), he has not acted contrary to the directive of the Torah. The Torah prohibits only violating the words of the Sages, and since the Sages never specifically prohibited a case of doubt, he has not violated their words. Therefore, one is not required to act stringently.

◈ מִצְוָה תצז: מִצְוַת מִנּוּי מֶלֶךְ עָלֵינוּ ◈

שֶׁנִּצְטַוֵּינוּ לְמַנּוֹת עָלֵינוּ מֶלֶךְ מִיִּשְׂרָאֵל[1] יְקַבְּצֵנוּ כֻלָּנוּ וְיַנְהִיגֵנוּ כְּחֶפְצוֹ, וְעַל זֶה נֶאֱמַר (דברים י״ז, ט״ו) שׂוֹם תָּשִׂים עָלֶיךָ מֶלֶךְ וְגוֹ׳, וְאָמְרוּ בַּסִּפְרִי (כאן) שׂוֹם תָּשִׂים עָלֶיךָ מֶלֶךְ, מִצְוַת עֲשֵׂה[2].

◈ Mitzvah 497 ◈
The Obligation to Appoint a King Over Ourselves

כִּי תָבֹא אֶל הָאָרֶץ אֲשֶׁר ה׳ אֱלֹהֶיךָ נֹתֵן לָךְ וִירִשְׁתָּהּ וְיָשַׁבְתָּה בָּהּ וְאָמַרְתָּ אָשִׂימָה עָלַי מֶלֶךְ כְּכָל הַגּוֹיִם אֲשֶׁר סְבִיבֹתָי. שׂוֹם תָּשִׂים עָלֶיךָ מֶלֶךְ אֲשֶׁר יִבְחַר ה׳ אֱלֹקֶיךָ בּוֹ מִקֶּרֶב אַחֶיךָ תָּשִׂים עָלֶיךָ מֶלֶךְ

When you come to the Land that HASHEM, your God, gives you, and possess it, and settle in it, and you will say, "I will set a king over myself, like all the nations that are around me." You shall surely set over yourself a king whom HASHEM, your God, shall choose; from among your brethren shall you set a king over yourself (Deuteronomy 17:14-15).

This mitzvah is the first in a series of six mitzvos (Mitzvos 497-499, 501-503) that deal with the institution of the Jewish monarchy. The monarchy effectively began when the Prophet Samuel appointed Saul as the first king over the Jewish people (*I Samuel* 10:1). With Samuel's subsequent appointment of David (ibid. 16:13), the institution of the monarchy became the eternal heritage of David's descendants. Nevertheless, during the reign of David's grandson, Rechavam, the northern ten tribes seceded from his kingdom and accepted the rule of a different king, Jerovam (see *I Kings* Ch. 12). From that time until the exile of the northern tribes, the Jewish people had two monarchs: the Judean king (who ruled over the tribes of Judah and Benjamin, known as the Kingdom of Judea) and the Israelite king (who ruled over the remaining ten tribes, known as the Kingdom of Israel).

Generally, the laws outlined in this and the coming mitzvos apply not only to Judean kings, but to Israelite kings as well, as long as they were installed by a prophet and are faithful to the Torah (*Rambam, Hil. Melachim* 1:8).

שֶׁנִּצְטַוֵּינוּ לְמַנּוֹת עָלֵינוּ מֶלֶךְ מִיִּשְׂרָאֵל — **We are commanded to appoint over ourselves a king from** among **the Jewish people,**[1] יְקַבְּצֵנוּ כֻלָּנוּ וְיַנְהִיגֵנוּ כְּחֶפְצוֹ — **who will gather us all together and lead us as per his will.** וְעַל זֶה נֶאֱמַר "שׂוֹם תָּשִׂים עָלֶיךָ מֶלֶךְ וְגוֹ׳ " — **Regarding this it is stated** (*Deuteronomy* 17:15): ***You shall surely set over yourself a king,* etc.**

Chinuch cites proof that this is an actual mitzvah-obligation:

וְאָמְרוּ בַּסִּפְרִי **[Our Sages] stated in** *Sifrei:* "שׂוֹם תָּשִׂים עָלֶיךָ מֶלֶךְ" — **The verse,** *You shall surely set over yourself a king,* מִצְוַת עֲשֵׂה — **is a mitzvah-obligation.**[2]

NOTES

1. The verse (*Deuteronomy* 17:15) states: מִקֶּרֶב אַחֶיךָ תָּשִׂים עָלֶיךָ מֶלֶךְ לֹא תוּכַל לָתֵת עָלֶיךָ אִישׁ נָכְרִי אֲשֶׁר לֹא אָחִיךָ הוּא, *from among your brethren shall you set a king over yourself; you cannot place over yourself a foreign man, who is not your brother.* A non-Jew or convert may thus not serve as king. See next mitzvah.

2. In the previous verse, the Torah states: כִּי תָבֹא אֶל הָאָרֶץ אֲשֶׁר ה׳ אֱלֹהֶיךָ נֹתֵן לָךְ וִירִשְׁתָּהּ וְיָשַׁבְתָּה בָּהּ וְאָמַרְתָּ אָשִׂימָה עָלַי מֶלֶךְ כְּכָל הַגּוֹיִם אֲשֶׁר סְבִיבֹתָי, *When you come to the Land that HASHEM, your God, gives you, and possess it, and settle in it, and you will say, "I will set a king*

over myself, like all the nations that are around me" (*Deuteronomy* 17:14). The Torah then goes on to say, *You shall surely set over yourself a king...* There is a dispute in the Gemara (*Sanhedrin* 20b) as to whether this is to be understood as a command to install a monarch, or if the Torah is simply telling us the laws pertaining to a king *should* we choose to appoint one. Chinuch (following *Rambam, Sefer HaMitzvos, Asei* 173) rules that we are commanded to appoint a king, and he cites *Sifrei* here, which states the same. See Insight for further discussion.

מִשָּׁרְשֵׁי הַמִּצְוָה כָּתַבְתִּי בְּכֶסֶף תַּלְוֶה בְּלָאו דְּנָשִׂיא ה׳ בְּסִימָן ע״ז[3] (מצוה ע״א), וְשָׁם הֶאֱרַכְתִּי בְּתוֹעֶלֶת הַנִּמְצָא לָעָם בִּהְיוֹת עֲלֵיהֶם אִישׁ אֶחָד לְרֹאשׁ וּלְקָצִין, כִּי לֹא יִתְקַיֵּם יִשּׁוּב הָעָם בְּשָׁלוֹם בִּלְתִּי זֶה[4], וְהִנֵּה תִּרְאֶה בְּסִפְרֵי הַנְּבוּאָה בָּא בִּקְלָלָה לִהְיוֹת אֲנָשִׁים רַבִּים לְרֹאשׁ בְּמָקוֹם אֶחָד, וּכְמוֹ שֶׁכָּתוּב[5].

מִדִּינֵי הַמִּצְוָה מַה שֶּׁאָמְרוּ זִכְרוֹנָם לִבְרָכָה (רמב״ם פ״א מהל׳ מלכים ה״ג) שֶׁאֵין מַעֲמִידִין מֶלֶךְ בְּיִשְׂרָאֵל בַּתְּחִלָּה אֶלָּא עַל פִּי בֵּית דִּין שֶׁל שִׁבְעִים זְקֵנִים וְעַל פִּי נָבִיא[6], כִּיהוֹשֻׁעַ שֶׁמִּנָּהוּ מֹשֶׁה רַבֵּנוּ וּבֵית דִּינוֹ, וּכְשָׁאוּל וְדָוִד שֶׁמִּנָּה אוֹתָם שְׁמוּאֵל הָרָמָתִי וּבֵית דִּינוֹ[7]. וּמַה שֶּׁאָמְרוּ

Underlying Purpose of the Mitzvah

מִשָּׁרְשֵׁי הַמִּצְוָה – **Among the underlying purposes of the mitzvah** כָּתַבְתִּי בְּכֶסֶף תַּלְוֶה בְּלָאו דְּנָשִׂיא ה׳ בְּסִימָן ע״ז – is that which **I have written in** *Parashas Im **Kesef Talveh**,* **regarding the prohibition of** cursing **a *Nasi,*** Mitzvah-prohibition **5, Chapter 77** of this work (Mitzvah 71).[3] וְשָׁם הֶאֱרַכְתִּי בְּתוֹעֶלֶת הַנִּמְצָא לָעָם – **There I discussed at length the benefit that emerges for the people** בִּהְיוֹת עֲלֵיהֶם אִישׁ אֶחָד לְרֹאשׁ וּלְקָצִין – **when there is one man over them** who serves **as a head and a commander;** כִּי לֹא יִתְקַיֵּם יִשּׁוּב הָעָם בְּשָׁלוֹם בִּלְתִּי זֶה – **for without this, peaceful national coexistence is not sustainable.**[4] וְהִנֵּה תִּרְאֶה בְּסִפְרֵי הַנְּבוּאָה בָּא בִּקְלָלָה לִהְיוֹת אֲנָשִׁים רַבִּים לְרֹאשׁ בְּמָקוֹם אֶחָד – **Indeed, you can see in the Books of the Prophets** how **it is deemed a curse for there to be many men** serving **as the leader in one place,** וּכְמוֹ שֶׁכָּתוּב – **as it is written** in Scripture.[5]

Laws of the Mitzvah

מִדִּינֵי הַמִּצְוָה – **Among the laws of the mitzvah** מַה שֶּׁאָמְרוּ זִכְרוֹנָם לִבְרָכָה – is **that which [our Sages], of blessed memory, have stated** (see *Rambam, Hil. Melachim* 1:3), שֶׁאֵין מַעֲמִידִין מֶלֶךְ בְּיִשְׂרָאֵל בַּתְּחִלָּה אֶלָּא עַל פִּי בֵּית דִּין שֶׁל שִׁבְעִים זְקֵנִים וְעַל פִּי נָבִיא – **that the initial appointment of a king among the Jewish people is done only on the directive of the *beis din* of seventy elders** (i.e., the Great Sanhedrin) **and the directive of a prophet,**[6] כִּיהוֹשֻׁעַ שֶׁמִּנָּהוּ מֹשֶׁה רַבֵּנוּ וּבֵית דִּינוֹ – **as was** the situation **with Joshua, whom Moses, our Teacher, and his court appointed** to lead the Jews after Moses, וּכְשָׁאוּל וְדָוִד שֶׁמִּנָּה אוֹתָם שְׁמוּאֵל הָרָמָתִי וּבֵית דִּינוֹ – **and as was with Saul and David, whom** the prophet **Samuel of Ramah and his court appointed** as kings over the Jewish people.[7]

וּמַה שֶּׁאָמְרוּ – Another law of this mitzvah is **that which [the Sages] stated** (*Rambam* ibid. 5; see

---

NOTES

3. Chinuch's numbering follows the original format of this work; see Mitzvah 494 note 4. Regarding the name *Im Kesef Talveh,* see Mitzvah 495 note 4.

4. Chinuch there explains that people's perspectives and opinions differ. Without an ultimate authority to make the final decisions, society would simply break down.

5. See *Judges* 9:2: מַה טּוֹב לָכֶם הַמְשֹׁל בָּכֶם שִׁבְעִים אִישׁ ... אִם מְשֹׁל בָּכֶם אִישׁ אֶחָד, *What is better for you, that seventy men rule over you ... or that one man rule over you?* See also *Proverbs* 28:2. [See also *Chibbur Yafeh Me-HaYeshuah* (*Rabbeinu Nissim Gaon*) Ch. 2.]

6. The requirement that the king be appointed by the Sanhedrin is stated in *Tosefta* (*Sanhedrin* 3:2). The involvement of a prophet is derived by *Sifrei* from the phrase אֲשֶׁר יִבְחַר ה׳ אֱלֹהֶיךָ, *whom HASHEM, your God, shall choose,* i.e., as communicated through His prophet. [See Mitzvah 498 note 1.]

7. See *Numbers* 27:15-23 for Moses' appointment of Joshua, and *I Samuel* 10:1 and 16:13, where Samuel's anointing of Saul and David is recorded. *Rambam* (*Hil. Melachim* 1:3) adds that in each of these instances, the Sanhedrin convened to take part in these appointments.

[Although Joshua was not anointed as a king, since he was the officially designated leader of the Jewish people, he had to be appointed in the manner of a king. In some respects, he had the same status as a king (see *Sanhedrin* 49a, cited below in note 18; see also *Bereishis Rabbah* 98:15). For further discussion, see *Nachalas Aharon* [Milevsky] §1, and footnote 3 to Chinuch in Machon Yerushalayim ed.]

(שם ה״ה) שֶׁאֵין מַעֲמִידִין אִשָּׁה בַּמַּלְכוּת, שֶׁנֶּאֱמַר מֶלֶךְ וְלֹא מַלְכָּה[8]. וּכְשֶׁמַּעֲמִידִין הַמֶּלֶךְ
הָיוּ מוֹשְׁחִין אוֹתוֹ בְּשֶׁמֶן הַמִּשְׁחָה[9], וּמֵאַחַר שֶׁנִּתְמַנָּה זָכָה בַּמַּלְכוּת לוֹ וּלְבָנָיו, כְּמוֹ שֶׁכָּתוּב
לְמַעַן יַאֲרִיךְ יָמִים עַל מַמְלַכְתּוֹ, הוּא וּבָנָיו בְּקֶרֶב יִשְׂרָאֵל[10]. הִנִּיחַ בֵּן קָטָן, מְשַׁמְּרִין לוֹ
הַמְּלוּכָה עַד שֶׁיִּגְדַּל כְּמוֹ שֶׁעָשָׂה יְהוֹיָדָע לְיוֹאָשׁ[11]. וְכָל הַקּוֹדֵם בְּנַחֲלָה קוֹדֵם לִירֻשַּׁת
הַמְּלוּכָה[12], וְהַבֵּן הַגָּדוֹל קוֹדֵם לַקָּטָן מִמֶּנּוּ[13]. וְלֹא הַמַּלְכוּת בִּלְבַד, אֶלָּא כָּל הַשְּׂרָרוֹת

Sifrei here), שֶׁאֵין מַעֲמִידִין אִשָּׁה בַּמַּלְכוּת — that we do not appoint a woman as the monarch, שֶׁנֶּאֱמַר "מֶלֶךְ" וְלֹא מַלְכָּה — for it is stated, *you shall surely set over yourself* a king, which implies, but you shall **not** set a queen over yourself as your leader.[8]

Chinuch now discusses the anointing of the king and how the kingship is a dynasty that passes from father to son:

וּכְשֶׁמַּעֲמִידִין הַמֶּלֶךְ הָיוּ מוֹשְׁחִין אוֹתוֹ בְּשֶׁמֶן הַמִּשְׁחָה — When they would appoint someone as king, they would anoint him with the anointment oil.[9] וּמֵאַחַר שֶׁנִּתְמַנָּה זָכָה בַּמַּלְכוּת לוֹ וּלְבָנָיו — Once he is appointed as king, he acquires the kingship for himself and his descendants, כְּמוֹ שֶׁכָּתוּב "לְמַעַן יַאֲרִיךְ יָמִים עַל מַמְלַכְתּוֹ הוּא וּבָנָיו בְּקֶרֶב יִשְׂרָאֵל" — as it is written (*Deuteronomy* 17:20): *so that he will prolong years over his kingdom, he and his sons amid Israel,* which indicates that the monarchy passes from father to son.[10]

Chinuch discusses the law in a situation where the king dies and leaves a son who is a minor, or he leaves a number of sons:

הִנִּיחַ בֵּן קָטָן — If, upon the king's death, he leaves a son who is a minor, too young to serve as king, מְשַׁמְּרִין לוֹ הַמְּלוּכָה עַד שֶׁיִּגְדַּל — we reserve the monarchy for him until he comes of age, כְּמוֹ שֶׁעָשָׂה יְהוֹיָדָע לְיוֹאָשׁ — as was done by Jehoyada, the Kohen Gadol, for Joash.[11] וְכָל הַקּוֹדֵם בְּנַחֲלָה קוֹדֵם לִירֻשַּׁת הַמְּלוּכָה — Another law is that anyone who has precedence with regard to inheritance of property (i.e., the closest kin) has precedence with regard to the hereditary succession of the monarchy.[12] וְהַבֵּן הַגָּדוֹל קוֹדֵם לַקָּטָן מִמֶּנּוּ — Furthermore, among the surviving sons of the king, an older son has precedence over one who is younger than he.[13]

Chinuch extends this concept to other areas:

וְלֹא הַמַּלְכוּת בִּלְבַד — It is not only the monarchy that is passed from father to son; אֶלָּא כָּל הַשְּׂרָרוֹת

NOTES

8. There were instances in Jewish history when women led the nation. For discussion of how this was permitted, see *Ramban, Rashba, Ritva,* and *Ran* to *Shevuos* 30a. See also *Minchas Chinuch* §2, and *Avnei Nezer, Yoreh Deah* 312:72-74.

9. This is the special anointment oil — *shemen hamishchah* — that was prepared by Moses in the Wilderness, as described in Mitzvah 107. The oil would be applied all around the king's head, in the shape of a crown (*Rashi, Kereisos* 5b; cf. *Rambam Commentary* to *Kereisos* 1:1). This anointment would take place alongside a flowing spring to symbolize that the king's monarchy should endure, like a spring that never dries up (*Kereisos* ibid.).

Chinuch writes above (Mitzvah 108, at notes 18-19) that only kings from the house of David were anointed with the *shemen hamishchah;* other kings were anointed with balsam oil.

10. Because the monarchy automatically passes on to the next generation, only the first king need be anointed; there is no need to anoint the son who ascends to

his late father's throne. However, if controversy arose as to which son should be appointed, the son who was chosen would be anointed (*Kereisos* ibid.; see Chinuch below).

11. As described in *II Kings* (Ch. 11), when the wicked Athaliah killed all of the members of the Davidic royal family, one infant prince, Joash, was secreted away in the Temple complex. He was quietly raised in the Temple compound for six years until the time came for Jehoyada, the Kohen Gadol, to introduce him as king to the Jewish people.

12. Thus, if there are no surviving sons, the monarchy passes on to the next of kin, as defined by the laws of inheritance (see Mitzvah 400 at note 22), such as the late king's brother (*Minchas Chinuch* §2).

13. As is evident in the verse (*II Chronicles* 21:3): וְאֶת הַמַּמְלָכָה נָתַן לִיהוֹרָם כִּי הוּא הַבְּכוֹר, *and the kingship he* (i.e., King Jehoshaphat) *gave to Jehoram, for he was the firstborn* (*Kereisos* 5b).

שֶׁהֵם בְּמַעֲשֶׂה אוֹ בְּשֵׁם כָּבוֹד מִן הַשֵּׁמוֹת הַנִּכְבָּדִים, וְכָל הַמִּנּוּיִין שֶׁבְּיִשְׂרָאֵל בִּירֻשָּׁה הֵם לוֹ לְאָדָם שֶׁזּוֹכֶה בָּהּ בְּנוֹ אַחֲרָיו וּבֶן בְּנוֹ וּבֶן בֶּן בְּנוֹ עַד לְעוֹלָם[14]. וְהוּא שֶׁיְּהֵא מְמַלֵּא מְקוֹם אֲבוֹתָיו בְּיִרְאַת שָׁמַיִם, אֲבָל כָּל שֶׁאֵין בּוֹ יִרְאַת שָׁמַיִם אַף עַל פִּי שֶׁחָכְמָתוֹ מְרֻבָּה אֵין צָרִיךְ לוֹמַר שֶׁאֵין מְמַנִּין אוֹתוֹ בְּמִנּוּי מִן הַמִּנּוּיִין שֶׁבְּיִשְׂרָאֵל, אֶלָּא שֶׁרָאוּי לְשָׂנְאָתָם וּלְהַרְחִיקָם, וַעֲלֵיהֶם אָמַר דָּוִד (תהלים ה׳, ו׳) שָׂנֵאתָ כָּל פֹּעֲלֵי אָוֶן[15].

וּמַה שֶּׁאָמְרוּ זִכְרוֹנָם לִבְרָכָה (סנהדרין י״ט ע״ב) שׂוֹם תָּשִׂים עָלֶיךָ מֶלֶךְ, שֶׁתְּהֵא אֵימָתוֹ עָלֶיךָ, כְּלוֹמַר, שֶׁנִּירָא אוֹתוֹ וְנַאֲמִין לִדְבָרָיו בְּכָל דָּבָר שֶׁלֹּא יְצַוֶּה כְּנֶגֶד הַתּוֹרָה[16], וּנְכַבְּדֵהוּ בְּתַכְלִית הַכָּבוֹד הָרָאוּי לְבָשָׂר וָדָם[17], וְכָל מִי שֶׁיַּעֲבֹר מִצְוַת מֶלֶךְ שֶׁהוּקַם עַל פִּי הַתּוֹרָה

שֶׁהֵם בְּמַעֲשֶׂה אוֹ בְּשֵׁם כָּבוֹד מִן הַשֵּׁמוֹת הַנִּכְבָּדִים – **rather,** with regard to **all positions of authority, whether** that authority is expressed **through deed or through any of the titles of honor** that one may receive (i.e., whether it is a practical position of authority or an honorary one), וְכָל הַמִּנּוּיִין שֶׁבְּיִשְׂרָאֵל – **and all appointments among the Jewish people,** בִּירֻשָּׁה הֵם לוֹ לְאָדָם – **they are** all **held by the** appointed **person as a heritage,** שֶׁזּוֹכֶה בָּהּ בְּנוֹ אַחֲרָיו – meaning **that his son is awarded the position after him,** וּבֶן בְּנוֹ וּבֶן בֶּן בְּנוֹ עַד לְעוֹלָם – **and his grandson, and great-grandson** after him, **forever.**[14] וְהוּא שֶׁיְּהֵא מְמַלֵּא מְקוֹם אֲבוֹתָיו בְּיִרְאַת שָׁמַיִם – **This,** however, **is provided that [this descendant] fills the place of his ancestors** (i.e., he is on a comparable level) **with respect to fear of Heaven.** אֲבָל כָּל שֶׁאֵין בּוֹ יִרְאַת שָׁמַיִם – **However, anyone who has no fear of Heaven,** אַף עַל פִּי שֶׁחָכְמָתוֹ מְרֻבָּה – **even if he has much knowledge,** אֵין צָרִיךְ לוֹמַר שֶׁאֵין מְמַנִּין אוֹתוֹ בְּמִנּוּי מִן הַמִּנּוּיִין שֶׁבְּיִשְׂרָאֵל – **not only may he not be appointed to any position** of authority **among the Jewish people,** אֶלָּא שֶׁרָאוּי לְשָׂנְאָתָם וּלְהַרְחִיקָם – **but it is** in fact **fitting to hate [such wicked people] and to distance them** from ourselves. וַעֲלֵיהֶם אָמַר דָּוִד שָׂנֵאתָ כָּל פֹּעֲלֵי אָוֶן – **Regarding [such people],** King **David said** (*Psalms* 5:6): ***You*** [i.e., Hashem] ***despise all evildoers.***[15]

Chinuch now discusses how the king's subjects must relate to him:

וּמַה שֶּׁאָמְרוּ זִכְרוֹנָם לִבְרָכָה – **Also** included in these laws **is that which [our Sages], of blessed memory, stated** (*Sanhedrin* 19b), "שׂוֹם תָּשִׂים עָלֶיךָ מֶלֶךְ" – that when the verse states, ***You shall surely set over yourself a king,*** שֶׁתְּהֵא אֵימָתוֹ עָלֶיךָ – the expression *over yourself* teaches **that his awe is to be upon you.** כְּלוֹמַר – **That is to say,** שֶׁנִּירָא אוֹתוֹ – **that we are to fear him,** וְנַאֲמִין לִדְבָרָיו בְּכָל דָּבָר שֶׁלֹּא יְצַוֶּה כְּנֶגֶד הַתּוֹרָה – **and adhere to his words in any matter that he commands, as long as it is not contrary to the Torah.**[16] וּנְכַבְּדֵהוּ בְּתַכְלִית הַכָּבוֹד הָרָאוּי לְבָשָׂר וָדָם – **We are to honor him with the utmost honor befitting a mortal.**[17] וְכָל מִי שֶׁיַּעֲבֹר מִצְוַת מֶלֶךְ שֶׁהוּקַם עַל פִּי הַתּוֹרָה – **Moreover, anyone who transgresses the command of a king who was appointed in accordance with Torah** law,

---

NOTES

14. That such positions are passed from father to son is derived from the verse: לְמַעַן יַאֲרִיךְ יָמִים עַל מַמְלַכְתּוֹ הוּא וּבָנָיו בְּקֶרֶב יִשְׂרָאֵל, *so that he will prolong years over his kingdom, he and his sons amid Israel* (*Deuteronomy* 17:20). The additional phrase, *amid Israel*, teaches that all appointments among the Jewish people are passed on to the following generation (*Sifrei* ad loc.).

15. Regarding the monarchy, if the descendants of the Davidic line in any particular era are all lacking in fear of Heaven, a custodian is placed on the throne until an upstanding descendant is born (*Meiri, Horayos* 11b ד״ה זה שאמרנו).

16. The double expression, שׂוֹם תָּשִׂים, *you shall surely place* (literally, *place, you shall place*), indicates that we must continually place his authority and awe upon ourselves (*Kesubos* 17a with *Rashi* ד״ה שום). If, however, he issues a command against the Torah, we are not to obey him, for when one must choose between the words of the Master (Hashem) and the words of the servant (the king), the words of the Master take precedence (*Rambam, Hil. Melachim* 3:9; see *Sanhedrin* 49a for a Scriptural source).

17. Literally, *flesh and blood.* That is, he is to be honored with the highest level of honor that a human being can be given.

אוֹ מוֹרֵד בְּשׁוּם עִנְיָן, הָרְשׁוּת בְּיַד מֶלֶךְ לְהָרְגוֹ וְאֵין עָלָיו צַד עָוֺן בְּכָךְ[18], עַד שֶׁאָמְרוּ זִכְרוֹנָם לִבְרָכָה (שבת נ״ו ע״א) **שֶׁאוּרִיָּה נִתְחַיֵּב בְּנַפְשׁוֹ כְּשֶׁאָמַר בִּפְנֵי דָּוִד וַאדֹנִי יוֹאָב** (שמואל ב׳ י״א, י״א), **שֶׁלֹּא הָיָה לוֹ לְהַזְכִּיר אֲדְנוּת לְשׁוּם אָדָם בִּפְנֵי הַמֶּלֶךְ[19]. וּמַה שֶּׁאָמְרוּ זִכְרוֹנָם לִבְרָכָה** (סנהדרין כ׳ ע״ב) **שֶׁרְשׁוּת בְּיַד הַמֶּלֶךְ לַעֲשׂוֹת לוֹ דֶּרֶךְ בְּאֶמְצַע הַשָּׂדוֹת וְהַכְּרָמִים[20], וְשֶׁהוּא יָכוֹל לָדוּן בְּנֵי אָדָם כְּפִי מַה שֶּׁיֵּרָאֶה לוֹ הָאֱמֶת וַאֲפִלּוּ בְּלֹא עֵדִים בְּרוּרִים[21]. וּמַה שֶּׁאָמְרוּ** (שם כ״ב ע״א) **שֶׁאֵין רוֹכְבִין עַל סוּסוֹ וְאֵין יוֹשְׁבִין עַל כִּסְאוֹ וְאֵין נוֹשְׂאִין אַלְמְנָתוֹ וְאֵין מִשְׁתַּמְּשִׁין בְּשַׁרְבִיטוֹ וְלֹא בְּכִתְרוֹ וְלֹא בְּכָל כְּלֵי תַשְׁמִישׁוֹ, וְכָל זֶה לְמַעֲלָתוֹ וְלִכְבוֹדוֹ,**

אוֹ מוֹרֵד בְּשׁוּם עִנְיָן – or who rebels against his authority **in any manner, הָרְשׁוּת בְּיַד מֶלֶךְ לְהָרְגוֹ – the king has the right to put him to death. וְאֵין עָלָיו צַד עָוֺן בְּכָךְ – In** doing **so, [the king] would not be** guilty of **wrongdoing in any way,**[18] **עַד שֶׁאָמְרוּ זִכְרוֹנָם לִבְרָכָה – to the extent that [our Sages], of blessed memory, have stated** (*Shabbos* 56a), **שֶׁאוּרִיָּה נִתְחַיֵּב בְּנַפְשׁוֹ כְּשֶׁאָמַר בִּפְנֵי דָּוִד וַאדֹנִי יוֹאָב – that Uriah was liable to death when he said before** King **David, "and my lord, Joab"** (*II Samuel* 11:11), **שֶׁלֹּא הָיָה לוֹ לְהַזְכִּיר אֲדְנוּת לְשׁוּם אָדָם בִּפְנֵי הַמֶּלֶךְ – for in the presence of the king it was not** proper **for him to ascribe lordship to any person** other than the king.[19]

Chinuch further discusses the king's privileges:

וּמַה שֶּׁאָמְרוּ זִכְרוֹנָם לִבְרָכָה – These laws **also** include **that which [our Sages], of blessed memory, stated** (*Sanhedrin* 20b), **שֶׁרְשׁוּת בְּיַד הַמֶּלֶךְ לַעֲשׂוֹת לוֹ דֶּרֶךְ בְּאֶמְצַע הַשָּׂדוֹת וְהַכְּרָמִים – that the king has the right to make a passage for himself through** privately owned **fields and vineyards.**[20] **וְשֶׁהוּא יָכוֹל לָדוּן בְּנֵי אָדָם כְּפִי מַה שֶּׁיֵּרָאֶה לוֹ הָאֱמֶת – Also** included is the law **that he is able to judge people as per what appears to him to be the truth, וַאֲפִלּוּ בְּלֹא עֵדִים בְּרוּרִים – even without clear** testimony of **witnesses.**[21]

Chinuch discusses laws related to the king's belongings and personal effects:

וּמַה שֶּׁאָמְרוּ שֶׁאֵין רוֹכְבִין עַל סוּסוֹ – Also included is the law **that [our Sages], of blessed memory, have stated** (ibid. 22a), **that [a commoner] may not ride upon [the king's] horse, וְאֵין יוֹשְׁבִין עַל כִּסְאוֹ – nor sit on his throne, וְאֵין נוֹשְׂאִין אַלְמְנָתוֹ – nor marry his widow** after his death, **וְאֵין מִשְׁתַּמְּשִׁין בְּשַׁרְבִיטוֹ וְלֹא בְּכִתְרוֹ וְלֹא בְּכָל כְּלֵי תַשְׁמִישׁוֹ – nor make use of his staff, his crown, or any of his personal effects. וְכָל זֶה לְמַעֲלָתוֹ וְלִכְבוֹדוֹ – This is all due to his stature and his**

NOTES

18. As the verse states with regard to Joshua (*Joshua* 1:18): כָּל אִישׁ אֲשֶׁר יַמְרֶה אֶת פִּיךָ וְלֹא יִשְׁמַע אֶת דְּבָרֶיךָ לְכֹל אֲשֶׁר תְּצַוֶּנּוּ יוּמָת, *Anyone who rebels against your command and does not hearken to your words in all that you command him, he shall be put to death* (*Sanhedrin* 49a).

Chinuch (citing *Rambam, Hil. Melachim* 3:8) indicates that the king merely has the *right* to put the rebel to death, but may choose not to do so. Although we will learn below (at note 23) that initially a king has no right to renounce or forgo his own honor, he is nevertheless permitted to pardon a rebel after the fact; for while he may not allow someone to cause him dishonor, once the affront has been committed it is the king's prerogative to pardon him (see *Minchas Chinuch* §5; *Maharatz Chayes, Toras Neviim* Ch. 7). [For an example, see *II Samuel* Ch. 16.]

19. Although Uriah was a soldier under the command of the general Joab, it was an affront to the king's honor for Uriah to refer to Joab with a title of authority while speaking to the king. Uriah was thus deserving of the death penalty (*Shabbos* 56a with *Rashi* ד״ה ואדוני יואב; cf. *Tosafos* ד״ה דאמר).

20. According to some, he may make a permanent path through the fields and vineyards of others in order to easily reach his own fields and vineyards (*Rashi, Sanhedrin* 20b). Other, however, maintain that this does not refer to permanently taking over land belonging to others. Rather, it means that when he and his men are traveling to fight a war, they may break down fences and go through private fields and vineyards, rather than go around them (*Rambam, Hil. Melachim* 5:3; *Yad Ramah, Sanhedrin* 20b ד״ה מתני׳).

21. In certain instances, a king may punish criminals despite the fact that they would not be punished when following the required procedural rules of *beis din*. Therefore, he can impose punishment even though there was no *hasraah* (forewarning), or even if there was only one witness to the act (*Rambam, Hil. Melachim* 3:10). The king's intent, however, must be to enforce law and order, not for his own honor (*Radvaz* there).

וּכְשֶׁהוּא מֵת כֵּלָיו נִשְׂרָפִין לִפְנֵי מִטָּתוֹ[22]. וּמַה שֶּׁאָמְרוּ (שם י״ט ע״ב) שֶׁמֶּלֶךְ שֶׁמָּחַל עַל כְּבוֹדוֹ אֵין כְּבוֹדוֹ מָחוּל[23], וְכָל הַדְּבָרִים הָאֵלּוּ הַכֹּל לְטוֹבַת הָעָם וּלְתוֹעַלְתָּם, וְדִינֵי הַמֶּלֶךְ עַל הָעָם הַכֹּל כְּמוֹ שֶׁמְּפֹרָשׁ בְּסֵפֶר שְׁמוּאֵל (א׳ ח׳, י״א-י״ז)[24]. וְיֶתֶר פְּרָטֵי הַמִּצְוָה מְבֹאָרִים בְּפֶרֶק שֵׁנִי מִסַּנְהֶדְרִין וּבְפֶרֶק רִאשׁוֹן מִכְּרֵיתוֹת וּבְפֶרֶק שְׁבִיעִי מִסּוֹטָה[25].

וְזֹאת מִן הַמִּצְווֹת הַמֻּטָּלוֹת עַל הַצִּבּוּר כֻּלָּן הַזְּכָרִים, כִּי לָהֶם יָאוּת לַעֲשׂוֹת עִנְיָנִים אֵלֶּה[26].

וְנוֹהֶגֶת בִּזְמַן שֶׁיִּשְׂרָאֵל עַל אַדְמָתָן, וּכְמוֹ שֶׁאָמְרוּ זִכְרוֹנָם לִבְרָכָה (סנהדרין כ׳ ע״ב)

---

honor. **וּכְשֶׁהוּא מֵת כֵּלָיו נִשְׂרָפִין לִפְנֵי מִטָּתוֹ** – **Moreover, when he dies, his** personal **effects are burned before his bier.**[22]

וּמַה שֶּׁאָמְרוּ שֶׁמֶּלֶךְ שֶׁמָּחַל עַל כְּבוֹדוֹ אֵין כְּבוֹדוֹ מָחוּל – **Also** included in these laws is **that which [our Sages] have stated** (ibid. 19b), **that if a king renounces his honor, his honor is not renounced,** i.e., his renouncement is ineffective.[23] **וְכָל הַדְּבָרִים הָאֵלּוּ הַכֹּל לְטוֹבַת הָעָם וּלְתוֹעַלְתָּם** – **All of these matters are entirely for the good of the nation and for their benefit,** as they reinforce the stature of the monarchy, which is critical for the proper functioning of society.

וְדִינֵי הַמֶּלֶךְ עַל הָעָם הַכֹּל כְּמוֹ שֶׁמְּפֹרָשׁ בְּסֵפֶר שְׁמוּאֵל – **The rights that the king has over the people** (i.e., their obligations to the king) **are all as is specified in the Book of *Samuel*** (*I Samuel* 8:11-17).[24]

וְיֶתֶר פְּרָטֵי הַמִּצְוָה מְבֹאָרִים בְּפֶרֶק שֵׁנִי מִסַּנְהֶדְרִין וּבְפֶרֶק רִאשׁוֹן מִכְּרֵיתוֹת וּבְפֶרֶק שְׁבִיעִי מִסּוֹטָה – These laws, **and the other details of the mitzvah, are set forth in the second chapter of** Tractate ***Sanhedrin*** (18a, 19a-20b, 22a)**, the first chapter of** Tractate ***Kereisos*** (5b), **and the seventh chapter of** Tractate ***Sotah*** (40b-41b).[25]

Applicability of the Mitzvah

וְזֹאת מִן הַמִּצְווֹת הַמֻּטָּלוֹת עַל הַצִּבּוּר כֻּלָּן הַזְּכָרִים – **This is one of the mitzvos that are incumbent upon the entire community,** collectively. However, only **men** are obligated, **כִּי לָהֶם יָאוּת לַעֲשׂוֹת עִנְיָנִים אֵלֶּה** – **for it is appropriate for them to be the ones involved in such matters.**[26]

וְנוֹהֶגֶת בִּזְמַן שֶׁיִּשְׂרָאֵל עַל אַדְמָתָן – **Furthermore, it applies** only **when the Jews are** dwelling **upon their Land** (Eretz Yisrael). **וּכְמוֹ שֶׁאָמְרוּ זִכְרוֹנָם לִבְרָכָה** – This is **in accordance with that which**

NOTES

22. This custom of burning the personal effects of a king after his death is described in Scripture, where the prophet informs King Zedekiah (*Jeremiah* 34:5): בְּשָׁלוֹם תָּמוּת וּכְמִשְׂרְפוֹת אֲבוֹתֶיךָ הַמְּלָכִים הָרִאשֹׁנִים אֲשֶׁר הָיוּ לְפָנֶיךָ כֵּן יִשְׂרְפוּ לָךְ, *You will die peacefully, and like the burnings for your fathers — the early kings who preceded you — so shall they make a burning for you.* Although the new king is not prohibited from using the personal effects of the deceased king, these items were nevertheless destroyed and not left for the next king to use, as burning them is considered a greater honor to the deceased king (*Minchas Chinuch* §3).

23. The king is not permitted to forgo the honor due him, nor may he do anything that will be a dishonor to his royal status. For example, he may not perform *chalitzah* with his late brother's widow (see Mitzvah 599), for attending the court proceedings and having her spit before him would be an affront to his honor (*Sanhedrin* 19b with *Rashi* ד״ה חליצה).

24. This includes the king's right to levy various taxes, confiscate property for the needs of the state, and forcibly draft his subjects into his service and army (see *Rambam, Hil. Melachim* Ch. 4, for a complete list).

Aside from the obligations that the people have toward the king, the king has certain responsibilities to the people. *Rambam* (ibid. 4:10) explains that the king must perform his activities for the sake of Heaven, supporting Torah values. He must champion justice, and weed out those who are corrupt. In addition, he serves as commander-in-chief of the army and leads it in battle.

25. These laws are codified in *Rambam, Hil. Melachim* Chs. 1-4.

26. The exemption of women applies specifically to the aspect of this mitzvah that relates to the installation of a king. Both men and women are obligated in the aspect of this mitzvah that relates to holding the king in reverence and according him honor (see *Minchas Chinuch* §7).

שָׁלֹשׁ מִצְוֹת נִצְטַוּוּ יִשְׂרָאֵל בִּכְנִיסָתָן לָאָרֶץ, לְמַנּוֹת עֲלֵיהֶן מֶלֶךְ, וְלִבְנוֹת בֵּית הַבְּחִירָה, וּלְהַכְרִית זַרְעוֹ שֶׁל עֲמָלֵק[27].

וְאַל[28] **תְּהַרְהֵר בְּנִי אַחֲרֵי דְּבָרַי לוֹמַר וְאֵיךְ יַחְשֹׁב אָבִי זֹאת הַמִּצְוָה מִן הַנּוֹהֲגוֹת לְדוֹרוֹת, וַהֲלֹא מִשֶּׁנִּמְשַׁח דָּוִד הַמֶּלֶךְ נִסְתַּלְּקָה זֹאת הַמִּצְוָה מִיִּשְׂרָאֵל שֶׁלֹּא יִהְיֶה לָהֶם לְמַנּוֹת עוֹד מֶלֶךְ, כִּי דָוִד וְזַרְעוֹ נְשִׂיאִים עֲלֵיהֶם לָעַד עַד כִּי יָבֹא שִׁילֹה**[29] **שֶׁיִּהְיֶה מִזַּרְעוֹ מֶלֶךְ לְעוֹלָם בִּמְהֵרָה בְיָמֵינוּ. שֶׁעִנְיַן הַמִּצְוָה אֵינוֹ לְמַנּוֹת מֶלֶךְ חָדָשׁ לְבַד, אֲבָל מֵעִנְיָנָהּ הוּא כָּל מַה שֶּׁזָּכַרְנוּ, לְמַנּוֹת מֶלֶךְ חָדָשׁ אִם תִּהְיֶה סִבָּה שֶׁנִּצְטָרֵךְ לוֹ, וְגַם כֵּן לְהַעֲמִיד הַמְּלוּכָה בְּיַד הַיּוֹרֵשׁ,**

[our Sages], of blessed memory, have stated (*Sanhedrin* 20b): **שָׁלֹשׁ מִצְוֹת נִצְטַוּוּ יִשְׂרָאֵל בִּכְנִיסָתָן לָאָרֶץ – The Jewish people were commanded to perform three mitzvos upon their entrance into the Land** of Israel: **לְמַנּוֹת עֲלֵיהֶן מֶלֶךְ** – (1) **to appoint a king upon themselves; וְלִבְנוֹת בֵּית הַבְּחִירָה** – (2) **to build the *Beis HaMikdash*** (Mitzvah 95); **וּלְהַכְרִית זַרְעוֹ שֶׁל עֲמָלֵק – and** (3) **to eradicate the offspring of Amalek** (Mitzvah 604).[27]

Count of the Mitzvah

As a rule, a commandment that was in effect only during a certain era is not counted as one of the 613 Mitzvos (*Rambam, Sefer HaMitzvos, Shoresh* 3).[28] Chinuch, anticipating a question that his son (for whom this work was written) may ask, addresses why the current mitzvah does not fall into that category:

וְאַל תְּהַרְהֵר בְּנִי אַחֲרֵי דְּבָרַי לוֹמַר – Do not doubt my words, my son, by asking: וְאֵיךְ יַחְשֹׁב אָבִי זֹאת הַמִּצְוָה מִן הַנּוֹהֲגוֹת לְדוֹרוֹת – How could my father count this mitzvah among those that are in force for all future **generations? וַהֲלֹא מִשֶּׁנִּמְשַׁח דָּוִד הַמֶּלֶךְ נִסְתַּלְּקָה זֹאת הַמִּצְוָה מִיִּשְׂרָאֵל – Why, once King David was anointed, this mitzvah ceased from** being an obligation upon **the Jewish people, שֶׁלֹּא יִהְיֶה לָהֶם לְמַנּוֹת עוֹד מֶלֶךְ – being that** after David was anointed **there would no longer be** a need **for them to appoint a king** ever again, **כִּי דָוִד וְזַרְעוֹ נְשִׂיאִים עֲלֵיהֶם לָעַד – for** King **David and his descendants are to be the rulers of [the Jewish people] forever, עַד כִּי יָבֹא שִׁילֹה – until the coming of Shiloh** (i.e., Mashiach),[29] **שֶׁיִּהְיֶה מִזַּרְעוֹ מֶלֶךְ לְעוֹלָם בִּמְהֵרָה בְיָמֵינוּ – who will** also **be of [David's] offspring, a king forever,** may he come **speedily in our days!** Why, then, is this not considered a mitzvah that applied only at a specific time (i.e., when David was anointed), which, as a rule, is not counted among the 613 Mitzvos?

Chinuch answers:

שֶׁעִנְיַן הַמִּצְוָה אֵינוֹ לְמַנּוֹת מֶלֶךְ חָדָשׁ לְבַד – This is not a question, **for the concept of the mitzvah is not limited to appointing a new king; אֲבָל מֵעִנְיָנָהּ הוּא כָּל מַה שֶּׁזָּכַרְנוּ – rather,** included **among its aspects is all that we mentioned** above: **לְמַנּוֹת מֶלֶךְ חָדָשׁ אִם תִּהְיֶה סִבָּה שֶׁנִּצְטָרֵךְ לוֹ** – that is, **to** once again **appoint a new king if the circumstances require it, וְגַם כֵּן לְהַעֲמִיד הַמְּלוּכָה בְּיַד הַיּוֹרֵשׁ – and also to establish the monarchy in the hands of the heir** to the throne.

NOTES

27. These mitzvos are to be performed in a specific order (though Chinuch does not list them in this order). First we are to appoint a king, who is tasked with eradicating Amalek. After the destruction of Amalek, the requirement to build the *Beis HaMikdash* comes into effect, as Scripture states (*Deuteronomy* 12:10-11): וְהֵנִיחַ לָכֶם מִכָּל אֹיְבֵיכֶם מִסָּבִיב וִישַׁבְתֶּם בֶּטַח. וְהָיָה הַמָּקוֹם אֲשֶׁר יִבְחַר ה' אֱלֹהֵיכֶם בּוֹ לְשַׁכֵּן שְׁמוֹ שָׁם שָׁמָּה תָבִיאוּ אֵת כָּל אֲשֶׁר אָנֹכִי מְצַוֶּה אֶתְכֶם, *He will give you rest from your enemies all around, and you will dwell securely. It shall be that the place where* HASHEM, *your God, will choose to rest His Name, there shall you bring everything that I command you* (*Sanhedrin* 20b; *Rambam, Hil. Melachim* 1:2).

28. Although circumstances, such as the absence of the *Beis HaMikdash,* may at times prevent us from performing certain mitzvos (such as bringing offerings) today, those mitzvos nevertheless do not fall into the category of mitzvos that were in effect only during a certain era. This is because they will be applicable once again when the *Beis HaMikdash* is rebuilt. Therefore, they are counted among the 613 Mitzvos.

29. Stylistic citations of *Ezekiel* 37:25 and *Genesis* 49:10 (see *Targum* and *Rashi* there).

וְלָתֵת מוֹרָאוֹ עָלֵינוּ וְנִתְנַהֵג עִמּוֹ בְּכָל דָּבָר כַּמִּצְוָה וְכַתּוֹרָה הַיְדוּעָה, וְזֶה בֶּאֱמֶת נוֹהֵג הוּא לְעוֹלָם.

וְלָתֵת מוֹרָאוֹ עָלֵינוּ – Furthermore, it includes **that we are to hold [the king] in reverence, וְנִתְנַהֵג עִמּוֹ בְּכָל דָּבָר כַּמִּצְוָה וְכַתּוֹרָה הַיְדוּעָה – and to act toward him in all matters as per the command and specific conduct** that the law requires. **וְזֶה בֶּאֱמֶת נוֹהֵג הוּא לְעוֹלָם – This, in truth, is applicable forever.** Thus, although the aspect of this mitzvah that requires us to institute the monarchy was accomplished long ago with Samuel's installation of David, the other aspects remain in force. It is therefore appropriate to count this obligation as one of the 613 Mitzvos.

◆ Insight: Why Were the Jewish People Faulted for Requesting a King?

For several centuries after the Jewish people entered Eretz Yisrael, they had no king, and were led by Judges. Eventually, the people came to the Prophet Samuel, the last of the Judges, and said to him (*I Samuel* 8:5): הִנֵּה אַתָּה זָקַנְתָּ וּבָנֶיךָ לֹא הָלְכוּ בִּדְרָכֶיךָ עַתָּה שִׂימָה לָּנוּ מֶלֶךְ לְשָׁפְטֵנוּ כְּכָל הַגּוֹיִם, *Behold! You are old and your sons did not follow in your ways. So now appoint for us a king to judge us, like all the nations.* Scripture relates (ibid. v. 6) that this request was wrong in Samuel's eyes, and he prayed to Hashem. Hashem said to Samuel (ibid. v. 7) that he should listen to the voice of the people, כִּי לֹא אֹתְךָ מָאָסוּ כִּי אֹתִי מָאֲסוּ מִמְּלֹךְ עֲלֵיהֶם, *for it is not you whom they have rejected, but it is Me Whom they have rejected from reigning over them.* Following Hashem's instructions, Samuel warned the people about the power that the king would wield over them, and he gave them a chance to reconsider. When they insisted on having a monarch, he anointed Saul as the first king of Israel. Later, though, Samuel admonished the people, saying (ibid. 12:17): וּדְעוּ וּרְאוּ כִּי רָעַתְכֶם רַבָּה... לִשְׁאוֹל לָכֶם מֶלֶךְ, *Recognize and see that your wickedness is great ... in requesting a king for yourselves.*

This incident is difficult to understand, in light of Chinuch's assertion that the verse (*Deuteronomy* 17:15), שׂוֹם תָּשִׂים עָלֶיךָ מֶלֶךְ, *You shall surely set over yourself a king,* is a mitzvah-obligation. How can the Jewish people be faulted for carrying out that which the Torah obligates them to do?

To be sure, the Gemara (*Sanhedrin* 20b) cites a dispute as to whether appointing a king is an actual Biblical obligation. There is an opinion that the Torah does not mean to *obligate* the people to appoint a king; rather, it means to *permit* them to do so. As the passage indicates (ibid. v. 14), they are to appoint a king when they say, *"I will set a king over myself, like all the nations that are around me."* According to one opinion, this means only that *if* they ever complain about being different from the other nations, they *may* appoint a king. However, the prevailing opinion — which is followed by *Rambam* (*Sefer HaMitzvos, Asei* 173, and *Hil. Melachim* 1:1) and Chinuch — is that there actually is a mitzvah-obligation to appoint a king (cf. *Abarbanel, Deuteronomy* 17:14). Why, then, were the people faulted when they asked for one?

Rambam (*Hil. Melachim* 1:2) addresses this question, and explains that the request for a king was sinful because the people expressed it as a grievance. They did not petition for a king because of the mitzvah, but rather, because they had grown tired of Samuel's leadership. *Ramban* (*Genesis* 49:10) takes the matter further, and explains that presenting such a request during Samuel's lifetime was an affront not only to Samuel's honor, but also to the honor of Hashem, in whose Name Samuel served. This is evident in Hashem's statement to Samuel, *it is not you whom they have rejected, but it is Me Whom they have rejected.*

Meiri (*Horayos* 11b ד"ה משיחה), however, takes issue with this, as Scripture itself states that the people petitioned Samuel for a king only after Samuel had grown old and it was clear that his sons were not fit to fill his role. Accordingly, it was obvious that the people were not rejecting Samuel, but merely looking for an appropriate successor. Rather, *Meiri* explains, the people did wrong because they asked for a king prematurely. The monarchy was reserved for the tribe of Judah (as stated in *Genesis* ibid.), and at that time there was not yet a candidate from Judah suited to be the king; it was some time later that David came of age. Had the people been patient, David would have been the first king and the monarchy would have remained with his descendants, as it ultimately did. Because they requested a king before the time was ripe, it was necessary to appoint Saul, and

indeed his kingship was not lasting, as it did not remain with his descendants (see *Meiri* ibid. at length).

Others take a different approach, and explain that the problem in the people's request lay in the type of governance they sought from this new form of leadership. The people were not looking for a king to enforce Torah law; rather, they sought a king who would rule them according to secular law, כְּכָל הַגּוֹיִם, *like all the nations*. They wanted this king to institute a body of customs and norms that would put them on some imagined par with their idolatrous neighbors, and it is to this that Hashem was alluding in the verse cited above: *but it is Me Whom they have rejected* (*Maharsha, Sanhedrin* 20b; *Aruch HaShulchan HeAsid, Hil. Melachim* 71:6-7).

Along similar lines, some suggest that the inappropriateness of the request was that they sought a king for the purpose of leading them in battle. This is borne out in their statement to Samuel (ibid. v. 20): וְהָיִינוּ גַם אֲנַחְנוּ כְּכָל הַגּוֹיִם וּשְׁפָטָנוּ מַלְכֵּנוּ וְיָצָא לְפָנֵינוּ וְנִלְחַם אֶת מִלְחֲמֹתֵנוּ, *And we shall also be like all the nations, and our king will judge us, and go out before us and fight our battles*. This indicated a lack of full trust in Hashem, for it is ultimately Hashem Who fights our battles, not a human king (*Yad Ramah* and *Meiri* to *Sanhedrin* 20b; see Mitzvah 525). Furthermore, their request highlighted a basic lack of appreciation and understanding of the true role of the Jewish king. In their view, the king would serve as a warrior chief, and his main qualification for the position would be his battlefield prowess. His character and righteousness would be secondary (*Ohr HaChaim, Deuteronomy* 17:14). However, such an approach is not the correct one. As *R' S. R. Hirsch* points out, the Torah specifically states (*Deuteronomy* ibid.) that the mitzvah to appoint a king takes effect, כִּי תָבֹא אֶל הָאָרֶץ וִירִשְׁתָּהּ ... וְיָשַׁבְתָּה בָּהּ, *when you come to the Land ... and possess it and settle in it*. That is, it applies only *after* the conquest of the land. Clearly, the main function of the king is not as a warrior. Granted, in times of war the king must mobilize the nation and serve as its commander-in-chief, but the primary purpose of his appointment is to fight *spiritual* battles and champion Torah values. The king is entrusted with the all-important role of securing Jewish life by upholding and enforcing a rulership greater than his own, the rule of the Kingdom of Heaven. For such a role, the character and righteousness of the individual are not secondary. Rather, they lie at the heart of his role as the Jewish monarch.

For yet another approach, see *Kli Yakar, Deuteronomy* 17:14.

מִצְוָה תצח: שֶׁלֹּא לְמַנּוֹת מֶלֶךְ עַל יִשְׂרָאֵל כִּי אִם מִבְּנֵי יִשְׂרָאֵל

שֶׁנִּמְנַעְנוּ מִלְּהָקִים עָלֵינוּ מֶלֶךְ אִישׁ שֶׁלֹּא יִהְיֶה מִזֶּרַע יִשְׂרָאֵל וַאֲפִלּוּ יִהְיֶה גֵּר צֶדֶק, וְעַל זֶה נֶאֱמַר (דברים י״ז, ט״ו) לֹא תוּכַל לָתֵת עָלֶיךָ אִישׁ נָכְרִי אֲשֶׁר לֹא אָחִיךָ הוּא[1], וְאָמְרוּ זִכְרוֹנָם לִבְרָכָה בְּסִפְרִי (כאן), לֹא תוּכַל לָתֵת עָלֶיךָ אִישׁ נָכְרִי, זוֹ מִצְוַת לֹא תַעֲשֶׂה. וּכְמוֹ כֵן שְׁאָר הַמִּנּוּיִין אֵין רָאוּי שֶׁנִּמַנֶּה עָלֵינוּ בְּדָבָר מֵהַדְּבָרִים לֹא מִנּוּי תּוֹרָה וְלֹא מִנּוּי מַלְכוּת[2] אִישׁ שֶׁיִּהְיֶה מִקְּהַל גֵּרִים עַד שֶׁתְּהֵא אִמּוֹ מִיִּשְׂרָאֵל[3] מִדִּכְתִיב שׂוֹם תָּשִׂים וְגוֹ׳,

---

Mitzvah 498

The Prohibition to Appoint Anyone Other Than a Person of Jewish Lineage as King Over Israel

שׂוֹם תָּשִׂים עָלֶיךָ מֶלֶךְ ... מִקֶּרֶב אַחֶיךָ תָּשִׂים עָלֶיךָ מֶלֶךְ לֹא תוּכַל לָתֵת עָלֶיךָ אִישׁ נָכְרִי אֲשֶׁר לֹא אָחִיךָ הוּא

You shall surely set over yourself a king ... From among your brethren shall you set a king over yourself; you may not place over yourself a foreign man, who is not your brother (*Deuteronomy* 17:15).

שֶׁנִּמְנַעְנוּ מִלְּהָקִים עָלֵינוּ מֶלֶךְ – **We are prohibited from appointing as king over us** אִישׁ שֶׁלֹּא יִהְיֶה מִזֶּרַע יִשְׂרָאֵל – **a man who is not of Jewish lineage,** וַאֲפִלּוּ יִהְיֶה גֵּר צֶדֶק – **even if he is a *ger tzedek*** (righteous convert). וְעַל זֶה נֶאֱמַר – **Regarding this it is stated** (*Deuteronomy* 17:15): "לֹא תוּכַל לָתֵת עָלֶיךָ אִישׁ נָכְרִי אֲשֶׁר לֹא אָחִיךָ הוּא" – ***you may not place over yourself a foreign man, who is not your brother.***[1]

Chinuch cites proof that this law is considered a mitzvah-prohibition:

וְאָמְרוּ זִכְרוֹנָם לִבְרָכָה בְּסִפְרִי – **[Our Sages], of blessed memory, have stated in *Sifrei*** (to the verse): "לֹא תוּכַל לָתֵת עָלֶיךָ אִישׁ נָכְרִי" – When Scripture states, ***you may not place over yourself a foreign man, who is not your brother,*** זוֹ מִצְוַת לֹא תַעֲשֶׂה – **this constitutes a mitzvah-prohibition.**

Chinuch shows that this prohibition applies in other situations as well:

וּכְמוֹ כֵן שְׁאָר הַמִּנּוּיִין – **Similarly with regard to other appointments,** אֵין רָאוּי שֶׁנִּמַנֶּה עָלֵינוּ בְּדָבָר מֵהַדְּבָרִים – **it is not appropriate to appoint** as leader **upon ourselves for any matter,** לֹא מִנּוּי תּוֹרָה וְלֹא מִנּוּי מַלְכוּת – **whether** it is **an appointment** that relates **to a Torah** leadership position **or an appointment** that relates **to the monarchy,**[2] אִישׁ שֶׁיִּהְיֶה מִקְּהַל גֵּרִים עַד שֶׁתְּהֵא אִמּוֹ מִיִּשְׂרָאֵל – **a man who is from the community of converts** (i.e., who either is himself a convert or descends from converts), **unless his mother is Jewish** from birth.[3] מִדִּכְתִיב "שׂוֹם תָּשִׂים וְגוֹ׳" –

NOTES

1. Even the son of a convert is disqualified, as are further generations, unless his mother was a Jewess from birth (*Rambam, Hil. Melachim* 1:4); see Chinuch below with note 3. [Others, however, argue that when it comes to appointing a king (as opposed to other appointments discussed below), *both* parents must be Jews from birth (*Tosafos, Sotah* 41b ד״ה אותו).]

We learned in the previous mitzvah that a king is installed by a prophet, who, through the power of prophecy, appoints the person of Hashem's choosing (see note 6 there). The question thus arises: Why is there a need for a prohibition against installing a "foreign man"? Surely, Hashem will not instruct the prophet to choose someone who is not qualified for the position! Commentators explain that while ideally the king is to be appointed through a prophet, if there is no prophet (such as in a generation that is unworthy of prophecy), this mitzvah requires that we choose someone who is of Jewish lineage (*Ramban, Deuteronomy* 17:15).

2. Positions of "Torah leadership" refer to those of a judge and the like. Positions related to "the monarchy" refer, for example, to government positions and local officers of the state who are placed throughout the land (*Yad HaLevi* to *Sefer HaMitzvos, Lo Saaseh* 362).

3. *Kesef Mishneh* (*Hil. Melachim* 1:4) explains this to mean that it is enough *even* for the mother to be Jewish

וְדִקְדְּקוּ זִכְרוֹנָם לִבְרָכָה (קידושין ע״ו ע״ב) כָּל שִׂימוֹת שֶׁאַתָּה מֵשִׂים עָלֶיךָ לֹא יִהְיוּ אֶלָּא מִקֶּרֶב אַחֶיךָ[4].

שֹׁרֶשׁ הַמִּצְוָה יָדוּעַ, כִּי מִהְיוֹת הַמְּמֻנֶּה לְרֹאשׁ נִשְׁמָע לַכֹּל בְּכָל אֲשֶׁר יְדַבֵּר, צָרִיךְ לִהְיוֹת עַל כָּל פָּנִים מִזֶּרַע יִשְׂרָאֵל שֶׁהֵם רַחֲמָנִים בְּנֵי רַחֲמָנִים, כְּדֵי שֶׁיְּרַחֵם עַל הָעָם שֶׁלֹּא לְהַכְבִּיד עֻלָּם בְּשׁוּם דָּבָר מִכָּל הַדְּבָרִים[5], וְיֶאֱהַב הָאֱמֶת וְהַצֶּדֶק וְהַיֹּשֶׁר, כַּיָּדוּעַ בְּכָל שֶׁהוּא מִמִּשְׁפַּחַת אַבְרָהָם אָבִינוּ עָלָיו הַשָּׁלוֹם שֶׁיֵּשׁ בָּהּ כָּל טוֹבוֹת אֵלּוּ, וּכְעֵין שֶׁאָמְרוּ חַכְמֵי הַטֶּבַע שֶׁטֶּבַע הָאָב צָפוּן בְּבָנָיו[6].

מִדִּינֵי הַמִּצְוָה מַה שֶּׁאָמְרוּ זִכְרוֹנָם לִבְרָכָה שֶׁאֵין מַעֲמִידִין אֶלָּא מִזֶּרַע יִשְׂרָאֵל רֹאשׁ שְׂרָרָה, וַאֲפִלּוּ מְמֻנֶּה עַל אַמַּת הַמַּיִם שֶׁמְּחַלֵּק מִמֶּנָּה לַשָּׂדוֹת[7].

This is derived **from that which is written:** ***You shall surely set*** *over yourself ... from among your brethren shall you set a king over yourself.* וְדִקְדְּקוּ זִכְרוֹנָם לִבְרָכָה – **[Our Sages], of blessed memory** (*Kiddushin* 76b), **expounded** this phrase to mean כָּל שִׂימוֹת שֶׁאַתָּה מֵשִׂים עָלֶיךָ – **that all appointments that you place upon yourselves** לֹא יִהְיוּ אֶלָּא מִקֶּרֶב אַחֶיךָ – **are to be** made **only from among your brethren.**[4]

Underlying Purpose of the Mitzvah

שֹׁרֶשׁ הַמִּצְוָה יָדוּעַ – **The underlying purpose of this mitzvah is** well **known,** כִּי מִהְיוֹת הַמְּמֻנֶּה לְרֹאשׁ נִשְׁמָע לַכֹּל בְּכָל אֲשֶׁר יְדַבֵּר – **for since one who is appointed as a leader is heeded by all** the people **in everything that he says,** צָרִיךְ לִהְיוֹת עַל כָּל פָּנִים מִזֶּרַע יִשְׂרָאֵל – **it is an absolute necessity that he be of Jewish lineage,** שֶׁהֵם רַחֲמָנִים בְּנֵי רַחֲמָנִים – a natural-born offspring of **those who are "merciful ones who descend from merciful ones,"** כְּדֵי שֶׁיְּרַחֵם עַל הָעָם – **so that he will** have a merciful nature and **act with mercy toward the people** that he leads, שֶׁלֹּא לְהַכְבִּיד עֻלָּם בְּשׁוּם דָּבָר מִכָּל הַדְּבָרִים – **and not increase their burden in any of the various matters** over which he has control.[5] וְיֶאֱהַב הָאֱמֶת וְהַצֶּדֶק וְהַיֹּשֶׁר – **He will love truth, justice, and uprightness,** כַּיָּדוּעַ בְּכָל שֶׁהוּא מִמִּשְׁפַּחַת אַבְרָהָם אָבִינוּ עָלָיו הַשָּׁלוֹם – **as is known with regard to all who are of the family of Abraham, our forefather, may peace be upon him,** שֶׁיֵּשׁ בָּהּ כָּל טוֹבוֹת אֵלּוּ – **which has all of these good** traits. וּכְעֵין שֶׁאָמְרוּ חַכְמֵי הַטֶּבַע שֶׁטֶּבַע הָאָב צָפוּן בְּבָנָיו – This is **along the lines of what the scientists say — that the nature of a father is inherent in his children.**[6]

Laws of the Mitzvah

מִדִּינֵי הַמִּצְוָה – **Among the laws of the mitzvah** מַה שֶּׁאָמְרוּ זִכְרוֹנָם לִבְרָכָה – is **that which [our Sages], of blessed memory, have stated** (see *Rambam, Hil. Melachim* 1:4; *Kiddushin* 76b), שֶׁאֵין מַעֲמִידִין אֶלָּא מִזֶּרַע יִשְׂרָאֵל רֹאשׁ שְׂרָרָה – **that we appoint only those who are of Jewish lineage to positions of authority** in every area, וַאֲפִלּוּ מְמֻנֶּה עַל אַמַּת הַמַּיִם שֶׁמְּחַלֵּק מִמֶּנָּה לַשָּׂדוֹת – **even** with respect to **the one placed in charge of the** public **irrigation channel, from which** water **is divided to** privately owned **fields.**[7]

NOTES

from birth, but certainly we may appoint to any position (including the monarchy) a man whose father is a Jew from birth, even if his mother is a convert (see also *Tosafos, Yevamos* 102a ד״ה לענין). See Insight.

4. The repetitive nature of the verse, *You shall surely set over yourself ... from among your brethren shall you set,* teaches that *any* position of authority may be filled only from among our brethren (*Rashi, Kiddushin* 76b ד״ה כל משימות; see *Rambam, Sefer HaMitzvos, Lo Saaseh* 362; see also *Hil. Melachim* 1:4).

5. One of the defining attributes of the Jewish people is that they are merciful, as the verse states (*Deuteronomy* 13:18): וְנָתַן לְךָ רַחֲמִים וְרִחַמְךָ, *and He will give you mercy and be merciful to you* (*Yevamos* 79a). Due to the great significance of the king's position, the Torah requires that he must have this attribute as an inborn trait.

6. *Rambam* (*Moreh Nevuchim* III, Ch. 50) suggests another reason: When the leader is of the same ethnicity as his nation, he will do his utmost to lead the nation with grace and compassion. If, however, he is from a different land, he will likely treat his subjects more harshly.

7. This is the person who assures that the water is

וְאָמְרוּ גַּם כֵּן שֶׁאֵין מַעֲמִידִין מֶלֶךְ וְלֹא כֹּהֵן גָּדוֹל לֹא סַפָּר וְלֹא בַּלָּן וְלֹא בּוּרְסִי, וְלֹא מִפְּנֵי שֶׁיִּהְיוּ פְּסוּלִים לְמַלְכוּת, אֶלָּא מִפְּנֵי שֶׁאֻמָּנוּתָן נְקַלָּה מְזַלְזְלִין בָּהֶם הָעָם לְעוֹלָם, וּמִי שֶׁיַּעֲשֶׂה בִּמְלָאכוֹת אֵלּוּ אֲפִלּוּ יוֹם אֶחָד נִפְסָל לְשְׂרָרוֹת אֵלּוּ.

וּבְמַלְכוּת יִשְׂרָאֵל כְּבָר זָכָה בּוֹ דָּוִד וְזַרְעוֹ לְעוֹלָם וְאֵין בְּיָדֵינוּ עוֹד לְשַׁנּוֹתָהּ, כְּמוֹ שֶׁאֵין בְּיָדֵינוּ עוֹד לְשַׁנּוֹת הַכְּהֻנָּה מִזֶּרַע אַהֲרֹן[8], שֶׁנֶּאֱמַר עָלָיו (שמואל ב׳ ז׳, ט״ז) כִּסְאֲךָ יִהְיֶה נָכוֹן עַד עוֹלָם, וּבְבֵאוּר אָמְרוּ זִכְרוֹנָם לִבְרָכָה (קהלת רבה פרשה ז׳) כֶּתֶר מַלְכוּת זָכָה בּוֹ דָוִד, וְכָל הַמַּאֲמִין בְּתוֹרַת מֹשֶׁה יוֹדֶה עַל זֶה[9]. וְיֶתֶר פְּרָטֵי הַמִּצְוָה מְבֹאָרִים בִּמְקוֹמוֹת מִיבָמוֹת וְסַנְהֶדְרִין וְסוֹטָה וְנִדָּה[10], וּכְבָר כָּתַבְתִּי קְצָת בְּדִינֵי הַמְּלוּכָה כְּמִנְהֲגֵי לְמַעְלָה

Chinuch now discusses factors other than lineage that can disqualify one from becoming king:

וְאָמְרוּ גַּם כֵּן — **[The Sages] further stated** (see *Rambam* ibid. 1:6; *Kiddushin* 82a) שֶׁאֵין מַעֲמִידִין מֶלֶךְ וְלֹא כֹּהֵן גָּדוֹל לֹא סַפָּר וְלֹא בַּלָּן וְלֹא בּוּרְסִי — **that one who is** either **a barber, a bathhouse attendant, or a tanner may not be appointed as king or as Kohen Gadol.** וְלֹא מִפְּנֵי שֶׁיִּהְיוּ פְּסוּלִים לְמַלְכוּת — This is **not because they are** intrinsically **unfit for the monarchy** or the high priesthood, אֶלָּא מִפְּנֵי שֶׁאֻמָּנוּתָן נְקַלָּה מְזַלְזְלִין בָּהֶם הָעָם לְעוֹלָם — **but rather,** because **since their professions are lowly, people will always disrespect them.** וּמִי שֶׁיַּעֲשֶׂה בִּמְלָאכוֹת אֵלּוּ אֲפִלּוּ יוֹם אֶחָד — **One who has engaged in** any of **these professions for even a single day** נִפְסָל לְשְׂרָרוֹת אֵלּוּ — **is** forever **disqualified from** serving in **these positions of authority.**

Chinuch now notes that with the appointment of David as king, the monarchy became the eternal heritage of his descendants. As such, we are further limited regarding whom we may appoint as king:

וּבְמַלְכוּת יִשְׂרָאֵל כְּבָר זָכָה בּוֹ דָּוִד וְזַרְעוֹ לְעוֹלָם — **Regarding the monarchy of Israel, King David and his descendants have acquired that** position **forever,** וְאֵין בְּיָדֵינוּ עוֹד לְשַׁנּוֹתָהּ — **and we no longer have the right to transfer it** to anyone else, כְּמוֹ שֶׁאֵין בְּיָדֵינוּ עוֹד לְשַׁנּוֹת הַכְּהֻנָּה מִזֶּרַע אַהֲרֹן — **just as we no longer have the ability to transfer the priesthood from the descendants of Aaron** to anyone else.[8] שֶׁנֶּאֱמַר עָלָיו "כִּסְאֲךָ יִהְיֶה נָכוֹן עַד עוֹלָם" — This is evident **from that which is stated with regard to [David]** (*II Samuel* 7:16): ***your throne will remain firm forever.*** וּבְבֵאוּר אָמְרוּ זִכְרוֹנָם לִבְרָכָה — Indeed, **[our Sages], of blessed memory, have explicitly stated** (*Koheles Rabbah* 7:2; see *Yoma* 72b; *Rambam, Hil. Talmud Torah* 3:1): כֶּתֶר מַלְכוּת זָכָה בּוֹ דָוִד — **David acquired the crown of monarchy,** meaning that it was granted to him as his permanent right. וְכָל הַמַּאֲמִין בְּתוֹרַת מֹשֶׁה יוֹדֶה עַל זֶה — **Anyone who believes in the Torah of Moses will acknowledge this.**[9] וְיֶתֶר פְּרָטֵי הַמִּצְוָה מְבֹאָרִים בִּמְקוֹמוֹת מִיבָמוֹת וְסַנְהֶדְרִין וְסוֹטָה וְנִדָּה — These laws **and the additional details of the mitzvah are set forth in** various **places in** Tractates ***Yevamos*** (45b), ***Sanhedrin*** (18a, 20a ff.), ***Sotah*** (41a), **and *Niddah*.**[10] וּכְבָר כָּתַבְתִּי קְצָת בְּדִינֵי הַמְּלוּכָה כְּמִנְהֲגֵי לְמַעְלָה

NOTES

divided in a fair manner, with each person taking water only on his assigned day (*Rashi, Kiddushin* 76b ד״ה גרגותא). Even though this position is not of great significance, it nevertheless falls under the category of שְׂרָרָה, *authority,* and must therefore be filled by someone of Jewish lineage.

8. See Mitzvah 491 at note 23, where Chinuch cites the Scriptural teaching that the priesthood remains the eternal heritage of Aaron and his sons. See also *Mechilta,* beginning of *Parashas Bo* ד״ה בארץ מצרים.

9. Chinuch's words here originate from *Rambam, Sefer HaMitzvos, Lo Saaseh* 362. *Rambam* goes on to note that once the Davidic line was chosen, anyone who is not of that line is deemed אִישׁ נָכְרִי, a *foreign man,* with respect to the throne.

With the statement, "Anyone who believes in the Torah of Moses will acknowledge this," Chinuch alludes that the idea that the monarchy belongs to the House of David touches on one of the basic principles of faith: the belief in the coming of Mashiach, who will be a king of the Davidic dynasty, descending from King Solomon; see *Rambam, Commentary to the Mishnah, Sanhedrin* 10:1 ד״ה היסוד הי״ב.

[Actually, there were times in the history of the Jewish people when kings not from the Davidic dynasty were appointed; see *Rambam, Hil. Melachim* 1:8. For discussion, see *R' Y. F. Perla, Sefer HaMitzvos of Rav Saadiah Gaon, Parashah* 7 (Vol. 3, p. 118b) ד״ה איברא דדברי הרמב״ם ז״ל; and *HaMaayan,* Vol. 23 no. 4, p. 36 ff.]

10. See 49b there with *Tosafos* ד״ה חדא. These laws are codified in *Rambam, Hil. Melachim* Ch. 1.

בְּסֵדֶר זֶה עֲשֵׂה ג' (מצוה תצ"ז).

וְנוֹהֵג אִסּוּר זֶה לְעִנְיַן מְלוּכָה בִּזְמַן שֶׁיִּשְׂרָאֵל עַל אַדְמָתָן בְּיִשּׁוּבָן[11], וְהִיא מִן הָאַזְהָרוֹת שֶׁהֵן עַל כְּלַל הַצִּבּוּר. וּלְעִנְיַן שְׁאָר שְׂרָרוֹת שֶׁבְּיִשְׂרָאֵל נוֹהֵג אִסּוּר זֶה בְּכָל מָקוֹם שֶׁהֵם, שֶׁאָסוּר לָהֶם מִן הַתּוֹרָה לְמַנּוֹת עַל הַצִּבּוּר אָדָם שֶׁאֵינוֹ מִבְּנֵי יִשְׂרָאֵל.

וּמִשֹּׁרֶשׁ הַמִּצְוָה אַתָּה דָּן שֶׁאָסוּר גַּם כֵּן לְמַנּוֹת עַל הַצִּבּוּר אֲנָשִׁים רְשָׁעִים וְאַכְזָרִים, וְהַמְמַנֶּה אוֹתָם מִפְּנֵי קֻרְבָה אוֹ מִיִּרְאָתוֹ לָהֶם אוֹ לְהַחֲנִיפָם לֹא תָסוּר רָעָה מִבֵּיתוֹ וְעַל קָדְקֳדוֹ חֲמָסוֹ שֶׁל אוֹתוֹ רָשָׁע יֵרֵד[12], וּמִי שֶׁלֹּא יִירָא מִכָּל אָדָם לְהוֹעִיל לָרַבִּים בְּכָל כֹּחוֹ, שְׂכָרוֹ יִהְיֶה אִתּוֹ מֵאֵת הַשֵּׁם תָּמִיד בָּעוֹלָם הַזֶּה, וְנַפְשׁוֹ בְּטוֹב תָּלִין לָעוֹלָם הַבָּא, וְזַרְעוֹ יִירַשׁ אָרֶץ[13].

בְּסֵדֶר זֶה עֲשֵׂה ג' – I have already written some of the laws of the monarchy, as is my custom, above in this *parashah*, Mitzvah-**obligation 3** (Mitzvah 497).

Applicability of the Mitzvah

וְנוֹהֵג אִסּוּר זֶה לְעִנְיַן מְלוּכָה – This prohibition, with regard to the monarchy, applies בִּזְמַן שֶׁיִּשְׂרָאֵל עַל אַדְמָתָן בְּיִשּׁוּבָן – when the Jewish people are settled on their Land (Eretz Yisrael).[11] **וְהִיא מִן הָאַזְהָרוֹת שֶׁהֵן עַל כְּלַל הַצִּבּוּר – [This mitzvah]** is one **of the prohibitions that apply to the entire community** of Jews, for the installation of a king is a communal responsibility.

וּלְעִנְיַן שְׁאָר שְׂרָרוֹת שֶׁבְּיִשְׂרָאֵל – With regard to other positions of authority among Israel, נוֹהֵג אִסּוּר זֶה בְּכָל מָקוֹם שֶׁהֵם – this prohibition applies wherever they are, not only in Eretz Yisrael, **שֶׁאָסוּר לָהֶם מִן הַתּוֹרָה לְמַנּוֹת עַל הַצִּבּוּר** – meaning **that it is Biblically prohibited for them to appoint over the community אָדָם שֶׁאֵינוֹ מִבְּנֵי יִשְׂרָאֵל – a person who is not of Jewish lineage.**

Chinuch extracts a broader lesson from the mitzvah:

וּמִשֹּׁרֶשׁ הַמִּצְוָה אַתָּה דָּן – You can learn from the underlying purpose of the mitzvah written above **שֶׁאָסוּר גַּם כֵּן לְמַנּוֹת עַל הַצִּבּוּר אֲנָשִׁים רְשָׁעִים וְאַכְזָרִים – that it is also prohibited to appoint over the community wicked and cruel men,** even if they are of Jewish descent; for if the Torah requires us to appoint people of Jewish lineage because they are naturally merciful, certainly we may not appoint those who are known to be cruel. **וְהַמְמַנֶּה אוֹתָם מִפְּנֵי קֻרְבָה – One who appoints [wicked people] because** they are **related** to him, **אוֹ מִיִּרְאָתוֹ לָהֶם אוֹ לְהַחֲנִיפָם – or because he fears them, or in order to flatter them, לֹא תָסוּר רָעָה מִבֵּיתוֹ** – will be punished that **evil will never depart from his home! וְעַל קָדְקֳדוֹ חֲמָסוֹ שֶׁל אוֹתוֹ רָשָׁע יֵרֵד – And upon his head will befall the wrongdoing of that wicked man**[12] whom he unjustly appointed, for he will be held responsible for that person's misconduct. **וּמִי שֶׁלֹּא יִירָא מִכָּל אָדָם – But one who fears no man, לְהוֹעִיל לָרַבִּים בְּכָל כֹּחוֹ** – and **makes every effort to help the public, שְׂכָרוֹ יִהְיֶה אִתּוֹ מֵאֵת הַשֵּׁם תָּמִיד בָּעוֹלָם הַזֶּה – his reward from Hashem will accompany him continually in this world, וְנַפְשׁוֹ בְּטוֹב תָּלִין לָעוֹלָם הַבָּא – and his soul will repose in goodness in the World to Come, וְזַרְעוֹ יִירַשׁ אָרֶץ – and his descendants will inherit the land.**[13]

NOTES

11. For it is only when we are settled in our land that we become obligated to install a king, as Chinuch stated in the previous mitzvah.

12. Stylistic citation of *Psalms* 7:17.

13. Stylistic citation of *Psalms* 25:13. That is, he will be at peace after his passing, and his children will find success in this world in his merit (*Malbim* ad loc.).

✑§ Insight: The Lineage of Rechavam, and of Agrippa

Scripture relates (*I Kings* 11:43) that after King Solomon's death, his son Rechavam inherited the throne. Rechavam's mother, Naamah, was an Ammonite by birth (ibid. 14:21), and had converted to Judaism (see *Bava Kamma* 38b). The question arises: Being that his mother was not of Jewish lineage, how could Rechavam have been appointed as king?

Now, *Rambam* (*Hil. Melachim* 1:4) rules that in order to be eligible to serve as king, it suffices if one's mother is of Jewish lineage (see Chinuch above, at note 3). Some commentators explain that if one's father is of Jewish lineage he is *certainly* eligible, even if his mother is not. Thus, according to *Rambam,* Rechavam was eligible for the throne even though his mother was not born Jewish, since his father was a born Jew (*Kesef Mishneh,* cited in note 3). *Tosafos* (*Sotah* 41b ד"ה אותו), however, maintain that in order for a person to be eligible for the throne, *both* of his parents must have been born Jews. According to their opinion, the question regarding the legitimacy of Rechavam's monarchy stands.

Some suggest that even according to those who require both parents to be of Jewish lineage, that requirement applies only at the beginning of a dynasty. This is because the verse of our mitzvah: שׂוֹם תָּשִׂים עָלֶיךָ מֶלֶךְ ... לֹא תוּכַל לָתֵת עָלֶיךָ אִישׁ נָכְרִי, *You shall surely set over yourself a king ... you may not place over yourself a foreign man,* is speaking of when a dynasty is first established. The prohibition against taking a "foreign man" as king does not apply when the dynasty passes from father to son, for under such circumstances, we are not the ones installing the king; rather, he is assuming the throne through the law of inheritance. Accordingly, Rechavam was eligible to serve as king, since he inherited the throne from his father (*Noda BiYehudah* I, *Choshen Mishpat* §1; *Teshuvos Chasam Sofer, Orach Chaim* §12). [For additional explanations, see *Be'er Sheva, Sotah* 41b ד"ה נתחייבו; *Minchas Chinuch* §1; and *Maharam Schik.*]

A related question pertains to a king of later times. In the latter part of the Second Temple Era, the Jewish people were ruled by the Herodian dynasty. Herod had been a Canaanite slave of the Hasmoneans who ruled Israel, but he killed the members of the Hasmonean family and usurped the throne (see *Bava Basra* 3b). One of Herod's descendants was King Agrippa. The Mishnah (*Sotah* 41a) relates that when Agrippa was reading the Torah to the assembled masses in fulfillment of the mitzvah of *Hakheil* (see Mitzvah 612), he reached the verse of this mitzvah, which prohibits installing אִישׁ נָכְרִי, *a "foreign" man,* as king. Being of Canaanite lineage, Agrippa realized that his occupancy of the throne was inappropriate, and his eyes welled with tears. The people, however, comforted him, saying, "Do not fear, Agrippa. You are our brother! You are our brother!" Since in actuality this statement was not true, the people were guilty of false flattery, for which they were severely punished by Heaven (ibid. 41b with *Tosafos* ד"ה אותו; see *Yerushalmi* there 7:7).

What exactly was the flaw in Agrippa's ancestry that disqualified him from the throne?

According to *Rashi* (*Sotah* 41a ד"ה אחינו אתה and 41b ד"ה אגרופה), Agrippa was technically fit to rule. Although his father descended from Herod, his mother was a born Jewess (which is why the people called him "our brother"), and thus he was not considered a "foreign" man. Nevertheless, since his father was a Canaanite slave (as were all of Herod's descendants who had no Jewish parent), he was unfit to be king due to his lowly status. [This is a Rabbinic disqualification] (see *Tosefta, Sanhedrin* 4:6, cited by *Smag, Lo Saaseh* 221; *Tosafos, Yevamos* 45b ד"ה כיון).

In explaining that Agrippa's flaw was due only to his lowly status, *Rashi* takes the position that the Biblical prohibition against installing one who is not of Jewish lineage is avoided even if one's mother alone is of Jewish lineage. This is consistent with the view of *Rambam* and Chinuch, as mentioned above. *Tosafos* (*Sotah* 41b ד"ה אותו), however, reject this position, for it is not plausible that the people would be punished so severely if Agrippa's flaw was merely that he was Rabbinically ineligible due to his lowly status. Therefore, *Tosafos* assert, this incident proves that when it comes to appointing a king, *both* parents must be of Jewish lineage. This was not the case with Agrippa, and he was thus Biblically unfit for the monarchy. [*Tosafos* concede, however, that this stringent standard applies only to a king. For lesser positions, a person may be appointed even if only his mother is a born Jew. This is evident from a statement of the Gemara (*Yevamos* 45b) that Rav Mari bar Rachel, whose father was not Jewish, was eligible to serve in a leadership position because his mother was of Jewish descent.]

Others explain that Agrippa's mother was not Jewish. According to this view, Agrippa was

halachically classified as a Canaanite slave like his father (for the son of a slave is also a slave unless his mother is Jewish). Nevertheless, the people called him "our brother," for a Canaanite slave is obligated to observe many of the mitzvos, and is therefore considered "our brother" with respect to mitzvah observance. However, when it comes to determining his status as a full-fledged Jew, and all the more so with respect to appointing him as king over the Jewish people, Agrippa was labeled אִישׁ נָכְרִי, *a "foreign" man*. Therefore, those who sought to comfort him by implying otherwise were guilty of condoning a Biblical violation and were punished in kind (*Tosafos* to *Yevamos* 45b ד"ה כיון and *Bava Basra* 3b ד"ה כל דאמר).

מִצְוָה תצט: שֶׁלֹּא יַרְבֶּה הַמֶּלֶךְ סוּסִים

שֶׁלֹּא יַרְבֶּה לוֹ הַמֶּלֶךְ שֶׁיִּמְלֹךְ עָלֵינוּ סוּסִים זוּלָתִי הַצְּרִיכִים לְמֶרְכַּבְתּוֹ וּמִרְכֶּבֶת פָּרָשָׁיו, וּכְמוֹ שֶׁכָּתוּב (דברים י״ז, ט״ז) לֹא יַרְבֶּה לוֹ סוּסִים. וְעִנְיַן הַמִּצְוָה שֶׁלֹּא יִהְיוּ לוֹ סוּסִים שֶׁיָּרוּצוּ לְפָנָיו לְכָבוֹד בְּעָלְמָא, וַאֲפִלּוּ עַל סוּס אֶחָד בָּטֵל יִהְיֶה עוֹבֵר עַל זֶה[1]. וְאָמְנָם אִם יִהְיוּ לוֹ סוּסִים בְּאִצְטַבְלָאוֹת שֶׁלּוֹ מוּכָנִים לַמִּלְחָמָה וּפְעָמִים שֶׁיִּרְכְּבוּ עֲלֵיהֶם פָּרָשָׁיו אֵין זֶה בִּכְלַל לָאו זֶה כְּלָל[2], שֶׁאֵין עִקַּר הָעִנְיָן אֶלָּא עַל הַצַּד שֶׁאָמַרְנוּ שֶׁלֹּא יַנְהִיג לְפָנָיו תָּמִיד סוּסִים בְּטֵלִים לְמַעְלָה וּלְכָבוֹד, אֲבָל יִהְיֶה לוֹ בְּהֵמָה אַחַת לְבַד לְמֶרְכַּבְתּוֹ[3].

Mitzvah 499
The Prohibition Upon a King to Have Too Many Horses

רַק לֹא יַרְבֶּה לּוֹ סוּסִים וְלֹא יָשִׁיב אֶת הָעָם מִצְרַיְמָה לְמַעַן הַרְבּוֹת סוּס וַה׳ אָמַר לָכֶם לֹא תֹסִפוּן לָשׁוּב בַּדֶּרֶךְ הַזֶּה עוֹד

Only he shall not have too many horses for himself, so that he will not return the people to Egypt in order to increase horses, for HASHEM has said to you, "You shall no longer return on this road again" (*Deuteronomy* 17:16).

In Mitzvah 497, the Torah commanded us, שׂוֹם תָּשִׂים עָלֶיךָ מֶלֶךְ, *You shall surely set over yourself a king*. Aside from the obligation to appoint a monarch, that mitzvah requires us to accord the king honor, awe, and obedience. The current mitzvah is the first of three mitzvos that deal with certain restrictions on the privileges of a Jewish monarch (see Mitzvos 501-502).

שֶׁלֹּא יַרְבֶּה לוֹ הַמֶּלֶךְ שֶׁיִּמְלֹךְ עָלֵינוּ סוּסִים – The Torah commands **that the king who rules over us shall not have too many horses for himself, זוּלָתִי הַצְּרִיכִים לְמֶרְכַּבְתּוֹ וּמִרְכֶּבֶת פָּרָשָׁיו** – meaning, horses **other than those needed for his chariot and the chariots of his cavalry, וּכְמוֹ שֶׁכָּתוּב "לֹא יַרְבֶּה לוֹ סוּסִים"** – **as it is written** (*Deuteronomy* 17:16): ***he shall not have too many horses for himself.***

וְעִנְיַן הַמִּצְוָה – The description of this mitzvah is שֶׁלֹּא יִהְיוּ לוֹ סוּסִים שֶׁיָּרוּצוּ לְפָנָיו לְכָבוֹד בְּעָלְמָא – that he may not have horses that simply **run before him for** the purpose of **honor alone. וַאֲפִלּוּ עַל סוּס אֶחָד בָּטֵל יִהְיֶה עוֹבֵר עַל זֶה** – In fact, **even for** keeping **one idle horse, he would transgress this** prohibition.[1] **וְאָמְנָם אִם יִהְיוּ לוֹ סוּסִים בְּאִצְטַבְלָאוֹת שֶׁלּוֹ מוּכָנִים לַמִּלְחָמָה – On the other hand, if he has** numerous **horses in his stables ready for battle** when needed, **וּפְעָמִים שֶׁיִּרְכְּבוּ עֲלֵיהֶם פָּרָשָׁיו – and at times his cavalry rides upon them, אֵין זֶה בִּכְלַל לָאו זֶה כְּלָל – that is not included in this prohibition at all.**[2] **שֶׁאֵין עִקַּר הָעִנְיָן אֶלָּא עַל הַצַּד שֶׁאָמַרְנוּ** – This is **because the essence** of this mitzvah **consists only of what we have said** earlier, **שֶׁלֹּא יַנְהִיג לְפָנָיו תָּמִיד סוּסִים בְּטֵלִים לְמַעְלָה וּלְכָבוֹד – that he not constantly have idle horses parade before him for prestige and honor. אֲבָל יִהְיֶה לוֹ בְּהֵמָה אַחַת לְבַד לְמֶרְכַּבְתּוֹ – Rather, he may have one animal alone for his chariot.**[3]

NOTES

1. The fact that even one idle horse is prohibited is derived from the phrase in the verse, לְמַעַן הַרְבּוֹת סוּס, *in order to increase horses,* where the word סוּס, literally, *horse,* is written in the singular (*Sanhedrin* 21b).

2. The verse prohibits only horses that are לוֹ, *for himself,* i.e., horses that have no purpose other than for his own glory. Those that have a military or practical use are permitted (*Sanhedrin* 21b). In fact, *Rambam* (*Commentary to the Mishnah, Sanhedrin* 2:4) writes that if the purpose of the multitude of horses is to frighten his enemies by virtue of military might (which, in earlier times, was largely dependent on the size of one's cavalry), it is permitted. Cf. *Ramban, Deuteronomy* 17:16.

3. Chinuch here is citing *Rambam* in *Sefer HaMitzvos*

וּכְבָר אָמַר הַכָּתוּב בְּטַעַם מִצְוָה זוֹ שֶׁהִיא לְבַל יָשִׁיב אֶת הָעָם מִצְרַיְמָה לְמַעַן הַרְבּוֹת סוּס וְגוֹ׳, כְּלוֹמַר שֶׁלֹּא יִשְׁלַח לְמִצְרַיִם מֵעַמּוֹ שֶׁיִּקְבְּעוּ דִּירָתָם בְּמִצְרַיִם לְגַדֵּל לוֹ שָׁם סוּסִים[4], שֶׁאֵין הָאִסּוּר רַק בִּקְבִיעוּת דִּירָה שָׁם, וּכְמוֹ שֶׁדָּרְשׁוּ זִכְרוֹנָם לִבְרָכָה (ירושלמי פ״י דסנהדרין ה״ח) לִישִׁיבָה אִי אַתָּה חוֹזֵר אֲבָל אַתָּה חוֹזֵר לִפְרַקְמַטְיָא. וְגַם שֶׁלֹּא יָרוּם לְבָבוֹ בְּהַרְבּוֹת לוֹ סוּסִים וְכֶסֶף וְזָהָב[5], כִּי הַסּוּסִים לְרֹב יָפְיָם וְקַלּוּתָם יִתְגָּאוּ בָּהֶם אֲדוֹנֵיהֶם.

דִּינֵי הַמִּצְוָה בְּפֶרֶק שֵׁנִי מִסַּנְהֶדְרִין[6].

וְנוֹהֵג אִסּוּר זֶה בִּזְמַן שֶׁאֶרֶץ יִשְׂרָאֵל בְּיִשּׁוּבָהּ שֶׁיִּהְיֶה לָנוּ מֶלֶךְ[7].

Underlying Purpose of the Mitzvah

וּכְבָר אָמַר הַכָּתוּב בְּטַעַם מִצְוָה זוֹ – **Scripture** itself **already states the purpose of this mitzvah,** שֶׁהִיא לְבַל "יָשִׁיב אֶת הָעָם מִצְרַיְמָה לְמַעַן הַרְבּוֹת סוּס וְגוֹ׳" – **which is,** ***so that he will not return the people to Egypt in order to increase horses,* etc.** כְּלוֹמַר שֶׁלֹּא יִשְׁלַח לְמִצְרַיִם מֵעַמּוֹ – **That is to say,** the purpose of the mitzvah is **so that he not send** members **of his nation to Egypt,** שֶׁיִּקְבְּעוּ דִּירָתָם בְּמִצְרַיִם לְגַדֵּל לוֹ שָׁם סוּסִים – **to take up residence in Egypt in order to raise horses for him there.**[4] שֶׁאֵין הָאִסּוּר רַק בִּקְבִיעוּת דִּירָה שָׁם – The concern is that they will remain there to live, **for the prohibition** against returning to Egypt (Mitzvah 500) **applies only if one establishes** his **residence there.** וּכְמוֹ שֶׁדָּרְשׁוּ זִכְרוֹנָם לִבְרָכָה – This is **as [our Sages], of blessed memory, expounded** (*Yerushalmi Sanhedrin* 10:8): לִישִׁיבָה אִי אַתָּה חוֹזֵר – **For** the purpose of **residence you may not return** to Egypt, אֲבָל אַתָּה חוֹזֵר לִפְרַקְמַטְיָא – **but you may return** there **to do business.**

Chinuch offers another possible reason for the prohibition upon a king to own idle horses:

וְגַם שֶׁלֹּא יָרוּם לְבָבוֹ בְּהַרְבּוֹת לוֹ סוּסִים וְכֶסֶף וְזָהָב – **An additional** purpose of this mitzvah **is so that his heart not become haughty due to his amassing of horses, silver, and gold;**[5] כִּי הַסּוּסִים לְרֹב יָפְיָם וְקַלּוּתָם – **for horses, due to their great beauty and agility,** יִתְגָּאוּ בָּהֶם אֲדוֹנֵיהֶם – cause **their owners to become prideful in** owning **them.**

Laws and Applicability of the Mitzvah

דִּינֵי הַמִּצְוָה בְּפֶרֶק שֵׁנִי מִסַּנְהֶדְרִין – **The laws of the mitzvah are** found **in the second chapter of** Tractate ***Sanhedrin.***[6]

וְנוֹהֵג אִסּוּר זֶה בִּזְמַן שֶׁאֶרֶץ יִשְׂרָאֵל בְּיִשּׁוּבָהּ – **This prohibition applies when Eretz Yisrael is settled,** i.e., when the Jewish people are living on their Land, שֶׁיִּהְיֶה לָנוּ מֶלֶךְ – as that is **when we can have a king.**[7]

NOTES

(*Lo Saaseh* 363), who writes that the king may have only one horse for his own riding purposes. It is difficult to understand, however, why the king's chariot cannot have multiple horses to increase its efficiency and speed. In fact, the Gemara (*Sanhedrin* 21b) seems to indicate that he may maintain any number of horses for his chariots, and he violates the prohibition only if he keeps one or more horses idle to be paraded before him for his honor. This is also the plain meaning of *Rambam's* words in *Hil. Melachim* 3:3 (*Yad HaLevi, Sefer HaMitzvos* loc. cit. §3; see also *Lechem Yehudah,* cited in *Sefer HaLikkutim,* Frankel ed. of *Rambam* ad loc.).

4. In ancient times, Egypt was a major exporter of horses. The Torah forbids Jewish monarchs from having unnecessary horses so that they should not come to rely on the Egyptian horses. Were the monarchs to rely on those horses, they might come to send their subjects to live there so as to secure that source of trade (*Rashi* to *Sanhedrin* 21b ד״ה הסוסים and to *Deuteronomy* 17:16 with *Mizrachi*). Residing in Egypt is prohibited under the next mitzvah; see further in Chinuch.

Scripture relates that King Solomon owned tens of thousands of horses in violation of the current prohibition (*I Kings* 5:6 with *Radak* ad loc.; see *Sanhedrin* 21b, which states that the number was even greater). The Talmud (ibid.) states that Solomon believed that he could amass horses without having to send Jews to live in Egypt. However, the Gemara explains, he was mistaken, for as Scripture indicates, he came to heavily rely upon the Egyptian imports (see *I Kings* 10:28-29).

5. The amassing of silver and gold by a king is a violation of Mitzvah 502. See there.

6. These laws are codified in *Rambam, Hil. Melachim* 3:3.

7. As Chinuch wrote in Mitzvah 497, the mitzvah-

וְזֹאת מִן הַמִּצְווֹת שֶׁהֵן עַל הַמֶּלֶךְ לְבַד. וּמֶלֶךְ הָעוֹבֵר עַל זֶה וְהוֹסִיף אֲפִלּוּ סוּס אֶחָד פָּנוּי לִהְיוֹת רָץ לְפָנָיו כְּדֶרֶךְ שֶׁשְּׁאָר מַלְכֵי אֻמּוֹת הָעוֹלָם עוֹשִׂים חַיָּב מַלְקוּת[8].

וְזֹאת מִן הַמִּצְווֹת שֶׁהֵן עַל הַמֶּלֶךְ לְבַד – This is one of the mitzvos that apply to the king alone, not to any other individual. **וּמֶלֶךְ הָעוֹבֵר עַל זֶה – A king who transgresses this** mitzvah, **וְהוֹסִיף אֲפִלּוּ סוּס אֶחָד פָּנוּי לִהְיוֹת רָץ לְפָנָיו – and adds even one idle horse** to his stables **to run before him, כְּדֶרֶךְ שֶׁשְּׁאָר מַלְכֵי אֻמּוֹת הָעוֹלָם עוֹשִׂים – as kings of the other nations do, חַיָּב מַלְקוּת – is liable to *malkus*.**[8]

NOTES

obligation to appoint a king applies only when we are settled in Eretz Yisrael.

8. As mentioned earlier (note 1), the Gemara (*Sanhedrin* 21b) explains that since the verse uses the singular term סוּס, *horse,* the prohibition is transgressed even with a single horse. Furthermore, since the plural term סוּסִים, *horses,* appears earlier in the verse, the prohibition is transgressed for each and every horse. Thus, if he were to add multiple horses, he would receive multiple sets of *malkus* (*Minchas Chinuch* §1; see *Kesef Mishneh, Hil. Melachim* 3:3 and other commentaries to *Rambam* there).

מִצְוָה תק: שֶׁלֹּא לִשְׁכֹּן בְּאֶרֶץ מִצְרַיִם לְעוֹלָם

שֶׁלֹּא נוֹסִיף לָשׁוּב בְּדֶרֶךְ מִצְרַיִם לְעוֹלָם, כְּלוֹמַר שֶׁלֹּא נֵלֵךְ לִקְבֹּעַ דִּירָתֵנוּ בְּמִצְרַיִם, וְעַל זֶה נֶאֱמַר (דברים י״ז, ט״ז) **וַה׳ אָמַר לָכֶם לֹא תֹסִפוּן לָשׁוּב בַּדֶּרֶךְ הַזֶּה עוֹד**[1]**. וְנִכְפְּלָה הַמְּנִיעָה בָּזֶה שָׁלֹשׁ פְּעָמִים, אָמְרוּ זִכְרוֹנָם לִבְרָכָה** (מכילתא בשלח י״ד י״ג) **בִּשְׁלֹשָׁה מְקוֹמוֹת הִזְהִירָה תּוֹרָה שֶׁלֹּא לָשׁוּב בְּאֶרֶץ מִצְרַיִם, בִּשְׁלָשְׁתָּן חָזְרוּ וּבִשְׁלָשְׁתָּן נֶעֶנְשׁוּ**[2]**. וּשְׁלֹשָׁה מְקוֹמוֹת אֵלּוּ אֶחָד מֵהֶם הוּא זֶה שֶׁזָּכַרְנוּ, וְהַשֵּׁנִי הוּא** (דברים כ״ח, ס״ח) **בַּדֶּרֶךְ אֲשֶׁר אָמַרְתִּי לְךָ לֹא תֹסִיף עוֹד וגו׳, וְהַשְּׁלִישִׁי** (שמות י״ד, י״ג) **כִּי אֲשֶׁר רְאִיתֶם אֶת מִצְרַיִם הַיּוֹם לֹא תֹסִפוּ וגו׳, וְאַף עַל פִּי שֶׁמַּשְׁמַן הַנִּגְלֶה שֶׁבּוֹ נִרְאֶה שֶׁיִּהְיֶה סִפּוּר, בָּאָה הַקַּבָּלָה עָלָיו שֶׁהוּא מְנִיעָה**[3]**.**

Mitzvah 500

The Prohibition to Ever Settle in Egypt

... וְלֹא יָשִׁיב אֶת הָעָם מִצְרַיְמָה לְמַעַן הַרְבּוֹת סוּס וַה׳ אָמַר לָכֶם לֹא תֹסִפוּן לָשׁוּב בַּדֶּרֶךְ הַזֶּה עוֹד

... so that he will not return the people to Egypt in order to increase horses, for HASHEM has said to you, "You shall no longer return on this road again" (*Deuteronomy* 17:16).

שֶׁלֹּא נוֹסִיף לָשׁוּב בְּדֶרֶךְ מִצְרַיִם לְעוֹלָם – We are commanded **to never again return on the road** back **to Egypt;** **כְּלוֹמַר שֶׁלֹּא נֵלֵךְ לִקְבֹּעַ דִּירָתֵנוּ בְּמִצְרַיִם** – **that is to say, that we are not to go and establish our residence in Egypt.** **וְעַל זֶה נֶאֱמַר** – **Regarding this it is stated** (*Deuteronomy* 17:16): **"וַה׳ אָמַר לָכֶם לֹא תֹסִפוּן לָשׁוּב בַּדֶּרֶךְ הַזֶּה עוֹד"** – ***for HASHEM has said to you, "You shall no longer return on this road again."***[1]

Chinuch notes that the mitzvah appears in other places in the Torah as well:

וְנִכְפְּלָה הַמְּנִיעָה בָּזֶה שָׁלֹשׁ פְּעָמִים – **This prohibition is repeated three times** in the Torah, as detailed below. **אָמְרוּ זִכְרוֹנָם לִבְרָכָה** – **[Our Sages], of blessed memory, have stated** (*Mechilta* to *Exodus* 14:13; *Yerushalmi Succah* 5:1): **בִּשְׁלֹשָׁה מְקוֹמוֹת הִזְהִירָה תּוֹרָה שֶׁלֹּא לָשׁוּב בְּאֶרֶץ מִצְרַיִם** – **In three places the Torah warns not to return to the land of Egypt;** **בִּשְׁלָשְׁתָּן חָזְרוּ וּבִשְׁלָשְׁתָּן נֶעֶנְשׁוּ** – on three occasions, **in** violation of **all three** of those prohibitions, **[Jews] returned** to Egypt, **and for all three they were punished.**[2]

וּשְׁלֹשָׁה מְקוֹמוֹת אֵלּוּ – **These three places** in which the Torah states this prohibition are as follows: **אֶחָד מֵהֶם הוּא זֶה שֶׁזָּכַרְנוּ** – **One of them is this** verse **that we** just **mentioned** (*Deuteronomy* 17:16). **וְהַשֵּׁנִי הוּא, "בַּדֶּרֶךְ אֲשֶׁר אָמַרְתִּי לְךָ לֹא תֹסִיף עוֹד וגו׳ "** – **The second is** where Hashem warns the Jewish people in the Tochachah (Admonition) that if they are sinful they will be returned to Egypt, ***on the road of which I said to you, "You shall never again** see it"* (ibid. 28:68). **וְהַשְּׁלִישִׁי, "כִּי אֲשֶׁר רְאִיתֶם אֶת מִצְרַיִם הַיּוֹם לֹא תֹסִפוּ וגו׳ "** – **And the third** is where the Jewish people were told before the Splitting of the Sea: ***For as you have seen Egypt today, you shall not** see them ever **again*** (*Exodus* 14:13). **וְאַף עַל פִּי שֶׁמַּשְׁמַן הַנִּגְלֶה שֶׁבּוֹ נִרְאֶה שֶׁיִּהְיֶה סִפּוּר** – **Now, although the plain meaning of [the verse] indicates that it is** simply **a narrative,** **בָּאָה הַקַּבָּלָה עָלָיו שֶׁהוּא מְנִיעָה** – the explanation that we have **received through the Oral Tradition** is **that it is** in fact conveying **a prohibition.**[3]

NOTES

1. "Return" in this context means to go back to Egypt so as to take up permanent residence (see below, after note 10). It is permitted, however, to travel to Egypt temporarily for business or other purposes; see Mitzvah 499, after note 4 (see *Yerushalmi Sanhedrin* 10:8; *Rambam, Hil. Melachim* 5:8).

2. As will be explained below (note 3), the three Scriptural verses prohibit returning to Egypt based on three different motivations. Jews ultimately returned there on account of each of those motivations, and thus violated each of the three prohibitions.

3. Chinuch would appear to be referring to the final

מִשָּׁרְשֵׁי הַמִּצְוָה לְפִי שֶׁאַנְשֵׁי מִצְרַיִם רָעִים וְחַטָּאִים וְהָאֵל בָּרוּךְ הוּא הוֹצִיאָנוּ מִשָּׁם וּגְאָלָנוּ בַּחֲסָדָיו מִיָּדָם לְזַכּוֹתֵנוּ לָלֶכֶת בְּדַרְכֵי הָאֱמֶת, וְרָצָה בְּטוּבוֹ הַגָּדוֹל עָלֵינוּ לְבִלְתִּי נָשׁוּב עוֹד לְהִטָּמַע בְּתוֹכָם כְּדֵי שֶׁלֹּא נִלְמֹד כְּפִרוּתֵיהֶם וְלֹא נֵלֵךְ בְּדַרְכֵיהֶם הַמְּגֻנִּים אֵצֶל תּוֹרָתֵנוּ הַשְּׁלֵמָה[4].

מִדִּינֵי הַמִּצְוָה מַה שֶּׁאָמְרוּ זִכְרוֹנָם לִבְרָכָה (סוכה נ״א ע״ב) שֶׁלֹּא הָעִיר מִצְרַיִם[5] לְבַדָּהּ הִיא בִּכְלַל הָאִסּוּר אֶלָּא אַף בְּכָל אַסְכַּנְדְּרִיָא אָסוּר לִשְׁכֹּן[6], וּמִיָּם אַסְכַּנְדְּרִיָא[7]

Underlying Purposes of the Mitzvah

מִשָּׁרְשֵׁי הַמִּצְוָה – Among the underlying purposes of the mitzvah is לְפִי שֶׁאַנְשֵׁי מִצְרַיִם רָעִים וְחַטָּאִים – that it is forbidden to return to Egypt **because the people of Egypt are wicked and sinful.** וְהָאֵל בָּרוּךְ הוּא הוֹצִיאָנוּ מִשָּׁם – **The Almighty, blessed is He, took us out from there,** וּגְאָלָנוּ בַּחֲסָדָיו מִיָּדָם – **and redeemed us from their control in His kindness,** לְזַכּוֹתֵנוּ לָלֶכֶת בְּדַרְכֵי הָאֱמֶת – **so as to enable us to merit going in the ways of truth.** וְרָצָה בְּטוּבוֹ הַגָּדוֹל עָלֵינוּ – **He desired, due to His great goodness toward us,** לְבִלְתִּי נָשׁוּב עוֹד לְהִטָּמַע בְּתוֹכָם – **that we not return again to become intermingled among them,** כְּדֵי שֶׁלֹּא נִלְמֹד כְּפִרוּתֵיהֶם – **so that we not learn their heretic views,** וְלֹא נֵלֵךְ בְּדַרְכֵיהֶם הַמְּגֻנִּים אֵצֶל תּוֹרָתֵנוּ הַשְּׁלֵמָה – **nor follow in their ways, which are held despicable by our perfect Torah.**[4]

Laws of the Mitzvah

מִדִּינֵי הַמִּצְוָה – Among the laws of the mitzvah is מַה שֶּׁאָמְרוּ זִכְרוֹנָם לִבְרָכָה – **that which [the Sages], of blessed memory, have stated** (*Succah* 51b), שֶׁלֹּא הָעִיר מִצְרַיִם לְבַדָּהּ הִיא בִּכְלַל הָאִסּוּר – **that not only is the city of Mitzrayim**[5] **included in the prohibition,** אֶלָּא אַף בְּכָל אַסְכַּנְדְּרִיָא אָסוּר לִשְׁכֹּן – **but,** in fact, **it is forbidden to settle in all of Alexandria as well.**[6] וּמִיָּם אַסְכַּנְדְּרִיָא

NOTES

verse cited, which, on the surface, seems merely like an assurance of Hashem that we would no longer go back to Egypt. However, the Oral Tradition teaches that the verse is to be understood as a prohibition. [Actually, the Torah does not state an *explicit* prohibition (i.e., "you shall not return to Egypt") in any of the three verses cited; nevertheless, all are to be understood as prohibitions. See further, *Ramban, Exodus* 14:13; *Maharsha, Succah* 51b.]

The Midrash and *Yerushalmi* that Chinuch cites list the three times that Jews returned to Egypt, and their disastrous results: The first was in the time of Sennacherib, king of Assyria, where the prophet laments the fate of the Ten Israelite Tribes who turned to Egypt for help against Sennacherib's upcoming invasion. The prophet states (*Isaiah* 31:1-3): *Woe to those who go down to Egypt for help, who rely on horses ... they will all perish*. [In this instance, the Jews violated the verse of this mitzvah, which prohibits returning to Egypt *in order to increase horses* (*Yefeh Mareh* to *Yerushalmi* loc. cit.).]

The second time that Jews returned to Egypt was after the assassination of Gedaliah ben Ahikam, whom the king of Babylonia had appointed governor of Eretz Yisrael. Many feared the wrath of the Babylonians and chose to flee to Egypt, ignoring the prophet's warning (*Jeremiah* 42:15-16): *if you turn your face to go to Egypt and you will come to dwell there, the very sword of which you are afraid will reach you there*. [In this instance, they violated the verse stated at the Splitting of the Sea, which warned the Jews not to turn back to Egypt out of fear (*Yefeh Mareh* ibid.).]

The third incident involved the tragic destruction of the Jewish community of Alexandria, Egypt, by the Roman Emperor, Trajan. [Historical sources record that this occurred in the years 114-117 C.E.] The Gemara (*Succah* 51b; *Yerushalmi* ibid.) attributes this tragedy to their having settled in Egypt in violation of the current mitzvah. [The Jews of Alexandria were fabulously wealthy (ibid.). Since they settled there to lead a life of luxury, they violated the verse in the Tochachah. That passage states that if the Jews fail to serve Hashem in affluence (see there, v. 47), they will be returned to Egypt in poverty (v. 68) – which indicates that it is prohibited to settle in Egypt for the purpose of gaining affluence (*Yefeh Mareh* ibid.).]

4. Egyptian society was most depraved, as is clear from the verse (*Leviticus* 18:3): כְּמַעֲשֵׂה אֶרֶץ מִצְרַיִם אֲשֶׁר יְשַׁבְתֶּם בָּהּ לֹא תַעֲשׂוּ, *Do not perform the practice of the land of Egypt in which you dwelled* (*Rambam, Hil. Melachim* 5:8; *Ramban, Deuteronomy* 17:16).

5. I.e., Memphis (situated on the Nile, south of present-day Cairo), which was the capital of ancient Egypt.

6. Chinuch seems to refer to the entire area that we call Egypt as "Alexandria." [This is what it is called in some

בְּאֹרֶךְ אַרְבַּע מֵאוֹת פַּרְסָה וּבְרֹחַב אַרְבַּע מֵאוֹת פַּרְסָה בְּאִסּוּר זֶה[8]. וְיֶתֶר פְּרָטֶיהָ מְבֹאָרִים[9].
וְנוֹהֵג אִסּוּר זֶה בְּכָל זְמַן בִּזְכָרִים וּנְקֵבוֹת[10].
וְעוֹבֵר עַל זֶה וְקָבַע דִּירָתוֹ שָׁם עָבַר עַל לָאו זֶה, אֲבָל אֵין לוֹקִין עַל לָאו זֶה לְפִי שֶׁבִּשְׁעַת הַכְּנִיסָה מֻתָּר הוּא, וּבְהִשְׁתַּקְּעוֹ שָׁם אֵין בּוֹ מַעֲשֶׂה[11]. וְכָתַב הָרַמְבַּ"ם ז"ל שֶׁיֵּרָאֶה לוֹ

בְּאֹרֶךְ אַרְבַּע מֵאוֹת פַּרְסָה וּבְרֹחַב אַרְבַּע מֵאוֹת פַּרְסָה בְּאִסּוּר זֶה – Proceeding inland **from the Sea of Alexandria,**[7] an area **the length of four hundred *parsaos* by a width of four hundred *parsaos* is included in this prohibition.**[8]
וְיֶתֶר פְּרָטֶיהָ מְבֹאָרִים – **The remaining details of [this mitzvah] are clear.**[9]

Applicability of the Mitzvah

וְנוֹהֵג אִסּוּר זֶה בְּכָל זְמַן בִּזְכָרִים וּנְקֵבוֹת – **This prohibition applies in all times, to** both **men and women.**[10]
וְעוֹבֵר עַל זֶה וְקָבַע דִּירָתוֹ שָׁם – **One who transgresses this and establishes his residence there,** in Egypt, **עָבַר עַל לָאו זֶה** – **has violated this prohibition. אֲבָל אֵין לוֹקִין עַל לָאו זֶה** – **However, one does not incur *malkus* for this prohibition, לְפִי שֶׁבִּשְׁעַת הַכְּנִיסָה מֻתָּר הוּא** – **since at the time of his entry** into Egypt **[the act] is permitted,** as one violates the prohibition only when he settles there, **וּבְהִשְׁתַּקְּעוֹ שָׁם אֵין בּוֹ מַעֲשֶׂה** – **and when [the person]** actually **settles there, [his violation] involves no action.**[11]

Chinuch now introduces a ruling of *Rambam* with regard to this prohibition:
וְכָתַב הָרַמְבַּ"ם ז"ל שֶׁיֵּרָאֶה לוֹ – ***Rambam,* of blessed memory, writes** (*Hil. Melachim* 5:8) **that it**

NOTES

editions of *Sefer HaMitzvos, Lo Saaseh* 46 (cf. Frankel and Kafich editions; see *Teshuvos Tzitz Eliezer* Vol. 14, 87:1 ד"ה ויש).]

7. I.e., the Mediterranean Sea (see *Rambam* ibid. 5:7). [The city of Alexandria is located on the Mediterranean, at the western tip of the Nile delta in Northern Egypt.]

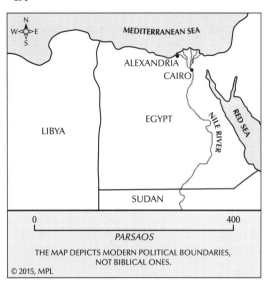

N
E
S
0
400
PARSAOS
THE MAP DEPICTS MODERN POLITICAL BOUNDARIES, NOT BIBLICAL ONES.
© 2015, MPL

8. [A *parsah* (pl. *parsaos*) is a linear measure equal to four *mil,* totaling approximately 2.3-2.9 miles.] This area of 400 by 400 *parsaos* is bordered on the north by the Mediterranean Sea, and extends southward toward Ethiopia, and westward toward the desert (*Rambam* ibid.). For further discussion, see *Even Sapir* [Y. Sapir], *Chikur Din,* Chs. 13-14.

9. These laws are codified in *Rambam, Hil. Melachim* 5:7-8.

10. I.e., it applies whether the *Beis HaMikdash* is standing or not. And it applies to women as well as men in accordance with the general rule pertaining to mitzvah-prohibitions. [See Insight for further discussion of when the prohibition applies.]

11. This is the position of *Rambam* (*Hil. Melachim* 5:8), who maintains that the act of traveling and entering into the land of Egypt is itself not forbidden, since one may go there temporarily for business or other purposes. It is only once one remains there with the intention of settling down that he has violated the prohibition. That violation, though, is passive, and as a rule one does not receive *malkus* for violating a prohibition unless his violation involves action. [*Rambam* and Chinuch imply that one would not be liable to *malkus* even if he were to enter Egypt initially with the intent of settling there (see also *Zohar HaRakia, Lo Saaseh* 186 §70). *Minchas Chinuch* (§3) wonders why in such a case the act of entry is not considered an action that would subject one to *malkus.* For a possible resolution, see end of Mitzvah 94 with note 15 there.]

שֶׁאִם כָּבַשׁ מֶלֶךְ יִשְׂרָאֵל עַל פִּי בֵּית דִּין[12] אֶרֶץ מִצְרַיִם שֶׁמֻּתָּר יִהְיֶה לָנוּ לִשְׁכֹּן בָּהּ. וְדִבְרֵי פִּי חָכָם חֵן[13].

---

seems to him שֶׁאִם כָּבַשׁ מֶלֶךְ יִשְׂרָאֵל עַל פִּי בֵּית דִּין אֶרֶץ מִצְרַיִם — **that if a Jewish king, with the sanction of** *beis din* **(i.e., the Great Sanhedrin),**[12] **conquered the land of Egypt,** שֶׁמֻּתָּר יִהְיֶה לָנוּ לִשְׁכֹּן בָּהּ — **it would** then **be permitted for us to dwell there.** וְדִבְרֵי פִּי חָכָם חֵן — *The words of a wise man win favor.*[13]

NOTES

12. A decision to wage an offensive war against a foreign adversary must be made by the king together with the Great Sanhedrin. See Introduction to Mitzvah 527.

13. Chinuch praises *Rambam's* ruling with a citation of *Ecclesiastes* 10:12.

Rambam there explains that the Torah forbade living in Egypt due to the negative influences of the non-Jewish inhabitants of the land, and this reason does not apply if it is under Jewish control.

⯊§ Insight: The Jewish Communities of Egypt

As Chinuch writes, our Sages point to three instances when Jews in large numbers went to settle in Egypt in violation of the current mitzvah, always with tragic consequences. Commentators note, however, that throughout our history, illustrious Jewish communities, led by great scholars and sages, were established in Egypt and flourished there. What was the basis for their actions, and why were they successful? Various arguments have been advanced to explain this matter.

Some authorities suggest that the Egyptians of antiquity were conquered and displaced over 2,500 years ago by the Assyrian king, Sennacherib (see *Tosefta, Kiddushin* 5:6). These authorities argue that the people who have lived in Egypt since that time are not the ones among whom the Torah forbids us to dwell (see *Mayim Chaim* [*Pri Chadash*] to *Hil. Melachim* 5:8; see also *Ritva, Yoma* 38a).

Others, however, reject this approach, arguing that the Torah focuses its prohibition on the *land*, not the people (*Sefer Yerei'im* §309). Furthermore, even if the prohibition depends on the people, the question of whether the ancient Egyptians were permanently dislocated from their land by Sennacherib is the subject of Tannaic debate (see *Tosefta* ibid. and *Yadayim* 2:8). These authorities argue that the halachah follows the opinion that the ancient Egyptians returned shortly after their exile (cf. *Rambam, Hil. Issurei Biah* 12:25). As proof that the prohibition remains in force, they cite the Gemara's statement (*Succah* 51b) that the spiritual flaw that led to the destruction of the Egyptian Jewish community of Alexandria was that community's violation of the current mitzvah-prohibition (see above, note 3). That community, though, was founded during the Second Temple period, many centuries *after* Sennacherib's conquest of ancient Egypt. It is thus clear that the prohibition remains in place — either because the original Egyptians returned to their land, or because it is prohibited to settle in that *land* regardless of whether its current inhabitants are those who lived there originally (*Sefer Yerei'im* ibid.; *Smag, Lo Saaseh* 227).

A different approach in defense of the Jewish communities of Egypt is that the Torah limits the prohibition by stating, לֹא תֹסִפוּן לָשׁוּב בַּדֶּרֶךְ הַזֶּה, *You shall no longer return on this road.* The words "on this road" imply that it is prohibited only to return to Egypt *from Eretz Yisrael* (see *Sefer Yerei'im* and *Smag* ibid.; *Rabbeinu Bachya* to the verse; cf. *Radvaz, Hil. Melachim* 5:7). Others go even further, and contend that it is prohibited only to follow, in reverse, the very same route through the Wilderness that the Jewish people took during their exodus from Egypt (see *Divrei Shaul* [Natanzon], beginning of *Parashas Masei*; see also *Ritva* ibid.; *Kaftor VaFerach* Ch. 5, with *Pirchei Tziyon* [R' Y. F. Perla] §110; cf. *Dei Hashev, Yoreh Deah* §15 ד"ה איברא דהרא"ה; *To'afos Re'eim* to *Sefer Yerei'im* ibid.).

Another defense offered for the Jewish communities of Egypt is that the prohibition to return to Egypt applies only when the Jewish people are settled in Eretz Yisrael. During the time of our dispersion and exile, though, the prohibition is not in force, and it is permitted to settle in Egypt, even if one's point of departure was Eretz Yisrael. Accordingly, the Jewish communities of Egypt that were founded after the destruction of the second *Beis HaMikdash* were not in violation of this

prohibition, for as long as the Jews are in a state of exile, all lands take on the same status (*Ritva* ibid.; *Knesses HaGedolah* to *Hil. Melachim* Ch. 5 [printed at the end of *Orach Chaim*]).

However, the approaches that we have cited do not resolve this issue according to *Rambam*. *Rambam* specifically writes (*Sefer HaMitzvos, Lo Saaseh* 46) that this prohibition applies לְעוֹלָם, *forever*, and he makes no exceptions based on the route taken, nor on whether or not Eretz Yisrael is in a settled state at the time — yet it is well known that *Rambam* himself spent many years living in Egypt! (*Bris Moshe* to *Smag, Lo Saaseh* 227; see also *Yad HaLevi* to *Sefer HaMitzvos* ibid.). [According to one account, *Rambam* would sign his personal letters with the postscript, "he who violates three prohibitions each day" (*Kaftor VaFerach* Ch. 5, citing a descendant of *Rambam*). However, many authorities have serious reservations as to the validity of this account (see *Hagahos Yaavetz* ad loc.; *Even Sapir* I, fol. 31a; *Yishrei Lev*, cited in *Sdei Chemed, Maareches Yud, Klal* 46 ד"ה וראיתי; see, however, *Sdei Chemed* there).]

To resolve *Rambam's* position, some explain as follows: Chinuch (in Mitzvah 499) cited the law that one is permitted to travel to Egypt for business purposes or the like, as long as he does not go with the intention of settling there (see also *Rambam, Hil. Melachim* 5:8). Accordingly, it is reasonable to assume that the original settlers had no intention of creating a permanent settlement in Egypt. Some had arrived there for business purposes, while others came to escape persecution. While it is questionable whether these individuals had the right to remain there, those who came in later times for the purpose of teaching Torah and strengthening the spirituality of these communities had a valid basis for doing so (see *Maharam Schik*, Mitzvah 503). *Rambam*, too, came to Egypt fleeing the sword of persecution, but ended up staying, insofar as he was needed to provide for the spiritual needs of the Jewish community. Moreover, once he was appointed the personal physician of the Sultan, *Rambam* was left with no choice but to stay (see *Radvaz* ibid., and *Aruch HaShulchan HeAsid, Hil. Melachim* 74:15; see also *Zohar HaRakia, Lo Saaseh* 186 §70).

מִצְוָה תקא: שֶׁלֹּא יַרְבֶּה לוֹ הַמֶּלֶךְ נָשִׁים

שֶׁלֹּא יַרְבֶּה לוֹ הַמֶּלֶךְ נָשִׁים הַרְבֵּה, וְעַל זֶה נֶאֱמַר (דברים י״ז, י״ז) וְלֹא יַרְבֶּה לוֹ נָשִׁים[1].

וְטַעַם הַמִּצְוָה מְבֹאָר בַּכָּתוּב, כִּי הַנָּשִׁים מְסִירוֹת לֵב בַּעְלֵיהֶן, כְּלוֹמַר שֶׁמְּפַתּוֹת אוֹתָם לַעֲשׂוֹת מַה שֶּׁאֵינוֹ רָאוּי, בְּהִתְמַדְתָּן עֲלֵיהֶם תַּחֲרוּת וְרִבּוּי דְּבָרִים וַחֲלַקְלַקּוֹת[2].

מִדִּינֵי הַמִּצְוָה מַה שֶּׁאָמְרוּ זִכְרוֹנָם לִבְרָכָה (סנהדרין כ״א ע״א) שֶׁעַד שְׁמוֹנֶה עֶשְׂרֵה נָשִׁים

Mitzvah 501

The Prohibition Upon a King to Have an Excessive Number of Wives

וְלֹא יַרְבֶּה לוֹ נָשִׁים וְלֹא יָסוּר לְבָבוֹ

And he shall not have too many wives, so that his heart not turn astray (*Deuteronomy* 17:17).

שֶׁלֹּא יַרְבֶּה לוֹ הַמֶּלֶךְ נָשִׁים הַרְבֵּה – The Torah commands **that the king not have an excessive number of wives.** וְעַל זֶה נֶאֱמַר "וְלֹא יַרְבֶּה לוֹ נָשִׁים" – **Regarding this it is stated** (*Deuteronomy* 17:17): ***And he shall not have too many wives.***[1]

Underlying Purpose of the Mitzvah

וְטַעַם הַמִּצְוָה מְבֹאָר בַּכָּתוּב – **The reason for the mitzvah is set forth in Scripture** itself, which states, *so that his heart not turn astray.* כִּי הַנָּשִׁים מְסִירוֹת לֵב בַּעְלֵיהֶן – **For wives** sometimes **turn the hearts of their husbands astray,** כְּלוֹמַר שֶׁמְּפַתּוֹת אוֹתָם לַעֲשׂוֹת מַה שֶּׁאֵינוֹ רָאוּי – **that is to say, they** sometimes **induce them to do improper things,** בְּהִתְמַדְתָּן עֲלֵיהֶם תַּחֲרוּת – **by involving them in rivalry,** וְרִבּוּי דְּבָרִים וַחֲלַקְלַקּוֹת – **and** with **overabundance of speech and equivocalness.** Having an excessive number of wives increases the risk of this occurring, and the Torah seeks to protect the king, "whose heart is the heart of the nation" (*Rambam, Hil. Melachim* 3:6), from having his heart led astray.[2]

Laws of the Mitzvah

מִדִּינֵי הַמִּצְוָה מַה שֶּׁאָמְרוּ זִכְרוֹנָם לִבְרָכָה – **Among the laws of the mitzvah** is **that which [our Sages], of blessed memory, stated** (*Sanhedrin* 21a), שֶׁעַד שְׁמוֹנֶה עֶשְׂרֵה נָשִׁים הוּא מֻתָּר

NOTES

1. Chinuch will define below what is considered an "excessive" number of wives.

2. Chinuch here describes a woman who is far from virtuous, who will stop at nothing in order to fulfill her materialistic desires. Obviously, this is not meant as a description of all women. However, kings who set their sights on having many wives accessible to them would often not pay proper attention to the moral and ethical standards of their wives, making it likely that a king would eventually marry someone fitting the description that Chinuch portrays. [While this is the underlying reason for the prohibition, the prohibition applies universally, even to a king who is on the highest spiritual level, and even if his wives are extremely righteous (see *Sanhedrin* 21a and Chinuch further).]

Others take a different approach in explaining the underlying purpose of this mitzvah. They suggest that the Torah's concern that the heart of the king would be "turned astray" is not necessarily due to the shortcomings of the wives. Rather, when a king has so many wives, he will be excessively involved in his physical drives, and his attention will be diverted from his lofty mission as the leader of all of Israel (*Ibn Ezra* and *R' S. R. Hirsch* to *Deuteronomy* 17:17; see *Rambam, Hil. Melachim* 3:6).

הוּא מֻתָּר לִשָּׂא וְלֹא יוֹתֵר[3], וַאֲפִלּוּ הֵן כַּאֲבִיגַיִל שֶׁהָיְתָה צִדְקָנִית וּזְרִיזָה וְטוֹבָה[4]. וְיֶתֶר פְּרָטֶיהָ בְּפֶרֶק שֵׁנִי מִסַּנְהֶדְרִין[5].

וְזֹאת מִן הַמִּצְווֹת שֶׁהֵן עַל הַמֶּלֶךְ לְבַדּוֹ, וְנוֹהֶגֶת בִּזְמַן שֶׁיֵּשׁ לָנוּ מֶלֶךְ.

וְאִם עָבַר עַל זֶה וְהוֹסִיף לִקַּח אַחַת עַל שְׁמוֹנֶה עֶשְׂרֵה, חַיָּב מַלְקוּת וְיֵשׁ לוֹ לְגָרְשָׁהּ[6].

לִשָּׂא – **that [the king] is permitted to marry up to eighteen wives,** וְלֹא יוֹתֵר – **but no more.**[3] וַאֲפִלּוּ הֵן כַּאֲבִיגַיִל – This is true **even if they are** as virtuous **as Abigail,** שֶׁהָיְתָה צִדְקָנִית וּזְרִיזָה וְטוֹבָה – **who was righteous, diligent, and good.**[4]

וְיֶתֶר פְּרָטֶיהָ בְּפֶרֶק שֵׁנִי מִסַּנְהֶדְרִין – These, **and the additional details of [this mitzvah], are** found **in the second chapter of** Tractate ***Sanhedrin*** (21a-b).[5]

Applicability of the Mitzvah

וְזֹאת מִן הַמִּצְווֹת שֶׁהֵן עַל הַמֶּלֶךְ לְבַדּוֹ – **This is one of the mitzvos that apply to the king alone,** וְנוֹהֶגֶת בִּזְמַן שֶׁיֵּשׁ לָנוּ מֶלֶךְ – **and it** therefore **applies** only **in** those **times when we have a king.** וְאִם עָבַר עַל זֶה – **If [the king] transgresses this** mitzvah, וְהוֹסִיף לִקַּח אַחַת עַל שְׁמוֹנֶה עֶשְׂרֵה – **and takes one additional wife over** the **eighteen** that he is permitted to have, חַיָּב מַלְקוּת וְיֵשׁ לוֹ לְגָרְשָׁהּ – **he is liable to *malkus*, and is** required **to divorce her.**[6]

NOTES

3. When admonishing King David after his failing with Batsheba (see *II Samuel* Ch. 11), the prophet recounts the many blessings Hashem had showered upon David. With regard to his wives, the prophet says in the name of Hashem (ibid. 12:8): וְאִם מְעָט וְאֹסִפָה לְּךָ כָּהֵנָּה וְכָהֵנָּה *and if this were not enough, I would have increased for you this much and this much again.* At that time, King David had six wives (see ibid. 3:2-5). Since Hashem indicated that He would have been willing to increase for David *this much and this much again,* the Sages derive that King David would have been permitted to marry an additional six wives corresponding to the wives he already had (*I would have increased for you this much*), plus another six (*and this much again*), for a total of twelve additional wives. Thus, in total, he was permitted to marry up to eighteen wives. King David serves as the model for all future kings, who are thus restricted to eighteen wives (*Sanhedrin* 21a).

4. Abigail was one of King David's wives (see *I Samuel* 25:40-42). Our Sages describe her as being virtuous and as having attained the spiritual height of prophecy (see *Megillah* 14a-b).

5. The laws are codified in *Rambam, Hil. Melachim* 3:2,6.

6. Chinuch implies that he is liable to *malkus* for the act of marrying this woman alone, even if they have not consummated the marriage (cf. *Rambam, Hil. Melachim* 3:2).

Minchas Chinuch (§2) adds that the woman whom the king marries (after his having already taken eighteen wives) is herself also liable to *malkus* for her participation in this forbidden union; cf. *Zera Avraham* [Luftbir] §22 ד״ה ונראה דהא״ה.

מִצְוָה תקב
שֶׁלֹּא יַרְבֶּה לוֹ הַמֶּלֶךְ כֶּסֶף וְזָהָב לְבַד מַה שֶּׁצָּרִיךְ לוֹ

שֶׁלֹּא יַרְבֶּה הַמֶּלֶךְ מָמוֹן רַב, כְּלוֹמַר שֶׁלֹּא יִהְיֶה תַּחַת יָדוֹ אֶלָּא כְּשִׁעוּר מַה שֶּׁהוּא צָרִיךְ לְמֶרְכַּבְתּוֹ וַעֲבָדָיו הַמְיֻחָדִים לוֹ[1]. וְעַל זֶה נֶאֱמַר (דברים י״ז, י״ז) וְכֶסֶף וְזָהָב לֹא יַרְבֶּה לוֹ.
מִשָּׁרְשֵׁי הַמִּצְוָה מַה שֶּׁמְּבֹאָר בַּכָּתוּב לְבִלְתִּי רוּם לְבָבוֹ וְגוֹ׳[2].
מִדִּינֵי הַמִּצְוָה מַה שֶּׁאָמְרוּ זִכְרוֹנָם לִבְרָכָה (סנהדרין כ״א ע״ב) שֶׁל עַצְמוֹ הוּא דְּאֵינוֹ מַרְבֶּה,

---

Mitzvah 502
The Prohibition Upon a King to Amass Silver and Gold Beyond What He Needs

...וְכֶסֶף וְזָהָב לֹא יַרְבֶּה לּוֹ מְאֹד

... and he shall not amass great amounts of silver and gold for himself (*Deuteronomy* 17:17).

שֶׁלֹּא יַרְבֶּה הַמֶּלֶךְ מָמוֹן רַב – The Torah commands **that the king not amass great amounts of money** for himself. כְּלוֹמַר שֶׁלֹּא יִהְיֶה תַּחַת יָדוֹ – **That is to say, he should not have** money **in his possession** אֶלָּא כְּשִׁעוּר מַה שֶּׁהוּא צָרִיךְ לְמֶרְכַּבְתּוֹ וַעֲבָדָיו הַמְיֻחָדִים לוֹ – **other than the amount that he needs for** expenses such as **his chariots and his personal servants.**[1] וְעַל זֶה נֶאֱמַר ״וְכֶסֶף וְזָהָב לֹא יַרְבֶּה לּוֹ״ – **Regarding this it is stated** (*Deuteronomy* 17:17): ***and he shall not amass great amounts of silver and gold for himself.***

Underlying Purpose of the Mitzvah

מִשָּׁרְשֵׁי הַמִּצְוָה מַה שֶּׁמְּבֹאָר בַּכָּתוּב – **Among the underlying purposes of the mitzvah is what is set forth in Scripture,** ״לְבִלְתִּי רוּם לְבָבוֹ וְגוֹ׳ ״ – ***so that his heart not become haughty,* etc.** (ibid. 17:20).[2]

Laws of the Mitzvah

מִדִּינֵי הַמִּצְוָה – **Among the laws of the mitzvah** מַה שֶּׁאָמְרוּ זִכְרוֹנָם לִבְרָכָה – is **that which [our Sages], of blessed memory, have stated** (*Sanhedrin* 21b): שֶׁל עַצְמוֹ הוּא דְּאֵינוֹ מַרְבֶּה – **It**

NOTES

1. He may also have what he needs for the upkeep of his palace, and for the support of his wives and children (*Yad HaLevi* to *Sefer HaMitzvos, Lo Saaseh* 365). [Perhaps, Chinuch mentions chariots and personal servants because these are things that ordinary people do not have. Maintaining a residence and supporting a family are expenses that are common to all people.] Moreover, the verse does not say that the king may have *no* wealth; it states that he may not *"amass great amounts"* of wealth. It is obvious that the position of king calls for him to have whatever is needed for a royal lifestyle, and to have funds on hand in order to deal with any expenses that may arise (see *R' S. R. Hirsch, Deuteronomy* 17:17; *Aruch HaShulchan HeAsid, Hil. Melachim* 72:9).

Chinuch's words here are based on *Sefer HaMitzvos* (ibid.). In *Hil. Melachim* (3:4), *Rambam* elaborates that the king may not amass silver and gold to place in his vaults and to take pride or glorify himself with it, but he may collect and possess funds that he needs to pay his officers and servants.

2. Although this verse appears a few verses after our verse, Chinuch applies it to our mitzvah. Accordingly, he understands that the reason a king is barred from amassing personal wealth is because excessive wealth leads to haughtiness (see *Rambam* ibid.). Others suggest that the reason for our prohibition is to protect the nation from being overly taxed by the king (*Ibn Ezra, Deuteronomy* 17:17; *Yad Ramah, Sanhedrin* 21b). See Insight for further discussion.

אֲבָל מַרְבֶּה הוּא לְצֹרֶךְ יִשְׂרָאֵל וּלְתוֹעַלְתָּם[3], כְּלוֹמַר לִשְׁמֹר אוֹתָם וְעָרֵיהֶם וּמְקוֹמוֹתָם מִן הָאוֹיְבִים[4]. וְיֶתֶר פְּרָטֶיהָ בְּסַנְהֶדְרִין (כ"א ע"ב)[5].

וּמֶלֶךְ הָעוֹבֵר עַל זֶה וְשָׂם מְגַמָּתוֹ לְמַלֹּאת אוֹצְרוֹת מָמוֹן לְהַשְׁלִים חֶפְצוֹ לְבַד, לֹא שֶׁתְּהֵא כַּוָּנָתוֹ לְתוֹעֶלֶת הָעָם וּשְׁמִירָתָם, עָבַר עַל לָאו זֶה. וְעָנְשׁוֹ גָּדוֹל מְאֹד, כִּי כָּל הָעָם תְּלוּיִים בַּמֶּלֶךְ, עַל כֵּן צָרִיךְ הוּא לְהָשִׂים כָּל הַשְׁגָּחָתוֹ בְּטוֹבַת עַמּוֹ וְלֹא בִּכְבוֹד עַצְמוֹ וְהַשְׁלָמַת תַּאֲווֹתָיו[6].

---

is only **his own** wealth **that he may not amass,** אֲבָל מַרְבֶּה הוּא לְצֹרֶךְ יִשְׂרָאֵל וּלְתוֹעַלְתָּם **– but he may amass** wealth **for the needs and benefit of the Jewish people.**[3] כְּלוֹמַר לִשְׁמֹר אוֹתָם וְעָרֵיהֶם וּמְקוֹמוֹתָם מִן הָאוֹיְבִים **– That is to say,** he may accumulate funds so that they will be available should the need arise **to defend them, their cities, and their** various **regions from** their **enemies.**[4]

וְיֶתֶר פְּרָטֶיהָ בְּסַנְהֶדְרִין – These laws **and the additional details of [this mitzvah]** can be found **in** Tractate ***Sanhedrin*** (21b).[5]

Applicability of the Mitzvah

וּמֶלֶךְ הָעוֹבֵר עַל זֶה **– A king who transgresses this** mitzvah, וְשָׂם מְגַמָּתוֹ לְמַלֹּאת אוֹצְרוֹת מָמוֹן **– and makes his objective to fill treasure houses with money,** לְהַשְׁלִים חֶפְצוֹ לְבַד **– so as to satisfy his** personal **desire** for wealth **alone,** לֹא שֶׁתְּהֵא כַּוָּנָתוֹ לְתוֹעֶלֶת הָעָם וּשְׁמִירָתָם **– as opposed to where his intention is for the benefit of the people and their security,** עָבַר עַל לָאו זֶה **– has transgressed this prohibition.** וְעָנְשׁוֹ גָּדוֹל מְאֹד **– His punishment** for doing so will be **very great,** כִּי כָּל הָעָם תְּלוּיִים בַּמֶּלֶךְ **– for the entire nation is dependent upon the king.** עַל כֵּן צָרִיךְ הוּא לְהָשִׂים כָּל הַשְׁגָּחָתוֹ בְּטוֹבַת עַמּוֹ **– Therefore, he must place his entire focus on the good of his people,** וְלֹא בִּכְבוֹד עַצְמוֹ וְהַשְׁלָמַת תַּאֲווֹתָיו **– and not upon** increasing **his own honor or satisfying his cravings.**[6]

NOTES

3. The verse stresses that *he shall not amass great amounts of silver and gold "for himself,"* which indicates that the prohibition applies only to personal wealth, not to what he amasses for the needs of the nation (*Sanhedrin* 21b). With regard to wealth amassed on behalf of the people, there is no concern that it will cause the king to become haughty (see *Meshech Chochmah, Deuteronomy* 17:20). In fact, amassing such wealth is considered a proper thing (*Rambam* ibid.).

4. He may have a reserve available for this in the treasury (*Rambam* ibid.).

5. These laws are codified in *Rambam, Hil. Melachim* 3:4.

6. *Rambam* (*Hil. Melachim* 3:4) writes that a king who violates this prohibition is subject to *malkus*. Chinuch here, however (in contrast to what he wrote in Mitzvos 499 and 501), makes no mention of this, and states only that the king's punishment will be "very great." This implies that he will be punished by Heaven, but is not subject to punishment in an earthly court. To explain Chinuch's view, some suggest that since there is no precise definition of how much money is considered "excessive," it is not practical to administer the necessary warning (*hasraah*) to him before he violates this prohibition. Furthermore, the king can always escape culpability by claiming that he is amassing the money for the needs of the nation (see *Heichal Melech,* fol. 76b; *Me'il HaEphod* §3; *Minchas Chinuch* §2; see, however, *Maharam Schik*).

Insight: The King's Share in the Spoils of War

Throughout the ages, kings have amassed wealth through the spoils that their victorious armies brought back from the battlefield. How the Jewish people are to apportion the spoils of their vanquished enemies is clearly outlined in the Gemara (*Sanhedrin* 20b): The entire treasury of the conquered monarch goes to the king. In addition, the king receives half of the remaining booty, with the other half being divided among the people (see *Rambam, Hil. Melachim* 4:9). It would thus seem that a Jewish king could amass large amounts of wealth from even a single successful military

campaign. How does such wealth not come into conflict with the current mitzvah, which prohibits him from amassing large amounts of wealth?

Some Rishonim explain that the prohibition for the king to amass large amounts of money is due to the fear that he will overly burden his Jewish subjects through heavy taxation. Wealth that comes from a conquered enemy does not present this concern, and may be kept by the king (*Yad Ramah* ibid. ד"ה וכסף וזהב; *Ran, Sanhedrin* 21b ד"ה לו). This, they suggest, is implied in our verse, which states וְכֶסֶף וְזָהָב לֹא יַרְבֶּה לּוֹ מְאֹד, *he shall not amass great amounts of gold and silver for himself*; as the term יַרְבֶּה, *amass*, indicates something that is being done actively by the king. Accordingly, the verse itself excludes wealth that falls to the king from other sources, such as spoils of war. In fact, they argue, it is clear that there are exceptions to this prohibition, for we find that when Hashem was pleased with Solomon's selfless request that He grant him wisdom to lead the Jewish people, He told Solomon that He would grant his request, adding: וְגַם אֲשֶׁר לֹא שָׁאַלְתָּ נָתַתִּי לָךְ גַּם עֹשֶׁר גַּם כָּבוֹד אֲשֶׁר לֹא הָיָה כָמוֹךָ אִישׁ בַּמְּלָכִים כָּל יָמֶיךָ, *even that which you did not request I have granted you — even riches and honor — all your days, such that there has never been any man among the kings like you* (*I Kings* 3:13). Now, if the king is prohibited from amassing all forms of great wealth— even that which comes from Heaven — how would this Divine promise be considered a blessing? Apparently, there is a type of wealth that is not included in the current mitzvah-prohibition (see *Yad Ramah; Yeshuos Malko, Kesavim* §17).

The language used by *Rambam* and Chinuch with regard to our mitzvah, however, seems to leave little room for such an exception. *Rambam* (*Sefer HaMitzvos, Lo Saaseh* 365) and Chinuch write that the king may not have money in his possession, other than the amount that he needs for his chariot and servants that are designated for him. This indicates that the issue is not so much the *amassing* of the wealth as much as it is *having* such wealth "in his possession." Similarly, in explaining our prohibition, *Rambam* (*Hil. Melachim* 3:4) writes that the king may not increase his wealth so as לְהָנִיחַ בְּגִנְזָיו וּלְהִתְגָּאוֹת בּוֹ אוֹ לְהִתְנָאוֹת בּוֹ, *to place in his vaults and to take pride or glorify himself with it*, again indicating that the issue is the very possession of a wealth-laden treasury, irrespective of how it was filled. Clearly then, even wealth that came to him from outside sources would be prohibited.

Rambam and Chinuch do, however, allow the king to amass wealth for the benefit of the Jewish people. Accordingly, the above question may be resolved by explaining that, according to *Rambam* and Chinuch, the spoils of war that fall to the king are not to be used by him personally, but are to be designated for the needs and expenses of the nation as a whole.

It would seem that the question of whether or not the king may personally keep his portion of the spoils of war hinges on how to understand the underlying reason for our mitzvah. As noted above, the authorities who maintain that the king may keep such spoils explain that the Torah's concern in the king's amassing of wealth is the welfare of the Jewish people. The Torah forbids the king from amassing unlimited wealth so that he not overly burden his subjects through taxation (see *Ibn Ezra, Deuteronomy* 17:17). Accordingly, there are no restrictions placed on wealth that comes from other sources. *Rambam* and Chinuch, though, explain that the reason a king may not amass great wealth is because such riches lead to arrogance (see above, note 2). According to their approach, the Torah's concern is not for the tax burden of the people, but rather for the king himself. A king who amasses great riches — irrespective of their source — could easily become "haughty over his brethren," as the Torah itself states later in the passage. Such a conceited individual is a dangerous leader. Moreover, in his inflated self-assessment, he will not merely view himself as being above his fellow country-men, but ultimately above the authority of Hashem Himself (see *Targum Yonasan* ad loc.). It thus follows that he is prohibited from keeping in his personal possession even excess funds that fall to him from sources such as spoils of war.

[Based on *Toras HaMelech* [*Arieli*], *Hil. Melachim* 3:4. See also *Yad HaLevi* to *Sefer HaMitzvos, Lo Saaseh* 365; *Minchas Chinuch* §1 with *Kometz Minchah*.]

מִצְוָה תקג

מִצְוָה עַל הַמֶּלֶךְ לִכְתֹּב סֵפֶר תּוֹרָה אֶחָד יָתֵר עַל שְׁאָר בְּנֵי יִשְׂרָאֵל

שֶׁמִּצְוָה עַל הַמֶּלֶךְ שֶׁיִּהְיֶה עַל יִשְׂרָאֵל לִכְתֹּב סֵפֶר תּוֹרָה מְיֻחָד לוֹ מִצַּד הַמְּלוּכָה שֶׁתִּהְיֶה עִמּוֹ תָּמִיד וְיִקְרָא בוֹ, מִלְּבַד סֵפֶר תּוֹרָה אַחֵר שֶׁמִּצְוָה עָלָיו לִכְתֹּב כְּכָל אֶחָד מִיִּשְׂרָאֵל כְּמוֹ שֶׁנִּכְתֹּב בַּמִּצְוָה הָאַחֲרוֹנָה שֶׁבַּסֵּפֶר בְּעֶזְרַת הַשֵּׁם (מצוה תרי״ג), וְעַל זֶה נֶאֱמַר (דברים י״ז, י״ח) וְכָתַב לוֹ אֶת מִשְׁנֵה הַתּוֹרָה הַזֹּאת וְגוֹ'[1].

מִשָּׁרְשֵׁי הַמִּצְוָה, לְפִי שֶׁהַמֶּלֶךְ בִּרְשׁוּת עַצְמוֹ לֹא יַעֲצִיבֵהוּ אָדָם עַל מַעֲשָׂיו וְלֹא יִגְעַר בּוֹ,

---

Mitzvah 503

The Obligation Upon a King to Write a Second Sefer Torah for Himself

וְהָיָה כְשִׁבְתּוֹ עַל כִּסֵּא מַמְלַכְתּוֹ וְכָתַב לוֹ אֶת מִשְׁנֵה הַתּוֹרָה הַזֹּאת עַל סֵפֶר מִלִּפְנֵי הַכֹּהֲנִים הַלְוִיִּם. וְהָיְתָה עִמּוֹ וְקָרָא בוֹ כָּל יְמֵי חַיָּיו לְמַעַן יִלְמַד לְיִרְאָה אֶת ה' אֱלֹהָיו לִשְׁמֹר אֶת כָּל דִּבְרֵי הַתּוֹרָה הַזֹּאת וְאֶת הַחֻקִּים הָאֵלֶּה לַעֲשֹׂתָם

It shall be that when he sits on the throne of his kingdom, he shall write for himself a second copy of this Torah in a scroll, from before the Kohanim, the Leviim. It shall be with him, and he shall read from it all the days of his life, so that he will learn to fear HASHEM, his God, to observe all the words of this Torah and these decrees, to perform them (*Deuteronomy* 17:18-19).

The very last mitzvah in the Torah, Mitzvah 613, requires each Jewish man to write a Sefer Torah (Torah scroll). As with other mitzvos, that mitzvah applies to the Jewish king as well. The current mitzvah requires the Jewish king to write an *additional* Sefer Torah, to be carried with him at all times.

שֶׁמִּצְוָה עַל הַמֶּלֶךְ שֶׁיִּהְיֶה עַל יִשְׂרָאֵל – **There is a mitzvah-obligation upon** every **king who rules over Israel** לִכְתֹּב סֵפֶר תּוֹרָה מְיֻחָד לוֹ מִצַּד הַמְּלוּכָה – **to write a special Sefer Torah for himself, in** his **capacity as the king;** שֶׁתִּהְיֶה עִמּוֹ תָּמִיד וְיִקְרָא בוֹ – **[that Sefer Torah] is to remain with him constantly and he is to read from it** regularly. מִלְּבַד סֵפֶר תּוֹרָה אַחֵר שֶׁמִּצְוָה עָלָיו לִכְתֹּב כְּכָל אֶחָד מִיִּשְׂרָאֵל – This is **aside from the other Sefer Torah that he is commanded to write like every** other **Jew,** כְּמוֹ שֶׁנִּכְתֹּב בַּמִּצְוָה הָאַחֲרוֹנָה שֶׁבַּסֵּפֶר בְּעֶזְרַת הַשֵּׁם – **as we will write, with Hashem's help, in the final mitzvah in this book** (Mitzvah 613). וְעַל זֶה נֶאֱמַר – **Regarding this it is stated** (*Deuteronomy* 17:18): "וְכָתַב לוֹ אֶת מִשְׁנֵה הַתּוֹרָה הַזֹּאת וְגוֹ'" – ***he shall write for himself a second copy of this Torah* etc.**[1]

Underlying Purpose of the Mitzvah

מִשָּׁרְשֵׁי הַמִּצְוָה – **Among the underlying purposes of the mitzvah** is לְפִי שֶׁהַמֶּלֶךְ בִּרְשׁוּת עַצְמוֹ – that the king requires a special Sefer Torah **because the king is under his own authority,** לֹא יַעֲצִיבֵהוּ אָדָם עַל מַעֲשָׂיו וְלֹא יִגְעַר בּוֹ – such that **no person can reproach him with regard to**

NOTES

1. He may keep one Torah deposited in a safe place, as all Jews do. The other one, which he must write specifically due to his position as king, is a small Sefer Torah that he is to carry upon his arm at all times (*Sanhedrin* 22a, with *Rashi* ד״ה כמו קמיע). He need not actually write it himself, but it must be written specifically for him after he assumes the throne (*Tosefta, Sanhedrin* 4:4; *Targum Yonasan* to *Deuteronomy* 17:18; see *Rambam, Hil. Sefer Torah* 7:2; see also *Minchas Chinuch* §1). [Our translation of the verse follows *Rambam, Hil. Melachim* 3:1; see *Even HaAzel* there.]

וּבְשֵׁבֶט פִּיו יַכֶּה אַרְצוֹ וּבְרוּחַ שְׂפָתָיו יָמִית מִי שֶׁיִּרְצֶה בְּכָל עַמּוֹ[2], עַל כֵּן בֶּאֱמֶת צָרִיךְ שְׁמִירָה גְּדוֹלָה וְזִכָּרוֹן טוֹב יַעֲמֹד נֶגְדּוֹ יַבִּיט אֵלָיו תָּמִיד לְמַעַן יִכְבֹּשׁ אֶת יִצְרוֹ וְיַטֶּה לִבּוֹ אֶל יוֹצְרוֹ[3], וְזֶהוּ שֶׁאָמְרוּ זִכְרוֹנָם לִבְרָכָה (סנהדרין כ״א ע״ב) יוֹצֵא לַמִּלְחָמָה וְסֵפֶר תּוֹרָה עִמּוֹ, יוֹשֵׁב בַּדִּין וְהוּא עִמּוֹ, מֵסֵב לֶאֱכֹל וְהוּא כְּנֶגְדּוֹ. כְּלַל הַדְּבָרִים, שֶׁלֹּא הָיָה זָז מִנֶּגֶד עֵינָיו אֶלָּא בְּעֵת שֶׁהוּא נִצְרָךְ לִנְקָבָיו אוֹ נִכְנָס לַמֶּרְחָץ[4].

מִדִּינֵי הַמִּצְוָה מַה שֶּׁאָמְרוּ זִכְרוֹנָם לִבְרָכָה (ירושלמי פ״ב דסנהדרין ה״ו) שֶׁסֵּפֶר תּוֹרָה שֶׁל מֶלֶךְ מִצְוָה עָלָיו לְהַגִּיהוֹ מִסֵּפֶר הָעֲזָרָה עַל פִּי בֵּית דִּין כְּדֵי שֶׁיְּכַוֵּן עַל פִּי[ו] מַעֲשָׂיו בְּיֹשֶׁר[5]. וְיֶתֶר פְּרָטֵי דִּינֵי סֵפֶר תּוֹרָה אֶכְתֹּב אוֹתָם בְּעֶזְרַת הַשֵּׁם בְּמִצְוָה אַחֲרוֹנָה שֶׁבַּסֵּפֶר[6].

---

any of **his actions, nor rebuke him** for his wrongdoings, וּבְשֵׁבֶט פִּיו יַכֶּה אַרְצוֹ – **and with the rod of his mouth he can strike** the residents of **his land,** וּבְרוּחַ שְׂפָתָיו יָמִית מִי שֶׁיִּרְצֶה בְּכָל עַמּוֹ – **and with the breath of his lips he can slay whomever he desires from** among **all of his people.**[2] עַל כֵּן בֶּאֱמֶת צָרִיךְ שְׁמִירָה גְּדוֹלָה – **Therefore, he definitely needs a major safeguard** from sin, וְזִכָּרוֹן טוֹב יַעֲמֹד נֶגְדּוֹ יַבִּיט אֵלָיו תָּמִיד – **and a powerful reminder to set before him that he can look at constantly,** לְמַעַן יִכְבֹּשׁ אֶת יִצְרוֹ וְיַטֶּה לִבּוֹ אֶל יוֹצְרוֹ – **so as to conquer his** evil **inclination and turn his heart toward his Creator.**[3] וְזֶהוּ שֶׁאָמְרוּ זִכְרוֹנָם לִבְרָכָה – **This is** the reason behind **what [our Sages], of blessed memory, have stated** (*Sanhedrin* 21b): יוֹצֵא לַמִּלְחָמָה וְסֵפֶר תּוֹרָה עִמּוֹ – When **he goes out to war, the** special **Sefer Torah is** to be **with him,** יוֹשֵׁב בַּדִּין וְהוּא עִמּוֹ – when **he sits in judgment, it is** to be **with him,** מֵסֵב לֶאֱכֹל וְהוּא כְּנֶגְדּוֹ – and when **he reclines to eat, it is** to be **opposite him.** כְּלַל הַדְּבָרִים – **The general rule is** שֶׁלֹּא הָיָה זָז מִנֶּגֶד עֵינָיו – **that [the Sefer Torah] does not move from his sight,** אֶלָּא בְּעֵת שֶׁהוּא נִצְרָךְ לִנְקָבָיו אוֹ נִכְנָס לַמֶּרְחָץ – **other than when he needs to** attend to **his bodily functions or enter the bathhouse.**[4]

Laws of the Mitzvah

מִדִּינֵי הַמִּצְוָה – **Among the laws of the mitzvah is** מַה שֶּׁאָמְרוּ זִכְרוֹנָם לִבְרָכָה – **that which [our Sages], of blessed memory, have stated** (see *Rambam, Hil Sefer Torah* 7:2; *Yerushalmi Sanhedrin* 2:6), שֶׁסֵּפֶר תּוֹרָה שֶׁל מֶלֶךְ – **that** with regard to **the Sefer Torah of a king,** מִצְוָה עָלָיו לְהַגִּיהוֹ מִסֵּפֶר הָעֲזָרָה עַל פִּי בֵּית דִּין – **it is a mitzvah upon him to** check it against and **correct it from the Sefer Torah of the** Temple **Courtyard, as directed by *Beis Din*,** כְּדֵי שֶׁיְּכַוֵּן עַל פִּי[ו] מַעֲשָׂיו בְּיֹשֶׁר – **so that he directs his actions correctly as per [that accurate Sefer Torah.]**[5]

וְיֶתֶר פְּרָטֵי דִּינֵי סֵפֶר תּוֹרָה – **As for the remaining details of the laws of a Sefer Torah,** אֶכְתֹּב אוֹתָם בְּעֶזְרַת הַשֵּׁם בְּמִצְוָה אַחֲרוֹנָה שֶׁבַּסֵּפֶר – **I will write them, with Hashem's help, in the last mitzvah of this work** (Mitzvah 613).[6]

NOTES

2. [Stylistic citation of *Isaiah* 11:4.] The king can exact punishment through his word (the "rod of his mouth" and "breath of his lips") alone, and need not justify his actions to anyone.

3. Carrying the Torah with him and constantly studying it reminds the king of his Torah obligations. This is conveyed in the verse that follows the verses of our mitzvah (*Deuteronomy* 17:20): וּלְבִלְתִּי סוּר מִן הַמִּצְוָה יָמִין וּשְׂמֹאול, *that he not turn from the commandments right or left* (*Chizkuni* ad loc.).

4. This is in keeping with the verse (*Deuteronomy* 17:19): וְהָיְתָה עִמּוֹ וְקָרָא בוֹ כָּל יְמֵי חַיָּיו, *It shall be with him, and he shall read from it all the days of his life* (*Rambam, Hil. Melachim* 3:1). He does not, however, carry it into those places where he may not read from it (*Sanhedrin* 21b). Rather, when he enters a bathhouse or the like, he leaves it at the door (*Tosefta, Sanhedrin* 4:4). In addition, he does not keep it upon his person when he goes to sleep (*Rambam, Hil. Sefer Torah* 7:3).

5. The Sefer Torah of the Temple Courtyard was written by Moses and was the one the king would read from in fulfillment of the mitzvah of *Hakheil* [Mitzvah 612] (*Rashi, Bava Basra* 14b ד״ה ספר). Moses gave it to the Kohanim and Sanhedrin of his day for safekeeping (see *Deuteronomy* 31:9), and it is to this Sefer Torah that our verse refers when it says: וְכָתַב לוֹ ... מִלִּפְנֵי הַכֹּהֲנִים הַלְוִיִּם, *he shall write ... from before the Kohanim, the Levites,* i.e., from the scroll that is before the Kohanim, in the Temple Courtyard (see *Chizkuni* and *R' S. R. Hirsch* to *Deuteronomy* 17:18). See *Hagahos HaGra* to *Sifrei* here.

6. The laws of the mitzvah for a king to write a second

וְזֹאת אַחַת מִן הַמִּצְוֹות שֶׁאָמַרְנוּ בִּתְחִלַּת הַסֵּפֶר שֶׁהֵן מֻטָּלוֹת עַל הַמֶּלֶךְ לְבַד[7].
וְאֵין צֹרֶךְ לִכְתֹּב בָּהּ בְּאֵיזֶה זְמַן הִיא נוֹהֶגֶת, שֶׁיָּדוּעַ הַדָּבָר שֶׁאֵין מַלְכוּת בְּיִשְׂרָאֵל אֶלָּא בִּזְמַן שֶׁאַרְצָם בְּיִשּׁוּבָהּ[8], תֶּחֱזֶינָה עֵינֵינוּ בִּמְהֵרָה בְּבִיאַת הַגּוֹאֵל וּמֶלֶךְ עָלֵינוּ בְּתוֹכָהּ.

Applicability of the Mitzvah

וְזֹאת אַחַת מִן הַמִּצְוֹות שֶׁאָמַרְנוּ בִּתְחִלַּת הַסֵּפֶר – This is one of the mitzvos about which **we said at the beginning of this work** **שֶׁהֵן מֻטָּלוֹת עַל הַמֶּלֶךְ לְבַד – that they apply to the king alone,** and to no one else.[7] **וְאֵין צֹרֶךְ לִכְתֹּב בָּהּ בְּאֵיזֶה זְמַן הִיא נוֹהֶגֶת – There is no need to write here in which time [this mitzvah] is applicable,** **שֶׁיָּדוּעַ הַדָּבָר שֶׁאֵין מַלְכוּת בְּיִשְׂרָאֵל אֶלָּא בִּזְמַן שֶׁאַרְצָם בְּיִשּׁוּבָהּ – for it is** well **known that the** institution of the **monarchy within Israel can exist only in** those **times when their land is settled** by the Jewish people.[8] **תֶּחֱזֶינָה עֵינֵינוּ בִּמְהֵרָה בְּבִיאַת הַגּוֹאֵל – May our eyes** merit to **quickly see the coming of the redeemer,** **וּמֶלֶךְ עָלֵינוּ בְּתוֹכָהּ – and a king** of Davidic descent presiding **over us in [that land].**

NOTES

Sefer Torah are codified in *Rambam, Hil. Melachim* 3:1 and *Hil. Sefer Torah* 7:2-3.

7. See Author's Introduction (Volume I), at note 97.

8. See Mitzvah 497, after note 25.

מִצְוָה תקד: שֶׁלֹּא יִהְיֶה לְשֵׁבֶט לֵוִי נַחֲלָה בָּאָרֶץ[1]

שֶׁלֹּא יִטֹּל כָּל שֵׁבֶט לֵוִי[2] חֵלֶק בָּאָרֶץ זוּלָתִי הֶעָרִים הַיְּדוּעוֹת וּמִגְרְשֵׁיהֶם[3] כְּמוֹ שֶׁמְּבֹאָר בַּכָּתוּב, וְעַל זֶה נֶאֱמַר (דברים י״ח, א׳) לֹא יִהְיֶה לַכֹּהֲנִים הַלְוִיִּם כָּל שֵׁבֶט לֵוִי חֵלֶק וְנַחֲלָה[4].

מִשָּׁרְשֵׁי הַמִּצְוָה, כְּדֵי שֶׁיִּהְיֶה כָּל עֵסֶק הַשֵּׁבֶט הַזֶּה בַּעֲבוֹדַת הָאֵל בָּרוּךְ הוּא[5] וְלֹא יִצְטָרְכוּ לַעֲבֹד אֶת הָאֲדָמָה, וּשְׁאָר הַשְּׁבָטִים נוֹתְנִין לָהֶם חֵלֶק מִכֹּל אֲשֶׁר לָהֶם[6] מִבְּלִי

Mitzvah 504

The Prohibition Upon the Tribe of Levi to Receive a Share in Eretz Yisrael

לֹא יִהְיֶה לַכֹּהֲנִים הַלְוִיִּם כָּל שֵׁבֶט לֵוִי חֵלֶק וְנַחֲלָה עִם יִשְׂרָאֵל אִשֵּׁי ה׳ וְנַחֲלָתוֹ יֹאכֵלוּן
There shall not for the Kohanim, the Leviim — the entire Tribe of Levi — a share and an inheritance with Israel; the fire-offerings of HASHEM and His inheritance they shall eat (*Deuteronomy* 18:1).

The Torah does not grant the Tribe of Levi, which includes the Kohanim and the Leviim, an expanse of land in Eretz Yisrael as their share. Instead, the Kohanim and Leviim dwelled in forty-eight cities that were scattered among the shares given to other tribes (see Mitzvah 408). This mitzvah prohibits the Tribe of Levi from taking a share in Eretz Yisrael outside of those forty-eight cities.[1]

שֶׁלֹּא יִטֹּל כָּל שֵׁבֶט לֵוִי חֵלֶק בָּאָרֶץ – The Torah commands **that the entire Tribe of Levi**[2] **shall not take a share in the Land** of Israel, זוּלָתִי הֶעָרִים הַיְּדוּעוֹת וּמִגְרְשֵׁיהֶם – **except for the** forty-eight **well-known cities and their open areas,**[3] כְּמוֹ שֶׁמְּבֹאָר בַּכָּתוּב – **as is set forth in Scripture** (*Numbers* 35:1-8). וְעַל זֶה נֶאֱמַר – **Regarding this** mitzvah **it is stated** (*Deuteronomy* 18:1): "לֹא יִהְיֶה לַכֹּהֲנִים הַלְוִיִּם כָּל שֵׁבֶט לֵוִי חֵלֶק וְנַחֲלָה" – ***There shall not be for the Kohanim, the Leviim — the entire Tribe of Levi — a share and an inheritance*** *with Israel*.[4]

Underlying Purpose of the Mitzvah

מִשָּׁרְשֵׁי הַמִּצְוָה – **Among the underlying purposes of the mitzvah** is כְּדֵי שֶׁיִּהְיֶה כָּל עֵסֶק הַשֵּׁבֶט הַזֶּה בַּעֲבוֹדַת הָאֵל בָּרוּךְ הוּא – **so that the entire occupation of this Tribe** of Levi **shall be the service of the Almighty, blessed is He.**[5] וְלֹא יִצְטָרְכוּ לַעֲבֹד אֶת הָאֲדָמָה – In order to ensure that the Leviim can focus on this pursuit, the Torah forbade them to occupy an expanse of land in Eretz Yisrael, so that **they will not need to work the land.** וּשְׁאָר הַשְּׁבָטִים נוֹתְנִין לָהֶם חֵלֶק מִכֹּל אֲשֶׁר לָהֶם מִבְּלִי

NOTES

1. This means that there could not be a specific portion of Eretz Yisrael allotted to the Tribe of Levi. Even if all the tribes agreed to give the Tribe of Levi a particular province, they were not allowed to take it (*Ohr HaChaim, Numbers* 18:20). [However, an individual Kohen or Levi was allowed to inherit a parcel of land from his maternal grandfather, who was a member of a different tribe, and keep it (see Mishnah, *Arachin* 33b). As to whether an individual Kohen or Levi was allowed to *purchase* land from a member of another tribe, see *Sifrei Zuta*, *Numbers* 18:24 with *Zayis Raanan; Ambuha DeSifrei* and *Sappirei Ephraim* to *Sifrei Zuta* loc. cit.; *R' Y. F. Perla, Sefer HaMitzvos of Rav Saadiah Gaon, Lo Saaseh* 234 (Vol. II, p. 254b).]

2. Chinuch alludes to the language of the verse, לֹא יִהְיֶה לַכֹּהֲנִים הַלְוִיִּם כָּל שֵׁבֶט לֵוִי, *There shall not be for the Kohanim, the Leviim — "the entire Tribe of Levi,"* which means to include the Kohanim and the Leviim.

3. That is, the area of 3,000 *amos* surrounding each of the Levitical cities. See Mitzvah 342.

4. As Chinuch explains at the beginning of the next mitzvah, the term "inheritance" refers to a share in Eretz Yisrael.

5. The Tribe of Levi was dedicated to service in the *Beis HaMikdash,* along with uninterrupted study of Torah and its dissemination among the general populace. See Mitzvos 342, 395, 408, and 450.

שֶׁיִּיגְעוּ הֵם בַּדָּבָר כְּלָל, כְּעִנְיָן שֶׁכָּתַבְתִּי לְמַעְלָה בְּמִצְוַת מַעֲשֵׂר בְּסֵדֶר וַיִּקַּח קֹרַח (מצוה שצ״ה)[7].

דִּינֵי הַמִּצְוָה כְּלוּלִים בִּפְשַׁט הַכָּתוּב לְפִי הַדּוֹמֶה[8].

וְנוֹהֶגֶת מִצְוָה זוֹ בַּלְוִיִּם[9] **בִּזְמַן שֶׁאֶרֶץ יִשְׂרָאֵל בְּיִשּׁוּבָהּ**[10].

שֶׁיִּיגְעוּ הֵם בַּדָּבָר כְּלָל – Rather, they are to live among **the other tribes,** who will **give them a share of all they have,**[6] **without [the Leviim] having to toil in [working the land] at all.** **כְּעִנְיָן שֶׁכָּתַבְתִּי לְמַעְלָה בְּמִצְוַת מַעֲשֵׂר** – This is **along the lines of what I wrote above, in the mitzvah of *maaser*** *rishon* (the first tithe), **בְּסֵדֶר וַיִּקַּח קֹרַח** – **in *Parashas Korach*** (Mitzvah 395).[7]

Laws of the Mitzvah

דִּינֵי הַמִּצְוָה כְּלוּלִים בִּפְשַׁט הַכָּתוּב לְפִי הַדּוֹמֶה – **The laws of the mitzvah, it seems, are contained in the simple** meaning **of the verse.**[8]

Applicability of the Mitzvah

וְנוֹהֶגֶת מִצְוָה זוֹ בַּלְוִיִּם – **This mitzvah applies to the Leviim**[9] **בִּזְמַן שֶׁאֶרֶץ יִשְׂרָאֵל בְּיִשּׁוּבָהּ** – **in a time that Eretz Yisrael is settled** by the Jewish nation as a whole. At that time, the Leviim may not take for themselves a share in Eretz Yisrael. When the Jewish people are in exile among the nations, however, even if there is a Jewish presence in Eretz Yisrael, this prohibition does not apply.[10]

NOTES

6. Each of the other tribes had to grant cities to the Tribe of Levi from within their own shares (Mitzvah 408), and had to give them a tithe (*terumah* or *maaser*) of all their produce (Mitzvos 507 and 395, respectively).

7. See also Mitzvah 342, at notes 24-27, where Chinuch cites *Rambam's* similar thoughts on the matter (*Hil. Shemittah VeYovel* 13:12).

8. That is, the Sages do not add anything to the laws of the mitzvah other than what is explicit in the verse — that the Tribe of Levi as a whole may not take an independent portion in Eretz Yisrael. [See, however, note 1, above, for certain specific laws regarding *individual* Leviim and Kohanim.]

The prohibition against the Tribe of Levi taking a share in Eretz Yisrael is codified in *Rambam, Hil. Shemittah VeYovel* 13:10-12.

9. In this context, "Leviim" refers to the entire Tribe of Levi, including the Kohanim (see *Chullin* 24b with *Rashi* ad loc. ד״ה וזה אחד מהם).

10. See *Sifrei Zuta* to *Numbers* 18:24 (cited in note 1).

Rambam (ibid. 13:11) rules that the prohibition against the Tribe of Levi taking a portion in Eretz Yisrael applies only within Eretz Yisrael proper. If, however, the borders of Eretz Yisrael were to be further expanded by a Jewish king, the Leviim were entitled to an equal share in those lands. *Raavad* (ad loc.) disagrees, maintaining that the Leviim received no share within those lands either. See *Minchas Chinuch* here (§2) and in Mitzvah 408 (§3). See also Insight to the next mitzvah.

Rambam there further indicates (see *Derech Emunah* ad loc. §51) that the prohibition *does* apply to the lands of the Kennite, Kenizzite, and Kadmonite nations [קֵינִי קְנִזִּי וְקַדְמֹנִי] (see, similarly, *Rashi* to *Deuteronomy* 18:2, citing *Sifrei* to *Numbers* 18:24). These lands were promised to Abraham as part of the future borders of Eretz Yisrael, but we will have no sovereignty there until the times of Mashiach (see *Genesis* 15:19 with *Rashi*). Since *Rambam* indicates that the Leviim are not permitted to take a share in those lands, evidently he holds that the exclusion of the Tribe of Levi from receiving a share in Eretz Yisrael will apply even in the times of Mashiach (*Minchas Chinuch* 408:2). Indeed, this appears to be *Rambam's* opinion earlier in the chapter (ibid. 13:1), as well as that of Chinuch in Mitzvah 408 (see note 22 there). *Smag* (*Lavin* §276), however, maintains that, in the time of Mashiach, the Tribe of Levi will receive its own portion in Eretz Yisrael, just like the other tribes. According to him, our prohibition cannot *possibly* apply to the lands of the Kennite, Kenizzite, and Kadmonite, since when these lands will belong to the Jewish people, i.e., in the times of Mashiach, the Leviim *will* receive their own share (see *Minchas Chinuch* ibid.). [For further discussion, see *Minchas Chinuch* here §3; *R' Y. F. Perla* ibid., p. 254a; and *Ambuha DeSifrei* ibid. ד״ה וראיתי עוד במנ״ח. For other understandings of *Rambam's* opinion, see *Maharam Schik* §505, and *Mirkeves HaMishneh, Hil. Sanhedrin* 19:4 (p. 312 in Feldheim ed. ד״ה ועיין לאוין ק״ע).]

מִצְוָה תקה: שֶׁלֹּא יִטֹּל שֵׁבֶט לֵוִי חֵלֶק בַּבִּזָּה

שֶׁלֹּא יִטֹּל כָּל שֵׁבֶט לֵוִי[1] חֵלֶק בַּבִּזָּה בְּמַה שֶּׁשָּׁלְלוּ יִשְׂרָאֵל בְּהִכָּנְסָם בָּאָרֶץ וּבְמַה שֶּׁיִּשְׁלְלוּ מֵאוֹיְבֵיהֶם אַחֲרֵי כֵן[2], וְעַל זֶה נֶאֱמַר (דברים י״ח, א׳) לֹא יִהְיֶה לַכֹּהֲנִים וְגוֹ׳ חֵלֶק וְנַחֲלָה, וְכֵן בָּא בְּסִפְרִי (כאן), חֵלֶק, בַּבִּזָּה, וְנַחֲלָה, בָּאָרֶץ[3].

Mitzvah 505
The Prohibition Upon the Tribe of Levi to Take a Share of the Spoils of War

לֹא יִהְיֶה לַכֹּהֲנִים הַלְוִיִּם כָּל שֵׁבֶט לֵוִי חֵלֶק וְנַחֲלָה עִם יִשְׂרָאֵל אִשֵּׁי ה׳ וְנַחֲלָתוֹ יֹאכֵלוּן
There shall not be for the Kohanim, the Leviim — the entire Tribe of Levi — a share and an inheritance with Israel; the fire-offerings of HASHEM and His inheritance they shall eat (*Deuteronomy* 18:1).

The previous mitzvah prohibited the Tribe of Levi from taking a share in Eretz Yisrael along with the other tribes. This mitzvah teaches a similar restriction regarding spoils of war.
שֶׁלֹּא יִטֹּל כָּל שֵׁבֶט לֵוִי חֵלֶק בַּבִּזָּה – The Torah commands **that the entire Tribe of Levi**[1] **shall not take a share of the spoils,** בְּמַה שֶּׁשָּׁלְלוּ יִשְׂרָאֵל בְּהִכָּנְסָם בָּאָרֶץ – both **in that which** the people of **Israel took as booty when they entered the Land** of Israel and defeated the Seven Canaanite Nations, וּבְמַה שֶּׁיִּשְׁלְלוּ מֵאוֹיְבֵיהֶם אַחֲרֵי כֵן – **and in that which they take as booty from** wars with **their enemies after that.**[2] וְעַל זֶה נֶאֱמַר – **Regarding this it is stated** (*Deuteronomy* 18:1): "לֹא יִהְיֶה לַכֹּהֲנִים וְגוֹ׳ חֵלֶק וְנַחֲלָה" – ***There shall not be for the Kohanim,*** *the Leviim ...* ***a share and an inheritance.*** Although this verse is the source for the prohibition against the Tribe of Levi taking a share in Eretz Yisrael (the previous mitzvah), the double expression (*a share and an inheritance*) indicates that the verse is referring to two types of "shares." וְכֵן בָּא בְּסִפְרִי – **And so it is presented in *Sifrei*** (to the verse): "חֵלֶק" בַּבִּזָּה – The term ***share*** prohibits the Tribe of Levi from taking a share **of the spoils** of war, "וְנַחֲלָה" בָּאָרֶץ – and the term ***and an inheritance*** prohibits them from taking a share **in the Land** of Israel.[3]

One of the principles that *Rambam* sets down with regard to counting the mitzvos (*Sefer HaMitzvos, Shoresh* §9) is that a לָאו שֶׁבִּכְלָלוֹת, "a generalized prohibition" — that is, a prohibition that encompasses several details — counts as only one among the 613 Mitzvos (unless the Sages tell us otherwise). One type of לָאו שֶׁבִּכְלָלוֹת is where the Torah issues a single prohibition (e.g., "you shall not ...") and applies it to several different subjects or things. For example, the Torah (*Leviticus* 2:11) states

---

NOTES

1. I.e., the Kohanim and the Leviim; see note 2 of the previous mitzvah.

2. For example, if a Jewish king subsequently conquers lands outside of Eretz Yisrael.

Rambam (*Sefer HaMitzvos, Lo Saaseh* 170; *Hil. Shemittah VeYovel* 13:10-11), however, indicates that this mitzvah applies only to booty taken in a war involving the conquest of Eretz Yisrael proper. [Presumably this includes the lands of the Kennite, Kenizzite, and Kadmonite, just like these lands are included in the prohibition upon the Leviim to take a share in Eretz Yisrael (see last note of the previous mitzvah). Indeed, it appears from *Rambam* (*Hil. Shemittah VeYovel* 13:11) that the two prohibitions share the same guidelines in this regard.]

3. Seemingly, since the verse first mentions "share" and then "inheritance," Chinuch should have counted the prohibition of taking a portion of the spoils *before* that of taking a share in Eretz Yisrael. However, Chinuch below will cite the verse (*Numbers* 18:20) that applies these same two prohibitions to the Kohanim, and there, the matter of not taking an inheritance comes before not taking a share of the spoils. Apparently, Chinuch followed the order of that verse in enumerating the prohibitions that appear in our verse (see *Chemdas Yisrael, Kuntres Ner Mitzvah* §44 [p. 29a]).

וְאַל יִקְשֶׁה עָלֶיךָ בְּזֶה הַלָּאו עִנְיַן לָאו שֶׁבִּכְלָלוֹת, שֶׁהֲרֵי כְּבָר בָּאוּ בַּכָּתוּב עַל שְׁנֵי עִנְיָנִים אֵלֶּה שְׁנֵי לָאוִין, וְהֵם לֹא יִהְיֶה לַכֹּהֲנִים הַלְוִיִּם וְגוֹ׳ חֵלֶק וְנַחֲלָה, וְאָמְרוּ עוֹד אַחַר כֵּן וְנַחֲלָה לֹא יִהְיֶה לּוֹ וְגוֹ׳[4]**.**

וְנִכְפְּלוּ[5] **שְׁנֵי הַלָּאוִין אֵלּוּ בְּעַצְמָם בַּכֹּהֲנִים, שֶׁנֶּאֱמַר בְּאַהֲרֹן** (במדבר י״ח, כ׳) **בְּאַרְצָם לֹא תִנְחָל וְחֵלֶק לֹא יִהְיֶה לְךָ בְּתוֹכָם, וְאָמְרוּ זִכְרוֹנָם לִבְרָכָה** (ספרי שם) **בְּאַרְצָם לֹא תִנְחָל, בִּשְׁעַת חִלּוּק הָאָרֶץ, וְחֵלֶק לֹא יִהְיֶה לְךָ בְּתוֹכָם, בַּבִּזָּה.**

---

that we may not bring either leaven or fruit-honey as a fire-offering to Hashem. This counts as one prohibition, which applies to both leaven and fruit-honey (Mitzvah 117). It would seem, then, that the prohibitions against the Tribe of Levi taking a share in Eretz Yisrael (the previous mitzvah) and taking a share of the spoils of war (this mitzvah) should have been counted as one mitzvah, since the Torah issues only one prohibition (*There shall not be* ...) and applies it to both of these details. Chinuch explains (based on *Rambam, Sefer HaMitzvos, Lo Saaseh* 170) why we nevertheless count them as two separate mitzvos:

וְאַל יִקְשֶׁה עָלֶיךָ בְּזֶה הַלָּאו עִנְיַן לָאו שֶׁבִּכְלָלוֹת – You should not have a difficulty regarding this mitzvah-**prohibition** of the Tribe of Levi taking a share in the spoils due to **the matter of "a generalized prohibition,"** which would seem to dictate that this should not be counted as a distinct mitzvah, but should be counted together with the mitzvah-prohibition of taking a share in Eretz Yisrael, **שֶׁהֲרֵי כְּבָר בָּאוּ בַּכָּתוּב עַל שְׁנֵי עִנְיָנִים אֵלֶּה שְׁנֵי לָאוִין – since, in fact,** ***two*** **prohibitions are expressed in Scripture with regard to these two matters.** **וְהֵם "לֹא יִהְיֶה לַכֹּהֲנִים הַלְוִיִּם וְגוֹ׳ חֵלֶק וְנַחֲלָה" – These are:** (1) ***There "shall not" be for the Kohanim, the Leviim... a share and an inheritance*** *with Israel* (our verse); **וְאָמְרוּ עוֹד אַחַר כֵּן "וְנַחֲלָה לֹא יִהְיֶה לּוֹ וְגוֹ׳ " – and** (2) **that which [Scripture] further states** in the **following** verse (v. 2), ***He*** [the Tribe of Levi] ***"shall not" have an inheritance, etc.*** By repeating the prohibition to take a share in Eretz Yisrael ("an inheritance") with the prohibitory term "shall not," the Torah indicates that each prohibition is to be regarded as a distinct mitzvah-prohibition.[4]

Chinuch further proves that these are two separate prohibitions from the manner in which they are issued elsewhere in the Torah:[5]

וְנִכְפְּלוּ שְׁנֵי הַלָּאוִין אֵלּוּ בְּעַצְמָם בַּכֹּהֲנִים – These very same two prohibitions are repeated elsewhere, specifically **with regard to the Kohanim,** and there they are expressed as two distinct prohibitions. **שֶׁנֶּאֱמַר בְּאַהֲרֹן – For it is stated with regard to Aaron** the Kohen (*Numbers* 18:20): **"בְּאַרְצָם לֹא תִנְחָל וְחֵלֶק לֹא יִהְיֶה לְךָ בְּתוֹכָם" –** ***In their Land "you shall have no" inheritance, and a share "you shall not have" among them,*** **וְאָמְרוּ זִכְרוֹנָם לִבְרָכָה – and [the Sages], of blessed memory, stated** (*Sifrei* to that verse) **"בְּאַרְצָם לֹא תִנְחָל" בִּשְׁעַת חִלּוּק הָאָרֶץ** – that the clause, ***In their Land you shall have no inheritance,*** teaches that the Kohanim can have no share in Eretz Yisrael **at the time of the distribution of the Land** among the tribes; **"וְחֵלֶק לֹא יִהְיֶה לְךָ בְּתוֹכָם" בַּבִּזָּה** – and the clause, ***And a share you shall not have among them,*** teaches that they can have no share **in the spoils** of war. Each prohibition is thus expressed separately ("*you shall have no* ..." and "*you shall not have* ...").

However, one should not conclude that since the two prohibitions were repeated for the Kohanim, there are actually *four* separate mitzvah-prohibitions – two for the Kohanim and two for the Leviim. Rather, there are *two*, issued to Leviim and Kohanim alike. Chinuch explains why the Torah needed to single out the Kohanim if they are part of the Tribe of Levi in any case:

NOTES

4. As *Rambam* (*Sefer HaMitzvos* ibid.) explains, the first "shall not" is referring primarily to taking a share in the spoils (*There shall not be for the Kohanim, the Leviim... "a share"*), while the second "shall not" is referring to taking a share in Eretz Yisrael (*He shall not have "an inheritance"*). See above, at note 3.

5. See *Rambam* ibid.

וְאַף עַל פִּי שֶׁהַכֹּהֲנִים בִּכְלַל שֵׁבֶט לֵוִי הָיוּ, נִכְפְּלָה הַמְּנִיעָה בָּהֶם לְחִזּוּק. וְכֵן כָּל מַה שֶּׁדּוֹמֶה לָזֶה בַּתּוֹרָה שֶׁתִּכְפֹּל הַלָּאוִין בִּמְקוֹמוֹת הַרְבֵּה, הַכֹּל לְחִזּוּק הָעִנְיָן[6] אוֹ לְהַשְׁלִים הַדִּין כְּשֶׁלֹּא יִהְיֶה שָׁלֵם מֵהַלָּאו הָאֶחָד. וְתָבִין מִמַּה שֶּׁכָּתַבְתִּי לְךָ בְּרֹאשׁ סֵפֶר אֵלֶּה הַדְּבָרִים לָמָּה יְחַסְּרֵנוּ הָאֵל בְּמָקוֹם אֶחָד וְיַשְׁלִימֶנּוּ בְּאַחֵר[7].

וְכָתַב הָרַמְבַּ"ם ז"ל (סה"מ ל"ת ק"ע), אִלּוּ מָנִינוּ אֵלּוּ הַלָּאוִין שֶׁהֵם בְּאַרְצָם לֹא תִנְחָל וְגוֹ' בַּכֹּהֲנִים תּוֹסֶפֶת עַל הַלָּאוִין הַנֶּאֱמָרִים בַּלְוִיִּם שֶׁהֵם לֹא יִהְיֶה לַכֹּהֲנִים הַלְוִיִּם וְגוֹ', הָיָה רָאוּי לָנוּ כְּמוֹ כֵן לְפִי זֶה הַהֶקֵּשׁ שֶׁנִּמְנֶה אִסּוּר הַגְּרוּשָׁה וַחֲלָלָה זוֹנָה עַל כֹּהֵן גָּדוֹל[8] בִּשְׁלֹשָׁה לָאוִין נוֹסָפִין עַל הַשְּׁלֹשָׁה שֶׁבָּאוּ עַל זֶה בְּכָל כֹּהֵן בֵּין גָּדוֹל בֵּין הֶדְיוֹט, וְאִם אָמַר אוֹמֵר שֶׁכֵּן הוּא הַדִּין, נְשִׁיבֵהוּ מִמַּה שֶּׁאָמְרוּ זִכְרוֹנָם לִבְרָכָה בְּקִדּוּשִׁין (ע"ז ע"ב)

וְאַף עַל פִּי שֶׁהַכֹּהֲנִים בִּכְלַל שֵׁבֶט לֵוִי הָיוּ – **Now, although the Kohanim were included in the Tribe of Levi,** נִכְפְּלָה הַמְּנִיעָה בָּהֶם לְחִזּוּק – **the prohibition was repeated for them** in order **to strengthen** the force and severity of the prohibition. וְכֵן כָּל מַה שֶּׁדּוֹמֶה לָזֶה בַּתּוֹרָה – **The same** applies to **anything similar to this in the Torah,** שֶׁתִּכְפֹּל הַלָּאוִין בִּמְקוֹמוֹת הַרְבֵּה – **which repeats prohibitions in *numerous* places;** הַכֹּל לְחִזּוּק הָעִנְיָן – it is **all to reinforce** the severity of **the matter.**[6] אוֹ לְהַשְׁלִים הַדִּין כְּשֶׁלֹּא יִהְיֶה שָׁלֵם מֵהַלָּאו הָאֶחָד – **Or,** sometimes, it is in order for the Torah **to complete** its discussion of **the law** regarding a particular prohibition **when it is** left **incomplete by the first** mention of that **prohibition.** וְתָבִין מִמַּה שֶּׁכָּתַבְתִּי לְךָ בְּרֹאשׁ סֵפֶר אֵלֶּה הַדְּבָרִים – **From what I have written for you in the Introduction to the Book of *Deuteronomy*, you can understand** לָמָּה יְחַסְּרֵנוּ הָאֵל בְּמָקוֹם אֶחָד וְיַשְׁלִימֶנּוּ בְּאַחֵר – **why the Almighty would omit** details of **[a particular prohibition] in one place** in the Torah **and complete** discussion of **it in another** place, rather than presenting all the details in one place.[7]

Chinuch cites *Rambam*'s proof that the prohibitions against the Kohanim taking a share of Eretz Yisrael and taking spoils of war cannot be counted as two additional mitzvos:

וְכָתַב הָרַמְבַּ"ם ז"ל – ***Rambam*, of blessed memory, writes** (ibid.): אִלּוּ מָנִינוּ אֵלּוּ הַלָּאוִין שֶׁהֵם "בְּאַרְצָם לֹא תִנְחָל וְגוֹ'" בַּכֹּהֲנִים – **Were we to count these prohibitions, namely, *In their Land you shall have no inheritance*,** *and a share you shall not have among them,* **etc.,** which are said **with regard to the Kohanim,** תּוֹסֶפֶת עַל הַלָּאוִין הַנֶּאֱמָרִים בַּלְוִיִּם שֶׁהֵם "לֹא יִהְיֶה לַכֹּהֲנִים הַלְוִיִּם וְגוֹ'" – as being **in addition to the prohibitions that are stated with regard to the Tribe of Levi** as a whole, **namely, *There shall not be for the Kohanim, the Leviim* ...** *a portion and an inheritance with Israel,* הָיָה רָאוּי לָנוּ כְּמוֹ כֵן לְפִי זֶה הַהֶקֵּשׁ – **it would have likewise been proper for us, based on that logic,** שֶׁנִּמְנֶה אִסּוּר הַגְּרוּשָׁה וַחֲלָלָה זוֹנָה עַל כֹּהֵן גָּדוֹל בִּשְׁלֹשָׁה לָאוִין – **to count the prohibitions** imposed **upon a Kohen Gadol** against marrying **a divorcee, a *chalalah*,** and **a *zonah***[8] (*Leviticus* 21:14), **as three** separate mitzvah-**prohibitions,** נוֹסָפִין עַל הַשְּׁלֹשָׁה שֶׁבָּאוּ עַל זֶה בְּכָל כֹּהֵן בֵּין גָּדוֹל בֵּין הֶדְיוֹט – **in addition to the three** mitzvah-prohibitions **that appear** in the Torah **about this with regard to all Kohanim** (ibid. v. 7; Mitzvos 266-268), **whether** one is a Kohen **Gadol or** an **ordinary** Kohen! וְאִם אָמַר אוֹמֵר שֶׁכֵּן הוּא הַדִּין – **And if anyone suggests that this is** indeed **the case,** that the Kohen Gadol was issued these prohibitions *in addition* to the prohibitions issued to all Kohanim, נְשִׁיבֵהוּ מִמַּה שֶּׁאָמְרוּ זִכְרוֹנָם לִבְרָכָה בְּקִדּוּשִׁין – **we will respond to him with**

NOTES

6. By repeating the prohibition in several contexts (for example, our prohibition in the context of the Tribe of Levi as a whole and then in the context of the Kohanim specifically), the Torah indicates that the sin of transgressing the prohibition is great (*Rambam, Sefer HaMitzvos, Shoresh* 9 [p. 155 in Frankel ed.]). See similarly, Mitzvah 362 at notes 7-8.

7. Chinuch there writes that the Torah contains within it all the wisdoms of the world, and that perhaps these are hidden in the organization of the Torah's passages and words. Accordingly, it is possible that Hashem arranged that a law should be incomplete in one place so that it can be repeated elsewhere, and in that arrangement there is an allusion to a hidden concept.

8. See Mitzvos 266 and 267 for the definitions of *zonah* and *chalalah*.

שֶׁאֵין כֹּהֵן גָּדוֹל חַיָּב בִּגְרוּשָׁה אֶלָּא אַחַת, וְאִלּוּ יִהְיֶה הַדִּין כֵּן יִתְחַיֵּב עָלֶיהָ שְׁתַּיִם, אַחַת מִשּׁוּם כֹּהֵן שֶׁהַגְּרוּשָׁה אֲסוּרָה עָלָיו, וְהַשֵּׁנִית מִצַּד שֶׁהוּא כֹּהֵן גָּדוֹל וְהִיא אֲסוּרָה עָלָיו בַּלָּאו הָאַחֵר. וּמִזֶּה הַמִּין בְּעַצְמוֹ הֵן הַמְּנִיעוֹת שֶׁבָּאוּ עַל הַכֹּהֲנִים בְּלֹא יִקְרְחוּ קָרְחָה בְּרֹאשָׁם וּפְאַת זְקָנָם לֹא יְגַלֵּחוּ וּבִבְשָׂרָם לֹא יִשְׂרְטוּ שָׂרָטֶת (ויקרא כ״א, ה׳)**, שֶׁכְּבָר**[9] **קָדְמוּ לְכָל יִשְׂרָאֵל בִּכְלָל בְּאוֹמְרוֹ לֹא תַקִּפוּ פְּאַת רֹאשְׁכֶם וְלֹא תָשִׂימוּ קָרְחָה וְגוֹ׳ וְשֶׂרֶט לָנֶפֶשׁ וְגוֹ׳** (ויקרא י״ט, כ״ח)**, וְאָמְנָם נִכְפְּלוּ אֵלּוּ בַּכֹּהֲנִים לְהַשְׁלִים הַדִּין כְּמוֹ שֶׁנִּתְבָּאֵר בְּסוֹף מַסֶּכֶת מַכּוֹת** (כ׳ ע״א־כ״א ע״א)[10]**,**

---

that which [the Sages], of blessed memory, stated in Tractate ***Kiddushin*** (77b), **שֶׁאֵין כֹּהֵן גָּדוֹל חַיָּב בִּגְרוּשָׁה אֶלָּא אַחַת – that a Kohen Gadol is liable to only one** set of *malkus* **for** marrying **a divorcee. וְאִלּוּ יִהְיֶה הַדִּין כֵּן – If the law were indeed [as he suggests],** that a Kohen Gadol is subject to multiple prohibitions, **יִתְחַיֵּב עָלֶיהָ שְׁתַּיִם – then [the Kohen Gadol] should be liable to *two*** sets of *malkus* **for** marrying **her: אַחַת מִשּׁוּם כֹּהֵן שֶׁהַגְּרוּשָׁה אֲסוּרָה עָלָיו – one** set of *malkus* **on account of** his being **a Kohen, to whom a divorcee is forbidden, וְהַשֵּׁנִית מִצַּד שֶׁהוּא כֹּהֵן גָּדוֹל וְהִיא אֲסוּרָה עָלָיו בַּלָּאו הָאַחֵר – and a second** set of *malkus* **due to his being a Kohen *Gadol*, which renders her forbidden to him by virtue of the other prohibition** (stated specifically for him), as well! Evidently, there is no additional prohibition for a Kohen Gadol to marry a divorcee or any of the other women forbidden to a Kohen. He is simply included in the prohibitions that apply to *all* Kohanim. The Torah restated these prohibitions with regard to the Kohen Gadol only in order to stress the severity of the prohibition. Similarly, although the Torah issues the prohibitions of taking a share in Eretz Yisrael or in the spoils of war with regard to the entire Tribe of Levi, it restates them with regard to the Kohanim in order to emphasize the severity of these prohibitions.

Rambam continues:

וּמִזֶּה הַמִּין בְּעַצְמוֹ הֵן הַמְּנִיעוֹת שֶׁבָּאוּ עַל הַכֹּהֲנִים – The following **prohibitions imposed upon the Kohanim are of the very same type: בְּ״לֹא יִקְרְחוּ קָרְחָה בְּרֹאשָׁם –** The prohibition of ***They shall not make a bald spot on their heads,*** **וּפְאַת זְקָנָם לֹא יְגַלֵּחוּ –** the prohibition of ***They shall not shave an edge of their beard,*** **וּבִבְשָׂרָם לֹא יִשְׂרְטוּ שָׂרָטֶת״ –** and the prohibition of ***In their flesh they shall not cut a gash*** (all stated in *Leviticus* 21:5). **שֶׁכְּבָר קָדְמוּ לְכָל יִשְׂרָאֵל בִּכְלָל**[9] **–** All of **these were previously** imposed **upon all of Israel as a whole, בְּאוֹמְרוֹ ״לֹא תַקִּפוּ פְּאַת רֹאשְׁכֶם״ – when [Scripture] stated, *You shall not round off the edge of your scalp*** *and you shall not destroy the edge of your beard* (*Leviticus* 19:27, Mitzvah 252); **״וְלֹא תָשִׂימוּ קָרְחָה וְגוֹ׳״ – *You shall not make a bald spot*** *between your eyes over a dead person* (*Deuteronomy* 14:1, Mitzvah 468); **״וְשֶׂרֶט לָנֶפֶשׁ וְגוֹ׳״ –** and *You shall not make* ***a cut*** *in your flesh* ***for the dead*** (*Leviticus* 19:28, Mitzvah 467). **וְאָמְנָם נִכְפְּלוּ אֵלּוּ בַּכֹּהֲנִים לְהַשְׁלִים הַדִּין – However, these** three prohibitions **were repeated in** the context of **the Kohanim in order** for the Torah **to complete** its discussion of **the laws** of these prohibitions, **כְּמוֹ שֶׁנִּתְבָּאֵר בְּסוֹף מַסֶּכֶת מַכּוֹת – as is set forth at the end of Tractate *Makkos*** (20a-21a).[10] They were *not* repeated in order to impose additional prohibitions upon a Kohen, so as

---

NOTES

9. Text follows Sefer HaChinuch, first ed. (Venice), as well as many later editions. See also *Sefer HaMitzvos, Lo Saaseh* 170.

10. The Gemara there teaches that the verse regarding the Kohanim (*Leviticus* 21:5) contains something new with regard to the first two of these three prohibitions:

(1) **Making a bald spot:** One is liable for *each and every* bald spot made in grief over a dead person. Additionally, one is liable not only for making a bald spot "between the eyes" (i.e., in the area on the top of the head that is opposite the area between the eyes), but anywhere on the head.

(2) **Destroying the corners of the beard:** One is liable only if one destroys it by way of *shaving*, i.e., with a razor, rather than with a tweezer or a plane used to smooth wood.

Sifra (to *Leviticus* 21:5) teaches what the third prohibition adds:

(3) **Making a cut:** One is liable for *each and every* cut made in grief over a dead person. [However, the Gemara (*Makkos* 20b), citing a different passage in *Sifra* (to *Leviticus* 19:28), indicates that this is actually derived from the verse pertaining to all Jews. See *Malbim* (to *Leviticus* 19:28) for a resolution.]

וּלְפִיכָךְ כֹּהֵן הָעוֹבֵר עַל אַחַת מֵאֵלֶּה אֵינוֹ מִתְחַיֵּב אֶלָּא מַלְקוּת אַחַת, וְהָבֵן זֶה הָעִקָּר וְשָׁמְרֵהוּ[11].

וּמִשָּׁרְשֵׁי הַמִּצְוָה, לְפִי שֶׁהֵם מְשָׁרְתֵי הַשֵּׁם לֹא נָאֶה לָהֶם לְהִשְׁתַּמֵּשׁ בְּכֵלִים הַחֲטוּפִים מִיַּד בְּנֵי אָדָם, לֹא יָבֹא בֵּית הַשֵּׁם רַק דָּבָר הַבָּא דֶּרֶךְ שָׁלוֹם וְיֹשֶׁר וֶאֱמוּנָה, וְלֹא שֶׁיִּדְאַג עָלָיו לֵב אִישׁ וְאִשָּׁה[12].

דִּינֵי הַמִּצְוָה[13].

וְנוֹהֶגֶת מִצְוָה זוֹ בִּזְמַן הַבַּיִת[14] בְּשֵׁבֶט הַלְוִיִּם[15].

---

to make him liable to two punishments for violating them. וּלְפִיכָךְ כֹּהֵן הָעוֹבֵר עַל אַחַת מֵאֵלֶּה אֵינוֹ מִתְחַיֵּב אֶלָּא מַלְקוּת אַחַת – **Accordingly, a Kohen who violates one of these** prohibitions **is liable to only one** set of ***malkus***. וְהָבֵן זֶה הָעִקָּר וְשָׁמְרֵהוּ – **Understand this principle and retain it** in your memory.[11]

Underlying Purpose of the Mitzvah

וּמִשָּׁרְשֵׁי הַמִּצְוָה – **Among the underlying purposes of the mitzvah** is לְפִי שֶׁהֵם מְשָׁרְתֵי הַשֵּׁם – that **since [the Kohanim and the Leviim] are the** devoted **servants of Hashem,** לֹא נָאֶה לָהֶם לְהִשְׁתַּמֵּשׁ בְּכֵלִים הַחֲטוּפִים מִיַּד בְּנֵי אָדָם – **it is unbecoming for them to use vessels** and garments **that were snatched** as spoils of war **from the possession of** other **people.** לֹא יָבֹא בֵּית הַשֵּׁם רַק דָּבָר הַבָּא דֶּרֶךְ שָׁלוֹם וְיֹשֶׁר וֶאֱמוּנָה – **Only an item that comes** into one's possession **by way of peace, integrity, and trustworthiness ought to enter the house of Hashem,** and be used by those who serve in it, וְלֹא שֶׁיִּדְאַג עָלָיו לֵב אִישׁ וְאִשָּׁה – **not one over which the heart of a man or woman agonizes** on account of having lost it to conquerors.[12]

Laws and Applicability of the Mitzvah

דִּינֵי הַמִּצְוָה – The **laws of the mitzvah ...**[13]

וְנוֹהֶגֶת מִצְוָה זוֹ בִּזְמַן הַבַּיִת – **This mitzvah applies in the time of the *Beis HaMikdash*,** when the Jewish nation is sovereign over Eretz Yisrael, and they obtain spoils of war from battles with their enemies.[14] בְּשֵׁבֶט הַלְוִיִּם – The mitzvah applies **to the Tribe of the Leviim.**[15]

NOTES

11. That is, that generally a prohibition is repeated in the Torah either to teach additional laws regarding the prohibition or to reinforce the prohibition, but not to impose additional penalties on the violator.

12. Chinuch thus provides different rationales for the two prohibitions: (1) The Tribe of Levi must not take a share in Eretz Yisrael, because this would force them to work the land and distract them from their Divine service (see previous mitzvah); and (2) they must not take from the spoils of war because it is unbecoming for them, as explained here. *Rambam* (*Hil. Shemittah VeYovel* 13:12), however, understands the rationale for the two prohibitions as one and the same: because the Tribe of Levi was set apart from the other tribes to be Hashem's devoted servants, they were also set apart from the other tribes with regard to their physical needs. Whereas the other tribes receive their sustenance through regular means — conquest, toil of the land, etc. — the Tribe of Levi receive their sustenance from "the portion of Hashem"; i.e., the portion that the other tribes ought to give Hashem from their possessions, but which Hashem passes on to the Tribe of Levi. See Mitzvah 342 with note 27.

[There is an allusion to *Rambam's* approach in the verse of our mitzvah. After stating that *There shall not be for the Kohanim, the Leviim ... a share and an inheritance with Israel* (referring to both prohibitions), the verse concludes, *the fire-offerings of HASHEM and His inheritance they shall eat.*]

13. These words appear in some editions of Sefer HaChinuch (e.g., first edition [Venice]), but without specifying what the laws are. Other editions omit this section altogether (Brunn ed., *Minchas Yitzchak* ed., and others). See previous mitzvah, at note 8.

The laws of this mitzvah are codified by *Rambam* in *Hil. Shemittah VeYovel* 13:10-12.

14. At other times, the Jewish people are not authorized to wage war (see end of Mitzvah 532).

15. This includes the Kohanim; see previous mitzvah, note 9.

וְהָעוֹבֵר עַל זֶה וְנוֹטֵל חֵלֶק מִן הַבִּזָּה עוֹבֵר עַל לָאו זֶה, וְאֵין בּוֹ מַלְקוּת לְפִי שֶׁאֶפְשָׁר לַעֲבֹר עָלָיו מִבְּלִי מַעֲשֶׂה[16], וְנִתָּן לְהִשָּׁבוֹן[17].

וְהָעוֹבֵר עַל זֶה – **[A person from the Tribe of Levi] who transgresses this** mitzvah **וְנוֹטֵל חֵלֶק מִן הַבִּזָּה** – **and takes a share of the spoils** **עוֹבֵר עַל לָאו זֶה** – **violates this** mitzvah-**prohibition,** **וְאֵין בּוֹ מַלְקוּת** – **but,** unlike most mitzvah-prohibitions, **there is no *malkus*** (lashes) **for** violating **it,** for two reasons: **לְפִי שֶׁאֶפְשָׁר לַעֲבֹר עָלָיו מִבְּלִי מַעֲשֶׂה** – First, **because it is possible to violate it without action;**[16] **וְנִתָּן לְהִשָּׁבוֹן** – **and** second, because **it is subject to being returned,** i.e., the spoils taken by the Levi can be returned to the nation at large, and the violation is thereby undone.[17]

NOTES

16. There is a general rule that one does not incur *malkus* for transgressing a mitzvah-prohibition in a manner that involves no action (see General Introduction, note 14). Chinuch in many places (e.g., Mitzvah 344) expands this rule, and maintains that one does not incur *malkus* for any prohibition that *can* be violated in a way that involves no action (see Insight to Mitzvah 68). In our case, it is possible for a Levi to *passively* violate the prohibition of taking booty, e.g., if someone were to put the object into the Levi's house, and the Levi would intend to acquire it (*Maayan HaChochmah,* Roedelheim ed., p. 94b). [One can acquire an object from someone else if it is placed within his home. This is one manifestation of what is called *kinyan chatzeir* — "acquisition by way of a courtyard." See *Rambam, Hil. Zechiyah U'Matanah* 4:8).] Therefore, the Levi never incurs *malkus* for violating this prohibition, even if he did commit the transgression with an action (for example, he took from the spoils himself).

17. As a general rule, one does not incur *malkus* for a violation of a mitzvah-prohibition that can be rectified through repayment (see General Introduction ibid.). See, similarly, Mitzvah 83 and Mitzvah 230 (at note 29).

Rambam (*Hil. Shemittah VeYovel* 13:10) rules that a Levi *does* incur *malkus* for taking a share of the spoils. While *Rambam* may well disagree with Chinuch's first reason for an exemption in this case (i.e., *Rambam* holds that one incurs *malkus* for any active violation of a prohibition, even if the prohibition can be violated without an action), it seems unusual that he would ignore the second reason, since he himself rules (in *Hil. Sanhedrin* 18:2) that there is no *malkus* for a prohibition that is subject to repayment! *Mirkeves HaMishneh* (*Hil. Sanhedrin* 19:4, p. 312 in Feldheim ed. ד״ה ועיין לאוין ק״ע) suggests that the spoils are not considered returnable since they were taken from the public rather than from an individual (see *Bava Basra* 35b, and *Derech Emunah* to *Rambam, Hil. Shemittah VeYovel* 13:49). For further discussion, see *R' Y. F. Perla, Sefer HaMitzvos of Rav Saadiah Gaon, Asei* 86-88, Vol. I, p. 311a ד״ה אבל מסוגיא; *Minchas Tzvi* to our mitzvah.

Insight: How Were the Spoils of the Midian War Different?

In note 10 of the previous mitzvah and note 2 of this mitzvah, we cited *Rambam* (*Hil. Shemittah VeYovel* 13:11), who says that the prohibitions upon the Tribe of Levi to receive a territorial portion or a portion in the spoils of war apply only to land in Eretz Yisrael and to spoils taken during wars waged for Eretz Yisrael. However, if a Jewish king wages war or conquers land outside of Eretz Yisrael, the Tribe of Levi is entitled to the spoils and land like all the other tribes. As also indicated there, *Raavad* disagrees with *Rambam*. One of the proofs *Raavad* provides is that in the battle against Midian (*Numbers* Ch. 31), which was not related to the conquest of Eretz Yisrael, the Tribe of Levi did not partake of the spoils like the other tribes. Instead, Hashem instructed that they be given a tribute (one-fiftieth) from the spoils divided among the rest of the nation (ibid. v. 30). Evidently, argues *Raavad,* the Tribe of Levi does not receive an equal share of the spoils even in wars not related to Eretz Yisrael. The tribute that they received in this case was a tithe of sorts, but even that was an exception, mandated specifically for this war by Divine command.

Kesef Mishneh (ad loc.) comes to *Rambam's* defense and turns *Raavad's* proof around. On the contrary, he says, the fact that in the battle against Midian the Leviim received anything at all is a *proof* to *Rambam's* view, since they are otherwise prohibited from taking *any* portion of the spoils, due to our mitzvah! Evidently, the Tribe of Levi was entitled to the spoils because the war took place outside of Eretz Yisrael. The fact that they received only a *small* measure of it was the exception, not that they *received* something at all. Indeed, in other wars waged outside of Eretz Yisrael (i.e., wars

unrelated to the conquest or protection of Eretz Yisrael), they would receive an equal share along with the other tribes.

Kesef Mishneh's approach is supported by *Ramban's* commentary to *Numbers* 31:28, who notes that the Leviim received a share (though a small one) from the spoils of Midian, but not from the war against Sichon and Og (see ibid. 21:21-35). *Ramban* explains that they were granted a portion of the booty from the war of Midian because that war was not part of the conquest of Eretz Yisrael, but rather was waged against the Midianites as retribution for their causing the Israelites to sin (see ibid. Ch. 25). The wars of Sichon and Og, on the other hand, were fought as part of the conquest of Eretz Yisrael. There, the Tribe of Levi did not receive any of the spoils. And even if the other tribes would have offered them a tribute from their own shares, they would have been forbidden to take it due to the prohibition of our mitzvah.

Meshech Chochmah (to ibid. 31:27) suggests that, in fact, the Tribe of Levi received an *equal* share in the spoils of Midian, since, as *Rambam* writes (above), they have the same status as the other tribes with respect to wars fought outside of Eretz Yisrael. Nevertheless, the spoils are shared only by those who serve in the war in some capacity: either in the fighting force, or in administrative or other duties (food, weapon supply, etc.). As such, those from the Tribe of Levi who served in any of those capacities received their share like all other Israelites. The relatively small portion (one-fiftieth) that the Torah instructed to give the Leviim was meant for those who did not serve at all, i.e., those between the ages of 25 and 50, who were charged with serving in the Mishkan and could not actively participate in the war effort. Such people would not receive *any* portion of the spoils if they were non-Leviim. However, since these Leviim fulfilled their duty in the Mishkan service, they were eligible for a tribute.

This brings us to another discussion; namely, whether the Tribe of Levi generally fought in the wars waged by the Jewish people. Regarding the war against Midian, the Torah states (ibid. 31:4): *A thousand from a tribe, a thousand from a tribe, for all the tribes of Israel shall you send to the legion.* *Rashi* (ad loc.) cites *Sifrei* to this verse, which explains the phrase *for all the tribes of Israel* to mean that the Tribe of Levi also sent a thousand of its men to battle (cf. *Gra* to *Sifrei* ad loc.). Accordingly, the Tribe of Levi fought the Midian war like everyone else (at least as far as combat was concerned, see *Meshech Chochmah* above).

The question is: what about other wars? *Rambam* (*Hilchos Shemittah VeYovel* 13:12) writes that the Tribe of Levi does *not* generally wage war along with the rest of Israel. However, there are a number of Biblical and Talmudic sources that seem to indicate that the Tribe of Levi — specifically, Kohanim — did participate in wars as a general rule. [The novelty with regard to Kohanim specifically is that, in addition to being from the Tribe of Levi, which might in itself exempt them from service, Kohanim are prohibited from coming into contact with a dead body (Mitzvah 263). Naturally, being on the battlefield, and particularly engaging in close combat, places a person at risk of doing so. For discussion of why this may not be an issue, see sources cited in *Teshuvos Beis David* §71.]

Scripture indicates in several places that Kohanim participated in wars, some even ranking among the prominent warriors of King David and King Solomon (see *Derech Emunah, Beur HaHalachah, Hil. Shemittah VeYovel* 13:12 ד"ה לא עורכין מלחמה). And the Talmud also indicates this. For example, in *Kiddushin* 21b, the Gemara debates whether a Kohen may take a *yefas toar* (a captive woman) as a wife (see Mitzvah 532). This is relevant only if Kohanim participated in wars, since the Torah permits taking a *yefas toar* only in the course of fighting a war (see *Rashi, Sanhedrin* 59a ד"ה לאו בני). How, then, does *Rambam* rule that the Tribe of Levi does not engage in warfare like the rest of Israel when all these sources indicate otherwise?

There are several approaches to explaining *Rambam*, one of which is the following: *Beur Ha-Halachah* (ibid.) suggests that *Rambam* means to say that the members of the Tribe of Levi were not *drafted* for war like the rest of Israel (other than for the war of Midian), since this would be disrespectful of their role as spiritual leaders of the nation. However, they were allowed to volunteer to go out to war (see also *Birkei Yosef, Even HaEzer* 6:6). For other possible approaches and further discussion, see *Mishnas Yaavetz, Hil. Shemittah VeYovel* 13:12, and *Teshuvos Divrei Shlomo* (Schneider), Vol. 1 §36; see also *Teshuvos Beis David* ibid.

מִצְוָה תקו: מִצְוַת מַתְּנוֹת זְרוֹעַ לְחָיַיִם וְקֵבָה לַכֹּהֵן[1]

שֶׁנִּצְטַוּוּ יִשְׂרָאֵל לָתֵת הַזְּרוֹעַ וְהַלְּחָיַיִם וְהַקֵּבָה מִכָּל בְּהֵמָה טְהוֹרָה שֶׁנִּזְבַּח לַכֹּהֵן, וְעַל זֶה נֶאֱמַר (דברים י״ח, ג׳) וְזֶה יִהְיֶה מִשְׁפַּט הַכֹּהֲנִים מֵאֵת הָעָם מֵאֵת זֹבְחֵי הַזֶּבַח אִם שׁוֹר אִם שֶׂה וְנָתַן לַכֹּהֵן הַזְּרֹעַ וְהַלְּחָיַיִם וְהַקֵּבָה.

כְּבָר אָמְרוּ זִכְרוֹנָם לִבְרָכָה (חולין קל״ד ע״ב) בְּטַעַם מִצְוָה זוֹ, כִּי בִּזְכוּת פִּנְחָס אֲבִיהֶם שֶׁקִּנֵּא לֵאלֹהָיו עַל דְּבַר כָּזְבִּי וּמָסַר נַפְשׁוֹ לַהֲרֹג נְשִׂיא שֵׁבֶט מִיִּשְׂרָאֵל עַל קְדֻשַּׁת הַשֵּׁם[2]

Mitzvah 506

The Obligation to Give the Foreleg, the Jaw, and the Stomach [of an Animal] to a Kohen

וְזֶה יִהְיֶה מִשְׁפַּט הַכֹּהֲנִים מֵאֵת הָעָם מֵאֵת זֹבְחֵי הַזֶּבַח אִם שׁוֹר אִם שֶׂה וְנָתַן לַכֹּהֵן הַזְּרֹעַ וְהַלְּחָיַיִם וְהַקֵּבָה

This shall be the due of the Kohanim from the people, from those who perform a slaughter, whether of an ox, or whether of the flock: He shall give the Kohen the foreleg, the jaw, and the stomach (*Deuteronomy* 18:3).

This is the first in a series of three mitzvos setting out three of the twenty-four gifts that the Torah grants the Kohanim (see *Rambam, Hil. Bikkurim* 1:1-8 for a list of all twenty-four gifts). In this mitzvah, the Torah requires that one who slaughters an animal give the foreleg, the jaw, and the stomach to a Kohen.[1] Collectively, these gifts are often referred to simply as *matanos* (*gifts*).

Unlike *terumah* (Mitzvah 507), the *matanos* portions themselves have no inherent sanctity. Rather, this mitzvah places a monetary obligation upon the owner of the animal to give these portions to the Kohen. This fact has a number of ramifications that will be discussed throughout the mitzvah.

שֶׁנִּצְטַוּוּ יִשְׂרָאֵל לָתֵת הַזְּרוֹעַ וְהַלְּחָיַיִם וְהַקֵּבָה מִכָּל בְּהֵמָה טְהוֹרָה שֶׁנִּזְבַּח לַכֹּהֵן – The Jewish people are commanded to give to a Kohen the foreleg, the jaw, and the stomach of any kosher domestic animal that we slaughter. **וְעַל זֶה נֶאֱמַר – Regarding this it is stated** (*Deuteronomy* 18:3): **"וְזֶה יִהְיֶה מִשְׁפַּט הַכֹּהֲנִים מֵאֵת הָעָם מֵאֵת זֹבְחֵי הַזֶּבַח אִם שׁוֹר אִם שֶׂה – *This shall be the due of the Kohanim from the people, from those who perform a slaughter, whether of an ox, or whether of the flock:*** **וְנָתַן לַכֹּהֵן הַזְּרֹעַ וְהַלְּחָיַיִם וְהַקֵּבָה" – *He shall give the Kohen the foreleg, the jaw, and the stomach.***

Underlying Purpose of the Mitzvah

כְּבָר אָמְרוּ זִכְרוֹנָם לִבְרָכָה בְּטַעַם מִצְוָה זוֹ – [The Sages], of blessed memory, have already stated (*Chullin* 134b) **in** expounding **the reason for this mitzvah,** **כִּי בִּזְכוּת פִּנְחָס אֲבִיהֶם – that** it is **in the merit of Pinchas, [the Kohanim's] forefather,** **שֶׁקִּנֵּא לֵאלֹהָיו עַל דְּבַר כָּזְבִּי – who,** when the Jewish people were in the Wilderness, **avenged** the honor of **his God in the incident of Cozbi,** the Midianite woman, whom the leader of the tribe of Shimon took publicly in an act of defiance; **וּמָסַר נַפְשׁוֹ לַהֲרֹג נְשִׂיא שֵׁבֶט מִיִּשְׂרָאֵל עַל קְדֻשַּׁת הַשֵּׁם – and [Pinchas] risked his life to kill the leader of a tribe of Israel** in full view of all of the people, despite the risk that they would avenge their leader's death, **as** an act of **sanctification of the Name** of Hashem.[2]

NOTES

1. The קֵבָה, which we have translated colloquially as "stomach," technically refers to the abomasum, the fourth compartment of the stomach of a ruminant animal, where digestion takes place. Chinuch will define the exact parameters of the other portions below.

2. The Torah relates (*Numbers* 25:1-8) that as the Jewish people approached Moab, the Moabites and their Midianite neighbors sent out their women to seduce

זָכוּ בָּנָיו הַכֹּהֲנִים לְעוֹלָם בְּמַתָּנָה זוֹ מֵאֵת הָאֵל[3]**, הַזְּרוֹעַ, כְּנֶגֶד וַיִּקַּח רֹמַח** (במדבר כ״ה, ז׳)**, הַלְּחָיַיִם, בִּזְכוּת שֶׁנִּתְפַּלֵּל עַל צַעֲרָן שֶׁל יִשְׂרָאֵל כְּמוֹ שֶׁכָּתוּב** (תהלים ק״ו, ל׳) **וַיַּעֲמֹד פִּינְחָס וַיְפַלֵּל**[4]**, וְהַקֵּבָה, כְּנֶגֶד וְאֶת הָאִשָּׁה אֶל קֳבָתָהּ** (במדבר כ״ה, ח׳)**. וְלָמַדְנוּ מִזֶּה שֶׁהַמְקַדֵּשׁ שֵׁם שָׁמַיִם בְּגָלוּי זוֹכֶה לוֹ וּלְדוֹרוֹתָיו בָּעוֹלָם הַזֶּה, מִלְּבַד זְכוּתוֹ שֶׁקַּיֶּמֶת לְנַפְשׁוֹ בָּעוֹלָם הַבָּא**[5]**.**

זָכוּ בָּנָיו הַכֹּהֲנִים לְעוֹלָם בְּמַתָּנָה זוֹ מֵאֵת הָאֵל – In this merit, **his offspring, the Kohanim, were granted this gift forever from the Almighty:**[3] **הַזְּרוֹעַ כְּנֶגֶד "וַיִּקַּח רֹמַח"** – **The foreleg** of the animal that is given to the Kohanim **corresponds to** the hand of Pinchas, which he used to slay the sinners, as Scripture states: ***And he took a spear** in his hand* (*Numbers* 25:7); **הַלְּחָיַיִם בִּזְכוּת שֶׁנִּתְפַּלֵּל עַל צַעֲרָן שֶׁל יִשְׂרָאֵל** – **the jaw,** alluding to the action of the mouth, is given **in the merit of his having prayed over the distress of the Jewish people,** who were being decimated by a plague, **כְּמוֹ שֶׁכָּתוּב "וַיַּעֲמֹד פִּינְחָס וַיְפַלֵּל"** – **as it is written** (*Psalms* 106:30): ***And Pinchas stood and prayed,** and the plague was halted;*[4] **וְהַקֵּבָה כְּנֶגֶד "וְאֶת הָאִשָּׁה אֶל קֳבָתָהּ"** – **and the stomach** that is given as part of the *matanos* **corresponds to** that which is described in the verse (*Numbers* 25:8): *He [Pinchas] followed the Israelite man into the tent and pierced them both, the Israelite man,* ***and the woman into her stomach.***

וְלָמַדְנוּ מִזֶּה – **We learn from this** reward that was given as a result of Pinchas's action **שֶׁהַמְקַדֵּשׁ שֵׁם שָׁמַיִם בְּגָלוּי זוֹכֶה לוֹ וּלְדוֹרוֹתָיו בָּעוֹלָם הַזֶּה** – **that one who publicly sanctifies the Name of Heaven achieves merit for himself and for his** future **generations in this world, מִלְּבַד זְכוּתוֹ שֶׁקַּיֶּמֶת לְנַפְשׁוֹ בָּעוֹלָם הַבָּא** – **aside from his merit that is reserved for his soul in the World to Come.**[5]

Laws of the Mitzvah

Chinuch sets out a detailed description of the foreleg and jaw of the *matanos* obligation:

NOTES

Jewish men for the purpose of subsequently luring them to idol worship. Many of the Jewish men indeed fell prey to these sins and Hashem punished Israel with a plague that took the lives of thousands. During this event, Zimri, the head of the tribe of Shimon, committed a public act of defiance, taking a Midianite woman in full view of Moses and the people. Pinchas arose and stabbed Zimri and the Midianite woman, Cozbi, killing them both, whereupon the plague immediately ceased.

3. When Aaron and his sons were anointed as Kohanim, they acquired the status of Kohanim for themselves and all children born after that point. Pinchas was already alive at that time but was not anointed, and therefore, although he was a grandson of Aaron, he and his subsequent children did not have the status of Kehunah. After Pinchas's heroic deed, however, Hashem granted him the Kehunah, for him and his children (*Zevachim* 101b).

Chinuch explains here that with this action Pinchas not only attained the status of Kohen for himself, but also brought to all Kohanim this special gift of the *matanos* (see *Ramban*, *Deuteronomy* 18:3). [Chinuch here refers to Pinchas as "their father" and the Kohanim as "his offspring" although he was the head of only one of the Kohanic families. Apparently Chinuch uses this term in the borrowed sense, reflecting the fact that Pinchas was among the most prominent of the earliest generations of Kohanim.]

4. The verse's plain meaning is that Pinchas exacted judgment (see *Ibn Ezra* and *Radak* ad loc.). However, in light of the similarity between וַיְפַלֵּל and וַיִּתְפַּלֵּל (*he prayed*), the Gemara interprets the verse as alluding also to the fact that Pinchas prayed, as indeed *Targum* renders the verse there.

5. This reason for the mitzvah is cited in the Gemara in the name of דּוֹרְשֵׁי חֲמוּרוֹת, *those who expound concealed verses* (see *Rashi* there). In Mitzvah 508 (at note 10), Chinuch follows a more basic approach, noting that the *matanos* provide the Kohanim with meat in addition to the basic staples provided for them by the *terumah*.

Other Rishonim suggest additional reasons for this mitzvah. *Ibn Ezra* (to the verse) writes that these parts are the choicest portions of the animal. *Rambam* (*Moreh Nevuchim* 3:39, cited in *Ramban* to the verse) writes that each of those portions is considered the "first" part of each section of the animal (the jaw is the first part of the body that one encounters, the foreleg is the first of the limbs of the animal, and the stomach is the first of the innards). And it is proper that the first of each thing be given to the servants of Hashem, the Kohanim. [Likewise, the following two mitzvos of Kohanic gifts refer to "first" portions; *terumah* is described as the first of the crops and *reishis hageiz* is the first of the fleece.]

מִדִּינֵי הַמִּצְוָה מַה שֶּׁאָמְרוּ זִכְרוֹנָם לִבְרָכָה (שם), אֵיזֶהוּ זְרוֹעַ, זֶה זְרוֹעַ יָמִין מִפֶּרֶק הָאַרְכֻּבָּה עַד כַּף שֶׁל יָד[6] שֶׁהֵן שְׁנֵי אֵבָרִים זֶה מְעֹרֶה בָּזֶה[7]. וְהַלְּחָיַיִם מִן הַפֶּרֶק שֶׁל לֶחִי עַד פִּיקָה שֶׁל גַּרְגֶּרֶת שֶׁהִיא טַבַּעַת גְּדוֹלָה[8] עִם הַלָּשׁוֹן שֶׁבֵּינֵיהֶם,

---

מִדִּינֵי הַמִּצְוָה מַה שֶּׁאָמְרוּ זִכְרוֹנָם לִבְרָכָה – Among the laws of the mitzvah is **that which [the Sages], of blessed memory, stated** (*Rambam, Hil. Bikkurim* 9:18; *Chullin* ibid.): **אֵיזֶהוּ זְרוֹעַ – What is** considered **the "foreleg"** with regard to this mitzvah? **זֶה זְרוֹעַ יָמִין מִפֶּרֶק הָאַרְכֻּבָּה עַד כַּף שֶׁל יָד – It is the right foreleg, from the joint of the lower leg,** up **until the shoulder blade,**[6] **שֶׁהֵן שְׁנֵי אֵבָרִים זֶה מְעֹרֶה בָּזֶה – which consist of** the **two** upper **limbs** of the leg that are **connected to each other.**[7] **וְהַלְּחָיַיִם מִן הַפֶּרֶק שֶׁל לֶחִי עַד פִּיקָה שֶׁל גַּרְגֶּרֶת – The "jaw"** refers to the portion that extends **from the joint of the jaw** down **to the opening of the trachea, שֶׁהִיא טַבַּעַת גְּדוֹלָה – which is "the great ring"** (cricoid cartilage),[8] **עִם הַלָּשׁוֹן שֶׁבֵּינֵיהֶם – including the tongue**

NOTES

6. Literally, *the spoon of the arm.* This describes the shoulder blade, because the socket of the shoulder blade is like a spoon into which the arm (i.e., foreleg) fits; see following note.

7. An animal's foreleg comprises three main sections: lower [metacarpus], middle [radius], and upper [humerus]. The Kohen's portion consists of the two upper sections of the leg: the middle bone [radius] and the upper bone [humerus]. It begins from the joint of the lower leg [carpus], and continues upward until the top of the upper leg, the shoulder blade. See Diagram below.

8. The back of the mouth cavity of the animal leads into the trachea. The trachea is encircled by many successive almost-complete rings of cartilage, with a thicker, complete ring at its top. This topmost ring is referred to in halachah as "the great ring." [The ring itself is not part of the Kohen's portion; the portion begins above this, at a point on the thyroid cartilage; see *Derech Emunah, Hil. Bikkurim* 9:156.] See Diagram.

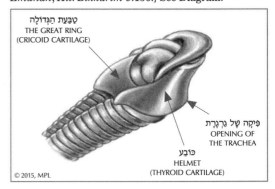

טַבַּעַת הַגְּדוֹלָה
THE GREAT RING
(CRICOID CARTILAGE)
פִּיקָה שֶׁל גַּרְגֶּרֶת
OPENING OF
THE TRACHEA
כּוֹבַע
HELMET
(THYROID CARTILAGE)
© 2015, MPL

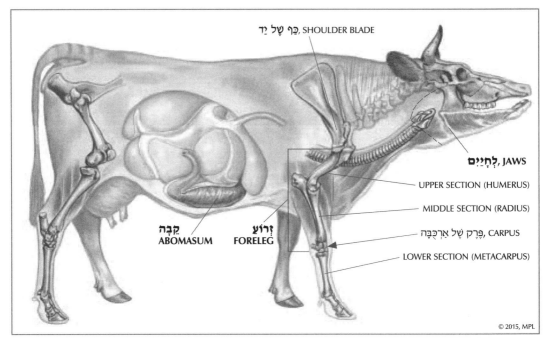

כַּף שֶׁל יָד, SHOULDER BLADE
לְחָיַיִם, JAWS
UPPER SECTION (HUMERUS)
MIDDLE SECTION (RADIUS)
פֶּרֶק שֶׁל אַרְכֻּבָּה, CARPUS
LOWER SECTION (METACARPUS)
קֵבָה
ABOMASUM
זְרוֹעַ
FORELEG
© 2015, MPL

וְהַקֵּבָה נוֹתְנִין אוֹתָהּ לַכֹּהֵן עִם חֵלֶב שֶׁבָּהּ, וּכְבָר נָהֲגוּ הַכֹּהֲנִים לְהָנִיחַ חֵלֶב הַקֵּבָה לַבְּעָלִים[9]. וְכֵן מַה שֶּׁאָמְרוּ (רמב״ם פ״ט מהל׳ ביכורים ה״ה) שֶׁאֵין חִיּוּב הַמַּתָּנוֹת אֶלָּא בִּבְהֵמָה טְהוֹרָה וְלֹא בְחַיָּה שֶׁנֶּאֱמַר אִם שׁוֹר אִם שֶׂה, וּבִכְלַל הַשֶּׂה וּמִינוֹ הַתַּיִשׁ[10].

וְעוֹד דָּרְשׁוּ זִכְרוֹנָם לִבְרָכָה (חולין קלב ע״א), אִם שׁוֹר[11], לְרַבּוֹת הַכּוֹי, וַאֲפִלּוּ לְמַאן דְּאָמַר בְּרִיָּה בִּפְנֵי עַצְמָהּ הִיא[12], אִם שֶׂה, לְרַבּוֹת הַכִּלְאַיִם, כְּגוֹן וָלָד הַבָּא מֵעֵז וָכֶבֶשׂ. וְאִם בָּא מִצְּבִי

---

between [these two points]. וְהַקֵּבָה נוֹתְנִין אוֹתָהּ לַכֹּהֵן עִם חֵלֶב שֶׁבָּהּ – **The stomach** (abomasum) **is given to the Kohen with the fat upon it,** וּכְבָר נָהֲגוּ הַכֹּהֲנִים לְהָנִיחַ חֵלֶב הַקֵּבָה לַבְּעָלִים – **but the Kohanim have already adopted the practice of leaving the fat of the stomach for the owner.**[9]

Chinuch sets out which animals are subject to this mitzvah:

וְכֵן מַה שֶּׁאָמְרוּ – **Also** included in the laws of the mitzvah is **that which [the Sages] stated** (*Rambam* ibid. 9:5), שֶׁאֵין חִיּוּב הַמַּתָּנוֹת אֶלָּא בִּבְהֵמָה טְהוֹרָה וְלֹא בְחַיָּה – **that the obligation of *matanos* applies only to kosher domestic animals, and not to nondomestic animals,** שֶׁנֶּאֱמַר ״אִם שׁוֹר אִם שֶׂה״ – **as it is stated** in the verse of this mitzvah: *This shall be the due of the Kohanim from the people, from those who perform a slaughter, **whether of an ox or whether of the flock.*** וּבִכְלַל הַשֶּׂה וּמִינוֹ הַתַּיִשׁ – **"The flock,"** mentioned in this verse refers not only to sheep **and its species** but **includes goats** as well. That is, the term "flock" includes all species of sheep and goats (that are domesticated). The Torah thus applies the mitzvah clearly to all the species of kosher domestic animals and to no others.[10]

Chinuch sets out the law of *matanos* as it pertains to animals of mixed parentage or unclear status. Chinuch begins this discussion with the status of an animal called the *koy*. The exact meaning of the term "*koy*" is disputed in the Gemara (*Chullin* 80a). Some maintain that it refers to a certain kind of mixed breed, while others maintain that it is a certain natural species of kosher animal whose classification as a "domestic" or "nondomestic" animal is in question. In this discussion, Chinuch first sets out the law of the *koy* according to the opinion that it refers to a specific natural species, and then explains how the *matanos* obligation pertains to mixed breeds:

וְעוֹד דָּרְשׁוּ זִכְרוֹנָם לִבְרָכָה – **[The Sages], of blessed memory, further expounded** the verse as follows (*Chullin* 132a): ״אִם שׁוֹר״ – The extra phrase, "*whether of*" in the verse ***whether of an ox,***[11] לְרַבּוֹת הַכּוֹי – comes **to include a *koy*;** we thus learn that one who slaughters a *koy* is obligated to give the *matanos* to a Kohen, וַאֲפִלּוּ לְמַאן דְּאָמַר בְּרִיָּה בִּפְנֵי עַצְמָהּ הִיא – **even according to the one who** says **that [a *koy*] is its own species.**[12] ״אִם שֶׂה״ לְרַבּוֹת הַכִּלְאַיִם – The extra phrase, "*whether of*" in the verse ***whether of the flock*** comes **to include a crossbreed,** כְּגוֹן וָלָד הַבָּא מֵעֵז וָכֶבֶשׂ – **such as the offspring of a goat and a sheep.** Both the goat and the sheep are subject to this mitzvah; this verse teaches that a mixed breed of these species is likewise subject to the mitzvah. וְאִם בָּא מִצְּבִי

NOTES

9. This fat is prohibited for consumption, as it is *cheilev* (see Mitzvah 147, at note 28). It can, however, be used for any purpose other than eating; for example, it may be fed to animals or sold to non-Jews (*Derech Emunah* ibid. 9:162).

Chinuch's observation that the Kohanim commonly leave the fat for the owner is cited directly from *Rambam* (*Hil Bikkurim* 9:19), and implies that this is the universal practice of Kohanim. *Shulchan Aruch* (61:4) indicates, however, that the custom in this matter varies from place to place (see *Taz* §7, ad loc.). For discussion, see *Beur HaHalachah* (of *Derech Emunah*) to *Rambam* ibid. ד״ה וכבר.

10. Oxen, sheep, and goats, are the only domestic animals that are kosher. This includes both the primary species as well as all related subspecies. For example, the category of "ox" includes all breeds of cattle (see *Rambam, Hil. Maachalos Asuros* 1:8).

11. The verse could have stated simply, *from those who perform a slaughter, of an ox or the flock.* The words אִם, *whether of,* in each phrase is apparently superfluous.

12. As stated earlier, one is obligated to give *matanos* only when slaughtering a domestic animal (*beheimah*), not a nondomestic animal (*chayah*). Now, with regard to other mitzvos the Sages were unsure how to classify the species of *koy*, i.e., whether as a domestic or nondomestic animal. The extra phrase in this verse is expounded to specifically include the species of *koy* as being subject to this mitzvah.

וְתִיָּשָׁה חַיָּב בַּחֲצִי מַתָּנוֹת לְבַד[13], מִשּׁוּם דִּכְתִיב אִם שֶׂה, וְדָרְשׁוּ זִכְרוֹנָם לִבְרָכָה (שם) אֲפִלּוּ
מִקְצָת שֶׂה[14], אֲבָל תַּיִשׁ הַבָּא עַל הַצְּבִיָּה אֵין הַוָּלָד חַיָּב בְּמַתָּנוֹת כְּלָל, מִשּׁוּם דִּמְסַפְּקָא לְהוּ
לְרַבָּנַן אִי חוֹשְׁשִׁין לְזֶרַע הָאָב אִי לָאו[15], וְכֵיוָן שֶׁכֵּן יֵשׁ לוֹ לְיִשְׂרָאֵל לוֹמַר לַכֹּהֵן הָבֵא רְאָיָה
דְּחוֹשְׁשִׁין לְזֶרַע הָאָב וְאֶתֵּן לְךָ חֲצִי הַמַּתָּנוֹת, וְאֵינוֹ יָכוֹל[16]. וּלְפִיכָךְ יֵשׁ לִי לִכְתֹּב דְּבַתַּיִשׁ
הַבָּא עַל הַצְּבִיָּה אֵין בָּהּ חִיּוּב מַתָּנוֹת כְּלָל[17]. כְּבָר כָּתַבְתִּי דַּעַת רַבֵּנוּ אַלְפָסִי זִכְרוֹנוֹ לִבְרָכָה

וְתִיָּשָׁה — **However, if it is an offspring of a male deer,** which is *not* subject to this mitzvah, **and a female goat,** which *is* subject to the mitzvah, — חַיָּב בַּחֲצִי מַתָּנוֹת לְבַד — then **one is obligated** to give a Kohen **only half of the *matanos*** from this offspring.[13] מִשּׁוּם דִּכְתִיב "אִם שֶׂה" — Even if this animal is only "half-goat," it is still subject to this mitzvah, **for it is written** *and whether of the flock,* וְדָרְשׁוּ זִכְרוֹנָם לִבְרָכָה אֲפִלּוּ מִקְצָת שֶׂה — **and [the Sages],** of blessed memory, **expounded** (*Chullin* ibid.) that **even** an animal that is only partly **"of the flock,"** i.e., it is part sheep or part goat, is also subject to the mitzvah.[14] אֲבָל תַּיִשׁ הַבָּא עַל הַצְּבִיָּה אֵין הַוָּלָד חַיָּב בְּמַתָּנוֹת כְּלָל — **However, if a male goat mated with a female deer, the offspring is not subject to the obligation of *matanos* at all.** מִשּׁוּם דִּמְסַפְּקָא לְהוּ לְרַבָּנַן אִי חוֹשְׁשִׁין לְזֶרַע הָאָב אִי לָאו — This is **because the Sages are unsure whether we concern ourselves with the seed of the father** in determining the offspring's identity **or not.** Since the mother is exempt (as she is a deer), and the father's status may not affect the identity of the offspring, we remain unsure whether there is any part of this animal that is subject to this mitzvah.[15] וְכֵיוָן שֶׁכֵּן — **And since it is so,** that even the partial obligation is in this case a matter of doubt, יֵשׁ לוֹ לְיִשְׂרָאֵל לוֹמַר לַכֹּהֵן הָבֵא רְאָיָה דְּחוֹשְׁשִׁין לְזֶרַע הָאָב — **the Yisrael** (non-Kohen) **can tell the Kohen** who requests the *matanos* of this animal, **"Bring a proof that we are concerned with the seed of the father** וְאֶתֵּן לְךָ חֲצִי הַמַּתָּנוֹת — and then **I will give you half of the *matanos*."** וְאֵינוֹ יָכוֹל — **And [the Kohen],** of course, **cannot** bring such a proof, since even the Sages remain unsure about this.[16] וּלְפִיכָךְ יֵשׁ לִי לִכְתֹּב דְּבַתַּיִשׁ הַבָּא עַל הַצְּבִיָּה אֵין בָּהּ חִיּוּב מַתָּנוֹת כְּלָל — **Therefore, it is appropriate for me to write that in a case of a male goat that mates with a female deer, there is no obligation to give *matanos* at all.**[17] כְּבָר כָּתַבְתִּי דַּעַת רַבֵּנוּ אַלְפָסִי זִכְרוֹנוֹ לִבְרָכָה

NOTES

13. This animal, by virtue of its goat mother, is considered at least "half-goat," and the owner is therefore obligated to give half of the *matanos*. See below, notes 15-18, for discussion of the father's influence on the status of this offspring.

14. That is, the Sages understood that when the verse described the animals that are included in this obligation, i.e., ox, sheep, or goat, it refers even to animals that are only partially identified as such. Thus, even a "part-goat" is subject to this mitzvah. Nevertheless, it is subject to the obligation only in proportion to its identity as one of the obligated animals. Therefore, if an animal is considered "half-goat," the owner is obligated to give half of the *matanos* to the Kohen. [This formula carries to future generations as well: if an animal that is considered a "half-goat" breeds with a full goat, the offspring is subject to at most three-quarters of the *matanos* (*Minchas Chinuch* §6).]

15. The mother's identity always affects that of the offspring. The Sages were unsure, however, whether the father's identity equally affects the halachic status of the offspring or not. If it does, this animal is half-deer by its mother and half-goat by its father, and would therefore be subject to the obligation of half of the *matanos*. If the father's identity does not affect the

halachic status of the offspring, then the offspring is halachically considered a full deer, and as such would be completely exempt from *matanos*.

16. As noted in the introduction to the mitzvah, *matanos* have no inherent sanctity (like *terumah* does), but are simply a monetary obligation upon the Yisrael to the Kohen. The doubtful status of the animal is therefore governed by the general principle that applies to questions of monetary liability: הַמּוֹצִיא מֵחֲבֵרוֹ עָלָיו הָרְאָיָה, *the one seeking to exact property from his fellow bears the burden of proof.* See following note.

17. Since in this case the Kohen cannot prove that the Yisrael has any obligation to him at all, as the status of this animal remains a matter of doubt, the Yisrael is completely exempt from giving the *matanos*.

With regard to the previous case, the offspring of a male deer and a female goat, there is, at the least, a clear part-obligation by virtue of the mother's identity, since, as noted, the mother's identity is certainly taken into account. Now, if we do not take the father's identity into account in determining the status of the animal, the offspring would be halachically considered a full goat by virtue of its mother and the owner would be obligated to give all of the *matanos* to the Kohen. If, on the other hand, we do take the father's identity into

וּמְפָרְשִׁים אֲחֵרִים בְּעִנְיַן חֲשַׁשׁ זֶרַע הָאָב בְּסֵדֶר קְדֹשִׁים תִּהְיוּ לָאו כ״ה בְּסִימָן רמ״ט (מצוה רמ״ד)[18]. **וְכֵן מֵעִנְיַן הַמִּצְוָה מַה שֶּׁאָמְרוּ זִכְרוֹנָם לִבְרָכָה** (רמב״ם שם הי״ד) **שֶׁמֻּתָּר לֶאֱכֹל מִן הַבְּהֵמָה עַד שֶׁלֹּא הוּרְמוּ מִמֶּנָּה הַמַּתָּנוֹת, שֶׁאֵין הֲלָכָה כְּרַבִּי יוֹחָנָן שֶׁאָמַר שֶׁהָאוֹכֵל מִמֶּנָּה קֹדֶם שֶׁהוּרְמוּ מַתְּנוֹתֶיהָ כְּאִלּוּ אוֹכֵל טְבָלִים, כִּי מְפֹרָשׁוֹת וּמְיֻחָדוֹת הֵן בְּמָקוֹם אֶחָד וּמִפְּנֵי כֵן אֵינָן טוֹבְלוֹת**[19]. **וְיֶתֶר פְּרָטֶיהָ בְּמַסֶּכֶת חֻלִּין בְּפֶרֶק הַזְּרוֹעַ הַמְיֻחָד בְּדִינֵי מִצְוָה זוֹ**[20].

וְנוֹהֶגֶת מִצְוָה זוֹ בִּבְהֵמוֹת שֶׁל חֻלִּין אֲבָל לֹא בְּשֶׁל מֻקְדָּשִׁין[21].

וּמְפָרְשִׁים אֲחֵרִים — I have already written the opinion of our Master, ***R' Yitzchak*** **Alfasi** (*Rif*), **of blessed memory, as well as** that of **other commentators,** **בְּעִנְיַן חֲשַׁשׁ זֶרַע הָאָב — with regard to** the issue of whether we **concern** ourselves **with the seed of the father,** **בְּסֵדֶר קְדֹשִׁים תִּהְיוּ לָאו כ״ה בְּסִימָן רמ״ט — in** ***Parashas Kedoshim*****, Mitzvah-prohibition 25, Chapter 249** of this work (Mitzvah 244).[18]

Before the required agricultural gifts (such as *terumah* and *maaser*) are separated from one's produce, the produce is forbidden as *tevel* (untithed produce; Mitzvah 284). Chinuch discusses whether the *tevel* prohibition applies to the *matanos* of this mitzvah:

וְכֵן מֵעִנְיַן הַמִּצְוָה מַה שֶּׁאָמְרוּ זִכְרוֹנָם לִבְרָכָה — Also pertinent to this mitzvah is **that which [the Sages], of blessed memory, stated** (*Rambam* ibid. 9:14), **שֶׁמֻּתָּר לֶאֱכֹל מִן הַבְּהֵמָה עַד שֶׁלֹּא הוּרְמוּ מִמֶּנָּה הַמַּתָּנוֹת — that it is permitted to eat from the** meat of an **animal** even **before its** ***matanos*** portions **were separated,** **שֶׁאֵין הֲלָכָה כְּרַבִּי יוֹחָנָן שֶׁאָמַר שֶׁהָאוֹכֵל מִמֶּנָּה קֹדֶם שֶׁהוּרְמוּ מַתְּנוֹתֶיהָ כְּאִלּוּ אוֹכֵל טְבָלִים — for the law does not follow R' Yochanan** (*Chullin* 132b), **who says that if one eats** the meat **of [the animal] before its** ***matanos*** **are separated, it is as if he is eating** ***tevel*****.** **כִּי מְפֹרָשׁוֹת וּמְיֻחָדוֹת הֵן בְּמָקוֹם אֶחָד —** The reason that it is different from untithed produce is **because [these portions of the animal] are separate and set apart in one place,** i.e., the foreleg, jaw, and stomach are clearly distinguishable from the rest of the animal, **וּמִפְּנֵי כֵן אֵינָן טוֹבְלוֹת — and, therefore, they do not render** the rest of the animal ***tevel*****.** The tithes of produce, by contrast, are indistinguishable from the rest of the produce until they are separated and designated as tithes; therefore, until they are separated, they render all of the produce *tevel*.[19]

וְיֶתֶר פְּרָטֶיהָ בְּמַסֶּכֶת חֻלִּין — These laws, **and the remaining the details of [the mitzvah],** appear **in Tractate** ***Chullin*****,** **בְּפֶרֶק הַזְּרוֹעַ הַמְיֻחָד בְּדִינֵי מִצְוָה זוֹ — in Chapter** ***Hazero'a*****,** the chapter **that is dedicated to the laws of this mitzvah.**[20]

Applicability of the Mitzvah

וְנוֹהֶגֶת מִצְוָה זוֹ בִּבְהֵמוֹת שֶׁל חֻלִּין אֲבָל לֹא בְּשֶׁל מֻקְדָּשִׁין — This mitzvah applies to unconsecrated animals, but not to [animals] consecrated as offerings.[21]

NOTES

account, the animal would be half-goat and half-deer, and the owner would be obligated to give half of the *matanos*. Since it is a monetary obligation, we can obligate the owner to give only the portion about which there is a clear obligation. Chinuch therefore writes in the previous case that the owner is obligated to give no more than half of the *matanos* to the Kohen.

18. [Regarding Chinuch's system of numbering the mitzvos, see Mitzvah 494 note 4.] The question of whether we concern ourselves with the father's seed is one that is debated in the Gemara at length (see, for example, *Chullin* 79a-80a). The Rishonim disagree as to the practical halachah with regard to this question. In this mitzvah, Chinuch follows the opinion that halachically, we must treat this question as a matter of standing doubt. In Mitzvah 244, however, Chinuch cites *Rif*, who maintains that the practical halachah follows the opinion that we do *not* take the father's identity into account at all. Accordingly, in this case, the law would be simple: If the mother is a goat, one gives *matanos*, and if the mother is a deer, one does not.

The opinion of Chinuch reflects that of *Rambam* (ibid. 9:5) and is followed by *Shulchan Aruch* (*Yoreh Deah* 61:18).

19. Nevertheless, it is still a mitzvah to separate *matanos* immediately after slaughtering the animal (see *Shulchan Aruch*, *Yoreh Deah* 61:5).

20. The laws of this mitzvah are codified in *Rambam, Hil. Bikkurim* Ch. 9, and *Shulchan Aruch, Yoreh Deah* §61.

21. It also applies only to animals that have been

וּבִזְכָרִים וּנְקֵבוֹת יִשְׂרְאֵלִים אֲבָל לֹא בְּכֹהֲנִים מִשּׁוּם דִּכְתִיב בְּהוּ מִשְׁפַּט הַכֹּהֲנִים מֵאֵת הָעָם, מִכְּלַל שֶׁאֵינָן בְּכֹהֲנִים, וְעוֹד דְּכֹהֲנִים לָא אִיקְרוּ עַם, וּכְמוֹ שֶׁכָּתוּב וְעַל הַכֹּהֲנִים וְעַל כָּל עַם הַקָּהָל יְכַפֵּר[22]. וְהַלְוִיִּם יֵשׁ בָּהֶם בְּעִנְיָן זֶה דִּין מְיֻחָד, שֶׁאֵין[23] הַכֹּהֲנִים נוֹטְלִים מֵהֶן הַמַּתָּנוֹת, לְפִי שֶׁנִּסְתַּפֵּק לְרַבּוֹתֵינוּ אִם נִקְרְאוּ עַם אִם לֹא, וּלְפִיכָךְ אֵין כֹּחַ בְּיָדָם לִטֹּל מֵהֶם מִסָּפֵק[24], וְאִם נָטְלוּ לֹא יַחֲזִירוּ[25].

וּלְעִנְיָן אִם נוֹהֲגוֹת עַכְשָׁו בַּזְּמַן הַזֶּה אִם לֹא[26], כְּבָר חָלְקוּ עַל זֶה הַרְבֵּה מִגְּדוֹלֵי הַמְפָרְשִׁים,

---

Chinuch sets out who is obligated to give *matanos*:

וּבִזְכָרִים וּנְקֵבוֹת יִשְׂרְאֵלִים אֲבָל לֹא בְּכֹהֲנִים – This mitzvah applies **to men and women** who are **Yisraelim, but not to Kohanim,** i.e., a Kohen need not give *matanos* of his animal to another Kohen, **מִשּׁוּם דִּכְתִיב בְּהוּ** – **because it is written regarding [*matanos*]:** **"מִשְׁפַּט הַכֹּהֲנִים מֵאֵת הָעָם"** – *This shall be* ***the due of the Kohanim from the people,*** **מִכְּלַל שֶׁאֵינָן בְּכֹהֲנִים** – **which implies that [the *matanos*]** obligation **does not apply to the Kohanim** themselves. **וְעוֹד דְּכֹהֲנִים לָא אִיקְרוּ עַם** – **Furthermore,** the term "the people" in the verse specifically excludes Kohanim, for **the Kohanim are not called "the people"** in Scripture, **וּכְמוֹ שֶׁכָּתוּב "וְעַל הַכֹּהֲנִים וְעַל כָּל עַם הַקָּהָל יְכַפֵּר"** – **as it is written** (*Leviticus* 16:33) regarding the Yom Kippur service: *[The Kohen Gadol will bring atonement]* ***upon the Kohanim, and upon all the people of the congregation shall he bring atonement.*** The verse clearly categorizes "the Kohanim" separately from "the people."[22]

וְהַלְוִיִּם יֵשׁ בָּהֶם בְּעִנְיָן זֶה דִּין מְיֻחָד – **Leviim,** however, **have a unique law with regard to this** mitzvah, **שֶׁאֵין הַכֹּהֲנִים נוֹטְלִים מֵהֶן הַמַּתָּנוֹת** – **for** although they are not eligible to receive *matanos*, as the verse clearly specifies Kohanim,[23] **the Kohanim do not take *matanos* from them** either. **לְפִי שֶׁנִּסְתַּפֵּק לְרַבּוֹתֵינוּ אִם נִקְרְאוּ עַם אִם לֹא** – The reason for this is **because our Sages** (*Chullin* 131b) **were unsure whether [Leviim] are called "the people"** by Scripture, **or not,** and therefore whether they are included in the category of those who are obligated to give *matanos*. **וּלְפִיכָךְ אֵין כֹּחַ בְּיָדָם לִטֹּל מֵהֶם מִסָּפֵק** – **Therefore, [the Kohanim] are not in a position to take from [the Leviim] on the basis of a doubt.**[24] **וְאִם נָטְלוּ לֹא יַחֲזִירוּ** – **However, if they did** improperly **take** the *matanos* from a Levi, **they need not return** them.[25]

Chinuch addresses whether this mitzvah applies nowadays:

וּלְעִנְיָן אִם נוֹהֲגוֹת עַכְשָׁו בַּזְּמַן הַזֶּה אִם לֹא – **As to the issue of whether** the obligation of **[*matanos*] applies now, in these times, or not,** i.e., outside Eretz Yisrael,[26] **כְּבָר חָלְקוּ עַל זֶה הַרְבֵּה מִגְּדוֹלֵי הַמְפָרְשִׁים** – **many of the great commentators have disagreed over this** matter,

---

NOTES

deemed kosher, meaning that their *shechitah* was performed correctly and they were not found to have any defect that forbids the animal for consumption (*Yoreh Deah* 61:6).

22. This, however, applies only when a Kohen slaughters an animal for his own use. If a Kohen slaughters an animal for sale, he must give the *matanos* to another Kohen; see *Yoreh Deah* 61:24.

23. *Shach, Yoreh Deah* 61:12.

24. As noted above (note 16), the rule that governs cases of monetary doubt is: הַמּוֹצִיא מֵחֲבֵרוֹ עָלָיו הָרְאָיָה, *the one seeking to exact property from his fellow bears the burden of proof.* Since the Kohen cannot prove that the Levi is obligated, he cannot demand *matanos* from him.

25. In a case where the Kohen already took possession of the *matanos*, it is the Levi who is "exacting property from his fellow," and the burden of proof falls on the Levi to show that he is exempt from giving. Since he cannot do this, the Kohen need not return the *matanos*.

Rama (*Yoreh Deah* 61:23) cites a dissenting view that maintains that in the case where the Kohen took possession of the *matanos*, he must return them; for discussion, see commentaries to *Yoreh Deah* there and 315:1.

26. The overwhelming consensus of halachic authorities is that the *matanos* obligation applies in Eretz Yisrael even nowadays, in the absence of the *Beis HaMikdash*. Thus, the discussion Chinuch cites here presumably pertains only to the question of whether the obligation applies outside of Eretz Yisrael (see *Minchas Chinuch* §16; *Maayan HaChochmah*, p. 117b in Roedelheim edition). See, however, Mitzvah 508 Insight B for further discussion.

וְהָעוֹלֶה מִן הַשְּׁמוּעָה בְּפֶרֶק הַזְּרוֹעַ עִם הַפֵּרוּשׁ הַטּוֹב שֶׁנּוֹהֲגוֹת הֵן הַיּוֹם[27], וְכֵן דַּעַת רַבֵּנוּ אַלְפָסִי זִכְרוֹנוֹ לִבְרָכָה[28] וְהָרַמְבַּ"ן ז"ל[29]. אֲבָל עַכְשָׁו אֵין בָּנוּ כֹּחַ עַל הַטַּבָּחִים לְהַכְרִיחָם לִתְּנָם[30], וְקוֹיֵ ה' יַחֲלִיפוּ כֹחַ[31].

וְשָׁם בְּפֶרֶק הַזְּרוֹעַ (קל"א ע"ב) אָמְרוּ זִכְרוֹנָם לִבְרָכָה שֶׁנּוֹתְנִין הַמַּתָּנוֹת לְכֹהֲנוֹת כְּמוֹ לַכֹּהֲנִים וַאֲפִלּוּ הֵן נְשׂוּאוֹת לְיִשְׂרָאֵל[32], וְכֵן אִתְּמַר הָתָם[33] כִּי אֲתָא עוּלָּא אֲמַר הָבוּ מַתְּנָתָא לְכָהַנְתָּא, אַלְמָא קָסָבַר עוּלָּא כֹּהֵן וַאֲפִלּוּ כֹּהֶנֶת, וְשָׁם (קל"ב ע"א) נֶאֱמַר עוֹד,

---

וְהָעוֹלֶה מִן הַשְּׁמוּעָה בְּפֶרֶק הַזְּרוֹעַ עִם הַפֵּרוּשׁ הַטּוֹב שֶׁנּוֹהֲגוֹת הֵן הַיּוֹם – **and what emerges from the** relevant **discussion in Chapter *Hazero'a*, with the proper interpretation** of the Gemara, **is that [the obligation] does apply nowadays.**[27] וְכֵן דַּעַת רַבֵּנוּ אַלְפָסִי זִכְרוֹנוֹ לִבְרָכָה – **This is the opinion of our Master, *R' Yitzchak Alfasi* (*Rif*), of blessed memory,**[28] וְהָרַמְבַּ"ן ז"ל – **and** of ***Ramban*, of blessed memory.**[29] אֲבָל עַכְשָׁו אֵין בָּנוּ כֹּחַ עַל הַטַּבָּחִים לְהַכְרִיחָם לִתְּנָם – In actual practice, **however, nowadays we do not have authority over the butchers,** and we are not able **to compel them to give [the *matanos*]** to the Kohanim.[30] "וְקוֹיֵ ה' יַחֲלִיפוּ כֹחַ" – ***But those whose hope is in HASHEM will have renewed strength*** (*Isaiah* 40:31).[31]

Chinuch discusses the eligibility of a Koheness (daughter of a Kohen; pl. Kohanos) to receive *matanos*: וְשָׁם בְּפֶרֶק הַזְּרוֹעַ אָמְרוּ זִכְרוֹנָם לִבְרָכָה – **There, in Chapter *Hazero'a*, [the Sages], of blessed memory, stated** שֶׁנּוֹתְנִין הַמַּתָּנוֹת לְכֹהֲנוֹת כְּמוֹ לַכֹּהֲנִים – **that we may give *matanos* to Kohanos just as** we give them **to the Kohanim,** וַאֲפִלּוּ הֵן נְשׂוּאוֹת לְיִשְׂרָאֵל – **and** this is so **even if they are married to Yisraelim.**[32] וְכֵן אִתְּמַר הָתָם – **This** is clear from that which **is stated there** (131b):[33] כִּי אֲתָא עוּלָּא אֲמַר הָבוּ מַתְּנָתָא לְכָהַנְתָּא – **When Ulla came** from Eretz Yisrael to Babylonia **he said, "Give *matanos* to a Koheness."** אַלְמָא קָסָבַר עוּלָּא כֹּהֵן וַאֲפִלּוּ כֹּהֶנֶת – And the Gemara concludes: **Thus, Ulla maintains** that when Scripture states that *matanos* are given to **a Kohen,** this includes **even a Koheness.** וְשָׁם נֶאֱמַר עוֹד – **And it is further stated there** (*Chullin* 132a):

NOTES

27. The Gemara (*Chullin* 132a) describes the practice of several Amoraim who lived outside of Eretz Yisrael who would indeed observe this mitzvah. Now, the Gemara (ibid. 136b) states that with regard to the mitzvah of *reishis hageiz* (the first fleece; Mitzvah 508), common practice follows the view of R' Ilai, who maintains that it does not apply outside of Eretz Yisrael. R' Ilai maintained the same about the *matanos* obligation as well, in apparent disagreement with the described practice of other Amoraim. The Rishonim debate whether in practice we follow R' Ilai also with regard to this mitzvah (*Rashi* and *Tosafos, Chullin* ad loc. ד"ה כרבי אילעי; *Ramban* loc. cit.; *Ran,* 46b *Rif* folio). For discussion, see Mitzvah 508 Insight A.

28. This is apparently based on an inference from *Rif, Chullin* fol. 46b; see *Beis Yosef, Yoreh Deah* 61:21 (סד"ה והר"ן).

29. *Chullin* 136b ד"ה ומכל מקום.

30. Chinuch speaks specifically about the butchers because, as the slaughterers of the animals, they are the ones required to actually give the gifts. Although the monetary obligation is the owner's, it is the one who slaughters the animals who must actually give the *matanos* to the Kohen (see *Yoreh Deah* 61:28).

31. After mentioning that we currently do not have the practical authority (אֵין בָּנוּ כֹּחַ, literally, *we do not have the strength ...*), Chinuch concludes with the words of Scripture, in prayer that those who hope to Hashem will gain renewed strength. [This is apparently a reference to that which the Gemara (ibid. 132b) relates, that certain Amoraim would penalize butchers who did not separate *matanos*; see further, Mitzvah 508 Insight A.]

32. This is in contrast to the law of *terumah*, which a Koheness who marries a Yisrael may no longer eat. The difference between *terumah* and *matanos* is that *terumah* food has inherent sanctity, whereas *matanos* do not have inherent sanctity, but are merely a monetary obligation, as noted earlier in this mitzvah. Upon marrying a Yisrael, a Koheness loses the level of Kohanic sanctity necessary to eat *terumah*, but *matanos* do not require any particular level of sanctity to eat; even a Yisrael may eat *matanos* if the Kohen gives them to him. Since a Koheness is also considered a Kohen with regard to this mitzvah, her marriage does not detract from her eligibility to receive *matanos* (see *Rashi*, *Chullin* 131b ד"ה לכהנת and *Rambam* ibid. 9:20).

33. The version of the Gemara that Chinuch cites differs slightly from the standard version of this Gemara, but is apparently the version of other Rishonim as well (see *Halachos Gedolos* §69; *Rif, Chullin* fol. 45a and *Rosh* 10:3).

רַב כַּהֲנָא אָכִיל בִּשְׁבִיל אִשְׁתּוֹ, וְכֵן רַב פַּפָּא וְרַב יֵימַר וְרַב אִידִי[34].
וְיִשְׂרָאֵל הָעוֹבֵר עַל זֶה וְשָׁחַט בְּהֶמְתּוֹ וְלֹא נָתַן הַמַּתָּנוֹת לְכֹהֵן אוֹ לְכֹהֶנֶת בִּטֵּל עֲשֵׂה זֶה. וְאָמְרוּ זִכְרוֹנָם לִבְרָכָה (שם קל"ד ע"ב) **שֶׁאִם אֵין עִמּוֹ כֹּהֵן אוֹ כֹּהֶנֶת מַעֲלֶה הַמַּתָּנוֹת בְּדָמִים וְאוֹכְלָן מִפְּנֵי הֶפְסֵד כֹּהֵן שֶׁאֵין בָּהֶן קְדֻשָּׁה, וְאַחַר כָּךְ נוֹתֵן הַדָּמִים לְכָל כֹּהֵן שֶׁיִּרְצֶה.**

רַב כַּהֲנָא אָכִיל בִּשְׁבִיל אִשְׁתּוֹ – **Rav Kahana,** who was a Yisrael, **ate** *matanos* **on account of his wife,** who was a Koheness, וְכֵן רַב פַּפָּא וְרַב יֵימַר וְרַב אִידִי – **and so** did **Rav Pappa, Rav Yeimar, and Rav Idi.**[34]

וְיִשְׂרָאֵל הָעוֹבֵר עַל זֶה – **A Yisrael who transgresses this** mitzvah, וְשָׁחַט בְּהֶמְתּוֹ וְלֹא נָתַן הַמַּתָּנוֹת לְכֹהֵן אוֹ לְכֹהֶנֶת – that is, **he slaughters his animal and does not give the** ***matanos*** **to a Kohen or Koheness,** בִּטֵּל עֲשֵׂה זֶה – **has violated this** mitzvah-**obligation.** וְאָמְרוּ זִכְרוֹנָם לִבְרָכָה שֶׁאִם אֵין עִמּוֹ כֹּהֵן אוֹ כֹּהֶנֶת – **[The Sages], of blessed memory, stated** (*Chullin* 134b) **that if there is no Kohen or Koheness with him** in his area to whom he can give the *matanos*, מַעֲלֶה הַמַּתָּנוֹת בְּדָמִים וְאוֹכְלָן – **he assesses the value of the** ***matanos*** **and** he may then **eat [the** ***matanos*****]** himself, מִפְּנֵי הֶפְסֵד כֹּהֵן – **on account of the loss to the Kohen.** Since the meat will spoil by the time a Kohen may come to claim them, it is better that he assess the monetary value of the *matanos* and then eat the meat himself. שֶׁאֵין בָּהֶן קְדֻשָּׁה – The Yisrael may eat them himself since **[the** ***matanos*****] have no sanctity;** וְאַחַר כָּךְ נוֹתֵן הַדָּמִים לְכָל כֹּהֵן שֶׁיִּרְצֶה – **and afterward, he gives the money to any Kohen that he wishes.**

NOTES

34. This Gemara demonstrates that a Koheness does not lose her eligibility to receive *matanos* with her marriage to a Yisrael. [The authorities further derive from this Gemara that not only may one give *matanos* to a Koheness, but one may give them directly to the husband of a Koheness as well, even if he is a Yisrael (see *Ran* to *Rif* fol. 45a, *Rambam* ibid., and *Yoreh Deah* 61:8).]

מִצְוָה תקז: מִצְוַת הַפְרָשַׁת תְּרוּמָה גְדוֹלָה[2,1]

שֶׁנִּצְטַוִּינוּ לְהַפְרִישׁ מִן הַדָּגָן וְהַתִּירוֹשׁ וְהַיִּצְהָר תְּרוּמָה וְנִתֵּן אוֹתָהּ לַכֹּהֵן וְהִיא הַנִּקְרֵאת תְּרוּמָה גְדוֹלָה[3], וְעַל זֶה נֶאֱמַר (דברים י״ח, ד׳) רֵאשִׁית דְּגָנְךָ תִּירֹשְׁךָ וְיִצְהָרְךָ וְגוֹ׳ תִּתֶּן לוֹ,

---

Mitzvah 507

The Obligation to Separate Terumah Gedolah

רֵאשִׁית דְּגָנְךָ תִּירֹשְׁךָ וְיִצְהָרֶךָ וְרֵאשִׁית גֵּז צֹאנְךָ תִּתֶּן לוֹ

The first of your grain, your wine, and your oil, and the first shearing of your sheep you shall give him (*Deuteronomy* 18:4).

Terumah, the subject of this mitzvah, is a portion of one's produce that one must separate and give to a Kohen. Unlike the Kohanic gifts of the previous and following mitzvos, the *terumah* portion is sanctified. As such, it may not be eaten by non-Kohanim, or even by Kohanim if either the *terumah* or the Kohen is *tamei*. The various regulations that apply to consumption of *terumah* have been set forth in Mitzvos 279-284.

Terumah is the first of the gifts that must be separated from one's harvested produce. The other agricultural gifts are the subject of earlier mitzvos: *Maaser rishon* ("the first tithe"; Mitzvah 395), *terumas maaser* (the *terumah* of *maaser;* Mitzvah 396), *maaser sheni* and *maasar ani* (Mitzvos 473 and 474). ***Maaser rishon*** is one-tenth of the produce that remains after *terumah* was removed; the owner separates it and gives it to a Levi. ***Terumas maaser*** is one-tenth of the *maaser rishon* that the Levi receives; he separates it and gives it to a Kohen. ***Maaser sheni*** and ***maasar ani*** apply in different years, as follows: During the first, second, fourth, and fifth year of each seven-year *shemittah* cycle, the owner separates *maaser sheni* ("the second tithe") after separating *maaser rishon*. He takes it to be eaten in Jerusalem, or he redeems it for its value and takes the money to Jerusalem to purchase food and eat it there. During the third and sixth year of the *shemittah* cycle, *maaser sheni* is substituted with *maasar ani* ("the pauper's tithe"), which is distributed to the poor.[1] The seventh year of this cycle is the *shemittah* year, during which all produce is rendered ownerless (Mitzvah 112) and is not subject to any *terumah* or *maaser* obligations at all.

While many of the laws of this mitzvah (such as the required amount and method of separating) are unique to *terumah*, most of the laws that Chinuch discusses in this mitzvah apply to all of these agricultural obligations.[2]

שֶׁנִּצְטַוִּינוּ לְהַפְרִישׁ מִן הַדָּגָן וְהַתִּירוֹשׁ וְהַיִּצְהָר תְּרוּמָה – **We are commanded to separate** a ***terumah*** portion **from the grain, wine, and oil** of one's produce, וְנִתֵּן אוֹתָהּ לַכֹּהֵן – **and give it to a Kohen;** וְהִיא הַנִּקְרֵאת תְּרוּמָה גְדוֹלָה – **this is** the portion that is **referred to as *terumah gedolah***, *the greater terumah*.[3] וְעַל זֶה נֶאֱמַר ״רֵאשִׁית דְּגָנְךָ תִּירֹשְׁךָ וְיִצְהָרְךָ וְגוֹ׳ תִּתֶּן לוֹ״ – **Regarding this** mitzvah **it is stated** (*Deuteronomy* 18:4): ***The first of your grain, your wine, and your oil ... you shall give him.***

NOTES

1. Because there are always two *maasros*, the obligation of *maaser* is often referred to in this mitzvah in the plural (*maasros*; sing. *maaser*). *Terumah*, by contrast, is often referred to in the singular since there is only one *terumah*.

2. See *Rambam, Commentary to the Mishnah, Terumos* 1:5.

3. This is in contrast to *terumas maaser*, the portion that the Levi takes from his *maaser*. *Terumah* is referred to as "*the greater terumah*" since it is the first of the agricultural gifts given from one's crop (see introduction). Alternatively, it can be the largest of all the other gifts, since the other gifts are limited to a tenth, whereas one may designate as large a percentage as he wants as *terumah*, as long as he does not give the entire crop (*Derech Emunah, Hil. Terumos* 3:1).

וְאָמְרוּ זִכְרוֹנָם לִבְרָכָה (רמב"ם פ"ג מהל' תרומות ה"א-ב) כִּי מִדִּין הַתּוֹרָה אֵין לָהּ שִׁעוּר אֶלָּא אֲפִלּוּ חִטָּה אַחַת פּוֹטֶרֶת כְּרִי גָּדוֹל, אֲבָל חֲכָמִים אָמְרוּ (תרומות פ"ד מ"ג) לְהַפְרִישׁ יוֹתֵר, וְאָמְרוּ מִי שֶׁיֵּשׁ לוֹ עַיִן בֵּינוֹנִית מַפְרִישׁ חֵלֶק אֶחָד מֵחֲמִשִּׁים[4], וְסָמְכוּ הַדָּבָר עַל לְשׁוֹן תְּרוּמָה, כְּלוֹמַר תְּרֵי מִמֵּאָה, דְּהַיְנוּ אֶחָד מֵחֲמִשִּׁים[5].

מִשָּׁרְשֵׁי הַמִּצְוָה, לְפִי שֶׁהַדָּגָן וְהַתִּירוֹשׁ וְהַיִּצְהָר הֵן עִקַּר מִחְיָתָן שֶׁל בְּרִיּוֹת, וְהָעוֹלָם כֻּלּוֹ לְהַקָּדוֹשׁ בָּרוּךְ הוּא הוּא, עַל כֵּן רָאוּי לָאָדָם לִזְכֹּר אֶת בּוֹרְאוֹ עַל הַבְּרָכָה אֲשֶׁר בֵּרְכוֹ[6] וְשֶׁיַּפְרִישׁ קְצָת מִמֶּנּוּ לִשְׁמוֹ בָּרוּךְ הוּא, וְיִתְּנֶנּוּ לִמְשָׁרְתָיו שֶׁהֵם הַכֹּהֲנִים הָעֲסוּקִים תָּמִיד בִּמְלֶאכֶת שָׁמַיִם טֶרֶם יִגַּע בּוֹ יַד אָדָם וְיֵהָנֶה מִמֶּנּוּ כְּלָל[7].

וּמִן הַיְסוֹד הַזֶּה אָמְרוּ זִכְרוֹנָם לִבְרָכָה שֶׁאֲפִלּוּ חִטָּה אַחַת פּוֹטֶרֶת אֶת הַכְּרִי,

---

וְאָמְרוּ זִכְרוֹנָם לִבְרָכָה – **The [Sages], of blessed memory, stated** (*Rambam, Hil. Terumos* 3:1-2), regarding the minimum measure of the *terumah* portion, כִּי מִדִּין הַתּוֹרָה אֵין לָהּ שִׁעוּר – **that by Biblical law there is no** minimum **amount,** אֶלָּא אֲפִלּוּ חִטָּה אַחַת פּוֹטֶרֶת כְּרִי גָּדוֹל – and **indeed even a single grain of wheat** given as *terumah* **discharges** the *terumah* obligation for **a large pile** of grain. אֲבָל חֲכָמִים אָמְרוּ לְהַפְרִישׁ יוֹתֵר – **However, the Sages said** (*Terumos* 4:3) **that one should separate more** than the Biblical minimum; וְאָמְרוּ מִי שֶׁיֵּשׁ לוֹ עַיִן בֵּינוֹנִית מַפְרִישׁ חֵלֶק אֶחָד מֵחֲמִשִּׁים – **and they said** specifically **that one who is of average generosity separates one-fiftieth** of the crop as *terumah*.[4] וְסָמְכוּ הַדָּבָר עַל לְשׁוֹן תְּרוּמָה – Although this is a Rabbinic standard, **[the Sages] found** Scriptural **support for it in the word *terumah*** itself; כְּלוֹמַר תְּרֵי מִמֵּאָה דְּהַיְנוּ אֶחָד מֵחֲמִשִּׁים – **that is,** the word *terumah* can be read as an acronym for the words ***"trei mime'ah,"*** *two from a hundred*, **which equals one-fiftieth.**[5]

Underlying Purpose of the Mitzvah

מִשָּׁרְשֵׁי הַמִּצְוָה – **Among the underlying purposes of the mitzvah** to give to the Kohen a portion of these three crops is לְפִי שֶׁהַדָּגָן וְהַתִּירוֹשׁ וְהַיִּצְהָר הֵן עִקַּר מִחְיָתָן שֶׁל בְּרִיּוֹת – **because grain, wine, and oil are people's primary** sources of **sustenance,** וְהָעוֹלָם כֻּלּוֹ לְהַקָּדוֹשׁ בָּרוּךְ הוּא הוּא – **and the entire world belongs to the Holy One, blessed is He;** עַל כֵּן רָאוּי לָאָדָם לִזְכֹּר אֶת בּוֹרְאוֹ עַל הַבְּרָכָה אֲשֶׁר בֵּרְכוֹ – **it is therefore proper for a person to acknowledge his Creator upon** benefiting from **the blessing with which He has blessed him.**[6] וְשֶׁיַּפְרִישׁ קְצָת מִמֶּנּוּ לִשְׁמוֹ בָּרוּךְ הוּא – **One should therefore separate some of [his crop] for His Name, blessed is He,** וְיִתְּנֶנּוּ לִמְשָׁרְתָיו שֶׁהֵם הַכֹּהֲנִים הָעֲסוּקִים תָּמִיד בִּמְלֶאכֶת שָׁמַיִם – **and give it to His servants, the Kohanim, who are constantly involved in Heavenly service,** i.e., the service of Hashem, טֶרֶם יִגַּע בּוֹ יַד אָדָם וְיֵהָנֶה מִמֶּנּוּ כְּלָל – **before people take any of it to benefit from it at all.**[7]

Chinuch points out that this reason is reflected in one of the central laws of the mitzvah:

וּמִן הַיְסוֹד הַזֶּה אָמְרוּ זִכְרוֹנָם לִבְרָכָה – **In light of this fundamental idea** we can understand that which **[the Sages], of blessed memory, have stated,** שֶׁאֲפִלּוּ חִטָּה אַחַת פּוֹטֶרֶת אֶת הַכְּרִי – that **even a single grain of wheat** given as *terumah* **discharges** the *terumah* obligation for **the**

NOTES

4. One-fiftieth is the standard *terumah* amount. The Mishnah there further states that a generous person gives one-fortieth and a miserly one gives one-sixtieth. By Rabbinic law one may not give less than one-sixtieth (*Rambam* ibid.; see also *Derech Emunah, Beur HaHalachah* to *Hil. Terumos* 3:1 ד"ה עין יפה).

5. This allusion is cited by many Rishonim, including *Rambam*, in his *Commentary to the Mishnah* (*Terumos* 4:3), and is found in *Zohar* (*Vayakhel*, p. 200a).

6. In applying this reason only to these three crops, Chinuch follows the opinion cited below that the Biblical obligation of *terumah* applies only to these; see further below, at note 9.

7. One must give the *terumah* as soon as the processing of the produce is complete, and one is forbidden to eat or benefit from any of the produce until *terumah* has been given. See Mitzvah 284 for the details of this prohibition.

כִּי זְכִירַת הָאַדְנוּת עַל הַדָּבָר אֵין הֶפְרֵשׁ בֵּין רַב לִמְעַט. אָמְנָם רַבּוֹתֵינוּ זִכְרוֹנָם לִבְרָכָה הוֹסִיפוּ בַּדָּבָר לָתֵת בּוֹ שִׁעוּר רָאוּי כְּדֵי שֶׁיִּתְעוֹרֵר לֵב הָאָדָם בָּעִנְיָן יוֹתֵר, כִּי בִּהְיוֹת הָאָדָם בַּעַל חֹמֶר לֹא יָשִׁית אֶל לִבּוֹ עַל הַדָּבָר הַמּוּעָט כְּמוֹ עַל הַמֻּרְבֶּה שֶׁיְּמַלֵּא עֵינָיו וְיָעִידוּ עָלָיו יוֹתֵר תְּנוּעוֹתָיו כְּדֶרֶךְ טֶבַע הָאָדָם וְהֶרְגֵּלוֹ שֶׁיִּשְׂמַח בְּמַאֲכָל רַב. וּכְבָר כָּתַבְתִּי עוֹד בְּטַעַם מְנוֹת הַכֹּהֲנִים בְּסֵדֶר וַיִּקַּח קֹרַח בְּמִצְוַת מַעֲשֵׂר וּמַעֲשֵׂר מִן הַמַּעֲשֵׂר בְּסִימָן שצ״א וְשצ״ב (מצוות שצ״ה־שצ״ו)[8].

דִּינֵי הַמִּצְוָה כְּגוֹן מַה שֶּׁנִּרְאֶה בַּגְּמָרָא[9] שֶׁעִקַּר חִיּוּב הַתְּרוּמָה דְּאוֹרַיְתָא וְכֵן הַמַּעַשְׂרוֹת הוּא בְּדָגָן[10] וְתִירוֹשׁ וְיִצְהָר לְבַד, לְפִי שֶׁהֵן עִקַּר מִחְיָתָן שֶׁל בְּרִיּוֹת. אֲבָל מִדִּבְרֵי סוֹפְרִים

---

entire pile, כִּי זְכִירַת הָאַדְנוּת עַל הַדָּבָר אֵין הֶפְרֵשׁ בֵּין רַב לִמְעַט – **because to acknowledge** Hashem's **authority upon one's produce, there is no difference between a large or a small** portion; any amount that one separates accomplishes the goal of acknowledging Hashem's ownership over it. אָמְנָם רַבּוֹתֵינוּ זִכְרוֹנָם לִבְרָכָה הוֹסִיפוּ בַּדָּבָר לָתֵת בּוֹ שִׁעוּר רָאוּי – **Still, our teachers,** the Sages, **of blessed memory, added to the** minimum, stating **that one should give a proper amount,** כְּדֵי שֶׁיִּתְעוֹרֵר לֵב הָאָדָם בָּעִנְיָן יוֹתֵר – **to further awaken Man's heart to this matter** of acknowledging Hashem in his blessings. כִּי בִּהְיוֹת הָאָדָם בַּעַל חֹמֶר – This awakening is necessary, **because since a person is comprised of a physical body,** לֹא יָשִׁית אֶל לִבּוֹ עַל הַדָּבָר הַמּוּעָט כְּמוֹ עַל הַמֻּרְבֶּה שֶׁיְּמַלֵּא עֵינָיו – **he does not take notice of a small thing** (such as a single kernel) **like** he does **of a large [amount] that "fills his eyes."** וְיָעִידוּ עָלָיו יוֹתֵר תְּנוּעוֹתָיו – **Thus, one's actions** that he performs with a larger amount **provide greater testimony about him** that he takes to heart the import of those actions, כְּדֶרֶךְ טֶבַע הָאָדָם וְהֶרְגֵּלוֹ שֶׁיִּשְׂמַח בְּמַאֲכָל רַב – **as** it **is the nature and tendency of Man to rejoice** and to be inspired **upon** seeing **a large amount of food.** The larger gift, representing a specific percentage of the crop, was therefore instituted by the Sages so that a person should be properly inspired to acknowledge Hashem's blessing.

וּכְבָר כָּתַבְתִּי עוֹד בְּטַעַם מְנוֹת הַכֹּהֲנִים בְּסֵדֶר וַיִּקַּח קֹרַח – **I have also written more on the reasons of the gifts** given **to the Kohanim in *Parashas Korach,*** בְּמִצְוַת מַעֲשֵׂר וּמַעֲשֵׂר מִן הַמַּעֲשֵׂר בְּסִימָן שצ״א וְשצ״ב – **in the mitzvah of *maaser* of the *maaser*** (i.e., *terumas maaser*), **Chapters 391 and 392** of this work (Mitzvos 395-396).[8]

Laws of the Mitzvah

Chinuch sets out which produce is subject to the *terumah* obligation by Biblical law and which by Rabbinic law:

דִּינֵי הַמִּצְוָה כְּגוֹן מַה שֶּׁנִּרְאֶה בַּגְּמָרָא – **The laws of the mitzvah** include, **for example,** the rule **that seems** to emerge **from the Gemara,**[9] שֶׁעִקַּר חִיּוּב הַתְּרוּמָה דְּאוֹרַיְתָא וְכֵן הַמַּעַשְׂרוֹת הוּא בְּדָגָן וְתִירוֹשׁ וְיִצְהָר לְבַד לְפִי שֶׁהֵן עִקַּר מִחְיָתָן שֶׁל בְּרִיּוֹת – **that the primary, Biblical *terumah* obligation, and likewise the** Biblical obligations of ***maasros,*** **apply only to grain,**[10] **wine, and oil,** which are mentioned in the verse, **for they are people's primary** source of **sustenance.** אֲבָל מִדִּבְרֵי סוֹפְרִים

NOTES

8. [Chinuch's numbering of the mitzvos follows the original format of this work; see Mitzvah 494 note 4.] In Mitzvos 395-396, Chinuch speaks of the special status of the tribe of Levi, and specifically of the Kohanim, since they are the servants of Hashem who serve Him in the *Beis HaMikdash*. Due to this special status, they merited the twenty-four Kohanic gifts. In Mitzvah 508, Chinuch further notes that the Kohanim do not have any portion in Eretz Yisrael as do the other tribes, so Hashem provided for them other sources of sustenance such as *terumah*; see there further (see also *Deuteronomy* 18:1-5).

9. See below, note 14.

10. "Grain" refers to the five primary species of grain: wheat, barley, oats, spelt, and rye (see Mishnah, *Challah* 1:1-2).

חַיָּב גַּם כֵּן כָּל שֶׁהוּא אֹכֶל אָדָם[11] וְנִשְׁמָר וְגִדּוּלוֹ מִן הָאָרֶץ[12], וְאַף עַל פִּי שֶׁמְּצָאנוּ בְּסִפְרִי[13] שֶׁסְּמָכוּ הַדָּבָר לַקְּרָא, אַסְמַכְתָּא בְּעָלְמָא הוּא, וּכְמוֹ שֶׁכָּתַבְתִּי בְּסֵדֶר וַיִּקַּח קֹרַח בְּמִצְוַת מַעֲשֵׂר (מצוה שצ״ה) שֶׁאָמְרוּ שָׁם, רֵאשִׁית דְּגָנְךָ וְגוֹ׳, מַה דָּגָן תִּירוֹשׁ וְיִצְהָר מַאֲכַל אָדָם וְגִדּוּלוֹ מִן הָאָרֶץ וְיֵשׁ לוֹ בְּעָלִים שֶׁנֶּאֱמַר דְּגָנְךָ, אַף כָּל כַּיּוֹצֵא בָּהֶן חַיָּב בִּתְרוּמָה וּמַעַשְׂרוֹת[14]. וְאָמְרוּ[15] זִכְרוֹנָם לִבְרָכָה שֶׁהַכַּרְשִׁינִין אַף עַל פִּי שֶׁאֵינָן מַאֲכַל אָדָם

חַיָּב גַּם כֵּן כָּל שֶׁהוּא – But by Rabbinic law there is an obligation upon any type of produce **that** meets these three criteria: **אֹכֶל אָדָם** – It is (1) **fit for human consumption** under normal conditions;[11] **וְנִשְׁמָר** – (2) it is **protected,** i.e., not ownerless; **וְגִדּוּלוֹ מִן הָאָרֶץ – and** (3) **it grows from the ground,** i.e., it has roots that derive sustenance from the ground.[12]

וְאַף עַל פִּי שֶׁמְּצָאנוּ בְּסִפְרִי שֶׁסְּמָכוּ הַדָּבָר לַקְּרָא – Now, **even though we find in *Sifrei*[13] that [the Sages] supported [these laws] with** verses from **Scripture,** i.e., they expounded various verses in ways that reflect these three criteria, **אַסְמַכְתָּא בְּעָלְמָא הוּא – [the Scriptural sources]** do not teach an actual Biblical obligation, but **are only Scriptural allusions** to a Rabbinic obligation, **וּכְמוֹ שֶׁכָּתַבְתִּי בְּסֵדֶר וַיִּקַּח קֹרַח בְּמִצְוַת מַעֲשֵׂר – as I wrote in *Parashas Korach,* in the mitzvah of *maaser*** (Mitzvah 395). **שֶׁאָמְרוּ שָׁם** – This refers to the following exposition **that [the Sages] stated there,** in *Sifrei*: **"רֵאשִׁית דְּגָנְךָ וְגוֹ׳"** – Scripture states that the *terumah* obligation applies to ***the first of your grain,*** *your wine, and your oil,* but this obligation may be extended to other foods, as follows: **מַה דָּגָן תִּירוֹשׁ וְיִצְהָר מַאֲכַל אָדָם וְגִדּוּלוֹ מִן הָאָרֶץ – Just as grain, wine, and oil,** which the verse mentions explicitly, **are** all **food for people and grow from the ground, "וְיֵשׁ לוֹ בְּעָלִים שֶׁנֶּאֱמַר "דְּגָנְךָ – and they** also **have an owner, as it is stated, "*your* grain,"** "*your* wine," and "*your* oil," indicating that they are not ownerless, **אַף כָּל כַּיּוֹצֵא בָּהֶן חַיָּב בִּתְרוּמָה וּמַעַשְׂרוֹת – so too, any** produce **that is similar to them** in these respects **is subject to the *terumah* and *maasros* obligations.** While this teaching might be understood as expanding the Biblical obligation, in truth it means only that Scripture provides support to a Rabbinic expansion of the obligation.[14]

Chinuch cites laws that provide some applications of the rule that produce is subject to the *terumah* obligation only if it is "food for human consumption." The following laws are cited directly from *Rambam, Hil. Terumos* 2:2-5, with minor modifications:[15]

וְאָמְרוּ זִכְרוֹנָם לִבְרָכָה – The [Sages], of blessed memory, stated (ibid. §2) **שֶׁהַכַּרְשִׁינִין אַף עַל פִּי שֶׁאֵינָן מַאֲכַל אָדָם – that vetch** (a legume used for animal fodder), **although it is** generally **not** used

---

NOTES

11. Chinuch elaborates on this below.

12. This excludes truffles and mushrooms, which lack roots and grow on the surface of the earth rather than *from* the earth.

13. The exposition that Chinuch will cite is also quoted by *Rambam* (*Hil. Terumos* 2:1), but does not appear in this form in our versions of *Sifrei* (to *Deuteronomy* 14:22); see there, where other Scriptural sources are brought for only some of these criteria. See also *Yerushalmi Maasros* 1:1 (1a-2b in Schottenstein edition), where various Scriptural sources are discussed.

14. Taken at face value, the cited *Sifrei* seems to be stating a Biblical law. However, as Chinuch noted, the Gemara indicates that only grain, wine, and oil are included in the Biblical obligation. There are various passages in the Gemara that indicate this (see *Tosafos, Bechoros* 54a ד״ה ושני and *Rosh Hashanah* 12a ד״ה תנא), but most explicit is *Bechoros* 54a, which states clearly that all other species aside from the three mentioned in the verse – grain, wine, and oil – are subject to *maasros* only by Rabbinic decree. Chinuch writes in Mitzvah 395 (at note 16) that the evidence from the Gemara compels us to interpret *Sifrei* as referring to a Rabbinic law, not a Biblical one, and the cited Scriptural derivations must be Scriptural allusions to a Rabbinic decree. As Chinuch notes in that mitzvah, however, *Rambam* (*Hil. Terumos* 2:1,6) accepts the laws mentioned in *Sifrei* as Biblical laws; see Mitzvah 395 for further discussion. [Even according to *Rambam* (ibid.), though, vegetables are subject to the obligation only by Rabbinic law; see Mitzvah 395 at note 15.]

15. The elucidation of the many laws cited from *Rambam, Hilchos Terumos*, throughout this mitzvah primarily follows the *Derech Emunah* commentary to these laws.

הוֹאִיל וְאוֹכְלִין אוֹתָן בִּשְׁנֵי רְעָבוֹן חַיָּבִין בִּתְרוּמָה וּמַעַשְׂרוֹת[16]. וְהַפִּיאָה[17] וְהָאֵזוֹב וְהַקּוֹרָנִית שֶׁזְּרָעָן תְּחִלָּה לְאָדָם חַיָּבִין בְּמַעֲשֵׂר, וְכֵן כָּל כַּיּוֹצֵא בָּהֶן. זְרָעָן לִבְהֵמָה אַף עַל פִּי שֶׁנִּמְלַךְ וְחָשַׁב עֲלֵיהֶן לְאָדָם כְּשֶׁהֵן מְחֻבָּרִין פְּטוּרִין, שֶׁמַּחֲשֶׁבֶת אָדָם בְּחִבּוּר אֵינָהּ כְּלוּם[18]. עָלוּ מֵאֲלֵיהֶן בְּחָצֵר, אִם חָצֵר הַמִּשְׁמֶּרֶת פֵּרוֹתֶיהָ הִיא הֲרֵי אֵלּוּ חַיָּבִין שֶׁסְּתָמָן לְאָדָם, וְאִם אֵינָהּ מִשְׁמֶּרֶת פְּטוּרִין. זֵרְעוֹנֵי גִנָּה שֶׁאֵינָן נֶאֱכָלִין כְּגוֹן זֶרַע לֶפֶת וְזֶרַע צְנוֹן וְזֶרַע בְּצָלִים וְכַיּוֹצֵא בָּהֶן פְּטוּרִין מִן הַתְּרוּמָה וּמִן הַמַּעַשְׂרוֹת מִפְּנֵי שֶׁאֵינָן מַאֲכַל אָדָם, אֲבָל הַקֶּצַח[19] חַיָּב בִּתְרוּמָה וּמַעַשְׂרוֹת[20].

---

as **food for people,** הוֹאִיל וְאוֹכְלִין אוֹתָן בִּשְׁנֵי רְעָבוֹן חַיָּבִין בִּתְרוּמָה וּמַעַשְׂרוֹת **– since people eat it in years of famine, it is subject to** the ***terumah*** **and** ***maasros*** obligations.[16]

The following law pertains to certain herbs that are sometimes planted for human consumption and other times for animal consumption:

וְהַפִּיאָה וְהָאֵזוֹב וְהַקּוֹרָנִית שֶׁזְּרָעָן תְּחִלָּה לְאָדָם חַיָּבִין בְּמַעֲשֵׂר **–** ***Pi'ah,***[17] **hyssop, and savory that one planted originally** for **human** consumption **are subject to** ***maaser*** and *terumah;* וְכֵן כָּל כַּיּוֹצֵא בָּהֶן **– and likewise all similar** plants, i.e., herbs that are at times planted for food and at times for fodder, if one planted them for food they are subject to the *maaser* and *terumah* obligations. זְרָעָן לִבְהֵמָה **– If** one planted these herbs **for animal** food, אַף עַל פִּי שֶׁנִּמְלַךְ וְחָשַׁב עֲלֵיהֶן לְאָדָם כְּשֶׁהֵן מְחֻבָּרִין פְּטוּרִין **– then, even if he** subsequently **reconsidered while they were attached** to the ground **and designated them** for **human** consumption, **they are exempt** from these obligations, שֶׁמַּחֲשֶׁבֶת אָדָם בְּחִבּוּר אֵינָהּ כְּלוּם **– because the designation that a person sets when** the plant is already growing, **attached to** the ground, **has no significance;** after the plant takes root, a change of designation has no effect.[18] עָלוּ מֵאֲלֵיהֶן בְּחָצֵר **– If [these herbs]** were not planted, but **grew on their own in a courtyard** from seeds that took root accidentally, אִם חָצֵר הַמִּשְׁמֶּרֶת פֵּרוֹתֶיהָ הִיא – then the law depends on the kind of courtyard in which they grew; **if the courtyard "protects its produce,"** i.e., the herbs are protected in the courtyard and not open to all passersby, הֲרֵי אֵלּוּ חַיָּבִין שֶׁסְּתָמָן לְאָדָם **– then they are subject** to *terumah* and *maaser,* **for those** herbs **that were not** explicitly **designated** for a specific purpose **are** considered to be designated for **human** consumption. וְאִם אֵינָהּ מִשְׁמֶּרֶת פְּטוּרִין **– But if [the courtyard] does not protect** its produce, **they are exempt from** these obligations. In this case, they are considered "ownerless" and as such are not subject to the *terumos* and *maasros* obligations.

Only a plant's "fruit" is subject to *terumah;* other parts of the plant are not, even if they happen to be edible. In the context of these laws, the "fruit" is defined as the portion of the plant for which the plant is grown. Chinuch next discusses the *terumah* obligation for *seeds* of plants that are grown primarily for their edible roots, bulbs, or leaves, but not for their seeds:

זֵרְעוֹנֵי גִנָּה שֶׁאֵינָן נֶאֱכָלִין – (*Rambam* ibid. §3) **Garden seeds that** usually **are not eaten,** כְּגוֹן זֶרַע לֶפֶת וְזֶרַע צְנוֹן וְזֶרַע בְּצָלִים וְכַיּוֹצֵא בָּהֶן **– such as turnip seeds, radish seeds, onion seeds, and the like,** פְּטוּרִין מִן הַתְּרוּמָה וּמִן הַמַּעַשְׂרוֹת מִפְּנֵי שֶׁאֵינָן מַאֲכַל אָדָם **– are exempt from** ***terumah*** **and** ***maasros*** **because they are not meant for human consumption,** אֲבָל הַקֶּצַח חַיָּב בִּתְרוּמָה וּמַעַשְׂרוֹת **– but** the seeds of ***ketzach*** (fennel)[19] **are subject to** the ***terumah*** **and** ***maasros*** obligations.[20]

NOTES

16. Some explain that this is a Rabbinic enactment, even according to the view that produce other than grain, wine, and oil is Biblically subject to *terumah.* For discussion, see *Derech Emunah, Beur HaHalachah* to *Hil. Terumos* 2:2 ד"ה הכרשינין.

17. In our text of *Rambam* (2:2) as well as in the Talmudic sources (*Niddah* 51a and Mishnah, *Maasros* 3:9), this word appears as סִיאָה, *pennyroyal* (*Rashi, Niddah* ibid. ד"ה הסיאה). It is possible that this is the correct version of the text of Chinuch as well (*Minchas Yitzchak* §5).

18. *Derech Emunah* 2:18,24.

19. See *Rashi,* to *Berachos* 40a ד"ה קצח; cf. *Derech Emunah* 2:31.

20. While *ketzach* has some features that make it difficult to eat, it is still considered food that is fit for human consumption since it has beneficial qualities as well (*Tos. Yom Tov, Eduyos* 5:3).

תְּמָרוֹת שֶׁל תִּלְתָּן וְשֶׁל חַרְדָּל וְשֶׁל פּוֹל הַלָּבָן וְשֶׁל צְלָף וְהַקַּפְרִיסִין שֶׁל צְלָף[21] פְּטוּרִין מִפְּנֵי שֶׁאֵינָן פְּרִי, בַּמֶּה דְּבָרִים אֲמוּרִים שֶׁזְּרָעָן לְזֶרַע, אֲבָל זְרָעָן לְיָרָק הֲרֵי אֵלּוּ חַיָּבִין[22], וְכֵן הָאֲבִיּוֹנוֹת שֶׁל צְלָף חַיָּבִין מִפְּנֵי שֶׁהֵן פְּרִי. כֶּסְבָּר שֶׁזְּרָעוֹ לְזֶרַע פָּטוּר מִן הַתְּרוּמָה וּמִן הַמַּעַשְׂרוֹת, זְרָעוֹ לְיָרָק מַפְרִישׁ תְּרוּמָה וּמַעַשְׂרוֹת מִן הַיָּרָק וּמִן הַזֶּרַע[23], וְכֵן הַשֶּׁבֶת זְרָעָהּ לְזֶרַע פָּטוּר זְרָעָהּ לְיָרָק מִתְעַשֶּׂרֶת זֶרַע וְיָרָק. הַגַּרְגִּיר שֶׁזְּרָעוֹ לְזֶרַע מִתְעַשֵּׂר לְזֶרַע וּלְיָרָק, שֶׁאִם לָקַח הַיָּרָק לְאָכְלוֹ מַפְרִישׁ מִמֶּנּוּ תְּרוּמָה וּמַעַשְׂרוֹת וְאַחַר כָּךְ אוֹכֵל, וּכְשֶׁיִּיבַשׁ וְיֶאֱסֹף הַזֶּרַע שֶׁלּוֹ מַפְרִישׁ מִן הַזֶּרַע.

וְכֵן מֵעִנְיַן הַמִּצְוָה מַה שֶּׁאָמְרוּ זִכְרוֹנָם לִבְרָכָה שֶׁאֵין חִיּוּב תְּרוּמוֹת וּמַעַשְׂרוֹת בְּפֵרוֹת

Chinuch discusses the *terumah* obligation for plants that are primarily grown for their seeds or berries, not for the other portions of the plant, such as the buds and leaves:

תְּמָרוֹת שֶׁל תִּלְתָּן וְשֶׁל חַרְדָּל וְשֶׁל פּוֹל הַלָּבָן וְשֶׁל צְלָף וְהַקַּפְרִיסִין שֶׁל צְלָף[21] – (*Rambam* ibid. §4) **The buds of fenugreek, mustard, white beans, and the caper bush, and the husks of the capers,** פְּטוּרִין מִפְּנֵי שֶׁאֵינָן פְּרִי – are exempt **because they are not** the true **"fruit"** of the plant, as these parts are generally not eaten. בַּמֶּה דְּבָרִים אֲמוּרִים שֶׁזְּרָעָן לְזֶרַע – **When does this apply? When they are planted for** the purpose of eating **the seeds** only. אֲבָל זְרָעָן לְיָרָק הֲרֵי אֵלּוּ חַיָּבִין – **However, if they were planted for** the purpose of eating **the greens** (i.e., leaves) of these plants, **they are subject to the** *terumah* **obligation.**[22] וְכֵן הָאֲבִיּוֹנוֹת שֶׁל צְלָף חַיָּבִין מִפְּנֵי שֶׁהֵן פְּרִי – **Also, the berries of the caper bush are** always **subject to the** *terumah* **obligation,** even if the capers were planted for the seeds, **because the berries are the** primary **"fruit"** of the caper.

Chinuch now discusses other plants that have edible seeds and leaves. He begins with plants in which the seeds are the primary edible component:

כֶּסְבָּר שֶׁזְּרָעוֹ לְזֶרַע פָּטוּר מִן הַתְּרוּמָה וּמִן הַמַּעַשְׂרוֹת – (*Rambam* ibid. §5) **Coriander that was planted for its seed is exempt from** ***terumah*** **and** ***maasros*** from its greens; זְרָעוֹ לְיָרָק מַפְרִישׁ תְּרוּמָה וּמַעַשְׂרוֹת מִן הַיָּרָק וּמִן הַזֶּרַע – **if it was planted for the greens, one must separate** ***terumah*** **and** ***maasros*** **from the greens and from the seeds.**[23] וְכֵן הַשֶּׁבֶת – The law is **the same for dill:** זְרָעָהּ לְזֶרַע פָּטוּר זְרָעָהּ לְיָרָק מִתְעַשֶּׂרֶת זֶרַע וְיָרָק – **if it was planted for its seeds, its** greens are **exempt; if it was planted for its greens, both its seeds and its greens are tithed.** הַגַּרְגִּיר שֶׁזְּרָעוֹ לְזֶרַע מִתְעַשֵּׂר לְזֶרַע וּלְיָרָק – On the other hand, **garden-rocket that was planted for its seeds is tithed from its seeds and its greens,** since the greens of this plant are always considered its primary "fruit." שֶׁאִם לָקַח הַיָּרָק לְאָכְלוֹ מַפְרִישׁ מִמֶּנּוּ תְּרוּמָה וּמַעַשְׂרוֹת וְאַחַר כָּךְ אוֹכֵל – How does one tithe the leaves and seeds of the same plant? **If one took the greens to eat them** before the seeds are edible, **he separates** ***terumah*** **and** ***maasros*** **from the greens and eats them;** וּכְשֶׁיִּיבַשׁ וְיֶאֱסֹף הַזֶּרַע שֶׁלּוֹ מַפְרִישׁ מִן הַזֶּרַע – **then, when** the rest of **[the plant] dries and he collects its seeds, he separates** *terumah* and *maasros* **from the seeds.**

Produce that is so unripe that it is inedible is exempt from *terumah* because it is not fit for human consumption. Here, Chinuch sets out the point when produce becomes edible and therefore subject to the *terumah* obligation:

וְכֵן מֵעִנְיַן הַמִּצְוָה מַה שֶּׁאָמְרוּ זִכְרוֹנָם לִבְרָכָה – **Also pertaining to this mitzvah is that which [the Sages], of blessed memory, stated** (see Mishnah, *Challah* 1:3), שֶׁאֵין חִיּוּב תְּרוּמוֹת וּמַעַשְׂרוֹת בְּפֵרוֹת

NOTES

21. Text emended in accordance with the cited *Rambam*.

22. In this case, not only the leaves but also the buds are subject to *terumah*. This is because the buds are considered more edible than the leaves, and since the person planted with the intent to eat an inferior part of the plant, any part superior to it is automatically included (*Derech Emunah* 2:38-39).

23. Since the seeds are the primary edible part of the coriander, even if one does not plan on eating them, they are still considered the "fruit" of the plant and subject to *terumah*.

עַד שֶׁיָּבִיאוּ שְׁלִישׁ[24]. וְכֵן מַה שֶּׁאָמְרוּ שֶׁהַלֶּקֶט וְהַשִּׁכְחָה וְהַפֵּאָה וְהָעוֹלֵלוֹת[25] שֶׁל יִשְׂרָאֵל אַף עַל פִּי שֶׁהֶעֱמִיד מֵהֶן כְּרִי בַּבַּיִת פְּטוּרִין מִן הַתְּרוּמָה וּמִן הַמַּעַשְׂרוֹת[26]. וְכֵן מַה שֶּׁאָמְרוּ שֶׁאֵין תּוֹרְמִין הַתְּרוּמָה לֹא בְמִדָּה וְלֹא בְמִנְיָן אֶלָּא בְּאֹמֶד, לְפִי שֶׁלֹּא נֶאֱמַר בָּהּ בַּתּוֹרָה שִׁעוּר, מַה שֶּׁאֵין כֵּן בְּמַעַשְׂרוֹת[27], וּכְבָר כָּתַבְתִּי בְּרֹאשׁ הַמִּצְוָה שֶׁעַיִן יָפָה מַפְרִישׁ אֶחָד מֵחֲמִשִּׁים[28] בְּאֹמֶד, וְלֹא יִתֵּן הַפֵּרוֹת בְּסַל וּבְקֻפָּה שֶׁמִּדָּתָן יְדוּעָה, אֲבָל תּוֹרֵם בָּהֶן חֶצְיָן אוֹ שְׁלִישָׁן[29].

עַד שֶׁיָּבִיאוּ שְׁלִישׁ – that there is no obligation of *terumos* or *maasros* on produce until it has grown one-third of its eventual growth.[24]

וְכֵן מַה שֶּׁאָמְרוּ – Also included in the mitzvah is **that which [the Sages] stated** (*Rambam* ibid. 2:9), **שֶׁהַלֶּקֶט וְהַשִּׁכְחָה וְהַפֵּאָה וְהָעוֹלֵלוֹת שֶׁל יִשְׂרָאֵל – that** the parts of the harvest that are left for the poor: ***leket, shich'chah, pe'ah,* and *oleilos***[25] **of** a field owned by **a Jew, אַף עַל פִּי שֶׁהֶעֱמִיד מֵהֶן כְּרִי בַּבַּיִת – even** at the stage **where** they were completely processed and **made into a pile in his house, פְּטוּרִין מִן הַתְּרוּמָה וּמִן הַמַּעַשְׂרוֹת – are exempt from *terumah* and *maasros*.**[26]

Chinuch cites a number of laws pertaining to the procedure for separating *terumah*:

וְכֵן מַה שֶּׁאָמְרוּ שֶׁאֵין תּוֹרְמִין הַתְּרוּמָה לֹא בְמִדָּה וְלֹא בְמִנְיָן אֶלָּא בְּאֹמֶד – Also included in the laws of the mitzvah **is that which [the Sages] stated** (*Rambam* ibid. 3:4), **that we do not separate *terumah* with a measure or count, but rather by estimation, לְפִי שֶׁלֹּא נֶאֱמַר בָּהּ בַּתּוֹרָה שִׁעוּר מַה שֶּׁאֵין כֵּן בְּמַעַשְׂרוֹת – for the Torah does not give a** minimum **amount [for *terumah*], in contrast to *maasros*,** for which the Torah sets the amount at one-tenth.[27] **וּכְבָר כָּתַבְתִּי בְּרֹאשׁ הַמִּצְוָה שֶׁעַיִן יָפָה מַפְרִישׁ אֶחָד מֵחֲמִשִּׁים בְּאֹמֶד – Now, I have already written in the beginning of the mitzvah that a** more **generous person gives a fiftieth;**[28] he is to separate this amount **by estimation. וְלֹא יִתֵּן הַפֵּרוֹת בְּסַל וּבְקֻפָּה שֶׁמִּדָּתָן יְדוּעָה – And,** when separating the *terumah*, **he should not put the produce in a basket or box that has a known measure, אֲבָל תּוֹרֵם בָּהֶן חֶצְיָן אוֹ שְׁלִישָׁן – but one may use them to take *terumah* by filling them** only to **half or a third** of their capacity.[29]

NOTES

24. This point in the development of the produce is known as עוֹנַת הַמַּעַשְׂרוֹת, *the stage of maasros*. See Mitzvah 395, where Chinuch notes another method to measure this stage, as well as indications that the Sages set out for when specific fruits reach this stage.

25. *Leket* (gleanings) refers to stalks of grain that fall to the ground during the harvest (Mitzvos 218-219); *shich'chah* (forgetting) refers to forgotten sheaves of grain (Mitzvos 592-593); *pe'ah* (edge) refers to the edge of the field, which one may not harvest (Mitzvos 216-217); *oleilos* refers to certain parts of the grapevine that may not be harvested (Mitzvah 220). All these portions of the crops are left for the poor.

26. The strongest level of the *terumah* and *maasros* obligations applies to the produce that is piled in one's house, at which point it is considered completely processed (see Mitzvah 395, at note 38). Nevertheless, the parts of the harvest left for the poor are exempt from *terumah* even in this form. This exemption is derived from Scripture (*Yerushalmi Maasros* 1b).

Chinuch specifically notes that the pile was made in the house. If the pile is made in the field, the Sages obligated the owner to give *terumah* and *maasros* even from this produce because those who see it would not be aware of the source of the produce and the reason for its exemption (see *Rambam* ibid. 2:9; see also *Minchas Yitzchak* §9).

27. From the fact that the Torah did not give any specific amount for *terumah,* it is understood that the Torah wished that *terumah* be given by estimation, not with an exact measure (see *Rambam Commentary* to *Terumos* 1:7, and *Derech Emunah* 3:33). Other Rishonim explain that the reason for this law is so that people should give generously, since people give more generously when they are not measuring exactly (*Rash*, *Terumos* ibid.). See *Derech Emunah* ibid. for other reasons.

28. At the beginning of the mitzvah (at note 4), Chinuch writes that a person of *average* generosity gives one-fiftieth. As noted there, the Mishnah writes that a generous person gives one-fortieth and a stingy person one-sixtieth. Apparently, Chinuch's description here of a generous person refers to one who is more generous than one described in the Mishnah as stingy. Some versions of Chinuch, however, read here עַיִן בֵּינוֹנִי, *a person of average generosity*.

29. One should not fill a container whose measure is known because it appears like he is taking *terumah* with an exact amount. If, however, he does not fill the container, it is permitted, because the amount is not precisely known (*Derech Emunah* 3:39-40).

וּמֻתָּר[30] לִתְרֹם שֶׁלֹּא מִן הַמֻּקָּף, וְאַף עַל פִּי כֵן תַּלְמִידֵי חֲכָמִים אֵין עוֹשִׂין כֵּן, כֵּן כָּתַב הָרַמְבַּ"ם ז"ל[31]. וּמַה שֶּׁאָמְרוּ שֶׁעוֹשֶׂה אָדָם שָׁלִיחַ יִשְׂרָאֵל לְהַפְרִישׁ תְּרוּמָה וּמַעַשְׂרוֹת שֶׁנֶּאֱמַר (במדבר י"ח, כ"ח) **כֵּן תָּרִימוּ גַם אַתֶּם, לְרַבּוֹת הַשָּׁלִיחַ שֶׁהוּא בֶּן בְּרִית כְּמוֹ כֵן[32], וְעוֹד דִּינִין רַבִּים בַּגְּמָרָא מֵעִנְיַן הַשְּׁלִיחוּת[33]. וּמַה שֶּׁאָמְרוּ שֶׁהַתְּרוּמָה נֶאֱכֶלֶת לַכֹּהֲנִים בֵּין גְּדוֹלִים בֵּין קְטַנִּים לָהֶם וְלִנְשֵׁיהֶם וּלְעַבְדֵיהֶם הַכְּנַעֲנִים וַאֲפִלּוּ לְבֶהֱמְתָּן, וְעוֹד דִּינִין רַבִּים בַּגְּמָרָא עַל זֶה כְּגוֹן אִשָּׁה שֶׁמָּרְדָה, וְהָעֶבֶד שֶׁבָּרַח[34], וְדִין גְּרוּשִׁין וְאֵרוּסִין וְכַמָּה כַּיּוֹצֵא**

Chinuch adds a law pertaining to separating *terumas maaser*:[30]

וּמֻתָּר לִתְרֹם שֶׁלֹּא מִן הַמֻּקָּף – **It is permitted to designate** *terumas maaser* even if the produce that one is designating it is **not in proximity** to the remaining produce that is being exempted by this designation. **וְאַף עַל פִּי כֵן תַּלְמִידֵי חֲכָמִים אֵין עוֹשִׂין כֵּן** – **Even so, Torah scholars do not do this;** rather, they are particular to designate *terumas maaser* only if it is in proximity to the rest of the produce. **כֵּן כָּתַב הָרַמְבַּ"ם ז"ל** – **So states *Rambam*, of blessed memory** (ibid. 3:20).[31]

וּמַה שֶּׁאָמְרוּ שֶׁעוֹשֶׂה אָדָם שָׁלִיחַ יִשְׂרָאֵל לְהַפְרִישׁ תְּרוּמָה וּמַעַשְׂרוֹת – **Also** included is **that which [the Sages] stated** (*Rambam* ibid. 4:1; *Kiddushin* 41a), **that a person may authorize a Jewish agent to separate *terumah* and *maasros*** on his behalf. **שֶׁנֶּאֱמַר "כֵּן תָּרִימוּ גַם אַתֶּם"** – This is learned **from that which is stated** (*Numbers* 18:28) with regard to the commandment to the Levi to separate *terumah* from his *maaser* (*terumas maaser*): ***So shall you, too, separate** the gift of* HASHEM; **לְרַבּוֹת הַשָּׁלִיחַ שֶׁהוּא בֶּן בְּרִית כְּמוֹ כֵן** – the word "too" **adds** that not only can the person himself separate *terumah*, but **one's agent who is also a member of the covenant,** e.g., a Jew, can also separate *terumah* for him.[32] **וְעוֹד דִּינִין רַבִּים בַּגְּמָרָא מֵעִנְיַן הַשְּׁלִיחוּת** – **Also** pertaining to this mitzvah are **the many laws** found **in the Gemara relating to agency (*shelichus*).**[33]

Who is eligible to eat *terumah*:

וּמַה שֶּׁאָמְרוּ שֶׁהַתְּרוּמָה נֶאֱכֶלֶת לַכֹּהֲנִים בֵּין גְּדוֹלִים בֵּין קְטַנִּים – There also is **that which [the Sages] stated** (*Rambam* ibid. 6:1), **that *terumah* may be eaten by Kohanim, both adults and minors; לָהֶם וְלִנְשֵׁיהֶם וּלְעַבְדֵיהֶם הַכְּנַעֲנִים וַאֲפִלּוּ לְבֶהֱמְתָּן** – not only is it permissible **to them,** but also **to their wives, their Canaanite slaves, and even their animals. וְעוֹד דִּינִין רַבִּים בַּגְּמָרָא עַל זֶה** – **There are many additional laws** discussed **in the Gemara relating to this** subject, i.e., who may eat *terumah*, **כְּגוֹן אִשָּׁה שֶׁמָּרְדָה וְהָעֶבֶד שֶׁבָּרַח** – **such as whether a woman,** the wife of a Kohen, **who rebelled** against her husband and no longer lives with him, **or a** Canaanite **slave** of a Kohen **who fled** from his master, may eat *terumah*,[34] **וְדִין גְּרוּשִׁין וְאֵרוּסִין וְכַמָּה כַּיּוֹצֵא**

NOTES

30. *Minchas Yitzchak* (§11) explains that the following law must refer to *terumas maaser*, as the cited law clearly does not apply to *terumah*; see following note.

31. *Terumah* must be designated in proximity to the produce that is being permitted through it (*Rambam* ibid. 3:17). *Maaser*, on the other hand, need not be designated in this way (*Rambam*, *Hil. Maaser* 1:6). *Terumas maaser* shares the same halachah as *maaser* and it need not be together with the rest of the produce during the designation. [For reasons for these guidelines, see Mitzvah 395 note 25 and Mitzvah 396 note 24.]

Although *terumas maaser* shares the same halachah as *maaser* and does not need to be in the proximity of the rest of the produce, it is the practice of Torah scholars to separate *terumas maaser* with the same restrictions as *terumah*, because *terumas maaser* could be confused with *terumah*, which *does* need to be separated in proximity to the rest of the produce (see *Beur HaHalachah, Hil. Maaser* 1:6 ד"ה וא"צ לעשר).

32. The word "too" in this verse appears superfluous. The Gemara expounds this as a reference to the agent of the produce's owner. This word also teaches that in order to serve as an agent, the agent must be similar to the owner, i.e., he also must be a member of the covenant. [This rule of agency applies in all other areas of Torah law as well (*Radvaz* to *Rambam* ad loc.).]

33. This includes such laws as who may serve as an agent, how one appoints a valid agent, and the halachah in the case that the agent did not follow his instructions exactly (see, for example, *Kiddushin* 42b; 48b; *Kesubos* 100a; *Rambam* discusses the laws of agency as it relates to *terumah* in *Hil. Terumos*, Chapter 4).

34. As long as the woman was not divorced and the slave was not freed, they may both eat *terumah* (*Rambam* ibid. 6:1).

בָּהֶן[35]. וְדִינֵי הַתְּרוּמָה בְּעִנְיַן בִּטּוּלָהּ שֶׁנָּתְנוּ לָהּ שִׁעוּר חֲכָמִים זִכְרוֹנָם לִבְרָכָה בְּאֶחָד וּמֵאָה[36], וְיֶתֶר רִבֵּי פְּרָטֶיהָ בְּמַסֶּכֶת תְּרוּמוֹת וּבְהַרְבֵּה מְקוֹמוֹת מֵהַתַּלְמוּד בְּפִזּוּר קְצָת מִדִּינֶיהָ[37].

וְנוֹהֶגֶת מִצְוַת הַתְּרוּמָה גַּם מִצְוַת הַמַּעַשְׂרוֹת מִן הַתּוֹרָה בְּאֶרֶץ יִשְׂרָאֵל וּבִזְמַן שֶׁיִּשְׂרָאֵל שָׁם.

בָּהֶן – **and the law of divorce and marriage** as they relate to allowing the woman to eat *terumah*, **and many** other laws **like them** that relate to this subject.[35]

וְדִינֵי הַתְּרוּמָה בְּעִנְיַן בִּטּוּלָהּ – **Also** included are **the laws of *terumah* with regard to nullification,** that is, if some *terumah* was mixed with other similar food and cannot be distinguished, שֶׁנָּתְנוּ לָהּ שִׁעוּר חֲכָמִים זִכְרוֹנָם לִבְרָכָה בְּאֶחָד וּמֵאָה – **where the Sages, of blessed memory, set the amount** necessary for the nullification of the *terumah* **at one hundred and one;** that is, one part *terumah* that is mixed with one hundred parts non-*terumah* is considered nullified. The *terumah* loses its special status and the entire mixture may be eaten by a non-Kohen.[36]

וְיֶתֶר רִבֵּי פְּרָטֶיהָ בְּמַסֶּכֶת תְּרוּמוֹת – **The rest of its many laws are found in Tractate *Terumos*,** וּבְהַרְבֵּה מְקוֹמוֹת מֵהַתַּלְמוּד בְּפִזּוּר קְצָת מִדִּינֶיהָ – **and some of the laws** are found **distributed in many places in the Talmud.**[37]

Applicability of the Mitzvah

וְנוֹהֶגֶת מִצְוַת הַתְּרוּמָה גַּם מִצְוַת הַמַּעַשְׂרוֹת מִן הַתּוֹרָה – **The mitzvah of *terumah* as well as the mitzvah of *maasros* apply by Biblical law** בְּאֶרֶץ יִשְׂרָאֵל וּבִזְמַן שֶׁיִּשְׂרָאֵל שָׁם – **in Eretz Yisrael, during the time that** all or most of **the Jewish people live there** (as explained below).

The *Terumah* Obligation in Eretz Yisrael Today

In connection with his discussion of the applicability of *terumah* nowadays, Chinuch embarks on a wide-ranging treatment of the halachic status of Eretz Yisrael and its surrounding lands, from the first conquest in the times of Joshua until the present era of the second exile.

The original conquest of Eretz Yisrael by Joshua and his generation (referred to as "those ascending from Egypt"),[38] marked the beginning of the first commonwealth. This period ended with the destruction of the first *Beis HaMikdash* and the exile of the Jewish people to Babylonia.[39] The second commonwealth began with the return from the Babylonian exile of a small minority of the Jewish people under the leadership of Ezra. Jewish control of Eretz Yisrael lasted until the destruction of the second *Beis HaMikdash* and the exile of the Jewish people by the Roman Empire.

The bulk of the following discussion is a direct citation of *Rambam* in the first chapter of *Hilchos Terumos.* Chinuch begins with the final ruling of *Rambam* in that chapter regarding the practical status of the *terumah* obligation in Eretz Yisrael today, and the dissenting view of *Raavad* (many of the ideas mentioned in this ruling will be explained and expanded upon in the subsequent discussion):

NOTES

35. The laws of marriage and divorce have specific applications to *terumah,* since the wife of a Kohen may eat *terumah* and if she is divorced she loses this permit. Chinuch elaborates somewhat on these and other related laws in Mitzvah 280.

36. Nevertheless, so as not to cause loss to Kohanim due to this nullification, the owner must remove an amount equal to the *terumah* that fell in and give that amount to a Kohen as *terumah* (see *Rambam* ibid. 13:1 with *Derech Emunah*).

37. The laws of *terumah* are codified in *Rambam, Hil. Terumos*, and in *Shulchan Aruch, Yoreh Deah* §331.

38. Those who come into Eretz Yisrael from any location are always referred to as "ascending," since Eretz Yisrael is considered the pinnacle of the world (*Kiddushin* 69a; see *Maharal*, *Chiddushei Aggados* there).

39. Although the ten tribes were exiled from Eretz Yisrael over 100 years before the destruction of the first *Beis HaMikdash,* the first commonwealth is considered to have lasted until the time of the Destruction with regard to these laws; see *Derech Emunah*, *Tziyun HaHalachah* 1:80.

וְכֵן כָּתַב הָרַמְבַּ״ם ז״ל סוֹף פֶּרֶק רִאשׁוֹן דְּהִלְכוֹת תְּרוּמוֹת וְזֶה לְשׁוֹנוֹ, הַתְּרוּמָה בַּזְּמַן הַזֶּה אֲפִלּוּ בְּמָקוֹם שֶׁהֶחֱזִיקוּ עוֹלֵי בָּבֶל וַאֲפִלּוּ בִּימֵי עֶזְרָא אֵינָהּ מִן הַתּוֹרָה אֶלָּא מִדִּבְרֵיהֶם, שֶׁאֵין לְךָ תְּרוּמָה שֶׁל תּוֹרָה אֶלָּא בְּאֶרֶץ יִשְׂרָאֵל וּבִזְמַן שֶׁהָיוּ שָׁם כָּל יִשְׂרָאֵל, שֶׁנֶּאֱמַר כִּי תָבֹאוּ[40], בִּיאַת כֻּלְּכֶם[41] כְּשֶׁהָיוּ בִּירֻשָּׁה רִאשׁוֹנָה, וּכְמוֹ שֶׁהֵם עֲתִידִים לַחֲזֹר בִּירֻשָּׁה שְׁלִישִׁית, וְלֹא כְּשֶׁהָיוּ בִּירֻשָּׁה בִּימֵי עֶזְרָא שֶׁהָיְתָה בִּיאַת מִקְצַתְכֶם, וּלְפִיכָךְ לֹא הָיְתָה מִן הַתּוֹרָה, וְכֵן הַדִּין נִרְאֶה לִי בְּמַעַשְׂרוֹת שֶׁאֵין חַיָּבִין בָּהֶן בַּזְּמַן הַזֶּה אֶלָּא מִדִּבְרֵיהֶם כִּתְרוּמָה[42], עַד כָּאן[43]. וְהָרַאֲבַ״ד ז״ל תָּפַס עָלָיו בְּעִנְיָן זֶה, וְזֶה לְשׁוֹנוֹ,

וְכֵן כָּתַב הָרַמְבַּ״ם ז״ל סוֹף פֶּרֶק רִאשׁוֹן דְּהִלְכוֹת תְּרוּמוֹת — ***Rambam*, of blessed memory, writes as follows at the end of the first chapter of *Hilchos Terumos*** (§26), וְזֶה לְשׁוֹנוֹ — **and this is a quote:** הַתְּרוּמָה בַּזְּמַן הַזֶּה — The law of ***terumah* nowadays,** אֲפִלּוּ בְּמָקוֹם שֶׁהֶחֱזִיקוּ עוֹלֵי בָּבֶל וַאֲפִלּוּ בִּימֵי עֶזְרָא — **even in the places** in Eretz Yisrael **that were taken by those ascending from Babylonia, and even during the era of Ezra,** i.e., throughout the second commonwealth, אֵינָהּ מִן הַתּוֹרָה אֶלָּא מִדִּבְרֵיהֶם — was not then, and **is not** now, **Biblical, but** only a **Rabbinic** obligation. שֶׁאֵין לְךָ תְּרוּמָה שֶׁל תּוֹרָה אֶלָּא בְּאֶרֶץ יִשְׂרָאֵל וּבִזְמַן שֶׁהָיוּ שָׁם כָּל יִשְׂרָאֵל — **For Biblically mandated *terumah* applies only in Eretz Yisrael and** only **when the entire Jewish people are there,** שֶׁנֶּאֱמַר "כִּי תָבֹאוּ" — **as it is stated** with regard to the *challah* obligation (*Numbers* 15:18): ***When you*** (the Jewish people) ***enter*** into the land;[40] בִּיאַת כֻּלְּכֶם — this wording implies that it is only **upon the entry of all of you** into Eretz Yisrael that there is an obligation.[41] כְּשֶׁהָיוּ בִּירֻשָּׁה רִאשׁוֹנָה — This refers to **the way [the Jewish people] existed during** the era of **the first conquest** in the times of Joshua, when the entire nation entered into Eretz Yisrael, וּכְמוֹ שֶׁהֵם עֲתִידִים לַחֲזֹר בִּירֻשָּׁה שְׁלִישִׁית — **and the way they will** exist upon their **return in the future during the third conquest,** when the Messiah will bring all of the Jewish people back to Eretz Yisrael; וְלֹא כְּשֶׁהָיוּ בִּירֻשָּׁה בִּימֵי עֶזְרָא שֶׁהָיְתָה בִּיאַת מִקְצַתְכֶם — **but not the way they existed during the conquest in Ezra's time, which was "an entry of** only **some of you,"** for when Ezra came to Eretz Yisrael, only a minority of the Jewish people came with him (see *Ezra* 2:64). וּלְפִיכָךְ לֹא הָיְתָה מִן הַתּוֹרָה — **Therefore,** since this second "conquest" did not fulfill the criteria of "the entry of all of you," during the period of Ezra **[the *terumah* obligation] was not Biblically mandated,** but was a Rabbinic requirement; and this is the rule nowadays as well. וְכֵן הַדִּין נִרְאֶה לִי בְּמַעַשְׂרוֹת — Not only is this the case with the *terumah* obligation, but **it appears to me that this is also the case with** the ***maasros*** obligations; שֶׁאֵין חַיָּבִין בָּהֶן בַּזְּמַן הַזֶּה אֶלָּא מִדִּבְרֵיהֶם כִּתְרוּמָה — meaning **that nowadays we are obligated to separate *maasros* only by Rabbinic law.**[42] עַד כָּאן — **Until here** is the citation from *Rambam*.[43] וְהָרַאֲבַ״ד ז״ל תָּפַס עָלָיו בְּעִנְיָן זֶה וְזֶה לְשׁוֹנוֹ — **However, *Raavad*, of blessed memory, objected to**

NOTES

40. [This should actually read בְּבֹאֲכֶם (*Derech Emunah* 1:228).] This verse introduces the mitzvah of *challah* (Mitzvah 385), the obligation to give a Kohen a portion of every dough that one prepares. The parameters of the *terumah* obligation are derived from the verse describing the *challah* obligation, since the verse itself equates *challah* with *terumah*: *Like the terumah-portion of the threshing-floor, so shall you separate it* (*Numbers* 15:20).

41. The plural possessive suffix ־כֶם, *your* (see previous note), indicates that it is the entry of the entire nation [to whom the plural form is addressed] that effects the obligation of *challah* (*Tos. HaRosh* to *Niddah* 47a).

42. Although the Scriptural rule was stated with regard to *challah*, and by extension to *terumah* (see note 40), *Rambam* states that it appears that this application would apply to *maasros* as well, since *terumah* and *maasros* share most of the criteria of their respective obligations (*Derech Emunah* 1:230).

43. Although *Rambam* maintains that the *sanctity* of Eretz Yisrael remained throughout the second commonwealth, and indeed remains from then for all time (see below, at note 65), in order for the *terumah* obligation to apply by Biblical law a second condition is necessary: that all or most of the Jewish people reside in Eretz Yisrael. Since that condition did not apply even with Ezra's ascent to Eretz Yisrael and throughout the second commonwealth, the *terumah* obligation has not been in force by Biblical law since the first exile.

אָמַר אַבְרָהָם[44], לֹא כִוֵּן לַהֲלָכָה יָפֶה, דְּהָא קַיְמָא לַן כְּרַבִּי יוֹחָנָן דְּאָמְרִינַן בִּיבָמוֹת (פ״א ע״א) תְּרוּמָה בַּזְּמַן הַזֶּה דְּאוֹרַיְתָא, כְּלוֹמַר בְּאֶרֶץ יִשְׂרָאֵל[45], וְהוּא עַצְמוֹ נִרְאֶה שֶׁכָּךְ כָּתַב בִּתְחִלַּת הַסֵּפֶר[46], וְאִם אִיתָא לְהָא מִלְּתָא בְּחַלָּה הוּא דְּאִיתָא[47], עַד כָּאן.

וְעַתָּה אִם הָאֱמֶת כְּדִבְרֵי הָרַאֲבָ״ד ז״ל יִהְיֶה לָנוּ לַחְשֹׁב בִּכְלַל מִצְוֹת הַנּוֹהֲגוֹת עַכְשָׁו בָּאָרֶץ מִדְּאוֹרַיְתָא זֹאת הַמִּצְוָה, וְגַם שִׁשָּׁה עוֹד שֶׁהֵם בְּעִנְיַן הַתְּרוּמָה בְּסֵדֶר אֱמֹר וְהֵן י״ד ט״ו י״ו י״ז י״ח י״ט מִן הַלָּאוִין (מצוות רע״ט-רפ״ד)[48], וְאַחַת שֶׁהִיא בְּכֶסֶף תַּלְוֶה[49] לָאו ו׳

Rambam*'s opinion on this and the following is a quote** of his gloss there: אָמַר אַבְרָהָם לֹא כִוֵּן לַהֲלָכָה יָפֶה – **Avraham says:**[44] **He** (*Rambam*) **did not arrive at the correct halachah** in this matter, דְּהָא קַיְמָא לַן כְּרַבִּי יוֹחָנָן דְּאָמְרִינַן בִּיבָמוֹת – **because it has been established** that the halachah accords **with R' Yochanan, as it is stated in *Yevamos (81a): תְּרוּמָה בַּזְּמַן הַזֶּה דְּאוֹרַיְתָא כְּלוֹמַר בְּאֶרֶץ יִשְׂרָאֵל – **The *terumah* obligation nowadays is Biblical; that is, in Eretz Yisrael.**[45] וְהוּא עַצְמוֹ נִרְאֶה שֶׁכָּךְ כָּתַב בִּתְחִלַּת הַסֵּפֶר – **And [*Rambam*] himself appears to have written so in the beginning of the book.**[46] וְאִם אִיתָא לְהָא מִלְּתָא בְּחַלָּה הוּא דְּאִיתָא – **And if this matter is true**, i.e., that the obligation nowadays is not Biblical, **it is only regarding** the ***challah*** obligation **that it is true,** but the obligation to separate *terumah* and *maasros* is surely Biblical even nowadays.[47] עַד כָּאן – **Until here** is the quote from *Raavad*.

At the end of the Author's Introduction to this work, in "The Order and Count of the Mitzvos," Chinuch sets the total number of mitzvos at 613, and divides them by various characteristics, such as when they apply, to whom, and under which circumstances. Chinuch writes that 369 of the mitzvos apply nowadays. Throughout the work, at the conclusion of each mitzvah, Chinuch points out whether that mitzvah applies nowadays or not. Here, Chinuch addresses his classification of a number of mitzvos in light of the above disagreement between *Rambam* and *Raavad*:

וְעַתָּה אִם הָאֱמֶת כְּדִבְרֵי הָרַאֲבָ״ד ז״ל – **Now, if the truth is like the opinion of *Raavad*, of blessed memory,** יִהְיֶה לָנוּ לַחְשֹׁב בִּכְלַל מִצְוֹת הַנּוֹהֲגוֹת עַכְשָׁו בָּאָרֶץ מִדְּאוֹרַיְתָא זֹאת הַמִּצְוָה – **we would have to count this mitzvah** of *terumah* **among the mitzvos that apply nowadays in Eretz Yisrael by Biblical law,** וְגַם שִׁשָּׁה עוֹד שֶׁהֵם בְּעִנְיַן הַתְּרוּמָה בְּסֵדֶר אֱמֹר – **as well as six others that pertain to *terumah* in *Parashas Emor*;** וְהֵן י״ד ט״ו י״ו י״ז י״ח י״ט מִן הַלָּאוִין – **they are,** in the count **of mitzvah-prohibitions** of that *parashah*, Mitzvos **14, 15, 16, 17, 18, and 19** (Mitzvos 279-284);[48] וְאַחַת שֶׁהִיא בְּכֶסֶף תַּלְוֶה לָאו ו׳ – **and** we would have to count an additional **one in**

NOTES

44. "*Raavad* " is an acronym for *Rav Avraham ben David*. Each of his glosses to *Rambam*'s *Mishneh Torah* open with the words "Avraham says."

45. The question of whether the *terumah* obligation is Biblical nowadays is debated in the Gemara there, as well as in *Yerushalmi Sheviis* (beginning of Chapter 6). The issue is also mentioned in numerous other places in the Talmud (see the various commentaries to the cited *Rambam*). *Raavad* maintains that the halachah follows the view of R' Yochanan, as he cites from *Yevamos*.

46. The commentators explain that this refers to what *Rambam* writes at the beginning of *Hil. Terumos* (1:1), that the *terumah* obligation applies by Biblical law whether the *Beis HaMikdash* is standing or not. In *Rambam*'s defense, however, they explain that this does not contradict *Rambam*'s position here, since it is not the absence of the *Beis HaMikdash* that removes the Biblical obligation, but the absence of the conquest of Eretz Yisrael by the majority of the Jewish people (see *Kesef Mishneh* and *Radvaz* ibid. 1:1, 26).

47. *Raavad* maintains that the sanctity of Eretz Yisrael returned with the second commonwealth and is still extant, as *Rambam* himself maintains. However, *Raavad* argues that this alone suffices to make a Biblical *terumah* obligation, even without the return of the majority of the nation. At most, *Raavad* says, the requirement of "the entry of all of you" pertains to the *challah* obligation, where that requirement is mentioned. But *terumah* is not equated with *challah* in respect to this law.

Many commentators to *Rambam* point to various sources in both *Talmud Bavli* and *Yerushalmi* that may serve as *Rambam*'s source for his ruling that the *terumah* obligation does not have Biblical force nowadays.

48. Chinuch uses the numbering of the original arrangement of this work, in which the mitzvah-obligations and mitzvah-prohibitions of each *parashah* were listed and numbered separately (see Mitzvah 494 note 4).

(מצוה ע״ב), **וּשְׁתַּיִם שֶׁהֵן בְּסֵדֶר וַיִּקַּח קֹרַח מִצְוַת מַעֲשֵׂר וּמַעֲשֵׂר מִן הַמַּעֲשֵׂר** (שצ״ה־ו׳). **אֲבָל אֲנִי דִּבְרֵי הָרַמְבַּ״ם ז״ל אָשִׂים בֵּין עֵינַי וּמִבּוֹרוֹ אֶשְׁאַב, כִּי הוּא סִבַּת זֶה הָעֵסֶק שֶׁל חֶשְׁבּוֹן הַמִּצְוֹת לִי וּלְכָל שֶׁבָּאוּ אַחֲרָיו**[50]**. וּמִכָּל מָקוֹם אֵין חוֹלֵק בָּעוֹלָם שֶׁנּוֹהֲגוֹת מִדְּרַבָּנָן אַף בְּאֶרֶץ שִׁנְעָר מִפְּנֵי שֶׁהִיא סְמוּכָה לְאֶרֶץ יִשְׂרָאֵל וְרֹב יִשְׂרָאֵל הוֹלְכִים וְשָׁבִים שָׁם**[51]**, וְגַם הִתְקִינוּ שֶׁיְּהוּ נוֹהֲגִין תְּרוּמוֹת וּמַעַשְׂרוֹת אַף בְּאֶרֶץ מִצְרַיִם וּבְאֶרֶץ בְּנֵי עַמּוֹן וּמוֹאָב**[52] **מִפְּנֵי שֶׁהֵן סְבִיבוֹת אֶרֶץ יִשְׂרָאֵל**[53]**.**

Parashas Im Kesef Talveh,[49] **Mitzvah-prohibition 6** (Mitzvah 72); **וּשְׁתַּיִם שֶׁהֵן בְּסֵדֶר וַיִּקַּח קֹרַח מִצְוַת מַעֲשֵׂר וּמַעֲשֵׂר מִן הַמַּעֲשֵׂר** – **as well as two** mitzvos **in *Parashas Korach*: the mitzvah of *maaser*** (Mitzvah 395), **and the mitzvah of *maaser* of the *maaser***, i.e., *terumas maaser* (Mitzvah 396). That is, following *Raavad's* approach there would be ten more mitzvos that must be classified as applying nowadays by Biblical law. **אֲבָל אֲנִי דִּבְרֵי הָרַמְבַּ״ם ז״ל אָשִׂים בֵּין עֵינַי וּמִבּוֹרוֹ אֶשְׁאַב** – **But** I did not follow this approach in classifying these mitzvos, because **I set the words of *Rambam*, of blessed memory, as the focus of my eyes, and I draw from his well, כִּי הוּא סִבַּת זֶה הָעֵסֶק שֶׁל חֶשְׁבּוֹן הַמִּצְוֹת לִי וּלְכָל שֶׁבָּאוּ אַחֲרָיו** – **because** it is **he** that **is the impetus of this endeavor of calculating the mitzvos for me and for everyone who comes after him.**[50]

Chinuch notes that there are certain areas outside of Eretz Yisrael where all agree that the Biblical obligation does not apply and a Rabbinic obligation does. The following section is quoted, with minor adjustments, from *Rambam, Hil. Terumos* 1:1-7:

וּמִכָּל מָקוֹם אֵין חוֹלֵק בָּעוֹלָם – **Nevertheless,** while there are differing opinions regarding the status of *terumah* in Eretz Yisrael nowadays, **there is no one in the world who disagrees** with the fact **שֶׁנּוֹהֲגוֹת מִדְּרַבָּנָן אַף בְּאֶרֶץ שִׁנְעָר** – (§1) **that [the *terumah* and *maasros* obligations] apply by Rabbinic law in the land of Shinar** [Babylonia]. **מִפְּנֵי שֶׁהִיא סְמוּכָה לְאֶרֶץ יִשְׂרָאֵל וְרֹב יִשְׂרָאֵל הוֹלְכִים וְשָׁבִים שָׁם** – The Sages enacted this obligation **because [Babylonia] is close to Eretz Yisrael and multitudes of Jewish people go back and forth** from Eretz Yisrael **[to Babylonia].**[51] **וְגַם הִתְקִינוּ שֶׁיְּהוּ נוֹהֲגִין תְּרוּמוֹת וּמַעַשְׂרוֹת אַף בְּאֶרֶץ מִצְרַיִם וּבְאֶרֶץ בְּנֵי עַמּוֹן וּמוֹאָב** – At a later point, **[the Sages] further instituted that *terumos* and *maasros* should apply in the land of Egypt and in the land of Ammon and Moab,**[52] **מִפְּנֵי שֶׁהֵן סְבִיבוֹת אֶרֶץ יִשְׂרָאֵל** – **because [these lands] surround Eretz Yisrael.**[53]

◈ The Sanctity and Halachic Status of Eretz Yisrael

Continuing his citation of *Rambam*, Chinuch sets out the various stages of the sanctity and halachic status of Eretz Yisrael, beginning with the first conquest during the times of Joshua, until today. Also included in this discussion are various other lands that were annexed to Eretz Yisrael during the time of King David, and the intermediate halachic status that these lands possess.

The Jewish people, under Joshua, were charged with the obligation to conquer the land from its

---

NOTES

49. This refers to the second part of *Parashas Mishpatim*; see Mitzvah 495 note 5.

50. *Rambam*'s count of the mitzvos in his *Sefer HaMitzvos* serves as the basis for the count of mitzvos in this work; see Author's Introduction, at the beginning of "The Order and Count of the Mitzvos."

51. This refers to the land to the northeast of Eretz Yisrael in the area of modern day Iraq. This obligation was enacted by the prophets who lived at the time of the destruction of the first *Beis HaMikdash* and who were exiled to Babylonia with the Jewish people. They were concerned that due to the proximity of Babylonia to Eretz Yisrael and the prevalent traffic of Jews from one place to another, if Babylonia would be exempt, people would come to neglect the *terumah* and *maasros* obligation in Eretz Yisrael itself (*Rambam* ibid. 1:1, with *Derech Emunah* §4,8).

52. Ammon and Moab are regions to the east of the Jordan River. [For further discussion about which specific area is referred to here, see *Derech Emunah* 1:10.]

53. In the generation after Ezra, when Jews began settling in the surrounding lands, the Sages of the time expanded the *terumah* and *maasros* obligations to these additional areas (*Derech Emunah* 1:9,12).

וְאֶרֶץ יִשְׂרָאֵל הָאֲמוּרָה בְּכָל מָקוֹם הֵן אֲרָצוֹת שֶׁכָּבַשׁ אוֹתָן מֶלֶךְ יִשְׂרָאֵל אוֹ שׁוֹפֵט אוֹ נָבִיא מִדַּעַת רֹב יִשְׂרָאֵל, וְזֶהוּ שֶׁיִּקְרְאוּ חֲכָמִים זִכְרוֹנָם לִבְרָכָה כִּבּוּשׁ רַבִּים[54], אֲבָל יָחִיד מִיִּשְׂרָאֵל אוֹ מִשְׁפָּחָה אוֹ שֵׁבֶט שֶׁנָּתְנוּ כָּבוֹד לְעַצְמָם וְכָבְשׁוּ מָקוֹם אֶחָד, וַאֲפִלּוּ הוּא תּוֹךְ תְּחוּמֵי הָאָרֶץ שֶׁנִּתְּנָה לְאַבְרָהָם אָבִינוּ, אֵינוֹ נִקְרָא אֶרֶץ יִשְׂרָאֵל[55]. וְהַמְּקוֹמוֹת שֶׁחָלַק יְהוֹשֻׁעַ לַשְּׁבָטִים אַף עַל פִּי שֶׁלֹּא נִכְבְּשׁוּ כֻּלָּם, דִּינָן כְּדִין אֶרֶץ יִשְׂרָאֵל כְּדֵי שֶׁלֹּא תִהְיֶה רְבָה כִּבּוּשׁ יָחִיד כְּשֶׁיַּעֲלֶה כָּל שֵׁבֶט וְשֵׁבֶט וְיִכְבֹּשׁ חֶלְקוֹ[56].

---

previous inhabitants, the seven Canaanite nations (see *Numbers* Ch. 34). As Chinuch explains here, the halachic status of Eretz Yisrael with regard to most mitzvos began only when these areas were conquered by the Jewish people:

וְאֶרֶץ יִשְׂרָאֵל הָאֲמוּרָה בְּכָל מָקוֹם – (§2) **In any instance that** the term **"Eretz Yisrael" is mentioned,** הֵן אֲרָצוֹת שֶׁכָּבַשׁ אוֹתָן מֶלֶךְ יִשְׂרָאֵל אוֹ שׁוֹפֵט אוֹ נָבִיא – **it refers to lands that were conquered by a king of Israel, or a Judge** who was the leader of the people, **or a prophet,** מִדַּעַת רֹב יִשְׂרָאֵל – **with the consent of the majority of the Jewish people.** וְזֶהוּ שֶׁיִּקְרְאוּ חֲכָמִים זִכְרוֹנָם לִבְרָכָה כִּבּוּשׁ רַבִּים – **It is this that the Sages, of blessed memory, call "conquest of the public."**[54] אֲבָל יָחִיד מִיִּשְׂרָאֵל אוֹ מִשְׁפָּחָה אוֹ שֵׁבֶט – **But an individual Jew, or** even **a family or tribe,** שֶׁנָּתְנוּ כָּבוֹד לְעַצְמָם וְכָבְשׁוּ מָקוֹם אֶחָד – **who pursued their own honor and conquered a place,** וַאֲפִלּוּ הוּא תּוֹךְ תְּחוּמֵי הָאָרֶץ שֶׁנִּתְּנָה לְאַבְרָהָם אָבִינוּ – **even if it is within the boundaries of the land given to our forefather Abraham,** אֵינוֹ נִקְרָא אֶרֶץ יִשְׂרָאֵל – **is not called Eretz Yisrael** with regard to Torah law.[55]

When the Jewish people first entered Eretz Yisrael, they did not conquer the entire land at once. But even before the land was conquered, Joshua divided the whole of Eretz Yisrael, and allotted specific portions to each tribe. After the portions were allotted, the individual tribes went and conquered the lands designated for them (*Joshua* Chs. 13-19).

The question arises, if even tribal conquest is considered "the conquest of an individual," as stated above, how were the areas conquered by the individual tribes considered part of Eretz Yisrael according to halachah? Chinuch addresses this issue:

וְהַמְּקוֹמוֹת שֶׁחָלַק יְהוֹשֻׁעַ לַשְּׁבָטִים – Regarding **the areas that Joshua allotted to the** individual **tribes,** אַף עַל פִּי שֶׁלֹּא נִכְבְּשׁוּ כֻּלָּם – **even though they were not all conquered** by the entire nation when they entered the land, דִּינָן כְּדִין אֶרֶץ יִשְׂרָאֵל – **their status is like that of** the rest of **Eretz Yisrael.** כְּדֵי שֶׁלֹּא תִהְיֶה רְבָה כִּבּוּשׁ יָחִיד כְּשֶׁיַּעֲלֶה כָּל שֵׁבֶט וְשֵׁבֶט וְיִכְבֹּשׁ חֶלְקוֹ – Indeed, it was for this very reason that Joshua allotted the entire land to the individual tribes, **so that when each tribe** subsequently **conquered its portion, it would *not* be considered *the conquest of an individual.*** By allotting the entire land, Joshua ensured that each tribe conquered it as emissaries of the whole nation. The conquered areas were therefore considered the conquest of the public, and thus acquired the special status of Eretz Yisrael.[56]

After being established as king of Israel, King David led campaigns that conquered areas neighboring Eretz Yisrael (see *II Samuel* Ch. 8). Chinuch sets out the status of those areas with regard to land-dependent mitzvos:

NOTES

54. In a number of places (*Gittin* 8b, 47a and *Avodah Zarah* 21a), the Sages discuss the status of areas that were brought under the control of Eretz Yisrael by the "conquest of an individual," and whether such areas should be considered part of Eretz Yisrael. Conversely, lands conquered by the nation as a whole or its representatives are considered "conquest of the public" and are certainly considered part of Eretz Yisrael. See further below.

55. Although God promised Abraham that He would give Eretz Yisrael to his offspring (*Genesis* 15:18-21), in order to attain the halachic status of Eretz Yisrael, the area must have been conquered by the Jewish people as a whole. The promise to Abraham will be completely fulfilled in the time of Mashiach (see *Derech Emunah* 1:24).

56. For discussion of this concept, see *Derech Emunah* 1:28; *Maadanei Eretz* to *Rambam, Hil. Terumos* 1:2, §4.

הָאָרֶץ שֶׁכָּבַשׁ דָּוִד, כְּגוֹן אֲרַם נַהֲרַיִם[57] וַאֲרַם צוֹבָה[58] כָּל יַד פְּרָת עַד בָּבֶל וְדַמֶּשֶׂק וְאַחְלַב[59] וְחָרָן וְכַיּוֹצֵא בָּהֶן, אַף עַל פִּי שֶׁבִּרְשׁוּת בֵּית דִּין הַגָּדוֹל כְּבָשָׁם, אֵינָם כְּאֶרֶץ יִשְׂרָאֵל לְכָל דָּבָר, אֶלָּא יָצְאוּ מִכְּלַל חוּצָה לָאָרֶץ וְלִכְלַל אֶרֶץ יִשְׂרָאֵל לֹא בָאוּ[60], וְהֵם הַנִּקְרָאִים בְּכָל מָקוֹם סוּרְיָא, וְיֵשׁ דְּבָרִים שֶׁדִּינָם כְּאֶרֶץ יִשְׂרָאֵל וְיֵשׁ שֶׁדִּינָם כְּחוּצָה לָאָרֶץ כְּמוֹ שֶׁתִּמְצָא בַּגְּמָרָא בִּמְקוֹמוֹת בְּפִזּוּר, וְהַטַּעַם מִפְּנֵי שֶׁכָּבַשׁ אוֹתָם קֹדֶם שֶׁיִּכְבֹּשׁ כָּל אֶרֶץ יִשְׂרָאֵל, שֶׁאִלּוּ תָּפַשׂ כָּל אֶרֶץ יִשְׂרָאֵל לִגְבוּלוֹתֶיהָ תְּחִלָּה[61] וְאַחַר כָּךְ כְּבָשָׁם הָיוּ כְּאֶרֶץ יִשְׂרָאֵל בְּכָל דָּבָר, וּלְעִנְיַן תְּרוּמוֹת וּמַעַשְׂרוֹת וּשְׁבִיעִית אָמְרוּ חֲכָמִים שֶׁיְּהוּ כְּאֶרֶץ יִשְׂרָאֵל[62], אֲבָל מִכָּל מָקוֹם בָּאָרֶץ הוּא הַחִיּוּב מִן הַתּוֹרָה בִּזְמַן שֶׁיִּשְׂרָאֵל שָׁם כְּמוֹ שֶׁאָמַרְנוּ לְדַעַת הָרַמְבַּ״ם ז״ל,

---

הָאָרֶץ שֶׁכָּבַשׁ דָּוִד – (§3-4) **The lands that King David conquered,** **כְּגוֹן אֲרַם נַהֲרַיִם וַאֲרַם צוֹבָה** – **such as Aram Naharayim,**[57] **Aram Tzovah,**[58] **כָּל יַד פְּרָת עַד בָּבֶל** – the area **along the entire bank of the Euphrates until Babylonia,** **וְדַמֶּשֶׂק וְאַחְלַב וְחָרָן וְכַיּוֹצֵא בָּהֶן** – including **Damascus, Halab,**[59] **Haran, and the like,** i.e., other lands in that area, **אַף עַל פִּי שֶׁבִּרְשׁוּת בֵּית דִּין הַגָּדוֹל כְּבָשָׁם** – **even though he conquered them with the consent of the Great Sanhedrin,** **אֵינָם כְּאֶרֶץ יִשְׂרָאֵל לְכָל דָּבָר** – **are not** considered **like Eretz Yisrael with regard to every matter.** **אֶלָּא יָצְאוּ מִכְּלַל חוּצָה לָאָרֶץ וְלִכְלַל אֶרֶץ יִשְׂרָאֵל לֹא בָאוּ** – **Rather, they are** somewhat **set apart from** the law of lands **outside Eretz Yisrael, yet they are not** completely **included in** the laws of **Eretz Yisrael.**[60] **וְהֵם הַנִּקְרָאִים בְּכָל מָקוֹם סוּרְיָא** – **These are** the lands that **in all instances** in the Talmud are **called "Surya,"** **וְיֵשׁ דְּבָרִים שֶׁדִּינָם כְּאֶרֶץ יִשְׂרָאֵל וְיֵשׁ שֶׁדִּינָם כְּחוּצָה לָאָרֶץ כְּמוֹ שֶׁתִּמְצָא בַּגְּמָרָא בִּמְקוֹמוֹת בְּפִזּוּר** – **and their laws are in some matters like** those of **Eretz Yisrael and in some matters like** those of **outside Eretz Yisrael, as you will find in various places in the Gemara.**

The conquest of Surya, having been undertaken by the king with the consent of the Great Sanhedrin, seems to have fulfilled all the criteria for "conquest of the public." Chinuch explains why Surya nevertheless does not have the Biblical status of Eretz Yisrael:

וְהַטַּעַם מִפְּנֵי שֶׁכָּבַשׁ אוֹתָם קֹדֶם שֶׁיִּכְבֹּשׁ כָּל אֶרֶץ יִשְׂרָאֵל – **The reason** that these areas are not considered like Eretz Yisrael **is because [King David] conquered them before the entire Eretz Yisrael was conquered;** **שֶׁאִלּוּ תָּפַשׂ כָּל אֶרֶץ יִשְׂרָאֵל לִגְבוּלוֹתֶיהָ תְּחִלָּה וְאַחַר כָּךְ כְּבָשָׁם** – **for if he would have first taken the entirety of Eretz Yisrael to** the extent of **all of its borders,**[61] **and afterward conquered [the various areas of Surya],** **הָיוּ כְּאֶרֶץ יִשְׂרָאֵל בְּכָל דָּבָר** – it would have been a true "conquest of the public" and **[those areas] would have been** classified **as Eretz Yisrael in every matter;** but since he conquered the areas of Surya before taking all of Eretz Yisrael proper, they do not have the status of Eretz Yisrael. **וּלְעִנְיַן תְּרוּמוֹת וּמַעַשְׂרוֹת וּשְׁבִיעִית אָמְרוּ חֲכָמִים שֶׁיְּהוּ כְּאֶרֶץ יִשְׂרָאֵל** – Nevertheless, **with regard to *terumos, maasros,* and *shemittah*** laws, **the Sages said that [the areas of Surya] should be** treated **like Eretz Yisrael,** and these laws should be observed there.[62]

Chinuch summarizes:

אֲבָל מִכָּל מָקוֹם בָּאָרֶץ הוּא הַחִיּוּב מִן הַתּוֹרָה בִּזְמַן שֶׁיִּשְׂרָאֵל שָׁם – **But in any case,** it is clear that **in Eretz Yisrael** proper **the** *terumah* **obligation is** of **Biblical** status **when** the majority of **the Jewish people reside there,** **כְּמוֹ שֶׁאָמַרְנוּ לְדַעַת הָרַמְבַּ״ם ז״ל** – **as we have stated according**

NOTES

57. Generally taken to be the northern part of Syria, east of the Euphrates.

58. This is a region in northern Syria, west of the Euphrates, near Aleppo.

59. *Derech Emunah, Tziyun HaHalachah* 1:53. Also known as Aleppo.

60. As Chinuch explains below, by Biblical law these lands do not have the status of Eretz Yisrael at all. It is only by Rabbinic law that they share some obligations of Eretz Yisrael.

61. I.e., those described in *Numbers* Ch. 34; see above, at note 55.

62. Since Surya is adjacent to Eretz Yisrael and was under the authority of Eretz Yisrael, it could be mistaken by people for Eretz Yisrael itself. The Sages were concerned that if it were exempt from all land-related mitzvos it could cause the neglect of those mitzvos in Eretz Yisrael (*Derech Emunah* 1:35).

וּבְאוֹתָן מְקוֹמוֹת מִדְּרַבָּנָן בְּכָל זְמַן. וְאָמְרוּ זִכְרוֹנָם לִבְרָכָה כָּל מָקוֹם שֶׁהֶחֱזִיקוּ בּוֹ יִשְׂרָאֵל כְּשֶׁעָלוּ מִגָּלוּת מִצְרַיִם וְנִתְקַדֵּשׁ עַל יַרְדֵּן, מִכֵּיוָן שֶׁגָּלוּ גָּלוּת רִאשׁוֹן בָּטְלָה אוֹתָהּ קְדֻשָּׁה[63] לְפִי שֶׁלֹּא קִדְּשׁוּהָ כִּי אִם בְּכִבּוּשׁ בִּלְבַד לְשָׁעָה[64], אֲבָל כְּשֶׁעָלוּ שֵׁנִית מִגָּלוּת בָּבֶל עִם עֶזְרָא הַסּוֹפֵר קִדְּשׁוּהָ קְדֻשָּׁה שְׁנִיָּה לְשַׁעְתָּהּ וְלֶעָתִיד לָבֹא, כְּלוֹמַר קְדֻשָּׁה הָעוֹמֶדֶת לְעוֹלָם[65], אֲבָל מִכָּל מָקוֹם אֵין חִיּוּב תְּרוּמוֹת וּמַעַשְׂרוֹת מִן הַתּוֹרָה שָׁם לְדַעַת הָרַמְבַּ״ם ז״ל אֶלָּא בִּזְמַן שֶׁיִּשְׂרָאֵל מְיֻשָּׁבִים שָׁם, וּכְמוֹ שֶׁכָּתַבְתִּי בְּסָמוּךְ. וּמִקְצָת מְקוֹמוֹת שֶׁהָיוּ שָׁם שֶׁהֶחֱזִיקוּ בָּהֶם בִּתְחִלָּה עוֹלֵי מִצְרַיִם וְלֹא הֶחֱזִיקוּ בָּהֶן בַּשְּׁנִיָּה עוֹלֵי בָבֶל,

---

to the opinion of *Rambam*, of blessed memory, וּבְאוֹתָן מְקוֹמוֹת מִדְּרַבָּנָן בְּכָל זְמַן – **and in those places,** i.e., the areas of Surya, **the obligation is always Rabbinic,** even when the majority of the Jewish people live in Eretz Yisrael.

❧ Differences Between the First and Second Commonwealth

Although Eretz Yisrael was sanctified, and therefore subject to all land-related mitzvos, by virtue of the first conquest during the times of Joshua, the sanctification of Eretz Yisrael today is not traced back to that era, but to the sanctification that occurred during the second commonwealth, as Chinuch explains here. This has ramifications with regard to certain places that were not sanctified at the start of the second commonwealth:

וְאָמְרוּ זִכְרוֹנָם לִבְרָכָה – **[The Sages], of blessed memory, stated** (*Rambam* ibid. §5): כָּל מָקוֹם שֶׁהֶחֱזִיקוּ בּוֹ יִשְׂרָאֵל כְּשֶׁעָלוּ מִגָּלוּת מִצְרַיִם – **All the places that the Jewish people took possession of when they ascended from the Egyptian exile** וְנִתְקַדֵּשׁ עַל יַרְדֵּן – **and which thereby became sanctified,** מִכֵּיוָן שֶׁגָּלוּ גָּלוּת רִאשׁוֹן בָּטְלָה אוֹתָהּ קְדֻשָּׁה – **as soon as they were exiled in the first exile** of the Jewish people with the destruction of the first *Beis HaMikdash*, the effect of **that** first **sanctification ended.**[63] לְפִי שֶׁלֹּא קִדְּשׁוּהָ כִּי אִם בְּכִבּוּשׁ בִּלְבַד לְשָׁעָה – The reason for this is **because** originally **it was sanctified only through conquest,** so the sanctity lasted only **for the time** that the effect of the conquest lasted.[64] אֲבָל כְּשֶׁעָלוּ שֵׁנִית מִגָּלוּת בָּבֶל עִם עֶזְרָא הַסּוֹפֵר – **However, when they ascended the second time** to Eretz Yisrael **from the Babylonian exile with Ezra the Scribe,** קִדְּשׁוּהָ קְדֻשָּׁה שְׁנִיָּה לְשַׁעְתָּהּ וְלֶעָתִיד לָבֹא – **they sanctified it with a second sanctification for the time** of the second commonwealth **as well as for future times;** כְּלוֹמַר קְדֻשָּׁה הָעוֹמֶדֶת לְעוֹלָם – **that is, a sanctification that remains forever.**[65] אֲבָל מִכָּל מָקוֹם אֵין חִיּוּב תְּרוּמוֹת וּמַעַשְׂרוֹת מִן הַתּוֹרָה שָׁם לְדַעַת הָרַמְבַּ״ם ז״ל – **But** although the sanctity of the land returned at that time, **nevertheless, there was no Biblical** obligation of ***terumos* and *maasros* there** at that time **according to *Rambam*, of blessed memory,** אֶלָּא בִּזְמַן שֶׁיִּשְׂרָאֵל מְיֻשָּׁבִים שָׁם וּכְמוֹ שֶׁכָּתַבְתִּי בְּסָמוּךְ – for those obligations existed **only when** the majority of **the Jewish people lived there, as I wrote above.** וּמִקְצָת מְקוֹמוֹת שֶׁהָיוּ שָׁם – **Now, there were some places there,** in Eretz Yisrael, שֶׁהֶחֱזִיקוּ בָּהֶם בִּתְחִלָּה עוֹלֵי מִצְרַיִם וְלֹא הֶחֱזִיקוּ בָּהֶן בַּשְּׁנִיָּה עוֹלֵי בָבֶל – **that those who ascended from Egypt took possession of, but those who ascended from Babylonia did not take possession of** when they

---

NOTES

63. The sanctity of the land ceased with regard to the land-related mitzvos, and any residents of the Land were then exempt from all land-related mitzvos. [The sanctity is considered to have ceased with regard to these mitzvos but not with regard to all matters; see *Derech Emunah* 1:52.]

64. That is, when the Jewish people first entered Eretz Yisrael there was no formal declaration of sanctification. The sanctity resulted from the conquest of the land from its previous inhabitants. Therefore, as soon as the effects of that conquest ended, the sanctification also ended. The second sanctification, however, was brought about differently, as Chinuch proceeds to explain (*Derech Emunah* 1:53).

65. The second sanctification did not come about through conquest, and therefore, it was not subject to removal by the loss of that conquest. Rather, the sanctification took effect through the general settling of Eretz Yisrael with the intention that through this settlement the land become sanctified for the mitzvos of Eretz Yisrael. This sanctification is tantamount to a verbal sanctification, which is not subject to change by the particular circumstances of sovereignty (*Derech Emunah* 1:56-57).

הִנִּיחוּם וְלֹא קִדְּשׁוּם, וּמִכָּל מָקוֹם לֹא פְּטָרוּ אוֹתָם מִתְּרוּמוֹת וּמַעַשְׂרוֹת כְּדֵי שֶׁיִּסְמְכוּ עֲלֵיהֶם עֲנִיֵּי עוֹלָם בַּשְּׁבִיעִית[66].

נִמְצָא כָּל הָעוֹלָם כֻּלּוֹ לְעִנְיַן מִצְוֹת הַתְּלוּיוֹת בָּאָרֶץ נֶחֱלָק לְשָׁלֹשׁ מַחְלָקוֹת, אֶרֶץ יִשְׂרָאֵל וְסוּרְיָא וְחוּצָה לָאָרֶץ[67], וְאֶרֶץ יִשְׂרָאֵל נֶחֱלֶקֶת לִשְׁנֵי חֲלָקִים, כָּל מָקוֹם שֶׁהֶחֱזִיקוּ בּוֹ עוֹלֵי בָּבֶל חֵלֶק אֶחָד, וְהַשְּׁאָר שֶׁהֶחֱזִיקוּ בּוֹ עוֹלֵי מִצְרַיִם בִּלְבַד חֵלֶק שֵׁנִי[68]. וְחוּצָה לָאָרֶץ נֶחֱלֶקֶת גַּם כֵּן לִשְׁנֵי חֲלָקִים, אֶרֶץ מִצְרַיִם וְשִׁנְעָר וְעַמּוֹן וּמוֹאָב מִצְוַת תְּרוּמוֹת וּמַעַשְׂרוֹת בָּהֶן מִדִּבְרֵי סוֹפְרִים, וּשְׁאָר כָּל הָאֲרָצוֹת אֵין תְּרוּמוֹת וּמַעַשְׂרוֹת נוֹהֲגוֹת בָּהֶן כְּלָל. וְאֵיזוֹ הִיא הָאָרֶץ שֶׁהֶחֱזִיקוּ בָּהּ עוֹלֵי מִצְרַיִם, מֵרֶקֶם שֶׁהִיא בְּמִזְרַח אֶרֶץ יִשְׂרָאֵל[69] עַד הַיָּם הַגָּדוֹל, וּמֵאַשְׁקְלוֹן

---

entered the Land **the second time** to establish the second commonwealth. הִנִּיחוּם וְלֹא קִדְּשׁוּם – **They** intentionally **left** these places **and did not sanctify them,** so that they should not be Biblically obligated in all land-related mitzvos, וּמִכָּל מָקוֹם לֹא פְּטָרוּ אוֹתָם מִתְּרוּמוֹת וּמַעַשְׂרוֹת – **but they still did not exempt them from** the ***terumos* and *maasros*** obligations. כְּדֵי שֶׁיִּסְמְכוּ עֲלֵיהֶם עֲנִיֵּי עוֹלָם בַּשְּׁבִיעִית – They did this **so that the poor of other places would be able to rely on them during *shemittah*.**[66]

Summation of the Status of the Various Locations and Borders of Eretz Yisrael

נִמְצָא כָּל הָעוֹלָם כֻּלּוֹ לְעִנְיַן מִצְוֹת הַתְּלוּיוֹת בָּאָרֶץ נֶחֱלָק לְשָׁלֹשׁ מַחְלָקוֹת – (§6) **It emerges that with regard to land-dependent mitzvos, the entire world can be divided into three categories:** אֶרֶץ יִשְׂרָאֵל וְסוּרְיָא וְחוּצָה לָאָרֶץ – (1) **Eretz Yisrael;** (2) **Surya; and** (3) **outside of Eretz Yisrael.**[67] וְאֶרֶץ יִשְׂרָאֵל נֶחֱלֶקֶת לִשְׁנֵי חֲלָקִים – **Eretz Yisrael** itself **is divided into two categories:** כָּל מָקוֹם שֶׁהֶחֱזִיקוּ בּוֹ עוֹלֵי בָּבֶל חֵלֶק אֶחָד – (a) **One** category **is any place taken by those who ascended from Babylonia;** וְהַשְּׁאָר שֶׁהֶחֱזִיקוּ בּוֹ עוֹלֵי מִצְרַיִם בִּלְבַד חֵלֶק שֵׁנִי – **and** (b) **the rest of the land that was taken** only **by those who ascended from Egypt** but not by those who ascended from Babylonia **is the second category** within Eretz Yisrael.[68] וְחוּצָה לָאָרֶץ נֶחֱלֶקֶת גַּם כֵּן לִשְׁנֵי חֲלָקִים – **Outside of Eretz Yisrael is also divided into two categories:** אֶרֶץ מִצְרַיִם וְשִׁנְעָר וְעַמּוֹן וּמוֹאָב – (a) **the lands of Egypt, Babylonia, Ammon, and Moab,** מִצְוַת תְּרוּמוֹת וּמַעַשְׂרוֹת בָּהֶן מִדִּבְרֵי סוֹפְרִים – **where the obligations of *terumos* and *maasros* exist by Rabbinic law;** וּשְׁאָר כָּל הָאֲרָצוֹת אֵין תְּרוּמוֹת וּמַעַשְׂרוֹת נוֹהֲגוֹת בָּהֶן כְּלָל – **and** (b) **the rest of the lands outside of Eretz Yisrael, where** the ***terumos* and *maasros*** obligations **do not apply at all.**

Chinuch sets out some demarcations of the first commonwealth boundaries:

וְאֵיזוֹ הִיא הָאָרֶץ שֶׁהֶחֱזִיקוּ בָּהּ עוֹלֵי מִצְרַיִם – (§7) **What is** the extent of **the land taken by those who ascended from Egypt?** מֵרֶקֶם שֶׁהִיא בְּמִזְרַח אֶרֶץ יִשְׂרָאֵל עַד הַיָּם הַגָּדוֹל – **From** the city of **Rekem in the east of Eretz Yisrael**[69] **to the Mediterranean Sea** in the west, וּמֵאַשְׁקְלוֹן

NOTES

66. In Eretz Yisrael proper, the *terumos* and *maasros* laws, as well as those of *leket, shich'chah,* and *pe'ah*, are not in effect during *shemittah*. The land is left fallow, and any produce that grows by itself is exempt from the usual obligations to the poor. As a result, the poor have much more limited access to produce during that year. To alleviate this situation, the generation of Ezra left certain areas without the sanctity of Eretz Yisrael, so that those places would not be subject to the *shemittah* laws. They then instituted the other agricultural obligations in those areas, so that the poor would receive the tithes of the poor (*maasar ani;* Mitzvah 474), as well as *leket, shich'chah* and *pe'ah* (*Derech Emunah* 1:59-60).

67. Surya is completely exempt by Biblical law from all land-related mitzvos, but is obligated by Rabbinic law in some, as noted above. Eretz Yisrael and outside of Eretz Yisrael are further divided into more categories, as Chinuch continues.

68. Those places included in the sanctification in the time of Ezra are sanctified by Biblical law for all time, although the *terumah* and *maasros* obligations do not apply when the majority of the Jewish people do not reside there. The places that were not taken in the second commonwealth were included in the first sanctification but not the second, and are therefore exempt from all land-related mitzvos by Biblical law, but subject to *terumah* and *maasros*, though not *shemittah*, by Rabbinic enactment.

69. This refers to a city in the area of Transjordan (*Derech Emunah* 1:68).

שֶׁהִיא לִדְרוֹם אֶרֶץ יִשְׂרָאֵל עַד עַכּוֹ שֶׁהִיא בַּצָּפוֹן[70]. וּמִי שֶׁהָיָה מְהַלֵּךְ מֵעַכּוֹ לִכְזִיב, כָּל הָאָרֶץ שֶׁהִיא עַל יְמִינוֹ שֶׁהִיא בְּמִזְרַח הַדֶּרֶךְ הֲרֵי הִיא בְּחֶזְקַת חוּצָה לָאָרֶץ, וּטְמֵאָה מִשּׁוּם אֶרֶץ הָעַמִּים[71] וּפְטוּרָה מִמַּעֲשֵׂר וּשְׁבִיעִית עַד שֶׁיִּוָּדַע לְךָ שֶׁאוֹתוֹ מָקוֹם הוּא מֵאֶרֶץ יִשְׂרָאֵל[72]. וְכָל הָאָרֶץ שֶׁעַל שְׂמֹאלוֹ שֶׁהוּא מַעֲרַב הַדֶּרֶךְ הֲרֵי הִיא בְּחֶזְקַת אֶרֶץ יִשְׂרָאֵל וּטְהוֹרָה מִשּׁוּם אֶרֶץ הָעַמִּים וְחַיֶּבֶת בְּמַעֲשֵׂר וּשְׁבִיעִית עַד שֶׁיִּוָּדַע לְךָ שֶׁאוֹתוֹ הַמָּקוֹם הוּא חוּצָה לָאָרֶץ[73]. וְכָל שֶׁשּׁוֹפֵעַ וְיוֹרֵד מִטּוּרֵי אַמְנוֹם וְלִפְנִים הוּא אֶרֶץ יִשְׂרָאֵל, מִטּוּרֵי אַמְנוֹם וְלַחוּץ הוּא חוּצָה לָאָרֶץ. וְהַנִּסִּין שֶׁבַּיָּם רוֹאִין אוֹתָם כְּאִלּוּ חוּט מָתוּחַ עֲלֵיהֶם מִטּוּרֵי אַמְנוֹם וְעַד נַחַל מִצְרַיִם[74],

---

שֶׁהִיא לִדְרוֹם אֶרֶץ יִשְׂרָאֵל עַד עַכּוֹ שֶׁהִיא בַּצָּפוֹן — **and from** the city of **Ashkelon in the south of Eretz Yisrael until** the city of **Acco in the north.**[70]

In the north of Eretz Yisrael there was a strip of land that was not part of Eretz Yisrael. Chinuch describes the demarcations of this land:

וּמִי שֶׁהָיָה מְהַלֵּךְ מֵעַכּוֹ לִכְזִיב — For **one traveling** north **from** the city of **Acco to** the city of **Keziv,** כָּל הָאָרֶץ שֶׁהִיא עַל יְמִינוֹ שֶׁהִיא בְּמִזְרַח הַדֶּרֶךְ הֲרֵי הִיא בְּחֶזְקַת חוּצָה לָאָרֶץ — **all the land to his right, east of the road, is assumed to be outside Eretz Yisrael;** וּטְמֵאָה מִשּׁוּם אֶרֶץ הָעַמִּים וּפְטוּרָה מִמַּעֲשֵׂר וּשְׁבִיעִית — **it is** therefore **impure with** regard to the Rabbinic law that **the land of the nations** is *tamei,*[71] **and is exempt from** the laws of *terumah,* ***maaser,*** **and *shemittah.*** עַד שֶׁיִּוָּדַע לְךָ שֶׁאוֹתוֹ מָקוֹם הוּא מֵאֶרֶץ יִשְׂרָאֵל — This assumption applies on the full length of the road, **unless one is informed that a particular spot is part of Eretz Yisrael.**[72] וְכָל הָאָרֶץ שֶׁעַל שְׂמֹאלוֹ שֶׁהוּא מַעֲרַב הַדֶּרֶךְ הֲרֵי הִיא בְּחֶזְקַת אֶרֶץ יִשְׂרָאֵל — **And all the land to his left, west of the road, is assumed to be** part of **Eretz Yisrael;** וּטְהוֹרָה מִשּׁוּם אֶרֶץ הָעַמִּים וְחַיֶּבֶת בְּמַעֲשֵׂר וּשְׁבִיעִית — **it is** therefore ***tahor*** **with regard to** the impurity of **the land of the nations, and is subject to** the laws of *terumah,* ***maaser,*** **and *shemittah.*** עַד שֶׁיִּוָּדַע לְךָ שֶׁאוֹתוֹ הַמָּקוֹם הוּא חוּצָה לָאָרֶץ — This assumption applies on the full length of the road, **unless one is informed that a particular place is outside Eretz Yisrael.**[73]

Further descriptions of the northern border, and the status of islands near Eretz Yisrael:

וְכָל שֶׁשּׁוֹפֵעַ וְיוֹרֵד מִטּוּרֵי אַמְנוֹם וְלִפְנִים הוּא אֶרֶץ יִשְׂרָאֵל — **All** the territory **that slopes from** the peak of **the mountains of Amnom inward,** i.e., south, toward Eretz Yisrael, **is included in Eretz Yisrael;** מִטּוּרֵי אַמְנוֹם וְלַחוּץ הוּא חוּצָה לָאָרֶץ — **and all** the territory **that slopes from** the peak of **the mountains of Amnom outward,** i.e., north, away from Eretz Yisrael, **is outside of Eretz Yisrael.** The northern border of Eretz Yisrael runs through the peak of the mountains of Amnom. וְהַנִּסִּין שֶׁבַּיָּם רוֹאִין אוֹתָם — **The islands in the** Mediterranean **sea are viewed** כְּאִלּוּ חוּט מָתוּחַ עֲלֵיהֶם מִטּוּרֵי אַמְנוֹם וְעַד נַחַל מִצְרַיִם — **as though a cord is stretched over them from** the west of **the mountains of Amnom** (the northwestern corner of Eretz Yisrael) **to Nachal Mitzrayim** (the southwestern corner):[74]

NOTES

70. Chinuch here does not draw complete borders of Eretz Yisrael, but only some of the indications of the borders in each direction (see *Derech Emunah* 1:68).

It should be noted that although Chinuch here sets Acco as a point in the north of Eretz Yisrael, the Land extended beyond Acco as well (except for the small area described next). Below, Chinuch indicates the furthest northern extent of Eretz Yisrael.

71. The nations of the world did not always bury their dead in marked graves or cemeteries, and consequently, any place in their lands might be a gravesite. The Sages therefore decreed that earth of lands outside Eretz Yisrael is *tamei,* because of a concern for corpses (which transmit *tumah*) buried in unmarked graves (*Rosh* to *Nazir* 54b; see *Tosafos* ibid. ד״ה ארץ and *Tosafos* to *Shabbos* 15b ד״ה ואאוירא).

72. The border of Eretz Yisrael in that place is a straight line between Acco and Keziv. For the most part, the road follows this line, but in some places it veers to the west or east. Hence, a traveler on this road may assume that the land to his right is outside of Eretz Yisrael, unless he is told by an expert that he is at a point where the road is to the west of the line and therefore the land immediately to the road's east is part of Eretz Yisrael (*Rashi, Gittin* 7b ד״ה עד שיודע).

73. See previous note.

74. Nachal Mitzrayim (literally, *the Brook of Egypt*), flows into the Mediterranean Sea. It marks the southwest border of Eretz Yisrael [see *Numbers* 34:5] (*Rashi, Gittin* 8a ד״ה נחל מצרים). According to many authorities, Nachal Mitzrayim is Wadi-El-Arish, but some identify

מִן הַחוּט וְלִפְנִים אֶרֶץ יִשְׂרָאֵל, מֵהַחוּט וְלַחוּץ חוּצָה לָאָרֶץ[75], וְזוֹ הִיא צוּרָתָהּ[76].
וְעוֹבֵר[77] עַל זֶה וְלֹא הוֹצִיא תְּרוּמָה מִדָּגָן תִּירוֹשׁ וְיִצְהָר שֶׁבָּאָרֶץ בִּזְמַן שֶׁיִּשְׂרָאֵל
שָׁם בָּטֵל עֲשֵׂה זֶה, וְעָנְשׁוֹ גָּדוֹל מְאֹד שֶׁאוֹכֵל טְבָלִים, וּכְבָר כָּתַבְתִּי בְּסֵדֶר אֱמֹר
אֶל הַכֹּהֲנִים בְּלָאו י"ט סִימָן ש"ה (מצוה רפ"ד) עֹנֶשׁ הָאוֹכֵל טֶבֶל[78]. וּבִשְׁאָר פֵּרוֹת
בָּטֵל מִצְוַת עֲשֵׂה דְּרַבָּנָן, וּבְדַעַת קְצָת הַמְּפָרְשִׁים גַּם בִּשְׁאָר פֵּרוֹת יֵשׁ בָּהֶן חִיּוּב
דְּאוֹרַיְתָא וּכְמוֹ שֶׁכָּתַבְנוּ[79]. וּבַזְּמַן הַזֶּה גַּם כֵּן מִי שֶׁלֹּא הִפְרִישׁ תְּרוּמָה מִפֵּרוֹת הָאָרֶץ
וְכֵן מִפֵּרוֹת סוּרְיָא וְכֵן מִפֵּרוֹת אוֹתָן מְקוֹמוֹת שֶׁכָּתַבְנוּ שֶׁחַיָּבִין בִּתְרוּמָה מִדְּרַבָּנָן

מִן הַחוּט וְלִפְנִים אֶרֶץ יִשְׂרָאֵל מֵהַחוּט וְלַחוּץ חוּצָה לָאָרֶץ — All the islands **from the cord inward,** i.e., east, toward Eretz Yisrael, belong to the territory of **Eretz Yisrael;** all the islands **from the cord outward** (i.e., west, away from Eretz Yisrael, **are outside of Eretz Yisrael.**[75]   וְזוֹ הִיא צוּרָתָהּ — **This is its shape.**[76]

This concludes Chinuch's citation of the first halachos in *Rambam, Hilchos Terumos*.[77] Chinuch continues with a summary of the level of violation for each of the areas mentioned above with regard to the *terumah* obligation:

וְעוֹבֵר עַל זֶה וְלֹא הוֹצִיא תְּרוּמָה מִדָּגָן תִּירוֹשׁ וְיִצְהָר — **One who violates this** mitzvah, **and does not,** before eating the produce, **take** *terumah* **from grain, wine, or oil**   שֶׁבָּאָרֶץ בִּזְמַן שֶׁיִּשְׂרָאֵל שָׁם — **in Eretz Yisrael, at a time when** the majority of **the Jewish people live there,**   בָּטֵל עֲשֵׂה זֶה — **has violated this mitzvah-obligation,**   וְעָנְשׁוֹ גָּדוֹל מְאֹד שֶׁאוֹכֵל טְבָלִים — **and his punishment is very severe, for** aside from violating this mitzvah-obligation **he is** also **eating** *tevel* (untithed) **produce,**   וּכְבָר כָּתַבְתִּי בְּסֵדֶר אֱמֹר אֶל הַכֹּהֲנִים בְּלָאו י"ט סִימָן ש"ה — **and I have already written in** *Parashas Emor*, **Mitzvah-prohibition 19, Chapter 305** of this work (Mitzvah 284),   עֹנֶשׁ הָאוֹכֵל טֶבֶל — **the punishment for one who eats** *tevel*.[78]   וּבִשְׁאָר פֵּרוֹת בָּטֵל מִצְוַת עֲשֵׂה דְּרַבָּנָן — **If** one neglects to take *terumah* **from other produce** aside from grain, wine, and oil, **he violates a Rabbinic mitzvah-obligation,**   וּבְדַעַת קְצָת הַמְּפָרְשִׁים גַּם בִּשְׁאָר פֵּרוֹת יֵשׁ בָּהֶן חִיּוּב דְּאוֹרַיְתָא וּכְמוֹ שֶׁכָּתַבְנוּ — **but according to some commentators** (*Rambam* ibid. 2:1), **other produce is also Biblically obligated, as we have written** (Mitzvah 395).[79]   וּבַזְּמַן הַזֶּה גַּם כֵּן מִי שֶׁלֹּא הִפְרִישׁ תְּרוּמָה מִפֵּרוֹת הָאָרֶץ — **Nowadays, too, one who does not separate** *terumah* **from produce of Eretz Yisrael,**   וְכֵן מִפֵּרוֹת סוּרְיָא וְכֵן מִפֵּרוֹת אוֹתָן מְקוֹמוֹת שֶׁכָּתַבְנוּ — **as well as from the produce of Surya, as well as from the produce of those places about which I have written**   שֶׁחַיָּבִין בִּתְרוּמָה מִדְּרַבָּנָן — **that there is a Rabbinic obligation of** *terumah,*

NOTES

it as the easternmost tributary of the Nile delta; see *Derech Emunah* 1:87 with *Tziyun HaHalachah*.

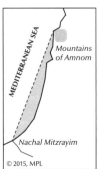

© 2015, MPL

75. See Diagram.

Although Chinuch mentions only islands, the sea itself that lies to the east of this line is also part of Eretz Yisrael. Chinuch specifies islands because produce, to which the laws of Eretz Yisrael (such as *terumah, maaser,* and *shemittah*) apply, grows on islands (*Derech Emunah* 1:84).

76. The description of the borders of the first commonwealth in *Rambam* conclude with these words, indicating that *Rambam* included some diagram of these borders, and apparently, Chinuch, too, included such a diagram. Most printed editions of *Rambam*, however, do not include any diagram here, as the original diagram was apparently lost. Some manuscript versions of *Rambam* in existence do contain diagrams, but their reliability is unclear.

77. Although Chinuch concludes his description of the borders of Eretz Yisrael here, *Rambam* continues to outline areas of Eretz Yisrael that were not part of the second commonwealth, and therefore were not sanctified as part of Eretz Yisrael (ibid. 1:8). Chinuch notes these areas as well in Mitzvah 84 (at note 50); see there with notes for descriptions of this area.

78. The punishment for eating *tevel* depends on which of the agricultural gifts have been neglected. The penalty for eating produce from which *terumah* has not been taken is death at the hands of Heaven; see Mitzvah 284 at note 12.

79. At note 20 there. See also above, note 14.

כְּגוֹן מִצְרַיִם וְשִׁנְעָר וְעַמּוֹן וּמוֹאָב בִּטֵּל עֲשֵׂה דְּרַבָּנָן[80], אֲבָל בְּפֵרוֹת שְׁאָר אֲרָצוֹת אֵין בָּהֶם חִיּוּב תְּרוּמוֹת לְעוֹלָם לֹא דְּאוֹרַיְתָא וְלֹא דְּרַבָּנָן.

כְּגוֹן מִצְרַיִם וְשִׁנְעָר וְעַמּוֹן וּמוֹאָב – **such as** the lands of **Mitzrayim, Babylonia, Ammon, and Moab,** בִּטֵּל עֲשֵׂה דְּרַבָּנָן – **has violated a Rabbinic mitzvah-obligation.**[80] אֲבָל בְּפֵרוֹת שְׁאָר אֲרָצוֹת אֵין בָּהֶם חִיּוּב תְּרוּמוֹת לְעוֹלָם – **However, the produce of any other lands is never subject to any *terumah* obligation,** לֹא דְּאוֹרַיְתָא וְלֹא דְּרַבָּנָן – **neither Biblical nor Rabbinic.**

NOTES

80. *Derech Emunah* (1:12) notes that today the common custom is not to consider these four lands subject to the *terumah* and *maasros* obligations even by Rabbinic law (see *Tziyun HaHalachah* §30 for various reasons). One who wishes to be stringent upon himself may take *terumah* from produce of those lands.

Insight: Must One Give Terumah if He Will Not Eat the Produce?

Chinuch's count of the 613 Mitzvos includes many kinds of mitzvah-obligations and prohibitions. With regard to mitzvah-obligations, there are some that represent actions that a person is commanded to do, such as putting on tefillin (Mitzvos 421-422) or eating matzah on Pesach (Mitzvah 10). Others, though, are a Torah-ordained *process*, rather than a positive obligation to take action. An example of the second kind of mitzvah-obligation is the mitzvah of *shechitah* (Mitzvah 451). There is certainly no obligation for a person to slaughter animals; rather, one who wishes to eat meat is commanded to first slaughter the animal according to the laws of this mitzvah. Although *shechitah* is counted as a "mitzvah-obligation," it is not an action that a person must do in all cases, but only a process that must be performed before eating meat (see Insight A to that mitzvah regarding the scope of that obligation).

With regard to the mitzvah to take *terumah* from produce, it is not immediately clear to which class of mitzvah-obligation it belongs. On the one hand, one could say that taking *terumah* is akin to *shechitah*: it is not a positive obligation to remove *terumah* from one's produce, but merely a mitzvah-process of permitting consumption of the food by taking off the required *terumah* portions and thus removing the *tevel* prohibition. However, it can also be argued that any person who has produce is commanded to perform the action of removing *terumah*, like any other mitzvah that requires positive, specific action.

The difference between these two approaches is illustrated in the case where the owner is not planning on eating (or selling) his produce. If taking *terumah* is an action that one is commanded to do, the fact that he does not wish to eat the rest of the produce is not pertinent, and he must separate the *terumah* in this case too. If, however, it is merely a process of permitting the produce for consumption, there would be no reason for a person to remove the *terumah* from produce that he does not wish to eat. [For another practical difference, relating to the blessing recited upon removing *terumah*, see *Magen Avraham* 8:2; *Beur HaGra, Orach Chaim* 8:1; *Pischei Teshuvah* to *Yoreh Deah* 328:2.]

This question is discussed by many later commentators, and support for both sides is found among the Rishonim. *Magen Avraham* (ibid.), *R' Akiva Eiger* (glosses to *Taz, Yoreh Deah* 1:17), and *Minchas Chinuch* (284:12), among others, maintain that separating *terumah* is simply a process to permit the rest of the produce; support for their position is found in *Rashi* (*Gittin* 47b ד"ה מדאורייתא) and *R' Avraham ben HaRambam* (*Bircas Avraham, Teshuvah* §14). Chinuch's wording in this mitzvah seems to indicate that this is his opinion as well. Chinuch writes (at note 78) that the punishment for one who violates this mitzvah is "very severe, for he is eating *tevel* produce." If this obligation was an independent one, regardless of whether the produce was eaten, one would be in violation of not separating *terumah* simply for failing to do so. Tying the omission of this action to the consumption of the produce indicates that the only context in which one stands in violation of this mitzvah is when one actually eats the untithed produce. It is thus similar to the mitzvah of *shechitah*, which one violates only upon eating meat that was not slaughtered according to halachah (*Mitzvas HaMelech, Asei* 133).

Taz (*Yoreh Deah* 1:17) maintains, however, that the *terumah* obligation is a positive obligation to

remove *terumah* from one's produce and not simply a halachic process of permitting produce. *Imrei Binah* (*Terumos U'Maasros* §3 ד"ה אולם זאת), in the course of a discussion of this very question, finds support for the approach of *Taz* in the words of *Tosefos Rid* (*Kiddushin* 58b ד"ה חטה). According to some Rishonim (but not Chinuch; see Insights to Mitzvos 385 and 395), aside from the obligation to separate *terumah*, there is an additional mitzvah-obligation to present that *terumah* to a Kohen. *Tosefos Rid*, following this approach, maintains that this affects a basic halachah in separating *terumah*. By Biblical law, one who removes even one kernel of grain as *terumah* exempts the entire crop from its *terumah* obligation (see above, at note 4). However, *Tosefos Rid* maintains, while the rest of the crop is indeed permitted, this individual has not yet completed even his *Biblical* obligation. For while he has rendered the remaining produce permitted, a Kohen must be given a respectable gift, and one kernel certainly falls short of this. He therefore cannot fulfill the additional requirement to give *terumah* to a Kohen with this amount (see also *Minchas Chinuch* §6).

Imrei Binah explains that if a person is required to give a certain minimum amount to the Kohen, this must mean that there is more to the obligation of removing *terumah* than merely permitting the remaining produce. *Tosefos Rid* must therefore maintain that one is required to separate *terumah* even when he is not planning to eat the remaining produce. Failure to do so would at the very least be a negation of the associated mitzvah-requirement to present the Kohen with a proper *terumah* gift.

Gra also takes this position (*Beur HaGra, Orach Chaim* 8:1 ד"ה מעומד), at least as it pertains to the very similar mitzvah of *challah* (Mitzvah 385). He brings proof from a halachah stated in *Yerushalmi* (*Challah* 3:1) and codified as halachah by *Rambam* (*Hil. Bikkurim* 6:16) and *Shulchan Aruch* (*Yoreh Deah* 324:14). The obligation of *challah* begins only when one kneads a certain minimum amount of flour for dough (see Mitzvah 385, at note 7). Theoretically, one can avoid the obligation altogether by making small batches of dough, each with less than the minimum amount of flour. The Sages, however, forbade a person to do this when his intention is to avoid the obligation to give *challah*. *Gra* argues that this prohibition is comprehensible only if there is a positive mitzvah to give *challah* to a Kohen, for in that case the person is looking to dodge this obligation. If, however, separating *challah* is simply a mitzvah-process to remove the prohibition from the dough, then there should be no reason that a person should not avoid the prohibition in the first place by making smaller batches of dough (see also *Teshuvos Be'er Moshe* [Denishevski], *Yoreh Deah* §1; cf. *Mitzvas HaMelech* ibid.). As mentioned above (note 40), *challah* shares many laws with *terumah*. It thus stands to reason that the mitzvah of *terumah* is likewise more than a mitzvah-process to remove the *tevel* prohibition from the produce.

מִצְוָה תקח: מִצְוַת רֵאשִׁית הַגֵּז שֶׁיִּנָּתֵן לַכֹּהֵן

שֶׁנִּצְטַוִּינוּ לָתֵת רֵאשִׁית גִּזַּת הַצֹּאן לַכֹּהֲנִים, וְעַל זֶה נֶאֱמַר (דברים י״ח, ד׳) וְרֵאשִׁית גֵּז צֹאנְךָ תִּתֶּן לוֹ[1]. וְעִנְיַן[2] הַמִּצְוָה הוּא שֶׁכָּל מִי שֶׁיֵּשׁ לוֹ חָמֵשׁ צֹאן, בֵּין זְכָרִים בֵּין נְקֵבוֹת בֵּין טְלָאִים בֵּין כְּבָשִׂים גְּדוֹלִים, אֲפִלּוּ גְּזָזָן כַּמָּה פְּעָמִים, בְּכָל פַּעַם חַיָּב לָתֵת מִן הַצֶּמֶר מַתָּנָה לַכֹּהֵן. וְאֵין לְמַתָּנָה זוֹ שִׁעוּר יָדוּעַ מִן הַתּוֹרָה, אֲבָל רַב וּשְׁמוּאֵל וְרַבִּי יוֹחָנָן אָמְרוּ בְּמַסֶּכֶת חֻלִּין (קל״ז ע״ב) רֵאשִׁית הַגֵּז בְּשִׁשִּׁים, כְּלוֹמַר שֶׁיִּתֵּן לוֹ חֵלֶק אֶחָד מִשִּׁשִּׁים[3].

Mitzvah 508
The Obligation to Give the Kohen the First of the Fleece

... וְרֵאשִׁית גֵּז צֹאנְךָ תִּתֶּן לוֹ

... and the first of the fleece of your flock you shall give him (*Deuteronomy* 18:4).

שֶׁנִּצְטַוִּינוּ לָתֵת רֵאשִׁית גִּזַּת הַצֹּאן לַכֹּהֲנִים – **We are commanded to give the first fleece** that one shears **of his sheep to the Kohanim.** וְעַל זֶה נֶאֱמַר – **Regarding this it is stated** (*Deuteronomy* 18:4): "וְרֵאשִׁית גֵּז צֹאנְךָ תִּתֶּן לוֹ" – ***and the first of the fleece of your flock you shall give him.***[1]

The words "first of the fleece" may be understood to mean that one must give the first fleece that he shears of *each sheep*, and afterward he can keep all the rest of the fleece of that sheep. Or, it can mean that he must give the fleece of the first sheep that he shears, and is then exempt from giving wool from the rest of the flock. Chinuch explains that neither of these interpretations is correct, and describes the correct parameters of the mitzvah:[2]

וְעִנְיַן הַמִּצְוָה הוּא – **The description of this mitzvah is** as follows: שֶׁכָּל מִי שֶׁיֵּשׁ לוֹ חָמֵשׁ צֹאן – **Anyone who has five sheep** (or more) to shear, בֵּין זְכָרִים בֵּין נְקֵבוֹת בֵּין טְלָאִים בֵּין כְּבָשִׂים גְּדוֹלִים – **whether** they are **males or females,** and **whether** they are **lambs or adult sheep,** אֲפִלּוּ גְּזָזָן כַּמָּה פְּעָמִים – and **even if he has** already **shorn them many times,** בְּכָל פַּעַם חַיָּב לָתֵת מִן הַצֶּמֶר מַתָּנָה לַכֹּהֵן – **each time** that he shears them **he is required to give** some **of the wool as a gift to a Kohen.** וְאֵין לְמַתָּנָה זוֹ שִׁעוּר יָדוּעַ מִן הַתּוֹרָה – **This gift has no set quantity under Biblical law,** אֲבָל רַב וּשְׁמוּאֵל וְרַבִּי יוֹחָנָן אָמְרוּ בְּמַסֶּכֶת חֻלִּין – **but Rav, Shmuel, and R' Yochanan state in Tractate *Chullin*** (137b) רֵאשִׁית הַגֵּז בְּשִׁשִּׁים – **that** the mitzvah of giving **the first fleece is set at "sixty,"** כְּלוֹמַר שֶׁיִּתֵּן לוֹ חֵלֶק אֶחָד מִשִּׁשִּׁים – **which means, that one should give [the Kohen]** no less than **one-sixtieth** of the shorn wool from each shearing.[3]

NOTES

1. This mitzvah is referred to as *reishis hageiz,* "the first of the fleece."

The basic obligation is to give a Kohen an amount of fleece (as described below) from each shearing of one's flock. The proper way to perform this mitzvah is to give the Kohen the first fleece that one shears, and not fleece sheared later in the process. If, however, one did not fulfill the mitzvah in the proper way, and he gave fleece from that which was sheared in the middle or the end of the shearing, he has still fulfilled the basic mitzvah (*Rambam, Hil. Bikkurim* 10:15; *Shulchan Aruch, Yoreh Deah* 333:11).

2. See *Tiferes Yaakov* to *Chullin* 135a.

3. Chinuch stated in the previous mitzvah that with respect to *terumah*, the Sages set the average amount at 1/50. And, as explained there (in note 4), they ordained three amounts: a miserly person gives 1/60, a person with average generosity gives 1/50, and a generous person gives 1/40. With regard to this mitzvah, however, the Sages set the amount at 1/60 for everyone. *Beur HaHalachah* (in *Derech Emunah, Hil. Bikkurim* 10:1 ד״ה שלא יפחות) writes that the reason for this difference is that *reishis hageiz* is less common, and involves less of a necessity, than *terumah,* which pertains to staple foods. Therefore, the Sages did not obligate anyone to give more than the minimum. Of course, if one gives more, he is deserving of Heavenly blessing.

וּלְפִי שֶׁהִזְכִּיר הַכָּתוּב לְשׁוֹן נְתִינָה בָּזֶה שֶׁאָמַר תִּתֶּן לוֹ, אָמְרוּ חֲכָמִים (שם קל״ה ע״א) **שֶׁמִּי שֶׁיֵּשׁ לוֹ גִּזּוֹת הַרְבֵּה וְרוֹצֶה לְחַלְּקָם לְהַרְבֵּה כֹּהֲנִים, לֹא יִתֵּן לְכָל אֶחָד פָּחוֹת מִמִּשְׁקַל חֲמִשָּׁה סְלָעִים מְלֻבָּן**[4] **כְּדֵי שֶׁיְּהֵא רָאוּי לַעֲשׂוֹת בּוֹ בֶּגֶד קָטָן**[5]**, לֹא שֶׁיְּלַבְּנֶנּוּ הַיִּשְׂרָאֵל וְאַחַר כָּךְ יִתְּנֶנּוּ לוֹ, אֶלָּא שֶׁיְּהֵא בּוֹ כָּל כָּךְ אַחַר שֶׁיְּלַבְּנֶנּוּ הַכֹּהֵן**[6] **כְּדֵי שֶׁיְּהֵא בּוֹ מַתָּנָה הַמּוֹעֶלֶת. וּכְמוֹ כֵן אָמְרוּ זִכְרוֹנָם לִבְרָכָה** (שם קל״ז ע״ב) **שֶׁאֵין חִיּוּב מִצְוָה זוֹ אֶלָּא בְּחָמֵשׁ צֹאן שֶׁתַּעֲלֶה הַגִּזָּה שֶׁלָּהֶן לְשִׁשִּׁים סְלָעִים, וְלֹא תְּהֵא כָּל אַחַת מֵהֶן פָּחוֹת מִמִּשְׁקַל שְׁנֵים עָשָׂר סֶלַע**[7]**.**

Having mentioned the overall amount of fleece that the owner must give to the Kohanim, Chinuch now sets out how he may divide this amount among individual Kohanim:

וּלְפִי שֶׁהִזְכִּיר הַכָּתוּב לְשׁוֹן נְתִינָה בָּזֶה שֶׁאָמַר ״תִּתֶּן לוֹ״ – Since Scripture uses the term "giving," in stating, *and the first of the fleece of your flock* ***you shall "give" him,*** it is understood that the amount given must be large enough to constitute a "gift." **אָמְרוּ חֲכָמִים – The Sages** therefore **said** (*Rambam, Hil. Bikkurim* 10:16) **שֶׁמִּי שֶׁיֵּשׁ לוֹ גִּזּוֹת הַרְבֵּה וְרוֹצֶה לְחַלְּקָם לְהַרְבֵּה כֹּהֲנִים – that if someone has a large amount of fleece and wishes to distribute it among many Kohanim, לֹא יִתֵּן לְכָל אֶחָד פָּחוֹת מִמִּשְׁקַל חֲמִשָּׁה סְלָעִים מְלֻבָּן – he should give each one no less than the weight of five *selaim* of cleansed** wool,[4] **כְּדֵי שֶׁיְּהֵא רָאוּי לַעֲשׂוֹת בּוֹ בֶּגֶד קָטָן – which is an amount** of wool **that can be used to make a small garment.**[5] **לֹא שֶׁיְּלַבְּנֶנּוּ הַיִּשְׂרָאֵל וְאַחַר כָּךְ יִתְּנֶנּוּ לוֹ** – This does not mean that **the Yisrael** (non-Kohen) **must cleanse it before giving it to the Kohen,** for the Yisrael may give it to the Kohen even before it is cleansed; **אֶלָּא שֶׁיְּהֵא בּוֹ כָּל כָּךְ אַחַר שֶׁיְּלַבְּנֶנּוּ הַכֹּהֵן – rather,** this means that he must give enough to each Kohen to ensure **that it will contain that amount** (i.e., the weight of five *selaim*) even **after the Kohen cleans it.**[6] **כְּדֵי שֶׁיְּהֵא בּוֹ מַתָּנָה הַמּוֹעֶלֶת** – He must give this amount to each Kohen **so that it should constitute a useful "gift,"** in fulfillment of the verse's words, "you shall give."

Chinuch sets out the amount of fleece that a person must have in order to be obligated in the mitzvah of *reishis hageiz*:

וּכְמוֹ כֵן אָמְרוּ זִכְרוֹנָם לִבְרָכָה – [The Sages], of blessed memory, also stated (*Chullin* 137b) **שֶׁאֵין חִיּוּב מִצְוָה זוֹ אֶלָּא בְּחָמֵשׁ צֹאן שֶׁתַּעֲלֶה הַגִּזָּה שֶׁלָּהֶן לְשִׁשִּׁים סְלָעִים – that the obligation of this mitzvah** applies **only when** one has **five sheep, whose fleece amounts to** at least the weight of **sixty *selaim.*** **וְלֹא תְּהֵא כָּל אַחַת מֵהֶן פָּחוֹת מִמִּשְׁקַל שְׁנֵים עָשָׂר סֶלַע – In addition,** the fleece of **each** sheep **shall be no less than the weight of twelve *selaim.***[7]

NOTES

4. Wool that is freshly sheared from a sheep naturally contains a considerable amount of foreign substance that adheres to the wool while attached to the sheep. All wool must thus be cleaned before it can be made into useful material.

The weight of five *selaim* refers to an amount of wool that weighs the same as five *sela* coins (a denomination of coin used in earlier times). This is approximately 3.5 oz., or 100 grams (*Derech Emunah* 10:117; cf. *Middos VeShiurei Torah* [Benisch], pp. 383-390, where other opinions regarding the contemporary weight of the *sela* are discussed). If the owner has less than ten *selaim*-weight of *reishis hageiz,* he may not give the fleece to more than one Kohen, because one of them would necessarily receive less than five *selaim*-weight. If he has less than fifteen *selaim*-weight of fleece, he may not distribute it to more than two Kohanim, etc. (see *Meiri, Chullin* 137b).

[Chinuch describes this rule as applying only to one who has a large amount of shorn fleece. This is because, as Chinuch will soon explain, the mitzvah of *reishis hageiz* begins when a person has 60 *selaim*-weight of fleece. Since the gift is one-sixtieth of his fleece, in order for him to have more than ten *selaim*-weight of *reishis hageiz*, he must be shearing at least 600 *selaim*-weight of wool (see *Derech Emunah* 10:113).]

5. The Gemara explains, based on a derivation from Scripture, that the small garment referred to here is the *Avneit,* the Sash worn by the Kohen while serving in the *Beis HaMikdash*. The amount of wool required to make the *Avneit* was no less than five *selaim*-weight (*Chullin* 138a with *Rashi*).

6. The cleansing process considerably lightens the weight of shorn wool. [*Derech Emunah* (10:117) writes that this process can remove up to half the weight of the wool. One should therefore give each Kohen ten *selaim*-weight of freshly shorn wool, to assure that he receives five *selaim*-weight of cleaned wool.]

7. That is, if five sheep produce a total of 60 *selaim*, but one of the sheep produces less than one-fifth of that

מִשָּׁרְשֵׁי הַמִּצְוָה כְּעִנְיַן מַה שֶּׁכָּתַבְתִּי בַּמַּעֲשֵׂר הַנִּתָּן לַלְוִיִּם בְּסֵדֶר וַיִּקַּח קֹרַח עֲשֵׂה ד' בְּסִימָן שצ"א (מצוה שצ"ה)[8]. וְהַכֹּהֲנִים כְּמוֹ כֵן שֶׁהֵם הַמְשָׁרְתִים תָּמִיד פְּנֵי הַשֵּׁם וְאֵין לָהֶם נַחֲלָה בַּקַּרְקָעוֹת וְלֹא בַּבִּזָּה, זִכָּה לָהֶם הַשֵּׁם יִתְבָּרַךְ כָּל צָרְךְ מִחְיָתָם עַל יְדֵי אֲחֵיהֶם, וְהִנֵּה נָתַן לָהֶם הַתְּרוּמָה וּמַעֲשֵׂר מִן הַמַּעֲשֵׂר שֶׁהֵם לַחְמָם וְיֵינָם[9], וּמַתְּנוֹת בְּהֵמָה שֶׁהֵם זְרוֹעַ וּלְחָיַיִם וְקֵבָה וְחֶלְקָם בְּקָדְשֵׁי מִקְדָּשׁ[10] שֶׁיֵּשׁ לָהֶם בָּשָׂר דֵּי סִפְקָם, וַעֲדַיִן חָסֵר לָהֶם מַלְבּוּשׁ, זִכָּה לָהֶם רֵאשִׁית הַגֵּז לְמַלְבּוּשֵׁיהֶם[11], וְעוֹד זִכָּה לָהֶם שְׂדֵה אֲחֻזָּה[12] וְגֶזֶל

Underlying Purpose of the Mitzvah

מִשָּׁרְשֵׁי הַמִּצְוָה – Among the underlying purposes of the mitzvah כְּעִנְיַן מַה שֶּׁכָּתַבְתִּי בַּמַּעֲשֵׂר הַנִּתָּן לַלְוִיִּם – is an idea **related to that which I wrote with regard to the *maaser*** (tithe) **that is given to the Leviim, בְּסֵדֶר וַיִּקַּח קֹרַח עֲשֵׂה ד' בְּסִימָן שצ"א – in *Parashas Korach*, Mitzvah-obligation 4, Chapter 391** of this work (Mitzvah 395),[8] that the Leviim are dedicated to the service of Hashem, and therefore receive *maaser* so they can remain completely focused on their holy service. **וְהַכֹּהֲנִים כְּמוֹ כֵן שֶׁהֵם הַמְשָׁרְתִים תָּמִיד פְּנֵי הַשֵּׁם – Similarly,** with regard to **the Kohanim, who constantly serve before Hashem** in the *Beis HaMikdash*, **וְאֵין לָהֶם נַחֲלָה בַּקַּרְקָעוֹת וְלֹא בַּבִּזָּה – and have no share in the lands** of Eretz Yisrael (Mitzvah 504), **nor in the spoils** of wars (Mitzvah 505), and are therefore very limited in their ability to provide for themselves, **זִכָּה לָהֶם הַשֵּׁם יִתְבָּרַךְ כָּל צָרְךְ מִחְיָתָם עַל יְדֵי אֲחֵיהֶם – Hashem, blessed be He, granted them all of their needs through** gifts they receive from **their brethren.**

Chinuch explains how all of their needs are met through the various gifts that Hashem bestowed upon the Kohanim:

וְהִנֵּה נָתַן לָהֶם הַתְּרוּמָה וּמַעֲשֵׂר מִן הַמַּעֲשֵׂר שֶׁהֵם לַחְמָם וְיֵינָם – Now, [Hashem] gave them *terumah* (Mitzvah 507), **and the tithe** given to the Kohanim by Leviim **of the tithe** that is given to the Leviim (*terumas maaser*, Mitzvah 396), **which constitute their bread and wine,** i.e., these gifts suffice for their basic sustenance;[9] **וּמַתְּנוֹת בְּהֵמָה – and the gifts from animals, שֶׁהֵם זְרוֹעַ וּלְחָיַיִם וְקֵבָה – which are the foreleg, the jaw, and the stomach** (Mitzvah 506), **וְחֶלְקָם בְּקָדְשֵׁי מִקְדָּשׁ – and their share in the *kodashim* of the Temple,**[10] **שֶׁיֵּשׁ לָהֶם בָּשָׂר דֵּי סִפְקָם – so that they have sufficient meat. וַעֲדַיִן חָסֵר לָהֶם מַלְבּוּשׁ – But** even with all these gifts **they still lack clothing; זִכָּה לָהֶם רֵאשִׁית הַגֵּז לְמַלְבּוּשֵׁיהֶם – [Hashem]** therefore **granted them *reishis hageiz*, to provide them with their clothing.**[11] **וְעוֹד זִכָּה לָהֶם שְׂדֵה אֲחֻזָּה וְגֶזֶל הַגֵּר וְהַחֲרָמִים וּפִדְיוֹן בְּכוֹרוֹת – He further granted them ancestral fields** that were consecrated by their owners;[12] monies given in

NOTES

amount, i.e., less than twelve *selaim*, then that sheep is not counted among the five, and the owner is exempt.

These amounts refer to the weight of the wool after it is cleaned (see previous note). [According to *Derech Emunah*, the weight of 12 *selaim* is, in contemporary terms, approximately half a pound (240 grams), and the weight of 60 *selaim* is approximately 2 pounds, 10 ounces (1200 grams, or 1.2 kg.). See note 4, however, for other opinions that maintain that the contemporary measure is less.] Less than this amount is not significant and cannot be what the verse describes as a "shearing" (*Derech Emunah* 10:86, 88, 90).

8. [See Mitzvah 494 note 4, regarding Chinuch's numbering of the mitzvos.]

9. *Terumah* and *terumas maaser* are given from all produce including grain and wine (see Mitzvah 507, at notes 9-14, for discussion of which types of produce are included in the Biblical *terumah* obligation).

10. The Kohanim are granted certain portions of the meat of many of the offerings brought in the *Beis HaMikdash*, such as *shelamim*, *chatas*, and *asham* offerings (see *Rambam, Hil. Bikkurim* 1:4-5).

11. This underlying purpose is from *Rambam* ibid. 10:5. It should be noted that this reason has practical ramifications as well, such as with regard to fleece that cannot be made into useful clothing, as Chinuch points out below, at note 17 (see *Beur HaHalachah* ibid. 10:5 ד"ה זיכה לו; see also *Chasam Sofer, Chullin* 136b ד"ה כר' אילעי).

12. If one consecrates his ancestral field to the *Beis HaMikdash* and does not redeem it before the *Yovel* (Jubilee) year, the field is given to the Kohanim as their eternal heritage (however, they must redeem the field from the *Beis HaMikdash* fund first); see Mitzvah 355.

הַגֵּר[13] וְהַחֲרָמִים[14] וּפִדְיוֹן בְּכוֹרוֹת[15] לִשְׁאָר הוֹצָאוֹת וּצְרָכִים שֶׁהָאָדָם צָרִיךְ[16].

מִדִּינֵי הַמִּצְוָה מַה שֶּׁאָמְרוּ זִכְרוֹנָם לִבְרָכָה (שם קל״ז ע״א) שֶׁאֵין חִיּוּב מִצְוָה זוֹ אֶלָּא גִּזַּת הַכְּבָשִׂים שֶׁצַּמְרָן רַךְ וְרָאוּי לִלְבֹּשׁ, אֲבָל הָיָה הַצֶּמֶר קָשֶׁה וְאֵינוֹ רָאוּי לִלְבִישָׁה פָּטוּר מֵרֵאשִׁית הַגֵּז, מִן הַטַּעַם שֶׁאָמַרְתִּי כִּי לְצֹרֶךְ לְבִישָׁה זָכוּ בָּזֶה הַכֹּהֲנִים, אֲבָל הָיָה הַצֶּמֶר אָדֹם אוֹ שָׁחֹר אוֹ שָׁחוּם חַיָּב בְּרֵאשִׁית הַגֵּז מִכֵּיוָן שֶׁרָאוּי לִלְבִישָׁה[17]. וְיֶתֶר פְּרָטֶיהָ מְבֹאָרִים בְּחֻלִּין בְּפֶרֶק י״א[18].

וְנוֹהֶגֶת מִצְוָה זוֹ בִּזְכָרִים וּנְקֵבוֹת[19], יִשְׂרְאֵלִים וּלְוִיִּם, בֵּין בִּפְנֵי הַבַּיִת בֵּין שֶׁלֹּא בִּפְנֵי הַבַּיִת,

---

return for a **theft from a convert;**[13] **properties declared "*cherem*";**[14] **and the redemption of the firstborn,**[15] לִשְׁאָר הוֹצָאוֹת וּצְרָכִים שֶׁהָאָדָם צָרִיךְ – so they will have sufficient resources **for other expenses and necessities that a person may need.**[16]

Laws of the Mitzvah

מִדִּינֵי הַמִּצְוָה – **Among the laws of the mitzvah** is מַה שֶּׁאָמְרוּ זִכְרוֹנָם לִבְרָכָה – **that which [the Sages], of blessed memory, stated** (*Chullin* 137a; *Rambam, Hil. Bikkurim* 10:4), שֶׁאֵין חִיּוּב מִצְוָה זוֹ אֶלָּא גִּזַּת הַכְּבָשִׂים שֶׁצַּמְרָן רַךְ וְרָאוּי לִלְבֹּשׁ – **that the obligation of this mitzvah applies only to fleece of sheep whose wool is soft and fit to wear,** אֲבָל הָיָה הַצֶּמֶר קָשֶׁה וְאֵינוֹ רָאוּי לִלְבִישָׁה – **but if the wool is hard and not fit to wear,** פָּטוּר מֵרֵאשִׁית הַגֵּז – **it is exempt from *reishis hageiz*.** מִן הַטַּעַם שֶׁאָמַרְתִּי – This is **due to the reason that I said** above for the mitzvah of *reishis hageiz*, כִּי לְצֹרֶךְ לְבִישָׁה זָכוּ בָּזֶה הַכֹּהֲנִים – **that this** gift **was granted to the Kohanim for the purpose of** their having garments **to wear;** therefore, wool that would not produce proper garments is not subject to the mitzvah. אֲבָל הָיָה הַצֶּמֶר אָדֹם אוֹ שָׁחֹר אוֹ שָׁחוּם חַיָּב בְּרֵאשִׁית הַגֵּז – **However, if the wool was** naturally **red, or black, or brown, it is** still **obligated in *reishis hageiz*,** מִכֵּיוָן שֶׁרָאוּי לִלְבִישָׁה – **since it is fit for wearing** regardless of its color.[17]

וְיֶתֶר פְּרָטֶיהָ – These, **and the rest of the details of [the mitzvah],** מְבֹאָרִים בְּחֻלִּין בְּפֶרֶק י״א – **are set forth in *Chullin*, Chapter 11.**[18]

Applicability of the Mitzvah

וְנוֹהֶגֶת מִצְוָה זוֹ בִּזְכָרִים וּנְקֵבוֹת – **This mitzvah applies to men and women,**[19] יִשְׂרְאֵלִים וּלְוִיִּם – and to both **Yisraelim and Leviim;** בֵּין בִּפְנֵי הַבַּיִת בֵּין שֶׁלֹּא בִּפְנֵי הַבַּיִת – it further applies **both**

NOTES

13. Under certain circumstances, if a person steals from a convert and the convert has died without an heir, he must repay the money to the Kohanim who are on duty in the *Beis HaMikdash* at that time; see *Numbers* 5:7-8, *Rambam, Hil. Gezeilah VaAveidah* 8:5-6.

14. A person may designate some of his property as "*cherem*" (literally, *condemned*, or *cursed*). In some of those cases, depending on how he expressed his vow, the property is given to the Kohanim (see Mitzvah 357).

15. A Yisrael must redeem his firstborn son by giving five silver *selaim* to a Kohen (Mitzvah 392). Also, a Yisrael must redeem the firstborn of his female donkey by giving a sheep (or the value of the firstborn donkey) to a Kohen (Mitzvah 22).

16. *Derech Emunah* points out (*Beur HaHalachah* 10:5 ד״ה זיכה לו) that the Leviim, too, receive no share in Eretz Yisrael or in any spoils of war, yet they do not receive any of these gifts. He explains that the *maaser* that the Leviim receive is a tenth of all the produce of the Yisraelim. This is a very large benefit, and is sufficient to provide for all of their needs, by eating what they need and selling the rest (*maaser* has no sanctity and may be eaten by Yisraelim as well). Kohanim, on the other hand, receive a much smaller amount from the produce; by Biblical law one may exempt himself from *terumah* with only one grain from his entire crop (Mitzvah 507, at note 4). *Terumas maaser* also represents only 1/100 of the crop. The Kohanim are therefore compensated with all the gifts listed here by Chinuch.

17. This refers only to naturally occurring colors. [A Yisrael may not dye the wool before giving *reishis hageiz*; if he does so, the wool is no longer subject to the requirement to be given to the Kohen and he has violated the mitzvah to give his fleece to the Kohen; see *Rambam* ibid. 10:6.]

18. The laws of *reishis hageiz* are codified in *Rambam, Hil. Bikkurim* Ch. 10, and *Shulchan Aruch, Yoreh Deah* §333.

19. This follows the general rule that women are obligated in mitzvah-obligations that are not time-specific.

וְדַוְקָא בְּאֶרֶץ יִשְׂרָאֵל, אֲבָל לֹא בְּחוּצָה לָאָרֶץ, וּכְדַאֲמַר רַב נַחְמָן בַּר יִצְחָק בְּחֻלִּין בְּפֶרֶק רֵאשִׁית הַגֵּז (קל״ו ע״ב), נָהוּג עָלְמָא כִּתְלָתָא סָבֵי, כְּרַבִּי אִילְעַאי בְּרֵאשִׁית הַגֵּז, כְּלוֹמַר דִּפָטַר בְּחוּצָה לָאָרֶץ[20] וְכוּ׳, כִּדְאִיתָא הָתָם[21].

וְעוֹבֵר עַל זֶה וְלֹא נָתַן רֵאשִׁית גִּזָּתוֹ לְכֹהֵן[22] כְּשֶׁיֵּשׁ לוֹ גִּזָּה הָרְאוּיָה עַל הָעִנְיָן שֶׁכָּתַבְנוּ[23] בִּטֵּל עֲשֵׂה זֶה.

---

in the time of the *Beis HaMikdash* and not in the time of the *Beis HaMikdash*. וְדַוְקָא בְּאֶרֶץ יִשְׂרָאֵל אֲבָל לֹא בְּחוּצָה לָאָרֶץ – It applies, however, **only in Eretz Yisrael, but not outside of Eretz Yisrael.** וּכְדַאֲמַר רַב נַחְמָן בַּר יִצְחָק בְּחֻלִּין בְּפֶרֶק רֵאשִׁית הַגֵּז – **This is in accordance with that which R' Nachman bar Yitzchak said in *Chullin*, Chapter *Reishis Hageiz*** (136b): נָהוּג עָלְמָא כִּתְלָתָא סָבֵי – Nowadays, **the** Jewish **world conducts itself in accordance with the** lenient **rulings of three elders:** כְּרַבִּי אִילְעַאי בְּרֵאשִׁית הַגֵּז – **Like R' Ilai with regard to** the ***reishis hageiz*** obligation; כְּלוֹמַר דִּפָטַר בְּחוּצָה לָאָרֶץ – **that is,** we follow R' Ilai **who exempts** one from this mitzvah **outside of Eretz Yisrael,**[20] וְכוּ׳ כִּדְאִיתָא הָתָם – **etc.,** (the Gemara continues with the two other rulings of elders mentioned by R' Nachman), **as appears** in the Gemara **there.**[21]

וְעוֹבֵר עַל זֶה וְלֹא נָתַן רֵאשִׁית גִּזָּתוֹ לְכֹהֵן – **One who transgresses this** mitzvah, **and does not give the first of his** shorn **fleece to a Kohen,**[22] כְּשֶׁיֵּשׁ לוֹ גִּזָּה הָרְאוּיָה עַל הָעִנְיָן שֶׁכָּתַבְנוּ – **when he has a proper shearing,** that is, when it is **in accordance with the description that we recorded** above,[23] בִּטֵּל עֲשֵׂה זֶה – **violates this** mitzvah-**obligation.**

NOTES

20. R' Ilai derives this (*Chullin* 136a) from a Scriptural source that connects *reishis hageiz* with *terumah*; and *terumah* applies only in Eretz Yisrael (see Mitzvah 507, at note 40).

21. This is likewise the ruling of *Rambam* (ibid. 10:1). For further discussion of the applicability of this mitzvah outside Eretz Yisrael, see Insight A.

22. See note 1 above.

23. That is, there are enough sheep, and the shearing produces the amount and quality of wool that Chinuch described in this mitzvah.

Insight A: The Obligation of Matanos and Reishis HaGeiz Outside of Eretz Yisrael

Terumah (Mitzvah 507), like many other Kohanic gifts, is an agricultural mitzvah and as such applies only in Eretz Yisrael. By contrast, the obligations of *matanos* (Mitzvah 506) and *reishis hageiz* (this mitzvah) are not agricultural mitzvos, since they relate only to various parts of the animals that the owner must give to the Kohen. It would therefore be reasonable to assume that this obligation, like the vast majority of the Torah's other non-agricultural mitzvos, should apply both inside and outside Eretz Yisrael (see *Kiddushin* 36b).

Chinuch, however, following *Rambam*, rules that while the *matanos* obligation does apply outside Eretz Yisrael, the *reishis hageiz* obligation does not (Mitzvah 506, at note 27, and 508, at note 21; *Rambam*'s rulings are in *Hil. Bikkurim* 9:1 and 10:1). In each of these mitzvos, Chinuch refers to the pertinent Gemaras upon which these rulings are based. In order to gain a more complete understanding of this difficult ruling it is important to place it in its proper context. Here, we trace the source of these halachos from the Mishnayos through the related discussions of the Gemara with the opinions of various Rishonim and halachic authorities on the matter.

The Mishnayos in *Chullin* (130a and 135b) state unequivocally that the obligation of *matanos* and *reishis hageiz* apply both inside and outside Eretz Yisrael. The Gemara (136a), however, cites the opinion of a dissenting Tanna, R' Ilai, who maintains that neither obligation applies outside of Eretz Yisrael. R' Ilai bases his exemption on a Scriptural source in which both obligations are linked to *terumah*, teaching that just as the *terumah* obligation, as an agricultural mitzvah, does not apply outside of Eretz Yisrael, so too the *matanos* and *reishis hageiz* obligations are limited to Eretz Yisrael only.

Does the halachah follow the Tanna of the Mishnah, who maintains that both mitzvos apply outside of Eretz Yisrael, or R' Ilai, who maintains that they do not? The answer to this question seems

to depend on the particular obligation. With regard to *reishis hageiz,* the Gemara (*Chullin* 136b) records a statement by R' Nachman bar Yitzchak that common custom is to follow R' Ilai. With regard to *matanos,* however, the Gemara (ibid. 132b) recounts a seemingly conflicting report. We are told that various Amoraim who lived in Babylonia, outside of Eretz Yisrael, would fine any butchers who would not give *matanos*. And the list of Amoraim who would do this included R' Nachman bar Yitzchak himself! Why is R' Nachman strict with regard to *matanos* but lenient with *reishis hageiz*? Or, put another way, if the halachah accords with R' Ilai, who maintains that there is a Scriptural link between these mitzvos and *terumah,* why would the halachah recognize this link only as it pertains to *reishis hageiz* and not to *matanos*?

There are three primary approaches among the Rishonim to resolve this difficulty. According to the first two approaches presented here, the contradiction is resolved in such a way that there is actually no difference between the two mitzvos. The last approach differentiates between the two mitzvos.

(1) *Rosh* writes (*Chullin* 11:1) that the original custom was to follow the ruling of the Mishnah that both mitzvos applied outside of Eretz Yisrael. It was at that point that R' Nachman bar Yitzchak would fine any butcher who did not give *matanos* in Babylonia. Later, however, the custom shifted, and it became standard to rule leniently regarding *both* mitzvos. At that point R' Nachman reversed his earlier ruling and reported the common custom to be lenient. Although his report mentioned only *reishis hageiz,* it logically applies to *matanos* as well since they are both derived from the same Scriptural source. According to this approach, nowadays neither *matanos* nor *reishis hageiz* applies outside Eretz Yisrael.

(2) Some explain that R' Nachman's own opinion is that even *reishis hageiz* applies outside Eretz Yisrael as well, in accordance with the ruling of the Mishnah. R' Nachman reported, though, that in actual practice, the masses did not follow this halachah, as they rather rely on the more lenient opinion of R' Ilai. R' Nachman reported this disapprovingly, as he himself did not approve of this practice (see *Tur, Yoreh Deah,* end of §333; *Rama* and *Beur HaGra* 333:1; cf. *Tur* ibid. §61). According to this approach, nowadays both *matanos* and *reishis hageiz* do apply outside Eretz Yisrael.

(3) The third approach is that of Chinuch and *Rambam,* and decides each mitzvah separately. R' Nachman maintained that the *matanos* obligation applies outside of Eretz Yisrael and he therefore fined butchers in Babylonia for not giving *matanos*. With regard to *reishis hageiz,* however, we follow R' Nachman's report about the common lenient custom, which *Rambam* and Chinuch understand to be R' Nachman's own opinion as well (see *Mahari Korkos, Hil. Bikkurim* 9:1).

In this third approach, our original question returns: Why do the Amoraim follow R' Ilai only with regard to *reishis hageiz* and not with regard to *matanos,* when both mitzvos share the same Scriptural link to *terumah*?

Ran (to *Rif, Chullin* 46b ד"ה גמ') suggests that although R' Ilai compared both *reishis hageiz* and *matanos* to *terumah,* the Amoraim were willing to make the comparison only for *reishis hageiz* because *reishis hageiz* resembles *terumah* in its essential characteristics. In the cases of both *terumah* and *reishis hageiz,* the Kohen's portion of produce or fleece, respectively, is mixed in with the owner's portion until the owner separates and designates them. By contrast, with regard to *matanos,* the foreleg, jaw, and stomach are always distinct, even before they are designated for the Kohen. They were never "mixed in" with the owner's portion and therefore do not need specific designation. Because *matanos* are so unlike *terumah,* the prevalent custom was not to draw R' Ilai's comparison with regard to this obligation. *Rambam* therefore rules like R' Ilai only with regard to *reishes hageiz,* but not *matanos*. [For another approach to the difference between these two mitzvos, see *Baal HaMaor* to *Rif, Chullin* fol. 46b.]

Although *Shulchan Aruch* (*Yoreh Deah* 61:21) cites both the stringent and the lenient opinions regarding the *matanos* obligation outside of Eretz Yisrael, it notes that common practice follows the more lenient view. With regard to *reishis hageiz, Shulchan Aruch* (ibid. 333:1) brings *only* the lenient opinion. *Rama* there mentions that there also is a stringent opinion but it is not consistent with common practice (see *Beur HaGra* ad loc.). In short, the common practice is to be lenient outside of Eretz Yisrael with regard to both *matanos* and *reishis hageiz*.

Nevertheless, throughout the generations punctilious individuals would give both *matanos* and *reishis hageiz* even outside Eretz Yisrael. Notably, *Chasam Sofer* would have an animal slaughtered

before Yom Tov and give the *matanos* and (*reishis hageiz*) to his brother-in-law, who himself was not a Kohen but was married to a Koheness (see Mitzvah 506, at note 32; *Teshuvos Chasam Sofer, Yoreh Deah* §301). Similarly, the Vilna Gaon had an animal slaughtered from which he gave the *matanos*, and he recited the *shehecheyanu* blessing upon doing so (*Maaseh Rav* §103; see also *Pischei Teshuvah* 61:8; *Aruch HaShulchan* 61:53).

⊷§ Insight B: Matanos and Reishis HaGeiz in Eretz Yisrael Nowadays

The question discussed above pertained only to whether we follow the opinion of R' Ilai, who exempts *matanos* and *reishis hageiz* outside of Eretz Yisrael, or the opinion of the Tanna of the Mishnah, who mandates it. Inside Eretz Yisrael itself, however, there should not be any question that the obligations apply, and that they apply whether the *Beis HaMikdash* is standing or not. As we shall see, however, the question of whether we follow R' Ilai's ruling does determine the general nature of these obligations, and this has ramifications even inside Eretz Yisrael.

As explained in the previous Insight, the reason that R' Ilai exempts lands outside of Eretz Yisrael from the obligations of *matanos* and *reishis hageiz* is that Scripture links these mitzvos to *terumah*. Now, according to *Rambam*, the mitzvah of *terumah* applies today only by Rabbinic decree; *Raavad* disagrees (Mitzvah 507, at notes 42-43). According to R' Ilai, then, *matanos* and *reishis hageiz* should apply on the same level that *terumah* does: if *terumah* is only a Rabbinic obligation, *matanos* and *reishis hageiz* are also only Rabbinic in nature — even in Eretz Yisrael.

It thus emerges, following *Rambam's* opinion regarding *terumah* (that it is not a Biblical obligation today), and his opinion on *matanos* and *reishis hageiz* (discussed in the previous Insight), as follows: With regard to *matanos*, we follow the Tanna of the Mishnah who *rejects* the linkage to *terumah*. Therefore, the obligation of *matanos* applies by Biblical law nowadays, both inside and outside of Eretz Yisrael. With regard to *reishis hageiz*, however, we follow R' Ilai, who *accepts* the linkage to *terumah*. Therefore, just as *terumah* applies in Eretz Yisrael only by Rabbinic law, so too *reishis hageiz* is only Rabbinically mandated even inside Eretz Yisrael (see *Minchas Chinuch* §3).

Some authorities go a step further and write that these obligations may not be in force today even by Rabbinic law (see *Beis Hillel, Yoreh Deah* 333:1). [Indeed, Chinuch himself is cited as one of these sources; see Mitzvah 506 note 26.] A number of reasons have been suggested for this. Some maintain this is because today we do not have Kohanim of proven Kohanic lineage, and therefore Kohanim cannot maintain a monetary claim to these gifts. Furthermore, instituting a widespread practice of giving these gifts might actually encourage people to falsely claim Kohanic lineage (see *Chazon Ish, Sheviis* 2:6 and *Yoreh Deah* 193:12 at length). [This reason applies only to *matanos* and *reishis hageiz*, which are primarily monetary obligations, and do not forbid the rest of the animal when they are not separated (see Mitzvah 506, at note 19). Furthermore, even when they are separated the portions themselves do not have inherent sanctity. *Terumah*, on the other hand, must always be separated because, until it is, the rest of the crop is forbidden as *tevel*. And when it is separated the *terumah* itself has sanctity and may not be eaten by a non-Kohen or one who is *tamei*.]

Chasam Sofer (*Chullin* 136b ד"ה כר' אלעאי) notes that perhaps the applicability of the *matanos* obligation today depends on the reason for the mitzvah. In this mitzvah, Chinuch writes (at note 10) that *matanos* are given to the Kohanim in recognition of the fact that they have no portion in Eretz Yisrael. Nowadays, unfortunately, the rest of the Jewish people also do not have their designated portion in Eretz Yisrael and therefore perhaps recompense is unnecessary. According to other reasons for the mitzvah, however (see Mitzvah 508, at note 2, and see note 5 there), the mitzvah would apply in all times. [It should be noted that this is no more than a theoretical suggestion. *Chasam Sofer* himself points out numerous times that we may not apply the reasons of the mitzvos to determine their practical applications (see *Teshuvos, Even HaEzer* I §17; II §155).]

The majority of authorities, however, maintain that both *matanos* and *reishis hageiz* certainly do apply in Eretz Yisrael (either by Biblical or Rabbinic law), even in current circumstances (*Pri Chadash, Kuntres Acharon, Yoreh Deah* §61; *Birkei Yosef, Yoreh Deah* 333:2; *Aruch HaShulchan* 333:2). See also *Minchas Tzvi* (Dzherkovski) to *Sefer HaChinuch*, in *Shibbolei HaLeket* §6, for a lengthy discussion of this issue.

מִצְוָה תקט

מִצְוָה לִהְיוֹת הַכֹּהֲנִים עוֹבְדִים בַּמִּקְדָּשׁ מִשְׁמָרוֹת מִשְׁמָרוֹת וּבַמּוֹעֲדִים עוֹבְדִים כְּאֶחָד[1]

שֶׁיִּהְיוּ הַכֹּהֲנִים וְהַלְוִיִּם עוֹבְדִים בַּמִּקְדָּשׁ לְמִשְׁמָרוֹת[2], כְּלוֹמַר לְכִתּוֹת יְדוּעוֹת,

---

Mitzvah 509

The Obligation Upon Kohanim and Leviim to Establish Mishmaros in the Beis HaMikdash and to Serve Together on the Festivals

וְכִי יָבֹא הַלֵּוִי מֵאַחַד שְׁעָרֶיךָ מִכָּל יִשְׂרָאֵל אֲשֶׁר הוּא גָּר שָׁם וּבָא בְּכָל אַוַּת נַפְשׁוֹ אֶל הַמָּקוֹם אֲשֶׁר יִבְחַר ה׳. וְשֵׁרֵת בְּשֵׁם ה׳ אֱלֹהָיו כְּכָל אֶחָיו הַלְוִיִּם הָעֹמְדִים שָׁם לִפְנֵי ה׳. חֵלֶק כְּחֵלֶק יֹאכֵלוּ לְבַד מִמְכָּרָיו עַל הָאָבוֹת

When the Levite will come from one of your cities, from all of Israel, where he dwells, and he comes when his heart fully desires to the place that HASHEM will choose, then he shall serve in the Name of HASHEM, his God, like all of his brethren, the Levites, who stand there before HASHEM. Portion for portion shall they eat, except for what was transacted by the forefathers (*Deuteronomy* 18:6-8).

The Kohanim, who are charged with the *avodah* (Temple service), did not all serve together at one time in the *Beis HaMikdash.* While the Jewish people were still in the Wilderness, Moses divided the families of the Kohanim into eight *mishmaros* (literally, *watches;* sing. *mishmar*). Later, after the families had grown larger, Samuel the Prophet and King David further divided them into a total of twenty-four *mishmaros,* with each *mishmar* serving for one week on a rotating basis, so that each one served approximately two weeks a year. Generally, a Kohen from a *mishmar* that was not on duty during a particular week was not allowed to take part in that week's *avodah* or take a share in the offerings brought that week. On the festivals, however, they would all serve together. Chinuch discusses these laws and how they are derived from the above verses.[1]

שֶׁיִּהְיוּ הַכֹּהֲנִים וְהַלְוִיִּם עוֹבְדִים בַּמִּקְדָּשׁ לְמִשְׁמָרוֹת – The Torah commands **that the Kohanim and Leviim shall serve in the *Beis HaMikdash* according to *mishmaros*,**[2] **כְּלוֹמַר לְכִתּוֹת יְדוּעוֹת** – **meaning,** they are to perform the *avodah* **in specific groups** into which they are divided, with each

---

NOTES

1. Although the verse refers to a Levi, *Sifrei* explains that since the verse speaks of one who *serves* in the *Beis HaMikdash,* it must be referring to a Kohen. [This is one of the twenty-four places in Scripture where the Torah refers to the Kohanim as Leviim; see *Yevamos* 86b.] See also *Rambam, Hil. Klei HaMikdash* 4:6. According to Chinuch, our mitzvah also applies to the Leviim, who assisted the Kohanim in their Temple service (see Mitzvah 394); see next note.

2. As Chinuch writes below (after note 4), the Leviim, like the Kohanim, were also divided into twenty-four *mishmaros* that rotated on a weekly basis, and they were all permitted to participate in the service on the festivals.

Minchas Chinuch (§2), however, strongly questions Chinuch's assertion that the Leviim are included in the mitzvah, for while it is indeed true that the Leviim were divided into *mishmaros* (as detailed in *I Chronicles* Chs. 24-26), this was an entirely voluntary arrangement. Furthermore, *Minchas Chinuch* asserts that, in the case of the Leviim, this division was not suspended on the festivals. For further discussion, see Insights to Mitzvah 389.

וְלֹא תִהְיֶה יַד הַכֹּל מִתְעַסֶּקֶת יַחַד בָּעֲבוֹדָה, חוּץ מִן הַיָּמִים טוֹבִים בִּלְבַד שֶׁהָיוּ הַכֹּל עוֹבְדִים יַחַד[3]**, כָּל הַבָּא יְמַלֵּא אֶת יָדוֹ לְשִׂמְחַת הָרֶגֶל**[4]**, וּבְסֵפֶר דִּבְרֵי הַיָּמִים** (א׳ כ״ד־כ״ו) **מְבֹאָר אֵיךְ חִלְּקוּ אוֹתָם דָּוִד וּשְׁמוּאֵל שֶׁעָשׂוּ מֵהֶן עֶשְׂרִים וְאַרְבָּעָה מִשְׁמְרוֹת כֹּהֲנִים וְעֶשְׂרִים וְאַרְבָּעָה מִשְׁמְרוֹת לְוִיִּם, כְּדֵי שֶׁתַּעֲבֹד כָּל מִשְׁמָרָה מֵהֶם שְׁתֵּי שַׁבָּתוֹת בְּשָׁנָה. וּבְמַסֶּכֶת סֻכָּה** (נ״ה ע״ב) **אָמְרוּ זִכְרוֹנָם לִבְרָכָה שֶׁבָּרְגָלִים הָיְתָה יַד הַכֹּל שָׁוָה, וְעַל זֶה נֶאֱמַר** (דברים י״ח, ו־ח׳) **וְכִי יָבֹא הַלֵּוִי וגו׳, וּבִכְלַל הַלֵּוִי הַכֹּהֵן כִּי הַלֵּוִי הָיָה אָב לְכָל הַשֵּׁבֶט, וּבָא בְּכָל אַוַּת נַפְשׁוֹ וגו׳ וְשֵׁרֵת בְּשֵׁם ה׳ אֱלֹהָיו כְּכָל אֶחָיו הַלְוִיִּם הָעֹמְדִים שָׁם וגו׳ חֵלֶק כְּחֵלֶק יֹאכֵלוּ. וּלְשׁוֹן סִפְרִי** (כאן)**, וּבָא בְּכָל אַוַּת נַפְשׁוֹ, יָכוֹל לְעוֹלָם, כְּלוֹמַר אֲפִלּוּ שֶׁלֹּא בָרְגָלִים,**

---

group serving at a different time; **וְלֹא תִהְיֶה יַד הַכֹּל מִתְעַסֶּקֶת יַחַד בָּעֲבוֹדָה – and that all** of the Kohanim and Leviim **not engage in the *avodah* together, חוּץ מִן הַיָּמִים טוֹבִים בִּלְבַד שֶׁהָיוּ הַכֹּל עוֹבְדִים יַחַד – with the sole exception of the** pilgrimage **festivals,** Pesach, Shavuos, and Succos, **when all** of them **would serve together.**[3] **כָּל הַבָּא יְמַלֵּא אֶת יָדוֹ –** During these festivals, **any** of the Kohanim and Leviim **who comes may perform** the *avodah,* **לְשִׂמְחַת הָרֶגֶל – due to the joy of the pilgrimage festival.**[4]

Chinuch elaborates:

וּבְסֵפֶר דִּבְרֵי הַיָּמִים מְבֹאָר אֵיךְ חִלְּקוּ אוֹתָם דָּוִד וּשְׁמוּאֵל – In the Book of *Chronicles* (*I Chronicles* Chs. 24-26), **it is set forth how** King **David and Samuel** the Prophet **divided [the Kohanim and Leviim]: שֶׁעָשׂוּ מֵהֶן עֶשְׂרִים וְאַרְבָּעָה מִשְׁמְרוֹת כֹּהֲנִים – They divided them into twenty-four *mishmaros* of Kohanim וְעֶשְׂרִים וְאַרְבָּעָה מִשְׁמְרוֹת לְוִיִּם – and twenty-four *mishmaros* of Leviim, כְּדֵי שֶׁתַּעֲבֹד כָּל מִשְׁמָרָה מֵהֶם שְׁתֵּי שַׁבָּתוֹת בְּשָׁנָה – so that each *mishmar* would serve for two weeks a year. וּבְמַסֶּכֶת סֻכָּה אָמְרוּ זִכְרוֹנָם לִבְרָכָה – And in Tractate *Succah*** (55b), **[the Sages], of blessed memory, stated שֶׁבָּרְגָלִים הָיְתָה יַד הַכֹּל שָׁוָה – that on the pilgrimage festivals all** the Kohanim and Leviim **served equally;** the division into *mishmaros* was not in effect at that time.

Chinuch cites the source for our mitzvah:

וְעַל זֶה נֶאֱמַר – Regarding this it is stated (*Deuteronomy* 18:6-8): **״וְכִי יָבֹא הַלֵּוִי וגו׳״ – *When the Levite will come ...*; וּבִכְלַל הַלֵּוִי הַכֹּהֵן כִּי הַלֵּוִי הָיָה אָב לְכָל הַשֵּׁבֶט – and** the expression **"the Levite" includes the Kohen, since the** original **Levite** (i.e., Levi, the son of Jacob) **was the father of the entire tribe,** which includes the Kohanim as well as the Leviim. **״וּבָא בְּכָל אַוַּת נַפְשׁוֹ וגו׳ וְשֵׁרֵת בְּשֵׁם ה׳ אֱלֹהָיו כְּכָל אֶחָיו הַלְוִיִּם הָעֹמְדִים שָׁם וגו׳ חֵלֶק כְּחֵלֶק יֹאכֵלוּ״ –** The verse continues: ***and he comes when his heart fully desires ... then he shall serve in the Name of HASHEM, his God, like all of his brethren, the Levites, who stand there*** *before* HASHEM. ***Portion for portion they shall eat*** (i.e., they are entitled to equal portions of the offerings), *except for what was transacted by the forefathers.* **וּלְשׁוֹן סִפְרִי – And** this is **a quote of *Sifrei*** (to the verse), with an elucidation of its words: **״וּבָא בְּכָל אַוַּת נַפְשׁוֹ״ –** "When Scripture states, ***and he comes when his heart fully desires,*** **יָכוֹל לְעוֹלָם – it might be** thought that this applies **at all times." כְּלוֹמַר אֲפִלּוּ שֶׁלֹּא בָרְגָלִים – That is to say,** one might think that he may come and serve at his heart's desire all year round, **even** at times **other than**

NOTES

3. Chinuch explains below (at notes 15-18) that this law applies specifically to the *avodah* of the special festival offerings. The *avodah* of voluntary offerings that people brought during the festivals (on Chol HaMoed), as well as the *avodah* of the *tamid* offerings, was performed by the *mishmar* on duty that week.

[The Pilgrimage Festivals were the sole exception in the sense that they were the only time that all the Kohanim and Leviim shared equally in the communal service. There was, however, another (more limited) exception to the rule of *mishmaros,* as Chinuch will explain below, before note 19.]

4. It is clear from Chinuch below (at note 20) that the permit for all Kohanim and Leviim to serve on the festivals is not merely an exception to the mitzvah of *mishmaros,* but is actually an integral part of the mitzvah. Thus, this mitzvah contains two elements: (a) those who serve shall be divided into *mishmaros*; (b) all must be allowed to serve on the festivals.

תַּלְמוּד לוֹמַר לְבַד מִמְכָּרָיו עַל הָאָבוֹת, מַה מָּכְרוּ אָבוֹת זֶה לָזֶה טֹל אַתָּה בְּשַׁבַּתְּךָ וַאֲנִי בְּשַׁבַּתִּי, כְּלוֹמַר הַסְכָּמָתָם בְּסֵדֶר מִשְׁמְרוֹת הָעֲבוֹדָה כָּל שָׁבוּעַ מִשְׁמָרָה[5], וְכֵן פֵּרְשׁוֹ הַתַּרְגּוּם, בַּר מִמַּטְרְתָא דְּיֵיתֵי בְּשַׁבַּתָּא דְּכֵן אַתְקִינוּ אֲבָהָתָא.

מִשָּׁרְשֵׁי מִצְוַת הַמִּשְׁמָרוֹת יְדוּעוֹת וּקְבוּעוֹת, לְפִי שֶׁכָּל הַמְּלָאכוֹת הַמֻּטָּלוֹת עַל מִסְפַּר אֲנָשִׁים יְדוּעִים נַעֲשׂוֹת כָּרָאוּי וְאֵין הָעַצְלָה וְהַיֵּאוּשׁ וְהַקַּפְּדָנוּת מְצוּיָה בָּהֶן[6], אֲבָל הַמֻּטָּלוֹת עַל הָרַבִּים מִבְּלִי שֶׁיִּהְיֶה בָּהֶם אֲנָשִׁים יְדוּעִים לַעֲשׂוֹתָהּ, פְּעָמִים יַטִּילוּ אוֹתָהּ קְצָתָן עַל קְצָתָן, וּפְעָמִים יַקְפִּידוּ אֵלּוּ עַל אֵלּוּ בָּעִנְיָן, אֵין לְהַאֲרִיךְ בִּדְבָרִים אֵלּוּ, יְדוּעוֹת הֵן בְּכָל אַנְשֵׁי מִנְיָן,

---

during the Pilgrimage Festivals. תַּלְמוּד לוֹמַר "לְבַד מִמְכָּרָיו עַל הָאָבוֹת" – **"[Scripture] therefore states:** ***except for what was transacted by the forefathers.*** מַה מָּכְרוּ אָבוֹת זֶה לָזֶה – **What transaction did the forefathers** (i.e., the early Kohanim and Leviim) **make with one another?** טֹל אַתָּה בְּשַׁבַּתְּךָ וַאֲנִי בְּשַׁבַּתִּי – One said to the other: **'You take** the right to perform *avodah* **during your week, and I** will take it **during my week.' "** כְּלוֹמַר הַסְכָּמָתָם בְּסֵדֶר מִשְׁמְרוֹת הָעֲבוֹדָה כָּל שָׁבוּעַ מִשְׁמָרָה – **That is to say, their consent to the arrangement of *mishmaros*,** in which **the *avodah*** of **each week** was reserved for **its *mishmar*,** is tantamount to a transaction. Therefore, the right for a Kohen or Levi to serve at will does not apply throughout the year, but is limited to the festivals.[5] וְכֵן פֵּרְשׁוֹ הַתַּרְגּוּם – **And so does *Targum* Onkelos explain [the phrase],** *except for what was transacted by the forefathers*: בַּר מִמַּטְרְתָא דְּיֵיתֵי בְּשַׁבַּתָּא דְּכֵן אַתְקִינוּ אֲבָהָתָא – No Kohen may perform *avodah* **except for the *mishmar* that comes on the Sabbath** (i.e., the *mishmar* of that week), **for so did the forefathers establish** – that each *mishmar* shall have the exclusive right to serve during its own week.

Underlying Purpose of the Mitzvah

מִשָּׁרְשֵׁי מִצְוַת הַמִּשְׁמָרוֹת יְדוּעוֹת וּקְבוּעוֹת – **Among the underlying purposes of the mitzvah** to have **specific, fixed *mishmaros*** is לְפִי שֶׁכָּל הַמְּלָאכוֹת הַמֻּטָּלוֹת עַל מִסְפַּר אֲנָשִׁים יְדוּעִים נַעֲשׂוֹת כָּרָאוּי – **because all tasks that are the responsibility of a specific group of people will be performed properly,** וְאֵין הָעַצְלָה וְהַיֵּאוּשׁ וְהַקַּפְּדָנוּת מְצוּיָה בָּהֶן – **as laziness, despair, and resentment are uncommon in [such a group].**[6] אֲבָל הַמֻּטָּלוֹת עַל הָרַבִּים – **On the other hand, when [a task] is the responsibility of the** general **public,** מִבְּלִי שֶׁיִּהְיֶה בָּהֶם אֲנָשִׁים יְדוּעִים לַעֲשׂוֹתָהּ – **without specific people among them** having been designated **to perform it,** it will often be neglected, פְּעָמִים יַטִּילוּ אוֹתָהּ קְצָתָן עַל קְצָתָן – for **at times some of [the people] will shift** the responsibility to perform **[the task] upon the rest,** וּפְעָמִים יַקְפִּידוּ אֵלּוּ עַל אֵלּוּ בָּעִנְיָן – **and at** other **times they will be resentful toward each other over the matter.** אֵין לְהַאֲרִיךְ בִּדְבָרִים אֵלּוּ – **There is no need to elaborate about these things,** יְדוּעוֹת הֵן בְּכָל אַנְשֵׁי מִנְיָן – since **they are well-known among all members of large groups.** Thus, to ensure that the *avodah* in the *Beis HaMikdash* be

---

NOTES

5. Thus, the institution of *mishmaros* emerges from these final words of the verse (see *Rambam, Sefer HaMitzvos, Asei* 36).

There seem to be some words missing from Chinuch here. The full quote of *Sifrei,* as cited by *Rambam* (ibid.; see also our version of *Sifrei*), is as follows: *It might be* thought that a Kohen or Levi is entitled *at all times* to serve according to his heart's desire. *[Scripture] therefore states: from one of your cities,* which means, *at a time when all of Israel is gathered in one city* (i.e., a Kohen or Levi may serve at his heart's desire only during the three Pilgrimage Festivals, when all of Israel comes to Jerusalem). *It might be* thought *that all the mishmaros are equal* even *with regard to the offerings brought on the festival that are not due to the festival* (such as voluntary offerings brought by individuals). *[Scripture] therefore states: except for what was transacted by the forefathers,* etc. (i.e., the original division into *mishmaros* included the right of the weekly *mishmar* to bring any non-festival offerings that happen to be brought during the festival; see note 3 above).

6. The source for this idea is *Ramban* (glosses to *Sefer HaMitzvos, Asei* 36). See end of this mitzvah.

אֲבָל בָּרֶגֶל מִפְּנֵי הַשִּׂמְחָה נִצְטַוּוּ לִהְיוֹת יַד הַכֹּל שָׁוָה בָּהֶן.

מִדִּינֵי הַמִּצְוָה מַה שֶּׁאָמְרוּ זִכְרוֹנָם לִבְרָכָה שֶׁבְּכָל מִשְׁמָר וּמִשְׁמָר הָיָה מְמֻנֶּה אִישׁ אֶחָד וְהוּא רֹאשׁ לְכָל אַנְשֵׁי הַמִּשְׁמָר, וְהוּא מְחַלֵּק אוֹתָן לְבָתֵּי אָבוֹת, וּבְכָל יוֹם וָיוֹם מִימֵי הַשָּׁבוּעַ מְחַלְּקִים רָאשֵׁי הָאָבוֹת בֵּינֵיהֶם אֲנָשִׁים יְדוּעִים לַעֲבוֹדָה, אִישׁ אִישׁ עַל עֲבוֹדָתוֹ[7], וּמִיּוֹם שַׁבָּת לְיוֹם שַׁבָּת מִתְחַלְּפִין הַמִּשְׁמָרוֹת[8] וְחוֹזְרִים חָלִילָה.

וּנְבִיאִים רִאשׁוֹנִים[9] תִּקְנוּ שֶׁיִּתְמַנּוּ מִיִּשְׂרְאֵלִים כְּמוֹ כֵן עֶשְׂרִים וְאַרְבָּעָה מִשְׁמָרוֹת, אֲנָשִׁים כְּשֵׁרִים וְיִרְאֵי חֵטְא, וְהֵם הַנִּקְרָאִים בְּכָל מָקוֹם בַּתַּלְמוּד אַנְשֵׁי מַעֲמָד, כְּלוֹמַר שֶׁהֵם שְׁלוּחֵי יִשְׂרָאֵל לַעֲמֹד עַל קָרְבְּנוֹת צִבּוּר, וּכְעִנְיָן שֶׁאָמְרוּ זִכְרוֹנָם לִבְרָכָה (תענית כ״ו ע״א)

---

carried out properly, the Torah commanded that the responsibility be assigned to a specific group each week, rather than left to all the Kohanim collectively. אֲבָל בָּרֶגֶל – **With regard to the Pilgrimage Festivals, however,** מִפְּנֵי הַשִּׂמְחָה – **due to the joy** of the holiday, נִצְטַוּוּ לִהְיוֹת יַד הַכֹּל שָׁוָה בָּהֶן – **[Kohanim and Leviim] were commanded that all should be equally entitled** to serve **on [those days].**

Laws of the Mitzvah

מִדִּינֵי הַמִּצְוָה – **Among the laws of the mitzvah** is מַה שֶּׁאָמְרוּ זִכְרוֹנָם לִבְרָכָה – **that which [the Sages], of blessed memory, stated** (*Rambam, Hil. Klei HaMikdash* 4:3,11; see *Tosefta, Taanis* 2:1), שֶׁבְּכָל מִשְׁמָר וּמִשְׁמָר הָיָה מְמֻנֶּה אִישׁ אֶחָד וְהוּא רֹאשׁ לְכָל אַנְשֵׁי הַמִּשְׁמָר – **that in each of the *mishmaros* there was one man who was appointed as the head of all members of the *mishmar*.** וְהוּא מְחַלֵּק אוֹתָן לְבָתֵּי אָבוֹת – **He would divide [the members of his *mishmar*] into** seven ***batei avos*** (family groups; sing., *beis av*) and assign to each *beis av* the duty for one day of the week. וּבְכָל יוֹם וָיוֹם מִימֵי הַשָּׁבוּעַ – **On each day of the week,** מְחַלְּקִים רָאשֵׁי הָאָבוֹת בֵּינֵיהֶם אֲנָשִׁים יְדוּעִים לַעֲבוֹדָה – **the heads of the** *batei* ***avos*** **would assign specific people** from **among [their *beis av*] for the *avodah*,** אִישׁ אִישׁ עַל עֲבוֹדָתוֹ – with **each person charged with his own *avodah*.**[7] וּמִיּוֹם שַׁבָּת לְיוֹם שַׁבָּת מִתְחַלְּפִין הַמִּשְׁמָרוֹת – **The *mishmaros* would change each** week on the **Sabbath day,**[8] until all of the *mishmaros* served, וְחוֹזְרִים חָלִילָה – **and the cycle would** then **repeat itself.**

Aside from the *mishmaros* of Kohanim and Leviim, there also were twenty-four *mishmaros* from among the Yisraelim, who were stationed in the *Beis HaMikdash.* Chinuch, citing *Rambam* (ibid. 6:1), presents the origin and purpose of this division:

וּנְבִיאִים רִאשׁוֹנִים תִּקְנוּ שֶׁיִּתְמַנּוּ מִיִּשְׂרְאֵלִים כְּמוֹ כֵן עֶשְׂרִים וְאַרְבָּעָה מִשְׁמָרוֹת – **The early prophets**[9] **instituted that from** among **the Yisraelim, as well, twenty-four *mishmaros* are to be appointed,** אֲנָשִׁים כְּשֵׁרִים וְיִרְאֵי חֵטְא – comprised of **people** who are **upstanding and fearful of sin.** וְהֵם הַנִּקְרָאִים בְּכָל מָקוֹם בַּתַּלְמוּד אַנְשֵׁי מַעֲמָד – **These are [the people] who are called, throughout the Talmud, "members of the *maamad*** (i.e., station)," כְּלוֹמַר שֶׁהֵם שְׁלוּחֵי יִשְׂרָאֵל לַעֲמֹד עַל קָרְבְּנוֹת צִבּוּר – **meaning that they are emissaries of** the nation of **Israel** who were posted **to stand over the communal offerings,** וּכְעִנְיָן שֶׁאָמְרוּ זִכְרוֹנָם לִבְרָכָה – **in accordance with what [the Sages],**

NOTES

7. In *Hil. Klei HaMikdash* (3:9), *Rambam* teaches that this arrangement applies to the Leviim. Each Levi was given a particular task to perform every time his *beis av* served. Chinuch, however, writes that this applies to Kohanim as well. For discussion of this dispute, see Insight A to Mitzvah 389.

Now, as is well known, the Kohanim actually decided by lottery who should perform each part of the *avodah.* For discussion of how this fits with Chinuch's words here, see Insight B to Mitzvah 389.

8. The outgoing *mishmar* would perform the *avodah* of the morning *tamid* and the Sabbath *mussaf* offerings, and the incoming *mishmar* would perform the *avodah* of the afternoon *tamid* (*Rambam, Hil. Temidin U'Mussafin* 4:9).

9. Samuel the Prophet and King David (*Taanis* 27a).

אֶפְשָׁר יְהֵא קָרְבָּנוֹ שֶׁל אָדָם קָרֵב וְהוּא אֵינוֹ עוֹמֵד עַל גַּבָּיו[10]. וְעַל כָּל מַעֲמָד הָיָה אֶחָד גָּדוֹל מְמֻנֶּה עַל כֻּלָּם, וְהוּא הַנִּקְרָא רֹאשׁ הַמַּעֲמָד[11]. וְכֵן הָיָה דַּרְכָּם שֶׁל אַנְשֵׁי הַמַּעֲמָד, בְּכָל שַׁבָּת וְשַׁבָּת מִתְקַבְּצִים, מִי שֶׁהוּא מֵהֶם בִּירוּשָׁלַיִם אוֹ סָבִיב לָהּ נִכְנַס לַמִּקְדָּשׁ, וּבֵין בִּירוּשָׁלַיִם בֵּין בִּשְׁאָר מְקוֹמוֹת מִתְקַבְּצִין בְּבֵית הַכְּנֶסֶת וּמַרְבִּין בִּתְפִלּוֹת[12] וּמִתְעַנִּין יוֹם שֵׁנִי וּשְׁלִישִׁי וּרְבִיעִי וַחֲמִישִׁי מִן הַשָּׁבוּעַ[13], וּשְׁאָר כָּל עִנְיָנָם בִּתְפִלָּה וּבִקְרִיאַת הַתּוֹרָה, כְּמוֹ שֶׁמְּפֹרָשׁ בְּמַסֶּכֶת תַּעֲנִית וּמְגִלָּה[14].

---

of blessed memory, stated (Mishnah, *Taanis* 26a): **אֶפְשָׁר יְהֵא קָרְבָּנוֹ שֶׁל אָדָם קָרֵב וְהוּא אֵינוֹ עוֹמֵד עַל גַּבָּיו – "Is it possible that a person's offering is brought, and he is not standing over it** (i.e., he is not present)?"[10] Since the communal offerings were brought on behalf of the entire nation, it was necessary that the nation be present at the time they were offered. And since the entire nation obviously cannot stand in the Courtyard, contingents of Yisraelim were designated to represent the entire nation. **וְעַל כָּל מַעֲמָד הָיָה אֶחָד גָּדוֹל מְמֻנֶּה עַל כֻּלָּם – For each *maamad* there was a prominent individual who was appointed over all of [the *maamad* members], וְהוּא הַנִּקְרָא רֹאשׁ הַמַּעֲמָד – and he is called "the head of the *maamad*."**[11]

Chinuch relates what these members of the *maamad* did during the week they were on duty: **וְכֵן הָיָה דַּרְכָּם שֶׁל אַנְשֵׁי הַמַּעֲמָד – This was the practice of the members of the *maamad*: בְּכָל שַׁבָּת וְשַׁבָּת מִתְקַבְּצִים – On each and every week,** at the beginning of the week, **[the members of that week's *maamad*] would gather together,** as follows: **מִי שֶׁהוּא מֵהֶם בִּירוּשָׁלַיִם אוֹ סָבִיב לָהּ נִכְנַס לַמִּקְדָּשׁ – Any one of them who was in Jerusalem or its surroundings,** who could arrive at the *Beis HaMikdash* in time to be present when the *tamid* offering was brought, **would enter the *Beis HaMikdash*.** In addition, the *maamad* had other members throughout Israel, **וּבֵין בִּירוּשָׁלַיִם בֵּין בִּשְׁאָר מְקוֹמוֹת מִתְקַבְּצִין בְּבֵית הַכְּנֶסֶת – and, both in Jerusalem and in other places, [the *maamad* members] would gather in the synagogue וּמַרְבִּין בִּתְפִלּוֹת – and pray extensively.**[12] **וּמִתְעַנִּין יוֹם שֵׁנִי וּשְׁלִישִׁי וּרְבִיעִי וַחֲמִישִׁי מִן הַשָּׁבוּעַ – They would fast on Monday, Tuesday, Wednesday, and Thursday of the week** during which they were on duty.[13] **וּשְׁאָר כָּל עִנְיָנָם בִּתְפִלָּה וּבִקְרִיאַת הַתּוֹרָה – The rest of their procedure, with regard to prayer and the Torah reading, כְּמוֹ שֶׁמְּפֹרָשׁ בְּמַסֶּכֶת תַּעֲנִית וּמְגִלָּה –** is **as detailed in Tractates *Taanis*** (26a-28b) **and *Megillah*** (30b, 31b).[14]

NOTES

10. The requirement that one be present when his offering is brought is derived from the verse concerning the *tamid* offering (*Numbers* 28:2): תִּשְׁמְרוּ לְהַקְרִיב לִי בְּמוֹעֲדוֹ, *You shall guard [the offering] to offer [it] to Me in its appointed time*. One "guards"' an offering by standing nearby when it is offered (see *Sifrei* ad loc.; *Rashi* to *Sotah* 8a ד״ה אקורבנייהו).

11. The head of the *maamad* would make sure that all the members were at their station in the *Beis HaMikdash* at the appointed time (*Aruch* ע׳ עמד). [For another duty that he had, see *Tamid* 33a and *Rambam, Hil. Temidin U'Mussafin* 6:5 with *Kesef Mishneh*.]

12. They recited special prayers that Hashem accept the communal offerings with favor, and for the salvation of the entire nation (see *Taanis* 27b; *Derech Chochmah, Beur HaHalachah* ibid. 6:5 ד״ה לתפלה). See next note.

[From *Rambam* (*Hil. Klei HaMikdash* 6:2-3) it would appear that only the members of the *maamad* who were distant from Jerusalem would go to the synagogue, while all those who were in or near Jerusalem would go to the *Beis HaMikdash*; see *Minchas Yitzchak* here, end of §4.]

13. Each day they prayed for something appropriate to that day. On Monday (when, during Creation, the upper and lower waters were separated; *Genesis* 1:6), they prayed for the safety of seafarers; on Tuesday (when dry land became visible and fit for travel; ibid. v. 9), they prayed for the safety of desert travelers; on Wednesday (when the מְאֹרֹת [luminaries] were placed in the sky, which can also be read as מְאֵרֹת [curses and misfortunes]; ibid. v. 14), they prayed that children be spared the curse of *askara* [diphtheria]; and on Thursday (when the first living creatures came into being; ibid. v. 20), they prayed for the well-being of pregnant and nursing women and their children (see *Taanis* 27b with *Rashi*; *Derech Chochmah* ibid. 6:23).

They did not fast on Friday, so as not to enter the Sabbath while hungry, and certainly they did not fast on the Sabbath itself. They also did not fast on Sunday, so as to avoid the difficult transition from a day of physical indulgence to a day of fasting (*Rambam* ibid. 6:3).

14. Aside from the regular morning and afternoon prayers (*Shacharis* and *Minchah*), the members of the *maamad* would recite the additional *Ne'ilah* prayer, as

וְאָמְרוּ זִכְרוֹנָם לִבְרָכָה (סוכה נ"ה ע"ב) בְּמִשְׁמָרוֹת כְּהֻנָּה וּלְוִיָּה שֶׁבָּרְגָלִים אֵין יַד הַכֹּל שָׁוֶה בָּהֶן כִּי אִם בְּקָרְבְּנוֹת הָרְגָלִים[15] וּבְחִלּוּק לֶחֶם הַפָּנִים[16] וּבְחִלּוּק שְׁתֵּי הַלֶּחֶם שֶׁל עֲצֶרֶת[17], אֲבָל נְדָרִים וּנְדָבוֹת[18] וּתְמִידִין אֵין מַקְרִיבִין אוֹתָם וַאֲפִלּוּ בָּרֶגֶל אֶלָּא מִשְׁמָר שֶׁזְּמַנּוֹ קָבוּעַ, שֶׁנֶּאֱמַר חֵלֶק כְּחֵלֶק יֹאכֵלוּ לְבַד וְגוֹ', כְּלוֹמַר חֵלֶק כְּחֵלֶק יֹאכֵלוּ בְּקָרְבְּנוֹת צִבּוּר, וְאֵינָם חֵלֶק כְּחֵלֶק בִּשְׁאָר דְּבָרִים שֶׁכְּבָר חִלְקוּ אוֹתָם הָאָבוֹת

Earlier, Chinuch mentioned that there is an exception to the rule that a Kohen may serve only during the time of his *mishmar*. That is, during each of the pilgrimage festivals, all of the Kohanim were allowed to participate in the offerings brought in honor of the festival. Chinuch elaborates on this law: וְאָמְרוּ זִכְרוֹנָם לִבְרָכָה — **[The Sages], of blessed memory, stated** (*Succah* 55b; see *Rambam* ibid. 4:4-5), בְּמִשְׁמָרוֹת כְּהֻנָּה וּלְוִיָּה שֶׁבָּרְגָלִים — **with regard to the *mishmaros* of the Kohanim and Leviim on the pilgrimage festivals,** that אֵין יַד הַכֹּל שָׁוֶה בָּהֶן כִּי אִם בְּקָרְבְּנוֹת הָרְגָלִים — the rule that **all** the *mishmaros* **serve equally on [the festivals]** pertains **only to** the *avodah* of **the** special **festival offerings,**[15] וּבְחִלּוּק לֶחֶם הַפָּנִים — **the distribution of the *Lechem HaPanim*,**[16] וּבְחִלּוּק שְׁתֵּי הַלֶּחֶם שֶׁל עֲצֶרֶת — **and the distribution of the Two Loaves of Shavuos.**[17] אֲבָל נְדָרִים וּנְדָבוֹת וּתְמִידִין אֵין מַקְרִיבִין אוֹתָם וַאֲפִלּוּ בָּרֶגֶל אֶלָּא מִשְׁמָר שֶׁזְּמַנּוֹ קָבוּעַ — **However, even on the pilgrimage festival,** the services of **the vow-offerings and gift-offerings** brought by individuals,[18] **as well as** the service of **the** regular communal *tamid* **offerings, were performed only by the *mishmar* whose time falls** on the festival, שֶׁנֶּאֱמַר — **as it is stated** (*Deuteronomy* 18:8): "חֵלֶק כְּחֵלֶק יֹאכֵלוּ לְבַד וְגוֹ' — *Portion for portion shall they eat, except* for what was transacted by the forefathers. כְּלוֹמַר — **That is to say:** "חֵלֶק כְּחֵלֶק יֹאכֵלוּ בְּקָרְבְּנוֹת צִבּוּר — **"Portion for portion shall they eat"** of the communal offerings of the festivals, as well as the personal offerings that are specific to the festivals; they may perform the *avodah* and receive a portion of those offerings. וְאֵינָם חֵלֶק כְּחֵלֶק בִּשְׁאָר דְּבָרִים — **But they are not** entitled to eat **"portion for portion" from other things** that are offered on the festivals; that is, they may not perform the *avodah* — and thus are not entitled to receive portions — of any offerings that are unrelated to the festival but happen to be offered during the festival, שֶׁכְּבָר חִלְקוּ אוֹתָם הָאָבוֹת — **because the forefathers have already divided**

NOTES

on Yom Kippur. According to *Rambam* (ibid. 6:4) there also was another prayer added daily between *Shacharis* and *Minchah* (cf. *Raavad* ad loc.).

They also had special Torah readings of passages from *Genesis* on each day. During the morning prayers they read these passages communally, and at the *Minchah* prayer each of them recited the passages individually (*Rambam* ibid.).

15. This includes the *chagigah, shalmei simchah,* and *olas re'iyah* offerings that every individual was obligated to bring on each pilgrimage festival [Mitzvos 88, 488, 489], as well as the communal *mussaf* offerings that were brought in honor of each festival [Mitzvos 299, 320, 322, 404] (see *Rashi, Succah* 55b ד"ה במה שאמור; *Rambam, Hil. Klei HaMikdash* 4:4 with *Derech Chochmah* §25; *Minchas Chinuch* §3).

16. The *Lechem HaPanim* (see Mitzvah 97) consisted of twelve loaves of bread that were baked on Friday, placed on the *Shulchan* in the *Beis HaMikdash* on the Sabbath, and left there until the following Sabbath, at which time they were distributed and eaten by the Kohanim. Normally, they were distributed only to the outgoing and incoming *mishmaros* of Kohanim, but on a Sabbath that coincided with a festival, they

were distributed among all the Kohanim.

Although the *Lechem HaPanim* is not related to any festival, a Scriptural exposition teaches that all Kohanim partake of the *Lechem HaPanim* during a festival (see *Succah* 55b-56a).

17. A special *minchah* offering consisting of two loaves of bread was baked on the day before Shavuos, and was used in the service on Shavuos and then eaten. The Kohen Gadol took one loaf, and the other was distributed among all the Kohanim. See Mitzvah 307.

18. Vow-offerings (*nedarim*) and gift-offerings (*nedavos*) are offerings that a person brings after he voluntarily obligated himself to do so. In the case of a vow-offering (*neder*), the vower declares, "It is hereby incumbent upon me to bring an offering," and he fulfills the vow by designating an animal as the offering and bringing it. In the case of a gift-offering (*nedavah*), the vower designates his animal as an offering at the moment of the vow, by declaring: "This animal is hereby consecrated as an offering."

It was permitted to bring these personal offerings on Chol HaMoed (but not on the Yom Tov days; *Beitzah* 19a). Since they were unrelated to the festival, their *avodah* was reserved for the *mishmar* on duty.

וְקָבְעוּ אוֹתָם כָּל מִשְׁמָר וּמִשְׁמָר בְּשַׁבַּתּוֹ. וְכֹהֵן שֶׁהָיָה לוֹ קָרְבָּן הֲרֵי זֶה בָּא לַמִּקְדָּשׁ וּמַקְרִיבוֹ בְּכָל עֵת שֶׁיִּרְצֶה, שֶׁנֶּאֱמַר וּבָא בְּכָל אַוַּת נַפְשׁוֹ, כְּלוֹמַר בַּקָּרְבָּן שֶׁהוּא שֶׁלּוֹ בְּכָל עֵת יָבֹא לְהַקְרִיבוֹ, וְהָעוֹר שֶׁלּוֹ. וְיֶתֶר פְּרָטֵי הַמִּצְוָה בְּמַסֶּכֶת תַּעֲנִית וּמְגִלָּה וּבְסוֹף סֻכָּה[19].

וְנוֹהֶגֶת מִצְוָה זוֹ בִּזְכָרֵי כְהֻנָּה וּלְוִיָּה בִּזְמַן הַבַּיִת.

וְעוֹבֵר עַל זֶה וּמָחָה בְּיַד חֲבֵרוֹ בָּרֶגֶל שֶׁלֹּא לַעֲבֹד בְּכָל אַוַּת נַפְשׁוֹ בִּטֵּל עֲשֵׂה זֶה[20].

וְהָרַמְבַּ״ן ז״ל הִשִּׂיג בְּזֹאת הַמִּצְוָה עַל הָרַמְבַּ״ם ז״ל וְאָמַר שֶׁהֱיוֹת הַכֹּהֲנִים עוֹבְדִים לְמִשְׁמָרוֹת אֵינוֹ בְּמַשְׁמַע הַכָּתוּב כְּלָל כְּדַעְתּוֹ שֶׁל הָרַב ז״ל, אֶלָּא הֲלָכָה לְמֹשֶׁה מִסִּינַי

---

them וְקָבְעוּ אוֹתָם כָּל מִשְׁמָר וּמִשְׁמָר בְּשַׁבַּתּוֹ – **and they established them** for **each *mishmar* in its week,** as was explained earlier.

There is a second exception to the rule that a Kohen may serve only during the time of his *mishmar.* Chinuch presents that law:

וְכֹהֵן שֶׁהָיָה לוֹ קָרְבָּן – **If a Kohen has an offering** of his own to bring, הֲרֵי זֶה בָּא לַמִּקְדָּשׁ וּמַקְרִיבוֹ בְּכָל עֵת שֶׁיִּרְצֶה – **he may come to the *Beis HaMikdash* and offer it whenever he wishes,** שֶׁנֶּאֱמַר ״וּבָא בְּכָל אַוַּת נַפְשׁוֹ״ – **as it is stated** (ibid. v. 6): ***and he comes when his heart fully desires,*** כְּלוֹמַר בַּקָּרְבָּן שֶׁהוּא שֶׁלּוֹ בְּכָל עֵת יָבֹא לְהַקְרִיבוֹ – **which means to say** that **for his own offering, he may come to offer it at any time** that his heart desires; וְהָעוֹר שֶׁלּוֹ – **and the hide** of the animal **is his,** unlike the usual arrangement, in which the Kohanim of the *mishmar* divide the hides of the offerings among themselves.

וְיֶתֶר פְּרָטֵי הַמִּצְוָה – These, **and the remaining details of the mitzvah,** בְּמַסֶּכֶת תַּעֲנִית וּמְגִלָּה וּבְסוֹף סֻכָּה – appear **in Tractates *Taanis*** (26a-28b), ***Megillah*** (30b, 31b), **and at the end of *Succah*** (55a-56b).[19]

Applicability of the Mitzvah

וְנוֹהֶגֶת מִצְוָה זוֹ בִּזְכָרֵי כְהֻנָּה וּלְוִיָּה בִּזְמַן הַבַּיִת – **This mitzvah applies to male Kohanim and Leviim in the time of the *Beis HaMikdash*.**

וְעוֹבֵר עַל זֶה – **One who transgresses this** commandment, וּמָחָה בְּיַד חֲבֵרוֹ בָּרֶגֶל שֶׁלֹּא לַעֲבֹד בְּכָל אַוַּת נַפְשׁוֹ – **and objects to his fellow** Kohen or Levi **on a pilgrimage festival, not** allowing him **to serve as he wishes,** בִּטֵּל עֲשֵׂה זֶה – **has violated this mitzvah-obligation.**[20]

Dispute Regarding the Mitzvah

וְהָרַמְבַּ״ן ז״ל הִשִּׂיג בְּזֹאת הַמִּצְוָה עַל הָרַמְבַּ״ם ז״ל – ***Ramban,* of blessed memory** (glosses to *Sefer HaMitzvos, Asei* 36), **takes issue with *Rambam,* of blessed memory, with regard to this mitzvah,** וְאָמַר שֶׁהֱיוֹת הַכֹּהֲנִים עוֹבְדִים לְמִשְׁמָרוֹת אֵינוֹ בְּמַשְׁמַע הַכָּתוּב כְּלָל כְּדַעְתּוֹ שֶׁל הָרַב ז״ל – **and says that for Kohanim to serve according to *mishmaros* is not indicated by the verse at all as the opinion of the Master** (*Rambam*), **of blessed memory;** אֶלָּא הֲלָכָה לְמֹשֶׁה מִסִּינַי

NOTES

19. The laws of the *mishmaros* and *maamados* are codified in *Rambam, Hil. Klei HaMikdash* 3:9, 4:3-11, and 6:1-8,11.

20. As mentioned earlier (note 4), Chinuch maintains that this mitzvah consists of two elements: (a) the Kohanim and Leviim are to be divided into *mishmaros;* and (b) all of them are to be allowed to serve on the festivals. Here, however, Chinuch makes no mention of the first element of the mitzvah. [Possibly, this is because the matter of creating *mishmaros* has already been fulfilled, and, therefore, this element can no longer be violated (see *Maayan HaChochmah,* Roedelheim ed., p. 118b, note 42; cf. *Chasam Sofer* to this mitzvah – printed after his commentary to Tractate *Kesubos*).]

Ramban (glosses to *Sefer HaMitzvos, Asei* 36) notes that while in *Sefer HaMitzvos* [as well as in his count of mitzvos at the beginning of *Mishneh Torah*] *Rambam* includes the component of establishing *mishmaros* in this mitzvah, in *Hil. Klei HaMikdash* (4:4), he presents the mitzvah only with regard to the requirement of having all the *mishmaros* serve on the pilgrimage festivals (see also his list of mitzvos at the beginning of *Hil. Klei HaMikdash* §11). For further discussion, see commentaries to *Sefer HaMitzvos* there; see also *Maayan HaChochmah* ibid.

הוּא שֶׁיְּחַלְּקוּ בֵּינֵיהֶם הָעֲבוֹדָה לְמִשְׁמָרוֹת, וּמֹשֶׁה רַבֵּנוּ הוּא שֶׁהִתְחִיל תְּחִלָּה לְחַלְּקָם וְהוּא עָשָׂה מֵהֶן שְׁמוֹנָה מִשְׁמָרוֹת, אַרְבָּעָה מֵאִיתָמָר וְסִיעָתוֹ וְאַרְבָּעָה מֵאֶלְעָזָר וְסִיעָתוֹ[21], כָּךְ הִיא הַקַּבָּלָה, וְזֶה שֶׁאָמַר הַכָּתוּב לְבַד מִמְכָּרָיו וְגוֹ׳ שְׁלִילוּת הוּא וְלֹא מִצְוָה כְּלָל, כְּלוֹמַר שֶׁיַּעַבְדוּ הַכֹּהֲנִים בְּכָל אַוַּת נַפְשָׁם בְּכָל עֵת בֵּין בַּחֹל בֵּין בָּרֶגֶל, לְבַד אִם רָצוּ וְהִסְכִּימוּ לְחַלֵּק בֵּינֵיהֶם הָעֲבוֹדָה לְמִשְׁמָרוֹת[22], וְקִבַּלְנוּ הֲלָכָה לְמֹשֶׁה מִסִּינַי שֶׁרָאוּי לַעֲשׂוֹת כֵּן כְּדֵי שֶׁתֵּעָשֶׂה הַמְּלָאכָה כְּסֵדֶר וּבִזְרִיזוּת, זֶהוּ תֹּרֶף דִּבְרֵי הָרַב ז״ל[23].

הוּא שֶׁיְּחַלְּקוּ בֵּינֵיהֶם הָעֲבוֹדָה לְמִשְׁמָרוֹת – rather, it is known through **the Oral Law transmitted to Moses at Sinai that the *avodah* shall be divided among them into *mishmaros*. וּמֹשֶׁה רַבֵּנוּ הוּא שֶׁהִתְחִיל תְּחִלָּה לְחַלְּקָם – Moses, our teacher, is the one who first started to divide them** in this way, **וְהוּא עָשָׂה מֵהֶן שְׁמוֹנָה מִשְׁמָרוֹת – and he** originally **made eight *mishmaros* of them, אַרְבָּעָה מֵאִיתָמָר וְסִיעָתוֹ – four** *mishmaros* **from Ithamar and his group** of Kohanim, **וְאַרְבָּעָה מֵאֶלְעָזָר וְסִיעָתוֹ – and four from Elazar and his group;**[21] **כָּךְ הִיא הַקַּבָּלָה – such is the** Oral **Tradition.**

Chinuch explains how *Ramban* interprets the verse that *Rambam* understands to be the source of our mitzvah:

וְזֶה שֶׁאָמַר הַכָּתוּב ״לְבַד מִמְכָּרָיו וְגוֹ׳ ״ – According to *Ramban,* **that which Scripture states,** ***except for what was transacted*** *by the forefathers,* **שְׁלִילוּת הוּא – is an exclusion** from the general procedure stated earlier in the verse, **וְלֹא מִצְוָה כְּלָל – and not a mitzvah at all. כְּלוֹמַר שֶׁיַּעַבְדוּ הַכֹּהֲנִים בְּכָל אַוַּת נַפְשָׁם בְּכָל עֵת בֵּין בַּחֹל בֵּין בָּרֶגֶל** – Rather, the verse **means to say that** it is a mitzvah-obligation that **the Kohanim shall serve whenever they desire, at any time, whether on a weekday or on a Pilgrimage Festival, לְבַד אִם רָצוּ וְהִסְכִּימוּ לְחַלֵּק בֵּינֵיהֶם הָעֲבוֹדָה לְמִשְׁמָרוֹת – unless they should desire and agree to divide the *avodah* among them according to *mishmaros.***[22] **וְקִבַּלְנוּ הֲלָכָה לְמֹשֶׁה מִסִּינַי שֶׁרָאוּי לַעֲשׂוֹת כֵּן – Indeed, we have received a tradition from Moses at Sinai that it is proper to do so, כְּדֵי שֶׁתֵּעָשֶׂה הַמְּלָאכָה כְּסֵדֶר וּבִזְרִיזוּת – in order that the service** in the *Beis HaMikdash* **be done orderly and speedily. זֶהוּ תֹּרֶף דִּבְרֵי הָרַב ז״ל – This is the essence of the words of the Master** (*Ramban*), **of blessed memory.**[23]

NOTES

21. Elazar and Ithamar were the third and fourth sons of Aaron the Kohen, respectively. The oldest two sons, Nadav and Avihu, died childless. [Although there were very few Kohanim in the time of Moses, he established that when the appropriate time would come, four *mishmaros* were to come from Elazar, and four from Ithamar (see *Ramban* there and *Meiri, Taanis* 27a ד״ה משמרות אלו). Later, when the number of Kohanim grew, they were further divided into a total of 24 *mishmaros.*]

22. The verse thus conveys a mitzvah-obligation to allow the Kohanim to serve whenever they want, and provides the *legal basis* for the arrangement of the *mishmaros,* but does not require that this arrangement be made.

23. See *Ramban* there for elaboration of his position. For further discussion of the dispute between *Rambam* and *Ramban,* see Insight A to Mitzvah 389.

מִצְוָה תקי: שֶׁלֹּא לִקְסֹם[1]

שֶׁנִּמְנַעְנוּ שֶׁלֹּא לִקְסֹם. וְכָתַב הָרַמְבַּ"ם ז"ל (בספר המצוות) שֶׁעִנְיַן הַקְּסִימָה הוּא הַמֵּנִיעַ כֹּחוֹ וּמַחֲשַׁבְתּוֹ לַחְשֹׁב בְּמִין מִמִּינֵי הַתְּנוּעָה, כַּאֲשֶׁר יַעֲשׂוּ בַּעֲלֵי הַכֹּחוֹת כֻּלָּם שֶׁיַּגִּידוּ מַה שֶּׁיִּתְחַדֵּשׁ קֹדֶם הֱיוֹתוֹ, וְאָמְנָם יִתְאַמֵּת לָהֶם זֶה בִּהְיוֹת כֹּחַ הַמַּחֲשָׁבָה וְהַשִּׂעוּר מֵהֶם חָזָק מְאֹד[2]. פֵּרוּשׁ לְפֵרוּשׁוֹ, כְּלוֹמַר שֶׁמִּתְבּוֹדְדִים בְּמַחְשַׁבְתָּם וְקוֹבְעִים כָּל הַכַּוָּנָה וְכָל הַהֶרְגֵּשׁ שֶׁלָּהֶם עַל אוֹתוֹ הָעִנְיָן שֶׁיַּחְפְּצוּ לָדַעַת, וּמִתּוֹךְ הַהִתְבּוֹדְדוּת וְהַקְּבִיעוּת הֶחָזָק

Mitzvah 510
The Prohibition to Practice Divination

לֹא יִמָּצֵא בְךָ ... קֹסֵם קְסָמִים

There shall not be found from among you ... one who practices divinations ... (*Deuteronomy* 18:10).

This mitzvah is the first in a series of mitzvos (510-515) that forbid us from engaging in various forms of fortunetelling and sorcery. These are in addition to similar prohibitions listed by Chinuch earlier, including the prohibitions against following superstitious omens (Mitzvah 249) and identifying favorable and unfavorable times for our endeavors (Mitzvah 250).[1] The current mitzvah prohibits the practice of divination, which is the foretelling of future events by means of various manipulations. Chinuch will give examples of these manipulations, and will describe the spiritual dangers of engaging in such acts.

The Torah (*Deuteronomy* 18:15 ff.) goes on to contrast these acts with true prophecy, which is reached through pure and positive spiritual attainment, and was conferred upon the most righteous individuals of their times (see Mitzvah 516). Moreover, as we will see below, unlike divination and the murky results it produces, the information received through prophecy is always accurate.

שֶׁנִּמְנַעְנוּ שֶׁלֹּא לִקְסֹם – **We are forbidden to practice divination.** וְכָתַב הָרַמְבַּ"ם ז"ל – ***Rambam*, of blessed memory, writes** (*Sefer HaMitzvos, Lo Saaseh* 31) שֶׁעִנְיַן הַקְּסִימָה הוּא הַמֵּנִיעַ כֹּחוֹ וּמַחֲשַׁבְתּוֹ – **that "divination" refers to manipulating one's energy and thoughts,** לַחְשֹׁב בְּמִין מִמִּינֵי הַתְּנוּעָה – **directing the thoughts through** the performance of **one of the various manipulations** described below, כַּאֲשֶׁר יַעֲשׂוּ בַּעֲלֵי הַכֹּחוֹת כֻּלָּם – **in the manner that all the diviners do** שֶׁיַּגִּידוּ מַה שֶּׁיִּתְחַדֵּשׁ קֹדֶם הֱיוֹתוֹ – when they wish **to inform what will happen before it occurs.** וְאָמְנָם יִתְאַמֵּת לָהֶם זֶה – **Now, this becomes known to them,** בִּהְיוֹת כֹּחַ הַמַּחֲשָׁבָה וְהַשִּׂעוּר מֵהֶם חָזָק מְאֹד – **since their power of thought and their awareness is very strong.**[2]

Chinuch explains:

פֵּרוּשׁ לְפֵרוּשׁוֹ – **The meaning of [*Rambam's*] explanation** כְּלוֹמַר שֶׁמִּתְבּוֹדְדִים בְּמַחְשַׁבְתָּם – **is that [those diviners] meditate in solitude,** וְקוֹבְעִים כָּל הַכַּוָּנָה וְכָל הַהֶרְגֵּשׁ שֶׁלָּהֶם עַל אוֹתוֹ הָעִנְיָן שֶׁיַּחְפְּצוּ לָדַעַת – **and they direct all their thoughts and emotions to the specific matter that they seek to know.** וּמִתּוֹךְ הַהִתְבּוֹדְדוּת וְהַקְּבִיעוּת הֶחָזָק – **By means of** this **solitude and intense**

NOTES

1. For whether such activities are truly effective or are mere fakery, see Insight to Mitzvah 62.

2. The diviner has the capacity to intently direct and focus his energies on a specific matter, enabling him to practice his forbidden craft (*Yad HaLevi* to *Sefer HaMitzvos, Lo Saaseh* 31; see also *Moreh Nevuchim* 2:37). Accordingly, *Rambam* refers to diviners as בַּעֲלֵי הַכֹּחוֹת, literally, *masters of powers,* i.e., those who are masters at being able to manipulate this intuitive spirit.

וְהִתְפַּשְּׁטוּת כָּל הַמַּחֲשָׁבָה מִכָּל עִנְיְנֵי הָעוֹלָם הַגּוּפָנִי תִּתְעָרֵב נַפְשָׁם עִם הָרוּחָנִים הַקּוֹלְטִים הָעֲתִידוֹת הַקְּרוֹבוֹת כַּיָּדוּעַ בֵּין הַחֲכָמִים. אֲבָל מִכָּל מָקוֹם אֵין כֹּחַ בָּהֶם לְעוֹלָם וְלֹא אֲפִלּוּ בְּשֵׁדִים לָדַעַת הָעֲתִידוֹת הָרְחוֹקוֹת[3], וְלֹא יַעֲלֶה אֶל הַמַּעֲלָה הַגְּדוֹלָה הַזֹּאת זוּלָתִי נְבִיאֵי אֱמֶת[4], וְגַם בָּעֲתִידוֹת הַקְּרוֹבוֹת לֹא יַשִּׂיגוּ בָּהֶן הַקּוֹסְמִין כָּל הָאֱמֶת אֲבָל יִתְקַיְּמוּ דִּבְרֵיהֶם בָּרֹב[5]. וּבְעִנְיָן הַזֶּה בְּעַצְמוֹ אֵין כָּל הָאֲנָשִׁים שָׁוִים בּוֹ, אֲבָל יֵשׁ מֵהֶם שֶׁיֵּשׁ לָהֶם יִתְרוֹן גָּדוֹל בְּעִנְיָנִים אֵלּוּ, כְּיִתְרוֹן בְּנֵי אָדָם בִּגְבוּרָה וְעִנְיָנִים אֲחֵרִים קְצָתָן עַל קְצָתָן. וְאֵלֶּה בַּעֲלֵי הַכֹּחוֹת אֵין פְּעֻלָּתָם בְּעִנְיָן הַזֶּה שָׁוָה, כִּי יֵשׁ מֵהֶם שֶׁיִּתְבּוֹדְדוּ בַּמִּדְבָּרוֹת לַחְשֹׁב בָּזֶה, וּמֵהֶם שֶׁיַּכֶּה בַּמַּטֶּה אֲשֶׁר בְּיָדוֹ בָּאָרֶץ מַכּוֹת מְמַהֵרוֹת זוֹ אַחַר זוֹ, וְיִצְעַק צְעָקוֹת מְשֻׁנּוֹת,

---

focus on the matter at hand, וְהִתְפַּשְּׁטוּת כָּל הַמַּחֲשָׁבָה מִכָּל עִנְיְנֵי הָעוֹלָם הַגּוּפָנִי – **and** by **freeing their mind of all matters pertaining to the physical world,** תִּתְעָרֵב נַפְשָׁם עִם הָרוּחָנִים הַקּוֹלְטִים הָעֲתִידוֹת הַקְּרוֹבוֹת – **their souls associate with the spirits that perceive the near future,** כַּיָּדוּעַ בֵּין הַחֲכָמִים – **as is known among the wise men** who are knowledgeable in such matters.

Chinuch goes on to discuss the extent of the accuracy of diviners:

אֲבָל מִכָּל מָקוֹם אֵין כֹּחַ בָּהֶם לְעוֹלָם – **However, [these diviners] nevertheless do not ever have the power,** וְלֹא אֲפִלּוּ בְּשֵׁדִים – **nor do even demons** have the power, לָדַעַת הָעֲתִידוֹת הָרְחוֹקוֹת – **to know the distant future.**[3] וְלֹא יַעֲלֶה אֶל הַמַּעֲלָה הַגְּדוֹלָה הַזֹּאת זוּלָתִי נְבִיאֵי אֱמֶת – **No one, other than the genuine prophets** of Hashem, **is able to rise to the great height** of being granted knowledge of the distant future.[4] וְגַם בָּעֲתִידוֹת הַקְּרוֹבוֹת – **Furthermore, even with regard to the near future,** לֹא יַשִּׂיגוּ בָּהֶן הַקּוֹסְמִין כָּל הָאֱמֶת – **the diviners will not perceive the entire truth.** That is, they will not know even short-term future events with perfect accuracy. אֲבָל יִתְקַיְּמוּ דִּבְרֵיהֶם בָּרֹב – **Nevertheless, for the most part, their words** and predictions **will come to be.**[5]

Chinuch notes that there are different levels of proficiency within the realm of this forbidden craft:

וּבְעִנְיָן הַזֶּה בְּעַצְמוֹ אֵין כָּל הָאֲנָשִׁים שָׁוִים בּוֹ – **Now, in this very matter** of accurately predicting the near future, **not all of the people** who engage **in it are equal.** אֲבָל יֵשׁ מֵהֶם שֶׁיֵּשׁ לָהֶם יִתְרוֹן גָּדוֹל בְּעִנְיָנִים אֵלּוּ – **Rather, there are** individuals **among them who have great superiority** over their fellows **in these matters,** כְּיִתְרוֹן בְּנֵי אָדָם בִּגְבוּרָה וְעִנְיָנִים אֲחֵרִים קְצָתָן עַל קְצָתָן – **just as some people have superiority over others in physical strength and** in **other matters.**

Chinuch details some of the techniques used by diviners:

וְאֵלֶּה בַּעֲלֵי הַכֹּחוֹת אֵין פְּעֻלָּתָם בְּעִנְיָן הַזֶּה שָׁוָה – **These diviners do not all employ the same techniques.** כִּי יֵשׁ מֵהֶם שֶׁיִּתְבּוֹדְדוּ בַּמִּדְבָּרוֹת לַחְשֹׁב בָּזֶה – **For some of them** simply **go into seclusion in the wilderness to meditate about this** future matter that they wish to know, וּמֵהֶם שֶׁיַּכֶּה בַּמַּטֶּה אֲשֶׁר בְּיָדוֹ בָּאָרֶץ מַכּוֹת מְמַהֵרוֹת זוֹ אַחַר זוֹ – **but** there also may be a practitioner **among them who,** after meditating for a while, **strikes the earth with a staff that is in his hand with quick successive blows,** וְיִצְעַק צְעָקוֹת מְשֻׁנּוֹת – **and** then **shouts out strange screams,**

NOTES

3. *Sheidim* (demons) are beings that resemble humans in certain ways and angels in others, and typically inhabit desolate areas (see *Chagigah* 16a; *Ramban, Leviticus* 17:7). The Gemara (ibid.) relates that they hear of future events as they are announced On High. However, such information always relates exclusively to events of the near future (*Ramban, Leviticus* 17:7). The same is true of diviners.

4. See Mitzvah 516, after note 3.

5. *Rambam* notes that a diviner will never be entirely accurate. Even the most skilled diviner will err in some of the details of his prediction. Hence, Scripture (*Isaiah* 47:13) describes diviners as being able to predict מֵאֲשֶׁר יָבֹאוּ עָלַיִךְ, *of what will happen to you* – about which our Sages say that they can predict only מֵאֲשֶׁר, *[some] of what* will happen, but not *all* of what will happen. They will be wrong about at least some of the details (*Bereishis Rabbah* 85:2). Genuine prophecy, on the other hand, will always come true in all of its details; see Mitzvah 517 with note 5.

וְיָנִיחַ מַחֲשַׁבְתּוֹ וְיַבִּיט לָאָרֶץ זְמַן אָרֹךְ[6] עַד שֶׁיָּבִין בְּמַה שֶּׁיִּהְיֶה, וְהֵעִיד הָרַמְבַּ״ם ז״ל שֶׁהוּא רָאָה זֶה בַּמַּעֲרָב פַּעַם אַחַת, וּמֵהֶם מִי שֶׁיְּיַשֵּׁר הַחוֹל וְיַעֲשֶׂה בּוֹ צוּרוֹת, וְזֶה יַעֲשׂוּ הַרְבֵּה בְּנֵי אָדָם בַּמַּעֲרָב, וּמֵהֶם מִי שֶׁיַּשְׁלִיךְ אֲבָנִים דַּקִּים בַּחֲתִיכַת עוֹר וְיַאֲרִיךְ לְהַבִּיט בָּם וְאַחַר כֵּן יְסַפֵּר דְּבָרִים, וּמֵהֶם מִי שֶׁיַּעֲשֶׂה מְלָאכָה זוֹ בְּשַׁעֲלֵי שְׂעוֹרִים[7] וְגַרְגִּיר מֶלַח וּפֶחָם מְעֹרָב בּוֹ, וְזֶה מְפֻרְסָם בֵּינֵינוּ יַעֲשׂוּ אוֹתוֹ תָּמִיד לְעֵינֵינוּ הַיִּשְׁמְעֵאלִים וְהַיִּשְׁמְעֵאלִיּוֹת[8], וּמֵהֶם מִי שֶׁיַּשְׁלִיךְ חֲגוֹרַת עוֹר בָּאָרֶץ וְיַבִּיט בָּהּ וְיַגִּיד. וְהַכַּוָּנָה בָּזֶה כֻּלּוֹ לְהָעִיר כֹּחַ נֶפֶשׁ הַמַּבִּיט[9]. וּמִכָּל עִנְיָנִים אֵלּוּ תַּרְחִיקֵנוּ תּוֹרָתֵנוּ הַשְּׁלֵמָה, וְעַל כָּל זֶה נֶאֱמַר (דברים י״ח, י׳) **לֹא יִמָּצֵא בְךָ וְגוֹ׳ קֹסֵם קְסָמִים וְגוֹ׳.**

וּכְבָר כָּתַבְתִּי בְּאַזְהָרַת לֹא תְנַחֲשׁוּ בְּסֵדֶר קְדֹשִׁים לָאו כ״ט בְּסִימָן רנ״ג (מצוה רמ״ט)[10] **בְּטַעַם אִסּוּר עִנְיָנִים אֵלּוּ מַה שֶּׁיָּדַעְתִּי[11].**

וְיָנִיחַ מַחֲשַׁבְתּוֹ וְיַבִּיט לָאָרֶץ זְמַן אָרֹךְ – and then **suspends his meditation and gazes at the earth for a long period,**[6] **עַד שֶׁיָּבִין בְּמַה שֶּׁיִּהְיֶה – until he perceives what will occur** in the future. **וְהֵעִיד הָרַמְבַּ״ם ז״ל שֶׁהוּא רָאָה זֶה בַּמַּעֲרָב פַּעַם אַחַת** – ***Rambam*, of blessed memory, testifies** (*Sefer HaMitzvos* ibid.) **that he** himself **once saw this** form of divination being practiced **in the West. וּמֵהֶם מִי שֶׁיְּיַשֵּׁר הַחוֹל וְיַעֲשֶׂה בּוֹ צוּרוֹת – Another one smooths out** some **sand and produces images in it; וְזֶה יַעֲשׂוּ הַרְבֵּה בְּנֵי אָדָם בַּמַּעֲרָב – this is done by many people in the West** as well. **וּמֵהֶם מִי שֶׁיַּשְׁלִיךְ אֲבָנִים דַּקִּים בַּחֲתִיכַת עוֹר – Another one throws pebbles at a piece of hide, וְיַאֲרִיךְ לְהַבִּיט בָּם וְאַחַר כֵּן יְסַפֵּר דְּבָרִים – and** then **gazes at length at [the pebbles], and afterward speaks matters** related to the future. **וּמֵהֶם מִי שֶׁיַּעֲשֶׂה מְלָאכָה זוֹ בְּשַׁעֲלֵי שְׂעוֹרִים – Another one practices this craft with handfuls of barley,**[7] **וְגַרְגִּיר מֶלַח וּפֶחָם מְעֹרָב בּוֹ – with a grain of salt and charcoal mixed in. וְזֶה מְפֻרְסָם בֵּינֵינוּ יַעֲשׂוּ אוֹתוֹ תָּמִיד לְעֵינֵינוּ הַיִּשְׁמְעֵאלִים וְהַיִּשְׁמְעֵאלִיּוֹת – This** latter form of divination **is well-known among us,** as **it is constantly done before our eyes by Ishmaelite men and women,** here in Spain.[8] **וּמֵהֶם מִי שֶׁיַּשְׁלִיךְ חֲגוֹרַת עוֹר בָּאָרֶץ – Another one throws a leather belt upon the ground, וְיַבִּיט בָּהּ וְיַגִּיד – and gazes at it and** then **tells** of the future.

וְהַכַּוָּנָה בָּזֶה כֻּלּוֹ לְהָעִיר כֹּחַ נֶפֶשׁ הַמַּבִּיט– The intent of all of these is to awaken the power of the spirit of the one who is gazing.[9] **וּמִכָּל עִנְיָנִים אֵלּוּ תַּרְחִיקֵנוּ תּוֹרָתֵנוּ הַשְּׁלֵמָה – Our perfect Torah distances us from all such matters, וְעַל כָּל זֶה נֶאֱמַר ״לֹא יִמָּצֵא בְךָ וְגוֹ׳ קֹסֵם קְסָמִים וְגוֹ׳ ״ – and regarding all this it is stated** (*Deuteronomy* 18:10): ***There shall not be found from among you ... one who practices divinations*, etc.**

Underlying Purpose of the Mitzvah

וּכְבָר כָּתַבְתִּי בְּאַזְהָרַת ״לֹא תְנַחֲשׁוּ״ – I have already written, in discussion of **the prohibition of *You shall not read omens*** (*Leviticus* 19:26), **בְּסֵדֶר קְדֹשִׁים לָאו כ״ט בְּסִימָן רנ״ג – in *Parashas Kedoshim*,** Mitzvah-**prohibition 29, Chapter 253** of this work (Mitzvah 249),[10] **בְּטַעַם אִסּוּר עִנְיָנִים אֵלּוּ מַה שֶּׁיָּדַעְתִּי – what I understand to be the** general **reason for** why **such matters are prohibited.**[11]

NOTES

6. This puts him into a self-induced trance (*Rambam, Sefer HaMitzvos* ibid.).

7. See *Ezekiel* 13:19 with *Radak* (second explanation).

8. In his introduction, Chinuch describes himself as being from Barcelona, Spain (see Vol. I, p. 30).

9. That is, these various manipulations have no intrinsic supernatural future-telling quality. They merely aid the diviner in focusing his thoughts upon the future matter that he wishes to know (*Rambam, Sefer HaMitzvos* ibid.).

10. Chinuch's numbering follows the original format of this work; see Mitzvah 494 note 4.

11. In Mitzvah 249 (The Prohibition to Follow Superstitious Omens), Chinuch explains that such practices are foolish, and it is inappropriate for the chosen people to be involved in such matters. Furthermore, these practices lead people to deny Divine Providence, as they cause them to think that all of life's occurrences are a matter of chance.

וְרָאִיתִי בְּסִפְרֵי הָרִאשׁוֹנִים בְּטַעַם אִסּוּר זֶה, לְפִי שֶׁכָּל עִנְיָנִים אֵלּוּ מַטְעִים הֶהָמוֹן, וְיַחְשְׁבוּ בִּשְׁבִיל שֶׁיִּצְדְּקוּ עֲלֵיהֶם קְצָת מִן הַדְּבָרִים שֶׁיַּגִּידוּ לָהֶם בַּעֲלֵי הַקֶּסֶם, שֶׁכָּל הַפְּעֻלּוֹת שֶׁהֵם בָּעוֹלָם סִבָּתָם הַמַּזָּלוֹת וְהַכֹּחוֹת[12], וּכְמְעַט יִקָּרְאוּ מִן הַכַּת הָרַע הָאוֹמְרִים עָזַב אֱלֹהִים אֶת הָאָרֶץ (יחזקאל ח׳, י״ב)[13], וּבְעַד זֶה הָעִנְיָן שֶׁהָיָה מְפֻרְסָם הַרְבֵּה בִּזְמַן הַנְּבִיאִים אָמַר הַנָּבִיא (הושע ד׳, י״ב) עַמִּי בְּעֵצוֹ יִשְׁאָל וּמַקְלוֹ יַגִּיד לוֹ.

דִּינֵי הַמִּצְוָה מְבֹאָרִים בִּמְקוֹמוֹת מִסַּנְהֶדְרִין וְתוֹסֶפְתָּא דְּשַׁבָּת וּבְסִפְרֵי[14].

וְנוֹהֵג אִסּוּר זֶה בְּכָל מָקוֹם וּבְכָל זְמַן, בִּזְכָרִים וּנְקֵבוֹת[15].

וְעוֹבֵר עַל זֶה וְעָשָׂה עַצְמוֹ קוֹסֵם עַל דֶּרֶךְ אֶחָד מִכָּל הָעִנְיָנִים שֶׁזָּכַרְנוּ אוֹ בְּעִנְיָן אַחֵר

Chinuch focuses on a reason for this specific prohibition:

וְרָאִיתִי בְּסִפְרֵי הָרִאשׁוֹנִים בְּטַעַם אִסּוּר זֶה – **I have seen in the works of the early authorities** that the **reason for this prohibition** in particular is לְפִי שֶׁכָּל עִנְיָנִים אֵלּוּ מַטְעִים הֶהָמוֹן – **because all such matters** of divination **mislead the masses,** וְיַחְשְׁבוּ בִּשְׁבִיל שֶׁיִּצְדְּקוּ עֲלֵיהֶם קְצָת מִן הַדְּבָרִים שֶׁיַּגִּידוּ לָהֶם בַּעֲלֵי הַקֶּסֶם – **leading them to think that since some of the things that the diviners predicted for them have proven true,** שֶׁכָּל הַפְּעֻלּוֹת שֶׁהֵם בָּעוֹלָם סִבָּתָם הַמַּזָּלוֹת וְהַכֹּחוֹת – **the cause of all of the world's happenings must be the constellations and the** celestial **powers,** as it is through them that the diviner draws his ability to foretell the future;[12] וּכְמְעַט יִקָּרְאוּ מִן הַכַּת הָרַע הָאוֹמְרִים עָזַב אֱלֹהִים אֶת הָאָרֶץ – **and [those who are mislead in this manner] are close to being considered part of the sect of wicked people who say, "God has forsaken the land"** (see *Ezekiel* 8:12).[13]

וּבְעַד זֶה הָעִנְיָן שֶׁהָיָה מְפֻרְסָם הַרְבֵּה בִּזְמַן הַנְּבִיאִים – It is **about this issue** of divination, **which was very prevalent in the time of the prophets,** אָמַר הַנָּבִיא ״עַמִּי בְּעֵצוֹ יִשְׁאָל וּמַקְלוֹ יַגִּיד לוֹ״ – that **the prophet stated** (*Hosea* 4:12): ***My people asks of its wood, and its rod relates to it.*** The prophet rebuked the Jewish people for turning to such objects (*its wood* or *its rod*) and using them for manipulations through which they attempted to divine the future, as described above.

Laws of the Mitzvah

דִּינֵי הַמִּצְוָה מְבֹאָרִים בִּמְקוֹמוֹת מִסַּנְהֶדְרִין וְתוֹסֶפְתָּא דְּשַׁבָּת וּבְסִפְרֵי – **The laws of the mitzvah are detailed in** various **places in** Tractate ***Sanhedrin*** (e.g., 65a-66a), in ***Tosefta*** **of** Tractate ***Shabbos*** (Chs. 7-8), **and in *Sifrei.***[14]

Applicability of the Mitzvah

וְנוֹהֵג אִסּוּר זֶה בְּכָל מָקוֹם וּבְכָל זְמַן – **This prohibition applies in every location and in all times,** בִּזְכָרִים וּנְקֵבוֹת – **to men and women.**[15]

וְעוֹבֵר עַל זֶה וְעָשָׂה עַצְמוֹ קוֹסֵם – **One who transgresses this** prohibition **and becomes a diviner,** עַל דֶּרֶךְ אֶחָד מִכָּל הָעִנְיָנִים שֶׁזָּכַרְנוּ אוֹ בְּעִנְיָן אַחֵר – whether **in one of the various manners that we**

NOTES

12. Above (after note 2), Chinuch stated that, through their meditation, the souls of the diviners associate with the spirits that perceive the near future. Those spirits are associated with the celestial bodies (*Ramban, Deuteronomy* 18:9; see also *Rambam, Sefer HaMitzvos, Lo Saaseh* 31).

13. This refers to people who completely deny Divine Providence, i.e., the principle that Hashem rewards righteousness and punishes evil (see *Ramban, Exodus* 13:16). [Chinuch points out below (at note 19) that Hashem will override the celestial signs when He wishes to reward (or punish) someone.]

14. These laws are codified in *Rambam, Hil. Avodah Zarah* 11:6-7; see also *Shulchan Aruch, Yoreh Deah* 179:1.

15. It applies in Eretz Yisrael and the Diaspora, and whether the *Beis HaMikdash* is standing or not. Additionally, it applies to women as well as men, in accordance with the general rule pertaining to mitzvah-prohibitions.

וְיַגִּיד לִבְנֵי אָדָם הַדְּבָרִים שֶׁיִּרְאֶה בְּקִסְמָיו חַיָּב מַלְקוּת, וְהוּא שֶׁעָשָׂה שׁוּם מַעֲשֶׂה בַּדָּבָר, שֶׁאֵין לוֹקִין עָלָיו מִבְּלִי מַעֲשֶׂה[16]. אֲבָל הַשּׁוֹאֵל מִן הַקּוֹסֵם אֵינֶנּוּ בְּחִיּוּב מַלְקוּת[17], וְאָמְנָם הוּא מְגֻנֶּה מְאֹד כָּל הַקּוֹבֵעַ מַחְשְׁבוֹתָיו וּמוֹצִיא עִתָּיו בַּהֲבָלִים אֵלֶּה, כִּי לַאֲשֶׁר חֲנָנוֹ הָאֵל דֵּעָה וְהִנְחִילוֹ דַּת הָאֱמֶת לֹא יָאוּת לוֹ לַחְשֹׁב בַּהֲבָלִים אֵלּוּ[18], רַק שֶׁיִּקְבַּע מַחְשְׁבוֹתָיו בַּעֲבוֹדַת הַבּוֹרֵא יִתְעַלֶּה וְלֹא יִירָא דִּבְרֵי קוֹסֵם, כִּי הַשֵּׁם בַּחֲסָדָיו יְשַׁנֶּה מַעֲרֶכֶת הַכּוֹכָבִים וִיבַטֵּל כֹּחַ הַמַּזָּלוֹת לְהֵטִיב לַחֲסִידָיו[19]. וְיָדוּעַ שֶׁאֲנַחְנוּ עַם הַקֹּדֶשׁ אֵין אָנוּ תַּחַת כּוֹכָב וּמַזָּל, ה׳ הוּא נַחֲלָתֵנוּ כַּאֲשֶׁר דִּבֵּר אֵלֵינוּ[20], וּכְעִנְיָן שֶׁמָּצִינוּ בָּאָבוֹת שֶׁשָּׂם הָאֵל מַעֲלָתָם לְמַעְלָה מִשָּׂרֵי מַעְלָה[21],

---

mentioned above, **or in some other manner,** וְיַגִּיד לִבְנֵי אָדָם הַדְּבָרִים שֶׁיִּרְאֶה בְּקִסְמָיו – **and he informs people of the matters that he sees through his divination,** חַיָּב מַלְקוּת – **is liable to *malkus*.** וְהוּא שֶׁעָשָׂה שׁוּם מַעֲשֶׂה בַּדָּבָר – **However, this** punishment **is** imposed **only if he did some action in this matter,** שֶׁאֵין לוֹקִין עָלָיו מִבְּלִי מַעֲשֶׂה – **for one does not incur *malkus* for** transgressing **[this prohibition] without** performing some **action.**[16]

Chinuch now addresses the law with regard to a person who seeks the services of a diviner:

אֲבָל הַשּׁוֹאֵל מִן הַקּוֹסֵם אֵינֶנּוּ בְּחִיּוּב מַלְקוּת – **However, one who requests of a diviner** to inform him of future events **is not liable to *malkus*.**[17] וְאָמְנָם הוּא מְגֻנֶּה מְאֹד כָּל הַקּוֹבֵעַ מַחְשְׁבוֹתָיו וּמוֹצִיא עִתָּיו בַּהֲבָלִים אֵלֶּה – **Nevertheless, anyone who sets his thoughts and spends his time on such vanities is** considered **extremely despicable,** כִּי לַאֲשֶׁר חֲנָנוֹ הָאֵל דֵּעָה וְהִנְחִילוֹ דַּת הָאֱמֶת לֹא יָאוּת לוֹ לַחְשֹׁב בַּהֲבָלִים אֵלּוּ – **because it is unbefitting for someone whom the Almighty graced with knowledge, and** to **whom He gave the True Faith as a heritage, to give thought to such vanities.**[18] רַק שֶׁיִּקְבַּע מַחְשְׁבוֹתָיו בַּעֲבוֹדַת הַבּוֹרֵא יִתְעַלֶּה – **Rather, he must focus his thoughts on the service of the Creator, exalted be He,** וְלֹא יִירָא דִּבְרֵי קוֹסֵם – **and not be fearful of the words of a diviner,** כִּי הַשֵּׁם בַּחֲסָדָיו יְשַׁנֶּה מַעֲרֶכֶת הַכּוֹכָבִים וִיבַטֵּל כֹּחַ הַמַּזָּלוֹת – **for Hashem, in His kindness, will change the system of** the influence of **the stars and nullify the power of the constellations** לְהֵטִיב לַחֲסִידָיו – in order **to bestow goodness upon His pious ones.**[19]

Chinuch now explains at length how the Jewish people are unaffected by the influence of these heavenly hosts:

וְיָדוּעַ שֶׁאֲנַחְנוּ עַם הַקֹּדֶשׁ אֵין אָנוּ תַּחַת כּוֹכָב וּמַזָּל – **It is known that we, the holy nation, are not under** the domain of **a star or a constellation.** ה׳ הוּא נַחֲלָתֵנוּ כַּאֲשֶׁר דִּבֵּר אֵלֵינוּ – **Hashem is our Heritage as He spoke to us,**[20] וּכְעִנְיָן שֶׁמָּצִינוּ בָּאָבוֹת – **and as we find regarding the forefathers,** Abraham, Isaac, and Jacob, שֶׁשָּׂם הָאֵל מַעֲלָתָם לְמַעְלָה מִשָּׂרֵי מַעְלָה – **whom the Almighty awarded a status above** that of **the ministering angels On High.**[21]

NOTES

16. As a general rule, one is liable to *malkus* only for a transgression that was performed by way of some action (rather than through speech or thought alone). [For clarification of Chinuch's view regarding "a prohibition that does not involve action," see Insight to Mitzvah 68.]

17. While the Torah forbids practicing divination, it does not specifically prohibit seeking the diviner's services. Accordingly, there is no penalty of *malkus* for doing so (aside from the fact that *asking* is not an action).

18. *Rambam* (*Hil. Avodah Zarah* 11:16) states that the Torah admonishes us not to seek such services with the verse (*Deuteronomy* 18:13): תָּמִים תִּהְיֶה עִם ה׳ אֱלֹהֶיךָ, *you shall be wholehearted with HASHEM, your God* (see also *Beur HaGra, Yoreh Deah* 179:3). [See further, Insight to Mitzvah 514.]

Rambam (ibid. §7) also states that a person receives *makkas mardus* (lashes of discipline) for involving himself in such pursuits (see also *Tur, Yoreh Deah* 179:1). See *Minchas Chinuch* §1 for further discussion.

19. See *Ramban* to the verse of this mitzvah, and to *Genesis* 17:1.

20. Stylistic citation of *Deuteronomy* 10:9. The Jewish people are under the direct supervision of Hashem Himself, and are thus unaffected by the influences of the celestial forces. In the words of our Sages, אֵין מַזָּל לְיִשְׂרָאֵל, *the [celestial] signs hold no sway over Israel* (*Shabbos* 156a). See Insight.

21. Every star and constellation has a ministering angel that controls it and gives it its influence over the world (*Ramban, Deuteronomy* 18:9). The forefathers — and, by extension, all of Israel who are their progeny — were elevated above those heavenly ministers and freed of their influence.

כְּעִנְיָן שֶׁכָּתוּב בְּיַעֲקֹב (בראשית ל״ב, כ״ט) **כִּי אִם יִשְׂרָאֵל יִהְיֶה שְׁמֶךָ כִּי שָׂרִיתָ עִם אֱלֹהִים וְגוֹ׳, כְּלוֹמַר שֶׁעֲשָׂאוֹ הָאֵל שַׂר עַל הַשָּׂרִים, וְכֵן יִצְחָק נִקְרָא יִשְׂרָאֵל, שֶׁנֶּאֱמַר** (בראשית מ״ו, ח׳) **אֵלֶּה בְּנֵי יִשְׂרָאֵל הַבָּאִים מִצְרַיְמָה יַעֲקֹב וּבָנָיו, וְכֵן אַבְרָהָם נִקְרָא יִשְׂרָאֵל כְּמוֹ שֶׁכָּתַבְתִּי בִּפְתִיחַת הַסֵּפֶר. וְזֶהוּ מַה שֶּׁכָּתוּב בְּעִנְיַן מַחֲלֹקֶת הַנָּבִיא אֵלִיָּהוּ עִם נְבִיאֵי הַבַּעַל, כְּמִסְפַּר שִׁבְטֵי בְנֵי יַעֲקֹב אֲשֶׁר נִקְרָא שְׁמוֹ יִשְׂרָאֵל**[26]**.**

"כְּעִנְיָן שֶׁכָּתוּב בְּיַעֲקֹב "כִּי אִם יִשְׂרָאֵל יִהְיֶה שְׁמֶךָ כִּי שָׂרִיתָ עִם אֱלֹהִים וְגוֹ׳ – This is **as it is written regarding Jacob,** after the struggle in which the angel of Esau was unable to defeat him (*Genesis* 32:29):[22] *Your name shall not always be called Jacob,* ***but Israel shall be your name, for you have striven with the divine*** *... and have overcome.* כְּלוֹמַר שֶׁעֲשָׂאוֹ הָאֵל שַׂר עַל הַשָּׂרִים – **That is to say, that [the Almighty] made [Jacob] a minister over the** divine **ministers,** placing him above their influences, and giving him control over them. This is why his name became "Israel."[23] וְכֵן יִצְחָק נִקְרָא יִשְׂרָאֵל – **Isaac was likewise called "Israel,"** "שֶׁנֶּאֱמַר "אֵלֶּה בְּנֵי יִשְׂרָאֵל הַבָּאִים מִצְרַיְמָה יַעֲקֹב וּבָנָיו – **as it is stated** (*Genesis* 46:8): ***These are the children of Israel who were coming to Egypt — Jacob and his sons.*** The verse speaks of the "children of Israel" and includes Jacob among those children. Accordingly, the term "Israel" in this verse must not refer to Jacob, but to Jacob's father, Isaac.[24] וְכֵן אַבְרָהָם נִקְרָא יִשְׂרָאֵל כְּמוֹ שֶׁכָּתַבְתִּי בִּפְתִיחַת הַסֵּפֶר – **Abraham, too, was called "Israel" as I have written in the Introduction to this book.**[25] Thus, all the forefathers were elevated above the divine ministers and made immune to their influences, and this immunity extends to their offspring, the Jewish people.

Under the reign of the wicked King Ahab, the northern tribes of Israel had been drawn after the idolatrous sect of *Baal*. Elijah the prophet, however, stood in the breach and took upon himself to prove to the nation the folly of their actions. He put forth a challenge to the four hundred and fifty false prophets of *Baal*: Elijah and the prophets of *Baal* would each erect an altar and place a slaughtered bull upon it. The one whose belief was true would be answered by Heaven, and his offering would be accepted (see *I Kings* Ch. 18). In the end, a fire came forth from Heaven and consumed Elijah's offering alone, upon which the people exclaimed (ibid. v. 39): *HASHEM — He is the God! HASHEM — He is the God!* Chinuch discusses a verse from that passage that refers to the altar that Elijah prepared for his offering, which he will relate to his discussion:

וְזֶהוּ מַה שֶּׁכָּתוּב בְּעִנְיַן מַחֲלֹקֶת הַנָּבִיא אֵלִיָּהוּ עִם נְבִיאֵי הַבַּעַל – **This is** the explanation of **what is written in discussion of the conflict between Elijah the Prophet and the** false **prophets of** ***Baal,*** כְּמִסְפַּר שִׁבְטֵי בְנֵי יַעֲקֹב אֲשֶׁר נִקְרָא שְׁמוֹ יִשְׂרָאֵל – where Scripture states that Elijah constructed

---

NOTES

22. See Mitzvah 3, where Chinuch discusses the symbolism of that struggle. [In quoting the following verse (*Genesis* 32:29), Chinuch includes a phrase from the similar verse, ibid. 35:10.]

23. The term שָׂרִיתָ (literally, *you have striven*) is understood as being derived from שַׂר, *minister*; the term אֱלֹהִים (literally, *the divine*) may also be understood similarly. The verse can thus be rendered: *for you have become a minister over ministers* (see *Chullin* 92a). This alludes to the fact that all such spiritual forces would now be placed under the power of Jacob. He was therefore given the name יִשְׂרָאֵל, *Israel*, which includes the words שַׂר אֵל, *minister over minister[s]*. Alternatively, as Chinuch indicates, שַׂר אֵל can be rendered, *minister of the Almighty.*

24. The verse is understood as follows: *These are the children of Israel* [i.e., Isaac] *who were coming to Egypt — Jacob and his sons* (see *Bereishis Rabbah* 63:3). [Jacob's sons can also be referred to as *the "children" of Isaac*, insofar as they are his grandchildren.]

25. In the Author's Introduction (Volume I of this edition, pp. 24-26), Chinuch cites the verse (*Exodus* 12:40): וּמוֹשַׁב בְּנֵי יִשְׂרָאֵל אֲשֶׁר יָשְׁבוּ בְּמִצְרָיִם שְׁלֹשִׁים שָׁנָה וְאַרְבַּע מֵאוֹת שָׁנָה, *The habitation of the Children of Israel during which they dwelled in Egypt was four hundred and thirty years.* He goes on to explain that these 430 years are counted from the time of the Covenant Between the Parts [בְּרִית בֵּין הַבְּתָרִים], which was when Hashem informed Abraham of the Egyptian exile (see *Genesis* 15:13). Therefore, when the verse speaks of the "habitation of the Children of Israel," it refers not only to the years in Egypt, but also to the earlier years when Abraham's child, Isaac, lived in various areas of Canaan. The Midrash explains that the phrase *Children of "Israel"* refers to the children of Abraham, as Abraham, too, was called "Israel" (*Bereishis Rabbah* 63:3).

שֶׁהוּא הָיָה מוֹכִיחָם לָמָּה הָיוּ פוֹנִים לַעֲבֹד הַכֹּחוֹת,[27]
וּמַנִּיחִין עֲבוֹדַת הָאָדוֹן ה׳ צְבָאוֹת
אֲשֶׁר בְּיָדוֹ לְבַטֵּל כָּל פְּעֻלַּת הַכֹּחוֹת וְהַמַּזָּלוֹת,
וְכָעִנְיָן שֶׁעָשָׂה בָּאָבוֹת

שֶׁשָּׁם הַמַּזָּלוֹת תַּחַת יָדָם, וְזֶהוּ אָמְרוּ בַּמָּקוֹם הַהוּא (מלכים י״ח, ל״א) כְּמִסְפַּר שִׁבְטֵי בְּנֵי
יַעֲקֹב אֲשֶׁר הָיָה דְבַר ה׳ אֵלָיו לֵאמֹר יִשְׂרָאֵל יִהְיֶה שְׁמֶךָ, כְּלוֹמַר שֶׁעֲשָׂאוֹ שַׂר עַל שָׂרִים
לְשַׁנּוֹת מַעֲרַכְתָּם וְכֹחָם בִּזְכוּתוֹ, כְּלוֹמַר וְיִשְׂרָאֵל שֶׁהֵם בְּנֵי יַעֲקֹב גַּם הֵם שָׂרִים עַל שָׂרֵי
מַעְלָה, וְעַל כֵּן הָיָה רָאוּי לָהֶם שֶׁלֹּא לַעֲבֹד בִּלְתִּי ה׳ לְבַדּוֹ, וְכֵן מָצִינוּ בִּיהוֹשֻׁעַ שֶׁגָּזַר
עַל הַשֶּׁמֶשׁ וְהַיָּרֵחַ לַעֲמֹד כְּמוֹ שֶׁכָּתוּב בִּיהוֹשֻׁעַ (י׳, י״ב) "שֶׁמֶשׁ בְּגִבְעוֹן דּוֹם וְיָרֵחַ בְּעֵמֶק"

___

his altar by taking twelve stones, **corresponding to the number of the tribes of the children of Jacob,** *whose name was called "Israel."*[26]

The question arises: Jacob had been given the name "Israel" many centuries earlier. Why then does the verse include this parenthetical phrase — i.e., that Jacob is also called "Israel," in the midst of its discussion of the conflict between Elijah and the prophets of *Baal*? Based on the above idea that the term "Israel" means "dominion over spiritual influences," Chinuch explains in rhyme:

שֶׁהוּא הָיָה מוֹכִיחָם לָמָּה הָיוּ פוֹנִים לַעֲבֹד הַכֹּחוֹת — **[Elijah] was admonishing them,** asking **why they had turned to worship the** celestial **powers,**[27]

וּמַנִּיחִין עֲבוֹדַת הָאָדוֹן ה׳ צְבָאוֹת — **and had forsaken the service of the Master, Hashem, God of Legions,**

אֲשֶׁר בְּיָדוֹ לְבַטֵּל כָּל פְּעֻלַּת הַכֹּחוֹת וְהַמַּזָּלוֹת — **with Whom rests the ability to nullify all activities of the powers and constellations,**

וְכָעִנְיָן שֶׁעָשָׂה בָּאָבוֹת — **as He did for the Forefathers,**

שֶׁשָּׁם הַמַּזָּלוֹת תַּחַת יָדָם — **under whose authority He placed the constellations** and all of their powers and influences. וְזֶהוּ אָמְרוּ בַּמָּקוֹם הַהוּא — **This is why [the verse] in that place** (*I Kings* 18:31), in the midst of recounting Elijah's conflict with the prophets of *Baal*, **states:** "כְּמִסְפַּר שִׁבְטֵי בְּנֵי יַעֲקֹב אֲשֶׁר הָיָה דְבַר ה׳ אֵלָיו לֵאמֹר יִשְׂרָאֵל יִהְיֶה שְׁמֶךָ" — *Elijah took twelve stones,* **corresponding to the number of the tribes of the children of Jacob, to whom the word of HASHEM came, saying, "Your name shall be Israel."** כְּלוֹמַר שֶׁעֲשָׂאוֹ שַׂר עַל שָׂרִים לְשַׁנּוֹת מַעֲרַכְתָּם וְכֹחָם בִּזְכוּתוֹ — The verse **means to say that [Hashem] had made [Jacob] a minister over** the celestial **ministers,** with the capability **to change** and override **their system** of influence **and their strength by virtue of his own merit.** כְּלוֹמַר וְיִשְׂרָאֵל שֶׁהֵם בְּנֵי יַעֲקֹב גַּם הֵם שָׂרִים עַל שָׂרֵי מַעְלָה — By extension, **this means that** the people of **Israel, who are the children of Jacob, are also ministers over the celestial ministers,** as they too share this illustrious title, "Israel"; וְעַל כֵּן הָיָה רָאוּי לָהֶם שֶׁלֹּא לַעֲבֹד בִּלְתִּי ה׳ לְבַדּוֹ — **and therefore it is** only **befitting for them to serve no one other than Hashem alone.** By reminding the people that Hashem had given Jacob the name "Israel," Elijah was informing them that they are above the celestial influences and powers that were worshiped by the practitioners of *Baal*.

Chinuch cites another example of a situation where a pious Jew had dominion over the celestial powers and influences:

וְכֵן מָצִינוּ בִּיהוֹשֻׁעַ שֶׁגָּזַר עַל הַשֶּׁמֶשׁ וְהַיָּרֵחַ לַעֲמֹד — **And so we find with Joshua, who decreed that the sun and the moon should stand still,** כְּמוֹ שֶׁכָּתוּב בִּיהוֹשֻׁעַ "שֶׁמֶשׁ בְּגִבְעוֹן דּוֹם וְיָרֵחַ בְּעֵמֶק"

___

NOTES

26. Chinuch here is referencing the verse that he will quote shortly (*I Kings* 18:31): וַיִּקַּח אֵלִיָּהוּ שְׁתֵּים עֶשְׂרֵה אֲבָנִים כְּמִסְפַּר שִׁבְטֵי בְּנֵי יַעֲקֹב אֲשֶׁר הָיָה דְבַר ה׳ אֵלָיו לֵאמֹר יִשְׂרָאֵל יִהְיֶה שְׁמֶךָ, *Elijah took twelve stones, corresponding to the number of the tribes of the children of Jacob, to whom* the word of HASHEM came, saying, "Your name shall be Israel."

27. All of idolatry, including *Baal,* is in essence a form of worshiping one of the celestial forces (see *Rambam, Hil. Avodah Zarah* 1:1).

אַיָּלוֹן", וְעָמְדוּ[28], וְכֵן כַּמָּה חֲסִידִים מִיִּשְׂרָאֵל שֶׁנִּשְׁתַּנּוּ מַעֲרֶכֶת הַמַּזָּלוֹת וְכֹחָם בִּזְכוּתָם, יֶאֱרַךְ הָעִנְיָן לְהָבִיא כַּמָּה מַעֲשִׂים שֶׁנַּעֲשׂוּ בְּיִשְׂרָאֵל בְּעִנְיָן זֶה[29].

אַיָּלוֹן" – as is written in the Book of ***Joshua*** (10:12): ***Sun, stand still at Gibeon, and moon, in the Valley of Ayalon,*** **וְעָמְדוּ – and they** indeed **stood still.**[28]
וְכֵן כַּמָּה חֲסִידִים מִיִּשְׂרָאֵל שֶׁנִּשְׁתַּנּוּ מַעֲרֶכֶת הַמַּזָּלוֹת וְכֹחָם בִּזְכוּתָם – Similarly, we find **that the system of the constellations and their power were changed** for **a number of pious Jews in their merit.** **יֶאֱרַךְ הָעִנְיָן לְהָבִיא כַּמָּה מַעֲשִׂים שֶׁנַּעֲשׂוּ בְּיִשְׂרָאֵל בְּעִנְיָן זֶה – The discussion would become** overly **lengthy,** however, if we were **to bring the numerous incidents of this sort that occurred among the Jewish people.**[29]

NOTES

28. Joshua commanded the sun and the moon to remain in place (over Gibeon and Ayalon, respectively), to allow the Jewish people enough time to completely defeat the Amorite kings against whom they were fighting. The verses go on to state that the sun and moon followed his orders, and remained in place for a full day. Thus, a righteous Jew has spiritual authority over the celestial powers.

29. However, suffice it to say that the natural place of the Jew is above the influence of the heavenly hosts and forces. Because of that, it is inappropriate for a Jew to seek the services of pagan diviners who attempt to control those forces.

Insight: Do Celestial Signs (Mazalos) Hold Sway Over Israel?

For the purposes of administrating this world, Hashem created a system involving successive levels of spiritual entities. He gave power and influence to these entities, which include higher beings such as angels, as well as various constellations and celestial bodies. These constellations and celestial bodies are referred to as *mazalos* (sing., *mazal*), related to the root נזל, *to flow,* for the spiritual decrees that begin on High, "flow" through them to bring about change in this world (see *Derech Hashem,* Section II, Ch. 7).

Scripture alludes to this system in various places and indicates that the nations of the world are bound by its influences (see *Ramban* to *Leviticus* 18:25, citing *Deuteronomy* 10:4 and *Daniel* 10:13, 20). With regard to the Jewish people, however, Chinuch writes that implicit in the name יִשְׂרָאֵל, *"Israel,"* is that the Jewish people are not bound by this system. Rather, they are under the direct guidance of Hashem, Who has placed us above the influence of these *mazalos.*

In truth, the question of whether the Jewish people are bound by the influence of *mazalos* is the subject of a Talmudic debate, with one opinion holding יֵשׁ מַזָּל לְיִשְׂרָאֵל, *the celestial signs do hold sway [even] over Israel,* and the other maintaining אֵין מַזָּל לְיִשְׂרָאֵל, *the celestial signs do not hold sway over Israel* (*Shabbos* 156a). Moreover, *Rashi* there explains that both opinions actually agree that Jews are influenced by *mazalos;* the difference of opinion revolves around the extent of that influence. According to the first opinion, *mazalos* hold such strong sway over the individual that even prayer and merit cannot undo their decrees; while according to the latter opinion, prayer and charitable acts have the power to prevail over that which one's *mazal* has in store for him (see also *Tosafos* to *Shabbos* 156a ד"ה אין מזל and to *Moed Katan* 28a ד"ה אלא; cf. *Abarbanel, Deuteronomy* 4:15 ד"ה היסוד הא' ff.).

Elsewhere (*Moed Katan* 28a), the Gemara cites a statement of Rava that would seem to ascribe great power to the celestial signs. Rava states that one's longevity, number of children, and financial wellbeing [חַיֵּי בְּנֵי וּמְזוֹנֵי] are all dependent on *mazal.* This, he says, explains why the great sage, Rabbah, lived a life full of challenges and losses, while his colleague, Rav Chisda, lived a life of tranquility and ease. Both were exceedingly righteous, but Rabbah's *mazal* was such that he was destined to experience a difficult life — notwithstanding his personal righteousness. Rava would thus seem to hold that יֵשׁ מַזָּל לְיִשְׂרָאֵל, the celestial signs do hold sway even over Israel; and, indeed, this is how some commentators explain his opinion (see opinion cited in *Ran* ad loc.; *Meiri, Shabbos* 156a). Others, however, suggest that Rava also agrees that a Jew is not ruled by *mazal,* which is, in fact, the opinion of a majority of Talmudic sages (see *Shabbos* 156a-b). Rava merely means to note that these

three particular areas (life, children, and sustenance) require *extra* merit to be changed (see *Ran* loc. cit.; *Rabbeinu Bachya, Deuteronomy* 31:14).

Chinuch in this mitzvah clearly follows the majority opinion, that *mazalos* do not hold sway over Israel, as do many other Rishonim (see *Teshuvos HaRashba* I, §148; *Ran, Moed Katan* 28a; *Rambam, Letter to the Sages of Marseilles; Meiri, Shabbos* 156a).

Tosafos (*Moed Katan* ibid.), however, suggest that the question of whether *mazalos* have an effect on Israel is not clear-cut, and that while sometimes *mazal* can be changed, at other times it cannot. As an example of an unchanging *mazal*, they cite the story of R' Elazar ben Pedas who was exceedingly poor and was informed in a dream that it would be impossible for his *mazal* to change unless Hashem would create the world anew (see *Taanis* 25a). *R' Eliyahu Dessler* (*Michtav MeEliyahu,* Vol. IV, p. 98 ff.) explains as follows: Every Jew has a unique life mission with respect to increasing spirituality and Godliness in the world. To fulfill that mission, one is given the appropriate tools and life circumstances that allow him to succeed. That set of circumstances and tools is referred to as his *mazal*. Although his life mission will not change, the tools and circumstances may; for as one progresses through life and succeeds in his mission, he is given new tools to further his work. In this respect, one's *mazal* can be said to be changeable, for it depends on his spiritual worthiness and readiness to make proper use of a different set of life circumstances toward the fulfillment of his overall life goal.

However, R' Dessler goes on to explain, sometimes [for reasons beyond our understanding] a person's task in life is such that the mission itself is to live the life of a Jew through hardship. His life's calling is to succeed in spite of — if not by way of — his very suffering! As in the case of R' Elazar ben Pedas, such *mazal* is unchanging, as it is built into the very fabric of Creation. Accordingly, R' Dessler explains, the question of whether or not *mazal* can be altered is ultimately not a debate; it is merely a question of to which *mazal* one is referring. The *mazal* of circumstantial factors that help support one's life-mission can change, while the form of *mazal* that lies at the very core of that mission cannot.

[It is important to note that according to all opinions, the effect of *mazalos* relates only to life's circumstances, such as intelligence, sustenance, and the like. They do not, however, determine whether one will be righteous or wicked. Even when *mazalos* invest a person with certain tendencies, the individual may choose how to channel those tendencies. In short, while one's physical circumstances may be predetermined, his spiritual stature is the product of his own free will, and hence he controls the ability to determine his destiny (see *Derashos HaRan* §8 ד"ה ואמנם שיהיה ff. and *Abarbanel* ibid.).]

מִצְוָה תקיא: שֶׁלֹּא לְכַשֵּׁף

שֶׁלֹּא נִשְׁתַּדֵּל בְּכָל מַעֲשֵׂה כִּשּׁוּף כְּלָל, וְעַל זֶה נֶאֱמַר (דברים י״ח, י׳) לֹא יִמָּצֵא בְךָ וְגוֹ׳ וּמְכַשֵּׁף. וְעִנְיַן הַכִּשּׁוּף יָדוּעַ לַכֹּל דֶּרֶךְ כְּלָל שֶׁיַּעֲשׂוּ בְּנֵי אָדָם תַּחְבּוּלוֹת בְּלִי מִסְפָּר בְּמִינֵי עֲשָׂבִים וַאֲבָנִים וְהַרְבֵּה מִן הַדְּבָרִים שֶׁמִּשְׁתַּמְּשִׁים בָּהֶן בְּנֵי אָדָם אֵלּוּ עִם אֵלּוּ[1], וּמֵהֶם שֶׁיְּכַוְּנוּ הַמַּעֲשִׂים הָרָעִים הָהֵם בְּעִתִּים יְדוּעִים וּבָחֳדָשִׁים מְכֻוָּנִין לְאוֹתָם מְלָאכוֹת. וּמִכָּל אֵלּוּ הַדְּבָרִים הַמְגֻנִּים וְהַמְכֹעָרִים תַּרְחִיקֵנוּ הַתּוֹרָה תַּכְלִית הָרִחוּק כִּי הֶבֶל הֵמָּה, וְאֵין רָאוּי לְעַם קָדוֹשׁ מַחֲזִיקֵי דַּת הָאֱמֶת לָתֵת מַחֲשָׁבָה בְּכִעוּרִין אֵלּוּ[2] רַק בַּעֲבוֹדָתוֹ יִתְעַלֶּה, כִּי הוּא יַשְׁלִים כָּל חֵפֶץ עַמּוֹ לְטוֹב בַּחֲסוֹתָם בִּשְׁמוֹ הַגָּדוֹל וְשׂוּמָם כָּל מִבְטֶחָם וּמִשְׁעַנְתָּם עַל חֲסָדָיו לְבַד[3].

Mitzvah 511
The Prohibition to Practice Sorcery

לֹא יִמָּצֵא בְךָ ... וּמְכַשֵּׁף
There shall not be found from among you ... a sorcerer (*Deuteronomy* 18:10).

The practice of sorcery has been introduced previously, in Mitzvah 62. That mitzvah prohibits allowing a sorcerer to avoid capital punishment. In the current mitzvah, the Torah sets forth a general prohibition against sorcery.

שֶׁלֹּא נִשְׁתַּדֵּל בְּכָל מַעֲשֵׂה כִּשּׁוּף כְּלָל – We are commanded **not to engage in any act of sorcery at all. וְעַל זֶה נֶאֱמַר ״לֹא יִמָּצֵא בְךָ וְגוֹ׳ וּמְכַשֵּׁף״ – Regarding this it is stated** (*Deuteronomy* 18:10): ***There shall not be found from among you ... a sorcerer.***

וְעִנְיַן הַכִּשּׁוּף יָדוּעַ לַכֹּל דֶּרֶךְ כְּלָל – The general **concept of sorcery is widely known; שֶׁיַּעֲשׂוּ בְּנֵי אָדָם תַּחְבּוּלוֹת בְּלִי מִסְפָּר –** namely, **that** there are **people** who **perform countless** forms of **manipulations בְּמִינֵי עֲשָׂבִים וַאֲבָנִים וְהַרְבֵּה מִן הַדְּבָרִים שֶׁמִּשְׁתַּמְּשִׁים בָּהֶן בְּנֵי אָדָם – with** various **types of herbs or stones and many** other such **items that** these **people use, אֵלּוּ עִם אֵלּוּ –** mixing **these with those** in order to bring about their desired results.[1] **וּמֵהֶם שֶׁיְּכַוְּנוּ הַמַּעֲשִׂים הָרָעִים הָהֵם בְּעִתִּים יְדוּעִים וּבָחֳדָשִׁים מְכֻוָּנִין לְאוֹתָם מְלָאכוֹת – There are those among them who specifically perform these wicked deeds at certain times or during specific months, which are particularly suitable for** the success of **such crafts.**

וּמִכָּל אֵלּוּ הַדְּבָרִים הַמְגֻנִּים וְהַמְכֹעָרִים תַּרְחִיקֵנוּ הַתּוֹרָה תַּכְלִית הָרִחוּק – The Torah distances us to the greatest extent from all such despicable and repugnant matters; כִּי הֶבֶל הֵמָּה – for they are nonsense, וְאֵין רָאוּי לְעַם קָדוֹשׁ מַחֲזִיקֵי דַּת הָאֱמֶת לָתֵת מַחֲשָׁבָה בְּכִעוּרִין אֵלּוּ – and it is not appropriate for the holy nation, upholders of the True Faith, to pay attention to such repugnant matters.[2] **רַק בַּעֲבוֹדָתוֹ יִתְעַלֶּה –** Rather, we are to place our thoughts **only on the service of [Hashem], exalted be He, כִּי הוּא יַשְׁלִים כָּל חֵפֶץ עַמּוֹ לְטוֹב – for He will satisfy all of the wishes of His people for the best בַּחֲסוֹתָם בִּשְׁמוֹ הַגָּדוֹל – when they take refuge in His great Name וְשׂוּמָם כָּל מִבְטֶחָם וּמִשְׁעַנְתָּם עַל חֲסָדָיו לְבַד – and place all of their trust and reliance on His kindness alone.**[3]

NOTES

1. In Mitzvah 62, Chinuch explains that every entity in this world has a higher, heavenly force that compels it to perform its designated function. In order to mingle the higher forces and produce an unnatural outcome that the sorcerer desires, he combines various physical items below with the aim of causing their spiritual counterparts to combine On High.

2. *Rambam* (*Hil. Avodah Zarah* 11:16) describes such acts as being "lies and falsehoods" through which pagans would attempt to fool and thereby control the masses. Others, however, argue and do ascribe real powers to such crafts (see Insight to Mitzvah 62).

3. Hence, after forbidding all such pagan practices, the Torah concludes by stating (*Deuteronomy* 18:13),

וּמִהְיוֹת הָעִנְיָנִים אֵלּוּ רְחוֹקִים מְאֹד וּכְעוּרִים לְפָנָיו בָּרוּךְ הוּא וּבָהֶם נִיצוֹץ מֵעִנְיְנֵי עֲבוֹדָה זָרָה[4], הִזְהִירָנוּ עַל זֶה בְּלָאו, וְחִיֵּב סְקִילָה[5] עַל הָעוֹבֵר וּמִשְׁתַּדֵּל בָּזֶה אִם הוּא מֵזִיד, וְחַטָּאת קְבוּעָה אִם הָיָה שׁוֹגֵג[6]. וְגַם מֵחֹמֶר הָעִנְיָן הִזְהִיר הַכָּתוּב בָּזֶה מִבִּשְׁאָר עֲבֵרוֹת עַל הַבֵּית דִּין שֶׁלֹּא לִמְחֹל לָעוֹבֵר עַל זֶה, וּכְמוֹ שֶׁנֶּאֱמַר (שמות כ״ב, י״ז) **מְכַשֵּׁפָה לֹא תְחַיֶּה[7].**

וּכְבָר דִּבַּרְתִּי מִשָּׁרְשֵׁי מִצְוָה זוֹ בְּלָאו דִמְכַשֵּׁפָה לֹא תְחַיֶּה בְּסֵדֶר וְאֵלֶּה הַמִּשְׁפָּטִים (מצוה ס״ב)[8].

Chinuch discusses the severity of this prohibition:

וּמִהְיוֹת הָעִנְיָנִים אֵלּוּ רְחוֹקִים מְאֹד וּכְעוּרִים לְפָנָיו בָּרוּךְ הוּא – Now, being that these matters are greatly distanced and repugnant before [Hashem], blessed is He, וּבָהֶם נִיצוֹץ מֵעִנְיְנֵי עֲבוֹדָה זָרָה – and because **they contain a taint of idolatry,**[4] **הִזְהִירָנוּ עַל זֶה בְּלָאו – He cautioned us against this with a** mitzvah-**prohibition** (i.e., the current mitzvah), **וְחִיֵּב סְקִילָה עַל הָעוֹבֵר וּמִשְׁתַּדֵּל בָּזֶה אִם הוּא מֵזִיד – and imposed** the penalty of ***sekilah*** (stoning)[5] **upon one who violates** this prohibition **and engages in such** sorcery, **if he** did so **intentionally, וְחַטָּאת קְבוּעָה אִם הָיָה שׁוֹגֵג – and** imposed the requirement to bring **a fixed-*chatas* offering if his** violation **was unintentional.**[6] **וְגַם מֵחֹמֶר הָעִנְיָן – In addition, due to the severity of the matter, הִזְהִיר הַכָּתוּב בָּזֶה מִבִּשְׁאָר עֲבֵרוֹת עַל הַבֵּית דִּין – Scripture warns *beis din* with regard to this** sin, more so **than with regard to other sins, שֶׁלֹּא לִמְחֹל לָעוֹבֵר עַל זֶה – not to grant clemency to those who violate it, וּכְמוֹ שֶׁנֶּאֱמַר ״מְכַשֵּׁפָה לֹא תְחַיֶּה״ – as it is stated** (*Exodus* 22:17): ***You shall not permit a sorceress to live.***[7]

Underlying Purpose of the Mitzvah

וּכְבָר דִּבַּרְתִּי מִשָּׁרְשֵׁי מִצְוָה זוֹ בְּלָאו ד״מְכַשֵּׁפָה לֹא תְחַיֶּה״ – I have already spoken about the underlying purpose of this mitzvah in the prohibition of *You shall not permit a sorceress to live,* בְּסֵדֶר וְאֵלֶּה הַמִּשְׁפָּטִים – in *Parashas Mishpatim* (Mitzvah 62).[8]

NOTES

תָּמִים תִּהְיֶה עִם ה׳ אֱלֹהֶיךָ, *You shall be wholehearted with* H*ASHEM*, *your God* (see *Rashi* there).

4. *Rambam* (*Hil. Avodah Zarah* 11:16) writes that sorcery was used as a way of luring people to idol worship; see also *Meiri, Sanhedrin* 56b ד״ה שבע מצוות and *Minchas Chinuch* §3.

5. See General Introduction, Section VI, for the circumstances in which capital punishment was carried out in earlier times.

6. This refers to the standard *chatas* offering, outlined in Mitzvah 121. [See there for why it is called a "fixed" *chatas* offering.]

The source for Chinuch's statement here, that an unintentional violation of this prohibition carries liability to a *chatas* offering, is *Rambam, Sefer HaMitzvos, Lo Saaseh* 34. However, many are puzzled by this ruling (see *Mishneh LaMelech, Hil. Shegagos* 1:2; *Minchas Chinuch* §1). It is clear that one who commits sorcery intentionally, with witnesses and *hasraah* (advance warning), is liable to *sekilah* (see *Sanhedrin* 67a). However, there is no Talmudic source for the idea that this sin carries the penalty of *kares* if done intentionally without witnesses or *hasraah*, and by extension, liability to a *chatas* if done unintentionally. The Mishnah (*Kereisos* 2a) and *Rambam* (*Hil. Shegagos* 1:4) do not list sorcery among the sins in that category. Some therefore suggest that the statement in *Sefer HaMitzvos* is a copyist's error (*Dina DeChayei, Lavin* §55). Indeed, these words do not appear in all versions of *Sefer HaMitzvos*; see glosses of *R' Chaim Heller* there.

7. With regard to other capital crimes, if *beis din* fails to impose the appropriate penalty, *beis din* has transgressed only a mitzvah-obligation (i.e., the obligation to impose whichever capital penalty that particular sin calls for; see Mitzvos 47, 50, 261, and 555). They do not, however, violate any mitzvah-prohibition. The case of the sorcerer though is an exception, as *beis din* violates a mitzvah-prohibition (Mitzvah 62) for not imposing the death penalty to the sorcerer (see *Rambam, Hil. Sanhedrin* 14:3; *Minchas Yitzchak* §1).

8. There Chinuch explains that sorcery is a corrupting force that undermines the basic natural laws of this world. One who engages in this practice shows contempt for God's perfect order of creation. In the related prohibition of following superstitious signs (Mitzvah 249), Chinuch writes that such beliefs lead a person away from belief in Hashem and His Divine Providence. In addition, sorcery was often used by people to realize their immoral desires, when they could not achieve them through natural means (see *Ibn Ezra* and *Baal HaTurim* to *Exodus* 22:17).

דִּינֵי הַמִּצְוָה בִּמְקוֹמוֹת בַּתַּלְמוּד בְּפִזּוּר, וְהָעִקָּר בְּפֶרֶק שְׁבִיעִי מִסַּנְהֶדְרִין[9]. וְכָל שֶׁהוּא דַּיָּן עַל זֶה, צָרִיךְ לָדַעַת חָכְמַת הַכִּשּׁוּף[10] כְּדֵי שֶׁיֵּדַע לְהַבְחִין בְּמַעֲשֶׂה הַנַּעֲשֶׂה אִם הוּא מִין מִמִּינֵי הַכִּשּׁוּף אוֹ אוּלַי הוּא מִן הַדְּבָרִים הַנַּעֲשִׂים בְּכֹחַ טֶבַע וּבִצְדָדִין הַמֻּתָּרִין[11], וְכָעִנְיָן שֶׁאָמְרוּ זִכְרוֹנָם לִבְרָכָה (שבת ס״ז ע״א) כָּל שֶׁיֵּשׁ בּוֹ מִשּׁוּם רְפוּאָה אֵין בּוֹ מִשּׁוּם דַּרְכֵי הָאֱמוֹרִי[12], וּכְבָר דִּבַּרְתִּי עַל זֶה שָׁם בְּלָאו דִּמְכַשֵּׁפָה כְּפִי כֹּחִי[13]. וּדְבָרִים אֵלּוּ צְרִיכִין עִיּוּן רַב כִּי הִנֵּה נִמְצָא בַּגְּמָרָא מַעֲשִׂים כַּמָּה שֶׁאִם לֹא יָדַעְנוּ אוֹתָם מִפִּיהֶם זִכְרוֹנָם לִבְרָכָה

Laws of the Mitzvah

דִּינֵי הַמִּצְוָה בִּמְקוֹמוֹת בַּתַּלְמוּד בְּפִזּוּר – **The laws of the mitzvah are scattered in** various **places in the Talmud,** וְהָעִקָּר בְּפֶרֶק שְׁבִיעִי מִסַּנְהֶדְרִין – **primarily in the seventh chapter of** Tractate ***Sanhedrin*** (67a-68a).[9]

Chinuch now describes the level of expertise required of judges who try such cases:

וְכָל שֶׁהוּא דַּיָּן עַל זֶה צָרִיךְ לָדַעַת חָכְמַת הַכִּשּׁוּף – **Anyone who is a judge on such** matters **must be versed in the study of sorcery,**[10] כְּדֵי שֶׁיֵּדַע לְהַבְחִין בְּמַעֲשֶׂה הַנַּעֲשֶׂה – **so as to be capable of differentiating, with regard to the act that was performed,** אִם הוּא מִין מִמִּינֵי הַכִּשּׁוּף אוֹ אוּלַי הוּא מִן הַדְּבָרִים הַנַּעֲשִׂים בְּכֹחַ טֶבַע וּבִצְדָדִין הַמֻּתָּרִין – **whether it is one of the** various **forms of sorcery,** which is prohibited, **or** whether **it is perhaps a matter brought about through natural forces and permissible means.**[11] וְכָעִנְיָן שֶׁאָמְרוּ זִכְרוֹנָם לִבְרָכָה – This distinction is **along the lines of that which [our Sages], of blessed memory, have stated** (*Shabbos* 67a): כָּל שֶׁיֵּשׁ בּוֹ מִשּׁוּם רְפוּאָה אֵין בּוֹ מִשּׁוּם דַּרְכֵי הָאֱמוֹרִי – **Any** practice **that has therapeutic value is not** prohibited **as "ways of the Amorites."**[12] וּכְבָר דִּבַּרְתִּי עַל זֶה שָׁם בְּלָאו דִ"מְכַשֵּׁפָה" כְּפִי כֹחִי – **I have already, to the best of my ability, spoken about this there, in the prohibition of,** *You shall not permit* ***a sorceress*** *to live* (*Exodus* 22:17; Mitzvah 62).[13]

Chinuch now warns that the fact that we see that certain practices are permitted does not allow us to permit other practices on this basis:

וּדְבָרִים אֵלּוּ צְרִיכִין עִיּוּן רַב – **These matters require careful examination,** כִּי הִנֵּה נִמְצָא בַּגְּמָרָא מַעֲשִׂים כַּמָּה – **for there actually are a number of incidents found in the Gemara** שֶׁאִם לֹא יָדַעְנוּ אוֹתָם מִפִּיהֶם זִכְרוֹנָם לִבְרָכָה – **that, had we not known them** to be permitted **from the words**

NOTES

9. The laws of this mitzvah are codified in *Rambam, Hil. Avodah Zarah* 11:15 and in *Shulchan Aruch, Yoreh Deah* 179:15-16.

10. Indeed, members of the Sanhedrin were expected to be versed in such matters (*Sanhedrin* 17a; *Rambam, Hil. Sanhedrin* 2:1).

11. The verse (*Deuteronomy* 18:9) states regarding the forbidden craft of sorcery: לֹא תִלְמַד לַעֲשׂוֹת כְּתוֹעֲבֹת הַגּוֹיִם הָהֵם, *you shall not learn to do in accordance with the abominations of those nations.* The Gemara (*Sanhedrin* 68a) derives from this verse that while one is prohibited to learn such things in order to "do" them, one *may* learn them in order to be able to understand them and rule in cases involving such matters.

12. The Amorites were one of the seven Canaanite nations that lived in Eretz Yisrael before the Jewish people. They were steeped in the forbidden practices of sorcery, superstitions, and the like. Mimicking their practices is forbidden under the general injunction of (*Leviticus* 18:3), וּבְחֻקֹּתֵיהֶם לֹא תֵלֵכוּ, *do not follow their traditions* (Mitzvah 262; see *Rashi, Shabbos* 67a ד״ה דרכי האמורי), and depending on the details of the act performed, could even be a violation of the current mitzvah, as Chinuch here indicates.

Nevertheless, one is permitted to employ their healing practices, if such practices are known to be effective. According to some, this refers to using their medications or ointments (*Rashi* there ד״ה שיש בו משום רפואה), while according to others it includes making use of their incantations as well (*Rosh, Shabbos* 6:19). [For more on which practices are permitted and which are forbidden, see *Teshuvos HaRashba* I §413, and *Shulchan Aruch, Orach Chaim* 301:27 with commentaries. See also note 14 below.]

13. Chinuch there (at notes 8-9) explains that ultimately Hashem's aim in prohibiting sorcery was to protect us from its detrimental results. Therefore, when such practices have proven therapeutic value, they are not included among the forbidden forms of sorcery. For further discussion, see sources cited at the end of the previous note and *Shulchan Aruch, Yoreh Deah* §179 with commentaries.

הָיִינוּ אוֹסְרִין אוֹתָם מִשּׁוּם חֲשַׁשׁ אִסּוּר זֶה. וּמִכָּל מָקוֹם אֲשֶׁר יִשָּׂא נַפְשׁוֹ לִכָּנֵס בְּתַחְבּוּלוֹת אֵלּוּ וִידַמֶּה דָּבָר לְדָבָר מֵהַדְּבָרִים שֶׁהִזְכִּירוּ זִכְרוֹנָם לִבְרָכָה, הֲרֵי הוּא כְּפוֹתֵחַ לוֹ פֶּתַח לָבוֹא בַּגֵּיהִנֹּם[14].

וְנוֹהֵג אִסּוּר זֶה בְּכָל מָקוֹם וּבְכָל זְמַן, בִּזְכָרִים וּנְקֵבוֹת[15].

---

of [our Sages], of blessed memory, הָיִינוּ אוֹסְרִין אוֹתָם מִשּׁוּם חֲשַׁשׁ אִסּוּר זֶה – **we would have forbade them due to a concern of** their being a violation of **this prohibition.** Seeing these incidents might lead a person to be lenient in similar situations. וּמִכָּל מָקוֹם אֲשֶׁר יִשָּׂא נַפְשׁוֹ לִכָּנֵס בְּתַחְבּוּלוֹת אֵלּוּ – **But** the truth is that **despite this** leniency of the Sages in those specific instances, **one who is interested in pursuing these techniques,** וִידַמֶּה דָּבָר לְדָבָר מֵהַדְּבָרִים שֶׁהִזְכִּירוּ זִכְרוֹנָם לִבְרָכָה – **and** goes and **compares** the **matter** that he seeks to permit **to** another **matter that [the Sages], of blessed memory,** specifically **mentioned** as being permitted, and thus allows himself to do the former act as well, הֲרֵי הוּא כְּפוֹתֵחַ לוֹ פֶּתַח לָבוֹא בַּגֵּיהִנֹּם – **is as though he has opened for himself an entrance into Gehinnom** (i.e., he is risking the possibility of transgressing a grave sin).[14]

Applicability of the Mitzvah

וְנוֹהֵג אִסּוּר זֶה בְּכָל מָקוֹם וּבְכָל זְמַן – **This prohibition applies in every location and in all times** בִּזְכָרִים וּנְקֵבוֹת – **to men and women.**[15]

NOTES

14. Although the Sages knew where to draw the line between permitted practices and those that are forbidden under the category of sorcery (see *Sanhedrin* 67b), others can easily err in this matter, and make incorrect comparisons between acts that are permitted and other similar acts which may very well be in violation of the current mitzvah.

15. I.e., it applies in Eretz Yisrael and the Diaspora, and whether the *Beis HaMikdash* is standing or not. In addition, it applies to both men and women in accordance with the general rule pertaining to mitzvah-prohibitions.

❧ מִצְוָה תקיב: שֶׁלֹּא לַחֲבֹר חֶבֶר ❧

שֶׁנִּמְנַעְנוּ מִלַּעֲשׂוֹת הַשְּׁבָעוֹת[1] עַל שׁוּם עִנְיָן, וְזֶה הָעִנְיָן הוּא שֶׁיֹּאמַר אָדָם דְּבָרִים[2] וְיֹאמַר לִבְנֵי אָדָם שֶׁאוֹתָם הַדְּבָרִים יוֹעִילוּ אוֹ יַזִּיקוּ לְאֶחָד מִכָּל הָעִנְיָנִים[3], וְעַל זֶה נֶאֱמַר (דברים י״ח, י׳-י״א) לֹא יִמָּצֵא בְךָ וְגוֹ׳ וְחֹבֵר חָבֶר. וּלְשׁוֹן סִפְרִי (כאן), אֶחָד חוֹבֵר אֶת הַנָּחָשׁ וְאֶחָד חוֹבֵר אֶת הָעַקְרָב, כְּלוֹמַר שֶׁיֹּאמַר עֲלֵיהֶם דְּבָרִים כְּדֵי שֶׁלֹּא יִשְּׁכֵהוּ לְפִי דַעְתּוֹ, וְכֵן הָאוֹמֵר דְּבָרִים עַל הַמַּכָּה כְּדֵי שֶׁיָּנוּחַ מֵעָלָיו הַכְּאֵב. וְיֵשׁ[4] שֶׁפֵּרְשׁוּ חֹבֵר חָבֶר,

---

☙ Mitzvah 512 ☜
The Prohibition to Cast Spells

לֹא יִמָּצֵא בְךָ ... חָבֵר וְחֹבֵר

There shall not be found among you ... and one who casts spells (Deuteronomy 18:10-11).

This mitzvah prohibits uttering incantations (i.e., charms or spells) to produce a magic-like effect. שֶׁנִּמְנַעְנוּ מִלַּעֲשׂוֹת הַשְּׁבָעוֹת עַל שׁוּם עִנְיָן — **We are prohibited from casting spells**[1] **over anything.** וְזֶה הָעִנְיָן הוּא שֶׁיֹּאמַר אָדָם דְּבָרִים — **This refers to when a person utters words,**[2] וְיֹאמַר לִבְנֵי אָדָם שֶׁאוֹתָם הַדְּבָרִים יוֹעִילוּ אוֹ יַזִּיקוּ לְאֶחָד מִכָּל הָעִנְיָנִים — **and tells people that those words will** be either **beneficial or detrimental in some way.**[3] וְעַל זֶה נֶאֱמַר "לֹא יִמָּצֵא בְךָ וְגוֹ׳ וְחֹבֵר חָבֶר" — **Regarding this it is stated** (*Deuteronomy* 18:10-11): *There shall not be found among you ... and one who casts spells.*

Chinuch cites examples of such charms: וּלְשׁוֹן סִפְרִי — **In the words of** *Sifrei* (ad loc.): אֶחָד חוֹבֵר אֶת הַנָּחָשׁ וְאֶחָד חוֹבֵר אֶת הָעַקְרָב — When the Torah states, *and one who casts spells,* it applies **"whether one charms a snake or one charms a scorpion,"** כְּלוֹמַר שֶׁיֹּאמַר עֲלֵיהֶם דְּבָרִים כְּדֵי שֶׁלֹּא יִשְּׁכֵהוּ לְפִי דַעְתּוֹ — meaning, that he utters words over [the creatures] so that they should not bite him, according to his erroneous **belief** that such charms are effective. וְכֵן הָאוֹמֵר דְּבָרִים עַל הַמַּכָּה כְּדֵי שֶׁיָּנוּחַ מֵעָלָיו הַכְּאֵב — **Similarly,** the verse refers to **one who utters words over a wound in order to relieve his pain.**

Until here, Chinuch has followed the approach of *Rambam* (*Sefer HaMitzvos, Lo Saaseh* 35; *Hil. Avodah Zarah* 11:10), who understands this mitzvah as being a prohibition against reciting "magical" incantations and spells.[4] Chinuch now cites a different interpretation of this mitzvah: וְיֵשׁ שֶׁפֵּרְשׁוּ "חֹבֵר חָבֶר" — **Some explain** the words *choveir chaver* (translated above as "one who

---

NOTES

1. Literally, *from adjuring* (i.e., to cause to accept an oath). [Sorcery was performed by adjuring spirits, compelling them to fulfill one's wishes (see *Ran, Sanhedrin* 67b). Here too, one has his wishes fulfilled through his incantations.]

2. In this context, the word דְּבָרִים can mean *anything* spoken. *Rambam* (*Hil. Avodah Zarah* 11:10) writes that the spellcaster utters combinations of sounds that have no meaning in any language.

3. An example of a charm with beneficial intent is an incantation that, it is claimed, will stop a snake or scorpion from harming someone (*Rambam, Hil. Avodah Zarah* 11:10). See further in Chinuch.

4. *Rambam* adds that such incantations are completely ineffective. [See, however, *Beur HaGra, Yoreh Deah* 179:13, who asserts that such incantations can in fact be effective. For further discussion, see Insight to Mitzvah 255.] Nevertheless, *Rambam* (ibid. 11:11) states that incantations may be recited for one who sustained a life-threatening sting or bite, in order to put the patient's mind at ease, even though these incantations have no real healing effect. Since the patient's condition can deteriorate if he is agitated, calming his nerves and providing encouragement may prove to be lifesaving. Hence, the prohibition is set aside (as are most of the Torah's laws) in order to save the person's life.

שֶׁמְּקַבֵּץ בְּתַחְבּוּלוֹתָיו וְהַשְׁבָּעוֹתָיו נְחָשִׁים אוֹ עַקְרַבִּים אוֹ שְׁאָר חַיּוֹת לְמָקוֹם אֶחָד[5]. וְהַכֹּל בִּכְלַל הָאִסּוּר.

וְאוּלַי בְּנִי תַּקְשֶׁה עָלַי בְּהָא דִּגְרְסִינַן בִּשְׁבוּעוֹת בְּפֶרֶק יְדִיעוֹת הַטֻּמְאָה (ט״ו ע״ב) שִׁיר שֶׁל פְּגָעִים בְּכִנּוֹרוֹת וּבִנְבָלִים, וְאוֹמֵר יֹשֵׁב בְּסֵתֶר עֶלְיוֹן עַד כִּי אַתָּה ה׳ מַחְסִי (תהלים צ״א)[6], וְאוֹמֵר ה׳ מָה רַבּוּ צָרָי עַד לַה׳ הַיְשׁוּעָה (שם ג׳)[7], וּפֵרוּשׁ פְּגָעִים, כְּלוֹמַר שֶׁאֲמִירַת אֵלּוּ הַמִּזְמוֹרִים תּוֹעִיל לִשְׁמֹר מִן הַנְּזָקִין, וְאָמְרוּ בִּבְרָכוֹת[8] רַבִּי יְהוֹשֻׁעַ בֶּן לֵוִי מְסַדֵּר לְהוּ

---

casts spells") שֶׁמְּקַבֵּץ בְּתַחְבּוּלוֹתָיו וְהַשְׁבָּעוֹתָיו נְחָשִׁים אוֹ עַקְרַבִּים אוֹ שְׁאָר חַיּוֹת לְמָקוֹם אֶחָד – to be referring to one **who, through his manipulations and incantations, gathers snakes, scorpions, or other creatures into one place.**[5] וְהַכֹּל בִּכְלַל הָאִסּוּר – **All** of the above activities **are included in this** mitzvah-**prohibition.**

Chinuch anticipates a question:

וְאוּלַי בְּנִי תַּקְשֶׁה עָלַי – **Perhaps, my son, you will question my** words, בְּהָא דִּגְרְסִינַן בִּשְׁבוּעוֹת בְּפֶרֶק יְדִיעוֹת הַטֻּמְאָה – **based on** something **that we learn in** Tractate ***Shevuos*****, in Chapter *Yedios Hatumah*** (15b). The Gemara states there that, as part of the procedure for expanding the Temple Courtyard or the city limits of Jerusalem, שִׁיר שֶׁל פְּגָעִים בְּכִנּוֹרוֹת וּבִנְבָלִים – they would sing **the "song of harmful spirits" with** the accompaniment of **harps and lyres.** וְאוֹמֵר "יֹשֵׁב בְּסֵתֶר עֶלְיוֹן" עַד "כִּי אַתָּה ה׳ מַחְסִי" – As the Gemara explains, this means that **they** would **chant** Psalm 91, beginning, ***He who sits in the refuge of the Most High*****, until** the words (verse 9), ***For You,* H*ASHEM*, *are my refuge;***[6] וְאוֹמֵר "ה׳ מָה רַבּוּ צָרָי" עַד "לַה׳ הַיְשׁוּעָה" – **and** then **they** would **chant** Psalm 3, beginning, ***H*ASHEM*, how numerous are my tormentors,*** and finishing with the words in the final verse, ***Salvation is* H*ASHEM*'s.**[7] וּפֵרוּשׁ פְּגָעִים – **Now, the meaning of** "song of **harmful spirits"** כְּלוֹמַר שֶׁאֲמִירַת אֵלּוּ הַמִּזְמוֹרִים תּוֹעִיל לִשְׁמֹר מִן הַנְּזָקִין – **is that the recitation of these** particular **psalms serves to protect from** spiritual **harm.** Such recitations, though, would seem to violate this mitzvah-prohibition against incantations! How could they be required as part of the process of sanctification? וְאָמְרוּ בִּבְרָכוֹת – **Furthermore, [the Sages] stated in** Tractate ***Berachos*****:**[8] רַבִּי יְהוֹשֻׁעַ בֶּן לֵוִי מְסַדֵּר לְהוּ

NOTES

5. According to this approach, the words חֹבֵר חָבֶר, *choveir chaver,* means "one who gathers together" [from the same root as the word חִבּוּר, *joining*], and refers to a person who charms animals and causes them to form packs (*Rashi, Sanhedrin* 65a ד״ה והתורה אמרה; *Smag, Lo Saaseh* 54). The charmer may intend to gather these creatures in order to engage them to fight with one another, or to move them to uninhabited areas where they will not harm anyone (*Rashi* there ד״ה ואפילו נחשים).

6. Psalm 91 was composed by Moses as part of his blessing to the Jewish people upon the completion of the *Mishkan* [Tabernacle]. It is therefore appropriate to include it in the procedure of Temple expansion (*Rashi, Shevuos* 15b ד״ה ושיר של פגעים).

As Chinuch goes on to say, this psalm, together with Psalm 3, is referred to as the "song of harmful spirits" because it has the ability to remove destructive forces. *Maharsha* explains that these "harmful spirits" are the damaging spiritual forces and forces of impurity that can exist in unsanctified places. In the process of expanding the areas of sanctification, this psalm was recited, since its verses speak of one who "sits in the refuge of the Most High," i.e., a place imbued with the Divine Presence, free of harmful spirits. The accompanying music too was meant to remove such negative forces, as we find that music has this ability [as with King Saul; see *I Samuel* 16:14-23].

7. This particular psalm was chosen, in part because it alludes to the scorn that we encountered from our adversaries when we came to build the Second Temple [see *Nehemiah* 3:34-37], and it serves as a prayer of sorts that such adversaries be removed (*Rashi, Shevuos* 15b ד״ה ואומר ה׳). Moreover, as Chinuch here notes, this psalm alludes to the removal of not only our physical adversaries, but our spiritual ones as well. It is therefore incorporated into the "song of harmful spirits."

According to Chinuch's understanding (which is consistent with the reading of that Gemara cited by *Hagahos HaGra* there), in each of these psalms, they would recite the first sixty words of the psalm concluding with the words mentioned, even though they stopped in the middle of a verse. This is an allusion to the verse (*Song of Songs* 3:8): *Behold Solomon's bed, "sixty" mighty warriors of the mightiest of Israel encircle it* (see *Ritva, Shevuos* 15b ד״ה יושב).

8. This passage is not found in Tractate *Berachos,* but rather in *Shevuos* (15b), immediately following the Gemara just cited by Chinuch. [However, both of these passages are cited in *Rif's* commentary to *Berachos* (fol. 3a).]

לְהָנֵי קְרָאֵי וְגָאנֵי[9], וְאֵין הַדָּבָר חָלִילָה דּוֹמֶה לְעִנְיַן חוֹבֵר חָבֶר שֶׁזָּכַרְנוּ, וּכְבָר אָמְרוּ זִכְרוֹנָם לִבְרָכָה (שם) עַל זֶה אָסוּר לְהִתְרַפֵּאת בְּדִבְרֵי תוֹרָה[10], אֲבָל הִזְכִּירוּ לוֹמַר מִזְמוֹרִים אֵלוּ שֶׁיֵּשׁ בָּהֶם דְּבָרִים יְעוֹרְרוּ הַנֶּפֶשׁ הַיּוֹדֵעַ אוֹתָם לַחֲסוֹת בַּה׳ וּלְהָשִׂים בּוֹ כָּל מִבְטָחוֹ וְלִקְבֹּעַ בִּלְבָבוֹ יִרְאָתוֹ וְלִסְמֹךְ עַל חַסְדּוֹ וְטוּבוֹ, וּמִתּוֹךְ הִתְעוֹרְרוּת עַל זֶה יִהְיֶה נִשְׁמָר בְּלִי סָפֵק מִכָּל נֶזֶק[11]. וְזֶה שֶׁהֵשִׁיבוּ בַּגְּמָרָא בְּעִנְיָן זֶה, דְּקָא פָּרִיךְ הָתָם וְהֵיכִי עֲבִיד רַבִּי יְהוֹשֻׁעַ כֵּן וְהָאָמַר רַבִּי יְהוֹשֻׁעַ אָסוּר לְהִתְרַפֵּאת בְּדִבְרֵי תוֹרָה, וְאָמְרוּ לְהָגֵן שָׁאנֵי. כְּלוֹמַר, לֹא אָסְרָה תוֹרָה שֶׁיֹּאמַר אָדָם דִּבְרֵי תוֹרָה לְעוֹרֵר נַפְשׁוֹ לְטוֹבָה כְּדֵי שֶׁיָּגֵן עָלָיו אוֹתוֹ הַזְּכוּת לְשָׁמְרוֹ[12].

לְהָנֵי קְרָאֵי וְגָאנֵי — **R' Yehoshua ben Levi would recite these** above-mentioned **verses** (Psalms 91 and 3) at bedtime, in order to ward off harmful spirits, **and** then **go to sleep.** This, too, begs the question: How are such recitations permitted — are they not forms of incantations?[9]

Chinuch answers these questions:

וְאֵין הַדָּבָר חָלִילָה דּוֹמֶה לְעִנְיַן חוֹבֵר חָבֶר שֶׁזָּכַרְנוּ — **These** examples of permitted recitations **are not** at all **comparable, Heaven forbid, to the matter of incantations that we discussed** above. וּכְבָר אָמְרוּ זִכְרוֹנָם לִבְרָכָה עַל זֶה — **Indeed, [our Sages], of blessed memory, have already stated** (ibid.) **regarding this:** אָסוּר לְהִתְרַפֵּאת בְּדִבְרֵי תוֹרָה — **It is forbidden to be healed through** the incantation of **words of Torah.**[10] Certainly then, that could not have been their intention with the recitation of these verses! אֲבָל הִזְכִּירוּ לוֹמַר מִזְמוֹרִים אֵלוּ — **However, they said that these psalms are to be recited** שֶׁיֵּשׁ בָּהֶם דְּבָרִים יְעוֹרְרוּ הַנֶּפֶשׁ הַיּוֹדֵעַ אוֹתָם — **because they contain words that inspire the spirit of one who internalizes their message** לַחֲסוֹת בַּה׳ וּלְהָשִׂים בּוֹ כָּל מִבְטָחוֹ — **to take refuge in Hashem and to place all of his trust in Him,** וְלִקְבֹּעַ בִּלְבָבוֹ יִרְאָתוֹ וְלִסְמֹךְ עַל חַסְדּוֹ וְטוּבוֹ — **as well as to implant in his heart fear of [Hashem] and to rely upon His kindness and goodness.** וּמִתּוֹךְ הִתְעוֹרְרוּת עַל זֶה — **As a result of becoming inspired in this manner,** יִהְיֶה נִשְׁמָר בְּלִי סָפֵק מִכָּל נֶזֶק — **he will undoubtedly be protected from all harm.**[11] וְזֶה שֶׁהֵשִׁיבוּ בַּגְּמָרָא בְּעִנְיָן זֶה — **This is what the Gemara** (ibid.) **means in its response regarding this issue;** דְּקָא פָּרִיךְ הָתָם — **for [the Gemara itself] asks there,** as we asked above: וְהֵיכִי עֲבִיד רַבִּי יְהוֹשֻׁעַ כֵּן — **How could R' Yehoshua have done this?** I.e., how could he have recited Scriptural passages for the purpose of protection? וְהָאָמַר רַבִּי יְהוֹשֻׁעַ אָסוּר לְהִתְרַפֵּאת בְּדִבְרֵי תוֹרָה — **Did not R' Yehoshua** himself **say** that **it is forbidden to be healed through** chanting **words of Torah?** וְאָמְרוּ לְהָגֵן שָׁאנֵי — **To which [the Gemara] replies:** Reciting Torah verses **for protection is different** than reciting them for healing, and is permitted. כְּלוֹמַר — The Gemara **means to say:** לֹא אָסְרָה תוֹרָה שֶׁיֹּאמַר אָדָם דִּבְרֵי תוֹרָה לְעוֹרֵר נַפְשׁוֹ לְטוֹבָה — **The Torah did not forbid a person to recite words of Torah in order to inspire his soul to goodness** (i.e., to recognize Hashem's benevolence and rely upon Him), כְּדֵי שֶׁיָּגֵן עָלָיו אוֹתוֹ הַזְּכוּת לְשָׁמְרוֹ — **so that this merit should protect him** from harm.[12]

NOTES

9. These psalms (§91 and §3) are in fact included in the order of the bedtime *Shema* that we recite

10. Using words of the Torah for "healing" is considered disgraceful to the Torah and verges upon heresy, as it reduces the sacred text to a mere therapeutic chant (see *Rambam, Hil. Avodah Zarah* 11:12, and *Shulchan Aruch, Yoreh Deah* 179:8). Chinuch argues that the same applies to reciting words of Torah for protection.

11. Thus, the "song of harmful spirits" is not chanted for *protection,* but rather, for *inspiration*; and naturally, Hashem protects those who are inspired to place their trust in Him. In this manner, the Torah is not being disgraced at all. To the contrary, such recitation of Torah verses is actually meritorious, as Chinuch now explains.

12. It is forbidden to chant Scriptural verses in an attempt at healing, as if the chant has curative value, because treating the sacred text as some therapeutic compilation is disgraceful to it. But it is permitted to recite verses as a means of inspiring one to seek refuge in Hashem, because the Torah was given to us in order that we should study and internalize its messages — one of which is that Hashem protects those who trust in Him. See similarly, *Perishah, Yoreh Deah* 179:17; *Toras Chaim, Shevuos* 15b.

[For further discussion of this subject, specifically with regard to reciting *Tehillim* (psalms) on behalf of ill people, see Insight.

מִשָּׁרְשֵׁי מִצְוָה זוֹ מַה שֶּׁכָּתַבְתִּי בַּמִּצְוָה הַקּוֹדֶמֶת לָהּ[13].
דִּינֵי הַמִּצְוָה בְּפֶרֶק שְׁבִיעִי מִשַּׁבָּת[14].
וְנוֹהֵג אִסּוּר זֶה בְּכָל מָקוֹם וּבְכָל זְמַן, בִּזְכָרִים וּנְקֵבוֹת[15].
וְעוֹבֵר עַל זֶה וְעָשָׂה הַשְּׁבָעוֹת בְּמֵזִיד חַיָּב מַלְקוּת[16].

Underlying Purpose of the Mitzvah

מִשָּׁרְשֵׁי מִצְוָה זוֹ – **Among the underlying purposes of this mitzvah** מַה שֶּׁכָּתַבְתִּי בַּמִּצְוָה הַקּוֹדֶמֶת לָהּ – **is that which I wrote in the previous mitzvah.**[13]

Laws of the Mitzvah

דִּינֵי הַמִּצְוָה בְּפֶרֶק שְׁבִיעִי מִשַּׁבָּת – **The laws of the mitzvah are** found **in the seventh chapter of** Tractate ***Shabbos.***[14]

Applicability of the Mitzvah

וְנוֹהֵג אִסּוּר זֶה בְּכָל מָקוֹם וּבְכָל זְמַן – **The prohibition applies in every location and in all times,** בִּזְכָרִים וּנְקֵבוֹת – **to men and women.**[15]

וְעוֹבֵר עַל זֶה וְעָשָׂה הַשְּׁבָעוֹת בְּמֵזִיד חַיָּב מַלְקוּת – **One who transgresses this** mitzvah-prohibition **and intentionally cast spells is liable to *malkus.***[16]

NOTES

13. In Mitzvah 511, Chinuch directs the reader to what he wrote in Mitzvah 62 (see Mitzvah 511 note 8). In Mitzvah 510, however, he discusses the underlying purpose at greater length.

14. [Chinuch here follows the reading found in *Rambam, Sefer HaMitzvos, Lo Saaseh* 35. Actually, though, these laws appear in the *sixth* chapter of *Shabbos*, fol. 67a-b.] These laws are codified in *Rambam, Hil. Avodah Zarah* 11:10-12 and in *Shulchan Aruch, Yoreh Deah* 179:5-12.

15. That is, it applies both in Eretz Yisrael and the Diaspora, whether the *Beis HaMikdash* is standing or not. In addition, it applies to both men and women in accordance with the general rule pertaining to mitzvah-prohibitions.

16. The charmer incurs *malkus* only if his incantations involved some action as well, even something as simple as pointing a finger. However, if all he did was chant his spell, he does not incur *malkus.* [See Insight to Mitzvah 68, regarding a transgression that does not involve action.] He does, however, incur *makkas mardus* (lashes of discipline), as does a person who solicits his services (*Rambam, Hil. Avodah Zarah* 11:10).

☙ Insight: Reciting Tehillim for the Sick

In light of the prohibition to use incantations, and the statement of the Sages that "it is forbidden to be healed through words of Torah" (*Shevuos* 15b), Chinuch discusses the custom of R' Yehoshua ben Levi to recite certain chapters of *Tehillim* (*Psalms*) for protection before going to sleep. This is a custom we follow to the present day, as those psalms (§91 and §3) are included in the order of the bedtime *Shema.* Chinuch explains that what this mitzvah prohibits is using verses (or any other formula) in some sort of "protective chant." The psalms recited before retiring, however, are recited for *inspiration,* and it is the inspiration that causes a person to be protected. By focusing on the message of those psalms, a person gains increased fear of Hashem, and increased recognition of His goodness and protectiveness. One who is inspired in this way merits Hashem's guardianship, and thus, he will undoubtedly be protected from harm. This, Chinuch explains, is what the Gemara means when it says (*Shevuos* 15b) that we are permitted to recite Scriptural verses לְהָגֵן, *for protection.*

Some Acharonim rely on this reasoning to explain the widespread custom of reciting *Tehillim* on behalf of ourselves, or on behalf of others such as the sick. While some chapters of *Tehillim* have the character of prayers, many are actually songs of praise to Hashem, descriptions of ways of righteousness, or simply discussions of King David's travails (which represent the personal and communal travails of all Jews). Thus, the majority of the psalms are not "prayers" in the conventional sense. It

would thus seem, at first glance, that the purpose of reciting these psalms is not to utter prayers, but rather, to invoke the "power" of *Tehillim* for the benefit of ourselves or others. But why does this not fall under the category of "healing through words of Torah"? And why is it not forbidden under the current mitzvah-prohibition?

Acharonim answer that we do not recite *Tehillim* as a chant or incantation at all. Rather, we recite the psalms in order to gain inspiration from their messages. By reading psalms that describe how Hashem delivers those who have faith in Him from trouble, we become inspired to greater levels of faith; and by virtue of this faith we fervently hope that we, too, will be worthy of His salvation. Likewise, when we recite *Tehillim* on behalf of another, we strengthen our faith in Hashem, and we fervently hope that in the merit of *our* being inspired to greater faith, He will spare the life of the ill person and heal him. Indeed, it is not only *permitted,* but actually *meritorious,* to do this, as it is a form of serving Hashem (*Perishah, Yoreh Deah* 179:17; *Toras Chaim, Shevuos* 15b).

A similar approach can be used to explain another teaching of the Sages (*Eruvin* 54a): חָשׁ בְּרֹאשׁוֹ יַעֲסֹק בַּתּוֹרָה שֶׁנֶּאֱמַר "כִּי לִוְיַת חֵן הֵם לְרֹאשֶׁךָ וכו'" חָשׁ בְּכָל גּוּפוֹ יַעֲסֹק בַּתּוֹרָה שֶׁנֶּאֱמַר "וּלְכָל בְּשָׂרוֹ מַרְפֵּא", One who feels pain in his head should study Torah, as it is stated (*Proverbs* 1:9): *For they* (i.e., words of Torah) *are a gracious accompaniment to your head* ... One who feels pain in his entire body should study Torah, as it is stated (ibid. 4:22): *and a cure for his entire flesh*. This cannot mean that one should rely on the recitation of Torah words as a curative measure, for doing so is clearly forbidden! Indeed, *Rambam* rules (*Hil. Avodah Zarah* 11:12) that one who chants Scriptural verses over a wound, or over a colicky baby, so as to heal the underlying ailment, is in violation of our prohibition (see also *Shulchan Aruch, Yoreh Deah* 179:8, and above, note 10). Rather, commentators explain that the Gemara means that a sick person should engage in Torah study *for the sake of the mitzvah,* and upon doing so, he may have in mind the prayerful request that Hashem should heal him in the merit of the mitzvah. This is a valid request, since Torah study is one of the mitzvos whose "fruits" or dividends a person enjoys in This World, though the principal reward is reserved for him in the World to Come [as stated in the Mishnah, *Peah* 1:1] (*Toras Chaim* ibid.; *Maharsha, Shabbos* 67a).

In this vein, R' Chaim Volozhiner (*Ruach Chaim, Avos* 1:1) relates an incident that occurred with *R' David HaLevi* of Lvov, the author of *Taz* on *Shulchan Aruch*: The *Taz* was in the midst of delivering a Torah lecture to his students when a woman entered, crying that her son was deathly ill. The *Taz* said to her, "Am I instead of God [Who heals the sick]?" She replied, "I am crying to the Torah that is within my master (i.e., you), for God and His Torah are one!" [See *Zohar, Acharei Mos* 73a.] Upon hearing this, the *Taz* said to her, "If so, I hereby grant your child [the merit of] the Torah that I am now learning with my students. Perhaps in this merit he will live, as it is stated (*Deuteronomy* 32:47): וּבַדָּבָר הַזֶּה תַּאֲרִיכוּ יָמִים, *for through this matter you shall prolong your days.*" Indeed, at that very moment, the child's fever broke and he was healed.

Thus, it is the *merit* of Torah study that brings about salvation. Regarding *Tehillim*, the same would apply: *Tehillim,* too, is part of the Torah, and reciting *Tehillim* is a form of Torah study. It is therefore the *merit* of reciting *Tehillim* that can bring healing for the sick and salvation for all people in crisis (*Halichos Shlomo, Tefillah* Ch. 8, *Dvar Halachah* §22).

מִצְוָה תקיג: שֶׁלֹּא לִשְׁאֹל בְּאוֹב

שֶׁלֹּא נִשְׁאַל בַּעַל אוֹב שֶׁיּוֹדִיעֵנוּ דָּבָר, וְעַל זֶה נֶאֱמַר (דברים י״ח, י׳-י״א) לֹא יִמָּצֵא בְךָ וְגוֹ׳ וְשֹׁאֵל אוֹב. וְעִנְיַן כִּשּׁוּף הַזֶּה הוּא שֶׁיֵּשׁ בְּנֵי אָדָם שֶׁעוֹשִׂין מְכַשְּׁפוּת שֶׁשְּׁמוֹ פִּיתוֹם[1], שֶׁהוּא מַעֲלֶה אֶת הַמֵּת מִבֵּין שֶׁחְיוֹ וְשׁוֹמֵעַ הַשּׁוֹאֵל מִן הַמֵּת תְּשׁוּבָה עַל שְׁאֵלוֹתָיו[2].

מִשָּׁרְשֵׁי הַמִּצְוָה מַה שֶּׁכָּתַבְתִּי בְּסָמוּךְ בְּעִנְיְנֵי הַכִּשּׁוּף[3].

דִּינֵי הַמִּצְוָה בְּסִפְרִי (כאן) וּבְסַנְהֶדְרִין (ס״ה ע״א-ע״ב)[4]. וְשָׁם בְּסַנְהֶדְרִין אָמְרוּ שֶׁהָעוֹשֶׂה

Mitzvah 513

The Prohibition to Consult an Ov-Sorcerer

לֹא יִמָּצֵא בְךָ ... וְשֹׁאֵל אוֹב

There shall not be found among you ... one who consults Ov (*Deuteronomy* 18:10-11).

The prohibition against practicing the sorcery of *Ov,* which entails conjuring up the spirit of the dead and communicating with it, was the subject of an earlier mitzvah (Mitzvah 255). The focus of this mitzvah is on those who seek their services, rather than on the practitioners themselves.

שֶׁלֹּא נִשְׁאַל בַּעַל אוֹב – **We are prohibited to consult an** ***Ov*****-sorcerer,** שֶׁיּוֹדִיעֵנוּ דָּבָר – to request of him **that he inform us of something** through his sorcery. וְעַל זֶה נֶאֱמַר ״לֹא יִמָּצֵא בְךָ וְגוֹ׳ וְשֹׁאֵל אוֹב״ – **Regarding this it is stated** (*Deuteronomy* 18:10-11): ***There shall not be found among you ... one who consults Ov.***

וְעִנְיַן כִּשּׁוּף הַזֶּה הוּא – **What this** particular form of **sorcery refers to is** as follows: שֶׁיֵּשׁ בְּנֵי אָדָם שֶׁעוֹשִׂין מְכַשְּׁפוּת שֶׁשְּׁמוֹ פִּיתוֹם – **There are individuals who perform sorcery that is referred to as "*Pitom,*"**[1] שֶׁהוּא מַעֲלֶה אֶת הַמֵּת מִבֵּין שֶׁחְיוֹ – **in which [the sorcerer] conjures up a dead** person's spirit, having it reside **under [the sorcerer's] armpit.** וְשׁוֹמֵעַ הַשּׁוֹאֵל מִן הַמֵּת תְּשׁוּבָה עַל שְׁאֵלוֹתָיו – **The inquirer of the dead** person's spirit then **hears the answer to his questions** coming forth from the sorcerer's armpit.[2]

Underlying Purpose of the Mitzvah

מִשָּׁרְשֵׁי הַמִּצְוָה – **Among the underlying purposes of this mitzvah** מַה שֶּׁכָּתַבְתִּי בְּסָמוּךְ בְּעִנְיְנֵי הַכִּשּׁוּף – **is that which I wrote above, with regard to the issue of sorcery.**[3]

Laws of the Mitzvah

דִּינֵי הַמִּצְוָה בְּסִפְרִי וּבְסַנְהֶדְרִין – **The laws of this mitzvah are in** ***Sifrei*** here **and in** Tractate ***Sanhedrin*** (65a-b).[4]

וְשָׁם בְּסַנְהֶדְרִין אָמְרוּ – **There, in** Tractate ***Sanhedrin,*** **[the Gemara] states** שֶׁהָעוֹשֶׂה

NOTES

1. This is another name for the sorcery of *Ov,* which Chinuch now describes (see also *Rashi, Sanhedrin* 65a ד״ה פיתום).

2. In Mitzvah 255, Chinuch explains that the sorcerer first performs various acts and burns certain incenses, and then conjures up the spirit of the dead, which comes to rest under the sorcerer's armpit (see *Rambam, Hil. Avodah Zarah* 6:1; cf. *Raavad* ad loc.). From there, it responds to the questions posed to it.

[See *I Samuel* Ch. 28, where Scripture describes how King Saul inquired of the *Ov* sorceress of En-dor (*Rashi, Sanhedrin* 65a ד״ה והנשאל). See Insight to Mitzvah 255 for a discussion of the basis for King Saul's actions, and for the various opinions as to whether such sorcery was real or contrived.]

3. See Mitzvah 510; see also Mitzvah 512 note 13.

4. These laws are codified in *Rambam, Hil. Avodah Zarah* 11:14.

כִּשׁוּף זֶה הוּא בִּסְקִילָה[5], וְהַשּׁוֹאֵל בָּהֶם בְּאַזְהָרָה, כְּלוֹמַר בְּחִיּוּב לָאו, וְאֵין בּוֹ מַלְקוּת לְפִי שֶׁאֵין בּוֹ מַעֲשֶׂה[6].

וְנוֹהֵג אִסּוּר זֶה בְּכָל מָקוֹם וּבְכָל זְמַן, בִּזְכָרִים וּנְקֵבוֹת[7].

כִּשׁוּף זֶה הוּא בִּסְקִילָה – **that one who performs this sorcery** (i.e., the sorcerer himself) intentionally **is** liable **to *sekilah*** (stoning) due to his transgression of Mitzvah 255;[5] וְהַשּׁוֹאֵל בָּהֶם בְּאַזְהָרָה – **but one who inquires of [the sorcerer]** who performs the *Ov* sorcery on his behalf **is subject** only **to an injunction,** כְּלוֹמַר בְּחִיּוּב לָאו – **meaning,** he is **liable for** having violated **a prohibition** (i.e., this mitzvah-prohibition). וְאֵין בּוֹ מַלְקוּת לְפִי שֶׁאֵין בּוֹ מַעֲשֶׂה – **However, there is no *malkus* for** the violation of **[this prohibition], since it does not involve an action.**[6]

Applicability of the Mitzvah

וְנוֹהֵג אִסּוּר זֶה בְּכָל מָקוֹם וּבְכָל זְמַן – **This prohibition applies in every location and in all times,** בִּזְכָרִים וּנְקֵבוֹת – **to men and women.**[7]

NOTES

5. See *Leviticus* 20:27. See General Introduction, Section VI, for the circumstances in which capital punishment was carried out in earlier times.

[As Chinuch writes at the end of Mitzvah 255, if there were no witnesses or there was no warning (*hasraah*), the transgressor is subject to *kares.* If he sinned unintentionally, he must bring a *chatas* offering.]

6. Inquiring of the *Ov* sorcerer involves only speech, and as a general rule, one does not incur *malkus* when one's violation involves no action.

Nevertheless, *Rambam* (*Hil. Avodah Zarah* 11:14) notes that if the inquirer were to perform some action based on the information he received from the sorcerer, then he would indeed be subject to *malkus,* since at that point his violation would involve an action (see *Minchas Chinuch* §2; see also Mitzvah 255, and *Minchas Yitzchak* there §2 with regard to whether Chinuch agrees with this latter point). Where no action was performed, although there is no penalty of *malkus,* the inquirer is subject to the Rabbinical punishment of *malkus mardus* (*Rambam* ibid.).

7. That is, it applies both in Eretz Yisrael and the Diaspora, whether the *Beis HaMikdash* is standing or not. In addition, it applies to both men and women in accordance with the general rule pertaining to mitzvah prohibitions.

מִצְוָה תקיד: שֶׁלֹּא לִשְׁאֹל בְּיִדְעוֹנִי

שֶׁלֹּא לִשְׁאֹל יִדְעוֹנִי. וְהָעִנְיָן הַזֶּה הוּא שֶׁמֵּשִׂים הַמְכַשֵּׁף עֶצֶם חַיָּה שֶׁשְּׁמָהּ יָדוּעַ לְתוֹךְ פִּיו, וְאוֹתוֹ הָעֶצֶם מְדַבֵּר עַל יְדֵי כְּשָׁפָיו[1]. וְזֹאת הַחַיָּה שֶׁשְּׁמָהּ יָדוּעַ רָאִיתִי בְּסֵפֶר מִן הַגְּאוֹנִים[2] שֶׁהִיא גְּדֵלָה בְּחֶבֶל גָּדוֹל שֶׁיּוֹצֵא מִן הָאָרֶץ כְּעֵין חֶבֶל הַקִּשּׁוּאִין וְהַדִּלּוּעִין, וְצוּרָתוֹ כְּצוּרַת אָדָם בְּכָל דָּבָר, בְּפָנִים וְגוּף וְיָדַיִם וְרַגְלַיִם, וּמִטַּבּוּרוֹ מְחֻבָּר לַחֶבֶל, וְאֵין כָּל בְּרִיָּה יְכוֹלָה לִקְרַב אֵלֶיהָ כִּמְלֹא הַחֶבֶל לְפִי שֶׁהִיא רוֹעָה סְבִיבוֹתֶיהָ כִּמְלֹא הַחֶבֶל וְטוֹרֶפֶת כָּל מַה שֶּׁיְּכוֹלָה לְהַשִּׂיג, וּכְשֶׁבָּאִין לְצוּדָהּ מוֹרִין בַּחִצִּים אֶל הַחֶבֶל עַד שֶׁנִּפְסָק וְהִיא מֵתָה מִיָּד. וּבִירוּשַׁלְמִי דְּכִלְאַיִם (פ״ח ה״ד) אָמְרוּ זִכְרוֹנָם לִבְרָכָה[3] בְּפֵרוּשׁ כִּי עִם אַבְנֵי הַשָּׂדֶה בְרִיתֶךָ

Mitzvah 514

The Prohibition to Consult a Yidoni-Socerer

לֹא יִמָּצֵא בְךָ ... וְשֹׁאֵל אוֹב וְיִדְּעֹנִי וְדֹרֵשׁ אֶל הַמֵּתִים
There shall not be found among you ... one who consults Ov or Yidoni (*Deuteronomy* 18:10-11).

In Mitzvah 256, Chinuch presented the prohibition against *practicing* the sorcery of *Yidoni.* This mitzvah prohibits seeking the services of one who engages in the sorcery of *Yidoni.* This parallels the previous mitzvah, which prohibits seeking the services of the *Ov* sorcerer.

שֶׁלֹּא לִשְׁאֹל יִדְעוֹנִי – We are commanded **not to consult a *Yidoni*-sorcerer.** וְהָעִנְיָן הַזֶּה הוּא – **The description of this** form of sorcery **is** as follows: שֶׁמֵּשִׂים הַמְכַשֵּׁף עֶצֶם חַיָּה שֶׁשְּׁמָהּ יָדוּעַ לְתוֹךְ פִּיו – **The sorcerer places the bone of a creature named "*yadua*" into his** own **mouth,** וְאוֹתוֹ הָעֶצֶם מְדַבֵּר עַל יְדֵי כְּשָׁפָיו – **and that bone speaks through his sorcery.**[1]

Chinuch describes the *yadua* creature:

וְזֹאת הַחַיָּה שֶׁשְּׁמָהּ יָדוּעַ רָאִיתִי בְּסֵפֶר מִן הַגְּאוֹנִים – **I have seen** the description of **this creature, whose name is *yadua,* in one of the books of the Geonim.**[2] שֶׁהִיא גְּדֵלָה בְּחֶבֶל גָּדוֹל שֶׁיּוֹצֵא מִן הָאָרֶץ – There it is explained **that [the *yadua*] develops from a large cord that protrudes from the earth,** כְּעֵין חֶבֶל הַקִּשּׁוּאִין וְהַדִּלּוּעִין – **like the cord** (i.e., vine) **of cucumbers and gourds.** וְצוּרָתוֹ כְּצוּרַת אָדָם בְּכָל דָּבָר – **It has the appearance of a man in all respects,** בְּפָנִים וְגוּף וְיָדַיִם וְרַגְלַיִם – **with** regard to its **face, body, hands, and feet.** וּמִטַּבּוּרוֹ מְחֻבָּר לַחֶבֶל – **From its navel it is attached to the cord** that connects it to the ground. וְאֵין כָּל בְּרִיָּה יְכוֹלָה לִקְרַב אֵלֶיהָ כִּמְלֹא הַחֶבֶל – **No creature is able to approach it within the length of** its **cord,** לְפִי שֶׁהִיא רוֹעָה סְבִיבוֹתֶיהָ כִּמְלֹא הַחֶבֶל – **for it pastures on** the vegetation in **its surroundings** up to **the length of** its **cord,** וְטוֹרֶפֶת כָּל מַה שֶּׁיְּכוֹלָה לְהַשִּׂיג – **and it** attacks and **tears up anything within its reach.** וּכְשֶׁבָּאִין לְצוּדָהּ מוֹרִין בַּחִצִּים אֶל הַחֶבֶל עַד שֶׁנִּפְסָק – **When they come to capture it, they** must **shoot arrows at the cord until it is severed,** וְהִיא מֵתָה מִיָּד – **and,** at that point, **it dies immediately.**

Chinuch cites a Talmudic reference to this creature:

וּבִירוּשַׁלְמִי דְּכִלְאַיִם אָמְרוּ זִכְרוֹנָם לִבְרָכָה – **In Talmud *Yerushalmi,*** Tractate ***Kilayim*** 8:4 (74a in Schottenstein edition),[3] **[our Sages], of blessed memory, stated** בְּפֵרוּשׁ "כִּי עִם אַבְנֵי הַשָּׂדֶה בְרִיתֶךָ" –

NOTES

1. In Mitzvah 256, Chinuch adds that the *Yidoni* sorcerer first burns various incenses, recites incantations, and performs other acts until he is overcome by a sort of epileptic seizure. At that point the bone that is in his mouth speaks of future events. [According to *Rambam* (*Hil. Avodah Zarah* 6:2), it is the sorcerer himself who speaks, not the bone.]

2. The following description of the *yadua* is cited by *Rash* (to *Kilayim* 8:5) in the name of *R' Meir, the son of R' Klonimus* of Speyer, Germany.

3. See note 14 there.

(איוב ה׳, כ״ג), **בַּר נָשׁ דְּטוּר הוּא וְהוּא חָיֵי מִן טַבּוּרֵיהּ, אִי פָּסִיק טַבּוּרֵיהּ לָא חָיֵי**[4].
שֹׁרֶשׁ מִצְוָה זוֹ וְכָל עִנְיָנָהּ בְּדִינֶיהָ וּבְחִיּוּבָהּ כְּעִנְיַן מִצְוַת אוֹב שֶׁכָּתַבְנוּ בְּסָמוּךְ (מצוה
תקי״ג)[5].

in explanation of the verse (*Job* 5:23), *For you shall have a treaty with the avnei ha'sadeh* (literally,
stones of the field), **בַּר נָשׁ דְּטוּר הוּא** — that **this** term **refers to the "man of the mountain,"** **וְהוּא**
חָיֵי מִן טַבּוּרֵיהּ — **which lives from its navel** cord. **אִי פָּסִיק טַבּוּרֵיהּ לָא חָיֵי** — **If its navel** cord **is
severed, it cannot live.**[4]

☙ Underlying Purpose, Laws, and Applicability of the Mitzvah ❧

שֹׁרֶשׁ מִצְוָה זוֹ וְכָל עִנְיָנָהּ — **The underlying purpose of this mitzvah and all of its aspects,** **בְּדִינֶיהָ**
וּבְחִיּוּבָהּ — **including its laws and the liability for** transgressing **it,** **כְּעִנְיַן מִצְוַת אוֹב שֶׁכָּתַבְנוּ**
בְּסָמוּךְ — **correspond to that which we wrote in the previous** mitzvah, **the mitzvah**-prohibition
of seeking the counsel of an ***Ov*** sorcerer.[5]

NOTES

4. The Scriptural term, אַבְנֵי הַשָּׂדֶה, *avnei ha'sadeh,* is interpreted as though it reads בְּנֵי הַשָּׂדֶה, *bnei ha'sadeh,* or
men of the field — a reference to this creature described
above (*Rabbeinu Bachya, Deuteronomy* 18:11). According to *Yerushalmi,* this creature lives in mountainous
regions, so *Yerushalmi* refers to it as the "man of the
mountain."

5. As with an *Ov* sorcerer, the *Yidoni* sorcerer himself
is subject to capital punishment (see Mitzvah 256),
while those who inquire of the sorcerer have merely
violated a standard Biblical prohibition (the current

mitzvah). Also, as with the sorcery of *Ov,* those who
violate this prohibition and inquire of *Yidoni* are
not liable to *malkus,* since such violations do not
involve action. See, however, note 6 to the previous
mitzvah.

This mitzvah-prohibition (like the previous one)
applies to both men and women, both in Eretz Yisrael
and the Diaspora, and whether the *Beis HaMikdash* is
standing or not.

The laws of this mitzvah are codified in *Rambam,
Hil. Avodah Zarah* 11:14.

⊸§ Insight: Consulting One Who Performs the Acts Prohibited in the Verse

In these mitzvos, the Torah forbids seeking out the services of an *Ov* or *Yidoni* sorcerer. One who
seeks out such services violates the Torah prohibitions of לֹא יִמָּצֵא בְךָ ... וְשֹׁאֵל אוֹב וְיִדְּעֹנִי, *There shall not
be found among you ... one who consults Ov or Yidoni. Ov* and *Yidoni,* however, are not the only forbidden practices mentioned in the verse. The Torah (*Deuteronomy* 18:10-11) states: *There shall not be
found among you ... one who practices divinations, a teller of auspicious times, one who reads omens,
a sorcerer, or one who casts spells.* The question thus arises: What is the law with regard to seeking
the services of one who practices one of the *other* forbidden activities mentioned earlier in the verse?
While the Torah certainly forbids *performing* these activities (see Mitzvos 249-250 and 510-512), does it
also forbid one from consulting one of these practitioners? This can have a practical application if the
practitioner is a non-Jew, who is therefore not bound by the prohibitions against engaging in these
practices. Would a Jew be in violation of any prohibition if he were to engage his services?

Yam Shel Shlomo (*Chullin* 8:13) rules that a Jew who seeks out the services of any of the forbidden occults is in fact in violation of a prohibition, regardless of who the practitioner is. In his
opinion, our verse's prohibition against one who "consults" [שָׁאַל] an *Ov* or *Yidoni* sorcerer is to be
applied to the *entire* verse, so that the verse is in effect stating that one may not seek the services
of *any* of these occults. Others come to the same conclusion, citing the verse (*Deuteronomy* 18:14):
כִּי הַגּוֹיִם הָאֵלֶּה אֲשֶׁר אַתָּה יוֹרֵשׁ אוֹתָם אֶל מְעֹנְנִים וְאֶל קֹסְמִים יִשְׁמָעוּ וְאַתָּה לֹא כֵן נָתַן לְךָ ה׳ אֱלֹהֶיךָ, *for these nations
that you are possessing — they hearken to tellers of auspicious times and to diviners, but as for you
— not so has* HASHEM, *your God, given to you.* In their opinion, the latter part of the verse serves as
a prohibition against seeking the services of the practitioners of any of these occults (*Sefer Yerei'im*
§335; see *Maharam Schik,* Mitzvah 510).

Some Rishonim, however, apply the Torah's prohibition against seeking the counsel of these

practitioners only to where it is explicitly stated, i.e., consulting an *Ov* or *Yidoni* sorcerer. In their opinion, the Torah does not express an explicit prohibition against seeking the services of any of the other practitioners mentioned in the verse (*Teshuvos HaRashba HaMeyuchasos LeRamban* §283; *Terumas HaDeshen, Pesakim U'Kesavim* §96). As for the above quoted verse (*For these nations…*), it may be interpreted as merely declaring the unique nature of the Jewish people who, due to their direct prophetic line of communication with Hashem, have no need to turn to such practices to divine the future. It is not, however, a prohibition against doing so (see *Chizkuni* and *Ohr HaChaim* ad loc.).

Rambam's stand on whether there is a prohibition to seek the counsel of the other occult practitioners (beyond *Ov* and *Yidoni*) is seemingly inconsistent, and ultimately the subject of debate. With regard to a *me'onein* (foreteller of auspicious times), it is apparent from *Rambam* (*Hil. Avodah Zarah* 11:9) that whoever acts upon the information received from the *me'onein* is subject to *malkus*. Similarly, with regard to the *menachesh* (one who reads omens), he indicates (ibid. 11:4) that anyone who guides his actions based on omens (not only the *menachesh* himself) has violated the prohibition, and receives *malkus*. Chinuch follows suit, and uses similar language both with regard to the *me'onein* (see Mitzvah 250 at note 15), and with regard to the *menachesh* (Mitzvah 249 at note 15). Accordingly, some suggest that *Rambam* [and Chinuch] hold that the client of any of the forbidden occult practitioners has violated a Biblical prohibition, as above (see *Lechem Mishneh, Hil. Avodah Zarah* 11:7; *Yam Shel Shlomo* ibid.).

On the other hand, with regard to the other occult prohibitions, *Rambam* does not indicate that one who consults with them violates a Biblical prohibition. If anything, he seems to indicate the opposite. For example, with regard to consulting a *koseim* (diviner), *Rambam* (*Sefer HaMitzvos, Lo Saaseh* 31; see also *Hil. Avodah Zarah* 11:7) writes that although doing so is "exceedingly objectionable," the client has *not* violated a prohibition! [Chinuch again follows suit, and states the same in Mitzvah 510 (at note 17).] Similarly, *Rambam* writes that one who goes to a *choveir chaver* (caster of spells) incurs only Rabbinically mandated *makkas mardus* for "participating in the idiocy of the *choveir*" (*Hil. Avodah Zarah* 11:10), indicating once again that the client (although not blameless) has not violated a Biblical prohibition.

Some suggest that the reason why *Rambam* and Chinuch rule that in some instances the client is in violation of a Biblical prohibition, while in others he is not, is based on the wording of the prohibitory verse. Our verse, which introduces the prohibitions against practicing divination, sorcery, and the casting of spells, is written in the singular form. Hence, only the practitioner himself violates the prohibition. In the case of the reader of omens (*menachesh*) and the foreteller of auspicious times (*me'onein*), however, the verse (*Leviticus* 19:26) uses the plural form: לֹא תְנַחֲשׁוּ וְלֹא תְעוֹנֵנוּ, *you* (plural) *may not read omens nor tell auspicious times*. Accordingly, both the practitioner and the client are bound by the verse (*Mishnas Chachamim, Yavin Shemuah* 46:1; see also *Teshuvos Radvaz* I, §485 [end]). In fact, from a careful reading of *Rambam*, it would seem that he may have taken the matter yet further, and understood that the prohibition of reading omens and auspicious times is not limited to one who is specifically skilled in such matters. Thus, there is no room for differentiation between the practitioner and client, as, for all practical purposes, the client, who accepts the belief and follows it, is *himself* a practitioner, and included in the prohibitions of לֹא תְנַחֲשׁוּ וְלֹא תְעוֹנֵנוּ, *you may not read omens nor tell auspicious times* (see *Radvaz* ibid.).

Many commentators, though, maintain that even if there is no specific Biblical prohibition against utilizing the services of many of the various occult practitioners, it is certainly not permitted to do so. In fact, the *Zohar* (*Tazria* 51a, cited by *Beis Yosef, Orach Chaim* 179:16) deems it to be a "great sin," even when doing so on behalf of the ill. [See, however, *Terumas HaDeshen* ibid.; *Teshuvas Nachalas Shivah* §76; and *Mishkenos Yaakov, Yoreh Deah* §41, cited by *Pischei Teshuvah, Yoreh Deah* 179:2, for another position on this matter.] Indeed some of these occult practices have idolatrous leanings [as Chinuch writes in Mitzvah 511 (at note 4)], and therefore must be treated with great severity (*Minchas Chinuch* 511:3; *Radvaz* ibid.). Finally, many assert that turning to any of these practitioners is contrary to the verse (*Deuteronomy* 18:13), תָּמִים תִּהְיֶה עִם ה' אֱלֹהֶיךָ, *You shall be wholehearted with* HASHEM, *your God* (see Mitzvah 510 note 18). Regarding this verse, *Sifrei* writes (ad loc.): Only if one is "wholehearted," is he then "with Hashem." *Malbim* (ad loc.) explains: If one places his trust in Hashem, and does not seek to divine the future — even in ways that may not be technically prohibited — he, in turn, can expect a more direct relationship with the Almighty, one in which Hashem will arrange the events of his life favorably.

מִצְוָה תקטו: שֶׁלֹּא לִדְרֹשׁ אֶל הַמֵּתִים

שֶׁלֹּא לִדְרֹשׁ אֶל הַמֵּתִים. וְעִנְיַן דְּרִישָׁה זוֹ הוּא שֶׁיֵּשׁ בְּנֵי אָדָם מַרְעִיבִין עַצְמָם וְהוֹלְכִים וְלָנִין בְּבֵית הַקְּבָרוֹת כְּדֵי שֶׁיָּבֹא לָהֶם הַמֵּת בַּחֲלוֹם וְיוֹדִיעֵם מַה שֶּׁיִּשְׁאֲלוּ עָלָיו[1], וְיֵשׁ אֲחֵרִים שֶׁלּוֹבְשִׁין בְּגָדִים יְדוּעִים וְאוֹמְרִים דְּבָרִים וּמַקְטִירִין קְטֹרֶת יְדוּעָה וִישֵׁנִים לְבַדָּם כְּדֵי שֶׁיָּבֹא הַמֵּת שֶׁהֵם רוֹצִים בּוֹ וִיסַפֵּר עִמָּהֶם בַּחֲלוֹם[2], וְעַל כָּל מְלָאכוֹת אֵלּוּ וְכַיּוֹצֵא בָּם נֶאֱמַר (דברים י״ח, י׳-י״א) לֹא יִמָּצֵא בְךָ וְגוֹ׳ וְדֹרֵשׁ אֶל הַמֵּתִים.

מִשָּׁרְשֵׁי הַמִּצְוָה מַה שֶּׁכָּתַבְתִּי בְּאִסּוּר כְּשׁוּף בְּסֵדֶר זֶה[3] (מצות תק״י-תקי״א) וּבְסֵדֶר מִשְׁפָּטִים (מצוה ס״ב).

Mitzvah 515
The Prohibition to Inquire of the Dead

לֹא יִמָּצֵא בְךָ ... וְדֹרֵשׁ אֶל הַמֵּתִים

There shall not be found among you ... or one who inquires of the dead (*Deuteronomy* 18:10-11).

שֶׁלֹּא לִדְרֹשׁ אֶל הַמֵּתִים – **We are commanded not to inquire of the dead.** וְעִנְיַן דְּרִישָׁה זוֹ הוּא – **What this "inquiry" refers to is** as follows: שֶׁיֵּשׁ בְּנֵי אָדָם מַרְעִיבִין עַצְמָם – **There are people who starve themselves** וְהוֹלְכִים וְלָנִין בְּבֵית הַקְּבָרוֹת – **and** then **go and sleep** overnight **in the cemetery,** כְּדֵי שֶׁיָּבֹא לָהֶם הַמֵּת בַּחֲלוֹם – **so that the** spirit of **a dead person will come to them in a dream** וְיוֹדִיעֵם מַה שֶּׁיִּשְׁאֲלוּ עָלָיו – **and inform them of what they ask of it.**[1]

Another example of how this forbidden craft was practiced: וְיֵשׁ אֲחֵרִים שֶׁלּוֹבְשִׁין בְּגָדִים יְדוּעִים– **There are others who wear certain types of garments,** וְאוֹמְרִים דְּבָרִים – **and say** certain **things,** וּמַקְטִירִין קְטֹרֶת יְדוּעָה – **and burn a specific type of incense,** וִישֵׁנִים לְבַדָּם – **and** then **sleep alone,** כְּדֵי שֶׁיָּבֹא הַמֵּת שֶׁהֵם רוֹצִים בּוֹ וִיסַפֵּר עִמָּהֶם בַּחֲלוֹם – **so that** the spirit of **the dead with whom they desire** to communicate **should come and tell them in a dream** the information that they wish to know.[2] וְעַל כָּל מְלָאכוֹת אֵלּוּ וְכַיּוֹצֵא בָּם נֶאֱמַר ״לֹא יִמָּצֵא בְךָ וְגוֹ׳ וְדֹרֵשׁ אֶל הַמֵּתִים״ – **With regard to all these deeds, and anything similar, it is stated** (*Deuteronomy* 18:10-11): ***There shall not be found among you ... or one who inquires of the dead.***

Underlying Purpose, Laws, and Applicability of the Mitzvah

מִשָּׁרְשֵׁי הַמִּצְוָה מַה שֶּׁכָּתַבְתִּי בְּאִסּוּר כְּשׁוּף – **Among the underlying purposes of the mitzvah is that which I wrote with regard to the prohibition against sorcery,** בְּסֵדֶר זֶה וּבְסֵדֶר מִשְׁפָּטִים – above, **in this *parashah*** (Mitzvos 510-511)[3] and in ***Parashas Mishpatim*** (Mitzvah 62).

NOTES

1. This is based on the Gemara's statement (*Sanhedrin* 65b) that one who starves himself and sleeps in the cemetery so as to cause a "spirit of impurity" to rest upon him has violated this prohibition. Chinuch, following *Rambam* (*Hil. Avodah Zarah* 11:13), explains that this "spirit of impurity" is the spirit of a dead person that comes in a dream and answers questions posed to it (see also *Yad Ramah, Sanhedrin* 65b; *Smag, Lo Saaseh* 56).

Others, however, explain that the "spirit of impurity" is that of a demon residing in the cemetery who is befriended by the one performing these acts (*Rashi, Sanhedrin* 65b ד״ה שתשרה), enabling him to communicate with the dead (*Bach, Yoreh Deah* 179:14). [For another interpretation, see *Levush, Yoreh Deah* 179:14.]

2. The source of this example is *Rambam* as well (*Hil. Avodah Zarah* 11:13), who concludes that, as a rule, any act that a person does so that the spirit of the dead should come and inform him of some matter is a transgression of this prohibition.

3. See Mitzvah 512 note 12.

וְדִינֵי הַמִּצְוָה בְּסַנְהֶדְרִין[4]. וְנוֹהֵג אִסּוּר זֶה בְּכָל מָקוֹם וּבְכָל זְמַן, בִּזְכָרִים וּנְקֵבוֹת[5]. וְעוֹבֵר עַל זֶה וְעָשָׂה שׁוּם מַעֲשֶׂה כְּדֵי שֶׁיָּבֹא הַמֵּת וְיוֹדִיעֵהוּ שׁוּם דָּבָר חַיָּב מַלְקוֹת[6].

וְדִינֵי הַמִּצְוָה בְּסַנְהֶדְרִין – **The laws of the mitzvah are found in** Tractate ***Sanhedrin*** (65b).[4] וְנוֹהֵג אִסּוּר זֶה בְּכָל מָקוֹם וּבְכָל זְמַן – **This prohibition applies in all locations and in all times** בִּזְכָרִים וּנְקֵבוֹת – **to men and women.**[5]

וְעוֹבֵר עַל זֶה וְעָשָׂה שׁוּם מַעֲשֶׂה – **One who transgresses this** prohibition, **and performs some action** כְּדֵי שֶׁיָּבֹא הַמֵּת וְיוֹדִיעֵהוּ שׁוּם דָּבָר – **so that the** spirit of the **dead will come and inform him of some matter,** חַיָּב מַלְקוֹת – **is liable to *malkus*.**[6]

NOTES

4. These laws are codified in *Rambam, Hil. Avodah Zarah* 11:13 and in *Shulchan Aruch, Yoreh Deah* 179:13-14.

5. That is, it applies both in Eretz Yisrael and the Diaspora, and whether the *Beis HaMikdash* is standing or not. In addition, it applies to women as well, in accordance with the general rule pertaining to mitzvah-prohibitions.

6. He is liable even if ultimately no spirit communicates with him, for the words of the verse, וְדֹרֵשׁ אֶל הַמֵּתִים, *one who inquires of the dead*, forbid the act of inquiring of the dead, even if he receives no response (*Mishnas Chachamim, Tzafnas Pane'ach* 49:2).

[Chinuch specifies that an action was performed, being that one is liable to *malkus* only if the prohibition involves an action (see Mitzvah 513, with note 6). The act is prohibited, however, whether or not an action was performed (see *Minchas Chinuch* here; see, however, *Beis Yosef, Yoreh Deah* 179:13-14).]

☙ Insight: Praying at Graves and Making Requests of the Departed

This mitzvah forbids being דֹּרֵשׁ אֶל הַמֵּתִים, *inquiring of the dead* (*Deuteronomy* 18:11), which, as Chinuch explains, is a craft that is performed by employing various techniques in order to have the spirit of the dead appear in a dream and answer one's questions. The question arises: What would the law be with regard to other forms of "communicating" with the spirits of those who have died? Indeed, is it permissible to pray at the gravesite of a departed loved one or righteous individual, beseeching him to utilize his influence in Heaven to assist us, or are such requests considered a form of "consulting the dead"?

One early authority, R' Chaim Paltiel (cited in *Bach, Yoreh Deah* 217:51), argued that such prayers are in fact problematic. R' Chaim Paltiel acknowledges the fact that the custom of praying at the gravesite of righteous ancestors certainly has ancient roots. We find that Caleb prayed at the burial place of the Patriarchs in Hebron for the spiritual strength not to be influenced by the scheme of the other spies, who sinned by falsely slandering Eretz Yisrael (see *Numbers* 13:22 with *Rashi*). Such burial places, explains R' Chaim Paltiel, are considered hallowed ground, because of the righteous people buried there, and are therefore preferred places for prayer. Nevertheless, R' Paltiel expresses concern that the common folk may not fully understand this. They may erroneously approach praying at such gravesites with the belief that the prayers are to be directed to the spirits of the dead, which may touch on the prohibition of being דֹּרֵשׁ אֶל הַמֵּתִים, *inquiring of the dead.* Therefore, in practice, he would dissuade people from going to pray at gravesites.

Other authorities (*Bach* ibid.; *Shach, Yoreh Deah* 179:15), however, take issue with this conclusion. They note that common custom certainly supports praying at the gravesites of one's ancestors. Praying at the gravesites of the righteous can be particularly beneficial, not only because it is hallowed ground (as mentioned above), but because such prayers evoke the merit of those who are buried there (*Maharil, Hil. Taanis*), and thus are more readily accepted (*Mishnah Berurah* 581:27). Accordingly, many argue that one should not discourage such practices (*Bach* and *Shach* ibid.). Nevertheless, these authorities caution that such prayers must be recited in an appropriate manner. They must not be directed to the dead themselves, but rather, must be addressed to Hashem alone (*Maharil* and *Bach* ibid.).

Others, however, take a lenient position on this matter as well, asserting that while praying to

the dead as though they have some power to answer prayers is certainly forbidden (and is in fact a form of idolatry), we are permitted to request of them to intercede in Heaven on our behalf. That is, according to this opinion, one is permitted to directly address the souls of the departed as long as he is merely asking them to be advocates before the Heavenly Throne. In this manner, it is clear that all prayers are directed to Hashem alone, and that the departed are simply being asked to intercede on our behalf to Hashem (see *Minchas Elazar* I, §68; *Gesher HaChaim* II, §26; *Pri Megadim, Eishel Avraham* 581:16). As support for this approach, these authorities note that in its description of Caleb's prayer in Hebron, the Gemara (*Sotah* 34b) indicates that he spoke *directly* to the spirits of the Patriarchs, saying: "*My ancestors! Request mercy for me that I be saved from [entanglement in] the plot of the spies.*" While some suggest that he was merely speaking expressively, attempting to invoke the merit of the Patriarchs, while in fact talking directly to Hashem (*Teshuvos Maharam Schik, Orach Chaim* §293), others disagree. They maintain that he was addressing our Forefathers directly, asking them to intercede in Heaven on his behalf (*Sefer Chassidim* §450; *Chadrei Deah, Yoreh Deah* §179 ד"ה ש"ך; *Minchas Elazar* ibid.). Furthermore, in later generations we find Sages of the Talmud acting in a similar manner. The Gemara (*Taanis* 23b) records how R' Mani, who was being harassed by some individuals, went to the burial place of his father and exclaimed, "Father, Father! These people are harassing me," effectively asking his father to beseech Heaven to put a stop to the persecution. In addition, some point out that common custom seems to support the idea of addressing the souls of the departed directly and asking them to intercede on our behalf, to the extent that there are prayers printed in *Maaneh Lashon* (an early collection of prayers related to death and dying), which say exactly that (*Maharam Schik* and *Minchas Elazar* ibid.; *Pri Megadim* ibid.).

Furthermore, *Zohar* (*Acharei* 71b) explains that praying at the gravesite of the righteous is fundamentally different from the practice of "inquiring of the dead." While inquiring of the dead involves employing pagan practices with the aim of bringing impure spirits upon oneself, praying at the gravesite of the righteous is a holy act. It involves approaching Hashem with humility and repentance, while asking the souls of the righteous to intercede on our behalf before Hashem as well. Furthermore, *Zohar* notes that enlisting these souls to pray for us cannot accurately be termed "inquiring of the *dead*," for the righteous are considered living even after their passing (see *Berachos* 18a). Accordingly, it is appropriate to inform the souls of the righteous of our suffering in this world, so that these "living" souls can then advocate on our behalf before the Heavenly Throne.

Although there are authorities who see the above *Zohar* and other citations as conclusive proof that one may direct requests to the souls of the departed, asking them to be advocates on our behalf (*Minchas Elazar* and *Gesher HaChaim* loc. cit.), others remain hesitant to support such practices (*Maharam Schik* ibid.; *Minchas Yitzchak* VIII §53). Still others remain steadfast in their insistence that while praying at the gravesites of the righteous is meritorious, such prayers must not be addressed to the departed, even to simply ask them to be advocates on our behalf. Rather one must address Hashem alone, with the hope that the holiness of the place and the merit of those buried there stand him in good stead (*Chayei Adam* 138:5; *Mishnah Berurah* 581:27).

[For further discussion, see *Darchei Teshuvah, Yoreh Deah* 179:36 and *Igros Moshe, Orach Chaim* V §43.6. For discussion of whether one may ask the angels on high to bring our prayers before the Heavenly Throne, see Introduction to *Otzar HaTefillos* §3; *Gesher HaChaim* II §26.]

מִצְוָה תקטז

מִצְוָה לִשְׁמֹעַ מִכָּל נָבִיא וְנָבִיא שֶׁיִּהְיֶה בְּכָל דּוֹר וָדוֹר אִם לֹא יוֹסִיף וְלֹא יִגְרַע בְּמִצְוֹת הַתּוֹרָה

שֶׁנִּצְטַוִּינוּ לִשְׁמֹעַ בְּקוֹל כָּל נָבִיא מֵהַנְּבִיאִים בְּכָל מַה שֶׁיְּצַוֵּנוּ[1], וַאֲפִלּוּ יְצַוֶּה אוֹתָנוּ לַעֲשׂוֹת בְּהֶפֶךְ מִצְוָה אַחַת מִן הַמִּצְווֹת אוֹ אֲפִלּוּ הַרְבֵּה מֵהֶם לְפִי שָׁעָה, חוּץ מֵעֲבוֹדָה זָרָה[2], שׁוֹמְעִין לוֹ, כִּי בֶּאֱמֶת אַחַר שֶׁהוּא נְבִיא אֱמֶת כָּל כַּוָּנוֹתָיו לְטוֹבָה

Mitzvah 516

The Obligation to Obey Each Prophet in Any Generation Provided That He Does Not Add to or Detract From the Torah's Commandments

נָבִיא מִקִּרְבְּךָ מֵאַחֶיךָ כָּמֹנִי יָקִים לְךָ ה׳ אֱלֹהֶיךָ אֵלָיו תִּשְׁמָעוּן

A prophet from your midst, from your brethren, like me, shall HASHEM, your God, establish for you — to him you shall hearken (*Deuteronomy* 18:15).

One of the Thirteen Principles of Faith enumerated by *Rambam* is that Hashem speaks to us through His prophets. How do we know if a person is an authentic prophet of Hashem? Chinuch explained in Mitzvah 424 that if an upright and devout person — meaning, one of exemplary character and good deeds who has devoted himself exclusively to the pursuit of spiritual perfection — prophetically predicts future events in detail several times, and everything comes true exactly as he predicted, he is established as a prophet. If he is wrong in even one minor detail, he is not a prophet, but perhaps a sorcerer with vague knowledge of the future who is externally devout (see *Rambam, Hil. Yesodei HaTorah* 10:1-3). A person can also be established as a prophet of Hashem if a previously established prophet testifies that he is a true prophet. In that case, the new prophet is not required to prove himself with predictions of future events (*Rambam* ibid. 10:5).

Once a person has been established as a prophet of Hashem, we are prohibited by Mitzvah 424 from challenging him, and are commanded by this mitzvah to obey his directives.

שֶׁנִּצְטַוִּינוּ לִשְׁמֹעַ בְּקוֹל כָּל נָבִיא מֵהַנְּבִיאִים בְּכָל מַה שֶׁיְּצַוֵּנוּ — We are commanded to hearken to the voice of each of the authentic **prophets in anything that he commands us.**[1] **וַאֲפִלּוּ יְצַוֶּה אוֹתָנוּ לַעֲשׂוֹת בְּהֶפֶךְ מִצְוָה אַחַת מִן הַמִּצְווֹת אוֹ אֲפִלּוּ הַרְבֵּה מֵהֶם לְפִי שָׁעָה — Moreover, even if he commands us to do the opposite of one of the mitzvos, or even** the opposite of **many of them, on a temporary basis, חוּץ מֵעֲבוֹדָה זָרָה — with the exception of idol worship, שׁוֹמְעִין לוֹ — we** are to **obey him.**[2] כִּי בֶּאֱמֶת אַחַר שֶׁהוּא נְבִיא אֱמֶת כָּל כַּוָּנוֹתָיו לְטוֹבָה — We need not suspect that he intends to

---

NOTES

1. The primary role of a prophet is to strengthen observance of the Torah. He urges the people to diligently fulfill the mitzvos, and warns them against violating any of the prohibitions. We are obviously commanded to heed his words in those areas. Additionally, a prophet may convey a message from Hashem about personal matters or seemingly mundane things. For example, he may tell us that he has received a prophecy that we are to travel to a certain place, or refrain from traveling there; that we are to go out to war, or refrain from going out; that we are to build a certain structure, or refrain from building it. In all such cases — whether the prophet's message pertains to Torah observance or any other matter — we are commanded by this mitzvah to obey his directives, as they are communications to us from Hashem (*Rambam, Hil. Yesodei HaTorah* 9:2).

2. We must obey a prophet's instruction to temporarily

וְכָל אֲשֶׁר יַעֲשֶׂה הוּא עוֹשֶׂה לְחַזֵּק הַדָּת וּלְהַאֲמִין בַּשֵּׁם בָּרוּךְ הוּא, וְעַל זֶה נֶאֱמַר (דברים י״ח, ט״ו) נָבִיא מִקִּרְבְּךָ מֵאַחֶיךָ כָּמֹנִי יָקִים לְךָ ה׳ אֱלֹהֶיךָ אֵלָיו תִּשְׁמָעוּן, וְכֵן אָמְרוּ בְּסִפְרִי (כאן), אֵלָיו תִּשְׁמָעוּן, אֲפִלּוּ יֹאמַר לְךָ לַעֲבֹר עַל אַחַת מִן הַמִּצְווֹת לְפִי שָׁעָה שְׁמַע לוֹ[3].

מִשָּׁרְשֵׁי הַמִּצְוָה, לְפִי שֶׁתַּכְלִית מַעֲלַת הָאָדָם הִיא הַשָּׂגַת הַנְּבוּאָה, וְאֵין לוֹ לְבֶן אָדָם בְּעוֹלָמוֹ אֲמִתַּת יְדִיעָה בִּדְבָרִים כַּאֲמִתַּת יְדִיעָתוֹ בִּנְבוּאָה שֶׁהִיא הַיְדִיעָה שֶׁאֵין אַחֲרֶיהָ

---

lead us astray, **for in truth, since he is** already known to us as **an authentic prophet** of Hashem, **all his intentions are** presumed to be **for the good,** וְכָל אֲשֶׁר יַעֲשֶׂה הוּא עוֹשֶׂה לְחַזֵּק הַדָּת וּלְהַאֲמִין בַּשֵּׁם בָּרוּךְ הוּא – **and everything that he does is** presumed to be **done for** the purpose of **strengthening the** Jewish **religion and** increasing **faith in Hashem, blessed is He.**

וְעַל זֶה נֶאֱמַר – **Regarding this it is stated** (*Deuteronomy* 18:15): "נָבִיא מִקִּרְבְּךָ מֵאַחֶיךָ כָּמֹנִי יָקִים לְךָ ה׳ אֱלֹהֶיךָ אֵלָיו תִּשְׁמָעוּן" – ***A prophet from your midst, from your brethren, like me, shall HASHEM, your God, establish for you – to him you shall hearken.*** וְכֵן אָמְרוּ בְּסִפְרִי – **And so have [the Sages] stated in *Sifrei*** (to the verse): "אֵלָיו תִּשְׁמָעוּן" – When it states, ***to him you shall hearken,*** it means: אֲפִלּוּ יֹאמַר לְךָ לַעֲבֹר עַל אַחַת מִן הַמִּצְווֹת לְפִי שָׁעָה שְׁמַע לוֹ – **even** if **he tells you to transgress one of the mitzvos on a temporary basis, hearken to him.**[3]

Underlying Purpose of the Mitzvah

מִשָּׁרְשֵׁי הַמִּצְוָה – **Among the underlying purposes of the mitzvah** is that a prophet is worthy of being obeyed, לְפִי שֶׁתַּכְלִית מַעֲלַת הָאָדָם הִיא הַשָּׂגַת הַנְּבוּאָה – **because the greatest height a person can attain is to experience prophecy.** וְאֵין לוֹ לְבֶן אָדָם בְּעוֹלָמוֹ אֲמִתַּת יְדִיעָה בִּדְבָרִים כַּאֲמִתַּת יְדִיעָתוֹ בִּנְבוּאָה – This is because **man in this world has no true knowledge of any matter** that is **comparable to the True Knowledge he acquires through prophecy,** שֶׁהִיא הַיְדִיעָה שֶׁאֵין אַחֲרֶיהָ

NOTES

set aside any mitzvah except for idolatry.

Now, if a prophet claims that one of the mitzvos has *permanently* been canceled and we should no longer observe it, we are not to believe him. Similarly, if he claims that a mitzvah has been changed and from now on we should observe it differently from the way we have been accustomed to by the Oral Tradition, we are not to believe him. This applies even if he was previously an established prophet. He is known to be stating a falsehood, for no prophet is on the level of Moses, so none can override the Torah that Moses taught us; and the Torah itself states in numerous places that its laws are everlasting and will not be canceled or changed! The false prophet is put to death (*Rambam* ibid. 8:3, 9:1).

If, on the other hand, a prophet states that one of the mitzvos has *temporarily* been suspended, and due to extraordinary circumstances we should act differently *at a particular time*, we are to obey him. In this case, he is not contradicting the Torah, but informing us of a one-time directive from Hashem; and since he has been established as a true prophet, we accept his words. The only exception is when the prophet tells us to engage in idolatry. Even if he claims that Hashem has permitted one specific instance of idol worship, he is known to be false. The Torah states explicitly (*Deuteronomy* 13:2-6) that any prophet who claims that we were commanded to worship an idol shall be put to death, for the prohibition of idolatry will never be suspended even temporarily (*Rambam* ibid. 9:2-5; see also *Meiri, Sanhedrin* 90a and *Ramban, Deuteronomy* 13:4).

3. In a classic application of this law, Elijah the Prophet brought offerings on Mount Carmel when he challenged the false prophets of *Baal* (*I Kings* Ch. 18; see Mitzvah 510, at note 27). This was essentially a forbidden act, since the *Beis HaMikdash* had been built, and it was prohibited to bring offerings anywhere else but there (see Mitzvah 439, and note 5 there). Elijah, however, had received a prophecy authorizing him to bring offerings on Mount Carmel that one time. As Scripture relates, all of Israel assembled at Mount Carmel, and the prophets of *Baal* and Elijah each erected altars and placed offerings on them. The prophets of *Baal* cried out to their deity from morning until mid-afternoon, but their offerings remained unburnt. Then, at the time of the afternoon *tamid* offering, Elijah prayed to Hashem that He should make it known that He is God in Israel and Elijah is His servant, and that Elijah had done this thing by His Word. A fire descended from Heaven and consumed Elijah's offerings, and upon seeing this all the people fell to the ground and proclaimed, *"HASHEM – He is the God! HASHEM – He is the God!"* See *Sanhedrin* 89b and *Rambam* ibid. 9:3. [See *Tosafos* (*Sanhedrin* 89b ד״ה אליהו and *Yevamos* 90b ד״ה וליגמר) for a somewhat different understanding of Elijah's authority to bring those offerings.]

פִּקְפּוּק כִּי הִיא תָּבֹא מִמַּעְיַן הָאֱמֶת[4], וּמְעַטִּים מִבְּנֵי הָעוֹלָם זוֹכִים בָּהּ וְעוֹלִים אֵלֶיהָ כִּי הַסֻּלָּם גָּדוֹל מְאֹד, רַגְלוֹ בָּאָרֶץ וְרֹאשׁוֹ מַגִּיעַ הַשָּׁמַיְמָה[5], וּמִי זֶה הָאִישׁ יְרֵא הַשֵּׁם יִזְכֶּה וְיַעֲלֶה בְּהַר ה׳ וְיָקוּם בִּמְקוֹם קָדְשׁוֹ[6] אֶחָד מֵאַלְפֵי רִבְבוֹת אֲנָשִׁים הוּא הַמַּשִּׂיג לְמַעֲלָה זוֹ וּבְדוֹר שֶׁרָאוּי לְכָךְ[7], עַל כֵּן צִוָּתָנוּ הַתּוֹרָה כִּי בְּהַגִּיעַ אִישׁ אֶחָד בַּדּוֹר אֶל הַמַּעֲלָה הַזֹּאת וְיִהְיֶה יָדוּעַ אֶצְלֵנוּ בְּעִנְיָנוֹ וּבְכֹשֶׁר מַעֲשֵׂהוּ כִּי נֶאֱמָן לְנָבִיא[8], שֶׁנִּשְׁמַע אֵלָיו בְּכָל אֲשֶׁר יְצַוֶּה כִּי הוּא הַיּוֹדֵעַ דֶּרֶךְ הָאֱמֶת וְיַדְרִיכֵנוּ בוֹ, וְלֹא נִשָּׂא נַפְשֵׁנוּ לְהַמְרוֹת פִּיו וְלַחֲלֹק עִמּוֹ כִּי הַמַּחֲלֹקֶת עָלָיו בְּשׁוּם דָּבָר הוּא טָעוּת גָּמוּר וְחֶסְרוֹן יְדִיעַת הָאֱמֶת[9].

פִּקְפּוּק – as [prophecy] is the only form of **knowledge that is not subject to** any **reservation** or doubt, **כִּי הִיא תָּבֹא מִמַּעְיַן הָאֱמֶת – since it comes from the Wellspring of Truth.**[4] **וּמְעַטִּים מִבְּנֵי הָעוֹלָם זוֹכִים בָּהּ וְעוֹלִים אֵלֶיהָ – Few human beings merit this** Knowledge **and ascend to** the level of perfection needed to attain **it, כִּי הַסֻּלָּם גָּדוֹל מְאֹד – for the ladder** of self-improvement leading to it **is very tall, רַגְלוֹ בָּאָרֶץ וְרֹאשׁוֹ מַגִּיעַ הַשָּׁמַיְמָה – its foot** being set **on earth while its head reaches the Heavens.**[5] **וּמִי זֶה הָאִישׁ יְרֵא הַשֵּׁם יִזְכֶּה וְיַעֲלֶה בְּהַר ה׳ וְיָקוּם בִּמְקוֹם קָדְשׁוֹ – Who is the man who fears Hashem** sufficiently **to merit to ascend the mountain of Hashem and stand in the place of His sanctity?**[6] **אֶחָד מֵאַלְפֵי רִבְבוֹת אֲנָשִׁים הוּא הַמַּשִּׂיג לְמַעֲלָה זוֹ – It is** no more than **one out of thousands upon tens of thousands of people who attains this** exalted **level, וּבְדוֹר שֶׁרָאוּי לְכָךְ – and** even that unique individual can attain it only if he lives **in a generation that is worthy of this** gift of prophecy![7]

עַל כֵּן צִוָּתָנוּ הַתּוֹרָה – The Torah therefore commands us כִּי בְּהַגִּיעַ אִישׁ אֶחָד בַּדּוֹר אֶל הַמַּעֲלָה הַזֹּאת – that when one man in a worthy **generation does** indeed **reach this** exalted **level, וְיִהְיֶה יָדוּעַ אֶצְלֵנוּ בְּעִנְיָנוֹ וּבְכֹשֶׁר מַעֲשֵׂהוּ כִּי נֶאֱמָן לְנָבִיא – and he is known to us, by** virtue of **his character and the quality of his deeds, to be trustworthy as a prophet,**[8] **שֶׁנִּשְׁמַע אֵלָיו בְּכָל אֲשֶׁר יְצַוֶּה – we are to hearken to him in everything that he commands** us, even if it involves a temporary contradiction of what the Torah teaches, **כִּי הוּא הַיּוֹדֵעַ דֶּרֶךְ הָאֱמֶת וְיַדְרִיכֵנוּ בוֹ – for he is the one who knows the Way of Truth and will guide us on it. וְלֹא נִשָּׂא נַפְשֵׁנוּ לְהַמְרוֹת פִּיו וְלַחֲלֹק עִמּוֹ – We should not take upon ourselves to disobey his word or to argue with him, כִּי הַמַּחֲלֹקֶת עָלָיו בְּשׁוּם דָּבָר הוּא טָעוּת גָּמוּר וְחֶסְרוֹן יְדִיעַת הָאֱמֶת – for arguing with him in regard to any matter is a complete error and** stems from **a lack of knowledge of the truth.**[9]

NOTES

4. Prophecy is not merely a message given to the prophet, but, more basically, a *revelation* of Heavenly wisdom to him. Sometimes, he may be granted this revelation simply to expand his intellect and deepen his knowledge of esoteric matters, not so that he should share it with others. And, sometimes, he may be instructed to transmit the prophecy to the people (*Rambam* ibid. 7:7; see also *Derech Hashem* III:3-4). In any event, the nature of genuine prophecy is that it is *absolutely* true. [See Mitzvah 510, at notes 3-5; and see further, Mitzvah 517 note 5.]

5. [Stylistic paraphrase of *Genesis* 28:12.] The rigorous demands of this ladder of self-perfection are discussed by *Rambam* in *Hil. Yesodei HaTorah* 7:1, *Shemoneh Perakim* Ch. 7, and *Moreh Nevuchim* II:36-38.

6. Stylistic paraphrase of *Psalms* 25:12 and 24:3.

7. The Gemara (*Sanhedrin* 11a) mentions certain individuals in Talmudic times who were worthy of having the Divine Spirit rest upon them but were not granted it because their generation was unworthy.

[Chinuch's statement that only one in "thousands upon tens of thousands of people" attains this level is difficult to understand, in light of the Gemara's comment (*Megillah* 14a) that the Jewish people, over the course of their history, had more than a million prophets. Perhaps, Chinuch refers to those who received prophecy that they were commanded to convey to the nation. Scripture records the words of only a select few prophets in this category.]

8. I.e., he has the personal qualifications of a prophet, as mentioned in the introduction to the mitzvah [and he has been proven to be a prophet, as explained there].

9. *Rambam* (ibid. 7:7, 9:3) indicates that the obligation to obey the prophet applies only when he issues an instruction in the Name of Hashem (see *Lechem Mishneh* to 9:3). This seems to be the opinion of *Ramban* (*Deuteronomy* 18:16), as well. *Tosafos* (*Yevamos* 90b ד״ה וליגמר מיניה, *Sanhedrin* 89b ד״ה אליהו), however, state that once a person is established as a prophet,

דִּינֵי הַמִּצְוָה מְבֹאָרִים בְּסוֹף סַנְהֶדְרִין[10].
וְנוֹהֶגֶת מִצְוָה זוֹ בִּזְכָרִים וּנְקֵבוֹת[11], בְּכָל זְמַן שֶׁיִּמָּצֵא נָבִיא בֵּינֵינוּ[12].
וְעוֹבֵר עַל זֶה וְלֹא יִשְׁמַע אֵלָיו חַיָּב מִיתָה בִּידֵי שָׁמַיִם, וּכְמוֹ שֶׁכָּתוּב (שם) וְהָיָה הָאִישׁ אֲשֶׁר לֹא יִשְׁמַע אֶל דְּבָרַי אֲשֶׁר יְדַבֵּר בִּשְׁמִי אָנֹכִי אֶדְרֹשׁ מֵעִמּוֹ[13]. וְאָמְרוּ חֲכָמֵינוּ זִכְרוֹנָם לִבְרָכָה בְּסַנְהֶדְרִין (פ״ט ע״א), שְׁלֹשָׁה מִיתָתָן בִּידֵי שָׁמַיִם, הָעוֹבֵר עַל דִּבְרֵי נָבִיא,

Laws of the Mitzvah

דִּינֵי הַמִּצְוָה מְבֹאָרִים בְּסוֹף סַנְהֶדְרִין – **The laws of the mitzvah are set out at the end of** Tractate ***Sanhedrin.***[10]

Applicability of the Mitzvah

וְנוֹהֶגֶת מִצְוָה זוֹ בִּזְכָרִים וּנְקֵבוֹת – **This mitzvah applies to** both **men and women,**[11] בְּכָל זְמַן שֶׁיִּמָּצֵא נָבִיא בֵּינֵינוּ – **in any period when a prophet is found among us.**[12]

וְעוֹבֵר עַל זֶה וְלֹא יִשְׁמַע אֵלָיו – **One who transgresses this [mitzvah] and does not obey** an instruction issued by **[a prophet]** חַיָּב מִיתָה בִּידֵי שָׁמַיִם – **is liable to death at the hands of Heaven,** וּכְמוֹ שֶׁכָּתוּב – **as it is stated** (*Deuteronomy* 18:19): ״וְהָיָה הָאִישׁ אֲשֶׁר לֹא יִשְׁמַע אֶל דְּבָרַי אֲשֶׁר יְדַבֵּר בִּשְׁמִי אָנֹכִי אֶדְרֹשׁ מֵעִמּוֹ״ – ***And it shall be that the man who will not hearken to My words that [the prophet] will speak in My Name, I*** (God) ***will exact from him.***[13]

Chinuch notes that this punishment actually applies in three cases:

וְאָמְרוּ חֲכָמֵינוּ זִכְרוֹנָם לִבְרָכָה בְּסַנְהֶדְרִין – **Our Sages, of blessed memory, stated in** Tractate ***Sanhedrin*** (89a): שְׁלֹשָׁה מִיתָתָן בִּידֵי שָׁמַיִם – There are **three** people **whose deaths** for prophecy-related offenses **are at the hands of Heaven:** הָעוֹבֵר עַל דִּבְרֵי נָבִיא – (1) **one who transgresses**

NOTES

we are obligated to obey even an instruction that he issues on his own. This applies even if it involves a temporary suspension of a law of the Torah, as long as its purpose is to ultimately strengthen observance of the Torah.

Chinuch states that we must hearken to "everything" that the prophet commands us, and he makes no mention of the prophet issuing his command in the Name of Hashem. *Minchas Chinuch* (§1) therefore infers that Chinuch follows the opinion of *Tosafos,* that we are obligated to heed even the prophet's own instructions. See also Mitzvah 517, at note 7.

[As for the requirement mentioned by *Tosafos,* that the purpose of such an instruction must be to strengthen Torah observance, this is implied by Chinuch's words, "for he is the one who knows the Way of Truth and will guide us on it." What Chinuch means is that whenever a trustworthy prophet issues an instruction, we may *assume* that its purpose is to guide us on the Way of Truth, even if at face value it appears contrary to the Torah (*Maharam Schik;* see *Meiri, Sanhedrin* 90a).]

10. The laws appear there on 89a-90a, which is the end of Chapter *Hanechnakin* (Ch. 10), the next to last chapter of the tractate. However, Rishonim of Chinuch's times (as well as current editions of the Mishnah) have the chapters in a different order, with *Hanechnakin* as the last chapter (Ch. 11), so these laws are actually at the end of the tractate.

The laws of the mitzvah, including how to identify a true prophet, are codified in *Rambam, Hil. Yesodei HaTorah* Chs. 7-10.

11. In accordance with the rule of mitzvah-obligations that are not time-specific (see General Introduction, VI).

12. The obligation also, obviously, applies in any location where we are instructed by a prophet to do something.

13. Chinuch's words here are based on *Rambam* (ibid. 9:2, and *Hil. Sanhedrin* 19:3) who states that one who "transgresses" the words of a prophet [הָעוֹבֵר עַל דְּבָרָיו] is liable to death at the hands of Heaven. This would include someone who disobeys the prophet for any personal reason. *Minchas Chinuch* (§2) notes, however, that the Mishnah (*Sanhedrin* 89a) uses the expression, וְהַמְוַותֵּר עַל דִּבְרֵי נָבִיא, *one who disregards the words of a prophet,* which *Rashi* explain to mean that the person *discards* the prophet's message and does not care about it. According to *Rashi,* it would seem that the punishment of death is reserved for someone who disobeys because he considers the prophet's words to have no value. A person who disobeys a prophet for a personal reason, such as lust, does not incur death, even though he has transgressed the mitzvah-obligation to hearken to the words of a prophet.

וְנָבִיא שֶׁעָבַר עַל דִּבְרֵי עַצְמוֹ[14], וְהַכּוֹבֵשׁ נְבוּאָתוֹ[15], וְכָל זֶה בְּמַשְׁמַע הַכָּתוּב, שֶׁאָמַר אֲשֶׁר לֹא יִשְׁמַע וְגוֹ', וְאָמְרוּ זִכְרוֹנָם לִבְרָכָה קְרִי בֵּהּ לֹא יִשָּׁמַע[16], לֹא יַשְׁמִיעַ[17].

---

the words of a prophet (as stated above); וְנָבִיא שֶׁעָבַר עַל דִּבְרֵי עַצְמוֹ – (2) **a prophet who transgresses his own words** of prophecy;[14] וְהַכּוֹבֵשׁ נְבוּאָתוֹ – **and** (3) **[a prophet] who suppresses his prophecy,** i.e., who fails to communicate Hashem's prophetic message to the people.[15] וְכָל זֶה בְּמַשְׁמַע הַכָּתוּב – **All** three of **these are** included **in the implication of the verse,** שֶׁאָמַר "אֲשֶׁר לֹא יִשְׁמַע וְגוֹ'" – **as it states:** ***asher lo yishma*** *(the man "who will not hearken" to My words ... I will exact from him),* וְאָמְרוּ זִכְרוֹנָם לִבְרָכָה – **and [the Sages], of blessed memory, stated** (ibid.): קְרִי בֵּהּ לֹא יִשָּׁמַע – **You may read this as,** *asher* ***lo yishama*** (who "will not be hearkened to" regarding My words),[16] לֹא יַשְׁמִיעַ – and you may also read it as, *asher* ***lo yashmia*** (who "will not make heard" My words).[17]

NOTES

14. Even if the prophet's words are contradicted by another prophet, he may not deviate from the prophecy that he himself received, and if he does he incurs death at the hands of Heaven (see *Teshuvos HaRashba* 1:11 and *Minchas Chinuch* §3). For an instance in which this punishment was imposed, see *I Kings* Ch. 13.

15. This refers to a case where the prophet was instructed in his prophecy to transmit it to the people (see above, note 4).

16. A Torah scroll has no vowels, and its reading is based on the Tradition received from Sinai. Since there are no vowels, the Sages were authorized to expound verses based on alternative vowelizing of the words, as long as these readings are consistent with the laws received in the Oral Torah (see Insight to Mitzvah 426). Here, the Oral Torah teaches that there are three sinners who are liable to the punishment mentioned in the verse, and the Sages showed that all three are alluded to in the various ways the verse can be vowelized.

One possible reading is לֹא יִשָּׁמַע, *lo yishama,* meaning, "will not be hearkened to." The verse thus imposes death on the *prophet* whose words are not heeded. Now, a prophet surely cannot be faulted if others ignore his words. Rather, according to this reading, the verse means that if the prophet does not heed his own words – thus *making* his words "not be hearkened to" – he is liable to death (see *Rashi, Sanhedrin* 89a ד"ה קרי ביה, with *Hagahos HaBach* and *Aruch LaNer* there; cf. *Tos. Yom Tov, Sanhedrin* 11:5).

17. According to this reading, the verse teaches that a prophet who fails to publicize his prophecy (when he has been instructed to do so) is liable to death. See *Gur Aryeh* to the verse and *Tos. Yom Tov* ibid.

[The case of a prophet who suppresses his prophecy is related to the case of one who does not hearken to a prophet's words (which is the explicit subject of the verse), because by suppressing the Word of God that was transmitted to him, the prophet causes people not to hearken to it (*Cheshbonos Shel Mitzvah [Aderes];* see *Lechem Mishneh, Hil. Yesodei HaTorah* 9:3).]

Insight: Was Jonah Guilty of Suppressing a Prophecy?

Chinuch states (at note 15) that if a prophet suppresses his prophecy, meaning, he fails to convey to the people a prophetic message that Hashem instructed him to convey, he is liable to death at the hands of Heaven. The Gemara (*Sanhedrin* 89a) mentions that Jonah is an example of such a prophet. Jonah was instructed by Hashem to go to the city of Nineveh and "call out against her, for their wickedness has ascended before Me," (*Jonah* 1:2), but he chose instead to flee to Tarshish "from before Hashem" (ibid. v. 3). Curiously, though, Jonah did not suffer death at the hands of Heaven. Hashem sent a mighty storm that threatened to break the ship that Jonah had taken, and his shipmates cast him into the sea, where he was swallowed by a giant fish. After he prayed to Hashem from the innards of the fish, Hashem commanded it to cast Jonah up onto dry land. Hashem then spoke to Jonah a second time and sent him to deliver His message of destruction to Nineveh, and this time, he carried out his mission and the people of Nineveh repented (see *Jonah* Chs. 1-3). Commentators wonder why Jonah was not punished with death for his initial sin. Moreover, being that the sin of suppressing prophecy is so severe as to be punishable by death, how could Jonah – a righteous prophet – have committed it in the first place?

Rashi (ibid. 1:3) cites a teaching of the Sages (*Mechilta,* introduction to *Parashas Bo*) that Jonah's intention was for the good of the Jewish people. He reasoned that if the people of Nineveh repented as a result of his prophecy, it would reflect badly on the Jews, who had been chastised by many

prophets and had not repented of their sins. He therefore attempted to avoid going to Nineveh. As the Midrash states (*Mechilta* ibid.): Jonah petitioned for the honor of the son (i.e., Israel), and did not petition for the honor of the Father (i.e., Hashem). In fact, according to one opinion in the Midrash (ibid.), Jonah boarded the ship *expecting* to be caught in a storm and cast into the sea, as he wanted to sacrifice his life for the sake of preserving the honor of the Jewish people.

Nevertheless, the question remains: Despite his rationalization, how could Jonah have defied the command of Hashem and suppressed his prophecy? Another basic question is, what did Jonah expect to gain by taking a ship to Tarshish? Did he actually think he could flee from God?

Rashi (citing *Mechilta* ibid.) addresses this last question as well, and explains that the spirit of prophecy rests upon a prophet only in Eretz Yisrael, but not outside the Land. Jonah reasoned that if he fled Eretz Yisrael, he would not experience prophecy, so he would be exempt from delivering Hashem's message. [This is implicit in the verse, which states that Jonah sought to flee מִלִּפְנֵי ה׳, "from *before* Hashem," not מִפְּנֵי ה׳, "from Hashem" (*Abarbanel* and *Malbim* ad loc.).] However, Hashem ultimately caused him to be cast back onto land in Eretz Yisrael, so that he *would* receive the prophecy.

This, however, seems to leave the matter unresolved: Since Jonah had already received the prophecy instructing him to deliver a message to Nineveh, was it not *too late* for him to flee Eretz Yisrael?

Radvaz (*Teshuvos*, Vol. II §842) offers two approaches to resolving all these difficulties. One approach is that in his initial prophecy, Jonah was not given a specific message to deliver to Nineveh. He was simply told, *"Go to Nineveh, the great city, and call out against it, for their wickedness has ascended before Me"* (*Jonah* 1:2). Jonah understood this as an instruction to deliver his own rebuke to Nineveh, not to convey a specific prophetic message from Hashem. Only later, when the fish cast him up, did Jonah receive a prophecy containing a specific message for Nineveh, for at that point it is stated (ibid. 3:2): *"Arise! Go to Nineveh, the great city, and call out against her* ***the proclamation that I tell you."*** Since the first prophecy lacked a specific message, Jonah reasoned that he would not be "suppressing a prophecy" if he did not go to Nineveh. For the good of the Jewish people, therefore, he tried to flee to Tarshish, where he would be unable to receive an actual prophecy that he would be forced to deliver to Nineveh (see also *Malbim, Jonah* 1:3).

The second approach of *Radvaz* is that there actually was a message for Nineveh in the initial prophecy, but a prophet is guilty of "suppressing a prophecy" only after he has already become an emissary of Hashem. If a prophet accepts a mission to prophesy to the people and he then fails to carry it out, he is guilty of suppressing a prophecy. Moreover, if he *once* prophesied to the people, he must from that point on deliver every prophecy that he is instructed to convey, and if he does not do so, he is guilty of suppressing a prophecy. It is permissible, however, for a prophet to decline to become Hashem's emissary in the first place. Thus, when Hashem revealed Himself to Moses at the Burning Bush and told him to go tell Pharaoh to set the Jews free, Moses initially refused, saying to Hashem (*Exodus* 4:13): *"Please, my Lord, send through whomever You will send"* [i.e., send anyone else but me (*Rashi*)]. Similarly, Jonah was entitled to refuse to become a prophet to the people. The initial prophecy, *"Go to Nineveh, the great city, and call out against it, for their wickedness has ascended before Me"* (*Jonah* 1:2), was the first prophecy Jonah had ever been instructed to convey (see *Yevamos* 98a; cf. *Pirkei DeRabbi Eliezer*, Ch. 10). He was therefore entitled to decline to become Hashem's emissary, so he fled to Tarshish. Hashem insisted, however, that he be the one to carry out this mission, so He caused him to be swallowed by the fish and cast up again (see also *Rabbeinu Bachya, Kad HaKemach* כפורים א).

According to these approaches, Jonah was not guilty of suppressing a prophecy. As mentioned, however, the Gemara cites Jonah as an example of one who suppresses his prophecy. Perhaps, *Radvaz* understands the Gemara to mean merely that if a prophet would do what Jonah did *after* receiving a specific message to deliver, and after becoming Hashem's emissary, he would be guilty of suppressing his prophecy. It does not mean that Jonah himself was guilty of this sin.

Others explain that Jonah was actually mistaken in his reasoning, but since he *thought* that he was not suppressing a prophecy, and his intention was for the good of the Jewish people, he was mercifully spared death at the hands of Heaven. His suffering in the innards of the fish sufficed to atone for the sin of running away from his mission (see *Chida* in *Chomas Anach, Jonah* 1:3).

For additional explanations of why Jonah may not have been guilty of suppressing a prophecy, see *Beer Yitzchak* [Mis] on the *haftarah* of Minchah of Yom Kippur, and *R' Chaim Shmulevitz* in *Sichos Mussar*, 5731:29. See also *Minchas Chinuch* §4, and *Radal* to *Pirkei DeRabbi Eliezer* Ch. 10.

מִצְוָה תקיז: שֶׁלֹּא לְהִתְנַבֵּאת בְּשֶׁקֶר

שֶׁנִּמְנַעְנוּ שֶׁלֹּא לְהִתְנַבֵּא בְּשֶׁקֶר, כְּלוֹמַר שֶׁלֹּא יֹאמַר שׁוּם אָדָם שֶׁנֶּאֶמְרוּ לוֹ דְּבָרִים בִּנְבוּאָה מֵהַשֵּׁם וְהַשֵּׁם לֹא אֲמָרָם[1], וְכֵן בִּכְלַל הַלָּאו אֲפִלּוּ אִם יֹאמַר דְּבָרִים שֶׁנֶּאֶמְרוּ בִּנְבוּאָה לְזוּלָתוֹ וְיֹאמַר בְּשֶׁקֶר שֶׁהוּא נִצְטַוָּה לְאָמְרָן[2], וְעַל זֶה נֶאֱמַר (דברים י״ח, כ׳) אַךְ הַנָּבִיא אֲשֶׁר יָזִיד לְדַבֵּר דָּבָר בִּשְׁמִי אֵת אֲשֶׁר לֹא צִוִּיתִיו לְדַבֵּר וְגוֹ׳, וְכֵן אָמְרוּ זִכְרוֹנָם לִבְרָכָה בְּסַנְהֶדְרִין (פ״ט ע״א), אֲשֶׁר יָזִיד לְדַבֵּר דָּבָר בִּשְׁמִי, זֶה הַמִּתְנַבֵּא מַה שֶּׁלֹּא שָׁמַע,

---

Mitzvah 517

The Prohibition to Prophesy Falsely

אַךְ הַנָּבִיא אֲשֶׁר יָזִיד לְדַבֵּר דָּבָר בִּשְׁמִי אֵת אֲשֶׁר לֹא צִוִּיתִיו לְדַבֵּר וַאֲשֶׁר יְדַבֵּר בְּשֵׁם אֱלֹהִים אֲחֵרִים וּמֵת הַנָּבִיא הַהוּא

But the prophet who flagrantly will speak a word in My Name, that which I have not commanded him to speak, or who will speak in the name of the gods of others — that prophet shall die (*Deuteronomy* 18:20).

This verse sets out the death sentence for two sinners — one who speaks a false prophecy in the Name of Hashem, and one who speaks a prophecy in the name of a false god. The current mitzvah refers to the first category, and the next mitzvah deals with the second category.

שֶׁנִּמְנַעְנוּ שֶׁלֹּא לְהִתְנַבֵּא בְּשֶׁקֶר – This mitzvah teaches **that we are prohibited to prophesy falsely.** כְּלוֹמַר שֶׁלֹּא יֹאמַר שׁוּם אָדָם שֶׁנֶּאֶמְרוּ לוֹ דְּבָרִים בִּנְבוּאָה מֵהַשֵּׁם וְהַשֵּׁם לֹא אֲמָרָם – **That is to say,** we are commanded **that no person may declare that** certain **things were said to him in a prophecy from Hashem, when** in truth **Hashem did not say them.**[1] וְכֵן בִּכְלַל הַלָּאו – **Also included in this prohibition is** another form of false prophecy: אֲפִלּוּ אִם יֹאמַר דְּבָרִים שֶׁנֶּאֶמְרוּ בִּנְבוּאָה לְזוּלָתוֹ – **Even if one relates things that** actually **were said in a prophecy to someone else,** וְיֹאמַר בְּשֶׁקֶר שֶׁהוּא נִצְטַוָּה לְאָמְרָן – **but [this person] falsely claims that *he* was** prophetically **commanded to say them** to the public, he has "prophesied falsely" and has transgressed this prohibition.[2] וְעַל זֶה נֶאֱמַר – **Regarding this it is stated** (*Deuteronomy* 18:20): "אַךְ הַנָּבִיא אֲשֶׁר יָזִיד לְדַבֵּר דָּבָר בִּשְׁמִי אֵת אֲשֶׁר לֹא צִוִּיתִיו לְדַבֵּר וְגוֹ׳" – ***But the prophet who flagrantly will speak a word in My Name, that which I have not commanded him to speak ...** that prophet shall die.*

Chinuch explains how both aspects of the prohibition are derived from the verse:

וְכֵן אָמְרוּ זִכְרוֹנָם לִבְרָכָה בְּסַנְהֶדְרִין – **So have [the Sages] stated in** Tractate ***Sanhedrin*** (89a): "אֲשֶׁר יָזִיד לְדַבֵּר דָּבָר בִּשְׁמִי" – When Scripture states, *But the prophet **who flagrantly will speak a word in My Name,*** זֶה הַמִּתְנַבֵּא מַה שֶּׁלֹּא שָׁמַע – **this is** a reference to **one who states a prophecy**

NOTES

1. Chinuch's statement that "no person" may do this implies that the prohibition applies even to a person who was never recognized as a prophet and has not provided any miraculous sign to establish his credentials as a prophet. Accordingly, *anyone* who claims to have received a prophecy, but actually did not receive it, transgresses this prohibition. This is also the opinion of *Sefer Yerei'im* (§241, cited by *Hagahos Maimoniyos, Hil. Avodah Zarah* 5:1), who cautions that a person should never say, *even in jest,* "God told me such and such." See also *Chazon Ish, Sanhedrin* 21:2 ד״ה ובדין נביא השקר.

Others, however maintain that the prohibition applies only to a *prophet,* i.e., someone who either was previously established as a prophet, or was in the process of establishing himself by invoking miraculous signs. In their view, this is implied by the verse, *But "the prophet" who flagrantly will speak a word in My Name,* etc. (*Meiri, Sanhedrin* 90a ד״ה כל מה שכתבנו; *R' Y. F. Perla, Sefer HaMitzvos of R' Saadiah Gaon, Onesh* 65 [Vol. III, p. 88a] ד״ה ולכן נראה, citing *Rambam's* Introduction to the Mishnah; *Haamek Davar* to the verse). See also *Minchas Chinuch* §4.

2. By misrepresenting the prophecy as his own, he is being a false prophet.

אֵת אֲשֶׁר לֹא צִוִּיתִיו, הוּא לֹא צִוִּיתִיו אֲבָל לַחֲבֵרוֹ צִוִּיתִיו, זֶה הַמִּתְנַבֵּא מַה שֶּׁלֹּא נֶאֱמַר לוֹ וְנֶאֱמַר לַחֲבֵרוֹ[4,3].

מִשָּׁרְשֵׁי הַמִּצְוָה לְפִי שֶׁיִּהְיֶה בָּזֶה חֻרְבָּן גָּדוֹל וְרָעָה רַבָּה בְּדָתֵנוּ הַמְקֻדֶּשֶׁת וְהַשְּׁלֵמָה, כִּי עִקַּר הָאֱמֶת מִבְּלִי סִיג הַמַּגִּיעַ אֶל בְּנֵי אָדָם הוּא עַל יְדֵי הַנְּבִיאִים[5], וְהַתּוֹרָה

---

that he did not hear at all, but invented; "אֵת אֲשֶׁר לֹא צִוִּיתִיו" – and when it then states, ***that which I have not commanded him*** *to speak,* הוּא לֹא צִוִּיתִיו אֲבָל לַחֲבֵרוֹ צִוִּיתִיו – which implies, **"I have not commanded *him*, but I have commanded his fellow** to speak it," זֶה הַמִּתְנַבֵּא מַה שֶּׁלֹּא נֶאֱמַר לוֹ וְנֶאֱמַר לַחֲבֵרוֹ – **this is** a reference to **one who states a prophecy that was not said to him, but was said to his fellow.**[3] Regarding each of these, the verse concludes, *that prophet shall die.*[4]

Underlying Purpose of the Mitzvah

מִשָּׁרְשֵׁי הַמִּצְוָה – **Among the underlying purposes of the mitzvah** is the idea that false prophecy cannot be allowed לְפִי שֶׁיִּהְיֶה בָּזֶה חֻרְבָּן גָּדוֹל וְרָעָה רַבָּה בְּדָתֵנוּ הַמְקֻדֶּשֶׁת וְהַשְּׁלֵמָה – **because this would result in terrible destruction and severe harm to our sacred and perfect religion.** כִּי עִקַּר הָאֱמֶת מִבְּלִי סִיג הַמַּגִּיעַ אֶל בְּנֵי אָדָם הוּא עַל יְדֵי הַנְּבִיאִים – **For the essential, unadulterated Truth that reaches people comes by way of the prophets,** who receive the Word of God,[5] וְהַתּוֹרָה

NOTES

3. If the verse refers only to one case, then the latter clause is redundant, since one who "flagrantly" speaks in Hashem's Name is obviously speaking something that he was not commanded. The Sages therefore expound the latter clause as referring to a second case, in which *he* was not commanded to say this prophecy but someone else was commanded to say it (*R' Y. F. Perla* ibid. p. 88b ד״ה ומה שכתב).

[There are various ways that a person may know something that was prophetically revealed to his fellow. First, perhaps the other fellow told it to him. Second, perhaps he inferred it from a prophetic message that the other one publicized (see *Sanhedrin* 89b with *Meiri* ד״ה אע״פ שהמתנבא). Third, if he is a true prophet, he is naturally aware of the other fellow's prophecy, for as a rule, a prophecy transmitted to one prophet is known to the other prophets of his time as well (*Sanhedrin* ibid.). Nevertheless, since the other prophet was commanded to publicize it and he was not, if he publicizes it he transgresses this prohibition.]

4. This verse sets out the punishment of a false prophet, but does not explicitly *prohibit* false prophecy. Now, there is a rule that the Torah never imposes a punishment without also issuing a prohibition, or a "warning," against the act. [Chinuch mentions this principle in the following mitzvah, and discusses it at length in Mitzvah 69.] Where does the Torah state the *prohibition* against prophesying falsely?

Smag (*Lo Saaseh* 34) suggests that this prohibition is included in the verse (*Leviticus* 19:11): וְלֹא תְשַׁקְּרוּ אִישׁ בַּעֲמִיתוֹ, *You shall not lie to each other.* Although that verse is a general prohibition against falsehood, it encompasses false prophecy. Being that the Torah, in our passage, specifies a punishment for prophesying falsely, we know that it is a sin, so the general prohibition against lying suffices as the "warning" against this act as well. [See the following mitzvah, and Mitzvah 48 (at note 10), where Chinuch applies this line of reasoning in other contexts. See also *Pri Chadash* to *Hil. Avodah Zarah* 5:4 (printed in *Sefer HaLikkutim* in Frankel ed.), for a similar suggestion.]

This, however, cannot be Chinuch's view here. In the next mitzvah, Chinuch notes that a verse containing a punishment (such as our verse) does not suffice to establish a prohibition, and he therefore searches for a verse that prohibits the act discussed there (i.e., prophesying in the name of a false god). Yet here, Chinuch does not address this issue at all. Evidently, Chinuch sees our verse itself as the source for the prohibition against prophesying falsely. Indeed, *Rambam* states this clearly in *Sefer HaMitzvos* (*Lo Saaseh* 27), though he does not explain how the verse conveys the prohibition. *Sefer Yerei'im* (§241) explains that the clause in this verse, לֹא צִוִּיתִיו לְדַבֵּר, *[that which] I have not commanded him to speak,* is the "warning" against prophesying falsely — for this clause can be understood to mean, "[that which] I have commanded him *not* to speak," referring to the false prophecy described in this verse (see *Toafos Re'eim* ad loc.; *R' Y. F. Perla* ibid., *Lo Saaseh* 34 [Vol. II, p. 36b] ד״ה ואמנם).

5. The nature of genuine prophecy is that it is *absolutely* true. In some instances, stargazers and sorcerers can predict future events, but they can never do so with complete accuracy, for there always is some "dross" in their knowledge (see Mitzvah 510, with note 5). The predictions of a true prophet, on the other hand, are borne out in *every detail.* The only exception is where the prophecy is one of impending punishment; such

תְּצַוֵּנוּ לְהַאֲמִין בָּהֶם וְלָלֶכֶת אַחַר עֲצָתָם הַנְּכוֹנָה וְדַעְתָּם הַשָּׁלֵם, וְעַל כֵּן בְּקוּם בְּנֵי בְלִיַּעַל לֵאמֹר דְּבָרִים שֶׁלֹּא צִוָּם הַשֵּׁם, יוֹצִיאוּ לַעַז בַּנְּבוּאָה שֶׁהִיא הָעִקָּר הַגָּדוֹל אֲשֶׁר בֵּינֵינוּ עַם הַקֹּדֶשׁ[6], וִיפַקְפֵּק בְּסִבָּתָם לֵב כָּל הָעָם אַף בִּנְבִיאֵי הָאֱמֶת. וְאִם יֹאמַר אָדָם גַּם כֵּן מַה שֶּׁנִּצְטַוָּה אָדָם אַחֵר עָלָיו, יֵשׁ בָּזֶה חָרְבָּה גְּדוֹלָה, כִּי הָאִישׁ הַזֶּה בְּאָמְרוֹ שֶׁהוּא נָבִיא וְנִצְטַוָּה בָּזֶה וְנִרְאֶה דְּבָרָיו מִתְקַיְּמִין כְּדִבְרֵי נְבִיאֵי הָאֱמֶת, נַחֲזִיק אוֹתוֹ כְּאִישׁ אֱלֹהִים קָדוֹשׁ שְׁלִיחַ הָאֵל וְנַאֲמִין אֵלָיו וְנִקַּח רְאָיָה בְּכָל הַנְהָגוֹתֵינוּ מִמַּעֲשָׂיו, וְאוּלַי אַחַר שֶׁאֵין זְכוּתוֹ וְעִנְיָנוֹ גָּדוֹל לִהְיוֹת הוּא שָׁלִיחַ בְּאוֹתָהּ נְבוּאָה שֶׁאָמַר, אֵינֶנּוּ רָאוּי לִסְמֹךְ בּוֹ בְּכָל אֲשֶׁר יַעֲשֶׂה וְיֹאמַר[7], וְיִטְעֶה הֶהָמוֹן בְּלֶכְתָּם אַחַר עֲצָתוֹ.

תְּצַוֵּנוּ לְהַאֲמִין בָּהֶם – **and** for this reason **the Torah commands us to trust [our prophets]** **וְלָלֶכֶת אַחַר עֲצָתָם הַנְּכוֹנָה וְדַעְתָּם הַשָּׁלֵם** – **and to follow their proper counsel and sound opinion.** **וְעַל כֵּן** – **Therefore,** **בְּקוּם בְּנֵי בְלִיַּעַל לֵאמֹר דְּבָרִים שֶׁלֹּא צִוָּם הַשֵּׁם** – **when lawless men stand up to say** in the Name of Hashem **things that Hashem has not commanded them** to say, and those things ultimately do not come true, **יוֹצִיאוּ לַעַז בַּנְּבוּאָה** – **they cast aspersions on** the authenticity of **prophecy,** **שֶׁהִיא הָעִקָּר הַגָּדוֹל אֲשֶׁר בֵּינֵינוּ עַם הַקֹּדֶשׁ** – **which is a major principle** of faith **among us, the holy nation,**[6] **וִיפַקְפֵּק בְּסִבָּתָם לֵב כָּל הָעָם אַף בִּנְבִיאֵי הָאֱמֶת** – **and as a result of their** evil, **the heart of the entire nation will** begin to **doubt even** the words of **the authentic prophets.**

Chinuch explains the reason for the second aspect of this mitzvah:

וְאִם יֹאמַר אָדָם גַּם כֵּן מַה שֶּׁנִּצְטַוָּה אָדָם אַחֵר עָלָיו יֵשׁ בָּזֶה חָרְבָּה גְּדוֹלָה – **Also, if a person would say something** prophetic **that another person was commanded to** tell the people but he himself was not commanded to tell, **this would be terribly destructive,** even though the prophecy would come true. **כִּי הָאִישׁ הַזֶּה בְּאָמְרוֹ שֶׁהוּא נָבִיא וְנִצְטַוָּה בָּזֶה** – **For when this person claims that he is a prophet and he received a command** from God **to** transmit **this** message to us, **וְנִרְאֶה דְּבָרָיו מִתְקַיְּמִין כְּדִבְרֵי נְבִיאֵי הָאֱמֶת** – **and we** then **see his words come true, like the words of the authentic prophets,** **נַחֲזִיק אוֹתוֹ כְּאִישׁ אֱלֹהִים קָדוֹשׁ שְׁלִיחַ הָאֵל** – **we will consider him** to be **confirmed as a holy man of God,** one chosen to be **a messenger of the Almighty,** **וְנַאֲמִין אֵלָיו וְנִקַּח רְאָיָה בְּכָל הַנְהָגוֹתֵינוּ מִמַּעֲשָׂיו** – **and we will** then **trust him** absolutely, **and will take lessons from his actions** as to how we should conduct ourselves **in all our affairs.** **וְאוּלַי אַחַר שֶׁאֵין זְכוּתוֹ וְעִנְיָנוֹ גָּדוֹל לִהְיוֹת הוּא שָׁלִיחַ בְּאוֹתָהּ נְבוּאָה שֶׁאָמַר** – **But it is possible** that **since he does not** actually **have** sufficient **greatness of merit and character to have been** designated **a messenger for** delivering **that prophecy that he related** to us, **אֵינֶנּוּ רָאוּי לִסְמֹךְ בּוֹ בְּכָל אֲשֶׁר יַעֲשֶׂה וְיֹאמַר** – **he is not worthy of being relied upon in everything that he does and says,**[7] **וְיִטְעֶה הֶהָמוֹן בְּלֶכְתָּם אַחַר עֲצָתוֹ** – **and he will mislead the masses when they follow his counsel.**

NOTES

a prophecy will not necessarily come true, since the people may repent and then Hashem will rescind His decree. But an authentic prophecy of good always comes true in every detail. For this reason, when a person presents himself as a prophet and makes a prediction of good, if he turns out to have been wrong in even one minor detail, he is proven to be a false prophet (*Rambam, Hil. Yesodei HaTorah* 10:1-4). [See further, Insight to Mitzvah 424.]

6. It is one of the Thirteen Principles of Faith that God communicates with us through His prophets, and all their words are His True Word. This underlies the Principle of Faith that the Torah that Hashem gave us through His prophet, Moses, is True (see *Rambam, Commentary to the Mishnah, Sanhedrin* 10:1, Principles 6-8; see also *Rambam's* Introduction to the Mishnah).

7. As mentioned in note 3, a person can know a prophecy that was received by another either by hearing it from him, or by inferring it from his words, or by virtue of being a prophet himself. Even if the person knows it through his own prophetic ability, he may be worthy only of attaining a prophetic revelation, but not of being God's messenger to the people. See Mitzvah 516 note 7.

דִּינֵי הַמִּצְוָה קְצָרִים וְהֵם בְּסַנְהֶדְרִין (פט, א)[8].
וְנוֹהֵג אִסּוּר זֶה בְּכָל מָקוֹם וּבְכָל זְמַן, בִּזְכָרִים וּנְקֵבוֹת[9].
וְעוֹבֵר עַל זֶה וְנִבָּא בְּשֶׁקֶר, כְּלוֹמַר שֶׁהִגִּיד דְּבָרִים בְּשֵׁם הָאֵל שֶׁלֹּא אָמַר לוֹ הָאֵל, וְכֵן הַמִּתְנַבֵּא מַה שֶּׁאָמַר הָאֵל לַחֲבֵרוֹ וְלֹא לוֹ, חַיָּב מִיתָה וּמִיתָתוֹ הִיא בְּחֶנֶק, שֶׁנֶּאֱמַר עַל זֶה וּמֵת הַנָּבִיא הַהוּא, וְאָמְרוּ זִכְרוֹנָם לִבְרָכָה (סנהדרין שם) **שֶׁכָּל מִיתָה הָאֲמוּרָה בַּתּוֹרָה סְתָם אֵינָהּ אֶלָּא חֶנֶק**[10].

Laws of the Mitzvah

דִּינֵי הַמִּצְוָה קְצָרִים וְהֵם בְּסַנְהֶדְרִין – The laws of the mitzvah are brief, and they are set out **in** Tractate ***Sanhedrin*** (89a).[8]

Applicability of the Mitzvah

וְנוֹהֵג אִסּוּר זֶה בְּכָל מָקוֹם וּבְכָל זְמַן – This prohibition applies in every location and in all times, בִּזְכָרִים וּנְקֵבוֹת – to both **men and women.**[9]

וְעוֹבֵר עַל זֶה וְנִבָּא בְּשֶׁקֶר – One who transgresses this prohibition **and prophesies falsely, כְּלוֹמַר שֶׁהִגִּיד דְּבָרִים בְּשֵׁם הָאֵל שֶׁלֹּא אָמַר לוֹ הָאֵל – that is, he relates things in the Name of the Almighty that the Almighty did not say to him** at all, **וְכֵן הַמִּתְנַבֵּא מַה שֶּׁאָמַר הָאֵל לַחֲבֵרוֹ וְלֹא לוֹ – and likewise, one who states a prophecy that the Almighty said to his fellow** as a message to the people **but** did **not** say **to him, חַיָּב מִיתָה – is liable to execution, וּמִיתָתוֹ הִיא בְּחֶנֶק – and his method of execution is *chenek*** (strangulation). **שֶׁנֶּאֱמַר עַל זֶה "וּמֵת הַנָּבִיא הַהוּא"** – This is **because it is stated regarding this** matter (*Deuteronomy* ibid.), ***that prophet shall die,*** **וְאָמְרוּ זִכְרוֹנָם לִבְרָכָה – and [our Sages], of blessed memory, have stated** (*Sanhedrin* ibid.) **שֶׁכָּל מִיתָה הָאֲמוּרָה בַּתּוֹרָה סְתָם אֵינָהּ אֶלָּא חֶנֶק – that any death** sentence **mentioned in the Torah** in which the manner of execution is **not specified is none other than *chenek.***[10]

NOTES

8. The laws are codified in *Rambam, Hil. Avodah Zarah* 5:7-8 and *Hil. Yesodei HaTorah* Ch. 9.

9. It applies in Eretz Yisrael and the Diaspora, whether the *Beis HaMikdash* is standing or not; and it applies to both men and women in accordance with the general rule concerning mitzvah-prohibitions. [Both men and women can attain prophecy, and Scripture mentions several female prophets. Obviously, then, both men and women can falsely present themselves as prophets.]

10. See Mitzvah 47 for how *chenek* is carried out.

Insight: The Prophet Who "Flagrantly" Speaks Falsely

As an example of a false prophet who incurs death at the hands of Heaven, the Gemara (*Sanhedrin* 89a) cites the case of Tzidkiyah ben Kenaanah, recorded in *I Kings* Ch. 22.

Ahab, king of Israel, asked Jehoshaphat, king of Judah, to join him in waging war against the people of Aram, in order to take back the city of Ramoth-gilead, which they had seized from Israel. Jehoshaphat agreed, on condition that they ask the prophets whether Hashem would grant them success. Ahab gathered 400 prophets, and all of them said unequivocally, "Go up, for my Lord will deliver it into the hand of the king." One of those prophets, Tzidkiyah ben Kenaanah, even made himself horns of iron and said, "Thus said Hashem: With these you shall gore Aram, until they are obliterated." Nevertheless, Jehoshaphat asked whether there was no other prophet of whom they could inquire. They brought him the prophet Michayhu ben Yimlah.

At first, Michayhu mimicked the words of the other prophets, but Jehoshaphat said, "I adjure you many times over that you speak to me nothing but the truth, in the Name of Hashem!" Michayhu then said that Ahab would be killed in the battle and the Israelite army would be scattered. When pressed as to how he could contradict all the other prophets, Michayhu replied that in his prophetic vision, he had seen the following: Hashem was sitting upon His throne with the Heavenly hosts

standing by Him, and Hashem said, "Who will lure Ahab to go up to war that he may fall in Ramoth-gilead?" [Ahab had sinned grievously by unjustly executing Naboth the Jezreelite, and had been doomed to die a violent death (see *I Kings* Ch. 21). The time had come to carry out that punishment.] A spirit came forward and said, "I will be a spirit of falsehood in the mouths of all his prophets." [This was the spirit of Naboth, who sought to avenge his death (see *Sanhedrin* 89a).] Hashem granted the spirit permission to do so. Thus, Michayhu said, when all the prophets predicted that Ahab would succeed in battle, it was because they had been tricked by the spirit of Naboth, and he (Michayhu) alone — who predicted failure — was conveying a true prophecy from Hashem. Tzidkiyah ben Kenaanah then came forward and struck Michayhu on the cheek, declaring him a liar. In the end, Michayhu's words were borne out, as Ahab was killed in the battle and the Israelites scattered.

This episode calls for clarification: Being that all 400 prophets, including Tzidkiyah, were misled by the spirit of Naboth, they thought that they were prophesying truthfully. Why, then, was Tzidkiyah considered guilty, and liable to death? Moreover, why is he alone, among the 400 men, singled out as a false prophet? The Gemara explains that there is a principle that, while Hashem may send similar prophetic visions to numerous prophets, never will two prophets convey that vision in the same words. Since 400 prophets all delivered the exact same message to Ahab and Jehoshaphat, it was evident that something was amiss. In fact, that is why Jehoshaphat, even after hearing a prediction of success from 400 prophets, insisted on calling for an additional prophet; he knew that they could not possibly be saying a genuine prophecy. All of the original 400 prophets except Tzidkiyah recognized this and became silent. They were not guilty of prophesying falsely, because they had indeed been misled by the spirit of Naboth, and when they realized it they stopped speaking. Tzidkiyah, however, insisted that his prophecy was truthful; he even made horns of iron and stated that Ahab would gore Aram until they were obliterated, and later, he struck Michayhu on the cheek. Since he stood by his prophecy and repeated it, when he already had evidence that it could not be a genuine prophecy from Hashem, he was guilty of prophesying falsely (*Sanhedrin* 89a, as elaborated by *Ohr HaChaim* to *Deuteronomy* 18:20; see also *Meiri* and *Maharsha* there).

Interestingly, even Michayhu was initially misled by the spirit of Naboth, for at first he mimicked the other prophets. Only when Jehoshaphat said, "I adjure you many times over that you speak to me nothing but the truth, in the Name of Hashem," did Michayhu prophesy truthfully. What brought about this change? *Ohr HaChaim* (ibid.) explains that it was because Jehoshaphat adjured him to speak "in the Name of Hashem." The initial false prophecy did not come from Hashem, but from the spirit of Naboth. Granted, Hashem gave the spirit permission to generate a falsehood, in order to punish Ahab. But never is falsehood spoken "in the Name of Hashem." When Michayhu was adjured to speak *in HASHEM's Name*, the spirit of Naboth left him and he received a true prophecy. Nevertheless, Hashem's plan to punish Ahab came to fruition, since Ahab believed Tzidkiyah and not Michayhu, and he went out to war against Aram.

Ohr HaChaim notes further that this episode is alluded to in the verses of the Torah passage containing our mitzvah. The verse states (*Deuteronomy* 18:20): אַךְ הַנָּבִיא אֲשֶׁר יָזִיד לְדַבֵּר דָּבָר בִּשְׁמִי אֵת אֲשֶׁר לֹא צִוִּיתִיו לְדַבֵּר... וּמֵת הַנָּבִיא הַהוּא, *But the prophet who flagrantly will speak a word in My Name, that which I have not commanded him to speak ... that prophet shall die.* The word "flagrantly" indicates that the punishment for prophesying falsely applies only to one who does so knowingly. If, however, a prophet is tricked by a spirit to say a falsehood, he is not subject to punishment. Further, when explaining how we can identify a false prophet who speaks "flagrantly," the Torah states (ibid. v. 22): אֲשֶׁר יְדַבֵּר הַנָּבִיא בְּשֵׁם ה' וְלֹא יִהְיֶה הַדָּבָר וְלֹא יָבֹא הוּא הַדָּבָר אֲשֶׁר לֹא דִבְּרוֹ ה' בְּזָדוֹן דִּבְּרוֹ הַנָּבִיא, *If the prophet will speak **in the Name of HASHEM** and that thing will not occur and not come about — that is the word that HASHEM has not spoken; the prophet has spoken it flagrantly.* A prophecy spoken "in the Name of Hashem" must always be true; never does falsehood emanate from Hashem. If, however, a prophet says something without attributing it to the Name of Hashem, it is possible that he has been misled by a false spirit, like the spirit of Naboth. [In this respect, too, Tzidkiyah was guilty; for although initially he said nothing more than the other prophets who were misled by that spirit, when he later made horns of iron, he said, *"Thus said HASHEM: With these you shall gore Aram."* The prophecy that he received could not have come *in the Name of HASHEM*, so this statement was a flagrant falsehood.]

⟪ מִצְוָה תקיח: שֶׁלֹּא לְהִתְנַבֵּאוֹת בְּשֵׁם עֲבוֹדָה זָרָה ⟫

שֶׁלֹּא לְהִתְנַבֵּא בְּשֵׁם עֲבוֹדָה זָרָה[1], כְּגוֹן שֶׁיֹּאמַר עֲבוֹדָה זָרָה פְּלוֹנִית צִוְּתָה לְעָבְדָהּ
וְתַבְטִיחַ גְּמוּל לְעוֹבְדֶיהָ וְתַפְחִיד מֵעֹנֶשׁ לְמִי שֶׁלֹּא יַעַבְדֶהָ, כְּמוֹ שֶׁהָיוּ אוֹמְרִים נְבִיאֵי
הַבַּעַל וְהָאֲשֵׁרָה כְּמוֹ שֶׁהֻזְכַּר בְּסִפְרֵי הַנְּבִיאִים[2]. וְכֵן בִּכְלָל זֶה אִם יֹאמַר שֶׁהָאֵל
צִוָּה לַעֲבֹד עֲבוֹדָה זָרָה פְּלוֹנִי[3]. וְלֹא בָּא עַל זֶה בַּכָּתוּב בְּאַזְהָרָה מְבֹאֶרֶת מְיֻחֶדֶת
בָּזֶה, אָמְנָם נִתְבָּאֵר בַּכָּתוּב עֹנֶשׁ הַמִּתְנַבֵּא בְּשֵׁם עֲבוֹדָה זָרָה שֶׁהוּא חַיָּב מִיתָה

⟪ Mitzvah 518 ⟫
The Prohibition to Prophesy
in the Name of Avodah Zarah

אַךְ הַנָּבִיא אֲשֶׁר יָזִיד לְדַבֵּר דָּבָר בִּשְׁמִי אֵת אֲשֶׁר לֹא צִוִּיתִיו לְדַבֵּר וַאֲשֶׁר יְדַבֵּר בְּשֵׁם
אֱלֹהִים אֲחֵרִים וּמֵת הַנָּבִיא הַהוּא

*But the prophet who flagrantly will speak a word in My Name, that which I
have not commanded him to speak, or who will speak in the name of the gods of
others — that prophet shall die (Deuteronomy 18:20).*

This verse mentions two types of sin: saying a false prophecy in the name of Hashem, and saying a
prophecy in the name of a false god (*avodah zarah*). The previous mitzvah dealt with the first category.
This mitzvah deals with the second category.
שֶׁלֹּא לְהִתְנַבֵּא בְּשֵׁם עֲבוֹדָה זָרָה — We are commanded **not to prophesy in the name of an *avodah
zarah*.**[1] כְּגוֹן שֶׁיֹּאמַר עֲבוֹדָה זָרָה פְּלוֹנִית צִוְּתָה לְעָבְדָהּ — **An example** of such prophesying **is where
one says, "Such-and-such an *avodah zarah* has commanded** us **to worship it,** וְתַבְטִיחַ גְּמוּל
לְעוֹבְדֶיהָ וְתַפְחִיד מֵעֹנֶשׁ לְמִי שֶׁלֹּא יַעַבְדֶהָ — **and it promises to reward those who worship it and
threatens to punish one who does not worship it,"** כְּמוֹ שֶׁהָיוּ אוֹמְרִים נְבִיאֵי הַבַּעַל וְהָאֲשֵׁרָה — **as**
the false **prophets of *Baal* and *asheirah* used to say** in the times when they existed, כְּמוֹ שֶׁהֻזְכַּר
בְּסִפְרֵי הַנְּבִיאִים — **as is mentioned in the Books of the Prophets.**[2] וְכֵן בִּכְלָל זֶה אִם יֹאמַר שֶׁהָאֵל
צִוָּה לַעֲבֹד עֲבוֹדָה זָרָה פְּלוֹנִי — **Also included in this** prohibition **is** a case **where one says that the
Almighty has commanded** us **to worship such-and-such an *avodah zarah*.**[3]

Chinuch focuses on the Scriptural source of the prohibition:
וְלֹא בָּא עַל זֶה בַּכָּתוּב בְּאַזְהָרָה מְבֹאֶרֶת מְיֻחֶדֶת בָּזֶה — **Scripture does not contain an explicit,
specific prohibition against this** matter of prophesying in the name of *avodah zarah*. אָמְנָם
נִתְבָּאֵר בַּכָּתוּב עֹנֶשׁ הַמִּתְנַבֵּא בְּשֵׁם עֲבוֹדָה זָרָה — **However, Scripture does set out the punishment of one who prophesies in the name of *avodah zarah*,** שֶׁהוּא חַיָּב מִיתָה — **which is that**

NOTES

1. See Mitzvah 517 note 1 for two opinions as to whether
that mitzvah (i.e., the prohibition to prophesy falsely)
applies to any person or only to an actual prophet.
The same two opinions exist regarding the current
mitzvah, which prohibits prophesying in the name
of an *avodah zarah*. See the sources cited there; and
Minchas Chinuch here §4.

2. *Baal* was an idol that for many generations had a
following among straying Jews (see *Judges* 2:11, 3:7;
I Kings 16:31-32; et al.). *Asheirah* refers to a tree designated for idol worship. There were many "prophets"
of *Baal* and *asheirah,* who worked to lure people into

idolatry. When Elijah brought offerings on Mount
Carmel to disprove the false prophets of his time (see
Mitzvah 516 note 3), he singlehandedly took on 450
prophets of *Baal* and 400 prophets of *asheirah* (*I Kings*
18:19,22). These prophets used to promise people that
their idols would give success to their followers (see
Ramban, Deuteronomy 18:20).

3. That is, even though the prophet speaks in the
Name of Hashem, if he claims that Hashem commanded us to worship an *avodah zarah,* he is considered a "prophet of *avodah zarah*." See Insight for
discussion. See also below, note 14.

שֶׁנֶּאֱמַר עַל זֶה (דְּבָרִים י״ח, כ׳) וַאֲשֶׁר יְדַבֵּר בְּשֵׁם אֱלֹהִים אֲחֵרִים וּמֵת הַנָּבִיא הַהוּא, וּמִיתָה זוֹ הִיא חֶנֶק כְּמוֹ שֶׁכָּתַבְתִּי בְּסָמוּךְ[4]. וּכְבָר יָדַעְנוּ הָעִקָּר שֶׁהוֹרוּנוּ זִכְרוֹנָם לִבְרָכָה לֹא עָנַשׁ אֶלָּא אִם כֵּן הִזְהִיר[5], וְעַל כֵּן נֹאמַר שֶׁיִּהְיֶה אַזְהָרַת הָעִנְיָן הַזֶּה בִּכְלַל וְשֵׁם אֱלֹהִים אֲחֵרִים לֹא תַזְכִּירוּ (שְׁמוֹת כ״ג, י״ג)[6] שֶׁכָּתַבְנוּ בְּכֶסֶף תַּלְוֶה[7] לְלָאו בִּפְנֵי עַצְמוֹ בְּעִנְיָן אַחֵר (מִצְוָה פ״ו)[8]. וְאֵין בְּנִמְנָע לִהְיוֹת לָאו אֶחָד מוֹנֵעַ דְּבָרִים רַבִּים[9], וְלֹא יִהְיֶה דִּינוֹ כְּדִין לָאו שֶׁבִּכְלָלוֹת מִכֵּיוָן שֶׁיִּתְבָּאֵר הָעֹנֶשׁ בְּכָל עִנְיָן וְעִנְיָן[10],

he is liable to execution, שֶׁנֶּאֱמַר עַל זֶה **– as it is stated regarding this** matter (*Deuteronomy* 18:20): "וַאֲשֶׁר יְדַבֵּר בְּשֵׁם אֱלֹהִים אֲחֵרִים וּמֵת הַנָּבִיא הַהוּא" – *But the prophet who flagrantly will speak … **or who will speak in the name of the gods of others – that prophet shall die.*** וּמִיתָה זוֹ הִיא חֶנֶק כְּמוֹ שֶׁכָּתַבְתִּי בְּסָמוּךְ **– This** penalty of **death,** in which the manner of death is not specified, **is** carried out through ***chenek*** (strangulation), **as I wrote just above,** in the previous mitzvah.[4] Thus, the punishment of a prophet of *avodah zarah* is stated explicitly. וּכְבָר יָדַעְנוּ הָעִקָּר שֶׁהוֹרוּנוּ זִכְרוֹנָם לִבְרָכָה **– And we already know the principle that [our Sages], of blessed memory, have taught us** (*Yoma* 81a, et al.): לֹא עָנַשׁ אֶלָּא אִם כֵּן הִזְהִיר **– [The Torah] did not punish unless it** also **warned** that the act is prohibited.[5] It follows that the Torah must contain a prohibition against prophesying in the name of *avodah zarah.* וְעַל כֵּן נֹאמַר **– Therefore, we will say** here שֶׁיִּהְיֶה אַזְהָרַת הָעִנְיָן הַזֶּה בִּכְלַל "וְשֵׁם אֱלֹהִים אֲחֵרִים לֹא תַזְכִּירוּ" **– that the warning against this matter is included in** the prohibition (*Exodus* 23:13), ***The name of alien gods you shall not mention.***[6] שֶׁכָּתַבְנוּ בְּכֶסֶף תַּלְוֶה לְלָאו בִּפְנֵי עַצְמוֹ בְּעִנְיָן אַחֵר – Now, this is a verse **that we recorded in** *Parashas Im **Kesef Talveh*** (Mitvzah 86)[7] **as a distinct prohibition pertaining to a different subject,**[8] וְאֵין בְּנִמְנָע לִהְיוֹת לָאו אֶחָד מוֹנֵעַ דְּבָרִים רַבִּים **– but nothing rules out having one prohibitive verse serve as a prohibition against several things.**[9] וְלֹא יִהְיֶה דִּינוֹ כְּדִין לָאו שֶׁבִּכְלָלוֹת **– [This verse] will not have the status of a "generalized prohibition,"** which is not punishable in *beis din,* מִכֵּיוָן שֶׁיִּתְבָּאֵר הָעֹנֶשׁ בְּכָל עִנְיָן וְעִנְיָן **– since a punishment is explicitly set out in regard to each one of the** prohibited **subjects** addressed by the verse.[10]

NOTES

4. *Minchas Chinuch* (§2) questions this, and argues that one who transgresses *this* mitzvah should be considered a מֵסִית, *inciter [to avodah zarah],* who is put to death through *sekilah.* See Insight for discussion.

5. The Torah never imposes a punishment unless it *prohibits* ("warns against") the act for which the punishment is incurred. Thus, whenever we see a punishment set out in the Torah, we must search for the prohibition, because we know that it exists. [See Mitzvah 69, at notes 5-9, where Chinuch discusses this principle at length.]

6. The warning is derived from this verse, since by prophesying in the name of *avodah zarah*, one mentions its name.

7. See Mitzvah 495 note 4 for the explanation of the name *"Parashas Im Kesef Talveh."*

8. There, Chinuch explained that the basic meaning of the verse, *The name of alien gods you shall not mention,* is that it prohibits *swearing* in the name of an *avodah zarah.*

9. Thus, a secondary meaning of the verse, *The name of alien gods you shall not mention,* will be that it prohibits *prophesying* in the name of an *avodah zarah.*

The verse therefore serves as (1) a prohibition against swearing in the name of an *avodah zarah* (Mitzvah 86); and (2) a prohibition against prophesying in the name of an *avodah zarah* (this mitzvah). [See also *Rambam, Sefer HaMitzvos, Lo Saaseh* 14 and 26.] These count as separate mitzvos because the punishments differ. One who swears in the name of an *avodah zarah* incurs *malkus,* while one who prophesies in the name of an *avodah zarah* incurs the death penalty.

[Other Rishonim, however, do not count them as separate mitzvos, but view them as different aspects of the same prohibition, since they are derived from the same verse (*Smag, Lo Saaseh* 32). For discussion, see *Mishneh LaMelech* in *Derech Mitzvosecha*, Part II, printed in Frankel ed. of *Sefer HaMitzvos*, p. 421.]

10. There is a principle that when a single verse is interpreted as prohibiting several different things, it is considered a לָאו שֶׁבִּכְלָלוֹת, *generalized prohibition.* The rule of such a prohibition is that one does not incur *malkus* (or another punishment of *beis din*) for violating any of the prohibitions that it includes. However, when a punishment is explicitly set out in the Torah, a violator does incur that punishment, even though the warning against the act is contained in a generalized prohibition. [See Mitzvah 248, beginning at note 8, where Chinuch discusses this at length. See also Insight

זֶהוּ דַּעַת הָרַמְבַּ"ם ז"ל (בספר המצוות)[11].

שֹׁרֶשׁ הַמִּצְוָה בְּכָל עִנְיַן עֲבוֹדָה זָרָה יָדוּעַ[12].

מִדִּינֵי הַמִּצְוָה מַה שֶּׁאָמְרוּ זִכְרוֹנָם לִבְרָכָה (סנהדרין פ"ט ע"א) **אֶחָד הָאוֹמֵר אָמְרָה לִי עֲבוֹדָה זָרָה פְּלוֹנִית אוֹ כּוֹכָב פְּלוֹנִי שֶׁמִּצְוָה לַעֲשׂוֹת כֵּן וְכֵן**[13] **אוֹ שֶׁלֹּא לַעֲשׂוֹת, אֲפִלּוּ כִּוֵּן אֶת הַהֲלָכָה לְטַמֵּא אֶת הַטָּמֵא וּלְטַהֵר אֶת הַטָּהוֹר, דִּינוֹ בְּמִיתָה בְּמֵזִיד**[14] **כְּשֶׁיֵּשׁ עֵדִים וְהַתְרָאָה**

זֶהוּ דַּעַת הָרַמְבַּ"ם ז"ל – This is the opinion of *Rambam,* of blessed memory (*Sefer HaMitzvos, Shoresh* 9 and *Lo Saaseh* 26).[11]

Underlying Purpose of the Mitzvah

שֹׁרֶשׁ הַמִּצְוָה בְּכָל עִנְיַן עֲבוֹדָה זָרָה יָדוּעַ – With regard to the entire subject of *avodah zarah,* the underlying purpose of the mitzvah is well known.[12]

Laws of the Mitzvah

Earlier, Chinuch addressed cases where one claims that an *avodah zarah* commanded that we are to worship it, or one claims that Hashem commanded us to worship an *avodah zarah.* Here, Chinuch discusses another type of prophecy in the name of an *avodah zarah*:

מִדִּינֵי הַמִּצְוָה – Among the laws of the mitzvah is **מַה שֶּׁאָמְרוּ זִכְרוֹנָם לִבְרָכָה – that which [the Sages], of blessed memory, stated** (*Rambam, Hil. Avodah Zarah* 5:6; see *Sanhedrin* 89a): **אֶחָד הָאוֹמֵר אָמְרָה לִי עֲבוֹדָה זָרָה פְּלוֹנִית אוֹ כּוֹכָב פְּלוֹנִי שֶׁמִּצְוָה לַעֲשׂוֹת כֵּן וְכֵן – Whether one says, "Such-and-such an *avodah zarah* or such-and-such a heavenly body told me that it is a mitzvah to do this or that,"**[13] **אוֹ שֶׁלֹּא לַעֲשׂוֹת – or** one says that the *avodah zarah* or the heavenly body told him that it is a mitzvah **not to do** this or that, **אֲפִלּוּ כִּוֵּן אֶת הַהֲלָכָה – even if** what **he** says **is in accordance with the halachah, לְטַמֵּא אֶת הַטָּמֵא וּלְטַהֵר אֶת הַטָּהוֹר –** for example, he instructs us **to deem *tamei* something that** actually **is *tamei*** according to Torah law, **or to deem *tahor* something that** actually **is *tahor,* דִּינוֹ בְּמִיתָה בְּמֵזִיד –** since he stated it in the name of an *avodah zarah,* **he is subject to execution** if he did this **intentionally.**[14] **כְּשֶׁיֵּשׁ עֵדִים וְהַתְרָאָה –** But this applies only

---

NOTES

to Mitzvah 273.] In our case, since the Torah explicitly imposes the death penalty on one who prophesies in the name of an *avodah zarah,* the punishment applies even though the warning is included in a generalized prohibition.

[Chinuch's language here (a punishment is explicitly set out in regard to each one of the prohibited subjects) is somewhat imprecise. Actually, the punishment of one who prophesies in the name of an *avodah zarah* is spelled out, but the punishment of one who swears in the name of an *avodah zarah* is not spelled out. Nevertheless, Chinuch states in Mitzvah 86 that a person who swears in the name of an *avodah zarah* incurs *malkus*. Presumably, the reason is because that is the primary subject of the prohibition. Thus, it is necessary only that the punishment for the *secondary* subject (prophesying in the name of an *avodah zarah*) be spelled out.]

11. In Mitzvah 248, Chinuch elaborates on this concept and cites the dissenting view of *Ramban* with respect to a generalized prohibition.

[According to *Sefer Yerei'im* (§242), the warning against prophesying in the name of an *avodah zarah* is derived from a different verse (*Deuteronomy* 6:14): לֹא תֵלְכוּן אַחֲרֵי אֱלֹהִים אֲחֵרִים, *you shall not follow after the gods of others*, for relating a prophecy in the name of an *avodah zarah* is surely a manner of "following after it." However, *Mechilta DeRashbi* explicitly interprets the verse, *The name of alien gods you shall not mention*, as warning against prophesying in the name of *avodah zarah*, in accordance with Chinuch and *Rambam*.]

12. As Chinuch writes in Mitzvah 26 (at note 6; quoting *Sifrei* to *Deuteronomy* 11:28): Anyone who believes in *avodah zarah* is considered as though he has denied the truth of the entire Torah. And, in Mitzvah 86 (at note 9), Chinuch writes that the Torah issued many prohibitions relating to *avodah zarah* in order to distance us from it as much as possible.

13. That is, he says that the *avodah zarah* instructed him in regard to one of the mitzvos of the Torah.

14. Chinuch (quoting *Rambam*) implies that this pertains even if the prophet states that the *avodah zarah* instructed us to do this because it is a mitzvah of Hashem. The very fact that he states something *in the name of* an idol makes him a prophet of *avodah zarah*. *Ramban* (*Deuteronomy* 18:20), however, asserts that

כַּיָּדוּעַ בְּכָל מָקוֹם[15]. וְיֶתֶר פְּרָטֶיהָ בְּסַנְהֶדְרִין בְּפֶרֶק י״א[16].
וְנוֹהֵג אִסּוּר זֶה בְּכָל מָקוֹם וּבְכָל זְמַן, בִּזְכָרִים וּנְקֵבוֹת[17].

---

when there are witnesses to the act **and** he received **a warning** before committing it, כַּיָּדוּעַ בְּכָל מָקוֹם – **as is known** to be the law **in every situation** of capital punishment.[15]

וְיֶתֶר פְּרָטֶיהָ בְּסַנְהֶדְרִין בְּפֶרֶק י״א – **The remaining details of [the mitzvah]** are set out **in** Tractate ***Sanhedrin*, Chapter 11** (89a, 90a).[16]

Applicability of the Mitzvah

וְנוֹהֵג אִסּוּר זֶה בְּכָל מָקוֹם וּבְכָל זְמַן – **This prohibition applies in every location and in all times,** בִּזְכָרִים וּנְקֵבוֹת – **to** both **men and women.**[17]

NOTES

this law applies only if the prophet states that the *avodah zarah itself* commands us to do this thing (e.g., the *avodah zarah* has decreed this thing *tamei* or *tahor*, or has commanded us to take a *lulav* on Succos). Since the prophet says that we are to do the mitzvah *for the sake of* an *avodah zarah,* he is a prophet of *avodah zarah.* But if he says that the idol instructed us to do this as a mitzvah of Hashem, he is not considered a prophet of *avodah zarah.* [See *Yad HaKetanah, Hil. Avodah Zarah* Ch. 4 §37.]

15. A person is never punished in *beis din* unless two witnesses saw the act, and he was warned about its consequences in advance. See General Introduction, Sec. VI, at note 15.

16. [Chinuch refers to Chapter *Hanechenakin,* which is Chapter 10 in our editions of Gemara *Sanhedrin.* See Mitzvah 516 note 10.] The laws of the mitzvah are codified in *Rambam, Hil. Avodah Zarah* 5:6-7.

17. It applies in Eretz Yisrael and the Diaspora, whether the *Beis HaMikdash* is standing or not. And it applies to both men and women in accordance with the general rule concerning mitzvah-prohibitions. See Mitzvah 517 note 9.

◆§ Insight: Who Is Considered a Prophet of Avodah Zarah?

At the beginning of this mitzvah, Chinuch defines two types of prophets of *avodah zarah.* One is a person who says that a certain *avodah zarah* has commanded us to worship it, and that it promises to reward those who worship it and punish those who do not. The other is a person who says that the Almighty has commanded us to worship a certain *avodah zarah.* Although this second type of person has not prophesied in the *name* of an *avodah zarah,* since he delivered a supposedly "prophetic" message that we are to accept an *avodah zarah,* he is considered a prophet of *avodah zarah.*

In including the second type of prophet in this mitzvah, Chinuch follows the approach of *Rambam* in *Sefer HaMitzvos* (*Lo Saaseh* 26). Commentators note, however, that *Rambam* seems to take a different approach in *Mishneh Torah.* There, in *Hilchos Avodah Zarah* (5:6), when he describes the law of "one who prophesies in the name of *avodah zarah," Rambam* mentions only a person who states that an *avodah zarah* itself spoke to him and issued a command; i.e., the first case mentioned by Chinuch. *Rambam* does not mention the case of a person who states that Hashem has commanded us to worship an *avodah zarah.* In fact, elsewhere in *Mishneh Torah* (*Hil. Yesodei HaTorah* 9:5), *Rambam* writes that a prophet who claims that Hashem commanded us to worship *avodah zarah* is a *false* prophet [for he has prophesied falsely in the Name of Hashem]. Thus, he transgresses the previous mitzvah, not this one. It would seem that in *Mishneh Torah, Rambam* retracted the opinion that he stated earlier in *Sefer HaMitzvos,* and maintains that only a person who actually speaks *in the name* of an *avodah zarah* is considered a prophet of *avodah zarah* (see *Yad HaLevi* to *Sefer HaMitzvos* ibid.). Chinuch, however, presents the mitzvah in accordance with *Sefer HaMitzvos,* as he often does. [See also *Rambam's Introduction to the Mishnah,* where he mentions both types of prophets. *Ramban* (*Deuteronomy* 13:2) likewise maintains that both types of prophets are included in this mitzvah.]

Minchas Chinuch (§2) raises another difficulty: If a "prophet" claims that we are commanded to worship an *avodah zarah,* then it seems that he is not in the category of a "prophet of *avodah zarah"* at all. If he tries to convince only one person to commit idolatry, he is considered a *meisis* (inciter), as discussed in Mitzvah 462. And if he tries to convince many people to commit idolatry, he

is considered a *madiach* (subverter), as discussed in Mitzvah 87. Either way, he is liable to *sekilah*, not *chenek*, like a "prophet of *avodah zarah*." This applies whether he claims to be a prophet or not, and whether he succeeded in convincing people to worship *avodah zarah* or not (see Chinuch in those mitzvos). *Rambam* states this clearly in *Hil. Avodah Zarah* (5:1-2). How can Chinuch, and *Rambam* in *Sefer HaMitzvos* (ibid.), state that if someone claims he was prophetically instructed that we should worship *avodah zarah* he is considered a "prophet of *avodah zarah*" and is liable to *chenek* (a less severe form of execution than *sekilah*)?

Moreover, *Rambam* seems to contradict himself within *Mishneh Torah* itself. In *Hil. Yesodei Ha-Torah* (9:5), *Rambam* states that a prophet who says that Hashem commanded us to worship *avodah zarah* is considered a *false* prophet (i.e., he violates the previous mitzvah), and is liable to *chenek*. But this contradicts *Rambam's* own ruling in *Hil. Avodah Zarah* (ibid.) that a prophet who incites people to worship *avodah zarah* is considered either a *meisis* or a *madiach* and is liable to *sekilah* (*Lechem Mishneh, Hil. Yesodei HaTorah* 9:1 and *Hil. Avodah Zarah* 5:1).

Some explain that a person becomes a *meisis* or a *madiach* only if he says, "*I* will go and worship *avodah zarah*," or "Let *us* go and worship *avodah zarah*" (see Mishnah, *Sanhedrin* 67a). This is because the definition of "inciting" or "subverting" to worship *avodah zarah* is that the person tries to *lure* people after himself into worshiping idols. Only in such a case is he liable to *sekilah*. If, however, he does not use himself as a lure, but states, "*You* should go and worship *avodah zarah*," he is not considered a *meisis* or a *madiach*. This applies even if he claims to be delivering a prophetic message to us. Thus, if someone states that he received a prophecy from an idol that we should worship it, but does not say that *he* will worship it, he is a prophet of *avodah zarah*. And if he claims that he received the prophecy from Hashem, then according to Chinuch (and *Rambam* in *Sefer HaMitzvos*), he is considered a prophet of *avodah zarah*; and according to *Rambam* in *Mishneh Torah*, he is considered a false prophet, as mentioned above. Either way, he is subject to the punishment of *chenek* and not *sekilah*. The only time he is subject to *sekilah* as either a *meisis* or a *madiach* is if he declares that he himself will worship an *avodah zarah* and he encourages others to do the same (*Pri Chadash* to *Hil. Yesodei HaTorah* 9:4, cited in *Sefer HaLikkutim* there; *Minchas Chinuch* 462:7).

For other explanations, see *Lechem Mishneh* and other commentators to *Rambam* ibid.; *Yad HaLevi* ibid.; *Maharam Schik*; *Chazon Ish, Sanhedrin* 21:2. See also *R' Y. F. Perla, Sefer HaMitzvos of R' Saadiah Gaon, Onesh* 65 [Vol. III, pp. 87b-88b].

מִצְוָה תקיט: שֶׁלֹּא נִמָּנַע מֵהֲרִיגַת נְבִיא שֶׁקֶר וְלֹא נָגוּר מִמֶּנּוּ

שֶׁלֹּא נִירָא מִלַּהֲרֹג נְבִיא הַשֶּׁקֶר וְלֹא נִפְחַד שֶׁיִּהְיֶה לָנוּ בָּזֶה שׁוּם עֹנֶשׁ[1], וַאֲפִלּוּ הָיָה מִתְנַבֵּא בְּקִיּוּם הַמִּצְוֹת, אַחַר שֶׁשֶּׁקֶר בְּפִיו אֵין לָנוּ עֹנֶשׁ בְּמִיתָתוֹ, אֲבָל הִיא עָלֵינוּ מִצְוָה[2]. וְעַל זֶה נֶאֱמַר (דברים י״ח, כ״ב) לֹא תָגוּר מִמֶּנּוּ, וּלְשׁוֹן סִפְרֵי (כאן), לֹא תָגוּר מִמֶּנּוּ, לֹא תִמְנַע עַצְמְךָ מִלְּלַמֵּד עָלָיו חוֹבָה[3].

Mitzvah 519
The Prohibition to Be Afraid to Execute a False Prophet

אֲשֶׁר יְדַבֵּר הַנָּבִיא בְּשֵׁם ה׳ וְלֹא יִהְיֶה הַדָּבָר וְלֹא יָבֹא הוּא הַדָּבָר אֲשֶׁר לֹא דִבְּרוֹ ה׳ בְּזָדוֹן דִּבְּרוֹ הַנָּבִיא לֹא תָגוּר מִמֶּנּוּ

If the prophet will speak in the Name of HASHEM *and that thing will not occur and not come about — that is the word that* HASHEM *has not spoken; the prophet has spoken it flagrantly, you shall not fear him* (*Deuteronomy* 18:22).

In Mitzvah 517, we learned that a false prophet is subject to execution. This mitzvah is a prohibition against being afraid to argue for the prophet's conviction or carry out his death sentence. Why does the Torah issue this additional prohibition? We learned in Mitzvah 516 that only the most upstanding and righteous individuals merited to receive prophecy from Hashem. Thus, any prophet who states a false prophecy, as well as any impostor who falsely claims to have received a prophecy, must be a man of prominence who is righteous enough to be a prophet, or at least is perceived to be so righteous. When such a person sins and states a false prophecy, people would naturally hesitate to execute him. The Torah therefore warns against being impressed by his stature and not judging him for his sin (*Rambam, Hil. Avodah Zarah* 5:9; *Mizrachi* to *Deuteronomy* 18:22).

שֶׁלֹּא נִירָא מִלַּהֲרֹג נְבִיא הַשֶּׁקֶר — **We are** commanded **not to be afraid to execute a false prophet,** וְלֹא נִפְחַד שֶׁיִּהְיֶה לָנוּ בָּזֶה שׁוּם עֹנֶשׁ — **and not to be worried that we will incur any punishment for this.**[1] וַאֲפִלּוּ הָיָה מִתְנַבֵּא בְּקִיּוּם הַמִּצְוֹת — **Even if he was saying prophecy about fulfilling the mitzvos** of Hashem, אַחַר שֶׁשֶּׁקֶר בְּפִיו אֵין לָנוּ עֹנֶשׁ בְּמִיתָתוֹ — **since he stated a lie** in his "prophecy," **we will not be punished for executing him;** אֲבָל הִיא עָלֵינוּ מִצְוָה — **to the contrary, [his execution] is a mitzvah upon us.**[2] וְעַל זֶה נֶאֱמַר "לֹא תָגוּר מִמֶּנּוּ" — **Regarding this it is stated** (*Deuteronomy* 18:22): ***you shall not fear him.*** וּלְשׁוֹן סִפְרֵי — **And, to quote *Sifrei*** (to the verse): "לֹא תָגוּר מִמֶּנּוּ", לֹא תִמְנַע עַצְמְךָ מִלְּלַמֵּד עָלָיו חוֹבָה — When it states, ***you shall not fear*** (*lo sagur*) ***him,*** it means: **you shall not hold yourself back from arguing for his conviction.**[3]

NOTES

1. As mentioned above (Mitzvah 517 note 1), some commentators maintain that the prohibition against saying false prophecy, and the death sentence for violating it, apply only to an actual prophet. *Beis din* might be concerned that executing a prophet is a sin that will cause Divine retribution. Even according to the opinion (cited there) that the prohibition and death sentence apply to anyone who *claims* to be a prophet, such a concern exists. No one could make such a claim unless he was an upstanding individual whom people would believe had received a prophecy from Hashem. *Beis din* might be afraid to sentence such an individual to death (see *R' S. R. Hirsch* and *Haamek Davar* to the verse).

2. It is a mitzvah-obligation upon *beis din* to carry out any sentence that the Torah imposes on a sinner, including execution (see Mitzvos 47, 50, 261, and 555). Here, the Torah adds a mitzvah-*prohibition* against being afraid to execute a false prophet due to his prominence.

This applies to a false prophet (the subject of Mitzvah 517), not to a prophet of *avodah zarah* (the subject of Mitzvah 518). A prophet of *avodah zarah* is viewed as an inferior, subversive person, so the Torah did not need to add a prohibition against being afraid to execute him (*Dina DeChayei* to *Smag, Lo Saaseh* 35; *Mishnas Chachamim, Yavin Shemuah* 31:1; see *Minchas Chinuch* §2).

3. The verse does not only prohibit *beis din* from being

מִשָּׁרְשֵׁי הַמִּצְוָה מַה שֶּׁכָּתַבְתִּי בְּסָמוּךְ בְּמִתְנַבֵּא בְּשֶׁקֶר[4]**.**
דִּינֵי הַמִּצְוָה קְצָרִים וְהֵם בְּסַנְהֶדְרִין[5]**.**
וְנוֹהֶגֶת מִצְוָה זוֹ בִּזְמַן הַבַּיִת שֶׁיִּשְׂרָאֵל בְּיִשּׁוּבָן, כִּי אָז בְּיָדֵינוּ לָדוּן דִּינֵי נְפָשׁוֹת. וְאָמְרוּ זִכְרוֹנָם לִבְרָכָה (סנהדרין ב׳ ע״א) **שֶׁאֵין דָּנִין נְבִיא הַשֶּׁקֶר אֶלָּא בְּבֵית דִּין שֶׁל שִׁבְעִים וְאֶחָד**[6]**.**

Underlying Purpose of the Mitzvah

מִשָּׁרְשֵׁי הַמִּצְוָה מַה שֶּׁכָּתַבְתִּי בְּסָמוּךְ בְּמִתְנַבֵּא בְּשֶׁקֶר – **Among the underlying purposes of the mitzvah is what I wrote above** (Mitzvah 517) **regarding a person who prophesies falsely.**[4]

Laws of the Mitzvah

דִּינֵי הַמִּצְוָה קְצָרִים – **The laws of the mitzvah are brief,** וְהֵם בְּסַנְהֶדְרִין – **and they are** set out **in** Tractate ***Sanhedrin.***[5]

Applicability of the Mitzvah

וְנוֹהֶגֶת מִצְוָה זוֹ בִּזְמַן הַבַּיִת שֶׁיִּשְׂרָאֵל בְּיִשּׁוּבָן – **This mitzvah applies in the time of the *Beis HaMikdash,* when the Jewish people are settled in their land,** כִּי אָז בְּיָדֵינוּ לָדוּן דִּינֵי נְפָשׁוֹת – **for that is when we have the power to judge capital cases** and execute a person who is liable to death, such as a false prophet. וְאָמְרוּ זִכְרוֹנָם לִבְרָכָה – **And, [the Sages], of blessed memory, have stated** (*Sanhedrin* 2a) שֶׁאֵין דָּנִין נְבִיא הַשֶּׁקֶר אֶלָּא בְּבֵית דִּין שֶׁל שִׁבְעִים וְאֶחָד – **that we do not judge a false prophet except in a court of seventy-one judges,** i.e., the Great Sanhedrin.[6]

NOTES

afraid to carry out the execution of a false prophet *after* he has been convicted. It also prohibits the judges — and all others — from holding back arguments for his conviction *during* the trial (*Rambam, Hil. Avodah Zarah* 5:9; see *R' Y. F. Perla, Sefer HaMitzvos of Rav Saadiah Gaon, Onesh* 66 [Vol. III, p. 178 ד״ה איברא]).

[The expression לֹא תָגוּר has two meanings: *do not be afraid,* and *do not hold in* (*Rashi, Deuteronomy* 1:17). Accordingly, when the verse of this mitzvah (ibid. 18:22) states, לֹא תָגוּר מִמֶּנּוּ, it teaches that (1) we must not be afraid to execute the false prophet; and (2) we must not hold back arguments for his conviction (see *Rashi* and *Sifsei Chachamim* to the verse; cf. *Mizrachi* there, *Maharam Schik*).]

4. Chinuch explained there that true prophecy is a foundation of our religion, and false prophecy undermines faith in that foundation. It is thus critical to prevent false prophets from practicing their deceit.

5. The laws of false prophecy, in general, are discussed in *Sanhedrin* 89a-b, but the Gemara does not discuss any specific law of *this* mitzvah. The laws are those mentioned by Chinuch above — one may not hold back an argument that would lead to the false prophet's conviction, and *beis din* may not refrain from executing him out of fear of retribution. These laws are codified in *Rambam, Hil. Avodah Zarah* 5:9.

6. The Great Sanhedrin does not exist nowadays and will be reinstated only in the times of Mashiach, so the mitzvah cannot apply until that time.

According to *Smak* (Mitzvah 13), this mitzvah applies nowadays as well. He explains that it prohibits us from being afraid of any person who tries to intimidate us into abandoning our faith and worshiping a false god. For discussion, see *R' Y. F. Perla* ibid.

מִצְוָה תקכ: מִצְוָה לְהָכִין שֵׁשׁ עָרֵי מִקְלָט[3,2,1]

לְהַבְדִּיל שֵׁשׁ עָרֵי מִקְלָט מֵעָרֵי הַלְוִיִּם שֶׁתִּהְיֶנָה מוּעָדוֹת לָנוּס שָׁמָּה מַכֵּה נֶפֶשׁ בִּשְׁגָגָה, וְשֶׁיְּתַקְּנוּ הַדְּרָכִים לְעֻמַּת הֶעָרִים וְיִתְיַשְּׁרוּ[4], וּכְעִנְיָן שֶׁאָמְרוּ[5] זִכְרוֹנָם

Mitzvah 520
The Obligation to Prepare Six Cities of Refuge

תָּכִין לְךָ הַדֶּרֶךְ וְשִׁלַּשְׁתָּ אֶת גְּבוּל אַרְצְךָ אֲשֶׁר יַנְחִילְךָ ה׳ אֱלֹהֶיךָ וְהָיָה לָנוּס שָׁמָּה כָּל רֹצֵחַ

Prepare the way for yourself, and divide into three parts the boundary of your Land that HASHEM, your God, causes you to inherit; and it shall be for any killer to flee there (*Deuteronomy* 19:3).

Unintentional killing is not subject to the death penalty, but when the killing involved some measure of negligence, the Torah decrees that the killer be exiled to a "city of refuge" (*ir miklat;* see Mitzvah 410). In addition to providing unintentional killers with atonement, exile to a city of refuge affords them legal protection from *go'alei hadam* (avenging relatives; sing. *go'eil hadam*).[1] In recognition of the strong emotions experienced by relatives of a person who was killed, the Torah declares that a *go'eil hadam* who exacts revenge before the killer reaches a city of refuge is exempt from the death penalty.[2] If, however, a *go'eil hadam* exacts vengeance within a city of refuge, he is liable for murder.

A sentence of exile can be served in any of the forty-eight Levitical cities (see Mitzvah 408), and all of them provide refuge from *go'alei hadam*. However, six of these cities were specifically designated as *arei miklat* (cities of refuge). [Chinuch will discuss some practical ramifications of this designation.] This mitzvah establishes a communal obligation to designate these six cities of refuge and to ensure that they can be reached quickly and safely.[3]

לְהַבְדִּיל שֵׁשׁ עָרֵי מִקְלָט מֵעָרֵי הַלְוִיִּם – We are commanded **to separate six cities of refuge from among the cities of the Leviim** **שֶׁתִּהְיֶנָה מוּעָדוֹת לָנוּס שָׁמָּה מַכֵּה נֶפֶשׁ בִּשְׁגָגָה** – **that should be available so that an unintentional killer can flee there.** **וְשֶׁיְּתַקְּנוּ הַדְּרָכִים לְעֻמַּת הֶעָרִים וְיִתְיַשְּׁרוּ** – **And** we are also commanded to ensure **that the roads leading to the cities** of refuge **are in good repair and straight,** so that it is easy for an unintentional killer to flee there,[4] **וּכְעִנְיָן**

NOTES

1. Literally, *redeemer of blood.* The *go'eil hadam* is a surviving relative of the victim who is fit to inherit him (*Rambam, Hil. Rotze'ach* 1:2). [There is some discussion as to how close of a relative one must be to qualify as a *go'eil hadam,* and whether there can be multiple *go'alei hadam* for a single victim; see *Teshuvos Tzemach Tzedek* [Nikolsburg] §111; *Mirkeves HaMishneh* and *Ohr Same'ach* to *Rambam* ibid.; *Chazon Ish, Sanhedrin* 19:2.]

2. This applies only in a case where the killing involved some degree of negligence. If it resulted from an accident that the killer had no reason to anticipate, he is exempt from exile, and if a *go'eil hadam* kills him, it is considered murder, for which the *go'eil hadam* is liable to execution (*Rambam, Hil. Rotze'ach* 6:1-3; see further, Mitzvah 410 note 1).

3. In addition to providing permanent refuge to unintentional killers, cities of refuge also provided temporary refuge to intentional killers while they awaited trial. For although a *go'eil hadam* is forbidden to exact revenge on a killer who is awaiting trial, if he does so outside the city of refuge, he is not liable for murder. If, however, he exacts revenge inside a city of refuge, he *is* liable for murder; see Mitzvah 408 note 5. Nevertheless, the primary focus of this mitzvah is providing refuge for unintentional killers, as Chinuch makes clear throughout the mitzvah.

4. We are first and foremost obligated to construct roads that lead from all other cities to the cities of refuge. In addition to actually constructing these roads, we are obligated to maintain them in good condition. This is all to ensure that unintentional killers can flee to a city of refuge without difficulty (see *Rambam, Hil. Rotze'ach* 8:5).

It emerges that this mitzvah has two components: (1) actually designating these six cities as cities of

לִבְרָכָה שֶׁמִּקְלָט מִקְלָט הָיוּ כּוֹתְבִין בְּפָרָשַׁת הַדְּרָכִים, וּמְפַנִּין הַדְּרָכִים שֶׁלֹּא יְהֵא בָּהֶן דָּבָר שֶׁיְּאַחֵר הַבּוֹרֵחַ מִן הַמְּרוּצָה[6], וְעַל זֶה נֶאֱמַר (דברים י״ט, ג׳) תָּכִין לְךָ הַדֶּרֶךְ וְשִׁלַּשְׁתָּ אֶת גְּבוּל אַרְצְךָ וְגוֹ׳[7].

שֹׁרֶשׁ מִצְוָה זוֹ יָדוּעַ וּבָרוּר, שֶׁהוּא כְּדֵי שֶׁלֹּא יוּמַת הַהוֹרֵג שׁוֹגֵג עַל יְדֵי גּוֹאֲלֵי הַדָּם[8].

מִדִּינֵי הַמִּצְוָה מַה שֶּׁאָמְרוּ זִכְרוֹנָם לִבְרָכָה כִּי שֵׁשׁ עָרִים אֵלֶּה שָׁלֹשׁ מֵהֶם הִבְדִּיל מֹשֶׁה רַבֵּנוּ עָלָיו הַשָּׁלוֹם בְּעֵבֶר הַיַּרְדֵּן, וְשָׁלֹשׁ הִבְדִּיל יְהוֹשֻׁעַ בְּאֶרֶץ כְּנַעַן[9],

---

שֶׁאָמְרוּ[5] זִכְרוֹנָם לִבְרָכָה – **in the same vein as that which [the Sages], of blessed memory, stated** (see *Rambam, Hil. Rotze'ach* 8:5) שֶׁמִּקְלָט מִקְלָט הָיוּ כּוֹתְבִין בְּפָרָשַׁת הַדְּרָכִים – **that "Refuge," "Refuge," was written** on signposts located **at crossroads** on the way to the cities of refuge, so that upon reaching a crossroad, a fleeing killer would immediately know in which direction to proceed. וּמְפַנִּין הַדְּרָכִים שֶׁלֹּא יְהֵא בָּהֶן דָּבָר שֶׁיְּאַחֵר הַבּוֹרֵחַ מִן הַמְּרוּצָה – **We** are **also** obligated to **clear the roads** leading to the cities of refuge, **so that nothing that might slow a fleeing [unintentional killer] from his swift pace remains in them.**[6] וְעַל זֶה נֶאֱמַר – **Regarding this** obligation, **it is stated** (*Deuteronomy* 19:3): "תָּכִין לְךָ הַדֶּרֶךְ וְשִׁלַּשְׁתָּ אֶת גְּבוּל אַרְצְךָ וְגוֹ׳" – ***Prepare the way for yourself, and divide into three parts the boundary of your Land*** *that HASHEM, your God, causes you to inherit; and it shall be for any killer to flee there.*[7]

Underlying Purpose of the Mitzvah

שֹׁרֶשׁ מִצְוָה זוֹ יָדוּעַ וּבָרוּר – **The underlying purpose of the mitzvah is obvious and clear;** שֶׁהוּא כְּדֵי שֶׁלֹּא יוּמַת הַהוֹרֵג שׁוֹגֵג עַל יְדֵי גּוֹאֲלֵי הַדָּם – **it is so that an unintentional killer will not** himself **die at the hands of** the ***go'alei hadam.***[8]

Laws of the Mitzvah

מִדִּינֵי הַמִּצְוָה – **Among the laws of the mitzvah** is מַה שֶּׁאָמְרוּ זִכְרוֹנָם לִבְרָכָה – **that which [the Sages], of blessed memory, stated** (see *Rambam, Hil. Rotze'ach* 8:2-3), כִּי שֵׁשׁ עָרִים אֵלֶּה – **that** with regard to **these six cities** of refuge, שָׁלֹשׁ מֵהֶם הִבְדִּיל מֹשֶׁה רַבֵּנוּ עָלָיו הַשָּׁלוֹם בְּעֵבֶר הַיַּרְדֵּן – **Moses, our teacher, peace be upon him, separated three of them in Transjordan,** וְשָׁלֹשׁ הִבְדִּיל יְהוֹשֻׁעַ בְּאֶרֶץ כְּנַעַן – **while Joshua separated** the remaining **three** cities **in the Land of Canaan.**[9]

NOTES

refuge, and (2) constructing and maintaining roads leading to them. See *Rambam's* list of mitzvos at the beginning of *Hil. Rotze'ach,* and see below, note 7.

5. Word emended based on *Minchas Yitzchak.*

6. For example, we are obligated to clear the roads of debris and obstacles, to level out hilly or depressed areas, and to build bridges over bodies of water (*Rambam* ibid. 8:5).

7. As mentioned in note 4, this mitzvah-obligation has two components: actually designating the cities, and building and maintaining roads that lead to them. The verse cited by Chinuch (based on *Sefer HaMitzvos, Asei* 182) is cited by *Rambam* in *Mishneh Torah* (*Hil. Rotze'ach* 8:5) as the source of the obligation to construct and maintain roads leading to the cities of refuge, but regarding the obligation to actually set aside cities of refuge, *Rambam* (ibid. §1) cites the previous verse, which states: *You shall separate three cities for yourselves in the midst of your Land, which HASHEM, your God, gives you to possess it.* See *Radvaz, Metzudas David* §481.

8. See above, note 1. As mentioned in the introduction to this mitzvah, a *go'eil hadam* who exacts revenge before an unintentional killer reaches a city of refuge is exempt from the death penalty (when the original death resulted from the killer's negligence). Nevertheless, since an unintentional killer does not really deserve to die (despite his negligence), and he can gain atonement through exile, the Torah commands that we take measures to ensure that he survives; namely, that we designate cities of refuge and facilitate travel to them.

9. "Transjordan" refers to the area east of the Jordan River that was conquered by Moses and the Jewish people from Sichon, king of the Amorites, and Og, king of Bashan (see *Numbers* 21:21-35). These territories were settled by the tribes of Reuben, Gad, and part of the tribe of Manasseh (see ibid. 32:33). "Land of Canaan" refers to the area to the west of the Jordan River that was conquered by Joshua and the Jewish people after

וְלֹא קָלְטוּ שֶׁל מֹשֶׁה עַד שֶׁהֻבְדְּלוּ הַשָּׁלֹשׁ שֶׁל יְהוֹשֻׁעַ[10], וְאִם כֵּן לָמָּה הִבְדִּילָן מֹשֶׁה, אָמַר
מִצְוָה שֶׁבָּאָה לְיָדִי אֲקַיְּמֶנָּה[11], וּבִימֵי מֶלֶךְ הַמָּשִׁיחַ נוֹסִיף עוֹד שָׁלֹשׁ, שֶׁנֶּאֱמַר וְיָסַפְתָּ לְךָ עוֹד
שָׁלֹשׁ עָרִים עַל הַשָּׁלֹשׁ הָאֵלֶּה[12].
וְאָמְרוּ זִכְרוֹנָם לִבְרָכָה שֶׁכָּל עָרֵי הַלְוִיִּם הָיוּ קוֹלְטוֹת, שֶׁנֶּאֱמַר וַעֲלֵיהֶם תִּתְּנוּ אַרְבָּעִים

וְלֹא קָלְטוּ שֶׁל מֹשֶׁה עַד שֶׁהֻבְדְּלוּ הַשָּׁלֹשׁ שֶׁל יְהוֹשֻׁעַ — **However, [the three cities] of Moses** (i.e., those designated by him) **did not** actually **provide refuge** for unintentional killers **until the three** cities **of Joshua were** later **separated.**[10] וְאִם כֵּן לָמָּה הִבְדִּילָן מֹשֶׁה — **If so, why did Moses** bother to **separate them?** אָמַר מִצְוָה שֶׁבָּאָה לְיָדִי אֲקַיְּמֶנָּה — **He said** to himself: **"Whatever mitzvah has come my way, I shall fulfill it."**[11]

Chinuch discusses three additional cities of refuge that the Jewish people will one day be required to separate:

וּבִימֵי מֶלֶךְ הַמָּשִׁיחַ נוֹסִיף עוֹד שָׁלֹשׁ — **In the days of the King Mashiach, we will add three more** cities of refuge, bringing the total to nine, שֶׁנֶּאֱמַר — **as it is stated** (*Deuteronomy* 19:9): ״וְיָסַפְתָּ לְךָ עוֹד שָׁלֹשׁ עָרִים עַל הַשָּׁלֹשׁ הָאֵלֶּה״ — *When HASHEM will broaden your boundary, as He swore to your forefathers ... When you observe this entire commandment to perform it — which I command you today ...* **then you shall add three more cities to these three.**[12]

Chinuch discusses the status of the forty-two Levitical cities that are not specifically referred to by the Torah as "cities of refuge":

וְאָמְרוּ זִכְרוֹנָם לִבְרָכָה — **[The Sages], of blessed memory, stated** (*Rambam, Hil. Rotze'ach* 8:9) שֶׁכָּל עָרֵי הַלְוִיִּם הָיוּ קוֹלְטוֹת — **that all** forty-eight **of the cities of the Leviim could provide refuge** for unintentional killers, שֶׁנֶּאֱמַר — **as it is stated** (*Numbers* 35:6-7): ״וַעֲלֵיהֶם תִּתְּנוּ אַרְבָּעִים״

NOTES

Moses died, and settled by the remaining nine and a half tribes. ["Canaan" was one of the seven nations that inhabited this land before the Jewish people conquered it. For reasons why it was referred to specifically as the Land of "Canaan," see *Vayikra Rabbah* 17:5.]

The Torah commands that three of the six cities of refuge be located in Transjordan and that the three remaining cities be located in the Land of Canaan (*Numbers* 35:14). Moses never entered the Land of Canaan, but before he died, he designated the three cities of refuge in Transjordan (*Deuteronomy* 4:41-43). After Moses died, the Jewish people, under the leadership of Joshua, crossed the Jordan River and began their conquest of the Land of Canaan. After conquering and dividing it, Joshua oversaw the designation of the three remaining cities of refuge; see *Joshua* Ch. 20 (see also *Rashi, Makkos* 9b ד״ה עד שלא, and *Ramban, Deuteronomy* 19:8).

10. The six cities of refuge function only as a complete unit. Therefore, the three cities designated by Moses did not provide refuge until the remaining three cities were designated by Joshua. See Mishnah, *Makkos* 9b, for the Scriptural source of this law.

11. Designating cities of refuge so that they can eventually provide refuge is considered a mitzvah. Although the complete mitzvah is to designate all six cities, Moses seized the opportunity to perform whatever part of the mitzvah that he could. The Gemara (*Makkos* 10a) cites this episode as proof of Moses'

tremendous desire to perform mitzvos. See also *Devarim Rabbah* 2:26-27.

12. After commanding the Jewish people to designate three cities of refuge in Eretz Yisrael (in addition to the three in Transjordan that Moses had already designated), the Torah commands the Jewish people to designate an *additional* three cities of refuge at some future point in time. The Torah describes that point as a time when the Jewish people will (a) take possession of the entire land promised to their forefathers; and (b) serve Hashem wholeheartedly. This refers to the times of Mashiach, when the previously unconquered lands of the Keini, Kenizi, and Kadmoni (promised to Abraham in the Covenant Between the Parts; *Genesis* 15:19) will be conquered, and when God will give the Jewish people *a single heart and a single path — to fear Me all the days* [*Jeremiah* 32:39] (see *Bereishis Rabbah* 44:23 and *Ramban* to *Deuteronomy* 19:8; see also *Rambam, Hil. Melachim* 11:2). [The three additional cities of refuge will be located in the newly conquered lands of the Keini, Kenizi, and Kadmoni (*Rambam, Hil. Rotze'ach* 8:4; see *Minchas Chinuch* §1).]

[For discussion regarding the need for cities of refuge during the era of Mashiach, a time when peace, goodwill, and righteousness will reign supreme, see *Shelah, Beis David* (§50 and §52 in Oz VeHadar ed.); *Minchas Chinuch* §1; *Nachal Eisan* 1:1 [6]; *Emunas Yehoshua,* Vol. VI, p. 1711.]

וּשְׁתַּיִם עִיר כָּל הֶעָרִים אֲשֶׁר תִּתְּנוּ לַלְוִיִּם וְגוֹ׳, הִקִּישָׁן הַכָּתוּב כֻּלָּן. אֲבָל הֶפְרֵשׁ זֶה הָיָה בֵּינֵיהֶם, שֶׁעָרֵי מִקְלָט קוֹלְטוֹת בֵּין לְדַעַת בֵּין שֶׁלֹּא לְדַעַת[13], וּשְׁאָר עָרֵי הַלְוִיִּם אֵינָם קוֹלְטוֹת אֶלָּא לְדַעַת. וְרוֹצֵחַ הַדָּר בְּעָרֵי מִקְלָט אֵינוֹ נוֹתֵן שְׂכַר בַּיִת, וּבִשְׁאָר הֶעָרִים נוֹתֵן שְׂכַר בַּיִת[14]. וְאָמְרוּ זִכְרוֹנָם לִבְרָכָה (רמב״ם פ״ח מהל׳ רוצח ה״ה) **שֶׁרֹחַב דֶּרֶךְ עִיר מִקְלָט צָרִיךְ שְׁלֹשִׁים וּשְׁתַּיִם אַמּוֹת[15]. וּבַחֲמִשָּׁה עָשָׂר בַּאֲדָר בֵּית דִּין שׁוֹלְחִין שְׁלוּחִים לְתַקֵּן אֶת הַדְּרָכִים[16], וְאִם נִתְרַשְּׁלוּ בַּדָּבָר כְּאִלּוּ שָׁפְכוּ דָּמִים[17].**

וּשְׁתַּיִם עִיר כָּל הֶעָרִים אֲשֶׁר תִּתְּנוּ לַלְוִיִּם וְגוֹ׳ – *The cities that you shall give to the Leviim: the six cities of refuge that you shall provide for a killer to flee there,* ***and in addition to them you shall give forty-two cities. All the cities that you shall give to the Leviim:*** *forty-eight cities.* **הִקִּישָׁן הַכָּתוּב כֻּלָּן** – In this verse, **Scripture made a *hekeish*** (comparison) **between [the six cities of refuge and the remaining Levitical cities],** which teaches that the remaining forty-two Levitical cities can also provide refuge.

Despite this *hekeish,* the fact that the Torah specifically identifies six cites as "cities of refuge" indicates that there must be *some* manner in which those cities differ from the rest of the Levitical cities: **אֲבָל הֶפְרֵשׁ זֶה הָיָה בֵּינֵיהֶם – However, these** following **differences existed between [the six cities of refuge and the remaining forty-two Levitical cities]: שֶׁעָרֵי מִקְלָט קוֹלְטוֹת בֵּין לְדַעַת בֵּין שֶׁלֹּא לְדַעַת** – (1) **The** six **cities of refuge provided refuge whether** the unintentional killer entered one of them **with awareness** of having reached asylum, **or whether** he entered the city **without** such **awareness,**[13] **וּשְׁאָר עָרֵי הַלְוִיִּם אֵינָם קוֹלְטוֹת אֶלָּא לְדַעַת – whereas the remaining** forty-two **Levitical cities provided refuge only** if the killer entered one of them **with** such **awareness; וְרוֹצֵחַ הַדָּר בְּעָרֵי מִקְלָט אֵינוֹ נוֹתֵן שְׂכַר בַּיִת – and** (2) **an** unintentional **killer who resided in** one of **the** six **cities of refuge was not required to pay rent for his housing** (i.e., the residents of the city were obligated provide him with free living accommodations), **וּבִשְׁאָר הֶעָרִים נוֹתֵן שְׂכַר בַּיִת – whereas, in the remaining** forty-two Levitical **cities, [a killer]** who lived there **was required to pay rent for his housing.**[14]

Chinuch returns to the topic of the roads leading into the cities of refuge and their upkeep: **וְאָמְרוּ זִכְרוֹנָם לִבְרָכָה – [The Sages], of blessed memory, stated** (*Rambam* ibid. §5) **שֶׁרֹחַב דֶּרֶךְ עִיר מִקְלָט צָרִיךְ שְׁלֹשִׁים וּשְׁתַּיִם אַמּוֹת – that a road** leading **to a city of refuge had to be** at least **thirty-two *amos* wide.**[15] **וּבַחֲמִשָּׁה עָשָׂר בַּאֲדָר בֵּית דִּין שׁוֹלְחִין שְׁלוּחִים לְתַקֵּן אֶת הַדְּרָכִים** – Each year, **on the fifteenth of Adar, *beis din* would send out agents of the court to repair the roads** leading to the cities of refuge,[16] **וְאִם נִתְרַשְּׁלוּ בַּדָּבָר כְּאִלּוּ שָׁפְכוּ דָּמִים – and if [*beis din*] was lax in this matter** and an unintentional killer was killed by a *go'eil hadam* as a result, **it is** considered **as though they** themselves **spilled blood.**[17]

NOTES

13. That is, either he was completely unaware of the fact that the city provides refuge to unintentional killers (*Rashi, Makkos* 10a ד״ה בין לדעת), or he was asleep when he entered the city (*Ritva* ad loc. ד״ה שלא לדעת).

14. See Insight to Mitzvah 410 for discussion of these differences.

15. [In contemporary measurements, an *amah* is between 18.9 and 22.7 in. (48-57.7 cm.).] In Biblical and Talmudic times, the standard width of a public thoroughfare was sixteen *amos.* A road leading to a city of refuge was supposed to be twice as wide, to ensure easy access to the city (see *Bava Basra* 100a-b).

16. These agents would first inspect these roads for damage, and would then attend to any road they had determined was in need of repair (*Rambam, Hil. Rotze'ach* 8:6).

Roads in Eretz Yisrael are most susceptible to damage during the winter months, when they are exposed to the winter rains. From the middle of Adar and on, heavy rains are rare. It is therefore logical to begin attending to road repairs at that time; see Mishnah, *Shekalim* 2a with commentaries.

17. If the flight of an unintentional killer to a city of refuge is impeded by poor road conditions and he is killed by a *go'eil hadam*, those responsible for maintenance of the roads bear some blame, since they did not take the required measures to ensure swift and easy escape to the cities of refuge.

וְאָמְרוּ זִכְרוֹנָם לִבְרָכָה (רמב"ם שם הי"א) **שֶׁכָּל עִיר הַקּוֹלֶטֶת, תְּחוּמָהּ**[18] **קוֹלֵט**[19]**. וְיֶתֶר פְּרָטֵי הַמִּצְוָה בְּסַנְהֶדְרִין וּמַכּוֹת וּשְׁקָלִים וְסוֹטָה**[20]**.**

וְנוֹהֶגֶת מִצְוָה זוֹ בִּזְמַן שֶׁיִּשְׂרָאֵל שְׁרוּיִם עַל אַדְמָתָן[21]**. וְהִיא מִן הַמִּצְווֹת הַמֻּטָּלוֹת עַל הַמֶּלֶךְ וְעַל הַצִּבּוּר כֻּלָּן**[22]**.**

Each of the forty-eight Levitical cities was surrounded in all directions by an area of non-residential land, consisting of open space and land set aside for the cultivation of fields and vineyards (Mitzvah 342). Chinuch discusses the status of this surrounding area with regard to providing refuge to unintentional killers:

וְאָמְרוּ זִכְרוֹנָם לִבְרָכָה – The [Sages], of blessed memory, also stated (*Rambam* ibid. §11) **שֶׁכָּל עִיר הַקּוֹלֶטֶת – that any city that provided refuge** for an unintentional killer (i.e., the forty-eight Levitical cities), **תְּחוּמָהּ קוֹלֵט – its *techum*** (perimeter)[18] also **provided refuge;** i.e., if a *go'eil hadam* kills an unintentional killer within its *techum,* he is liable for murder, just as if he killed him in the city proper.[19]

וְיֶתֶר פְּרָטֵי הַמִּצְוָה בְּסַנְהֶדְרִין וּמַכּוֹת וּשְׁקָלִים וְסוֹטָה – These **and the remaining details of the mitzvah are** found **in** Tractates ***Sanhedrin, Makkos*** (Chapter 2), ***Shekalim*** (2a), **and *Sotah.***[20]

Applicability of the Mitzvah

וְנוֹהֶגֶת מִצְוָה זוֹ בִּזְמַן שֶׁיִּשְׂרָאֵל שְׁרוּיִם עַל אַדְמָתָן – This mitzvah applies only **when the Jewish people are settled upon their land** (Eretz Yisrael),[21] **וְהִיא מִן הַמִּצְווֹת הַמֻּטָּלוֹת עַל הַמֶּלֶךְ וְעַל הַצִּבּוּר כֻּלָּן – and it is among the mitzvos that are incumbent upon the king and the community as a whole.**[22]

NOTES

18. In our context, "*techum*" refers to the mandated non-residential area that surrounded each Levitical city (*Minchas Chinuch* 410:14; *Divrei Malkiel* Vol. II §5; *Siach Yitzchak, Makkos* 12a). According to Chinuch (Mitzvah 342) and *Rambam* (*Shemittah VeYovel* 13:2), this area measured 3,000 *amos* in each direction; others maintain that it measured only 2,000 *amos* in each direction (*Rashi* to *Numbers* 35:4,5 and to *Sotah* 27b ד"ה שדות וכרמים).

19. See *Sifrei Zuta* to *Numbers* 35:27 for a source for this law.

Even though the *techum* provides refuge for an unintentional killer, his sentence of exile must be fulfilled in the city proper; he may not live in the *techum* (*Rambam, Hil. Rotze'ach* 8:11).

20. [It is unclear which Gemaras in *Sanhedrin* and *Sotah* Chinuch means to reference. His words are based on *Sefer HaMitzvos, Asei* 182.] The laws of this mitzvah are codified in *Rambam, Hil. Rotze'ach* Ch. 8.

21. The cities of refuge provide refuge only when all six of them (including the three in Transjordan) are under the control of the Jewish people (see *Beur HaGra, Choshen Mishpat* 425:2, citing *Sifrei*), and there is obviously no mitzvah to build and maintain roads to the cities of refuge unless they can provide refuge for unintentional killers from *go'alei hadam.*

22. Whenever the Sages speak about this obligation, they identify *beis din* as the party responsible for it. Apparently, Chinuch maintains that this is true only when the Jewish people are not ruled by a king; but when there is a king, the responsibility to maintain the roads leading to the cities of refuge is primarily his.

Insight: Chatzi Shiur (Half-measure) With Regard to Mitzvah-Obligations

When it comes to forbidden food items, such as *cheilev* (forbidden fats; Mitzvah 147), one does not transgress a mitzvah-prohibition and is not liable to *malkus* unless he eats at least a *kezayis* (olive's volume). Nevertheless, it is Biblically forbidden to eat even a *chatzi shiur* (literally, *half-measure;* i.e., less than a *kezayis*) of a forbidden item (*Yoma* 73b; *Rambam, Hil. Maachalos Asuros* 14:2). According to many authorities, the concept that *chatzi shiur* is Biblically forbidden is not limited to prohibitions involving forbidden foods, but applies to other prohibitions as well (see *Teshuvos Chacham Tzvi* §86; *Teshuvos Rama MiFano* §36; *Maggid Mishneh, Hil Geneivah* 1:2; *Beur Halachah* 340:1 ד"ה על ב'). For example, although one who cuts hair on the Sabbath does not transgress the mitzvah-prohibition

against performing *melachah* on the Sabbath and is not liable to *kares* unless he removes two hairs, it is nevertheless Biblically forbidden to remove even one hair (*Mishnah Berurah* 340:3).

The commentators discuss whether a similar rule applies to mitzvah-obligations. For example, in order to fulfill the mitzvah-obligation of eating matzah on Pesach (Mitzvah 10), one must eat a *kezayis*. What if a person has a medical condition that prevents him from eating a full *kezayis* of matzah? Is such a person obligated to eat whatever amount he can, even though he will not fulfill the actual mitzvah, or is eating less than a *kezayis* no different from not eating at all? Some authorities maintain that there is a mitzvah to eat a *chatzi shiur* of a mitzvah item, just as there is a prohibition against eating a *chatzi shiur* of a forbidden item, while others maintain that *chatzi shiur* is significant only with regard to prohibitions (see *Sdei Chemed* מערכת ח' כלל יב and *Teshuvos B'Tzeil HaChochmah* Vol. V §64 for a list of many authorities on both sides of this issue). [*Chida* (*Machazik Berachah, Orach Chaim* 475:5 ד"ה ולי ההדיוט; *Chaim Sha'al* 1:4) proposes an interesting argument as to why *chatzi shiur* ought to be significant with regard to mitzvah-obligations as well. There is a general rule that Hashem's measure of beneficence is greater than His measure of retribution [מִדָּה טוֹבָה מְרוּבָּה מִמִּדַּת פּוּרְעָנוּת]; see, for example, *Yoma* 76a. Therefore, if a person is punished for *chatzi shiur* of a mitzvah-prohibition, then he surely should be rewarded for *chatzi shiur* of a mitzvah-obligation!]

One of the sources that is cited in support of the view that fulfilling a *chatzi shiur* of a mitzvah is significant is from a Gemara cited by Chinuch in this mitzvah. The Torah states that of the six *arei miklat* (cities of refuge), three are supposed to be east of the Jordan River (in Transjordan) and three are supposed to be west of the Jordan River (in the Land of Canaan). The Torah relates that Moses designated the three cities in Transjordan before he died, and the Gemara (*Makkos* 10a) notes that Moses did so even though these cities could not provide refuge for unintentional killers until the three remaining cities were designated. Why, then, did he do so? Because he said to himself, "Whatever mitzvah comes to my hands, I shall fulfill it."

Now, the fact that the cities of refuge could not provide refuge (which was their purpose) until all of them were designated clearly indicates that one does not fulfill a separate mitzvah by designating each city, but rather, that designating all six cities should be viewed as one mitzvah. Therefore, by separating the three cities in Transjordan, Moses fulfilled only part of a mitzvah. [Indeed, when citing the Gemara regarding Moses and the *arei miklat, Rambam* (*Commentary, Avos* 4:2) comments: If Moses, a paragon of virtue, was so eager to add a mere *half-mitzvah* to his list of spiritual accomplishments, how much more should the rest of us strive to fulfill mitzvos?] The fact that Moses viewed designating three *arei miklat* as a mitzvah should be proof that there is significance to *chatzi shiur* even with regard to mitzvah-obligations (*Chikrei Lev, Kuntres Konein LeCheiker* (printed at the back of *Yore Deah* Vol. II) p. 318b; *Marcheshes* 3:5 [2]).

Yad David (Sinzheim; *Makkos* 10b ד"ה מצוה שבאה) offers a simple way of deflecting this proof. He writes that the entire question as to whether fulfilling only part of a mitzvah has any significance is limited to cases where that is all that will be fulfilled, for example, where a person will eat only half a *kezayis* of matzah. When, however, a mitzvah is fulfilled by more than one person, once the entire mitzvah is completed, each component of the mitzvah is considered to be a significant part of the mitzvah, and each person is deemed to have performed a mitzvah-activity. For example, with regard to the mitzvah-obligation to build a fence around one's roof (Mitzvah 546), if two people own a house together and each of them builds half of a fence, once the fence is completed, every part of the fence is considered part of the mitzvah, and therefore, each person is considered to have participated in the mitzvah of building a fence. The same applies to the mitzvah of designating cities of refuge. Although Moses fulfilled only half of the mitzvah when he designated the three cities in Transjordan, he knew that the Jewish people would eventually designate the remaining three cities, at which point, his efforts would be part of a completed mitzvah. Perhaps, that is why Moses viewed designating some of the cities as a mitzvah. If so, there is no proof that a *chatzi shiur* of a mitzvah-obligation is significant in cases where that is all that will be fulfilled.

מִצְוָה תקכא: שֶׁלֹּא לְרַחֵם עַל הַמַּזִּיק בְּדִינֵי קְנָסוֹת

שֶׁנִּמְנַעְנוּ מִלַּחֲמֹל עַל מִי שֶׁהָרַג חֲבֵרוֹ אוֹ חִסֵּר אֶחָד מֵאֵבָרָיו[1], שֶׁלֹּא יֹאמַר הַדַּיָּן עָנִי זֶה שֶׁכָּרַת יַד חֲבֵרוֹ אוֹ סִמֵּא עֵינוֹ לֹא בְּכַוָּנָה עָשָׂה זֶה[2], וְיַחְמֹל עָלָיו וִירַחֲמֵהוּ מִלְּשַׁלֵּם לוֹ כְּדֵי רִשְׁעָתוֹ[3,4], עַל זֶה נֶאֱמַר (דברים י״ט, כ״א) וְלֹא תָחוֹס עֵינְךָ נֶפֶשׁ בְּנֶפֶשׁ וְגוֹ׳[5].

Mitzvah 521

The Prohibition to Have Compassion on an Assailant in Punitive Judgments

לֹא תָחוֹס עֵינֶךָ נֶפֶשׁ בְּנֶפֶשׁ עַיִן בְּעַיִן שֵׁן בְּשֵׁן יָד בְּיָד רֶגֶל בְּרָגֶל

Your eye shall not pity; life for life, eye for eye, tooth for tooth, hand for hand, foot for foot (*Deuteronomy* 19:21).

שֶׁנִּמְנַעְנוּ מִלַּחֲמֹל עַל מִי שֶׁהָרַג חֲבֵרוֹ – **We** (the Jewish courts) **are prohibited to have mercy on someone who murdered his fellow,** אוֹ חִסֵּר אֶחָד מֵאֵבָרָיו – **or** on someone **who maimed one of [his fellow's] limbs.**[1] שֶׁלֹּא יֹאמַר הַדַּיָּן – In the case of someone who maimed his fellow's limb, this means **that a judge should not,** for example, **say** to himself, עָנִי זֶה שֶׁכָּרַת יַד חֲבֵרוֹ אוֹ סִמֵּא עֵינוֹ לֹא בְּכַוָּנָה עָשָׂה זֶה – **"This poor fellow who cut off his fellow's hand or who blinded [his fellow's] eye did not do so intentionally,"**[2] וְיַחְמֹל עָלָיו וִירַחֲמֵהוּ מִלְּשַׁלֵּם לוֹ כְּדֵי רִשְׁעָתוֹ – **and** to therefore **have pity on [the assailant] and absolve him from paying [the victim] "according to his wickedness,"**[3] i.e., the full amount that the Torah requires him to pay.[4] עַל זֶה נֶאֱמַר – **Regarding this it is stated** (*Deuteronomy* 19:21): "וְלֹא תָחוֹס עֵינְךָ נֶפֶשׁ בְּנֶפֶשׁ וְגוֹ׳" – ***Your eye shall not pity; life for life,*** *eye for eye, tooth for tooth, hand for hand, foot for foot.*[5]

NOTES

1. That is, *beis din* is forbidden to have compassion on a murderer and exempt him from the death penalty, or to have compassion on someone who maimed his fellow and exempt him from the full payment he is required to pay; see note 4.

2. Chinuch's words are based on *Sefer HaMitzvos, Lo Saaseh* 279. From the translations of *Sefer HaMitzvos* available to us, it appears that in *Rambam's* example, the judge contemplates two reasons for treating the assailant leniently: (1) He is poor and cannot afford to pay; (2) he injured his fellow unintentionally. See also *Rambam, Hil. Choveil U'Mazik* 1:4 and *Hil. Sanhedrin* 20:4.

3. Stylistic citation of *Deuteronomy* 25:2.

4. A person who injures his fellow is obligated to pay: (1) נֶזֶק, *damages* – payment for any permanent physical damage; (2) צַעַר, *pain* – payment for the victim's suffering; (3) רִפּוּי, *healing* – payment of the victim's medical expenses incurred as a result of the injury; (4) שֶׁבֶת, *unemployment* – payment for loss of income due to the victim's inability to work while recuperating; and (5) בֹּשֶׁת, *humiliation* – payment for the embarrassment that the victim suffered when being struck (Mishnah, *Bava Kamma* 83b; see Mitzvah 49).

5. The expression "eye for eye" refers to monetary payment for damaging an eye. The same is true for the other similar expressions in the verse (see *Sifrei* to the verse). The verse therefore commands *beis din* not to take pity on someone who causes damage to someone else's limb, but rather, to exact from him full payment for the damages.

This verse that Chinuch cites is written in the context of *zomemin* witnesses (a certain type of false witness; see Mitzvah 524), and it is therefore puzzling how it can serve as a source for a prohibition against having compassion on a murderer or on someone who maims his fellow. *Chazon Ish* (*Sanhedrin* 21:1) suggests that a copyist mistakenly added a few extra words (נֶפֶשׁ בְּנֶפֶשׁ וגו׳) into the text, making it appear as though Chinuch is citing the verse dealing with *zomemin* witnesses, when in reality, Chinuch means to cite an entirely different verse (*Deuteronomy* 25:12), which states: לֹא תָחוֹס עֵינֶךָ, *Your eye shall not pity.* That verse is speaking about a woman who assaults a man who had been fighting with her husband, and the beginning of the verse teaches that the woman is obligated to pay damages for humiliating her victim (see *Rashi* to the verse). The Torah's subsequent warning not to have pity on her can therefore serve as a source for a general prohibition against having pity on an assailant and exempting him from paying damages. See Insight B for further discussion.

וְנִכְפְּלָה הַמְּנִיעָה בָּזֶה בְּמָקוֹם אַחֵר שֶׁנֶּאֱמַר (שם, י״ג) לֹא תָחוֹס עֵינְךָ עָלָיו וּבִעַרְתָּ דַם הַנָּקִי[6].

שֹׁרֶשׁ מִצְוָה זוֹ יָדוּעַ, שֶׁאִם לֹא נִיַּסֵּר הַמַּזִּיקִין וּנְבַעֵר הָרָע מִקִּרְבֵּנוּ, אִישׁ אֶת רֵעֵהוּ חַיִּים בְּלָעוֹ[7] וְלֹא יִתְיַשְּׁבוּ הַמְּדִינוֹת[8], אֵין הַצֹּרֶךְ לְהַאֲרִיךְ בּוֹ הַדִּבּוּר.

דִּינֵי הַמִּצְוָה קְצָרִים, מְבֹאָרִים בִּלְשׁוֹן הַכָּתוּב.

וְנוֹהֵג אִסּוּר זֶה בִּזְכָרִים כִּי לָהֶם לַעֲשׂוֹת הַמִּשְׁפָּט[9], וּבִזְמַן הַבַּיִת[10].

וְנִכְפְּלָה הַמְּנִיעָה בָּזֶה בְּמָקוֹם אַחֵר — **The prohibition regarding this** matter **is repeated in another place** in the Torah with regard to a murderer, שֶׁנֶּאֱמַר — **as it is stated** (*Deuteronomy* 19:13): "לֹא תָחוֹס עֵינְךָ עָלָיו וּבִעַרְתָּ דַם הַנָּקִי" — *Your eye shall not pity him; you shall remove the innocent blood from Israel.*[6]

☞ Underlying Purpose of the Mitzvah ☜

שֹׁרֶשׁ מִצְוָה זוֹ יָדוּעַ — **The underlying purpose of this mitzvah is well known;** it is to ensure that society functions smoothly. שֶׁאִם לֹא נִיַּסֵּר הַמַּזִּיקִין וּנְבַעֵר הָרָע מִקִּרְבֵּנוּ — **For if we would not punish those who cause damage, and** we would not **eliminate evil from our midst,** אִישׁ אֶת רֵעֵהוּ חַיִּים בְּלָעוֹ — **each person would swallow his fellow alive,**[7] וְלֹא יִתְיַשְּׁבוּ הַמְּדִינוֹת — **and countries would not be settled** peacefully.[8] אֵין הַצֹּרֶךְ לְהַאֲרִיךְ בּוֹ הַדִּבּוּר — This is self-evident; **there is** therefore **no need to speak at length about it.**

☞ Laws of the Mitzvah ☜

דִּינֵי הַמִּצְוָה קְצָרִים — **The laws of the mitzvah are few;** מְבֹאָרִים בִּלְשׁוֹן הַכָּתוּב — they are all **set out in the language of the verse.**

☞ Applicability of the Mitzvah ☜

וְנוֹהֵג אִסּוּר זֶה בִּזְכָרִים כִּי לָהֶם לַעֲשׂוֹת הַמִּשְׁפָּט — **This prohibition applies** only **to men, for it is they who are tasked with carrying out justice,**[9] וּבִזְמַן הַבַּיִת — **and** it applies **only in the time of the *Beis HaMikdash*.**[10]

NOTES

6. That is, "You shall not have pity on him, but rather, you shall carry out his deserved punishment, thereby removing the guilt for the innocent blood that was shed."

Of all capital cases, this prohibition applies only to the case of a murderer (see *Minchas Chinuch* §3; see, however, *Mishnas Chachamim,* cited by *Minchas Chinuch* 519:2). See Mitzvah 62 for a similar prohibition with regard to one who transgresses the capital offense of engaging in sorcery.

7. Based on *Avos* 3:2.

8. Without the fear of being punished by the courts, many people would resort to criminal behavior, which would lead to a general breakdown of society.

9. As Chinuch has mentioned numerous times. See, for example, Mitzvah 77.

10. Capital cases can be adjudicated only when the Great Sanhedrin convenes in the Chamber of Hewn Stone (*Lishkas HaGazis*) in the *Beis HaMikdash*. Therefore, the prohibition against having pity on a murderer and refraining from executing him certainly does not apply when the *Beis HaMikdash* is not standing. It is, however, possible to try a person for causing bodily harm even when the *Beis HaMikdash* is not standing. It is therefore difficult to understand Chinuch's statement that this mitzvah applies only when the *Beis HaMikdash* is standing.

[Certain types of payment can be collected only by judges who have received *semichah,* a special type of ordination that traces itself back to Moses (see Mitzvah 491). In Mitzvah 49, Chinuch (based on *Sefer HaMitzvos, Asei* 236) seems to indicate that judges who have not received *semichah* cannot exact any of the five types of payment that an assailant must make (see *Minchas Chinuch* there, §25). Therefore, nowadays, when we do not have judges with *semichah,* beis din cannot force an assailant to pay any damages. However, in *Mishneh Torah* (Hil. Sanhedrin 5:10), Rambam rules that even judges who have not received *semichah* are authorized to collect payment for medical expenses (רִפּוּי) and lost income (שֶׁבֶת).]

וְהַדַּיָּן הָעוֹבֵר עַל זֶה וְהֶעְלִים עֵינוֹ מִלַּעֲנֹשׁ הַמְחֻיָּב כְּפִי רִשְׁעָתוֹ, עָבַר עַל לָאו זֶה[11], אֲבָל אֵין בּוֹ מַלְקוּת לְפִי שֶׁאֵין בּוֹ מַעֲשֶׂה[12]. וְעָנְשׁוֹ גָּדוֹל מְאֹד מִן הַטַּעַם שֶׁזְּכַרְנוּ שֶׁיֵּשׁ בַּדָּבָר חֻרְבָּן בְּיִשּׁוּב הָעוֹלָם, וְאַף בְּחוּצָה לָאָרֶץ אַף עַל פִּי שֶׁאֵין בָּנוּ כֹּחַ לָדִין דִּינֵי נְפָשׁוֹת חַיָּבִין כָּל בֵּית דִּין לַעֲנֹשׁ הַמְחֻיָּבִין כְּפִי רִשְׁעָתָן כַּאֲשֶׁר תַּשִּׂיג יָדָם הֵן בְּמָמוֹן אוֹ בְּגוּף אִם יוּכְלוּ לָהֶם כְּפִי שֶׁיִּרְאוּ שֶׁהַשָּׁעָה צְרִיכָה[13], שֶׁאִי אֶפְשָׁר לְקִיּוּם הָעָם אִם אֵין הַשֵּׁבֶט נָטוּי תָּמִיד עַל גֵּו כְּסִילִים[14,15].

וְהַדַּיָּן הָעוֹבֵר עַל זֶה – **A judge who transgresses this** mitzvah וְהֶעְלִים עֵינוֹ מִלַּעֲנֹשׁ הַמְחֻיָּב כְּפִי רִשְׁעָתוֹ – **and turns a blind eye to punishing the guilty party "according to his wickedness,"** עָבַר עַל לָאו זֶה – **transgresses this mitzvah-prohibition.**[11] אֲבָל אֵין בּוֹ מַלְקוּת לְפִי שֶׁאֵין בּוֹ מַעֲשֶׂה – **There is, however, no liability to *malkus* for this** transgression, **because it does not involve** any **action.**[12] וְעָנְשׁוֹ גָּדוֹל מְאֹד מִן הַטַּעַם שֶׁזְּכַרְנוּ – Nevertheless, **the punishment** at the hands of Heaven **for [a judge who transgresses this prohibition] is very great, for the reason that we have mentioned;** שֶׁיֵּשׁ בַּדָּבָר חֻרְבָּן בְּיִשּׁוּב הָעוֹלָם – namely, **that this matter** of neglecting to punish wrongdoers **leads to the destruction of society.**

Chinuch notes that even nowadays, when its authority is severely limited, *beis din* serves an important role:

וְאַף בְּחוּצָה לָאָרֶץ אַף עַל פִּי שֶׁאֵין בָּנוּ כֹּחַ לָדִין דִּינֵי נְפָשׁוֹת – **Even outside of Eretz Yisrael, although we do not have the authority to try capital cases,** חַיָּבִין כָּל בֵּית דִּין לַעֲנֹשׁ הַמְחֻיָּבִין כְּפִי רִשְׁעָתָן כַּאֲשֶׁר תַּשִּׂיג יָדָם – **every *beis din* is** nevertheless **obligated to punish guilty parties "according to their wickedness," in whatever manner they are able,** הֵן בְּמָמוֹן אוֹ בְּגוּף אִם יוּכְלוּ לָהֶם – **whether with monetary sanctions or** even **with corporal punishment if [*beis din*] is able to do so,** כְּפִי שֶׁיִּרְאוּ שֶׁהַשָּׁעָה צְרִיכָה – **all according to what [*beis din*] deems necessary according to the needs of the hour.**[13] שֶׁאִי אֶפְשָׁר לְקִיּוּם הָעָם – **For it is impossible for the** Jewish **nation to thrive** אִם אֵין הַשֵּׁבֶט נָטוּי תָּמִיד עַל גֵּו כְּסִילִים – **if the rod** of punishment **is not constantly hanging over the backs of fools,**[14] deterring them from wrongdoing.[15]

NOTES

11. Chinuch's language indicates that judges who fail to carry out the prescribed punishment of a murderer or an assailant transgress this prohibition regardless of whether they do so out of compassion, or for some other reason. Accordingly, the example he gives above, of a judge who treats an assailant leniently out of compassion, simply describes a likely reason why a judge would be lenient. There are, however, several other ways of understanding the nature of this prohibition; see Insight A.

12. The standard punishment for intentional transgression of a mitzvah-prohibition is *malkus,* but there are several exceptions to this rule. One of the categories excluded from *malkus* is לָאו שֶׁאֵין בּוֹ מַעֲשֶׂה, *a transgression that does not involve action.* Since refraining from punishing someone is passive, judges who transgress this mitzvah-prohibition are not liable to *malkus.*

13. The Torah gives authority to the courts to impose measures that go beyond the strict letter of the law if they perceive a compelling need to do so for the benefit of society (see *Sanhedrin* 46a and *Rambam, Hil. Sanhedrin* 24:4-10). Under this power, if the need arises, even judges who have not received *semichah* can administer punishments that usually require fully ordained judges. The exact parameters of this authority, including what type of *beis din* is authorized to make use of it, is subject to much discussion; see *Shulchan Aruch, Choshen Mishpat* §2 with commentaries. See also *HaOnshin Acharei Chasimas HaTalmud* for a history of how this power was employed by various communities throughout the generations.

14. Stylistic paraphrase of *Proverbs* 26:3.

15. See *Teshuvos HaRashba* Vol. 3 §393, where this idea is developed at length.

Insight A: What Does This Mitzvah Forbid?

In this mitzvah, the Torah establishes a mitzvah-prohibition against having pity on a murderer. When discussing this prohibition, *Ramban* (*Commentary* to *Deuteronomy* 19:13; glosses to *Sefer HaMitzvos, Prohibitions that Rambam Omitted* §13) explains: With regard to most people who have

been sentenced to death, if *beis din* fails to carry out their punishment, the judges are in violation of a mitzvah-obligation (see end of *Mitzvah* 47), but have not transgressed a mitzvah-prohibition. However, with regard to a murderer, the Torah added a mitzvah-prohibition, so that judges who fail to execute a convicted murderer transgress a mitzvah-obligation *and* a mitzvah-prohibition.

In *Ramban's* view, then, the mitzvah-prohibition against having pity on a murderer is a prohibition against failing to execute a convicted murderer, regardless of whether the judges do so out of pity for the murderer or for some other reason (see *Chazon Ish, Sanhedrin* 21:1, and *Chidushei HaGriz al HaRambam*, p. 140 ד"ה בסה"מ). This also appears to be the position of Chinuch, for at the end of the mitzvah, he writes: "A judge who violates this prohibition and turns a blind eye to punishing the guilty party according to his wickedness transgresses this mitzvah-prohibition." The fact that Chinuch does not specify that the judge did so out of compassion seems to indicate that, in his view, judges transgress this prohibition regardless of why they fail to carry out the punishment.

Rambam, though, seems to have understood the essence of this mitzvah-prohibition differently. In *Hil. Sanhedrin* 14:3, he writes that, as a rule, if *beis din* fails to execute someone who has been sentenced to death, the judges are in violation of a mitzvah-obligation, but have not transgressed a mitzvah-prohibition. The one exception, *Rambam* writes, is the case of someone who was convicted of sorcery; if *beis din* fails to carry out his punishment, the judges transgress a mitzvah-obligation *and* a mitzvah-prohibition (*Mitzvah* 62). If *Rambam* maintained, like *Ramban*, that judges who fail to execute a convicted murderer are automatically guilty of transgressing a mitzvah-prohibition, then he should have listed the case of a murderer as a second exception to the general rule. *Rambam's* omission of this case indicates that he must have had a different understanding of the mitzvah-prohibition against having pity on a murderer.

Some commentators (*Seder Mishnah* [Te'omim], *Hil. Sanhedrin* 14:3; *Ner Mitzvah* [Sid] 3:19; see also *Dina DeChayei, Lav* 198 and *Lav* 202) explain that according to *Rambam*, judges are not in violation of the mitzvah-prohibition against having pity on a murderer unless they refrain from executing him out of compassion. If, however, they fail to execute him for some other reason, they transgress only the mitzvah-obligation that applies to all capital cases, but do not transgress our mitzvah-prohibition. According to this understanding, the case of sorcery is the only case where judges *automatically* transgress a mitzvah-prohibition if they fail to impose capital punishment. Therefore, although it is possible for judges to transgress a mitzvah-prohibition if they refrain from executing a murderer out of compassion, it is still understandable why *Rambam* did not list the case of a murderer as an exception to the general rule, since judges do not *automatically* transgress a mitzvah-prohibition for failing to execute a convicted murderer.

The *Brisker Rav, R' Yitzchak Zev Soloveitchik* (*Chidushei HaGriz* ibid.), suggests a different way to understand our mitzvah according to *Rambam*. In his view, *Rambam* maintains that the focus of the mitzvah is the attitude of the judges toward the murderer; that is, the Torah forbids the judges to relate to the murderer with an *attitude* of compassion. According to this understanding of the mitzvah, what the Torah forbids is the judges' compassion for the murderer — i.e., the attitude that can *lead* them to be lenient with him — not their actual failure to punish him. *Rambam's* understanding of the mitzvah is thus completely different from *Ramban's* understanding of it. Whereas *Ramban* explains that this mitzvah prohibits judges from failing to execute a convicted murderer, *Rambam* explains that it prohibits judges from letting themselves feel compassionate toward him.

What emerges from this explanation is that, according to *Rambam*, judges who refrain from executing a murderer *never* transgress a mitzvah-prohibition for their failure to carry out his punishment. The only case where judges transgress a mitzvah-prohibition for *actually failing to impose* capital punishment is that of a convicted sorcerer, and it is therefore understandable why *Rambam* listed the case of a sorcerer as the only exception to the general rule.

◆§ Insight B: What Verse Is the Actual Source of This Mitzvah?

Chinuch cites two verses as sources for this mitzvah: (1) *Deuteronomy* 19:21, which states: וְלֹא תָחוֹס עֵינֶךָ נֶפֶשׁ בְּנֶפֶשׁ עַיִן בְּעַיִן שֵׁן בְּשֵׁן יָד בְּיָד רֶגֶל בְּרָגֶל, *Your eye shall not pity; life for life, eye for eye, tooth for tooth, hand for hand, foot for foot*; and (2) *Deuteronomy* 19:13, which states: לֹא תָחוֹס עֵינְךָ עָלָיו וּבִעַרְתָּ דַם הַנָּקִי מִיִּשְׂרָאֵל, *Your eye shall not pity him; you shall remove the innocent blood from Israel*.

As mentioned above (note 5), it is difficult to understand how the first verse can serve as a source

for a prohibition against having compassion on a murderer or an assailant, since it is speaking about *zomemin* witnesses. *Chazon Ish* therefore suggests that our text contains a copyist's error, and in reality, the first verse that Chinuch cites is not the verse about *zomemin* witnesses, but an entirely different one, namely, *Deuteronomy* 25:12 (see note 5 for further details).

However, a strong argument can be made that Chinuch did indeed mean to cite the verse dealing with *zomemin* witnesses. In earlier editions of Chinuch, in which the mitzvah-obligations and mitzvah-prohibitions of each *parashah* were presented separately (as we have pointed out repeatedly throughout this work; see General Introduction, note 7), there also was a difference in the ordering of the mitzvah-prohibitions of *Parashas Shoftim*. In those earlier editions, our mitzvah is found *after* the next two mitzvah-prohibitions, the prohibition against moving a property boundary and the prohibition against rendering judgment based on a single witness (Mitzvos 522 and 523 in current editions).

Now, the verses for those two mitzvos are *Deuteronomy* 19:14 and 19:15, respectively. It would appear that the only way to understand Chinuch's original arrangement is if the first verse that Chinuch cites in this mitzvah is indeed *Deuteronomy* 19:21, the verse dealing with *zomemin* witnesses. If, however, Chinuch does not mean to cite the verse dealing with *zomemin* witnesses, but rather, *Deuteronomy* 25:12, it is difficult to understand the rationale behind Chinuch's original placement of our mitzvah. Granted, Chinuch also quotes *Deuteronomy* 19:13, but if he based the position of this mitzvah on that verse, he should have placed it *before* the prohibitions against moving a property boundary and rendering judgment based on a single witness (which are based on vv. 14 and 15). And if Chinuch based the position of this mitzvah on *Deuteronomy* 25:12, a verse that he cites according to the emendation suggested by *Chazon Ish*, then this mitzvah should be in *Parashas Ki Seitzei*, where that verse is found, and not here in *Parashas Shoftim*.

In conclusion, the original arrangement of Chinuch strongly indicates that Chinuch indeed meant to cite the *zomemin* witnesses verse as a source for our mitzvah. [See also Kafich and Frankel eds. of *Sefer HaMitzvos, Lo Saaseh* 279, and notes to Heller ed. ad loc.] This, however, requires further study, since it remains unclear how a verse dealing with the punishment for *zomemin* witnesses can serve as a source for a prohibition against having pity on a murderer or an assailant.

מִצְוָה תקכב: שֶׁלֹּא לְהַשִּׂיג גְּבוּל

שֶׁלֹּא נַסִּיג גְּבוּל[1]. וְהָעִנְיָן הוּא שֶׁלֹּא נְשַׁנֶּה גְּבוּל שֶׁיִּהְיֶה בֵּינֵינוּ וּבֵין זוּלָתֵנוּ עַד שֶׁיִּתָּכֵן לַמְשַׁקֵּר שֶׁיֹּאמַר שֶׁאֶרֶץ זוּלָתוֹ הִיא שֶׁלּוֹ, וְכֵן אִם שִׁנָּה סִימָנֵי הַגְּבוּל וּקְבָעָם בְּתוֹךְ קַרְקַע שֶׁל חֲבֵרוֹ וְיֹאמַר שֶׁלֹּא שִׁנָּהוּ וְשֶׁהַקַּרְקַע הוּא שֶׁלּוֹ עַד הַגְּבוּל[2], עַל כָּל זֶה נֶאֱמַר (דברים י״ט, י״ד) לֹא תַסִּיג גְּבוּל רֵעֲךָ וְגוֹ׳[3].

Mitzvah 522
The Prohibition to Change a [Property] Boundary

לֹא תַסִּיג גְּבוּל רֵעֲךָ אֲשֶׁר גָּבְלוּ רִאשֹׁנִים בְּנַחֲלָתְךָ אֲשֶׁר תִּנְחַל בָּאָרֶץ אֲשֶׁר ה׳ אֱלֹהֶיךָ נֹתֵן לְךָ לְרִשְׁתָּהּ

You shall not change a boundary of your fellow, which the early ones marked, in your inheritance that you shall inherit, in the Land that HASHEM, your God, gives you to possess it (*Deuteronomy* 19:14):

שֶׁלֹּא נַסִּיג גְּבוּל – We are commanded **not to change a** property **boundary.**[1] **וְהָעִנְיָן הוּא שֶׁלֹּא נְשַׁנֶּה גְּבוּל שֶׁיִּהְיֶה בֵּינֵינוּ וּבֵין זוּלָתֵנוּ – The definition** of this prohibition **is that we are not to make changes to a boundary** marker **that lies between us** (i.e., our land) **and our fellow** (i.e., his land), **עַד שֶׁיִּתָּכֵן לַמְשַׁקֵּר שֶׁיֹּאמַר שֶׁאֶרֶץ זוּלָתוֹ הִיא שֶׁלּוֹ – to the extent that a liar will be able to claim that his fellow's land is** really **his. וְכֵן אִם שִׁנָּה סִימָנֵי הַגְּבוּל וּקְבָעָם בְּתוֹךְ קַרְקַע שֶׁל חֲבֵרוֹ – Likewise, if one changed** the location of **the boundary markers** between his land and that of his fellow **and fixed them** farther back than they had previously been, **in his fellow's land, וְיֹאמַר שֶׁלֹּא שִׁנָּהוּ וְשֶׁהַקַּרְקַע הוּא שֶׁלּוֹ עַד הַגְּבוּל – and,** when confronted, **he will claim that he did not adjust [the boundary], and** thus, **that the land until the boundary** markers **belongs to him,** he is guilty of transgressing this prohibition.[2] **עַל כָּל זֶה נֶאֱמַר – Regarding all this, it is stated** (*Deuteronomy* 19:14): **"לֹא תַסִּיג גְּבוּל רֵעֲךָ וְגוֹ׳" – *You shall not move a boundary of your fellow,* etc.**[3]

Even without this verse, one who takes possession of his fellow's property transgresses a mitzvah-prohibition; if he does so by force, in the open, he transgresses the mitzvah-prohibition of *You shall not rob* (*Leviticus* 19:13; Mitzvah 229), and if he does so stealthily, he transgresses the mitzvah-prohibition of *You shall not steal* (*Levitcus* 19:11; Mitzvah 224).[4] Chinuch cites *Sifrei* (to the verse) to explain what our mitzvah adds:

NOTES

1. As Chinuch will soon teach, although moving property boundaries is forbidden everywhere, this specific mitzvah-prohibition is limited to land in Eretz Yisrael.

2. The phrase לֹא תַסִּיג גְּבוּל has two interpretations: *You shall not change* (i.e., destroy) *a boundary* (*Targum Onkelos, Ibn Ezra, Sefer Yerei'im* §129 [258]); and, *You shall not* ***move*** *a boundary* (*Rashi*). Chinuch apparently means to cite both interpretations. First, he says (based on *Onkelos*) that one may not "change" a boundary marker (i.e., damage it) to the extent that he can falsely claim that the property line (which is now unmarked) is somewhere else. Then he says (based on *Rashi*) that one may not "move back" a boundary marker, which, when he denies moving it, *automatically* gives him a claim to more land than he actually owns.

3. This prohibition applies to changing any border markers that lie between properties. The verse specifies border markers "that the early ones marked," because it is much easier, and therefore more common, to change ancient border markers, about which no one currently has firsthand knowledge (*Ramban* to the verse). One who transgresses this mitzvah-prohibition is also subject to a Divine curse, as the Torah states (*Deuteronomy* 27:17): אָרוּר מַסִּיג גְּבוּל רֵעֵהוּ, *Accursed is one who moves the boundary of his fellow.* See below, note 7.

See *Sifrei* for additional prohibitions that are derived from this verse; see also *Ramban* to the verse.

[Colloquially, the term הַשָּׂגַת גְּבוּל, *hasagas gevul,* refers to infringing upon someone else's livelihood in a way forbidden by halachah. Though forbidden, such behavior is not subject to this mitzvah-prohibition, which refers exclusively to stealing land by changing border markers. See Insight.]

4. The Torah differentiates between stealing stealthily

וְאָמְרוּ בְּסִפְרִי (כאן)**, לֹא תַסִּיג גְּבוּל, וַהֲלֹא כְּבָר נֶאֱמַר לֹא תִגְזֹל וּמַה תַּלְמוּד לוֹמַר לֹא תַסִּיג**[5]**, מְלַמֵּד שֶׁכָּל הָעוֹקֵר תְּחוּמוֹ שֶׁל חֲבֵרוֹ עוֹבֵר בִּשְׁנֵי לָאוִין**[6]**, יָכוֹל אַף בְּחוּצָה לָאָרֶץ, תַּלְמוּד לוֹמַר בְּנַחֲלָתְךָ אֲשֶׁר תִּנְחַל, בְּאֶרֶץ יִשְׂרָאֵל עוֹבֵר בִּשְׁנֵי לָאוִין, בְּחוּצָה לָאָרֶץ עוֹבֵר בְּלָאו אֶחָד**[7]**. נִמְצָא**[8] **הָעִנְיָן כֵּן, הַמַּשִּׂיג גְּבוּל אֲפִלּוּ מְלֹא אֶצְבַּע אִם בְּחָזְקָה עָשָׂה עָבַר עַל לֹא תִגְזֹל, וְאִם בְּסֵתֶר עוֹבֵר עַל לֹא תִגְנֹב, וְזֶה יִהְיֶה בְּחוּצָה לָאָרֶץ, וּבְאֶרֶץ יִשְׂרָאֵל עוֹבֵר בִּשְׁנֵי לָאוִין**[9]**.**

וְאָמְרוּ בְּסִפְרִי – [The Sages] stated in *Sifrei*: "לֹא תַסִּיג גְּבוּל" – The Torah states: ***You shall not move a boundary*** *of your fellow.* **וַהֲלֹא כְּבָר נֶאֱמַר "לֹא תִגְזֹל" – Now, it was already stated** earlier in the Torah (*Leviticus* 19:13): ***You shall not rob,*** which establishes a prohibition against taking someone else's property, including moving a property boundary. **וּמַה תַּלְמוּד לוֹמַר "לֹא תַסִּיג" – What, then, does [the verse] teach by stating: *You shall not move a boundary*?**[5] **מְלַמֵּד שֶׁכָּל הָעוֹקֵר תְּחוּמוֹ שֶׁל חֲבֵרוֹ עוֹבֵר בִּשְׁנֵי לָאוִין – It teaches that anyone who uproots the property boundary of his fellow transgresses *two* mitzvah-prohibitions,** *You shall not rob,* and *You shall not move a boundary.*[6]

Sifrei continues:

יָכוֹל אַף בְּחוּצָה לָאָרֶץ – It might be thought **that** this applies **even outside of Eretz Yisrael,** i.e., even one who moves a property boundary outside of Eretz Yisrael transgresses two mitzvah-prohibitions. **תַּלְמוּד לוֹמַר "בְּנַחֲלָתְךָ אֲשֶׁר תִּנְחַל" – [Scripture]** therefore **states** further in the verse: ***in your inheritance that you shall inherit,*** which refers to Eretz Yisrael, clearly indicating that the prohibition of *You shall not move a boundary* does not apply outside of Eretz Yisrael. **בְּאֶרֶץ יִשְׂרָאֵל עוֹבֵר בִּשְׁנֵי לָאוִין –** Therefore, **[one who changes a boundary] in Eretz Yisrael transgresses *two* mitzvah-prohibitions,** *You shall not rob,* and *You shall not move a boundary,* **בְּחוּצָה לָאָרֶץ עוֹבֵר בְּלָאו אֶחָד** – while **[one who does so] outside of Eretz Yisrael transgresses** only **one mitzvah-prohibition,** *You shall not rob.*[7]

Chinuch summarizes:[8]

נִמְצָא הָעִנְיָן כֵּן – Thus, the sum of the matter is: **הַמַּשִּׂיג גְּבוּל אֲפִלּוּ מְלֹא אֶצְבַּע** – Regarding **one who moved a property boundary even by** only **a thumb's width,** **אִם בְּחָזְקָה עָשָׂה עָבַר עַל "לֹא תִגְזֹל" – if he did so by force,** in the open, **he transgresses** the mitzvah-prohibition of ***You shall not rob,*** **וְאִם בְּסֵתֶר עוֹבֵר עַל "לֹא תִגְנֹב" – and if he did so stealthily, he transgresses** the mitzvah-prohibition of ***You shall not steal.*** **וְזֶה יִהְיֶה בְּחוּצָה לָאָרֶץ – This is** all regarding one who moves a boundary **outside of Eretz Yisrael;** **וּבְאֶרֶץ יִשְׂרָאֵל עוֹבֵר בִּשְׁנֵי לָאוִין – but [one who does so] in Eretz Yisrael transgresses two mitzvah-prohibitions,** for he transgresses *You shall not move a boundary* in addition to either *You shall not rob* or *You shall not steal.*[9]

NOTES

(גְּנֵבָה) and open robbery (גְּזֵלָה), with each type of theft subject to a separate mitzvah-prohibition. These prohibitions apply to the unlawful taking of any type of property, whether movable objects or land (see *Minchas Chinuch* §1 and *Emek HaNetziv,* in explanation of *Sifrei* to the verse). Cf. *Tosafos, Bava Metzia* 61a ד״ה אלא לאו דגזל.

5. *Sifrei* is specifically addressing a person who forcefully changed a property boundary. A similar question could be asked regarding a person who stealthily changes a property boundary, since such a person is guilty of transgressing the mitzvah-prohibition of *You shall not steal.*

6. One who performs an action that is subject to two mitzvah-prohibitions is liable to more punishment than one who performs an action that is subject to only one mitzvah-prohibition. [In our case, this means that a transgressor is liable to more punishment at the hands of Heaven, because as Chinuch writes below, one who moves a property boundary does not receive *malkus.*]

One who stealthily changes a property boundary also transgresses two mitzvah-prohibitions, but rather than transgressing *You shall not rob,* he transgresses *You shall not steal.*

7. For a possible reason that the Torah assigns greater severity to moving a boundary in Eretz Yisrael, see *Sefer HaBatim, Sefer HaMitzvah,* p. 414 in Hirschler ed.

Even one who moves a boundary outside of Eretz Yisrael is subject to the Divine curse mentioned above, in note 3, since the verse in which the curse is written does not specify Eretz Yisrael (*Aruch HaShulchan, Choshen Mishpat* 376:1).

8. Based on *Rambam, Hil. Geneivah* 7:11.

9. Although it is forbidden to take any amount of

שֹׁרֶשׁ הַמִּצְוָה בְּכָל עִנְיַן גֶּזֶל יָדוּעַ הוּא, כִּי הוּא דָּבָר שֶׁהַשֵּׂכֶל מֵעִיד עָלָיו וְתוֹעֶלֶת הַכֹּל הִיא[10].

דִּינֵי הַמִּצְוָה קְצָרִים[11].

וְנוֹהֵג בְּכָל מָקוֹם[12] וּבְכָל זְמַן, בִּזְכָרִים וּנְקֵבוֹת[13]. וְעוֹבֵר עַל זֶה עָבַר עַל לָאו, אֲבָל אֵין לוֹקִין עָלָיו מִן הַכְּלָל הַיָּדוּעַ לָנוּ שֶׁלָּאו הַנִּתָּן לְתַשְׁלוּמִין אֵין לוֹקִין עָלָיו[14].

Underlying Purpose and Laws of the Mitzvah

שֹׁרֶשׁ הַמִּצְוָה בְּכָל עִנְיַן גֶּזֶל יָדוּעַ הוּא – **The underlying purpose of the** Torah's **commandments regarding all matters relating to stealing is well known,** כִּי הוּא דָּבָר שֶׁהַשֵּׂכֶל מֵעִיד עָלָיו וְתוֹעֶלֶת הַכֹּל הִיא – **for it is something attested to by logic, and it is to everyone's benefit.**[10]
דִּינֵי הַמִּצְוָה קְצָרִים – **The laws of the mitzvah are few.**[11]

Applicability of the Mitzvah

וְנוֹהֵג בְּכָל מָקוֹם וּבְכָל זְמַן – **[This prohibition] applies in every location**[12] **and in all times,** בִּזְכָרִים וּנְקֵבוֹת – **to** both **men and women.**[13]
וְעוֹבֵר עַל זֶה עָבַר עַל לָאו – **One who violates this** law **transgresses a mitzvah-prohibition,** אֲבָל אֵין לוֹקִין עָלָיו – **but does not incur *malkus* on account of it,** מִן הַכְּלָל הַיָּדוּעַ לָנוּ שֶׁלָּאו הַנִּתָּן לְתַשְׁלוּמִין אֵין לוֹקִין עָלָיו – **based on the rule that is known to us that one does not incur *malkus* for** transgressing **a mitzvah-prohibition that is subject to repayment** (i.e., a prohibition that carries monetary liability).[14]

NOTES

someone else's property, one does not transgress the mitzvah-prohibitions of *You shall not rob* or *You shall not steal* unless he takes at least a *perutah*'s worth, which is the smallest amount that is considered to have monetary value according to halachah (see Mitzvah 229, after note 2, and Mitzvah 224 note 19). *Minchas Chinuch* §3 writes that the fact that the mitzvah-prohibition against moving a boundary applies only in Eretz Yisrael seems to indicate that it is not simply a monetary prohibition. He therefore entertains the possibility that it should apply even if it involves less than a *perutah's* worth of land. *R' Y. F. Perla* (in his glosses to *Minchas Chinuch,* cited in notes to Machon Yerushalayim ed.), however, contends that *Sifrei* seems to indicate otherwise, for if this were true, *Sifrei* should have answered that this is what the prohibition of *You shall not move a border* adds to the prohibitions of *You shall not rob* and *You shall not steal,* instead of answering that it comes merely to add a second prohibition to an already forbidden action.

10. As Chinuch notes in Mitzvah 229, lack of respect for property rights leads to lawlessness and the breakdown of society.

11. This mitzvah-prohibition is codified in *Rambam, Hil. Geneivah* 7:11 and *Shulchan Aruch, Choshen Mishpat* §376.

12. These words are clearly a copyist's error, for, as Chinuch himself just wrote, this mitzvah-prohibition applies only in Eretz Yisrael (*Minchas Chinuch* §5).

13. That is, whether or not the *Beis HaMikdash* is standing. It applies to both men and women, in accordance with the general rule that applies to mitzvah-prohibitions.

14. The standard punishment for intentional transgression of a mitzvah-prohibition is *malkus*, but there are several exceptions to this rule. One exception is any mitzvah-prohibition that is subject to repayment; see General Introduction, note 14, and above, Mitzvah 229 note 29.

Insight: Hasagas Gevul — Encroaching on Someone's Livelihood

This mitzvah establishes a mitzvah-prohibition against moving a boundary that lies between properties owned by different people. Based on the language of the verse, this prohibition is known as the prohibition of הַשָּׂגַת גְּבוּל, *hasagas gevul* (moving a boundary). In addition to transgressing a mitzvah-prohibition, one who is guilty of *hasagas gevul* is subject to the curse set forth in *Deuteronomy* 27:17.

In colloquial usage, however, the term *hasagas gevul* is most often used to refer to encroaching

upon someone's trade. [In the language of the Gemara, engaging in such activity is referred to as יוֹרֵד לְתוֹךְ אֻמָּנָתוֹ שֶׁל חֲבֵירוֹ, *encroaching upon the trade of one's fellow.*] *Radvaz* (*Teshuvos* Vol. IV §1126) maintains that when used in this sense, *hasagas gevul* is purely a borrowed term; in the Torah, the term refers exclusively to stealing land by moving a property marker. This is clearly the case with regard to the mitzvah-prohibition against *hasagas gevul,* since the Torah states (*Deuteronomy* 19:14): *You shall not move a boundary of your fellow … in the Land that* HASHEM, *Your God, gives you to possess it,* which clearly indicates that the Torah is speaking about moving property markers. And even with regard to the curse against one who is guilty of *hasagas gevul,* which is written in a later verse, although there is no indication that the verse is speaking about moving property boundaries, it is reasonable to assume that the Torah refers to the same act that it labeled as *hasagas gevul* in an earlier verse. *Maharshal* (*Teshuvos* §89 and *Beur to Smag, Lav* 153, based on *Roke'ach*), on the other hand, maintains that although the mitzvah-prohibition against *hasagas gevul* is limited to moving property markers, the curse applies to other forms of *hasagas gevul* as well, including encroaching upon someone else's trade.

Regardless of that dispute, encroaching upon someone else's livelihood is considered a severe transgression, and refraining from doing so is considered one of the pillars upon which the entire Torah rests. The Gemara (*Makkos* 24a) relates that in *Psalm* 15, King David lists eleven requirements that serve as the basis for the fulfillment of all of the 613 mitzvos, and one of them is refraining from encroaching on someone else's trade.

There is a fundamental disagreement in the Gemara (*Bava Basra* 21b) as to what activities are included in the prohibition against encroaching upon another's trade. The basic halachah is that the only situation where setting up a rival business is forbidden is for a resident of another city to set up a business in a city where a local resident had already set up a similar business. It is, however, permitted for a resident of the same city to set up a rival business (see *Shulchan Aruch, Choshen Mishpat* 156:5). [It should be noted, however, that even in situations where it is permitted to open up a rival business, it is still considered an act of piety not to do so (*Shulchan Aruch HaRav, Hil. Hefker VeHasagas Gevul* §13.]

According to some authorities, the previous halachah applies only in a situation where setting up a competing business would merely *decrease* the profits of the first business. If, however, setting up a competing business would *destroy* the profits of the first business, even a resident of the same city may not open a rival business (see *Teshuvos Chasam Sofer, Choshen Mishpat* §79 ד"ה והרב"י).

A similar distinction was used by *Rama* (*Teshuvos HaRama* §10 ד"ה היסוד הפשוט הראשון) in a case involving the renowned sage, R' Meir Katzenellenbogen (known as *Maharam Padua*). *Maharam Padua* had partnered with a non-Jewish printer to publish a new edition of *Rambam,* in which he had invested much time and money. Another non-Jewish printer, jealous that *Maharam Padua* had not partnered with him, decided to print a similar edition of *Rambam.* The second printer was extremely wealthy, and in an attempt to bankrupt his rival, he announced that he would sell his edition at an extremely low price, one that *Maharam Padua* and his partner could not possibly match. Facing the possibility of financial ruin, *Maharam Padua* turned to *Rama* to see if he had any recourse.

Rama ruled in favor of *Maharam Padua,* stating that setting up such destructive competition is forbidden. To ensure that the rival printer's stratagem would not be successful, *Rama* issued a ban, under the penalty of excommunication, for any Jew to buy the competing edition of *Rambam,* until *Maharam Padua's* entire stock was sold out. *Rama* based his ruling on four independent arguments, one of which was an application of the rule mentioned above. *Rama* argued that since the rival printer was offering his edition at a low price that was impossible for his competitors to match, it was virtually certain that anyone who wished to buy a *Rambam* would buy his edition. Therefore, by selling his edition of *Rambam,* the second printer would put *Maharam Padua* out of business. In such a situation, *Rama* maintained that it is forbidden (even for a non-Jew) to set up a rival business, even though it is ordinarily permitted for a fellow resident of a city to compete with an already existing business. [See there for *Rama's* other arguments.]

מִצְוָה תקכג: שֶׁלֹּא לַחְתֹּךְ הַדִּין עַל פִּי עֵד אֶחָד

שֶׁנִּמְנַעְנוּ שֶׁלֹּא נַעֲמִיד גְּבוּלֵי הָעֹנֶשׁ בְּגוּף הַנֶּעֱנָשׁ, וְכֵן שֶׁלֹּא נוֹצִיא מָמוֹן, עַל פִּי עֵדוּת עֵד אֶחָד, וַאֲפִלּוּ הוּא בְּתַכְלִית הַכַּשְׁרוּת וְהַחָכְמָה אוֹ אֲפִלּוּ נָבִיא, וְעַל זֶה נֶאֱמַר (דברים י״ט, ט״ו) לֹא יָקוּם עֵד אֶחָד בְּאִישׁ לְכָל עָוֹן וּלְכָל חַטָּאת[1].

מִשָּׁרְשֵׁי הַמִּצְוָה, לְפִי שֶׁיֵּצֶר לֵב הָאָדָם רַע[2] וְלִפְעָמִים יַעֲלֶה בְּלִבּוֹ טִינָא עַל חֲבֵרוֹ[3], וַאֲפִלּוּ יִהְיֶה הָאָדָם בְּתַכְלִית הַכֹּשֶׁר לֹא יִנָּצֵל מֵחֵטְא לִפְעָמִים, וְאַף כִּי יַעֲמֹד אָדָם יָמִים רַבִּים

Mitzvah 523

The Prohibition to Render Judgment Based Upon the Testimony of a Single Witness

לֹא יָקוּם עֵד אֶחָד בְּאִישׁ לְכָל עָוֹן וּלְכָל חַטָּאת בְּכָל חֵטְא אֲשֶׁר יֶחֱטָא עַל פִּי שְׁנֵי עֵדִים אוֹ עַל פִּי שְׁלֹשָׁה עֵדִים יָקוּם דָּבָר

A single witness shall not stand up against a man for any punishment or penalty, regarding any sin that he may commit; according to two witnesses or according to three witnesses shall a matter be confirmed (*Deuteronomy* 19:15).

שֶׁנִּמְנַעְנוּ שֶׁלֹּא נַעֲמִיד גְּבוּלֵי הָעֹנֶשׁ בְּגוּף הַנֶּעֱנָשׁ – This mitzvah teaches **that we** (the Jewish courts) **are forbidden to mete out corporal punishment** (capital punishment or *malkus*), וְכֵן שֶׁלֹּא נוֹצִיא מָמוֹן – **or to exact money,** עַל פִּי עֵדוּת עֵד אֶחָד – **based on the testimony of a single witness,** וַאֲפִלּוּ הוּא בְּתַכְלִית הַכַּשְׁרוּת וְהַחָכְמָה אוֹ אֲפִלּוּ נָבִיא – **even if [that witness] is exceptionally righteous and wise, or even** if he is **a prophet.** וְעַל זֶה נֶאֱמַר – **Regarding this it is stated** (*Deuteronomy* 19:15): "לֹא יָקוּם עֵד אֶחָד בְּאִישׁ לְכָל עָוֹן וּלְכָל חַטָּאת" – ***A single witness shall not stand up against a man for any punishment or penalty.***[1]

Underlying Purpose of the Mitzvah

מִשָּׁרְשֵׁי הַמִּצְוָה – **Among the underlying purposes of the mitzvah** is the following idea: לְפִי שֶׁיֵּצֶר לֵב הָאָדָם רַע וְלִפְעָמִים יַעֲלֶה בְּלִבּוֹ טִינָא עַל חֲבֵרוֹ – **Being that the instinct of man's heart is evil**[2] **and hateful thoughts concerning his fellow will sometimes enter his heart,**[3] וַאֲפִלּוּ יִהְיֶה הָאָדָם בְּתַכְלִית הַכֹּשֶׁר לֹא יִנָּצֵל מֵחֵטְא לִפְעָמִים – **and** that **even a person who is exceptionally righteous will not avoid sinning from time to time,** וְאַף כִּי יַעֲמֹד אָדָם יָמִים רַבִּים בְּדַרְכֵי הַיֹּשֶׁר – **and** that **even if a person remains on the paths of upstanding behavior for a long time,**

NOTES

1. As Chinuch explains below (after note 6), the word עָוֹן refers to corporal punishment, and the word חַטָּאת refers to monetary penalties. See *Maskil LeDavid* to the verse; see, however, *Sifrei* to the verse.

According to Chinuch (based on *Rambam, Sefer HaMitzvos, Lo Saaseh* 268), this verse is understood as a command to the courts not to render judgment in these areas of law on the basis of the testimony of a single witness, i.e., they are not to allow the testimony of a single witness to "stand"; see *Rabbeinu Bachya* to the verse.

In contrast to Chinuch, *Yerei'im* §205 [244] and *Smag* (*Lav* 213) understand that this verse establishes a mitzvah-prohibition for a single witness to testify against another person in cases where two witnesses are necessary; see *Pesachim* 113b. This view is cited in *Sefer Chafetz Chaim, Pesichah, Lavin* §10. For discussion of these two ways of understanding the verse, see *Sdei Chemed, Maareches Lamed* §132.

2. Based on *Genesis* 8:21.

3. Literally, *mud will enter his heart.* See *Targum* to *Jeremiah* 38:6. [The expression, "mud entering the heart," is used to describe various types of impure thoughts; see *Sanhedrin* 75b and *Chagigah* 15b.]

בְּדַרְכֵי הַיֹּשֶׁר אֵינוֹ מִן הַנִּמְנָע לְהִתְהַפֵּךְ בְּמַחֲשַׁבְתּוֹ וּלְהַרְשִׁיעַ, שֶׁהֲרֵי אָמְרוּ זִכְרוֹנָם לִבְרָכָה (ברכות כ״ט ע״א) **כִּי יוֹחָנָן שִׁמֵּשׁ בִּכְהֻנָּה גְּדוֹלָה וּלְבַסּוֹף נַעֲשָׂה צְדוֹקִי**[4]**, גַּם אָמְרוּ בַּחֲנַנְיָה בֶּן עַזּוּר שֶׁהָיָה תְּחִלָּה נְבִיא אֱמֶת וּלְבַסּוֹף נַעֲשָׂה נְבִיא שֶׁקֶר**[5]**, עַל כֵּן הוּא רָאוּי וְכָשֵׁר הַדָּבָר שֶׁלֹּא לִסְמֹךְ עַל לֵב אָדָם לַעֲנֹשׁ חֲבֵרוֹ עַל פִּיו, וַאֲפִלּוּ יִהְיֶה הַנֶּעֱנָשׁ רָשָׁע גָּמוּר וְהֶדְיוֹט שֶׁבַּהֶדְיוֹטוֹת וְהַמֵּעִיד חָכָם גָּדוֹל שֶׁבְּיִשְׂרָאֵל. אֲבָל בִּהְיוֹת הַמְּעִידִים שְׁנַיִם אֲנָשִׁים כְּשֵׁרִים, חֲזָקָה בְּכָל זֶרַע יִשְׂרָאֵל שֶׁלֹּא יַסְכִּימוּ שְׁנַיִם לְהָעִיד בְּשֶׁקֶר, וּגְדוֹלָה חֲזָקָה בְּכָל הַדְּבָרִים**[6]**.**

מִדִּינֵי הַמִּצְוָה מַה שֶּׁאָמְרוּ זִכְרוֹנָם לִבְרָכָה (כתובות פ״ז ע״ב) **בְּעֵד אֶחָד דִּלְכָל עָוֹן וּלְכָל חַטָּאת הוּא דְּאֵינוֹ קָם, כְּלוֹמַר שֶׁלֹּא נַעֲנִישׁ שׁוּם אָדָם עַל פִּי עֵד אֶחָד בְּעֹנֶשׁ גּוּף אוֹ בְּעֹנֶשׁ מָמוֹן,**

אֵינוֹ מִן הַנִּמְנָע לְהִתְהַפֵּךְ בְּמַחֲשַׁבְתּוֹ וּלְהַרְשִׁיעַ – **it is not impossible that his attitude will change and he will** begin to **do evil,** שֶׁהֲרֵי אָמְרוּ זִכְרוֹנָם לִבְרָכָה – **for [the Sages], of blessed memory, said** (*Berachos* 29a) כִּי יוֹחָנָן שִׁמֵּשׁ בִּכְהֻנָּה גְּדוֹלָה וּלְבַסּוֹף נַעֲשָׂה צְדוֹקִי – **that Yochanan served as Kohen Gadol** for many years, **but in the end became a Sadducee,**[4] גַּם אָמְרוּ בַּחֲנַנְיָה בֶּן עַזּוּר שֶׁהָיָה תְּחִלָּה נְבִיא אֱמֶת וּלְבַסּוֹף נַעֲשָׂה נְבִיא שֶׁקֶר – **and [the Sages] also said** (see *Sanhedrin* 90a) **that originally, Hananiah the son of Azur was a** true **prophet, but in the end became a false prophet.**[5] עַל כֵּן הוּא רָאוּי וְכָשֵׁר הַדָּבָר שֶׁלֹּא לִסְמֹךְ עַל לֵב אָדָם לַעֲנֹשׁ חֲבֵרוֹ עַל פִּיו – **It is therefore fitting and proper not to rely on the** integrity of **a person's heart to punish his fellow based** solely **on his [testimony],** וַאֲפִלּוּ יִהְיֶה הַנֶּעֱנָשׁ רָשָׁע גָּמוּר וְהֶדְיוֹט שֶׁבַּהֶדְיוֹטוֹת – **even if the one who faces punishment is a thoroughly wicked man and the lowest of the lowly,** וְהַמֵּעִיד חָכָם גָּדוֹל שֶׁבְּיִשְׂרָאֵל – **and the one testifying** against him **is the greatest sage among the Jewish people.** אֲבָל בִּהְיוֹת הַמְּעִידִים שְׁנַיִם אֲנָשִׁים כְּשֵׁרִים – **However, where the witnesses are *two* upstanding people,** we are not concerned for false testimony, חֲזָקָה בְּכָל זֶרַע יִשְׂרָאֵל שֶׁלֹּא יַסְכִּימוּ שְׁנַיִם לְהָעִיד בְּשֶׁקֶר – because **there is a legal presumption that two** upstanding **Jews would not agree to testify falsely** together, וּגְדוֹלָה חֲזָקָה בְּכָל הַדְּבָרִים – **and** since the power of **legal presumption is great in all areas** of Jewish law, we rely on the testimony of two valid witnesses.[6]

Laws of the Mitzvah

מִדִּינֵי הַמִּצְוָה – **Among the laws of the mitzvah** is מַה שֶּׁאָמְרוּ זִכְרוֹנָם לִבְרָכָה בְּעֵד אֶחָד – **that which [the Sages], of blessed memory, stated** (*Kesubos* 87b) **regarding** the acceptability of the testimony of **a single witness,** דִּלְכָל עָוֹן וּלְכָל חַטָּאת הוּא דְּאֵינוֹ קָם – namely, **that** it is only **"for any punishment or any penalty" that [a single witness] may not stand;** כְּלוֹמַר שֶׁלֹּא נַעֲנִישׁ שׁוּם אָדָם עַל פִּי עֵד אֶחָד בְּעֹנֶשׁ גּוּף אוֹ בְּעֹנֶשׁ מָמוֹן – **that is, we are not to mete out corporal**

NOTES

4. Yochanan the Kohen Gadol was part of the Hasmonean dynasty that ruled during the Second Temple Era. [See *Berachos* 29a, where his exact identity is disputed.] He was righteous for many years, but ultimately joined the Sadducees, a heretical sect that was active during that period.

The Sages (ibid.) cite Yochanan's tragic spiritual fall in support of their warning (*Avos* 2:4) that a person should never become complacent and trust his own righteousness.

5. Hananiah the son of Azur lived in the days of the prophet Jeremiah. Scripture (*Jeremiah* 28:2-4) tells us that Hananiah prophesied falsely that the Babylonian exile foretold by Jeremiah would not come to pass. The Sages teach that Hananiah was originally a true prophet and only later became a false prophet. Now, as we learned in Mitzvah 516, a person can become a prophet only after having reached great spiritual heights. Thus, the story of Hananiah is another example of a person who was exceedingly righteous, but nevertheless suffered a great fall.

6. See *Rambam, Hil. Yesodei HaTorah* 7:7 and 8:3.

According to Chinuch, the reason a single witness is not believed is that we are concerned that he might be lying; see *Minchas Chinuch* §2. Others contend that since each person has a presumption of righteousness, there is no real concern that a single witness is lying. In their view, the law that a single witness is not believed is a Scriptural decree, much like the law that disqualifies relatives from serving together as witnesses (*Ketzos HaChoshen* 30:9, citing *Teshuvos Meyuchasos LeRamban* §94; see *Tosafos HaRosh, Gittin* 10b ד״ה אי לאו דכותי). For further discussion, see *Tashbetz* 1:77 and *Shaarei Torah* [Lev], *Eidus* 1:1.

זְהוּ פֵּרוּשׁ עָוֹן וְחַטָּאת, אֲבָל קָם הוּא לִשְׁבוּעָה, כְּלוֹמַר שֶׁמְּחַיֵּב הוּא שְׁבוּעָה לְאוֹתוֹ שֶׁמֵּעִיד עָלָיו[7], כְּגוֹן שֶׁאָמַר אֶחָד לַחֲבֵרוֹ תֵּן לִי מָנֶה שֶׁהִלְוִיתִיךָ, אָמַר לוֹ אֵין לְךָ בְּיָדִי כְּלוּם, וְעֵד אֶחָד מֵעִיד כְּדִבְרֵי הַתּוֹבֵעַ, חַיָּב הַנִּתְבָּע לִשָּׁבַע[8]. וּמַה שֶּׁאָמְרוּ גַּם כֵּן שֶׁאַף עַל פִּי שֶׁעֵד אֶחָד לֹא הֶאֱמִינַתּוּ תּוֹרָה לַעֲנֹשׁ עַל פִּיו חֲבֵרוֹ בְּגוּף אוֹ בְּמָמוֹן, מִכָּל מָקוֹם נֶאֱמָן הוּא בְּאִסּוּרִין[9], וּכְמוֹ שֶׁאָמְרוּ זִכְרוֹנָם לִבְרָכָה בְּהַרְבֵּה מְקוֹמוֹת בַּגְּמָרָא עֵד אֶחָד נֶאֱמָן בְּאִסּוּרִין, כְּלוֹמַר שֶׁיָּעִיד בָּשָׂר זֶה אוֹ יַיִן זֶה אָסוּר הוּא אוֹ כָּשֵׁר נֶאֱמָן[10],

---

punishment or to assess monetary penalties to anyone on the basis of the testimony of **a single witness,** זְהוּ פֵּרוּשׁ עָוֹן וְחַטָּאת **— which is the meaning of** the phrase, **"for any punishment or any penalty";** אֲבָל קָם הוּא לִשְׁבוּעָה **— but, [a single witness]** ***does*** **stand for** the purpose of requiring a litigant to take **an oath,** כְּלוֹמַר שֶׁמְּחַיֵּב הוּא שְׁבוּעָה לְאוֹתוֹ שֶׁמֵּעִיד עָלָיו **— meaning that** in monetary cases, **[a single witness] obligates the person against whom he testifies to take an oath** to exempt himself from paying.[7] כְּגוֹן שֶׁאָמַר אֶחָד לַחֲבֵרוֹ תֵּן לִי מָנֶה שֶׁהִלְוִיתִיךָ **— For example, if one said to his fellow, "Give me the** ***maneh*** (100 *dinars*) **that I lent you,"** אָמַר לוֹ אֵין לְךָ בְּיָדִי כְּלוּם **— and [the defendant] responded, "I owe you nothing,"** וְעֵד אֶחָד מֵעִיד כְּדִבְרֵי הַתּוֹבֵעַ **— and a single witness testifies in support of the claimant's words,** חַיָּב הַנִּתְבָּע לִשָּׁבַע **— the defendant is obligated to take an oath** to refute the witness' testimony, or else he must pay.[8]

Chinuch discusses another area of law in which a single witness is believed: וּמַה שֶּׁאָמְרוּ גַּם כֵּן **— There is also that which [the Sages] said,** שֶׁאַף עַל פִּי שֶׁעֵד אֶחָד לֹא הֶאֱמִינַתּוּ תּוֹרָה לַעֲנֹשׁ עַל פִּיו חֲבֵרוֹ בְּגוּף אוֹ בְּמָמוֹן **— that even though the Torah does not believe a single witness with regard to meting out corporal punishment or levying monetary penalties on the basis of his testimony,** מִכָּל מָקוֹם נֶאֱמָן הוּא בְּאִסּוּרִין **— [a single witness] is nevertheless believed with regard to** Torah **prohibitions,**[9] וּכְמוֹ שֶׁאָמְרוּ זִכְרוֹנָם לִבְרָכָה בְּהַרְבֵּה מְקוֹמוֹת בַּגְּמָרָא **— as [the Sages], of blessed memory, stated in numerous places in the Gemara** (*Gittin* 2b, 3a, and *Chullin* 10b): עֵד אֶחָד נֶאֱמָן בְּאִסּוּרִין **— "A single witness is believed with regard to prohibitions."** כְּלוֹמַר שֶׁיָּעִיד בָּשָׂר זֶה אוֹ יַיִן זֶה אָסוּר הוּא אוֹ כָּשֵׁר נֶאֱמָן **— This means that** if, for example, **[a single witness] testifies that some meat or wine is forbidden or permitted, he is believed.**[10]

NOTES

7. The phrase "for any punishment or any penalty" is unnecessary, since the Torah could have simply written, "A single witness may not stand," and we would have known that *beis din* cannot render *any* judgment on the basis of his testimony. Therefore, the Sages understood that this phrase means to imply that there is something for which the testimony of a single witness *is* effective, namely, obligating a defendant in monetary cases to take an oath to exempt himself from paying (*Mizrachi* and *Gur Aryeh* to the verse).

8. If the defendant swears that he does not owe the plaintiff anything, he is exempt from paying. If, however, he refuses to take an oath (or if he is unable to take an oath; see below, after note 31), he must pay the amount he is accused of owing.

[One could have interpreted the verse as teaching that the one who is *supported* by the witness swears and is thereby able to exact payment from the defendant. However, since all Biblically required oaths are taken only to *exempt* oneself from paying, the verse is understood to be referring to an oath taken by the defendant to exempt himself from paying, and not to an oath taken by the plaintiff to exact money from the defendant.]

Chinuch's example of the testimony of a single witness requiring a defendant to take an oath is a case where the plaintiff himself claims with certainty, independently of the witness' testimony, that the defendant owes him money. The commentators debate whether the testimony of a single witness requires a defendant to take an oath even in cases where the plaintiff does not make a definite claim; see *Shulchan Aruch, Choshen Mishpat* 75:23 and 87:1 with *Beur HaGra* in both places.

There is also debate as to whether the testimony of a single witness can *exempt* a person from an obligation to make an oath. See Insight for discussion.

9. אִסּוּרִין refers to laws that deal with questions of permitted or forbidden status, as opposed to questions of monetary or criminal law.

10. According to *Rashi* (*Gittin* 2b and *Yevamos* 88a), this principle is self-evident; it does not require a Scriptural source. If not for this principle, a person would be forbidden to eat food prepared by others — even by his own wife — since he could not accept anyone's word that the food was permitted! Since this is obviously not true, a single witness is evidently believed with regard to matters of prohibition. *Tosafos* (*Gittin* ibid. ד"ה עד א'),

וְכֵן כָּל כַּיּוֹצֵא בָּזֶה בְּכָל הָאִסּוּרִין שֶׁבַּתּוֹרָה[11]. וּכְמוֹ כֵן אָמְרוּ זִכְרוֹנָם לִבְרָכָה שֶׁבְּדִינֵי מָמוֹנוֹת מְקַבְּלִין עֵדוּת מְיֻחֶדֶת[12], כֵּיצַד, אֶחָד אוֹמֵר בְּפָנַי הִלְוָהוּ וְאֶחָד אוֹמֵר בְּפָנַי הוֹדָה לוֹ, מִצְטָרְפִין[13]. וְעוֹד אָמְרוּ זִכְרוֹנָם לִבְרָכָה שֶׁאִם הֵעִיד אֶחָד בְּבֵית דִּין זֶה וְאֶחָד בְּבֵית דִּין אַחֵר, יָבֹא בֵּית דִּין אֵצֶל בֵּית דִּין וְיִצְטָרְפוּ עֵדוּתָן[14], וְכִדְאָמְרִינַן בְּרֵישׁ פֶּרֶק גֵּט פָּשׁוּט

וְכֵן כָּל כַּיּוֹצֵא בָּזֶה בְּכָל הָאִסּוּרִין שֶׁבַּתּוֹרָה – The same applies to similar cases involving all of the other prohibitions in the Torah.[11]

Although monetary cases cannot be resolved with less than two witnesses, the standards for what constitutes a "set" of two witnesses are less stringent for monetary cases than they are for capital cases: **וּכְמוֹ כֵן אָמְרוּ זִכְרוֹנָם לִבְרָכָה – [The Sages], of blessed memory, also stated** (see *Rambam, Hil. Eidus* 4:2-3) **שֶׁבְּדִינֵי מָמוֹנוֹת מְקַבְּלִין עֵדוּת מְיֻחֶדֶת – that in monetary cases, we accept the testimony of isolated witnesses.**[12] **כֵּיצַד – How so? אֶחָד אוֹמֵר בְּפָנַי הִלְוָהוּ וְאֶחָד אוֹמֵר בְּפָנַי הוֹדָה לוֹ – If one** witness **says, "[Reuven] lent money to [Shimon] in my presence," while another** witness **says, "[Shimon]** (the borrower from the first witness' testimony) **admitted** that he owes money to **[Reuven]," מִצְטָרְפִין – [the witnesses] combine** to exact money from Shimon.[13]

וְעוֹד אָמְרוּ זִכְרוֹנָם לִבְרָכָה – [The Sages], of blessed memory, further stated (*Rambam* ibid. 4:6) **שֶׁאִם הֵעִיד אֶחָד בְּבֵית דִּין זֶה וְאֶחָד בְּבֵית דִּין אַחֵר – that if one** witness **testifies in** front of **a certain *beis din*, and another** witness testifies **in** front of **another *beis din*, יָבֹא בֵּית דִּין אֵצֶל בֵּית דִּין וְיִצְטָרְפוּ עֵדוּתָן** – then the judges of **one of the** two ***batei din* should come to the other *beis din*** to form a larger *beis din*, **and** they should then **combine the testimony** that was said in front of each *beis din* and issue a verdict on the basis of that testimony.[14] **וְכִדְאָמְרִינַן בְּרֵישׁ פֶּרֶק גֵּט פָּשׁוּט** – This

---

NOTES

on the other hand, maintain that the credibility of a single witness with regard to prohibitions is derived from Scripture. With regard to a *zavah* (a woman who experiences a discharge of uterine blood at an irregular point in her cycle; Mitzvah 182), who is forbidden to her husband until she counts seven clean days and immerses in a *mikveh*, the Torah states (15:28): וְסָפְרָה לָּהּ שִׁבְעַת יָמִים וְאַחַר תִּטְהָר *She must count seven* (clean) *days **for herself** and afterward she can become purified.* As the Gemara (*Kesubos* 72a) explains, the expression "*for herself*" teaches that a woman may count these clean days privately, which indicates that she is believed regarding the count. This, in turn, teaches that a single witness is believed with regard to all prohibitions.

There is much discussion about the parameters of a single witness' credibility in the realm of prohibitions. See *Shulchan Aruch, Yoreh Deah* §127 with commentaries, where this topic is discussed at length.

11. An exception to this rule are areas of halachah that are classified as דָּבָר שֶׁבְּעֶרְוָה, *matters concerning ervah* [forbidden relationships], which include all matters involving marriage, divorce, and adultery. As a general rule, such matters cannot be resolved with fewer than two witnesses (*Yevamos* 88a, *Gittin* 2b, *Kiddushin* 66a).

12. The classic case of "isolated witnesses" is when two people see the same event but do not see each other. Such testimony is not sufficient to convict in capital cases (see Mitzvah 411), but *is* sufficient to resolve monetary cases. Moreover, as Chinuch immediately explains, an even greater degree of "isolation" is acceptable in monetary cases, so that it is sometimes possible for *beis din* to exact money based on the testimony of two witnesses who did not even see the same event.

13. Although two witnesses are required to exact money, these witnesses do not have to testify about the same event; even if one witness testifies about an actual loan and another witness testifies about an admission of debt, *beis din* can combine their testimony and exact money from a defendant. [*Beis din* can exact money both on the basis of witnesses to an actual loan (עֵדֵי הַלְוָאָה) and on the basis of witnesses to an admission of indebtedness (עֵדֵי הוֹדָאָה).]

The law that the testimonies of a loan-witness and an admission-witness can be combined is not based on the assumption that the admission was to the very loan about which the other witness testified. Indeed, *beis din* combines such testimony and exacts money even in cases where the admission could not possibly have been to the loan attested to by the other witness; e.g., a single witness testified that on a certain date Shimon admitted to owing Reuven money, and a second witness testified that Shimon borrowed money from Reuven on a later date, so that the admission preceded the loan (see *Rambam, Hil. Eidus* 4:3). Rather, the reason that both types of testimony can be combined is that when it comes to monetary obligations, we are not concerned about the *source* of the debt, but the *indebtedness* itself, and as long as two witnesses attest to the fact that Shimon owes Reuven money, that is sufficient for *beis din* to force Shimon to pay Reuven. [See Insight to Mitzvah 411.]

14. Neither *beis din* could render judgment on its own,

(קס"ה ע"ב), שְׁלַחוּ לֵיהּ חַבְרַיָּא לְרַבִּי יִרְמְיָה, עֵד אֶחָד בִּכְתָב וְעֵד אֶחָד עַל פֶּה מַהוּ שֶׁיִּצְטָרְפוּ[15], שְׁנַיִם שֶׁהֵעִידוּ אֶחָד בְּבֵית דִּין זֶה וְאֶחָד בְּבֵית דִּין אַחֵר מַה הוּא שֶׁיָּבוֹא בֵּית דִּין זֶה אֵצֶל בֵּית דִּין זֶה וְיִצְטָרְפוּ[16], שְׁנַיִם שֶׁהֵעִידוּ בְּבֵית דִּין זֶה וְחָזְרוּ וְהֵעִידוּ בְּבֵית דִּין זֶה מַהוּ שֶׁיָּבוֹא אֶחָד מִכָּל בֵּית דִּין וְיִצְטָרְפוּ[17], שְׁלַח לְהוּ, אֲנִי אֵינִי כְּדֵי שֶׁאַתֶּם שְׁלַחְתֶּם לִי, אֲבָל דַּעַת תַּלְמִידְכֶם נוֹטָה שֶׁיִּצְטָרְפוּ[18], וְכֵן הֲלָכָה.

---

is **as we say at the beginning of Chapter** ***Get Pashut*** (*Bava Basra* 165b): שְׁלַחוּ לֵיהּ חַבְרַיָּא לְרַבִּי יִרְמְיָה – **The scholars of the academy sent** the following inquiry **to R' Yirmiyah:** עֵד אֶחָד בִּכְתָב וְעֵד אֶחָד עַל פֶּה מַהוּ שֶׁיִּצְטָרְפוּ – **Can a witness who testified in writing** (i.e., he signed a document) **combine with a witness who testified orally?**[15] שְׁנַיִם שֶׁהֵעִידוּ אֶחָד בְּבֵית דִּין זֶה וְאֶחָד בְּבֵית דִּין אַחֵר – Others reported that the inquiry to R' Yirmiyah was as follows: In a case where **two witnesses testify,** with **one** of them giving testimony **in a certain** ***beis din*** **and the other** giving testimony **in another** ***beis din,*** so that neither *beis din* can resolve the issue on its own, מַה הוּא שֶׁיָּבוֹא בֵּית דִּין זֶה אֵצֶל בֵּית דִּין זֶה וְיִצְטָרְפוּ – **can** judges of **one of the** two ***batei din*** **come to the other** ***beis din*** to form a larger *beis din* **and combine** the testimony they each heard, in order to issue a verdict?[16] שְׁנַיִם שֶׁהֵעִידוּ בְּבֵית דִּין זֶה וְחָזְרוּ וְהֵעִידוּ בְּבֵית דִּין זֶה – Still others reported that the inquiry to R' Yirmiyah was as follows: In a case where **two [witnesses] testified in a certain** ***beis din*** **and [the same two witnesses] then testified in another** ***beis din,*** and the same two witnesses repeated their testimony in front of a third *beis din,* and then two members of each *beis din* went overseas, leaving behind only one member of each *beis din,* מַהוּ שֶׁיָּבוֹא אֶחָד מִכָּל בֵּית דִּין וְיִצְטָרְפוּ – **can a single judge from each** ***beis din*** (i.e., the remaining judge from each of the three *batei din*) **join together** to form a new *beis din* that can render a verdict on the basis of the testimonies that were given in front of the three original *batei din?*[17] שְׁלַח לְהוּ – Whatever the inquiry was, **[R' Yirmiyah] sent** the following response **to [his colleagues]:** אֲנִי אֵינִי כְּדֵי שֶׁאַתֶּם שְׁלַחְתֶּם לִי – **"I am not worthy of being sent this question.** אֲבָל דַּעַת תַּלְמִידְכֶם נוֹטָה שֶׁיִּצְטָרְפוּ – **But,** if you insist on hearing my opinion, **your disciple**[18] **is inclined to say that they should be able to join together."** וְכֵן הֲלָכָה – **And,** as is evident

---

NOTES

since each *beis din* heard only the testimony of one witness. Nevertheless, a joint *beis din* comprised of the judges from both *batei din* can pass judgment, since there are two witnesses to the matter, each of whom testified in front of some of the judges of the joint *beis din.* [See *Sma* 30:34 and *Nesivos HaMishpat, Beurim* 30:8 for discussion as to whether the joint *beis din* must be comprised of all six judges from the original two *batei din,* or if two judges (a majority) from each *beis din* suffices.]

As we have already seen, witnesses in monetary cases are not required to observe an event together. Moreover, they are not required to testify at the same time (*Rambam, Hil. Eidus* 4:4). This ruling takes that law one step further; even testimonies that were given in front of different *batei din* can be combined (see *Bava Basra* 165b).

15. One witness signed on a loan document that states that Shimon borrowed money from Reuven, and another witness gave oral testimony that Shimon borrowed money from Reuven. Can the testimony of these two witnesses be combined in order to exact money from Shimon? The uncertainty in this case is that perhaps the testimony of "isolated witnesses" in monetary cases is acceptable only where the two witnesses give the same *type* of testimony, i.e., they both testify orally or both sign as witnesses to a contract (see *Bava Basra* 165b).

16. See above, note 14.

17. The Gemara (*Sanhedrin* 30a) records a dispute as to whether the two witnesses in a monetary case must testify at the same time. The halachah follows the view that there is no such requirement (see above, note 14), but the current version of the inquiry to R' Yirmiyah was posed according to the view that there is such a requirement. On the one hand, perhaps all that is necessary is that both witnesses testify at the same time, but not that all of the judges accept the witnesses' testimony at the same time. If so, the remaining judges from the three original *batei din* can join together to issue a verdict, even though each judge heard the witnesses' testimony at different times, since in each of three *batei din,* the witnesses gave their testimony together. On the other hand, an argument can be made that not only is there a requirement for the two witnesses to testify together, but also for the judges to accept the testimony of the witnesses together. If so, the remaining judges from the original *batei din* cannot join together to issue a verdict, since each judge heard the witnesses' testimony at different times (see *Bava Basra* ibid.).

18. He referred to himself as a "disciple," as an expression of humility.

וּמַה שֶּׁאָמְרוּ בִּכְתֻבּוֹת פֶּרֶק הָאִשָּׁה שֶׁנִּתְאַלְמְנָה (כ״א ע״ב) שֶׁעֵד וְדַיָּן אֵין מִצְטָרְפִין בְּמַה שֶּׁהוּא דְּאוֹרַיְתָא[19].

וּמַה שֶּׁאָמְרוּ זִכְרוֹנָם לִבְרָכָה שֶׁבִּשְׁנֵי מְקוֹמוֹת הֶאֱמִינָה הַתּוֹרָה עֵד אֶחָד, בְּסוֹטָה שֶׁלֹּא תִשְׁתֶּה מֵי הַמָּרִים[20], וּבְעֶגְלָה עֲרוּפָה[21] שֶׁלֹּא תֵעָרֵף, כְּלוֹמַר אִם מֵעִיד אֶחָד שֶׁהוּא יוֹדֵעַ בַּהֲרִיגַת הַנִּרְצָח אֵין עוֹרְפִין אֶת הָעֶגְלָה[22] שֶׁהַתּוֹרָה אָמְרָה (דברים כ״א, א׳) לֹא נוֹדַע,

---

from the Gemara's conclusion there, **so is the halachah.** In all three of these cases, either the witnesses or the judges can combine so that money can be exacted from the defendant.

וּמַה שֶּׁאָמְרוּ בִּכְתֻבּוֹת פֶּרֶק הָאִשָּׁה שֶׁנִּתְאַלְמְנָה – There is **also that which [the Sages] stated in** Tractate ***Kesubos*, Chapter *Ha'ishah Shenisalmenah*** (*Kesubos* 21b), **שֶׁעֵד וְדַיָּן אֵין מִצְטָרְפִין בְּמַה שֶּׁהוּא דְּאוֹרַיְתָא** – **that a witness and a judge cannot combine** to give testimony **in a matter that concerns Biblical law.**[19]

Chinuch discusses other cases in which a single witness' testimony is sufficient:

וּמַה שֶּׁאָמְרוּ זִכְרוֹנָם לִבְרָכָה – **And** there is **that which [the Sages], of blessed memory, stated** (*Rambam, Hil Eidus* 5:2) **שֶׁבִּשְׁנֵי מְקוֹמוֹת הֶאֱמִינָה הַתּוֹרָה עֵד אֶחָד** – **that in two situations, the Torah believed a single witness: בְּסוֹטָה שֶׁלֹּא תִשְׁתֶּה מֵי הַמָּרִים** – (1) **in the case of a *sotah*, so that she does not drink the bitter waters;**[20] **וּבְעֶגְלָה עֲרוּפָה שֶׁלֹּא תֵעָרֵף** – **and** (2) **in the case of an *eglah arufah*** (decapitated calf; Mitzvah 530),[21] **so that [a calf] is not decapitated, כְּלוֹמַר אִם מֵעִיד אֶחָד שֶׁהוּא יוֹדֵעַ בַּהֲרִיגַת הַנִּרְצָח** – **meaning that if a single witness testifies that he has knowledge about the victim's murder, אֵין עוֹרְפִין אֶת הָעֶגְלָה** – **we do not decapitate the calf.**[22] **שֶׁהַתּוֹרָה אָמְרָה "לֹא נוֹדַע"** – This is **because** in setting forth the requirement to decapitate a

---

NOTES

19. The "judge" in this case refers to a person who was part of a *beis din* that accepted testimony that Shimon owes Reuven money but was unable to exact money from Shimon before the other judges left. The "witness" is a person who actually witnessed an event in which Shimon became indebted to Shimon (e.g., the witness saw Shimon borrow money from Reuven). If the judge testifies in front of a *beis din* that he was part of another *beis din* that accepted testimony that Shimon owes Reuven money, his testimony cannot be combined with that of the witness to issue a verdict against Shimon. The reason for this is that the two testimonies are fundamentally different; whereas the witness testified that he actually saw an event that creates a monetary obligation, the judge only testified that he was part of a *beis din* that accepted testimony to that effect (see *Rambam, Hil. Eidus* 4:6 with *Kesef Mishneh*). [Many commentators explain the Gemara in *Kesubos* differently; see Rishonim there.]

Chinuch limits this disqualification to Biblical matters; for Rabbinic matters, such as the certification of documents (i.e., attesting to the validity of signatures on a document), the testimonies of a witness and a judge can be combined. The source for this distinction is unclear; see *Minchas Yitzchak* §4 for discussion.

20. A *sotah* is a woman who was warned by her husband (in front of two witnesses) not to be secluded with a specific man and was found to have disregarded that warning (i.e., two witnesses testified that after being warned, she secluded herself with that man). Such a woman is forbidden to her husband under suspicion of adultery unless she drinks specially prepared waters (מֵי הַמָּרִים, *the bitter waters*) that miraculously test her fidelity (see Mitzvah 365). If after disregarding her husband's warning, even one witness testifies that she indeed committed adultery with the man about whom she was warned, the witness is believed, and she is not given the bitter waters to drink. Rather, her husband must divorce her, just like any man whose wife is found to have committed adultery (Mishnah *Sotah* 31a; *Rambam, Hil. Sotah* 1:14). See Mishnah ibid. with *Rashi,* for the source that a single witness is believed in this case.

The credibility of a single witness in this case is novel, because, in general, the rule is that a דָּבָר שֶׁבְּעֶרְוָה, *a matter relating to ervah,* requires two witnesses (see above, note 11) However, in a case where a woman was warned against secluding herself with a specific man and disregarded that warning, there is strong circumstantial evidence that she indeed committed adultery, and the Torah therefore made an exception to its rule and accepted the testimony of a single witness [though she is not subject to capital punishment unless there were two witnesses] (see *Rashi* ad loc. ד״ה לא היתה שותה).

21. If a murder victim is found between towns and it is not known who killed him, a measurement is made to determine the town nearest to the corpse. The elders of that town bring a calf to an untilled valley, where they kill it by chopping its neck from the back. The elders then wash their hands over the dead calf, and make a statement in which they declare that they are in no way responsible for the murder. The Kohanim who are present then pray for atonement.

22. If even a single witness claims to have knowledge about the murder, the procedure described in the

וַהֲרֵי נוֹדַע לְאִישׁ אֶחָד[23]. וַחֲכָמִים הֶאֱמִינוּ עֵד אֶחָד שֶׁיָּעִיד בְּאִשָּׁה שֶׁמֵּת בַּעְלָהּ כְּדֵי שֶׁלֹּא תִתְעַגֵּן[24], וְאָמְרוּ זִכְרוֹנָם לִבְרָכָה (יבמות פ״ח ע״א) בְּטַעַם זֶה[25] שֶׁהִיא מְדַקְדֶּקֶת אַחַר הָאֱמֶת בָּזֶה, שֶׁאִם תִּנָּשֵׂא וְאַחַר כָּךְ יָבֹא בַּעְלָהּ, תֵּצֵא מִזֶּה וּמִזֶּה[26] וְהַוָּלָד מַמְזֵר[27,28,29].

---

calf, **the Torah states** (*Deuteronomy* 21:1): *If a corpse will be found ... **it was not known** who smote him*, which indicates that there were no witnesses at all; וַהֲרֵי נוֹדַע לְאִישׁ אֶחָד – **but** in a case where there is a single witness, **it is known to one person;** therefore, in such a situation, there is no obligation to decapitate a calf.[23]

וַחֲכָמִים הֶאֱמִינוּ עֵד אֶחָד שֶׁיָּעִיד בְּאִשָּׁה שֶׁמֵּת בַּעְלָהּ כְּדֵי שֶׁלֹּא תִתְעַגֵּן – In addition to these two cases, in which the credibility of a single witness is derived from Scripture, **the Sages gave credibility to a single witness who testifies that a woman's husband died, so that [the woman] not remain an *agunah*.**[24] וְאָמְרוּ זִכְרוֹנָם לִבְרָכָה בְּטַעַם זֶה – **[The Sages], of blessed memory, stated** (see *Yevamos* 88a) **in explanation of this**[25] שֶׁהִיא מְדַקְדֶּקֶת אַחַר הָאֱמֶת בָּזֶה – **that a woman is careful to** independently **investigate the truth regarding this matter** before remarrying, שֶׁאִם תִּנָּשֵׂא וְאַחַר כָּךְ יָבֹא בַּעְלָהּ – **for if she gets married** to another man, **and her husband,** who was presumed dead, **then returns,** the law is that תֵּצֵא מִזֶּה וּמִזֶּה וְהַוָּלָד מַמְזֵר – **she must leave this one and that one** (i.e., she is forbidden to both men),[26] **and** any **child** she has from either one of them **is** considered **a *mamzer*.**[27] To avoid these and other severe consequences,[28] a woman will conduct her own investigation into her missing husband's fate, and will remarry only after concluding that he indeed died. On the basis of this presumption, together with the testimony of a single witness, the Sages permitted the woman to remarry.[29]

NOTES

previous note is not carried out. See further, Mitzvah 530 note 4

23. *Sotah* 47b. [For discussion as to why *Rambam* does not list the credibility of a single witness in the realm of prohibitions along with the credibility of a single witness in the areas of *sotah* and *eglah arufah*, see *Imrei Binah, Dinei Eidus* §29.]

24. [Literally, *so that she will not be restrained* (see *Rashi* to *Ruth* 1:13; *Radak, Shorashim* עגה).] An *agunah* is a woman who is perpetually bound to a husband with whom she no longer lives, because there is insufficient evidence of his death or a valid divorce.

A woman whose husband goes missing may not remarry unless there is sufficient evidence of his death. Under the usual guidelines for matters concerning marriage and divorce, two witnesses should be required (see above, note 11). However, the Sages accepted the testimony of a single witness, to alleviate the plight of women who, without this law, might be forced to spend the rest of their lives alone (see *Yevamos* 88a). See further.

25. The Sages do not have the ability to simply uproot a halachah when doing so will result in *active* transgression of Torah law (see *Yevamos* 90a), even for the noblest of purposes. Therefore, it is necessary to explain why the Sages allowed a woman to marry on the basis of a single witness.

26. A woman who willingly commits adultery is permanently forbidden to both her husband and the adulterer (*Sotah* 27b). If, however, the adultery was unintentional, these prohibitions do not apply (*Yevamos* 56b). When a woman remarries on the basis of a single witness' testimony and her husband returns alive, she cannot be blamed for her adulterous relationship with the second man, since she was permitted to rely on the single witness' testimony. Nevertheless, in this case, the Sages decreed that she is forbidden to both men (see Rishonim to Mishnah, *Yevamos* 87b). [This was in the woman's best interest, for it is these laws that allowed the Sages to rely on the testimony of a single witness to permit the woman to remarry; see note 29.]

27. A child conceived from the second husband before the first one returned and divorced her is a *mamzer* according to Biblical law, since it was born from an adulterous relationship. [A child born from an adulterous relationship is a *mamzer,* even if the adultery was unintentional.] A child born from the first husband after his return is a *mamzer* according to Rabbinic law. [Authorities debate the status of a child from the first husband after the second husband gave a *get,* and the status of a child from the second husband after the first one gave a *get.* See *Tosafos, Yevamos* 87b ד״ה הולד; *Rambam, Hil. Geirushin* 10:7 with *Maggid Mishneh; Chelkas Mechokeik* 4:17; and *Beis Shmuel* 4:27.]

28. See Mishnah, *Yevamos* 87b.

29. As mentioned in note 26, some of the consequences that a woman faces if her missing husband returns alive are Rabbinic. That is, the Sages developed a system of penalties to increase the likelihood that a woman will conduct her own investigation before remarrying. Once sufficiently confident that a woman would conduct her own investigation, the Sages allowed for the woman

וְאָמְרוּ זִכְרוֹנָם לִבְרָכָה שֶׁבְּכָל מָקוֹם שֶׁיּוֹעִיל עֵדוּת עֵד אֶחָד מוֹעִיל גַּם כֵּן עֵדוּת אִשָּׁה וּפָסוּל[30], חוּץ מֵעֵד אֶחָד שֶׁל שְׁבוּעָה שֶׁאֵין מְחַיְּבִין שְׁבוּעָה אֶלָּא בְּעֵדוּת עֵד כָּשֵׁר[31].

וְכֵן מַה שֶּׁאָמְרוּ שֶׁפְּעָמִים יְשַׁלֵּם הַנִּתְבָּע מָמוֹן עַל פִּי עֵד אֶחָד, כֵּיצַד, הָאוֹמֵר לַחֲבֵרוֹ מָנֶה לִי בְּיָדְךָ וַהֲרֵי עֵד אֶחָד מֵעִיד עָלָיו[32], וְהַנִּטְעָן אוֹמֵר כֵּן הוּא אֲבָל אַתָּה חַיָּב לִי מָנֶה כְּנֶגֶד אוֹתוֹ מָנֶה, הֲרֵי זֶה מְחֻיָּב שְׁבוּעָה בִּשְׁבִיל עֵדוּת הָעֵד, וְאֵינוֹ יָכוֹל לִשָּׁבַע

Chinuch briefly addresses who is qualified to testify in cases where a single witness suffices: **וְאָמְרוּ זִכְרוֹנָם לִבְרָכָה – [The Sages], of blessed memory, also stated** (*Rambam* ibid. 5:3) **שֶׁבְּכָל מָקוֹם שֶׁיּוֹעִיל עֵדוּת עֵד אֶחָד – that in any situation where the testimony of a single witness is effective** (e.g., to preclude a *sotah* from drinking the bitter waters, to testify that a woman's husband has died so she can remarry, or to remove the *eglah arufah* requirement), **מוֹעִיל גַּם כֵּן עֵדוּת אִשָּׁה וּפָסוּל – the testimony of a woman or a disqualified witness** (e.g., a relative) **is effective as well;**[30] **חוּץ מֵעֵד אֶחָד שֶׁל שְׁבוּעָה – with the exception of** the case of **a single witness who creates an obligation to take an oath, שֶׁאֵין מְחַיְּבִין שְׁבוּעָה אֶלָּא בְּעֵדוּת עֵד כָּשֵׁר – for we obligate** a litigant to take **an oath only on account of a valid witness.**[31]

As mentioned above (after note 6), in monetary cases, the testimony of a single witness creates an obligation for the person against whom he is testifying to take an oath. This means that if the defendant refuses to take the oath, he must pay the claim. Chinuch begins a lengthy discussion about the law regarding a defendant who does not refuse to take the oath, but is *unable* to take it:

וְכֵן מַה שֶּׁאָמְרוּ שֶׁפְּעָמִים יְשַׁלֵּם הַנִּתְבָּע מָמוֹן עַל פִּי עֵד אֶחָד – Also pertaining to this mitzvah is **that which [the Sages] stated** (see *Rambam, Hil. To'ein VeNitan* 4:8), **that sometimes a defendant *is* required to pay money on the basis of** the testimony of **a single witness. כֵּיצַד – How so? הָאוֹמֵר לַחֲבֵרוֹ מָנֶה לִי בְּיָדְךָ וַהֲרֵי עֵד אֶחָד מֵעִיד עָלָיו –** If **one says to his fellow, "You owe me a *maneh*," and a single witness testifies in support of [that claim],**[32] **וְהַנִּטְעָן אוֹמֵר כֵּן הוּא אֲבָל אַתָּה חַיָּב לִי מָנֶה כְּנֶגֶד אוֹתוֹ מָנֶה – to which the defendant says, "It is true** that I borrowed a *maneh* from you and never repaid it, **but you owe me a** different ***maneh* that cancels out that *maneh*,"** the defendant is required to pay the *maneh* to the claimant. **הֲרֵי זֶה מְחֻיָּב שְׁבוּעָה בִּשְׁבִיל עֵדוּת הָעֵד –** The reason is because, in order to deflect the claim against him, **this** defendant **is required** by law **to take an oath on account of the testimony of the** single **witness** that supports the claim, **וְאֵינוֹ יָכוֹל לִשָּׁבַע**

NOTES

to remarry on the basis of the testimony of a single witness.

Chinuch's language seems to indicate that the presumption that a woman will conduct a private investigation into her husband's fate is reason enough to rely on the testimony of a single witness. That is, although the testimony of a single witness is not sufficient proof to allow a woman to remarry, that testimony together with the private investigation that the woman will presumably conduct does constitute sufficient proof, and is considered just as reliable as two witnesses; see *Ritva, Yevamos* 88a ד״ה מתוך חומר. [An alternative explanation as to how the Sages could rely on a single witness is that a single witness is sufficient for any matter whose truth is likely to be revealed [מִילְתָא דַעֲבִידָא לְאִגַּלּוּיֵי], for it is unlikely that a person will lie if his lie would, in all likelihood, be exposed. Whether or not someone is alive falls into this category, because if a missing person is actually alive, it is likely that he will someday return (*Rambam, Hil. Geirushin* 12:15). See *Otzar HaPoskim, Even HaEzer,* beginning of 17:3, for a comprehensive discussion of these and other explanations.]

30. See *Rambam, Hil. Sotah* 1:15 and *Hil. Rotze'ach* 9:12.

31. As Chinuch wrote above (at note 7), the law that a single witness creates an obligation to take an oath is derived from the verse, *A single witness shall not stand up against any man for any punishment or penalty,* which implies that a single witness *does* stand to obligate a litigant to take an oath. The end of that verse, which states, *according to two witnesses or according to three witnesses shall a matter be confirmed,* certainly refers to valid witnesses. It stands to reason, then, that the single witness mentioned in the first part of the verse as a contrast to the "two or three witnesses" mentioned later also refers to a valid witness. Thus, the implication of the first part of the verse, that a single witness can obligate a litigant to take an oath, refers to a valid witness (*Noda BiYehudah* I, *Even HaEzer* §33 ד״ה והנה הספרי).

32. This refers to a case where the witness not only testified that the loan occurred, but also that the loan had not been repaid (*Maggid Mishneh* and *Kesef Mishneh;* see also *Shulchan Aruch, Choshen Mishpat* 75:13). See next note.

לְהַכְחִישׁ הָעֵד שֶׁהֲרֵי הוּא מוֹדֶה בְּמַה שֶּׁהָעֵד מֵעִיד בּוֹ, וְהַדִּין הוּא כֵּן שֶׁכָּל מְחֻיָּב לַחֲבֵרוֹ שְׁבוּעָה וְאֵינוֹ יָכוֹל לִשָּׁבַע שֶׁמְּשַׁלֵּם[33].

וְאֵין נִשְׁבָּעִין בְּהַעֲדַת עֵד אֶחָד לְעוֹלָם אֶלָּא אִם כֵּן יַכְחִישׁ הַנִּשְׁבָּע אֶת הָעֵד וִיכַפֵּר בְּעֵדוּתוֹ וְיִשָּׁבַע עַל זֶה[34]. וּמִפְּנֵי טַעַם זֶה כָּתַב הָרַמְבַּ"ם ז"ל (פ"ד מטוען ונטען ה"ח) שֶׁשְּׁטָר שֶׁיֵּשׁ בּוֹ עֵד אֶחָד וְהַנִּתְבָּע טוֹעֵן שֶׁפְּרָעוֹ, שֶׁעַכְשָׁו אֵינוֹ מַכְחִישׁ עֵדוּת הָעֵד שֶׁמֵּעִיד בַּהַלְוָאָה,

---

לְהַכְחִישׁ הָעֵד – **but he is unable to swear to deny** the testimony of **the witness,** שֶׁהֲרֵי הוּא מוֹדֶה בְּמַה שֶּׁהָעֵד מֵעִיד בּוֹ – **since he concedes the** essential **content of the witness' testimony** (i.e., that he borrowed the money and did not repay it); וְהַדִּין הוּא כֵּן שֶׁכָּל מְחֻיָּב לַחֲבֵרוֹ שְׁבוּעָה וְאֵינוֹ יָכוֹל לִשָּׁבַע שֶׁמְּשַׁלֵּם – **and the law is that anyone who is obligated to take an oath to** refute the claim of **his fellow and is unable to swear must pay.**[33]

Chinuch anticipates a question: Granted, the defendant cannot take an oath to refute the testimony of the single witness, since he concedes that he borrowed the money and did not repay it, but why is he not given the option of swearing that his counter-claim (that the lender owes him a corresponding amount) is true instead?

וְאֵין נִשְׁבָּעִין בְּהַעֲדַת עֵד אֶחָד לְעוֹלָם – The reason the defendant cannot exempt himself by swearing in support of his counter-claim is that **we never** accept **an oath in response to the testimony of a single witness** to exempt the defendant אֶלָּא אִם כֵּן יַכְחִישׁ הַנִּשְׁבָּע אֶת הָעֵד וִיכַפֵּר בְּעֵדוּתוֹ וְיִשָּׁבַע עַל זֶה – **unless [the defendant]** directly **contradicts the witness by denying** the content of **[the witness'] testimony and takes an oath supporting that [denial].** In the absence of that specific oath, the defendant is required to pay.[34]

Other cases governed by this principle:

וּמִפְּנֵי טַעַם זֶה כָּתַב הָרַמְבַּ"ם ז"ל – **It is on these grounds that *Rambam*, of blessed memory, wrote** (ibid.) שֶׁשְּׁטָר שֶׁיֵּשׁ בּוֹ עֵד אֶחָד וְהַנִּתְבָּע טוֹעֵן שֶׁפְּרָעוֹ – **that** in a situation where a plaintiff produces **a** loan **document signed by a single witness** as proof of the defendant's indebtedness **and the defendant claims to have repaid [the loan],** שֶׁעַכְשָׁו אֵינוֹ מַכְחִישׁ עֵדוּת הָעֵד שֶׁמֵּעִיד בַּהַלְוָאָה – **in which case, he is not contradicting the testimony of the witness, who** merely **attested to the**

NOTES

33. This rule is based on the following understanding of the single-witness oath: Like two witnesses, a single witness creates a monetary obligation for the defendant, but in contrast to the monetary obligation created by two witnesses, the obligation created by a single witness is not absolute. Rather, the defendant can exempt himself from paying by taking an oath to refute the witness' testimony. If, however, the defendant cannot take the oath — for whatever reason — the monetary obligation created by the single witness remains in place and the defendant must pay (*Nesivos HaMishpat, Kelalei Migo* §28; *Tumim* 94:2, and *Terumas HaKeri* 75:2; see *Teshuvos Rivash* §392 ד"ה ומה שכתבת וטענת). Cf. *Ketzos HaChoshen* 87:9.

Under normal circumstances, someone who borrows money orally (without a written document), even in the presence of two witnesses, is able to say that he is exempt from paying because the lender owes him a corresponding amount. This is because one who takes an undocumented loan is believed with a claim of repayment (*Rambam, Hil. Malveh VeLoveh* 11:1), and therefore, under the principle of *migo,* he is also believed when he claims that the lender owes him a corresponding amount. [The principle of *migo* states that if a litigant could have prevailed with a stronger claim, he is believed with a weaker claim too, since if he had wanted to lie he could have simply advanced the stronger claim.] In our case, however, the defendant is *not* believed to claim that the lender owes him a corresponding amount. This is because we are dealing with a case where the witness not only testified regarding the original loan, but also that the loan had not been repaid, i.e., he was with the borrower from the time of the loan until now. Thus, the borrower could not have prevailed with a claim of repayment, and is therefore also not believed with a claim that the lender owes him a corresponding amount of money (*Maggid Mishneh; Kesef Mishneh*).

34. When a single witness testifies that there is a monetary obligation, the Torah gives credibility to the witness and requires the defendant to pay unless the defendant takes a very specific oath, namely, one that directly refutes the testimony of the witness. In the case at hand, where the single witness testified that a loan occurred and was not repaid, the defendant must pay unless he swears that the loan never occurred, or that even though it did occur, it was repaid.

שֶׁמְּשַׁלֵּם[35], וַחֲלוּקִין עָלָיו אֲחֵרִים[36]. וְכֵן כַּפְרָן[37] שֶׁבָּא עָלָיו עֵד אֶחָד וְטָעַן שֶׁפָּרַע אוֹ שֶׁהֶחֱזִיר הַפִּקָּדוֹן, בְּכָל זֶה אָמְרִינַן שֶׁהוּא מְחֻיָּב שְׁבוּעָה וְאֵינוֹ יָכוֹל לִשָּׁבַע וּמְשַׁלֵּם[38].

occurrence of the **loan** and not whether it was repaid, שֶׁמְּשַׁלֵּם – **that [the defendant] must pay** the amount written in the document, since he is unable to take an oath that contradicts the testimony of the witness, and the rule is that one who is required to take an oath but is unable to do so must pay.[35] וַחֲלוּקִין עָלָיו אֲחֵרִים – In this case, though, **others disagree with [*Rambam*],** and maintain that the defendant *is* believed to say that he repaid the loan.[36]

וְכֵן כַּפְרָן שֶׁבָּא עָלָיו עֵד אֶחָד וְטָעַן שֶׁפָּרַע אוֹ שֶׁהֶחֱזִיר הַפִּקָּדוֹן – **Similarly, a "denier"** (i.e., one who initially denied that he borrowed money or was entrusted with a deposit),[37] **against whom a single witness** subsequently **came** and testified that he *did* borrow money or *was* given a deposit for safekeeping, **and** the denier then changed his story and **claimed that** although he borrowed money or was given a deposit, **he repaid** the loan **or returned the deposit,** and therefore owes nothing, בְּכָל זֶה אָמְרִינַן שֶׁהוּא מְחֻיָּב שְׁבוּעָה וְאֵינוֹ יָכוֹל לִשָּׁבַע וּמְשַׁלֵּם – **in** this and **all** cases like **this, we say that the defendant is required to take an oath but is unable to swear, and** therefore **must pay.**[38]

NOTES

35. *Rambam's* ruling is based on two assumptions: (1) If a lender produces a loan document signed by a single witness, the borrower is not believed with a claim of repayment. [This is because there is a legal presumption that a borrower would not repay the loan unless the lender returns the note to him. Therefore, the lender's possession of the note is proof that the loan was not repaid.] (2) A single signature on a contract is considered valid testimony, and can therefore create an obligation for a defendant to take an oath. [Although written testimony is generally invalid, signatures on a שְׁטָר, *legal document,* qualify as valid testimony. According to *Rambam,* even a document with a single signature is considered a שְׁטָר, so it constitutes valid testimony of a single witness.]

Therefore, if a lender produces a loan document with a single signature, the borrower is obligated to pay the loan unless he takes an oath that contradicts the testimony of the witness, i.e., he swears that the loan never occurred. In our case, the borrower cannot take that oath, because he claimed that he *repaid* the loan, and thus concedes that the loan did, in fact, occur. Since he cannot take the mandated oath, he is required to pay (see *Sma* 51:4 and *Aruch HaShulchan* ad loc. §1). [As in the previous case, the defendant does not have the option to simply swear in support of his counterclaim (in this case, that he repaid the loan); the only way for him to avoid payment is by taking the specific oath prescribed by the Torah, i.e., one that contradicts the single witness's testimony.]

36. Each of the two assumptions on which *Rambam's* ruling is based (see previous note) is disputed by others. Some challenge the notion that a single signature on a loan document is considered valid testimony. In their view, the signature of a single witness on a document has the status of ordinary written testimony, which is invalid. Others argue that even if a single signature on a document is considered valid testimony (i.e., even a document with a single signature is considered a שְׁטָר), a borrower is nevertheless believed to simply claim that he repaid the loan, just like a borrower is believed to claim that he repaid an undocumented loan. That is, when a loan document is signed by only one witness, the lender's possession of the document is not considered evidence that the loan has not been repaid (see *Beur HaGra, Choshen Mishpat* 51:8 and *Maggid Mishneh, Hil. Malveh VeLoveh* 14:10). [See *Beur HaGra* ibid. for a practical difference between these two lines of reasoning.]

37. *Maggid Mishneh, Hil. To'ein VeNitan* 4:8.

38. If there are no witnesses to a loan (all the following applies to a case involving a deposit, as well), an alleged borrower is believed if he claims that the loan never occurred or that he borrowed the money but repaid it. Indeed, even if a person first claims to have never borrowed the money and then changes his claim and says that he borrowed the money but repaid it, he is still exempt from paying (see *Shulchan Aruch, Choshen Mishpat* 79:9). If there are two witnesses to an undocumented loan, a person is not believed if he contradicts the witnesses and says that he never borrowed the money, but he *is* believed if he says that he repaid the loan. If an alleged borrower claims that he did not borrow money and two witnesses *then* come and testify that he did borrow money, he is obligated to pay no matter what, i.e., even if he changes his claim to one of repayment (the reason why he is not believed in this case will be explained in note 44).

Now, the rule is that whenever two witnesses create a monetary obligation, a single witness creates an obligation to take an oath [which is, in essence, an obligation for the defendant to pay unless he takes the required oath; see above, note 33]. Therefore, in a case where a person first denies having borrowed the money and a *single* witness then testifies that the loan occurred, the defendant is obligated to pay unless he takes an oath to contradict the testimony of the witness, i.e., he swears that the loan never occurred. When

וּבִגְמָרָא בָּבָא בַּתְרָא בְּפֶרֶק חֶזְקַת הַבָּתִּים (ל״ג ע״ב-ל״ד ע״א) מַעֲשֶׂה בְּאֶחָד שֶׁחָטַף לָשׁוֹן שֶׁל כֶּסֶף מֵחֲבֵרוֹ בִּפְנֵי עֵד אֶחָד, וְאָמַר כֵּן הוּא הָאֱמֶת שֶׁחֲטַפְתִּיהָ מִמֶּנּוּ אֲבָל שֶׁלִּי חָטַפְתִּי, וַאֲתָא לְקַמֵּיהּ דְּרַבִּי אַמִי וַאֲמַר הֵיכִי לִידַיְינוּהּ דַּיָּינֵי לְהַאי דִּינָא, לְשַׁלֵּם לֵיכָּא תְּרֵי סָהֲדֵי[39], לְפַטְרֵיהּ אִיכָּא חַד סָהֲדָא[40], לִישְׁתְּבַע דְּלָא חֲטַף הָא קָא מוֹדֶה וְאָמַר אִין חֲטַפִי[41], וַהֲוָה יְתִיב רַבִּי אַבָּא קַמֵּיהּ וַאֲמַר הָוֵה לֵיהּ מְחֻיָּב שְׁבוּעָה, כְּלוֹמַר מִפְּנֵי עֵדוּת הָעֵד, וְאֵינוֹ יָכוֹל לִשָּׁבַע

Chinuch presents the classic case in which the rule that "one who is obligated to take an oath but cannot swear must pay" is invoked:

וּבִגְמָרָא בָּבָא בַּתְרָא בְּפֶרֶק חֶזְקַת הַבָּתִּים – **In Tractate *Bava Basra*, Chapter *Chezkas Habatim*** (33b-34a), the Gemara relates the following: מַעֲשֶׂה בְּאֶחָד שֶׁחָטַף לָשׁוֹן שֶׁל כֶּסֶף מֵחֲבֵרוֹ בִּפְנֵי עֵד אֶחָד **– There was an incident where someone snatched a bar of silver from his fellow in front of a single witness,** who then testified about the incident. וְאָמַר כֵּן הוּא הָאֱמֶת שֶׁחֲטַפְתִּיהָ מִמֶּנּוּ אֲבָל שֶׁלִּי חָטַפְתִּי – In response to the claim against him, **[the defendant] said, "It is true that I snatched [the silver] from him, but it was *my* [silver] that I snatched!"** וַאֲתָא לְקַמֵּיהּ דְּרַבִּי אַמִי וַאֲמַר הֵיכִי לִידַיְינוּהּ דַּיָּינֵי לְהַאי דִּינָא – **The [incident] came before R' Ami** for a ruling, **who,** uncertain how to rule, **said, "How are judges supposed to judge this case?,"** and then proceeded to point out difficulties with several possible rulings. לְשַׁלֵּם לֵיכָּא תְּרֵי סָהֲדֵי – **"Should [the defendant] be made to pay?** That does not seem to be an option, for **there are not two witnesses** that he grabbed the silver, and in general two witnesses are required to exact money from a defendant."[39] לְפַטְרֵיהּ אִיכָּא חַד סָהֲדָא – **"Should [the defendant] be exempted** from paying based on his counter-claim that the silver is his? That, too, is problematic because **there is a single witness** who testifies that he grabbed it, which weakens the defendant's claim."[40] לִישְׁתְּבַע דְּלָא חֲטַף הָא קָא מוֹדֶה וְאָמַר אִין חֲטַפִי – **"Should** we have **[the defendant] take an oath that he did not snatch** the silver to refute the testimony of the single witness? That is not an option, for **[the defendant]** already **admitted** the truth of the witness' testimony **by saying, 'Indeed, I snatched** it,' and cannot possibly take an oath to contradict his previous claim."[41] Having pointed out flaws with each possible verdict, R' Ami was unsure of how to proceed. וַהֲוָה יְתִיב רַבִּי אַבָּא קַמֵּיהּ וַאֲמַר – **R' Abba was sitting in [R' Ami's] presence and said:** הָוֵה לֵיהּ מְחֻיָּב שְׁבוּעָה כְּלוֹמַר מִפְּנֵי עֵדוּת הָעֵד וְאֵינוֹ יָכוֹל לִשָּׁבַע – **"[The defendant[is obligated to**

NOTES

the defendant instead retracts his original claim and says that he paid up the loan, he concedes that the loan occurred, and can no longer take the mandated oath. He must therefore pay, in keeping with the general rule that a defendant who is unable to take the mandated oath must pay.

39. Had two witnesses testified that the defendant grabbed the silver, he would have been forced to return it, despite claiming that it belongs to him. This is because of the basic legal presumption that the person in possession of an object is its owner. Therefore, if two witnesses had seen the silver in the claimant's possession, we would have presumed that it belongs to him, unless the defendant could prove his claim that it actually belongs to him.

40. Had there been *no* witnesses that the defendant grabbed the silver, it would have remained in the possession of the one who grabbed it, because his claim that the silver belongs to him would have been accepted under the principle of *migo* (see above, note 33): Had he wished to lie, he could have simply denied grabbing it, in which case the court would have presumed that it belongs to him because it is currently in his possession.

Now, the principle of *migo* is based on the assumption that a liar would choose the strongest claim available to him. Therefore, the strength of the defendant's claim is diminished in a case where there is a single witness who says that he grabbed the silver. For had he denied grabbing it, he would have been required to take an oath to refute the testimony of the single witness who says that he *did* grab it; and it is thus possible that he chose to claim that the silver was his in order to avoid taking the oath. In sum, when a single witness testifies that he grabbed the silver, the claim that the silver is his own is a weak one (*Rashbam, Bava Basra* 34a ד״ה לפטריה).

41. If the defendant had denied taking the silver, he would have been required to take an oath to refute the witness's testimony, just like any defendant who contradicts the testimony of a single witness. In our case, though, the defendant admitted to having taken the silver, which disqualifies him from swearing that he did not grab it.

שֶׁהֲרֵי אֵינוֹ מַכְחִישׁ דִּבְרֵי הָעֵד, וְכָל הַמְחֻיָּב שְׁבוּעָה וְאֵינוֹ יָכוֹל לִשָּׁבַע מְשַׁלֵּם[42], וְכֵן הַדִּין בְּכָל כַּיּוֹצֵא בָּזֶה.

וּמִי[43] שֶׁתָּבַע חֲבֵרוֹ מָנֶה הִלְוִיתִיךָ, וְכָפַר בּוֹ וְאָמַר לוֹ לֹא הִלְוִיתַנִי כְּלוּם מֵעוֹלָם, וְהֵבִיא עֵד אֶחָד שֶׁלָּוָה מִמֶּנּוּ בְּפָנָיו, הוֹאִיל וְאִלּוּ הָיוּ שְׁנַיִם הָיָה מֻחְזָק כַּפְרָן וְדִינוֹ שֶׁיְּשַׁלֵּם[44], הֲרֵי זֶה נִשְׁבָּע עַל פִּי עֵד אֶחָד, שֶׁכָּל מָקוֹם שֶׁשְּׁנַיִם מְחַיְּבִין אוֹתוֹ מָמוֹן, אֶחָד מְחַיְּבוֹ שְׁבוּעָה[45]. חָזַר וְאָמַר פָּרַעְתִּי, מְשַׁלֵּם בְּלֹא שְׁבוּעָה, לְפִי שֶׁהוּא מְחֻיָּב שְׁבוּעָה מִפְּנֵי עֵדוּת הָעֵד, וְאֵינוֹ יָכוֹל לִשָּׁבַע שֶׁהֲרֵי אֵינוֹ מַכְחִישׁוֹ בְּעֵדוּת הַהַלְוָאָה אֶלָּא שֶׁאוֹמֵר פָּרַעְתִּי,

---

take an oath" — meaning, on account of the testimony of the single **witness — "but is unable to swear,"** שֶׁהֲרֵי אֵינוֹ מַכְחִישׁ דִּבְרֵי הָעֵד **— since he is not denying the words of the witness,** וְכָל הַמְחֻיָּב שְׁבוּעָה וְאֵינוֹ יָכוֹל לִשָּׁבַע מְשַׁלֵּם **— "and** the law is that **anyone who is obligated to take an oath but is unable to swear must pay."**[42]

וְכֵן הַדִּין בְּכָל כַּיּוֹצֵא בָּזֶה **— This is the law for any similar case.**

Chinuch returns to a case he mentioned above, and explains it in greater detail:[43]

וּמִי שֶׁתָּבַע חֲבֵרוֹ מָנֶה הִלְוִיתִיךָ **— If one claims to his fellow, "I lent you a *maneh*,"** וְכָפַר בּוֹ וְאָמַר לוֹ לֹא הִלְוִיתַנִי כְּלוּם מֵעוֹלָם **— and [the defendant] denies [the claim], and says to [the claimant], "I never borrowed anything from you,"** וְהֵבִיא עֵד אֶחָד שֶׁלָּוָה מִמֶּנּוּ בְּפָנָיו **— and [the claimant]** then **brings a single witness that [the defendant] borrowed** a *maneh* **in his presence,** הוֹאִיל וְאִלּוּ הָיוּ שְׁנַיִם הָיָה מֻחְזָק כַּפְרָן וְדִינוֹ שֶׁיְּשַׁלֵּם — the law is that **since if two witnesses had been** brought following the defendant's denial of the loan, **[the defendant] would be presumed a liar** with regard to that money **and would be required to pay,**[44] הֲרֵי זֶה נִשְׁבָּע עַל פִּי עֵד אֶחָד — in our case, where only a single witness attests to the loan, **[the defendant] is obligated to take an oath based on the testimony of the single witness,** שֶׁכָּל מָקוֹם שֶׁשְּׁנַיִם מְחַיְּבִין אוֹתוֹ מָמוֹן **— for** the rule is that **in any situation where two [witnesses] would obligate [a defendant] to pay,** אֶחָד מְחַיְּבוֹ שְׁבוּעָה **— a single [witness] requires him to take an oath** to refute the testimony.[45] חָזַר וְאָמַר פָּרַעְתִּי — Therefore, **if** following the testimony of the single witness, **[the defendant] changed his claim and said,** "Indeed, I borrowed a *maneh,* but **I repaid** it," מְשַׁלֵּם בְּלֹא שְׁבוּעָה **— he must pay, without** being given the opportunity to take **an oath,** לְפִי שֶׁהוּא מְחֻיָּב שְׁבוּעָה מִפְּנֵי עֵדוּת הָעֵד **— because he is obligated to take an oath on account of the testimony of the witness,** וְאֵינוֹ יָכוֹל לִשָּׁבַע שֶׁהֲרֵי אֵינוֹ מַכְחִישׁוֹ בְּעֵדוּת הַהַלְוָאָה **— but is unable to swear, since he is not contradicting the [witness] with regard to the testimony about the loan,** אֶלָּא שֶׁאוֹמֵר פָּרַעְתִּי **— only claiming,**

NOTES

42. As explained above (note 33), this rule teaches that the testimony of a single witness requires a defendant to pay unless he takes an oath to refute the testimony. Therefore, if he is unable to take that oath — for whatever reason — he must pay.

43. See *Maggid Mishneh, Hil. To'ein VeNitan* 4:9. Cf. *Gidulei Terumah* to *Sefer HaTerumos* 12:2 [pp. 290-291 in Machon Yerushalayim ed.].

44. When two witnesses come and testify that the loan occurred, the defendant certainly does not prevail with his original claim that he did not borrow the money, since that claim is contradicted by two witnesses. One might have thought, though, that the defendant can still prevail by changing his original claim and saying that he repaid the loan, since a defendant is typically believed when claiming to have repaid an oral loan, even if the loan was made in front of witnesses. However, this is not so, for once a defendant's claim is found to be false based on the testimony of two witnesses, he is presumed to be a liar with regard to that money [הֻחְזַק כַּפְרָן לְאוֹתוֹ מָמוֹן], and no longer has any credibility with respect to *any* claim regarding that money, even a claim that would otherwise have been believed (see *Bava Metzia* 17a and *Rambam, Hil. To'ein VeNitan* 6:1). Therefore, once two witnesses come and testify that the loan occurred, in contradiction of the defendant's original claim, the defendant is required to pay, since he is no longer believed with any claim about this loan.

45. That is, in any case where two witnesses require a defendant to pay, a single witness requires a defendant to either take an oath to refute the testimony or to pay. Since in a case like ours, the testimony of two witnesses would create an obligation to pay, a single witness's testimony creates an obligation to either take an oath that the loan did not occur or to pay. See next note.

וּכְבָר אָמַרְנוּ שֶׁכָּל מְחֻיָּב שְׁבוּעָה שֶׁאֵינוֹ יָכוֹל לִשָּׁבַע מְשַׁלֵּם[46]. וְיֶתֶר פְּרָטֵי הַמִּצְוָה רַבִּים מְבֹאָרִין בִּמְקוֹמוֹת מְפֻזָּרִין בִּיבָמוֹת וּכְתֻבּוֹת וְסוֹטָה וְגִטִּין וְקִדּוּשִׁין וּבְכָל סֵדֶר נְזִיקִין[47].

וְנוֹהֶגֶת מִצְוָה זוֹ לְעִנְיַן דִּינֵי מָמוֹנוֹת[48] שֶׁנּוֹהֲגִין הַיּוֹם בְּכָל מָקוֹם וְכָל זְמַן[49], בִּזְכָרִים כִּי לָהֶם לַעֲשׂוֹת מִשְׁפָּט. וְעוֹבֵר עַל זֶה וְהֵקִים גְּבוּלֵי הָעֹנֶשׁ זוּלָתִי בִּצְדָדִין שֶׁפֵּרַשְׁנוּ הֵן בְּגוּף הֵן בְּמָמוֹן בְּעֵד אֶחָד, עָבַר עַל לָאו זֶה.

"I repaid it," **וּכְבָר אָמַרְנוּ שֶׁכָּל מְחֻיָּב שְׁבוּעָה שֶׁאֵינוֹ יָכוֹל לִשָּׁבַע מְשַׁלֵּם – and we have already stated that anyone who is obligated to take an oath and is unable to swear must pay.**[46] **וְיֶתֶר פְּרָטֵי הַמִּצְוָה רַבִּים** – These **and the many remaining details of the mitzvah מְבֹאָרִין בִּמְקוֹמוֹת מְפֻזָּרִין בִּיבָמוֹת וּכְתֻבּוֹת וְסוֹטָה וְגִטִּין וְקִדּוּשִׁין וּבְכָל סֵדֶר נְזִיקִין – are set forth in scattered places in** Tractates ***Yevamos, Kesubos, Sotah, Gittin, Kiddushin,* and throughout the Order of *Nezikin.***[47]

Applicability of the Mitzvah

וְנוֹהֶגֶת מִצְוָה זוֹ לְעִנְיַן דִּינֵי מָמוֹנוֹת שֶׁנּוֹהֲגִין הַיּוֹם בְּכָל מָקוֹם וְכָל זְמַן – This mitzvah, with regard to those monetary cases that can be adjudicated nowadays,[48] **applies in every location and in all times,**[49] **בִּזְכָרִים כִּי לָהֶם לַעֲשׂוֹת מִשְׁפָּט** – but only **to men, for it is their duty to carry out justice. וְעוֹבֵר עַל זֶה וְהֵקִים גְּבוּלֵי הָעֹנֶשׁ זוּלָתִי בִּצְדָדִין שֶׁפֵּרַשְׁנוּ הֵן בְּגוּף הֵן בְּמָמוֹן בְּעֵד אֶחָד – One who transgresses this [prohibition] and administers** any **punishment, whether corporal or monetary, based on** the testimony **of a single witness, other than in those cases that we have mentioned, עָבַר עַל לָאו זֶה – transgresses this mitzvah-prohibition.**

NOTES

46. Had the defendant stuck with his original claim that the loan never occurred, he could have exempted himself from paying by taking an oath to refute the testimony of the single witness. However, since he now claims to have repaid the loan, he admits that he indeed borrowed the money, and can no longer take an oath to refute the witness's testimony. Since he cannot take that oath, he must pay, just like any defendant who is required to take an oath to refute a single witness but is unable to do so.

[When a single witness contradicts a defendant's claim, the defendant is not "presumed a liar" with regard to that money. Therefore, in our case, one might have thought that even after the single witness testifies, the defendant can prevail by changing course and claiming to have repaid the loan. However, since the testimony of two witnesses would force the defendant to pay, and the rule is that "in any situation where two witnesses require a defendant to pay, a single witness requires him to take an oath," the defendant *cannot* prevail with a claim of repayment.]

Rashba (*Teshuvos,* Vol. II §206) disagrees with this ruling, which is based on *Rambam* (*Hil. To'ein VeNitan* 4:9). In his view, the rule that "in any situation where two witnesses require a defendant to pay, a single witness requires him to take an oath" is limited to cases where it is the testimony of the two witnesses itself, without the contribution of any outside factors, which obligates the defendant to pay. In our case, however, it is not the testimony of the two witnesses per se that obligates the defendant to pay, but rather, the fact that their testimony causes the defendant to be presumed a liar, which, in turn, destroys the credibility of any further claims. In a case like this, *Rashba* argues, the defendant can still prevail by claiming to have repaid the loan.

47. This mitzvah-prohibition is codified in *Rambam, Hil. Eidus* 5:1. The cases in which the testimony of a single witness is accepted are discussed in various places throughout *Mishneh Torah* and *Shulchan Aruch.*

48. There are two categories of monetary payments: *compensations* and *fines.* Payments that correspond exactly to the amount of damage or to a person's indebtedness are considered *compensation.* Payments that are either a fixed sum regardless of the amount of the damage (e.g., the 100 *zuz* paid by the מוֹצִיא שֵׁם רַע, *man who defames* his wife; Mitzvah 553) or that exceed the amount of the damage (e.g., כֶּפֶל, *the double payment* of a thief; see Mitzvah 54) are considered *fines.* Under Biblical law, *all* monetary cases must be adjudicated by judges who have received *semichah* (a special type of ordination that can be traced back to Moses; see Mitzvah 491). However, non-ordained judges are empowered as the agents of ordained judges to preside over monetary cases that (a) involve compensation, and (b) occur with regularity. Therefore, nowadays, when we do not have judges who have received *semichah,* the jurisdiction of *beis din* even in monetary cases is limited to compensatory payments that occur with regularity, such as cases involving loans (see *Bava Kamma* 84b).

49. That is, they apply both in Eretz Yisrael and the Diaspora, and whether or not the *Beis HaMikdash* is standing.

◈⧉ Insight: Can a Single Witness Exempt a Defendant From Swearing?

One of the areas in which the testimony of a single witness is effective is in requiring a defendant to take an oath. If Reuven claims that Shimon owes him $100 and Shimon denies this, but a single witness supports Reuven's claim, Shimon is obligated to take a Biblical oath to support his denial. If Shimon refuses to take the oath, he must pay the entire claim (see above, at note 7).

Rishonim disagree whether a single witness can only obligate a defendant to take an oath, or whether he can also exempt a defendant from doing so. For example, if Reuven claims that Shimon owes him $100 and Shimon admits to owing $50, the law is that Shimon is obligated to take a Biblical oath that he does not owe the remaining $50. [A defendant who partially admits to a plaintiff's claim is obligated to take a Biblical oath known as a שְׁבוּעַת מוֹדֶה בְּמִקְצָת, *oath of partial admission*; see Mitzvah 58, after note 20.] What if a single witness then testifies that Shimon does *not* owe Reuven the remaining $50? According to some Rishonim, a single witness only has the power to *create* an obligation to swear, but not to remove such an obligation. They therefore rule that Shimon would be obligated to take an oath, even though a single witness supports him. Others maintain that just as a single witness can create an obligation to swear, so too, he can remove such an obligation. According to them, Shimon would be exempt from paying the remaining $50, even without swearing (see *Beis Yosef, Choshen Mishpat* 75:3 and 84:7, for a list of authorities on both sides of this issue). Both opinions are cited in *Shulchan Aruch, Choshen Mishpat* 87:6, and *Rama* there rules that a single witness can indeed exempt a defendant from taking an oath.

The preceding applies where the obligation to take the oath was based on a factor such as a partial admission. The law may be different where the obligation to take the oath stemmed from the testimony of a single witness. *Ran* (*Bava Metzia* 2b ד"ה ולחזי זוזי) writes that in this case, a single witness who supports the defendant *can* exempt him from swearing, even according to those who maintain that a single witness generally cannot exempt from an oath. This is because the rule is that wherever a single witness is believed, his testimony is discarded if a second witness contradicts him. This is true even if the second witness does not have any special credibility regarding the matter he is testifying about. [For example, a single witness is believed to testify that a woman's husband died, allowing her to remarry, but a single witness does not have any special credibility to testify that a woman's husband is still alive. Nevertheless, if a single witness testifies that a woman's husband died and another testifies that he is still alive, we do not allow the woman to remarry, because the witness who testified that the husband died is contradicted by another witness.] Therefore, even if the Torah did not give a single witness special credibility with regard to removing an obligation to swear, he can still contradict a single witness who testifies that someone owes his fellow money, and we cannot require the defendant to swear.

Usually, the preceding rule applies only if the contradicting witness testified before *beis din* issued a ruling on the basis of the first witness' testimony. If, however, *beis din* had already issued a ruling, the rule is that the first witness is treated with the force of two witnesses, and a single witness can no longer contradict him. For example, if a single witness testified that a woman's husband died and *beis din* ruled that she is permitted to remarry, and a second witness then comes and testifies that the woman's husband is still alive, he is not believed to contradict the first witness, and the woman remains permitted to remarry. However, *Ran* contends that this rule is limited to cases like that, where *beis din* completes its role in the case by issuing a ruling. [Once *beis din* rules that a woman is permitted to remarry, there is nothing left for the judges to do.] In the case of swearing, though, *beis din's* role is not completed once they rule that the defendant must swear; they still have to administer the oath, or force the defendant to pay if he refuses to swear. Therefore, *Ran* argues, a second witness can contradict the first witness and exempt the defendant from swearing even if *beis din* already ruled that the defendant is obligated to swear on the basis of the first witness's testimony. Thus, even if one maintains that, in general, a single witness does not have the power to exempt a defendant from swearing, a single witness *can* exempt a defendant from taking an oath that was based on a single witness's testimony.

Shach (*Choshen Mishpat* 87:15), however, disagrees with *Ran*, and maintains that there is no difference between a case where *beis din* ruled that a woman can remarry and a case where *beis din* ruled that a defendant is obligated to swear. In his view, even in the case of swearing, as soon as *beis din*

issues a ruling, the first witness is treated with the force of two witnesses, and a second witness can no longer simply contradict him. Therefore, the only way that a single witness can now exempt the defendant from swearing is if a single witness has the power to remove an obligation to swear, just as he has the power to create such an obligation. Therefore, *Shach* maintains, whether or not a single witness can exempt a defendant from a single-witness oath, after *beis din* has already obligated the defendant to swear, *does* depend on the general question of whether or not a single witness has the power to remove an obligation to swear.

מִצְוָה תקכד

מִצְוָה לַעֲשׂוֹת לְעֵדִים זוֹמְמִים כְּמוֹ שֶׁדִּמּוּ לַעֲשׂוֹת

שֶׁנִּצְטַוִּינוּ לַעֲשׂוֹת לָעֵדִים אֲשֶׁר הֵעִידוּ עֵדוּת שֶׁקֶר כְּפִי מַה שֶּׁבִּקְשׁוּ לְהַזִּיק בְּעֵדוּתָם לַאֲשֶׁר הֵעִידוּ עָלָיו הֵן בְּמָמוֹן הֵן בְּמַלְקוּת הֵן בְּמִיתָה[1], וְעַל זֶה נֶאֱמַר (דברים י״ט, י״ט) ״וַעֲשִׂיתֶם לוֹ כַּאֲשֶׁר זָמַם לַעֲשׂוֹת לְאָחִיו,[2]״ וְזֶהוּ דִּין עֵדִים[3] זוֹמְמִים הַנִּזְכָּר בַּגְּמָרָא בְּהַרְבֵּה מְקוֹמוֹת. וְעִנְיַן הַהֲזָמָה הוּא שֶׁיָּבוֹאוּ שְׁנֵי עֵדִים וְיַכְחִישׁוּ הָרִאשׁוֹנִים עַל עֵדוּתָן כְּגוֹן שֶׁיֹּאמְרוּ לָהֶם,

---

Mitzvah 524

The Obligation to Do to Zomemin Witnesses Exactly What They Sought to Do [to the Defendant]

וַעֲשִׂיתֶם לוֹ כַּאֲשֶׁר זָמַם לַעֲשׂוֹת לְאָחִיו וּבִעַרְתָּ הָרָע מִקִּרְבֶּךָ

You shall do to him as he conspired to do to his brother, and you shall destroy the evil from your midst (*Deuteronomy* 19:19).

שֶׁנִּצְטַוִּינוּ לַעֲשׂוֹת לָעֵדִים אֲשֶׁר הֵעִידוּ עֵדוּת שֶׁקֶר – We (i.e., the Jewish courts) **are commanded to inflict upon witnesses who testified falsely כְּפִי מַה שֶּׁבִּקְשׁוּ לְהַזִּיק בְּעֵדוּתָם לַאֲשֶׁר הֵעִידוּ עָלָיו – the exact harm they sought to inflict with their testimony upon the one whom they testified against, הֵן בְּמָמוֹן הֵן בְּמַלְקוּת הֵן בְּמִיתָה – whether it is a monetary payment, *malkus*, or death.**[1] **וְעַל זֶה נֶאֱמַר – Regarding this it is stated** (*Deuteronomy* 19:19): **״וַעֲשִׂיתֶם לוֹ כַּאֲשֶׁר זָמַם לַעֲשׂוֹת לְאָחִיו״ – *You shall do to him*** (the false witness) ***as he conspired to do to his brother.***[2] **וְזֶהוּ דִּין עֵדִים זוֹמְמִים הַנִּזְכָּר בַּגְּמָרָא בְּהַרְבֵּה מְקוֹמוֹת – This is the law of *zomemin*** (conspiring) **witnesses,**[3] **which is mentioned in many places throughout the Gemara.**

Chinuch explains that in order for the law of *zomemin* witnesses to apply, the witnesses must be contradicted by other witnesses in a very specific manner:

וְעִנְיַן הַהֲזָמָה הוּא – The description of *hazamah* (the process by which witnesses are rendered *zomemin*) **is שֶׁיָּבוֹאוּ שְׁנֵי עֵדִים וְיַכְחִישׁוּ הָרִאשׁוֹנִים עַל עֵדוּתָן – that** at least **two** other **witnesses come** to *beis din* **and contradict the testimony of the first** set of **[witnesses], כְּגוֹן שֶׁיֹּאמְרוּ לָהֶם – such**

NOTES

1. If the false witnesses testified that someone is liable to pay a certain amount of money, they are required to pay him that amount; if they testified that someone is liable to *malkus* (e.g., they testified that he transgressed a mitzvah-prohibition that carries this penalty), they themselves receive *malkus*; and if they testified that someone is liable to the death penalty (e.g., they testified that he committed murder; see Mitzvah 34), they themselves are executed in the manner in which they sought to have the defendant executed. [In cases involving monetary payment, the false witnesses divide the payment. By contrast, in cases involving *malkus,* each witness receives a full set of *malkus,* and in cases involving capital punishment, each witness is executed (Mishnah, *Makkos* 5a; *Rambam, Hil Eidus* 18:1).]

2. The previous verse states: *The judges shall inquire thoroughly, and behold! the testimony was false testimony; he testified falsely against his fellow.* Thus, this verse commands us to do unto a false witness that which he sought to have done to the defendant. [The Torah does not state explicitly how we must establish the falsehood of the witnesses for them to be subject to reciprocal punishment. Chinuch will soon address this issue.]

3. The term עֵדִים זוֹמְמִין, *zomemin* (conspiring) *witnesses*, is derived from the language of Scripture, which states: וַעֲשִׂיתֶם לוֹ כַּאֲשֶׁר זָמַם לַעֲשׂוֹת לְאָחִיו, *You shall do to him* (the false witness) *as he conspired* (זָמַם, *zamam*) *to do to his brother.*

אֵיךְ אַתֶּם מְעִידִים עַל דָּבָר פְּלוֹנִי וַהֲלֹא בְּאוֹתוֹ יוֹם שֶׁאַתֶּם אוֹמְרִים שֶׁהָיָה הַמַּעֲשֶׂה הַהוּא לֹא הֱיִיתֶם אַתֶּם בְּאוֹתוֹ הַמָּקוֹם שֶׁאַתֶּם אוֹמְרִים שֶׁנַּעֲשָׂה שָׁם, אֲבָל עִמָּנוּ הֱיִיתֶם בְּמָקוֹם אַחֵר, זוֹ הִיא עִקַּר הֲזָמַת הָעֵדוּת[4], וְהַתּוֹרָה צִוְּתָנוּ לְהַאֲמִין הָעֵדִים הָאַחֲרוֹנִים עַל הָרִאשׁוֹנִים[5] בֵּין שֶׁהָרִאשׁוֹנִים שְׁנַיִם אוֹ אֲפִלּוּ מֵאָה אוֹ יוֹתֵר, דִּלְעִנְיַן עֵדוּת תְּרֵי כְּמֵאָה וּמֵאָה כִּתְרֵי[6].

מִשָּׁרְשֵׁי הַמִּצְוָה לְיַסֵּר כָּל אִישׁ אֲשֶׁר מְלָאוֹ לִבּוֹ לְהָעִיד בְּדָבָר אֲשֶׁר אֵינוֹ יוֹדֵעַ אוֹתוֹ בֶּאֱמֶת וּבְבֵרוּר, בַּעֲבוּר הֱיוֹת הַדָּבָר עִנְיָן שֶׁכָּל אֲשֶׁר לַבְּרִיּוֹת תָּלוּי עָלָיו הֵן מָמוֹן הֵן גּוּף[7]. וּבַאֲשֶׁר תַּאֲמִין הַתּוֹרָה הָאַחֲרוֹנִים עַל הָרִאשׁוֹנִים לֹא יָדַעְנוּ טַעַם בָּרוּר בָּזֶה[8],

---

that [the second set] says to [the first set]: אֵיךְ אַתֶּם מְעִידִים עַל דָּבָר פְּלוֹנִי – **"How could you have testified about such-and-such an incident?** וַהֲלֹא בְּאוֹתוֹ יוֹם שֶׁאַתֶּם אוֹמְרִים שֶׁהָיָה הַמַּעֲשֶׂה הַהוּא – **Why, on the very day on which you say the incident occurred,** לֹא הֱיִיתֶם אַתֶּם בְּאוֹתוֹ הַמָּקוֹם שֶׁאַתֶּם אוֹמְרִים שֶׁנַּעֲשָׂה שָׁם – **you were not at the location where you say [the incident] occurred,** אֲבָל עִמָּנוּ הֱיִיתֶם בְּמָקוֹם אַחֵר – **but were with us in another location!"** זוֹ הִיא עִקַּר הֲזָמַת הָעֵדוּת – **This is the essence of the *hazamah* of testimony,**[4] וְהַתּוֹרָה צִוְּתָנוּ לְהַאֲמִין הָעֵדִים הָאַחֲרוֹנִים עַל הָרִאשׁוֹנִים – and in cases like this, **the Torah commands us to believe the second** set of **witnesses over the first** set of **[witnesses],**[5] בֵּין שֶׁהָרִאשׁוֹנִים שְׁנַיִם אוֹ אֲפִלּוּ מֵאָה אוֹ יוֹתֵר – regardless of **whether the first [witnesses] were** only **two or even if they were a hundred or more** than a hundred, דִּלְעִנְיַן עֵדוּת תְּרֵי כְּמֵאָה וּמֵאָה כִּתְרֵי – **for when it comes to testimony,** the rule is that **two** witnesses **are** given as much weight **as a hundred** witnesses, **and a hundred** witnesses **are** given only as much weight **as two** witnesses.[6]

Underlying Purpose of the Mitzvah

מִשָּׁרְשֵׁי הַמִּצְוָה – **Among the underlying purposes of the mitzvah** is לְיַסֵּר כָּל אִישׁ אֲשֶׁר מְלָאוֹ לִבּוֹ לְהָעִיד בְּדָבָר אֲשֶׁר אֵינוֹ יוֹדֵעַ אוֹתוֹ בֶּאֱמֶת וּבְבֵרוּר – **to punish any man whose heart is brazen enough to testify about something that he does not know with accurate and clear** knowledge. בַּעֲבוּר הֱיוֹת הַדָּבָר עִנְיָן שֶׁכָּל אֲשֶׁר לַבְּרִיּוֹת תָּלוּי עָלָיו – Such punishment is very important, **since [testimony] is something that can affect everything that belongs to people,** הֵן מָמוֹן הֵן גּוּף – **both** their **money and** their **body.**[7]

Chinuch addresses why, in cases of *hazamah,* the second set is believed over the first set:

וּבַאֲשֶׁר תַּאֲמִין הַתּוֹרָה הָאַחֲרוֹנִים עַל הָרִאשׁוֹנִים – **Now, regarding that which the Torah believes the last** set of **[witnesses] over the first** set of **[witnesses],** לֹא יָדַעְנוּ טַעַם בָּרוּר בָּזֶה – **we do**

NOTES

4. That is, only this specific type of contradictory testimony qualifies as *hazamah,* which renders the first set of witnesses *zomemin,* and subjects them to reciprocal punishment. See next note.

5. In most instances where one set of witnesses contradicts another set, *beis din* must discard the testimony of *all* the witnesses, because neither set is believed more than the other; see below, at note 11. With regard to *hazamah,* however, the Torah commands us to accept the testimony of the second set of witnesses over that of the first set. The reason for this will be discussed below.

6. [See Mishnah, *Makkos* 5b, for the source of this rule.] This rule teaches that with regard to testimony, controversy is not settled by the majority. The maximum level of credibility that witnesses can attain is already assigned to a set of two witnesses. Therefore, a set of two witnesses and a set of a hundred witnesses are deemed equally credible. As Chinuch explains, in cases involving *hazamah,* where the Torah commands us to accept the testimony of the second set over that of the first set, the ramification of this rule is that even if the witnesses in the first set far outnumber those in the second set, the testimony of the second set is nevertheless accepted. [In a case of regular contradictory testimony, where neither set is believed over the other, this rule dictates that the testimony of both sets is discarded even though one set is comprised of far more witnesses than the other set.]

7. By instituting severe consequences for false testimony, the Torah deters people from using the court system as an instrument to wrongly harm people.

אָכֵן הִגִּיד לִי אֶחָד מִן הַחֲכָמִים קְצַת טַעֲנָה בַּדָּבָר, כִּי הַתּוֹרָה תַּאֲמִין עֵדִים, וְאֵין סָפֵק שֶׁאִלּוּ יָעִידוּ שְׁנֵי עֵדִים כְּשֵׁרִים עַל שְׁלֹשָׁה אֲנָשִׁים אוֹ יוֹתֵר שֶׁהָרְגוּ אֶת הַנֶּפֶשׁ שֶׁנֶּאֱמָנִים הַשְּׁנַיִם הַמְּעִידִים וַאֲפִלּוּ יַכְחִישׁוּם הַמְרֻבִּים, מִפְּנֵי שֶׁאֵלּוּ הֵם עֵדִים וְהָאֲחֵרִים בַּעֲלֵי דָבָר[9], וּבְעֵדִים זוֹמְמִין כְּמוֹ כֵן, אַחַר שֶׁהָאַחֲרוֹנִים מְעִידִים עַל הָעֵדִים עַצְמָן לוֹמַר לָהֶם עִמָּנוּ הֱיִיתֶם שֶׁזֶּהוּ עִקַּר הֲזָמָה, חָזְרוּ הָרִאשׁוֹנִים בַּעֲלֵי דָבָר וְהָאַחֲרוֹנִים עֵדִים[10].

---

not know a clear reason for this.[8] אָכֵן הִגִּיד לִי אֶחָד מִן הַחֲכָמִים קְצַת טַעֲנָה בַּדָּבָר – **However, one of the sages related to me somewhat of a rationale regarding this matter,** as follows: כִּי הַתּוֹרָה תַּאֲמִין עֵדִים – It is axiomatic **that the Torah gives credibility to** two **witnesses,** and *beis din* is therefore commanded to act upon their testimony. וְאֵין סָפֵק שֶׁאִלּוּ יָעִידוּ שְׁנֵי עֵדִים כְּשֵׁרִים עַל שְׁלֹשָׁה אֲנָשִׁים אוֹ יוֹתֵר שֶׁהָרְגוּ אֶת הַנֶּפֶשׁ – **Now, there is no doubt that if two valid witnesses would testify that three or more people murdered a person,** שֶׁנֶּאֱמָנִים הַשְּׁנַיִם הַמְּעִידִים וַאֲפִלּוּ יַכְחִישׁוּם הַמְרֻבִּים – **then the two [witnesses] would be believed** and the murderers would be put to death, **even though [the witnesses] are outnumbered by those who contradict them** (i.e., the defendants who maintain their innocence). מִפְּנֵי שֶׁאֵלּוּ הֵם עֵדִים וְהָאֲחֵרִים בַּעֲלֵי דָבָר – **The reason** for this **is that [the two people]** who testified about the murder **are "witnesses,"** who are given credibility in all legal proceedings, **while the others** (the defendants), are not considered "witnesses," but rather, **"parties to the matter,"** who are never given credibility regarding that very matter.[9] וּבְעֵדִים זוֹמְמִין כְּמוֹ כֵן – **Now, in the case of *zomemin* witnesses, too,** אַחַר שֶׁהָאַחֲרוֹנִים מְעִידִים עַל הָעֵדִים עַצְמָן – **since the last [witnesses] are testifying** not about the alleged incident but **about the witnesses themselves** (i.e., their location at the time of the incident), לוֹמַר לָהֶם עִמָּנוּ הֱיִיתֶם שֶׁזֶּהוּ עִקַּר הֲזָמָה – **by saying to them, "You were with us** at a different location at the time of the alleged incident," **which is the definition of *hazamah*** as explained above, חָזְרוּ הָרִאשׁוֹנִים בַּעֲלֵי דָבָר וְהָאַחֲרוֹנִים עֵדִים – therefore, with regard to the testimony of the second set of witnesses, **the first [witnesses] are now considered "parties to the matter,"** i.e., the principals, **while the last [set of witnesses] are witnesses** to the matter. The last set of witnesses are therefore believed over the first set, just like witnesses to any alleged incident are always believed over the principals.[10]

NOTES

8. In cases involving ordinary contradictory testimony, we do not believe one set of witnesses over the other. In the words of the Gemara (see, for example, *Yevamos* 93b), this is a matter of simple logic: מַאי חָזֵית דִּסְמַכְתְּ אַהָנֵי סְמוֹךְ אַהָנֵי, *Why do you see fit to rely on these [witnesses]? Rely on these [instead]!* Since this logic should seemingly apply to cases of *hazamah* as well, it is difficult to explain why the Torah commands us to believe the second set of witnesses over the first set.

9. See *Makkos* 6a.

10. In a case of *hazamah,* the witnesses in the second set do not claim any knowledge about whether or not the alleged incident occurred, only that the first set of witnesses could not have been there to see it, because they were in a different location at the time that it was supposed to have occurred. Since their testimony pertains to the location of the first set of witnesses, and not details of the event itself, the first witnesses are considered "parties to the matter" (i.e., the matter of where they were located at the time in question), and are not believed about it. Only the second set is believed about this matter.

[This explanation of why the second set of witnesses is believed over the first set is also suggested by *Rabbeinu Nissim Gaon* (*Sefer HaMafte'ach* to *Kesubos,* printed in *Teshuvos HaGeonim* [Jerusalem 1942] pp. 195-196); *Ramban* and *Rabbeinu Bachya* to the verse; *Rambam, Commentary* to *Makkos* 1:4; and *Tur, Choshen Mishpat* §38). It is thus unclear why Chinuch attributes it to "one of the sages," which seems to refer to a contemporary of his.]

As Chinuch writes, this rationale provides only "somewhat of an explanation" for the credibility of the second set of witnesses over the first set. This is because the location of the first set of witnesses at the time of the alleged incident does not really have a legal ramification outside of the alleged incident, and it is therefore, extremely novel to classify the first set of witnesses as "parties to the matter." At its core, then, the Torah's command to believe the second set of witnesses remains an anomaly that eludes logical explanation (see *Sanhedrin* 27a), and the rationale presented by Chinuch merely lessens the anomaly, by explaining how *hazamah* differs from ordinary contradictory testimony (see *Chidushei Chasam Sofer, Bava Basra* 31b ד״ה ועיין רמב״ן; *Teshuvos Divrei Chaim* Vol. I, *Choshen Mishpat* §11; *Chidushei R' Shmuel,*

מִדִּינֵי הַמִּצְוָה מַה שֶּׁאָמְרוּ זִכְרוֹנָם לִבְרָכָה שֶׁעִנְיַן הַהֲזָמָה הִיא בָּעֵדִים בְּעַצְמָן כְּמוֹ שֶׁאָמַרְנוּ, כְּגוֹן שֶׁיֹּאמְרוּ לָהֶם עִמָּנוּ הֱיִיתֶם בְּמָקוֹם פְּלוֹנִי. אֲבָל בְּעִנְיַן הַכְחָשָׁה אֵין מַאֲמִינִין אֵלּוּ עַל אֵלּוּ וּתְהֵא עֵדוּת כֻּלָּם בְּטֵלָה[11], וּמַהוּ עִנְיַן הַהַכְחָשָׁה, כְּגוֹן שֶׁמְּעִידִין בָּעֵדוּת בְּעַצְמוֹ, שֶׁהַכַּת הָרִאשׁוֹנָה אוֹמֶרֶת הָיָה דָּבָר פְּלוֹנִי וְהָאַחֲרוֹנָה אוֹמֶרֶת לֹא הָיָה[12], אוֹ שֶׁיָּבֹא מִכְּלַל דִּבְרֵיהֶם שֶׁלֹּא הָיָה[13]. וּמַה שֶּׁאָמְרוּ זִכְרוֹנָם לִבְרָכָה שֶׁאֵין עֵדִים זוֹמְמִין נֶהֱרָגִין וְלֹא מְשַׁלְּמִין מָמוֹן וְלֹא לוֹקִין עַד שֶׁיּוּזְמוּ שְׁנֵיהֶם[14],

Laws of the Mitzvah

מִדִּינֵי הַמִּצְוָה – **Among the laws of the mitzvah is** מַה שֶּׁאָמְרוּ זִכְרוֹנָם לִבְרָכָה – **that which [the Sages], of blessed memory stated** (see *Rambam, Hil. Eidus* 18:2), שֶׁעִנְיַן הַהֲזָמָה הִיא בָּעֵדִים בְּעַצְמָן כְּמוֹ שֶׁאָמַרְנוּ – **that the definition of *hazamah* is that it is** contradictory testimony **directed at the witnesses themselves,** not at the content of their testimony, **as we** already **mentioned,** כְּגוֹן שֶׁיֹּאמְרוּ לָהֶם עִמָּנוּ הֱיִיתֶם בְּמָקוֹם פְּלוֹנִי – **such that [the second set of witnesses] says to [the first set of witnesses], "You were with us at such-and-such location** at the time that the alleged incident was supposed to have occurred." אֲבָל בְּעִנְיַן הַכְחָשָׁה אֵין מַאֲמִינִין אֵלּוּ עַל אֵלּוּ – **However, when it comes to** ordinary **contradictory testimony, we do not believe these** (the second set of witnesses) **more than those** (the first set of witnesses), וּתְהֵא עֵדוּת כֻּלָּם בְּטֵלָה – **and** in such a case, **all of their testimony** (that of the first *and* that of the second set) **is invalidated,** since each set is given equal credibility.[11] וּמַהוּ עִנְיַן הַהַכְחָשָׁה – **And what is the essence of** ordinary **contradictory testimony?** כְּגוֹן שֶׁמְּעִידִין בָּעֵדוּת בְּעַצְמוֹ – It is testimony **such that [the second set of witnesses] testifies regarding** the actual content of **the testimony** of the first set; שֶׁהַכַּת הָרִאשׁוֹנָה אוֹמֶרֶת הָיָה דָּבָר פְּלוֹנִי – for example, **if the first set** of witnesses **says that a certain incident occurred,** וְהָאַחֲרוֹנָה אוֹמֶרֶת לֹא הָיָה – **and the second** set **says that the incident did not occur,**[12] אוֹ שֶׁיָּבֹא מִכְּלַל דִּבְרֵיהֶם שֶׁלֹּא הָיָה – **or if it emerges from their words that [the incident] did not occur.**[13]

Chinuch mentions an important limit to when *zomemin* witnesses can receive reciprocal punishment: וּמַה שֶּׁאָמְרוּ זִכְרוֹנָם לִבְרָכָה – **Also** included in this mitzvah is **that which [the Sages], of blessed memory, stated** (see *Rambam, Hil. Eidus* 20:1), שֶׁאֵין עֵדִים זוֹמְמִין נֶהֱרָגִין וְלֹא מְשַׁלְּמִין מָמוֹן וְלֹא לוֹקִין עַד שֶׁיּוּזְמוּ שְׁנֵיהֶם – **that *zomemin* witnesses are not executed, nor are they required to pay money, nor do they receive *malkus,* unless *both* [witnesses] are rendered *zomemin.***[14]

NOTES

Kesubos p. 106; see also *R' S. R. Hirsch* to the verse).

For further discussion regarding why the Torah commands us to accept the second set of witnesses, see *Derashos HaRan* §11 and *Teshuvos Melameid LeHo'il* Vol. III §101.

11. It is impossible for *beis din* to render judgment in such a case, since they have no way of determining which of the two sets of witnesses is telling the truth (*Rambam, Hil. Eidus* 18:2). Even if additional witnesses would come and testify in support of one of the first two sets of witnesses, *beis din* would still be unable to render judgment, since the rule is that the testimony of a hundred witnesses carries no more weight than that of two witnesses (see above, at note 6).

12. For example, witnesses testify that Reuven killed Shimon on a certain day in a certain place, and other witnesses say that they were together with Reuven and Shimon that entire day, and Reuven did not kill Shimon (see *Rambam, Hil. Eidus* 18:2 with *Lechem Mishneh*).

13. For example, witnesses testify that Reuven killed Shimon on a certain day in a certain place, and other witnesses testify that they were together with Shimon (the alleged murder victim), on that very day in a different place [which is far away from the first place], making it impossible for the first witnesses' testimony to be true [since Shimon could not have been in both places on the same day] (*Rambam* ibid.).

14. The verse that introduces the reciprocal penalty for *zomemin* witnesses states (*Deuteronomy* 19:18): וְהִנֵּה עֵד שֶׁקֶר הָעֵד, *and behold the witness is a false witness.* The Sages (*Sotah* 2b) teach that whenever the Torah speaks of an עֵד, *witness,* without specifying a *single* witness, it actually means *two* witnesses (i.e., a *set*). Thus, when the verse says *and behold the "witness" is a false witness,* it means that *both* witnesses have been rendered *zomemin.* Therefore, when the Torah then states: *You shall do to him as he conspired to do to his brother,* it refers specifically to a case where both witnesses were rendered *zomemin* (*Rashi, Makkos* 5b ד״ה שהרי אמרו).

Chinuch speaks of a case where the first set was

וּמַה שֶּׁאָמְרוּ זִכְרוֹנָם לִבְרָכָה (כתובות ל״ג ע״א) שֶׁעֵדִים זוֹמְמִין אֵין צְרִיכִין הַתְרָאָה אֶלָּא
מִכֵּיוָן שֶׁהֻזְמוּ נִדּוֹנִין,¹⁵ וְעֵדִים שֶׁהֻכְחֲשׁוּ תְּחִלָּה וּלְבַסּוֹף הֻזְמוּ הֲרֵי אֵלּוּ גַּם כֵּן נִדּוֹנִין,
שֶׁכֵּן אָמְרוּ זִכְרוֹנָם לִבְרָכָה (ב״ק ע״ד ע״א) הַכְחָשָׁה תְּחִלַּת הֲזָמָה הִיא,¹⁶ וּמַה שֶּׁאָמְרוּ

In general, *beis din* does is not empowered to administer corporal punishment unless the transgressor was forewarned about the consequences of his actions. Chinuch discusses whether this requirement applies to the reciprocal punishment of *zomemin* witnesses: וּמַה שֶּׁאָמְרוּ זִכְרוֹנָם לִבְרָכָה — There is **also that which [the Sages], of blessed memory, stated** (*Kesubos* 33a), שֶׁעֵדִים זוֹמְמִין אֵין צְרִיכִין הַתְרָאָה — **that** *zomemin* **witnesses do not require** *hasraah* (forewarning) to be punished; אֶלָּא מִכֵּיוָן שֶׁהֻזְמוּ נִדּוֹנִין — **rather, as long as they have been rendered** *zomemin,* even if they were not warned prior to giving their false testimony, **they receive** reciprocal **punishment.**[15]

As mentioned above, the Torah prescribes reciprocal punishment only for witnesses who have been subjected to *hazamah,* but not for witnesses whose testimony has simply been contradicted by other witnesses. Chinuch discusses a case where witnesses first were contradicted and then were subjected to *hazamah.* I.e., after two witnesses (Reuven and Shimon) stated their testimony, two other witnesses (Levi and Yehudah) came and said that the incident never occurred, and then two additional witnesses (Yissachar and Zevulun) came and said that they have no knowledge regarding the actual incident, but the original witnesses (Reuven and Shimon) were with them in an entirely different location at the time they claim to have witnessed it: וְעֵדִים שֶׁהֻכְחֲשׁוּ תְּחִלָּה וּלְבַסּוֹף הֻזְמוּ הֲרֵי אֵלּוּ גַּם כֵּן נִדּוֹנִין — **If witnesses first had** their testimony **contradicted and then were subjected to** *hazamah,* **these [witnesses] also receive** reciprocal **punishment,** just like witnesses who were subjected only to *hazamah.* שֶׁכֵּן אָמְרוּ זִכְרוֹנָם לִבְרָכָה — This is **because [the Sages], of blessed memory, stated** (*Bava Kamma* 74a) that הַכְחָשָׁה תְּחִלַּת הֲזָמָה הִיא — ordinary **contradiction is** considered **the beginning of the** *hazamah* **process.**[16]

The rule is that all testimony that affects a person (e.g., subjects him to monetary payment or to corporal punishment) must be given in his presence (see *Bava Kamma* 112b). Chinuch discusses how this rule applies to the different types of contradictory testimony: וּמַה שֶּׁאָמְרוּ — **Also** included in the mitzvah is **that which [the Sages] stated** (*Rambam, Hil.*

NOTES

comprised of two witnesses, and teaches that both of them must be rendered *zomemin* for either of them to receive reciprocal punishment. In a case where the first set is comprised of three or more witnesses, reciprocal punishment cannot be given to *any* of the witnesses unless *all* of them have been rendered *zomemin* (Mishnah, *Makkos* 5b; see there for the Scriptural source of this law).

15. Since the witnesses sought to have the defendant punished even though he received no warning, the requirement to *do to him as he conspired to do to his brother* mandates that they too must be subjected to punishment even if they did not receive a warning (*Kesubos* 33a; see there for another reason). See Mitzvah 462, at note 11.

16. Once the testimony of the original witnesses was contradicted by other witnesses, it was rendered ineffective, since *beis din* cannot convict on the basis of contradicted testimony; see above, at note 11. One could

therefore have argued that a *hazamah* that follows a contradiction should not subject the false witnesses to reciprocal punishment, for the concept of reciprocal punishment applies only to testimony that would have been valid in the absence of *hazamah.* Nevertheless, the witnesses *are* liable to reciprocal punishment, because when witnesses are first contradicted and then subjected to *hazamah,* we view the ordinary contradiction as the beginning of the *hazamah* process. Therefore, the testimony of the original witnesses was *not* rendered irrelevant before the *hazamah* process began. [Both an ordinary contradiction and *hazamah* are ways in which testimony is discredited, only that an ordinary contradiction partially discredits the testimony (i.e., it is discredited only because of uncertainty as to which set of witnesses is telling the truth) while *hazamah* discredits it *completely* (i.e., it is definitely discredited). Thus, the contradicting witnesses are viewed as having begun a process that was ultimately completed with the *hazamah.*]

(רמב"ם פי"ח מהל' עדות ה"ה) **שֶׁאֵין מְזַמְּמִין הָעֵדִים אֶלָּא בִּפְנֵיהֶם אֲבָל מַכְחִישִׁין אוֹתָם שֶׁלֹּא בִּפְנֵיהֶם**[17]**.**

וְאִם הוֹצִיאוּ בְּעֵדוּתָם מָמוֹן, מַחֲזִירִין בֵּית דִּין הַמָּמוֹן לִבְעָלָיו וּמְשַׁלְּמִין הָעֵדִים כֶּסֶף הַמָּמוֹן שֶׁחָשְׁבוּ לְהַפְסִידוֹ[18]**. אֲבָל בְּדִינֵי נְפָשׁוֹת אֵינוֹ כֵן, שֶׁאִם נֶהֱרַג אֶחָד עַל פִּיהֶם וְהֻזְּמוּ אַחַר כֵּן אֵינָם נֶהֱרָגִים, שֶׁכֵּן בָּאָה הַקַּבָּלָה, לֹא הָרְגוּ נֶהֱרָגִין, הָרְגוּ אֵינָם נֶהֱרָגִין**[19]**.**

Eidus 18:5), שֶׁאֵין מְזַמְּמִין הָעֵדִים אֶלָּא בִּפְנֵיהֶם – **that we can render witnesses *zomemin* only in their presence,** אֲבָל מַכְחִישִׁין אוֹתָם שֶׁלֹּא בִּפְנֵיהֶם – **but we can contradict** the testimony of **witnesses** (i.e., we can accept ordinary contradictory testimony) even **when they are not present.**[17]

Witnesses who were rendered *zomemin* before a verdict was issued on the basis of their testimony are not subject to any type of reciprocal punishment (*Makkos* 5b; *Rambam* 18:2). Witnesses who were rendered *zomemin* after the verdict was issued but before it was carried out are subject to *all* types of reciprocal punishment. Witnesses who were rendered *zomemin* after the verdict was carried out are subject to some reciprocal punishments but not to others, as Chinuch proceeds to explain:

וְאִם הוֹצִיאוּ בְּעֵדוּתָם מָמוֹן – **If [*beis din*] exacted money** from a defendant **on the basis of the testimony of [witnesses who were then rendered *zomemin*],** מַחֲזִירִין בֵּית דִּין הַמָּמוֹן לִבְעָלָיו – ***beis din* returns the money** they exacted **to its** rightful **owner** (i.e., the defendant), וּמְשַׁלְּמִין הָעֵדִים כֶּסֶף הַמָּמוֹן שֶׁחָשְׁבוּ לְהַפְסִידוֹ – **and** additionally, **the** *zomemin* **witnesses pay** the defendant **the amount of money they had sought to make him lose.**[18] אֲבָל בְּדִינֵי נְפָשׁוֹת אֵינוֹ כֵן – **With regard to capital cases, however, this is not [the law];** rather, the law is שֶׁאִם נֶהֱרַג אֶחָד עַל פִּיהֶם וְהֻזְּמוּ אַחַר כֵּן – **that if someone was put to death on the basis of** the testimony of **[witnesses] and [those witnesses] were then rendered *zomemin*,** אֵינָם נֶהֱרָגִים – **the [witnesses] are *not* put to death,** שֶׁכֵּן בָּאָה הַקַּבָּלָה – **for this is the tradition we have received:** לֹא הָרְגוּ נֶהֱרָגִין – **If [the witnesses] had not killed [the defendant]** (i.e., he had not yet been killed based on their testimony) by the time they were rendered *zomemin,* **they** themselves **are executed;** הָרְגוּ אֵינָם נֶהֱרָגִין – but **if [the witnesses] had** already **killed [the defendant]** (i.e., he had already been executed on the basis of their testimony) by the time they were rendered *zomemin,* **they are *not* executed.**[19]

Logic dictates that if witnesses are executed for merely seeking to have a defendant executed, then they should surely be put to death for actually having him executed. Chinuch suggests a rationale for the counterintuitive law that teaches otherwise:

NOTES

17. Since *zomemin* witnesses are liable to punishment, they cannot be rendered *zomemin* by testimony that was given when they were not present. By contrast, regular contradictory testimony does not subject witnesses to punishment; it only invalidates their testimony. Therefore, there is no requirement for such testimony to be given in the presence of the original witnesses.

Although *hazamah* testimony that was given in the absence of the original witnesses cannot subject those witnesses to punishment, it is certainly no less effective than ordinary contradictory testimony. Therefore, in such a case, although the witnesses are not subject to reciprocal punishment, their testimony is nevertheless invalidated (*Kesubos* 20a; *Rambam, Hil. Eidus* 18:5).

18. That is, with regard to monetary cases, once a verdict has been handed down, the witnesses are liable to reciprocal punishment whenever they are rendered *zomemin,* whether before the verdict has been carried out or afterward. See next note.

19. That is, with regard to capital cases, witnesses are liable to reciprocal punishment only if they were rendered *zomemin* after the verdict had been issued, but before the verdict had actually been carried out. The Mishnah (*Makkos* 5b) and *Rambam* (*Hil. Eidus* 20:2) provide Scriptural sources for this law, but as Chinuch writes, this law is known primarily through the Oral Tradition (see also *Rambam* ibid.).

In distinguishing between monetary and capital cases with regard to witnesses who were rendered *zomemin* after the verdict had already been carried out, Chinuch follows the opinion of *Rambam* (ibid.). *Tosafos* (*Bava Kamma* 4b ד"ה ועדים זוממין) also make a similar distinction. By contrast, several Rishonim maintain that even in monetary cases, witnesses do not receive reciprocal punishment if they were rendered *zomemin* after the verdict had been carried out (*Ritva, Makkos* 3a ד"ה ופרכינן; *Shitah Mekubetzes* to *Bava Kamma* 4b). See below, note 27, regarding cases involving *malkus.*

וְיֵשׁ לוֹמַר קְצָת טַעַם לַדָּבָר כִּי אֱלֹהִים נִצָּב בַּעֲדַת הַדַּיָּנִין[20], וְלוּלֵי שֶׁנִּתְחַיֵּב הַנִּדּוֹן בְּמַעֲשָׂיו הָרָעִים לֹא נִגְזַר עָלָיו מַעֲשֵׂה הַמִּשְׁפָּט, אֲבָל וַדַּאי רָאוּי הָיָה לְכָךְ[21] וְגִלְגְּלוּ עָלָיו דִּינוֹ מִן הַשָּׁמַיִם עַל יַד זֶה הָרָשָׁע[22], וְעַל כַּיּוֹצֵא בָּזֶה נֶאֱמַר (משלי ט״ז, ד׳) וְגַם רָשָׁע לְיוֹם רָעָה[23], וְאַחַר שֶׁנִּתְגַּלָּה הַדָּבָר לְעֵינֵינוּ כִּי זֶה הָאִישׁ בֶּן מָוֶת הָיָה, לֹא רָצְתָה הַתּוֹרָה שֶׁנַּהֲרֹג הָעֵדִים עָלָיו, וְהַמָּשָׁל בָּזֶה, מִי שֶׁהָרַג אֶת הַטְּרֵפָה[24] שֶׁאֵינוֹ נֶהֱרָג עָלָיו[25], גַּם זֶה כְּמוֹ כֵן, מִכֵּיוָן שֶׁיָּדַעְנוּ עַל הַדֶּרֶךְ שֶׁאָמַרְנוּ שֶׁנִּתְחַיֵּב בְּבֵית דִּין שֶׁל מַעְלָה אֵין לוֹ דָּמִים[26,27].

וְיֵשׁ לוֹמַר קְצָת טַעַם לַדָּבָר – Now, it is possible to give a bit of a rationale for this matter, as follows: **כִּי אֱלֹהִים נִצָּב בַּעֲדַת הַדַּיָּנִין – For God stands** (is present) **in the assembly of judges,**[20] and prevents them from shedding innocent blood. **וְלוּלֵי שֶׁנִּתְחַיֵּב הַנִּדּוֹן בְּמַעֲשָׂיו הָרָעִים לֹא נִגְזַר עָלָיו מַעֲשֵׂה הַמִּשְׁפָּט – Therefore,** in a case where the defendant was executed, we are confident that **had he not been worthy** of death **on account of his wicked deeds, the verdict would not have been carried out upon him. אֲבָל וַדַּאי רָאוּי הָיָה לְכָךְ – But** since the punishment *was* carried out, **he surely must have deserved it,**[21] **וְגִלְגְּלוּ עָלָיו דִּינוֹ מִן הַשָּׁמַיִם עַל יַד זֶה הָרָשָׁע – only his punishment was brought about by Heaven through these wicked people** (the *zomemin* witnesses).[22] **וְעַל כַּיּוֹצֵא בָּזֶה נֶאֱמַר – Regarding situations like this, it is stated** (*Proverbs* 16:4): **"וְגַם רָשָׁע לְיוֹם רָעָה"** – *Everything HASHEM made, [He made] for His sake,* ***even the evildoer for the day of retribution.***[23] **וְאַחַר שֶׁנִּתְגַּלָּה הַדָּבָר לְעֵינֵינוּ כִּי זֶה הָאִישׁ בֶּן מָוֶת הָיָה – And since it is clear to us that this man** (the executed defendant) **was** truly **deserving of death, לֹא רָצְתָה הַתּוֹרָה שֶׁנַּהֲרֹג הָעֵדִים עָלָיו – the Torah did not want us to execute the** ***zomemin*** **witnesses on his account. וְהַמָּשָׁל בָּזֶה מִי שֶׁהָרַג אֶת הַטְּרֵפָה שֶׁאֵינוֹ נֶהֱרָג עָלָיו – This is analogous** to the case of **someone who murders a** ***tereifah,***[24] where the law is **that [the murderer] is not put to death on account of** killing **[the** ***tereifah*****]** since the *tereifah* was going to die soon anyway.[25] **גַּם זֶה כְּמוֹ כֵן – In this case, too, מִכֵּיוָן שֶׁיָּדַעְנוּ עַל הַדֶּרֶךְ שֶׁאָמַרְנוּ שֶׁנִּתְחַיֵּב בְּבֵית דִּין שֶׁל מַעְלָה – since we know, based on that which I have said, that [the defendant] was liable** to death **in the Heavenly Court, אֵין לוֹ דָּמִים – "he has no blood,"**[26] i.e., one who kills him is not held accountable for full-fledged murder.[27]

NOTES

20. Paraphrase of *Psalms* 82:1; see *Sanhedrin* 7a.

21. Since God is present during the proceedings of *beis din,* it is inconceivable that they would execute someone who is undeserving of death. Therefore, if a death sentence was carried out by *beis din*, we can be sure that the defendant deserved to die for some transgression. [As in all cases of *hazamah,* the presumption is that the *first* set of witnesses testified falsely. However, we take the defendant's execution as proof that he must have committed some other transgression that made him deserving of death.]

22. Although the defendant surely deserved his fate, as explained in the previous note, the witnesses are still guilty of severe wrongdoing for testifying falsely. Furthermore, even if someone deserves to die for his sins, killing him or causing him to be killed (without a proper trial and conviction) is still a grievous sin. Chinuch therefore refers to the witnesses as "wicked people."

23. That is, the verse teaches that all of God's creations serve a purpose for Him. Even the wicked, who consistently flout His will, serve a purpose, in that God makes use of their wicked deeds to punish those who deserve punishment. In our case, too, God employed the wickedness of the *zomemin* witnesses to punish the defendant. [See *Metzudos David* to the *Mishlei* verse and *Sforno* to *Exodus* 21:13, who understand the *Mishlei* verse like Chinuch.]

24. In this context, *tereifah* refers to a person who suffers from a physical ailment or injury that will certainly cause his death (see *Rambam, Hil. Rotze'ach* 2:8).

25. One who murders a *tereifah* is not liable to the death penalty, which is the usual punishment for murder (*Sanhedrin* 78a). This is because a *tereifah* will certainly die as a result of his ailment or injury (if he does not die due to some other cause first), which somewhat lessens the severity of murdering him. Nevertheless, murdering a *tereifah* is still a terrible sin, for which a person is liable to death at the hands of Heaven (*Meiri, Sanhedrin* 57b; *Chidushei HaGriz* to *Hil. Rotze'ach* 1:13, in explanation of *Rambam, Hil. Rotze'ach* 2:8).

26. Stylistic citation of *Exodus* 22:1 and *Numbers* 35:27.

27. Here too, the fact that the defendant was certainly liable to death lessens the severity of the false testimony against him, to the point that the Torah did not see fit to have the *zomemin* witnesses executed. See *Rabbeinu Bachya* and *Recanati* to the verse, who explain similarly; see also *Ramban* to the verse for a slightly different explanation of why witnesses who are rendered *zomemin* after the defendant has already been killed are not executed. For further discussion as

וְיֶתֶר פְּרָטֵי הַמִּצְוָה מְבֹאָרִים בְּמַסֶּכֶת מַכּוֹת (פרק ראשון)[28].

וְנוֹהֶגֶת מִצְוָה זוֹ בְּאֶרֶץ יִשְׂרָאֵל בִּזְמַן שֶׁיֵּשׁ לָנוּ בֵּית דִּין סָמוּךְ[29], לְפִי שֶׁתַּשְׁלוּמִין שֶׁל עֵדִים זוֹמְמִין קְנָס הוּא[30], וְיָדוּעַ שֶׁאֵין דָּנִין דִּינֵי קְנָסוֹת אֶלָּא בְּבֵית דִּין סָמוּךְ[31].

וּבֵית דִּין הָרָאוּי לָדוּן דִּינֵי קְנָסוֹת שֶׁלֹּא עָשָׂה לְעֵדִים זוֹמְמִים כַּאֲשֶׁר זָמְמוּ לַעֲשׂוֹת לַאֲחִיהֶם בִּטֵּל עֲשֵׂה זֶה[32].

וְיֶתֶר פְּרָטֵי הַמִּצְוָה מְבֹאָרִים בְּמַסֶּכֶת מַכּוֹת – These **and the remaining details of the mitzvah are set forth in Tractate *Makkos*** (Chapter 1).[28]

Applicability of the Mitzvah

וְנוֹהֶגֶת מִצְוָה זוֹ בְּאֶרֶץ יִשְׂרָאֵל בִּזְמַן שֶׁיֵּשׁ לָנוּ בֵּית דִּין סָמוּךְ – **This mitzvah applies** only **in Eretz Yisrael, at a time when we have courts** made up **of judges who have received *semichah*,**[29] לְפִי שֶׁתַּשְׁלוּמִין שֶׁל עֵדִים זוֹמְמִין קְנָס הוּא – **for the payment imposed upon *zomemin* witnesses** is considered **a fine,**[30] וְיָדוּעַ שֶׁאֵין דָּנִין דִּינֵי קְנָסוֹת אֶלָּא בְּבֵית דִּין סָמוּךְ – **and it is well known that cases involving fines can be adjudicated only in a court** that is made up **of** judges who have **received *semichah*.**[31]

וּבֵית דִּין הָרָאוּי לָדוּן דִּינֵי קְנָסוֹת – **A *beis din* that is qualified to adjudicate penalties** שֶׁלֹּא עָשָׂה לְעֵדִים זוֹמְמִים כַּאֲשֶׁר זָמְמוּ לַעֲשׂוֹת לַאֲחִיהֶם – **that did not do to *zomemin* witnesses exactly what they conspired to do to their "brother,"** בִּטֵּל עֲשֵׂה זֶה – **has violated this mitzvah-obligation.**[32]

NOTES

to why reciprocal punishment is limited to cases where witnesses are rendered *zomemin* before the verdict is carried out, see *Meiri, Makkos* 3a; *Kesef Mishneh, Hil. Eidus* 20:2; and *Maharal, Be'er HaGolah* 2:2.

Kesef Mishneh (*Hil. Eidus* 20:2) contends that Chinuch's rationale for this law would not apply to cases involving *malkus*. [That is, God's Presence during judicial proceedings guarantees only that *beis din* will not *execute* a completely innocent person; see, however, *Tosafos Yom Tov, Makkos* 1:9.] Accordingly, the reciprocal punishment of *malkus* should be administered to witnesses even if they were rendered *zomemin* after the defendant had already received *malkus* (*Minchas Chinuch* §4). This, indeed, is how *Rambam* (*Hil. Eidus* 20:2) rules. [For discussion, see *Minchas Chinuch* §4 and *Chidushei R' Chaim HaLevi* to *Rambam* ibid.]. Others maintain that cases involving *malkus* are treated like capital cases in this regard, i.e., witnesses receive *malkus* only if they were rendered *zomemin* before the verdict has been carried out (see *Raavad* to *Hil. Eidus* 20:2, as explained by *Radvaz* and *Kesef Mishneh* there; see *Ritva, Makkos* 3a and *Tosafos, Bava Kamma* 4b ועדים זוממין).

28. These laws are codified in *Rambam, Hil. Eidus* Chs. 18-21.

[The Machon Yerushalayim ed. contains an additional sentence of text before this sentence. That sentence does not appear in most editions and manuscripts of Chinuch.]

29. *Semichah* is a special type of ordination that can be traced back to Moses; see Mitzvah 491. It does not exist nowadays.

30. There are two categories of monetary payments: *compensations* and *fines*. As explained above, Mitzvah 523 note 48, any payment that does not correspond exactly to the amount of damage that a person caused is considered a fine. Now, Chinuch mentioned above (at note 18) that in monetary cases, *zomemin* witnesses are obligated to pay whether they were rendered *zomemin* before the verdict was carried out or afterward. In either case, the payment is considered a *fine*. When they are rendered *zomemin* before the verdict has been enforced, their payment is certainly a fine, since they had not yet caused any damage to the defendant. And even when they are rendered *zomemin* after the verdict has been enforced, their payment is still considered a fine, since, in addition to the witnesses' payment, the exacted money is returned to the defendant, so that ultimately they did not cause any damage. [See Insight.]

31. See Mitzvah 523 note 48. [It goes without saying that the reciprocal punishments of *malkus* or capital punishment cannot be administered in the absence of fully ordained judges, since such cases require fully ordained judges to be tried in the first place.] See Insight for further discussion regarding laws of *hazamah* nowadays.

Chinuch states that this mitzvah is limited to Eretz Yisrael. This is difficult to understand, for although *semichah* can be conferred only in Eretz Yisrael, judges who have received *semichah* in Eretz Yisrael are empowered to adjudicate all cases even outside of Eretz Yisrael (see Mitzvah 491). Therefore, this mitzvah should seemingly apply even outside of Eretz Yisrael, provided that the presiding judges had received *semichah*.

32. See Mitzvah 521 Insight B.

⇛ Insight: Hazamah Nowadays

Chinuch described two types of contradictory testimony. Ordinary contradictory testimony (known as הַכְחָשָׁה, *hach'chashah*) is when one set of witnesses testifies about a certain event and a second set of witnesses contradicts the actual testimony of the first set. For example, a set of witnesses testifies that Reuven borrowed money from Shimon on a certain date, and a second set of witnesses testifies that no such loan took place. The second type of contradictory testimony, known as *hazamah,* is where the second set of witnesses does not contradict the actual testimony of the first set, but testifies that the first set could not possibly have seen the alleged event because they were with them (the second set) in a different location at the time that the event was supposed to have occurred. Although *beis din* cannot render judgment on the basis of testimony that has been subjected to either type of contradictory testimony, there is a fundamental difference between them. In cases of ordinary contradictory testimony, neither set of witnesses is believed over the other; therefore, since we have no way of determining which set is telling the truth, all of the testimony is discarded. By contrast, in the case of *hazamah,* the Torah teaches that the testimony of the second set is believed over the first set, and that the witnesses of the first set, known as *zomemin* witnesses, are liable to reciprocal punishment; e.g., if they testified that a person owes a certain amount of money, they are required to pay that amount to the person against whom they testified.

Nowadays, *beis din* cannot impose reciprocal punishment upon *zomemin* witnesses even in cases involving monetary payment, because (as Chinuch explained at note 30) the payment of *zomemin* witnesses is classified as a fine (קְנָס), and *beis din* is not authorized to collect fines nowadays. Nevertheless, there are still several practical ramifications to the fact that *hazamah* completely discredits the first set of witnesses.

(1) A person who is found to have testified falsely is disqualified to serve as a witness. However, when two sets of witnesses contradict each other with ordinary contradictory testimony, the halachah is that all of the witnesses retain their status as valid witnesses and can testify in future cases, despite the fact that one of the sets of witnesses was definitely guilty of testifying falsely (*Shulchan Aruch, Choshen Mishpat* 31:1). Since neither set is given more credibility than the other, there is doubt as to which of the witnesses testified falsely. In general, when an event occurs that *may* have changed a person's halachic status, the principle of *chazakah* (legal presumption) teaches that the person's status remains unchanged. In our case, too, both sets of witnesses were previously qualified to testify, but following the contradictory testimonies, their fitness is in doubt. The principle of *chazakah* therefore teaches that we maintain the previous situation and allow all of the witnesses to testify in future cases (*Rashbam, Bava Basra* 31b ד"ה זו באה בפני עצמה).

All this is true only with regard to cases involving ordinary contradictory testimony, because in such cases, the Torah does not give more credibility to either of the two sets of witnesses, thus creating a situation of doubt. By contrast, in cases involving *hazamah,* the Torah gives credibility to the second set of witnesses over the first set. This is true regardless of whether *beis din* is actually empowered to punish the *zomemin* witnesses. Therefore, even nowadays, when *beis din* is not authorized to administer reciprocal punishment, if witnesses are subjected to *hazamah,* they are considered with certainty to be false witnesses, and are therefore disqualified from serving as witnesses in future cases (*Shulchan Aruch, Choshen Mishpat* 34:8).

(2) If *beis din* exacted money from a person based on the testimony of witnesses and a second set of witnesses then came and subjected the first set of witnesses to *hazamah,* the law is that the money is returned to the victim and the *zomemin* witnesses must also pay that amount to the victim (see above, at note 18). Nowadays, when *beis din* does not have the authority to exact payment from *zomemin* witnesses, the money that was exacted on the basis of their testimony is simply returned, but they themselves are exempt from paying. However, in a situation where it is impossible to recover the exacted money from the person who collected it (e.g., he left town and his whereabouts are unknown), the *zomemin* witnesses *are* obligated to pay. For in such a case, since the money was exacted on the basis of the witnesses' testimony and cannot be recovered, the *zomemin* witnesses are considered to have caused a loss to the person against whom they testified, and are required to pay under the law of *garmi* (causative damage), which teaches that a person is liable for certain indirect damages (*Rama, Choshen Mishpat* 1:4; see *Nesivos HaMishpat, Chidushim* 38:2; see Mitzvah 236 note 24 for more about the law of *garmi*). This is true in cases of *hazamah,* because the Torah

gives credibility to the second set of witnesses over the first, and we can therefore hold the *zomemin* witnesses responsible for the money that was exacted on the basis of their testimony. By contrast, in cases of ordinary contradictory testimony, where the Torah does not give more credibility to either set of witnesses, we cannot force the first set of witnesses to pay for causing damage, for it is possible that they are the ones telling the truth, in which case, the defendant was properly required to pay (*Shach, Choshen Mishpat* 38:2).

(3) As mentioned previously, nowadays *beis din* is not authorized to collect any payment that is categorized as a fine. However, the law is that if a person who is owed a fine takes matters into his own hands and seizes the amount he is owed, he is allowed to keep that money (*Shulchan Aruch, Choshen Mishpat* 1:5). Consequently, although the payment of *zomemin* witnesses is considered a fine and cannot be imposed by *beis din* nowadays, if the person against whom the *zomemin* witnesses testified seizes payment from the *zomemin* witnesses, he is allowed to keep that money (*Beis Yosef, Choshen Mishpat,* end of §38, in explanation of *Tur; Sma* 38:3; *Shach* 38:2).

[Whether seizure of payment from *zomemin* witnesses is effective is actually subject to a dispute among Rishonim, which was discussed in the Insight to Mitzvah 51. *Rosh* (*Bava Kamma* 1:20) maintains that seizure of payment categorized as a fine is effective in all cases, even where the one who seizes it stands to profit, e.g., he seized the double payment (*keifel*) of a thief. *Ramah* (*R' Meir HaLevi,* cited by *Rosh* ibid.), on the other hand, maintains that seizure of payment categorized as a fine is effective only in cases where the victim suffered a *loss.* In order to mitigate his loss, the Sages authorized him to seize the amount the other party would have been penalized if there were an ordained *beis din* in the area. But in a case where the victim will not suffer any *loss* due to our inability to enforce the fine, he is not permitted to seize it himself. In our case, the victim of the *zomemin* witnesses does not suffer any loss, since any money that was exacted on the basis of their false testimony is returned to him. Therefore, seizure of that payment would be effective only according to *Rosh,* but not according to *Ramah.* For the actual halachah, see *Gra, Choshen Mishpat* 38:4, and *Sma* 1:18.]

מִצְוָה תקכה: שֶׁלֹּא לַעֲרֹץ מִפְּנֵי הָאוֹיֵב בַּמִּלְחָמָה[2,1]

שֶׁנִּמְנַעְנוּ שֶׁלֹּא לַעֲרֹץ וּלְפַחֵד מִן הָאוֹיְבִים בְּעֵת הַמִּלְחָמָה וְשֶׁלֹּא נִבְרַח מִפְּנֵיהֶם,[3]

Mitzvah 525

The Prohibition to Be Afraid of the Enemy During War

כִּי תֵצֵא לַמִּלְחָמָה עַל אֹיְבֶךָ וְרָאִיתָ סוּס וָרֶכֶב עַם רַב מִמְּךָ לֹא תִירָא מֵהֶם כִּי ה׳ אֱלֹהֶיךָ עִמָּךְ הַמַּעַלְךָ מֵאֶרֶץ מִצְרָיִם

If you go out to battle against your enemy and you see horse and chariot – a people more numerous than you – you shall not fear them, for HASHEM, your God, is with you, Who brought you up from the land of Egypt (*Deuteronomy* 20:1).

לֹא תַעֲרֹץ מִפְּנֵיהֶם כִּי ה׳ אֱלֹהֶיךָ בְּקִרְבֶּךָ אֵל גָּדוֹל וְנוֹרָא

You shall not tremble before them, for HASHEM, your God, is among you, a great and awesome God (ibid. 7:21).

לֹא תִּירָאוּם כִּי ה׳ אֱלֹהֵיכֶם הוּא הַנִּלְחָם לָכֶם

You shall not fear them, for HASHEM, your God – He shall wage war for you (ibid. 3:22).

When it was necessary for the Jewish people to wage war, only the most righteous individuals were chosen to fight in the army. As Chinuch teaches in Mitzvah 526, anyone who was "afraid of a transgression that he had committed" was disqualified, lest his sins cause him and others to fall in battle. The cited verses teach that those who did go out to war were prohibited to let fear take hold in their hearts, but were required to place their trust in Hashem, Who wages war for His people.

This prohibition is stated in the Torah several times. Two of the verses appear earlier, in *Parashas Devarim* (3:22) and *Parashas Eikev* (7:21), and those are the verses that *Rambam* cites in *Sefer HaMitzvos* (*Lo Saaseh* 58) as the sources of this mitzvah. Chinuch, as is his usual style, begins this mitzvah by loosely quoting from *Sefer HaMitzvos,* and he thus cites those verses. Nevertheless, Chinuch places the mitzvah here in *Parashas Shoftim*, where the prohibition is stated for the third time (*Deuteronomy* 20:1). The reason is because this is where the Torah speaks at length about the process of war and sets out several related mitzvos (Mitzvos 526-529).

We will learn in Mitzvos 526-527 that there are two categories of wars: מִלְחֶמֶת מִצְוָה, *an obligatory war,* referring to a war that the Torah requires us to wage, and מִלְחֶמֶת הָרְשׁוּת, *a discretionary war,* referring to a war that the king and the Sanhedrin decide to wage.[1] This mitzvah applies in all cases. Regardless of why the war was begun, a soldier is prohibited to be afraid of the enemy (*Rambam, Hil. Melachim* 7:1).

It should be noted that while *Rambam* counts the cited verses as a mitzvah-prohibition, *Raavad* (glosses to *Rambam's* list of mitzvos at the beginning of *Mishneh Torah*) and *Ramban* (glosses to *Sefer HaMitzvos, Lo Saaseh* 58) argue that they are not meant as a prohibition at all. Rather, they are meant to provide *encouragement* to those who go out to battle. Their meaning is: You *need* not fear your enemies, for Hashem is with you and He shall wage war for you.[2]

שֶׁנִּמְנַעְנוּ שֶׁלֹּא לַעֲרֹץ וּלְפַחֵד מִן הָאוֹיְבִים בְּעֵת הַמִּלְחָמָה – We are prohibited to tremble and be frightened of our **enemies at the time of battle, וְשֶׁלֹּא נִבְרַח מִפְּנֵיהֶם – and** certainly **we are**

NOTES

1. For details, see Mitzvah 526 after note 17.

2. See further, *Ramban* to *Deuteronomy* 20:4,8.

אֲבָל הַחוֹבָה עָלֵינוּ לְהִתְגַּבֵּר כְּנֶגְדָּם וּלְהִתְחַזֵּק וְלַעֲמֹד בִּפְנֵיהֶם, וְעַל זֶה נֶאֱמַר (דברים ז׳, כ״א), **לֹא תַעֲרֹץ מִפְּנֵיהֶם, וְנִכְפְּלָה הַמְּנִיעָה בְּמָקוֹם אַחֵר** (שם ג׳, כ״ב) **בְּאָמְרוֹ לֹא תִירָאוּם**[4].

מִשָּׁרְשֵׁי הַמִּצְוָה שֶׁיֵּשׁ לְכָל אֶחָד מִיִּשְׂרָאֵל לָשׂוּם לַה׳ יִתְבָּרַךְ מִבְטַחוֹ, וְלֹא יִירָא עַל גּוּפוֹ בְּמָקוֹם שֶׁיּוּכַל לָתֵת כָּבוֹד לַה׳ בָּרוּךְ הוּא וּלְעַמּוֹ[5].

דִּינֵי הַמִּצְוָה כְּגוֹן מַה שֶּׁהִזְהִירוּ זִכְרוֹנָם לִבְרָכָה שֶׁלֹּא יַחְשֹׁב אָדָם בְּעֵת הַמִּלְחָמָה לֹא בְּאִשְׁתּוֹ וְלֹא בְּבָנָיו וְלֹא בְּמָמוֹנוֹ[6]**, אֶלָּא יְפַנֶּה לִבּוֹ מִכָּל דָּבָר לַמִּלְחָמָה.**

---

not to flee from them.[3] אֲבָל הַחוֹבָה עָלֵינוּ לְהִתְגַּבֵּר כְּנֶגְדָּם – **Rather, our duty is to be courageous against them** וּלְהִתְחַזֵּק וְלַעֲמֹד בִּפְנֵיהֶם – **and to strengthen ourselves to stand** firmly **before them.** וְעַל זֶה נֶאֱמַר ״לֹא תַעֲרֹץ מִפְּנֵיהֶם״ – **Regarding this it is stated** (*Deuteronomy* 7:21): ***You shall not tremble before them,*** *for HASHEM, your God, is among you, a great and awesome God;* וְנִכְפְּלָה הַמְּנִיעָה בְּמָקוֹם אַחֵר – **and this prohibition is repeated elsewhere,** בְּאָמְרוֹ ״לֹא תִירָאוּם״ – **as [the Torah] states** (ibid. 3:22): ***You shall not fear them,*** *for HASHEM, your God – He shall wage war for you.*[4]

Underlying Purpose of the Mitzvah

מִשָּׁרְשֵׁי הַמִּצְוָה – **Among the underlying purposes of the mitzvah** is to teach us the concept שֶׁיֵּשׁ לְכָל אֶחָד מִיִּשְׂרָאֵל לָשׂוּם לַה׳ יִתְבָּרַךְ מִבְטַחוֹ – **that every Jewish person should place his trust** solely **in Hashem, blessed be He,** וְלֹא יִירָא עַל גּוּפוֹ בְּמָקוֹם שֶׁיּוּכַל לָתֵת כָּבוֹד לַה׳ בָּרוּךְ הוּא וּלְעַמּוֹ – **and should not be concerned about his physical** safety **in a situation where he is able to give honor to Hashem, blessed is He, and to His nation.**[5]

Laws of the Mitzvah

דִּינֵי הַמִּצְוָה כְּגוֹן מַה שֶּׁהִזְהִירוּ זִכְרוֹנָם לִבְרָכָה – **The laws of the mitzvah** include, **for example, that which [the Sages], of blessed memory, warned** (*Rambam, Hil. Melachim* 7:15), שֶׁלֹּא יַחְשֹׁב אָדָם בְּעֵת הַמִּלְחָמָה לֹא בְּאִשְׁתּוֹ וְלֹא בְּבָנָיו וְלֹא בְּמָמוֹנוֹ – **that during battle a person must not think about his wife, nor about his children, nor about his possessions;**[6] אֶלָּא יְפַנֶּה לִבּוֹ מִכָּל דָּבָר לַמִּלְחָמָה – **rather, one must clear his mind of** thoughts about **any** personal **matter** in order **to**

NOTES

3. Fleeing from battle is an obvious demonstration of fear and thus is included in the prohibition (see *Sefer HaMitzvos, Lo Saaseh* 58).

4. As mentioned in the introduction to this mitzvah, Chinuch here quotes *Rambam's Sefer HaMitzvos,* which cites these verses as the source of this mitzvah-prohibition. Our passage in *Parashas Shoftim* (*Deuteronomy* 20:1) states similarly: כִּי תֵצֵא לַמִּלְחָמָה עַל אֹיְבֶךָ וְרָאִיתָ סוּס וָרֶכֶב עַם רַב מִמְּךָ לֹא תִירָא מֵהֶם כִּי ה׳ אֱלֹהֶיךָ עִמָּךְ הַמַּעַלְךָ מֵאֶרֶץ מִצְרָיִם, *If you go out to battle against your enemy and you see horse and chariot – a people more numerous than you – you shall not fear them, for HASHEM, your God, is with you, Who brought you up from the land of Egypt.*

Rambam in *Hilchos Melachim* (7:15) points to yet another verse here, in *Parashas Shoftim,* as a source of this mitzvah. After stating the above prohibition against being afraid of the enemy, the Torah teaches that at the time of war a Kohen shall go out to the battlefield and urge the soldiers to be brave and rely on Hashem (see Mitzvah 526). The Torah states (ibid. v. 3) that one of the things the Kohen tells the soldiers is: אַתֶּם קְרֵבִים הַיּוֹם לַמִּלְחָמָה עַל אֹיְבֵיכֶם אַל יֵרַךְ לְבַבְכֶם אַל תִּירְאוּ וְאַל תַּחְפְּזוּ וְאַל תַּעַרְצוּ מִפְּנֵיהֶם, *You are coming near to the battle against your enemies; let your heart not be faint, do not be afraid, do not panic, and do not tremble before them. Rambam* in *Hil. Melachim* cites this verse as the source of the mitzvah-prohibition against fearing the enemy. See also *Smag, Lo Saaseh* 231.

5. Since Israel's defeat would result in a desecration of Hashem's Name, one must do all he can, to the point of endangering his own life, to help vanquish Israel's enemies. He is thus to banish from his heart any thought of danger and any concern about his own welfare, in order to fully devote himself to the sanctification of Hashem's Name. His attitude should be that he is on a mission for Hashem and his life is in Hashem's hands (*Maharam Schik;* see *Rambam, Hil. Melachim* 7:15, part of which Chinuch will immediately cite). See Insight.

6. He is to banish all thoughts of his family and finances, and not concern himself with who will care for them in the event that he is killed. Dwelling on these things would cause him to be disheartened and thus rob him of the ability to fight effectively (see *Birchas Peretz* [*R' Y. Y. Kanievski*], *Parashas Shoftim* ד״ה אכן לומר).

וְעוֹד יַחְשֹׁב שֶׁכָּל דְּמֵי יִשְׂרָאֵל תְּלוּיִין עָלָיו וַהֲרֵי הוּא כְּאִלּוּ שָׁפַךְ דְּמֵי כֻלָּן אִם יִפְחַד וְיָשׁוּב אָחוֹר יְמִינוֹ[8,7], וּכְעִנְיָן שֶׁכָּתוּב (שם כ׳, ח׳) וְלֹא יִמַּס אֶת לְבַב אֶחָיו כִּלְבָבוֹ[9], וּמְפֹרָשׁ בְּדִבְרֵי קַבָּלָה (ירמיה מ״ח, י׳) אָרוּר עֹשֶׂה מְלֶאכֶת ה׳ רְמִיָּה וְאָרוּר מֹנֵעַ חַרְבּוֹ מִדָּם[10]. וְאָמְרוּ זִכְרוֹנָם לִבְרָכָה שֶׁכָּל הַנִּלְחָם בְּכָל לִבָּבוֹ וְכַוָּנָתוֹ לְקַדֵּשׁ הַשֵּׁם מֻבְטָח הוּא שֶׁלֹּא יִמְצָא נֵזֶק[11] וְיִזְכֶּה לוֹ וּלְבָנָיו לִהְיוֹת לָהֶם בַּיִת נָכוֹן בְּיִשְׂרָאֵל וְיִזְכֶּה לְחַיֵּי הָעוֹלָם הַבָּא, וּכְעִנְיָן שֶׁכָּתוּב (שמואל א׳ כ״ה, כ״ח-כ״ט) כִּי עָשֹׂה יַעֲשֶׂה ה׳ לַאדֹנִי בַּיִת נֶאֱמָן כִּי מִלְחֲמוֹת ה׳ אֲדֹנִי נִלְחָם וְגוֹ׳[12].

---

focus on **the battle** at hand. **וְעוֹד יַחְשֹׁב שֶׁכָּל דְּמֵי יִשְׂרָאֵל תְּלוּיִין עָלָיו – Moreover, one must bear in mind that the blood of all of Israel is dependent upon him, וַהֲרֵי הוּא כְּאִלּוּ שָׁפַךְ דְּמֵי כֻלָּן – and he will be** considered **as though he spilled all their blood אִם יִפְחַד וְיָשׁוּב אָחוֹר יְמִינוֹ – if he becomes frightened and "draws back his right hand"**[7] from doing battle and Israel is defeated.[8] **וּכְעִנְיָן שֶׁכָּתוּב** – This is **in accordance with that which is written** (ibid. 20:8) that, before battle, appointed officers would announce to the soldiers: **"וְלֹא יִמַּס אֶת לְבַב אֶחָיו כִּלְבָבוֹ"** – *"Who is the man who is fearful and fainthearted? Let him go and return to his house, **and let him not melt the heart of his fellows, like his heart.**"*[9] **וּמְפֹרָשׁ בְּדִבְרֵי קַבָּלָה – And,** regarding one who allows fear to take hold of him during battle, **it is stated explicitly in the words of the Prophets** (*Jeremiah* 48:10): **"אָרוּר עֹשֶׂה מְלֶאכֶת ה׳ רְמִיָּה וְאָרוּר מֹנֵעַ חַרְבּוֹ מִדָּם"** – ***Cursed be the one who carries out the mission of HASHEM deceitfully! Cursed be the one who withholds his sword from bloodshed!***[10]

Chinuch turns to the reward of a soldier who fights valiantly:

וְאָמְרוּ זִכְרוֹנָם לִבְרָכָה – On the other hand, **[the Sages], of blessed memory, have stated** (see *Rambam* ibid.) **שֶׁכָּל הַנִּלְחָם בְּכָל לִבָּבוֹ – that whoever does battle with all his heart, וְכַוָּנָתוֹ לְקַדֵּשׁ הַשֵּׁם – and his intention** in doing so **is to sanctify the Name of Hashem, מֻבְטָח הוּא שֶׁלֹּא יִמְצָא נֵזֶק – is assured that he will encounter no harm,**[11] **וְיִזְכֶּה לוֹ וּלְבָנָיו לִהְיוֹת לָהֶם בַּיִת נָכוֹן בְּיִשְׂרָאֵל – and he will merit, on behalf of himself and his children, to have a house** (i.e., a dynasty) that is **firmly established among** the people of **Israel, וְיִזְכֶּה לְחַיֵּי הָעוֹלָם הַבָּא – and he will** surely **merit** eternal **life in the World to Come. וּכְעִנְיָן שֶׁכָּתוּב** – This is **in accordance with what is written** about King David (*I Samuel* 25:28-29): **"כִּי עָשֹׂה יַעֲשֶׂה ה׳ לַאדֹנִי בַּיִת נֶאֱמָן כִּי מִלְחֲמוֹת ה׳ אֲדֹנִי נִלְחָם וְגוֹ׳ "** – ***For HASHEM shall certainly make for my lord an enduring house, for my lord fights the wars of HASHEM,*** *and nothing bad shall be found in you in all your days ... May my lord's soul be bound up in the bond of life, with HASHEM, your God.*[12]

NOTES

7. I.e., fails to fight with all of his strength and capability. [Stylistic paraphrase of *Lamentations* 2:3.]

8. If even a single soldier allows himself to be overcome by fear, he may dishearten his fellows and cause the entire army to suffer defeat. This in turn might cause many innocent people to be killed. The deaths of all the victims would be blamed on the individual whose cowardice triggered the defeat. A soldier must bear this in mind in order to infuse himself with courage and embolden himself to fight with all his strength.

9. This is one of the warnings that was issued to the soldiers before they engaged in battle (see the following mitzvah). The verse demonstrates that a soldier who shows fear in battle will demoralize his companions. Thus, if a soldier does not go home but remains on the battlefield, he must bear in mind that allowing himself to become fearful would endanger the entire army and nation. [For other interpretations of this verse, see Mitzvah 526 notes 13 and 15.]

10. The "mission of Hashem" with which a soldier is charged is to wage war bravely and vigorously, so as to ensure victory. One who "withholds his sword from bloodshed" on account of fear is considered a deceitful warrior, since his cowardice is liable to cause the entire army to fail in its mission.

11. *Rambam* (ibid.) adds a clause, stating that this applies if one does battle "with all his heart, *without fear,* etc." See above, note 5.

[*Ramban* (*Deuteronomy* 20:4,8) explains that, in order to merit Hashem's guarantee of protection, one must have full faith in Him. A person who is fearful displays a lack of faith (*bitachon*), and thus is bound by the ordinary rules of warfare, in which people fall in battle. When the Jewish army fights the wars of Hashem with absolute faith in His salvation, it is guaranteed that no man will be lost. *Ramban* states that this is why a person who was "fearful and fainthearted" was sent home from the war.]

12. This was said to King David by Avigail (who would later become his wife), when she pleaded with him to

וְיֶתֶר פְּרָטֵי הַמִּצְוָה בְּפֶרֶק שְׁמִינִי מְסוֹטָה[13].

וְנוֹהֶגֶת מִצְוָה זוֹ בִּזְכָרִים כִּי לָהֶם לְהִלָּחֵם[14] בִּזְמַן שֶׁיִּשְׂרָאֵל עַל אַדְמָתָן[15].

וְעוֹבֵר עַל זֶה וְהִתְחִיל לַחְשֹׁב וּלְהַרְהֵר וּלְהַבְהִיל עַצְמוֹ בַּמִּלְחָמָה[16] עָבַר עַל לָאו זֶה, וְעָנְשׁוֹ גָּדוֹל מְאֹד כְּמוֹ שֶׁכָּתַבְנוּ[17].

Chinuch concludes:

וְיֶתֶר פְּרָטֵי הַמִּצְוָה בְּפֶרֶק שְׁמִינִי מְסוֹטָה – These, **and the remaining details of the mitzvah,** are discussed **in Chapter Eight of** Tractate ***Sotah.***[13]

Applicability of the Mitzvah

וְנוֹהֶגֶת מִצְוָה זוֹ בִּזְכָרִים – **This mitzvah applies to men,** but not to women, כִּי לָהֶם לְהִלָּחֵם – **since** the duty **to wage war** with Israel's enemies **rests** only **upon [men];**[14] בִּזְמַן שֶׁיִּשְׂרָאֵל עַל אַדְמָתָן – and it applies **during the time when the Jewish people are** settled **upon their land.**[15] וְעוֹבֵר עַל זֶה – **One who transgresses this** mitzvah, וְהִתְחִיל לַחְשֹׁב וּלְהַרְהֵר וּלְהַבְהִיל עַצְמוֹ בַּמִּלְחָמָה – **and begins to think** about the dangers of war, **and** proceeds **to dwell** on these thoughts **and to** thus **unnerve himself during battle,**[16] עָבַר עַל לָאו זֶה – **has violated this mitzvah-prohibition,** וְעָנְשׁוֹ גָּדוֹל מְאֹד כְּמוֹ שֶׁכָּתַבְנוּ – **and his punishment is very severe, as we have written** above.[17]

NOTES

spare the life of Naval (her husband at that time), who had committed a capital crime by delivering an insult to the king. According to *Rashi*, when Avigail said, *and nothing bad shall be found in you,* she meant that it would be a stain on David's record if he killed Naval. *Rambam* (whose words Chinuch quotes here), however, seems to understand this phrase to mean that, in the merit of David "fighting the wars of Hashem" — with all his heart, for the sake of sanctifying the Name of Hashem — he was assured that no harm would befall him. Thus, this passage mentions all the blessings that *Rambam* lists for one who fights with all his heart: a guarantee of safety, an enduring dynasty, and eternal life.

13. The laws are codified in *Rambam, Hil. Melachim* 7:15.

14. Since only men join the fighting, only they are subject to the prohibition against becoming frightened in battle.

As mentioned in the introduction to the mitzvah, there are two categories of wars: מִלְחֶמֶת מִצְוָה, *an obligatory war,* and מִלְחֶמֶת הָרְשׁוּת, *a discretionary war.* Chinuch states in Mitzvah 526 (at note 19) that women do take part in מִלְחֲמוֹת מִצְוָה, *obligatory wars*. *Minchas Chinuch* therefore wonders why the prohibition against being frightened would not apply to them as well. Numerous commentators explain, however, that even in an obligatory war, women do not join the fighting, but perform only rear-echelon duties (see *Radvaz, Hil. Melachim* 7:4; *Rashash, Sotah* 44b). Since this prohibition applies specifically to those whose fear would demoralize the fighting force, it does not apply to women (*Minchas Yitzchak*; *Toafos Re'eim* §432; *Minchah Chareivah, Sotah* 44b ד״ה אפילו).

15. The Jewish people have no army and no authority to wage war when they are not settled in their homeland (see end of Mitzvah 532). [An army existed in the times of Joshua, when they entered the Land in order to conquer it. Presumably, the soldiers of that time were prohibited to be fearful in battle. However, Chinuch refers here to the mitzvah-prohibition as it applies throughout the generations, for only such commandments are counted among the 613 Mitzvos. In this context, the mitzvah applies only when the Jewish people are settled in Eretz Yisrael.]

16. Chinuch indicates that one transgresses this prohibition only if he actively causes himself to be frightened. If, however, he is simply unable to shake his natural fear of war, he is not in violation of this prohibition (*Maharam Schik*; *Birchas Peretz* ibid.; see also *Rambam, Hil. Melachim* 7:15).

Chinuch also implies (here, and at the beginning of the mitzvah) that the prohibition to be frightened applies only during the actual battle. Before the battle begins, it is permissible to be afraid. Thus, before battle the officers warn the soldiers that anyone who is frightened should return home, and those who heed their warning have *not* transgressed this prohibition. It is only those who remain on the battlefield that are subject to the prohibition (*Birchas Peretz* ibid.; *Meshech Chochmah, Deuteronomy* 20:3; see also *Rambam* ibid.; cf. *Ramban,* glosses to *Sefer HaMitzvos, Lo Saaseh* 58; see Mitzvah 526 note 15).

17. That is, he is subject to the curse mentioned in Scripture for "one who carries out the mission of Hashem deceitfully" (see Chinuch above, at note 10).

[There is no *malkus* penalty for this violation, since it does not involve action. Even if one should flee the battlefield he would not incur *malkus*, since the

NOTES

transgression can be committed without action, by simply dwelling on frightening thoughts. Chinuch's position is that when a prohibition *can* be violated without action, it is not subject to *malkus* even when violated through action (see Mitzvah 344, at notes 24-25; Insight B to Mitzvah 11, and Insight to Mitzvah 68).]

❧ Insight: What Type of Fear Does the Torah Prohibit?

As mentioned in the introduction to the mitzvah, while *Rambam* and Chinuch interpret the verse, *You shall not fear them, for HASHEM, your God, is with you,* as a prohibition against being afraid of an enemy army, *Raavad* and *Ramban* understand it as an assurance that we *need* not be afraid of the enemy, for Hashem fights our wars. Accordingly, *Ramban* omits this prohibition from his count of the 613 Mitzvos. [*Ramban* replaces this with another battle-related prohibition, as explained in Mitzvah 526 note 16.]

Minchas Chinuch questions the opinion of *Rambam* and Chinuch who count this verse as a mitzvah-prohibition: We will learn in Mitzvah 526 that the Torah exempts a number of people from fighting in wars, and before the Jewish people engaged in battle, a designated Kohen would announce these exemptions. One of them is (*Deuteronomy* 20:8): מִי הָאִישׁ הַיָּרֵא וְרַךְ הַלֵּבָב יֵלֵךְ וְיָשֹׁב לְבֵיתוֹ וְלֹא יִמַּס אֶת לְבַב אֶחָיו כִּלְבָבוֹ, *Who is the man who is fearful and fainthearted? Let him go and return to his house, and let him not melt the heart of his fellows, like his heart.* The Gemara explains (*Sotah* 44b, according to R' Yose HaGlili) that this verse exempts two types of people who are "fearful": (1) A person who committed sins and is afraid that he may die in battle on account of them; and (2) a person who is simply afraid of war. These exemptions are indicated by the two clauses of the verse. The first clause, מִי הָאִישׁ הַיָּרֵא וְרַךְ הַלֵּבָב יֵלֵךְ וְיָשֹׁב לְבֵיתוֹ, *Who is the man who is fearful and fainthearted? Let him go and return to his house,* refers to a person who is afraid of his sins. The second clause, וְלֹא יִמַּס אֶת לְבַב אֶחָיו כִּלְבָבוֹ, *and let him not melt the heart of his fellows, like his heart,* refers to a person who simply lacks the courage to wage war. Scripture teaches that both of these people are sent home (see Mitzvah 526 note 13).

The Gemara further explains that a person who committed *any* transgression would be sent home "on account of his sins." *Minchas Chinuch* therefore asks: If in fact a person who is afraid of the enemy transgresses a mitzvah-prohibition, why is the second part of the verse needed to exempt the fearful person from battle? He would automatically be sent home on account of having transgressed the prohibition against being afraid! *Minchas Chinuch* sees the necessity for the additional verse as supporting the view of *Ramban* that being afraid to go to war is *not* a transgression.

R' Y. Y. Kanievski (*Bircas Peretz, Parashas Shoftim*) offers several answers to *Minchas Chinuch's* question. First, *Rambam* and Chinuch indicate that the prohibition against being afraid applies only *during* the battle (see note 16). The Kohen's announcement exempting "the man who is fearful and fainthearted," however, is made *before* the battle commences. At that point, a person who is frightened of the enemy has not committed a transgression, so he would not be sent home on account of his sins, but he is sent home on account of his fear.

Second, *Rambam* and Chinuch indicate that one transgresses the prohibition only if he *causes* himself to be frightened by dwelling on thoughts of the enemy's strength and the like (see note 16). One who is naturally afraid of war does not commit any transgression, for the Torah does not demand of a person to be like an angel and squelch his instinctive human fear. Thus, such a person would not be sent home on account of his sins, but he is sent home on account of his natural fear.

Beyond these relatively straightforward answers, however, R' Kanievski notes that we need to explore the meaning of the mitzvah "not to be afraid." Does the Torah mean to command the warriors to *have faith* (*bitachon*) that Hashem will spare them from any harm, meaning that they must internalize the conviction that there is *nothing to fear*? Or, does it mean to command them to fight *without concern* for their own well-being, meaning that they must be willing to fearlessly *sacrifice their lives* for the sake of Hashem's honor? [Chinuch actually mentions both of these points in his description of the underlying purpose of this mitzvah. He states that every Jewish person (1) should place his trust solely in Hashem; and (2) should not be concerned about his physical safety in a situation where he is able to give honor to Hashem. Evidently, the mitzvah requires a person not only to have faith in Hashem, but also to be prepared to sacrifice his life. But are these two ideas not contradictory? If one has faith that Hashem will save him, why need he be ready to

sacrifice his life? And if he is ready to sacrifice his life, is this not a contradiction to having faith in Hashem?]

R' Kanievski explains as follows: War is inherently dangerous, and one who goes out to battle must certainly recognize that he is endangering his life; that is what war is about — one fights to kill or be killed. The Torah acknowledges this danger, when it states that before the army advanced against the enemy, the designated Kohen would tell the troops, *Who is the man who has built a new house and has not inaugurated it? Let him go and return to his house, lest he die in the war and another man will inaugurate it* (*Deuteronomy* 20:5; see next mitzvah). It is natural for a person to be afraid of the inherent danger of war, and a person who experiences this fear does not commit any transgression. What the Torah prohibits in this mitzvah is for a person who is not naturally unnerved by war to become frightened by the apparent superiority of an enemy army. In this vein, it states (ibid. v. 1): *If you go out to battle against your enemy and you see horse and chariot — a people more numerous than you — you shall not fear them, for HASHEM, your God, is with you, Who brought you up from the land of Egypt.* The Torah demands that a soldier have faith in Hashem and recognize that the size or strength of the enemy force will not determine who wins the war, nor who lives and who dies. Hashem fights our wars, and He alone determines the outcome.

Thus, the mission of war requires that a soldier be prepared to die in battle; one who is not ready to fight to the end even if it means dying is guilty of "*carrying out the mission of HASHEM deceitfully.*" At the same time, this mitzvah-prohibition requires that a person have faith in Hashem, and not be deterred from fighting bravely by the superficial impression that the enemy is stronger. As the Mishnah (*Sotah* 42a) states in discussing this idea: *They come with the strength of flesh and blood, but you come with the strength of the Omnipresent!*

It emerges that there are two different types of fear, one that is permitted and one that is prohibited. To be afraid of the inherent dangers of war is natural for many people, and does not indicate a lack of faith in Hashem; such fear is not prohibited. A person who experiences such fear is still sent home from the battlefield, so that he should *not melt the heart of his fellows like his heart.* On the other hand, to be frightened by the size and power of the enemy army indicates that one does not fully recognize the truth that *HASHEM, your God, is with you.* This is the fear that our mitzvah prohibits. It is thus understandable that, although a person who committed any sin was exempted from war by the verse, *Who is the man who is fearful and fainthearted,* the Torah needed to add the clause, *and let him not melt the heart of his fellows like his heart,* to exempt a person who had a natural fear of warfare (*Bircas Peretz*; for another explanation, see *Chidushei HaGriz* stencil to *I Samuel* 25:28).

Interestingly, *Rabbeinu Yonah* (*Shaarei Teshuvah* 3:31) sees in the verse, *you shall not fear them, for HASHEM, your God, is with you,* a general prohibition for a person to let himself be overcome by fear in *any* situation of danger. The verse calls for a person to place his trust in Hashem and have faith in His salvation, knowing that He can save him from any perilous situation, no matter how hopeless it may seem. In other words, this prohibition requires us to gird ourselves with *bitachon* in Hashem when faced with any form of danger, even if it seems inescapable by natural means (see *Maharam Schik* here).

מִצְוָה תקכו: מִצְוָה לִמְשֹׁחַ כֹּהֵן לְמִלְחָמָה[1,2]

שֶׁנִּצְטַוִּינוּ לִמְשֹׁחַ כֹּהֵן אֶחָד בְּשֶׁמֶן הַמִּשְׁחָה[3] וּלְמַנּוֹתוֹ לִהְיוֹת מְדַבֵּר עִם הָעָם בִּשְׁעַת מִלְחָמָה, וְזֶה הַכֹּהֵן נִקְרָא מְשׁוּחַ מִלְחָמָה[4].

Mitzvah 526

The Obligation to Anoint a Kohen for Battle

וְהָיָה כְּקָרָבְכֶם אֶל הַמִּלְחָמָה וְנִגַּשׁ הַכֹּהֵן וְדִבֶּר אֶל הָעָם. וְאָמַר אֲלֵהֶם שְׁמַע יִשְׂרָאֵל אַתֶּם קְרֵבִים הַיּוֹם לַמִּלְחָמָה עַל אֹיְבֵיכֶם אַל יֵרַךְ לְבַבְכֶם אַל תִּירְאוּ וְאַל תַּחְפְּזוּ וְאַל תַּעַרְצוּ מִפְּנֵיהֶם. כִּי ה' אֱלֹהֵיכֶם הַהֹלֵךְ עִמָּכֶם לְהִלָּחֵם לָכֶם עִם אֹיְבֵיכֶם לְהוֹשִׁיעַ אֶתְכֶם

It shall be that when you draw near to the battle, the Kohen shall approach and speak to the people. He shall say to them, "Hear O Israel, you are coming near to the battle against your enemies; let your heart not be faint, do not be afraid, do not panic, and do not tremble before them. For HASHEM, your God, is the One Who goes with you, to fight for you with your enemies, to save you" (*Deuteronomy* 20:2-4).

When the Torah states that "*the* Kohen" shall approach and speak to the people, it refers to a specific Kohen who has been designated for this purpose. This indicates that the community is required to appoint a Kohen who will carry out the duty of inspiring the army to fight courageously.[1] The designated Kohen is called מְשׁוּחַ מִלְחָמָה, *The Anointed for Battle.* This mitzvah-obligation, which requires us to appoint such a Kohen, complements the previous mitzvah-prohibition, which forbids the soldiers from being fearful and cowardly in battle.[2]

In subsequent verses in the passage, Scripture teaches that in addition to encouraging the troops to fight courageously, the Kohen would announce a number of exemptions from battle, and would order anyone who had such an exemption to turn back from the field. Chinuch lists these exemptions below, and explains that they all refer to people who might be distracted from the mission of war due to events in their private lives, and not fight with all their might. Thus, the task of the Kohen Anointed for Battle was to take the various steps necessary to ensure that every soldier in Hashem's army would fight bravely and vigorously in defense of His honor (see *Rambam, Sefer HaMitzvos, Asei* 191).

שֶׁנִּצְטַוִּינוּ לִמְשֹׁחַ כֹּהֵן אֶחָד בְּשֶׁמֶן הַמִּשְׁחָה – We are commanded to anoint one Kohen with the sacred **anointing oil,**[3] **וּלְמַנּוֹתוֹ לִהְיוֹת מְדַבֵּר עִם הָעָם בִּשְׁעַת מִלְחָמָה – and to appoint him to speak to the people at the time of battle. וְזֶה הַכֹּהֵן נִקְרָא מְשׁוּחַ מִלְחָמָה – This Kohen is called "The Anointed for Battle."**[4]

NOTES

1. See *Sotah* 42a, where the Gemara proves through Scriptural exegesis that this is in fact an obligation.

2. The Mishnah (*Sotah* 42a) explains that the four expressions in the verse, *let your heart not be faint, do not be afraid, do not panic, and do not tremble before them,* correspond to four tactics that armies would employ in order to psychologically weaken the opposing troops. They would clash shields, blow trumpets, shout, and stamp their horses' hooves. The Kohen admonished the Jewish troops not to be cowed by any of these tactics.

3. We learned in Mitzvah 107 that Moses was commanded to prepare a special mixture of oil known as *shemen hamishchah,* "anointing oil," for the purpose of anointing kings and Kohanim Gedolim. This oil was also used to anoint the "Kohen Anointed for Battle" (see *Sotah* 42a and *Kesef Mishneh, Hil. Klei HaMikdash* 1:7; see also Mitzvah 108, at note 17).

[*Minchas Chinuch* (107:7) maintains that the anointment is essential to the designation of this Kohen. As such, during the Second Temple Era, when there was no *shemen hamishchah* (*Yoma* 52b, *Horayos* 11b-12a), the position of "Anointed for Battle" did not exist (see *Tos. Yeshanim, Yoma* 39a). However, *Dvar Avraham* (Vol. II, 22:2) maintains that anointment is part of the mitzvah of designating such a Kohen, but is not essential; a Kohen could be appointed to this position even without being anointed.]

4. Chinuch, following *Rambam* (*Sefer HaMitzvos, Asei* 191; *Hil. Melachim* 7:1), does not mention any duty of the Anointed Kohen other than to speak to the soldiers

וּמִן הַמִּצְוָה זוֹ שֶׁיֹּאמַר הַכֹּהֵן הַמָּשׁוּחַ אֶל הָעָם בִּשְׁעַת הַמִּלְחָמָה שְׁלֹשָׁה כְּתוּבִים הַנִּזְכָּרִים בַּתּוֹרָה (דברים כ׳, ה׳-ז׳), מִי הָאִישׁ וְגוֹ׳[5] וּמִי הָאִישׁ וְגוֹ׳[6] וּמִי הָאִישׁ וְגוֹ׳[7], וְיוֹסִף עוֹד מִשֶּׁלּוֹ דְּבָרִים אֲחֵרִים[8] יְעוֹרְרוּ בְּנֵי אָדָם לְמִלְחָמָה וְיִשָּׂאוּם לְסַכֵּן בְּנַפְשָׁם לַעֲזוֹר דַּת הָאֵל וּלְשָׁמְרָהּ וּלְהִנָּקֵם מֵהַסְּכָלִים הַמַּפְסִידִים סִדְרֵי הַמְּדִינוֹת[9].

In the verses cited above, Scripture states explicitly that the Kohen Anointed for Battle urges the people not to be afraid of the enemy. Chinuch explains that he must deliver additional messages:

וּמִן הַמִּצְוָה זוֹ – **This mitzvah includes** the requirement שֶׁיֹּאמַר הַכֹּהֵן הַמָּשׁוּחַ אֶל הָעָם בִּשְׁעַת הַמִּלְחָמָה – **that,** in addition to exhorting them not to be afraid, **the Kohen Anointed** for Battle **shall say to the people at the time of battle** שְׁלֹשָׁה כְּתוּבִים הַנִּזְכָּרִים בַּתּוֹרָה – the following **three verses that are mentioned in the Torah** in this context (*Deuteronomy* 20:5-7): "מִי הָאִישׁ וְגוֹ׳" – (1) ***Who is the man*** *who has built a new house and has not inaugurated it? Let him go and return to his house, lest he die in the war and another man will inaugurate it.*[5] וּמִי הָאִישׁ וְגוֹ׳ – (2) ***And who is the man*** *who has planted a vineyard and not redeemed it? Let him go and return to his house, lest he die in the war, and another man will redeem it.*[6] "וּמִי הָאִישׁ וְגוֹ׳" – (3) ***And who is the man*** *who has betrothed a woman and not married her? Let him go and return to his house, lest he die in the war and another man will marry her.*[7]

וְיוֹסִף עוֹד מִשֶּׁלּוֹ דְּבָרִים אֲחֵרִים – After reciting these verses, **[the Anointed Kohen] adds other words of his own,**[8] יְעוֹרְרוּ בְּנֵי אָדָם לְמִלְחָמָה – choosing words **that motivate people to battle** courageously, וְיִשָּׂאוּם לְסַכֵּן בְּנַפְשָׁם – **and** that **inspire them to place themselves in danger** לַעֲזוֹר דַּת הָאֵל וּלְשָׁמְרָהּ – in order **to help** defend **the Law of the Almighty and preserve it,** וּלְהִנָּקֵם מֵהַסְּכָלִים הַמַּפְסִידִים סִדְרֵי הַמְּדִינוֹת – **and to take revenge from the fools who disrupt the** preordained **order of the countries** of the world.[9]

Chinuch stated that the Kohen Anointed for Battle recites the three verses that set out exemptions

NOTES

before battle. Others maintain that the Anointed Kohen actually directed the war (*Rosh Commentary, Nazir,* end of 47b; *Aruch HaShulchan HeAsid, Hil. Melachim* 76:1, based on *Rashi, Yoma* 73b ד״ה וכל בני ישראל אתו; see *Parashas Derachim* §11 ד״ה מעתה). [Chinuch at the end of Mitzvah 527 (at note 21) implies that the king or other leaders directed the war.]

5. This exemption includes one who purchases a house or receives it as a gift or an inheritance (*Sotah* 43a; *Rambam, Hil. Melachim* 7:5).

Yerushalmi (*Sotah* 8:4) states that the exemption applies only to one who built (or acquired) a house that it is a mitzvah to inaugurate, i.e., a house in Eretz Yisrael, whose construction is a fulfillment of the mitzvah to settle Eretz Yisrael (*Korban HaEidah* and *Pnei Moshe* ad loc.). A house built outside of Eretz Yisrael does not generate an exemption (*Rambam* ibid. 7:14). [Based on this, *Minchas Chinuch* (§5) notes that there is no mitzvah to celebrate the inauguration of a new house built outside of Eretz Yisrael.]

6. The fruit produced by a newly planted tree or grapevine in its first three years is prohibited for benefit under the prohibition of *orlah* (Mitzvah 246; *Leviticus* 19:23). The fruit of the fourth year must either be taken to Jerusalem and eaten there, or redeemed for money that is taken to Jerusalem and used to buy food that is eaten there; this produce is known as *revai* (Mitzvah 247; ibid. v. 24). When the verse speaks of one who has not "redeemed" his vineyard, it refers to one who has not yet harvested and redeemed (or taken to Jerusalem) the produce of the fourth year. Thus, he has not yet had the opportunity to eat the first permissible crop of his vineyard (*Rashi* to the verse; see Chinuch below, after note 11; cf. *Ibn Ezra* and *Ramban* to the verse).

[This exemption is not limited to one who planted a vineyard, but includes one who planted an orchard of any other fruit tree and has not yet been able to eat of its produce (*Minchas Chinuch* §6, from *Sotah* 43b; see there for further details). Like the previous exemption, it applies only to one who planted a vineyard or orchard in Eretz Yisrael (*Rambam* ibid.).]

7. Marriage is accomplished in two stages, *erusin* and *nisuin.* To effect *erusin* ("betrothal"), the husband gives the wife an object of value, such as a ring, in the presence of witnesses; from that point, they are legally married, but certain privileges and responsibilities of marriage are not yet in effect. To effect *nisuin,* the husband formally brings the wife into his domain, usually in the *chuppah* ceremony; at that point, the marriage is completed. Our verse refers to a man who has performed *erusin* but not *nisuin,* and it exempts him from participating in battle.

8. He adds his own words of encouragement to the verses that he is mandated to recite. See Insight for discussion.

9. [Since the purpose of Israel's wars, whether offensive or defensive in nature, is to preserve God's Will, those who fight against them seek, in essence, to upset the order that God has decreed for His world.]

וְכֵן אָמְרוּ זִכְרוֹנָם לִבְרָכָה בְּמַסֶּכֶת סוֹטָה (מ״ג ע״א) וְדִבְּרוּ הַשּׁוֹטְרִים, כֹּהֵן מְדַבֵּר וְשׁוֹטֵר מַשְׁמִיעַ.[10]

שֹׁרֶשׁ מִצְוָה זוֹ יָדוּעַ, כִּי בִּשְׁעַת מִלְחָמָה צְרִיכִים אַנְשֵׁי הַמִּלְחָמָה חִזּוּק, וּמִפְּנֵי שֶׁהָאָדָם נִשְׁמָע יוֹתֵר כְּשֶׁהוּא נִכְבָּד, צִוְּתָה הַתּוֹרָה לִהְיוֹת הַמְּמֻנֶּה לְחַזֵּק בִּדְבָרִים טוֹבִים מִן הַכֹּהֲנִים שֶׁהֵם מִבְחַר הָעָם.[11] וְהָעִנְיָן לִהְיוֹת מַחֲזִירִין מִן הַמִּלְחָמָה מִי שֶׁנָּטַע כֶּרֶם וְלֹא אָכַל מִמֶּנּוּ אוֹ אֵרַשׂ אִשָּׁה וְלֹא לְקָחָהּ אוֹ בָּנָה בַּיִת וְלֹא שָׁכַן בּוֹ[12] וְכֵן הַיָּרֵא מֵעֲבֵרוֹת שֶׁבְּיָדוֹ[13],

---

for the man who built a new house, planted a vineyard, or betrothed a woman. A simple reading of the Scriptural passage, however, indicates that this is not part of the Kohen's duty, for Scripture states (ibid. v. 5): *Then the* officers *shall speak to the people, saying, "Who is the man who has built a new house,* etc." Chinuch addresses this point:

וְכֵן אָמְרוּ זִכְרוֹנָם לִבְרָכָה בְּמַסֶּכֶת סוֹטָה – **And so have [the Sages], of blessed memory, stated in Tractate** ***Sotah*** (43a): "וְדִבְּרוּ הַשּׁוֹטְרִים" – When Scripture states, ***Then the officers shall speak*** *to the people,* etc., כֹּהֵן מְדַבֵּר וְשׁוֹטֵר מַשְׁמִיעַ – this means that **the Kohen** Anointed for Battle **speaks** these words initially, **and the officers** repeat them aloud, to **make them heard** by the people.[10]

Underlying Purpose of the Mitzvah

שֹׁרֶשׁ מִצְוָה זוֹ יָדוּעַ – **The underlying purpose of this mitzvah is** well **known:** כִּי בִּשְׁעַת מִלְחָמָה צְרִיכִים אַנְשֵׁי הַמִּלְחָמָה חִזּוּק – It is **because at a time of battle, the soldiers need encouragement,** וּמִפְּנֵי שֶׁהָאָדָם נִשְׁמָע יוֹתֵר כְּשֶׁהוּא נִכְבָּד – **and since** a message delivered by **a prominent person is more** likely to be **heeded,** צִוְּתָה הַתּוֹרָה לִהְיוֹת הַמְּמֻנֶּה לְחַזֵּק בִּדְבָרִים טוֹבִים – **the Torah commands that the one appointed to encourage** the troops **with positive words should be** מִן הַכֹּהֲנִים שֶׁהֵם מִבְחַר הָעָם – one **of the Kohanim, who are the choicest of the nation** and the most respected among them.[11]

Chinuch examines the Torah's rationale for exempting certain groups of people from fighting:

וְהָעִנְיָן לִהְיוֹת מַחֲזִירִין מִן הַמִּלְחָמָה – **As for the idea that we are** commanded **to send back from the** field of **battle** מִי שֶׁנָּטַע כֶּרֶם וְלֹא אָכַל מִמֶּנּוּ – **anyone who has planted a vineyard but not** yet **eaten from it,** אוֹ אֵרַשׂ אִשָּׁה וְלֹא לְקָחָהּ – **or who has betrothed a woman but not** yet fully **married her,** אוֹ בָּנָה בַּיִת וְלֹא שָׁכַן בּוֹ – **or who has built a** new **house but not** yet **lived in it,**[12] וְכֵן הַיָּרֵא מֵעֲבֵרוֹת שֶׁבְּיָדוֹ – **as well as one who is fearful of sins that he has committed,**[13]

NOTES

10. All these verses are recited by the Kohen. However, he does not need to shout and make himself heard by the entire army. Rather, he recites the verses to the officers around him, and they in turn announce the verses for all to hear.

Rambam (ibid. 7:2-3; based on *Sotah* 42a-b) explains that the Kohen Anointed for Battle actually addresses the army on two occasions, first when the troops are massed at the border of Eretz Yisrael, and again when they reach the battlefield. At the border, he recites only the three verses of exemption that Chinuch cited. The entire army (including those who were exempted) then proceeds to the battlefield, and when they reach there, the Kohen begins his second speech with words of encouragement. He recites the verses that precede the three verses of exemption (ibid. vv. 3-4): *Hear O Israel, you are coming near to the battle against your enemies; let your heart not be faint, do not be afraid, do not panic, and do not tremble before them. For* HASHEM, *your God, is the One Who goes with you, to fight for you with your enemies, to save you.* He then continues with the three verses of exemption that he had previously recited at the border. Everything he says is repeated aloud for all to hear. Afterward, an officer of the army announces a fourth exemption (contained in v. 8): *Who is the man who is fearful and fainthearted? Let him go and return to his house, and let him not melt the heart of his fellows like his heart.* Other officers repeat this verse aloud, and at this point all those who have been exempted return home (see *Kesef Mishneh* ad loc.). [For a somewhat different understanding of the procedure, see *Rashi, Sotah* 42b ד״ה שמעו and 43a ד״ה ואלו שאין זזין.]

11. In fact, the Kohen who is designated as "The Anointed for Battle" becomes elevated over the other Kohanim and, in certain respects, attains a status similar to that of the Kohen Gadol. [See *Horayos* 12b and *Yoma* 72b-73a; *Rambam, Hil. Klei HaMikdash* 4:19; see also Mitzvah 108 note 17.]

12. See above, notes 5-7.

13. This is one interpretation of the phrase (ibid. v. 8),

גַּם זֶה הַדָּבָר רָאוּי וְכָשֵׁר, כִּי כָּל אֵלּוּ בְּנֵי אָדָם חֲלוּשִׁים מְאֹד מִבּוֹא בְּמִלְחָמָה, כִּי מַחֲשַׁבְתָּם נִתְפֶּסֶת הַרְבֵּה עַל הַדְּבָרִים הַנִּזְכָּרִים בַּכָּתוּב[14], וְאֵלּוּ יָנִיאוּ לֵב חַבְרֵיהֶם, וּכְעִנְיָן שֶׁכָּתוּב בְּפֵרוּשׁ וְלֹא יִמַּס אֶת לְבַב אֶחָיו[15], וְכֵן הַיָּרֵא מֵעֲבֵרוֹת שֶׁבְּיָדוֹ רָאוּי לְהַחֲזִירוֹ פֶּן יִסָּפוּ אֲחֵרִים בַּעֲוֹנוֹ[16], וְכָל דַּרְכֵי הַתּוֹרָה יֹשֶׁר וֶאֱמוּנָה[17].

גַּם זֶה הַדָּבָר רָאוּי וְכָשֵׁר – this too is an appropriate and correct thing. **כִּי כָּל אֵלּוּ בְּנֵי אָדָם חֲלוּשִׁים מְאֹד מִבּוֹא בְּמִלְחָמָה** – We send back the one who planted a vineyard, betrothed a woman, or built a new house **because all these people are much too weak** of heart **to** effectively **engage in battle,** **כִּי מַחֲשַׁבְתָּם נִתְפֶּסֶת הַרְבֵּה עַל הַדְּבָרִים הַנִּזְכָּרִים בַּכָּתוּב – since their thoughts are heavily focused on the things** that are **mentioned in the verse** (i.e., their new vineyard, wife, or house), and this distracts them from the battle at hand.[14] **וְאֵלּוּ יָנִיאוּ לֵב חַבְרֵיהֶם – These** people will thus **dissuade the hearts of their fellows** from fighting if they remain on the battlefield. **וּכְעִנְיָן שֶׁכָּתוּב בְּפֵרוּשׁ** – This is **along the lines of what is written explicitly** regarding a person who is fearful and fainthearted (ibid. v. 8): **"וְלֹא יִמַּס אֶת לְבַב אֶחָיו"** – *Let him go and return to his house,* ***and let him not melt the heart of his fellows*** *like his heart.*[15] **וְכֵן הַיָּרֵא מֵעֲבֵרוֹת שֶׁבְּיָדוֹ רָאוּי לְהַחֲזִירוֹ – It is similarly appropriate to send back one who is fearful of sins that he has committed,** **פֶּן יִסָּפוּ אֲחֵרִים בַּעֲוֹנוֹ – lest others be swept away on account of his sins.**[16] **וְכָל דַּרְכֵי הַתּוֹרָה יֹשֶׁר וֶאֱמוּנָה – Thus, all the ways of the Torah are just and true.**[17]

NOTES

מִי הָאִישׁ הַיָּרֵא וְרַךְ הַלֵּבָב, *Who is the man who is fearful and fainthearted?* (see above, end of note 10). In Mitzvah 525 (at note 9), Chinuch cited another interpretation, that the verse refers literally to a person who is afraid of war. Both interpretations are correct, as they emerge from different parts of the verse, as explained in the Insight to Mitzvah 525.

[In adopting both interpretations of "fearful and fainthearted" as halachah, Chinuch follows the opinion of R' Yose HaGlili in the Mishnah (*Sotah* 44a). This opinion is disputed by R' Akiva, who understands the verse as exempting *only* a man who literally is afraid of war. *Rambam* (*Hil. Melachim* 7:15) rules in accordance with R' Akiva, that the verse refers only to a person who is afraid of war (see *Kesef Mishneh* there and *Lechem Mishneh* 7:7). *Minchas Chinuch* (§4) wonders why Chinuch deviates here from *Rambam's* opinion, which he generally follows. However, *Meiri* (*Sotah* 44a) also disagrees with *Rambam* in this case and rules in accordance with R' Yose HaGlili.]

14. *Rabbeinu Bachya* (*Deuteronomy* 20:9) explains that a vineyard [i.e., a source of income], a wife, and a house represent the most fundamental desires of every man. Those preoccupied with such deep-seated needs are unable to give their fullest attention to battle. They thus constitute a danger to their fellows, as Chinuch proceeds to explain.

15. While this verse is written regarding the man who is fearful, Chinuch sees it as a reason for all the exemptions.

According to *Ramban* (glosses to *Sefer HaMitzvos, Prohibitions Omitted by Rambam* §10; see also commentary to *Deuteronomy* 20:8), the verse, *and let him not melt the heart of his fellows like his heart,* constitutes a mitzvah-*prohibition* for a person who is weak-hearted to remain on the field of battle. *Minchas Chinuch* (§8) expresses uncertainty as to whether the other three types of people who are exempt are also prohibited to remain on the battlefield if they desire. However, based on Chinuch's reasoning that they are sent home because they might weaken the other soldiers, it would seem that they, too, are *required* to turn back. See also *Rashi, Deuteronomy* 20:7, cited by *Minchas Chinuch*.

16. I.e., lest his sins cause God to remove His protection from the army that includes him in its ranks.

17. Chinuch seems to be hinting to the following: One might think it is unfair to allow people who have been blessed with a new vineyard, wife, or house, as well as those who have committed sins, to return home, while others who did not merit these blessings and are virtuous must go to war. According to what Chinuch has explained, however, this is not unfair at all. To the contrary, these people are sent home for the benefit of the entire army, which will now be able to fight courageously and will be blessed with Hashem's protection.

It is of note that, although Scripture states that each of these people should return "to his house," they actually were required to participate in the war effort by performing rear-echelon duties, such as repairing the roads and supplying the army with food (Mishnah, *Sotah* 43a; see Gemara there, 44a, for the Scriptural source of this law). [Thus, they were merely sent back from the danger zone, so that they should be assured of *eventually* returning home. Certain other groups, however, were entirely exempt, as stated there in *Sotah*.]

מִדִּינֵי[19,18] **הַמִּצְוָה מַה שֶּׁאָמְרוּ זִכְרוֹנָם לִבְרָכָה** (שם מ"ד ע"ב) **שֶׁאֵין מַחֲזִירִין מֵעוֹרְכֵי הַמִּלְחָמָה אֵלּוּ הַנִּזְכָּרִים בַּכָּתוּב אֶלָּא בְּמִלְחֶמֶת הָרְשׁוּת, אֲבָל בְּמִלְחֶמֶת מִצְוָה הַכֹּל יוֹצְאִין אֲפִלּוּ חָתָן מֵחֶדְרוֹ וְכַלָּה מֵחֻפָּתָהּ**[20]**, וּמַה שֶּׁאָמְרוּ שֶׁאַחַר שֶׁחָזְרוּ בְּמִלְחֶמֶת הָרְשׁוּת כָּל הַחוֹזְרִים, שֶׁהַנִּשְׁאָרִים מְתַקְּנִין אֶת הַמַּעֲרָכוֹת וּפוֹקְדִין שָׂרֵי צְבָאוֹת בְּרֹאשׁ הָעָם**[21]**,**

Laws of the Mitzvah

In discussing when the Jewish people are authorized to wage war, the Mishnah (*Sotah* 44b) identifies two categories of war: מִלְחֶמֶת מִצְוָה, *an obligatory war,* and מִלְחֶמֶת הָרְשׁוּת, *a discretionary war.* An obligatory war is one that the Torah mandates; this includes the original war that Joshua waged in order to conquer the Land of Israel from the seven Canaanite nations, wars against Amalek (see Mitzvah 604), and defensive wars (see Mitzvah 425).[18] A discretionary war is one that the king, sanctioned by the Great Sanhedrin, decides to wage in order to destroy neighboring enemies and preempt their aggression, and to expand the borders of Eretz Yisrael (see *Sotah* ibid. and *Rambam, Hil. Melachim* 5:1-2 with *Lechem Mishneh*).[19] Chinuch discusses which of these wars is subject to the exemptions from battle that are set forth above:

מִדִּינֵי הַמִּצְוָה – Among the laws of the mitzvah is **מַה שֶּׁאָמְרוּ זִכְרוֹנָם לִבְרָכָה – that which [the Sages], of blessed memory, stated** (*Sotah* 44b; *Rambam* ibid. 7:4), **שֶׁאֵין מַחֲזִירִין מֵעוֹרְכֵי הַמִּלְחָמָה אֵלּוּ הַנִּזְכָּרִים בַּכָּתוּב אֶלָּא בְּמִלְחֶמֶת הָרְשׁוּת – that these** people **who are mentioned in Scripture are sent back from the legions of battle only in** the case of **a discretionary war, אֲבָל בְּמִלְחֶמֶת מִצְוָה הַכֹּל יוֹצְאִין – but in** the case of **an obligatory war, everyone goes out** to battle, **אֲפִלּוּ חָתָן מֵחֶדְרוֹ וְכַלָּה מֵחֻפָּתָהּ – even a bridegroom from his chamber and a bride from her *chuppah*.**[20]

Chinuch describes what took place on the battlefield after the exempted people were sent back, including steps taken to prevent any of the remaining soldiers from retreating in panic:

וּמַה שֶּׁאָמְרוּ – Another law is **that which [the Sages] stated** (*Sotah* 44a; *Rambam* ibid.), **שֶׁאַחַר שֶׁחָזְרוּ בְּמִלְחֶמֶת הָרְשׁוּת כָּל הַחוֹזְרִים – that after all those who were exempt from** fighting in Israel's **discretionary wars turned back, שֶׁהַנִּשְׁאָרִים מְתַקְּנִין אֶת הַמַּעֲרָכוֹת – those who remained** at the battlefield **were organized into regiments, וּפוֹקְדִין שָׂרֵי צְבָאוֹת בְּרֹאשׁ הָעָם – and military officers were appointed** to stand **at the head of the people** in those regiments.[21]

NOTES

18. Chinuch states in Mitzvah 425 (at note 16) that a defensive war fought against an invading army is considered a מִלְחֶמֶת מִצְוָה, *obligatory war* (or, *war of mitzvah*). For discussion, see *Minchas Yitzchak* 527:4.

19. Some of the wars that King David fought were in the latter category, such as when he conquered *Aram Tzovah* and annexed it to Eretz Yisrael (see *II Samuel* Ch. 10; *Sotah* 44b with *Rashi* ד"ה ומלחמת בית דוד).

20. This is not to say that a bride goes out to fight, for women do not join in battle (see end of Mitzvah 525). Rather, they perform rear-echelon duties, such as supplying the troops with food and drink (see Mitzvah 525 note 14).

The distinction between these two types of wars is derived from Scripture. The passage that teaches the various exemptions begins (*Deuteronomy* 20:1): כִּי תֵצֵא לַמִּלְחָמָה עַל אֹיְבֶךָ, *If you go out to battle against your enemy.* The expression "*If* you go out" implies that we are speaking about a discretionary war. The exemptions are stated only regarding this case, not regarding an obligatory war (*Sifrei* to *Deuteronomy* ibid., as explained by *Malbim* there; *Rashi, Sotah* 35b ד"ה ה"ג ושבית שביו; cf. *Emek HaNetziv* and *Sifrei DeVei Rav* to *Sifrei*). [Most authorities understand this to mean that *none* of the exemptions applies to an obligatory war (see *Raavad* and *Lechem Mishneh, Hil. Melachim* 7:1). Some suggest, however, that the exemption of the person who is afraid of his sins applies in all cases, since his involvement would serve only to endanger the lives of his fellows (*Minchah Chareivah, Sotah* 44b).]

Rambam (*Hil. Melachim* 7:1) states that even in the case of an obligatory war, there was a requirement to designate a Kohen Anointed for Battle. Commentators explain that although in that case the Kohen did not announce any exemptions, he did deliver words of encouragement to the soldiers so that they not be afraid (see *Raavad, Kesef Mishneh,* and *Lechem Mishneh* ad loc.). [In *Sefer HaMitzvos* (*Asei* 191), however, *Rambam* states that in an obligatory war there was no speech delivered at all, neither words of encouragement nor an announcement of exemptions.]

21. These officers were mighty warriors whose duty was to uplift and encourage anyone who faltered during the battle, and to inspire the entire army to fight with valor (*Rashi, Sotah* 44a ד"ה מעמידין זקיפין מלפניהם).

וּמַעֲמִידִין מֵאֲחוֹרֵי כָּל מַעֲרָכָה שׁוֹטְרִים חֲזָקִים וּכַשִּׁילִין שֶׁל בַּרְזֶל בִּידֵיהֶם, וְכָל הַמְבַקֵּשׁ לַחֲזוֹר מִן הַמִּלְחָמָה הָרְשׁוּת בְּיָדָם לַחְתֹּךְ אֶת שׁוֹקָיו מִפְּנֵי שֶׁתְּחִלַּת נְפִילָה נִיסָה[22]. וְיֶתֶר פְּרָטֶיהָ מְבֹאָרִים בְּמַסֶּכֶת סוֹטָה (פרק שמיני)[23].

וְנוֹהֶגֶת מִצְוָה זוֹ בִּזְכָרִים[24] בִּזְמַן שֶׁאֶרֶץ יִשְׂרָאֵל בִּישׁוּבָהּ[25], וְזוֹ מִן הַמִּצְוֹת הַמֻּטָּלוֹת עַל הַצִּבּוּר כֻּלָּם[26].

וְאִם עָבְרוּ הָעָם עַל זֶה שֶׁלֹּא מִנּוּ בֵּינֵיהֶם כֹּהֵן מָשִׁיחַ עַל הָעִנְיָן שֶׁזָּכַרְנוּ וְלֹא דִבֵּר אֶל הָעָם הַדְּבָרִים הַנִּזְכָּרִים בַּכָּתוּב, בִּטְּלוּ עֲשֵׂה זֶה[27].

וּמַעֲמִידִין מֵאֲחוֹרֵי כָּל מַעֲרָכָה שׁוֹטְרִים חֲזָקִים – Also, strong guards were stationed at the rear of each regiment **וּכַשִּׁילִין שֶׁל בַּרְזֶל בִּידֵיהֶם – with iron axes in their hands,** **וְכָל הַמְבַקֵּשׁ לַחֲזוֹר מִן הַמִּלְחָמָה – and** if **anyone would try to turn back** and flee **from the battle,** **הָרְשׁוּת בְּיָדָם לַחְתֹּךְ אֶת שׁוֹקָיו – [these guards] were authorized to sever his legs;** **מִפְּנֵי שֶׁתְּחִלַּת נְפִילָה נִיסָה – for the beginning of** an army's **downfall is** her soldiers' **flight.**[22]

וְיֶתֶר פְּרָטֶיהָ מְבֹאָרִים בְּמַסֶּכֶת סוֹטָה – These, **and the remaining details of [the mitzvah], are explained in Tractate *Sotah*** (Ch. 8).[23]

Applicability of the Mitzvah

וְנוֹהֶגֶת מִצְוָה זוֹ בִּזְכָרִים – This mitzvah applies only **to men,**[24] **בִּזְמַן שֶׁאֶרֶץ יִשְׂרָאֵל בִּישׁוּבָהּ** – and only **when Eretz Yisrael is in its settled state.**[25] **וְזוֹ מִן הַמִּצְוֹת הַמֻּטָּלוֹת עַל הַצִּבּוּר כֻּלָּם** – In addition, **this is** one **of the mitzvos that are incumbent upon the entire community** of Israel.[26]

וְאִם עָבְרוּ הָעָם עַל זֶה – If the people of Israel **transgress this** mitzvah, **שֶׁלֹּא מִנּוּ בֵּינֵיהֶם כֹּהֵן מָשִׁיחַ עַל הָעִנְיָן שֶׁזָּכַרְנוּ – and they do not appoint among themselves a Kohen who is anointed for the purpose that we have mentioned,** **וְלֹא דִבֵּר אֶל הָעָם הַדְּבָרִים הַנִּזְכָּרִים בַּכָּתוּב** – **so** that **[no Kohen] says to the people** before battle **the things that are mentioned in Scripture,** **בִּטְּלוּ עֲשֵׂה זֶה – they have violated this mitzvah-obligation.**[27]

NOTES

22. The disorderly flight of a few soldiers can cause a whole army to collapse. Since a soldier who flees endangers the entire army, he is in the category of a רוֹדֵף, *rodeif* (pursuer), i.e., one whose actions threaten another with mortal danger. Since a *rodeif* may be injured (or even killed) in order to save the lives of his potential victims (see Mitzvos 600-601; *Sanhedrin* 72a-73a), the guards are authorized to smite those who attempt to flee (*Meromei Sadeh* to *Sotah* 44a; *Meshech Chochmah* to *Deuteronomy* 20:3).

23. The laws are codified in *Rambam, Hil. Melachim* Ch. 7.

24. Since women do not go out to battle, as Chinuch stated at the end of Mitzvah 525.

25. See Mitzvah 525 note 15.

26. The nation as a whole bears responsibility to ensure that a Kohen is anointed for the purpose of battle. [Chinuch seems to hold that the appointing of a specific Kohen for this purpose was done by the people, not by the king or the Sanhedrin (*Bigdei Kehunah* [Shachor], *Kuntres Mashuach Milchamah* §4). For another opinion, see *Meromei Sadeh, Sotah* 42a.]

27. The obligation is violated only when a battle actually takes place without an anointed Kohen in place to deliver the Torah's message to the soldiers. When there was no war, the nation was not obligated to have a Kohen Anointed for Battle (*Chasdei David* to *Tosefta Horayos* 2:9, p. 940; *Mirkeves HaMishneh, Hil. Klei HaMikdash* 4:19).

Insight: Adding to the Message That the Torah Mandates

In the passage discussing the duties of the Kohen Anointed for Battle (*Deuteronomy* 20:1-9), the Torah clearly sets out the message that he is commanded to tell the army assembled for war: First, he must urge the soldiers not to let themselves be frightened by the enemy army, even if it is more numerous and seems more powerful, because Hashem is the One Who fights for Israel. Then, he is to announce which people are exempt from battle and order them to turn back from the field.

Chinuch (at note 8) states, however, that after delivering these messages that the Torah mandates, the Kohen would add his own words of encouragement, to motivate the soldiers to fight bravely and not hesitate to place themselves in danger for the sake of defending the Law of God.

Chinuch's words are taken from *Rambam's Sefer HaMitzvos* (*Asei* 191) and are apparently based on the Mishnah, *Sotah* 42a. In describing the message that the Kohen was commanded to deliver to the army, the Mishnah quotes the various verses in this Scriptural passage and then it expounds each verse. For example, after quoting *Deuteronomy* 20:3, *He shall say to them, "Hear O Israel, you are coming near to the battle against your enemies,"* the Mishnah explains: *"Against your enemies* — and not against your brothers! This is not Judah against Simon or Simon against Benjamin, where if you fall into their hands they will show you mercy [as actually occurred when they fought each other; see *II Chronicles* 28:15]. Rather, you go to war against your enemies, where if you fall into their hands they will show you no mercy." The Mishnah similarly expounds the other verses in the passage. The plain meaning of the Mishnah is that when the Kohen Anointed for Battle spoke to the army he would expound the verses in such a manner (see *Meiri* there). Thus, he added explanations to the verses that the Torah requires him to recite, using them to deliver an inspirational message.

Minchas Chinuch (§3) wonders, though, how anyone can suggest that the Kohen actually added his own words to the verses that the Torah instructs him to speak. We find in another case where the Torah sets out a specific message — namely, *Bircas Kohanim*, The Priestly Blessing (Mitzvah 378) — that one may not add to it. The Gemara (*Rosh Hashanah* 28b) teaches that if a Kohen augments the prescribed verses of *Bircas Kohanim* with his own blessings, he has added a component to one of the Torah's commandments and has transgressed the prohibition of *bal tosif* ("not to add"; Mitzvah 454). By the same token, *Minchas Chinuch* argues, if the Kohen Anointed for Battle should add his personal thoughts to the text that the Torah orders him to recite to the army, he would violate the prohibition of *bal tosif*! As for the Mishnah that cites expositions of the verses, *Minchas Chinuch* explains that the Mishnah means merely to teach *us* the inner meaning of those verses; it does not mean that the Kohen actually said those interpretations when he addressed the army (see also *Be'er Sheva, Sotah* 42a ד"ה ולא על אחיכם; and see *Toras HaKenaos* there).

Numerous commentators explain, however, that the Kohen would not violate *bal tosif* for adding his own message, because the Torah itself indicates that he *should* add to the prescribed text. The passage states (ibid. vv. 2-3): וְהָיָה כְּקָרְבְכֶם אֶל הַמִּלְחָמָה וְנִגַּשׁ הַכֹּהֵן וְדִבֶּר אֶל הָעָם. וְאָמַר אֲלֵהֶם שְׁמַע יִשְׂרָאֵל וגו', *It shall be that when you draw near to the battle, the Kohen shall approach and speak to the people. And he shall say to them, "Hear O Israel," etc.* The expression, *the Kohen shall approach and speak to the people,* followed by *and he shall say to them* etc., seems redundant. It is therefore understood to mean that the Kohen shall speak to the people in his own words *in addition* to saying to them the precise verses set out in the passage (*Haamek Davar* to the verse; *Minchas Yitzchak*; see similarly, *Minchah Chareivah, Sotah* 42a). Since the Torah indicates that the Kohen should embellish the message of the prescribed verses, when he does so he is *fulfilling* the mitzvah, not adding to it! This is different from the case of *Bircas Kohanim*, where the Torah states (*Numbers* 6:23): כֹּה תְבָרְכוּ אֶת בְּנֵי יִשְׂרָאֵל, ***This is how*** *you shall bless the Children of Israel;* meaning, the Kohanim shall recite the blessing specifically in *this* way, not adding anything to the prescribed verses.

According to this explanation, the Mishnah cited above can be understood plainly, to mean that when the Kohen spoke to the army he would expound the verses, either in the manner set out in the Mishnah, or in some other manner (*Minchas Yitzchak; Minchah Chareivah* ibid.). [For another resolution to *Minchas Chinuch's* question, see *Maharam Schik*.]

It is of note, however, that although *Rambam* states in *Sefer HaMitzvos* that the Kohen Anointed for Battle would add his own words of encouragement to the Torah verses that he recited, *Rambam* omits this point when he sets down the duties of the Kohen Anointed for Battle in *Hilchos Melachim* (7:3). There, *Rambam* states only that the Kohen recited the Scriptural verses, and he makes no mention about the Kohen adding personal words of encouragement.

◈ מִצְוָה תקכז ◈

מִצְוָה לַעֲשׂוֹת בְּמִלְחֶמֶת הָרְשׁוּת כְּמִשְׁפַּט הַכָּתוּב

שֶׁנִּצְטַוֵּינוּ בְּהִלָּחֲמֵנוּ בְּעִיר אַחַת מִצַּד הָרְשׁוּת שֶׁנִּרְצֶה לְהִלָּחֵם בָּהּ, וְזוֹ הִיא שֶׁנִּקְרֵאת מִלְחֶמֶת הָרְשׁוּת, שֶׁנַּבְטִיחַ אוֹתָם שֶׁלֹּא נַהַרְגֵם אִם יַשְׁלִימוּ עִמָּנוּ וְיִהְיוּ לָנוּ לַעֲבָדִים, כְּלוֹמַר מַעֲלִים מַס לְמַלְכֵּנוּ וּכְבוּשִׁים תַּחַת יָדֵינוּ, וְאִם לֹא יַשְׁלִימוּ עִמָּנוּ עַל הָעִנְיָן הַנִּזְכָּר אָנוּ מְצֻוִּים

◈ Mitzvah 527 ◈

The Obligation to Follow the Torah's Instructions for Conducting a Discretionary War

---

כִּי תִקְרַב אֶל עִיר לְהִלָּחֵם עָלֶיהָ וְקָרָאתָ אֵלֶיהָ לְשָׁלוֹם

When you draw near to a city to wage war against it, you shall call out to it for peace (Deuteronomy 20:10).

We learned in the previous mitzvah that there are two categories of wars fought by the Jewish people: מִלְחֶמֶת מִצְוָה, *an obligatory war,* and מִלְחֶמֶת הָרְשׁוּת, *a discretionary war.* An obligatory war is one that the Torah mandates, such as the original war that the Israelites, under the leadership of Joshua, waged in order to conquer the Land of Israel from the seven Canaanite nations. A discretionary war is one that the king, sanctioned by the Great Sanhedrin, decides to wage in order to destroy neighboring enemies and preempt their aggression, or to expand the borders of Eretz Yisrael (see *Sotah* 44b and *Rambam, Hil. Melachim* 5:1-2 with *Lechem Mishneh*).

The Torah passage that begins with the verse cited above contains various instructions about how to conduct war. This includes, for example, that when we initiate war we must always begin with an offer of peace. In this mitzvah, Chinuch focuses primarily on the rules governing discretionary wars. The next mitzvah pertains specifically to conflict with the seven Canaanite nations.

שֶׁנִּצְטַוֵּינוּ בְּהִלָּחֲמֵנוּ בְּעִיר אַחַת מִצַּד הָרְשׁוּת שֶׁנִּרְצֶה לְהִלָּחֵם בָּהּ — **We have been commanded,** regarding a case **when we wage war against a city based on our own decision to engage it in battle,** וְזוֹ הִיא שֶׁנִּקְרֵאת מִלְחֶמֶת הָרְשׁוּת — **which is** the type of war **that is called a "discretionary war,"** שֶׁנַּבְטִיחַ אוֹתָם שֶׁלֹּא נַהַרְגֵם אִם יַשְׁלִימוּ עִמָּנוּ וְיִהְיוּ לָנוּ לַעֲבָדִים — **that we must assure [the city's residents] that we will not kill them if they surrender to us and** undertake to **become our servants,** כְּלוֹמַר מַעֲלִים מַס לְמַלְכֵּנוּ וּכְבוּשִׁים תַּחַת יָדֵינוּ — **that is,** they agree **to pay taxes to our king and be subservient to us.**[1] וְאִם לֹא יַשְׁלִימוּ עִמָּנוּ עַל הָעִנְיָן הַנִּזְכָּר — **And, if they do not surrender to us according to the terms** just **described,** אָנוּ מְצֻוִּים — **we are** further **commanded to** conduct war

---

NOTES

1. "Paying taxes to the king" means that they must be prepared to surrender whatever property the king demands, or whatever annual tax he imposes on them, and they must also be willing to perform the king's work free of charge when he needs it, such as to build fortifications for him. "Being subservient to us" means that they will live as subjects of the Jewish people and have no positions of authority among us (*Rambam, Hil. Melachim* 6:1 and *Sefer HaMitzvos,*

Asei 190; cf. *Ramban, Deuteronomy* 20:11). According to *Rambam* (ibid.), they also must accept upon themselves to observe the Seven Noahide Laws (see note 9 below).

[Chinuch states below (at note 7) that the obligation to offer peace applies even in the case of an obligatory war. The following law, however, applies only to a discretionary war, as Chinuch explains below.]

לַהֲרֹג מֵהֶם כָּל זָכָר שֶׁבָּעִיר הַהִיא שֶׁהִגִּיעַ לְפִרְקוֹ[2] וְנִקַּח לָנוּ הַטַּף וְהַנָּשִׁים וְכָל שְׁלָלָהּ, וְעַל זֶה כֻּלּוֹ יֹאמְרוּ זִכְרוֹנָם לִבְרָכָה מִלְחֶמֶת הָרְשׁוּת[3]. וְאָמְרוּ בְּסִפְרֵי (כאן), אִם אָמְרוּ מְקַבְּלִין אָנוּ עָלֵינוּ מִסִּים וְלֹא שִׁעְבּוּד, שִׁעְבּוּד וְלֹא מִסִּים, אֵין שׁוֹמְעִין לָהֶם עַד שֶׁיְּקַבְּלוּ עֲלֵיהֶם זוֹ וָזוֹ[4].

מִשָּׁרְשֵׁי הַמִּצְוָה לְפִי שֶׁמִּדַּת הָרַחֲמָנוּת הִיא מִדָּה טוֹבָה וְרָאוּי לָנוּ זֶרַע הַקֹּדֶשׁ לְהִתְנַהֵג בָּהּ בְּכָל עִנְיָנֵינוּ גַּם עִם הָאוֹיְבִים עוֹבְדֵי עֲבוֹדָה זָרָה, לְמַעֲלָתֵנוּ אֲנַחְנוּ, לֹא מִצַּד הֱיוֹתָם הֵם רְאוּיִים לְרַחֲמִים וָחֶסֶד, וְגַם כִּי יֵשׁ בַּדָּבָר הַזֶּה תּוֹעֶלֶת לָנוּ לִהְיוֹת לְמַלְכֵּנוּ עֲבָדִים יַעַבְדוּהוּ לְהַעֲלוֹת לוֹ מַס תָּמִיד וְלַעֲשׂוֹת מְלַאכוֹתָיו אִם יִצְטָרֵךְ

---

with them in a specific manner: לַהֲרֹג מֵהֶם כָּל זָכָר שֶׁבָּעִיר הַהִיא שֶׁהִגִּיעַ לְפִרְקוֹ – We are **to kill every adult male of that city** who remains there to fight, but we may not kill any male child or any female, whether adult or child;[2] וְנִקַּח לָנוּ הַטַּף וְהַנָּשִׁים וְכָל שְׁלָלָהּ – **rather, we** may **take the children and women** of the city **for ourselves** as servants, **as well as** take **all of its booty.** וְעַל זֶה כֻּלּוֹ יֹאמְרוּ זִכְרוֹנָם לִבְרָכָה מִלְחֶמֶת הָרְשׁוּת – **Regarding all this, [the Sages], of blessed memory, state** that it represents the laws of a **"discretionary war."**[3]

Chinuch addresses a case of conditional surrender:

וְאָמְרוּ בְּסִפְרֵי – **[The Sages] have stated in** ***Sifrei*** (to *Deuteronomy* 20:11): אִם אָמְרוּ מְקַבְּלִין אָנוּ עָלֵינוּ מִסִּים וְלֹא שִׁעְבּוּד – **If [the residents of the enemy city] say,** in reply to our offer of peace, **"We undertake** to pay **taxes** to your king **but not** to be **subservient** to you," שִׁעְבּוּד וְלֹא מִסִּים – or, "We undertake to be **subservient** to you **but not** to pay **taxes** to your king," אֵין שׁוֹמְעִין לָהֶם עַד שֶׁיְּקַבְּלוּ עֲלֵיהֶם זוֹ וָזוֹ – **we do not heed them,** and we proceed to wage war **unless they undertake** both **this and that,** i.e., taxes and subservience.[4]

Underlying Purpose of the Mitzvah

מִשָּׁרְשֵׁי הַמִּצְוָה – **Among the underlying purposes of the mitzvah is** that it is appropriate to extend an offer of peace to an enemy לְפִי שֶׁמִּדַּת הָרַחֲמָנוּת הִיא מִדָּה טוֹבָה – **because the attribute of mercy is a worthy trait** וְרָאוּי לָנוּ זֶרַע הַקֹּדֶשׁ לְהִתְנַהֵג בָּהּ בְּכָל עִנְיָנֵינוּ – **and it is appropriate for us, the holy seed** of our forefathers, **to implement [this trait] in all our interactions,** גַּם עִם הָאוֹיְבִים עוֹבְדֵי עֲבוֹדָה זָרָה – **even** when dealing **with** our **enemies** who are **pagan idol worshipers,** לְמַעֲלָתֵנוּ אֲנַחְנוּ – **due to** ***our*** **eminence,** לֹא מִצַּד הֱיוֹתָם הֵם רְאוּיִים לְרַחֲמִים וָחֶסֶד – **not because they are** necessarily **worthy of** being treated with **mercy and kindness.**

וְגַם כִּי יֵשׁ בַּדָּבָר הַזֶּה תּוֹעֶלֶת לָנוּ – **This matter also provides us a** practical **benefit,** לִהְיוֹת לְמַלְכֵּנוּ עֲבָדִים יַעַבְדוּהוּ – in **that our king will have subjects** available **who will serve him** לְהַעֲלוֹת לוֹ מַס תָּמִיד – by **paying taxes to him regularly** וְלַעֲשׂוֹת מְלַאכוֹתָיו אִם יִצְטָרֵךְ – **and** being ready **to**

NOTES

2. *Rambam, Hil. Melachim* 6:4. [We also may not kill an adult male who surrenders or flees before the war begins (see *Tosafos, Sotah* 35b ד״ה לרבות).]

3. These laws are explicitly stated in the Scriptural passage (ibid. vv. 10-14): כִּי תִקְרַב אֶל עִיר לְהִלָּחֵם עָלֶיהָ וְקָרָאתָ אֵלֶיהָ לְשָׁלוֹם וְהָיָה אִם שָׁלוֹם תַּעַנְךָ וּפָתְחָה לָךְ וְהָיָה כָּל הָעָם הַנִּמְצָא בָהּ יִהְיוּ לְךָ לָמַס וַעֲבָדוּךָ. וְאִם לֹא תַשְׁלִים עִמָּךְ וְעָשְׂתָה עִמְּךָ מִלְחָמָה וְצַרְתָּ עָלֶיהָ. וּנְתָנָהּ ה׳ אֱלֹהֶיךָ בְּיָדֶךָ וְהִכִּיתָ אֶת כָּל זְכוּרָהּ לְפִי חָרֶב. רַק הַנָּשִׁים וְהַטַּף וְהַבְּהֵמָה וְכֹל אֲשֶׁר יִהְיֶה בָעִיר כָּל שְׁלָלָהּ תָּבֹז לָךְ וְאָכַלְתָּ אֶת שְׁלַל אֹיְבֶיךָ אֲשֶׁר נָתַן ה׳ אֱלֹהֶיךָ לָךְ, *When you draw near to a city to wage war against it, you shall call out to it for peace. It shall be that if it responds to you in peace and opens for you, then the entire people found within it shall be as tribute for you, and they shall serve you. But if it does not make peace with you, but makes war with you, you shall besiege it.* HASHEM *shall deliver it into your hand, and you shall smite all its men by the blade of the sword. Only the women, the children, the animals, and everything that will be in the city — all its booty — you may plunder for yourselves; you shall consume the booty of your enemies, which* HASHEM, *your God, gave you.*

4. We will learn below (see note 14) that this applies only if the enemy people wish to remain in their place of residence that we are conquering; in order to remain settled there, they must accept our terms of surrender. If, however, they wish to flee to a different country, we allow them safe passage with no conditions attached.

מִבְּלִי שֶׁיּוֹצִיא בָּהֶם הוֹצָאָה שֶׁל כְּלוּם[5], וּבַהֲמִיתֵנוּ אוֹתָם לֹא יִהְיֶה בַּדָּבָר תּוֹעֶלֶת אַחַר שֶׁהֵם רוֹצִים לַעֲמֹד כְּבוּשִׁים תַּחְתֵּינוּ, אֲבָל יִהְיֶה בַּדָּבָר הַשְׁחָתָה וְהוֹרָאָה עָלֵינוּ בְּמִדַּת הָאַכְזָרִיּוּת וְיַחְסְדֵנוּ שׁוֹמֵעַ[6], וּלְהוֹעִיל עַל כָּל שֶׁזְּכַרְנוּ נִצְטַוִּינוּ בָּזֶה.

מִדִּינֵי הַמִּצְוָה מַה שֶׁאָמְרוּ זִכְרוֹנָם לִבְרָכָה שֶׁדִּין קְרִיאַת הַשָּׁלוֹם הוּא בְּכָל מָקוֹם, כְּלוֹמַר בֵּין בְּמִלְחֶמֶת מִצְוָה בֵּין בְּמִלְחֶמֶת רְשׁוּת[7], וּמִלְחֶמֶת מִצְוָה הִיא כְּגוֹן שִׁבְעָה עֲמָמִין וַעֲמָלֵק[8], וְהַכֹּל אִם הִשְׁלִימוּ עִמָּנוּ, כְּלוֹמַר שֶׁקִּבְּלוּ עֲלֵיהֶם מַס וַעֲבָדוּת וּכְמוֹ כֵן שֶׁקִּבְּלוּ עֲלֵיהֶם שֶׁבַע מִצְוֹת[9], אֵין הוֹרְגִין מֵהֶם כָּל נְשָׁמָה וְיִהְיוּ לְמַס וַעֲבָדוּנוּ,

───

perform his tasks if he needs them, מִבְּלִי שֶׁיּוֹצִיא בָּהֶם הוֹצָאָה שֶׁל כְּלוּם — **without him having to spend anything on [those tasks].**[5] וּבַהֲמִיתֵנוּ אוֹתָם לֹא יִהְיֶה בַּדָּבָר תּוֹעֶלֶת — **If,** on the other hand, **we would kill them** even when they are prepared to surrender on our terms, **there would be no benefit in the matter,** אַחַר שֶׁהֵם רוֹצִים לַעֲמֹד כְּבוּשִׁים תַּחְתֵּינוּ — since they are willing **to remain subservient to us** and do not pose a threat; אֲבָל יִהְיֶה בַּדָּבָר הַשְׁחָתָה — **rather, such behavior would be** an act of **wanton destruction** וְהוֹרָאָה עָלֵינוּ בְּמִדַּת הָאַכְזָרִיּוּת — **and** would **indicate about us** that we are afflicted with **the trait of cruelty,** וְיַחְסְדֵנוּ שׁוֹמֵעַ — **and** anyone **who heard** about such behavior **would shame us.**[6] וּלְהוֹעִיל עַל כָּל שֶׁזְּכַרְנוּ נִצְטַוִּינוּ בָּזֶה — **It is** in order **to achieve all** the goals **we mentioned** that **we have been commanded about this matter** of making an overture of peace before waging war.

☙ Laws of the Mitzvah ☙

מִדִּינֵי הַמִּצְוָה — **Among the laws of the mitzvah is** מַה שֶׁאָמְרוּ זִכְרוֹנָם לִבְרָכָה — **that which [the Sages],** of blessed memory, **stated** (Rambam, Hil. Melachim 6:1), שֶׁדִּין קְרִיאַת הַשָּׁלוֹם הוּא בְּכָל מָקוֹם — **that the law requiring** us to make **an offer of peace applies in every event,** כְּלוֹמַר בֵּין בְּמִלְחֶמֶת מִצְוָה בֵּין בְּמִלְחֶמֶת רְשׁוּת — **that is, both in** a case of **an obligatory war and in** the case of **a discretionary war.**[7] וּמִלְחֶמֶת מִצְוָה הִיא כְּגוֹן שִׁבְעָה עֲמָמִין וַעֲמָלֵק — **An example of an "obligatory war" is** a war fought against **the seven** Canaanite **nations or** against **Amalek.**[8] וְהַכֹּל — **In all** cases, אִם הִשְׁלִימוּ עִמָּנוּ — **if,** after we make an offer of peace, **[the enemy] surrenders to us,** כְּלוֹמַר שֶׁקִּבְּלוּ עֲלֵיהֶם מַס וַעֲבָדוּת — **meaning that they undertake** the payment of **taxes** to our king **and subservience** to us, וּכְמוֹ כֵן שֶׁקִּבְּלוּ עֲלֵיהֶם שֶׁבַע מִצְוֹת — **and they also undertake** to abide by **the Seven** Noahide **Laws,**[9] אֵין הוֹרְגִין מֵהֶם כָּל נְשָׁמָה — **we do not kill a single soul among them,** וְיִהְיוּ לְמַס וַעֲבָדוּנוּ — **and they shall** remain alive to **be taxpayers** to our king **and to serve us.**

NOTES

5. See above, note 1.

6. Stylistic paraphrase of Proverbs 25:10.

7. This is the opinion of Rambam and Ramban (Deuteronomy 20:10). According to Rashi (Numbers 21:22, Deuteronomy 20:10), however, the obligation to offer peace applies only in the case of a discretionary war, not in the case of an obligatory war. For discussion, see Mizrachi and Gur Aryeh to Rashi (loc. cit.), and Lechem Mishneh, Hil. Melachim 6:1. See also Minchas Chinuch §4, and Chazon Ish, Yoreh Deah 157.

8. Chinuch speaks here about wars of offense; that is where we make overtures of peace. In Mitzvah 425 (at note 16), Chinuch also calls a defensive war against invaders a מִלְחֶמֶת מִצְוָה, obligatory war. Obviously, though, the obligation to offer peace does not apply in that case. See further, Minchas Yitzchak §4, and Chazon Ish ibid. 157:5.

9. Rambam maintains that whenever we make an offer of peace, whether to the seven Canaanite nations or to another enemy, the terms of surrender include that they shall abide by the Noahide Laws, which include the prohibition of idolatry as well as other basic principles of morality. Ramban (ibid.), however, argues that it is only the seven Canaanite nations who must undertake to observe the Noahide Laws. This is because they live in Eretz Yisrael, and the Torah stipulates that we may not let idol worshipers [and those who flout the other Noahide Laws] reside in Eretz Yisrael (see Mitzvah 94, with note 4). Outside of Eretz Yisrael, the terms of surrender are simply that they must accept paying taxes and servitude, as that is all that is stated in this Scriptural passage. For further discussion, see Lechem Mishneh ibid. [See also Insight to Mitzvah 93.]

אֲבָל כְּשֶׁלֹּא הִשְׁלִימוּ יֵשׁ חִלּוּק בֵּין מִלְחֶמֶת מִצְוָה לִרְשׁוּת, שֶׁבְּמִלְחֶמֶת מִצְוָה אֵין מְחַיִּין מֵהֶם כָּל נְשָׁמָה[10], וּבְמִלְחֶמֶת הָרְשׁוּת מַנִּיחִין מֵהֶן הַטַּף וְהַנָּשִׁים, כְּמוֹ שֶׁכָּתַבְנוּ בְּסָמוּךְ. וְכֵן מַנִּיחִין רוּחַ אַחַת בְּעִיר מָצוֹר בְּמִלְחֶמֶת רְשׁוּת שֶׁיִּבְרְחוּ מִשָּׁם,[11] סִפְרֵי, וְיָלְפִינָן זֶה מִדִּכְתִיב (במדבר ל״א, ז׳) וַיִּצְבְּאוּ עַל מִדְיָן כַּאֲשֶׁר צִוָּה ה׳ וְגו׳,[12] וּבְמִלְחֶמֶת שִׁבְעָה עֲמָמִין מַקִּיפִין אוֹתָם מִכָּל צַד,[13] וּמִכָּל מָקוֹם מוֹדִיעִים אוֹתָם תְּחִלָּה שֶׁאִם רְצוֹנָם לְהַנִּיחַ הָעִיר וְשֶׁיֵּלְכוּ לָהֶם, הָרְשׁוּת בְּיָדָם.[14]

אֲבָל כְּשֶׁלֹּא הִשְׁלִימוּ יֵשׁ חִלּוּק בֵּין מִלְחֶמֶת מִצְוָה לִרְשׁוּת — **If, on the other hand, they do not surrender** to us, **there is a difference between** how we proceed to wage **an obligatory war and** how we proceed to wage **a discretionary war,** as follows: שֶׁבְּמִלְחֶמֶת מִצְוָה אֵין מְחַיִּין מֵהֶם כָּל נְשָׁמָה — In the case of **an obligatory war, we do not leave a single one of them alive,**[10] וּבְמִלְחֶמֶת הָרְשׁוּת מַנִּיחִין מֵהֶן הַטַּף וְהַנָּשִׁים — **but in** the case of **a discretionary war, we** kill only the men who wage war and we **leave** all **their children and women** alive, כְּמוֹ שֶׁכָּתַבְנוּ בְּסָמוּךְ — **as we wrote above.**

Aside from offering the enemy an opportunity to surrender peacefully, we are obligated to take other steps to spare their lives:

וְכֵן מַנִּיחִין רוּחַ אַחַת בְּעִיר מָצוֹר בְּמִלְחֶמֶת רְשׁוּת שֶׁיִּבְרְחוּ מִשָּׁם — **Also** among the laws of conducting warfare is that **in** the case of **a discretionary war, when laying siege to a city we leave one side** of the city **open, so that [the residents] can flee through there.**[11] סִפְרֵי — This rule is taught in *Sifrei,* וְיָלְפִינָן זֶה מִדִּכְתִיב — where **[the Sages] derive it from that which is written** (*Numbers* 31:7): "וַיִּצְבְּאוּ עַל מִדְיָן כַּאֲשֶׁר צִוָּה ה׳ וְגו׳" — *They laid siege to Midian as* HASHEM *had commanded, etc.*[12] וּבְמִלְחֶמֶת שִׁבְעָה עֲמָמִין מַקִּיפִין אוֹתָם מִכָּל צַד — **But in** the case of **a war against the seven** Canaanite **nations,** which is an obligatory war, **we surround [the enemy city]** completely, **on all sides,** so that the residents cannot escape.[13] וּמִכָּל מָקוֹם מוֹדִיעִים אוֹתָם תְּחִלָּה — **In any event, we notify them,** **in advance** of laying siege, שֶׁאִם רְצוֹנָם לְהַנִּיחַ הָעִיר וְשֶׁיֵּלְכוּ לָהֶם הָרְשׁוּת בְּיָדָם — **that if they wish to abandon the city and go away** to settle elsewhere, **they may** do so and avoid war altogether.[14]

NOTES

10. See the introduction to the next mitzvah.

11. According to *Ramban* (glosses to *Sefer HaMitzvos,* Additional Mitzvah-obligations §5), this rule is not part of the current mitzvah. Rather, there is a specific mitzvah-obligation to leave one side of a city open when laying siege in a discretionary war.

Ramban offers two reasons for this requirement: (1) so that we will learn to act benevolently toward our enemies even *during* a war; (2) so that the enemy, knowing that he has a means of escape, will not fight with all his vigor.

12. The verse indicates that the Jewish people had been commanded by Hashem to conduct the siege in a specific way. The Oral Tradition teaches that the command was to leave one side open for people to escape if they desired (see *Sifrei* to the verse and *Rambam, Hil. Melachim* 6:7; see also *Sifrei* to *Deuteronomy* 20:10 with *Emek HaNetziv*). [See *Minchas Yitzchak* for further discussion.]

13. This is Chinuch's understanding of *Rambam, Hil. Melachim* 6:7 (see also *Radvaz* there, and *Ramban* ibid.). *Minchas Chinuch* (§5) argues, however, that *Rambam's* language indicates that we leave one side open for escape even in the case of an obligatory war.

[The reason why, according to Chinuch, we close off all sides is that in the case of an obligatory war, once the battle commences we may not let anyone survive, as was just stated (*Minchas Yitzchak;* cf. *Minchas Chinuch* to *Ramban's* Additional Mitzvah-obligations §5).]

14. That is, if the people of the city wish to flee from the area coming under Jewish control, they may do so and are given safe passage. In this case, they are not required to accept upon themselves the payment of taxes or servitude, nor to abide by the Noahide Laws. Those requirements pertain only when the enemy people wish to remain in their place, which from this point forward will be under Jewish control. But if they wish to abandon their city and go elsewhere, we let them escape and do not demand anything of them (see *Avnei Nezer, Yoreh Deah* 454:6, 457:5; and *Mitzvas HaMelech* [Cziment], *Asei* 187, 3:3-5).

In fact, when the Jewish people were about to enter Eretz Yisrael in the times of Joshua, they sent messages to the inhabitants of the Land notifying them that they had three options. They could either (1) flee the land; (2) surrender and accept servitude; or (3) remain and fight. One of the seven Canaanite nations, the Girgashite, actually chose to leave the Land and settle in Africa, and its people were spared. Among the other nations, one sect, the people of Gibeon, surrendered and accepted servitude, and they were designated as

וְכֵן מֵעִנְיָן זֶה מַה שֶּׁאָמְרוּ גַּם כֵּן דְּבֵין מִלְחֶמֶת רְשׁוּת אוֹ מִצְוָה מֻתָּר לַחֲלוּצֵי הַצָּבָא כְּשֶׁיִּכָּנְסוּ בִּגְבוּל הַגּוֹיִם וְהֵם רְעֵבִים וְאֵין בְּיָדָם צֵדָה לֶאֱכֹל, אוֹכְלִין אֲפִלּוּ מַאֲכָלוֹת אֲסוּרִים, כְּגוֹן נְבֵלוֹת וּטְרֵפוֹת וַחֲזִירִים וְלִשְׁתּוֹת יֵין נֶסֶךְ[15]. וְכֵן דָּרְשׁוּ זִכְרוֹנָם לִבְרָכָה (חולין י״ז ע״א) וּבָתִּים מְלֵאִים כָּל טוּב, אֲפִלּוּ קָדְלֵי דַחֲזִירֵי הֻתְּרוּ לָנוּ[16].

וְעַל זֶה נֶאֱמַר (דברים כ׳, י׳-י״א) כִּי תִקְרַב אֶל עִיר וְגוֹ׳ עַד גְּמַר הַפָּרָשָׁה[17].

וְיֶתֶר פְּרָטֵי הַמִּצְוָה בְּפֶרֶק שֵׁנִי מִסַּנְהֶדְרִין וּשְׁמִינִי מִסּוֹטָה[18].

וְנוֹהֶגֶת מִצְוָה זוֹ בִּזְמַן שֶׁיִּשְׂרָאֵל עַל אַדְמָתָן[19], בִּזְכָרִים שֶׁהֵם רְאוּיִם לְמִלְחָמָה[20],

---

Chinuch discusses other laws that apply during war:

וְכֵן מֵעִנְיָן זֶה מַה שֶּׁאָמְרוּ גַּם כֵּן – **Also pertaining to this matter** of war **is that which [the Sages] additionally stated** (see *Rambam, Hil. Melachim* 8:1), דְּבֵין מִלְחֶמֶת רְשׁוּת אוֹ מִצְוָה – **that whether** we are engaged in **a discretionary or an obligatory war,** מֻתָּר לַחֲלוּצֵי הַצָּבָא כְּשֶׁיִּכָּנְסוּ בִּגְבוּל הַגּוֹיִם וְהֵם רְעֵבִים וְאֵין בְּיָדָם צֵדָה – **it is permissible for the soldiers, after they enter the borders of the** other **nations, when they are hungry and have no** kosher **provisions,** לֶאֱכֹל אוֹכְלִין אֲפִלּוּ מַאֲכָלוֹת אֲסוּרִים – **to eat** whatever **foods** they find there, including **even food items that are** normally **prohibited,** כְּגוֹן נְבֵלוֹת וּטְרֵפוֹת וַחֲזִירִים – **such as *neveilah*** meat, ***tereifah*** meat, **and swine** meat, וְלִשְׁתּוֹת יֵין נֶסֶךְ – **and to drink *nesech* wine.**[15] וְכֵן דָּרְשׁוּ זִכְרוֹנָם לִבְרָכָה – **For this is how [the Sages]** (*Chullin* 17a), **of blessed memory, expounded** the passage, *When HASHEM, your God, brings you to the Land ... to give you ... houses filled with every good thing ... and you shall eat and be satisfied* (*Deuteronomy* 6:10-11): "וּבָתִּים מְלֵאִים כָּל טוּב" – The phrase, ***houses filled with every good thing,*** teaches that אֲפִלּוּ קָדְלֵי דַחֲזִירֵי הֻתְּרוּ לָנוּ – **even bacon was permitted to us** (i.e., to our army) when we were in the process of conquering Eretz Yisrael.[16]

Chinuch cites the verses that serve as the source of this mitzvah:

וְעַל זֶה נֶאֱמַר – **Regarding this** matter of conducting war in a specific manner, as described above, **it is stated** (*Deuteronomy* 20:10): "כִּי תִקְרַב אֶל עִיר וְגוֹ׳" עַד גְּמַר הַפָּרָשָׁה – ***When you draw near to a city*** *to wage war against it, you shall call out to it for peace,* **etc., until the end of the passage.**[17]

Chinuch concludes:

וְיֶתֶר פְּרָטֵי הַמִּצְוָה – These **and the remaining details of the mitzvah** are set forth בְּפֶרֶק שֵׁנִי מִסַּנְהֶדְרִין וּשְׁמִינִי מִסּוֹטָה – **in Chapter Two of** Tractate ***Sanhedrin*** (20b) **and** Chapter **Eight of** Tractate ***Sotah*** (44b).[18]

Applicability of the Mitzvah

וְנוֹהֶגֶת מִצְוָה זוֹ בִּזְמַן שֶׁיִּשְׂרָאֵל עַל אַדְמָתָן – **This mitzvah applies in times when the Jewish people are** settled **on their land,**[19] בִּזְכָרִים שֶׁהֵם רְאוּיִם לְמִלְחָמָה – and it applies **to men, for they are**

NOTES

wood-choppers and water carriers for the Altar and the assembly [see *Joshua* 9:27]. All the other Canaanites chose war and were wiped out [see *Joshua* 11:19-20] (*Yerushalmi Sheviis* 6:1, 45b in Schottenstein ed.; see *Rambam, Hil. Melachim* 6:5 and *Ramban, Deuteronomy* 20:10; see further, Mitzvah 528 notes 4-5).

15. This does not refer to a situation where the soldiers are in peril of starving to death, for in a case of mortal danger *anyone* (not only a soldier) may eat prohibited foods in order to save his life. Rather, it refers to a situation where the soldiers are simply hungry and have no kosher food. The Torah grants them a special permit to eat nonkosher food during the war, when they are suffering from hunger in enemy territory and no kosher food is available (*Kesef Mishneh* and *Radvaz, Hil. Melachim* 8:1). See Insight for discussion.

16. And, the same applies during all subsequent wars. See Insight.

17. See above, note 3, where the verses relevant to this mitzvah were cited.

18. The laws are codified in *Rambam, Hil. Melachim* 5:1-3, 6:1-7, 8:1.

19. See Mitzvah 525 note 15.

וְהִיא מִן הַמִּצְוֹות הַמֻּטָּלוֹת עַל הַצִּבּוּר וְיוֹתֵר עַל הַמֶּלֶךְ וְעַל רָאשֵׁי הָעָם.[21]

וְאִם עָבְרוּ עַל זֶה וְלֹא שָׁלְחוּ אֶל הָעִיר לִקְרֹא אֵלֶיהָ לְשָׁלוֹם וּלְהִתְנַהֵג עִמָּהֶם עַל הָעִנְיָן שֶׁזָּכַרְנוּ, בִּטְּלוּ עֲשֵׂה זֶה.

---

the ones who are **suited to wage war.**[20] **וְהִיא מִן הַמִּצְוֹות הַמֻּטָּלוֹת עַל הַצִּבּוּר** – **This is** one **of the mitzvos that are incumbent upon the community** as a whole, **וְיוֹתֵר עַל הַמֶּלֶךְ וְעַל רָאשֵׁי הָעָם** – **but especially on the king and the leaders of the people,** for they are the ones who decide when to wage a discretionary war, and who have the practical authority to offer peace to an enemy and carry out the other directives mentioned above.[21]

וְאִם עָבְרוּ עַל זֶה – **If they transgress this** obligation **וְלֹא שָׁלְחוּ אֶל הָעִיר לִקְרֹא אֵלֶיהָ לְשָׁלוֹם** – **and do not send** a message **to a city calling to it for peace** before engaging it in battle, **וּלְהִתְנַהֵג עִמָּהֶם עַל הָעִנְיָן שֶׁזָּכַרְנוּ** – **and** do not **treat [the enemy] in the manner we have described** when the enemy does choose war, **בִּטְּלוּ עֲשֵׂה זֶה** – **they have violated this mitzvah-obligation.**

NOTES

20. Women did not participate in discretionary wars at all, and filled only supportive roles in obligatory wars; see Mitzvah 525 note 14.

21. See Mitzvah 526 note 4.

☙ Insight: The Permit for Soldiers to Eat Nonkosher Food During War

Chinuch rules (after note 14) that during any war, whether an obligatory war or a discretionary war, Jewish soldiers in enemy territory who are hungry and have no kosher provisions are permitted to eat whatever foods they find, including nonkosher items. This is derived from the verse (*Deuteronomy* 6:10-11): *When HASHEM, your God, brings you to the Land ... to give you ... houses filled with every good thing ... and you shall eat and be satisfied.* The phrase, *houses filled with every good thing,* teaches that anything found in the enemy's houses is permitted for consumption. Chinuch's ruling follows the opinion of *Rambam* (*Hil. Melachim* 8:1). Now, the verse he cites is actually speaking about the initial conquest of Eretz Yisrael in the time of Joshua, as it states, *When HASHEM, your God, brings you to the Land,* etc. However, *Rambam* maintains that the rule stated in the verse applies during all wars; hungry soldiers who have nothing else to eat may partake of nonkosher foods. As explained in note 15, this does not refer to a situation of mortal danger, for in that case *anyone* may eat nonkosher. It is a special permit granted for soldiers who are simply suffering from hunger.

One might wonder, though: *Why* does the Torah provide soldiers with this dispensation? It seems to contradict the basic rule that no prohibition of the Torah may be overridden except in a case of mortal danger!

Some suggest that the Torah permits this because if the soldiers would have to search for kosher food, they would be distracted from the task of warfare and might be vulnerable to counterattack by the enemy (*Radvaz* to *Hil. Melachim* 8:1). Others, however, note that *Rambam* (ibid. 8:1-2) sets down this permit together with the similar permit for a soldier to take a *yefas toar* (woman of beautiful form) as a captive and marry her. As Chinuch explains in Mitzvah 532 (at note 7), the Torah granted soldiers that dispensation in recognition of the strength of man's evil inclination; for if it had not permitted the *yefas toar* to him, he might marry her in sin. Here, too, the Torah recognized that soldiers at war who have no kosher provisions might be overcome by the evil inclination and eat nonkosher food; to save them from sinning in this way, it gave them a special permit to eat whatever they find. This, however, applies only while they are in enemy territory and have nothing kosher to eat. In all other situations, soldiers too must eat only kosher food (*Avi Ezri* to *Hil. Melachim* 8:1; *Maharatz Chayes* to *Chullin* 17a; *Meshech Chochmah* ibid.).

The preceding reflects how *Rambam* and Chinuch understand the verse, *When HASHEM, your God, brings you to the Land ... to give you ... houses filled with every good thing ... and you shall eat and be satisfied. Ramban* (*Deuteronomy* 6:10) has a very different understanding of the verse. According to *Ramban,* the verse provides a dispensation that applied only during the period of the initial conquest of the Land, as a plain reading of its words indicates. And, *Ramban* contends, this

dispensation was not limited to the soldiers actively engaged in warfare. Rather, the conquering Jews were granted a permit to *enjoy* the booty seized from the Canaanites to their heart's content, even though it included foods that are normally prohibited. This permit applied to *all* the people; they were allowed to savor whatever foods they found in the cities that they conquered. The permit remained in place until all the booty had been consumed, or (according to another opinion) until the seven years of conquest ended. At the end of that period, all the prohibitions against consuming nonkosher food returned to full force.

According to *Ramban's* approach, the dispensation did not apply during any subsequent war. Moreover, according to *Ramban*, in later wars even soldiers engaged in battle are not permitted to eat nonkosher food. Of course, if their lives are endangered by the lack of kosher food, they may eat anything they need to in order to save their lives. But when they are simply hungry, they must eat only kosher provisions.

Another point of contention is that *Rambam* and Chinuch state that the permit (which in their view applies to soldiers in all times) includes the right to drink *nesech* wine. *Ramban* argues that the permit (which in his view applied only during the conquest of Eretz Yisrael) was limited to ordinary nonkosher foods, but did not include any item related to idolatry, such as *nesech* wine (i.e., wine used as a libation for an idol). This is because the Torah (*Deuteronomy* 7:25-26) expressly forbade the Jews who entered Eretz Yisrael to derive any benefit from items related to idolatry.

As mentioned, *Ramban* argues that the plain meaning of the verse, *When HASHEM, your God, brings you to the Land*, etc., indicates that the permit applied only during the initial conquest of Eretz Yisrael. On what basis do *Rambam* and Chinuch extend this permit to all subsequent wars? Numerous commentators explain that there is a similar verse in the passage of our mitzvah that pertains to all wars. The verse states (*Deuteronomy* 20:14): וְאָכַלְתָּ אֶת שְׁלַל אֹיְבֶיךָ אֲשֶׁר נָתַן ה' אֱלֹהֶיךָ לָךְ, *you shall consume the booty of your enemies, which HASHEM, your God, gave you.* Obviously, this does not mean that we *must* consume the booty. Rather, it means that we *may* consume it. But why would one think otherwise? The verse must be referring to nonkosher foods, and it comes to teach that they are permitted for consumption in all wars (see *Aderes Eliyahu* and *Meshech Chochmah* to the verse, and *Kli Chemdah* to *Deuteronomy* 6:10 §2).

For further discussion of this topic, see *Minchas Chinuch* §6, *Minchas Yitzchak,* and the many sources cited in *Sefer HaMafte'ach* (Frankel) to *Rambam* ibid.

∞ מִצְוָה תקכח ∞
שֶׁלֹּא לְהַחֲיוֹת אֶחָד מִכָּל שִׁבְעָה עֲמָמִין

∞ Mitzvah 528 ∞
The Prohibition to Let Any of the
Seven Canaanite Nations Survive

רַק מֵעָרֵי הָעַמִּים הָאֵלֶּה אֲשֶׁר ה׳ אֱלֹהֶיךָ נֹתֵן לְךָ נַחֲלָה לֹא תְחַיֶּה כָּל נְשָׁמָה. כִּי הַחֲרֵם תַּחֲרִימֵם הַחִתִּי וְהָאֱמֹרִי הַכְּנַעֲנִי וְהַפְּרִזִּי הַחִוִּי וְהַיְבוּסִי כַּאֲשֶׁר צִוְּךָ ה׳ אֱלֹהֶיךָ. לְמַעַן אֲשֶׁר לֹא יְלַמְּדוּ אֶתְכֶם לַעֲשׂוֹת כְּכֹל תּוֹעֲבֹתָם אֲשֶׁר עָשׂוּ לֵאלֹהֵיהֶם וַחֲטָאתֶם לַה׳ אֱלֹהֵיכֶם

But from the cities of these peoples that HASHEM, your God, gives you as inheritance, you shall not allow any person to live. Rather you shall utterly destroy them: the Hittite, the Amorite, the Canaanite, the Perizzite, the Hivvite, and the Jebusite, as HASHEM, your God, has commanded you. This is so that they will not teach you to act according to all their abominations that they performed for their gods so that you will sin to HASHEM, your God (Deuteronomy 20:16-18).

The seven Canaanite nations who inhabited Eretz Yisrael at the time when the Israelites entered the Land were the very embodiment of paganism and its associated depraved behavior. Their wicked practices were deemed by the Torah to be abominable, and included such rites as the passing of their children through fire as offerings to their gods (see *Deuteronomy* 12:31).

According to *Rambam* (*Hil. Melachim* 6:4, cited in the previous mitzvah), the current mitzvah teaches that, when engaged in war with these nations, we are not to let any of them survive. Now, we learned in the previous mitzvah that the nation of Israel may not engage anyone in conflict without first offering them the opportunity to flee, as well as the opportunity to remain and accept subservience to us. Only when an enemy rejects these choices and opts to stand up and fight us do we commence warfare. As Chinuch stated there, this applies even to the seven Canaanite nations. Had these nations chosen to leave the Land, they would have been afforded safe passage without any conditions attached. In fact, one of those seven nations did choose to leave and settle elsewhere.[1] Had the others agreed to be subservient to us and to abide by the Seven Noahide Laws, which represent basic principles of morality, they would have been allowed to live peacefully in the Land. However, only one small sect chose to do so.[2] All the other Canaanite people rejected our overtures of peace and instead waged war against the Israelites, effectively sealing their own fate.

Rambam states further (*Hil. Avodah Zarah* 10:1, as elaborated by *Minchas Chinuch* 93:1) that outside the context of war it is prohibited to kill any person, including a member of the Canaanite nations. Thus, this mitzvah has no application in our times (see also *Hil. Melachim* 5:4 and *Sefer HaMitzvos, Asei* 187). Chinuch has a broader definition of the mitzvah, but as Chinuch notes below (and at greater length in Mitzvah 425), these Canaanite nations no longer exist. Their nation states were eradicated in antiquity, and the individuals who survived were absorbed into the other nations of the world. Although, according to Chinuch, the mitzvah would theoretically be relevant if one could positively identify surviving members of those nations, in the practical sense it has no applicability nowadays. [See Mitzvah 425, where Chinuch discusses this further.]

NOTES

1. See below, notes 4 and 5.   2. See Mitzvah 527 note 14.

שֶׁהֻזְהַרְנוּ בְּלֹא תַעֲשֶׂה שֶׁלֹּא נְחַיֶּה אֶחָד מִשִּׁבְעָה עֲמָמִים[3] בְּכָל מָקוֹם שֶׁנִּמְצָאֵם וְנוּכַל לְהָרְגָם בְּלִי סַכָּנָה לְנַפְשׁוֹתֵינוּ[4], וְשִׁבְעָה עֲמָמִים הֵן, הַכְּנַעֲנִי וְהַפְּרִזִּי וְהַחִוִּי וְהַיְבוּסִי וְהַחִתִּי וְהַגִּרְגָּשִׁי[5] וְהָאֱמוֹרִי, וַעֲלֵיהֶם נֶאֱמַר (דברים כ׳, ט״ז) לֹא תְחַיֶּה כָּל נְשָׁמָה.

וְאַף עַל פִּי שֶׁהָאֱמֶת כִּי דָוִד הַמֶּלֶךְ הָרַג מֵהֶם רַבִּים עַד אֲשֶׁר כִּמְעַט כִּלָּה אוֹתָם וְאִבֵּד זִכְרָם, עֲדַיִן נִשְׁאֲרוּ מֵהֶן קְצָת שֶׁטָּבְעוּ בֵּין הָאֻמּוֹת[6].

שֶׁהֻזְהַרְנוּ בְּלֹא תַעֲשֶׂה – We have been warned by force of **a mitzvah-prohibition** שֶׁלֹּא נְחַיֶּה אֶחָד מִשִּׁבְעָה עֲמָמִים בְּכָל מָקוֹם שֶׁנִּמְצָאֵם וְנוּכַל לְהָרְגָם בְּלִי סַכָּנָה לְנַפְשׁוֹתֵינוּ **– not to let any of the Seven Nations** of Canaan **survive** as long as they persist in their worship of *avodah zarah*,[3] **wherever we find them and are able to eliminate them without endangering our own lives,** and when we have the legal authority to do so.[4] וְשִׁבְעָה עֲמָמִים הֵן **– These seven nations consist of** הַכְּנַעֲנִי וְהַפְּרִזִּי וְהַחִוִּי וְהַיְבוּסִי וְהַחִתִּי וְהַגִּרְגָּשִׁי וְהָאֱמוֹרִי **–** (1) **the Canaanite,** (2) **the Perizzite,** (3) **the Hivvite,** (4) **the Jebusite,** (5) **the Hittite,** (6) **the Girgashite,**[5] **and** (7) **the Amorite.** וַעֲלֵיהֶם נֶאֱמַר **– Regarding these** nations **it is stated** (*Deuteronomy* 20:16): "לֹא תְחַיֶּה כָּל נְשָׁמָה" **–** ***you shall not allow any person to live.***

וְאַף עַל פִּי שֶׁהָאֱמֶת כִּי דָוִד הַמֶּלֶךְ הָרַג מֵהֶם רַבִּים **– Now, although the fact is that King David** already **killed many of them,** עַד אֲשֶׁר כִּמְעַט כִּלָּה אוֹתָם וְאִבֵּד זִכְרָם **– to the point that he nearly destroyed [these nations] and eradicated their memory** from the earth, עֲדַיִן נִשְׁאֲרוּ מֵהֶן קְצָת שֶׁטָּבְעוּ בֵּין הָאֻמּוֹת **– some of them** survived those wars and **still remained** alive, **absorbed among the** other **nations.**[6]

NOTES

3. Chinuch in Mitzvah 93, at note 10. If, however, they abandon *avodah zarah,* they may be left alone.

4. Chinuch in Mitzvah 425, at note 19. According to Chinuch, the mitzvah could *theoretically* apply nowadays, in very limited circumstances. In the practical sense, though, it has no application, as mentioned in the introduction. As further noted there, *Rambam* maintains that our mitzvah was applicable only in the context of war. Thus, as long as the Seven Nations actively fought us, this mitzvah was in effect. However, once they put down their arms, we were discharged of our obligation to destroy them and in fact became *forbidden* to kill them. [See further, note 6.]

Chinuch's assertion that the mitzvah applies "wherever we find them," meaning even outside of Eretz Yisrael, is also disputed. As was mentioned above (Mitzvah 527 note 14), *Yerushalmi* states that the Girgashite, one of the seven Canaanite nations, heeded Joshua's warning of the impending invasion of the Land of Canaan by the Jewish forces, and they fled the Land to settle in Africa. Being that they were left alone at that point, many conclude that the mitzvah to destroy the Seven Nations applied only to those who remained within the ancestral boundaries of Eretz Yisrael (and persisted in their worship of *avodah zarah*). The point of the mitzvah was to clear Eretz Yisrael of their wicked influence, so it did not apply to those who no longer resided in the Land (see *Rashi, Sotah* 35b, end; *Kiryas Sefer, Hil. Avodah Zarah, Azharah* 42; *Avnei Nezer, Yoreh Deah* 454:6 and 457:5; see also discussion in *Mitzvas HaMelech* [Cziment], *Asei* 187, 2:2 and 3:3-5, and *Ein HaMelech* §1).

5. The Girgashite is listed among the seven Canaanite nations in *Deuteronomy* 7:1, which describes the land that the Jewish people would inherit; but the Girgashite is notably absent from the verse of this mitzvah (*Deuteronomy* 20:17, cited above in the introduction). According to *Rambam's* view that the mitzvah applies only in the context of war with the Canaanite nations, the reason for this omission is obvious: The Girgashite actually fled Eretz Yisrael before the Jews entered (see previous note). Being that the mitzvah never took on practical relevance in regard to the Girgashite, even during the initial conquest of the Land, Scripture prophetically omits that nation from the verse discussing this mitzvah.

6. Chinuch thus indicates that if we could positively identify these people the current mitzvah would apply. Realistically, though, this is impossible. And, as has been mentioned, according to *Rambam* and other Rishonim, the mitzvah would not apply even in that case, since we do not have the authority to wage war with them. *Rambam* also states (*Hil. Melachim* 5:4) that the mitzvah has no relevance nowadays because these nations were already eradicated. [That is, since they no longer have their own national identities, the mitzvah has been fulfilled, and would no longer apply even in the context of war (see *Mitzvas HaMelech* ibid. 3:5).]

The text here follows the *Minchas Yitzchak* edition.

וְכָל עִנְיַן מִצְוָה זוֹ כָּתַבְתִּי לְמַעְלָה בַּאֲרֻכָּה בְּסֵדֶר וָאֶתְחַנַּן עֲשֵׂה ח׳ בְּסִימָן תכ״ג (מצוה תכ״ה)[7] **וְקָחֶנּוּ מִשָּׁם.**

וְכָל עִנְיַן מִצְוָה זוֹ כָּתַבְתִּי לְמַעְלָה בַּאֲרֻכָּה – I have already written everything about this mitzvah at length above, **בְּסֵדֶר וָאֶתְחַנַּן עֲשֵׂה ח׳ בְּסִימָן תכ״ג – in Mitzvah-obligation 8 of *Parashas Va'eschanan*, Chapter 423** of this work (Mitzvah 425),[7] **וְקָחֶנּוּ מִשָּׁם – and you may take** all **[the information] from there.**

NOTES

7. Chinuch's numbering of the mitzvos follows the original format of this work; see Mitzvah 494 note 4.

מִצְוָה תקכט

שֶׁלֹּא לְהַשְׁחִית אִילָנֵי מַאֲכָל בְּמָצוֹר וְכֵן כָּל הַשְׁחָתָה בִּכְלַל הַלָּאו

שֶׁנִּמְנַעְנוּ מִלִּכְרֹת הָאִילָנוֹת כְּשֶׁנָּצוּר עַל עִיר כְּדֵי לְהָצֵר לְאַנְשֵׁי הָעִיר וּלְהַכְאִיב לִבּוֹתָם[1], וְעַל זֶה נֶאֱמַר (דברים כ׳, י״ט) לֹא תַשְׁחִית אֶת עֵצָהּ וְגוֹ׳ וְאֹתוֹ לֹא תִכְרֹת[2]. וּכְמוֹ כֵן נִכְנָס תַּחַת זֶה הַלָּאו שֶׁלֹּא לַעֲשׂוֹת שׁוּם הֶפְסֵד, כְּגוֹן לִשְׂרֹף אוֹ לִקְרֹעַ בֶּגֶד אוֹ לְשַׁבֵּר כְּלִי לְבַטָּלָה, וּבְכָל עִנְיָנִים אֵלּוּ וּבְכָל כַּיּוֹצֵא בָּם שֶׁיִּהְיֶה בָּהֶם הַשְׁחָתָה יֹאמְרוּ זִכְרוֹנָם לִבְרָכָה תָּמִיד בַּגְּמָרָא (קידושין ל״ב ע״א) וְהָא קָא עָבַר מִשּׁוּם בַּל תַּשְׁחִית[3].

Mitzvah 529

The Prohibition to Destroy Fruit Trees During a Siege or to Do Any Other Wasteful Destruction

כִּי תָצוּר אֶל עִיר יָמִים רַבִּים לְהִלָּחֵם עָלֶיהָ לְתָפְשָׂהּ לֹא תַשְׁחִית אֶת עֵצָהּ לִנְדֹּחַ עָלָיו גַּרְזֶן כִּי מִמֶּנּוּ תֹאכֵל וְאֹתוֹ לֹא תִכְרֹת

When you besiege a city for many days to wage war against it to seize it, you shall not destroy [any of] its trees by swinging an axe against it, for from it you shall eat, and you shall not cut it down (*Deuteronomy* 20:19).

שֶׁנִּמְנַעְנוּ מִלִּכְרֹת הָאִילָנוֹת כְּשֶׁנָּצוּר עַל עִיר – The Torah states **that when we lay siege to a city, we are prohibited to cut down the** fruit **trees** surrounding the city כְּדֵי לְהָצֵר לְאַנְשֵׁי הָעִיר וּלְהַכְאִיב לִבּוֹתָם – **in order to oppress the residents of the** besieged **city and to cause their hearts distress.**[1] וְעַל זֶה נֶאֱמַר – **Regarding this it is stated** (*Deuteronomy* 20:19): "לֹא תַשְׁחִית אֶת עֵצָהּ וְגוֹ׳ וְאֹתוֹ לֹא תִכְרֹת" – *When you besiege a city ... **do not destroy [any of] its trees** ... for from it you shall eat, **and you shall not cut it down.***[2]

Chinuch expands the scope of the prohibition:

וּכְמוֹ כֵן נִכְנָס תַּחַת זֶה הַלָּאו שֶׁלֹּא לַעֲשׂוֹת שׁוּם הֶפְסֵד – **This prohibition also includes** a warning **that we shall not do anything wasteful,** כְּגוֹן לִשְׂרֹף אוֹ לִקְרֹעַ בֶּגֶד אוֹ לְשַׁבֵּר כְּלִי לְבַטָּלָה – **such as to burn or tear a garment, or to break a vessel, needlessly.** וּבְכָל עִנְיָנִים אֵלּוּ – **Regarding all of these things,** וּבְכָל כַּיּוֹצֵא בָּם שֶׁיִּהְיֶה בָּהֶם הַשְׁחָתָה – **and all similar** things **that involve wasteful destruction,** יֹאמְרוּ זִכְרוֹנָם לִבְרָכָה תָּמִיד בַּגְּמָרָא – **[the Sages], of blessed memory, often state in the Gemara** (e.g., *Kiddushin* 32a): "וְהָא קָא עָבַר מִשּׁוּם "בַּל תַּשְׁחִית – **But one** who does this **violates** the prohibition of ***bal tashchis*** ("not to destroy")![3]

NOTES

1. Cutting down fruit trees for the purpose of oppressing the city's residents is considered wasteful and is thus forbidden. This is the view of *Rambam* (*Sefer HaMitzvos, Lo Saaseh* 57). *Ramban* (to verse, and in his glosses to *Sefer HaMitzvos,* Additional Mitzvah-Obligation 6), however, states that only wanton destruction is forbidden, but to destroy trees for the sake of intensifying the siege is considered a valid purpose, and is permitted (*Minchas Chinuch* §1).

2. The verse refers only to fruit trees, as it states, *for from it you shall eat.* The next verse states explicitly, *Only a tree that you know is not a food tree, it you may destroy and cut down, and build a fortification against the city.*

3. The Gemara applies the prohibition of *bal tashchis* to various cases of destructive activity. This indicates that the prohibition pertains to all wasteful actions, and is not limited to destroying fruit trees during a siege (*Kesef Mishneh, Hil. Melachim* 6:8). Some suggest that this added rule is derived from the fact that the verse repeats the prohibition, stating: *you shall not destroy [any of] its trees,* and *you shall not cut it down.* The repetition is understood to expand the prohibition to all sorts of wasteful activity (*Tosafos Yom Tov, Bava Kamma* 8:6; see *R' Y. F. Perla, Sefer HaMitzvos of Rav Saadiah Gaon, Lo Saaseh* 249 [Vol. II, pp. 259a-b]). [As for why the Torah sets out the prohibition in the context of a siege, see *R' S. R. Hirsch* cited in the Insight to Mitzvah 532.]

וּמִכָּל מָקוֹם אֵין מַלְקִין אֶלָּא בְּקוֹצֵץ אִילָנֵי מַאֲכָל שֶׁהוּא מְפֹרָשׁ בַּכָּתוּב, אֲבָל בִּשְׁאָר הַהַשְׁחָתוֹת מַכִּין אוֹתוֹ מַכַּת מַרְדּוּת[4].

שֹׁרֶשׁ הַמִּצְוָה יָדוּעַ, שֶׁהוּא כְּדֵי לְלַמֵּד נַפְשֵׁנוּ לֶאֱהֹב הַטּוֹב וְהַתּוֹעֶלֶת וּלְהִדָּבֵק בּוֹ, וּמִתּוֹךְ כָּךְ תִּדְבַּק בָּנוּ הַטּוֹבָה וְנַרְחִיק מִכָּל דָּבָר רַע וּמִכָּל דְּבַר הַשְׁחָתָה, וְזֶהוּ דֶּרֶךְ הַחֲסִידִים וְאַנְשֵׁי מַעֲשֶׂה אוֹהֲבִים שָׁלוֹם וּשְׂמֵחִים בְּטוֹב הַבְּרִיּוֹת וּמְקָרְבִים אוֹתָן לַתּוֹרָה, וְלֹא יְאַבְּדוּ אֲפִלּוּ גַּרְגֵּר שֶׁל חַרְדָּל בָּעוֹלָם, וְיֵצֵר עֲלֵיהֶם בְּכָל אֲבַדּוֹן וְהַשְׁחָתָה שֶׁיִּרְאוּ, וְאִם יוּכְלוּ לְהַצִּיל יַצִּילוּ כָּל דָּבָר מֵהַשְׁחִית בְּכָל כֹּחָם[5], וְלֹא כֵן הָרְשָׁעִים אֲחֵיהֶם[6] שֶׁל מַזִּיקִין

Chinuch qualifies this rule:

וּמִכָּל מָקוֹם אֵין מַלְקִין אֶלָּא בְּקוֹצֵץ אִילָנֵי מַאֲכָל – **Nevertheless,** the punishment of ***malkus*** (lashes) **is imposed only for cutting down fruit trees,** שֶׁהוּא מְפֹרָשׁ בַּכָּתוּב – **since this is** the only form of wastefulness that is **expressed openly in the verse;** אֲבָל בִּשְׁאָר הַהַשְׁחָתוֹת – **but with** respect to one who does **other types of wasteful destruction,** מַכִּין אוֹתוֹ מַכַּת מַרְדּוּת – **we** (i.e., the court) **administer** ***makkas mardus*** **to him.**[4]

Underlying Purpose of the Mitzvah

שֹׁרֶשׁ הַמִּצְוָה יָדוּעַ – **The underlying purpose of the mitzvah is** well **known.** שֶׁהוּא כְּדֵי לְלַמֵּד נַפְשֵׁנוּ לֶאֱהֹב הַטּוֹב וְהַתּוֹעֶלֶת – **It is in order to train ourselves to love** and appreciate **that which is good and productive,** וּלְהִדָּבֵק בּוֹ – **and to cleave to it;** וּמִתּוֹךְ כָּךְ תִּדְבַּק בָּנוּ הַטּוֹבָה – **for through this, goodness will adhere to us,** וְנַרְחִיק מִכָּל דָּבָר רַע וּמִכָּל דְּבַר הַשְׁחָתָה – **and we will be distanced from all things evil and all things destructive.**

וְזֶהוּ דֶּרֶךְ הַחֲסִידִים וְאַנְשֵׁי מַעֲשֶׂה – **This is the way of the pious ones and the men of** good **deeds:** אוֹהֲבִים שָׁלוֹם – **They love peace,** וּשְׂמֵחִים בְּטוֹב הַבְּרִיּוֹת וּמְקָרְבִים אוֹתָן לַתּוֹרָה – **they rejoice in the good** fortune **of** all **the** people that God **created, and** seek to **bring them closer to Torah** observance, וְלֹא יְאַבְּדוּ אֲפִלּוּ גַּרְגֵּר שֶׁל חַרְדָּל בָּעוֹלָם – **and they will not** needlessly **destroy** anything **of** God's **world,** not **even** something as tiny as **a mustard seed.** וְיֵצֵר עֲלֵיהֶם בְּכָל אֲבַדּוֹן וְהַשְׁחָתָה שֶׁיִּרְאוּ – **They are pained by any loss or destruction that they see,** וְאִם יוּכְלוּ לְהַצִּיל – **and if they can rescue** something from destruction, יַצִּילוּ כָּל דָּבָר מֵהַשְׁחִית בְּכָל כֹּחָם – **they will act with all their might to rescue anything,** no matter how insignificant, **from being** needlessly **destroyed.**[5]

וְלֹא כֵן הָרְשָׁעִים אֲחֵיהֶם שֶׁל מַזִּיקִין – **But the wicked ones,** who are **the "brothers of demons,"**[6] **are**

NOTES

4. [*Makkas mardus* are "lashes of discipline," and are somewhat different from *malkus*; see General Introduction, at note 16, and Mitzvah 496 note 69.] Chinuch implies (here and at the end of the mitzvah) that any act of destruction is a violation of *bal tashchis* on the Biblical level, yet not all such acts carry the penalty of *malkus.* Only cutting down fruit trees, which is the act that Scripture *explicitly* forbids, is subject to *malkus.* All other forms of destructive activity, which are derived through the implication of the repetitive verse (see note 3), are punished with *makkas mardus.* This is Chinuch's understanding of *Rambam, Hil. Melachim* 6:10 (*Minchas Chinuch* §2).

Others understand *Rambam* to hold that the Biblical prohibition applies only to cutting down fruit trees, and all other forms of wasteful activity are prohibited Rabbinically. That is why the other forms of wastefulness are punishable only with *makkas mardus* (*Teshuvos R' Yechiel Bassan* §101, cited in *Mishneh LaMelech, Hil. Melachim* 6:8). It is of note, however, that in *Sefer HaMitzvos* (ibid.), *Rambam* writes that any form of needless destruction is punishable with *malkus.* [See also *Tosafos, Bava Metzia* 32b ד״ה מדברי with *Rashash.*]

5. A person who is benevolent and peaceful appreciates every person and every item that God created. He seeks to benefit people and to preserve all of Creation; and he is pained by any loss of life or destruction of something useful.

6. Demons (*mazikin;* literally, *damagers*) are by their nature harmful to Man and his possessions. The wicked, who revel in the corruption of society, are thus their "brothers."

שְׂמֵחִים בְּהַשְׁחָתַת עוֹלָם וְהֵמָּה מַשְׁחִיתִים אֶת עַצְמָם, בְּמִדָּה שֶׁאָדָם מוֹדֵד בָּהּ מוֹדְדִין לוֹ, כְּלוֹמַר בָּהּ הוּא נִדְבָּק לְעוֹלָם[7], וּכְעִנְיָן שֶׁכָּתוּב (משלי י״ז, ה׳) שָׂמֵחַ לְאֵיד לֹא יִנָּקֶה[8], וְהֶחָפֵץ בַּטּוֹב וְשָׂמֵחַ בּוֹ, נַפְשׁוֹ בְּטוֹב תָּלִין לְעוֹלָם[9], זֶה יָדוּעַ וּמְפֻרְסָם.

מִדִּינֵי הַמִּצְוָה מַה שֶּׁאָמְרוּ זִכְרוֹנָם לִבְרָכָה (ב״ק צ״א ע״ב) שֶׁלֹּא אָסְרָה תּוֹרָה שֶׁלֹּא לָקֹץ אִילָנֵי מַאֲכָל אֶלָּא בְּקוֹצֵץ אוֹתָם דֶּרֶךְ הַשְׁחָתָה, אֲבָל וַדַּאי מֻתָּר לָקֹץ אוֹתָם אִם יִמָּצֵא בַּדָּבָר תּוֹעֶלֶת, כְּגוֹן שֶׁיִּהְיוּ דְּמֵי אוֹתוֹ הָעֵץ יְקָרִים[10] וְזֶה רָצָה לְמָכְרוֹ, אוֹ לְסַלֵּק בִּקְצִיצָתָן נֵזֶק כְּגוֹן שֶׁהָיָה מַזִּיק אִילָנוֹת אֲחֵרִים טוֹבִים מִמֶּנּוּ[11], אוֹ מִפְּנֵי שֶׁמַּזִּיק בִּשְׂדוֹת אֲחֵרִים[12], בְּכָל צְדָדִין אֵלּוּ וּבְכָל כַּיּוֹצֵא בּוֹ מֻתָּר.

---

not so: שְׂמֵחִים בְּהַשְׁחָתַת עוֹלָם – **They rejoice in the destruction of society,** וְהֵמָּה מַשְׁחִיתִים אֶת עַצְמָם – **and they** thus **corrupt themselves** as well. How so? בְּמִדָּה שֶׁאָדָם מוֹדֵד בָּהּ מוֹדְדִין לוֹ – Because, as our Sages teach (Mishnah, *Sotah* 8b), **with the measure that one measures** out his actions, **they** (the Heavenly Court) **measure for him** in return, כְּלוֹמַר בָּהּ הוּא נִדְבָּק לְעוֹלָם – meaning **to say, he is eternally attached to [that measure].**[7] Thus, since the wicked revel in the destruction and degradation of God's world, they themselves are met with destructive forces. וּכְעִנְיָן שֶׁכָּתוּב "שָׂמֵחַ לְאֵיד לֹא יִנָּקֶה" – This is **in accordance with that which is written** (*Proverbs* 17:5): ***One who rejoices in [another's] misfortune will not be exonerated.***[8] וְהֶחָפֵץ בַּטּוֹב וְשָׂמֵחַ בּוֹ – **As for one who desires good, and rejoices in it,** נַפְשׁוֹ בְּטוֹב תָּלִין לְעוֹלָם – **his soul will eternally reside with good.**[9] זֶה יָדוּעַ וּמְפֻרְסָם – All **this is** well **known and is common knowledge.**

Laws of the Mitzvah

מִדִּינֵי הַמִּצְוָה – **Among the laws of the mitzvah** is מַה שֶּׁאָמְרוּ זִכְרוֹנָם לִבְרָכָה – **that which [the Sages], of blessed memory, stated** (*Bava Kamma* 91b; *Rambam, Hil. Melachim* 6:8), שֶׁלֹּא אָסְרָה תּוֹרָה שֶׁלֹּא לָקֹץ אִילָנֵי מַאֲכָל אֶלָּא בְּקוֹצֵץ אוֹתָם דֶּרֶךְ הַשְׁחָתָה – **that the Torah did not prohibit cutting down fruit trees except when one cuts them down in a wasteful manner,** אֲבָל וַדַּאי מֻתָּר לָקֹץ אוֹתָם אִם יִמָּצֵא בַּדָּבָר תּוֹעֶלֶת – **but it is certainly permissible to cut them down if there is a benefit in doing so.** כְּגוֹן שֶׁיִּהְיוּ דְּמֵי אוֹתוֹ הָעֵץ יְקָרִים וְזֶה רָצָה לְמָכְרוֹ – **For example,** if **the timber of that tree is** more **valuable** than its fruit,[10] **and this** person **wishes to sell [the timber];** אוֹ לְסַלֵּק בִּקְצִיצָתָן נֵזֶק – **or** if **by cutting down [the fruit tree] one** intends **to prevent** it from causing **damage,** כְּגוֹן שֶׁהָיָה מַזִּיק אִילָנוֹת אֲחֵרִים טוֹבִים מִמֶּנּוּ – **such as,** if **[this tree] was harmful to other trees** that are **more valuable than it;**[11] אוֹ מִפְּנֵי שֶׁמַּזִּיק בִּשְׂדוֹת אֲחֵרִים – **or** if he wishes to cut it down **because it is causing damage in fields of others.**[12] בְּכָל צְדָדִין אֵלּוּ וּבְכָל כַּיּוֹצֵא בּוֹ מֻתָּר – **In all these circumstances and in all similar** situations, **it is permitted** to cut down a fruit tree.[13]

NOTES

7. The Mishnah teaches that God rewards and punishes a person with the same *middah* (literally, *measure*; i.e., mode of behavior) that he himself adopts. One who acts kindly is rewarded with similar kindness, and one who acts harmfully will himself suffer similar harm. Chinuch explains that this is because when a person chooses to conduct himself with a certain *middah*, he attaches himself to that *middah,* and therefore, he either enjoys or suffers its consequences.

8. I.e., he will suffer that very misfortune (*Metzudas David*).

9. Stylistic paraphrase of *Psalms* 25:13.

10. *Rashi, Bava Kamma* 91b ד״ה ואם היה מעולה בדמים.

11. E.g., this tree is depriving a more valuable tree of nourishment (see *Bava Kamma* 92a).

12. The Gemara (*Bava Basra* 26a) cites an incident in which birds nested in Rava bar Rav Chanan's fruit trees, and from there they flew into his neighbor's orchard and ate its produce. Those fruit trees were considered to be damaging the orchard, and Rava bar Rav Chanan was ordered to remove them (*Kesef Mishneh, Hil. Melachim* 6:8).

13. *Rosh* (*Bava Kamma* 8:15) adds that it is permitted to cut down a fruit tree when the space that it occupies is needed for another [more important] purpose. For discussion of this topic, see *Teshuvos Mahari Bassan*

וְכָל אִילַן סְרָק אָמְרוּ זִכְרוֹנָם לִבְרָכָה (שם) שֶׁמֻּתָּר לָקֹץ וַאֲפִלּוּ בְּשֶׁאֵינוֹ צָרִיךְ לוֹ[14], וְכָל אִילַן מַאֲכָל שֶׁהוּא זָקֵן מְאֹד עַד שֶׁאֵינוֹ עוֹשֶׂה אֶלָּא מְעַט פֵּרוֹת שֶׁאֵין רָאוּי לִטְרֹחַ בּוֹ בִּשְׁבִילָן[15], וְאָמְרוּ זִכְרוֹנָם לִבְרָכָה בְּזַיִת, כָּל שֶׁהִיא עוֹשָׂה פָּחוֹת מֵרֹבַע זֵיתִים[16] מֻתָּר לָקֹץ אוֹתָהּ, וּבְדֶקֶל שֶׁיַּעֲשֶׂה פָּחוֹת מִקַּב תְּמָרִים[17].

וְדֶרֶךְ כְּלָל אָסְרוּ זִכְרוֹנָם לִבְרָכָה לַעֲשׂוֹת כָּל דָּבָר שֶׁל הַשְׁחָתָה, וְהַמַּשְׁחִית שׁוּם דָּבָר מִתּוֹךְ חֵמָה אָמְרוּ עָלָיו (שבת ק״ה ע״ב) שֶׁהוּא כְּעוֹבֵד עֲבוֹדָה זָרָה, שֶׁכֵּן דַּרְכּוֹ

Chinuch now addresses the status of trees that do not produce fruit:
וְכָל אִילַן סְרָק – With regard to **any non-fruit tree,** אָמְרוּ זִכְרוֹנָם לִבְרָכָה שֶׁמֻּתָּר לָקֹץ – **[our Sages], of blessed memory, have stated** (*Rambam* ibid. §9) **that it is permissible** for one **to cut** it **down** וַאֲפִלּוּ בְּשֶׁאֵינוֹ צָרִיךְ לוֹ – **even if he has no need for it.**[14] וְכָל אִילַן מַאֲכָל שֶׁהוּא זָקֵן מְאֹד – It is **also** permissible to cut down **any fruit tree that is very aged,** עַד שֶׁאֵינוֹ עוֹשֶׂה אֶלָּא מְעַט פֵּרוֹת – and is **so** feeble **that it yields only a small amount of fruit,** שֶׁאֵין רָאוּי לִטְרֹחַ בּוֹ בִּשְׁבִילָן – **since it is not worthwhile to bother with [this tree] for the sake of [those fruits].**[15]

Chinuch discusses the amount of fruit that determines whether a tree is worth maintaining:
וְאָמְרוּ זִכְרוֹנָם לִבְרָכָה בְּזַיִת – **[Our Sages], of blessed memory, have stated** (ibid.) that **with regard to an olive tree,** כָּל שֶׁהִיא עוֹשָׂה פָּחוֹת מֵרֹבַע זֵיתִים – **if it yields less than a quarter-*kav***[16] of fruit per season, מֻתָּר לָקֹץ אוֹתָהּ – **it is permissible to cut it down;** וּבְדֶקֶל שֶׁיַּעֲשֶׂה פָּחוֹת מִקַּב תְּמָרִים – **and with regard to a date-palm,** it may be cut down **if it yields less than a *kav* of dates.**[17]

Chinuch discusses the evil of acting destructively in anger:
וְדֶרֶךְ כְּלָל אָסְרוּ זִכְרוֹנָם לִבְרָכָה לַעֲשׂוֹת כָּל דָּבָר שֶׁל הַשְׁחָתָה – **[Our Sages], of blessed memory, forbade** us **in general to do anything destructive;** וְהַמַּשְׁחִית שׁוּם דָּבָר מִתּוֹךְ חֵמָה אָמְרוּ עָלָיו – **and with regard to one who destroys anything out of anger, they said** (*Shabbos* 105b) שֶׁהוּא כְּעוֹבֵד עֲבוֹדָה זָרָה – **that he is** viewed **as one who worships *avodah zarah*.** How so? שֶׁכֵּן דַּרְכּוֹ

NOTES

§101; *Teshuvos Chikrei Lev, Mahadura Basra,* Vol. I, *Yoreh Deah* §11; *Teshuvos Yabia Omer,* Vol. V, *Yoreh Deah* §12. See also Insight to Mitzvah 492.

14. This does not mean that one may destroy the tree without *any* purpose. A non-fruit tree is no different from any other item that may not be wantonly destroyed, as Chinuch mentioned above. Just as it is forbidden to needlessly tear a garment or break a vessel, so is it prohibited to cut down a non-fruit tree with no cause. Rather, Chinuch [citing *Rambam*] means that unlike a fruit tree, which may be cut down only for a purpose that is more valuable than its fruit, a non-fruit tree may be cut down for any sort of purpose. For example, one may cut down the tree for firewood (*Teshuvos Chikrei Lev* ibid. ד״ה וברר מן דין; cf. *Teshuvos Mahari Bassan* ibid.).

15. The prohibition against cutting down fruit trees applies only to trees that produce enough fruit to make it worth the cost and bother of maintaining them. Thus, an aged tree that will never again yield a significant crop may be cut down. However, a tree that yields little fruit because of its youth may not be cut down. This is because its yield will increase as it matures, making it worthwhile to maintain even now (*Teshuvos Shevet Sofer, Yoreh Deah* §94).

16. A *kav* is a measure equal to the volume of 24 eggs. Thus, a quarter-*kav* equals the volume of six eggs.

17. An olive tree, whose fruit is very valuable, is worth maintaining for a yield of a quarter-*kav* of fruit. A date palm, however, requires a yield of a *kav* to make it worth maintaining (*Meiri* to *Bava Kamma* ibid.).

With regard to other species of trees, *Rambam* (*Commentary* to *Sheviis* 4:10) states that they may be felled if they yield less than a *kav* of fruit. A grapevine, however, may be cut down only if it yields no fruit at all (*Rosh, Bava Kamma* 8:15). This is because, unlike other trees, a detached vine is never usable as timber and its value is only for its fruit. Thus, it yields nothing of value when detached, and may be cut down only if it produces no fruit at all (*Yam Shel Shlomo, Bava Kamma* 8:62).

[Some state that the measures of a quarter-*kav* and a *kav* for the various types of trees refer to the amount by which the owner of the tree *profits* after subtracting the expense of maintaining the tree (*Shitah Mekubetzes, Bava Kamma* 91b; *Teshuvos Shevet Sofer* ibid.).]

שֶׁל הַיֵּצֶר הָרַע, הַיּוֹם אוֹמֵר לוֹ עֲשֵׂה כֵּן, וְאִם יַאֲמִין אוֹתוֹ, לְמָחָר יֹאמַר לוֹ לֵךְ עֲבֹד עֲבוֹדָה זָרָה[18], כְּלוֹמַר שֶׁכָּל אָדָם חַיָּב לִגְעֹר בְּיִצְרוֹ וְלִכְבֹּשׁ תַּאֲוָתוֹ עַד שֶׁיַּגְבִּיר נֶפֶשׁ הַמַּשְׂכֶּלֶת עַל נֶפֶשׁ הַמִּתְאַוָּה[19] עַד שֶׁתִּהְיֶה לָהּ לְאָמָה וְהִיא גְּבֶרֶת לְעוֹלָם וָעֶד[20]. וְאָמְנָם הֵבִיאוּ בַּגְּמָרָא (שם) מַעֲשִׂים בִּקְצָת הַחֲכָמִים שֶׁמַּרְאִים עַצְמָן כְּעוּסִים כְּדֵי לְיַסֵּר בְּנֵי בֵיתָם וּלְזָרְזָן וּמַשְׁלִיכִין מִיָּדָם שׁוּם מַאֲכָל אוֹ שׁוּם דָּבָר[21], וּמִכָּל מָקוֹם הַשְׁגָּחָתָם הָיְתָה בָּהֶם לְעוֹלָם שֶׁלֹּא יַשְׁלִיכוּ דָּבָר שֶׁיְּהֵא נִשְׁחָת בָּזֶה[22].

שֶׁל הַיֵּצֶר הָרַע – Because this is the way of the evil inclination: הַיּוֹם אוֹמֵר לוֹ עֲשֵׂה כֵּן – Today he tells [a person] to **perform this** sin, such as breaking something to vent his anger, **וְאִם יַאֲמִין אוֹתוֹ – and if [the person] trusts him** and acts on his suggestion, **לְמָחָר יֹאמַר לוֹ לֵךְ עֲבֹד עֲבוֹדָה זָרָה** – then **tomorrow he will tell him** to **go worship *avodah zarah*** and the person will listen.[18] **כְּלוֹמַר שֶׁכָּל אָדָם חַיָּב לִגְעֹר בְּיִצְרוֹ וְלִכְבֹּשׁ תַּאֲוָתוֹ** – This teaching of the Sages **means to say that every person must,** when challenged, **fight back at his** evil **inclination and suppress his desire** to sin, **עַד שֶׁיַּגְבִּיר נֶפֶשׁ הַמַּשְׂכֶּלֶת עַל נֶפֶשׁ הַמִּתְאַוָּה – until he makes his "intelligent soul" overpower his "desirous soul,"**[19] **עַד שֶׁתִּהְיֶה לָהּ לְאָמָה וְהִיא גְּבֶרֶת לְעוֹלָם וָעֶד – to the extent that [the desirous soul] will become its maidservant, and [the intelligent soul] will be the mistress forever.**[20]

Chinuch discusses incidents that seem to contradict this point:

וְאָמְנָם הֵבִיאוּ בַּגְּמָרָא מַעֲשִׂים בִּקְצָת הַחֲכָמִים – Now, the Gemara (ibid.) **cites incidents involving some Sages, שֶׁמַּרְאִים עַצְמָן כְּעוּסִים כְּדֵי לְיַסֵּר בְּנֵי בֵיתָם וּלְזָרְזָן – who would portray themselves as** being **angry in order to rebuke the members of their household and admonish them** against certain behaviors, **וּמַשְׁלִיכִין מִיָּדָם שׁוּם מַאֲכָל אוֹ שׁוּם דָּבָר – and they would throw from their hands an article of food, or some other object,** to display their "anger."[21] This would seem to indicate that it is permitted to destroy things in "anger," at least in order to give rebuke. **וּמִכָּל מָקוֹם הַשְׁגָּחָתָם הָיְתָה בָּהֶם לְעוֹלָם שֶׁלֹּא יַשְׁלִיכוּ דָּבָר שֶׁיְּהֵא נִשְׁחָת בָּזֶה – However,** in truth, **[the Sages] were always careful not to throw** down **something that would** actually **be ruined by this.**[22]

NOTES

18. The *yetzer hara* (evil inclination) does not immediately attempt to induce a person to transgress a sin as severe as idolatry. Rather, he begins with a "minor" sin, such as provoking one to lose his temper [which is prohibited; *Rambam, Hil. Dei'os* 2:3], and then progresses to more severe sins, eventually leading to idolatry (see *Shabbos* 105b). Thus, once a person breaks something in a fit of anger, he is on the road to *avodah zarah*.

[The Gemara (*Shabbos* 129a) does, however, permit destroying vessels for the sake of one's genuine well-being; for example, an ill person who needs warmth is allowed to burn furniture for heat, when no firewood is available. Breaking things in order to vent one's anger is not considered a legitimate need, for although it may help a person calm down, it inevitably leads to greater sins (*Yichusei Tannaim VaAmoraim* ערך חילפא).]

19. Chinuch has stated numerous times that man is comprised of two conflicting elements: a spiritual element that strives for growth and elevation, and a physical element that craves sensual pleasure (see Author's Introduction [Vol. I, pp. 12-17], and Mitzvos 95, 313 and 421). Here, Chinuch refers to these two elements as man's "intelligent soul" and his "desirous soul."

20. Man's physical element was placed in him in order to assist him and enable his spiritual pursuits. Its ultimate mission is to serve his spiritual element in the manner that a maidservant serves her mistress. However, the *yetzer hara* instigates man to digress from his mission and follow his sensual desires. In order to reach the state for which he was created, in which his spiritual soul has mastery over his desirous soul, one must fiercely battle his *yetzer hara* until he vanquishes it. By subduing the *yetzer hara* in relatively small matters, such as the instinct to shatter vessels in a fit of temper, one begins on the path of gaining complete control over his physicality. But if one relinquishes control in these "small" matters, he risks progressing to ever greater sins. [See *Shaarei Teshuvah* 3:82.]

21. The Gemara (*Shabbos* 105b) relates how Rav Yehudah tore off the border of a garment to demonstrate his displeasure with something that had been done, Rav Acha bar Yaakov broke utensils, Rav Sheishess threw fish brine at his maidservant, and R' Abba broke the lid of a pitcher.

Chinuch states that they would *portray* themselves as angry, not that they actually became angry. One may project himself as being angry in order to rebuke the members of his household, but even then one should not allow himself to truly become angry (*Rambam, Hil. Dei'os* 2:3). In any event, these Sages would destroy things to show their displeasure.

22. For example, when tearing off the border of a

וְיֶתֶר פְּרָטֵי הַמִּצְוָה בְּבָבָא בַּתְרָא פֶּרֶק שֵׁנִי[23].
וְנוֹהֵג אִסּוּר זֶה בְּכָל מָקוֹם וּבְכָל זְמַן, בִּזְכָרִים וּנְקֵבוֹת[24].
וְעוֹבֵר עַל זֶה וְהִשְׁחִית אִילָנֵי מַאֲכָל עָבַר עַל לָאו זֶה וְחַיָּב מַלְקוּת[25], וְעַל שְׁאָר הַשְׁחָתָה בְּכָל שְׁאָר דְּבָרִים שֶׁאֵינָן מְפֹרָשִׁין מַכִּין אוֹתוֹ מַכַּת מַרְדּוּת[26].

וְיֶתֶר פְּרָטֵי הַמִּצְוָה בְּבָבָא בַּתְרָא פֶּרֶק שֵׁנִי – These, **and the remaining details of the mitzvah,** are explained **in the second chapter of** Tractate ***Bava Basra*** (26a).[23]

Applicability of the Mitzvah

וְנוֹהֵג אִסּוּר זֶה בְּכָל מָקוֹם וּבְכָל זְמַן – **This prohibition applies in every location and in all times,** בִּזְכָרִים וּנְקֵבוֹת – to both **men and women.**[24]

Chinuch reiterates his position regarding the punishment for violating this prohibition:

וְעוֹבֵר עַל זֶה וְהִשְׁחִית אִילָנֵי מַאֲכָל – **One who transgresses this** matter **and** needlessly **destroys fruit trees** עָבַר עַל לָאו זֶה וְחַיָּב מַלְקוּת – **violates this prohibition, and is liable to *malkus.***[25] וְעַל שְׁאָר הַשְׁחָתָה – **But with regard to other** forms of **destruction** בְּכָל שְׁאָר דְּבָרִים שֶׁאֵינָן מְפֹרָשִׁין – **pertaining to any other objects that are not** mentioned **expressly** in our verse, מַכִּין אוֹתוֹ מַכַּת מַרְדּוּת – if one does them **we administer *makkas mardus* to him.**[26]

NOTES

garment, they would tear it at the seam, so that it could be sewn together again (see *Kiddushin* 32a). Similarly, in each of the other cases cited in the previous note, the object in question was not ruined permanently; or, it was something that already had no value.

[Others explain that the Sages actually ruined items of value, but the reason these actions were permitted was because the benefit of bringing disobedient members of the household into line outweighed the loss of the objects. Just as one may cut down a fruit tree whose timber is more valuable than its fruit, so is it permitted to tear a garment for the worthwhile purpose of correcting someone's behavior (*Sefer Yerei'im* §382 [297]; *Smag, Lo Saaseh* 229).]

23. See also *Bava Kamma* 91b-92a. The laws are codified in *Rambam, Hil. Melachim* 6:8-10.

24. That is, it applies in Eretz Yisrael and the Diaspora, and whether the *Beis HaMikdash* is standing or not; and it applies to both men and women, in accordance with the general rule pertaining to mitzvah-prohibitions.

25. In addition, one who cuts down a fruit tree places himself in mortal danger (*Taz, Yoreh Deah* 116:6, citing *Tzavaas R' Yehudah HeChassid* §45). Indeed, the Gemara relates (*Bava Kamma* 91b, *Bava Basra* 26a) that R' Chanina attributed the premature death of his son to the fact that the son cut down a fig tree before its time. [For discussion of this incident, see *She'eilas Yaavetz,* Vol. I §76, and *Teshuvos Chasam Sofer, Yoreh Deah* §102.]

26. See above, note 4. According to *Ramban* (glosses to *Sefer HaMitzvos,* Additional Mitzvah-Obligation 6), aside from the mitzvah-prohibition, there also is a mitzvah-obligation associated with cutting down fruit trees. The verse of the mitzvah states, ... כִּי תָצוּר אֶל עִיר לֹא תַשְׁחִית אֶת עֵצָהּ לִנְדֹּחַ עָלָיו גַּרְזֶן כִּי מִמֶּנּוּ תֹאכֵל וְאֹתוֹ לֹא תִכְרֹת, *When you besiege a city ... you shall not destroy [any of] its trees by swinging an axe against it, for from it you shall eat, and you shall not cut it down.* The phrase, *for from it you shall eat,* is a mitzvah-obligation. This does not mean that one *must* eat from the fruit; rather, it means to imply: you may *only* eat from it, but not cut it down. This is a לָאו הַבָּא מִכְּלַל עֲשֵׂה, *a prohibition derived from the implication of an obligation.* Thus, according to *Ramban,* one who cuts down a fruit tree transgresses both a mitzvah-prohibition and a mitzvah-obligation. See also *Sifrei* to the verse.

Insight: Cutting Down a Tree That *May* Be Fruit-producing

The passage of this mitzvah prohibits cutting down a fruit tree, and explicitly permits cutting down a non-fruit tree for the purpose of building a fortification. In this context, it states (*Deuteronomy* 20:20): רַק עֵץ אֲשֶׁר תֵּדַע כִּי לֹא עֵץ מַאֲכָל הוּא אֹתוֹ תַשְׁחִית וְכָרָתָּ וּבָנִיתָ מָצוֹר עַל הָעִיר אֲשֶׁר הִוא עֹשָׂה עִמְּךָ מִלְחָמָה עַד רִדְתָּהּ, *Only a tree that you know is not a food tree, it you may destroy and cut down, and build a fortification against the city, until it is conquered.* Now, the verse limits this permit to a tree that we *know* is not a food tree — clearly implying that if we are in doubt whether a tree produces fruit we may not cut it down. Many commentators point out that this presents a difficulty to a noted opinion of *Rambam.*

As is well known, any case of doubt in regard to a matter of Biblical law is governed by the principle

of סְפֵיקָא דְאוֹרַיְתָא לְחֻמְרָא, *An uncertainty regarding a Biblical matter is to be treated stringently.* That is, if one is uncertain whether something is prohibited, and the issue involves a potential Biblical violation, one must act stringently (see Mitzvah 496, at note 47). While this principle is universally agreed upon, there is disagreement among the Rishonim regarding its source. *Rambam* (Hil. Issurei Bi'ah 15:29, Hil. Tumas Meis 9:12) maintains that this is a Rabbinic enactment. That is, according to *Rambam*, Biblical law itself does not obligate us to be stringent in cases of uncertainty; it is the Sages who decreed that such cases be treated stringently. Other Rishonim disagree with *Rambam* and maintain that the requirement to be stringent in situations of uncertainty regarding Biblical law is itself a Biblical requirement (*Rashba, Toras HaBayis* 4:1; *Ran* to *Rif, Kiddushin* fol. 15b ד"ה גרסי'). [See Insight to Mitzvah 128 for discussion of this dispute.]

The verse regarding our mitzvah would seem to refute *Rambam's* view. If, in fact, Biblical law allows us to be lenient in situations of doubt, why does the Torah state that we may cut down only a tree that we *know* is not a food tree? Under Biblical law, this should be permitted even if we are *unsure* whether it is a food tree!

To resolve *Rambam's* position, numerous commentators explain that the verse does not refer to a case where we are uncertain about which species a certain tree belongs to; rather, it refers to a tree that certainly is of the fruit-producing variety, but we are in doubt whether it *still* produces fruit. As Chinuch mentioned (at note 15), when a food tree has aged to the point that it no longer produces enough fruit to make it worthwhile for the owner to cultivate it, the tree may be cut down. In a case of uncertainty about this point, even *Rambam* will agree that Biblical law prohibits cutting down the tree until we know that it has stopped producing a worthwhile crop. This is because of the principle of *chazakah*, which states that the law presumes that things remain unchanged until proven otherwise. Since the tree was originally a fruit-producing one that was forbidden to be cut down, it is presumed to remain a fruit-producing tree, and to remain prohibited for cutting down, until we determine that it has stopped producing fruit. Thus, the verse states, *Only a tree that you know is not a food tree, it you may destroy and cut down.*

Commentators note further that this interpretation is supported by *Sifrei* (cited in *Bava Kamma* 91b), which expounds the verse as follows: רַק עֵץ אֲשֶׁר תֵּדַע, *Only a tree that you know* — "this refers to a food tree"; כִּי לֹא עֵץ מַאֲכָל הוּא, *that it is not a food tree* — "this refers to a non-food tree." Regarding *both* of these trees, the verse concludes: אֹתוֹ תַשְׁחִית וְכָרָתָּ, *it you may destroy and cut down.* On the surface, *Sifrei's* exposition is perplexing. How can we interpret the words *Only a tree that you know* as referring to a food tree, when the verse immediately states, *that it is not a food tree*?! It must be that *Sifrei* means that the first part of the verse refers to a tree that is of a fruit-producing variety but has ceased to produce fruit. It is regarding such a tree that the verse stipulates *that you know,* meaning, we may not cut it down unless we *know* that it no longer produces fruit. But in a case where we are uncertain as to whether a certain tree *ever* produced fruit, we may cut it down even if we are unable to resolve our uncertainty. This is referred to with the words *that it is not a food tree.* Why is cutting down the latter type of tree permitted? Because when there is no *chazakah* that the tree is a fruit-producing one, Biblical law allows us to be lenient in a case of uncertainty, as *Rambam* states!

In other words, the commentators explain, *Sifrei* was disturbed by the very question raised above: Why does the verse stipulate *that you know,* when Biblical law allows for leniency in cases of doubt? *Sifrei* therefore explains that the first part of the verse must be referring to a tree that once *did* produce fruit, so it is under a *chazakah* of being prohibited to be cut down until we *know* that it stopped producing fruit. Only the latter part of the verse refers to a tree that never produced fruit.

It thus emerges that not only is the verse not difficult according to *Rambam's* opinion, but *Sifrei's* exposition actually provides *proof* to *Rambam's* opinion. For according to the view of the other Rishonim, that Biblical law demands stringency in cases of doubt, the meaning of the verse is clear: We may not cut down *any* tree unless we *know* that it is a non-fruit tree. There is thus no need to expound the two clauses of the verse as speaking about two different kinds of trees. According to *Rambam,* however, the verse is difficult, for we ought to be permitted (by Biblical law) to cut down even a tree whose nature is in doubt. It is because of this difficulty that *Sifrei* finds it necessary to explain that the verse speaks of two different kinds of trees, and when it states *that you know,* it refers to a tree that once produced fruit — for in such a case we must *know* that it stopped producing fruit before we may cut it down (see *Smag, Lo Saaseh* 229; *Teshuvos Chasam Sofer, Yoreh Deah* §102;

Maayan HaChochmah, p. 121a-b in Roedelheim ed.; *Malbim* to the verse; see, however, *Rashi, Bava Kamma* 91b ד"ה זה עץ מאכל).

Maharam Schik has another approach to explain why, according to *Rambam's* opinion, the verse requires us to *know* that something is not a fruit tree before we may cut it down. He assumes that this stipulation applies even when we are uncertain whether a tree is of a fruit-producing variety or not. Although Biblical law generally allows us to be lenient in cases of uncertainty, in the specific case of cutting down a fruit tree the Torah demands stringency. This is because, as was explained in note 25 above, cutting down a fruit tree is not only prohibited, but actually dangerous, as it places a person at risk of dying prematurely. Biblical law allows for leniency in a case of a possible *prohibition,* but not in a case of possible *mortal danger!* As our Sages state (*Chullin* 10a), סַכַּנְתָּא חֲמִירָא מֵאִיסּוּרָא, a question of *danger is treated more stringently than* a question of *a prohibition.* Where there is a potential threat to life, we must certainly be stringent. This is why the Torah stresses that we must *know* that something is not a fruit tree before we cut it down. By stating this, the Torah teaches that cutting down a fruit tree involves mortal danger, and must be avoided even in cases of uncertainty.

For additional resolutions of *Rambam's* opinion, see *HaKesav VeHaKabbalah, Haamek Davar,* and *Kli Chemdah* (end) to the verse.

מִצְוָה תקל: מִצְוַת עֲרִיפַת הָעֶגְלָה בְּנַחַל[1]

שֶׁנִּצְטַוִּינוּ בַּעֲרִיפַת עֶגְלָה[2] בְּנַחַל אֵיתָן, פֵּרוּשׁ אֵיתָן, שֶׁמֵּימָיו שׁוֹטְפִין בְּחָזְקָה[3].

Mitzvah 530

The Obligation to Perform the Eglah Arufah (Decapitated Calf) Procedure by a Stream

כִּי יִמָּצֵא חָלָל בָּאֲדָמָה אֲשֶׁר ה׳ אֱלֹהֶיךָ נֹתֵן לְךָ לְרִשְׁתָּהּ נֹפֵל בַּשָּׂדֶה לֹא נוֹדַע מִי הִכָּהוּ. וְיָצְאוּ זְקֵנֶיךָ וְשֹׁפְטֶיךָ וּמָדְדוּ אֶל הֶעָרִים אֲשֶׁר סְבִיבֹת הֶחָלָל. וְהָיָה הָעִיר הַקְּרֹבָה אֶל הֶחָלָל וְלָקְחוּ זִקְנֵי הָעִיר הַהִוא עֶגְלַת בָּקָר אֲשֶׁר לֹא עֻבַּד בָּהּ אֲשֶׁר לֹא מָשְׁכָה בְּעֹל. וְהוֹרִדוּ זִקְנֵי הָעִיר הַהִוא אֶת הָעֶגְלָה אֶל נַחַל אֵיתָן אֲשֶׁר לֹא יֵעָבֵד בּוֹ וְלֹא יִזָּרֵעַ וְעָרְפוּ שָׁם אֶת הָעֶגְלָה בַּנָּחַל. וְנִגְּשׁוּ הַכֹּהֲנִים בְּנֵי לֵוִי כִּי בָם בָּחַר ה׳ אֱלֹהֶיךָ לְשָׁרְתוֹ וּלְבָרֵךְ בְּשֵׁם ה׳ וְעַל פִּיהֶם יִהְיֶה כָּל רִיב וְכָל נָגַע. וְכֹל זִקְנֵי הָעִיר הַהִוא הַקְּרֹבִים אֶל הֶחָלָל יִרְחֲצוּ אֶת יְדֵיהֶם עַל הָעֶגְלָה הָעֲרוּפָה בַנָּחַל. וְעָנוּ וְאָמְרוּ יָדֵינוּ לֹא שָׁפְכָה אֶת הַדָּם הַזֶּה וְעֵינֵינוּ לֹא רָאוּ. כַּפֵּר לְעַמְּךָ יִשְׂרָאֵל אֲשֶׁר פָּדִיתָ ה׳ וְאַל תִּתֵּן דָּם נָקִי בְּקֶרֶב עַמְּךָ יִשְׂרָאֵל וְנִכַּפֵּר לָהֶם הַדָּם.

If a corpse will be found on the land that HASHEM, your God, gives you to inherit it, fallen in the field, it was not known who smote him, your elders and judges shall go out and measure toward the cities that are around the corpse. It shall be that the city nearest the corpse, the elders of that city shall take a calf, with which no work has been done, which has not pulled with a yoke. The elders of that city shall bring the calf down to a mighty stream, which cannot be worked and cannot be sown, and they shall decapitate it by the stream. The Kohanim, the offspring of Levi, shall approach, for them has HASHEM, your God, chosen to minister to Him, and to bless with the Name of HASHEM, and according to their word shall be every grievance and every plague. All of the elders of that city, who are the closest to the corpse, shall wash their hand over the calf that was decapitated by the stream. They shall speak up and say, "Our hands have not spilled this blood, and our eyes did not see. Atone for Your people Israel that You have redeemed, O HASHEM: Do not place innocent blood in the midst of Your people Israel!" Then the blood shall be atoned for them (*Deuteronomy* 21:1-8).

In the above passage, the Torah describes the *eglah arufah* (decapitated calf) procedure, which comes to atone for certain murders. If the corpse of a murder victim is found in Eretz Yisrael and it is not known who killed him, measurements must be made by members of the Great Sanhedrin to determine the town that is closest to the corpse. The elders of the closest town[1] are obligated to bring a calf to the banks of a strongly flowing stream, where they kill it by striking the back of its neck with a cleaver. They then wash their hands at the site of the decapitation, and make a declaration in which they state that they bear no responsibility for the murder. Kohanim who are present (see v. 5) then pray for atonement.

שֶׁנִּצְטַוִּינוּ בַּעֲרִיפַת עֶגְלָה בְּנַחַל אֵיתָן – **We are commanded,** under specific circumstances, **to decapitate a calf[2] at an *eisan* stream,** **פֵּרוּשׁ אֵיתָן שֶׁמֵּימָיו שׁוֹטְפִין בְּחָזְקָה** – with **the meaning**

NOTES

1. This refers to the local *beis din* of twenty-three (minor sanhedrin). If a town does not have a *beis din* of twenty-three (e.g., its population is too small; see Mitzvah 491 note 6), it does not become obligated to bring an *eglah arufah,* even if it is the town closest to the corpse (*Rambam, Hil. Rotze'ach* 9:4; see also Insight).

2. As Chinuch will explain below, there are several steps to the *eglah arufah* procedure, one of which is

וְעִנְיַן הַמִּצְוָה הוּא כְּשֶׁנִּמְצָא בְּשָׂדֶה אוֹ בַדֶּרֶךְ הָרוּג וְלֹא נוֹדַע מִי הִכָּהוּ[4] וּכְמוֹ שֶׁבָּא מְפֹרָשׁ בַּכָּתוּב[5], וְעַל זֶה נֶאֱמַר (דברים כ״א, א׳) כִּי יִמָּצֵא חָלָל וְגוֹ׳ עַד גְּמַר הַפָּרָשָׁה, וְזֶהוּ עִנְיַן עֶגְלָה עֲרוּפָה הַנִּזְכָּר בַּגְּמָרָא[6].

מִשָּׁרְשֵׁי הַמִּצְוָה, כְּדֵי שֶׁיִּתְעוֹרֵר לֵב כָּל הָעָם בִּרְאוֹתָם אֶת הַמַּעֲשֶׂה הַגָּדוֹל הַזֶּה אֲסִיפַת זִקְנֵי הָעִיר וּגְדוֹלֶיהָ, וְיִקְחוּ פָּרָה שֶׁהִיא בְּהֵמָה גְדוֹלָה[7] וְיֵלְכוּ בַּאֲסִיפָה וּבְהָמוֹן, שֶׁהַכֹּל חֲפֵצִים לִרְאוֹת עִנְיָנִים אֵלֶּה, אֶל מִחוּץ לָעִיר, וּלְקוֹל עֲרִיפָתָהּ יֶחֶרְדוּ כָּל הַשּׁוֹמְעִים[8]

---

of *eisan* being that the water [of the stream] flows strongly.[3]

וְעִנְיַן הַמִּצְוָה הוּא – **The description of** when **the mitzvah is** applicable is כְּשֶׁנִּמְצָא בְּשָׂדֶה אוֹ בַדֶּרֶךְ הָרוּג – **when a murder victim is found in a field or on the road,** וְלֹא נוֹדַע מִי הִכָּהוּ – **and it is unknown who killed him,**[4] וּכְמוֹ שֶׁבָּא מְפֹרָשׁ בַּכָּתוּב – **as Scripture explicitly conveys.**[5] וְעַל זֶה נֶאֱמַר "כִּי יִמָּצֵא חָלָל וְגוֹ׳" עַד גְּמַר הַפָּרָשָׁה – **Regarding this** obligation, **it is stated** (*Deuteronomy* 21:1), ***If a corpse will be found*** *on the land that* H*ASHEM*, *your God, gives you to inherit it, fallen in the field, it was not known who smote him* **etc., until the end of the passage** (v. 9). וְזֶהוּ עִנְיַן עֶגְלָה עֲרוּפָה הַנִּזְכָּר בַּגְּמָרָא – **This** (the procedure described in those verses) **is the topic of *eglah arufah*** (decapitated calf) **that is mentioned in** various places in **the Gemara.**[6]

Underlying Purpose of the Mitzvah

מִשָּׁרְשֵׁי הַמִּצְוָה – **Among the underlying purposes of the mitzvah** is כְּדֵי שֶׁיִּתְעוֹרֵר לֵב כָּל הָעָם בִּרְאוֹתָם אֶת הַמַּעֲשֶׂה הַגָּדוֹל הַזֶּה – **so that the hearts of the entire nation will be aroused when they see this remarkable procedure,** which consists of אֲסִיפַת זִקְנֵי הָעִיר וּגְדוֹלֶיהָ – **the gathering of the town's elders and its leaders,** וְיִקְחוּ פָּרָה שֶׁהִיא בְּהֵמָה גְדוֹלָה – **who** then **take a cow, which is a large animal,**[7] וְיֵלְכוּ בַּאֲסִיפָה וּבְהָמוֹן שֶׁהַכֹּל חֲפֵצִים לִרְאוֹת עִנְיָנִים אֵלֶּה אֶל מִחוּץ לָעִיר – **and go together with a throng** of people – **for everyone desires to see these matters – out of town** to a strongly flowing stream.[8] וּלְקוֹל עֲרִיפָתָהּ יֶחֶרְדוּ כָּל הַשּׁוֹמְעִים – **All those listening**

NOTES

decapitating a calf. Although all of these steps are included in the mitzvah, Chinuch describes the mitzvah as an obligation to decapitate a calf, since that is the central component of the procedure.

3. The Torah states that the calf must be decapitated at a נַחַל אֵיתָן. The term נַחַל can refer either to a stream or to a valley. Chinuch follows *Rambam* (*Hil. Rotze'ach* 9:2), who translates נַחַל here as "stream." Accordingly, the word אֵיתָן, *strong,* describes the flow of the water. Others (*Rashi, Deuteronomy* 21:4; *Rashbam, Bava Basra* 55a ד״ה הנחל; *Rash, Peah* 2:1) maintain that נַחַל here refers to a "valley." According to that understanding, the word אֵיתָן teaches that the ground of the valley must be hard (*Rashi* ibid.). For further discussion of these two views, see *Teshuvos Maharik* §158 and *Teshuvos Chacham Tzvi* §32.

Meiri (*Sotah* 44b ד״ה ואחר שהביאו and *Niddah* 8b) writes that according to *Rambam,* the decapitation takes place on the bank of the stream, and not in the stream itself. See also *Nachal Eisan* (*R' Chaim Kanievski*) 12:3 [4] at length.

4. That is, not even one witness has testified that he saw the murderer kill the victim. If, however, even one person has given such testimony, the procedure is not carried out (see Mitzvah 523, at note 22), even if that one person would usually be disqualified from giving testimony (*Rambam, Hil. Rotze'ach* 9:12). [See *Nachal Eisan* 4:2 [11] for discussion as to whether it is sufficient for the single witness to merely have seen the murder, or whether the witness must have the ability to recognize the murderer if he would see him again.]

5. When introducing the obligation to perform this procedure, the Torah writes (*Deuteronomy* 21:1), *If a corpse will be found on the land that* H*ASHEM*, *your God, gives you to inherit it, fallen in the field,* ***it was not known who smote him,*** etc.

6. As Chinuch mentions later, it is discussed primarily in the ninth chapter of *Sotah,* which is called Chapter *Eglah Arufah.*

7. Chinuch's reference to a פָּרָה, *cow,* is surprising, since this term usually refers to an adult cow that is at least two years old (see *Parah* 1:1 and *Rambam, Hil. Parah Adumah* 1:1), while an *eglah arufah* must be a female calf that is *younger* than two years old; see *Rambam, Hil. Rotze'ach* 10:2 (*Hagahos Tzava Rav*). [It would seem that Chinuch uses "cow" merely to describe the *species* of animal, which is "large" in comparison to a sheep or goat; and a calf is likewise larger than a lamb or kid.]

8. There is seemingly no source that indicates that the stream cannot be in the city itself. Therefore, Chinuch's

וְיִתְעוֹרֵר רַעְיוֹנָם עַל הַדָּבָר, וְכָל הַיּוֹדֵעַ בַּדָּבָר מִיָּד יֶהֱמֶה לְבָבוֹ וְתָעִיר מַחֲשַׁבְתּוֹ לְהַגִּיד מַה שֶּׁהוּא יוֹדֵעַ לִפְנֵי הַזְּקֵנִים, וּמִתּוֹךְ כָּךְ יְבַעֲרוּ הָרָעִים וְהָרוֹצְחִים מִקִּרְבָּם[9]. וּמִלְּבַד הַיְדִיעָה יֵשׁ תּוֹעֶלֶת רַב בְּמַעֲשֶׂה הַגָּדוֹל הַזֶּה לְהֵרָאוֹת וּלְפַרְסֵם בֶּהָמוֹן פִּרְסוּם גָּדוֹל כִּי חֵפֶץ הַזְּקֵנִים וְאַנְשֵׁי הַדַּעַת יִהְיֶה לִמְצֹא הָרוֹצֵחַ לִנְקֹם מִמֶּנּוּ נִקְמַת הַנִּרְצָח[10], וְכֵן מָצָאתִי לְהָרַמְבַּ״ם ז״ל (מורה נבוכים ח״ג פ״מ)[11].

מִדִּינֵי הַמִּצְוָה מַה שֶּׁאָמְרוּ זִכְרוֹנָם לִבְרָכָה (סוטה מ״ה ע״ב) שֶׁיְּרוּשָׁלַיִם אֵינָהּ מְבִיאָה עֶגְלָה עֲרוּפָה לְפִי שֶׁנֶּאֱמַר בָּזֶה בָּאֲדָמָה אֲשֶׁר ה׳ אֱלֹהֶיךָ נֹתֵן לְךָ, וִירוּשָׁלַיִם לֹא נִתְחַלְּקָה לַשְּׁבָטִים[12,13].

---

will surely **tremble at the sounds emitted** by the calf **during its decapitation,** וְיִתְעוֹרֵר רַעְיוֹנָם עַל הַדָּבָר **– and their thoughts will be stirred to** think **about the matter,** i.e., the murder, וְכָל הַיּוֹדֵעַ בַּדָּבָר מִיָּד יֶהֱמֶה לְבָבוֹ וְתָעִיר מַחֲשַׁבְתּוֹ **– and immediately the heart of anyone who has any knowledge regarding the matter will be moved and his mind stirred** לְהַגִּיד מַה שֶּׁהוּא יוֹדֵעַ לִפְנֵי הַזְּקֵנִים **– to relate what he knows to the elders** of the city. וּמִתּוֹךְ כָּךְ יְבַעֲרוּ הָרָעִים וְהָרוֹצְחִים מִקִּרְבָּם **– As a result of this, [the Jewish people] will succeed in removing the evildoers and the murderers from their midst.**[9] וּמִלְּבַד הַיְדִיעָה **– Aside from the knowledge** regarding the murder that can emerge from carrying out this mitzvah and can lead to justice being carried out, יֵשׁ תּוֹעֶלֶת רַב בְּמַעֲשֶׂה הַגָּדוֹל הַזֶּה **– there is great benefit in performing this remarkable procedure,** לְהֵרָאוֹת וּלְפַרְסֵם בֶּהָמוֹן פִּרְסוּם גָּדוֹל **– in** simply **demonstrating and publicizing with great fanfare in front of the masses** כִּי חֵפֶץ הַזְּקֵנִים וְאַנְשֵׁי הַדַּעַת יִהְיֶה לִמְצֹא הָרוֹצֵחַ **– that it is the desire of the elders and wise people** of the city **to find the murderer,** לִנְקֹם מִמֶּנּוּ נִקְמַת הַנִּרְצָח **– in order to take vengeance on him for the murder victim.**[10] וְכֵן מָצָאתִי לְהָרַמְבַּ״ם ז״ל **– And so did I find in** the writings of ***Rambam,* of blessed memory** (*Moreh Nevuchim* III:40).[11]

Laws of the Mitzvah

Chinuch mentions several cases where the regular laws of *eglah arufah* do not apply:

מִדִּינֵי הַמִּצְוָה **– Among the laws of the mitzvah** is מַה שֶּׁאָמְרוּ זִכְרוֹנָם לִבְרָכָה **– that which [the Sages], of blessed memory, stated** (*Sotah* 45b), שֶׁיְּרוּשָׁלַיִם אֵינָהּ מְבִיאָה עֶגְלָה עֲרוּפָה **– that** the city of **Jerusalem does not bring an *eglah arufah*** when it is the closest town to a corpse, לְפִי שֶׁנֶּאֱמַר בָּזֶה ״בָּאֲדָמָה אֲשֶׁר ה׳ אֱלֹהֶיךָ נֹתֵן לְךָ״ **– because it is stated in** the passage of **this** mitzvah: *If a corpse will be found* ***on the land that HASHEM, your God, gives you*** *to inherit it,* which limits the mitzvah to land that was included in the original division of Eretz Yisrael among the tribes, to then be passed down from generation to generation as an inheritance, וִירוּשָׁלַיִם לֹא נִתְחַלְּקָה לַשְּׁבָטִים **– and Jerusalem was not apportioned among the tribes,**[12] so it is not considered land that Hashem gave "to inherit it."[13]

NOTES

description of the elders of the city going out of the city to decapitate the calf requires further study (*Nachal Eisan* 11:3 [1]).

9. If there are valid witnesses to the murder and the murderer was forewarned about the consequences of his action, *beis din* can execute him. And even in situations where *beis din* cannot execute the murderer, it is still possible, in certain circumstances, for a Jewish king or the *go'eil hadam* (avenging relative) to kill the murderer (*Moreh Nevuchim* III:40).

10. That is, by performing an elaborate public ceremony whose purpose is to reveal the identity of the murderer, the elders demonstrate that they sincerely desire to bring the murderer to justice. When the residents see this, they will come to realize the severity of murder, and do everything in their power to prevent it.

11. Chinuch refers to the first idea he mentioned, that the purpose of the *eglah arufah* procedure is to publicize the matter, so that the identity of the murderer can be revealed. The added benefit of demonstrating the elders' desire to carry out justice is Chinuch's addition.

12. Tannaim dispute whether Jerusalem was given to a specific tribe when Eretz Yisrael was apportioned in the time of Joshua (see *Megillah* 26a). The halachah follows the view that Jerusalem was *not* apportioned to a specific tribe, but remained the property of the nation as a whole (*Rambam, Hil. Tumas Tzaraas* 14:11, *Hil. Rotze'ach* 9:4).

13. According to its plain meaning, the verse refers to the site where the corpse was *found,* not to the town that is required to bring the *eglah arufah.* Nevertheless, the Sages understood that the verse implies that the

וְכֵן אִם נִמְצָא סָמוּךְ לַסְּפָר אוֹ לְעִיר שֶׁרֻבָּהּ גּוֹיִם[14] אֵין מְבִיאִין עֶגְלָה, שֶׁחֲזָקָה הִיא שֶׁהַגּוֹיִם הֲרָגוּהוּ[15].

הָיוּ[16] שָׁם שְׁתֵּי עֲיָרוֹת, אַחַת קְרוֹבָה וְאַחַת אֵינָהּ קְרוֹבָה אֲבָל יֵשׁ בָּהּ רִבּוּי אֲנָשִׁים יוֹתֵר מִן הַקְּרוֹבָה, הוֹלְכִין אַחַר הָרְחוֹקָה שֶׁיֵּשׁ בָּהּ רֹב[17], שֶׁכֵּן אָמְרוּ זִכְרוֹנָם לִבְרָכָה בַּגְּמָרָא

וְכֵן אִם נִמְצָא סָמוּךְ לַסְּפָר – **Likewise, if** a corpse **is found near the border** of Eretz Yisrael אוֹ לְעִיר שֶׁרֻבָּהּ גּוֹיִם – **or** near **a town that is** inhabited **mostly** by **idolaters,**[14] אֵין מְבִיאִין עֶגְלָה – **we do not bring an** ***eglah*** *arufah* (ibid. 45b), שֶׁחֲזָקָה הִיא שֶׁהַגּוֹיִם הֲרָגוּהוּ – **because** in such cases, **it is presumed that the idolaters killed [the person],** and we are not commanded to bring an *eglah arufah* to atone for a murder committed by an idolater.[15]

The reason that an *eglah arufah* is brought by the town closest to the corpse is that there is a presumption that the murderer came from there.[16] This is based on the principle known as קָרוֹב, *proximity,* which teaches that when there is uncertainty regarding where something came from, we presume that it came from the closest possible location. There is, however, another rule for determining where something came from — the rule of רוֹב, *majority,* which dictates that when there is uncertainty as to where something came from, we presume that it came from the place where the majority of such things are found. Chinuch discusses how to resolve cases in which these two principles are in conflict: הָיוּ שָׁם שְׁתֵּי עֲיָרוֹת – If **there were two towns** near the corpse, אַחַת קְרוֹבָה – **one** is **closest to [the corpse],** וְאַחַת אֵינָהּ קְרוֹבָה אֲבָל יֵשׁ בָּהּ רִבּוּי אֲנָשִׁים יוֹתֵר מִן הַקְּרוֹבָה – **and the other is not closest** to the corpse, **but has a larger population than the closest** town, הוֹלְכִין אַחַר הָרְחוֹקָה שֶׁיֵּשׁ בָּהּ רֹב – **we follow the farther** town **that has more** people (the "majority") in determining where the murderer came from.[17] שֶׁכֵּן אָמְרוּ זִכְרוֹנָם לִבְרָכָה בַּגְּמָרָא – **For this is what [the Sages], of blessed memory, stated in the Gemara** (*Bava Basra* 23b):

NOTES

town that is obligated to bring the *eglah arufah* must also be subject to inheritance (*Tiferes Tzion, Sotah* 45b; *Nachal Eisan* 6:11 [1,4]). Therefore, Jerusalem, which does not fit this description, does not become obligated to bring an *eglah arufah* even if it is the closest city to the corpse.

Rambam (*Hil. Rotze'ach* 9:5) rules that in a situation where Jerusalem is the closest town to the corpse, the next closest town brings an *eglah arufah* instead. See *Tosefta, Sotah* 9:3.

14. That is, no town lies between the corpse and the border of Eretz Yisrael, or between the corpse and the city with a majority population of idolaters (*Meir* to *Sotah* 44b ד״ה ואמר אח״כ שהיו בית דין הגדול).

15. If the corpse is found near a border of Eretz Yisrael that adjoins a land of idolaters, there is no obligation to bring an *eglah arufah,* even if a town on the other side of the corpse (in Eretz Yisrael) is closer to the corpse than the border. And if the corpse is found near a town that is inhabited mostly by idolaters, there is no obligation to bring an *eglah arufah* even if there are Jewish towns on the other sides of the corpse that are closer to the corpse (*Nachal Eisan* 6:3 [2]). In both these cases, the proximity of idolaters on one side creates a presumption that the murderer was an idolater, and there is no obligation to bring an *eglah arufah*.

Chinuch's reason for these laws is taken from *Rambam, Hil. Rotze'ach* 9:5. The Gemara (*Sotah* 45b), however, derives these laws from Scripture. See *Nachal Eisan* ibid. for discussion.

Although Chinuch seems to equate this case to the previous case, their laws are not identical. As Chinuch clearly writes, in cases where a corpse is found near the border or near a town that is inhabited mostly by idolaters, there is no obligation for *any* city to bring an *eglah arufah*. By contrast, in a case where Jerusalem is the closest city to the corpse, only Jerusalem is exempt from bringing an *eglah arufah,* but the next closest city is obligated to bring one instead. See above, note 13. See, however, *R' Y. F. Perla, Sefer HaMitzvos of Rav Saadiah Gaon, Parashah* 8 (Vol. III, p. 122b ד״ה אלא דעיקר דברי).

16. See *Bava Basra* 23b with *Tosafos* ד״ה בדליכא.

17. Therefore, the closest town (which is smaller) certainly does not bring an *eglah arufah.* [This refers even to a city that has a *beis din.*] Rishonim disagree as to whether the larger city, which is farther away, is required to bring an *eglah arufah* instead in this case; see Insight for discussion.

Since the principle of "majority" is superior to the principle of "proximity," we are forced to explain that when the Torah commands the "town nearest the corpse" to bring an *eglah arufah,* it is speaking about a case where the principle of "majority" cannot help us determine where the murderer came from; i.e., all cities in the vicinity of the corpse have the same population as the closest city (see *Bava Basra* 23b and *Rambam* ibid.).

(ב״ב כ״ג ע״ב), רֹב וְקָרוֹב, הַלֵּךְ אַחַר הָרֹב, וְאַף עַל פִּי שֶׁרֹב וְקָרוֹב שְׁנֵיהֶם דְּאוֹרַיְתָא, כְּלוֹמַר שֶׁהַתּוֹרָה תִּצַוֵּנוּ לָחוּשׁ עַל הַקָּרוֹב וְעַל הָרֹב[18], הָרֹב עָדִיף. וּמֵהֵיכָן מוֹדְדִין[19], מֵחָטְמוֹ שֶׁל הָרוּג[20]. וְדִין עֲרִיפָתָהּ שֶׁהוּא בְּקוֹפִיץ מֵאַחֲרֶיהָ[21], וְדִין רְחִיצַת הַיָּדַיִם[22], וְדִין נִמְצָא הַגּוּף בְּמָקוֹם אֶחָד וְהָרֹאשׁ בְּמָקוֹם אַחֵר[23].

רֹב וְקָרוֹב הַלֵּךְ אַחַר הָרֹב — Where a conflict arises between the principles of **"majority" and "proximity,"** we follow the concept of **"majority."** וְאַף עַל פִּי שֶׁרֹב וְקָרוֹב שְׁנֵיהֶם דְּאוֹרַיְתָא — For even though the principles of **"majority" and "proximity"** are both of Biblical origin, כְּלוֹמַר שֶׁהַתּוֹרָה תִּצַוֵּנוּ לָחוּשׁ עַל הַקָּרוֹב וְעַל הָרֹב — meaning, that the Torah commanded us to consider both **"proximity" and "majority"** when determining where something came from,[18] הָרֹב עָדִיף — nevertheless, the principle of **"majority" is superior.**

Chinuch mentions several additional laws pertaining to the *eglah arufah* procedure:

וּמֵהֵיכָן מוֹדְדִין — **From where** (i.e., from what part of the corpse) **do we measure** to the nearest town?[19] מֵחָטְמוֹ שֶׁל הָרוּג — **From the nose of the murder victim.**[20]

וְדִין עֲרִיפָתָהּ שֶׁהוּא בְּקוֹפִיץ מֵאַחֲרֶיהָ — There **also** is **the law regarding** how **the decapitation of [the calf]** is performed, namely **that it is** performed **with a cleaver, from behind [the calf].**[21] וְדִין רְחִיצַת הַיָּדַיִם — **And** there is **the law of the "washing of the hands,"** i.e., that after the calf has been decapitated, the elders of the city must wash their hands at the site of the decapitation.[22] וְדִין נִמְצָא הַגּוּף בְּמָקוֹם אֶחָד וְהָרֹאשׁ בְּמָקוֹם אַחֵר — **And** there is **the law concerning** a case where most of **the** murder victim's **body was found in one place, but its head was found elsewhere** (i.e., the victim had been decapitated).[23]

NOTES

18. The principle of "proximity" is learned from our mitzvah, where the Torah commands the city closest to the corpse to bring an *eglah arufah,* based on the presumption that the murderer came from there. The principle of "majority" is learned from the verse (*Exodus* 23:2): אַחֲרֵי רַבִּים לְהַטֹּת, which is interpreted to mean, *after the majority it shall be decided* (see *Chullin* 11a; see also Insight to Mitzvah 78).

19. When two towns are virtually the same distance from the corpse, the body part from which the measurement is made could make a difference in determining which of the two is actually closest to the corpse (see *Rashi* to *Sanhedrin* 88a ד״ה ממקום שנעשה חלל and *Meiri* ad loc.).

20. The measurement must be made from the "main" part of the corpse, defined as the part of the body that performs the function most critical to life. Since breathing is considered the most critical bodily function, the measurement is made from the corpse's nose (see *Sotah* 45b with רש״י ד״ה עיקר חיותא).

21. That is, the calf is struck with a cleaver at the back of its neck (*Kesubos* 37b). The word, וְעָרְפוּ, which the Torah uses to convey this obligation, is understood to mean, *and they shall remove the part of the body called the "oref"* (Ibn Ezra to the verse; *Radak, Sefer HaShorashim* ע׳ ערף; see *Rashi* to the verse with *Sifsei Chachamim*). In Scriptural terminology, עוֹרֶף, *oref,* usually refers to the back of the head opposite the face (see *Chullin* 19b), but the Sages derive exegetically that here it refers to the back of the neck (see *Sotah* 46b and *Kesubos* 37b with *Tosafos* ד״ה מה להלן). Thus, the Torah

commands that the calf be decapitated with a blow to the back of its neck.

The obligation to use a cleaver is indicated by the plain meaning of the verse, for since a cleaver is used to cut thick pieces of meat and bone, it is the instrument that is naturally used for such a blow (see *Bechoros* 10b with *Rashi* ד״ה בקופיץ).

22. As stated in *Deuteronomy* 21:6. By washing their hands at the site where the calf was decapitated, the elders symbolically declare that their hands are clean of any responsibility for the murder (*Chizkuni* and *R' S. R. Hirsch* to *Deuteronomy* ibid.).

23. The law that Chinuch alludes to does not concern the measurement from the corpse to the surrounding towns to determine which city is obligated to bring an *eglah arufah*. Rather, it concerns the burial of the murder victim (see *Sotah* 45b). The law is that an unattended corpse "acquires" ownership of the place where he died, and is buried there, regardless of who owns that site. Therefore, in our case, the murder victim is buried where it is found. In the case of an unattended corpse that has been decapitated so that its head and the rest of its body are not together, the body is brought to the head, and the entire corpse is buried where the head was found (*Rambam, Hil. Rotze'ach* 9:9). The reason for this is that we presume that he died at the spot where his head was found, and that as he was fleeing his attacker, his momentum carried his body further after his head had been severed (*Sotah* ibid.; see *Yerushalmi Sotah* 9:4 for exceptions to this rule).

[As mentioned previously (at note 20), the

וְדִין מַה שֶׁאָמְרוּ חָלָל וְלֹא חָנוּק[24], בָּאֲדָמָה וְלֹא טָמוּן בְּגַל[25], נֹפֵל וְלֹא תָלוּי בְּאִילָן[26], בַּשָּׂדֶה וְלֹא צָף עַל פְּנֵי הַמַּיִם[27], וְיֶתֶר פְּרָטֶיהָ מְבֹאָרִים בְּפֶרֶק אַחֲרוֹן מִמַּסֶּכֶת סוֹטָה[28]. וְנוֹהֵג מִצְוָה זוֹ בְּאֶרֶץ יִשְׂרָאֵל בִּזְמַן שֶׁהִיא בְּיִשּׁוּבָהּ[29] וְכֵן בְּעֵבֶר הַיַּרְדֵּן[30].

In introducing the *eglah arufah* procedure, the Torah states (*Deuteronomy* 21:1): *If a chalal* (corpse) *will be found on the land that HASHEM, your God, gives you to inherit it, fallen in the field* etc. Chinuch mentions several laws that are derived from this verse:

וְדִין מַה שֶׁאָמְרוּ – There is **the law that [the Sages] stated** (*Sotah* 45b): **"חָלָל" וְלֹא חָנוּק** – An *eglah arufah* is brought only if the murder victim is **"a *chalal*,"** i.e., he was killed by a sharp metal instrument, **but not** if he was **strangled** to death;[24] **"בָּאֲדָמָה" וְלֹא טָמוּן בְּגַל** – it is brought only if the corpse is found **"on the land,"** i.e., out in the open, **but not** if it was found **covered by a pile** of stones;[25] **"נֹפֵל" וְלֹא תָלוּי בְּאִילָן** – it is brought only if the corpse was found **"fallen,"** i.e., in a lying position, **but not** if it was found **hanging from a tree;**[26] **"בַּשָּׂדֶה" וְלֹא צָף עַל פְּנֵי הַמַּיִם** – and only if it was found **"in the field," but not** if it was found **floating on the water.**[27]

וְיֶתֶר פְּרָטֶיהָ מְבֹאָרִים בְּפֶרֶק אַחֲרוֹן מִמַּסֶּכֶת סוֹטָה – These, **and the additional details of the mitzvah, are set forth in the final chapter of** Tractate ***Sotah*** (44b-47b).[28]

Applicability of the Mitzvah

וְנוֹהֵג מִצְוָה זוֹ בְּאֶרֶץ יִשְׂרָאֵל בִּזְמַן שֶׁהִיא בְּיִשּׁוּבָהּ – **This mitzvah applies in Eretz Yisrael at a time when it is settled** by the Jewish people (i.e., when the *Beis HaMikdash* is standing),[29] **וְכֵן בְּעֵבֶר**

NOTES

measurement to determine which city is obligated to bring an *eglah arufah* is made from the nose of the corpse. Since we presume that the person died at the spot where his head was found, the measurement can be made from the head of the corpse without first bringing the rest of the body to the head.]

24. The term חָלָל, *chalal* (as opposed to the more generic הָרוּג, *murdered person*), refers specifically to a corpse killed by a sharp metal instrument, such as a sword (*Rashi* 45b ד״ה חלל). Therefore, by referring to the corpse as a חָלָל, the Torah teaches that an *eglah arufah* is brought only for a corpse killed by a sharp metal instrument, and not for a corpse killed in any other way (see *Malbim* to *Deuteronomy* 21:1). See, however, *Meiri* (*Sotah* 45b) for a different understanding of this exposition.

25. By stating "on the land," the verse implies that the corpse was found *on* the land, i.e., lying exposed on the surface of the field, and not *within* the land, buried underground or covered (see *Rashi* to 45a ד״ה בשדה and ד״ה התם מענייניה דקרא). [A pile of stones is merely an example. The same applies if the corpse is covered by anything (see *Sotah* 45a).]

26. Hanging from a tree is merely an example. Any corpse not found in a *lying* position does not create a requirement to bring an *eglah arufah* (*Rashash, Sotah* 44b ד״ה נופל ולא תלוי; *Dvar Avraham* 1:6).

This law does not speak of a corpse that died by being hanged, for such a case is already excluded from the *eglah arufah* requirement by the word *chalal*; see note 24. Rather, we are speaking about a case where the corpse was found hanging from a tree, but it is apparent that it was killed by a sharp metal instrument (*Yerushalmi Sotah* 9:2).

27. The phrase "in the field" implies that the corpse was found lying on the surface of the field. By using this expression, the Torah teaches that there is no obligation to bring an *eglah arufah* in any case where the corpse was not found in direct contact with the ground, e.g., it was floating on the water (see *Sotah* 44b). [The earlier case of a corpse found hanging from a tree refers to a case where the feet of the corpse were touching the ground, not dangling in the air. Therefore, it cannot be excluded on the basis of the present exposition, which teaches that the corpse must be in contact with the ground (*Rashash* ibid.).]

As in the previous case (see previous note), we are not speaking about a corpse that died by drowning, for such a case is already excluded by the word *chalal*. Rather, the corpse was found floating in the water, but it is apparent that it was killed by a sharp metal instrument (see *Yerushalmi Sotah* 9:2).

[See *R' S. R. Hirsch, Deuteronomy* 21:1, who suggests a rationale for all these exceptions to the *eglah arufah* obligation.]

28. These laws are codified by *Rambam* in *Hil. Rotze'ach* Chs. 9-10.

29. As Chinuch explains in Mitzvah 531, this mitzvah applies only when it is possible for *beis din* to judge capital cases, i.e., when the Great Sanhedrin convenes in the Chamber of Hewn Stone (*Lishkas HaGazis*) in the *Beis HaMikdash*.

The source for Chinuch's assertion that *eglah arufah*, which is not a capital case, should be limited to times when *beis din* can judge capital cases is not readily

וְחִיּוּבָהּ עַל הַזְּכָרִים וְיוֹתֵר עַל גְּדוֹלֵי הָעִיר, וּכְעִנְיָן שֶׁכָּתוּב וְלָקְחוּ זִקְנֵי הָעִיר הַהִיא³¹. וּמַה שֶּׁאָמַר הַכָּתוּב תְּחִלָּה וְיָצְאוּ זְקֵנֶיךָ וְשֹׁפְטֶיךָ, עַל זִקְנֵי יְרוּשָׁלַיִם הוּא מְדַבֵּר, שֶׁכֵּן אָמְרוּ זִכְרוֹנָם לִבְרָכָה (סוטה מ״ד ע״ב) שֶׁחֲמִשָּׁה זְקֵנִים שֶׁל בֵּית דִּין הַגָּדוֹל שֶׁבִּירוּשָׁלַיִם הָיוּ יוֹצְאִין וּמוֹדְדִין³², וַעֲלֵיהֶם מִצְוַת הַמְּדִידָה. וְעַל זִקְנֵי הָעִיר מִצְוַת הָעֶגְלָה וּרְחִיצַת הַיָּדַיִם³³

הַיַּרְדֵּן — and it **also** applies **in Transjordan** at such a time.[30] וְחִיּוּבָהּ עַל הַזְּכָרִים וְיוֹתֵר עַל גְּדוֹלֵי הָעִיר — **The obligation of** [this mitzvah] **is incumbent upon the men** of the town closest to the corpse, **but even more so upon the leaders of the town,** וּכְעִנְיָן שֶׁכָּתוּב ״וְלָקְחוּ זִקְנֵי הָעִיר הַהִיא״ — **in keeping with that which is written** in the *eglah arufah* passage (*Deuteronomy* 21:3): *It shall be that the town nearest the corpse,* ***the elders of that town shall take*** *a calf,* etc.[31]

Having mentioned that the "elders of that town" play a crucial role in the *eglah arufah* procedure, Chinuch clarifies that not all mentions of "elders" in the *eglah arufah* passage refer to the elders of the town closest to the corpse:

וּמַה שֶּׁאָמַר הַכָּתוּב תְּחִלָּה ״וְיָצְאוּ זְקֵנֶיךָ וְשֹׁפְטֶיךָ״ — **That which the verse first states:** *your elders and judges shall go out* and *measure toward the cities that are around the corpse,* etc., עַל זִקְנֵי יְרוּשָׁלַיִם הוּא מְדַבֵּר — **refers to the elders of Jerusalem,** i.e., judges from the Great Sanhedrin, שֶׁכֵּן אָמְרוּ זִכְרוֹנָם לִבְרָכָה — **for so said** [the Sages], **of blessed memory** (*Sotah* 44b): שֶׁחֲמִשָּׁה זְקֵנִים שֶׁל בֵּית דִּין הַגָּדוֹל שֶׁבִּירוּשָׁלַיִם הָיוּ יוֹצְאִין וּמוֹדְדִין — **that five elders from the Great Court** (i.e., the Great Sanhedrin) that convened **in Jerusalem would go out and measure** to determine which town must bring an *eglah arufah*.[32] וַעֲלֵיהֶם מִצְוַת הַמְּדִידָה — **It is** incumbent **upon** [the elders of the Great Sanhedrin] to perform **the mitzvah of measuring** from the corpse, וְעַל זִקְנֵי הָעִיר מִצְוַת הָעֶגְלָה — **but it is** incumbent **upon the elders of the town** closest to the corpse to perform **the mitzvah associated with the calf,** i.e., bringing it to the river and decapitating it, וּרְחִיצַת הַיָּדַיִם — **the washing of the hands,**[33]

NOTES

apparent (see *Minchas Chinuch* 531:10 and §2). Some suggest that since the Torah limits the obligation to bring an *eglah arufah* to cities that have a *beis din* of twenty-three (see above, note 1), which is the type of *beis din* required to try capital cases, it indicates that we are supposed to treat the *eglah arufah* procedure like a capital case (see *Nachal Eisan* 1:3 [1]). See *Rashash, Sotah* 47b ד״ה ת״ר משרבו for an alternative explanation.

30. "Transjordan" refers to the territories east of the Jordan River that were conquered by Moses and the Jewish people from Sihon, king of the Amorites, and Og, king of Bashan (see *Numbers* 21:21-35). These territories were given to the tribes of Reuben and Gad, and half of the tribe of Manasseh (ibid. 32:33). With regard to many laws, Transjordan is treated the same as Eretz Yisrael (see *Tashbetz* Vol. III §199-200).

The verse introducing the laws of *eglah arufah* states: *If a corpse will be found on the land that HASHEM, your God, gives you to inherit it.* This refers specifically to Eretz Yisrael, which was divided among most of the tribes, and Transjordan, which was divided among the tribes of Reuben and Gad and half of Manasseh (see *Tosefta, Sotah* 9:1 with *Minchas Bikkurim,* and *Sifrei* to the verse).

According to its plain explanation, the verse speaks about where a corpse must be *found* for there to be an obligation to bring an *eglah arufah.* It therefore teaches that if a corpse is found outside of Eretz Yisrael, there is no obligation to bring an *eglah arufah,* even if the city

closest to the corpse is *inside* Eretz Yisrael. However, as mentioned above (see note 13), the Sages understand that this verse also comes to define which cities are subject to the obligation to bring an *eglah arufah.* Accordingly, the verse also teaches that a city outside of Eretz Yisrael is not obligated to bring an *eglah arufah* even if it is the city closest to a corpse found *inside* Eretz Yisrael (see *Nachal Eisan* 1:2 [2]; see, however, *Minchas Chinuch* 531:11).

31. All the men of the city closest to the corpse are obligated to see to it that an *eglah arufah* is brought (e.g., the calf is bought with their money; see *Rambam, Hil. Rotze'ach* 9:2). However, as Scripture states, all the steps of the *eglah arufah* procedure that follow the measurements from the corpse to the surrounding cities (which is performed by members of the Great Sanhedrin) must be carried out by the elders of the city closest to the corpse.

32. The *eglah arufah* passage is addressed to the Jewish people as a whole. When setting forth the obligation to measure from the corpse to the surrounding cities, the Torah states (*Deuteronomy* 21:2): *your elders and judges shall go out and measure toward the cities that are around the corpse.* The Sages (44b) teach that the phrase "*your elders and judges*" is a reference to "the select among your judges," i.e., the Great Sanhedrin. See ibid. for the source that *five* judges from the Great Sanhedrin must perform the measurement.

33. See above, note 22.

וּקְרִיאַת אוֹתָם הַכְּתוּבִים, שֶׁנֶּאֱמַר יָדֵינוּ לֹא שָׁפְכוּ אֶת הַדָּם הַזֶּה וְעֵינֵינוּ לֹא רָאוּ[34], כְּלוֹמַר, לֹא בָא לְיָדֵינוּ הַנֶּהֱרָג וּפְטַרְנוּהוּ בְּלֹא מְזוֹנוֹת, וְעֵינֵינוּ לֹא רָאוּ אוֹתוֹ יוֹצֵא מֵעִירֵנוּ וּפְטַרְנוּהוּ בְּלֹא לְוָיָה[35].

וּקְרִיאַת אוֹתָם הַכְּתוּבִים — **and the recitation of those passages** that the Torah commands to be recited after the decapitation, שֶׁנֶּאֱמַר "יָדֵינוּ לֹא שָׁפְכוּ אֶת הַדָּם הַזֶּה וְעֵינֵינוּ לֹא רָאוּ" — **as it is stated** (ibid. 21:7): *They* (the elders of the city) *shall speak up and say, "Our hands have not spilled this blood, and our eyes did not see."*[34] כְּלוֹמַר לֹא בָא לְיָדֵינוּ הַנֶּהֱרָג וּפְטַרְנוּהוּ בְּלֹא מְזוֹנוֹת — **This** declaration **means to say: "The murdered person did not come to** our hands for assistance, **with us sending him away without food,** וְעֵינֵינוּ לֹא רָאוּ אוֹתוֹ יוֹצֵא מֵעִירֵנוּ וּפְטַרְנוּהוּ בְּלֹא לְוָיָה — **and** our eyes did **not see him leave our town and let him depart without escorting him** on his way."[35]

NOTES

34. In contrast to the measurements from the corpse, which the Torah delegates to "the select among your judges," i.e., members of the Great Sanhedrin, with regard to these other activities, the Torah states that they are to be performed by זִקְנֵי הָעִיר הַהִיא, *the elders of that city* (i.e., the city closest to the corpse).

35. Simply understood, in this declaration, the elders of the city proclaim that they did not murder the victim themselves, nor did they witness his murder without coming to his rescue. This, however, cannot be the actual meaning of the declaration, for we certainly do not suspect that the members of the elders are guilty of actual murder. Rather, the elders declare that they do not bear even *indirect* responsibility for the murder. By stating that their hands did not spill blood, they declare that they did not send the victim away without food, which might have caused him to turn to robbery as a means of support, resulting in him being killed by one of his intended victims. And by stating that their eyes

did not see, they declare that they did not see him leave town without providing him with an escort, leaving him more susceptible to being attacked (Mishnah, *Sotah* 45b with *Rashi*; see *Tiferes Yisrael* to that Mishnah). See *Yerushalmi Sotah* 9:6 and *Moreh Nevuchim* III:40 for alternative understandings of the elders^ declaration.

Obviously, if the elders *were* guilty of sending away the murder victim without food or escort, they cannot make this declaration. See *Nachal Eisan* (15:2 [14-15]) for discussion of whether this would rule out bringing an *eglah arufah* altogether.

[The verse that follows this declaration states (*Deuteronomy* 21:8): *Atone for Your people Israel that You have redeemed, O HASHEM: Do not place innocent blood in the midst of Your people Israel!* Those words are not part of the elders' declaration, but rather, a prayer for atonement that is recited by the Kohanim who are present at the procedure (Mishnah, *Sotah* 46a; see ibid. v. 5).]

☙ **Insight: Is the Eglah Arufah Procedure Always Limited to the Closest City?**

As Chinuch taught above (at note 17), when the principles of "majority" and "proximity" are in conflict, we follow the principle of "majority." Therefore, when two cities are in the vicinity of a murder victim and the one that is closer to the corpse has a smaller population, we follow the larger city in determining where the murderer came from. All agree that since the principle of "majority" tells us that the murderer presumably came from the larger city, the smaller city does not perform the *eglah arufah* procedure even though it is closest to the corpse, but Rishonim disagree whether the larger but more distant city *does* do so.

According to *Rambam* (*Hil. Rotze'ach* 9:6) and several other Rishonim (*Smag, Asei* 78; *Meiri, Sotah* 45b), in a case like this, the larger city *is* required to perform the *eglah arufah* procedure. *Tosefos Rid* (*Bava Basra* 23b), on the other hand, contends that even the larger city is not required to do so. In his view, the larger city cannot possibly perform the *eglah arufah* procedure, because the Torah clearly limits the *eglah arufah* requirement to the "city *closest* to the corpse." [*Rambam* and all those who maintain that the larger city does perform the *eglah arufah* procedure might counter that when the Torah mentions "the city closest to the corpse," it does not mean to limit the requirement to the closest city, but rather to teach a general rule that the *eglah arufah* requirement applies to whichever city is most likely to be where the murderer originated from.] There is some controversy as to what Chinuch's opinion is regarding this matter; see *Minchas Chinuch* §8 and *Nachal Eisan* 6:8 [3].

Even *Tosefos Rid* must concede that there are times when a city is obligated to perform the *eglah*

arufah procedure even though it is not the closest city to the corpse. The rule is that a city that does not have a *beis din* (i.e., a *beis din* of twenty-three; see above, note 1) is never obligated to perform the *eglah arufah* procedure even if it is the closest city to the corpse (Mishnah, *Sotah* 44b). In such a case, however, the Gemara (ibid. 45b) rules that the next closest city must perform the procedure, even though it is not the closest city to the corpse. *Tosefta* 9:3 rules similarly with regard to Jerusalem, which is also excluded from the obligation to perform the *eglah arufah* procedure (see above, at note 12). That is, if Jerusalem is the closest city to the place where the murder victim is found, the next closest city performs the *eglah arufah* procedure, even though it is not the closest city to the corpse.

Afikei Yam (1:26), however, explains that the cases of Jerusalem and a city without a *beis din* are fundamentally different from the case where the principles of "majority" and "proximity" are in conflict. In the case where these principles conflict, *Tosefos Rid* argues that the larger but more distant city cannot be required to perform the *eglah arufah* procedure because it in no way fulfills the requirement to be "the city *closest* to the corpse." However, in the cases of Jerusalem and a city without a *beis din,* the next closest city *does* fulfill the requirement to be "the city closest to the corpse." This is because when the Torah mentions the "city closest to the corpse," it refers to the city that is closest to the corpse among a specific category of cities; namely, the cities that are included in the initial measurement taken by *beis din* after the corpse is discovered. Now, *beis din* includes in this measurement all the cities in the vicinity of the corpse that can potentially perform the *eglah arufah* procedure, but excludes cities that can never do so; e.g., Jerusalem and cities that do not have a *beis din* of twenty-three judges. In the case where one city is nearer to the corpse but the next city is larger, both cities can potentially become obligated in the *eglah arufah* procedure, and therefore, both are included in the initial measurement of *beis din*. Since they are both included in the measurement, only the one that is closer to the corpse qualifies as the "city closest to the corpse." Therefore, the larger city does not perform the *eglah arufah* procedure instead of the smaller city. By contrast, Jerusalem and cities that have no *beis din* can never become obligated to perform the *eglah arufah* procedure, and are therefore always completely excluded from the initial measurements of *beis din*. Therefore, the next closest city, which is the closest to the corpse of the *qualifying* cities, fulfills the requirement of being "the city closest to the corpse," and can be required to perform the *eglah arufah* procedure.

מִצְוָה תקלא: שֶׁלֹּא לַעֲבֹד וְלִזְרֹעַ בְּנַחַל אֵיתָן

שֶׁנִּמְנַעְנוּ מִלַּעֲבֹד וְלִזְרֹעַ בְּנַחַל אֵיתָן, הוּא הַנַּחַל[1] שֶׁנֶּעֶרְפָה שָׁם הָעֶגְלָה[2], וְעַל זֶה נֶאֱמַר (דברים כ״א, ד׳) אֲשֶׁר לֹא יֵעָבֵד בּוֹ וְלֹא יִזָּרֵעַ[3].

מִשָּׁרְשֵׁי הַמִּצְוָה מַה שֶּׁכָּתַבְתִּי בְּסֵדֶר זֶה בְּמִצְוַת עֲרִיפַת הָעֶגְלָה עֲשֵׂה אַחֲרוֹן

Mitzvah 531

The Prohibition to Perform Work or to Sow in a Nachal Eisan (the Place Where an Eglah Arufah Was Decapitated)

וְהוֹרִדוּ זִקְנֵי הָעִיר הַהִוא אֶת הָעֶגְלָה אֶל נַחַל אֵיתָן אֲשֶׁר לֹא יֵעָבֵד בּוֹ וְלֹא יִזָּרֵעַ

The elders of that city shall bring the calf down to a mighty stream, which may not be worked and may not be sown (*Deuteronomy* 21:4).

The previous mitzvah established a mitzvah-obligation to carry out a specific procedure, which includes decapitating a calf (*eglah arufah*), when a murder victim is found and it is not known who killed him. This mitzvah establishes a mitzvah-prohibition against performing certain types of work at the location where the *eglah arufah* procedure was carried out.

שֶׁנִּמְנַעְנוּ מִלַּעֲבֹד וְלִזְרֹעַ בְּנַחַל אֵיתָן – **We are forbidden to perform work or to sow in a *nachal eisan*,** הוּא הַנַּחַל שֶׁנֶּעֶרְפָה שָׁם הָעֶגְלָה – **which is the stream**[1] **at which the *eglah arufah* was decapitated.**[2] וְעַל זֶה נֶאֱמַר – **Regarding this it is stated** (*Deuteronomy* 21:4): "אֲשֶׁר לֹא יֵעָבֵד בּוֹ וְלֹא יִזָּרֵעַ" – *The elders of that city shall bring the calf down to a mighty stream,* ***which may not be worked and may not be sown.***[3]

Underlying Purpose of the Mitzvah

מִשָּׁרְשֵׁי הַמִּצְוָה – **Among the underlying purposes of the mitzvah** is an idea consistent with מַה שֶּׁכָּתַבְתִּי בְּסֵדֶר זֶה בְּמִצְוַת עֲרִיפַת הָעֶגְלָה – **that which I wrote** earlier **in this *parashah* in** the explanation of **the mitzvah of decapitating the *eglah arufah*** (Mitzvah 530), עֲשֵׂה אַחֲרוֹן

NOTES

1. See previous mitzvah, at note 3, with the accompanying note.

2. According to several commentators, the prohibition against performing work or sowing in a *nachal eisan* applies to land that is adjacent to the stream and not to the stream itself, which could not be worked or sown in any event (*Meiri, Niddah* 8b; *Tiferes Yisrael* 9:5). Others explain that the intent of the Torah is to forbid working or sowing the ground of the stream itself in the event that the stream dries up (*Malbim* to the verse; *Maharatz Chayes, Sotah* 45b).

The Torah does not specify how much land is forbidden to be worked or sown. *Talmud Yerushalmi* (*Sotah* 9:5) cites a dispute about this matter. According to one view, the prohibition applies to the exact spot where the calf was decapitated and to an additional four *amos,* while another view maintains that fifty *amos* beyond the spot of the decapitation are subject to the prohibition. [In contemporary measurements, an *amah* is between 18.9 and 22.76 in. (48-57.6 cm.).] *Yerushalmi* does not specify whether these measurements represent the amount of land that is forbidden in each direction, or whether they represent a total, with the carcass of the calf in the middle; see *Dvar Shaul, Sotah* 71:29. See *Nachal Eisan* (16:3 [1]), who maintains that the first possibility is correct.

3. The Gemara (*Sotah* 46b) records a dispute regarding the exact meaning of the phrase, אֲשֶׁר לֹא יֵעָבֵד וְלֹא יִזָּרֵעַ. All agree that it should be understood as a reference to the future (*which may not be worked and may not be sown*), and establishes a prohibition against performing work or sowing in a *nachal eisan.* However, according to one opinion, the phrase should *also* be understood as a reference to the past (*"which was not worked and was not sown"*). According to this opinion, in addition to establishing a prohibition, the verse also describes the required characteristics of a *nachal eisan,* i.e., it must never have been worked or sown. Chinuch does not mention such a requirement, indicating that he rules in accordance with the view that the verse should be understood as referring exclusively to the future. Cf. *Rashi* to the verse.

שֶׁבַּסֵּדֶר (מצוה תק״ל)[4] שֶׁעִנְיַן הָעֲרִיפָה לְפַרְסֵם עִנְיַן הָרְצִיחָה כְּדֵי לְעוֹרֵר הֶהָמוֹן עַל הַדָּבָר, וְיַכְנִיסוּ יִרְאָה בְּלִבָּם עַל הַדָּבָר הָרַע הַזֶּה[5]. וְגַם מְנִיעַת הָעֲבוֹדָה וְהַזְּרִיעָה שָׁם לְעוֹלָם מִן הַטַּעַם הַזֶּה בְּעַצְמוֹ הִיא לְפִי הַדּוֹמֶה עַל צַד הַפָּשׁוּט, כְּדֵי לְהַזְכִּיר לְעוֹלָם בְּלֵב כָּל עוֹבְרֵי דֶרֶךְ כִּי עַל דְּבַר שֶׁנִּרְצַח אִישׁ אֶחָד בַּדֶּרֶךְ נֶעֶרְפָה הָעֶגְלָה בַּמָּקוֹם הַהוּא וְנִשְׁאַר חָרֵב לְעוֹלָם, וְיָנִיעוּ לְבָבָם עִם זֶה לְהַרְחִיק עִנְיַן הָרְצִיחָה מְאֹד[6]. וְאִם תַּקְשֶׁה בְּטַעַם זֶה כִּי הַנַּחַל לֹא מְקוֹם זֶרַע, נָשִׁיב שֶׁרָאוּי הוּא לְכָךְ אַחַר שֶׁתִּמְנָעֵנוּ הַתּוֹרָה מִלִּזְרֹעַ בּוֹ[7].

שֶׁבַּסֵּדֶר – which is the **last mitzvah-obligation in this *parashah*** (*Parashash Shoftim*);[4] שֶׁעִנְיַן הָעֲרִיפָה לְפַרְסֵם עִנְיַן הָרְצִיחָה – namely, **that the purpose of decapitating** the calf **is to publicize the episode of the murder** for which the calf was decapitated, כְּדֵי לְעוֹרֵר הֶהָמוֹן עַל הַדָּבָר – **in order to arouse the masses** to reflect **about the matter** וְיַכְנִיסוּ יִרְאָה בְּלִבָּם עַל הַדָּבָר הָרַע הַזֶּה **– so that fear will be instilled into their hearts about this evil matter.**[5] וְגַם מְנִיעַת הָעֲבוֹדָה וְהַזְּרִיעָה שָׁם לְעוֹלָם מִן הַטַּעַם הַזֶּה בְּעַצְמוֹ הִיא לְפִי הַדּוֹמֶה עַל צַד הַפָּשׁוּט – **It would seem that according to the simple** (i.e., non-esoteric) **perspective, the permanent restriction against performing work or sowing in [the *nachal eisan*] is also for that very same reason;** כְּדֵי לְהַזְכִּיר לְעוֹלָם בְּלֵב כָּל עוֹבְרֵי דֶרֶךְ – namely, **so that there will always be a reminder for passersby** כִּי עַל דְּבַר שֶׁנִּרְצַח אִישׁ אֶחָד בַּדֶּרֶךְ – **that because a person was murdered on the road,** נֶעֶרְפָה הָעֶגְלָה בַּמָּקוֹם הַהוּא וְנִשְׁאַר חָרֵב לְעוֹלָם – **a calf was decapitated at that location, and [that location] was** then **left permanently desolate.** וְיָנִיעוּ לְבָבָם עִם זֶה לְהַרְחִיק עִנְיַן הָרְצִיחָה מְאֹד – **As a result of this** reminder, **[passersby] will be stirred to greatly distance** themselves from **anything associated with murder.**[6]

וְאִם תַּקְשֶׁה בְּטַעַם זֶה – **And should you challenge this reason** כִּי הַנַּחַל לֹא מְקוֹם זֶרַע – by asking **that a stream is not a place fit for** planting **seed,** נָשִׁיב שֶׁרָאוּי הוּא לְכָךְ אַחַר שֶׁתִּמְנָעֵנוּ הַתּוֹרָה מִלִּזְרֹעַ בּוֹ – **we will respond that it** obviously ***is* fit for** planting **[seed]** to some extent, **since the Torah forbids sowing in it.**[7]

NOTES

4. Chinuch refers to the original format of this work, according to which all of the mitzvah-obligations of a *parashah* were listed before the mitzvah-prohibitions of that *parashah*; see Mitzvah 494 note 4.

5. In the previous mitzvah, Chinuch wrote that by involving themselves in the *eglah arufah* procedure, the elders of the city demonstrate their sincere desire to bring the murderer to justice. When people see this, they will reflect upon the severity of murder; see there, note 10.

6. The fact that the Torah commanded us to decapitate a calf and to leave desolate the place where the decapitation took place underscores the severity of murder. Reflecting upon this will inspire people to do all they can to avoid causing the loss of life.

7. That is, the Torah obviously did not prohibit something that is impossible to do.

As mentioned above (note 2), several commentators understand that this prohibition applies to land that is adjacent to the stream. Although such land is not optimal for planting crops, it is possible to sow there. Chinuch's words here are understandable according to this view. He means to ask: How can we say that the prohibition of sowing in the *nachal eisan* is intended as a *reminder* of the *eglah arufah* procedure? Why since that land is not suitable for sowing, its barrenness will not be a reminder of anything at all! Chinuch answers that the prohibition must refer to an area that is at least *somewhat* usable (such as the riverbank), for otherwise the Torah would not have prohibited sowing there. Thus, its being left barren *will* cause people to remember the incident.

Minchas Yitzchak, however, emends the text of Chinuch to read: נָשִׁיב שֶׁרָאוּי הוּא לְכָךְ אַחַר כָּךְ שֶׁתִּמְנָעֵנוּ הַתּוֹרָה מִלִּזְרֹעַ בּוֹ, *we will respond that it is fit for* planting *[seed]* ***afterward*** (i.e., after the stream dries up), and *that* is why *the Torah forbids sowing in it.* That is, the Torah's prohibition applies to the streambed itself (in accordance with the second view cited in note 2), and is intended for a future time, if and when the stream dries up. At that point, leaving it barren will serve as a reminder of the earlier *eglah arufah* event. [For another explanation of Chinuch's words, see *Dvar Shaul, Sotah* 71:27.]

[According to those who maintain that *nachal eisan* refers to a valley whose ground is hard (see Mitzvah 530 note 3), it is certainly understandable how it is possible to sow there.]

דִּינֵי הַמִּצְוָה מַה שֶּׁאָמְרוּ זִכְרוֹנָם לִבְרָכָה (סוטה מ״ו ע״ב) מַה זְּרִיעָה בְּגוּפָהּ שֶׁל קַרְקַע אַף עֲבוֹדָה שֶׁאָסְרָה תּוֹרָה הִיא בְּגוּפָהּ שֶׁל קַרְקַע כְּגוֹן חוֹרֵשׁ וְחוֹפֵר וְכַיּוֹצֵא בָּאֵלּוּ, אֲבָל מֻתָּר לִסְרֹק שָׁם פִּשְׁתָּן וְלַעֲשׂוֹת שָׁם כָּל עֲבוֹדָה שֶׁאֵינָהּ בְּגוּף הַקַּרְקַע[8]. וְיֶתֶר פְּרָטֶיהָ בְּסוֹף מַסֶּכֶת סוֹטָה[9].

וְאַף עַל פִּי שֶׁכָּתַבְתִּי לְמַעְלָה שֶׁמִּצְוַת דִּין עֶגְלָה עֲרוּפָה אֵינוֹ נוֹהֵג אֶלָּא בִּזְמַן הַבַּיִת כְּשֶׁאָנוּ דָּנִין דִּינֵי נְפָשׁוֹת[10], אִסּוּר הָעֲבוֹדָה בְּנַחַל אֵיתָן נוֹהֵג הוּא לְפִי הַדּוֹמֶה לְעוֹלָם אִלּוּ יָדַעְנוּ בְּקַבָּלָה אֲמִתִּית שֶׁיֵּשׁ שָׁם בְּאַרְצֵנוּ נַחַל שֶׁעָרְפוּ בּוֹ עֶגְלָה בִּזְמַן שֶׁהָיְתָה הָאָרֶץ בְּיִשּׁוּבָהּ[11], כִּי לֹא הִזְכִּיר הַכָּתוּב בְּאִסּוּר הָעֲבוֹדָה בְּאוֹתוֹ מָקוֹם זְמַן,

---

Laws of the Mitzvah

דִּינֵי הַמִּצְוָה – **The laws of the mitzvah** include מַה שֶּׁאָמְרוּ זִכְרוֹנָם לִבְרָכָה – **that which [the Sages], of blessed memory, stated** (*Sotah* 46b): The Torah forbids both "working" and "sowing" the *nachal eisan* to teach that מַה זְּרִיעָה בְּגוּפָהּ שֶׁל קַרְקַע – **just like "sowing" is** an activity **performed with the ground itself,** אַף עֲבוֹדָה שֶׁאָסְרָה תּוֹרָה הִיא בְּגוּפָהּ שֶׁל קַרְקַע – **so too,** the **"work" that the Torah forbids refers to** work performed **with the ground itself,** כְּגוֹן חוֹרֵשׁ וְחוֹפֵר וְכַיּוֹצֵא בָּאֵלּוּ – **such as, plowing, digging, and the like.** אֲבָל מֻתָּר לִסְרֹק שָׁם פִּשְׁתָּן – **It is, however, permitted to comb flax there,** וְלַעֲשׂוֹת שָׁם כָּל עֲבוֹדָה שֶׁאֵינָהּ בְּגוּף הַקַּרְקַע – **or to perform any** other type of **work there that is not** performed ***with*** **the land itself,** but is merely performed *on* the land.[8]

וְיֶתֶר פְּרָטֶיהָ בְּסוֹף מַסֶּכֶת סוֹטָה – These **and remaining details of [the mitzvah]** are found **at the end of Tractate *Sotah*** (45b-46b).[9]

Applicability of the Mitzvah

וְאַף עַל פִּי שֶׁכָּתַבְתִּי לְמַעְלָה שֶׁמִּצְוַת דִּין עֶגְלָה עֲרוּפָה אֵינוֹ נוֹהֵג אֶלָּא בִּזְמַן הַבַּיִת – **Although I wrote above** in Mitzvah 530 **that the mitzvah of** carrying out **the *eglah arufah* procedure applies only when the *Beis HaMikdash* is standing,** כְּשֶׁאָנוּ דָּנִין דִּינֵי נְפָשׁוֹת – **when we** have the ability to **try capital cases,**[10] אִסּוּר הָעֲבוֹדָה בְּנַחַל אֵיתָן נוֹהֵג הוּא לְפִי הַדּוֹמֶה לְעוֹלָם – **the prohibition against performing work in a *nachal eisan* should seemingly apply forever,** and therefore, we would be bound by its strictures even nowadays, אִלּוּ יָדַעְנוּ בְּקַבָּלָה אֲמִתִּית – **if we knew based on an accurate tradition** שֶׁיֵּשׁ שָׁם בְּאַרְצֵנוּ נַחַל שֶׁעָרְפוּ בּוֹ עֶגְלָה בִּזְמַן שֶׁהָיְתָה הָאָרֶץ בְּיִשּׁוּבָהּ – **of a stream in our land** (Eretz Yisrael) **at which an *eglah* *arufah* had been decapitated when the land was** fully **settled** (i.e., the *Beis HaMikdash* was standing) and the mitzvah of *eglah arufah* applied.[11] כִּי לֹא הִזְכִּיר הַכָּתוּב בְּאִסּוּר הָעֲבוֹדָה בְּאוֹתוֹ מָקוֹם זְמַן – **For when** setting forth **the prohibition against performing work in [a *nachal eisan*], Scripture does not mention** that the prohibition is limited

---

NOTES

8. Had the Torah meant to forbid all work, it could simply have mentioned the all-inclusive term, "work," without singling out "sowing." By mentioning sowing, the Torah teaches that only work that resembles "sowing," i.e., work that is performed with the land itself, is forbidden (*Sotah* 46b).

9. These laws are codified in *Rambam, Hil. Rotze'ach* 10:9.

10. No court can try capital cases unless the Great Sanhedrin convenes in the Chamber of Hewn Stone (*Lishkas HaGazis*) in the *Beis HaMikdash.* According to Chinuch, the mitzvah of performing the *eglah arufah* procedure applies only when *beis din* has jurisdiction over capital cases; therefore, it applies only when the *Beis HaMikdash* is standing and the Great Sanhedrin convenes there. See Mitzvah 530 note 29 for further explanation.

11. That is, as long as the *eglah arufah* procedure was carried out at a time when the mitzvah applied, i.e., the *Beis HaMikdash* was still standing, it remains forbidden to perform work at that location forever, even when the *Beis HaMikdash* is no longer standing.

וְאִם כֵּן יֵשׁ לָנוּ לְכָתְבָהּ עִם הַמִּצְווֹת הַנּוֹהֲגוֹת הַיּוֹם בְּאַרְצֵנוּ[12].

וְנוֹהֵג אִסּוּר זֶה בִּזְכָרִים וּנְקֵבוֹת[13]. וְעוֹבֵר עַל זֶה וְזוֹרֵעַ בְּנַחַל אֵיתָן חַיָּב מַלְקוּת[14], וְכֵן אָמְרוּ זִכְרוֹנָם לִבְרָכָה שָׁם בִּגְמָרָא מַכּוֹת (כ״ב ע״א) כְּשֶׁזָּכְרוּ שָׁם מְחֻיְּבֵי מַלְקוּת, אָמְרוּ וְהָא אִיכָּא זוֹרֵעַ בְּנַחַל אֵיתָן, וְאַזְהָרְתֵיהּ מֵהָכָא אֲשֶׁר לֹא יֵעָבֵד בּוֹ וְלֹא יִזָּרֵעַ[15]. הִנֵּה הִתְבָּאֵר לָנוּ מִזֶּה שֶׁזֶּה שֶׁאָמַר הַכָּתוּב לֹא יֵעָבֵד וְלֹא יִזָּרֵעַ שֶׁהַכֹּל אַזְהָרָה אַחַת, כְּלוֹמַר שֶׁהָעוֹבֵד וְהַזּוֹרֵעַ שָׁם לֹא עָבַר אֶלָּא לָאו אֶחָד וְלֹא נְחַיְּבֵהוּ בִּשְׁנֵי לָאוִין בַּעֲבוֹדָה וּבִזְרִיעָה[16],

---

to a specific time, וְאִם כֵּן יֵשׁ לָנוּ לְכָתְבָהּ עִם הַמִּצְווֹת הַנּוֹהֲגוֹת הַיּוֹם בְּאַרְצֵנוּ – **and we should therefore include it among the mitzvos that apply in our land** (Eretz Yisrael) even **nowadays.**[12]

וְנוֹהֵג אִסּוּר זֶה בִּזְכָרִים וּנְקֵבוֹת – **This prohibition applies to** both **men and women.**[13] וְעוֹבֵר עַל זֶה וְזוֹרֵעַ בְּנַחַל אֵיתָן – **One who transgresses this** prohibition **and sows** or performs a similar type of work **at a** ***nachal eisan*** חַיָּב מַלְקוּת – **is liable to** ***malkus.***[14] וְכֵן אָמְרוּ זִכְרוֹנָם לִבְרָכָה שָׁם בִּגְמָרָא מַכּוֹת – **And so did [the Sages], of blessed memory, state in Tractate** ***Makkos*** (22a), כְּשֶׁזָּכְרוּ שָׁם מְחֻיְּבֵי מַלְקוּת אָמְרוּ – for **when they mentioned there** various **people who are liable to** ***malkus,*** **they stated:** וְהָא אִיכָּא זוֹרֵעַ בְּנַחַל אֵיתָן – **But, there is** also **one who sows in a** ***nachal eisan,*** וְאַזְהָרְתֵיהּ מֵהָכָא – **whose** Scriptural **warning is from here:** "אֲשֶׁר לֹא יֵעָבֵד בּוֹ וְלֹא יִזָּרֵעַ" – *a mighty stream,* ***which may not be worked and may not be sown.***[15]

Chinuch points out that this Gemara teaches *two* important points regarding our mitzvah:

הִנֵּה הִתְבָּאֵר לָנוּ מִזֶּה – **This [Gemara] has clarified for us** שֶׁזֶּה שֶׁאָמַר הַכָּתוּב "לֹא יֵעָבֵד וְלֹא יִזָּרֵעַ" – **that that which the verse states,** *a mighty stream that* ***may not be worked and may not be sown,*** שֶׁהַכֹּל אַזְהָרָה אַחַת – **is all** considered **a single prohibition,** כְּלוֹמַר שֶׁהָעוֹבֵד וְהַזּוֹרֵעַ שָׁם לֹא עָבַר אֶלָּא לָאו אֶחָד – **meaning that someone who performs work** ***and*** **sows** in a *nachal eisan* **transgresses only a single mitzvah-prohibition,** וְלֹא נְחַיְּבֵהוּ בִּשְׁנֵי לָאוִין בַּעֲבוֹדָה וּבִזְרִיעָה – **and we do not hold him liable for** transgressing ***two*** separate **mitzvah-prohibitions,** one **for performing work and** another for **sowing.**[16]

NOTES

12. The fact that we do not observe this prohibition nowadays is simply because of a technical issue; i.e., we do not know where *eglah arufah* procedures have been carried out in the past. The mitzvah, however, is in full force, and it should therefore be counted among mitzvos that apply even nowadays, since there is nothing intrinsic to the mitzvah that prevents it from being applicable.

As mentioned in the previous mitzvah (note 30), the mitzvah of bringing an *eglah arufah* applies only to cities in Eretz Yisrael, and only for a corpse found in Eretz Yisrael. From the fact that Chinuch characterizes the prohibition against working a *nachal eisan* as a prohibition that applies only in Eretz Yisrael, it is clear that he holds that the *nachal eisan* at which the *eglah arufah* procedure is performed must also be located in Eretz Yisrael. The source for this requirement, though, is unclear, and indeed, *Minchas Chinuch* (§8) assumes that the *nachal eisan* can be located even outside of Eretz Yisrael.

13. In keeping with the general rule that applies to mitzvah-prohibitions; see General Introduction.

14. *Malkus* (lashes) is the standard punishment for the intentional violation of a mitzvah-prohibition; see General Introduction.

15. The Mishnah there (*Makkos* 21b) teaches that a person who plows a single furrow, and in the process he covered seeds that were lying on the ground, can incur liability to eight sets of *malkus* for transgressing eight distinct mitzvah-prohibitions. [See there for details.] The Gemara (cited by Chinuch) wonders why the Mishnah does not discuss a case where a person plowed in a *nachal eisan,* in which case, he would be liable to a *ninth* set of *malkus* for transgressing the prohibition against sowing in a *nachal eisan.* It is clear from the Gemara's question that the Scriptural phrase, אֲשֶׁר לֹא יֵעָבֵד בּוֹ וְלֹא יִזָּרֵעַ, *[a mighty stream] which may not be worked and may not be sown,* is a mitzvah-prohibition against performing work at a *nachal eisan* that carries liability to *malkus.*

16. If the verse contained two distinct mitzvah-prohibitions, one for performing work in a *nachal eisan* and another for sowing in a *nachal eisan,* then one who sowed and also performed some other type of work in a *nachal eisan* would be guilty of having transgressed *two* separate mitzvah-prohibitions and would be liable to two sets of *malkus.* If so, the Mishnah could have listed liability to *two* extra sets of *malkus,* since in the case under discussion (covering seeds while plowing a furrow in a *nachal eisan;* see previous note), the person

וְלָמַדְנוּ שָׁם גַּם כֵּן שֶׁיֵּשׁ בַּדָּבָר חִיּוּב מַלְקוּת.

וְלָמַדְנוּ שָׁם גַּם כֵּן שֶׁיֵּשׁ בַּדָּבָר חִיּוּב מַלְקוּת — **We have also learned** from the Gemara **there that this matter,** i.e., sowing or performing work by a *nachal eisan,* **carries liability to** *malkus.*

NOTES

is guilty of both plowing and sowing in a *nachal eisan.* Since the Gemara asks only that the Mishnah should have included *one* additional set of *malkus,* we see that the verse contains only one mitzvah-prohibition. Therefore, one who performs work and sows in a *nachal eisan* is liable to only a single set of *malkus,* just like anyone who transgresses a single transgression multiple times without receiving a separate *hasraah* (warning) before each transgression.

In general, the fact that the Torah uses separate prohibitory expressions for two actions (*You shall not do such and such, and you shall not do such and such*) indicates that the prohibitions are considered distinct. In our case, however, this is not so, for as Chinuch explained

above (at note 8), the Torah's mention of "sowing" helps define what activities are included in the prohibition against performing "work." Therefore, the prohibition against sowing in a *nachal eisan* is understood to be part of a larger prohibition against performing work, and not a separate mitzvah-prohibition (*Shaar HaMelech, Hil. Rotze'ach* 10:9, cited by *Minchas Chinuch* §3).

Chinuch's words here are based on *Rambam* in *Sefer HaMitzvos* (*Lo Saaseh* 309). See, however, *R' Y. F. Perla, Sefer HaMitzvos of Rav Saadiah Gaon, Lo Saaseh* 269 (Vol. II, p. 329a), who questions the proof from the Gemara in *Makkos,* and cites several authorities who count the prohibitions against performing work and sowing as distinct prohibitions.

פרשת כי תצא

Parashas Ki Seitzei

כִּי תֵצֵא יֵשׁ בָּהּ עֶשְׂרִים וְשֶׁבַע מִצְווֹת עֲשֵׂה
וְאַרְבָּעִים וָשֶׁבַע מִצְווֹת לֹא תַעֲשֶׂה

***Parashas Ki Seitzei* contains twenty-seven Mitzvah-Obligations and forty-seven Mitzvah-Prohibitions**

CONTAINS SEVENTY-FOUR MITZVOS:
MITZVOS 532-604

549. **שֶׁלֹּא לֶאֱכֹל כִּלְאֵי הַכֶּרֶם בְּאֶרֶץ יִשְׂרָאֵל – The Prohibition to Eat Kilayim of the Vineyard [Grown] In Eretz Yisrael**

550. **שֶׁלֹּא לַעֲשׂוֹת מְלָאכָה בִּשְׁנֵי מִינֵי בְהֵמָה – The Prohibition to Work Two Species of Animals Together**

551. **שֶׁלֹּא לִלְבֹּשׁ שַׁעַטְנֵז – The Prohibition to Wear Shaatnez**

The remaining mitzvos of *Parashas Ki Seitzei* (§552-604) appear in Volume 10.

מִצְוָה תקלב: מִצְוַת דִּין יְפַת תֹּאַר[1]

שֶׁנִּצְטַוִּינוּ בְּאֵשֶׁת יְפַת תֹּאַר לַעֲשׂוֹת לָהּ כְּמִשְׁפָּט הַכָּתוּב בְּפָרָשָׁה זוֹ, שֶׁנֶּאֱמַר (דברים כ״א, י״א) וְרָאִיתָ בַּשִּׁבְיָה אֵשֶׁת יְפַת תֹּאַר וְגוֹ׳. יְפַת תֹּאַר, כְּלוֹמַר שֶׁתִּהְיֶה יָפָה בְּעֵינָיו.[2]

Mitzvah 532
The Obligation Regarding the Yefas Toar

כִּי תֵצֵא לַמִּלְחָמָה עַל אֹיְבֶיךָ וּנְתָנוֹ ה׳ אֱלֹהֶיךָ בְּיָדֶךָ וְשָׁבִיתָ שִׁבְיוֹ. וְרָאִיתָ בַּשִּׁבְיָה אֵשֶׁת יְפַת תֹּאַר וְחָשַׁקְתָּ בָהּ וְלָקַחְתָּ לְךָ לְאִשָּׁה. וַהֲבֵאתָהּ אֶל תּוֹךְ בֵּיתֶךָ וְגִלְּחָה אֶת רֹאשָׁהּ וְעָשְׂתָה אֶת צִפָּרְנֶיהָ. וְהֵסִירָה אֶת שִׂמְלַת שִׁבְיָהּ מֵעָלֶיהָ וְיָשְׁבָה בְּבֵיתֶךָ וּבָכְתָה אֶת אָבִיהָ וְאֶת אִמָּהּ יֶרַח יָמִים וְאַחַר כֵּן תָּבוֹא אֵלֶיהָ וּבְעַלְתָּהּ וְהָיְתָה לְךָ לְאִשָּׁה

When you go out to war against your enemy, and HASHEM, your God, delivers him into your hands, and you capture his captivity; and you see among the captivity a woman who is beautiful of form, and you desire her, you may take her to yourself for a wife. You shall bring her to the midst of your house; she shall shave her head and let her nails grow. She shall remove the garment of her captivity from upon herself and sit in your house, and she shall weep for her father and her mother for a full month; thereafter you may come to her and live with her, and she shall be a wife to you (*Deuteronomy* 21:10-13).

In this passage, the Torah sets out the unique law of a *"yefas toar"* (woman of beautiful form). It creates a special dispensation under which a Jewish soldier who captured a woman in war may bring her home, have her carry out a specific thirty-day protocol of mourning, and then marry her. Although Scripture mentions only the mourning protocol, Chinuch will note that before the soldier may marry this woman, she must consent to convert to Judaism and become his wife.[1] If she agrees to convert and marries him, she is entitled to the same marital rights as any other Jewish woman. If she refuses to convert, he must set her free.

Chinuch will also explain that while the Torah *allows* the soldier to do this because it recognizes that in the heat of battle he may be seized by desire, all the Torah's stipulations in this passage are designed to cool his passion and ultimately discourage him from marrying the *yefas toar.*

שֶׁנִּצְטַוִּינוּ בְּאֵשֶׁת יְפַת תֹּאַר – We are commanded regarding a woman who is a *yefas toar,* לַעֲשׂוֹת לָהּ כְּמִשְׁפָּט הַכָּתוּב בְּפָרָשָׁה זוֹ – to act with her in accordance with the protocol set forth in this Torah **passage, שֶׁנֶּאֱמַר – as it is stated** (*Deuteronomy* 21:11): "וְרָאִיתָ בַּשִּׁבְיָה אֵשֶׁת יְפַת תֹּאַר וְגוֹ׳ " – *When you go out to war against your enemy ...* ***and you see among the captivity a woman who is beautiful of form*** *(a "yefas toar"), and you desire her, you may take her to yourself for a wife,* **etc.** The passage then sets out the procedure for taking such a woman as a wife.

Before explaining the mitzvah, Chinuch sets aside a misconception:

"יְפַת תֹּאַר" – When Scripture mentions *a woman who is* ***beautiful of form,*** **כְּלוֹמַר שֶׁתִּהְיֶה יָפָה בְּעֵינָיו** – it **means to say** only **that she is beautiful in [her captor's] eyes,** i.e., appealing to him personally, not that she is objectively beautiful.[2]

NOTES

1. A Jewish man is prohibited to marry a non-Jewish woman (Mitzvah 427; see *Rambam, Hil. Issurei Bi'ah* 12:1-2), and this prohibition applies even in the case of a *yefas toar* (*Rambam, Hil. Melachim* 8:7; see note 19 below). [Likewise, cohabitation with a non-Jewess outside the context of marriage is prohibited; see *Rambam, Hil. Issurei Bi'ah* ibid., and Mitzvah 427 with notes 6-7.] See Chinuch below, at note 11.

2. *Sifrei* (to the verse) expounds the clause of the verse, *and you desire her,* to indicate that the expression, *beautiful of form,* refers even to an unattractive woman who is desired by this man.

וְעִנְיַן הַצִּוּוּי בָּהּ שֶׁיְּבִיאֶנָּה הַיִּשְׂרָאֵל אֶל בֵּיתוֹ וִיצַוֶּה אוֹתָהּ לְגַלֵּחַ רֹאשָׁהּ וּלְגַדֵּל צִפָּרְנֶיהָ[3] וּלְהָסִיר מֵעָלֶיהָ הַכְּסוּת הַנָּאָה שֶׁהֵבִיאָה מִבֵּיתָהּ[4], שֶׁכֵּן דַּרְכָּן שֶׁל גּוֹיִם הָאֲרוּרִים שֶׁבְּנוֹתֵיהֶן מִתְקַשְּׁטוֹת בַּמִּלְחָמָה לִזְנוֹת[5], וְיַרְשֶׁה אוֹתָהּ לִבְכּוֹת אָבִיהָ וְאִמָּהּ חֹדֶשׁ יָמִים כִּרְצוֹנָהּ[6].

אֵלּוּ הֵם הַדְּבָרִים הַמְפֹרָשִׁים בַּכָּתוּב בְּדִין אֵשֶׁת יְפַת תֹּאַר, וּמִן הַדּוֹמֶה שֶׁעַל כָּל אֵלֶּה יָבוֹא חִיּוּב הָעֲשֵׂה.

Chinuch proceeds to describe the mitzvah in some detail:

וְעִנְיַן הַצִּוּוּי בָּהּ – The description of the commandment regarding [the *yefas toar*] is as follows: **שֶׁיְּבִיאֶנָּה הַיִּשְׂרָאֵל אֶל בֵּיתוֹ – The Israelite** soldier who wishes to marry her **must** first **bring her to his house** **וִיצַוֶּה אוֹתָהּ לְגַלֵּחַ רֹאשָׁהּ וּלְגַדֵּל צִפָּרְנֶיהָ – and command her to shave her head and let her fingernails grow,** as it is stated (ibid. v. 12), *You shall bring her to the midst of your house; she shall shave her head and let her nails grow;*[3] **וּלְהָסִיר מֵעָלֶיהָ הַכְּסוּת הַנָּאָה שֶׁהֵבִיאָה מִבֵּיתָהּ – and** he shall also command her **to remove from herself the handsome garment that she brought** with her **from her house** (i.e., the fine garment she was wearing when captured), as it is stated (ibid. v. 13), *She shall remove the garment of her captivity from upon herself.* She must instead dress in garments of mourning.[4]

Chinuch interrupts to explain why the Torah assumes that the captive woman was wearing a fine garment:

שֶׁכֵּן דַּרְכָּן שֶׁל גּוֹיִם הָאֲרוּרִים – For this is the way of the accursed, idolatrous **nations,** **שֶׁבְּנוֹתֵיהֶן מִתְקַשְּׁטוֹת בַּמִּלְחָמָה לִזְנוֹת – that their daughters adorn themselves during war** and go out to the battlefield in order **to seduce** the enemy soldiers.[5]

Chinuch returns to the protocol of this mitzvah:

וְיַרְשֶׁה אוֹתָהּ לִבְכּוֹת אָבִיהָ וְאִמָּהּ חֹדֶשׁ יָמִים כִּרְצוֹנָהּ – And [the Jewish soldier] shall allow [his captive] to sit in his house and **weep for her father and mother for a month's time, as she desires;** as it is stated (ibid.), *and she shall weep for her father and her mother for a full month.*[6]

Chinuch concludes:

אֵלּוּ הֵם הַדְּבָרִים הַמְפֹרָשִׁים בַּכָּתוּב בְּדִין אֵשֶׁת יְפַת תֹּאַר – These are the things that are written **expressly in Scripture in the context of a woman** taken as a ***yefas toar,*** **וּמִן הַדּוֹמֶה שֶׁעַל כָּל אֵלֶּה יָבוֹא חִיּוּב הָעֲשֵׂה – and it would seem that the requirement of this mitzvah-obligation encompasses all of these** details; if a soldier omits any of them, he has violated the mitzvah-obligation.

NOTES

3. The verse actually states, וְעָשְׂתָה אֶת צִפָּרְנֶיהָ, literally, *and she shall tend to her nails. Sifrei* cites a dispute as to what this means. Chinuch (following *Rambam, Hil. Melachim* 8:5) rules in accordance with R' Akiva, who explains that she must let them grow long. R' Eliezer argues that she must cut them short. [See also *Yevamos* 48a.]

4. *Sifrei* to the verse.

5. *Sifrei* to the verse. The young women would participate in the war effort by dressing provocatively and letting themselves be seen by the enemy soldiers, in order to distract them from the battle and make them vulnerable to defeat (*Aderes Eliyahu* to *Deuteronomy* 21:13).

6. Her parents were not necessarily killed in the battle; what she mourns is her separation from them (*Sforno* to the verse; see *Tosafos, Yevamos* 48b ד״ה רבי אליעזר). She is given a month of grieving to find solace and adjust to her new situation (*Rambam, Moreh Nevuchim* III, Ch. 41; see Insight).

[Sifrei cites two interpretations of the words, *she shall weep for her father and her mother* (see also *Yevamos* 48b). Chinuch follows the opinion of R' Eliezer, who understands the verse literally. R' Akiva, however, understands "*her father and her mother*" as a reference to the idols she worshiped before her capture, which she revered like parents. According to R' Akiva, she is given a month's time to mourn the pagan practices that she will be forced to abandon (see *Emek HaNetziv* to *Sifrei,* and *Rambam, Hil. Melachim* 8:5).]

וּמִשָּׁרְשֵׁי הַמִּצְוָה אָמְרוּ זִכְרוֹנָם לִבְרָכָה לְפִי שֶׁלֹּא הִתִּירָה הַתּוֹרָה יְפַת תֹּאַר בַּשִּׁבְיָה אֶלָּא כְּנֶגֶד יֵצֶר הָרַע, שֶׁאִם לֹא הִתִּירָהּ הַכָּתוּב יִשָּׂאֶנָּה בְּאִסּוּר לְתֹקֶף יֵצֶר לֵב הָאָדָם רַע בְּעִנְיַן הַחֵשֶׁק[7], וְעַל כֵּן סָתַם הַכָּתוּב דֶּלֶת בְּפָנָיו לַהֲבִאישָׁהּ בְּעֵינָיו, וְצִוָּה לְגַלֵּחַ רֹאשָׁהּ כְּדֵי לְאַבֵּד תֹּאַר שַׂעֲרוֹתֶיהָ הַנָּאִים וּלְגַדֵּל צִפָּרְנֶיהָ כְּדֵי לְנַוֵּל תֹּאַר יָדֶיהָ, וְשֶׁיַּרְשֶׁה אוֹתָהּ לִבְכּוֹת חֹדֶשׁ רִאשׁוֹן לְנַוֵּל פָּנֶיהָ וּלְכַלּוֹת בְּדִמְעוֹת עֵינֶיהָ, גַּם חִיֵּב הַכָּתוּב שֶׁתֵּשֵׁב עִמּוֹ בְּבֵיתוֹ בַּעֲשׂוֹתָהּ כָּל זֶה בַּחֹדֶשׁ הָרִאשׁוֹן[8], וְהַכֹּל לְהַמְאִיסָהּ בְּעֵינָיו שֶׁיְּהֵא נִכְנָס וְיוֹצֵא נִתְקָל בָּהּ וְרוֹאֶה בְּנִוּוּלָהּ[9].

Underlying Purpose of the Mitzvah

וּמִשָּׁרְשֵׁי הַמִּצְוָה אָמְרוּ זִכְרוֹנָם לִבְרָכָה – **Regarding the underlying purposes of the mitzvah, [the Sages], of blessed memory, have stated** (*Kiddushin* 21b) לְפִי שֶׁלֹּא הִתִּירָה הַתּוֹרָה יְפַת תֹּאַר בַּשִּׁבְיָה אֶלָּא כְּנֶגֶד יֵצֶר הָרַע – that we must **consider that the Torah permitted a** ***yefas toar*** to a soldier who took her **in captivity only in recognition of the strength of** man's **evil inclination.** שֶׁאִם לֹא הִתִּירָהּ הַכָּתוּב יִשָּׂאֶנָּה בְּאִסּוּר – **For if Scripture would not have permitted her** to him, it is likely that **he would marry her in sin,** לְתֹקֶף יֵצֶר לֵב הָאָדָם רַע בְּעִנְיַן הַחֵשֶׁק – **due to the overwhelming passion of the evil inclination in man's heart,** specifically **with regard to** his **desire** for illicit relationships. It is in recognition of this pitfall that the Torah created a specific permit.[7]

Considering that the Torah permitted the *yefas toar* to the soldier only out of necessity, and it would certainly be preferable that he overcome his evil inclination, Chinuch proceeds to explain the underlying purpose of the *yefas toar's* mourning protocol:

וְעַל כֵּן סָתַם הַכָּתוּב דֶּלֶת בְּפָנָיו לַהֲבִאישָׁהּ בְּעֵינָיו – **Therefore,** being that Scripture permitted the *yefas toar* to a soldier only as a response to his evil inclination, **Scripture** largely **"closed the door"** of this permit **before him,** by legislating conditions **to make her** appear **repulsive in his eyes.** וְצִוָּה לְגַלֵּחַ רֹאשָׁהּ – **[The Torah] commands** that the captive woman is **to shave her head,** כְּדֵי לְאַבֵּד תֹּאַר שַׂעֲרוֹתֶיהָ הַנָּאִים – **in order to ruin the** attractive **form of her beautiful hair;** וּלְגַדֵּל צִפָּרְנֶיהָ – **and** she is **to let her fingernails grow,** כְּדֵי לְנַוֵּל תֹּאַר יָדֶיהָ – **in order to disfigure the** attractive **form of her hands;** וְשֶׁיַּרְשֶׁה אוֹתָהּ לִבְכּוֹת חֹדֶשׁ רִאשׁוֹן – **and that [her captor] allow her to weep for the first month** after she is brought to his house, לְנַוֵּל פָּנֶיהָ וּלְכַלּוֹת בְּדִמְעוֹת עֵינֶיהָ – in order **to disfigure** the features of **her face and to dim her eyes with tears.** גַּם חִיֵּב הַכָּתוּב שֶׁתֵּשֵׁב עִמּוֹ בְּבֵיתוֹ בַּעֲשׂוֹתָהּ כָּל זֶה בַּחֹדֶשׁ הָרִאשׁוֹן – **Scripture further obligates that she live with him in his house while she performs all these** actions, **during the first month** of her captivity,[8] וְהַכֹּל לְהַמְאִיסָהּ בְּעֵינָיו – **all** in order **to make her** seem **repulsive in his eyes,** שֶׁיְּהֵא נִכְנָס וְיוֹצֵא נִתְקָל בָּהּ וְרוֹאֶה בְּנִוּוּלָהּ – by ensuring **that whenever he enters and exits [his house], he will trip over her and see her disfigurement.**[9]

NOTES

7. Being that the idolatrous women would act provocatively in the battle zone, it was inevitable that female prisoners would represent an overwhelming temptation to the soldiers. In order to avoid the near certainty that some Jews would engage in illicit relations with these women, the Torah legislated a law, allowing a soldier to marry a captive woman under a controlled set of circumstances. As Chinuch will explain, these circumstances are designed to make her repulsive to him, so that his passions will subside and he will set her free.

This is implied by Scripture's description of the captive woman as "beautiful." By including this term, the Torah indicates that it permits the non-Jewish captive only reluctantly, because of the soldier's passion for her beauty (*Rashi, Kiddushin* 21b ד"ה דברה תורה וד"ה יפת תואר).

8. [Chinuch implies that the *yefas toar* procedure must begin immediately upon the woman's arrival at her captor's house. Scripture does not state this explicitly, but that is the simple understanding of the passage.] Moreover, reason dictates that it will be effective only if this is so. If the process would be postponed, her captor might grow accustomed to her presence and then would not be repulsed by any of the steps she subsequently takes (*Minchas Chinuch* §10).

9. *Sifrei* (to v. 13) teaches that if he has more than one house [or room; *Malbim*], she must be brought to the one that he uses most. This is derived from the fact that

וְאָמְרוּ מִן הַמְפָרְשִׁים[11] שֶׁהֶתֵּר יְפַת תֹּאַר בִּיאָה רִאשׁוֹנָה הִיא בְּגֵיוּתָהּ, וּקְרוֹבִים דִּבְרֵיהֶם אַחַר שֶׁהַהֶתֵּר שֶׁלָּהּ הוּא מִפְּנֵי תֹּקֶף יֵצֶר הָרַע[12]. אֲבָל מֵהֶם[13] שֶׁאָמְרוּ שֶׁאֵינָהּ מֻתֶּרֶת כְּלָל עַד לְאַחַר כָּל הַמַּעֲשִׂים הָאֵלּוּ שֶׁזָּכַרְנוּ, וּמִפְּשַׁט הַכְּתוּבִים נִרְאֶה כֵּן[14], גַּם בִּירוּשַׁלְמִי (פ״ב דמכות ה״ו) **חָלְקוּ עַל זֶה[15].**

Even after the *yefas toar* has completed her thirty-day period of mourning, her captor is not permitted to marry her unless she first converts to Judaism.[10] Now, as has been explained thus far, the Torah addresses the soldier's evil inclination by permitting him to bring home a female captive, put her through the process described above, convert her, and then marry her. There is a debate among the Rishonim whether this is all that is permitted, or the Torah grants the soldier an additional dispensation. Chinuch cites the two opinions:

וְאָמְרוּ מִן הַמְפָרְשִׁים – Some commentators say[11] **שֶׁהֶתֵּר יְפַת תֹּאַר בִּיאָה רִאשׁוֹנָה הִיא בְּגֵיוּתָהּ – that the permit regarding a *yefas toar*** includes a dispensation for **an initial act of cohabitation** with her **while she is** still **a non-Jew,** before she undergoes the lengthy process described above and converts. **וּקְרוֹבִים דִּבְרֵיהֶם – The words of [these commentators] are logical, אַחַר שֶׁהַהֶתֵּר שֶׁלָּהּ הוּא מִפְּנֵי תֹּקֶף יֵצֶר הָרַע – since the dispensation for** cohabiting with **her is** granted only **because of the strength of** man's **evil inclination,** so it stands to reason that there is an immediate permit of some sort at the time that the soldier is gripped by his evil inclination.[12] **אֲבָל מֵהֶם שֶׁאָמְרוּ – However, some [commentators]**[13] disagree and **say שֶׁאֵינָהּ מֻתֶּרֶת כְּלָל עַד לְאַחַר כָּל הַמַּעֲשִׂים הָאֵלּוּ שֶׁזָּכַרְנוּ – that [a *yefas toar*] is not permitted** to her captor **at all until after** she has completed **all the actions that we have mentioned. וּמִפְּשַׁט הַכְּתוּבִים נִרְאֶה כֵּן – And** although we noted that the first opinion seems logical, **this** latter opinion **seems** to emerge **from the plain meaning of the verses** in the passage.[14]

גַּם בִּירוּשַׁלְמִי חָלְקוּ עַל זֶה – This issue **is debated** by the Talmudic Sages **as well, in *Yerushalmi*** (*Makkos* 2:6).[15]

NOTES

after having stated (v. 12), *you shall bring her to the midst of your house,* Scripture repeats (v. 13), *She shall … "sit in your house" and she shall weep.* The repetition teaches that she must sit and weep in the room that her captor uses most, where he will see her constantly and become disgusted (*Mizrachi, Malbim,* and *Sifsei Chachamim* ad loc.).

[See Insight for another explanation of the purpose of these requirements.]

10. See above, note 1.

11. *Rambam* ibid. 8:2; *Rabbeinu Tam,* cited in *Tosafos, Kiddushin* 22a and *Sanhedrin* 21a.

12. Being that the Torah's permit is designed to address the overwhelming temptation that a soldier faces while in battle, it is only logical that the permit applies at that time, at least in a limited sense. If the captive would be entirely prohibited to the soldier until she completed her lengthy process of mourning and conversion followed by marriage, his *yetzer hara* would remain unchecked and he would be likely to cohabit with her illicitly beforehand. It thus stands to reason that the Torah grants a dispensation for a single act of cohabitation even before she undergoes the prescribed *yefas toar* procedure. Following this initial contact, however, he may not cohabit with her again until he carries out the entire procedure, ending with her conversion and their marriage (*Tosafos, Kiddushin* 22a ד״ה שלא; see *Minchas Chinuch* §2).

13. *Rashi, Kiddushin* 22a, as understood by *Tosafos* ibid. [See, however, alternative interpretations of *Rashi* in *Tosefos Rid, Pnei Yehoshua,* and *Meromei Sadeh* there, and *Mizrachi* to *Deuteronomy* 21:11.]

14. After describing the entire procedure, the Torah states (in v. 13): ***thereafter** you may come to her and live with her.* This implies that the soldier may not cohabit with her at all until the end of the *yefas toar* process (*Ramban* ad loc.).

As for the question of how the Torah has addressed the soldier's temptation, this view maintains that the soldier's knowledge that the captive will be completely permitted to him in a month's time enables him to control his *yetzer hara* in the interim (*Tosafos* ibid.). [See *Tosafos* and *Ritva* there (to 21b) for further discussion of this view.]

Chinuch below, at notes 18 and 24 (and the beginning of Mitzvah 533), adopts the first opinion.

15. *Yerushalmi* cites a dispute about this matter between Rav and R' Yochanan. Rav permits an initial cohabitation immediately, while R' Yochanan prohibits it until the entire procedure has been completed.

דִּינֵי הַמִּצְוָה מַה שֶּׁאָמְרוּ זִכְרוֹנָם לִבְרָכָה שֶׁאֵשֶׁת יְפַת תֹּאַר בֵּין בְּתוּלָה בֵּין בְּעוּלָה בֵּין אֵשֶׁת אִישׁ[16]. וְאֵין מֻתָּר לִקַּח שְׁתַּיִם, שֶׁנֶּאֱמַר בָּהּ, וְלֹא בָּהּ וּבַחֲבֶרְתָּהּ.

וּמַה[17] שֶּׁאָמְרוּ (קידושין כ״ב ע״א) **שֶׁלֹּא יִלְחָצֶנָּה בַּמִּלְחָמָה אֶלָּא יְיַחֲדֶנָּה לוֹ בַּבַּיִת, שֶׁלֹּא תְּהֵא סָבוּר שֶׁהִתִּירַתָּהּ הַתּוֹרָה בְּכָל עִנְיָן וַאֲפִלּוּ בְּפִרְסוּם[18].**

וּצְרִיכָה לְהִתְגַּיֵּר קֹדֶם שֶׁיִּשָּׂאֶנָּה לוֹ לְאִשָּׁה[19], וְאַחַר הַגֵּרוּת נוֹשְׂאָהּ בִּכְתֻבָּה וְקִדּוּשִׁין

Laws of the Mitzvah

דִּינֵי הַמִּצְוָה – The laws of the mitzvah include **מַה שֶּׁאָמְרוּ זִכְרוֹנָם לִבְרָכָה – that which [the Sages], of blessed memory, stated** (*Rambam* ibid. 8:3), **שֶׁאֵשֶׁת יְפַת תֹּאַר – that a woman** taken as a ***yefas toar*** is permitted to her captor **בֵּין בְּתוּלָה בֵּין בְּעוּלָה – whether** she is **a maiden or she** previously **had relations** with another man, **בֵּין אֵשֶׁת אִישׁ –** and **even** if at the time of her capture she was **the wife of** another (non-Jewish) **man.**[16] **וְאֵין מֻתָּר לִקַּח שְׁתַּיִם –** Another law (ibid.) is that **[a soldier] is not permitted to take two** captive women as wives, **שֶׁנֶּאֱמַר "בָּהּ" – for it is stated,** *and you desire **her**, you may take her to yourself for a wife*, which implies that the soldier may take only *her*, i.e., one woman, **וְלֹא בָּהּ וּבַחֲבֶרְתָּהּ – but not her and her fellow** captive.

Chinuch above cited two opinions as to whether the Torah permits a soldier a single act of cohabitation with his captive before she undergoes the *yefas toar* procedure and converts to Judaism. Now, the passage of the mitzvah states (v. 12), *You shall bring her to the midst of your house,* and the Gemara (*Kiddushin* 22a) expounds this to mean that a soldier "may not subjugate her during battle." According to the stringent opinion cited above, this means that the captive is entirely prohibited to the soldier until she is brought to his house and completes the process described in the passage.[17] According to the other opinion, however, the Gemara means something else. Chinuch, apparently adopting that opinion, proceeds to explain the Gemara's statement:

וּמַה שֶּׁאָמְרוּ – There **also** is **that which [the Sages] stated** (*Kiddushin* 22a), **שֶׁלֹּא יִלְחָצֶנָּה בַּמִּלְחָמָה – that [a soldier] may not subjugate [a *yefas toar*] during battle; אֶלָּא יְיַחֲדֶנָּה לוֹ בַּבַּיִת –** meaning that what he is permitted is, **rather,** only to **seclude her for himself in a house. שֶׁלֹּא תְּהֵא סָבוּר שֶׁהִתִּירַתָּהּ הַתּוֹרָה בְּכָל עִנְיָן וַאֲפִלּוּ בְּפִרְסוּם –** The Sages teach us here **that** although an initial cohabitation with the *yefas toar* is permitted even in the battle zone, **you should not think that the Torah permits her** to the soldier **in any setting,** meaning **even in** a **public** area. Rather, the cohabitation may be performed only in a secluded place.[18]

After describing the *yefas toar's* thirty-day protocol of mourning, the Torah concludes (v. 13), *thereafter ... she shall be a wife to you.* Chinuch points out that before the captor may marry her, she must fulfill another condition not mentioned in the Scriptural passage:

וּצְרִיכָה לְהִתְגַּיֵּר קֹדֶם שֶׁיִּשָּׂאֶנָּה לוֹ לְאִשָּׁה – [The *yefas toar*] must also convert to Judaism **before [the soldier] may take her as a wife.**[19] **וְאַחַר הַגֵּרוּת נוֹשְׂאָהּ בִּכְתֻבָּה וְקִדּוּשִׁין – After the conversion,**

NOTES

16. Since Scripture describes the captive as אֵשֶׁת יְפַת תֹּאַר, which literally means, *a "wife" who is beautiful of form,* we derive that the captive is permitted even if she had been married at the time of her capture (*Sifrei;* cited in *Kiddushin* 21b). [Under the Noahide laws, the marriage is terminated once she leaves her husband's home never to return, even without a formal divorce (see *Rambam, Hil. Melachim* 9:7-8).] For further discussion, see *Rambam, Hil. Melachim* 8:3; *Tosafos, Kiddushin* 21b ד״ה אשת and *Sanhedrin* 52b ד״ה פרט לאשת אחרים; *Mizrachi* and *Gur Aryeh* to *Deuteronomy* 21:11; *Shaar HaMelech, Hil. Issurei Bi'ah* 12:2.

17. See *Tosafos, Kiddushin* 22a ד״ה שלא.

18. This is Chinuch's understanding of *Rambam, Hil. Melachim* 8:3; see *Moreh Nevuchim* III, Ch. 41. Others explain the rule that "he may not subjugate her during battle" to mean that the soldier may not cohabit with the captive against her will, only with her consent (*Sefer Yerei'im,* end of §20). See *Ritva, Kiddushin* 21b, for additional explanations, including another interpretation of *Rambam's* opinion.

19. Although the passage does not mention this requirement, it is obvious, since under Torah law marriage is possible only with a Jewish woman (see *Rambam* ibid. 8:7 and *Minchas Chinuch* §16 ד״ה והנה לדברי הכל; see also *Kiddushin* 21b).

[A captive woman who expresses a willingness to convert to Judaism at the outset is exempted from

וְדִינָהּ כְּדִין בְּנוֹת יִשְׂרָאֵל[20]. וְאִם[21] לֹא רָצְתָה לְהִתְגַּיֵּר מְגַלְגֵּל עִמָּהּ שְׁנֵים עָשָׂר חֹדֶשׁ וּמְשַׁלְּחָהּ לְנַפְשָׁהּ[22], וְאַחַר חֹדֶשׁ הַבְּכִיָּה מַמְתִּין לָהּ שְׁנֵי חֳדָשִׁים עוֹד[23]. וְאִם נִתְעַבְּרָה מִבִּיאָה רִאשׁוֹנָה, הַוָּלָד גּוֹי וְאֵינוֹ בְּנוֹ לְשׁוּם דָּבָר מִכָּל הַדְּבָרִים, וּכְמוֹ שֶׁאָמְרוּ זִכְרוֹנָם לִבְרָכָה

---

he marries her with a *kesubah* (i.e., marriage contract), **and** with ***kiddushin*** and *chuppah*, וְדִינָהּ כְּדִין בְּנוֹת יִשְׂרָאֵל – **and her status is** the same **as that of** all married **Jewish women.**[20]

As a rule, conversion cannot be forced upon anyone, and is valid only if done willingly. Chinuch maintains that this holds true even in the case of a *yefas toar.*[21] He therefore discusses the procedure in the event that she does not consent to convert:

וְאִם לֹא רָצְתָה לְהִתְגַּיֵּר – **If** after thirty days **[the woman] does not want to convert,** מְגַלְגֵּל עִמָּהּ שְׁנֵים עָשָׂר חֹדֶשׁ – **[her captor] bears with her for** up to **twelve months;** וּמְשַׁלְּחָהּ לְנַפְשָׁהּ – **and** if after this time she still refuses to convert, **he sends her** out **to her freedom.**[22]

Chinuch sets out an additional requirement for marriage when the woman does agree to convert:

וְאַחַר חֹדֶשׁ הַבְּכִיָּה – **After the month of weeping,** מַמְתִּין לָהּ שְׁנֵי חֳדָשִׁים עוֹד – **[the captor] must wait an additional two months** in order **to** marry **her.**[23]

Chinuch above took the position that a soldier is permitted an initial act of cohabitation with his captive before he brings her to his house and puts her through the *yefas toar* procedure. He now discusses the status of a child conceived from that cohabitation:

וְאִם נִתְעַבְּרָה מִבִּיאָה רִאשׁוֹנָה – **If [a *yefas toar*] became pregnant from the first act of cohabitation** that she had with her Jewish captor before he brought her to his house, הַוָּלָד גּוֹי וְאֵינוֹ בְּנוֹ לְשׁוּם דָּבָר מִכָּל הַדְּבָרִים – **the child** that she conceived **is a non-Jewish** child, **and is not** considered **[the captor's] son with regard to any matter** of halachah. וּכְמוֹ שֶׁאָמְרוּ זִכְרוֹנָם לִבְרָכָה – This is **as**

NOTES

the *yefas toar* procedure. She may simply convert immediately like any other person and then marry her captor. The procedure is required only for a captive who does not initially wish to convert. She is given thirty days to mourn her family, and then is asked to convert (*Yevamos* 47b; *Rambam* ibid. 8:5; see further, *Minchas Chinuch* §7). See Insight.]

20. Once she has converted, she is a regular Jewess. As such, she must be married through the standard process of *kiddushin* and *chuppah*, which can be done only with her consent (see *Sefer HaMiknah, Kiddushin* 22a, to *Rashi* ד"ה ליקוחין; see, however, *Ramban, Deuteronomy* 21:13-14). Upon marriage, she is granted a *kesubah*, for she has the same financial and conjugal rights as any other wife (see above, Mitzvah 46, regarding a wife's marital rights). See also Mitzvah 534, at note 3.

21. This is the view of *Rambam,* ibid. 8:5-7. [See, however, *Rashi, Kiddushin* 22a ד"ה ליקוחין יש לך בה; *Tosafos* there 21b ד"ה בביאה שניה; *Ritva* there; *Ramban* to *Deuteronomy* 21:12.]

22. That is, after the initial thirty-day period of mourning, the captor may keep her in his house for an additional eleven months, during which he attempts to persuade her to convert to Judaism. If he is unsuccessful, he must set her free (*Rambam* ibid. 8:7; see *Kesef Mishneh* there). [At that time, however, she must at least abandon the worship of idols and accept observance of the Seven Noahide Laws (*Rambam* ibid.; see also ibid. 8:9).]

23. A total of three months must elapse between the time that the captor brings her home and the time that he marries her, for the following reason: It is possible that when the *yefas toar* is brought home she is pregnant from a previous non-Jewish husband. If she immediately marries her Jewish captor and later gives birth, it will not be known whether this child is the Jew's son or the previous husband's son. However, a woman's pregnancy is generally discerned after three months. By postponing her marriage until a total of three months has elapsed from when the Jewish soldier brings her home, we are able to determine whether or not she was pregnant at the time of her marriage to him, and thus, whether or not a child born later was fathered by him (*Sifrei* to v. 13; *Rambam, Hil. Melachim* 8:6 and *Hil. Geirushin* 11:21).

Now, since (according to *Rambam* and Chinuch) the Jewish captor is permitted to cohabit with his captive in the battle zone, it is also possible that a pregnancy discerned during these three months is the result of her initial cohabitation with the Jewish captor. However, as Chinuch will explain, being that the woman had not yet converted at the time of their initial cohabitation, a child conceived from that cohabitation would, halachically, not have the Jewish father's lineage. Thus, the three-month wait always serves to determine whether the child is of Jewish lineage (see *Kesef Mishneh* to *Hil. Melachim* 8:6).

[See *Minchas Chinuch* §6 for discussion of whether the waiting period is imposed even on a woman who at the time of her capture was unmarried, or was not of childbearing age. See also *Maggid Mishneh, Hil. Geirushin* 11:21, and *Birkei Yosef, Even HaEzer* 13:4.]

(קידושין ס״ח ע״ב) **בִּנְךָ הַבָּא מִן הַגּוֹיָה אֵינוֹ בִּנְךָ אֶלָּא בְּנָהּ**[24]**, וְתָמָר אֲחוֹת אַבְשָׁלוֹם**[25] **מִבִּיאָה רִאשׁוֹנָה שֶׁל יְפַת תֹּאַר הָיְתָה**[26]**, וְאַבְשָׁלוֹם אָחִיהָ נוֹלַד אַחַר הַנִּשּׂוּאִין**[27]**, וְנִמְצֵאת תָּמָר אֲחוֹת אַבְשָׁלוֹם מֵאִמּוֹ**[28] **וּמֻתֶּרֶת לְהִנָּשֵׂא לְאַמְנוֹן**[29]**, וְכֵן הוּא אוֹמֵר** (שמואל ב׳ י״ג, י״ג) **דַּבֶּר נָא אֶל הַמֶּלֶךְ כִּי לֹא יִמְנָעֵנִי מִמֶּךָּ**[30]**. וְיֶתֶר פְּרָטֵי הַמִּצְוָה בְּקִדּוּשִׁין פֶּרֶק רִאשׁוֹן וּבְסַנְהֶדְרִין**[31]**.**

[the Sages], of blessed memory, stated (*Kiddushin* 68b), based on Scripture: **בִּנְךָ הַבָּא מִן הַגּוֹיָה אֵינוֹ בִּנְךָ אֶלָּא בְּנָהּ – Your son who comes from** your cohabitation with **a non-Jewish woman is not** considered ***your*** **son, but *her* son.**[24]

Chinuch points out an application of the law he just stated. King David had a daughter Tamar by his wife Maachah, and a son Amnon by his wife Achinoam. Thus, Tamar and Amnon were not related maternally. Scripture (*II Samuel* Ch. 13) relates that Amnon desired Tamar, and she agreed to marry him if he secured permission from their father David. It seems odd that Tamar thought David would sanction the marriage, when she and Amnon were paternal siblings. Chinuch cites the Gemara's explanation of this matter (*Sanhedrin* 21a):

וְתָמָר אֲחוֹת אַבְשָׁלוֹם – Tamar, whom Scripture describes as **"the sister of Absalom,"**[25] **מִבִּיאָה רִאשׁוֹנָה שֶׁל יְפַת תֹּאַר הָיְתָה – was** born **from [King David's] initial cohabitation with a *yefas toar,***[26] **וְאַבְשָׁלוֹם אָחִיהָ נוֹלַד אַחַר הַנִּשּׂוּאִין – and her brother Absalom was born after the marriage** of their mother to King David.[27] **וְנִמְצֵאת תָּמָר אֲחוֹת אַבְשָׁלוֹם מֵאִמּוֹ – Thus, it emerges** that **Tamar was** halachically considered **Absalom's maternal sister,** but not his paternal sister;[28] **וּמֻתֶּרֶת לְהִנָּשֵׂא לְאַמְנוֹן – she was** therefore **permitted to be married to Amnon.**[29] **וְכֵן הוּא אוֹמֵר – This is** the meaning of **what [Scripture] states** that Tamar told Amnon (*II Samuel* 13:13): **"דַּבֶּר נָא אֶל הַמֶּלֶךְ כִּי לֹא יִמְנָעֵנִי מִמֶּךָּ" –** *Therefore, **speak please to the king, for he will not withhold me from you.***[30]

Chinuch concludes:

וְיֶתֶר פְּרָטֵי הַמִּצְוָה בְּקִדּוּשִׁין פֶּרֶק רִאשׁוֹן וּבְסַנְהֶדְרִין – These, **and the remaining details of the mitzvah,** are explained **in the first chapter of** Tractate ***Kiddushin*** (21b-22a) **and in** various places in Tractate ***Sanhedrin.***[31]

NOTES

24. I.e., he is a non-Jewish child, and is not halachically recognized as the Jew's son.

If a Jewish man fathers a child with a non-Jewish woman, the Torah does not recognize the child as having his father's lineage for any matter; he is not considered Jewish, and will not inherit the father's estate. This is derived from a Scriptural verse that indicates that a son born to a Jew from a non-Jewish woman is considered "her" son, not "his" son (see *Kiddushin* 68b for details). Thus, a child that the *yefas toar* conceived before her conversion is non-Jewish even if he was fathered by the Jewish captor.

[This pertains to a case where she does not convert while pregnant. If she converts before the child is born, such that he is born to a Jewish mother, he is considered a Jew. Nevertheless, since his mother was a non-Jewess at the time of his conception, he is recognized as *her* child but not as the captor's child. Thus, he will not inherit his father (see *Yevamos* 97b, end, with *Rashi* ד״ה אבל חייבין).]

25. See *II Samuel* 13:1. Absalom was born to King David from Maachah, so he and Tamar shared the same father *and* mother.

26. Maachah, the mother of Tamar and Absalom, was a *yefas toar.* According to Chinuch, she conceived Tamar through her initial cohabitation with David, before she converted to Judaism. [For another approach, see *Tosafos, Sanhedrin* 21a ד״ה דאי and *Kiddushin* 22a ד״ה שלא.]

27. I.e., Absalom was conceived after Maachah had converted to Judaism and married King David.

28. Since King David fathered Tamar before Maachah converted, Tamar was halachically not considered his daughter (see note 24). She and Absalom were thus halachic siblings through their mother, but not through their father. [Although Tamar was conceived before Maachah's conversion, she was born after her conversion. Thus, Tamar was born Jewish and was halachically considered Maachah's daughter and Absalom's *maternal* sister (see end of note 24).]

29. Since Tamar was halachically not recognized as King David's daughter, she was not Amnon's paternal sister. She also was not his maternal sister, since they were born to different mothers. Thus, she could have married him.

30. Had Amnon agreed to marry Tamar, David would have consented. Amnon, however, forced himself upon her, leading Absalom to have him assassinated (ibid. vv. 28-29). This incident ultimately led to Absalom's ill-fated rebellion.

31. The laws are codified in *Rambam, Hil. Melachim* 8:2-9.

וְנוֹהֶגֶת מִצְוָה זוֹ בִּזְמַן שֶׁיִּשְׂרָאֵל עַל אַדְמָתָן, כִּי אָז הָיָה לָהֶן רְשׁוּת וִיכֹלֶת בְּיָדָם לְהִלָּחֵם. וְעוֹבֵר עַל זֶה וְלֹא עָשָׂה הַמַּעֲשִׂים שֶׁזָּכַרְנוּ בִּטֵּל עֲשֵׂה זֶה.[32]

❧ Applicability of the Mitzvah ❧

וְנוֹהֶגֶת מִצְוָה זוֹ בִּזְמַן שֶׁיִּשְׂרָאֵל עַל אַדְמָתָן – **This mitzvah applies** only **when the Jewish people are** settled **in their land,** כִּי אָז הָיָה לָהֶן רְשׁוּת וִיכֹלֶת בְּיָדָם לְהִלָּחֵם – **for** only **then did they have** the **authority and the capacity to wage war** and take captives.

וְעוֹבֵר עַל זֶה וְלֹא עָשָׂה הַמַּעֲשִׂים שֶׁזָּכַרְנוּ – **One who transgresses this** mitzvah, **and does not perform** all of **the actions that we mentioned** above when taking a *yefas toar* for himself, בִּטֵּל עֲשֵׂה זֶה – **has violated this** mitzvah-**obligation.**[32]

NOTES

32. As Chinuch asserted above (after note 6), the mitzvah encompasses *all* the steps set out in the Scriptural passage.

❧§ Insight: Setting a Moral Standard for the Nation

Chinuch cites the teaching of the Sages (*Kiddushin* 21b) that the Torah permitted a *yefas toar* to a soldier in recognition of the strength of man's evil inclination. A superficial glance at this mitzvah might give the impression that the Torah sanctions unbridled behavior by soldiers on the battlefield. Rishonim point out, however, that the truth is the exact opposite. The purpose of this mitzvah is to *control* the behavior of Jewish soldiers in battle. When the tension of war finds release in the exhilaration of victory, troops of other armies tend to act with reckless abandon, and they abuse female prisoners without restraint. The Torah, however, places strict guidelines on how a soldier must treat his captive. At the same time that the Torah recognizes that a soldier in the heat of war may be caught up by heightened passions, and therefore provides him a special dispensation, it places a clear limit on his exercising those passions and commands him to treat his captive with dignity and compassion.

Chinuch explained that many of the laws of this mitzvah are designed to subdue the soldier's desire for the *yefas toar* and cause him to send her away. *Rambam* (*Moreh Nevuchim* III, Ch. 41), however, explains that the underlying purpose of these laws is to develop virtuous behavior and a high moral standard among the Jewish people, particularly in its soldiers. Thus, the Torah teaches that even when a soldier who sees a *yefas toar* is gripped by uncontrollable desire, he may not subjugate her on the battlefield; rather, he must take her to a private place for the permitted cohabitation. [And, according to *Sefer Yerei'im* (cited in note 18), he may not cohabit with her against her will, even in privacy.] The other laws, *Rambam* explains, similarly demand that he treat his captive in a dignified manner.

After the initial contact at the time of battle, the Torah prohibits him to cohabit with her again until he has given her thirty days to mourn her parents and her previous lifestyle. During that time, he must let her display her mourning by growing her hair and fingernails even in his house, and he must let her cry, so that she can release her emotions and ultimately find solace by crying herself out. Throughout this thirty-day mourning period, he must allow her to practice idolatry as had been her custom (see above, note 6), even to the point of letting her do so openly in his house. And, for that entire time, he may not attempt to convert her to Judaism and may not even discuss religion with her. It is only after the period of mourning has passed that he may try — for up to twelve months — to persuade her to convert. And if, after that time, she refuses, he is forbidden to convert her or marry her forcibly, to keep her as a servant, or to sell her (see Mitzvos 533-534). Rather, he is obligated to set her free. Thus, although she is non-Jewish, and was taken as a prisoner, since the captor cohabited with her during the war, the Torah requires him to treat her with compassion and dignity. In setting this standard for a soldier's treatment of his prisoner, the Torah impresses upon its people that they must behave in a benevolent manner even at a time when others would act brutally. This sets the

tone for virtuous behavior in all areas of life (*Rambam* ibid.; see similarly, *Rabbeinu Bachya,* introduction to *Parashas Ki Seitzei*).

R' S. R. Hirsch notes that this is not the only instance in which the Torah uses the context of war to set an unexpectedly high moral standard. We learned in Mitzvah 529 about the prohibition of *bal tashchis,* which forbids us to wastefully destroy something at *any* time. The Torah, however, chooses to express this prohibition (*Deuteronomy* 20:19) by telling us that when we lay siege to a city we should not cut down the fruit trees around it. Similarly, in ibid. 23:10, the Torah states that when we go out as a camp against our enemies, וְנִשְׁמַרְתָּ מִכֹּל דָּבָר רָע, *you shall beware of anything evil.* This verse teaches that "a person should not think immoral thoughts by day, and thus come to *tumah* [through a seminal emission] by night" (*Avodah Zarah* 20b). The warning applies in all settings, yet the Torah chooses to express it in the context of an army camp. Likewise, Mitzvah 565 requires a man who had a seminal emission to leave "the camp of the Leviim," which refers to the Temple Mount in Jerusalem. The Torah (ibid. 23:11), however, expresses this mitzvah as a requirement upon a soldier who experiences such an emission to leave the army camp.

In all these cases, the Torah teaches that the Jewish people must adhere to the highest levels of morality and spiritual purity *even* when they are part of an army at war. Principled and honorable behavior is expected of us under the extraordinary conditions that exist on a battlefield, where the morality of other nations tends to erode. Certainly, we must infer, the Torah demands of us to abide by these standards — and even higher ones — in ordinary times when we are more readily able to control our actions and thoughts (*R' Hirsch, Commentary* to *Deuteronomy* 21:10; see also *Ramban, Deuteronomy* 23:10).

מִצְוָה תקלג: שֶׁלֹּא לִמְכֹּר אֵשֶׁת יְפַת תֹּאַר

שֶׁלֹּא לִמְכֹּר אֵשֶׁת יְפַת תֹּאַר אַחַר שֶׁיָּבֹא עָלֶיהָ הַחוֹשֵׁק בָּהּ בִּיאָה אַחַת[1], וְעַל זֶה נֶאֱמַר (דברים כ״א, י״ד) וְהָיָה אִם לֹא חָפַצְתָּ בָּהּ וְשִׁלַּחְתָּהּ לְנַפְשָׁהּ וּמָכֹר לֹא תִמְכְּרֶנָּה בַּכָּסֶף[2].

מִשָּׁרְשֵׁי הַמִּצְוָה לְלַמֵּד נַפְשֵׁנוּ מִדּוֹת טוֹבוֹת וִיקָרוֹת[3], וּכְבָר כָּתַבְתִּי בְּהַרְבֵּה מְקוֹמוֹת כִּי הַנֶּפֶשׁ הַיְקָרָה רְאוּיָה לְקַבֵּל הַטּוֹבוֹת וְעָלֶיהָ יָחוּלוּ הַבְּרָכוֹת לְעוֹלָם[4], וְכִי חָפֵץ הָאֵל בְּטוֹב עַמּוֹ

Mitzvah 533
The Prohibition to Sell a Yefas Toar

וְהָיָה אִם לֹא חָפַצְתָּ בָּהּ וְשִׁלַּחְתָּהּ לְנַפְשָׁהּ וּמָכֹר לֹא תִמְכְּרֶנָּה בַּכָּסֶף
But it shall be that if you do not desire her, then you shall send her on her own, but you may not sell her for money (*Deuteronomy* 21:14).

After setting out the protocol for marrying a *yefas toar* in the previous mitzvah, in this mitzvah the Torah prohibits a man who decides against marrying his female captive to sell her into slavery. Chinuch will explain at what point in the procedure this prohibition takes effect:

שֶׁלֹּא לִמְכֹּר אֵשֶׁת יְפַת תֹּאַר – We are commanded **not to sell a woman** who was taken as a ***yefas toar*** אַחַר שֶׁיָּבֹא עָלֶיהָ הַחוֹשֵׁק בָּהּ בִּיאָה אַחַת – **after the one who desired her has performed one act of cohabitation with her.**[1] וְעַל זֶה נֶאֱמַר – **Regarding this it is stated** (*Deuteronomy* 21:14): "וְהָיָה אִם לֹא חָפַצְתָּ בָּהּ וְשִׁלַּחְתָּהּ לְנַפְשָׁהּ וּמָכֹר לֹא תִמְכְּרֶנָּה בַּכָּסֶף" – ***But it shall be that if you do not desire her, then you shall send her on her own, but you may not sell her for money.***[2]

Underlying Purpose of the Mitzvah

מִשָּׁרְשֵׁי הַמִּצְוָה – **Among the underlying purposes of the mitzvah** is לְלַמֵּד נַפְשֵׁנוּ מִדּוֹת טוֹבוֹת וִיקָרוֹת – **to instill in ourselves good and valuable character traits.**[3] וּכְבָר כָּתַבְתִּי בְּהַרְבֵּה מְקוֹמוֹת – **I have already written in many places** in this work כִּי הַנֶּפֶשׁ הַיְקָרָה רְאוּיָה לְקַבֵּל הַטּוֹבוֹת – **that a precious soul** that has developed admirable traits **is worthy of receiving the goodness** of God, וְעָלֶיהָ יָחוּלוּ הַבְּרָכוֹת לְעוֹלָם – **and** His **blessings shall come to rest upon it forever.**[4] וְכִי חָפֵץ הָאֵל בְּטוֹב עַמּוֹ – **Thus, since the Almighty desires the good of His people** and

---

NOTES

1. In the previous mitzvah (at note 11), Chinuch cited a dispute as to when the captor becomes permitted to cohabit with the *yefas toar.* Some say that he has no permit until she completes the process of mourning described there and converts to Judaism, while others say that he is permitted a single act of cohabitation beforehand. Chinuch there (at notes 18 and 24) follows the latter opinion. Accordingly, Chinuch states here that once the captor performed the initial act of cohabitation, even in the battle zone, he becomes prohibited to sell her (see *Sifrei* to the verse; *Rambam, Sefer HaMitzvos, Lo Saaseh* 263; *Ramban, Deuteronomy* 21:14, end; *Minchas Chinuch* §1; see, however, *Minchas Chinuch* §2, who suggests that *Rambam* takes a different position in *Hil. Melachim* 8:6).

In addition to being prohibited, the sale of a *yefas toar* is entirely ineffective, and the seller must return the buyer's money (*Rambam, Hil. Melachim* ibid.; see *R' Akiva Eiger* ad loc.).

2. The verse concludes: *you shall not enslave her, since you have afflicted her. Sifrei* understands the phrase, *since you have afflicted her,* to mean, "once you have cohabited with her." According to Chinuch, this stipulation applies even to the prohibition against selling her that is mentioned earlier in the verse. See *Minchas Chinuch* §1.

Although the verse explicitly prohibits only selling her for money, *Sifrei* expounds the repetitious expression, וּמָכֹר לֹא תִמְכְּרֶנָּה, literally, *but selling, you may not sell her,* as teaching that it is also prohibited to gift her to another master for free.

3. See Insight to Mitzvah 532 regarding the basic law of the *yefas toar.*

4. By cultivating in oneself God's Attributes and thus making one's essence a personification of goodness, one becomes worthy of receiving His blessing. [This theme is mentioned repeatedly in Sefer HaChinuch, and is discussed at length in Mitzvos 66, 74, 430, and 611, among other places.]

הִכְתִּירָם בְּכָל מִדָּה חֲמוּדָה וּמְהֻדֶּרֶת, וְאֵין סָפֵק כִּי מִמִּדַּת הַנְּבָלִים הַפְּחוּתִים בְּתַכְלִית לִמְכֹּר הָאִשָּׁה אַחַר שֶׁהִשְׁכִּיבוּהָ בְּחֵיקָם, יָדוּעַ הַדָּבָר, אֵין לְהַאֲרִיךְ בּוֹ.

וְעִנְיַן יְפַת תֹּאַר וּקְצָת דִּינֶיהָ וּמְקוֹם בֵּאוּרָן בַּגְּמָרָא, וְהַזְּמַן שֶׁדִּין יְפַת תֹּאַר נוֹהֵג, הַכֹּל כָּתוּב בְּמִצְוָה רִאשׁוֹנָה שֶׁבְּסֵדֶר זֶה (תקל״ב)[5].

---

seeks to endow them with His blessing, הִכְתִּירָם בְּכָל מִדָּה חֲמוּדָה וּמְהֻדֶּרֶת – **He has crowned them with every desirable and glorious character trait,** in order to make them worthy of that blessing. וְאֵין סָפֵק כִּי מִמִּדַּת הַנְּבָלִים הַפְּחוּתִים בְּתַכְלִית – **Now, there is no doubt that it is** representative **of the traits of the most despicable, degenerate [people]** לִמְכֹּר הָאִשָּׁה אַחַר שֶׁהִשְׁכִּיבוּהָ בְּחֵיקָם – **to sell a woman** into slavery **after having had her lie in their lap.** Since selling this woman is the antithesis of goodness, God has prohibited us from doing so. יָדוּעַ הַדָּבָר אֵין לְהַאֲרִיךְ בּוֹ – **This matter is obvious** and **there is no** need **to dwell on it.**

Laws and Applicability of the Mizvah

וְעִנְיַן יְפַת תֹּאַר – **The protocol** that the Torah sets out **for** marrying **a** ***yefas toar,*** וּקְצָת דִּינֶיהָ – **as well as some of the laws pertaining to her,** וּמְקוֹם בֵּאוּרָן בַּגְּמָרָא – **the place in the Talmud where [the laws] are explained,** וְהַזְּמַן שֶׁדִּין יְפַת תֹּאַר נוֹהֵג – **and the time** period **in which the law of** ***yefas toar*** **applies,** הַכֹּל כָּתוּב בְּמִצְוָה רִאשׁוֹנָה שֶׁבְּסֵדֶר זֶה – **are all written in the first mitzvah of this** ***parashah*** (Mitzvah 532).[5]

5. Chinuch does not mention a punishment of *malkus* for violating this transgression. *Rambam* (*Hil. Bechoros* 6:5) states that since the sale of a *yefas toar* does not take effect and the seller must refund the payment (see above, note 1), by attempting to sell her he has not done anything of import, and therefore he does not incur *malkus*. [However, some texts of *Sefer HaMitzvos* (*Lo Saaseh* 263) state that the seller does incur *malkus*. See footnote in Heller ed. there.] For discussion, and other reasons why the seller might be exempt from *malkus*, see *Mishneh LaMelech, Hil. Bechoros* ibid.; *Maayan HaChochmah,* p. 122b in Roedelheim ed.; and *Minchas Chinuch* §2. See also Mitzvah 534 note 7.

מִצְוָה תקלד

שֶׁלֹּא לְהַעֲבִיד בְּאֵשֶׁת יְפַת תֹּאַר אַחַר שֶׁבָּא עָלֶיהָ כְּמוֹ בְּשִׁפְחָה

שֶׁלֹּא נַעֲבֹד בְּאֵשֶׁת יְפַת תֹּאַר אַחַר בִּיאָה עָלֶיהָ, וְעַל זֶה נֶאֱמַר (דברים כ״א, י״ד) **לֹא תִתְעַמֵּר בָּהּ תַּחַת אֲשֶׁר עִנִּיתָהּ**[1]**. פֵּרוּשׁ מִתְעַמֵּר לְשׁוֹן שִׁמּוּשׁ, וְכֵן אָמְרוּ בְּסִפְרִי** (כאן)**, לֹא תִתְעַמֵּר בָּהּ, לֹא תִשְׁתַּמֵּשׁ בָּהּ**[2]**. וְהָעִנְיָן הוּא שֶׁלֹּא נַעֲמִידֶהָ כִּפִלֶּגֶשׁ**[3] **אוֹ שִׁפְחָה לַעֲבְדוּת. וְאֵין עִנְיַן הַכָּתוּב שֶׁלֹּא נִשְׁתַּמֵּשׁ בָּהּ בְּכָל שִׁמּוּשׁ שֶׁהַנָּשִׁים עוֹשׂוֹת לְבַעְלֵיהֶן, אֲבָל הַכָּתוּב**

Mitzvah 534

The Prohibition to Work a Yefas Toar Like a Maidservant

לֹא תִתְעַמֵּר בָּהּ תַּחַת אֲשֶׁר עִנִּיתָהּ
You shall not enslave her, since you have afflicted her (*Deuteronomy* 21:14).

Having established in the previous mitzvah that it is prohibited to sell a *yefas toar* into slavery after cohabiting with her, the Torah in this mitzvah prohibits enslaving her for one's own needs:

שֶׁלֹּא נַעֲבֹד בְּאֵשֶׁת יְפַת תֹּאַר אַחַר בִּיאָה עָלֶיהָ – We are commanded **not to work with a woman** who was taken as a ***yefas toar*****, after having cohabited with her.** **וְעַל זֶה נֶאֱמַר** – **Regarding this it is stated** (*Deuteronomy* 21:14): **"לֹא תִתְעַמֵּר בָּהּ תַּחַת אֲשֶׁר עִנִּיתָהּ"** – ***You shall not be "mis'amer" with her, since you have afflicted her.***[1] **פֵּרוּשׁ מִתְעַמֵּר לְשׁוֹן שִׁמּוּשׁ** – **The meaning of "*mis'amer*" is** that it is **an expression of "making use."** Thus, the verse forbids a captor to make use of a *yefas toar* for his own needs, in the manner of a maidservant. **וְכֵן אָמְרוּ בְּסִפְרִי** – **And so did [the Sages] state in *Sifrei*** (to the verse): **לֹא תִתְעַמֵּר בָּהּ** – The phrase ***you shall not be mis'amer with her*** means, **לֹא תִשְׁתַּמֵּשׁ בָּהּ** – **you shall not make use of her.**[2]

Chinuch elaborates:

וְהָעִנְיָן הוּא שֶׁלֹּא נַעֲמִידֶהָ כִּפִלֶּגֶשׁ – **The point** of this prohibition **is that one may not designate [a *yefas toar*] as a concubine,**[3] **אוֹ שִׁפְחָה לַעֲבְדוּת** – **nor as a maidservant to** remain in **slavery** with him. **וְאֵין עִנְיַן הַכָּתוּב שֶׁלֹּא נִשְׁתַּמֵּשׁ בָּהּ בְּכָל שִׁמּוּשׁ שֶׁהַנָּשִׁים עוֹשׂוֹת לְבַעְלֵיהֶן** – **The point of the verse is not, however,** to say **that one may not use her for all the services that wives** commonly **perform for their husbands.** Once he marries her (as discussed in Mitzvah 532), he surely may have her do whatever household chores a wife normally performs. **אֲבָל הַכָּתוּב**

NOTES

1. The phrase, *since you have afflicted her,* means, "once you have cohabited with her" (*Sifrei*; see Mitzvah 533 notes 1-2).

2. The word מִתְעַמֵּר has several possible meanings; see *Targum Onkelos* and *Ramban* to the verse. Chinuch follows *Sifrei,* which interprets this term as an expression of "making use" (see also Mishnah and Gemara, *Sanhedrin* 85b). Accordingly, the verse prohibits a captor from enslaving a *yefas toar* for his service.

Rambam (*Hil. Melachim* 8:6) states that one transgresses this prohibition the first time that he makes use of the *yefas toar* in the manner of a maidservant; i.e., he holds her in his jurisdiction and has her perform a menial task.

3. A concubine (in earlier times) was a woman who was designated as one's mate but was not formally married with *kiddushin,* and was not granted a *kesubah* guaranteeing her husband's financial support (*Sanhedrin* 21a). It is prohibited for a common person to take a concubine, though a king was permitted to have concubines (*Rambam* ibid. 4:4). Even a king, however, may not designate a *yefas toar* as his concubine, for that would be a form of enslavement, which the Torah prohibits in this case. As we learned in Mitzvah 532 (at note 20), a *yefas toar* may be married only through the standard process of *kiddushin* and *chuppah*, with her consent.

יֶאֱסֹר מִלַּעֲשׂוֹתָהּ שִׁפְחָה כְּמוֹ שֶׁאָסַר מִלְּמָכְרָהּ גַּם כֵּן לְשִׁפְחָה, וְהַכַּוָּנָה אַחַת[4]. וּכְמוֹ כֵן בְּגוֹנֵב נֶפֶשׁ מֵאֶחָיו שֶׁכָּתוּב בּוֹ (שם כ״ד, ז׳) וְהִתְעַמֶּר בּוֹ, פֵּרְשׁוּ זִכְרוֹנָם לִבְרָכָה (סנהדרין פ״ה ע״ב) שֶׁיַּכְנִיסֶנּוּ לִרְשׁוּתוֹ וְיִשְׁתַּמֵּשׁ בּוֹ[5].

בְּשֹׁרֶשׁ מִצְוָה זוֹ יַגִּיד עָלָיו רֵעוֹ הַסָּמוּךְ (תקל״ג)[6], וּשְׁאָר הָעִנְיָן כָּתוּב בְּמִצְוָה רִאשׁוֹנָה שֶׁבַּסֵּדֶר (תקל״ב)[7].

יֶאֱסֹר מִלַּעֲשׂוֹתָהּ שִׁפְחָה – Rather, the verse prohibits him **from making her into a maidservant** for himself, **כְּמוֹ שֶׁאָסַר מִלְּמָכְרָהּ גַּם כֵּן לְשִׁפְחָה – just as it similarly prohibits** him (in the previous mitzvah) **from selling her as a maidservant** to another person; **וְהַכַּוָּנָה אַחַת – the intent** behind both prohibitions **is one** and the same.[4]

Chinuch cites another instance in which the term *mis'amer* is used this way:

וּכְמוֹ כֵן בְּגוֹנֵב נֶפֶשׁ מֵאֶחָיו – Scripture **likewise** employs this term **in the context of one who kidnaps a person of his brethren, שֶׁכָּתוּב בּוֹ "וְהִתְעַמֶּר בּוֹ" – where it is written** (*Deuteronomy* 24:7): *If a man is found kidnaping a person of his brethren among the Children of Israel,* ***and he enslaves him*** (*vehis'amer*), **פֵּרְשׁוּ זִכְרוֹנָם לִבְרָכָה** – and **[the Sages], of blessed memory** (*Sanhedrin* 85b) **explain** this to mean **שֶׁיַּכְנִיסֶנּוּ לִרְשׁוּתוֹ וְיִשְׁתַּמֵּשׁ בּוֹ – that one** is considered to have "enslaved" the victim when he **brings him into his possession and makes use of him** for some task.[5]

Underlying Purpose, Laws, and Applicability of the Mitzvah

בְּשֹׁרֶשׁ מִצְוָה זוֹ "יַגִּיד עָלָיו רֵעוֹ" הַסָּמוּךְ – Regarding the underlying purpose of this mitzvah, we can apply the dictum, ***Its companion testifies about it*** (*Job* 36:33), referring to **the preceding** mitzvah, which, as stated, has the same intent as this one.[6]

וּשְׁאָר הָעִנְיָן כָּתוּב בְּמִצְוָה רִאשׁוֹנָה שֶׁבַּסֵּדֶר – As far as **the remainder of the subject** of *yefas toar,* it **is** all **written in the first mitzvah of this *parashah*** (Mitzvah 532).[7]

NOTES

4. The Torah sets out two complementary prohibitions against making the *yefas toar* into a slave after having cohabited with her. The previous mitzvah forbids selling her into slavery, and this mitzvah forbids enslaving her for oneself.

5. The verse concludes that if, after enslaving the victim, the kidnaper sells him, he is liable to the death penalty. See *Rambam, Hil. Geneivah* 9:2. [Cf. *Targum Onkelos* to that verse.]

6. As Chinuch explained there, turning a woman into a slave after having cohabited with her is despicable behavior, and is the antithesis of the goodness that God wants us to develop in our character.

7. *Ramban* (*Deuteronomy* 21:14) states that one who transgresses this prohibition incurs *malkus.* However, Chinuch (and *Rambam*) make no mention of liability to *malkus* for transgressing this prohibition. This leads *Minchas Chinuch* (§3) to conclude that in their opinion it does not carry the penalty of *malkus. Minchas Chinuch* wonders, though, why this transgression should *not* be punishable by *malkus,* like every standard prohibition in the Torah that is violated through action. *Maayan HaChochmah* (p. 122b in Roedelheim ed.) suggests that the reason is because it is a transgression that is subject to restitution, for the captor can reimburse his captive the value of the work she performed for him. As a rule, a transgression that can be rectified through restitution is excluded from *malkus* (see General Introduction, note 14; and Mitzvah 229 note 29). See also Mitzvah 533 note 5.

מִצְוָה תקלה: מִצְוַת דִּין תְּלִיָּה לְמִי שֶׁיִּתְחַיֵּב לִתָּלוֹת

שֶׁנִּצְטַוִּינוּ לִתְלוֹת מִי שֶׁיִּתְחַיֵּב תְּלִיָּה בְּבֵית דִּין, וְיָדוּעַ שֶׁכָּל הַנִּתְלִין נִסְקָלִין תְּחִלָּה[1], וְעַל זֶה נֶאֱמַר (דברים כ״א, כ״ב) וְתָלִיתָ אֹתוֹ עַל עֵץ. וְדִין הַתְּלִיָּה הוּא בִּמְגַדֵּף וְעוֹבֵד עֲבוֹדָה זָרָה לְבַדָּם כְּדִבְרֵי חֲכָמִים בְּפֶרֶק נִגְמַר הַדִּין (סנהדרין מ״ה ע״ב) דִּפְלִיגֵי עֲלֵיהּ דְּרַבִּי אֱלִיעֶזֶר דְּאָמַר כָּל הַנִּסְקָלִין נִתְלִין[2].

Mitzvah 535

The Obligation [Upon Beis Din] to Hang an Executed Person Who Is Liable to Hanging

וְכִי יִהְיֶה בְאִישׁ חֵטְא מִשְׁפַּט מָוֶת וְהוּמָת וְתָלִיתָ אֹתוֹ עַל עֵץ

If a man shall have committed a sin whose judgment is death, he shall be put to death, and you shall hang him on a gallows (*Deuteronomy* 21:22).

In Temple times, those who committed certain capital offenses could be subject to court-administered execution. Such executions were very rare, insofar as numerous conditions would need to be met before they could be administered (see General Introduction, Section VI). When they were administered, depending on the capital crime that was committed, the sinner could be subject to one of four different execution methods: (1) *sekilah* (stoning; Mitzvah 555), (2) *sereifah* (burning; Mitzvah 261), (3) *hereg* (the sword; Mitzvah 50), or (4) *chenek* (strangulation; Mitzvah 47).

The verse here requires the corpse of one "whose judgment is death" to be hanged on the gallows after his execution. We will learn below that this requirement does not apply to all those who are executed. Rather, it applies only to those who are executed through *sekilah*, and, even in such instances, only to those who had committed certain specific offenses.

שֶׁנִּצְטַוִּינוּ לִתְלוֹת מִי שֶׁיִּתְחַיֵּב תְּלִיָּה בְּבֵית דִּין – **We are commanded to hang** the corpse of **one who is subject to hanging by the court.** וְיָדוּעַ שֶׁכָּל הַנִּתְלִין נִסְקָלִין תְּחִלָּה – **Now, it is known that all those who are** subject to being **hanged are** those who were **first stoned,** for the requirement to hang the corpse of a person executed by the court applies only to the corpses of those who were put to death by *sekilah.*[1] וְעַל זֶה נֶאֱמַר "וְתָלִיתָ אֹתוֹ עַל עֵץ" – **Regarding this** requirement **it is stated** (*Deuteronomy* 21:22): ***and you shall hang him on a gallows.***

Chinuch notes that the obligation to hang the corpse of those who have been executed by *sekilah* does not apply to all who have been executed by *sekilah,* but rather, only to those who are put to death for one of two specific crimes:

וְדִין הַתְּלִיָּה הוּא בִּמְגַדֵּף וְעוֹבֵד עֲבוֹדָה זָרָה לְבַדָּם – **The requirement of hanging** the corpse of those executed by *sekilah* **applies to** the corpse of **a blasphemer and an idolater alone.** כְּדִבְרֵי חֲכָמִים בְּפֶרֶק נִגְמַר הַדִּין – This is **in accordance with the opinion of the Sages, in Chapter *Nigmar HaDin*** (*Sanhedrin* 45b), דִּפְלִיגֵי עֲלֵיהּ דְּרַבִּי אֱלִיעֶזֶר דְּאָמַר כָּל הַנִּסְקָלִין נִתְלִין – **who argue with R' Eliezer who says that *all* those who receive *sekilah* are** then **hanged.**[2]

NOTES

1. See next note.

2. There are a total of 18 offenses (listed by *Rambam* in *Hil. Sanhedrin* 15:10) for which the transgressor may be subject to *sekilah*. R' Eliezer maintains that the corpse of one who is executed for any one of those offenses is subsequently hanged, while the Sages argue that only two of these offenders are subject to hanging: the blasphemer (i.e., one who curses the Name of Hashem; Mitzvah 70) and the idolater (Mitzvos 26, 28, and 29).

The law that a blasphemer is hanged after his execution is derived from the verse that follows the verse of our mitzvah. That verse, which speaks of the obligation to bury the hanged corpse before nightfall, states

מִשָּׁרְשֵׁי מִצְוַת אַרְבַּע מִיתוֹת בֵּית דִּין כָּתַבְתִּי קְצָת בְּסֵדֶר מִשְׁפָּטִים עֲשֵׂה ד׳ בְּסִימָן מ״ב (מצוה מ״ז)[4,3], וְשָׁם כָּתַבְתִּי מַחֲלֹקֶת הָרַמְבַּ״ן ז״ל עִם הָרַמְבַּ״ם ז״ל בְּעִנְיָן זֶה[5]. וְעוֹד נֹאמַר כִּי דִּין הַתְּלִיָּה כְּדֵי לְהַגְבִּיהַּ הַנִּדּוֹן וּלְפַרְסְמוֹ לְעֵין כֹּל, גַּם בִּרְאוֹתָם עֵסֶק זְקִיפַת הָעֵץ וּקְשִׁירַת הַנִּדּוֹן עָלָיו, תִּכָּנֵס יִרְאָה וָפַחַד בְּלִבָּם[6].

מִדִּינֵי הַמִּצְוָה מַה שֶּׁאָמְרוּ זִכְרוֹנָם לִבְרָכָה שֶׁמִּצְוַת הַנִּתְלִין אַחַר שֶׁסּוֹקְלִין אוֹתוֹ מְשַׁקְּעִין קוֹרָה בָּאָרֶץ וְהָעֵץ יוֹצֵא מִמֶּנָּה[7], וּמַקִּיפִין שְׁתֵּי יָדָיו זוֹ עַל זוֹ

Underlying Purpose of the Mitzvah

מִשָּׁרְשֵׁי מִצְוַת אַרְבַּע מִיתוֹת בֵּית דִּין כָּתַבְתִּי קְצָת בְּסֵדֶר מִשְׁפָּטִים עֲשֵׂה ד׳ בְּסִימָן מ״ב – **I have written some of the underlying purposes of the mitzvos of the four** methods of **court-administered execution, in *Parashas Mishpatim*, Mitzvah-obligation 4, Chapter 42** of this work (Mitzvah 47);[3] namely, that they are meant to maintain law and order and promote a functioning society.[4] וְשָׁם כָּתַבְתִּי מַחֲלֹקֶת הָרַמְבַּ״ן ז״ל עִם הָרַמְבַּ״ם ז״ל בְּעִנְיָן זֶה – **I also recorded there the dispute between *Ramban*, of blessed memory, and *Rambam*, of blessed memory, in this matter.**[5]

וְעוֹד נֹאמַר – With regard to our mitzvah, **we can say further** כִּי דִּין הַתְּלִיָּה כְּדֵי לְהַגְבִּיהַּ הַנִּדּוֹן וּלְפַרְסְמוֹ לְעֵין כֹּל – **that** the purpose of **the law of hanging** the offender after death **is in order to lift** the corpse of **the one who was convicted and display it to all.** גַּם בִּרְאוֹתָם עֵסֶק זְקִיפַת הָעֵץ וּקְשִׁירַת הַנִּדּוֹן עָלָיו – **Moreover, when they see the activity** surrounding **the erecting of the gallows and the tying of the one who was executed onto it,** תִּכָּנֵס יִרְאָה וָפַחַד בְּלִבָּם – **fear and fright will enter their hearts,** and they will make sure to distance themselves from such sins.[6]

Laws of the Mitzvah

מִדִּינֵי הַמִּצְוָה מַה שֶּׁאָמְרוּ זִכְרוֹנָם לִבְרָכָה – **Among the laws of the mitzvah is that which [our Sages], of blessed memory, stated** (*Rambam, Hil. Sanhedrin* 15:7,9; see *Sanhedrin* 46a), שֶׁמִּצְוַת הַנִּתְלִין – **that the mitzvah of hanging** is done as follows: אַחַר שֶׁסּוֹקְלִין אוֹתוֹ מְשַׁקְּעִין קוֹרָה בָּאָרֶץ – **After they stone [the sinner] they sink a beam into the ground** וְהָעֵץ יוֹצֵא מִמֶּנָּה – **with** a piece of **wood protruding from it.**[7] וּמַקִּיפִין שְׁתֵּי יָדָיו זוֹ עַל זוֹ – **They** then **tie his two hands**

NOTES

(*Deuteronomy* 21:23): קָבוֹר תִּקְבְּרֶנּוּ בַּיּוֹם הַהוּא כִּי קִלְלַת אֱלֹהִים תָּלוּי, *you shall surely bury him on that day, for a hanging person is a curse of God*. The final phrase is expounded to mean, *he is hanged because he cursed God,* thus teaching that the corpse of the blasphemer is subject to hanging (*Sanhedrin* 45b with *Rashi* ד״ה כי קללת). Now, Scripture utilizes a general expression when introducing this hanging requirement, and states, *If a man shall have committed a sin "whose judgment is death,"* without qualifying to which capital sinner it is referring. This broadens the requirement to hang the corpse beyond the case of the blasphemer alone. R' Eliezer and the Sages disagree as to how far this law extends. R' Eliezer, who utilizes a broader method of Scriptural exegesis [רִבּוּי וּמִעוּט], applies this requirement to all whose execution is similar to that of the blasphemer, i.e., to *anyone* who is executed by *sekilah*. The Sages, though, use a narrower form of Scriptural exegesis [כְּלָל וּפְרָט], and therefore extend this requirement only to one most like the blasphemer; namely, one who is both subject to *sekilah* and denies the fundamental basis of faith through his offense. Accordingly, the Sages apply the hanging requirement to the idolater alone (*Sanhedrin* ibid.).

3. [Chinuch's numbering follows the original format of this work; see Mitzvah 494 note 4.]

4. Chinuch adds there that different capital crimes are liable to different forms of execution, depending on the nature of each one.

5. Chinuch explains there that *Rambam* counts each of the four court-administered capital punishments as a separate mitzvah, but *Ramban* maintains that there is merely one overriding requirement to administer capital punishment, based on (*Deuteronomy* 13:6) וּבִעַרְתָּ הָרָע מִקִּרְבֶּךָ, *and you shall destroy the evil in your midst*. The various means of execution are, in *Ramban's* opinion, merely details of this requirement (see end of Mitzvah 47).

6. *Ramban* (*Deuteronomy* 21:22) offers a different approach. Unlike Chinuch, who sees the obligation to hang the executed man as a lesson to the assembled masses, he suggests that it is part of his punishment, due to the heinous nature of the crime that he committed.

7. They do not use a living tree, since (as Chinuch

וְתוֹלִין אוֹתוֹ סָמוּךְ לִשְׁקִיעַת הַחַמָּה וּמַתִּירִין אוֹתוֹ מִיָּד[8], וְקוֹבְרִין אוֹתוֹ עִם הָעֵץ שֶׁנִּתְלָה בּוֹ, וְעִם הָאֶבֶן שֶׁנִּסְקַל בּוֹ, שֶׁלֹּא יֹאמְרוּ הַבְּרִיּוֹת זֶה הָעֵץ שֶׁנִּתְלָה בּוֹ פְּלוֹנִי[9].

וְאִם הֱלִינוּהוּ שָׁם עוֹבְרִין בְּלֹא תַעֲשֶׂה כְּמוֹ שֶׁנִּכְתֹּב בְּסֵדֶר זֶה (מצוה תקל״ו) **בְּעֶזְרַת הַשֵּׁם. וְיֶתֶר פְּרָטֶיהָ בְּפֶרֶק שִׁשִּׁי מִסַּנְהֶדְרִין[10].**

וְנוֹהֶגֶת מִצְוָה זוֹ בִּזְמַן הַבַּיִת שֶׁהָיָה כֹּחַ בְּיָדֵינוּ לָדוּן דִּינֵי נְפָשׁוֹת, וּבִזְכָרִים דַּוְקָא כִּי לָהֶם לַעֲשׂוֹת הַמִּשְׁפָּט[11].

---

together, וְתוֹלִין אוֹתוֹ סָמוּךְ לִשְׁקִיעַת הַחַמָּה – **and hang him** by his tied hands upon that protruding piece of wood **close to sunset,** וּמַתִּירִין אוֹתוֹ מִיָּד – **and then untie him immediately** and take him down.[8] וְקוֹבְרִין אוֹתוֹ עִם הָעֵץ שֶׁנִּתְלָה בּוֹ – **They then bury him together with the gallows upon which he was hanged,** וְעִם הָאֶבֶן שֶׁנִּסְקַל בּוֹ – **and together with the stone with which he was stoned,** שֶׁלֹּא יֹאמְרוּ הַבְּרִיּוֹת זֶה הָעֵץ שֶׁנִּתְלָה בּוֹ פְּלוֹנִי – **so that people should not say, "Those are the gallows upon which So-and-so was hanged,"** or "That is the stone with which So-and-so was stoned."[9]

Chinuch elaborates on the obligation to take the body down from the gallows immediately after hanging it:

וְאִם הֱלִינוּהוּ שָׁם – If they leave him to hang **there overnight,** עוֹבְרִין בְּלֹא תַעֲשֶׂה – **they violate a** mitzvah-**prohibition,** כְּמוֹ שֶׁנִּכְתֹּב בְּסֵדֶר זֶה בְּעֶזְרַת הַשֵּׁם – **as we will write** later **in this** ***parashah*** (Mitzvah 536)**, with Hashem's help.**

וְיֶתֶר פְּרָטֶיהָ בְּפֶרֶק שִׁשִּׁי מִסַּנְהֶדְרִין – These **and the additional details of [this mitzvah]** can be found **in the sixth chapter of** Tractate ***Sanhedrin*** (45b-46b).[10]

Applicability of the Mitzvah

וְנוֹהֶגֶת מִצְוָה זוֹ בִּזְמַן הַבַּיִת – **This mitzvah applied in the times of the** ***Beis HaMikdash,*** שֶׁהָיָה כֹּחַ בְּיָדֵינוּ לָדוּן דִּינֵי נְפָשׁוֹת – **when we had the authority to judge capital cases.**

וּבִזְכָרִים דַּוְקָא כִּי לָהֶם לַעֲשׂוֹת הַמִּשְׁפָּט – It applies **to men alone, for it is they who are** obligated **to carry out judgment.**[11]

NOTES

notes below) the wood upon which the executed man is hanged must be buried with him, and we derive from Scripture that the burial of the wood must be done right away, without requiring additional intervening steps. If a living tree would be used, it would first need to be chopped down before it could be buried along with the executed man (*Sanhedrin* 46b).

8. Even hanging the corpse for a short time suffices to fulfill the mitzvah (*Sanehdrin* 46b with *Yad Ramah*) [and to instill fear in the hearts of people]. Now, there is a mitzvah-obligation to bury the corpse that very day (Mitzvah 537), as well as a mitzvah-prohibition against leaving the corpse on the gallows overnight (see Mitzvah 536). The hanging of the corpse is therefore done toward the end of the day, so that those involved will realize that they have a limited amount of time to take him back down and bury him before nightfall. Were the corpse hanged earlier in the day, those involved might forget about it over the course of the day, and thereby unwittingly transgress the requirement of burial (*Rashi, Sanhedrin* 46b ד״ה משהין אותו).

9. Chinuch (from *Rambam, Hil. Sanhedrin* 15:9) explains that the reason these items are buried is in order to preserve the dignity of the executed man (see *Lechem Mishneh* ad loc.). [These items are not actually placed in his grave, rather, they are buried nearby, i.e., within four *amos* (*Sanhedrin* 45b with *Rashi* ד״ה בתפיסתו).] See Insight for another reason why the gallows and the stone are buried.

10. These laws are codified in *Rambam, Hil. Sanhedrin* 15:6-9.

11. That is, only men can serve on a *beis din* (see Mitzvah 77, after note 40).

It should be noted that while both men and women can be subject to the punishment of *sekilah* for blaspheming or worshiping *avodah zarah,* we learn, based on a Scriptural derivation, that the corpse of a woman is not hanged (*Sanhedrin* 46a; *Rambam, Hil. Sanhedrin* 15:6).

✦§ **Insight:** *And Cast Into the Depths of the Sea All Their Sins*

R' Moshe Cordovero, in *Tomer Devorah* (1:9), writes that one of the ways in which Hashem's Providence manifests itself in the world is that when the Jewish people sin, He turns their enemies against them and thus brings suffering upon them. Ultimately though, once they have received their punishment and have repented from their sins, Hashem does not merely alleviate their suffering, but He also punishes those who so enthusiastically made then suffer. This, he notes, is the meaning of the dream of Nebuchadnezzar (see *Daniel*, Ch. 2), in which he saw a large statue consisting of various materials, including gold, silver, copper, iron, and earthenware. The dream concludes with the crushing destruction of the statue brought about by a great stone that was "hewn without human hands." Daniel, who was asked to interpret the dream, explained that the different materials in the figure represent the various kingdoms over the ages that would dominate and inflict suffering upon the Jewish people, and the stone that crushed them represents the ultimate retribution and destruction that would be visited upon those peoples by the Hand of God.

Tomer Devorah notes further that the concept that those who bring suffering upon the Jews will be destroyed is alluded to in the verse (*Deuteronomy* 32:23), חִצַּי אֲכַלֶּה בָּם, *My arrows I shall consume against them*. The "arrows" refer to the various sources of affliction sent to punish the Jews. While the simple meaning of the verse is that Hashem will, so to speak, "use up" all of His various "arrows" against them, by afflicting them in many different ways, the Sages (*Sifrei* ad loc.) interpret the expression *I shall consume* to mean that Hashem will ultimately "consume" (i.e., destroy) those who afflict the Jews.

Tomer Devorah finds an allusion to this in the law cited by Chinuch that the stone used to execute a sinful person, as well as the gallows upon which he is hanged after his execution, are buried with him. Chinuch, following *Rambam* (*Hil. Sanhedrin* 15:9), explains that these items are buried in order to preserve the dignity of the executed man. *Tomer Devorah*, however, sees in the burial and ultimate destruction of these instruments an application of the above idea — that once a Jew has received his Divinely ordained measure of punishment, the source of that punishment (whether human or inanimate) is destroyed.

All in all, Hashem never vengefully punishes His people. Rather, the goal of all suffering visited upon the Jews is to provide them with the spiritual correction they require. After that is accomplished, the enemies of the Jews, who chose to inflict the suffering and did so vengefully, are punished for their deeds. [Although Hashem had decreed that the Jews suffer on account of their sins, those who inflicted the suffering did not do so out of respect of Hashem's decree, but rather, out of *hatred* of Hashem, which manifests itself in hatred of His people. Hence, they in turn must face His vengeance (*Ramban, Deuteronomy* 32:40; see further, *Rambam* and *Raavad, Hil. Teshuvah* 6:5).]

This, in fact, is how *Tomer Devorah* interprets the verse that lies at the core of the *tashlich* service, traditionally recited on Rosh Hashanah at a body of water. The verse (*Micah* 7:19) states: וְתַשְׁלִיךְ בִּמְצֻלוֹת יָם כָּל חַטֹּאתָם, *You will cast all their sins into the depths of the sea*. The "depths of the sea," he explains, refers to the foes of the Jews (see *Isaiah* 57:20), who brought suffering to the Jewish people. The same Divine Attribute of Judgment that allowed the enemies of the Jews to bring suffering upon them, due to their sins, will now turn against those nations and "cast all their sins" (i.e., the sins of the Jews) upon them. That is, those enemies will be punished for their role in inflicting the suffering, even though the Jews deserved to suffer for their sins.

In our interpersonal relationships too, *Tomer Devorah* goes on to note, we must take this idea to heart. If we ever see a sinful Jew beset by suffering, we must not view him as someone who is rejected by Hashem. Rather, we must recognize that it is Hashem's desire to cleanse such an individual and set him on the proper path. We, too, must therefore not reject him, but rather embrace him, and do whatever we can to alleviate his suffering.

מִצְוָה תקלו

שֶׁלֹּא יָלִין הַצָּלוּב עַל הָעֵץ וְכֵן הַמֵּת בְּבֵיתוֹ אֶלָּא לִכְבוֹדוֹ

שֶׁלֹּא נַעֲזֹב הַתָּלוּי שֶׁיָּלִין[1] עַל הָעֵץ, שֶׁנֶּאֱמַר (דברים כ״א, כ״ג) לֹא תָלִין נִבְלָתוֹ עַל הָעֵץ, וּלְשׁוֹן סִפְרִי (כאן), לֹא תָלִין נִבְלָתוֹ עַל הָעֵץ, זוֹ מִצְוַת לֹא תַעֲשֶׂה.

כָּל עִנְיַן הַמִּצְוָה כָּתוּב בְּמִצְוַת עֲשֵׂה ג׳ שֶׁבְּסֵדֶר זֶה (תקל״ז), וְאֵין לְהַאֲרִיךְ בְּמַה שֶּׁאֵין צֹרֶךְ בּוֹ[2].

Mitzvah 536

The Prohibition to Leave One Hanging on the Gallows Overnight, or to Leave Any Corpse Unburied Overnight Except for the Sake of His Honor

לֹא תָלִין נִבְלָתוֹ עַל הָעֵץ כִּי קָבוֹר תִּקְבְּרֶנּוּ בַּיּוֹם הַהוּא כִּי קִלְלַת אֱלֹהִים תָּלוּי וְלֹא תְטַמֵּא אֶת אַדְמָתְךָ אֲשֶׁר ה׳ אֱלֹהֶיךָ נֹתֵן לְךָ נַחֲלָה

His corpse shall not remain for the night on the gallows; rather, you shall surely bury him on that day, for a hanging person is a curse of God, and you shall not contaminate your land, which HASHEM, your God, gives you as an inheritance (*Deuteronomy* 21:23).

The previous mitzvah conveys the requirement to hang the corpses of those who were executed for certain sins. In the above verse, the Torah sets forth two additional laws: (1) that the body may not be left hanging on the gallows overnight; and (2) that it be buried that day. These two laws are the subjects of this and the following mitzvah, respectively. Chinuch will also teach that these laws are not limited to executed sinners, but apply to any deceased Jew.

שֶׁלֹּא נַעֲזֹב הַתָּלוּי שֶׁיָּלִין עַל הָעֵץ – We are commanded **not to leave** the body of **one who was hanged to remain overnight**[1] **on the gallows,** שֶׁנֶּאֱמַר ״לֹא תָלִין נִבְלָתוֹ עַל הָעֵץ״ – **as it is stated** (*Deuteronomy* 21:23): ***His corpse shall not remain for the night on the gallows.***

Chinuch shows that this verse is conveying an actual mitzvah-prohibition:

וּלְשׁוֹן סִפְרִי – **In the words of** ***Sifrei:*** ״לֹא תָלִין נִבְלָתוֹ עַל הָעֵץ״ – When the verse states, ***His corpse shall not remain for the night on the gallows,*** זוֹ מִצְוַת לֹא תַעֲשֶׂה – **this constitutes a mitzvah-prohibition.**

כָּל עִנְיַן הַמִּצְוָה כָּתוּב בְּמִצְוַת עֲשֵׂה ג׳ שֶׁבְּסֵדֶר זֶה – **All of the details of** this **mitzvah are written in the third mitzvah-obligation of this** ***parashah*** (Mitzvah 537). וְאֵין לְהַאֲרִיךְ בְּמַה שֶּׁאֵין צֹרֶךְ בּוֹ – The details are not repeated here, since **one should not elaborate unnecessarily.**[2]

Chinuch notes that this mitzvah is not limited to leaving the sinner hanging overnight on the gallows, but, in fact, applies to leaving any human corpse unburied:

NOTES

1. We have translated שֶׁיָּלִין as "to remain *overnight*," which is the simple meaning, and is how *Minchas Chinuch* understands this term. See Insight to Mitzvah 537 for discussion of whether this actually refers to leaving the corpse unburied the *entire* night.

2. The particulars of this mitzvah, including when and to whom it is applicable, are detailed in Mitzvah 537 (the mitzvah-obligation to bury the deceased on the day of death), which, in current editions of Chinuch, follows this mitzvah. [In the original format of this work (see Mitzvah 494 note 4), that mitzvah appeared before the current mitzvah.]

וְשָׁם כָּתוּב שֶׁאַף הַמֵּלִין מֵתוֹ שֶׁלֹּא לִכְבוֹדוֹ עוֹבֵר בְּלָאו.[3]

וְשָׁם כָּתוּב — **There,** in Mitzvah 537, **it is written**   שֶׁאַף הַמֵּלִין מֵתוֹ שֶׁלֹּא לִכְבוֹדוֹ עוֹבֵר בְּלָאו — **that one who leaves his deceased** relative unburied **overnight,** where the delay is **not for the honor of [the dead person], has also transgressed a prohibition,** i.e., he violates *this* mitzvah-prohibition.[3]

NOTES

3. In Mitzvah 537, Chinuch teaches that the mitzvah-obligation to bury the dead on the day of death applies to *any* Jew. The same also applies to this mitzvah-prohibition against leaving a body unburied overnight (see note 4 there).

However, as with the mitzvah-obligation, the prohibition applies only when it is similar to leaving the corpse hanging on the gallows. It is thus permissible to delay the burial for the honor of the deceased, such as in order to make proper funeral arrangements or to allow for the arrival of relatives (see *Sifrei* to this verse; *Sanhedrin* 47a; *Shulchan Aruch, Yoreh Deah* 357:1).

One who violates this prohibition does not incur *malkus,* since the violation is passive and involves no action; see General Introduction note 14 (*Minchas Chinuch* §4).

מִצְוָה תקלז

מִצְוַת קְבוּרָה לַנֶּהֱרָג עַל פִּי בֵּית דִּין וְכֵן לְכָל מֵת

לִקְבֹּר מִי שֶׁנִּתְלָה בַּיּוֹם הַהוּא, שֶׁנֶּאֱמַר (דברים כ״א, כ״ג) כִּי קָבוֹר תִּקְבְּרֶנּוּ בַּיּוֹם הַהוּא וְגוֹ׳, וּלְשׁוֹן סִפְרִי (כאן), כִּי קָבוֹר תִּקְבְּרֶנּוּ בַּיּוֹם הַהוּא, מִצְוַת עֲשֵׂה[1].

מִשָּׁרְשֵׁי הַמִּצְוָה מַה שֶּׁהִזְכִּירוּ זִכְרוֹנָם לִבְרָכָה בַּמִּשְׁנָה בְּפֶרֶק נִגְמַר הַדִּין (סנהדרין מ״ו ע״א) שֶׁאָמְרוּ שָׁם, כִּי קִלְלַת אֱלֹהִים תָּלוּי, כְּלוֹמַר, שֶׁלֹּא יֹאמְרוּ הַבְּרִיּוֹת מִפְּנֵי מָה זֶה תָּלוּי, מִפְּנֵי שֶׁקִּלֵּל אֶת הַשֵּׁם, וְנִמְצָא בְּהַזְכִּירָם זֶה וּבְהַעֲלוֹתָם הַדָּבָר בְּפִיהֶם

Mitzvah 537

The Obligation to Bury One Executed by Beis Din, or Any Deceased Person [on the Day of Death]

לֹא תָלִין נִבְלָתוֹ עַל הָעֵץ כִּי קָבוֹר תִּקְבְּרֶנּוּ בַּיּוֹם הַהוּא כִּי קִלְלַת אֱלֹהִים תָּלוּי וְלֹא תְטַמֵּא אֶת אַדְמָתְךָ אֲשֶׁר ה׳ אֱלֹהֶיךָ נֹתֵן לְךָ נַחֲלָה

His corpse shall not remain for the night on the gallows; rather, you shall surely bury him on that day, for a hanging person is a curse of God, and you shall not contaminate your land, which HASHEM, *your God, gives you as an inheritance* (*Deuteronomy* 21:23).

The previous mitzvah (Mitzvah 536) prohibits leaving the corpse of a sinner (i.e., a specific type of sinner who was executed and his corpse was hung) hanging on the gallows overnight, and by extension prohibits leaving any deceased Jew unburied overnight. The current mitzvah conveys the mitzvah-*obligation* to bury the sinner — as well as any deceased Jew — on the day of death.

לִקְבֹּר מִי שֶׁנִּתְלָה בַּיּוֹם הַהוּא – We are obligated **to bury one who was** executed and then **hanged** by *beis din* **on the same day** as his execution, **שֶׁנֶּאֱמַר ״כִּי קָבוֹר תִּקְבְּרֶנּוּ בַּיּוֹם הַהוּא וְגוֹ׳ ״** – **as it is stated** (*Deuteronomy* 21:23): ***rather, you shall surely bury him on that day.***

Chinuch shows that this verse is conveying an actual mitzvah-obligation:

וּלְשׁוֹן סִפְרִי – **In the words of *Sifrei:*** **״כִּי קָבוֹר תִּקְבְּרֶנּוּ בַּיּוֹם הַהוּא״** – When the verse states, ***rather you shall surely bury him on that day,*** **מִצְוַת עֲשֵׂה** – **this constitutes a mitzvah-obligation.**[1]

Underlying Purpose of the Mitzvah

מִשָּׁרְשֵׁי הַמִּצְוָה – **Among the underlying purposes of the mitzvah** **מַה שֶּׁהִזְכִּירוּ זִכְרוֹנָם לִבְרָכָה** **בַּמִּשְׁנָה בְּפֶרֶק נִגְמַר הַדִּין** – **is that which [our Sages], of blessed memory, mentioned in the Mishnah in Chapter *Nigmar HaDin*** (*Sanhedrin* 46a), **שֶׁאָמְרוּ שָׁם** – **where they said** as follows: **״כִּי קִלְלַת אֱלֹהִים תָּלוּי״** – When the verse states, ***for a hanging person is a curse of God,*** **כְּלוֹמַר** – **it means to say** that such a person shall not be left on the gallows, **שֶׁלֹּא יֹאמְרוּ הַבְּרִיּוֹת מִפְּנֵי מָה זֶה תָּלוּי מִפְּנֵי שֶׁקִּלֵּל אֶת הַשֵּׁם** – **so that people not ask, "Why was this one hanged?,"** to which others will reply, **"Because he blasphemed Hashem!"** **וְנִמְצָא בְּהַזְכִּירָם זֶה וּבְהַעֲלוֹתָם הַדָּבָר בְּפִיהֶם** **– It will emerge that by their mention of this** hanging **and their discussion of the matter,**

NOTES

1. See Insight for discussion of at what point in time this obligation is violated.

שֶׁהֵם מְחַלְּלִים שֵׁם שָׁמַיִם וְגוֹמְלִים רַע לְנַפְשָׁם[2]**, וְהָאֵל שֶׁחָפֵץ בְּטוֹבַת בְּרִיּוֹתָיו מְנָעָם מִזֶּה מִפְּנֵי כָּךְ.**

מִדִּינֵי הַמִּצְוָה מַה שֶּׁאָמְרוּ זִכְרוֹנָם לִבְרָכָה שֶׁאֵין מִצְוָה זוֹ בְּנִתְלֶה לְבַד אֶלָּא אַף כָּל הֲרוּגֵי בֵּית דִּין מִצְוָה לְקָבְרָן בְּיוֹם הֲרִיגָתָם[3]**, גַּם בִּכְלַל הַמִּצְוָה לִקְבֹּר כָּל מֵת מִיִּשְׂרָאֵל בְּיוֹם מוֹתוֹ**[4]**, וּמִפְּנֵי כֵן יִקְרְאוּ זִכְרוֹנָם לִבְרָכָה הַמֵּת שֶׁאֵין לוֹ מִי שֶׁיִּתְעַסֵּק בִּקְבוּרָתוֹ מֵת מִצְוָה,**

שֶׁהֵם מְחַלְּלִים שֵׁם שָׁמַיִם – **they are** further **profaning the Name of Heaven,** וְגוֹמְלִים רַע לְנַפְשָׁם – **and** consequently **bringing evil upon themselves.**[2] וְהָאֵל שֶׁחָפֵץ בְּטוֹבַת בְּרִיּוֹתָיו – **The Almighty, Who desires goodness for His creatures,** מְנָעָם מִזֶּה מִפְּנֵי כָּךְ – **restrained them from** engaging in **this** type of talk **for this** reason.

Laws of the Mitzvah

מִדִּינֵי הַמִּצְוָה – **Among the laws of the mitzvah** מַה שֶּׁאָמְרוּ זִכְרוֹנָם לִבְרָכָה – **is that which [our Sages], of blessed memory, stated** (see *Rambam, Hil. Sanhedrin* 15:8), שֶׁאֵין מִצְוָה זוֹ בְּנִתְלֶה לְבַד – **that this mitzvah is not limited to one who was hanged,** אֶלָּא אַף כָּל הֲרוּגֵי בֵּית דִּין – **but rather** it applies to **all who were executed by *beis din,*** מִצְוָה לְקָבְרָן בְּיוֹם הֲרִיגָתָם – meaning, that **there is a mitzvah to bury them on the day of their execution.**[3]

Chinuch now explains that this mitzvah is not limited to the corpses of executed individuals: גַּם בִּכְלַל הַמִּצְוָה – **Also included in the mitzvah** לִקְבֹּר כָּל מֵת מִיִּשְׂרָאֵל בְּיוֹם מוֹתוֹ – is the obligation **to bury any deceased Jew on the day of his death.**[4] וּמִפְּנֵי כֵן – **It is due to this** obligation יִקְרְאוּ זִכְרוֹנָם לִבְרָכָה הַמֵּת שֶׁאֵין לוֹ מִי שֶׁיִּתְעַסֵּק בִּקְבוּרָתוֹ מֵת מִצְוָה – **that [our Sages], of blessed memory, refer to a corpse that has no one to be involved in its burial** by the term ***"meis mitzvah"***

NOTES

2. The blasphemy that this executed person committed was a blatant desecration of the Name of God, and discussing his deed only adds to that desecration.

As we learned in Mitzvah 535, there are two capital offenses for which the body of the sinner is hanged after execution: blasphemy and idolatry. The desecration of Hashem's Name that arises from discussing the crime of the hanged sinner applies to an idolater as well, for idolatry is referred to as "blasphemy" [*Numbers* 15:30] (see *Rambam, Sefer HaMitzvos, Lo Saaseh* 66). Moreover, to speak about what deity the idolater worshiped, how he worshiped it, and the supposed miraculous results of the worship, only furthers the desecration of Hashem's Name (*Ramban, Deuteronomy* 21:22).

3. The obligation to bury other sinners executed by *beis din* is actually based on the same general obligation that requires one to bury *any* deceased Jew, which will immediately be discussed by Chinuch. Nevertheless, Chinuch [based on *Rambam, Sefer HaMitzvos, Asei* 231; *Hil. Sanhedrin* 15:8] separates the obligation to bury those who were executed from the general obligation to bury a deceased Jew. Some suggest that this is because the obligation to bury the sinner is the responsibility of *beis din,* while that of burying any other Jew is the responsibility of his relatives (see *Teshuvos Shaagas Aryeh HaChadashos* §6).

4. This is based on the phrase in our verse (*Deuteronomy* 21:23): כִּי קָבוֹר תִּקְבְּרֶנּוּ, *for you shall surely bury him.* From the double expression, קָבוֹר תִּקְבְּרֶנּוּ (literally, *bury, you shall bury*), the Gemara (*Sanhedrin* 46b) derives that the prohibition to leave the deceased unburied (Mitzvah 536) applies not only to the body of a sinner, but to that of any deceased Jew as well. While the Talmud is specifically discussing the *prohibition,* Chinuch (based on *Rambam, Sefer HaMitzvos, Asei* 231) understands that the current requirement [which emerges from those very same words cited in the Gemara — קָבוֹר תִּקְבְּרֶנּוּ, *you shall surely bury him*] conveys a mitzvah-*obligation* to bury *any* deceased Jew, and not merely a sinner (see also *Ramban,* glosses to *Sefer HaMitzvos, Shoresh* §1 [p. 46 in Frankel ed.], and commentary to *Deuteronomy* 21:22). Indeed, in some versions of the Gemara, this is explicitly stated (see marginal gloss of R' Y. Pick there, citing *Yalkut Shimoni* to this verse).

Others, however, argue that while the *prohibition* to leave a body unburied applies to all deceased Jews, the mitzvah-obligation to bury a Jewish corpse on the day of death applies only to the hanged sinner who is the subject of the verse. They point out that this is implied by *Rambam* in *Hil. Sanhedrin* 15:8 (*Teshuvos HaRadvaz* I §311; see *Minchas Chinuch* §1; cf. *Lechem Mishneh, Hil. Eivel* 4:8 and 12:1). For an extensive list of commentators who discuss this matter, see *Sefer HaMafte'ach* to *Rambam* [Frankel ed.], *Hil. Sanhedrin* 15:8.

כְּלוֹמַר שֶׁמִּצְוָה עַל הַכֹּל לְקָבְרוֹ מִצַּד הַצִּוּוּי הַזֶּה[5]. וְאָמְרוּ זִכְרוֹנָם לִבְרָכָה בַּמִּשְׁנָה הַנִּזְכֶּרֶת, שֶׁשְּׁנֵי קְבָרוֹת הָיוּ נִתְקָנִין לְבֵית דִּין, אֶחָד לַנִּסְקָלִים וְלַנִּשְׂרָפִים שֶׁדִּינָם חָמוּר, וְאֶחָד לַנֶּהֱרָגִין וְלַנֶּחֱנָקִין שֶׁדִּינָם קַל[6], וְאַחַר שֶׁנִּתְאַכֵּל בְּשַׂר הַנִּדּוֹן לְשָׁם מְלַקְּטִין אֶת הָעֲצָמוֹת וְקוֹבְרִין אוֹתָם בְּקִבְרוֹת אֲבוֹתֵיהֶן[7]. וְיֶתֶר פְּרָטֶיהָ בַּפֶּרֶק הַנִּזְכָּר[8].

וְנוֹהֶגֶת מִצְוָה זוֹ לְעִנְיַן הֲרוּגֵי בֵּית דִּין בִּזְמַן שֶׁנּוֹהֵג דִּינֵי נְפָשׁוֹת, וּלְעִנְיַן שְׁאָר מֵתֵי יִשְׂרָאֵל בְּכָל מָקוֹם וּבְכָל זְמַן[9] בִּזְכָרִים וּנְקֵבוֹת שֶׁמִּצְוָה לְקָבְרָם בְּיוֹם מִיתָה[10].

(literally, *a mitzvah corpse*), כְּלוֹמַר שֶׁמִּצְוָה עַל הַכֹּל לְקָבְרוֹ מִצַּד הַצִּוּוּי הַזֶּה – **meaning, that it is a mitzvah upon all to bury him, due to this command** to bury every Jew on the day of death.[5]

Chinuch returns to the subject of the burial of those executed by *beis din*:

וְאָמְרוּ זִכְרוֹנָם לִבְרָכָה בַּמִּשְׁנָה הַנִּזְכֶּרֶת – **[Our Sages], of blessed memory, also stated in the Mishnah that was referenced** earlier (*Sanhedrin* 46a), שֶׁשְּׁנֵי קְבָרוֹת הָיוּ נִתְקָנִין לְבֵית דִּין – **that there were two burial places designated for** those executed by ***beis din*****:** אֶחָד לַנִּסְקָלִים וְלַנִּשְׂרָפִים – **one for those** executed **through *sekilah* or *sereifah*,** שֶׁדִּינָם חָמוּר – **for their** death **sentence is** more **harsh,** וְאֶחָד לַנֶּהֱרָגִין וְלַנֶּחֱנָקִין – **and another for those** executed **through *hereg* or *chenek*,** שֶׁדִּינָם קַל – **for their** death **sentence is** relatively **lighter.**[6]

וְאַחַר שֶׁנִּתְאַכֵּל בְּשַׂר הַנִּדּוֹן לְשָׁם– **After the flesh of the executed individual had decomposed there,** in the burial place designated for executed sinners, מְלַקְּטִין אֶת הָעֲצָמוֹת וְקוֹבְרִין אוֹתָם בְּקִבְרוֹת אֲבוֹתֵיהֶן – **they would collect his bones and bury them in the burial place of his ancestors.**[7]

וְיֶתֶר פְּרָטֶיהָ בַּפֶּרֶק הַנִּזְכָּר – These **and the remaining details of [the mitzvah]** can be found **in the chapter** of Tractate *Sanhedrin* **that was mentioned** above, Chapter *Nigmar HaDin* (46a-47a).[8]

Applicability of the Mitzvah

וְנוֹהֶגֶת מִצְוָה זוֹ לְעִנְיַן הֲרוּגֵי בֵּית דִּין – **This mitzvah applies, with regard to those executed by *beis din*,** בִּזְמַן שֶׁנּוֹהֵג דִּינֵי נְפָשׁוֹת – only **when** the judgment of **capital cases was in force,** i.e., when the Sanhedrin was in place and such executions were carried out. וּלְעִנְיַן שְׁאָר מֵתֵי יִשְׂרָאֵל – **With regard to other deceased Jews,** however, בְּכָל מָקוֹם וּבְכָל זְמַן – the obligation applies **in every location and in all times,**[9] בִּזְכָרִים וּנְקֵבוֹת – **to men and women,** שֶׁמִּצְוָה לְקָבְרָם בְּיוֹם מִיתָה – meaning **that there is a mitzvah to bury [deceased Jews] on the day of** their **death.**[10]

NOTES

5. The term *meis mitzvah* refers to a deceased Jew for whom there is no one to take on the responsibility of burial; for example, a corpse lying in a field. Anyone who encounters such a corpse is obligated to bury it, including a Kohen, who normally may not come in contact with the dead. Chinuch (from *Rambam, Sefer HaMitzvos* ibid.) explains that this corpse derives its name — *meis "mitzvah"* — from the current mitzvah-obligation.

Even if one chances upon the *meis mitzvah* a number of days after his passing, there is a mitzvah-obligation to bury him that very day (*Teshuvos Shaagas Aryeh HaChadashos* 6:2; cf. *Teshuvos HaRadvaz* ibid.).

6. As a rule, it is forbidden to bury someone wicked next to someone righteous, or for that matter even next to someone less wicked. Accordingly, those executed with the more severe death penalties of *sekilah* and *sereifah* — whose crimes are deemed more severe — are buried apart from those who are executed with the relatively lighter death penalties of *hereg* and *chenek* (*Sanhedrin* 47a).

7. Mishnah, *Sanhedrin* (46a). As a result of his execution and the decomposition of his corpse, the sinner attains atonement, and may now be buried alongside his righteous ancestors (*Rashi* there ד״ה נתעכל הבשר).

8. These laws are codified in *Rambam, Hil. Sanhedrin* 15:7-8, and in *Shulchan Aruch, Yoreh Deah* §357 and §362.

9. I.e., it applies in Eretz Yisrael and the Diaspora, and whether the *Beis HaMikdash* is standing or not.

10. The obligation to bury an executed sinner is incumbent upon *beis din*. The obligation to bury any deceased Jew is incumbent upon his relatives, whether male or female (*Teshuvos Shaagas Aryeh HaChadashos* §6).

וְעוֹבֵר עַל זֶה וְהֵלִין אֶת הַמֵּת שֶׁלֹּא לִכְבוֹדוֹ בִּטֵּל עֲשֵׂה זֶה[11]**, מִלְּבַד שֶׁעָבַר עַל לָאו כְּמוֹ שֶׁנִּכְתֹּב בְּסֵדֶר זֶה בְּעֶזְרַת הַשֵּׁם** (מצוה תקל״ו)[12].

וְעוֹבֵר עַל זֶה וְהֵלִין אֶת הַמֵּת שֶׁלֹּא לִכְבוֹדוֹ – One who transgresses this and leaves the deceased unburied for the night, where the delay is **not for the honor of [the dead person], בִּטֵּל עֲשֵׂה זֶה – has violated this** mitzvah-**obligation.**[11] **מִלְּבַד שֶׁעָבַר עַל לָאו –** This is **aside** from the fact **that he has transgressed a** mitzvah-**prohibition, כְּמוֹ שֶׁנִּכְתֹּב בְּסֵדֶר זֶה בְּעֶזְרַת הַשֵּׁם – as we will write in this *parashah*, with the help of Hashem** (Mitzvah 536).[12]

NOTES

11. If, however, the burial is delayed for reasons that relate to the honor of the deceased, this mitzvah-obligation is not violated, just as there is no violation of the previous mitzvah (the prohibition against leaving a body unburied) under such circumstances (see note 2 there).

See Insight for discussion of Chinuch's words here.

12. In the original format of Chinuch, all of the mitzvah-obligations of each *parashah* were listed before the mitzvah-prohibitions of the *parashah*. Thus, the current mitzvah appeared before the mitzvah-prohibition against leaving the deceased unburied overnight (see Mitzvah 494 note 4).

☙ Insight: When Is the Prohibition of Leaving a Corpse Unburied Transgressed?

The verse that sets out the previous mitzvah and this one (i.e., the mitzvah-prohibition to leave a corpse unburied and the mitzvah-obligation to bury it) states as follows: לֹא תָלִין נִבְלָתוֹ עַל הָעֵץ כִּי קָבוֹר תִּקְבְּרֶנּוּ בַּיּוֹם הַהוּא, *His corpse shall not remain for the night on the gallows; rather, you shall surely bury him on that day.* This verse mentions two different time frames: it prohibits leaving a corpse "for the night," which would seem to mean that the burial must take place before daybreak *the next morning*; but then it commands that the corpse be buried "on that day," which indicates that the burial must take place before sunset *that evening*. How are these seemingly contradictory clauses to be understood?

There are three basic approaches to this question:

(1) *Minchas Chinuch* and numerous other commentators explain that the two mitzvos actually have two different time limits. The mitzvah-*obligation* to bury the corpse requires that burial take place (if possible) on the day of death, before sunset. If the day ends without the corpse having been buried, those responsible for the burial violate this obligation. On the other hand, the mitzvah-*prohibition* to leave a corpse unburied forbids leaving it overnight, meaning, until daybreak the next morning. It is only when daylight arrives that this prohibition is violated.

This interpretation of the mitzvos is based on the fact that with regard to the mitzvah-*prohibition* the verse uses the expression לֹא תָלִין, which throughout the Torah means "to leave over *all* night." For example, with regard to paying wages (Mitzvah 230), where the Torah states (*Leviticus* 19:13): לֹא תָלִין פְּעֻלַּת שָׂכִיר אִתְּךָ עַד בֹּקֶר, *You shall not let a worker's wage remain overnight until morning,* the phrase לֹא תָלִין clearly refers to holding back the wage all night (see *Bava Metzia* 110b). Similarly, in regard to the disqualification of *kodashim* (Mitzvah 90), where the Torah states (*Exodus* 23:18): וְלֹא יָלִין חֵלֶב חַגִּי עַד בֹּקֶר, *nor may the fat of My festive offering remain overnight until morning,* the phrase וְלֹא יָלִין clearly refers to leaving it all night. Here, too, when the Torah states לֹא תָלִין נִבְלָתוֹ, *His corpse shall not remain for the night,* it means to issue a prohibition against leaving a corpse unburied *all* night, with a violation occurring only at daybreak. With regard to the mitzvah-*obligation,* however, the Torah states that we must bury the corpse *on that day,* which means before sunset on the day of death. Thus, each of these mitzvos has its own time frame (see *Teshuvos HaRadvaz* I §311; *Shulchan Aruch HaRav* §495, *Kuntres Acharon* 3; *Minchas Chinuch* §1; *Rashash, Sanhedrin* 46b; see also *Sefer Yerei'im* §384 [252]).

(2) *Teshuvos Ginas Veradim* (*Yoreh Deah, Klal* 8 §2-3, by the 17th-century Egyptian scholar, *R' Avraham HaLevi;* cited in *Gilyon Maharsha, Yoreh Deah* 357:1) takes issue with the preceding explanation. He insists that despite the fact that elsewhere in the Torah the phrase לֹא תָלִין [or לֹא יָלִין] means the entire night, here it means something else. Since the Torah specifically sets forth a mitzvah-obligation to bury the deceased *on that day,* with a violation occurring at nightfall,

it follows that the mitzvah-prohibition stated in the same verse is also violated immediately upon nightfall. Moreover, he demonstrates that the phrase לֹא תָלִין does not by definition refer to leaving something the entire night; rather, in each of the cases where it is understood that way, that is because the Torah specifically indicates that it is speaking about the entire night, with a violation occurring only when morning arrives. Here, however, those reasons do not apply. Thus, in his opinion, when the Torah writes לֹא תָלִין נִבְלָתוֹ, it means simply, *His corpse shall not remain "at night."* The prohibition is thus transgressed as soon as *part* of the night has passed. In short, according to *Ginas Veradim,* both the mitzvah-obligation and the mitzvah-prohibition are violated at the *beginning* of the night. See also *Chochmas Adam,* end of *Hil. Aveilus, Hanhagas Chevrah Kaddisha* §12.

Me'il HaEphod (537:3) sides with *Ginas Veradim,* and marshals a number of earlier commentators who, in his opinion, take the same position. One of them is Chinuch, who, at the end of this mitzvah writes: וְעוֹבֵר עַל זֶה וְהֵלִין אֶת הַמֵּת ... בִּטֵּל עֲשֵׂה זֶה מִלְּבַד שֶׁעָבַר עַל לָאו. *One who transgresses this and leaves the deceased unburied for the night . . . has violated this mitzvah-obligation, aside from having transgressed a mitzvah-prohibition.* Now, if the term וְהֵלִין refers to leaving "overnight," this sentence would mean that both of the mitzvos are violated when *morning* comes. This would be quite difficult to understand, because, as we have explained, the mitzvah-obligation is transgressed earlier, when *night* falls. However, if וְהֵלִין refers to leaving "at night," Chinuch's words are readily understood. He means to say that not only the mitzvah-obligation, but even the mitzvah-prohibition, is transgressed at the *beginning* of the night. [See also *Magen Avraham* 72:2 with *Hagahos R' Akiva Eiger.*]

(3) *Teshuvos Avnei Nezer* (*Orach Chaim* 406:1) takes the opposite approach in interpreting Chinuch's words. He explains Chinuch's expression וְהֵלִין to mean "leaves *overnight,*" and since Chinuch indicates that the mitzvah-obligation and the mitzvah-prohibition are violated at the same time, he infers that the mitzvah-obligation is *also* violated only in the morning. For although the Torah commands that the corpse be buried "on that day," since the Torah sets out a parallel mitzvah-prohibition that allows for burial all night, we may infer that in this case, "on that day" includes the following night! Thus, *Avnei Nezer* argues, even the mitzvah-obligation requires only that the corpse be buried before the next morning.

Let us return to the first approach mentioned above, that the mitzvah-obligation is violated at nightfall but the mitzvah-prohibition is violated in the morning. This is the opinion of *Minchas Chinuch,* but accordingly, Chinuch's language is somewhat problematic, since (as *Ginas Veradim* points out) when speaking about the time of a violation, Chinuch equates the obligation with the prohibition. Perhaps, we may deflect this difficulty as follows: Chinuch chose to say that one who leaves the body unburied "overnight" violates the mitzvah-obligation simply because he wanted to point out that, in such a case, the person violates the mitzvah-prohibition as well. Chinuch would agree, however, that one violates the mitzvah-obligation even if he leaves the body unburied for *part* of the night.

[See above, note 4, where it was explained that the mitzvah-prohibition to leave a corpse "for the night" surely applies to every deceased person, but there is disagreement as to whether the mitzvah-obligation to bury "on that day" pertains to every deceased person or only to those executed by *beis din.*]

מִצְוָה תקלח: מִצְוַת הֲשָׁבַת אֲבֵדָה[2,1]

לְהָשִׁיב הָאֲבֵדָה לִבְעָלֶיהָ, שֶׁנֶּאֱמַר (דברים כ״ב, א׳) הָשֵׁב תְּשִׁיבֵם לְאָחִיךָ, וּבְבֵאוּר אָמְרוּ זִכְרוֹנָם לִבְרָכָה (בבא מציעא ל׳ ע״א, ל״ב ע״א) הֲשָׁבַת אֲבֵדָה עֲשֵׂה הוּא. וְנִכְפְּלָה הַמִּצְוָה בְּמָקוֹם אַחֵר בַּתּוֹרָה שֶׁנֶּאֱמַר כִּי תִפְגַּע שׁוֹר אָחִיךָ וְגוֹ׳ הָשֵׁב תְּשִׁיבֵם לְאָחִיךָ[3].

שֹׁרֶשׁ מִצְוָה זוֹ יָדוּעַ, כִּי יֵשׁ בָּזֶה תּוֹעֶלֶת הַכֹּל וְיִשּׁוּב הַמְּדִינָה, שֶׁהַשִּׁכְחָה בַּכֹּל הִיא מְצוּיָה,

---

Mitzvah 538
The Obligation to Return a Lost Object

לֹא תִרְאֶה אֶת שׁוֹר אָחִיךָ אוֹ אֶת שֵׂיוֹ נִדָּחִים וְהִתְעַלַּמְתָּ מֵהֶם הָשֵׁב תְּשִׁיבֵם לְאָחִיךָ
You shall not see the ox of your brother or his sheep or goat far away from their place, and hide yourself from them; you shall surely return them to your brother (*Deuteronomy* 22:1).

The Torah obligates a person who finds an object to pick it up and make every effort to return it to its owner. This is known as the mitzvah of *hashavas aveidah* (returning a lost object). The Torah further issues a prohibition against shirking this duty by walking away from the object or, worse yet, taking the object for oneself. This obligation and its corresponding prohibition are the subject of the next two mitzvos.

Chinuch will touch on many of the conditions that must be met in order for these mitzvos to be in effect.[1] When these conditions are in place, the finder is obligated to pick up the object. If he knows who the owner is, he should return it to him directly.[2] If he does not know who the owner is, he announces in public that he has found the object, and the owner can claim it by providing an identifying mark (*siman;* pl. *simanim*). Chinuch will address what constitutes a valid *siman*.

Until the owner is found, the finder must guard the object to ensure that it is not stolen or lost, and must also properly maintain it so that it is not ruined. He may not use it for his own needs. He is not obligated, however, to incur any financial expense or loss on account of tending to the lost object. All these guidelines will be elaborated on below.

לְהָשִׁיב הָאֲבֵדָה לִבְעָלֶיהָ – We are commanded **to return a lost object to its owner,** שֶׁנֶּאֱמַר – **as it is stated** (*Deuteronomy* 22:1): "הָשֵׁב תְּשִׁיבֵם לְאָחִיךָ" – ***You shall surely return them to your brother.*** וּבְבֵאוּר אָמְרוּ זִכְרוֹנָם לִבְרָכָה – **Indeed, [the Sages], of blessed memory, stated explicitly** (*Bava Metzia* 30a and 32a) הֲשָׁבַת אֲבֵדָה עֲשֵׂה הוּא – that **returning a lost object is a** mitzvah-**obligation.** וְנִכְפְּלָה הַמִּצְוָה בְּמָקוֹם אַחֵר בַּתּוֹרָה – **The mitzvah is repeated elsewhere in the Torah,** שֶׁנֶּאֱמַר כִּי תִפְגַּע שׁוֹר אָחִיךָ וְגוֹ׳ הָשֵׁב תְּשִׁיבֵם לְאָחִיךָ – **as it is stated: "If you encounter the ox of your brother, etc., you shall surely return them to your brother."**[3]

Underlying Purpose of the Mitzvah

שֹׁרֶשׁ מִצְוָה זוֹ יָדוּעַ – **The underlying purpose of this mitzvah is evident,** כִּי יֵשׁ בָּזֶה תּוֹעֶלֶת הַכֹּל וְיִשּׁוּב הַמְּדִינָה – **for in** fulfillment of **this** mitzvah **there is benefit for everyone, and a fostering of a thriving society.** שֶׁהַשִּׁכְחָה בַּכֹּל הִיא מְצוּיָה – This is **because forgetting** or losing objects

NOTES

1. See *Tiferes Yisrael,* Introduction to *Bava Metzia* Ch. 2, for a list of these conditions. See also *Shulchan Aruch, Choshen Mishpat* 259:2.

2. *Tur, Choshen Mishpat* 267:1.

3. This citation appears to be a copyist's error. Presumably, Chinuch is referring to the verse in *Exodus* (23:4): כִּי תִפְגַּע שׁוֹר אֹיִבְךָ אוֹ חֲמֹרוֹ תֹּעֶה הָשֵׁב תְּשִׁיבֶנּוּ לוֹ, *If you encounter an ox of your enemy or his donkey wandering, you shall surely return it to him* (*Me'il HaEphod*; see also *Rambam, Sefer HaMitzvos, Asei* 204, with *Tziyunim* [in Frankel ed.] ad loc.).

גַּם בְּהֶמְתָּם וְכָל חַיָּתָם בּוֹרְחִים[4] תָּמִיד הֵנָּה וָהֵנָּה, וְעִם הַמִּצְוָה הַזֹּאת שֶׁהִיא בְּעַמֵּנוּ יִהְיוּ נִשְׁמָרוֹת הַבְּהֵמוֹת וְהַכֵּלִים בְּכָל מָקוֹם שֶׁיִּהְיוּ בְּאַרְצֵנוּ הַקְּדוֹשָׁה כְּאִלּוּ הֵן תַּחַת יַד הַבְּעָלִים[5], וְכָל פִּקּוּדֵי ה' יְשָׁרִים מְשַׂמְּחֵי לֵב[6].

מִדִּינֵי הַמִּצְוָה מַה שֶּׁאָמְרוּ זִכְרוֹנָם לִבְרָכָה (שם כ"א ע"א) שֶׁיֵּשׁ מְצִיאוֹת שֶׁהָאָדָם מוֹצֵא בְּעִנְיָן וּבְמָקוֹם שֶׁאֵינוֹ חַיָּב לַהֲשִׁיבָן לְבַעֲלֵיהֶן אֶלָּא זוֹכֶה בָּהֶן לְעַצְמוֹ, שֶׁלֹּא חִיְּבָנוּ הַתּוֹרָה בְּאֵלּוּ[7].

---

happens to everyone. גַּם בְּהֶמְתָּם וְכָל חַיָּתָם בּוֹרְחִים תָּמִיד הֵנָּה וָהֵנָּה – **In addition, [people's] animals, both domestic and nondomestic,**[4] **are always running off this way and that way,** and inevitably some get lost. וְעִם הַמִּצְוָה הַזֹּאת שֶׁהִיא בְּעַמֵּנוּ – **With this mitzvah** of *hashavas aveidah* **that our nation has,** however, יִהְיוּ נִשְׁמָרוֹת הַבְּהֵמוֹת וְהַכֵּלִים בְּכָל מָקוֹם שֶׁיִּהְיוּ בְּאַרְצֵנוּ הַקְּדוֹשָׁה כְּאִלּוּ הֵן תַּחַת יַד הַבְּעָלִים – **the animals and objects** that do become lost **will be protected, wherever they may be in our Holy Land, as if they were in the possession of** their **owner.**[5] וְכָל פִּקּוּדֵי ה' יְשָׁרִים מְשַׂמְּחֵי לֵב – **Indeed, all the orders of Hashem are upright; they gladden the heart.**[6]

Laws of the Mitzvah

מִדִּינֵי הַמִּצְוָה – **Among the laws of the mitzvah** is מַה שֶּׁאָמְרוּ זִכְרוֹנָם לִבְרָכָה – **that which [the Sages], of blessed memory, stated** (*Bava Metzia* 21a), שֶׁיֵּשׁ מְצִיאוֹת שֶׁהָאָדָם מוֹצֵא בְּעִנְיָן וּבְמָקוֹם שֶׁאֵינוֹ חַיָּב לַהֲשִׁיבָן לְבַעֲלֵיהֶן – **that there are** certain **lost objects that a person finds in a circumstance or location** such **that he is not obligated to return them to their owner,** אֶלָּא זוֹכֶה בָּהֶן לְעַצְמוֹ – **but rather, he** may **acquire them for himself,** שֶׁלֹּא חִיְּבָנוּ הַתּוֹרָה בְּאֵלּוּ – **because the Torah did not obligate us** to return **these [lost objects].**[7]

Chinuch proceeds to present a list of items that one need not return to their owner, but may take for himself. Their common denominator is that they have no *siman* (identifying mark) by which to recognize and distinguish them. As Chinuch will later explain, it is assumed that someone who loses an object that has no *siman* despairs of recovering it, because he knows that even if it is found, he will be unable

---

NOTES

4. Stylistic paraphrase of *Numbers* 35:3.

5. Toward the end of the mitzvah (at note 45), Chinuch will teach that the mitzvah to return lost objects applies both in Eretz Yisrael as well as outside of it. It is not readily clear, therefore, why Chinuch specifies that lost objects *in Eretz Yisrael* will be protected by way of our mitzvah, and not objects elsewhere. [Perhaps, Chinuch's intention can be explained based on the approach of *R' S. R. Hirsch* (commentary to *Deuteronomy* 1:3) to the mitzvos that appear in the Book of *Deuteronomy*. He explains that these mitzvos were given to the Jewish people prior to their entry into Eretz Yisrael because they govern aspects of Jewish life that were mostly irrelevant in the Wilderness, but became uniquely relevant to the building of a healthy society in Eretz Yisrael. This included the social organization of the populace, which demanded that everyone accept to preserve and protect each individual's property as if it were his own (see *R' Hirsch's* commentary to our verse). Thus, while it is true that our mitzvah applies even outside of Eretz Yisrael, there is special significance in how it affects the integrity of the community in Eretz Yisrael. This may also account for Chinuch's earlier statement that our mitzvah facilitates "a fostering of a thriving society."]

6. Stylistic citation of *Psalms* 19:9.

While this phrase is applicable to all mitzvos, Chinuch apparently cites it here because fulfillment of our mitzvah directly gladdens the heart of man, for a person who loses an object and has no means of recovering it is saddened by the loss. With the mitzvah of *hashavas aveidah* in place, however, he knows that whoever finds it will do his utmost to return it to him. [Notably, the only other place Chinuch cites this phrase is in Mitzvah 557. There, too, fulfillment of the mitzvah provides comfort to a person experiencing emotional pain (see there).]

7. Although the Torah did not obligate us to return these finds, if the finder knows who the owner is, it is praiseworthy to go beyond the requirement of the law (לִפְנִים מִשּׁוּרַת הַדִּין) and return the lost item to its owner. The same is true regarding most, if not all, of the exemptions that Chinuch mentions later in the mitzvah. See *Bava Metzia* 24b; *Rambam, Hil. Gezeilah VaAveidah* 11:7; *Shulchan Aruch* ibid. 259:5; *Aruch HaShulchan, Choshen Mishpat* 259:7; and *Shulchan Aruch HaRav, Hil. Metziah U'Pikadon* §18-20. See also note 42 below.

וּכְמוֹ[9,8] שֶׁאָמְרוּ בַּמִּשְׁנָה, אֵלּוּ מְצִיאוֹת שֶׁלּוֹ, מָצָא פֵּרוֹת מְפֻזָּרִין[10] מָעוֹת מְפֻזָּרוֹת[11] כְּרִיכוֹת בִּרְשׁוּת הָרַבִּים, פֵּרוּשׁ עֲמָרִים[12], עִגּוּלֵי דְבֵלָה[13] כִּכָּרוֹת שֶׁל נַחְתּוֹם[14] וּמַחֲרוּזוֹת שֶׁל דָּגִים[15]

---

to prove that it is his. By abandoning hope of recovering the item, the owner effectively forfeits his ownership over it (see below, at note 28).

The items listed below have no *siman* because they are all of a standard size, shape, and weight, etc., so they have no unique physical characteristics. They also cannot be identified by the location in which they were found, since they were found on the ground. We can presume that the owner did not put them there on purpose. Rather, he must have dropped them there, and he does not know exactly where this happened.[8]

There is another condition that must be met in order for the finder to be able to take a lost object for himself: He must know (or be reasonably sure) that the owner is already aware that he has lost it and has *already* abandoned hope of recovering it. Otherwise, the item has not yet become ownerless and he may not take it for himself. The items listed below meet this condition because the owner is aware of the loss almost as soon as it happens. In some cases this is because the item is important to him (whether because it is expensive or because it is a food), so he is constantly checking to make sure he still has it. In other cases, the item is heavy, so he quickly notices that his load is lighter than before. In any event, by the time a finder discovers the item, the owner is surely aware of his loss and has already abandoned hope of recovering it, since it has no *siman*. The finder is therefore allowed to keep it.[9]

Chinuch cites the Mishnah that lists these items:

וּכְמוֹ שֶׁאָמְרוּ בַּמִּשְׁנָה – As [the Sages] stated in the Mishnah (ibid.): **אֵלּוּ מְצִיאוֹת שֶׁלּוֹ – These finds belong to [the finder]: מָצָא פֵּרוֹת מְפֻזָּרִין – If one found scattered produce;**[10] **מָעוֹת מְפֻזָּרוֹת – scattered coins;**[11] **כְּרִיכוֹת בִּרְשׁוּת הָרַבִּים – bundles in a public domain, פֵּרוּשׁ עֲמָרִים** – "bundles," **meaning, small sheaves** of grain;[12] **עִגּוּלֵי דְבֵלָה – round cakes of pressed figs;**[13] **כִּכָּרוֹת שֶׁל נַחְתּוֹם – loaves of a commercial baker;**[14] **וּמַחֲרוּזוֹת שֶׁל דָּגִים – strings of fish;**[15]

NOTES

8. *Tos. Yom Tov, Bava Metzia* 2:1. [See note 20, below, for an exception.]

9. Our presentation of the second condition follows the opinion of Abaye in the Gemara (*Bava Metzia* 21b), which is the accepted halachah.

[If one unlawfully took an object about which it could *not* be assumed that the owner had abandoned hope of recovering it, then even if the owner *later* abandons hope of recovering it, the finder may not keep it (*Shulchan Aruch* ibid. 262:3). It must be returned to the owner (for although it has no *siman*, he might have witnesses that he dropped the object). Until someone claims it, some say that the finder may use it, while others say that it must remain untouched under his protection. For discussion, see *Rambam* ibid. 15:1; *Raavad, Maggid Mishneh,* and *Kesef Mishneh* ad loc.; *Shulchan Aruch* ibid. 260:9 with commentaries, and *Rama* 260:10.]

10. Typically, produce has no identifying marks on it, and since it is scattered about, the owner cannot know the amount that was found (*Tiferes Yisrael, Bava Metzia* 2:1). Thus, it has no *siman* at all. In addition, the owner is surely aware that he has lost it (because it is heavy or because it is a food) and has abandoned hope of recovering it (see *Rambam* ibid. 15:8 with *Kesef Mishneh*, and *Shulchan Aruch* ibid. 262:7 with *Be'er HaGolah*; cf. *Sma* and *Beur HaGra* ad loc.). Both conditions mentioned in the introductory paragraph are thus fulfilled, and the finder may therefore take the object for himself.

11. Scattered coins also have no *siman*. In addition, since a person is constantly checking his purse to make sure that he still has his money, the finder can be sure that the owner is already aware that he has lost it and has abandoned hope of recovering it (*Bava Metzia* 21b). Thus, here too, both conditions are met.

12. "In a public domain" means that the sheaves were found in a public place where many people walk. Chinuch will elaborate on this case below.

13. Fig cakes were generally of a standard size; thus, they have no *siman*.

14. Loaves of a commercial baker are of a standard size, shape, and weight. [By contrast, homemade loaves, which are different from each other and therefore identifiable, must be returned; see Mishnah ibid. 24b-25a.]

15. That is, fish that were sold on a string. There was a standard amount of fish on each string, as well as a standard way in which the string was tied (ibid. 23b).

וַחֲתִיכוֹת שֶׁל בָּשָׂר[16] וְגִזֵּי צֶמֶר הַבָּאוֹת מִמְּדִינָתָן[17] וַאֲנִיצֵי פִשְׁתָּן[18] וּלְשׁוֹנוֹת שֶׁל אַרְגָּמָן[19]. וְאָמְרוּ בַּגְּמָרָא (שם כ״ג ע״א) אָמַר רַב זְבִיד הִלְכְתָא כְּרִיכוֹת בִּרְשׁוּת הָרַבִּים הֲרֵי אֵלּוּ שֶׁלּוֹ[20], בִּרְשׁוּת הַיָּחִיד אִי דֶּרֶךְ נְפִילָה הֲרֵי אֵלּוּ שֶׁלּוֹ[21] וְאִי דֶּרֶךְ הַנָּחָה חַיָּב לְהַכְרִיז[22], וְשָׁם בֵּאֲרוּ כֵּיצַד הוּא דֶּרֶךְ הַנָּחָה אוֹ דֶּרֶךְ נְפִילָה[23].

וַחֲתִיכוֹת שֶׁל בָּשָׂר – **pieces of meat;**[16] וְגִזֵּי צֶמֶר הַבָּאוֹת מִמְּדִינָתָן – **fleeces of wool brought from their province;**[17] וַאֲנִיצֵי פִשְׁתָּן – **bundles of flax;**[18] וּלְשׁוֹנוֹת שֶׁל אַרְגָּמָן – **and "tongues" of purple-dyed wool.**[19]

Chinuch elaborates on the case of "sheaves found in a public domain":

וְאָמְרוּ בַּגְּמָרָא – **It is further stated in the Gemara** (ibid. 23a): אָמַר רַב זְבִיד – **Rav Zevid said:** הִלְכְתָא – The **halachah** is that כְּרִיכוֹת בִּרְשׁוּת הָרַבִּים – with regard to **small sheaves** found **in the public domain,** הֲרֵי אֵלּוּ שֶׁלּוֹ – **these belong to [the finder],** as the Mishnah stated.[20] בִּרְשׁוּת הַיָּחִיד – If they are found **in the private domain,** the rule is as follows: אִי דֶּרֶךְ נְפִילָה – **If** they lie **in a way indicating that they had fallen** from the owner, הֲרֵי אֵלּוּ שֶׁלּוֹ – **they belong to [the finder].**[21] וְאִי דֶּרֶךְ הַנָּחָה – **However, if** they lie **in a way indicating that they had been placed** there deliberately by the owner, חַיָּב לְהַכְרִיז – **[the finder] must announce** his find.[22] וְשָׁם בֵּאֲרוּ – **[The Sages] explain there** כֵּיצַד הוּא דֶּרֶךְ הַנָּחָה – **how** one can tell whether they are situated in **a way indicating that they had been placed** there deliberately by the owner, אוֹ דֶּרֶךְ נְפִילָה – **or** in **a way indicating that they had fallen** from him.[23]

NOTES

16. Meat was generally cut in a standard way and had a standard weight; thus, the pieces had no *siman* (ibid.).

Fig cakes, bread, fish, and meat are all food items, so the owner is quickly aware of their loss (*Rosh, Bava Metzia* 2:2; see *Pilpula Charifta* §4). Alternatively, they are all heavy (*Ramban, Bava Metzia* 21b).

17. That is, wool that has been sheared but has not been processed any further, i.e., raw wool. It is therefore identical to all wool brought from that province.

18. This refers to flax that has been beaten and combed, and is ready for spinning. It generally has no distinguishing *siman*.

The fleeces of wool and bundles of flax were heavy, so their owner would quickly be aware that he had dropped them (*Rosh* and *Ramban* ibid.).

19. That is, wool that was combed, drawn out into tongue-shaped strips, and dyed purple. Since purple wool commonly came in this shape, anyone losing a tongue of purple wool would despair of recovering it. And since it is expensive, the owner quickly realizes that it is lost (*Rosh* ibid.; see also *Ramban* ibid.).

20. As will be clarified below, this applies regardless of whether the sheaves were dropped on the ground, or purposely placed there and then forgotten. [A person carrying sheaves will often put them on the ground in order to rest.] We will further see that the case here is that the sheaves are unmarked, meaning that they have no *siman* of their own. The only *siman* to be considered is the location in which they are found (which is generally a valid *siman*; see *Bava Metzia* 22b with *Rambam* ibid. 15:10), but even that *siman* cannot be used. If they were dropped, the owner does not know where he dropped them. And even if they were put down on purpose, the location where they were put down is no longer relevant, because the people and animals walking in the public domain kick the sheaves and move them away from their original location. The owner therefore has no way to prove that they are his, and abandons hope of recovering them.

In any event, their owner will soon realize that he lost the sheaves. They are heavy, so if he dropped them he will soon realize that he is no longer holding them. And if he put them down on purpose, he will soon remember that he forgot them there.

21. The location cannot be used as a *siman* since the owner is unaware of the place where they fell. And since these sheaves lack any *siman* of their own, the owner can never identify them. Therefore, they belong to the finder.

22. Since the sheaves were found in a *private* domain, there is no heavy traffic, so the sheaves were likely not kicked away from their original location. The owner can therefore prove that they are his by stating the location in which they were found (see *Tosafos, Bava Metzia* 22b ד״ה אי).

23. The Gemara there does not directly inform us as to how one can tell whether *sheaves* were dropped or purposely left in place. However, the Mishnah (*Bava Metzia* 25b) states that a utensil that is found covered in a garbage heap is presumed to have been placed there on purpose. Similarly, the Mishnah (ibid. 30b) teaches that a donkey or cow found grazing by the road is presumed to have been left there intentionally by the owner. Chinuch apparently means that similar common-sense guidelines would apply to sheaves as well (see *Minchas Yitzchak* §3).

וְזֶה בְּדָבָר שֶׁאֵין בּוֹ סִימָן[24], אֲבָל בְּדָבָר שֶׁיֵּשׁ בּוֹ סִימָן בֵּין בִּרְשׁוּת הָרַבִּים בֵּין בִּרְשׁוּת הַיָּחִיד בֵּין דֶּרֶךְ נְפִילָה בֵּין דֶּרֶךְ הַנָּחָה חַיָּב לְהַכְרִיז[25]. חוּץ מִן הַדְּבָרִים הַנִּמְצָאִים בְּזוּטוֹ שֶׁל יָם וּבִשְׁלוּלִיתוֹ שֶׁל נָהָר, שֶׁבְּאוֹתָן הַמְּקוֹמוֹת אַף עַל גַּב דְּאִית בֵּהּ סִימָן רַחֲמָנָא שַׁרְיֵהּ, וְדִקְדְּקוּ זֶה (שם כ״ב ע״א) מִמַּה שֶּׁאָמַר הַכָּתוּב אֲשֶׁר תֹּאבַד מִמֶּנּוּ וּמְצָאתָהּ, מִי שֶׁאֲבוּדָה מִמֶּנּוּ וּמְצוּיָה אֵצֶל כָּל אָדָם[26], כְּלוֹמַר בַּשְּׁוָקִים וּבַדְּרָכִים אוֹתָהּ אַתָּה חַיָּב לְהָשִׁיב, יָצְאתָה זֹאת שֶׁל נָהָר שֶׁאֲבוּדָה מִמֶּנּוּ וּמִכָּל אָדָם שֶׁאֵין אַתָּה חַיָּב לַהֲשִׁיבָהּ אֶלָּא הַמּוֹצֵא זוֹכֶה בָּהּ[27].

Chinuch cites the Gemara further:

וְזֶה בְּדָבָר שֶׁאֵין בּוֹ סִימָן – All **this** is true, **however,** only **regarding an object that has no identifying mark** of its own.[24] אֲבָל בְּדָבָר שֶׁיֵּשׁ בּוֹ סִימָן – **But if** the find was **an object that *has* an identifying mark** of its own, בֵּין בִּרְשׁוּת הָרַבִּים בֵּין בִּרְשׁוּת הַיָּחִיד – then **whether it is** found **in the public domain or in the private domain,** בֵּין דֶּרֶךְ נְפִילָה בֵּין דֶּרֶךְ הַנָּחָה – and **whether** it is found **in a way indicating that it had fallen or** in **a way indicating that it had been placed** there deliberately by the owner, חַיָּב לְהַכְרִיז – **[the finder] must announce** his find.[25] חוּץ מִן הַדְּבָרִים הַנִּמְצָאִים בְּזוּטוֹ שֶׁל יָם וּבִשְׁלוּלִיתוֹ שֶׁל נָהָר – Thus, one must always announce a find that has an identifying mark, **except objects found in** the sea or river, having been swept away by **the tides of the sea or** by **the flooding of the river.** שֶׁבְּאוֹתָן הַמְּקוֹמוֹת – If an object is found **in those places,** אַף עַל גַּב דְּאִית בֵּהּ סִימָן – **even though [the object]** ***has*** **an identifying mark,** רַחֲמָנָא שַׁרְיֵהּ – **the Merciful One permitted** the finder to keep **it.** וְדִקְדְּקוּ זֶה מִמַּה שֶּׁאָמַר הַכָּתוּב – **[The Sages] deduce this** (ibid. 22b) **from that which Scripture states** regarding the mitzvah of *hashavas aveidah* (*Deuteronomy* 22:3): "אֲשֶׁר תֹּאבַד מִמֶּנּוּ וּמְצָאתָהּ" – *And so shall you do for any lost object of your brother* ***that is lost "from him" and you have found it.*** מִי שֶׁאֲבוּדָה מִמֶּנּוּ וּמְצוּיָה אֵצֶל כָּל אָדָם – This teaches that **that which is lost *from him*,** i.e., the owner, **but is accessible to all people,**[26] כְּלוֹמַר בַּשְּׁוָקִים וּבַדְּרָכִים – **which is to say,** it was found **in the marketplaces or on the roadways** (for example), אוֹתָהּ אַתָּה חַיָּב לְהָשִׁיב – only ***that*** **are you obligated to return;** יָצְאתָה זֹאת שֶׁל נָהָר – **excluded, then,** is **this** case **of** an object swept away by **a river** or the sea, שֶׁאֲבוּדָה מִמֶּנּוּ וּמִכָּל אָדָם – **which was lost from him and all others** as well; שֶׁאֵין אַתָּה חַיָּב לַהֲשִׁיבָהּ – the law is **that you are not obligated to return [such an object].** אֶלָּא הַמּוֹצֵא זוֹכֶה בָּהּ – **Rather, the finder** may **acquire it** for himself.[27]

Earlier, Chinuch mentioned that one may keep an object that had clearly fallen from the owner if it has no identifying mark. Chinuch now explains why this is so:

NOTES

24. I.e., the only *siman* it might have is the location in which it was found, as above. However, it has no identifying mark in and of itself.

25. Since the item has its own *siman*, the owner does not abandon hope. He expects a fellow Jew to pick it up and announce the find, and thereby allow him to identify and recover it.

26. The word מִמֶּנּוּ, *from him,* is seemingly superfluous. If the object is lost, it is obviously lost from him, its owner! The verse is therefore understood as emphasizing that the obligation to return lost objects applies only to objects that are lost specifically *to him*, the owner (because he does not know where he lost them), but they are still accessible to other people (see *Rashi* ad loc.).

27. Under ordinary circumstances, an object swept away by a flood is lost to everyone. Therefore, even if one finds it by sheer chance, he is not obligated to return it.

There seems to be a dispute among the Rishonim as to how to understand this Biblical decree, particularly, the idea of רַחֲמָנָא שַׁרְיֵהּ, "the Merciful One permitted it." *Ramban* (*Bava Metzia* 27a ד״ה מתני׳), *Rashba* (ibid. 21b ד״ה זוטו של ים), and *Rosh* (ibid., Ch. 2 §6), understand this to mean that the Torah declared ownerless (*hefker*) any object lost to all, regardless of whether the owner actually abandoned hope of recovering it. This seems to be the view of *Tosafos* as well (ibid. 22b ד״ה איסורא). According to *Rabbeinu Chananel* (to Gemara ibid. 21b) and *Rambam* (ibid. 11:10), however, the Torah is telling us that since it is lost to everyone, we can be *certain* that the owner abandoned hope of recovering it. [Even if the owner protests that he has *not* despaired of it, we do not accept his protest (see *Ritva* ibid. 24a ד״ה מפני שהבעלים מתיאשים; cf. his statements on 21b ת״ש נטל נהר).]

וְטַעַם הֱיוֹת הָאָדָם זוֹכֶה בִּמְצִיאָה שֶׁאֵין בָּהּ סִימָן אָמְרוּ זִכְרוֹנָם לִבְרָכָה (שם כ״ג ע״א) לְפִי שֶׁבַּעְלָהּ מִתְיָאֵשׁ מִמֶּנָּה, כְּלוֹמַר שֶׁמְּסַלֵּק דַּעְתּוֹ וּזְכוּתוֹ מֵעָלֶיהָ אַחַר שֶׁאֵין לוֹ בָּהּ סִימָן, אוֹ אֲפִלּוּ בְּשֶׁיֵּשׁ בָּהּ סִימָן כְּשֶׁנָּפְלָה בְּמָקוֹם שֶׁהַבְּעָלִים מִתְיָאֲשִׁים מִמֶּנָּה עַל כָּל פָּנִים כְּגוֹן שְׁוָקִים שֶׁרֻבָּן גּוֹיִם, וַהֲרֵי הַמּוֹצְאָהּ כְּזוֹכֶה מִן הַהֶפְקֵר[28].

וְדִינֵי הַדְּבָרִים שֶׁאָדָם חַיָּב לְהַכְרִיז[29], וְכֵיצַד יַעֲשֶׂה הַהַכְרָזָה[30], וְאֵי זֶה דָּבָר יִהְיֶה

וְטַעַם הֱיוֹת הָאָדָם זוֹכֶה בִּמְצִיאָה שֶׁאֵין בָּהּ סִימָן — As for **the reason that a person** may **acquire a find that has no identifying mark,** אָמְרוּ זִכְרוֹנָם לִבְרָכָה — **[the Sages], of blessed memory, stated** (ibid. 23a) לְפִי שֶׁבַּעְלָהּ מִתְיָאֵשׁ מִמֶּנָּה — that this is **because its owner despairs of it,** כְּלוֹמַר שֶׁמְּסַלֵּק דַּעְתּוֹ וּזְכוּתוֹ מֵעָלֶיהָ — **which is to say that he removes his mental** attachment to it **and his rights over it,** אַחַר שֶׁאֵין לוֹ בָּהּ סִימָן — **since he has no identifying mark on it** by which he can claim it. אוֹ אֲפִלּוּ בְּשֶׁיֵּשׁ בָּהּ סִימָן — **Or,** sometimes, an owner despairs of the object **even if it has an identifying mark,** כְּשֶׁנָּפְלָה בְּמָקוֹם שֶׁהַבְּעָלִים מִתְיָאֲשִׁים מִמֶּנָּה עַל כָּל פָּנִים — i.e., **when it fell in a place where the owner nevertheless despairs of it,** for other reasons, כְּגוֹן שְׁוָקִים שֶׁרֻבָּן גּוֹיִם — **such as** when he dropped it in **marketplaces where most** of the passersby **are idolaters,** in which case the owner will assume that an idolater found it. Since the idolater will likely not return it to its owner even though it has an identifying mark, the owner surely despairs of it. וַהֲרֵי הַמּוֹצְאָהּ כְּזוֹכֶה מִן הַהֶפְקֵר — In either case, since the owner despairs of it, **the person who finds it is like one who acquires** something **from *hefker*** (a state of ownerlessness), since the person who lost the object has forfeited his ownership over it.[28]

Chinuch touches on numerous laws relating to *hashavas aveidah*:

וְדִינֵי הַדְּבָרִים שֶׁאָדָם חַיָּב לְהַכְרִיז — **The laws** of the mitzvah also include the types **of objects that a person** (i.e., a finder) **is obligated to announce,** so that the one who lost it can come forward and claim it.[29] וְכֵיצַד יַעֲשֶׂה הַהַכְרָזָה — **Also, how one is to make the announcement** regarding his find.[30] וְאֵי זֶה דָּבָר יִהְיֶה סִימָן שֶׁנָּשִׁיב הָאֲבֵדָה לִבְעָלֶיהָ בּוֹ — The laws of the mitzvah **also** include **what**

NOTES

28. This explanation, that the object becomes ownerless when the owner despairs of it, follows *Rashi* (*Bava Metzia* 21a ד״ה מצא; see discussion in *Chazon Ish, Bava Kamma* [*Nezikin*] 18:1). According to *Nesivos HaMishpat* (262:3; see also *Ketzos HaChoshen* 406:2), a lost object does *not* become ownerless upon the owner's despair. Instead, the legal state of *ye'ush* (literally, *abandoning hope*) that results from the owner's despair permits the finder to acquire the lost object for himself. However, until someone actually acquires the object, it remains technically under the ownership of the one who lost it. [See *Nesivos HaMishpat* there for the practical differences between *ye'ush* and true ownerlessness [*hefker*]. See also *Shulchan Aruch HaRav, Hil. Metziah U'Pikadon* §18.]

29. The essential rule in this regard is that a finder must pick up any lost object that has a *siman* and announce his find, unless it has obviously been left there for a very long time, in which case the owner has surely despaired of recovering it (see *Shulchan Aruch* ibid. 262:5).

Note that we refer here to an object that was obviously dropped by the owner, or was put down and inadvertently left in an unprotected location (like the sheaves discussed above, at notes 12 and 20-23). If the item looks like it was put down and it is in a protected location, the finder should not take it even if it does not have a *siman*, since it is likely not lost and the owner intends to retrieve it from there. See *Shulchan Aruch* ibid. 260:9-10 and *Rama* there for details regarding this law.

30. The Gemara (*Bava Metzia* 28b) teaches that there was a "claimants' stone" (אֶבֶן טוֹעַן) in Jerusalem, and anyone who lost something or found something would go there. The finder would announce his find, and the owner would state what the *siman* is and take the object. Also, the Gemara (ibid.) teaches that anyone who found a lost object would announce it on each of the three Pilgrimage Festivals (Pesach, Shavuos, and Succos), and after the final festival, for another seven days, so that one would have three days to travel home and check his belongings, three days to return, and one day to announce the loss of his object and provide its identifying marks. When the *Beis HaMikdash* was destroyed, and there was no longer any pilgrimage to Jerusalem, the Sages instituted that they should announce lost objects in the synagogues and study halls. When the law of the land became that lost objects were confiscated and given to the king, they instituted that finders should merely inform their neighbors. Nowadays, when this is not the law of the land, we revert back to announcing lost objects in the synagogues and study halls; see *Shulchan Aruch* ibid. 267:3.

The finder announces which object he found, and the claimant must give its *simanim* (ibid. 267:4).

סִימָן שֶׁנָּשִׁיב הָאֲבֵדָה לִבְעָלֶיהָ בּוֹ[31], וּמַה שֶּׁאָמְרוּ בָּזֶה דְּמִדָּה וּמִנְיָן וּמִשְׁקָל וּמָקוֹם הָוֵי סִימָן[32], וְדִין זֶה אוֹמֵר מִדַּת אָרְכּוֹ וְזֶה אוֹמֵר מִדַּת רָחְבּוֹ[33] אוֹ זֶה אוֹמֵר אָרְכּוֹ וְרָחְבּוֹ וְזֶה מִשְׁקְלוֹתָיו[34], וְדִין רָאָה סֶלַע שֶׁנָּפְלָה מֵחֲבֵרוֹ וּנְטָלָהּ לִפְנֵי יֵאוּשׁ[35], אוֹ לְאַחַר יֵאוּשׁ, כְּלוֹמַר אַחַר שֶׁשָּׁמַע חֲבֵרוֹ שֶׁאָמַר וַוי לֵיהּ עַל מַה שֶּׁאָבַד אוֹ כַּיּוֹצֵא בָּזֶה[36], וְדִין מַה שֶּׁאָמְרוּ

---

feature of the lost object **constitutes an identifying mark by which we return the lost object to its owner;**[31] וּמַה שֶּׁאָמְרוּ בָּזֶה – **and that which [the Sages] said about this** matter of identifying marks, דְּמִדָּה וּמִנְיָן וּמִשְׁקָל וּמָקוֹם הָוֵי סִימָן – namely, **that size, amount, weight, and location are** valid **identifying marks.**[32] וְדִין זֶה אוֹמֵר מִדַּת אָרְכּוֹ וְזֶה אוֹמֵר מִדַּת רָחְבּוֹ – **Another law** relates to a case where two people claim a lost object; **this** claimant **states the measure of its length and that** claimant **states the measure of its width,**[33] אוֹ זֶה אוֹמֵר אָרְכּוֹ וְרָחְבּוֹ וְזֶה מִשְׁקְלוֹתָיו – **or this** claimant **states** both **its length and width, and that** claimant states **its weight.**[34]

וְדִין רָאָה סֶלַע שֶׁנָּפְלָה מֵחֲבֵרוֹ – **Also** included in the laws of the mitzvah is **the law** of someone **who saw that a *sela* coin fell from his fellow** וּנְטָלָהּ לִפְנֵי יֵאוּשׁ – **and took it** for himself **before** the owner **despaired** of it;[35] אוֹ לְאַחַר יֵאוּשׁ – **or** he waited a while and then took it for himself **after** the owner expressly **despaired** of it, כְּלוֹמַר אַחַר שֶׁשָּׁמַע חֲבֵרוֹ שֶׁאָמַר וַוי לֵיהּ עַל מַה שֶּׁאָבַד – **which is to say,** that he picked it up **after he heard his fellow say, "Woe," to himself over his loss,** אוֹ כַּיּוֹצֵא בָּזֶה – **or** any statement **similar to that,** which indicates that he has abandoned hope of recovering it.[36] וְדִין מַה שֶּׁאָמְרוּ – **Another law is that which [the Sages] stated** (see *Bava Metzia* 27a),

---

NOTES

31. There are three levels of *simanim*: (1) Very distinctive [סִימָן מֻבְהָק בְּיוֹתֵר], e.g., a hole near a particular letter in a document, or a scratch in a very specific place on an object; (2) distinctive [סִימָן מֻבְהָק], e.g., the precise length, width, size, or weight of the object; (3) and general [סִימָן שֶׁאֵינוֹ מֻבְהָק], e.g., the color of the object. We give an object back to anyone who provides *simanim* of the first or second level (*Rambam* ibid. 13:3 and 5, with *Maggid Mishneh*; for discussion, see *Shach, Choshen Mishpat* 267:2).

32. I.e., they are considered distinctive identifying marks (*Rambam* ibid. 13:5).

33. The Gemara (ibid. 28a) states that it is given to the one who provides its length. This is because the person who provides its width may simply be gauging that measurement by looking at the other claimant who is standing before him, who is the true owner, and estimating how wide a garment of his would be. [The Gemara refers to a garment that was worn in the manner that we wear a *tallis* today; the width of the garment hung down the wearer's back, while the length was wrapped around the body. Thus, it was easier for an observer to gauge the garment's width than its length (*Sma, Choshen Mishpat* 267:13). Accordingly, *Shach* (ibid. 267:10) states that nowadays a judge must base his ruling on the type of garment and the manner in which it is generally worn.]

34. The Gemara (ibid.) states that it is given to the one who provides its weight. Since it is unusual to weigh a garment, knowledge of its weight constitutes greater proof of ownership than knowledge of its other measurements (see *Tosafos* 23b ד״ה מדמשקל).

35. According to several Rishonim, the *sela* coin had a *siman* by which it could be identified, e.g., it was in a pouch (*Ritva* and *R' Peretz* cited in *Shitah Mekubetzes* to *Bava Metzia* 26b; see also *Shulchan Aruch* ibid. 259:1-2; cf. *Rashi, Bava Metzia* 26b ד״ה נטלה). Thus, although we assume that a person immediately realizes that he dropped the coin, and if it has no *siman* we say that he surely despaired of it (see note 11, above), in our case we do not automatically assume that he despairs of it, since it has a *siman* by which it can be retrieved. The bystander is therefore obligated to pick it up and return it to him (see note 2 above). The Gemara (ibid. 26b) states that if the bystander instead picks it up with the intention of taking it for himself, he transgresses three Biblical commandments: (1) לֹא תִגְזֹל, *You shall not rob* (*Leviticus* 19:13; Mitzvah 229). Since the owner had not yet despaired of recovering his coin when the finder picked it up, it was still considered in the owner's possession at that time. By taking the coin with intent to steal it, it is as if the finder took the coin from the owner's house – in violation of the Biblical prohibition against stealing (*Ritva* ibid. ד״ה עובר); (2) הָשֵׁב תְּשִׁיבֵם, *You shall surely return them,* i.e., he failed to fulfill our mitzvah-obligation to return the lost article; and (3) לֹא תוּכַל לְהִתְעַלֵּם, *You shall not hide yourself* (*Deuteronomy* 22:3), i.e., he violated the mitzvah-prohibition against ignoring a lost article (Mitzvah 539); that is, ignoring the owner's potential loss.

36. [See Gemara ibid. 23a; *Rambam* ibid. 14:3.] In this case, the bystander waited near the coin until he heard the owner make a statement indicating that he was abandoning hope of recovering it, and the bystander then took it for himself. The Gemara (ibid. 26b) states that, in this case, he has violated only the mitzvah-prohibition of ignoring a lost object (Mitzvah 539),

שֶׁאֲבֵדָה שֶׁאֵין בָּהּ שָׁוֶה פְּרוּטָה שֶׁאֵין חַיָּב לְהִטַּפֵּל בָּהּ וְלֹא לַהֲשִׁיבָהּ[37], וּמַה שֶּׁאָמְרוּ דְּמִשֶּׁרַבּוּ הָרַמָּאִים אוֹמְרִים לוֹ הָבֵא עֵדִים שֶׁאֵין אַתָּה רַמַּאי וְטֹל[38], וְדִין כָּל דָּבָר שֶׁעוֹשֶׂה וְאוֹכֵל

שֶׁאֲבֵדָה שֶׁאֵין בָּהּ שָׁוֶה פְּרוּטָה – **that** if **a lost object does not have the value of** even **a *perutah,*** שֶׁאֵין חַיָּב לְהִטַּפֵּל בָּהּ וְלֹא לַהֲשִׁיבָהּ – **[the finder] is not obligated to tend to it, nor to return it.**[37] וּמַה שֶּׁאָמְרוּ – **Also,** there is **that which [the Sages] stated** (ibid. 28b), דְּמִשֶּׁרַבּוּ הָרַמָּאִים – **that when dishonest people became prevalent** it was not enough for the person claiming the object to provide identifying marks; rather, אוֹמְרִים לוֹ הָבֵא עֵדִים שֶׁאֵין אַתָּה רַמַּאי וְטֹל – **they would say to [the claimant], "Bring witnesses that you are not a dishonest person, and** then you may **take** the object based on the identifying marks."[38]

As stated in the introduction to the mitzvah, whenever a person is obligated to pick up and return a find to its owner, he is also obligated to maintain it so that he can eventually return it intact. He is not required, however, to bear the *expense* of maintaining it. Thus, upon returning the lost object to its owner, the finder may demand reimbursement for any maintenance expense he had incurred (see *Rambam* ibid. 13:11-19). As we shall see below, most inanimate objects are low-maintenance, as they require nothing more than an occasional airing or light usage to keep them from deteriorating or rotting. However, in the case of animals, the maintenance costs can add up considerably, since animals need to be fed. If the finder then presents a feed bill to the owner that is equal to, say, half the value of the animal, he would effectively not be returning the animal intact [i.e., in terms of its value] (Mishnah ibid. 28b with *Rashi*). Chinuch cites the Sages' solution to this matter:

וְדִין כָּל דָּבָר שֶׁעוֹשֶׂה וְאוֹכֵל – The Sages (ibid.) discuss **the law** of **any** lost **object that works and**

NOTES

which he transgresses immediately by virtue of his ignoring the owner's potential loss (see end of previous note). However, he is not guilty of stealing, because he picked up the coin after *ye'ush*, when it was no longer in the owner's possession (see note 28 above).

He also did not violate our mitzvah-obligation, for he did not walk away from the lost object, but stood there watching it; thus, although he had no *intention* of fulfilling the mitzvah, technically he could have fulfilled it at any point. As for the fact that he can no longer fulfill the mitzvah now that the owner expressed *ye'ush* (and thus forfeited his ownership over the coin), that does not constitute a violation of the mitzvah on the bystander's part, since this was not due to his actions (*Ran, Bava Metzia* 30a ד״ה קרא למאי אתא; for further clarification of *Ran's* approach, see *Chidushei HaGrach al HaShas* §267). [See *Ramban* and *Rashba* to *Bava Metzia* 30a (cited by *Ran* ibid.) for another explanation as to why the bystander violates the prohibition but not the mitzvah-obligation.]

37. That is, he need not pick it up, and if he did, he need not return it to the owner; he may keep it for himself (*Chazon Yechezkel* on *Tosefta, Bava Metzia* 2:5). [For alternative interpretations of this dual phrasing, which is taken from *Rambam* ibid. 11:12 and *Rif, Bava Metzia* 15a, see *Halachah LeMoshe* (*R' C. M. Amarillo*) to *Rambam* there, and *Magen Shaul* (*R' Chananya Shaul*), *Leshonos HaRambam, Hil. Gezeilah VaAveidah* 13:1 (p. 24b).]

An item worth less than a *perutah,* the smallest coin used in Talmudic times, is not considered significant (see *Sma, Choshen Mishpat* 262:1), and the Gemara (ibid. 27a) derives from Scripture that there is no obligation to return insignificant objects. The authorities debate, however, whether the value of an object is determined based on its value in the marketplace or based on its value to the person who lost it. This question would be relevant if the lost article was, for example, a single shoe (of a pair), a prescription lens, or a family picture, which in the marketplace might be worthless but to its owner may be worth a lot. According to *Nesivos HaMishpat* (148:1), the determining factor is the item's value in the marketplace, but according to *Chazon Ish* (*Bava Kamma* [*Nezikin*] 6:3) one must assess how much the item would be worth to the owner. The majority of contemporary authorities seem to accept this latter view. See *Mishpat HaAveidah* 262:1, *Moznei Tzedek* §2-4 with *Shaarei Tzedek*. See also there §1 (with *Shaarei Tzedek*) for the current equivalent of a *perutah*.

38. The original law was that a claimant who gave identifying marks was given the article unless he was *known* to be a dishonest person; in that case, providing a *siman* was insufficient proof (Mishnah, ibid. 28b; *Rambam* ibid. 13:4). [This is because it often happens that a person is aware of the distinctive features of his neighbor's possessions. If a dishonest person then hears his neighbor bemoaning the loss of his object and also hears that an object of that type has been found, he may falsely claim the object based on the *simanim* he knows (see *Rashi* ad loc. ד״ה חיישינן לרמאי; for an alternative explanation, see *Yerushalmi Bava Metzia* 2:7).] When dishonesty became more prevalent, we could no longer trust even the general populace based solely on a *siman*, and every person claiming a lost object would have to bring witnesses that he is of upright character.

אוֹ הָאוֹכֵל וְאֵינוֹ עוֹשֶׂה מַה דִּינָם[39]**, וְכַמָּה זְמַן יְטַפֵּל בְּפָרָה וַחֲמוֹר וּבַעֲגָלִים וּסְיָחִין וְאַוָּזִין וְתַרְנְגוֹלִין**[40]**, וְדִין סְפָרִים אוֹ תְּפִלִּין אוֹ כֵּלִים שֶׁל צֶמֶר וּפִשְׁתָּן אוֹ כֵּלִים אֲחֵרִים אֵיךְ יִתְנַהֵג בָּהֶם**[41]**, וּמַה שֶּׁאָמְרוּ שֶׁיֵּשׁ צְדָדִים שֶׁלֹּא יִתְחַיֵּב הַמּוֹצֵא לְהָשִׁיב הָאֲבֵדָה**

---

thereby covers the expense of what it **eats,** for example, an ox or donkey, אוֹ הָאוֹכֵל וְאֵינוֹ עוֹשֶׂה – **and** the law of **[an object] that eats but does not work,** such that its work cannot cover the expense of the food it eats, for example, a calf or rooster; מַה דִּינָם – specifically, **what their law is** with regard to the finder's obligation to take care of them until their owner claims them. Basically, an animal that can earn its keep should be maintained by the finder, and an animal that cannot earn its keep should be sold and the money from the sale should be returned to the owner instead.[39] וְכַמָּה זְמַן יְטַפֵּל בְּפָרָה וַחֲמוֹר וּבַעֲגָלִים וּסְיָחִין וְאַוָּזִין וְתַרְנְגוֹלִין – However, there are some specific guidelines, depending on the particular type of animal and other factors. Thus, the Sages there (ibid.) delineate **how long [a finder] must care for a cow, a donkey, calves, young donkeys, geese, and chickens.**[40] וְדִין סְפָרִים אוֹ תְּפִלִּין אוֹ כֵּלִים שֶׁל צֶמֶר וּפִשְׁתָּן אוֹ כֵּלִים אֲחֵרִים – **An additional** discussion by the Sages (ibid. 29b) pertains to the **law of books,** ***tefillin,*** **garments of wool or linen, and general utensils,** אֵיךְ יִתְנַהֵג בָּהֶם – in terms of **how [the finder] should treat them** until they are claimed.[41] וּמַה שֶּׁאָמְרוּ שֶׁיֵּשׁ צְדָדִים שֶׁלֹּא יִתְחַיֵּב הַמּוֹצֵא לְהָשִׁיב הָאֲבֵדָה – Finally, the laws of the mitzvah include

---

NOTES

39. In other words: If one found a calf, rooster, or the like, which must be fed but cannot do anything to earn its keep (work, lay eggs, etc.), he should sell it, and when the owner claims it, he gives the owner the amount for which it was sold. [The finder must be careful to record the *simanim* of the animal, so that the owner can later identify it and claim the money (*Nachalas Moshe, Bava Metzia* ad loc.).] If, however, the object is something that can be put to work and fed from the money it earns, such as a grown ox or donkey, then the finder should have it work and feed it rather than sell it. The reason is that the owner is more comfortable with the animal he knows and trained for his needs (*Rashi* ad loc.). Therefore, even though it is somewhat of a burden on the finder to work or rent out the animal, we do not allow him to sell it, since returning the money would not be the same as returning the animal. [Nevertheless, the Sages did not obligate the finder to maintain the animal indefinitely. See next note.]

If the animal earns more than it consumes, the finder must pass on that difference to the owner when he retrieves the animal (*Rambam* ibid. 13:15).

40. Cows and donkeys, which can be worked or rented out to earn their food, must be kept for twelve months, after which time they may be sold (*Rashi* ad loc. ד״ה שם דמיהן; cf. *Rambam* ibid.). Hens, which lay eggs and thus cover the expense of their food, are similarly kept for twelve months.

Calves and young donkeys that can be fed from surrounding pastures are kept for three months, since little expense is incurred in maintaining them. [The expense is also offset to some extent by the increase in their value resulting from their growth (see *Shitah Mekubetzes* ad loc.).] If pasture is scarce, however, and they must be fattened from feed, then they should be kept for only one month.

Small roosters and geese are similarly kept for thirty days (one month), but large ones, which eat a lot, are sold after three days (*Rashi* 28b ד״ה רברבי; cf. *Rambam* ibid. 13:16; see *Hagahos HaGra, Bava Metzia* ad loc.).

41. As mentioned, a finder is obligated to maintain the article he found so that he can return it to the owner intact. Therefore, if one found books (i.e., parchment scrolls), he should read from them once every thirty days, to air them out and prevent their decay. [If he does not know how to read, he should just roll them from beginning to end to air them out.] However, he may not linger on any specific part of the scroll for too long, since this might lead to its damage. For further details, see Gemara ibid. 29b; *Rambam* ibid. 13:13, and *Shulchan Aruch* ibid. 267:20.

A person who finds *tefillin* may sell them immediately, since they are readily available in the marketplace, and it is of no consequence to the owner whether he gets his own *tefillin* back or he has to buy a new pair with the proceeds (Gemara ibid., with *Sma, Choshen Mishpat* 267:30). [Whether this rule is applicable to all found objects that are easily replaced, or only to *tefillin,* is a matter of some discussion; see *Sma* ibid. and *Shach* 267:16. In any event, *Minchas Elazar* (*Teshuvos* IV §9) maintains that nowadays *tefillin* are not "easily replaced," since many people today are particular about where they purchase their *tefillin* and who the scribe is, etc. Thus, lost *tefillin* nowadays should not be sold.]

Regarding wool and linen garments: The Gemara (ibid.) distinguishes between wool and linen garments with regard to their maintenance: one type of garment should be shaken out once every thirty days (as stated in the Mishnah there), and the other type of garment should not be shaken out at all. Which type of garment has which guideline, however, is a subject of dispute. *Rashi* (ad loc.) maintains that wool garments are more

כְּגוֹן זָקֵן וְאֵינָהּ לְפִי כְּבוֹדוֹ[42] אוֹ כֹּהֵן וְהִיא בְּבֵית הַקְּבָרוֹת[43], וְיֶתֶר פְּרָטֵי הַמִּצְוָה, בְּבָבָא מְצִיעָא בְּפֶרֶק שֵׁנִי[44].

וְנוֹהֶגֶת בְּכָל מָקוֹם וּבְכָל זְמַן, בִּזְכָרִים וּנְקֵבוֹת[45].

וְעוֹבֵר עַל זֶה וּמָצָא מְצִיאָה שֶׁחַיָּב לַהֲשִׁיבָהּ עַל הָעִנְיָן שֶׁזָּכַרְנוּ וְלֹא הֱשִׁיבָהּ בִּטֵּל עֲשֵׂה זֶה,

---

that which [the Sages] stated (ibid. 30a-b), **that there are circumstances under which the finder is not obligated to return the lost object,** כְּגוֹן זָקֵן וְאֵינָהּ לְפִי כְּבוֹדוֹ – **such as** where the finder is **a sage and it is not befitting his honor** to pick up this particular object and return it,[42] אוֹ כֹּהֵן וְהִיא בְּבֵית הַקְּבָרוֹת – **or** where the finder is **a Kohen and [the object] is in a cemetery,** which he is forbidden to enter.[43]

וְיֶתֶר פְּרָטֵי הַמִּצְוָה – All these laws, **and the rest of the details of the mitzvah,** בְּבָבָא מְצִיעָא בְּפֶרֶק שֵׁנִי – can be found **in** Tractate ***Bava Metzia*, Chapter 2.**[44]

Applicability of the Mitzvah

וְנוֹהֶגֶת בְּכָל מָקוֹם וּבְכָל זְמַן – This mitzvah **applies in every location and in all times,** בִּזְכָרִים וּנְקֵבוֹת – **to** both **men and women.**[45]

וְעוֹבֵר עַל זֶה – **One who transgresses this** mitzvah, וּמָצָא מְצִיאָה שֶׁחַיָּב לַהֲשִׁיבָהּ עַל הָעִנְיָן שֶׁזָּכַרְנוּ – **and comes across a find that he is obligated to return based on the guidelines that we have mentioned** וְלֹא הֱשִׁיבָהּ – **but does not return it,** בִּטֵּל עֲשֵׂה זֶה – **has violated this**

NOTES

prone than linen to being stretched and torn, and therefore only linen ones should be shaken out. However, most Rishonim hold that the reverse is true, and only *wool* garments should be shaken out. *Shulchan Aruch* (ibid. 267:18-19) rules in accordance with the majority view; see there as to the manner in which one is to shake out the wool garment. It should also be spread out periodically in order to prevent its disintegration. Linen garments are simply left untouched until their owner claims them.

With regard to utensils: The general guideline is that they are to be used from time to time in order to preserve them, but they may not be used in a way that might damage them. The exception is utensils made of gold or glass, which do not tarnish or decay and, therefore, should not be used at all (see Gemara ibid. 29b-30a; *Rambam* ibid. 13:12, and *Shulchan Aruch* ibid. 267:19).

42. According to *Rambam*, this refers to any respectable elder, as well (ibid. 11:13; see *Even HaAzel* ad loc.; *Shulchan Aruch HaRav, Hil. Metziah U'Pikadon* §36). Such an elder or sage is not obligated to pick up a lost article in a public area if it would be beneath his dignity to pick it up even if it were his own. For example, he might not pick up his own sock in a public area; thus, if he finds a sock that belongs to someone else, he is also not obligated to pick it up (see *Rambam* ibid., and *Shulchan Aruch* ibid. 263:1).

Other Rishonim, however, maintain that this exception refers only to a Torah sage, and is due to the honor of his Torah scholarship. All other people, distinguished as they may be, must perform the mitzvah. And if they feel it is beneath their dignity to pick up the object, they must at least financially compensate the owner for his loss [which they could have prevented] (*Ritva, Bava Metzia* ad loc.; see also *Ramban* cited by *Ran* to *Bava Metzia* 33a; *Rosh, Bava Metzia* Ch. 2 §21).

In any event, the exemption for a sage (or an elder, according to *Rambam*), reflects the letter of the law. *Rambam* (ibid. 11:17, based on *Bava Metzia* 30b) writes that one who conducts himself in a good and righteous way and goes *beyond* the requirement of the law (לִפְנִים מִשּׁוּרַת הַדִּין) will return a lost object to its owner even if it is beneath his dignity. *Rosh* (ibid.) agrees with this idea in concept, but maintains that a Torah sage must not degrade himself by actually retrieving the lost article. He may, if he wishes, choose to financially compensate the owner for his loss. For the practical halachah, see *Shulchan Aruch* ibid. 263:3 with *Rama*, and *Erech Lechem* ad loc.

43. By entering a cemetery, a Kohen will almost certainly contract *tumah* from a human corpse, which is forbidden to him (Mitzvah 263). [Essentially, the Gemara is teaching that the mitzvah-obligation to return a lost object does not override the mitzvah-prohibition for a Kohen to contract *tumah* from a corpse (see Gemara there).]

44. The laws of *hashavas aveidah* are codified in *Rambam, Hil. Gezeilah VaAveidah* Chs. 11-16,18; and in *Shulchan Aruch, Choshen Mishpat* §259-267.

45. I.e. the mitzvah applies in Eretz Yisrael and the Diaspora, and whether the *Beis HaMikdash* is standing or not. And it applies to women as well as men, in accordance with the general rule pertaining to mitzvah-obligations that are not time-specific.

מִלְּבַד שֶׁעָבַר עַל לָאו כְּמוֹ שֶׁנִּכְתֹּב בְּסֵדֶר זֶה בַּלָּאוִין (מצוה תקל״ט) בְּעֶזְרַת הַשֵּׁם[46].

mitzvah-**obligation.** מִלְּבַד שֶׁעָבַר עַל לָאו — This is **aside from** the fact **that he transgressed a** mitzvah-**prohibition,** i.e., the prohibition against hiding one's eyes from a lost object (Mitzvah 539), כְּמוֹ שֶׁנִּכְתֹּב בְּסֵדֶר זֶה בַּלָּאוִין — **as we will write in this** *parashah,* **in** our presentation of the *parashah's* mitzvah-**prohibitions,** בְּעֶזְרַת הַשֵּׁם — **with the help of Hashem.**[46]

NOTES

46. In the original order of Chinuch, all the mitzvah-obligations in each *parashah* were presented before all of its mitzvah-prohibitions (see Mitzvah 494 note 4, and General Introduction, note 7). Chinuch therefore states that he presents the mitzvah-prohibition against ignoring a lost object along with all the other mitzvah-prohibitions in the *parashah.* A further ramification of the original order is that the mitzvah-prohibition under discussion (Mitzvah 539) did not appear immediately after our mitzvah (538), but much later in the *parashah.* This explains why Chinuch indicates that he will not be presenting that mitzvah-prohibition immediately after our mitzvah, but only at some later time. [Notably, several of the later editions that adopted the current order of the mitzvos also modified the text to read, כְּמוֹ שֶׁנִּכְתֹּב בְּלָאו שֶׁלּוֹ בְּסָמוּךְ, *As we will soon write in its [corresponding] mitzvah-prohibition* (see Brunn and Minchas Yitzchak editions, for example).]

Chinuch indicates here that whenever one violates our mitzvah-obligation by failing to return a lost item, he has violated the mitzvah-prohibition of *You shall not hide your eyes* as well. Note, however, that there are cases where one can violate the mitzvah-prohibition but not the mitzvah-obligation; see note 36 above.

◆§ Insight: Aveidas Gufo — Saving One's Fellow From Physical or Spiritual Loss

Although the basic definition of our mitzvah refers to returning a lost object to its owner, the Gemara (*Bava Metzia* 31a) indicates that the mitzvah includes not only returning someone else's *lost* items, but also saving and rescuing his possessions from damage or other loss (such as saving another's field from flooding). The Sages and later authorities further expand the mitzvah to include not only helping a person recover his lost *material* possessions, but also helping him recover his body or soul. The following are some examples of this:

(1) Saving another from danger: As Chinuch teaches in Mitzvah 237, a person who sees his fellow in danger (e.g., drowning in the river) is obligated to rescue him, as the verse states (*Leviticus* 19:16): לֹא תַעֲמֹד עַל דַּם רֵעֶךָ, *Do not stand by the blood of your fellow.* Although there is a special verse and a distinct mitzvah for this requirement, the Gemara in *Sanhedrin* (73a) indicates that saving someone's life is essentially a form of *hashavas aveidah.* This is because when a person's life is danger, his life is potentially lost to him (the Gemara refers to this as אֲבֵדַת גּוּפוֹ, *the loss of his body*). Saving him is therefore akin to giving him back his life. [See below for a possible explanation of the significance of classifying this as a form of *hashavas aveidah.*]

(2) Helping a person who is lost to find his way: The Gemara in *Bava Kamma* (81b) teaches that if one sees his fellow lost in the vineyards, he is obligated to help him find his way back to the city or the road. The Gemara explains that this is a Biblical obligation, rooted in the mitzvah of *hashavas aveidah.* [Presumably, this extends to bringing a missing person back to his family. Accordingly, when one assists in a search for a missing person, he is engaging in the mitzvah of *hashavas aveidah.*] The Scriptural source for both the requirement to help a lost person find his way and the requirement to save another's life (see above) is from the phrase (*Deuteronomy* 22:2), וַהֲשֵׁבֹתוֹ לוֹ, which in the context of the verse means, *and you shall return [the lost item] to [its owner].* The Sages (*Sanhedrin* and *Bava Kamma* ibid.), however, expound the phrase to mean, *and you shall return him* (i.e., the lost person or the person in danger) *to himself.*

(3) Saving one's fellow from sin (spiritual danger): As Chinuch taught in Mitzvah 239, a person who sees a fellow Jew engaged in improper conduct is obligated to admonish him until the sinner abandons his sin (this is the mitzvah of *tochachah,* reproof). Several Acharonim note that, in addition, the person witnessing his fellow's misconduct is subject to the prohibition of לֹא תַעֲמֹד עַל דַּם רֵעֶךָ, *Do not stand by the blood of your fellow,* as well as the obligation of וַהֲשֵׁבֹתוֹ לוֹ, *and you shall return him to himself.* For if these two verses require one to save his fellow's body, all the more so do they

require him to save his fellow's soul! [*Minchas Chinuch* 239:6; *Maharam Schik* §240; see also *Teshuvos Maharashdam, Yoreh Deah* §204.]

(4) Providing medical treatment to an ill person: *Rambam* (*Commentary to the Mishnah, Nedarim* 4:4) writes that included in the exposition of וַהֲשֵׁבֹתוֹ לוֹ is an obligation to provide medical treatment to an ill person, thereby helping him recover his health (see also *Shulchan Aruch, Yoreh Deah* 336:2 with *Shach* and *Taz*). [The Rishonim debate whether providing medical treatment to someone else's animal, too, is a fulfillment of *hashavas aveidah* (i.e., the typical *hashavas aveidah* pertaining to someone else's material possessions). See *Rashba* and *Ran*, and *Tosafos* and *Rosh*, to *Nedarim* 41b.]

There is an interesting discussion regarding the Gemara's classification of rescuing a person from danger as *hashavas aveidah* (see above). It relates to the exemption known as זָקֵן וְאֵינָהּ לְפִי כְּבוֹדוֹ (*zakein ve'einah lefi kevodo;* literally, *an elder and it is not befitting his honor*), which Chinuch mentions above (at note 42). This law, as it pertains to *hashavas aveidah,* states that if a distinguished individual finds an item that would be beneath his dignity to retrieve, he is exempt from the obligation to return it (see note 42 for details). *R' Shlomo Kluger* (*Chochmas Shlomo* to *Shulchan Aruch, Choshen Mishpat* 426:1) reasons that just as there is an exemption of *zakein ve'einah lefi kevodo* with respect to returning a lost object, there should be such an exemption with respect to saving a person from danger, since that, too, is a form of *hashavas aveidah*. Accordingly, if it would be necessary for the distinguished individual to do something that is beneath his dignity in order to assist the person in danger, he would not be obligated to intervene. [Surely, one who conducts himself in a good and righteous way and goes beyond the requirement of the law (לִפְנִים מִשּׁוּרַת הַדִּין) would rescue his fellow even if it is beneath his dignity, as is true regarding *hashavas aveidah* as well (see note 42). However, perhaps he is not obligated to do so.] Although R' Kluger maintains that this is a logical conclusion, he ultimately hesitates to declare it a definitive ruling.

R' Moshe Feinstein (*Igros Moshe, Yoreh Deah* II 174:3), however, rejects *R' Kluger's* suggestion outright. R' Feinstein points out that the principle of *zakein ve'einah lefi kevodo* — in the context of a typical *hashavas aveidah* — is measured by how the finder would deal with the situation if it were his own object. If he would forgo his own object because the embarrassment of retrieving it is too great, he is not required to embarrass himself to save someone else's property. But if he would pick up the object if it were his own, he must do the same for his fellow, even if returning the object causes minor embarrassment (see *Bava Metzia* 30b). When it comes to saving a life, one would certainly do whatever possible to save his own life, even if it will cause him great embarrassment. Therefore, the same standard applies to others, and one is required to rescue another in danger even if it will cause him great embarrassment. [For further discussion, see *Kli Chemdah* to *Deuteronomy* 22:1 (*Ki Seitzei* §6); *Teshuvos Minchas Yitzchak*, Vol. V, 7:17-18; and *Teshuvos Tzitz Eliezer*, Vol. IX, §17, Ch. 11 (citing *R' Y. S. Elyashiv* and others).]

❧ מִצְוָה תקלט: שֶׁלֹּא לְהִתְעַלֵּם מִן הָאֲבֵדָה ❧

שֶׁלֹּא נַעֲלִים עַיִן[1] מֵאֲבֵדַת אָחִינוּ אֲבָל נִקָּחֶהָ וּנְשִׁיבָה אֵלָיו, וְעַל זֶה נֶאֱמַר (דברים כ"ב, ג')
לֹא תוּכַל לְהִתְעַלֵּם.

כָּל עִנְיַן הַמִּצְוָה כָּתוּב בְּמִצְוַת עֲשֵׂה ד' (מצוה תקל"ח) שֶׁבְּסֵדֶר זֶה[2].

❧ Mitzvah 539 ❧
The Prohibition to Ignore a Lost Object

וְכֵן תַּעֲשֶׂה לַחֲמֹרוֹ וְכֵן תַּעֲשֶׂה לְשִׂמְלָתוֹ וְכֵן תַּעֲשֶׂה לְכָל אֲבֵדַת אָחִיךָ אֲשֶׁר תֹּאבַד
מִמֶּנּוּ וּמְצָאתָהּ לֹא תוּכַל לְהִתְעַלֵּם

So shall you do for his donkey, so shall you do for his garment, and so shall you do for any lost object of your brother that is lost from him and you have found it; you shall not hide yourself (Deuteronomy 22:3)

שֶׁלֹּא נַעֲלִים עַיִן מֵאֲבֵדַת אָחִינוּ — **We are** commanded **not to turn a blind eye**[1] **toward a lost object** that belongs to **our brother,** אֲבָל נִקָּחֶהָ וּנְשִׁיבָה אֵלָיו — **but rather, we should take it and return it to him.** וְעַל זֶה נֶאֱמַר — **Regarding this it is stated** (*Deuteronomy* 22:3): "לֹא תוּכַל לְהִתְעַלֵּם" — *You shall not hide yourself.*

כָּל עִנְיַן הַמִּצְוָה — **The entire matter of the mitzvah,** including its underlying purpose, laws, and applicability, כָּתוּב בְּמִצְוַת עֲשֵׂה ד' שֶׁבְּסֵדֶר זֶה — **is written in Mitzvah-obligation 4 of this parashah** (Mitzvah 538).[2]

NOTES
1. Literally, *hide one's eyes.*
2. See Mitzvah 494 note 4 regarding Chinuch's original numbering of his work.

מִצְוָה תקמ: שֶׁלֹּא לְהַנִּיחַ בֶּהֱמַת חֲבֵרוֹ רוֹבֶצֶת תַּחַת מַשָּׂאָהּ

שֶׁהֻזְהַרְנוּ שֶׁאִם נִרְאֶה אֶחָד מִיִּשְׂרָאֵל שֶׁנָּפַל לוֹ חֲמוֹרוֹ אוֹ בְּהֵמָה[1] אַחֶרֶת מִכֹּבֶד הַמַּשָּׂא אוֹ בְּסִבָּה אַחֶרֶת, אוֹ שֶׁהוּא בְּעַצְמוֹ רוֹבֵץ תַּחַת מַשָּׂאוֹ[2], שֶׁלֹּא לְהַנִּיחוֹ בַּדֶּרֶךְ וְנֵלֵךְ, אֲבָל נַעַזְרֵהוּ וְנָקִים עִמּוֹ בְּהֶמְתּוֹ[3] וְנַעֲמֹד שָׁם עַד שֶׁיְּתַקֵּן מַשָּׂאוֹ אוֹ עַל גַּבּוֹ אוֹ עַל בְּהֶמְתּוֹ[4], וְעַל זֶה נֶאֱמַר (דברים כ״ב, ד׳) לֹא תִרְאֶה אֶת חֲמוֹר אָחִיךָ וְגוֹ׳, וְאָמְרוּ בְּסִפְרֵי (כאן)

Mitzvah 540
The Prohibition to Ignore the Animal of One's Fellow That Has Fallen Under Its Load

לֹא תִרְאֶה אֶת חֲמוֹר אָחִיךָ אוֹ שׁוֹרוֹ נֹפְלִים בַּדֶּרֶךְ וְהִתְעַלַּמְתָּ מֵהֶם הָקֵם תָּקִים עִמּוֹ

You shall not see the donkey of your brother or his ox falling on the road and hide yourself from them; you shall surely stand them up with him (*Deuteronomy* 22:4).

Three mitzvos pertain to one who encounters the animal of one's fellow that has faltered beneath its load. In Mitzvah 80, we are commanded to assist in removing the load that is weighing down his animal, causing it to falter. This is known as *perikah*, unloading. The present mitzvah is a corresponding mitzvah-prohibition that forbids us from ignoring the plight of one whose animal has faltered while traveling. The next mitzvah, Mitzvah 541, obligates one to further assist the owner in reloading the animal. That obligation is known as *te'inah*, loading.

שֶׁהֻזְהַרְנוּ שֶׁאִם נִרְאֶה אֶחָד מִיִּשְׂרָאֵל שֶׁנָּפַל לוֹ חֲמוֹרוֹ אוֹ בְּהֵמָה אַחֶרֶת – **We are cautioned, that if we see a Jew whose donkey or other animal**[1] **has fallen,** מִכֹּבֶד הַמַּשָּׂא אוֹ בְּסִבָּה אַחֶרֶת – **due to the weight of its load or for some other reason,** אוֹ שֶׁהוּא בְּעַצְמוֹ רוֹבֵץ תַּחַת מַשָּׂאוֹ – **or,** if we see **that [our fellow Jew] has himself collapsed beneath his load,**[2] שֶׁלֹּא לְהַנִּיחוֹ בַּדֶּרֶךְ וְנֵלֵךְ – **that we not abandon him on the road and go** on our way. אֲבָל נַעַזְרֵהוּ וְנָקִים עִמּוֹ בְּהֶמְתּוֹ – **Rather, we must assist him and stand his animal up together with him,**[3] וְנַעֲמֹד שָׁם עַד שֶׁיְּתַקֵּן מַשָּׂאוֹ – **and remain there until he adjusts his load,** אוֹ עַל גַּבּוֹ אוֹ עַל בְּהֶמְתּוֹ – **either upon himself or upon his animal.**[4] וְעַל זֶה נֶאֱמַר ״לֹא תִרְאֶה אֶת חֲמוֹר אָחִיךָ וְגוֹ׳ ״ – **Regarding this it is stated** (*Deuteronomy* 22:4): ***You shall not see the donkey of your brother*** *or his ox falling on the road and hide yourself from them;* וְאָמְרוּ בְּסִפְרֵי – **and as [the Sages] have stated in *Sifrei*** (ad loc.):

NOTES

1. In Mitzvah 80 (at note 7; based on Mishnah, *Bava Kamma* 54b), Chinuch states that the verse of the mitzvah refers specifically to a donkey and an ox because these animals were commonly used for transporting loads. The mitzvah, however, applies to all animals. See next note; see also Mitzvah 541 note 1.

2. Although the verse speaks only of an animal that was overwhelmed by its load, Chinuch (from *Rambam, Sefer HaMitzvos, Lo Saaseh* 270; see also *Asei* 203) also applies this mitzvah to a *person* who is suffering beneath the load he is carrying. See also *Rambam's* list of the mitzvos in his introduction to *Mishneh Torah, Asei* 202; *Teshuvos HaRashba,* Vol. 1 §252 and 256-257. See, however, *Tos. Rabbeinu Peretz, Bava Kamma* 54b.

3. The verse concludes הָקֵם תָּקִים עִמּוֹ, *you shall surely stand them up "with him."* This indicates that one is required to *assist* the animal's owner. If, however, the owner is unwilling to participate in unloading or reloading the load, these mitzvos do not apply. Nevertheless, if the owner is not present, or if he is weak or infirm and unable to help, one is required to tend to the animal for him (*Rambam, Hil. Rotze'ach U'Shemiras HaNefesh* 13:8).

[In many instances, even when one is exempt from the mitzvah of assisting the owner, he is nevertheless obligated to help unload the animal, due to the obligation to alleviate an animal's pain (*tzaar baalei chaim*); see *Rama, Choshen Mishpat* 272:9. For further discussion of the laws of *tzaar baalei chaim,* see Mitzvah 550, at note 7, and Insight to Mitzvah 452. See also Insight to Mitzvah 80.]

4. Moreover, as Chinuch writes in Mitzvah 80 (at note 19), one is required to escort the traveler as he resumes his journey, to ensure that his animal will not falter further.

לֹא תִרְאֶה אֶת חֲמוֹר וְגוֹ׳, מִצְוַת לֹא תַעֲשֶׂה.

וְהִנֵּה הָעוֹבֵר עַל זֶה וְלֹא סִיֵּעַ חֲבֵרוֹ בַּדֶּרֶךְ עוֹבֵר עַל לֹא תַעֲשֶׂה זֶה, וְעַל עֲשֵׂה הַנִּזְכָּר בְּכֶסֶף תַּלְוֶה ג׳ בְּסִימָן ס״ח (מצוה פ׳)[6,5]**, וְשָׁם בֵּאַרְנוּ שֹׁרֶשׁ מִצְוָה זוֹ וְכָל עִנְיָנָהּ כְּמִנְהָגֵנוּ בְּסֵפֶר זֶה, תִּרְאֶנּוּ מִשָּׁם.**[7]

״לֹא תִרְאֶה אֶת חֲמוֹר וְגוֹ׳ ״ מִצְוַת לֹא תַעֲשֶׂה – ***You shall not see*** **etc., is a mitzvah-prohibition.** That is, the opening words of the verse are not merely introducing the mitzvah-obligation at the end of the verse, requiring one to assist in loading the animal. Rather, these words constitute an actual mitzvah-prohibition.

וְהִנֵּה הָעוֹבֵר עַל זֶה וְלֹא סִיֵּעַ חֲבֵרוֹ בַּדֶּרֶךְ – **Now, one who transgresses this** prohibition, **and does not assist his fellow** who is traveling **on the way, עוֹבֵר עַל לֹא תַעֲשֶׂה זֶה וְעַל עֲשֵׂה הַנִּזְכָּר בְּכֶסֶף תַּלְוֶה ג׳ בְּסִימָן סח** – **transgresses this mitzvah-prohibition, as well as the third mitzvah-obligation mentioned in** *Parashas Im* ***Kesef Talveh,*** **in Chapter 68** (Mitzvah 80),[5] the mitzvah of *perikah* (unloading).[6] **וְשָׁם בֵּאַרְנוּ שֹׁרֶשׁ מִצְוָה זוֹ וְכָל עִנְיָנָהּ** – **There,** in Mitzvah 80, **we explained the underlying purpose of this mitzvah, as well as its complete description, כְּמִנְהָגֵנוּ בְּסֵפֶר זֶה** – **as is our practice in this work; תִּרְאֶנּוּ מִשָּׁם** – **you can apply** here **[the information] that** you find **there.**[7]

NOTES

5. *Parashas Im Kesef* is the second part of *Parashas Mishpatim*; see Mitzvah 495 note 4. [Chinuch refers to Mitzvah 80 as Chapter 68 based on the original numbering of this work; see Mitzvah 494 note 4 and Mitzvah 538 note 46.]

6. From the fact that Chinuch here focuses specifically on a situation where one's fellow requires assistance *unloading* his animal (as is evident from Chinuch's citation of Mitzvah 80), commentators deduce that Chinuch maintains that the current mitzvah-prohibition applies only when one ignores the plight of the wayfarer who is in need of help in *unloading* his animal. It does not, however, apply if one ignores one's fellow's need for assistance in *reloading* the animal. Thus, one who fails to assist his fellow reload his animal has transgressed only a mitzvah-*obligation* – Mitzvah 541 (see *Minchas Chinuch* §1; *Maayan HaChochmah, Lo Saaseh* 324 [Roedelheim ed., p. 124a]). [This, however, requires further study, since the verse of this mitzvah is discussing *te'inah,* not *perikah*; see *Bava Metzia* 32a [end] (see *Minchas Chinuch* ibid.). See Insight.]

7. Literally, *see it from there.*

☙ Insight: The Mitzvah of Te'inah

At the end of this mitzvah, Chinuch writes that one who did not assist a wayfarer whose animal has faltered has not only transgressed this prohibition, but also failed to fulfill the mitzvah-obligation of *perikah,* the requirement to assist in unloading the burden of a faltering animal. This is based on *Rambam, Sefer HaMitzvos, Asei* 202 (see also *Mechilta* cited there in *Lo Saaseh* 270). It seems odd, however, that *Rambam* and Chinuch do not mention that he has transgressed the mitzvah-obligation of *te'inah,* the requirement to assist with *reloading* the animal, which is the subject of the continuation of this very verse; see *Bava Metzia* 32a and next mitzvah (see *Maayan HaChochmah, Lo Saaseh* 324 [Roedelheim ed., p. 124a]; *Minchas Chinuch* §1). This is even more puzzling considering the fact that, when presenting this prohibition, Chinuch (at notes 3-4), and *Rambam* (*Sefer HaMitzvos, Lo Saaseh* 270) do make mention of the obligation to perform *te'inah.* Now, although commentators (cited above, note 6) understand that our mitzvah-*prohibition* is not addressing one who fails to perform *te'inah,* there is no question that by failing to fulfill that requirement he has transgressed a mitzvah-*obligation* (i.e., *te'inah*)! Why, then, does Chinuch, when he writes that one who ignores the plight of the traveler transgresses this prohibition and the mitzvah-obligation of *perikah,* not mention that he also trangresses the mitzvah-obligation of *te'inah*?

This matter may be understood with an explanation offered by *Chasam Sofer* to this mitzvah (printed after his commentary to Tractate *Kesubos*), in resolution of a similar difficulty in *Rambam* in *Mishneh Torah. Rambam* (*Hil. Rotze'ach U'Shemiras HaNefesh* 13:2) writes that one who ignores the plight of a traveler in distress transgresses a mitzvah-obligation, as well as the prohibition against

ignoring him. Now, these words imply that one transgresses a *single* mitzvah-obligation. But why should he transgress only *one* mitzvah-obligation? When one sees a traveler in distress, he is obligated to perform *two* mitzvah-obligations: the mitzvah of *perikah* and the mitzvah of *te'inah*! [See *Minchas Chinuch* and *Maayan HaChochmah* ibid.; *Maaseh Roke'ach* to *Rambam* ad loc.] *Chasam Sofer* answers that while indeed one who assists the traveler unload and reload has fulfilled two mitzvos, nevertheless, one who neglects to do so, and leaves the traveler on his own, has transgressed only the obligation to assist with unloading. This is because the obligation to assist with reloading begins only *after* the animal has been unloaded. Thus, one who entirely ignores the traveler's plight has never incurred an obligation to *reload*. Accordingly, he has transgressed only one mitzvah-obligation. Therefore, while one is certainly obligated to perform *perikah* and then *te'inah*, *Rambam* and Chinuch do not include the mitzvah of *te'inah* among the mitzvos one transgresses by ignoring the traveler's plight, since one who totally ignores the traveler has transgressed only the mitzvos pertaining to *perikah,* as the mitzvah of *te'inah* does not begin until after the animal has been unloaded.

[For another approach, see *Yaskil Avdi*, Vol. 4, *Choshen Mishpat* 10:4. See also *Kiryas Sefer* to the cited *Rambam*.]

מִצְוָה תקמא: מִצְוַת הֲקָמַת מַשָּׂא לְיִשְׂרָאֵל

שֶׁנִּצְטַוִּינוּ לַעֲזוֹר אֶת אַחֵינוּ כְּשֶׁיִּהְיוּ צְרִיכִים לָתֵת הַמַּשָּׂא עַל הַבְּהֵמָה אוֹ עַל הָאִישׁ וְאֵין מִי שֶׁיַּעַזְרֵם עַל הַדָּבָר[1], וְעַל זֶה נֶאֱמַר (דברים כ״ב, ד׳) הָקֵם תָּקִים עִמּוֹ, וְזֶה יִקְרְאוּ זִכְרוֹנָם לִבְרָכָה טְעִינָה. וְאָמְרוּ זִכְרוֹנָם לִבְרָכָה (בבא מציעא ל״ב ע״א) שֶׁנּוֹטְלִין שָׂכָר עַל הַטְּעִינָה, אֲבָל עַל הַפְּרִיקָה, כְּלוֹמַר לַעֲזוֹר אֶת אָחִיו לִפְרוֹק הַמַּשָּׂא מֵעָלָיו אוֹ מֵעַל בְּהֶמְתּוֹ, הַחִיּוּב הַזֶּה הוּא עָלֵינוּ לַעֲשׂוֹתוֹ בְּחִנָּם[2].

וּמִשָּׁרְשֵׁי מִצְוָה זוֹ וּקְצָת דִּינֶיהָ כָּתַבְתִּי בְּמִצְוַת פְּרִיקָה בְּסֵדֶר אִם כֶּסֶף תַּלְוֶה עֲשֵׂה ג׳

Mitzvah 541
The Obligation to Help a Fellow Jew Reload a Burden

הָקֵם תָּקִים עִמּוֹ
You shall surely stand them up with him (*Deuteronomy* 22:4).

The Torah (Mitzvah 80) obligates a person to assist in unloading an animal that he encounters struggling beneath its load (*perikah;* see introduction to the previous mitzvah). This mitzvah obligates him to assist with reloading the animal (*te'inah*).

שֶׁנִּצְטַוִּינוּ לַעֲזוֹר אֶת אַחֵינוּ – **We are commanded to assist our brethren** כְּשֶׁיִּהְיוּ צְרִיכִים לָתֵת הַמַּשָּׂא עַל הַבְּהֵמָה אוֹ עַל הָאִישׁ – **when they need to place a load upon an animal or a person,** וְאֵין מִי שֶׁיַּעַזְרֵם עַל הַדָּבָר – **and there is nobody** else **who can assist him in this matter.**[1] וְעַל זֶה נֶאֱמַר – **Regarding this it is stated** (*Deuteronomy* 22:4): "הָקֵם תָּקִים עִמּוֹ" – ***you shall surely stand them up with him.*** וְזֶה יִקְרְאוּ זִכְרוֹנָם לִבְרָכָה טְעִינָה – **This is what [the Sages], of blessed memory, refer to as *te'inah.***

וְאָמְרוּ זִכְרוֹנָם לִבְרָכָה – **Now, [the Sages], of blessed memory, stated** (*Bava Metzia* 32a) שֶׁנּוֹטְלִין שָׂכָר עַל הַטְּעִינָה – **that compensation may be taken for *te'inah.*** אֲבָל עַל הַפְּרִיקָה – **However, with regard to *perikah,*** כְּלוֹמַר לַעֲזוֹר אֶת אָחִיו לִפְרוֹק הַמַּשָּׂא מֵעָלָיו אוֹ מֵעַל בְּהֶמְתּוֹ – **which is** the requirement **to help one's fellow remove a load from upon himself or from upon his animal,** הַחִיּוּב הַזֶּה הוּא עָלֵינוּ לַעֲשׂוֹתוֹ בְּחִנָּם – **that is an obligation we are required to perform without charge.**[2]

Underlying Purpose and Laws of the Mitzvah

וּמִשָּׁרְשֵׁי מִצְוָה זוֹ וּקְצָת דִּינֶיהָ כָּתַבְתִּי בְּמִצְוַת פְּרִיקָה – **I have written about the underlying purpose of this mitzvah, and some of its laws, in the mitzvah of *perikah,*** בְּסֵדֶר אִם כֶּסֶף תַּלְוֶה עֲשֵׂה ג׳

NOTES

1. With regard to the mitzvah of *perikah* (see Mitzvah 80, with note 3), Chinuch indicates that the obligation to assist one whose animal has faltered applies only in the case of a traveler who experiences distress while away from his home; presumably he is speaking of such a case here as well.

2. The Gemara (*Bava Metzia* 32a) derives this law through the following reasoning: Why is it necessary for the Torah to teach that there is a mitzvah of *perikah*? Why, if there is a mitzvah to assist with reloading an animal, when the animal is not suffering and there is no concern that it may die and the owner will incur a loss, certainly there must be an obligation to assist with unloading it, when these concerns exist! It must be that, with the mitzvah of *perikah,* the Torah wishes to impose an obligation that is greater than the mitzvah of *te'inah*; namely, that while one who assists with reloading an animal may charge for his services, if he assists with unloading the animal, he may not request compensation. [Nevertheless, one is entitled to a certain amount of compensation for his loss of income when performing *perikah* (see *Choshen Mishpat* 272:6 and 265:1 with commentaries for the particulars).]

With regard to whether one may accept compensation for *perikah* if it is offered, see *Perishah* and *Derishah, Choshen Mishpat* 272:11; *Sma* ad loc. §17.

בְּסִימָן ס"ח (מצוה פ')[3], וְכָל עִנְיָנָהּ תַּגִּיד עָלֶיהָ חֲבֶרְתָּהּ[4].

בְּסִימָן סח – in the third obligation listed in *Parashas Im Kesef Talveh,* Chapter 68 (Mitzvah 80).[3] **וְכָל עִנְיָנָהּ תַּגִּיד עָלֶיהָ חֲבֶרְתָּהּ – All of the particulars of [this mitzvah] will be** understood **through** the study of **its companion mitzvah.**[4]

NOTES

3. *Parashas Im Kesef* is the second part of *Parashas Mishpatim*; see Mitzvah 495 note 4. [Chinuch refers to Mitzvah 80 as Chapter 68 based on the original numbering of this work; see Mitzvah 494 note 4.]

4. Literally, *its comrade tells about it* (stylistic citation of *Job* 36:33).

מִצְוָה תקמב: שֶׁלֹּא תַעְדֶּה אִשָּׁה עֲדִי אִישׁ[1]

שֶׁלֹּא יִלְבְּשׁוּ הַנָּשִׁים מַלְבּוּשֵׁי הָאֲנָשִׁים וְלֹא יִזְדַּיְּנוּ בְּזִיּוּנָם, וְעַל זֶה נֶאֱמַר (דברים כ״ב, ה׳) לֹא יִהְיֶה כְלִי גֶבֶר עַל אִשָּׁה, וְתִרְגֵּם אֻנְקְלוֹס לָא יְהֵא תִקּוּן זֵין דִּגְבַר עַל אִתְּתָא[2]. וּמִן הַדּוֹמֶה כִּי מִפְּנֵי כֵן פֵּרֵשׁ הַכָּתוּב בִּכְלֵי זַיִן, לְפִי שֶׁהֵם הַכֵּלִים הַמְיֻחָדִים לְגַמְרֵי לַאֲנָשִׁים, שֶׁאֵין דֶּרֶךְ אִשָּׁה בָּעוֹלָם לָצֵאת בִּכְלֵי זַיִן[3], אֲבָל הוּא הַדִּין שֶׁאָסוּר לָהֶם מִדְּאוֹרַיְתָא

Mitzvah 542
The Prohibition Upon a Woman to Wear Men's Clothing

לֹא יִהְיֶה כְלִי גֶבֶר עַל אִשָּׁה
A man's apparel shall not be upon a woman (*Deuteronomy* 22:5)

The following two mitzvos discuss the prohibitions generally known as *lo yilbash*, which forbid one gender from wearing garments or accessories typically worn by the other gender. This mitzvah focuses on women wearing men's clothing, while the next mitzvah focuses on men wearing women's clothing.[1]

שֶׁלֹּא יִלְבְּשׁוּ הַנָּשִׁים מַלְבּוּשֵׁי הָאֲנָשִׁים – **Women are** commanded **not to wear men's clothes,** that is, garments that are typically worn only by men, וְלֹא יִזְדַּיְּנוּ בְּזִיּוּנָם – **and not to arm themselves with [men's] weapons,** such as a sword. וְעַל זֶה נֶאֱמַר – **Regarding this it is stated** (*Deuteronomy* 22:5): "לֹא יִהְיֶה כְלִי גֶבֶר עַל אִשָּׁה" – ***A man's apparel shall not be upon a woman,*** which refers not only to clothing but to any form of male accessories or gear, including weapons, וְתִרְגֵּם אֻנְקְלוֹס – **as Onkelos translated** this verse: לָא יְהֵא תִקּוּן זֵין דִּגְבַר עַל אִתְּתָא – ***"Weapons of a man shall not adorn a woman."***[2]

The word כְּלִי in the verse (usually translated as *utensil*) signifies a broad range of objects, including vessels, tools, clothing, etc. Accordingly, as indicated above, our prohibition encompasses any item typically worn by men — clothing, adornments, and weapons. Chinuch explains why Onkelos translated the term here as *specifically* referring to weapons:

וּמִן הַדּוֹמֶה כִּי מִפְּנֵי כֵן פֵּרֵשׁ הַכָּתוּב בִּכְלֵי זַיִן – **It seems that it is for the following** reason **that [Onkelos] explains the verse as referring to weapons:** לְפִי שֶׁהֵם הַכֵּלִים הַמְיֻחָדִים לְגַמְרֵי לַאֲנָשִׁים – It is **because they are the articles that are completely unique to men,** שֶׁאֵין דֶּרֶךְ אִשָּׁה בָּעוֹלָם לָצֵאת בִּכְלֵי זַיִן – **for it is not the way of** any **woman in the world to go out bearing weapons.** Thus, it is the most clear-cut example of the prohibition, since weapons are "unique to men" in every location. By contrast, other articles that are generally considered male garb are, in some locations, worn by women as well as men. This would make it permissible for women to wear them there.[3] Onkelos therefore chose the simple, universal, example. אֲבָל הוּא הַדִּין שֶׁאָסוּר לָהֶם מִדְּאוֹרַיְתָא

NOTES

1. The term *lo yilbash* is taken from the second half of our verse, וְלֹא יִלְבַּשׁ גֶּבֶר שִׂמְלַת אִשָּׁה, *and a man shall not wear (lo yilbash) a woman's garment*, which is the source of the next mitzvah, but it is colloquially used in regard to both mitzvah-prohibitions (see, for example, title of *Shulchan Aruch, Yoreh Deah* §182).

2. This reflects the opinion of R' Eliezer ben Yaakov in *Nazir* 59a, who maintains that the prohibitions of *lo yilbash* pertain not only to clothing, but to all types of adornments or other items typically worn or sported by the other gender. *Rambam* rules like R' Eliezer ben Yaakov in *Hil. Avodah Zarah* 12:10 (see also *Sefer HaMitzvos, Lo Saaseh* 39-40; for discussion of *Rambam's* ruling, see *Beis Yosef, Yoreh Deah* 182:5). *Rashi* to the verse, however, seems to follow the opinion of the Tanna Kamma in that Gemara, according to whom the Torah forbade only *disguising* oneself as a member of the opposite gender and mingling with them for promiscuous purposes (see *Mizrachi* ad loc.). In terms of practical halachah, *Shulchan Aruch* (*Yoreh Deah* 182:5) follows the ruling of *Rambam*, as per the opinion of R' Eliezer ben Yaakov; see also *Rama* ad loc.

3. As Chinuch will indicate immediately below and at the end of the mitzvah, what defines "male garb"

לָצֵאת בְּמַלְבּוּשִׁים שֶׁדֶּרֶךְ הָאֲנָשִׁים בְּאוֹתוֹ הַמָּקוֹם לְהִשְׁתַּמֵּשׁ בָּהֶם, כְּגוֹן שֶׁתָּשִׂים בְּרֹאשָׁהּ מִצְנֶפֶת אוֹ שְׁאָר כֵּלִים הַמְיֻחָדִים לְאִישׁ[4].

מִשָּׁרְשֵׁי הַמִּצְוָה לְהַרְחִיק מֵאֻמָּתֵנוּ הַקְּדוֹשָׁה דְּבַר עֶרְוָה וְכָל עִנְיָן וְכָל צַד שֶׁיִּהְיֶה הַכִּשָּׁלוֹן בְּאוֹתוֹ דָּבָר מָצוּי מִתּוֹכוֹ, וּכְעִנְיָן שֶׁיֹּאמְרוּ זִכְרוֹנָם לִבְרָכָה (סנהדרין צ״ג ע״א) עַל דֶּרֶךְ מָשָׁל, שֶׁאֱלֹקֵינוּ שׂוֹנֵא זִמָּה הוּא, כְּלוֹמַר שֶׁלְּאַהֲבָתֵנוּ הִרְחִיקָנוּ מִן הַזִּמָּה[5] שֶׁהִיא דָּבָר מְכֹעָר בְּיוֹתֵר וְיִקַּח לֵב הָאָדָם וּמַדִּיחוֹ מִדֶּרֶךְ טוֹבָה וּמַחֲשָׁבָה רְצוּיָה לְדֶרֶךְ רָעָה וּמַחֲשָׁבָה שֶׁל שְׁטוּת. וְאֵין סָפֵק כִּי אִם יִהְיוּ מַלְבּוּשֵׁי הָאֲנָשִׁים וְהַנָּשִׁים שָׁוִים, יִתְעָרְבוּ אֵלּוּ עִם אֵלּוּ תָּמִיד וּמָלְאָה הָאָרֶץ זִמָּה[6].

לָצֵאת בְּמַלְבּוּשִׁים שֶׁדֶּרֶךְ הָאֲנָשִׁים בְּאוֹתוֹ הַמָּקוֹם לְהִשְׁתַּמֵּשׁ בָּהֶם – **However, it is likewise Biblically forbidden for [women] to go out wearing clothing that, in that locale, is typically worn** only **by men;** even one article of clothing, כְּגוֹן שֶׁתָּשִׂים בְּרֹאשָׁהּ מִצְנֶפֶת – **such as to don a turban** (a typically male attire in those days) **on her head,** אוֹ שְׁאָר כֵּלִים הַמְיֻחָדִים לְאִישׁ – **or any other articles** of clothing or accessories **that are unique to men.**[4]

Underlying Purpose of the Mitzvah

מִשָּׁרְשֵׁי הַמִּצְוָה – **Among the underlying purposes of the mitzvah** is לְהַרְחִיק מֵאֻמָּתֵנוּ הַקְּדוֹשָׁה דְּבַר עֶרְוָה – **to keep immorality away from our holy nation,** וְכָל עִנְיָן וְכָל צַד שֶׁיִּהְיֶה הַכִּשָּׁלוֹן בְּאוֹתוֹ דָּבָר מָצוּי מִתּוֹכוֹ – **and** thus to forbid **any matter and any situation through which** it is **common** for people to experience **failure in that area.** וּכְעִנְיָן שֶׁיֹּאמְרוּ זִכְרוֹנָם לִבְרָכָה עַל דֶּרֶךְ מָשָׁל – This is **along the lines of what [the Sages], of blessed memory, stated** (*Sanhedrin* 93a), **by way of a metaphor,** שֶׁאֱלֹקֵינוּ שׂוֹנֵא זִמָּה הוּא – **that our God hates immorality,** כְּלוֹמַר שֶׁלְּאַהֲבָתֵנוּ הִרְחִיקָנוּ מִן הַזִּמָּה – **which is to say, that out of His love for us, He distanced us from immorality,**[5] שֶׁהִיא דָּבָר מְכֹעָר בְּיוֹתֵר – **as it is a most ugly thing.** וְיִקַּח לֵב הָאָדָם – **Furthermore, it grabs a man's heart,** וּמַדִּיחוֹ מִדֶּרֶךְ טוֹבָה וּמַחֲשָׁבָה רְצוּיָה לְדֶרֶךְ רָעָה וּמַחֲשָׁבָה שֶׁל שְׁטוּת – **and makes him stray from a good path and a desirable mindset onto a bad path and a mindset of folly.** The Torah therefore forbade not only acts of immorality, but even things that might lead to immorality. וְאֵין סָפֵק כִּי אִם יִהְיוּ מַלְבּוּשֵׁי הָאֲנָשִׁים וְהַנָּשִׁים שָׁוִים – **And there is no doubt that if men and women would wear similar clothing,** יִתְעָרְבוּ אֵלּוּ עִם אֵלּוּ תָּמִיד – it would lead to a situation where **they would constantly mingle with each other,** וּמָלְאָה הָאָרֶץ זִמָּה – **and the land would be full of immorality.**[6] By forbidding the genders from dressing like each other

---

NOTES

in regard to our prohibition [as well as what defines "female garb" in regard to the prohibition with respect to men] depends on local norms (see also *Rambam, Sefer HaMitzvos* and *Hil. Avodah Zarah* ibid.; *Teshuvos HaRashba*, Vol. V §121; *Shulchan Aruch* ibid.; for what defines "local norms," see note 9 below). It is thus possible that a certain article of clothing is typically worn by men around the world, but in some places it is worn by women as well. In those places, our prohibition would not apply. Weapons, on the other hand, are an example of "male garb" to which the prohibition is relevant everywhere, since no woman in the world goes out bearing weapons. [When it is necessary for a woman to carry a weapon for her safety, it may be permissible; see *Terumas HaDeshen, Teshuvos* §197, and *Igros Moshe, Orach Chaim* IV §75.]

4. See *Rambam, Hil. Avodah Zarah* 12:10; *Shulchan Aruch* ibid. 182:5 with *Rama*.

At the beginning of the mitzvah, Chinuch stated that the prohibition is for women to *wear* male garb, but here he phrases the issue as *going out* with male garb, which would seem to imply that there is no prohibition against women wearing such garments in private. *Panim Yafos* (to our verse) indeed maintains that the prohibition for women to wear male garb applies only if she walks among men while dressed in that fashion. [Regardless, *Panim Yafos* says this only regarding women wearing men's clothing, not vice versa, as he himself makes clear.] In practice, the halachic authorities forbid a woman from wearing men's garb even in private; see *Teshuvos BeTzeil HaChochmah,* Vol. 5 §126, and *Teshuvos Minchas Yitzchak,* Vol. 2 §108.

5. Presumably, Chinuch says, "by way of a metaphor," because the Sages used an emotion (hate) with respect to Hashem.

6. Stylistic citation of *Leviticus* 19:29.

וְעוֹד אָמְרוּ בְּטַעַם מִצְוָה זוֹ שֶׁהִיא לְהַרְחִיק כָּל עִנְיַן עֲבוֹדָה זָרָה שֶׁדַּרְכָּן שֶׁל עוֹבְדֵי עֲבוֹדָה זָרָה הָיָה בְּכָךְ. וְאֵלֶּה שְׁנֵי הַטְּעָמִים מְצָאתִים בְּסִפְרֵי הָרַמְבַּ"ם ז"ל אַחַר כָּתְבִי אוֹתָם[7].

דִּינֵי הַמִּצְוָה קְצָרִים, בִּפְשַׁט הַכְּתוּבִים הֵם נִכְלָלִים[8].

וְנוֹהֵג אִסּוּר זֶה בְּכָל מָקוֹם וּבְכָל זְמַן[9] בִּנְקֵבוֹת. וְאִשָּׁה הָעוֹבֶרֶת עַל זֶה וְלָבְשָׁה הַמַּלְבּוּשִׁים הַמְיֻחָדִים בַּאֲנָשִׁים לְבַד בְּאוֹתוֹ הַמָּקוֹם שֶׁהִיא בּוֹ, חַיֶּבֶת מַלְקוּת[10].

(even in regard to one article of clothing), the Torah ensures a separation between the genders and an atmosphere of purity and holiness.

Chinuch provides a second underlying purpose to the mitzvah:

וְעוֹד אָמְרוּ בְּטַעַם מִצְוָה זוֹ – It has further been said regarding the reason for this mitzvah **שֶׁהִיא לְהַרְחִיק כָּל עִנְיַן עֲבוֹדָה זָרָה – that it is to distance any matter of idolatry,** **שֶׁדַּרְכָּן שֶׁל עוֹבְדֵי עֲבוֹדָה זָרָה הָיָה בְּכָךְ – for that was the mode** of conduct **of idolaters** in earlier times, to wear clothing or gear worn by the opposite gender. **וְאֵלֶּה שְׁנֵי הַטְּעָמִים מְצָאתִים בְּסִפְרֵי הָרַמְבַּ"ם ז"ל אַחַר כָּתְבִי אוֹתָם – I found these two reasons in the books of *Rambam*, of blessed memory, after I wrote them** here.[7]

Laws of the Mitzvah

דִּינֵי הַמִּצְוָה קְצָרִים – The laws of the mitzvah are brief; **בִּפְשַׁט הַכְּתוּבִים הֵם נִכְלָלִים – they are covered by the simple meaning of the Scriptural verses.**[8]

Applicability of the Mitzvah

וְנוֹהֵג אִסּוּר זֶה בְּכָל מָקוֹם וּבְכָל זְמַן – This prohibition applies in every location and in all times,[9] **בִּנְקֵבוֹת** – and only **to women,** for it is they who are commanded not to wear male garb. **וְאִשָּׁה הָעוֹבֶרֶת עַל זֶה – A woman who transgresses this** prohibition **וְלָבְשָׁה הַמַּלְבּוּשִׁים הַמְיֻחָדִים בַּאֲנָשִׁים לְבַד בְּאוֹתוֹ הַמָּקוֹם שֶׁהִיא בּוֹ – and dons garments** or accessories **that are unique to men alone in the locale where she is** at that time **חַיֶּבֶת מַלְקוּת – is liable to *malkus*.**[10]

NOTES

7. See *Moreh Nevuchim* 3:37 (with *Shem Tov* §4 ad loc.), and *Sefer HaMitzvos, Lo Saaseh* 40. [In *Moreh Nevuchim* (ibid.), *Rambam* cites a book of idolatry that urges men to wear colorful, feminine garments when their horoscope sign coincides with Venus, and women to don weapons and armor when their horoscope coincides with Mars.]

Teshuvos Arugas HaBosem (*Yoreh Deah* 138:4) notes that the two reasons provided by *Rambam* and Chinuch are alluded to in the conclusion of our verse: *for it is an "abomination" unto HASHEM your God [that is perpetrated by] whoever does these things.* Both immorality and idolatry are deemed an "abomination" in the Torah; see *Leviticus* 18:26-30 and *Deuteronomy* 7:26, respectively. *Arugas HaBosem* (ibid.) suggests that there is a practical difference between the two reasons (see there). However, *Minchas Chinuch* (543:3) maintains that we cannot determine the practical halachos of the mitzvah based on the reasons proposed by the Rishonim. Both reasons may be true, and there may be other reasons that *Rambam* and Chinuch did not mention (see also *Teshuvos Minchas Yitzchak* ibid.).

8. In the next mitzvah, however, Chinuch mentions that some laws are discussed in Tractate *Nazir* (59a), which is equally relevant to this mitzvah. The laws of this mitzvah are codified in *Rambam, Hil. Avodah Zarah* 12:10, and in *Shulchan Aruch, Yoreh Deah* 182:5.

9. I.e., in Eretz Yisrael and the Diaspora, and whether the *Beis HaMikdash* is standing or not.

10. The halachic authorities debate whether a garment is deemed to be particular to men or women based on the manner in which *Jews* dress, or perhaps even if non-Jews of both genders wear a certain garment, it is considered to be gender-neutral and Jews of either gender may wear it. See *Perishah, Yoreh Deah* 182:5; *Teshuvos Levushei Mordechai* (Vol. 1, *Yoreh Deah* §100 ד"ה בדבר); *Teshuvos Maharsham* (Vol. 2 §243 והנה מ"ש); *Seridei Aish* (Vol. 2, end of §81).

The halachic authorities also debate whether it is permitted to wear the clothing of the other gender if there is no intent to look like the other gender. For example, if it is raining and the only available coat is one that belongs to the other gender. See *Bach, Taz, and Shach, Yoreh Deah* 182:5; *Yad HaKetanah, Hil. Avodah Zarah* Ch. 6 §82 (p. 279b) and *Chochmas Adam* 90:3, *Binas Adam* §74; *Igros Moshe, Yoreh Deah* II §61 ד"ה ובאם כוונת צביעתו. A related dispute pertains to dressing like the other gender on Purim or other festive occasions. See *Rama, Orach Chaim* 696:8 with *Mishnah Berurah* ad loc. §30; *Aruch HaShulchan, Orach Chaim* 696:12; *Teshuvos Be'er Moshe*, Vol. 8, §7-8. [See also Insight to the next mitzvah for another related dispute.]

מִצְוָה תקמג: שֶׁלֹּא יַעְדֶּה הָאִישׁ עֲדִי אִשָּׁה

שֶׁלֹּא יִלְבְּשׁוּ הָאֲנָשִׁים מַלְבּוּשֵׁי הַנָּשִׁים, וְעַל זֶה נֶאֱמַר (דברים כ״ב, ה׳) וְלֹא יִלְבַּשׁ גֶּבֶר שִׂמְלַת אִשָּׁה.

מִשָּׁרְשֵׁי הַמִּצְוָה מַה שֶּׁכָּתוּב בַּמִּצְוָה הַקּוֹדֶמֶת.

דִּינֵי הַמִּצְוָה מַה שֶּׁאָמְרוּ זִכְרוֹנָם לִבְרָכָה (נזיר נ״ט ע״א; מכות כ׳ ע״ב) שֶׁאֵין הָאִסּוּר וְהַמַּלְקוּת בִּלְבוּשׁ לְבַד, דְּהוּא הַדִּין בְּתִקּוּן שֶׁלָּהֶם, שֶׁכָּל הַמְתַקֵּן עַצְמוֹ בְּתִקּוּנִים הַמְיֻחָדִים לַנָּשִׁים חַיָּב מַלְקוּת, כְּגוֹן הַמְלַקֵּט שְׂעָרוֹת לְבָנוֹת מִתּוֹךְ שְׁחוֹרוֹת מֵרֹאשׁוֹ אוֹ מִזְּקָנוֹ, וְכֵן הַצּוֹבֵעַ שַׂעֲרוֹתָיו כְּדֶרֶךְ שֶׁנָּשִׁים צוֹבְעוֹת אוֹתָן[1], וְכֵן תִּרְגֵּם אֻנְקְלוֹס וְלָא יְתַקַּן גְּבַר

Mitzvah 543
The Prohibition Upon a Man to Wear Women's Clothing

וְלֹא יִלְבַּשׁ גֶּבֶר שִׂמְלַת אִשָּׁה
And a man shall not wear a woman's garment (*Deuteronomy* 22:5)

This mitzvah is the counterpart to the previous mitzvah, which prohibits women to wear men's clothing. Chinuch taught there that the prohibition upon women to wear men's clothing is not limited to clothing, but includes male accessories and gear, as well. As Chinuch will indicate below, the prohibition upon men to wear women's clothing is also not limited to clothing alone. Aside from feminine accessories, the mitzvah-prohibition includes even grooming practices that women typically engage in to beautify themselves.

As mentioned in the introduction to the previous mitzvah, these two mitzvah-prohibitions are colloquially referred to as "the (general) prohibition of *lo yilbash*," based on the verse of our mitzvah.

שֶׁלֹּא יִלְבְּשׁוּ הָאֲנָשִׁים מַלְבּוּשֵׁי הַנָּשִׁים – **Men are** commanded **not to wear women's clothing.** וְעַל זֶה נֶאֱמַר – **Regarding this it is stated** (*Deuteronomy* 22:5): "וְלֹא יִלְבַּשׁ גֶּבֶר שִׂמְלַת אִשָּׁה" – ***And a man shall not wear a woman's garment.***

Underlying Purpose of the Mitzvah

מִשָּׁרְשֵׁי הַמִּצְוָה – **Among the underlying purposes of the mitzvah** מַה שֶּׁכָּתוּב בַּמִּצְוָה הַקּוֹדֶמֶת – are **[the two reasons] cited in the previous mitzvah** regarding the prohibition upon women to wear men's clothing. The reasons proposed there apply to both prohibitions.

Laws of the Mitzvah

דִּינֵי הַמִּצְוָה – **The laws of the mitzvah** include מַה שֶּׁאָמְרוּ זִכְרוֹנָם לִבְרָכָה – **that which [the Sages], of blessed memory, indicated** (*Nazir* 59a; *Makkos* 20b), שֶׁאֵין הָאִסּוּר וְהַמַּלְקוּת בִּלְבוּשׁ לְבַד – **that the prohibition** of wearing women's clothing, **and the *malkus*** for violating this prohibition, **are not limited to clothing;** דְּהוּא הַדִּין בְּתִקּוּן שֶׁלָּהֶם – **the same applies to** any type of **grooming** practice that is typical **of [women].** שֶׁכָּל הַמְתַקֵּן עַצְמוֹ בְּתִקּוּנִים הַמְיֻחָדִים לַנָּשִׁים חַיָּב מַלְקוּת – That is to say, **that any** man **who grooms himself by means of cosmetic practices that are unique to women is liable to *malkus*.** כְּגוֹן הַמְלַקֵּט שְׂעָרוֹת לְבָנוֹת מִתּוֹךְ שְׁחוֹרוֹת מֵרֹאשׁוֹ אוֹ מִזְּקָנוֹ – **For example, if he plucks white hairs from among** the **dark** hairs **of his head or of his beard,** וְכֵן הַצּוֹבֵעַ שַׂעֲרוֹתָיו כְּדֶרֶךְ שֶׁנָּשִׁים צוֹבְעוֹת אוֹתָן – **or if he dyes his hair in the manner that women dye theirs.**[1] וְכֵן תִּרְגֵּם אֻנְקְלוֹס – **Onkelos,** too, **translated** the verse **in this vein:** וְלָא יְתַקַּן גְּבַר

NOTES

1. See *Rambam, Hil. Avodah Zarah* 12:10; cf. *Raavad* cited in note 7 below. Regarding the example of dyeing

בְּתִקּוּנֵי אִתְּתָא. וּמַה שֶּׁאָמְרוּ זִכְרוֹנָם לִבְרָכָה שֶׁטֻּמְטוּם וְאַנְדְּרוֹגִינוּס[2] אֵינוֹ עוֹטֵף רֹאשׁוֹ כְּאִשָּׁה וְאֵינוֹ מְגַלֵּחַ רֹאשׁוֹ כְּאִישׁ[3] וְאִם עָשָׂה כֵּן אֵינוֹ לוֹקֶה, וְכֵן בְּכָל מָקוֹם נוֹתְנִין עֲלֵיהֶם חֻמְרֵי הָאֲנָשִׁים וְהַנָּשִׁים[4], וְאִם עָבְרוּ אֵינָם לוֹקִין לְפִי שֶׁהֵן סָפֵק[5], אֲבָל אִם עָבְרוּ בְּאִסּוּר שֶׁאִישׁ וְאִשָּׁה שָׁוִין בּוֹ בָּזֶה אֵין צָרִיךְ לוֹמַר שֶׁלּוֹקִין עָלָיו.

בְּתִקּוּנֵי אִתְּתָא – "And a man shall not groom himself with the cosmetic practices of a woman."

The previous mitzvah prohibits a woman to dress as a man or to adorn herself with a weapon, and our mitzvah forbids a man to dress or groom himself in the manner of a woman. Chinuch now discusses the law regarding people whose halachic status as male or female is in doubt:

וּמַה שֶּׁאָמְרוּ זִכְרוֹנָם לִבְרָכָה – Another law **is that which [the Sages], of blessed memory, stated** (see *Rambam, Hil. Avodah Zarah* 12:10, and 12:4), **שֶׁטֻּמְטוּם וְאַנְדְּרוֹגִינוּס אֵינוֹ עוֹטֵף רֹאשׁוֹ כְּאִשָּׁה – that a *tumtum* or an *androgynus*[2] may not wrap his head in the manner of a woman** (i.e., he may not wear a head covering that is typically worn only by women), since he may in fact be male. **וְאֵינוֹ מְגַלֵּחַ רֹאשׁוֹ כְּאִישׁ – He also may not shave his head** (i.e., cut his hair) **like a man,** since he may in fact be female.[3] **וְאִם עָשָׂה כֵּן אֵינוֹ לוֹקֶה – However,** although both of these acts are prohibited to these types of people, **if one does so he does not incur *malkus*,** for it is not certain that he sinned, since he may actually be of the gender to whom the clothing or the practice is appropriate. **וְכֵן בְּכָל מָקוֹם – And so it is in all places,** that is, with regard to all matters that apply only to men or only to women: **נוֹתְנִין עֲלֵיהֶם חֻמְרֵי הָאֲנָשִׁים וְהַנָּשִׁים – we impose the stringencies of** both **men and women upon [the *tumtum* and the *androgynous*];[4]** **וְאִם עָבְרוּ אֵינָם לוֹקִין – yet, if they transgress** and do not follow these stringencies, **they do not incur *malkus*** (if *malkus* is relevant), **לְפִי שֶׁהֵן סָפֵק – because their** halachic **status** as a male or female **is in doubt,** and, as such, we cannot be sure that they, in fact, violated any prohibition.[5] **אֲבָל אִם עָבְרוּ בְּאִסּוּר שֶׁאִישׁ וְאִשָּׁה שָׁוִין בּוֹ – However, if they transgress a prohibition in which men and women are equally** forbidden (for example, the prohibition to wear *shaatnez* [Mitzvah 551]), such that no matter which gender they are, they are bound by the prohibition, **בָּזֶה אֵין צָרִיךְ לוֹמַר שֶׁלּוֹקִין עָלָיו** – then, **in that** case, **it goes without saying that they incur *malkus* for it.**

NOTES

hair, which appears in *Rambam* (ibid.) but is not mentioned in the Gemara (*Makkos* 20b), see *Kesef Mishneh* ad loc.; *Igros Moshe*, *Yoreh Deah* I §82 ד״ה ומסתבר. For other examples of cosmetic practices that are unique to women and may thus be included in the mitzvah-prohibition, see *Rosh's* commentary to *Nazir* 59a (cf. *Rambam* ibid. 12:9; see discussion in *Beis Yosef, Yoreh Deah* 182:5).

Chinuch's language "in the manner that women dye their hair" implies that a man *may* dye his hair in a manner that is *not* typical of women. Accordingly, since women typically dye their white hairs to match their natural hair color in order to look younger, a man is prohibited to do the same. However, he would be allowed to dye his hair white (or gray) in order to look more distinguished, since women would never dye their hair in that fashion (see *Beis Yosef, Yoreh Deah* §182; *Taz, Yoreh Deah* 182:7; see also Insight).

2. A *tumtum* is one whose gender cannot be ascertained. An *androgynos* is a person who possesses the signs of both genders (a hermaphrodite), whose halachic status as either a man or a woman remains unresolved by the Sages (see *Bikkurim* Ch. 4).

3. *Rambam's* ruling, which Chinuch cites here, seems puzzling: If an *androgynus* or *tumtum* may not dress like a woman *or* like a man, who *should* he dress like?! Notably, *Rama* (*Yoreh Deah* 182:5) cites only the first half of *Rambam's* ruling, that an *androgynus* or a *tumtum* must not wrap his head like a woman, but omits the part about not cutting his hair like a man (see, however, *Shach* ad loc.). For discussion and possible explanations of *Rambam's* ruling, see *Yad HaKetanah* (*Hil. Avodah Zarah* Ch. 6 §82.); *Chadrei Deah, Yoreh Deah* §182; and *Chasdei David* to *Tosefta, Bikkurim* 2:3, end.

4. Thus, they may not remove their sideburns (Mitzvah 251) or shave their beards with a razor (Mitzvah 252), although these prohibitions apply only to men. Similarly, if they are children of a Kohen, they may not contract *tumah* from a corpse (Mitzvah 263), a prohibition limited to male Kohanim. On the other hand, they are forbidden to partake of *kodshei kodashim* (most-holy offerings), which may be eaten only by male Kohanim (see Mitzvah 201 note 20). For other examples, see Mishnah, *Bikkurim* 4:2-3.

5. *Rambam* ibid. 12:4.

וְיֶתֶר פְּרָטֶיהָ מְבֹאָרִים בְּמַסֶּכֶת נָזִיר פֶּרֶק שְׁנֵי נְזִירִים (נ״ט ע״א)[6].

וְנוֹהֵג אִסּוּר זֶה בְּכָל מָקוֹם וּבְכָל זְמַן[7] בִּזְכָרִים.

וְעוֹבֵר עַל זֶה וְלָבַשׁ מַלְבּוּשֵׁי הַנָּשִׁים אוֹ שֶׁתִּקֵּן עַצְמוֹ בְּתִקּוּנֵי הַנָּשִׁים כְּגוֹן שֶׁלִּקֵּט שְׂעָרוֹת לְבָנוֹת מִתּוֹךְ שְׁחוֹרוֹת אוֹ שֶׁצָּבַע אֲפִלּוּ שַׂעֲרָה אַחַת, חַיָּב מַלְקוּת מִשֶּׁיְּלַקֵּט אוֹתָהּ אוֹ יִצְבָּעֶנָּה[8].

וְיֶתֶר פְּרָטֶיהָ – The above laws **and the remaining details of [this mitzvah]** **מְבֹאָרִים בְּמַסֶּכֶת נָזִיר פֶּרֶק שְׁנֵי נְזִירִים** – **are set forth in Tractate *Nazir*, Chapter *Shnei Nezirim*** (59a).[6]

Applicability of the Mitzvah

וְנוֹהֵג אִסּוּר זֶה בְּכָל מָקוֹם וּבְכָל זְמַן – **This prohibition applies in every location and in all times,**[7] **בִּזְכָרִים** – and only **to men,** for it is they who are forbidden to dress or groom themselves like women. **וְעוֹבֵר עַל זֶה** – **One who transgresses this** prohibition **וְלָבַשׁ מַלְבּוּשֵׁי הַנָּשִׁים** – **and wears garments of women** has violated this mitzvah and is liable to *malkus*. **אוֹ שֶׁתִּקֵּן עַצְמוֹ בְּתִקּוּנֵי הַנָּשִׁים** – **Similarly, if one** transgresses this prohibition and **grooms himself by means of cosmetic practices** that are typical **of women,** **כְּגוֹן שֶׁלִּקֵּט שְׂעָרוֹת לְבָנוֹת מִתּוֹךְ שְׁחוֹרוֹת** – **for example, he plucked white hairs from among dark** ones on his head or beard, **אוֹ שֶׁצָּבַע אֲפִלּוּ שַׂעֲרָה אַחַת** – **or he dyed** his hair, **even** if only **one hair,** **חַיָּב מַלְקוּת מִשֶּׁיְּלַקֵּט אוֹתָהּ אוֹ יִצְבָּעֶנָּה** – **he is liable to *malkus* as soon as he plucks [that one hair] or dyes it.**[8]

NOTES

6. See also *Makkos* 20b and *Shabbos* 94b. The laws of the mitzvah are codified in *Rambam, Hil. Avodah Zarah* 12:9-10, and in *Shulchan Aruch, Yoreh Deah* §182 as well as 156:2.

7. I.e. in Eretz Yisrael and the Diaspora, and whether the *Beis HaMikdash* is standing or not.

8. *Rambam* ibid. 12:10. That is to say, that even if a person has many white hairs on his head, such that plucking one hair has no visible impact on his appearance, he is liable as soon as he plucks out the first hair. The reason for this is that, although plucking out one hair in this case does not *accomplish* one's goal of looking younger, it is still an *act* of female beautification (see *Beis Yosef, Yoreh Deah* 182:6).

Raavad (ad loc.) disagrees with this ruling, but the commentators differ in their interpretation of his argument. Some understand *Raavad* as saying that, indeed, plucking or dyeing even a single white hair is Biblically prohibited, but one does not receive *malkus* unless he plucks or dyes enough hairs to make a difference in his appearance (*Teshuvos Mahari Ashkenazi, Yoreh Deah* §19; *Erech Shai, Yoreh Deah* 182:6; and *Teshuvos Divrei Chaim*, Vol. II, *Yoreh Deah* §62). Others explain *Raavad* as saying that plucking just one hair is forbidden only by *Rabbinic* decree, so there is no *malkus* for it (*Aruch LaNer* to *Makkos* 20b ד״ה בחול אסור, and *Erech Shai* to *Yoreh Deah* 182:6). Finally, some maintain that, according to *Raavad*, the entire matter of a man grooming himself like a woman is a Rabbinic decree, so even if one dyes *all* of his hair he would not incur *malkus* (*Teshuvos Levush Mordechai, Yoreh Deah* 24:2; *Teshuvos Minchas Elazar* Vol. 4 §23; see also *Mas'as HaMelech* to *Rambam* ibid. [§75]). According to *Teshuvos Avnei Zikaron* (Pfeffer), Vol. III 39:1, *Kesef Mishneh* (to *Rambam* ibid.) proposes the first and third explanations as the possible intention of *Raavad*. For further discussion, see Insight.

☙ Insight: The Debate Regarding the Man With the Half-White Beard

Chinuch taught that our prohibition is not limited to men wearing women's clothing, but includes also a man grooming himself in ways that are typical of women. For example, if a man's hair turns white, he may not dye it black (i.e., his original hair color) or pluck out individual white hairs, since this is a feminine grooming practice. The halachic authorities debate whether an exception can be made in cases where a man's white hair makes it difficult for him to find a marriage partner or a job, or where it causes him great embarrassment.

Darchei Teshuvah (*Yoreh Deah* 182:17) writes about a young rabbi in his time (late 1800's) whose hair and beard turned entirely white on one side, while his other side remained entirely black. Naturally, his unusual appearance attracted attention wherever he went, and this caused him great

embarrassment. He turned to all the great halachic authorities of his generation, asking if he was permitted to dye the white half of his hair so that he would regain his normal appearance. As can be inferred from a reading of the responsa (cited below), two primary arguments were made in favor of allowing him to dye his hair.

First, several statements of the Rishonim indicate that a man may employ cosmetic practices that are typically used by women if his appearance is embarrassing to him. For example, a Baraisa cited in *Shabbos* (50b) states that a man may not scrape crusts of filth or crusts of a wound from his skin in order to beautify himself, as that is a transgression of *lo yilbash* (*Rashi* ad loc.). Nevertheless, if these scabs cause him discomfort, he is permitted to remove them. *Tosafos* (ad loc. ד"ה בשביל צערו) note that "discomfort" refers not only to physical discomfort, but to emotional discomfort as well, such as being embarrassed to appear in public. So too, it was argued, the man with the half-white beard should be allowed to dye his hair black, as his unusual appearance was clearly causing him great emotional distress (see *Teshuvos Mahari Ashkenazi, Yoreh Deah* §19; *Minchas Pittim, Yoreh Deah* §182; *Seridei Eish*, Vol. II 81:2 [Mosad HaRav Kook ed., 2003]).

Another case for leniency made at the time was based on *Teshuvos HaRashba* (Vol. V §271, cited by *Beis Yosef, Yoreh Deah* 182:4), who says that, although it is forbidden for a man to shave his armpits or pubic hair, as that is a feminine practice, it is permissible to do this for medical purposes (e.g., the individual has a rash in that area). *Rashba's* initially reasons that there is a specific permit for medical situations, but then he states a more general concept: whenever the cosmetic act is performed for a purpose other than beautification, it is not defined as a feminine practice and is therefore permitted. As such, the case was made that since the purpose of dyeing the hair black in this instance was not for beautification (i.e., to look younger), but to prevent humiliation, it should be permitted (see *Shoel U'Meishiv*, Vol. I §210; see related discussions in note 10 of the previous mitzvah).

Some of the authorities, however, refuted these arguments. Regarding the first reasoning, some contended that the embarrassment caused by the half-white beard does not compare to the humiliation a person might experience from having crusted wounds or filth on his skin. The latter is a condition that is repulsive and disgusting to people, and is a very real concern. The former, on the other hand, is a passing curiosity. People may initially find the half-white/half-black beard amusing or perhaps bizarre, but they generally become accustomed to it, and then it no longer causes embarrassment (*Teshuvos Mahari Ashkenazi* ibid.; see, however, *Minchas Elazar*, Vol. IV §23).

With respect to the second reasoning (the one based on *Teshuvos HaRashba*), some pointed out that shaving one's armpits, even when done for beautification purposes, is forbidden only due to a Rabbinic decree; it is not included in the Biblical prohibition (see *Rambam, Hil. Avodah Zarah* 12:9). Since it is a Rabbinic decree, they forbade shaving the armpits only when one's intention is to beautify himself like a woman. Dyeing hair, on the other hand, is a type of feminine embellishment that is forbidden on a Biblical level, as *Rambam* indicates (ibid. 12:10) [and as Chinuch teaches, as well]. An act that is prohibited on a *Biblical* level is prohibited regardless of one's intention. So, although the individual with the half-white beard was not seeking to look younger, but to avoid embarrassment, he would still not be allowed to dye his hair black (*Sho'el U'Meishiv* ibid.). [*Sho'el U'Meishiv* acknowledges, however, that although *Rambam* clearly holds that it is Biblically forbidden for a man to dye his hair black, the majority of halachic authorities maintain that it is only a Rabbinic decree (among them, possibly *Raavad*, see note 8). According to them, *Rashba's* principle should apply to dyeing hair, as well.]

After deliberating the two sides, *Shoel U'Meishiv* seems to lean toward a strict ruling, but concedes that one *may* rely on the majority who say that dyeing hair for a man is only a Rabbinic decree and, accordingly, he may dye his hair black under these circumstances (see also *Minchas Elazar* ibid.). Other authorities maintained that the man's predicament was not grounds for leniency. As an alternative to dyeing the white half of his hair *black*, they suggested that he dye the black half of his hair *white*, turning *completely* white. As indicated in note 1, the prohibition states that one may not dye his hair "in the manner that women do," which is to return it to its original color in order to look younger, or to change it to a more attractive color. No woman, however, would dye her hair *white*, so there is no issue whatsoever with a man dyeing his hair white (*Erech Shai, Yoreh Deah* 182:6; *Mahari Ashkenazi* ibid.; *Divrei Chaim*, Vol. II, *Yoreh Deah* 62). Others add that any color that women

would generally not use to dye their hair is permissible (*Maharam Schik, Yoreh Deah* §173; see *Sdei Chemed, Maareches HaLamed* §116 ד״ה ולא ילבש ff.).

Thus far, the arguments for permitting the dyeing of the half-white beard were based on the premise that, as far as the actual act is concerned, it is an act of "feminine beautification" (since it is generally unique to women), except that there is place for leniency due to the embarrassment the person is experiencing, or because one's intention is not for beautification (see above). *Teshuvos Avnei Zikaron* (Vol. III, 39:6) posits, however, that dyeing the half-white beard is *inherently* different from the typical circumstance in which women dye their hair. Women typically dye their hair as they grow older and their hair begins to turn grey or white, or if they want their hair to have a different color. What the dyeing does is create an *unnatural* appearance for the woman — naturally, she would look her age, and the dye makes her look younger; or the dye changes her natural hair color. That is the definition of beautification: it comes to *improve* one's natural appearance. In the case at hand, however, the man was not interested in looking differently than his natural appearance. On the contrary, he was a young man who naturally had dark hair, but whose hair unnaturally turned white. Changing it back to its original color is not beautification at all; it is merely removing an imperfection. *Avnei Zikaron* argues that it should therefore be permitted. [*Avnei Zikaron* addresses the Baraisa in *Shabbos* 50b, which seems to indicate that removing scabs *is* a transgression of *lo yilbash* unless it causes one discomfort. He explains that, in fact, the accepted ruling follows a second Baraisa cited there in the Gemara, according to which anything done simply to maintain a person's natural appearance (e.g., getting rid of a wart or a pimple) is permissible.]

With regard to dyeing one's hair in order to make it easier to find a marriage partner or a job, essentially much of the discussion and rulings above are relevant to these circumstances, as well. Several authorities rule that it is permissible to dye one's hair for these purposes (*Avnei Zikaron* ibid.; *Levush Mordechai, Yoreh Deah* 24:1; *Seridei Eish*, Vol. II, 81:11; *Igros Moshe, Yoreh Deah* II §61 ד״ה ובאם כוונת צביעתו; *Be'er Moshe*, Vol. 8, 8:6; *Minchas Yitzchak*, Vol. 6, §81; cf. *Shevet HaLevi*, Vol. 3, *Yoreh Deah* 111:3). They note, however, that it is permitted only if one's hair has prematurely turned white and the purpose of dyeing the hair is to make him look his age. Otherwise, aside from the possible transgression of *lo yilbash*, it is misleading to his prospective employer or match, as it will give the impression that he is younger than he actually is, and that is forbidden (see Mitzvah 337, The Prohibition to Commit Fraud When Buying or Selling).

מִצְוָה תקמד: שֶׁלֹּא לִקַּח הָאֵם עַל הַבָּנִים

שֶׁלֹּא נִקַּח קֵן צִפּוֹר הָאֵם וְהָאֶפְרוֹחִים אוֹ הַבֵּיצִים בִּכְלָלוֹ, אֶלָּא שֶׁנְּשַׁלַּח הָאֵם, וְעַל זֶה נֶאֱמַר (דברים כ״ב, ו׳) **לֹא תִקַּח הָאֵם עַל הַבָּנִים**[1].

Mitzvah 544

The Prohibition to Take the Mother Bird With Her Young

כִּי יִקָּרֵא קַן צִפּוֹר לְפָנֶיךָ בַּדֶּרֶךְ בְּכָל עֵץ אוֹ עַל הָאָרֶץ אֶפְרֹחִים אוֹ בֵיצִים וְהָאֵם רֹבֶצֶת עַל הָאֶפְרֹחִים אוֹ עַל הַבֵּיצִים לֹא תִקַּח הָאֵם עַל הַבָּנִים. שַׁלֵּחַ תְּשַׁלַּח אֶת הָאֵם וְאֶת הַבָּנִים תִּקַּח לָךְ לְמַעַן יִיטַב לָךְ וְהַאֲרַכְתָּ יָמִים

Should a bird's nest chance to be before you, on the path, in any tree, or on the ground — chicks or eggs — and the mother [bird] is sitting on the chicks or on the eggs, you shall not take the mother [bird] together with the young. You shall surely send away the mother [bird] and the young take for yourself, so that it will be good for you and you will merit long life (Deuteronomy 22:6-7).

The above Scriptural passage discusses the mitzvah of *shiluach hakein* (שִׁלּוּחַ הַקֵּן, *the sending away of [the mother from] the nest*). It begins with the prohibition of לֹא תִקַּח הָאֵם עַל הַבָּנִים, which Chinuch understands to mean, "*You shall not take the mother [bird]* ***with*** *the young.*" If one takes the entire nest, i.e., the mother bird *and* her chicks or eggs, he violates this prohibition according to Chinuch. In order to benefit from the nest, one must perform the mitzvah-obligation of sending away the mother first — the subject of the next mitzvah — and then he may take the chicks or the eggs for himself.

שֶׁלֹּא נִקַּח קֵן צִפּוֹר הָאֵם וְהָאֶפְרוֹחִים אוֹ הַבֵּיצִים בִּכְלָלוֹ — We are commanded **not to take a bird's nest in its entirety;** that is, **the mother** bird **with the chicks or the eggs.** **אֶלָּא שֶׁנְּשַׁלַּח הָאֵם** — **Rather,** as the verse continues to say, **we must send away the mother** bird, and then we may take the young (Mitzvah 545). **וְעַל זֶה נֶאֱמַר** — **Regarding this it is stated** (*Deuteronomy* 22:6): **"לֹא תִקַּח הָאֵם עַל הַבָּנִים"** — ***You shall not take the mother [bird] together with the young.***[1]

NOTES

1. Chinuch follows *Rambam* (*Sefer HaMitzvos, Lo Saaseh* 306, and *Commentary to the Mishnah, Makkos* 3:1 החלק הרביעי) in explaining that the prohibition is to take the mother bird *together* with her young, apparently rendering the expression עַל הַבָּנִים as ***together with*** [עַל] *the young* (see *Chizkuni* to this verse). *Rashi* (to the verse), however, explains the expression עַל הַבָּנִים to mean ***while*** *she is on* [עַל] *the young* (see *Mizrachi* there), or ***from upon*** [עַל] *her young* (*Minchas Chinuch* §1; see also *HaKesav VeHaKabbalah* to the verse). According to *Rashi's* interpretation, one who takes even the mother bird alone while she is resting on her young violates the prohibition. Notably, *Teshuvos Chacham Tzvi* §83 asserts that *Rambam* and Chinuch's interpretation reflects the verse's simple meaning. For further discussion, see *Chacham Tzvi* and *Minchas Chinuch* ibid., and *Tiferes Yaakov* to *Chullin* 139a ד״ה ודע.

[Although according to *Rambam* and Chinuch one would need to have taken the mother bird *with* her young in order to transgress this prohibition, *Chacham Tzvi* (ibid.) indicates that even they would agree that taking the mother by herself *as* she is sitting on her young is forbidden. However, it is not on account of our prohibition, but by virtue of the mitzvah-*obligation* to send away the mother. This is because that mitzvah delineates the proper way by which a person can benefit from the nest: It is by sending away the mother and taking the young. Any other manner, be it taking the young without sending away the mother or taking (only) the mother as she is sitting on her young, is a violation of the mitzvah-obligation.]

מִשָּׁרְשֵׁי הַמִּצְוָה וּקְצָת דִּינֶיהָ וְכָל עִנְיָנָהּ כָּתַבְתִּי בַּעֲשֵׂה ו׳ שֶׁבְּסֵדֶר זֶה (מצוה תקמ״ה)[2] **תִּרְאֶנּוּ מִשָּׁם.**

וְשָׁם דִּבַּרְנוּ גַּם כֵּן עַל הַלָּאו הַזֶּה שֶׁהוּא נִתָּק לַעֲשֵׂה דְשַׁלֵּחַ תְּשַׁלַּח אֶת הָאֵם[3]**. וּכְבָר לִמְּדוּנוּ זִכְרוֹנָם לִבְרָכָה בְּמַסֶּכֶת מַכּוֹת פֶּרֶק אֵלּוּ הֵן הַלּוֹקִין** (ט״ו ע״ב) **שֶׁכָּל מִצְוַת לֹא תַעֲשֶׂה שֶׁיֵּשׁ בָּהּ קוּם עֲשֵׂה, קִיֵּם עֲשֵׂה שֶׁבָּהּ פָּטוּר, לֹא קִיֵּם עֲשֵׂה שֶׁבָּהּ וְאִי אֶפְשָׁר לוֹ לְקַיְּמוֹ עוֹד חַיָּב מַלְקוּת**[4]**.**

Underlying Purpose and Laws of the Mitzvah

מִשָּׁרְשֵׁי הַמִּצְוָה וּקְצָת דִּינֶיהָ וְכָל עִנְיָנָהּ – Some of the underlying purposes of the mitzvah and some of its laws, as well as its overall concept, כָּתַבְתִּי בַּעֲשֵׂה ו׳ שֶׁבְּסֵדֶר זֶה – I have written in Mitzvah-**obligation 6 of this *parashah*,** *Parashas Ki Teitzei* (Mitzvah 545);[2] **תִּרְאֶנּוּ מִשָּׁם – see [the discussion] there.**

וְשָׁם דִּבַּרְנוּ גַּם כֵּן עַל הַלָּאו הַזֶּה – There, we also mentioned about this mitzvah-prohibition שֶׁהוּא נִתָּק לַעֲשֵׂה דְ״שַׁלֵּחַ תְּשַׁלַּח אֶת הָאֵם״ – that it is remedied by the performance of the mitzvah-**obligation of *You shall surely send away the mother [bird],***[3] **וּכְבָר לִמְּדוּנוּ זִכְרוֹנָם לִבְרָכָה בְּמַסֶּכֶת מַכּוֹת פֶּרֶק אֵלּוּ הֵן הַלּוֹקִין – and [our Sages], of blessed memory, have taught us in Tractate *Makkos*, Chapter *Eilu Hein HaLokin*** (15b), **שֶׁכָּל מִצְוַת לֹא תַעֲשֶׂה שֶׁיֵּשׁ בָּהּ קוּם עֲשֵׂה – that** in the case of **any mitzvah-prohibition that has in it a** mitzvah-**obligation,** i.e., any prohibition whose violation may be remedied by performing a mitzvah-obligation, **קִיֵּם עֲשֵׂה שֶׁבָּהּ פָּטוּר – if [the transgressor] fulfilled its** mitzvah-**obligation, he is exempt** from *malkus*. **לֹא קִיֵּם עֲשֵׂה שֶׁבָּהּ וְאִי אֶפְשָׁר לוֹ לְקַיְּמוֹ עוֹד – If he did not fulfill its** mitzvah-**obligation,** which is to say, that **it is no longer *possible* for him to fulfill it, חַיָּב מַלְקוּת – he is liable to *malkus*.**[4]

What Chinuch just quoted is actually a Baraisa that appears in the Gemara there somewhat differently:

NOTES

2. As noted repeatedly in this edition, in the original format of Chinuch, all the mitzvah-obligations of each *parashah* preceded all the mitzvah-prohibitions of that *parashah* (see Mitzvah 494 note 4). In that format, our mitzvah (which is a mitzvah-prohibition) appeared after the mitzvah-obligation to send away the mother.

3. The Torah links certain prohibitions with mitzvah-obligations that "remedy" the transgression. A prohibition of this type is known as a לָאו הַנִּיתָּק לַעֲשֵׂה, *a prohibition that can be remedied through [fulfillment of] an obligation.*

The prohibition of *You shall not take the mother [bird]...* is likewise classified as a "prohibition remedied by a mitzvah-obligation," since it is followed by the mitzvah-obligation to send the mother away. Now, on a basic level, that mitzvah-obligation does not come to "remedy" our prohibition. Rather, it delineates the proper way of how one may benefit from birds he finds in a nest. After warning not to take the nest in its entirety, the Torah instructs to instead send away the mother and take only the young. However, the Sages (Mishnah, *Chullin* 141a) taught that the mitzvah-obligation can also serve as a remedy in a case where the person had already violated the prohibition and took the mother with her young. The Torah informs him that he can still rectify his sin by sending away the mother at that point, and be spared the punishment of *malkus*. It is as though the verse also stated, "You shall not take the mother bird… but if you did take her, you shall surely send her away…"

4. If he has not yet fulfilled the mitzvah-obligation, but it is still possible for him to fulfill it, his *malkus* is pending; i.e., he is not formally exempt from *malkus*, but he does not receive *malkus* as long as he can still remedy his transgression (see *Minchas Chinuch* §8). [Chinuch below illustrates all these scenarios in the context of *shiluach hakein*.]

Chinuch's explanation, that "not fulfilling the mitzvah-obligation" means that it is no longer *possible* to fulfill the mitzvah-obligation, and that as long as it is possible to fulfill it one is not liable, follows the opinion of *Rambam* (*Sefer HaMitzvos*, *Lo Saaseh* 306, *Hil. Shechitah* 13:1-3). See also Mitzvah 593. *Rashi*, however, gives a much more limited time-frame for fulfilling the mitzvah-obligation. In *Makkos* (15a ד״ה הניחא), he states that if one violates the prohibition, he is warned by *beis din* to perform the corrective mitzvah-obligation or suffer the penalty of *malkus*. If he fulfills the mitzvah-obligation immediately, he avoids punishment. Otherwise, *beis din* administers *malkus* to him, even though it is still possible for him to fulfill the mitzvah-obligation at a later time (cf. *Rashi* to *Chullin* 141a ד״ה קיימו; see also *Ran, Chullin Rif* fol. 48b).

וּכְדְאִתְּמַר הָתָם דְּאָמַר לֵיהּ רַבִּי יוֹחָנָן לְתַנָּא[5] תְּנֵי קִיְּמוֹ וְלֹא קִיְּמוֹ, וְזוֹ הִיא הַגִּרְסָא הַנְּכוֹנָה[6].

[In the case of] any prohibition that has in it a mitzvah-obligation — if [the transgressor] fulfilled its mitzvah-obligation (קִיֵּם עֲשֵׂה שֶׁבָּהּ)*, he is not liable [to malkus]; but if he nullified its mitzvah-obligation* (בִּטֵּל עֲשֵׂה שֶׁבָּהּ)*, he is liable.* The Gemara notes an inconsistency in the text of the Baraisa, in that it contrasts "fulfillment'" with "nullification." In other words, the Baraisa first rules that a transgressor of a prohibition who *fulfills* the associated mitzvah-obligation is exempt from *malkus*, indicating that the transgressor needs to actively rectify his sin by performing the mitzvah-obligation. While it is not essential that he do so *immediately* (according to Chinuch), once the mitzvah-obligation can no longer be fulfilled for whatever reason, he becomes liable to *malkus*. The latter part of the Baraisa, however, states that if the transgressor *nullifies* the mitzvah-obligation, he is then liable to *malkus*. This implies that he is liable only if he *does* something that makes it impossible for him to fulfill the mitzvah-obligation; but if he stays passive and neither fulfills nor nullifies the mitzvah-obligation, he remains exempt from *malkus* even if the mitzvah-obligation can no longer be fulfilled!

The Gemara's general approach to this difficulty is to emend the Baraisa so that the two clauses are consistent. However, the Gemara cites two opinions as to the correct way to emend the Baraisa. One view is that the Baraisa should read בִּטְּלוֹ וְלֹא בִטְּלוֹ, *"he nullified it" or "he did not nullify it."* That is: *[In the case of] any prohibition that has in it a mitzvah-obligation — if* ***he nullified [the mitzvah-obligation],*** *he is liable [to malkus]; if* ***he did not nullify it,*** *he is not liable.* The other view is that the Baraisa should read קִיְּמוֹ וְלֹא קִיְּמוֹ, *"he fulfilled it" or "he did not fulfill it."* That is: *[In the case of] any prohibition that has in it a mitzvah-obligation — if* ***he fulfilled [the mitzvah-obligation]*** *he is not liable to lashes;* ***if he did not fulfill*** *it he is liable.* Thus, Chinuch set down the law earlier in accordance with the emendation of קִיְּמוֹ וְלֹא קִיְּמוֹ, as he proceeds to explain:

וּכְדְאִתְּמַר הָתָם – The criteria for remedying the prohibition with the mitzvah-obligation is indeed "fulfillment" of the mitzvah-obligation, **for it is stated** in the Gemara **there** (*Makkos* 15b) **דְּאָמַר לֵיהּ רַבִּי יוֹחָנָן לְתַנָּא** – **that** the Amora, **R' Yochanan, said to the teacher of** this **Baraisa:**[5] **תְּנֵי קִיְּמוֹ וְלֹא קִיְּמוֹ** – **Teach** the text of the Baraisa as follows: If **[the transgressor] fulfilled [the mitzvah-obligation],** he is not liable to *malkus* for his transgression of the prohibition; **and** if **he did not fulfill [the mitzvah-obligation],** he is liable. **וְזוֹ הִיא הַגִּרְסָא הַנְּכוֹנָה** – **This is the correct version** of the Gemara there; i.e., it was R' Yochanan who maintained that the criteria is whether one can still fulfill the mitzvah-obligation or not, not the other Amora mentioned there (Reish Lakish).[6]

NOTES

5. The term תַּנָּא, *Tanna*, usually refers to a Sage of the Mishnaic period whose view is recorded in a Mishnah or Baraisa. In the present context, however, it refers to a scholar in the Amoraic period who was assigned to memorize the exact wording of the various Mishnaic traditions and recite them verbatim to the assembled students. [During this period, the Oral Law was still studied without resort to written texts.] The Rosh Yeshivah (in this case R' Yochanan) would then expound on the laws recited by the scholar.

6. According to *Rashi* (*Makkos* ad loc.), it is Reish Lakish who emends the Baraisa to *"he fulfilled it" or "he did not fulfill it,"* whereas R' Yochanan maintains that the criteria is *"he nullified it" or "he did not nullify it." Ramban* and *Ritva* (ad loc.), however, find *Rashi's* textual reading and explanation of the Gemara to be untenable (see also *Tosafos* ad loc. ד"ה מידי הוא טעמא). They therefore follow a different (older) version of the Gemara, according to which it is R' Yochanan who emends the Bararisa to *"he fulfilled it" or "he did not fulfill it"* (see also *Rabbeinu Chananel, Makkos* ad loc., and *Ran, Chullin Rif* fol. 48b). Chinuch is informing us here that in his opinion, this version of the Gemara is the correct one.

The significance of these two versions is that, as a general rule, if there is a halachic dispute between R' Yochanan and Reish Lakish, the halachah follows R' Yochanan. Accordingly, if we were to follow *Rashi's* text of the Gemara, then we would rule that the criteria is "nullification," since that is the position of R' Yochanan (see *Kesef Mishneh, Hil. Shechitah* 13:1). By contrast, according to Chinuch's version (i.e., *Ramban's* and *Ritva's*), R' Yochanan is of the opinion that the criteria is "fulfillment." The halachah, therefore, follows that opinion (see *Meiri* ad loc. ד"ה והקשו והרי לאו).

וּמִן הַדַּעַת הַזּוֹ לָמַדְנוּ שֶׁכָּל זְמַן שֶׁמֵּתָה הָאֵם אוֹ שִׁלְּחָהּ אָדָם אַחֵר שֶׁחַיָּב, וְאַף עַל פִּי שֶׁעַכְשָׁו לֹא בִּטֵּל הוּא הָעֲשֵׂה בְּיָדָיו, שֶׁהֲרֵי לֹא הֱמִיתָהּ הוּא אֶלָּא שֶׁמֵּתָה מֵאֵלֶיהָ, וְאֵין צָרִיךְ לוֹמַר שֶׁאִם הֱמִיתָהּ הוּא בְּיָדָיו שֶׁחַיָּב לְכֻלֵּי עָלְמָא. אֲבָל כָּל זְמַן שֶׁשִּׁלְּחָהּ קֹדֶם שֶׁתָּמוּת אַף עַל פִּי שֶׁלֹּא שִׁלְּחָהּ בְּשָׁעָה שֶׁלְּקָחָהּ מִן הַקֵּן לֹא בִטֵּל הַלָּאו וְלֹא הָעֲשֵׂה מִכֵּיוָן שֶׁהַתּוֹרָה נִתְּקוֹ לַעֲשֵׂה וַהֲרֵי קִיְּמוֹ[7]. וְאַף עַל פִּי כֵן אֵין רָאוּי לַעֲשׂוֹת כֵּן, דְּשֶׁמָּא תָמוּת הָאֵם אוֹ הַמְשַׁלֵּחַ קֹדֶם שִׁלּוּחַ וְלֹא יוּכַל לִתְקֹן[8], וְעוֹד שֶׁהַזְּרִיזִין מַקְדִּימִין לְמִצְוֹת[9],

Chinuch applies the rule of "if he fulfilled it, he is exempt from *malkus*, but if he did not fulfill it, he is liable to *malkus*" to a case where a person took the mother bird with her young, in violation of our prohibition:

וּמִן הַדַּעַת הַזּוֹ לָמַדְנוּ – We can **infer from this opinion** **שֶׁכָּל זְמַן שֶׁמֵּתָה הָאֵם אוֹ שִׁלְּחָהּ אָדָם אַחֵר – that if the mother bird died** before the person had a chance to send her away, **or** if **another person** took the mother from him and *he* **sent her away, שֶׁחַיָּב – he is liable** (i.e., the one who had *originally* taken the mother bird with her young). **וְאַף עַל פִּי שֶׁעַכְשָׁו לֹא בִּטֵּל הוּא הָעֲשֵׂה בְּיָדָיו – And although now he is not** guilty of **actively *nullifying* the** mitzvah-**obligation, שֶׁהֲרֵי לֹא הֱמִיתָהּ הוּא אֶלָּא שֶׁמֵּתָה מֵאֵלֶיהָ – for he did not kill [the mother bird] himself; rather, she died on her own** (or someone grabbed her from him and sent her away), nevertheless, he is liable, since he committed the sin by taking the mother in the first place, and now he can no longer fulfill the mitzvah-obligation to remedy it. **וְאֵין צָרִיךְ לוֹמַר שֶׁאִם הֱמִיתָהּ הוּא בְּיָדָיו – It goes without saying that if he actually killed her,** such that he *himself* nullified the mitzvah-obligation, **שֶׁחַיָּב לְכֻלֵּי עָלְמָא – he is liable** to *malkus* **according to all opinions.**

Chinuch illustrates a case where our prohibition *is* remedied by the mitzvah-obligation to send away the mother:

אֲבָל כָּל זְמַן שֶׁשִּׁלְּחָהּ קֹדֶם שֶׁתָּמוּת – However, as long as one sent [the mother bird] away before she dies, אַף עַל פִּי שֶׁלֹּא שִׁלְּחָהּ בְּשָׁעָה שֶׁלְּקָחָהּ מִן הַקֵּן – even though he did not send her away at the time that he took her from the nest, which is what he should have done, **לֹא בִטֵּל הַלָּאו וְלֹא הָעֲשֵׂה – he has not violated the prohibition** (against taking the mother bird with her young), **nor** did he violate **the** mitzvah-**obligation** (to send the mother bird away), **מִכֵּיוָן שֶׁהַתּוֹרָה נִתְּקוֹ לַעֲשֵׂה – being that the Torah remedied** one's transgression of **[the prohibition] with** his fulfillment of **the** mitzvah-**obligation, וַהֲרֵי קִיְּמוֹ – and he has** indeed **fulfilled [the mitzvah-obligation].**[7]

וְאַף עַל פִּי כֵן אֵין רָאוּי לַעֲשׂוֹת כֵּן – Nevertheless, although one can remedy his taking of the mother bird by subsequently sending her away, **it is not proper to do so,** i.e., to take the mother with the intention of sending her away later, **דְּשֶׁמָּא תָמוּת הָאֵם אוֹ הַמְשַׁלֵּחַ קֹדֶם שִׁלּוּחַ – since it is possible that the mother bird may die, or the person** himself **may die, before** he gets a chance to **send** her away, **וְלֹא יוּכַל לִתְקֹן –** in which case **he would be unable to remedy**[8] his transgression by fulfilling the mitzvah-obligation. **וְעוֹד שֶׁהַזְּרִיזִין מַקְדִּימִין לְמִצְוֹת – In addition,** one should not delay the mitzvah of sending away the mother bird (*shiluach hakein*) at all, since **the conscientious ones are early to** perform **mitzvos,** i.e., they perform the mitzvos as soon as they possibly can.[9]

NOTES

7. Chinuch seems to be saying that as long as one ended up sending away the mother, he has not *violated* the prohibition. In other words, not only is he exempt from *malkus*, it is as though he never violated the prohibition in the first place! See Gemara, *Chullin* 141a with *Minchas Yitzchak* 228:6 ד״ה המנ״ח ז״ל כתב. [See, similarly, *Rashi* to *Bava Metzia* 62a ד״ה פוטרין with *Chasam Sofer; Hagahos Imrei Baruch* to *Shulchan Aruch, Choshen Mishpat* 34:7; *Sfas Emes, Yoma* 85b ד״ה אר״י; *Limudei Hashem* (*R' Yehudah Najar*), *Limud* 49 ד״ה שוב מצאתי. Cf. *Lechem Mishneh, Hil. Gezeilah VaAveidah* 14:6, explaining *Rambam* there; *Shaagas Aryeh* §81. For discussion, see *Kli Chemdah, Ki Seitzei* 8:1-3.]

8. Stylistic citation of *Ecclesiastes* 1:15.

9. See *Pesachim* 4a.

וְדָבָר בְּעִתּוֹ מַה טוֹב[10].

וְדָבָר בְּעִתּוֹ מַה טוֹב – Indeed, a thing in its proper **time, how good it is!**[10]

---

10. Stylistic citation of *Proverbs* 15:23.

Chinuch seems to be saying that the only reasons to send away the mother bird immediately are to ensure that one not lose the opportunity, and in order to be conscientious. But as far as the *requirement* of the mitzvah goes, it makes no difference whether one sends the mother away immediately or at some later point in time. This is difficult to understand, for at the beginning of the next mitzvah Chinuch states that proper fulfillment of the mitzvah-obligation requires that the mother bird be sent away *first*, before one takes the young. Thus, while sending the mother away afterward is *also* a fulfillment of the mitzvah, and that suffices for the person to avoid a violation, it is not the *correct* way to fulfill the mitzvah – quite aside from the other concerns that Chinuch mentions here. Thus, Chinuch's words here require further study.

מִצְוָה תקמה: מִצְוַת שִׁלּוּחַ הַקֵּן

לְשַׁלֵּחַ הָאֵם מִן הַקֵּן קֹדֶם שֶׁיִּקַּח הַבָּנִים, שֶׁנֶּאֱמַר (דברים כ״ב, ז׳) **שַׁלֵּחַ תְּשַׁלַּח אֶת הָאֵם וְאֶת הַבָּנִים תִּקַּח לָךְ[1].**

Mitzvah 545
The Obligation of Shiluach HaKein

שַׁלֵּחַ תְּשַׁלַּח אֶת הָאֵם וְאֶת הַבָּנִים תִּקַּח לָךְ לְמַעַן יִיטַב לָךְ וְהַאֲרַכְתָּ יָמִים
You shall surely send away the mother and take the young for yourself, so that it will be good for you and you will merit long life (*Deuteronomy* 22:7).

The previous mitzvah taught that if one comes upon a nest and finds the mother bird sitting on her young (chicks or eggs), he is prohibited from taking the mother bird together with her young. Rather, as this current mitzvah teaches, one must send away the mother, and then he may take the young for himself. This is the mitzvah of *shiluach hakein* (*the sending away of [the mother from] the nest*).

לְשַׁלֵּחַ הָאֵם מִן הַקֵּן קֹדֶם שֶׁיִּקַּח הַבָּנִים – We are commanded **to send away the mother** bird **from the nest before taking** her **young,** **שֶׁנֶּאֱמַר** – **as it is stated** (*Deuteronomy* 22:7): **"שַׁלֵּחַ תְּשַׁלַּח אֶת הָאֵם וְאֶת הַבָּנִים תִּקַּח לָךְ"** – ***You shall surely send away the mother [bird] and take the young for yourself.***[1]

Underlying Purpose of the Mitzvah

There are several approaches to understanding the rationale behind the mitzvah of *shiluach hakein.* As Chinuch will state below, some view the mitzvah as a decree without a known reason. Others maintain that it does have a discernible rationale, and they provide several explanations. *Rambam* (*Moreh Nevuchim* III:48) and *Ramban* (to our verse), though each one proposes his own explanation, both link the mitzvah of *shiluach hakein* with the prohibition to slaughter an animal and its child on the same day (Mitzvah 294).[2] One of the ideas that *Ramban* suggests is that taking the mother bird along with the chicks, ostensibly in order to slaughter both, represents a destruction of the species, similar to slaughtering an animal and its child in one day. Multiple generations of a species – in particular, a mother and child – are symbolic of the propagation of the species, and slaughtering both at once thus represents disregard for the species as a whole.

NOTES

1. Chinuch makes two points in defining the mitzvah: (1) The mother must be sent away and only the young may be taken, and not vice versa [the prohibition of the previous mitzvah forbade only taking *both*, see note 1 there]; (2) the mother must be sent away *first*, i.e., before one takes the young (see the last note of the previous mitzvah). [See below, where Chinuch discusses the reasons for the mitzvah, for possible explanation of these two aspects.]

Chinuch also indicates here that one is obligated in the mitzvah of *shiluach hakein* only if he wants the chicks or the eggs. Thus, Chinuch says that "before taking the young" he must send away the mother. If he has no interest in the young, he is not obligated in the mitzvah at all. [As discussed at length in the Insight, however, this is a subject of broad dispute among the authorities; see there.] Chinuch also does not mention anything about actually *taking* the young, indicating that if, after sending away the mother bird, the person changes his mind and does not want the young, he has nevertheless fulfilled the mitzvah of *shiluach hakein.* He is not *obligated* to take the young in order to complete the mitzvah. See note 11 below, for discussion, as well as for a dissenting opinion.

2. As Chinuch cited in the Introduction to the Book of *Deuteronomy* (Vol. 7, pp. 309-311) from *Ramban,* most of the mitzvos that appear in *Deuteronomy* are merely expansions of mitzvos that were taught in earlier Books of the Torah. *Ramban* begins his commentary on the mitzvah of *shiluach hakein* by noting that the fundamentals of this mitzvah, too, were already established earlier, in the prohibition to slaughter a mother and her offspring on the same day [אֹתוֹ וְאֶת בְּנוֹ]. In essence, it is the same prohibition but extended to birds.

מִשָּׁרְשֵׁי הַמִּצְוָה לָתֵת אֶל לִבֵּנוּ שֶׁהַשְׁגָּחַת הָאֵל בָּרוּךְ הוּא עַל בְּרִיּוֹתָיו בְּמִין הָאָדָם
בִּפְרָט, כְּמוֹ שֶׁכָּתוּב כִּי עֵינָיו עַל כָּל דַּרְכֵי אִישׁ וְגוֹ'[3], וּבִשְׁאָר מִינֵי בַּעֲלֵי חַיִּים בַּמִּינִין
דֶּרֶךְ כְּלָל[4], כְּלוֹמַר שֶׁחֶפְצוֹ בָּרוּךְ הוּא בְּקִיּוּם הַמִּין, וְעַל כֵּן לֹא יִכְלֶה לְעוֹלָם מִין מִכָּל
מִינֵי הַנִּבְרָאִים, כִּי בְּהַשְׁגָּחַת הַחַי וְקַיָּם לָעַד בָּרוּךְ הוּא עַל הַדָּבָר יִמָּצֵא בּוֹ הַקִּיּוּם,
וּבְהַנִּיחַ הָאָדָם דַּעְתּוֹ עַל זֶה יָבִין דַּרְכֵי ה' וְיִרְאֶה כִּי הַמְשָׁכַת קִיּוּם הַמִּינִין בָּעוֹלָם

◆§ Chinuch's approach

Chinuch in Mitzvah 294 expresses the same idea, but he explains that it is intended to teach us a positive lesson; namely, that Hashem desires and therefore directs the continued existence of all the species in Creation. As we refrain from slaughtering an animal and its child, we acknowledge and internalize Hashem's wondrous care and guidance over the world. Chinuch explains the mitzvah of *shiluach hakein* in a similar vein:

מִשָּׁרְשֵׁי הַמִּצְוָה — **Among the underlying purposes of the mitzvah** is לָתֵת אֶל לִבֵּנוּ — **for us to impress upon our hearts** the fact שֶׁהַשְׁגָּחַת הָאֵל בָּרוּךְ הוּא עַל בְּרִיּוֹתָיו — **that the Almighty's supervision, blessed is He,** is trained **on** all of **His creations.** בְּמִין הָאָדָם בִּפְרָט, כְּמוֹ שֶׁכָּתוּב "כִּי עֵינָיו עַל כָּל דַּרְכֵי אִישׁ וְגוֹ' " — **In regard to mankind,** it is trained on each person **individually, as it is written:** *For His eyes are upon all of man's ways,* and He sees all his steps.[3] וּבִשְׁאָר מִינֵי בַּעֲלֵי חַיִּים בַּמִּינִין דֶּרֶךְ כְּלָל — **And in regard to** all **other species of living creatures,** such as animals, though His supervision is not trained on each animal individually, it is trained **on the species in general** (i.e., Hashem supervises over each species as a whole).[4] כְּלוֹמַר שֶׁחֶפְצוֹ בָּרוּךְ הוּא בְּקִיּוּם הַמִּין — **That is to say, that [Hashem], blessed is He, desires the continuity of** each and every **species,** and so He supervises and watches over each species in order to ensure its survival. וְעַל כֵּן לֹא יִכְלֶה לְעוֹלָם מִין מִכָּל מִינֵי הַנִּבְרָאִים — **It follows, therefore,** that **no species among all the species of creatures** in the world **will ever become extinct,** כִּי בְּהַשְׁגָּחַת הַחַי וְקַיָּם לָעַד בָּרוּךְ הוּא עַל הַדָּבָר יִמָּצֵא בּוֹ הַקִּיּוּם — **for a thing's** continued **existence** does not depend on natural factors (which might in fact threaten its existence), but **on the Providence of He Who lives and endures forever** (i.e., Hashem), **blessed is He,** and He ensures the survival of each species that He created.

The ultimate purpose of the mitzvah is for the person to take this philosophical idea and to internalize it, such that it becomes a belief that guides his life and inspires him to a greater commitment to Hashem's Torah. For this he will receive the reward mentioned in our verse (*So that it will be good for you and you will merit long life*), as Chinuch explains now:

וּבְהַנִּיחַ הָאָדָם דַּעְתּוֹ עַל זֶה — **When,** in performing the mitzvah of *shiluach hakein,* which is meant to ensure the continued existence of the species, **a person sets his mind on this** principle and contemplates it, יָבִין דַּרְכֵי ה' — **he will** come to **recognize the ways of Hashem;** וְיִרְאֶה כִּי הַמְשָׁכַת — קִיּוּם הַמִּינִין בָּעוֹלָם — **and he will see that the continued existence of the** various **species in the**

NOTES

3. Chinuch presumably refers to the verse in *Job* 34:21, though the word כָּל does not appear there. See Mitzvah 169 at note 15.

4. This concept, that animals experience Divine Providence over the species as a whole but not over individual members of the species, is expressed by several Rishonim (*Moreh Nevuchim* III:17; *Ramban* and *Rabbeinu Bachya* to *Genesis* 18:19; *Kad HaKemach*, השגחה; *Sefer HaIkkarim* 4:7). Chinuch himself has mentioned it in Mitzvos 291, 294, 451, and primarily in Mitzvah 169 (at notes 15-28). In brief, this means that while Hashem's knowledge certainly embraces every detail of creation, His specific manipulation of events in regard to animals involves only the species as a whole. Individual animals are given to the laws of nature that

Hashem has set in place. In regard to man, however, there is Divine manipulation of events in every detail of an individual's life. For further clarification, see Mitzvah 169 with notes 24 and 26; see there also for a dissenting opinion regarding animals and the like.

Rambam (ibid. Chs. 18 and 51), as well as *Ramban* and *Rabbeinu Bachya* (ibid.), note, however, that even as it pertains to people, not every individual merits Hashem's Providence (i.e., so that he would not be given to the laws of nature). It depends on the person's deeds. Regarding animals and other creations, however, Divine Providence is directed exclusively toward the species as a whole (see further sources cited in Mitzvah 169, note 28). Chinuch below (at notes 6-7) indicates this as well.

שֶׁלֹּא כָלָה וְאָבַד אֶחָד מִכֻּלָּם מִבֵּיצֵי כִנִּים וְעַד קַרְנֵי רְאֵמִים[5] **מִיּוֹם שֶׁנִּבְרְאוּ הַכֹּל בְּמַאֲמָרוֹ וְחֶפְצוֹ עַל זֶה. וּכְמוֹ כֵן יֵדַע הָאָדָם כִּי אֲשֶׁר יִשְׁמֹר מִצְוֹת בּוֹרְאוֹ וְיַיְשִׁיר כָּל דְּרָכָיו וְהוּא נְקִי כַפַּיִם וּבַר לֵבָב**[6] **תִּהְיֶה הַשְׁגָּחַת הָאֵל עָלָיו וְיִתְקַיֵּם גּוּפוֹ זְמַן רַב בָּעוֹלָם הַזֶּה וְנַפְשׁוֹ לָעַד לָעוֹלָם הַבָּא**[7]**, וּכְגוֹן זֶה יֹאמְרוּ זִכְרוֹנָם לִבְרָכָה** (סנהדרין צ׳ ע״א) **מִדָּה כְּנֶגֶד מִדָּה**[8]**, כִּי בִּהְיוֹת זֶה הָאִישׁ נוֹתֵן דַּעְתּוֹ כִּי הַקִּיּוּם וְהַטּוֹבָה בְּהַשְׁגָּחַת הָאֵל בַּדְּבָרִים וְלֹא בְּסִבָּה אַחֶרֶת, יִזְכֶּה הוּא גַּם כֵּן שֶׁיִּפְנֶה עָלָיו הָאֵל לְטוֹבָה וִיקַיֵּם אוֹתוֹ**[9]**.**

---

world, שֶׁלֹּא כָלָה וְאָבַד אֶחָד מִכֻּלָּם, מִבֵּיצֵי כִנִּים וְעַד קַרְנֵי רְאֵמִים, מִיּוֹם שֶׁנִּבְרְאוּ – such **that not even one of them, from** the lowly species of lice called **"eggs of lice" to the** mighty **horned *re'eim*,**[5] **has ever become extinct or eradicated since the day they were created** as a species (in the six days of Creation), **הַכֹּל בְּמַאֲמָרוֹ וְחֶפְצוֹ עַל זֶה** – is **all due to [Hashem's] Utterance and Will that this** should be. **וּכְמוֹ כֵן יֵדַע הָאָדָם** – **The person should** then apply this idea to mankind, for whom Hashem's supervision is trained upon each *individual*, and **likewise recognize כִּי אֲשֶׁר יִשְׁמֹר מִצְוֹת בּוֹרְאוֹ וְיַיְשִׁיר כָּל דְּרָכָיו** – **that if one observes the mitzvos of his Creator and sets all his ways** on the **straight** path, **וְהוּא נְקִי כַפַּיִם וּבַר לֵבָב** – **and he is** a person **with "clean hands** (i.e., honest in his dealings) **and a pure heart,"**[6] **תִּהְיֶה הַשְׁגָּחַת הָאֵל עָלָיו** – **the Almighty's Providence will be trained upon him** to protect him. **וְיִתְקַיֵּם גּוּפוֹ זְמַן רַב בָּעוֹלָם הַזֶּה** – **His physical self will thus endure for a long time in this world** (i.e., he will enjoy a long, healthy life), **וְנַפְשׁוֹ לָעַד לָעוֹלָם הַבָּא** – **while his soul** will endure **forever in the World to Come.**[7]

Chinuch highlights the "measure for measure" factor that emerges according to his approach to *shiluach hakein* (i.e., the reward of meriting Hashem's Providence in return for *recognizing* Hashem's Providence):

וּכְגוֹן זֶה יֹאמְרוּ זִכְרוֹנָם לִבְרָכָה – **Regarding** a reward **such as this, [our Sages], of blessed memory, would cite** the expression (*Sanhedrin* 90a) **מִדָּה כְּנֶגֶד מִדָּה** – **"measure for measure";** that is to say, that Hashem repays (either reward or punishment) exactly in correspondence with the nature of the deed.[8] **כִּי בִּהְיוֹת זֶה הָאִישׁ נוֹתֵן דַּעְתּוֹ** – The reward a person receives for performing *shiluach hakein* and internalizing its message is indeed "measure for measure," **for as this person focuses his mind** on the idea **כִּי הַקִּיּוּם וְהַטּוֹבָה בְּהַשְׁגָּחַת הָאֵל בַּדְּבָרִים וְלֹא בְּסִבָּה אַחֶרֶת** – **that the existence and welfare** of everything in the world comes about only **through the Almighty's Providence over** these **things, and not due to any other cause, יִזְכֶּה הוּא גַּם כֵּן שֶׁיִּפְנֶה עָלָיו הָאֵל לְטוֹבָה וִיקַיֵּם אוֹתוֹ** – **he, too, will merit that the Almighty will turn** His Providence **toward him, to** bestow **good** upon him **and grant him an** enduring **existence.**[9]

NOTES

5. The רְאֵם, *re'eim*, is a tall beast with beautiful horns (see *Rashi* to *Deuteronomy* 33:17). [Some suggest that it is a reindeer.] As for the "eggs of lice" being a species of lice, rather than *literally* eggs of lice (nits), see *Shabbos* 107b, and *Rashi* to *Avodah Zarah* 3b ד״ה ביצי כנים.

6. Stylistic citation of *Psalms* 24:4.

7. As indicated in the introductory paragraph to this segment, Chinuch appears to be alluding to the reward described at the end of our verse: לְמַעַן יִיטַב לָךְ וְהַאֲרַכְתָּ יָמִים, *So that it will be good for you and you will merit long life.* See also *Chasam Sofer* to the verse.

8. See similarly above, Mitzvah 529, at note 7.

9. Throughout his presentation here, Chinuch indicates that the long and good life that the Torah promises in reward for *shiluach hakein* is not attained by merely performing the *act* of sending away the mother. One must perform the act and at the same time contemplate and internalize the *message* that it carries. To the extent that he will strengthen himself in faith in Hashem and His Providence through his performance of the mitzvah, he will be rewarded with a long and good life — measure for measure. And he will merit having children — also, measure for measure — as Chinuch teaches below. However, if one performs the act of *shiluach hakein* without internalizing the message of faith that it carries, though he will surely receive reward as he would for performing *any* mitzvah, he might not receive the reward of long life and children that is unique to this mitzvah.

[In addition, there are other Divine considerations that are at play whenever the Torah spells out a reward for observance of a mitzvah. Hashem, in His infinite understanding, may hold back a person's reward if He sees that it is better for that individual not to receive it at this time, or if that individual is not worthy for other

וּבִשְׂכַר הַקִּיּוּם וְהַיְכֹלֶת שֶׁהוּא מַאֲמִין בַּבּוֹרֵא בָּעִנְיָן זֶה אָמְרוּ זִכְרוֹנָם לִבְרָכָה בַּמִּדְרָשׁ
(דברים רבה, כי תצא פיסקא ו') שֶׁהָאָדָם זוֹכֶה לְבָנִים בִּשְׂכַר מִצְוָה זוֹ, כְּלוֹמַר שֶׁיִּמָּשֵׁךְ קִיּוּמוֹ,
שֶׁבָּנִים הֵם קִיּוּם הָאָדָם וְזִכְרוֹ. וְדִקְדְּקוּ הַדָּבָר לְפִי הַדּוֹמֶה מֵאָמְרוֹ שַׁלֵּחַ תְּשַׁלַּח אֶת הָאֵם
וְאֶת הַבָּנִים תִּקַּח לָךְ, כְּלוֹמַר בָּנִים תִּקַּח לְנַפְשֶׁךָ[10], שֶׁהָיָה יָכוֹל לוֹמַר תְּשַׁלַּח הָאֵם וְלֹא וְאֶת
הַבָּנִים תִּקַּח לָךְ[11].

Chinuch cites a Midrash, which teaches that one who performs *shiluach hakein* will merit having children. Chinuch explains that this is essentially a reward of "continuity," and that this too is "measure for measure" for the recognition of Hashem's Providence that one attains through this mitzvah: וּבִשְׂכַר הַקִּיּוּם וְהַיְכֹלֶת שֶׁהוּא מַאֲמִין בַּבּוֹרֵא בָּעִנְיָן זֶה — It is precisely **in reward for** one's recognition that Hashem preserves **the continuity** of all creation, **and for his belief in the absolute power of the Creator in this regard,** אָמְרוּ זִכְרוֹנָם לִבְרָכָה בַּמִּדְרָשׁ — that **[the Sages], of blessed memory, stated in the Midrash** (*Devarim Rabbah* 6:6) שֶׁהָאָדָם זוֹכֶה לְבָנִים בִּשְׂכַר מִצְוָה זוֹ — that **a person merits having children as a reward for** performing **this mitzvah** of *shiluach hakein*. כְּלוֹמַר שֶׁיִּמָּשֵׁךְ קִיּוּמוֹ — In light of what we are saying, **this** essentially **means that his existence will endure** (through his children), שֶׁבָּנִים הֵם קִיּוּם הָאָדָם וְזִכְרוֹ — since one's **children are his continuity and his remembrance** (i.e., he will be remembered through them).

Chinuch explains how the Midrash derived the reward of having children: וְדִקְדְּקוּ הַדָּבָר לְפִי הַדּוֹמֶה מֵאָמְרוֹ — **[The Sages]** (ibid.) **derived the matter, it seems, from that which [the verse] states:** שַׁלֵּחַ תְּשַׁלַּח אֶת הָאֵם וְאֶת הַבָּנִים תִּקַּח לָךְ — *You shall surely send away the mother and take the young* (literally, *sons*) *for yourself,* כְּלוֹמַר בָּנִים תִּקַּח לְנַפְשֶׁךָ — which **is** expounded **to mean,** that as a reward for sending away the mother bird **you will "take"** (i.e., acquire) **sons for yourself,** i.e., you will have children.[10] שֶׁהָיָה יָכוֹל לוֹמַר תְּשַׁלַּח הָאֵם — **The reason the verse** is expounded this way, and not understood literally to mean that after sending away the mother bird you may take the young birds for yourself, is **because the verse could** just as well **have said, "Send away the mother,"** וְלֹא "וְאֶת הַבָּנִים תִּקַּח לָךְ" — **without** saying, **"and take the young for yourself,"** since it is self-evident that the young may be taken after one has fulfilled his obligation to send away the mother. The Sages therefore interpreted it to mean that one *merits children* as a reward for sending away the mother.[11]

Thus far, Chinuch has explained that the purpose of our mitzvah is for us to strengthen our belief in Hashem's Providence over Creation. If we perform the mitzvah and internalize this belief, Hashem

---

NOTES

reasons. See *Imrei Shefer* (R' Shlomo Kluger) to *Deuteronomy* 22:6, specifically regarding *shiluach hakein*. See also *Rabbeinu Yonah, Shaarei Teshuvah* 3:30; *Chazon Ish, Sheviis* 18:4; and *Mishnah Berurah* 158:38.]

10. The Midrash itself cites the phrase *and take the young for yourself* as its source. However, this requires explanation, since the simple reading of the verse comes to teach that one may take the chicks or the eggs ("the young") after sending away their mother. How does the Midrash know to interpret the phrase differently? It is this point that Chinuch is coming to clarify here, as he now explains.

11. *Chasam Sofer* (*Teshuvos, Orach Chaim* §100 ד"ה והנה בתשו' חכם צבי) infers from Chinuch's explanation of the Midrash that, in Chinuch's opinion, the mitzvah of *shiluach hakein* does not include picking up the chicks or the eggs (see, similarly, end of note 1, above). For if it *were* a part of the obligation, then the phrase *and take the young for yourself* is not superfluous; it is

necessary in order to teach this component of the mitzvah! Evidently, Chinuch understands that according to its simple reading, the verse would simply mean that one *may* take the young, which is indeed superfluous. This is also the opinion of *Ibn Ezra* (*Yesod Mora, Shaar* 9) and *Teshuvos Chacham Tzvi* (§83).

Other authorities, however, maintain that fulfillment of the mitzvah requires that the person pick up and *acquire* the offspring after sending away the mother (see *Shulchan Aruch, Yoreh Deah* 292:4 with *Levushei Serad; Chazon Ish, Yoreh Deah* 175:2; see also *Aruch HaShulchan, Yoreh Deah* 292:4). [According to these authorities, the Midrash's exposition of the verse requires a different explanation than Chinuch's. See *Eitz Yosef* and *Chidushei HaRadal* ad loc. for possible alternatives. For additional homiletic explanations of this Midrash — specifically, why the reward of children is "measure for measure" for performing *shiluach hakein* — see the Kleinman ed. of *Midrash Rabbah* ad loc.]

וּמִן הַשֹּׁרֶשׁ הַזֶּה אָמְרוּ זִכְרוֹנָם לִבְרָכָה (ברכות ל״ג ע״ב) שֶׁהָאוֹמֵר בִּתְפִלָּתוֹ רַחֲמֵנוּ שֶׁאַתָּה הַמְרַחֵם כִּי עַל קַן צִפּוֹר יַגִּיעוּ רַחֲמֶיךָ, שֶׁמְּשַׁתְּקִין אוֹתוֹ, שֶׁאֵין הָעִנְיָן רַחֲמִים אֶלָּא כְּדֵי לְזַכּוֹתֵנוּ עַל הָעִנְיָן שֶׁזָּכַרְתִּי, וְאָמְרוּ בְּטַעַם זֶה בַּגְּמָרָא (שם) מִפְּנֵי שֶׁעוֹשֶׂה מִדּוֹתָיו שֶׁל הַקָּדוֹשׁ בָּרוּךְ הוּא רַחֲמִים וְאֵינָן אֶלָּא גְּזֵרוֹת[12]. וְאֵין הָעִנְיָן לוֹמַר שֶׁאֵין הַקָּדוֹשׁ בָּרוּךְ הוּא מְרַחֵם חָלִילָה, שֶׁהֲרֵי הוּא נִקְרָא רַחוּם, וְאָמְרוּ זִכְרוֹנָם לִבְרָכָה (שבת קל״ג ע״ב) מָה הַקָּדוֹשׁ בָּרוּךְ הוּא רַחוּם אַף אַתָּה הֱיֵה מְרַחֵם, אֲבָל כַּוָּנָתָם לוֹמַר שֶׁאֵין מִדַּת הָרַחֲמָנוּת בּוֹ חָלִילָה כְּמוֹ בְּנֵי אָדָם שֶׁהָרַחֲמָנוּת בָּהֶם מֻכְרָח בְּטִבְעָם שֶׁשָּׂם בָּהֶם הַבּוֹרֵא בָּרוּךְ הוּא, אֲבָל הָרַחֲמָנוּת אֵלָיו מֵחֶפְצוֹ הַפָּשׁוּט

---

rewards us "measure for measure," by shining His Providence upon us and granting us continuity through long life and children. One might contend, however, that the purpose of the mitzvah is not as Chinuch suggests. Rather, Hashem commanded us to send away the mother bird before taking her young simply out of compassion for her; that is, so that she should not see her young being taken, or worse, slaughtered. Chinuch cites a ruling by the Sages which indicates that the reason for the mitzvah is not compassion, but rather to teach us a lesson, as he had explained:

וּמִן הַשֹּׁרֶשׁ הַזֶּה אָמְרוּ זִכְרוֹנָם לִבְרָכָה – **On account of this underlying reason** that I presented for the mitzvah of *shiluach hakein*, **[our Sages], of blessed memory, stated** (*Berachos* 33b) שֶׁהָאוֹמֵר בִּתְפִלָּתוֹ – **that if one says in his prayer,** רַחֲמֵנוּ שֶׁאַתָּה הַמְרַחֵם כִּי עַל קַן צִפּוֹר יַגִּיעוּ רַחֲמֶיךָ – "Hashem, **have mercy on us, as You are the Compassionate One, for Your mercy extends even to a bird's nest** as evident by the mitzvah of *shiluach hakein*," שֶׁמְּשַׁתְּקִין אוֹתוֹ – **we silence him.** שֶׁאֵין הָעִנְיָן רַחֲמִים – The reason we do so is **because** although Hashem is certainly the Compassionate One, **the idea** behind *shiluach hakein* **is not** Hashem's **mercy** on the mother bird, אֶלָּא כְּדֵי לְזַכּוֹתֵנוּ עַל הָעִנְיָן שֶׁזָּכַרְתִּי – **but** is **in order to bring us merit, in the manner that I indicated** above, i.e., to bring us to contemplate Hashem's Providence over creation, and ultimately over ourselves.

וְאָמְרוּ בְּטַעַם זֶה בַּגְּמָרָא – **[The Sages] expressed this reason in the Gemara** (ibid.) as follows: מִפְּנֵי שֶׁעוֹשֶׂה מִדּוֹתָיו שֶׁל הַקָּדוֹשׁ בָּרוּךְ הוּא רַחֲמִים – We silence the person who prays this way **because he renders the Attributes of the Holy One, blessed is He,** with which He governs the world, into Attributes of **Mercy,** וְאֵינָן אֶלָּא גְּזֵרוֹת – **while,** in truth, **they are nothing but decrees.**[12] וְאֵין הָעִנְיָן לוֹמַר שֶׁאֵין הַקָּדוֹשׁ בָּרוּךְ הוּא מְרַחֵם חָלִילָה – **Now, this does not mean to say that the Holy One, blessed is He, does not have compassion** on His creatures, **Heaven forbid** the thought, שֶׁהֲרֵי הוּא נִקְרָא רַחוּם – **for** in many places in the Torah, **[Hashem] is described as "Compassionate"** (e.g., *Exodus* 34:6); וְאָמְרוּ זִכְרוֹנָם לִבְרָכָה – **and,** in fact, we are required to *emulate* Hashem's compassion, as **[our Sages], of blessed memory, stated** (*Sifrei* to *Deuteronomy* 11:22; *Shabbos* 133b): מָה הַקָּדוֹשׁ בָּרוּךְ הוּא רַחוּם אַף אַתָּה הֱיֵה מְרַחֵם – **Just as the Holy One, blessed is He, is compassionate, so too, you should be compassionate.** אֲבָל כַּוָּנָתָם לוֹמַר – **Rather,** when the Sages negated the idea that Hashem governs the world with compassion, **their intention** was **to say** שֶׁאֵין מִדַּת הָרַחֲמָנוּת בּוֹ חָלִילָה כְּמוֹ בְּנֵי אָדָם – **that the trait of compassion** that we attribute **to [Hashem] is not, Heaven forbid** the thought, **the same as** the trait of compassion that **people** have. שֶׁהָרַחֲמָנוּת בָּהֶם מֻכְרָח בְּטִבְעָם שֶׁשָּׂם בָּהֶם הַבּוֹרֵא בָּרוּךְ הוּא – **For in [people], the** trait of **compassion is instinctive in their nature, as imparted to them by the Creator, blessed is He.** They are therefore compelled to act out of compassion when faced with a situation that evokes their sympathy. אֲבָל הָרַחֲמָנוּת אֵלָיו מֵחֶפְצוֹ הַפָּשׁוּט – **[Hashem's] compassion, on the other hand,** draws **from His**

NOTES

12. The term "decrees" in this context will be explained by Chinuch below.

[We translated the word מִדּוֹתָיו here as "His Attributes" because this seems to be Chinuch's understanding of the term (see also *Maharal, Tiferes Yisrael* Ch. 6). *Rashi* (*Berachos* ad loc.), however, understands the word מִדּוֹתָיו in this context as "His mitzvos." This seems also to be the understanding of *Rambam* cited below, at note 21.]

שֶׁחִיְּבָה חָכְמָתוֹ לְרַחֵם מִפְּנֵי שֶׁהִיא מִדָּה טוֹבָה, וְכָל הַטּוֹבוֹת נִמְצָאוֹת מֵאִתּוֹ, וְאָמְרוּ כִּי בְּצִוּוּתוֹ אוֹתָנוּ עַל זֶה לֹא מִצַּד הֶכְרֵחַ מִדַּת הָרַחֲמָנוּת צִוָּנוּ בַּדָּבָר שֶׁהֲרֵי הִתִּיר לָנוּ הַשְּׁחִיטָה בָּהֶן, כִּי כָל הַמִּינִין לְצֹרֶךְ הָאָדָם הֵן נִבְרָאִין[13], אֲבָל הַצַּוָּאָה עַל זֶה וּבְאוֹתוֹ וְאֶת בְּנוֹ שֶׁהִיא כַּיּוֹצֵא בָהּ וּבִשְׁאָר מִצְוֹת רַבּוֹת אֵינוֹ אֶלָּא כִּגְזֵרָה לְפָנָיו שֶׁגָּזַר עַל זֶה בְּחֶפְצוֹ הַפָּשׁוּט, וְאִלּוּ רָצָה בְּהֵפֶךְ מִזֶּה לֹא יַכְרִיחֶנּוּ דָּבָר וְלֹא יְמַנְעֶנּוּ סִבָּה חָלִילָה כָּמוֹנוּ אֲנַחְנוּ הַבְּנוּיִים בְּכֹחַ הַטְּבָעִים, שֶׁמִּדַּת הָרַחֲמָנוּת תְּעַכְּבֵנוּ מִלְּהַשְׁחִית אוֹ תַּכְרִיחֵנוּ לְהֵטִיב לִפְעָמִים, זֶהוּ עִנְיַן אָמְרָם אֵינָן אֶלָּא גְּזֵרוֹת[14] וּמִשֹּׁרֶשׁ הָעִנְיָן מַה שֶּׁזָּכַרְנוּ.

transcendent Will (i.e., a will that is not influenced by any emotion, compulsion, or impulse); שֶׁחִיְּבָה חָכְמָתוֹ לְרַחֵם מִפְּנֵי שֶׁהִיא מִדָּה טוֹבָה – that is to say, **that His Wisdom dictated** that it is proper **to act mercifully because it is a good trait,** וְכָל הַטּוֹבוֹת נִמְצָאוֹת מֵאִתּוֹ – **and** as **all good** things **emanate from [Hashem],** so does the good trait of compassion. However, Hashem does not do things, or command us to do things, "out of compassion," as though He is compelled by a sense of sympathy or pity. Rather, He acts *with* compassion and commands us to act with compassion when, in His infinite Wisdom, He determines that compassion is warranted.

Chinuch explains that this is what the Sages meant when they said, "… while, in truth, [Hashem's Attributes] are nothing but decrees":

וְאָמְרוּ – **Thus, [the Sages] stated** כִּי בְּצִוּוּתוֹ אוֹתָנוּ עַל זֶה – **that when [Hashem] commanded us about this** mitzvah of *shiluach hakein,* לֹא מִצַּד הֶכְרֵחַ מִדַּת הָרַחֲמָנוּת צִוָּנוּ בַּדָּבָר – **He did not command us in the matter out of an instinctive sense of compassion** for the birds, שֶׁהֲרֵי הִתִּיר לָנוּ הַשְּׁחִיטָה בָּהֶן – **for** if so, out of that same sense of compassion He would have forbidden us to slaughter and eat birds altogether, and **the fact** of the matter **is that He *permitted* us to slaughter** and eat **them;** כִּי כָל הַמִּינִין לְצֹרֶךְ הָאָדָם הֵן נִבְרָאִין – **the reason being that all the species** of living and non-living things **were created for** the purpose of serving **the needs of man.**[13] One cannot suggest, then, that Hashem forbade us to take the mother bird with her young, even when we might need both, simply because He has pity on her. אֲבָל הַצַּוָּאָה עַל זֶה – **Rather, the command against [taking the mother with her young],** וּבְאוֹתוֹ וְאֶת בְּנוֹ שֶׁהִיא כַּיּוֹצֵא בָהּ – **and** the command against slaughtering **[an animal] and its offspring** on the same day (Mitzvah 294), **which is similar to [this command],** וּבִשְׁאָר מִצְוֹת רַבּוֹת – **as well as many other** similar **mitzvos** that seem to be rooted in compassion, אֵינוֹ אֶלָּא כִּגְזֵרָה לְפָנָיו שֶׁגָּזַר עַל זֶה בְּחֶפְצוֹ הַפָּשׁוּט – **are** actually **but a decree** from **before [Hashem],** that is to say, **that He decreed so by virtue of His transcendent Will,** for reasons that are specific to each mitzvah. וְאִלּוּ רָצָה בְּהֵפֶךְ מִזֶּה – **Had He desired the opposite of this,** i.e., that we should take the entire nest, or slaughter the mother animal and its child on the same day, etc., לֹא יַכְרִיחֶנּוּ דָּבָר וְלֹא יְמַנְעֶנּוּ סִבָּה חָלִילָה – **nothing would have compelled Him** otherwise, **and no factor would have prevented Him, Heaven forbid** the thought, from implementing His Will, כָּמוֹנוּ אֲנַחְנוּ הַבְּנוּיִים בְּכֹחַ הַטְּבָעִים – **as it would us, who are composed of natural tendencies,** שֶׁמִּדַּת הָרַחֲמָנוּת תְּעַכְּבֵנוּ מִלְּהַשְׁחִית – such **that** our inborn **sense of compassion may prevent us from destroying** precious things, אוֹ תַּכְרִיחֵנוּ לְהֵטִיב לִפְעָמִים – **or, at times,** even **compel us to do good.** With regard to Hashem, it is not so. זֶהוּ עִנְיַן אָמְרָם אֵינָן אֶלָּא גְּזֵרוֹת – **This is the meaning of [the Sages'] statement,** that **[Hashem's Attributes] are nothing but "decrees."** That is to say, that Hashem's Attributes (including that of mercy) are not expressions of impulses or sentiments, but are rather expressions of His Wisdom, which decrees that in a particular situation a certain action or trait is good.[14] וּמִשֹּׁרֶשׁ הָעִנְיָן מַה שֶּׁזָּכַרְנוּ – **As for the rationale** as **to** why **the matter** of sending

NOTES

13. [Though we may benefit from animals and birds for our needs, we must not cause them unnecessary pain or anguish (צַעַר בַּעֲלֵי חַיִּים); see Mitzvah 451, at notes 14-15, specifically regarding the requirement to be sensitive to their pain during slaughter, as well as Insight to Mitzvah 452; see also Mitzvah 540 note 3 and Mitzvah 550, at notes 7-8. This concept will come up again below.]

14. See a similar explanation by *Ran* to *Rif, Megillah*

(והרמב"ן) [וְהָרַמְבַּ"ם][15] **ז"ל** (מורה נבוכים חלק ג פרק מ"ח) **כָּתַב בְּטַעַם מִצְוָה זוֹ וּבְטַעַם אֹתוֹ וְאֶת בְּנוֹ לְפִי שֶׁיֵּשׁ לַבְּהֵמוֹת דְּאָגָה גְּדוֹלָה בִּרְאוֹתָן צַעַר בְּנֵיהֶן כְּמוֹ לִבְנֵי אָדָם**[16]**, כִּי אַהֲבַת הָאֵם לַבֵּן אֵינֶנּוּ דָּבָר נִמְשָׁךְ אַחַר הַשֵּׂכֶל, אֲבָל הוּא מִפְּעֻלּוֹת כֹּחַ הַמַּחֲשָׁבָה הַמְּצוּיָה בַּבְּהֵמוֹת כַּאֲשֶׁר הִיא מְצוּיָה בָּאָדָם**[17,18]**. וְאָמַר הָרַמְבַּ"ם ז"ל בְּעִנְיָן זֶה, וְאַל תָּשִׁיב מִלִּין**[19] **מִמַּאֲמַר הַחֲכָמִים (האומרים) [הָאוֹמֵר]**[20] **עַל קַן צִפּוֹר וְכוּ'** (ברכות דף ל"ג ע"א)[21,22]**,**

---

away the mother bird is "good," it is **what we indicated** above, i.e., that through its performance we recall Hashem's Providence over Creation.

☙ *Rambam's* approach

Chinuch cites *Rambam*, however, who does explain that the rationale behind *shiluach hakein* is Hashem's compassion on the birds:

(והרמב"ן) [וְהָרַמְבַּ"ם][15] ז"ל כָּתַב בְּטַעַם מִצְוָה זוֹ וּבְטַעַם אֹתוֹ וְאֶת בְּנוֹ – ***Rambam*, of blessed memory** (*Moreh Nevuchim* III:48), **wrote** the following idea to explain **the reason for this mitzvah** of *shiluach hakein* **and the reason for the** prohibition to slaughter an **animal and its offspring** on the same day: **לְפִי שֶׁיֵּשׁ לַבְּהֵמוֹת דְּאָגָה גְּדוֹלָה בִּרְאוֹתָן צַעַר בְּנֵיהֶן כְּמוֹ לִבְנֵי אָדָם** – It is in order to ensure that we not slaughter the offspring in the presence of the mother, **since animals have great anguish when they see the suffering of their young, just as people do.**[16] **כִּי אַהֲבַת הָאֵם לַבֵּן אֵינֶנּוּ דָּבָר נִמְשָׁךְ אַחַר הַשֵּׂכֶל** – **For the love of a mother toward her child is not a matter that stems from intelligence,** which only human beings possess. **אֲבָל הוּא מִפְּעֻלּוֹת כֹּחַ הַמַּחֲשָׁבָה הַמְּצוּיָה בַּבְּהֵמוֹת כַּאֲשֶׁר הִיא מְצוּיָה בָּאָדָם** – **Rather, it is a function of** simple, instinctive **thought, which exists in animals** just **as it exists in people.**[17] In any event, the reason for these two mitzvos (this mitzvah and Mitzvah 294) is that Hashem has compassion on the animals and the birds, and therefore He forbade us to cause them this sort of distress.[18]

Chinuch above cited the Gemara in *Berachos*, which seems to *negate* the idea that *shiluach hakein* has something to do with compassion toward the mother. *Rambam* considers the challenge to his explanation from that Gemara:

וְאָמַר הָרַמְבַּ"ם ז"ל בְּעִנְיָן זֶה – ***Rambam*, of blessed memory, says about this:** **וְאַל תָּשִׁיב מִלִּין** – **Do not reply** with **words** of rebuttal,[19] **מִמַּאֲמַר הַחֲכָמִים (האומרים) [הָאוֹמֵר][20] עַל קַן צִפּוֹר וְכוּ'** – quoting **from the statement of the Sages** (*Berachos* 33b) that **if one says** to Hashem in prayer, "Just as Your mercy extends **to a bird's nest**, so, too, may You have mercy on us," we silence him. And the Gemara (ibid.) explains that we silence him because he effectively "renders the

---

NOTES

fol. 16a. Regarding Chinuch's general theme, that Hashem's Attributes are not to be understood as we perceive human character traits, see also Mitzvah 611, and *Daas Tevunos* §46 (with notes by R' Chaim Friedlander, p. 34) and §80.

15. Emendation follows *Minchas Yitzchak* edition; see also *Me'il HaEphod*.

16. That is, the Torah commands not to slaughter the mother animal and her offspring on the same day for fear that one may come to slaughter the offspring in the presence of the mother. Similarly, the Torah commands to send away the mother bird before taking her young, lest one come to *slaughter* her young in her presence (*Rambam* ibid., as explained by *Ramban* to our verse). [*Rambam* (ibid.) concludes that if the Torah was so concerned about the pain and anguish of animals and birds, how much more so with regard to people!]

17. *Ramban* (to *Leviticus* 17:12) writes: The animal "soul" (i.e., intellect) is a complete "soul" in a certain respect. Thus, an animal has the sense to flee from harm and to go after that which is advantageous for it. It has the capacity of recognizing those to whom it is accustomed, and even love for them, such as the love of dogs for their masters ... and similarly, doves possess knowledge and recognition of people.

18. Notably, *Rambam's* approach already appears in the Midrash (*Devarim Rabbah* 6:1), which states: Just as Hashem has compassion over people, He has compassion over animals. From where do we know this? For it is stated… (*Leviticus* 22:28): *You may not slaughter it and its offspring on the same day.* And just as Hashem has compassion over animals, so He has compassion over birds, as it is stated, *Should a bird's nest chance to be before you,* etc.

19. Stylistic paraphrase of *Job* 35:4.

20. Emendation follows *Minchas Yitzchak* edition.

כִּי זוֹ סְבָרַת מִי שֶׁיִּרְאֶה שֶׁאֵין טַעַם לַמִּצְוֹת אֶלָּא חֵפֶץ הַבּוֹרֵא, וְאָנוּ מַחֲזִיקִים בַּסְּבָרָא הַשֵּׁנִית שֶׁהִיא שֶׁיֵּשׁ בְּכָל הַמִּצְווֹת טַעַם[23,24].

---

mitzvos[21] of the Holy One, blessed is He, into acts of mercy, when in truth they are nothing but decrees." Now, you might argue that this indicates that the mitzvah of *shiluach hakein* is *not* due to Hashem's compassion over the birds.[22] כִּי זוֹ סְבָרַת מִי שֶׁיִּרְאֶה שֶׁאֵין טַעַם לַמִּצְוֹת אֶלָּא חֵפֶץ הַבּוֹרֵא – However, this is not a refutation to what I have said, **for that** statement in the Gemara **is** based on **the approach of [the Sages], who maintain that there is no** rational **reason for the mitzvos** *whatsoever*, and that we are not supposed to seek explanations for them; **rather,** we are to perceive them strictly as reflecting **the** incomprehensible **Will of the Creator.** Surely, then, these Sages reject the idea that *shiluach hakein* is rooted in compassion, since they reject the idea of mitzvos having rationale altogether! Thus, when they say, "[The mitzvos] are nothing but decrees," they mean that all the mitzvos are decrees from Hashem without reasons that we are capable of comprehending. וְאָנוּ מַחֲזִיקִים בַּסְּבָרָא הַשֵּׁנִית – **We** (i.e., *Rambam* himself), **however, follow the other approach of the Sages,** שֶׁהִיא שֶׁיֵּשׁ בְּכָל הַמִּצְווֹת טַעַם – **which is that there** ***is*** **a** rational **reason for all the mitzvos,** and that it is our duty to seek them out so as to enhance our performance of the mitzvos.[23] Accordingly, we may suggest that the reason for *shiluach hakein* (as well as the prohibition to slaughter an animal and its offspring on one day) is rooted in compassion.[24]

NOTES

21. See note 12 above.

22. See *Ibn Crescas* to *Moreh Nevuchim* ad loc.

23. By way of background: In *Moreh Nevuchim* (III, Chs. 26 and 31), *Rambam* presents a debate regarding the idea of seeking reasons for mitzvos. Some of "the Torah scholars," he writes, maintain that one must not seek any rational reason for the mitzvos, as they were given to us by decree of the King, and as far as we are concerned, they are based on nothing but Hashem's unfathomable Will. "The majority of Sages" (*Rambam's* words), however, are of the opinion that all mitzvos have a rational reason, i.e., a purpose and benefit that is comprehensible to man. And although some of the reasons are hidden from us (i.e., the *chukim*), due to the profundity of those reasons and the feebleness of our minds, we are still urged to pursue them and understand them to the best of our ability.

[Those who maintain that the mitzvos should be viewed simply as decrees of Hashem still distinguish between *mishpatim* (מִשְׁפָּטִים), ordinances, and *chukim* (חֻקִּים), decrees. *Mishpatim* are the civil laws of the Torah and the like (e.g., Do not steal, Do not kill, Honor your elders), which have a universal acceptance, as they are necessary for society to function smoothly. *Chukim* are all the mitzvos that one observes only because Hashem commanded us in them (e.g., Do not wear *shaatnez*, Do not eat meat and milk together). We must observe all mitzvos, they say, without seeking reasons but simply because they are Hashem's command. The "majority of the Sages," however, maintain that even the *chukim* have rational reasons, except that their reasons are not readily understood; and in some cases, not accessible to man at all (except to rare individuals, such as Moses, King Solomon, and R' Akiva). However, the reasons will be revealed to all in the Days to Come (see further, below, in *Ramban's* thesis on the matter). Essentially, then, according to the latter opinion, *mishpatim* are the mitzvos whose purpose is readily understood by most people, and *chukim* are mitzvos whose purpose is not understood by most people (*Moreh Nevuchim* ibid.).]

24. One might wonder, though: How will *Rambam* accommodate the ruling of the Mishnah that if someone says in prayer, "Just as Your mercy extends to a bird's nest, so, too, may You have mercy on us," we silence him? What is wrong with saying that, if in fact Hashem's mercy *is* the reason for this mitzvah? The answer would seem to be that *Rambam* follows the other explanation in the Gemara there (*Berachos* 33b), which is, that saying, "Your mercy extends to a bird's nest," implies that Hashem has mercy on birds and not on other creatures, when in fact His mercy extends to *all* creatures (see *Meiri* to *Berachos* ad loc.; cf. *Maharal, Tiferes Yisrael* Ch. 6, and *Tos. Yom Tov* to *Berachos* 5:3). [Notably, however, when *Rambam* in *Hil. Tefillah* (9:7) cites the law of "one who says, 'Your mercy extends ...,' we silence him," he actually mentions the reason, "because he renders Hashem's mitzvos into acts of mercy, etc." (see *Lechem Mishneh* and *Rabbeinu Manoach* ad loc.). Indeed, *Tos. Yom Tov* (ibid.) notes this apparent discrepancy between *Rambam's* opinion in *Moreh Nevuchim* and his opinion in *Hil. Tefillah*. See also *Shem Tov* to *Moreh Nevuchim* ad loc.]

In any event, *Rambam* here clearly understands the statement of the Sages, that "[the mitzvos] are nothing but decrees," as reflecting the opinion that mitzvos are Divine decrees without reason. This is also the understanding of *Rashi* (to *Berachos* ad loc.) and *Rabbeinu Yonah* (*Berachos, Rif* fol. 23b). However, Chinuch will later cite *Ramban*, who explains this statement in a manner that is consistent with the opinion that mitzvos have reasons.

וְהֻקְשָׁה עָלָיו מַה שֶּׁמָּצָא בִּבְרֵאשִׁית רַבָּה (פרשה מ״ד פיסקא א׳) וְכִי מָה אִכְפַּת לוֹ לְהַקָּדוֹשׁ בָּרוּךְ הוּא בֵּין שׁוֹחֵט מִן הַצַּוָּאר לְשׁוֹחֵט מִן הָעֹרֶף, הָא לֹא נִתְּנוּ הַמִּצְוֹות אֶלָּא לִצְרֹף בָּהֶן אֶת הַבְּרִיּוֹת, שֶׁנֶּאֱמַר (משלי ל׳, ה׳) כָּל אִמְרַת אֱלוֹהַ צְרוּפָה[26,25]. וְהָרַמְבַּ״ן ז״ל תֵּרֵץ הַקֻּשְׁיוֹת וּבֵרֵר הָעִנְיָן בֵּרוּר שָׁלֵם וְנֶחְמָד, וְזֶה לְשׁוֹנוֹ שֶׁכָּתַב בְּפֵרוּשׁ הַתּוֹרָה שֶׁלּוֹ. זֶה הָעִנְיָן שֶׁכָּתַב הָרַמְבַּ״ם ז״ל בַּמִּצְוֹות שֶׁיֵּשׁ לָהֶם טַעַם, דָּבָר מְבֹאָר הוּא מְאֹד, כִּי בְּכָל אַחַת טַעַם וְתוֹעֶלֶת וְתִקּוּן לָאָדָם[27] מִלְּבַד שְׂכָרָן מֵאֵת הַמְצַוֶּה עֲלֵיהֶם יִתְבָּרַךְ,

---

In *Moreh Nevuchim* III:26, *Rambam* acknowledges another statement of the Sages that seems to contradict his preferred approach, that the mitzvos have reasons:

וְהֻקְשָׁה עָלָיו מַה שֶּׁמָּצָא בִּבְרֵאשִׁית רַבָּה – **[*Rambam*] had difficulty,** though, **with what he found** written **in *Bereishis Rabbah*** (44:1): וְכִי מָה אִכְפַּת לוֹ לְהַקָּדוֹשׁ בָּרוּךְ הוּא בֵּין שׁוֹחֵט מִן הַצַּוָּאר לְשׁוֹחֵט מִן הָעֹרֶף – **Of what concern is it to the Holy One, blessed is He, whether one slaughters** an animal **from the** front of the **neck,** as required by the Torah (Mitzvah 451), **or one slaughters from the back of the neck?** Surely none at all! הָא לֹא נִתְּנוּ הַמִּצְוֹות אֶלָּא לִצְרֹף בָּהֶן אֶת הַבְּרִיּוֹת – **Rather,** it must be concluded that **the mitzvos were given only in order to purify the people through them,** שֶׁנֶּאֱמַר ״כָּל אִמְרַת אֱלוֹהַ צְרוּפָה״ – **as it is stated** (*Proverbs* 30:5): ***Every word of God purifies.***[25] *Rambam* understands this to mean that Hashem commanded us with the mitzvos for no other reason than to test us ("to purify us") whether we obey or disobey His Will. Evidently, then, the mitzvos do *not* have rational underlying purposes, but are simply Hashem's decrees that we must obey![26]

❧ *Ramban's* approach

Ramban (to the verse of the mitzvah) addresses this issue at length and resolves the difficulties *Rambam* raises. Chinuch cites the greater part of *Ramban's* presentation:

וְהָרַמְבַּ״ן ז״ל תֵּרֵץ הַקֻּשְׁיוֹת וּבֵרֵר הָעִנְיָן בֵּרוּר שָׁלֵם וְנֶחְמָד – ***Ramban,* of blessed memory, resolved the** apparent **difficulties** that *Rambam* raised, **and clarified the issue in a perfect and delightful** manner. וְזֶה לְשׁוֹנוֹ שֶׁכָּתַב בְּפֵרוּשׁ הַתּוֹרָה שֶׁלּוֹ – **The following is a quote of what he wrote in his Commentary to the Torah** (ibid.): זֶה הָעִנְיָן שֶׁכָּתַב הָרַמְבַּ״ם ז״ל בַּמִּצְוֹות שֶׁיֵּשׁ לָהֶם טַעַם דָּבָר מְבֹאָר הוּא מְאֹד – **This idea that *Rambam*, of blessed memory, wrote regarding the mitzvos,** i.e., **that they do have a** rational **reason, is a very clear matter,** כִּי בְּכָל אַחַת טַעַם וְתוֹעֶלֶת וְתִקּוּן לָאָדָם – **for,** indeed, **every one of the mitzvos has a reason, and a benefit and usefulness for man,**[27] מִלְּבַד שְׂכָרָן מֵאֵת הַמְצַוֶּה עֲלֵיהֶם יִתְבָּרַךְ – **in addition to the reward** that one will receive **for** fulfilling **them,** which will come **from the One Who commanded them, blessed be He.** That is, in addition to the reward we will receive for obeying Hashem's Will and performing His mitzvos, the

---

NOTES

25. The literal meaning of the verse, כָּל אִמְרַת אֱלוֹהַ צְרוּפָה, is that Hashem's Word itself is pure. The Midrash expounds it, however, to mean that it purifies *us*. [This verse, and similar verses, will come up later as well. There, too, we will translate the term as per the Midrash's homiletical interpretation.]

26. [See, similarly, *Rashi* to *Berachos* 33b ד״ה מדותיו and *Megillah* 25a ד״ה ואינן אלא.] "To purify us" (as in purifying gold or silver) is thus understood as follows: Just like a refiner of precious metals determines whether a piece of gold or silver is pure or impure, so too the mitzvos reveal whether a person is committed to Hashem's Will or not (*Shem Tov* to *Moreh Nevuchim* ad loc.; *Maharal, Tiferes Yisrael,* beginning of Ch. 7).

Rambam (ibid.) concludes from this Midrash that although all mitzvos have reasons, that is true only regarding the general mitzvah (e.g., that an animal must be slaughtered before being eaten). The specific laws of a mitzvah (e.g., whether one slaughter from the back or the front of the neck), however, do not necessarily have reasons. [Notably, *Rambam* could have explained this Midrash as reflecting the other school of thought that he mentioned above, which maintains that the mitzvos are not based on rational reasons. Apparently, this distinction between the general mitzvah and its specifics seemed more satisfactory to him.] Further below, Chinuch will cite *Ramban*'s interpretation of this Midrash, according to which even the specific laws of a mitzvah have reasons.

27. *Ramban* to *Exodus* 20:23 (end) writes: With regard to God's mitzvos, there are many reasons for each one, because there are a great number of benefits in each one, for the body and for the soul. See also *Ramban* to *Leviticus* 19:19.

וּכְבָר אָמְרוּ זִכְרוֹנָם לִבְרָכָה (סנהדרין כ״א ע״ב) מִפְּנֵי מָה לֹא נִתְגַּלּוּ טַעֲמֵי תוֹרָה וְכוּ׳,[28] וְדָרְשׁוּ זִכְרוֹנָם לִבְרָכָה (פסחים קי״ט ע״א), וְלִמְכַסֶּה עָתִיק (ישעיה כ״ג, י״ח),[29] זֶה (המכסה) [הַמְגַלֶּה][30] דְּבָרִים שֶׁכִּסָּה עַתִּיק יוֹמַיָּא,[31] וּמַאי נִיהוּ טַעֲמֵי תוֹרָה,[32] וּכְבָר דָּרְשׁוּ בְּפָרָה אֲדֻמָּה (במדבר רבה פרשה י״ט פיסקא ג׳) שֶׁאָמַר שְׁלֹמֹה עַל הַכֹּל עָמַדְתִּי, וּפָרָשַׁת פָּרָה אֲדֻמָּה חָקַרְתִּי וְשָׁאַלְתִּי וּפִשְׁפַּשְׁתִּי אָמַרְתִּי אֶחְכָּמָה וְהִיא רְחוֹקָה מִמֶּנִּי (קהלת ז׳, כ״ג).[33] וְאָמַר רַבִּי יוֹסֵי בְּרַבִּי חֲנִינָא

---

mitzvos themselves provide benefit for us, physically or spiritually, and this is the primary reason that they were given to us.

Ramban quotes various statements of the Sages that prove that the mitzvos have reasons: וּכְבָר אָמְרוּ זִכְרוֹנָם לִבְרָכָה — **[Our Sages], of blessed memory, have thus expressed** the following question (*Sanhedrin* 21b): מִפְּנֵי מָה לֹא נִתְגַּלּוּ טַעֲמֵי תוֹרָה וְכוּ׳ — **Why were the reasons for the** mitzvos of the **Torah not revealed?** The Sages (ibid.) provide an answer to this question, but the implication of the question is that the mitzvos do have reasons, except that they were not generally revealed to us in the Torah.[28] וְדָרְשׁוּ זִכְרוֹנָם לִבְרָכָה — **In addition, [the Sages], of blessed memory** (*Pesachim* 119a), **expounded the verse** (*Isaiah* 23:18): "וְלִמְכַסֶּה עָתִיק" — *For the goods ... will be for those who sit before HASHEM, to eat and be sated, and for the cover of the ancient.*[29] What does it mean "for the cover of the ancient"? זֶה (המכסה) [הַמְגַלֶּה][30] דְּבָרִים שֶׁכִּסָּה עַתִּיק יוֹמַיָּא — **This is** referring to **one who reveals matters that** Hashem, Who is called **"the Ancient of Days,"**[31] **covered** (i.e., concealed). וּמַאי נִיהוּ טַעֲמֵי תוֹרָה — **And what are those** concealed matters? **The reasons for the** mitzvos of the **Torah.**[32] The Sages here praise one who "uncovers" the reasons for the mitzvos. It is evident from this passage as well that the mitzvos have reasons, and that we are urged to uncover them.

Ramban cites the Midrash, which indicates that even what we refer to as *chukim* (decrees with no known reason; sing., *chok*) actually have reasons, except that Hashem concealed them to the broader public, but revealed them to certain individuals: וּכְבָר דָּרְשׁוּ בְּפָרָה אֲדֻמָּה — **[The Sages]** (*Bamidbar Rabbah* 19:3; *Tanchuma, Chukas* §6) **have thus expounded in regard to** the *parah adumah* (red cow; see Mitzvah 397), שֶׁאָמַר שְׁלֹמֹה עַל הַכֹּל עָמַדְתִּי — **that** the wise King **Solomon said, "I have mastered** the reasons for **everything;** וּפָרָשַׁת פָּרָה אֲדֻמָּה חָקַרְתִּי וְשָׁאַלְתִּי וּפִשְׁפַּשְׁתִּי — **but** while **I have investigated and inquired and examined the passage of** *parah adumah,* I could not plumb the depth of its meaning." King Solomon expressed this in the following verse (*Ecclesiastes* 7:23): "אָמַרְתִּי אֶחְכָּמָה וְהִיא רְחוֹקָה מִמֶּנִּי" — *I said I could gain wisdom, but it is beyond me.* Evidently, even *parah adumah,* which is the epitome of a *chok*,[33] has a reason, and King Solomon attempted to uncover it, though he was unsuccessful. וְאָמַר רַבִּי יוֹסֵי בְּרַבִּי חֲנִינָא — **Further** (*Bamidbar Rabbah* 19:6; *Tanchuma* ibid. §8), the Midrash states: **R' Yose the**

NOTES

28. The Gemara's answer there is that if the reasons for mitzvos had been revealed to us, people would rationalize that they do not apply in this or that situation (see Mitzvah 159, at notes 6 and 7). However, the reasons do exist and we are encouraged to seek them out in order to better appreciate the Will of the Creator and what He desires of us (see Mitzvah 159, notes 13-14). Since the reasons are not explicit in the Torah, however, we cannot be *sure* of the reasons, so we will not be led to rationalize (see *Maharsha, Chidushei Aggados* to *Pesachim* 119a ד״ה טעמי).

29. The simple translation of וְלִמְכַסֶּה עָתִיק in the context of the verse is, *and for elegant clothing* (i.e., that those who sit before Hashem will be rewarded with elegant clothing). However, for the purpose of expounding the verse, the Gemara reads the phrase

more literally as, *and for the cover of the ancient.*

30. Emendation follows *Minchas Chinuch* edition (Vilna), in accordance with *Pesachim* and *Ramban* ibid.

31. See *Daniel* 7:13 and 7:22.

32. Thus, Hashem concealed the reasons for the mitzvos in the Torah, so that people would not rationalize that they do not apply in certain cases (as indicated in the Gemara in *Sanhedrin*; see note 28). However, a sage who merits to gain insight into the mitzvos and shares those insights with others will be rewarded (see *Maharsha* ibid.).

33. The Torah begins the passage of *parah adumah* (*Numbers* 19:1-22) with the phrase, זֹאת חֻקַּת הַתּוֹרָה, *This is the decree (chok) of the Torah.*

אָמַר לוֹ הַקָּדוֹשׁ בָּרוּךְ הוּא לְמֹשֶׁה, לְךָ אֲנִי מְגַלֶּה טַעַם פָּרָה, אֲבָל לְאַחֵר חֻקָּה, דִּכְתִיב (זכריה י״ד, ו׳) וְהָיָה בַּיּוֹם הַהוּא לֹא יִהְיֶה אוֹר יְקָרוֹת וְקִפָּאוֹן[34], קִפָּאוֹן[35], דְּבָרִים הַמְכֻסִּין מִכֶּם בָּעוֹלָם הַזֶּה עֲתִידִין לִהְיוֹת צוֹפִין[36] לָעוֹלָם הַבָּא כְּהָדֵין סַמְיָא דְּצָפֵי, דִּכְתִיב (ישעיה מ״ב, ט״ז) וְהוֹלַכְתִּי עִוְרִים בְּדֶרֶךְ לֹא יָדָעוּ, וּכְתִיב (שם) אֵלֶּה הַדְּבָרִים עֲשִׂיתִם וְלֹא עֲזַבְתִּים, שֶׁכְּבָר עֲשִׂיתִים לְרַבִּי עֲקִיבָא, כְּלוֹמַר שֶׁרַבִּי עֲקִיבָא יְדָעָם בָּעוֹלָם הַזֶּה. הִנֵּה בֵּאֲרוּ שֶׁאֵין מְנִיעַת טַעֲמֵי תוֹרָה מִמֶּנּוּ אֶלָּא עִוָּרוֹן בְּשִׂכְלֵנוּ[37] וְשֶׁכְּבָר נִתְגַּלָּה טַעַם הַחֲמוּרָה שֶׁבָּהֶן לְחַכְמֵי יִשְׂרָאֵל,

---

son of R' Chanina said: אָמַר לוֹ הַקָּדוֹשׁ בָּרוּךְ הוּא לְמֹשֶׁה **— The Holy One, blessed is He, said to Moses,** לְךָ אֲנִי מְגַלֶּה טַעַם פָּרָה אֲבָל לְאַחֵר חֻקָּה **— "To you I reveal the reason for** ***parah** adumah,* **but to anyone else** it shall remain **a 'decree'** (i.e., a law without a known reason)." Here we see again that even *parah adumah* has a reason, but that it was revealed only to Moses. Eventually, the reason for *parah adumah,* and certainly of other mitzvos, will be revealed to all, דִּכְתִיב "וְהָיָה בַּיּוֹם הַהוּא לֹא יִהְיֶה אוֹר יְקָרוֹת וְקִפָּאוֹן" **— as it is written** (*Zechariah* 14:6): ***It will be on that day, the light will not be heavy, vekipaon.***[34] "קִפָּאוֹן" — The term ***vekipaon*** is related to the root קפא (*kafa*), which means "lightweight and afloat."[35] The verse is thus expounded as follows: דְּבָרִים הַמְכֻסִּין מִכֶּם בָּעוֹלָם הַזֶּה עֲתִידִין לִהְיוֹת צוֹפִין לָעוֹלָם הַבָּא — All **matters** of Torah (the ultimate "light") **that are** "heavy," submerged, and thus **concealed from you in this world** — that is, the reasons for the mitzvos — **will float** to the surface and become visible[36] to you **in the World to Come.** כְּהָדֵין סַמְיָא דְּצָפֵי — You will be **like a blind person who** regains his eyesight and **can** now **see** things that he could not see before, דִּכְתִיב "וְהוֹלַכְתִּי עִוְרִים בְּדֶרֶךְ לֹא יָדָעוּ" **— as it is written** regarding the Future Redemption (*Isaiah* 42:16): ***I will lead the blind on a way they never knew ...*** *I will turn darkness into light before them;* which is to say, I will reveal to them the secrets of the Torah. וּכְתִיב "אֵלֶּה הַדְּבָרִים עֲשִׂיתִם וְלֹא עֲזַבְתִּים" **— Furthermore,** although Hashem will not reveal the reasons for the Torah to the *masses* of people until the Future Era, He has already revealed them to certain great individuals, as **it is written** at the end of that verse: ***These are the things I will do*** (*asisim*; literally, *I did*) ***and not forsake them.*** Clearly the verse means that Hashem will do those things in the Future Era, as the beginning of the verse implies. Yet, instead of saying, *e'eseh* (*I will do*, i.e., I *will* reveal the reasons to them), the verse expresses the term in the past tense, *asisim* (*I did,* i.e., I *already* revealed the reasons to them), שֶׁכְּבָר עֲשִׂיתִים לְרַבִּי עֲקִיבָא **— because, in fact,** Hashem **already "did [these things]" for R' Akiva** in *this* world. כְּלוֹמַר שֶׁרַבִּי עֲקִיבָא יְדָעָם בָּעוֹלָם הַזֶּה **— That is to say, that R' Akiva knew [the reasons for the mitzvos]** already **in this world.**

הִנֵּה בֵּאֲרוּ **— You see,** then, that **[the Sages] stated clearly** שֶׁאֵין מְנִיעַת טַעֲמֵי תוֹרָה מִמֶּנּוּ אֶלָּא עִוָּרוֹן בְּשִׂכְלֵנוּ **— that the withholding of reasons for the** mitzvos of the **Torah from us is not** because the reasons do not exist, or because Hashem does not want us to pursue them, **but** as a result of **"blindness" in our intellect,**[37] וְשֶׁכְּבָר נִתְגַּלָּה טַעַם הַחֲמוּרָה שֶׁבָּהֶן לְחַכְמֵי יִשְׂרָאֵל **— and that,** in fact, the

---

NOTES

34. The literal interpretation of the verse is: *It will be on that day* (i.e., the Future Era), *the light will not be [either] very bright* [יְקָרוֹת] *or very dim* [וְקִפָּאוֹן] (see commentaries ad loc.). However, according to the homiletic interpretation here, יְקָרוֹת means "heavy" or "weighty" (as in *Bava Metzia* 21b). The word וְקִפָּאוֹן (*vekipaon*) according to this exposition will be immediately explained.

35. *Rashi* (*Pesachim* 50a) finds a source for this interpretation from the verse (*II Kings* 6:6), וַיָּצֶף הַבַּרְזֶל, *And he made the iron float,* which *Targum* (ad loc.) translates as וּקְפָא בַּרְזְלָא.

36. See *Matnos Kehunah* to *Bamidbar Rabbah* ad loc.

37. This is a reference to the metaphor of the blind person who regains his eyesight (see above). The fact that a blind person cannot see things around him is not because they do not exist; they *do* exist, except that he lacks the ability to see them. Once he regains his eyesight, he is able to see what was already there before. The same is true with regard to the reasons for the mitzvos. Though we cannot completely fathom most of them, and some of them not at all, it does not mean that they are not there. The reasons exist, but we are intellectually, or spiritually, blind and cannot perceive them — until the Future Era, when Hashem will open our eyes.

וְכָאֵלֶּה רַבּוֹת בְּדִבְרֵיהֶם וּבַתּוֹרָה וּבַמִּקְרָא דְּבָרִים רַבִּים, וְהָרַמְבַּ"ם ז"ל הִזְכִּיר מֵהֶם. אֲבָל[38] אֵלּוּ הַהַגָּדוֹת אֲשֶׁר נִתְקַשּׁוּ עַל הָרַב כְּפִי דַּעְתּוֹ עִנְיָן אַחֵר לָהֶם, שֶׁרָצוּ לוֹמַר שֶׁאֵין הַתּוֹעֶלֶת בַּמִּצְווֹת לְהַקָּדוֹשׁ בָּרוּךְ הוּא בְּעַצְמוֹ יִתְבָּרֵךְ, אֲבָל הַתּוֹעֶלֶת בָּאָדָם עַצְמוֹ לִמְנֹעַ מִמֶּנּוּ נֵזֶק אוֹ אֱמוּנָה רָעָה אוֹ מִדָּה מְגֻנָּה אוֹ לִזְכֹּר נִסִּים וְנִפְלְאוֹת הַבּוֹרֵא יִתְבָּרֵךְ לָדַעַת אֶת ה׳, וְזֶהוּ לְצָרֵף בָּהֶם, שֶׁיִּהְיוּ כְּכֶסֶף צָרוּף, כִּי הַצּוֹרֵף הַכֶּסֶף אֵין מַעֲשֵׂהוּ בְּלֹא טַעַם, אֲבָל לְהוֹצִיא מִמֶּנּוּ כָּל סִיג, וְכֵן הַמִּצְווֹת לְהוֹצִיא מִמֶּנּוּ כָּל אֱמוּנָה רָעָה וּלְהוֹדִיעֵנוּ הָאֱמֶת וּלְזָכְרוֹ

---

reasons **were already revealed to the Sages of Israel, even for [the mitzvos] that are the most difficult** to understand. וְכָאֵלֶּה רַבּוֹת בְּדִבְרֵיהֶם – **There are many other statements like these in the words of [the Sages]** that indicate that the mitzvos have reasons. וּבַתּוֹרָה וּבַמִּקְרָא דְּבָרִים רַבִּים – **In the Torah and in** the other Books of **Scripture, too,** there are **many statements** that indicate this, וְהָרַמְבַּ"ם ז"ל הִזְכִּיר מֵהֶם – **some of which** ***Rambam*****, of blessed memory, mentions** in *Moreh Nevuchim* (III:26).

Thus far, *Ramban* proved that the mitzvos have understandable reasons. He now turns to his next discussion. *Rambam* (cited above) quoted two passages from the Sages that apparently contradict his view that the mitzvos have reasons.[38] *Ramban* shows how those passages are in fact consistent with that view: אֲבָל אֵלּוּ הַהַגָּדוֹת אֲשֶׁר נִתְקַשּׁוּ עַל הָרַב כְּפִי דַּעְתּוֹ – **But these Aggadic teachings that posed difficulty for the Rabbi** (*Rambam*) **according to his understanding** of the matter, עִנְיָן אַחֵר לָהֶם – in my opinion **have a different meaning** from what he thought. When the Sages say in the Midrash, "Of what concern is it for the Holy One, blessed is He, whether one slaughters… Rather the mitzvos were given only to purify us through them," they did not mean to say that there is no purpose at all to the mitzvos other than compliance with Hashem's Will. שֶׁרָצוּ לוֹמַר שֶׁאֵין הַתּוֹעֶלֶת בַּמִּצְווֹת לְהַקָּדוֹשׁ בָּרוּךְ הוּא בְּעַצְמוֹ יִתְבָּרֵךְ – What **they meant to say** was **that there is no** purpose or **benefit for the Holy One, blessed be He,** ***Himself*** in our performance of **the mitzvos,** אֲבָל הַתּוֹעֶלֶת בָּאָדָם עַצְמוֹ – **but** rather, **the benefit is for man himself,** לִמְנֹעַ מִמֶּנּוּ נֵזֶק אוֹ אֱמוּנָה רָעָה אוֹ מִדָּה מְגֻנָּה – either **to prevent harm from** befalling **him, or** to prevent him from developing **a wrong belief or a contemptible** character **trait,** אוֹ לִזְכֹּר נִסִּים וְנִפְלְאוֹת הַבּוֹרֵא יִתְבָּרֵךְ לָדַעַת אֶת ה׳ – **or to** help him **remember the miracles and wonders of the Creator, blessed be He,** so that he should come **to know Hashem.** וְזֶהוּ לְצָרֵף בָּהֶם – **This is** the meaning of the Midrash's expression (*Bereishis Rabbah* 44:1), that the mitzvos were given **"to purify** (or refine) us **through them";** שֶׁיִּהְיוּ כְּכֶסֶף צָרוּף – **that is, that** Hashem gave us the mitzvos so that, through performing them and reflecting on their underlying purposes, we **should become** purified and refined **like refined silver.** Indeed, the Midrash's expression "to purify us" itself demonstrates that Hashem designed the mitzvos with a purpose and a benefit for us in mind, כִּי הַצּוֹרֵף הַכֶּסֶף אֵין מַעֲשֵׂהוּ בְּלֹא טַעַם – **for when one refines silver, his action is not without reason** or purpose, אֲבָל לְהוֹצִיא מִמֶּנּוּ כָּל סִיג – **but** rather it is in order **to remove any impurity from it** and thus turn it into a better product. וְכֵן הַמִּצְווֹת – **Likewise,** with regard to **the mitzvos,** Hashem did not give us random mitzvos, without reason or purpose, just to test our obedience. Rather, He gave us specially designed mitzvos לְהוֹצִיא מִמֶּנּוּ כָּל אֱמוּנָה רָעָה וּלְהוֹדִיעֵנוּ הָאֱמֶת וּלְזָכְרוֹ

NOTES

38. Briefly, the two passages were: (1) The Gemara in *Berachos* (33b) regarding one who prays that Hashem's mercy should extend to His people as it extends to a bird's nest (as evident from the mitzvah of *shiluach hakein*). We silence him because he implies that Hashem commanded us in *shiluach hakein* out of compassion for the birds, while in reality mitzvos are "decrees." See above, at notes 19-22.

(2) The Midrash in *Bereishis Rabbah* (44:1) regarding the law of slaughtering an animal from the front of the neck, where the Sages assert that there is really no difference to Hashem whether one slaughters from the front of the neck or the back of the neck (which *Rambam* understands to mean that there is no rationale for this law). Rather, this law, as well as all the mitzvos of the Torah, were meant "to purify us through them" (which *Rambam* understands to mean that the mitzvos are decrees, without any reason other than to test our obedience to Hashem). See above, at notes 25-26.

תָּמִיד[39]. וּלְשׁוֹן זֶה הַהַגָּדָה עַצְמָהּ בִּילַמְּדֵנוּ[40] בְּפָרָשָׁה זֹאת הַחַיָּה (ראה תנחומא שמיני פיסקא ח׳), וְכִי מָה אִכְפַּת לֵיהּ לְהַקָּדוֹשׁ בָּרוּךְ הוּא בֵּין שׁוֹחֵט בְּהֵמָה וְאוֹכֵל לְנוֹחֵר וְאוֹכֵל, כְּלוּם אַתָּה מוֹעִילוֹ אוֹ כְּלוּם אַתָּה מַזִּיקוֹ, אוֹ מָה אִכְפַּת לוֹ בֵּין אוֹכֵל טְהוֹרוֹת אוֹ טְמֵאוֹת, אִם חָכַמְתָּ חָכַמְתָּ לָּךְ, הָא לֹא נִתְּנוּ הַמִּצְווֹת אֶלָּא לְצָרֵף בָּהֶן אֶת הַבְּרִיּוֹת, שֶׁנֶּאֱמַר (תהלים י״ב, ז׳) אִמְרוֹת ה׳ אֲמָרוֹת טְהֹרוֹת, אִמְרַת ה׳ צְרוּפָה (שם י״ח, ל״א), לָמָּה, שֶׁיִּהְיֶה מָגֵן עָלֶיךָ. הִנֵּה מְפֹרָשׁ בְּכָאן שֶׁבָּאוּ לוֹמַר שֶׁאֵין הַתּוֹעָלוֹת אֵלָיו יִתְבָּרַךְ שֶׁיִּצְטָרֵךְ לְאוֹרָה כְּמַחְשָׁב מִן

תָּמִיד – **in order to remove from us any improper belief** that we might have, **and to have us know the truth and remember it constantly.** As a result, we will become more refined.[39]

Ramban proves his interpretation of the Midrash from a parallel Midrash:

וּלְשׁוֹן זֶה הַהַגָּדָה עַצְמָהּ בִּילַמְּדֵנוּ בְּפָרָשָׁה זֹאת הַחַיָּה – This same Aggadic teaching is mentioned **in** *Midrash Yelamedeinu* (see *Tanchuma, Shemini* §8),[40] **in the Scriptural passage** beginning with ***These are the creatures*** *that you may eat* (*Leviticus* 11:2), **and** there **the language** is as follows: **וְכִי מָה אִכְפַּת לֵיהּ לְהַקָּדוֹשׁ בָּרוּךְ הוּא בֵּין שׁוֹחֵט בְּהֵמָה וְאוֹכֵל לְנוֹחֵר וְאוֹכֵל – Of what concern is it to the Holy One, blessed is He, whether one slaughters an animal** through *shechitah* **and eats** it, **or stabs** it **and eats** it? **כְּלוּם אַתָּה מוֹעִילוֹ אוֹ כְּלוּם אַתָּה מַזִּיקוֹ – Do you benefit Him at all** if you do *shechitah*, **or harm Him** if you do not?! **אוֹ מָה אִכְפַּת לוֹ בֵּין אוֹכֵל טְהוֹרוֹת אוֹ טְמֵאוֹת – Likewise, of what concern is it to [Hashem] whether one eats "clean"** (kosher) things **or "unclean"** (nonkosher) things? **"אִם חָכַמְתָּ חָכַמְתָּ לָּךְ"** – Rather, as King Solomon said (*Proverbs* 9:12): ***If you have become wise, you have become wise for your own good;*** in other words, you benefit only yourself if you conduct yourself wisely and obey Hashem's mitzvos. **הָא לֹא נִתְּנוּ הַמִּצְווֹת אֶלָּא לְצָרֵף בָּהֶן אֶת הַבְּרִיּוֹת – Indeed, the mitzvos were given only in order to purify the people through them,** **שֶׁנֶּאֱמַר "אִמְרוֹת ה׳ אֲמָרוֹת טְהֹרוֹת, אִמְרַת ה׳ צְרוּפָה" – as it is stated** (*Psalms* 12:7), ***The words of HASHEM are purifying words,*** and (ibid. 18:31), ***The word of HASHEM purifies.*** **לָמָּה – For what purpose** does Hashem want you to become purified and refined? **שֶׁיִּהְיֶה מָגֵן עָלֶיךָ – So that** you shall be worthy and **He will protect you,** as the latter verse (ibid. 18:31) concludes, *He is a shield for all who take refuge in Him.*

Ramban explains what he intended to prove from *Yelamedeinu's* version of the Aggadic teaching:

הִנֵּה מְפֹרָשׁ בְּכָאן – It is abundantly **clear here** in the Midrash, in the way it concludes the question, "Do you benefit Him at all (if you do) or harm Him (if you do not)?," **שֶׁבָּאוּ לוֹמַר שֶׁאֵין הַתּוֹעָלוֹת אֵלָיו יִתְבָּרַךְ – that** when the Sages exclaimed, "Of what concern is it to Hashem whether one slaughters the animal from the back of the neck or the front?," they did not mean to say that Hashem did not give the mitzvos for any particular benefit. Rather, **they meant to say that the benefit** that is gained from the mitzvos **is not for [Hashem], blessed be He.** **שֶׁיִּצְטָרֵךְ לְאוֹרָה כְּמַחְשָׁב מִן הַמְּנוֹרָה** – Take, for example, the mitzvah to light the Menorah in the *Beis HaMikdash* (Mitzvah 98). It is not **that [Hashem] needs light** in the *Beis HaMikdash*, **as** might be erroneously **thought from** His command that we

---

NOTES

39. In other words, "to purify us" does not mean to determine whether we are committed to Hashem's Will or not, as *Rambam* understood (see note 26 above). Rather, it means to purify and *refine* our character. The purpose of the mitzvos is to rid us of our flaws (in character traits, beliefs, etc.) and bring out a more elevated form of ourselves (see also *Meiri* to *Berachos* 33b; *Ibn Crescas* to *Moreh Nevuchim* III:26 §1-2). *Ramban* will explain below (at note 47) how this applies specifically to the law of slaughtering from the front of the neck.

[Interestingly, *Rambam,* at the end of *Hil. Temurah,* also indicates that the mitzvos are essentially ways through which Hashem brings us to perfection, by refining our outlook and correcting our actions (see also *Abarbanel* cited in note 60 below). However, it seems that he applies this idea only to the general mitzvah, not to the specific laws of the mitzvah, which is why he explains this Midrash differently than *Ramban* (see note 26 above).]

40. *Midrash Yelamedeinu*, cited often by the early commentators, is no longer extant, although its contents frequently overlap with our *Midrash Tanchuma*. The particular Midrash that *Ramban* quotes here is found in *Tanchuma, Shemini* §8.

הַמְּנוֹרָה[41] וְיִצְטָרֵךְ לְמַאֲכַל הַקָּרְבָּנוֹת וְרֵיחַ הַקְּטֹרֶת כַּנִּרְאֶה מִפְּשׁוּטֵיהֶן[42]. וַאֲפִלּוּ הַזֵּכֶר לְנִפְלְאוֹתָיו[43] שֶׁצִּוָּה לַעֲשׂוֹת לִזְכֹּר יְצִיאַת מִצְרַיִם וּמַעֲשֵׂה בְרֵאשִׁית[44], אֵין הַתּוֹעֶלֶת רַק שֶׁנֵּדַע אֲנַחְנוּ הָאֱמֶת וְנִזְכֶּה בּוֹ[45]. עַד שֶׁנִּהְיֶה רְאוּיִין לִהְיוֹת מָגֵן עָלֵינוּ, כִּי כְבוֹדֵנוּ וְסִפּוּרֵנוּ בִּתְהִלּוֹתָיו מֵאֶפֶס וָתֹהוּ נֶחְשְׁבוּ לוֹ[46]. וְהֵבִיא רְאָיָה מִן הַשּׁוֹחֵט מִן הַצַּוָּאר וְהָעֹרֶף לוֹמַר שֶׁכֻּלָּן לָנוּ וְלֹא לְהַקָּדוֹשׁ בָּרוּךְ הוּא, לְפִי שֶׁלֹּא יִתָּכֵן לוֹמַר בַּשְּׁחִיטָה שֶׁיְּהֵא בָהּ תּוֹעֶלֶת וְכָבוֹד לַבּוֹרֵא יִתְבָּרֵךְ בַּצַּוָּאר יוֹתֵר מִן הָעֹרֶף אוֹ הַנָּחוֹר, אֶלָּא לָנוּ הֵם

— **should light the Menorah** there.[41] וְיִצְטָרֵךְ לְמַאֲכַל הַקָּרְבָּנוֹת וְרֵיחַ הַקְּטֹרֶת כַּנִּרְאֶה מִפְּשׁוּטֵיהֶן **Likewise,** with regard to the mitzvos of the offerings and the incense (*ketores*; Mitzvah 103) in the *Beis HaMikdash*, it is not **that He needs the food from the offerings and the aroma of the incense,** **as it might seem from a superficial understanding of** the passages describing [**these things**].[42] וַאֲפִלּוּ הַזֵּכֶר לְנִפְלְאוֹתָיו שֶׁצִּוָּה לַעֲשׂוֹת — **And even** with respect to **the commemorations of His wonders**[43] that **He commanded us to observe,** לִזְכֹּר יְצִיאַת מִצְרַיִם וּמַעֲשֵׂה בְרֵאשִׁית — such as the many mitzvos that we do in order **to commemorate the Exodus from Egypt or the act of Creation,**[44] אֵין הַתּוֹעֶלֶת רַק שֶׁנֵּדַע אֲנַחְנוּ הָאֱמֶת וְנִזְכֶּה בּוֹ — **the benefit** in all these mitzvos is not for Hashem, **but rather that *we* should know the truth** about the Exodus or the Creation, **and** that **we should gain merit through** our knowledge of it,[45] עַד שֶׁנִּהְיֶה רְאוּיִין לִהְיוֹת מָגֵן עָלֵינוּ — until **we will become worthy that [Hashem] will protect us.** כִּי כְבוֹדֵנוּ וְסִפּוּרֵנוּ בִּתְהִלּוֹתָיו מֵאֶפֶס וָתֹהוּ נֶחְשְׁבוּ לוֹ — The idea of recounting Hashem's miracles is certainly not for *His* benefit, however, **for the honor** given Him **by us, and our recounting of His praises, are considered as nothingness and emptiness to Him.**[46]

Ramban highlights the significance of the Midrash's example of *shechitah* in its citation of the verse, *If you have become wise, you have become wise for your own good*:

וְהֵבִיא רְאָיָה מִן הַשּׁוֹחֵט מִן הַצַּוָּאר וְהָעֹרֶף — [The Midrash] thus **brought a proof from** the contrast between **one who slaughters** an animal **from the** front of **the neck and** one who does so from **the back of the neck,** which seems to make no difference as far as Hashem is concerned, לוֹמַר שֶׁכֻּלָּן לָנוּ וְלֹא לְהַקָּדוֹשׁ בָּרוּךְ הוּא — **to show that *all* of** [the mitzvos] **are for our** benefit **and not for the** benefit of the **Holy One, blessed is He.** לְפִי שֶׁלֹּא יִתָּכֵן לוֹמַר בַּשְּׁחִיטָה — **For,** whereas regarding some of the mitzvos (such as the ones mentioned earlier) one might mistakenly believe that it is for the benefit of Hashem, **it is *impossible*** to **say regarding** ritual **slaughter** שֶׁיְּהֵא בָהּ תּוֹעֶלֶת וְכָבוֹד לַבּוֹרֵא יִתְבָּרֵךְ בַּצַּוָּאר יוֹתֵר מִן הָעֹרֶף — **that there is** greater **benefit or honor for the Creator, blessed be He,** if we slaughter the animal **in the front of the neck than** if we slaughter it **from the back of the neck** (as stated in *Bereishis Rabbah* ibid.), אוֹ הַנָּחוֹר — **or** that there is any greater honor for Him if we slaughter rather than kill the animal via **stabbing** (as stated in *Midrash Yelamedeinu* [*Tanchuma*] ibid.). אֶלָּא לָנוּ הֵם — **Evidently, [the laws of *shechitah*] are for *our*** benefit,

---

NOTES

41. The Gemara (*Shabbos* 22b) states: Does Hashem need the Menorah's light? Is it not so that during the entire forty years that the Children of Israel traveled in the Wilderness they traveled only by His light? Rather, [the light of the Menorah] is a testimony for all mankind that the Divine Presence dwells with Israel.

42. Such as the phrase that appears often in the passages of the offerings (e.g., Leviticus 1:9): רֵיחַ נִיחֹחַ לַה׳, *a satisfying aroma to Hashem*. [See Mitzvah 95 (beginning at note 16), where Chinuch discusses the idea posited here by *Ramban* — that Hashem has no benefit from our fulfillment of His mitzvos; rather, the mitzvos are intended to refine us and make us better people, worthy of Hashem's Providence. That discussion focuses specifically on the offerings and other services in the *Beis HaMikdash*.]

43. Stylistic paraphrase of *Psalms* 111:4.

44. The mitzvos associated with the Pesach festival are among those that commemorate the Exodus (see below, at note 51, for additional examples). A primary example of a mitzvah that commemorates the act of Creation is observing the Sabbath; see *Exodus* 20:11.

45. *Sfas Emes* (to *Psalms* ibid. [Ohr Etzion ed.]) writes: In addition to the great wonders that Hashem did for us, He gave us ways to remember them; i.e., He gave us mitzvos by which we can recall and thus continue to be inspired by those wonders.

46. Stylistic citation of *Isaiah* 40:17.

לְהַדְרִיכֵנוּ בִּנְתִיבוֹת הָרַחֲמִים גַּם בְּעֵת הַשְּׁחִיטָה[47]**. וְהֵבִיא רְאָיָה אַחֶרֶת** (ראה תנחומא שם)**, אוֹ מָה אִכְפַּת לוֹ בֵּין אוֹכֵל טְהוֹרוֹת וְהֵם הַמַּאֲכָלִים הַמֻּתָּרִין, לְאוֹכֵל טְמֵאִים, וְהֵם הַמַּאֲכָלִים הָאֲסוּרִים שֶׁאָמְרָה בָּהֶם הַתּוֹרָה** (ויקרא י״א, ח) **טְמֵאִים הֵם לָכֶם, רַק שֶׁהוּא לְהִיוֹתֵנוּ נְקִיֵּי הַנֶּפֶשׁ חֲכָמִים מַשְׂכִּילֵי הָאֱמֶת**[48]**. וְאָמְרָם אִם חָכַמְתָּ חָכַמְתָּ לָּךְ**[49]**, הִזְכִּירוּ כִּי הַמִּצְוֹת הַמַּעֲשִׂיּוֹת כְּגוֹן שְׁחִיטַת הַצַּוָּאר לְלַמְּדֵנוּ הַמִּדּוֹת הַטּוֹבוֹת, וְהַמִּצְוֹת הַגְּזוּרוֹת בְּמִינִים לְזַקֵּק אֶת נַפְשׁוֹתֵינוּ, וּכְמוֹ שֶׁאָמְרָה תּוֹרָה** (שם כ׳, כ״ה) **וְלֹא תְשַׁקְּצוּ אֶת נַפְשֹׁתֵיכֶם בַּבְּהֵמָה וּבָעוֹף וּבְכֹל אֲשֶׁר תִּרְמֹשׂ הָאֲדָמָה אֲשֶׁר הִבְדַּלְתִּי לָכֶם לְטַמֵּא, אִם כֵּן כֻּלָּם הֵם לְתוֹעַלְתֵּנוּ בִּלְבַד, וְזֶה כְּמוֹ שֶׁאָמַר אֱלִיהוּא** (איוב ל״ה, ו׳) **אִם חָטָאתָ מַה תִּפְעָל בּוֹ וְרַבּוּ**

לְהַדְרִיכֵנוּ בִּנְתִיבוֹת הָרַחֲמִים גַּם בְּעֵת הַשְּׁחִיטָה — so as **to guide us in the paths of compassion even while** we are engaged in **the slaughter** of an animal.[47] So too, *all* the mitzvos of the Torah are intended *solely* for our benefit, even those that may seem like they benefit Hashem in some way.

The other example in *Midrash Yelamedeinu* illustrates the same idea:

וְהֵבִיא רְאָיָה אַחֶרֶת — In this vein, **[*Midrash Yelamedeinu*] brought another proof,** saying: אוֹ מָה אִכְפַּת לוֹ בֵּין אוֹכֵל טְהוֹרוֹת וְהֵם הַמַּאֲכָלִים הַמֻּתָּרִין — **And of what concern is it to [Hashem] whether one eats clean** things, **meaning the permitted** (kosher) **foods,** לְאוֹכֵל טְמֵאִים וְהֵם הַמַּאֲכָלִים הָאֲסוּרִים שֶׁאָמְרָה בָּהֶם הַתּוֹרָה טְמֵאִים הֵם לָכֶם — **or unclean** things, **meaning the forbidden** (nonkosher) **foods, about which the Torah said** (*Leviticus* 11:8): *But this you shall not eat ... **they are "unclean" to you***? Surely this mitzvah is not for Hashem's benefit! רַק שֶׁהוּא לְהִיוֹתֵנוּ נְקִיֵּי הַנֶּפֶשׁ חֲכָמִים מַשְׂכִּילֵי הָאֱמֶת — **Rather,** the reason that Hashem commanded us to refrain from nonkosher food **is so we should be pure in spirit, wise, and discerning of the truth.**[48] וְאָמְרָם "אִם חָכַמְתָּ חָכַמְתָּ לָּךְ" — **In citing** the verse, ***If you have become wise, you have "become wise" for your own good,*** to express the idea that the mitzvos of *shechitah* and refraining from nonkosher food are for our benefit, הִזְכִּירוּ כִּי הַמִּצְוֹת הַמַּעֲשִׂיּוֹת כְּגוֹן שְׁחִיטַת הַצַּוָּאר — **[the Sages] indicated that** the benefit for us from these mitzvos is a spiritual benefit ("become wise"): **The mitzvos that involve action, such as slaughtering at the** front of the **neck,** לְלַמְּדֵנוּ הַמִּדּוֹת הַטּוֹבוֹת — are in order **to teach us good** character **traits** (e.g., to be compassionate);[49] וְהַמִּצְוֹת הַגְּזוּרוֹת בְּמִינִים לְזַקֵּק אֶת נַפְשׁוֹתֵינוּ — **and the mitzvos that are instituted in regard to species**, such as, "You may eat this kind of animal, but not that kind of animal," are in order **to purify our souls,** וּכְמוֹ שֶׁאָמְרָה תּוֹרָה — **as the Torah says** regarding prohibited foods (*Leviticus* 20:25): "וְלֹא תְשַׁקְּצוּ אֶת נַפְשֹׁתֵיכֶם בַּבְּהֵמָה וּבָעוֹף וּבְכֹל אֲשֶׁר תִּרְמֹשׂ הָאֲדָמָה אֲשֶׁר הִבְדַּלְתִּי לָכֶם לְטַמֵּא" — ***And you shall not render your souls abominable through animals and birds, and through anything that creeps on the ground, which I have set apart for you to render unclean.*** Conversely, *refraining* from eating such foods *purifies* our souls. אִם כֵּן כֻּלָּם הֵם לְתוֹעַלְתֵּנוּ בִּלְבַד — In any event, these mitzvos are certainly only for our benefit. **If so,** then evidently **all [the mitzvos] are solely for our benefit,** and not for Hashem's. וְזֶה כְּמוֹ שֶׁאָמַר אֱלִיהוּא — **It is as Elihu said** to Job (*Job* 35:6): "אִם חָטָאתָ מַה תִּפְעָל בּוֹ וְרַבּוּ

NOTES

47. Although we are permitted to slaughter an animal for our benefit, we must nevertheless be sensitive to its pain (see note 13 above). And it is less painful for an animal to have its throat slit than to be killed by stabbing or decapitation from the rear of the neck, as explained in Mitzvah 451.

48. See *Ramban* to *Leviticus* 11:13, where he writes that the ingesting of nonkosher birds or animals can impart the bad character traits of those birds or animals. See also *Ramban* to *Exodus* 22:30 and *Deuteronomy* 14:3.

The text in *Ramban* is וְרָמַז שֶׁהוּא לִהְיוֹתֵנוּ נְקִיֵּי הַנֶּפֶשׁ חֲכָמִים מַשְׂכִּילֵי הָאֱמֶת, *And [the Torah] alluded* (by use of the words, *they are "unclean" to you*) *that it* (i.e., the prohibition against eating certain animals) *is in order that we should be of pure soul — wise people who are discerning of the truth.*

[Chinuch has a somewhat different understanding of the reasons for these mitzvos; namely, that they provide health benefits. For discussion of the views of *Ramban* and Chinuch, see Insight to Mitzvah 73.]

49. And this is how slaughtering at the front of the neck or not eating nonkosher meat make a person "wise."

פְּשָׁעֶיךָ מַה תַּעֲשֶׂה לוֹ, וְאָמַר (שם, ז׳) **אוֹ מַה מִיָּדְךָ יִקָּח, וְזֶה דָבָר מֻסְכָּם בְּכָל דִּבְרֵי רַבּוֹתֵינוּ. וְשָׁאֲלוּ בִּירוּשַׁלְמִי בִּנְדָרִים** (פ״ט ה״א) **אִם פּוֹתְחִין לְאָדָם בִּכְבוֹד הַמָּקוֹם בִּדְבָרִים שֶׁבֵּינוֹ לְבֵין הַמָּקוֹם, וְהֵשִׁיבוּ עַל הַשְּׁאֵלָה הַזֹּאת, אֵי זֶהוּ כְּבוֹד הַמָּקוֹם, כְּגוֹן סֻכָּה שֶׁאֵינִי עוֹשֶׂה, לוּלָב שֶׁאֵינִי נוֹטֵל, תְּפִלִּין שֶׁאֵינִי נוֹשֵׂא, וְהַיְנוּ כְּבוֹד הַמָּקוֹם מַשְׁמַע דִּלְנַפְשֵׁיהּ הוּא דִּמְהַנֵּי**[50]**, כְּהָדָא אִם צָדַקְתָּ מַה תִּתֶּן לוֹ אוֹ מַה מִיָּדְךָ יִקָּח, וְחָטָאתָ מַה תִּפְעָל בּוֹ וְרַבּוּ פְּשָׁעֶיךָ מַה תַּעֲשֶׂה לוֹ. הִנֵּה בֵּאֲרוּ שֶׁאֲפִלּוּ הַסֻּכָּה וְהַלּוּלָב וּתְפִלִּין שֶׁצִּוָּה בָּהֶן שֶׁיִּהְיוּ לְאוֹת עַל יָדְךָ וּלְזִכָּרוֹן בֵּין עֵינֶיךָ כִּי בְּיָד חֲזָקָה הוֹצִיאֲךָ ה׳ מִמִּצְרַיִם**[51]**, אֵינָן לִכְבוֹד הַשֵּׁם יִתְבָּרַךְ**

״פְּשָׁעֶיךָ מַה תַּעֲשֶׂה לוֹ״ – ***If you have sinned, how have you affected Him? If your transgressions multiply, what have you done to Him?*** **וְאָמַר ״אוֹ מַה מִיָּדְךָ יִקָּח״** – **And** as **he** similarly **said** (ibid. v. 7): *If you were righteous, what have you given Him,* ***or what has He received from your hand?*** **וְזֶה דָבָר מֻסְכָּם בְּכָל דִּבְרֵי רַבּוֹתֵינוּ** – **This** explanation, that the mitzvos are for our benefit, and that this is the intention of the Midrashim cited, **is** the **accepted approach in all the works of our teachers.**

Ramban goes on to bring support for his explanation from a passage in *Talmud Yerushalmi* pertaining to the annulment of vows (*nedarim*; sing. *neder*). As Chinuch teaches in Mitzvah 30 (at notes 38-55) and in Mitzvah 406 (at notes 26 39), a vow can be nullified by an expert sage or a *beis din* if they find an "opening" (grounds) to do so. Such an "opening" is provided when the vow was based on a misunderstanding of some sort, or upon some fact that was overlooked. *Yerushalmi* discusses a possible "opening" for vows related to one's service of Hashem:

וְשָׁאֲלוּ בִּירוּשַׁלְמִי בִּנְדָרִים – **[The Sages] inquired in *Yerushalmi Nedarim*** (9:1) **אִם פּוֹתְחִין לְאָדָם בִּכְבוֹד הַמָּקוֹם בִּדְבָרִים שֶׁבֵּינוֹ לְבֵין הַמָּקוֹם** – **whether an "opening" can be provided to a person based on the honor of the Omnipresent** (Hashem), **in matters** (i.e., vows) **that are between [a person] and the Omnipresent.** In other words: If a person made a vow that adversely affects his service of Hashem, can an "opening" be made to the effect that the person would not have made the vow had he realized that it causes dishonor to Hashem? **וְהֵשִׁיבוּ עַל הַשְּׁאֵלָה הַזֹּאת** – **[The Sages] responded to this query** as follows: **אֵי זֶהוּ כְּבוֹד הַמָּקוֹם** – **What sort of** vow would involve **"the honor of the Omnipresent"?** **כְּגוֹן סֻכָּה שֶׁאֵינִי עוֹשֶׂה, לוּלָב שֶׁאֵינִי נוֹטֵל, תְּפִלִּין שֶׁאֵינִי נוֹשֵׂא** – **Something like** "I vow **that I will not make a *succah*** on Succos," or **"I will not take a *lulav*** on Succos," or **"I will not put on *tefillin*."** **וְהַיְנוּ כְּבוֹד הַמָּקוֹם** – But **are these** really things that involve **the honor of the Omnipresent?** **מַשְׁמַע דִּלְנַפְשֵׁיהּ הוּא דִּמְהַנֵּי** – Why, **it is implied** in Scripture **that [observing the mitzvos] benefits [the person] himself,** *not* Hashem,[50] **כְּהָדָא ״אִם צָדַקְתָּ מַה תִּתֶּן לוֹ אוֹ מַה מִיָּדְךָ יִקָּח״** – **as the following** verse states (*Job* 35:7): ***If you were righteous, what have you given Him, or what has He received from your hand?*** **״וְחָטָאתָ מַה תִּפְעָל בּוֹ וְרַבּוּ פְּשָׁעֶיךָ מַה תַּעֲשֶׂה לוֹ״** – And the preceding verse (ibid. v. 6) states as well: ***If you have sinned, how have you affected Him? If your transgressions multiply, what have you done to Him?***

הִנֵּה בֵּאֲרוּ – **You see** that **[the Sages] made clear** **שֶׁאֲפִלּוּ הַסֻּכָּה וְהַלּוּלָב** – **that even** mitzvos that might be *perceived* as benefiting Hashem (by bringing honor to His Name), such as making **the *succah*** **and** taking **the *lulav,*** **וּתְפִלִּין שֶׁצִּוָּה בָּהֶן שֶׁיִּהְיוּ ״לְאוֹת עַל יָדְךָ וּלְזִכָּרוֹן בֵּין עֵינֶיךָ ... כִּי בְּיָד חֲזָקָה הוֹצִיאֲךָ ה׳ מִמִּצְרַיִם״** – **and** putting on ***tefillin,* about which [Hashem] commanded that they be *a sign on your arm and a reminder between your eyes ... for with a strong hand HASHEM took you out of Egypt*** (*Exodus* 13:9),[51] **אֵינָן לִכְבוֹד הַשֵּׁם יִתְבָּרַךְ** – **were *not*** intended **for the honor of Hashem,**

NOTES

50. See *Pnei Moshe* and *Korban HaEidah* ad loc.

51. Regarding the obligation to sit in the *succah*, too, the Torah states (*Leviticus* 23:43): לְמַעַן יֵדְעוּ דֹרֹתֵיכֶם כִּי בַסֻּכּוֹת הוֹשַׁבְתִּי אֶת בְּנֵי יִשְׂרָאֵל בְּהוֹצִיאִי אוֹתָם מֵאֶרֶץ מִצְרָיִם, *So that your generations will know that I sheltered the Children of Israel in booths when I took them from the land of Egypt.* And the mitzvah of *lulav* is also related to this idea, that Hashem took us out of Egypt and performed miracles for us; see *Moreh Nevuchim* III:43. [One might therefore mistakenly believe that these mitzvos are meant to bring honor to Hashem.]

אֲבָל לְרַחֵם עַל נַפְשׁוֹתֵינוּ. וּכְבָר סִדְּרוּ לָנוּ בִּתְפִלַּת יוֹם הַכִּפּוּרִים, אַתָּה הִבְדַּלְתָּ אֱנוֹשׁ מֵרֹאשׁ וַתַּכִּירֵהוּ לַעֲמֹד לְפָנֶיךָ כִּי מִי יֹאמַר לְךָ מַה תַּעֲשֶׂה וְאִם יִצְדַּק מַה יִּתֶּן לְךָ, וְכֵן אָמַר בַּתּוֹרָה (דברים י׳, י״ג) לְטוֹב לָךְ, וְכֵן (שם ו׳, כ״ד) וַיְצַוֵּנוּ ה׳ אֱלֹהֵינוּ לַעֲשׂוֹת אֶת הַחֻקִּים הָאֵלֶּה לְטוֹב לָנוּ כָּל הַיָּמִים, וְהַכַּוָּנָה בְּכֻלָּם לְטוֹב לָנוּ וְלֹא לוֹ יִתְעַלֶּה[52], אֲבָל כָּל מַה שֶּׁנִּצְטַוִּינוּ שֶׁיִּהְיוּ נַפְשׁוֹתֵינוּ צְרוּפוֹת וּמְזֻקָּקוֹת בְּלֹא סִיגֵי מַחֲשָׁבוֹת רָעוֹת וּמִדּוֹת מְגֻנּוֹת[53]. וְכֵן מַה שֶּׁאָמְרוּ לְפִי שֶׁעוֹשֶׂה גְּזֵרוֹתָיו שֶׁל הַקָּדוֹשׁ בָּרוּךְ הוּא רַחֲמִים וְאֵינָן אֶלָּא גְּזֵרוֹת, לוֹמַר שֶׁלֹּא חָס הָאֵל עַל קַן צִפּוֹר וְלֹא הִגִּיעוּ רַחֲמָיו עַל אוֹתוֹ וְאֶת בְּנוֹ, שֶׁאֵין רַחֲמָיו מַגִּיעוֹת בְּבַעֲלֵי נֶפֶשׁ הַבַּהֲמִית[54] לִמְנֹעַ אוֹתָנוּ מִלַּעֲשׂוֹת בָּהֶם צְרָכֵינוּ

---

blessed be He. אֲבָל לְרַחֵם עַל נַפְשׁוֹתֵינוּ – **Rather,** Hashem gave them to us in order **to bestow mercy upon our souls,** so that we should cling to Him through our recognition of His kindness to us, and thus merit His protection.

Ramban cites a passage from the prayer liturgy that echoes the idea that Hashem gains nothing from our mitzvos:

וּכְבָר סִדְּרוּ לָנוּ בִּתְפִלַּת יוֹם הַכִּפּוּרִים – **Thus, [our Sages] formulated for us in the Yom Kippur prayers** (*Ne'ilah* service) the following declaration: אַתָּה הִבְדַּלְתָּ אֱנוֹשׁ מֵרֹאשׁ וַתַּכִּירֵהוּ לַעֲמֹד לְפָנֶיךָ – ***You separated Man from the outset, and You distinguished him to stand before You,*** כִּי מִי יֹאמַר לְךָ מַה תַּעֲשֶׂה וְאִם יִצְדַּק מַה יִּתֶּן לְךָ – ***for who can say to You, "What are You doing?" and if one is righteous, what does he*** *thereby* ***give You?***

Ramban notes that this concept is expressed in several Scriptural verses, as well:

וְכֵן אָמַר בַּתּוֹרָה "לְטוֹב לָךְ" – **Similarly, it says in the Torah** (*Deuteronomy* 10:13): *to observe the commandments ...* ***"for your benefit."*** וְכֵן "וַיְצַוֵּנוּ ה׳ אֱלֹהֵינוּ לַעֲשׂוֹת אֶת הַחֻקִּים הָאֵלֶּה לְטוֹב לָנוּ כָּל הַיָּמִים" – **Likewise,** the verse states (ibid. 6:24): ***HASHEM commanded us to perform all these decrees ... "for our good," all the days.*** וְהַכַּוָּנָה בְּכֻלָּם לְטוֹב לָנוּ וְלֹא לוֹ יִתְעַלֶּה – **The intent in all [these verses] is** that the mitzvos are **for *our* benefit, not for** the benefit of **[Hashem], exalted be He.**[52] אֲבָל כָּל מַה שֶּׁנִּצְטַוִּינוּ – **Rather, whatever we were commanded** was given to us שֶׁיִּהְיוּ נַפְשׁוֹתֵינוּ צְרוּפוֹת וּמְזֻקָּקוֹת – in order **that our souls should be purified and refined,** בְּלֹא סִיגֵי מַחֲשָׁבוֹת רָעוֹת וּמִדּוֹת מְגֻנּוֹת – **without the imperfections of bad thoughts and contemptible** character **traits.**

Ramban has thus explained that all the mitzvos *are* intended to benefit us in some way, and when the Sages state that it is of no concern to the Holy One, blessed is He, whether we slaughter from the front of the neck or from the back of the neck, they mean only that *HASHEM* derives no benefit from the mitzvos. He now goes on to resolve *Rambam's* other difficulty:[53]

וְכֵן מַה שֶּׁאָמְרוּ – **In a similar vein,** we can explain **[the Sages'] statement** (*Berachos* 33b), לְפִי שֶׁעוֹשֶׂה גְּזֵרוֹתָיו שֶׁל הַקָּדוֹשׁ בָּרוּךְ הוּא רַחֲמִים וְאֵינָן אֶלָּא גְּזֵרוֹת – that one who says, "Your mercy extends even to a bird's nest," is to be silenced, **because he** thereby **implies that the decrees** (i.e., the mitzvos) **of the Holy One, blessed is He, are** based on His Attribute of **Mercy, while** in truth **they are exclusively decrees.** The Sages did not mean to say that the mitzvos have no reason whatsoever, as *Rambam* understood. לוֹמַר שֶׁלֹּא חָס הָאֵל עַל קַן צִפּוֹר – Rather, they meant **to say that the Almighty did not** command us in the mitzvah of *shiluach hakein* because He **has compassion on the birds,** וְלֹא הִגִּיעוּ רַחֲמָיו עַל אוֹתוֹ וְאֶת בְּנוֹ – **nor did** He command us not to slaughter an animal and its offspring on the same day because **His mercy extends to [the animal] and its offspring.** שֶׁאֵין רַחֲמָיו מַגִּיעוֹת בְּבַעֲלֵי נֶפֶשׁ הַבַּהֲמִית לִמְנֹעַ אוֹתָנוּ מִלַּעֲשׂוֹת בָּהֶם צְרָכֵינוּ – **For,** in fact, while Hashem certainly cares for all of His creations, **He does not extend His mercy to animals** and the like,[54] insofar as **to**

NOTES

52. See *Ramban's* commentary to *Deuteronomy* 6:20 (6:24 in some prints) ד״ה והנה אנחנו חייבים, and 10:12-13.

53. See note 38 above.

54. Literally, *those [creatures] that possess an animal soul.* [See *Ramban* to *Genesis* 1:22 and 2:7 for his explanation of the term "animal soul."]

שֶׁאִם כֵּן הָיָה אוֹסֵר הַשְּׁחִיטָה‎[55], אֲבָל טַעַם הַמְּנִיעָה לְלַמֵּד אוֹתָנוּ מִדַּת הָרַחֲמָנוּת וְשֶׁלֹּא נִתְאַכְזֵר, כִּי הָאַכְזָרִיּוּת תִּתְפַּשֵּׁט בְּנֶפֶשׁ הָאָדָם, כַּיָּדוּעַ בְּטַבָּחִים שׁוֹחֲטֵי הַשְּׁוָרִים הַגְּדוֹלִים (וְהַחֲמוֹדִים) [וְהַיַּחְמוּרִים]‎[56] שֶׁהֵם אַנְשֵׁי דָמִים זוֹבְחֵי אָדָם אַכְזָרִיִּים מְאֹד‎[57], וּמִפְּנֵי זֶה אָמְרוּ (קידושין פ״ב ע״א) טוֹב שֶׁבַּטַּבָּחִים שֻׁתָּפוֹ שֶׁל עֲמָלֵק‎[58]. וְהִנֵּה הַמִּצְוֹת הָאֵלֶּה בַּבְּהֵמָה וּבָעוֹף אֵינָן רַחֲמִים עֲלֵיהֶן אֲבָל גְּזֵרוֹת בָּנוּ לְהַדְרִיכֵנוּ וּלְלַמֵּד אוֹתָנוּ הַמִּדּוֹת הַטּוֹבוֹת‎[59], עַד כָּאן בְּפֵרוּשֵׁי הָרַמְבַּ״ן ז״ל‎[60].

---

prevent us from fulfilling our needs through them, שֶׁאִם כֵּן הָיָה אוֹסֵר הַשְּׁחִיטָה – **for if so, He would have prohibited the slaughtering** of animals altogether.[55] אֲבָל טַעַם הַמְּנִיעָה – **Rather, the reason for the** Torah's **prohibition** of taking the mother bird with her young or slaughtering an animal and its child is לְלַמֵּד אוֹתָנוּ מִדַּת הָרַחֲמָנוּת וְשֶׁלֹּא נִתְאַכְזֵר – in order **to teach** *us* **the trait of mercy, and that we should not become cruel.** כִּי הָאַכְזָרִיּוּת תִּתְפַּשֵּׁט בְּנֶפֶשׁ הָאָדָם – Not only that we should not become cruel toward animals, but also that we should not become cruel toward *people*, **since cruelty spreads through a man's character,** escalating from cruelty toward animals to cruelty toward people, כַּיָּדוּעַ בְּטַבָּחִים שׁוֹחֲטֵי הַשְּׁוָרִים הַגְּדוֹלִים (וְהַחֲמוֹדִים) [וְהַיַּחְמוּרִים]‎[56] – **as is known regarding animal slaughterers who slaughter large oxen and fallow-deer,** שֶׁהֵם אַנְשֵׁי דָמִים זוֹבְחֵי אָדָם אַכְזָרִיִּים מְאֹד – **that they are** often **bloody men, "murderers of people,"**[57] and are **very cruel,** וּמִפְּנֵי זֶה אָמְרוּ טוֹב שֶׁבַּטַּבָּחִים שֻׁתָּפוֹ שֶׁל עֲמָלֵק – **on account of which [the Sages] said** (*Kiddushin* 82a) that even **the best of animal slaughterers is an associate of Amalek.**[58] וְהִנֵּה הַמִּצְוֹת הָאֵלֶּה בַּבְּהֵמָה וּבָעוֹף אֵינָן רַחֲמִים עֲלֵיהֶן – In any event, **as stated** earlier, **these mitzvos pertaining to animals** (i.e., the slaughter of mother and offspring on the same day) **and birds** (i.e., *shiluach hakein*) **are not** Hashem's expression of **compassion for [the animals and the birds];** אֲבָל גְּזֵרוֹת בָּנוּ לְהַדְרִיכֵנוּ וּלְלַמֵּד אוֹתָנוּ הַמִּדּוֹת הַטּוֹבוֹת – **rather, they are "decrees"** directed **toward us, to guide us and to teach us good character traits.** *That* is the meaning of the expression in the Gemara, "while [the mitzvos] are nothing but decrees."[59] עַד כָּאן בְּפֵרוּשֵׁי הָרַמְבַּ״ן ז״ל – **Until here** is the presentation **in the commentary of *Ramban*,** of blessed memory.[60]

NOTES

55. *Rambam* in his *Commentary to the Mishnah* (*Berachos* 5:3) and in *Hil. Tefillah* (9:7) makes this point as well.

As Chinuch explained at the beginning of the mitzvah, Hashem's compassion is not an emotional response to someone or something in distress. Hashem is not "moved" by a situation to the extent that He is "compelled" to act out of sympathy. Rather, Hashem acts with compassion toward all His creations because that is the right thing to do according to His Infinite Wisdom. Thus, when His Wisdom dictates otherwise (as in allowing people to use animals or birds for their needs) He does *not* extend His mercy. [Nevertheless, if people's needs can be obtained through compassionate means, such as by slaughtering animals rather than by stabbing them, or slaughtering them from the front of the neck rather than from the back of the neck, then His Wisdom dictates that, in this regard, compassion is warranted.]

56. Emendation follows *Ramban*, Artscroll ed. [*Minchas Yitzchak* and *Minchas Chinuch* (Vilna) editions have חֲמוֹרִים, *donkeys*.]

57. Stylistic citation from *Hosea* 13:2.

58. Amalek was the first nation to attack the Jewish people after the Exodus from Egypt. The Jews were a beleaguered nation with no land, and had just escaped prolonged bondage. Nothing motivated Amalek to wage war with them other than cruelty and callousness (see *Tos. Ri HaZaken* to *Kiddushin* ad loc.; *Tos. Yom Tov* and *Tiferes Yisrael* to Mishnah, *Kiddushin* 4:14; cf. *Rashi* to *Kiddushin* ad loc.). The Mishnah means to illustrate the idea that while the occupation of slaughterers may be a worthy and necessary one, they are at great risk of being affected in terms of their sensitivity and compassion toward others, and in that sense, they become associated with the trait of callousness and cruelty that Amalek represents.

59. In other words: The term גְּזֵרוֹת (*decrees*) is generally understood to mean that it is a mitzvah without a reason. This seems to be the way *Rambam* interpreted this statement in the Gemara, that "the mitzvos are nothing but גְּזֵרוֹת." He therefore concluded that the statement reflects the opinion among the Sages that the mitzvos do not have reasons. *Ramban*, however, explains that what is meant by גְּזֵרוֹת is that they are decrees of the King to His subjects in order to teach them good character traits (*middos*) and refine their character. [They are "decrees" in that they are "imposed upon" the person for his own good, though he may not appreciate the benefit that doing the mitzvah brings him (see *Ramban* to *Leviticus* 18:6 and 19:19; see also *Meiri, Berachos* 33b).]

60. To summarize *Rambam* and *Ramban*'s point of

וְהִנֵּה הֶאֱרַכְתִּי לִכְתֹּב לְךָ בְּנִי כָּל זֶה
לְהָעִיד עַל כָּל שָׁרְשֵׁי סִפְרִי עֵדִים נֶאֱמָנִים
שְׁנֵי עַמּוּדֵי עוֹלָם חֲכָמִים גְּדוֹלִים וּנְבוֹנִים
בַּעֲלֵי שֵׂכֶל מְזֻקָּק וּבְסִתְרֵי הַתּוֹרָה מְקֻבָּלִים,
כִּי הִנְּךָ רוֹאֶה בְּעֵינֶיךָ דַּעַת שְׁנֵיהֶם
כִּי יֵשׁ בְּמִצְוֹת הַתּוֹרָה טַעַם לְהוֹעִיל בְּנֵי אָדָם בְּדֵעוֹתֵיהֶם
לְהַכְשִׁירָם וּלְהַרְגִּילָם לְהַכְשִׁיר בָּהֶן כָּל פְּעֻלּוֹתֵיהֶם[61],

Chinuch's conclusion

After citing *Rambam*, and especially *Ramban,* at length, Chinuch explains his motivation for doing so:

וְהִנֵּה הֶאֱרַכְתִּי לִכְתֹּב לְךָ בְּנִי כָּל זֶה – **Now, I wrote all this for you, my son,** citing *Rambam* and *Ramban* **at** great **length,**

לְהָעִיד עַל כָּל שָׁרְשֵׁי סִפְרִי עֵדִים נֶאֱמָנִים – **in order to draw testimony from** these **reliable witnesses regarding all the underlying purposes** that I propose **in my work;**

שְׁנֵי עַמּוּדֵי עוֹלָם חֲכָמִים גְּדוֹלִים וּנְבוֹנִים – namely, *Rambam* and *Ramban,* **two pillars of the world, great and wise sages,**

בַּעֲלֵי שֵׂכֶל מְזֻקָּק וּבְסִתְרֵי הַתּוֹרָה מְקֻבָּלִים – **men of a** highly **refined intellect, and recipients of the tradition of the secrets of the Torah.**

כִּי הִנְּךָ רוֹאֶה בְּעֵינֶיךָ דַּעַת שְׁנֵיהֶם – **For you can see with your** own **eyes** that it is **the opinion of both of them,**

כִּי יֵשׁ בְּמִצְוֹת הַתּוֹרָה טַעַם לְהוֹעִיל בְּנֵי אָדָם בְּדֵעוֹתֵיהֶם – **that there is a reason** and purpose **to the mitzvos of the Torah;** namely, **to positively affect people's sensitivities,**

לְהַכְשִׁירָם וּלְהַרְגִּילָם לְהַכְשִׁיר בָּהֶן כָּל פְּעֻלּוֹתֵיהֶם – so as **to make them** more **refined, and to ingrain in them** these sensitivities **so that all their actions will become** more **refined.**[61]

NOTES

contention: *Rambam* understood the Gemara's statement that the mitzvos are גְּזֵרוֹת ("decrees") to mean that they are decrees without rationales. Since this contradicts his thesis that the mitzvos have reasons, *Rambam* said that this opinion in the Gemara reflects a variant viewpoint that maintains that there are no reasons for the mitzvos. *Rambam,* however, accepts the opinion that the mitzvos do have rational reasons. And, with regard to the mitzvah to send away the mother bird, *Rambam* explains that it was given to show compassion for the mother, as animals feel the pain of losing their young as people do.

Ramban disagrees: When the Gemara says that the mitzvos are "decrees," it does not mean that they are without reason. Rather, it means that they are directed toward *us*, as opposed to being an expression of Hashem's compassion or the like. The reason a person is silenced for saying, "Your mercy extends even to a bird's nest," is not because he has uttered a statement that is *philosophically* incorrect (i.e., that mitzvos have reasons), but because he is mistaken in his understanding of this particular mitzvah; that is, he incorrectly ascribes it to compassion for the mother bird.

[For an extensive discussion of both *Rambam's* and *Ramban's* approaches, see *Maharal, Tiferes Yisrael* Chs. 6 and 7. Notably, *Abarbanel* (to our verse) comment that *Ramban* "utters truth," but that everything he says is simply an explanation of *Rambam's* words. In other words, *Rambam* also did not mean to say that Hashem commanded us in *shiluach hakein* simply because He has compassion for the birds. It is so that *we* should develop that same sensitivity and that same trait of compassion! See note 39 above.]

Chinuch himself began this discussion by proposing yet another reason for *shiluach hakein*: that it is intended to remind us of Hashem's Providence over all creation and, most importantly, ourselves. We thus find four possible approaches to *shiluach hakein* discussed here in this mitzvah: (1) It is a mitzvah without reason, like all other mitzvos (*Berachos* 33b, as understood by *Rambam* and others); (2) it is Hashem showing compassion for the birds (*Rambam*); (3) it is so that we should not become callous and cruel (*Ramban*); and (4) it is to recall Hashem's Providence over creation (Chinuch). And above, at note 2, we cited *another* approach mentioned by *Ramban,* which is related to Chinuch's approach: it is to prevent us from doing something that is destructive to the species. For yet another, esoteric reason mentioned in the *Zohar*, see Insight.

61. Chinuch indicates here ("it is the opinion of both of them…") that he agrees with *Abarbanel's* assertion, that there is actually no dispute at all between

וְשֶׁאֵין הַתּוֹעֶלֶת בַּעֲשִׂיָּתָן חָלִילָה לַבּוֹרֵא בָּרוּךְ הוּא, וְאִם אָמְנָם כִּי יֵשׁ מִן הַמִּצְוֹות שֶׁלֹּא הִשַּׂגְנוּ בְּטַעֲמָן בִּמְעוּט שִׂכְלֵנוּ מֵרֹב עָמְקָן וְתַכְלִית גָּדְלָן, לֹא נִמְנַע מִמֶּנּוּ מֵהַגִּיד בָּהֶן כָּל אֲשֶׁר נַשִּׂיג לִמְצֹא מִן הַתּוֹעֶלֶת שֶׁיֵּשׁ לוֹ לָאָדָם בַּעֲשִׂיָּתָן. וְזֶה דַּרְכִּי בְּכָל שִׂיחָתִי בְּסִפְרִי זֶה שֶׁיֵּשׁ בַּמִּצְוֹות תּוֹעֶלֶת מָצוּי לָנוּ אַךְ לֹא אֶל הַמְצַוֶּה בָּהֶן, וְאִם תִּתֵּן לִבְּךָ בַּדְּבָרִים תִּמְצָא זֹאת הַכַּוָּנָה בְּכֻלָּן, וְהַרְבֵּה יָגַעְתִּי בְּמִקְצָתָן לְהַשִּׂיג בַּעֲנִיּוּת דַּעְתִּי לִרְאוֹת בָּהֶן מְעַט קָט[62] מֵרֹב הַתּוֹעָלוֹת שֶׁבָּהֶן, וּכְתַבְתִּיו עַל כָּל אַחַת[63], וְזֶה חֶלְקִי מִכָּל עֲמָלִי[64].

מִדִּינֵי הַמִּצְוָה מַה שֶּׁאָמְרוּ זִכְרוֹנָם לִבְרָכָה (חולין קל״ט ע״ב) **כִּי יִקָּרֵא קַן צִפּוֹר לְפָנֶיךָ**

וְשֶׁאֵין הַתּוֹעֶלֶת בַּעֲשִׂיָּתָן חָלִילָה לַבּוֹרֵא בָּרוּךְ הוּא – **Likewise**, it is clear from both *Rambam* and *Ramban's* presentations **that the benefit of observing [the mitzvos] is *not*, Heaven forbid** the thought, **for the Creator, blessed is He;** rather, it is exclusively for *our* benefit. **וְאִם אָמְנָם כִּי יֵשׁ מִן הַמִּצְוֹות שֶׁלֹּא הִשַּׂגְנוּ בְּטַעֲמָן בִּמְעוּט שִׂכְלֵנוּ** – **And while it is true that there are some mitzvos whose** true **reason we have not** yet **grasped, due to our limited intellect, מֵרֹב עָמְקָן וְתַכְלִית גָּדְלָן** – and also **due to the profundity and absolute exaltedness of those mitzvos, לֹא נִמְנַע מִמֶּנּוּ מֵהַגִּיד בָּהֶן כָּל אֲשֶׁר נַשִּׂיג** – **we were** nevertheless **not prevented from conveying whatever we *can* grasp of [the reasons for those mitzvos], לִמְצֹא מִן הַתּוֹעֶלֶת שֶׁיֵּשׁ לוֹ לָאָדָם בַּעֲשִׂיָּתָן** – **to uncover some of the benefits that a person gains from their performance.**

וְזֶה דַּרְכִּי בְּכָל שִׂיחָתִי בְּסִפְרִי זֶה – **This, indeed, is the approach I take throughout my discourse in this work of mine, שֶׁיֵּשׁ בַּמִּצְוֹות תּוֹעֶלֶת מָצוּי לָנוּ אַךְ לֹא אֶל הַמְצַוֶּה בָּהֶן** – that is, **that there is benefit in the mitzvos for us, but not for the One Who commanded us in them. וְאִם תִּתֵּן לִבְּךָ בַּדְּבָרִים תִּמְצָא זֹאת הַכַּוָּנָה בְּכֻלָּן** – **If you will set your heart to** understand **the ideas** I propose, **you will discern this intent in all of them. וְהַרְבֵּה יָגַעְתִּי בְּמִקְצָתָן לְהַשִּׂיג בַּעֲנִיּוּת דַּעְתִּי** – **In some of [the mitzvos], I** had to **toil greatly, with my limited intellect, to gain** some **understanding, לִרְאוֹת בָּהֶן מְעַט קָט מֵרֹב הַתּוֹעָלוֹת שֶׁבָּהֶן** – and **to detect** even **a small trifle**[62] **of their great many benefits. וּכְתַבְתִּיו עַל כָּל אַחַת** – But, ultimately, **I wrote [an idea] for each** of the mitzvos.[63] **וְזֶה חֶלְקִי מִכָּל עֲמָלִי** – **May this be my reward for all my efforts.**[64]

Laws of the Mitzvah

מִדִּינֵי הַמִּצְוָה – **Among the laws of the mitzvah is מַה שֶּׁאָמְרוּ זִכְרוֹנָם לִבְרָכָה** – **that which [the Sages], of blessed memory, stated** (*Chullin* 139b), expounding the verse: **"כִּי יִקָּרֵא קַן צִפּוֹר לְפָנֶיךָ**

NOTES

Rambam and *Ramban* regarding the purpose of this mitzvah, and that the focus is only the refinement of *our* character (see previous note).

62. Stylistic paraphrase of *Ezekiel* 16:47.

63. Except, notably, for the mitzvah of *parah adumah* (Mitzvah 397; see there with Insight).

64. Stylistic paraphrase of *Ecclesiastes* 2:10. In his humility, Chinuch expresses these sentiments in several places in this work. See, primarily, the Afterword to the Book of *Vayikra/Leviticus* (Vol. 6).

Rambam writes at the end of *Hil. Me'ilah* (loosely translated): It is appropriate for a person to contemplate the laws of the holy Torah and know their ultimate purpose to the best of his ability. If he cannot find a reason or a rationale for a practice, he should nevertheless not regard it lightly. Nor should he attempt to propose a reason at all cost, even if it is far-fetched, for this too can be a denigration of Hashem's Word. One's thoughts and perceptions concerning the mitzvos should not be like his thoughts concerning other ordinary matters.

Numerous later authorities stress the importance of performing the mitzvos with simple faith in the One Who gave us the mitzvos. They explain that, though one should certainly investigate the reasons behind the mitzvos, this falls under the category of *learning* Torah; the reasons of the mitzvos are a part of Torah just as are the laws of the mitzvos. Studying the reason can thus enlighten and inspire us. But our *performance* of the mitzvos should not depend on our understanding the reasons behind them. One who fulfills the mitzvos only because he understands their purpose is, ultimately, not following the dictates of Hashem, but *his own* dictates. Rather, when a person performs a mitzvah, he should approach it with utter humility and acceptance of Hashem's Will (see *Beis HaLevi, Genesis* 17:1; *R' S. R. Hirsch,* Introduction to *Horeb*; *R' Yechezkel Abramski* in *Peninei Rabbeinu Yechezkel*, p. 41, cited in Mitzvah 159 note 14).

בַּדֶּרֶךְ, מַה דֶּרֶךְ שֶׁאֵין קָנוּי לְךָ אַף כָּל וְכוּ׳[65], מִכָּאן אָמְרוּ יוֹנֵי שׁוֹבָךְ וְיוֹנֵי עֲלִיָּה[66] וְצִפֳּרִין שֶׁקִּנְּנוּ בִּטְפִיחִין[67] וּבְשִׁיחִין וּבְבוֹרוֹת וּבִמְעָרוֹת וְתַרְנְגוֹלִין וְאַוָּזִין שֶׁקִּנְּנוּ בְּפַרְדֵּס[68] חַיָּב לְשַׁלֵּחַ[69], קִנְּנוּ בְּתוֹךְ הַבַּיִת[70] וְכֵן יוֹנִים דּוֹרְסִיּוֹת[71] פָּטוּר מִלְּשַׁלֵּחַ[72], וְאָמַר רַב יְהוּדָה הַמּוֹצֵא קֵן בַּיָּם[73] חַיָּב לְשַׁלֵּחַ, שֶׁבִּכְלַל לְשׁוֹן בַּדֶּרֶךְ הוּא, שֶׁנֶּאֱמַר (ישעיה מ״ג, ט״ז) **הַנּוֹתֵן בַּיָּם דָּרֶךְ.**

"בַּדֶּרֶךְ" — ***Should a bird's nest chance to be before you, on the path*** ... *You shall surely send away the mother,* etc. מַה דֶּרֶךְ שֶׁאֵין קָנוּי לְךָ אַף כָּל וְכוּ׳ — The words "on the path" come to teach that **just as** it is true regarding **a path,** which is a public area, **that [the nest]** found there **is not owned by you** (i.e., you do not own the *contents* of the nest — the birds)**, so too, wherever** you may find the nest, the mitzvah of *shiluach hakein* applies only if you have no ownership of the birds.[65] מִכָּאן אָמְרוּ — **From here [the Sages] said:** יוֹנֵי שׁוֹבָךְ וְיוֹנֵי עֲלִיָּה — Regarding wild (i.e., ownerless) **doves** that nested in one's **birdhouse and** wild **doves** that nested in one's dove **loft,**[66] וְצִפֳּרִין שֶׁקִּנְּנוּ בִּטְפִיחִין וּבְשִׁיחִין וּבְבוֹרוֹת וּבִמְעָרוֹת — **as well as** wild **birds that nested in containers** placed in wall niches for this purpose,[67] **or in ditches, pits, or caves** (on one's property), וְתַרְנְגוֹלִין וְאַוָּזִין שֶׁקִּנְּנוּ בְּפַרְדֵּס — **and hens and geese that** escaped from one's house, which renders them ownerless (*hefker*),[68] and have subsequently **nested in an orchard,** חַיָּב לְשַׁלֵּחַ — if he wishes to take their young, **he is obligated to send away** the mother.[69] קִנְּנוּ בְּתוֹךְ הַבַּיִת — However, **if [the hens or geese]** never escaped, but rather **nested in** his **house,**[70] וְכֵן יוֹנִים דּוֹרְסִיּוֹת — **and similarly,** if the doves whose young he wishes to take are thoroughly domesticated doves that he breeds in his house, known as ***yonim dorsios,***[71] פָּטוּר מִלְּשַׁלֵּחַ — **one is exempt from sending away** the mother, because the birds are his (even though, in theory, they can fly away too).[72]

Chinuch cites another law that appears in that Gemara:

וְאָמַר רַב יְהוּדָה — **Rav Yehudah said** in the name of Rav: הַמּוֹצֵא קֵן בַּיָּם חַיָּב לְשַׁלֵּחַ — **If one found a nest in the sea,**[73] **he is obligated to send away** the mother bird before taking her young, שֶׁבִּכְלַל לְשׁוֹן בַּדֶּרֶךְ הוּא — **for** although the verse states *on the path, in any tree, or on the ground,* **[the sea] is included in the term "on the path,"** שֶׁנֶּאֱמַר "הַנּוֹתֵן בַּיָּם דָּרֶךְ" — **as it is stated** (*Isaiah* 43:16):

NOTES

65. The text in our Gemara is slightly different, but as explained by *Rashi* it has the same meaning. See *Dikdukei Soferim* there §2.

66. See *Rashi* ad loc., as emended by *Rashash*. [A dove loft is a raised structure in which pigeons or doves are kept.]

67. *Rashi* to *Beitzah* 24a ד״ה בטפיחין.

68. See *Rashi, Chullin* 138b ד״ה שקננו בפרדס, and *Tosafos, Chullin* 139a ד״ה כיון דמרדו. [The concept of ownership is applicable only to items that one can hold and retain for himself. Items that are beyond one's control to retain are deemed *hefker* (ownerless). For example, if one's barrel of honey breaks and the owner has no way of saving the honey, the honey is deemed *hefker* and anyone who rescues it may keep it for himself (see *Bava Kamma* 115b-116b for this and other examples). In the same vein, if one's bird escapes to the wild, it is no longer deemed his possession, since he is powerless to retain it.]

69. In all these instances, the birds are *hefker* — either because they came from the wild, or because they are no longer in the custody of their owner. Thus, they are similar to a nest one finds "on the path," and are subject to *shiluach hakein*.

The novelty in the cases that the Baraisa mentions is that these birds are not simply ownerless birds that nested in the wild (like a nest found on the path). Rather, they are either wild birds that nested on one's property (e.g., doves that nested in a birdhouse or a loft), or they are birds that were actually his at one point (e.g., hens and geese that nested in an orchard). Regardless, since he does not *currently* own them, he is obligated in *shiluach hakein* if he wants their young. [One does not acquire wild doves that nest in his birdhouse or loft, since they leave their nest at will; see *Chullin* 141b and *Aruch HaShulchan, Choshen Mishpat* 370:2 (and 4). See also *Tiferes Yisrael, Chullin* 12:1 §3 regarding a case where the escaped hens or geese came back to nest in their former owner's orchard.]

70. *Rashi* ibid. ד״ה שקננו בתוך הבית.

71. This name refers to the place where these doves were raised (see *Chullin* 139b). [The Gemara (ibid.) notes that some referred to these domesticated doves as יוֹנֵי הַרְדְּסִיאוֹת — *yonei hardesios,* or Herodian doves; they were named after King Herod, who was the first to raise and domesticate them.]

72. There may be other factors that come into play in determining whether one is obligated in *shiluach hakein* in these cases. See note 12 in the Schottenstein ed. of *Chullin* 138b and sources cited there.

73. E.g., atop a tree that had been swept away by the sea (*Rashi* ad loc.).

הָיְתָה הָאֵם מְעוֹפֶפֶת עַל הַקֵּן וְאֵין כְּנָפֶיהָ נוֹגְעוֹת בַּקֵּן פָּטוּר מִלְּשַׁלֵּחַ, הָיְתָה רוֹבֶצֶת עַל בֵּיצִים מוּזָרוֹת[74] פָּטוּר מִלְּשַׁלֵּחַ, שֶׁנֶּאֱמַר אֶפְרֹחִים אוֹ בֵיצִים, מָה אֶפְרוֹחִים בְּנֵי קְיָמָא אַף בֵּיצִים כְּמוֹ כֵן, שִׁלְּחָהּ וְחָזְרָה[75] אֲפִלּוּ כַּמָּה פְּעָמִים[76] חַיָּב לְשַׁלֵּחַ, שֶׁנֶּאֱמַר שַׁלֵּחַ תְּשַׁלַּח[77].

וְיֶתֶר פְּרָטֵי הַמִּצְוָה מְבֹאָרִים בְּפֶרֶק אַחֲרוֹן מֵחֻלִּין[78].

וְנוֹהֶגֶת בְּכָל מָקוֹם וּבְכָל זְמַן בִּזְכָרִים וּנְקֵבוֹת[79].

So said HASHEM, ***He Who made a path through the sea,*** etc. Accordingly, a nest found at sea is also considered to be "on the path."

Chinuch cites an additional law. In presenting the mitzvah of *shiluach hakein*, the Torah describes the mother bird as רוֹבֶצֶת עַל הָאֶפְרֹחִים אוֹ עַל הַבֵּיצִים, *"sitting" on the chicks or on the eggs.* What would the law be if the mother bird was not sitting in the nest, but rather hovering over it? The Mishnah (*Chullin* 140b) teaches that as long as her wings are touching the nest (i.e., the eggs or the chicks in the nest, not the *material* of the nest such as the twigs; see *Ran* to *Rif, Chullin* fol. 48a), one is obligated to send her away before taking her young. The Mishnah then goes on to discuss a case where the mother bird lifted herself completely off her young, so that her wings are no longer touching the nest:

הָיְתָה הָאֵם מְעוֹפֶפֶת עַל הַקֵּן – **If the mother** bird **was flying above the nest,** וְאֵין כְּנָפֶיהָ נוֹגְעוֹת בַּקֵּן – **and her wings were *not* touching the nest,** פָּטוּר מִלְּשַׁלֵּחַ – **one is exempt from sending** her **away.**

Another law stated in that Mishnah:

הָיְתָה רוֹבֶצֶת עַל בֵּיצִים מוּזָרוֹת – **If [the mother bird] was sitting upon infertile eggs,**[74] פָּטוּר מִלְּשַׁלֵּחַ – **one is exempt from sending** her **away,** שֶׁנֶּאֱמַר "אֶפְרֹחִים אוֹ בֵיצִים" – **for it is stated, *chicks or eggs,*** indicating that the verse refers only to chicks or eggs that can be compared to each other. מָה אֶפְרוֹחִים בְּנֵי קְיָמָא אַף בֵּיצִים כְּמוֹ כֵן – **Just as chicks are viable, so too** must the **eggs** be viable (i.e., capable of producing chicks), which excludes infertile eggs.

Chinuch cites one additional law (from the Mishnah, *Chullin* 141a):

שִׁלְּחָהּ וְחָזְרָה – If **one sent [the mother bird] away and she returned** to the nest before he took the young,[75] אֲפִלּוּ כַּמָּה פְּעָמִים – **even** if this happened **several times,** חַיָּב לְשַׁלֵּחַ – **he is** still **obligated to send** her **away** (again),[76] שֶׁנֶּאֱמַר "שַׁלֵּחַ תְּשַׁלַּח" – **for it is stated, *You shall surely send*** *away the mother [bird].*[77]

Chinuch concludes:

וְיֶתֶר פְּרָטֵי הַמִּצְוָה – These laws **and the remaining details of the mitzvah** מְבֹאָרִים בְּפֶרֶק אַחֲרוֹן מֵחֻלִּין – **are set forth in** Chapter *Shiluach HaKein*, which is **the final chapter of** Tractate ***Chullin.***[78]

Applicability of the Mitzvah

וְנוֹהֶגֶת בְּכָל מָקוֹם וּבְכָל זְמַן – **[This mitzvah] applies in every location and in all times,** בִּזְכָרִים וּנְקֵבוֹת – **to** both **men and women.**[79]

NOTES

74. I.e., eggs that were not fertilized by a male, and are thus incapable of producing chicks (*Rashi, Chullin* 64b ד״ה ביצים מוזרות). [The word מוּזָרוֹת is derived from the root מזר, which means to *spin* or *twist* yarn. These eggs become rotten with the passage of time, developing within them what resembles spun yarn (*Ran* to *Rif, Chullin* fol. 22a; see also *Tiferes Yisrael* to *Chullin* 12:3, *Boaz* §1).]

75. *Meiri* ad loc. See *Shach, Yoreh Deah* 292:9.

76. See *Dvar Avraham* (Vol. II 8:6 ד״ה והנה) for an analysis of whether each "sending" constitutes a separate fulfillment of the mitzvah.

77. As explained in the Gemara there, the Mishnah derives its ruling from the word שַׁלֵּחַ itself, not from the repetitive phraseology of the verse (שַׁלֵּחַ תְּשַׁלַּח). [The word שַׁלֵּחַ, *sending away,* is the "infinitive absolute" form of the verb שלח, which can mean both one time or many times (see *Rambam, Commentary to the Mishnah* ibid.; see also *Toras Chaim* to *Chullin* ad loc.).]

78. The laws of *shiluach hakein* are codified by *Rambam* in *Hil. Shechitah* Ch. 13; and by *Shulchan Aruch* in *Yoreh Deah* §292.

79. I.e., it applies both in Eretz Yisrael and in the Diaspora, and whether the *Beis HaMikdash* is standing or not. And it applies to women as well as men,

וְעוֹבֵר עַל זֶה וְלָקַח הָאֵם בְּעוֹדָהּ עַל הַבָּנִים בִּטֵּל עֲשֵׂה זֶה[80] **מִלְּבַד שֶׁעָבַר עַל לָאו דְּלֹא תִקַּח הָאֵם**[81]**, וְאִם מֵתָה הָאֵם קֹדֶם שֶׁיְּשַׁלְּחֶנָּה אוֹ שֶׁשִּׁלְּחָהּ אָדָם אַחֵר אֵין לוֹ תַּקָּנָה לְקַיֵּם הָעֲשֵׂה וּלְתַקֵּן הַלָּאו**[82]**, אֲבָל אִם שִׁלְּחָהּ הוּא קֹדֶם שֶׁתָּמוּת נִתְקַן לָאוֵיהּ בְּכָךְ וּפָטוּר, שֶׁזֶּה הַלָּאו נִתָּק הוּא אֶל הָעֲשֵׂה, וּכְמוֹ שֶׁנִּכְתֹּב בְּלָאו ח׳** (מצוה תקמ״ד) **הַבָּא עַל זֶה בְּעֶזְרַת הַשֵּׁם**[83]**.**

וְעוֹבֵר עַל זֶה – One who transgresses this mitzvah **וְלָקַח הָאֵם בְּעוֹדָהּ עַל הַבָּנִים – and takes the mother bird while she is** sitting **on her young,** instead of sending her away and taking the chicks or the eggs, **בִּטֵּל עֲשֵׂה זֶה – has violated this** mitzvah-**obligation;**[80] **מִלְּבַד שֶׁעָבַר עַל לָאו דְּ״לֹא תִקַּח הָאֵם״ – aside from** the fact **that he has** also **violated the** mitzvah-**prohibition of** ***You shall not take the mother [bird]*** *with the young* (Mitzvah 544), for which he is liable to *malkus*.[81]

As discussed in Mitzvah 544, if one violated the prohibition by taking the mother bird with her young, he can rectify the violation by sending the mother bird away *afterward*. Chinuch discusses when such rectification is possible:

וְאִם מֵתָה הָאֵם קֹדֶם שֶׁיְּשַׁלְּחֶנָּה – If the mother bird died in his hand, **before he** could **send her away,** **אוֹ שֶׁשִּׁלְּחָהּ אָדָם אַחֵר – or if someone** ***else*** took the mother bird from his hand and **sent her away,** **אֵין לוֹ תַּקָּנָה לְקַיֵּם הָעֲשֵׂה וּלְתַקֵּן הַלָּאו – he can no** longer **remedy** his sin **by fulfilling the** mitzvah-**obligation** of sending the mother away now **and thus rectifying** his violation of **the** mitzvah-**prohibition.** Thus, he receives *malkus*.[82] **אֲבָל אִם שִׁלְּחָהּ הוּא קֹדֶם שֶׁתָּמוּת – However, if he himself sends away [the mother bird] before she dies,** **נִתְקַן לָאוֵיהּ בְּכָךְ וּפָטוּר – his** violation of the **prohibition is thereby rectified, and he is exempt** from *malkus*. **שֶׁזֶּה הַלָּאו נִתָּק הוּא אֶל הָעֲשֵׂה – This is because the prohibition of [*Do not take the mother bird*] is** a mitzvah-prohibition that is **remedied through** the fulfillment of **the** accompanying mitzvah-**obligation,** **וּכְמוֹ שֶׁנִּכְתֹּב בְּלָאו ח׳ הַבָּא עַל זֶה בְּעֶזְרַת הַשֵּׁם – as we shall write, with the help of Hashem, in Mitzvah-prohibition 8** of this *parashah* (Mitzvah 544), **which** is the mitzvah that **discusses this** prohibition.[83]

NOTES

in accordance with the rule that pertains to mitzvah-obligations that are not time-specific. [In fact, the Gemara in *Kiddushin* (34a) cites *shiluach hakein* as a primary example of a mitzvah-obligation that is not time-specific.]

80. As explained in note 1 above, although the mitzvah-prohibition (i.e., Mitzvah 544) forbids only taking the nest in its entirety (the mother bird *with* the young), our mitzvah adds a requirement: The mother bird shall be sent away, and this should be done before taking the young. Accordingly, Chinuch writes here that one who takes the mother while she is still sitting on her young, even if he left the young in the nest, has violated the mitzvah. [Another scenario in which one has violated the mitzvah-obligation, but not the mitzvah-prohibition, is if he took the chicks without first sending away the mother.]

However, if the mother is not sitting on (or at least touching) her young, one may take her, as Chinuch indicated earlier. Similarly, if one sent the mother away and she returned after he took the young, he may take her as well. In short, the mitzvah is violated only if one takes the mother "while she is sitting on her young."

It emerges, then, that according to Chinuch, taking the mother without taking her young is a violation of this mitzvah, but it is not a violation of the mitzvah-prohibition (see *Teshuvos Chacham Tzvi* §83; and *Teshuvos Yehudah Yaaleh* Vol. I, *Yoreh Deah* §104). Chinuch's next statement is therefore puzzling, as will be discussed in the next note.

81. As indicated in the previous note, Chinuch's assertion that one violates the prohibition for taking the mother alone seems very problematic, since Chinuch stated clearly in the previous mitzvah that the prohibition forbids only taking the nest in its entirety! *Teshuvos Yehudah Yaaleh* (ibid.) maintains that these two statements by Chinuch cannot be reconciled, and that Chinuch evidently changed his mind here and adopted the view that the prohibition forbids even taking the mother alone and leaving the young. [Actually, Chinuch wrote Mitzvah 544 *after* writing Mitzvah 545 (see note 83, below), so if Chinuch modified his opinion, it would be in Mitzvah 544.]

82. See Mitzvah 544 with note 4.

83. See there for extensive explanation of this matter.

Chinuch's language "as we shall write" (as opposed to "as we have written") and his reference to that mitzvah as "Mitzvah-prohibition 8 of the *parashah*" reflects his original arrangement of the mitzvos. See note 2 of the previous mitzvah.

~§ **Insight: Is There a Mitzvah if the Person Has No Use for the Eggs or the Chicks?**

It is a prevalent custom among God-fearing Jews to seek to fulfill the mitzvah of *shiluach hakein*. Some simply wish to perform this rare and cherished mitzvah. Others hope to merit the *segulos* (supernatural benefits; sing. *segulah*) associated with the mitzvah. As Chinuch mentions (at notes 6-10), the Torah promises one who performs *shiluach hakein* long life and children. Other, perhaps less-known, *segulos* are meriting to find a mate (*Yalkut Shimoni* to *Deuteronomy* 21:15); meriting to acquire a new home (*Tanchuma, Ki Seitzei* §1 [end], cited by *Rashi* to *Deuteronomy* 22:8); meriting wealth and blessing (*Devarim Rabbah* 6:7 with *Eitz Yosef* and *Radal*); meriting protection from harm, specifically from hazards associated with travel (*Devarim Rabbah* 6:5-6 with *Radal* ד"ה כדי שתנצל); and hastening the Redemption and the rebuilding of the *Beis HaMikdash* (*Devarim Rabbah* 6:7; *Baal HaTurim* to our verse; see also *Zohar* cited below). In any event, the conventional understanding seems to be that *shiluach hakein* is a mitzvah that should be pursued and performed, even if one has no intention of using the birds or the eggs — as is usually the case nowadays. However, this is actually a subject of broad dispute among the commentators, which hinges in part on the reasons proposed for our mitzvah.

Teshuvos Chavas Yair (§67, cited briefly in *Pischei Teshuvah, Yoreh Deah* 292:1) is of the opinion that there is a mitzvah to perform *shiluach hakein* regardless of whether the person is interested in the birds or not. If one comes across a nest and he sees the mother bird sitting on the young (in the words of the verse, *Should a bird's nest chance to be before you…*), he is obligated to send her away. [He possibly would not be required to pick up the eggs or the chicks if he is not interested in them; see discussion in note 11 above. Note that, according to *Chavas Yair's* approach, not only is one obligated in the mitzvah even if he will not *benefit* from the birds; he is obligated even if he will thereby incur a monetary loss (*Teshuvos Chasam Sofer, Orach Chaim* §100; *Meromei Sadeh, Chullin* 139b).]

Chasam Sofer (ibid.), however, maintains that there is no mitzvah to perform *shiluach hakein* for its own sake, as, for example, is the mitzvah to put on *tefillin* (Mitzvos 421-422). It is rather a mitzvah like *shechitah* (Mitzvah 451), where, if a person wants to eat the meat of an animal, he must slaughter the animal as the Torah prescribes; if he does not want to eat the meat, the mitzvah does not apply to him. So too, if a person wants to take the contents of a nest (for consumption, etc.), he must follow the procedure set forth in the Torah, which is to send away the mother first and then take the young. However, if he has no interest in the contents of the nest, the mitzvah of *shiluach hakein* does not apply to him and he may simply continue on his way. [As indicated in notes 1 and 11 above, it appears that this is Chinuch's opinion, as well.]

Chasam Sofer adds that this is especially true according to *Ramban's* explanation of the underlying purpose of the mitzvah (*Ramban's Commentary* to the verse, cited above, at note 55). *Ramban* explains that, although we are permitted to benefit from birds and animals for our legitimate needs, such as for food, we must be careful to do so in a compassionate manner. Therefore, we must not take the entire nest, i.e., the mother bird and her young, or take the young while the mother watches them being taken and possibly slaughtered, for that is an act of cruelty. Rather, we try to minimize the mother's distress by sending her away first. According to this explanation, reasons *Chasam Sofer*, if the person has no need for the eggs or the chicks, he should *not* perform *shiluach hakein*, for there is no greater cruelty than to send away the mother and separate her from her young for no reason! Not only will this not be a fulfillment of the mitzvah of *shiluach hakein*, *Chasam Sofer* adds, it will also constitute an act of *tzaar baalei chaim* (causing unnecessary pain to animals), which is a Biblical transgression (see Mitzvah 451, at notes 15-16). [See also *Torah Temimah* to the verse of our mitzvah, §68.]

Interestingly, *Ralbag* (to our verse) suggests that the best course of action, even when a person comes across a nest and *wants* the birds, is to leave the nest alone. In presenting the reason for the mitzvah, *Ralbag* explains that, generally speaking, the chicks or the eggs are not fit to be eaten, and Hashem knows that if a person is required to send away the mother bird (which is the one bird in the nest that he would actually benefit from), he will probably leave the nest alone altogether. That, says *Ralbag*, is in fact the best thing to do, for this allows the mother bird to raise and nurture her young to maturity, which is the ideal plan of Creation (see also *Rambam, Moreh Nevuchim* III:48). It goes without saying that, according to *Ralbag*, one is not obligated to perform *shiluach hakein* if he

does *not* want the birds. One would actually fulfill the will of the Torah more devotedly if he does not disturb the nest and continues on his way.

One of the sources that *Chavas Yair* cites in support of his position, that a person *is* required to send away the mother bird in any event, is *Zohar* (*Zohar Chadash, Rus* ד״ה ויהי בימי, cited by *Rabbeinu Bachya* to *Deuteronomy* 22:7). In contrast to the approaches proposed by *Rambam* and *Ramban*, which explain the mitzvah in terms of compassion on the mother, *Zohar* actually interprets the mitzvah as an act of *cruelty* to the mother bird, but whose purpose, ironically, is to arouse the Mercy of Heaven. The mother bird, which is chased away from her chicks, wanders crying and full of distress throughout the world, and arouses pity upon herself and upon others that are hurt as she is. As a result, Hashem's pity is aroused toward the nest that was abandoned and destroyed, toward the Jewish people, who wander without rest among the nations, and over the fact that the *Shechinah* is so far from its dwelling place. According to *Zohar's* explanation, *Chavas Yair* points out, it follows that the mitzvah of *shiluach hakein* rests upon the person whether he wants the birds or not. Whenever he has the opportunity to send away the mother bird and thereby arouse Divine Mercy on the world and the Jewish people, he is obligated to do so. *Mishnas Chachamim*, cited by *Pischei Teshuvah* (ibid.), adds that if one comes across a nest and does not perform the mitzvah, he will be punished in a time of Divine anger. [*Chasam Sofer* deals with *Chavas Yair's* reference to *Zohar*; see there (ibid.). Other sources that explain the mitzvah based on the approach of *Zohar* are *Yaaros Devash*, Vol. II, *Derush* 6; and *Gra* in his *Commentary* to *Mishlei* 30:17, *Imrei Noam* to *Berachos* 33b, and *Kol Eliyahu*, *Parashas Vayeira*.]

In terms of practical halachah, many authorities side with *Chasam Sofer*, while others side with *Chavas Yair*. [*Shale'ach Teshalach*, a very informative work on the subject of *shiluach hakein*, lists at length the proponents of both sides of this dispute, from the Rishonim to contemporary authorities (*Dinei Shiluach HaKein* §2).] However, even those who side with *Chasam Sofer* do not necessarily accept his suggestion that performing *shiluach hakein* when one has no need for the birds constitutes *tzaar baalei chaim*. They simply maintain that one is not *obligated* to perform the mitzvah in this case, but it is certainly meritorious to do so (see sources cited in *Shale'ach Teshalach* ibid.).

מִצְוָה תקמו: מִצְוַת מַעֲקֶה[2,1]

לְהָסִיר הַמִּכְשׁוֹלִים וְהַנְּגָפִים מִכָּל מִשְׁכְּנוֹתֵינוּ, וְעַל זֶה נֶאֱמַר (דברים כ״ב, ח׳) **וְעָשִׂיתָ מַעֲקֶה לְגַגֶּךָ. וְהָעִנְיָן הוּא שֶׁנִּבְנֶה קִיר סְבִיב הַגַּגּוֹת וּסְבִיב הַבּוֹרוֹת וְהַשִּׁיחִין וְדוֹמֵיהֶן כְּדֵי שֶׁלֹּא תִּכָּשֵׁל בְּרִיָּה לִפֹּל בָּהֶם אוֹ מֵהֶם, וּבִכְלַל מִצְוָה זוֹ לִבְנוֹת וּלְתַקֵּן כָּל כֹּתֶל וְכָל גָּדֵר שֶׁיִּהְיֶה קָרוֹב לָבוֹא תַּקָּלָה מִמֶּנּוּ**[3].

Mitzvah 546

The Obligation of Maakeh (Removing Hazards)

כִּי תִבְנֶה בַּיִת חָדָשׁ וְעָשִׂיתָ מַעֲקֶה לְגַגֶּךָ וְלֹא תָשִׂים דָּמִים בְּבֵיתֶךָ כִּי יִפֹּל הַנֹּפֵל מִמֶּנּוּ
If you build a new house, you shall make a fence for your roof, and you shall not place blood in your house, if one should fall from it (*Deuteronomy* 22:8).

In earlier times, rooftops of homes were generally flat and were commonly used for various purposes, such as putting fruit out to dry in the sun. In order to avoid the risk of people falling from these rooftops, the Torah imposes a mitzvah-obligation to make a protective fence or railing (*maakeh*) around them.[1] However, Chinuch will teach below that this mitzvah is not limited to building a protective fence around the rooftop. It requires us to design and build our homes and properties in such a way that they do not pose *any* danger. It also requires us to ensure that our property remains safe at all times. If we become aware of a hazard on our property, we must take measures to remove it.[2]

The verse that teaches this mitzvah-obligation also issues a counterpart mitzvah-prohibition: *You shall not place blood in your house*. That prohibition is the subject of Mitzvah 547.

לְהָסִיר הַמִּכְשׁוֹלִים וְהַנְּגָפִים מִכָּל מִשְׁכְּנוֹתֵינוּ – We are commanded **to remove stumbling blocks and hazards from all of our dwelling places.** **וְעַל זֶה נֶאֱמַר** – **Regarding this it is stated** (*Deuteronomy* 22:8): **"וְעָשִׂיתָ מַעֲקֶה לְגַגֶּךָ"** – ***And you shall make a fence for your roof.*** **וְהָעִנְיָן הוּא שֶׁנִּבְנֶה קִיר סְבִיב הַגַּגּוֹת** – **The idea** of this mitzvah **is that we are** required **to build a** protective **wall** or fence **around the rooftops** of our homes, **וּסְבִיב הַבּוֹרוֹת וְהַשִּׁיחִין וְדוֹמֵיהֶן** – **as well as around pits, ditches, and similar** hazards on our property, **כְּדֵי שֶׁלֹּא תִּכָּשֵׁל בְּרִיָּה לִפֹּל בָּהֶם אוֹ מֵהֶם** – **so that people will not accidentally fall into them** (in the case of pits and the like) **or** fall ***from* them** (in the case of rooftops). **וּבִכְלַל מִצְוָה זוֹ לִבְנוֹת וּלְתַקֵּן כָּל כֹּתֶל וְכָל גָּדֵר שֶׁיִּהְיֶה קָרוֹב לָבוֹא תַּקָּלָה מִמֶּנּוּ** – **Included in this mitzvah** is an obligation **to rebuild or repair any** existing **wall or fence from which harm is likely to come about;** for example, a wall or fence that is likely to collapse or that has something jutting out of it that could cause harm.[3]

NOTES

1. Nowadays, most rooftops are not used at all, especially the slanted rooftops common in many parts of the world. According to many authorities, a rooftop that is not used at all does not require a *maakeh* [even if people go up there occasionally for repairs] (*Shulchan Aruch HaRav, Hil. Shemiras Guf V'Nefesh* §1; *Aruch HaShulchan, Choshen Mishpat* 427:5; *Chazon Ish, Choshen Mishpat, Likkutim* 18:1; for further discussion, see *Sefer HaBayis* [Lerner] 11:18 with footnote 32).

2. *Sefer Chareidim* (16:22) writes that every time a person checks his property to make sure that his *maakeh* is intact and that there are no hazards present, he fulfills this mitzvah.

3. Other hazards that may be present on one's property and one is obligated to remove are a rickety ladder, a vicious dog, and the like (see *Bava Kamma* 15b). [*Yad HaLevi* (to *Rambam, Sefer HaMitzvos, Asei* 184) mentions also ice on one's property, where people might slip and hurt themselves, such as on the sidewalk or steps. This mitzvah requires the owner of the property to remove the ice (by shoveling, spreading salt, etc.).]

As mentioned in the introduction to this mitzvah, Chinuch here expands the mitzvah-obligation of *maakeh* to include not only building a fence around a rooftop, but also building a fence around a pit or a ditch, as well as removing all other hazards from one's property. This is how *Rambam* presents the mitzvah in *Sefer HaMitzvos* (ibid.). *Rambam's* language in

וְזֶה שֶׁהִזְכִּיר הַכָּתוּב לְגַגֶּךָ, דִּבֵּר הַכָּתוּב בַּהֹוֶה[4]**, וּלְשׁוֹן סִפְרִי** (כאן)**, וְעָשִׂיתָ מַעֲקֶה, מִצְוַת עֲשֵׂה**[5]**.**

מִשָּׁרְשֵׁי[6] **הַמִּצְוָה, לְפִי שֶׁעִם הֱיוֹת הַשֵּׁם בָּרוּךְ הוּא מַשְׁגִּיחַ בִּפְרָטֵי בְּנֵי אָדָם וְיוֹדֵעַ כָּל מַעֲשֵׂיהֶם**[7] **וְכָל אֲשֶׁר יִקְרֶה לָהֶם טוֹב אוֹ רַע בִּגְזֵרָתוֹ וּבְמִצְוָתוֹ לְפִי זְכוּתָן אוֹ חִיּוּבָן,**

Chinuch explains why the Torah specifically addresses the hazard of a rooftop:

וְזֶה שֶׁהִזְכִּיר הַכָּתוּב "לְגַגֶּךָ" – **This that Scripture** specifically **mentions** making a fence ***for your roof,*** even though one must build a fence around pits and ditches too (and one must also remove other hazards), דִּבֵּר הַכָּתוּב בַּהֹוֶה – is because **Scripture** typically **speaks about the common reality,** and a rooftop is a very common hazard.[4]

One might argue that the requirement to build a fence around a rooftop or a pit is merely a safety measure that the Torah imposes, but that it should not be considered a mitzvah-obligation. Chinuch cites *Sifrei* to demonstrate that it is indeed a mitzvah-obligation:

וּלְשׁוֹן סִפְרִי – **The language of *Sifrei*** (to our verse) is: "וְעָשִׂיתָ מַעֲקֶה" – The directive, ***You shall make a fence** for your roof,* מִצְוַת עֲשֵׂה – is **a mitzvah-obligation.**[5]

Underlying Purpose of the Mitzvah

One might ask: Why are we required to remove hazards from our homes? If a person will be harmed through them, it was evidently decreed upon him by Heaven; and if it was not decreed by Heaven, then he will not be harmed! Chinuch addresses this question:[6]

מִשָּׁרְשֵׁי הַמִּצְוָה – **Among the underlying purposes of the mitzvah** is the following: לְפִי שֶׁעִם הֱיוֹת הַשֵּׁם בָּרוּךְ הוּא מַשְׁגִּיחַ בִּפְרָטֵי בְּנֵי אָדָם וְיוֹדֵעַ כָּל מַעֲשֵׂיהֶם – **To be sure, Hashem, blessed is He, supervises** even **the** minute **details of** the lives of all **human beings and is aware of all their activities,**[7] וְכָל אֲשֶׁר יִקְרֶה לָהֶם טוֹב אוֹ רַע בִּגְזֵרָתוֹ וּבְמִצְוָתוֹ – **and everything that happens to [people],** whether **good or bad, is by His decree and by His command,** לְפִי זְכוּתָן אוֹ חִיּוּבָן – **in**

NOTES

Mishneh Torah (*Hil. Rotze'ach* 11:4), however, is a bit ambiguous. According to some, *Rambam* means to say that our mitzvah-obligation pertains specifically to a rooftop, as the verse states, *You shall make a fence for your "roof."* All other hazards, even a pit or a ditch, fall under the Torah's general directive (*Deuteronomy* 4:9): רַק הִשָּׁמֶר לְךָ וּשְׁמֹר נַפְשְׁךָ מְאֹד, *Only be careful and guard your soul well.* They are also included in the mitzvah-prohibition of *You shall not place blood in your house* (Mitzvah 547), but they are not included in the mitzvah-obligation of *maakeh* (see *Chayei Adam* 15:24). Others understand *Rambam* (in *Mishneh Torah*) as saying that our mitzvah does include building a fence around a pit or a ditch, but not the removal of other hazards (*Minchas Chinuch* §10-11; *Dvar Avraham,* Vol. I, 37:3-4). [The significance of whether a particular hazard is included in the mitzvah-obligation or not is whether one recites a blessing when removing that hazard, as one does when building a *maakeh* around a rooftop (see Insight). See cited sources for discussion.] In any event, it is unclear how these commentators would reconcile *Rambam's* definition of the mitzvah in *Sefer HaMitzvos* with what he wrote in *Mishneh Torah*.

4. *Pesikta Zutrasa* (to the verse), cited by *R' Y. F. Perla, Sefer HaMitzvos of Rav Saadiah Gaon, Asei* 77 (Vol. I, p. 298b).

5. Thus, most authorities rule that one must recite a blessing when building a *maakeh* (... *Who sanctified us with His commandments, and commanded us to build a maakeh*). This is because it is a mitzvah act, similar to taking a *lulav*. See Insight.

6. In the course of his presentation, Chinuch will touch on a fundamental aspect of Jewish thought: How to reconcile Hashem's supervision and providence over the world with the seemingly random occurrences that come about through the laws of nature. This is a very wide-ranging subject with varying views among the Rishonim and Acharonim. For a comprehensive treatment of this matter, see *Sifsei Chaim, Emunah V'Hashgachah* I. See also Mitzvah 169, notes 24-28, and sources cited there.

7. Hashem is certainly aware of everything that happens to *any and all* things. As Chinuch goes on to explain, however, Hashem actively *judges* individual people and guides occurrences in this world in accordance with their merits or misdeeds. Other individual creatures are not subject to such guidance and providence, though Hashem does supervise each *species* as a whole, as Chinuch explains in Mitzvah 169 (at note 26), Mitzvah 294 (at note 7), and Mitzvah 545 (at note 4).

וּכְעִנְיָן שֶׁאָמְרוּ זִכְרוֹנָם לִבְרָכָה (חולין ז׳ ע״ב) אֵין אָדָם נוֹקֵף אֶצְבָּעוֹ מִלְּמַטָּה אֶלָּא אִם כֵּן מַכְרִיזִין עָלָיו מִלְּמַעְלָה[8], אַף עַל פִּי כֵן צָרִיךְ הָאָדָם לִשְׁמֹר עַצְמוֹ מִן הַמִּקְרִים הַנְּהוּגִים בָּעוֹלָם, כִּי הָאֵל בָּרָא עוֹלָמוֹ וּבְנָאוֹ עַל יְסוֹדוֹת עַמּוּדֵי הַטֶּבַע[9], וְגָזַר שֶׁיִּהְיֶה הָאֵשׁ שׂוֹרֶפֶת וְהַמַּיִם מְכַבִּין הַלֶּהָבָה, וּכְמוֹ כֵן יְחַיֵּב הַטֶּבַע שֶׁאִם תִּפֹּל אֶבֶן גְּדוֹלָה עַל רֹאשׁ אִישׁ שֶׁתְּרַצֵּץ אֶת מֹחוֹ אוֹ אִם יִפֹּל הָאָדָם מֵרֹאשׁ הַגַּג הַגָּבוֹהַּ לָאָרֶץ שֶׁיָּמוּת, וְהוּא בָּרוּךְ הוּא חָנַן גּוּפוֹת בְּנֵי אָדָם וַיִּפַּח בְּאַפָּיו נִשְׁמַת חַיִּים[10] בַּעֲלַת דַּעַת לִשְׁמֹר הַגּוּף מִכָּל פֶּגַע וְנָתַן שְׁנֵיהֶם הַנֶּפֶשׁ וְגוּפָהּ בְּתוֹךְ גַּלְגַּל הַיְסוֹדוֹת[11] וְהֵמָּה יְנַהֲגוּם וְיִפְעֲלוּ בָם פְּעֻלּוֹת. וְאַחַר שֶׁהָאֵל שִׁעְבֵּד גּוּף הָאָדָם לַטֶּבַע, כִּי כֵן חִיְּבָה חָכְמָתוֹ, מִצַּד שֶׁהוּא בַּעַל חֹמֶר, צִוָּהוּ לִשְׁמֹר מִן הַמִּקְרֶה, כִּי הַטֶּבַע שֶׁהוּא מָסוּר בְּיָדוֹ יַעֲשֶׂה פְּעֻלָּתוֹ עָלָיו אִם לֹא יִשָּׁמֵר מִמֶּנּוּ[12].

---

accordance with their merit or liability, וּכְעִנְיָן שֶׁאָמְרוּ זִכְרוֹנָם לִבְרָכָה – **as [our Sages], of blessed memory, stated** (*Chullin* 7b): אֵין אָדָם נוֹקֵף אֶצְבָּעוֹ מִלְּמַטָּה אֶלָּא אִם כֵּן מַכְרִיזִין עָלָיו מִלְּמַעְלָה – **A person does not** so much as **stub his finger down below,** on Earth, **unless [the Heavenly Court] has first proclaimed** (i.e., decreed) this **upon him from Above.**[8] אַף עַל פִּי כֵן צָרִיךְ הָאָדָם לִשְׁמֹר עַצְמוֹ מִן הַמִּקְרִים הַנְּהוּגִים בָּעוֹלָם – **Nevertheless, a person must protect himself** and others **from** the bad **incidences that naturally occur in the world,** such as the possibility of falling from an unprotected rooftop. כִּי הָאֵל בָּרָא עוֹלָמוֹ וּבְנָאוֹ עַל יְסוֹדוֹת עַמּוּדֵי הַטֶּבַע – This is **because the Almighty created His world and founded it upon principles of nature;** that is, He designed the world so that it is generally governed by rules of nature. Obviously, the rules of nature *themselves* were designed by the Almighty.[9] וְגָזַר שֶׁיִּהְיֶה הָאֵשׁ שׂוֹרֶפֶת וְהַמַּיִם מְכַבִּין הַלֶּהָבָה –**Thus, He decreed that fire should burn and** that **water** should **extinguish a flame.** וּכְמוֹ כֵן יְחַיֵּב הַטֶּבַע שֶׁאִם תִּפֹּל אֶבֶן גְּדוֹלָה עַל רֹאשׁ אִישׁ שֶׁתְּרַצֵּץ אֶת מֹחוֹ – **Likewise,** by His design, the laws of **nature dictate that if a large rock falls on a man's head, it will crush his brains,** אוֹ אִם יִפֹּל הָאָדָם מֵרֹאשׁ הַגַּג הַגָּבוֹהַּ לָאָרֶץ שֶׁיָּמוּת – **and** that **if a person falls from a high rooftop to the ground, he will die.** וְהוּא בָּרוּךְ הוּא חָנַן גּוּפוֹת בְּנֵי אָדָם – **However, [the Almighty], blessed is He, had compassion on man's body** and did not want that it should be defenseless, וַיִּפַּח בְּאַפָּיו נִשְׁמַת חַיִּים בַּעֲלַת דַּעַת לִשְׁמֹר הַגּוּף מִכָּל פֶּגַע – **so He blew into [man's] nostrils a life-soul**[10] **possessed of** the **intelligence** with which man is able **to protect his body from all harm.** וְנָתַן שְׁנֵיהֶם הַנֶּפֶשׁ וְגוּפָהּ בְּתוֹךְ גַּלְגַּל הַיְסוֹדוֹת – **[Hashem]** then **placed both of them – the soul and its body – within the sphere of the** natural **elements** (i.e., the physical universe),[11] וְהֵמָּה יְנַהֲגוּם וְיִפְעֲלוּ בָם פְּעֻלּוֹת – **and [those elements and their laws] govern [the body and the soul]** that constitute the human being, **and act upon them.** וְאַחַר שֶׁהָאֵל שִׁעְבֵּד גּוּף הָאָדָם לַטֶּבַע – **Since the Almighty subjected man's body to** the laws of **nature,** כִּי כֵן חִיְּבָה חָכְמָתוֹ מִצַּד שֶׁהוּא בַּעַל חֹמֶר – **for so did His Wisdom dictate, due to the fact that [man]** himself **is composed of** a **physical** body, צִוָּהוּ לִשְׁמֹר מִן הַמִּקְרֶה – **He commanded [man] to guard** his body **against** natural **occurrences.** כִּי הַטֶּבַע שֶׁהוּא מָסוּר בְּיָדוֹ יַעֲשֶׂה פְּעֻלָּתוֹ עָלָיו אִם לֹא יִשָּׁמֵר מִמֶּנּוּ – **For, if he does not guard his body from those natural** occurrences, **then the laws of nature to which he is** otherwise **beholden will act upon him.**[12]

NOTES

8. That is, Hashem decrees that the person should injure himself in order to awaken him to repent for his misdeeds and receive atonement for them (see *Meiri* ad loc.).

9. Many Kabbalistic sources point out that the word הַטֶּבַע, *the [laws of] nature*, has the same numerical value as the Divine Name אֱלֹהִים, *God*. This is because the laws of nature are merely a vehicle through which Hashem governs and manifests Himself in the world (see, for example, *Reishis Chochmah, Shaar HaAhavah* Ch. 11 §78; *Pri Tzaddik, Parashas Korach*, end of §4; see also *Daas Torah* [R' Yerucham Levovitz], *Parashas Haazinu*, p. 135, citing *Kuzari* [perhaps in reference to *Maamar Rishon* §76, in the context of *Kuzari's* discourse on God and the laws of nature, where he in fact touches on the ideas that Chinuch presents here (ibid. §71-79)]).

10. Stylistic citation of *Genesis* 2:7.

11. Chinuch is presumably alluding to the four "elements" that, by traditional teaching, constitute the basic material from which the physical world is formed: fire, air, earth (dust), and water.

12. In other words: Hashem placed man in a world that

וְאָמְנָם יִהְיוּ קְצָת מִבְּנֵי אָדָם אֲשֶׁר הַמֶּלֶךְ חָפֵץ בִּיקָרָם[13] לְרֹב חֲסִידוּתָם וּדְבֵקוּת נַפְשָׁם בִּדְרָכָיו בָּרוּךְ הוּא, הֵמָּה הַחֲסִידִים הַגְּדוֹלִים אֲשֶׁר מֵעוֹלָם אַנְשֵׁי הַשֵּׁם[14] כְּמוֹ הָאָבוֹת הַגְּדוֹלִים וְהַקְּדוֹשִׁים וְהַרְבֵּה מִן הַבָּנִים שֶׁהָיוּ אַחֲרֵיהֶם כְּמוֹ דָּנִיֵּאל חֲנַנְיָה מִישָׁאֵל וַעֲזַרְיָה וְדוֹמֵיהֶם, שֶׁמָּסַר הָאֵל הַטֶּבַע בִּידֵיהֶם[15], וּבִתְחִלָּתָם הָיָה הַטֶּבַע אָדוֹן עֲלֵיהֶם, וּבְסוֹפָן לְגֹדֶל הִתְעַלּוּת נַפְשָׁם נֶהְפַּךְ הוּא שֶׁיִּהְיוּ הֵם אֲדוֹנִים עַל הַטֶּבַע, כַּאֲשֶׁר יָדַעְנוּ בְּאַבְרָהָם אָבִינוּ שֶׁהִפִּילוּהוּ בְּכִבְשַׁן הָאֵשׁ וְלֹא הֻזַּק[16], וְאַרְבַּעַת הַחֲסִידִים הַנִּזְכָּרִים שֶׁשָּׂמוּ אוֹתָם לְגוֹ אַתּוּן נוּרָא יָקִידְתָּא וּשְׂעַר רָאשֵׁיהוֹן לָא אִתְחָרַךְ[17]. וְרֹב בְּנֵי אָדָם בְּחֶטְאָם לֹא זָכוּ אֶל הַמַּעֲלָה הַגְּדוֹלָה הַזֹּאת,

---

Chinuch notes that there are exceptionally pious people whom Hashem elevates above the laws of nature:

וְאָמְנָם יִהְיוּ קְצָת מִבְּנֵי אָדָם אֲשֶׁר הַמֶּלֶךְ חָפֵץ בִּיקָרָם – **Now, there are indeed some individuals whom the King** (Hashem) **holds dear,**[13] לְרֹב חֲסִידוּתָם וּדְבֵקוּת נַפְשָׁם בִּדְרָכָיו בָּרוּךְ הוּא – **due to the intensity of their piety and the devotion of their souls to the ways of [Hashem], blessed is He.** הֵמָּה הַחֲסִידִים הַגְּדוֹלִים אֲשֶׁר מֵעוֹלָם אַנְשֵׁי הַשֵּׁם – **These are the great pious ones of old, men of renown,**[14] כְּמוֹ הָאָבוֹת הַגְּדוֹלִים וְהַקְּדוֹשִׁים – **such as our great and holy forefathers,** Abraham, Isaac, and Jacob, וְהַרְבֵּה מִן הַבָּנִים שֶׁהָיוּ אַחֲרֵיהֶם כְּמוֹ דָּנִיֵּאל חֲנַנְיָה מִישָׁאֵל וַעֲזַרְיָה וְדוֹמֵיהֶם **– as well as many of their descendants who came after them, such as Daniel, Chananiah, Mishael, and Azariah, and** others **like them,** שֶׁמָּסַר הָאֵל הַטֶּבַע בִּידֵיהֶם – **to whom the Almighty gave** control over the laws of **nature.**[15] וּבִתְחִלָּתָם הָיָה הַטֶּבַע אָדוֹן עֲלֵיהֶם – To be sure, they were not born this way. **At the outset of their** lives, Hashem assigned **nature** to be **master over them** just like everyone else, וּבְסוֹפָן לְגֹדֶל הִתְעַלּוּת נַפְשָׁם נֶהְפַּךְ הוּא שֶׁיִּהְיוּ הֵם אֲדוֹנִים עַל הַטֶּבַע – **but eventually, due to their great spiritual elevation, the matter was reversed,** and Hashem made it so **that they should be masters over** the laws of **nature.** כַּאֲשֶׁר יָדַעְנוּ בְּאַבְרָהָם אָבִינוּ שֶׁהִפִּילוּהוּ בְּכִבְשַׁן הָאֵשׁ וְלֹא הֻזַּק – **We know this about Abraham, our forefather, who was cast** by Nimrod **into the fiery furnace but was not harmed,**[16] וְאַרְבַּעַת הַחֲסִידִים הַנִּזְכָּרִים שֶׁשָּׂמוּ אוֹתָם לְגוֹ אַתּוּן נוּרָא יָקִידְתָּא – **as well as** about **the four pious ones mentioned** above (Daniel, Chananiah, Mishael, and Azariah), **who were similarly thrown** by Nebuchadnezzar of Babylon **into a burning furnace of fire** but were not harmed at all, וּשְׂעַר רָאשֵׁיהוֹן לָא אִתְחָרַךְ – **and** even **the hair on their heads was not singed.**[17]

Indeed, these great individuals were not subject to the laws of nature. However, most people are not on that level, so the mitzvah to prevent natural accidents remains in place:

וְרֹב בְּנֵי אָדָם בְּחֶטְאָם לֹא זָכוּ אֶל הַמַּעֲלָה הַגְּדוֹלָה הַזֹּאת – **Most people, however, due to their sins,**

NOTES

is governed by the laws of nature, and he is therefore required to utilize his intelligence and all means at his disposal to protect himself and others from naturally occurring harm. Of course, Hashem's Will ultimately determines the outcome of a person's efforts (or lack of them), and nothing can override that Will. This, however, does not exempt a person from acting within the framework of the natural laws of cause and effect (see *Orchos Chaim* by *R' Aharon MiLunel*, Vol. II [Berlin ed.], *Din Shiluach HaKein* [§33] ד"ה טעם המצוה זאת, and other sources cited in footnote 4 in the Machon Yerushalayim edition of *Minchas Chinuch;* for a lengthy treatment of this matter, see *Sifsei Chaim* ibid., pp. 96-114).

13. Literally, *whom the King desires to honor* (stylistic paraphrase of *Esther* 6:9).

14. Stylistic paraphrase of *Genesis* 6:4.

15. See note 17 below.

16. Abraham's father, Terach, who was a manufacturer and seller of idols, complained to Nimrod (the Mesopotamian king at that time) that Abraham had smashed his wares, so Nimrod had Abraham thrown into a fiery furnace. Abraham was miraculously saved from the fire. See *Bereishis Rabbah* 38:13; *Rashi* to *Genesis* 11:28.

17. Stylistic citation of *Daniel* 3:21, 27.

Actually, only three of the four – Chananiah, Mishael, and Azariah – were cast into a furnace by Nebuchadnezzar for refusing to bow down to an idol, and emerged unscathed, as recorded in *Daniel* ibid. Daniel was not present at that event; see *Sanhedrin* 93a. Nevertheless, Daniel, too, was supernaturally saved from certain death. He was cast into a den of starving lions and emerged unhurt, as recorded in *Daniel* 6:1-25 (see *Minchas Yitzchak*).

וְעַל כֵּן תְּצִוָּנוּ הַתּוֹרָה לִשְׁמֹר מִשְׁכְּנוֹתֵינוּ וּמְקוֹמוֹתֵינוּ לְבַל יִקְרֶנוּ מָוֶת בִּפְשִׁיעוּתֵינוּ וְלֹא נְסַכֵּן נַפְשׁוֹתֵינוּ עַל סָמַךְ הַנֵּס, וְאָמְרוּ זִכְרוֹנָם לִבְרָכָה (תורת כהנים אמר פרשתא ח׳) שֶׁכָּל הַסּוֹמֵךְ עַל הַנֵּס אֵין עוֹשִׂין לוֹ נֵס[18].

וְעַל הַדֶּרֶךְ הַזֶּה תִּרְאֶה רֹב עִנְיְנֵי הַכְּתוּבִים בְּכָל מָקוֹם, כִּי גַּם בְּהִלָּחֵם יִשְׂרָאֵל מִלְחֶמֶת מִצְוָה עַל פִּי ה׳ הָיוּ עוֹרְכִין מִלְחַמְתָּן וּמְזַיְּנִין עַצְמָן וְעוֹשִׂין כָּל עִנְיָנָם כְּאִלּוּ יִסְמְכוּ בְּדַרְכֵי הַטֶּבַע לְגַמְרֵי[19], וְכֵן רָאוּי לַעֲשׂוֹת לְפִי הָעִנְיָן שֶׁזְּכַרְנוּ, וַאֲשֶׁר לֹא יַחֲלֹק עַל הָאֱמֶת מֵרֹעַ לֵב יוֹדֶה בָּזֶה.

מִדִּינֵי הַמִּצְוָה מַה שֶּׁאָמְרוּ זִכְרוֹנָם לִבְרָכָה (רמב״ם הלכות רוצח ושמירת נפש י״א:א־ב)

---

do not merit this exalted level and *are* subject to the laws of nature. וְעַל כֵּן תְּצִוָּנוּ הַתּוֹרָה לִשְׁמֹר מִשְׁכְּנוֹתֵינוּ וּמְקוֹמוֹתֵינוּ לְבַל יִקְרֶנוּ מָוֶת בִּפְשִׁיעוּתֵינוּ – **The Torah therefore commands us to safeguard our dwellings and our property so that no fatality should occur** to anyone **due to our negligence,** וְלֹא נְסַכֵּן נַפְשׁוֹתֵינוּ עַל סָמַךְ הַנֵּס – **and** that **we should not put our lives** or the lives of others **at risk while relying on a miracle.** Meaning, we must not neglect our responsibility to safeguard our property, rationalizing that Hashem will surely protect us from harm. וְאָמְרוּ זִכְרוֹנָם לִבְרָכָה – **Indeed, [the Sages], of blessed memory, stated** (*Sifra* to *Leviticus* 22:32) שֶׁכָּל הַסּוֹמֵךְ עַל הַנֵּס אֵין עוֹשִׂין לוֹ נֵס – **that anyone who relies on a miracle, a miracle will** surely **not be done for him.**[18]

וְעַל הַדֶּרֶךְ הַזֶּה תִּרְאֶה רֹב עִנְיְנֵי הַכְּתוּבִים בְּכָל מָקוֹם – **You will see** that **most of the narratives throughout Scripture follow this path.** כִּי גַּם בְּהִלָּחֵם יִשְׂרָאֵל מִלְחֶמֶת מִצְוָה עַל פִּי ה׳ – For example, **even when** the nation of **Israel would fight an obligatory war on Hashem's command,** knowing that Hashem would deliver their enemies into their hands, הָיוּ עוֹרְכִין מִלְחַמְתָּן וּמְזַיְּנִין עַצְמָן וְעוֹשִׂין כָּל עִנְיָנָם כְּאִלּוּ יִסְמְכוּ בְּדַרְכֵי הַטֶּבַע לְגַמְרֵי – **they would** nevertheless **wage their war, arm themselves, and conduct all their** combat **affairs as if they were relying entirely on the ways of nature.**[19] וְכֵן רָאוּי לַעֲשׂוֹת לְפִי הָעִנְיָן שֶׁזְּכַרְנוּ – **And** indeed, **so is it proper to do,** to conduct our lives within the framework of nature and its laws, while at the same time know that ultimately, Hashem runs the world, **as we have indicated.** This is all the Will of Hashem. וַאֲשֶׁר לֹא יַחֲלֹק עַל הָאֱמֶת מֵרֹעַ לֵב יוֹדֶה בָּזֶה – **Any** intellectually honest person **who does not dispute the truth out of spite will agree to this.**

Laws of the Mitzvah

מִדִּינֵי הַמִּצְוָה – **Among the laws of the mitzvah** is מַה שֶּׁאָמְרוּ זִכְרוֹנָם לִבְרָכָה – **that which [our Sages], of blessed memory, stated** (see *Rambam, Hil. Rotze'ach U'Shemiras Nefesh* 11:1-2),

---

NOTES

18. *Sifra* continues to say that a miracle is performed only for those who actually do *not* rely on a miracle, such as Chananiah, Mishael, and Azariah, who were ready to die in the fire and sanctify Hashem's Name. As *Malbim* (ad loc.) explains, a person who is willing to have his body consumed in fire for the sanctification of Hashem's Name demonstrates that he has elevated his physical body to a spiritual purpose (i.e., to be a vessel for serving Hashem). As such, his body transcends the laws of the physical world that Hashem set in place, and is now directly and entirely under Hashem's Providence, which is the *source* of all miracles. [See *Taanis* (18b) for an account of some pious individuals who were in a similar situation as Chananiah, Mishael, and Azariah, but insisted that they were not worthy of a miracle like them. The Gemara concludes there that in the merit of that declaration itself, they too were ultimately saved (see *Hamaspik L'Ovdei Hashem* [*R' Avraham ben HaRambam*], pp. 136-137 in Feldheim ed.).]

It follows, then, that *relying* on a miracle demonstrates the opposite — that this person believes that Hashem's Providence should serve his body and save it from all harm (instead of his body being in the service of Hashem). If anything, this further entrenches his body in the physical world and binds it to its physical laws.

19. *Ramban* (to *Job* 36:7) brings several examples of this. See also *Sifsei Chaim* (*Emunah V'Hashgachah* I, pp. 100-108) for an elaboration of this matter.

שֶׁאֵין חִיּוּב הַמַּעֲקֶה אֶלָּא בְּבַיִת שֶׁיֵּשׁ בָּהּ דִּירָה, אֲבָל בֵּית הָאוֹצָרוֹת וּבֵית הַבָּקָר וְכַיּוֹצֵא בָּהֶן וְכָל בַּיִת שֶׁאֵין בּוֹ אַרְבַּע אַמּוֹת עַל אַרְבַּע אַמּוֹת פָּטוּר מִן הַמַּעֲקֶה[20], וְכֵן בָּתֵּי כְנֵסִיּוֹת וּבָתֵּי מִדְרָשׁוֹת לְפִי שֶׁאֵינָן עֲשׂוּיִין לְדִירָה[21], וּמַה שֶּׁאָמְרוּ זִכְרוֹנָם לִבְרָכָה

שֶׁאֵין חִיּוּב הַמַּעֲקֶה אֶלָּא בְּבַיִת שֶׁיֵּשׁ בָּהּ דִּירָה – **that the obligation of** making **a** protective **fence** around a rooftop of one's house applies **only in a house that has** livable **dwelling quarters.** אֲבָל בֵּית הָאוֹצָרוֹת וּבֵית הַבָּקָר וְכַיּוֹצֵא בָּהֶן – **However, a storage house, a cattle barn, or the like,** וְכָל בַּיִת שֶׁאֵין בּוֹ אַרְבַּע אַמּוֹת עַל אַרְבַּע אַמּוֹת – **or any house whose dimensions are less than four** ***amos*** **by four** ***amos***, such that it is not fit for dwelling, פָּטוּר מִן הַמַּעֲקֶה – **does not require a fence** around its rooftop.[20] וְכֵן בָּתֵּי כְנֵסִיּוֹת וּבָתֵּי מִדְרָשׁוֹת – **The same** applies to **synagogues and study halls,** i.e., they do not require a fence around their rooftops, לְפִי שֶׁאֵינָן עֲשׂוּיִין לְדִירָה – **since they are not made for dwelling.**[21]

Chinuch discusses the law of a house whose rooftop is lower than the public domain, such that there is no danger of someone falling from the roof onto the public domain, but only from the public domain onto the rooftop:

וּמַה שֶּׁאָמְרוּ זִכְרוֹנָם לִבְרָכָה – **Another** law **is that which [the Sages], of blessed memory, stated**

NOTES

20. The Gemara (*Succah* 3a-b) teaches that a house that is less than four-by-four *amos* (cubits) is not considered a house, as it is unfit for dwelling. Since the Torah's injunction to put up a fence is stated regarding a "house" (*If you build a new "house," you shall make a fence for your roof*), if it is less than four cubits squared it is not included in the obligation (*Meiri* to *Succah* ad loc.). Apparently, *Rambam* (whom Chinuch cites here) reasons that the same applies to a storage house or cattle barn, since they, too, are unfit for dwelling. [*Rambam* may also have based his ruling on *Mechilta* cited in *Midrash HaGadol* to our verse.]

Other Rishonim, however, maintain that the requirement of *maakeh* applies to the roof of a storage house and barn as well (*Smag, Asei* §79; *Yerei'im* §234 [45]). For discussion, see *Kesef Mishneh* to *Rambam* ibid.; *Sma, Choshen Mishpat* 427:2; *Emek HaNetziv* on *Sifrei* to the verse ד״ה מנין הבונה בית התבן (p. 258).

21. Based on *Chullin* 136a (see *Rashi* ad loc., second explanation). [*Sma* (ibid. §5) maintains that even those authorities who require a *maakeh* around rooftops of barns and storehouses (*Smag* and *Yerei'im* cited in previous note) would agree that synagogues and study halls are exempt, due to *Rashi's* first explanation there (that synagogues and study halls have no real owners). See also *Aruch HaShulchan, Choshen Mishpat* 427:2.]

One might wonder: Why should the requirement of a *maakeh* depend upon the structure's definition as a "house" and its suitability for dwelling? Is there no danger of a fall from the roof of a structure that does not have the dimensions or qualifications of a "house"?! Furthermore, pits and ditches are not a "house" at all, yet they require a *maakeh,* because they pose a danger. So why should rooftops of storehouses be different?

Chazon Ish (*Choshen Mishpat, Likkutim* 18:1-2) explains as follows: In truth, a rooftop is not considered a genuine hazard, because anyone who walks on it is fully aware of the danger and naturally exercises caution. It is unlike a pit or similar obstacles, which the average pedestrian does not have the foresight to avoid. Accordingly, if not for the specific mitzvah-obligation to make a fence on the roof, it would not have been required, just as no special protection is required for one who climbs a ladder or a tree, for instance. Nevertheless, the Torah teaches that the rooftop of a "house" requires a *maakeh*, perhaps as a *superior* degree of protection. A structure that is not a "house," however, is not included in this requirement, and its roof is thus treated like a ladder or tree, which do not require any safeguarding (see also *Emek Berachah, Chol HaMoed* §6, p. 121).

Others suggest that indeed, if the rooftop is used on a regular basis, it does constitute a hazard (unlike *Chazon Ish*, who says that even regular use does not make it a bona fide hazard). And in that case, a *maakeh* is mandatory, whether the structure has dwelling quarters or not. The difference between a "house" and other structures is only with respect to a rooftop that is used infrequently, in which case it does not pose a hazard. The Torah requires a *maakeh* around the rooftop of a house even in that case, but not around the rooftops of non-residential structures (see *Maharam Schik* 547:2; *Emek HaNetziv* ibid. ד״ה מן המעקה, p. 260).

Finally, others indicate that the difference between a residential and a non-residential house is precisely the extent to which their rooftops are generally used. The rooftops of residential homes are used regularly and therefore present a hazard, whereas the rooftops of non-residential structures are rarely used and do *not* present a hazard (*Sma* ibid. §2; *Shulchan Aruch HaRav, Hil. Shemiras Guf V'Nefesh* §1).

שֶׁאִם הָיְתָה רְשׁוּת הָרַבִּים גְּבוֹהָה מִגַּגּוֹ אֵין זָקוּק לַמַּעֲקֶה, שֶׁנֶּאֱמַר כִּי יִפֹּל הַנֹּפֵל מִמֶּנּוּ, וְלֹא בְּתוֹכוֹ²², וְשִׁעוּר גֹּבַהּ מַעֲקֶה עֲשָׂרָה טְפָחִים.²³

וְהִרְבָּה דְבָרִים אָסְרוּ זִכְרוֹנָם לִבְרָכָה כְּדֵי לְהִשָּׁמֵר מִן הַנְּזָקִים וּמִן הַמִּקְרִים הָרָעִים, שֶׁאֵין רָאוּי לוֹ לְאָדָם שֶׁיֵּשׁ בּוֹ דֵעָה לְסַכֵּן בְּנַפְשׁוֹ וְעַל כֵּן רָאוּי שֶׁיִּתֵּן לִבּוֹ לְכָל הַדְּבָרִים שֶׁאֶפְשָׁר לְהַגִּיעַ לוֹ נֶזֶק בָּהֶם, וְהָעוֹבֵר עֲלֵיהֶם חַיָּב מַכַּת מַרְדּוּת דְּרַבָּנָן²⁴, מֵהֶן מַה שֶּׁאָמְרוּ שֶׁלֹּא יַנִּיחַ אָדָם פִּיו עַל הַסִּילוֹן וְיִשְׁתֶּה, וְכֵן לֹא יִשְׁתֶּה מִן הַנְּהָרוֹת וְהָאֲגַמִּים

(Bava Kamma 51a), שֶׁאִם הָיְתָה רְשׁוּת הָרַבִּים גְּבוֹהָה מִגַּגּוֹ — that if the public domain was *higher* than one's rooftop, such that someone might fall from the public domain onto the rooftop, אֵין זָקוּק לַמַּעֲקֶה — it does not require a fence, שֶׁנֶּאֱמַר "כִּי יִפֹּל הַנֹּפֵל מִמֶּנּוּ" — as it is stated: *If you build a new house, you shall make a fence for your roof, and you shall not place blood in your house,* **if one should** fall *"from it,"* וְלֹא בְּתוֹכוֹ — which implies that the obligation to build a fence applies only when the concern is that one may fall *off* one's property **and not** *into* **it.**[22]

Chinuch teaches the height requirement of a *maakeh*:

וְשִׁעוּר גֹּבַהּ מַעֲקֶה — Whenever a fence is required, **the** minimum **measurement of the height of the fence is** עֲשָׂרָה טְפָחִים — **ten** *tefachim* (handbreadths), which is generally high enough to prevent someone from falling.[23]

Related to the mitzvah-obligation of *maakeh*, in which we are commanded to remove all types of hazards from our property, we are also commanded to safeguard our health in other ways:

וְהִרְבָּה דְבָרִים אָסְרוּ זִכְרוֹנָם לִבְרָכָה כְּדֵי לְהִשָּׁמֵר מִן הַנְּזָקִים וּמִן הַמִּקְרִים הָרָעִים — There are **many things that [the Sages], of blessed memory, restricted in order to prevent harm and bad incidents.** שֶׁאֵין רָאוּי לוֹ לְאָדָם שֶׁיֵּשׁ בּוֹ דֵעָה לְסַכֵּן בְּנַפְשׁוֹ — For it does not befit an intelligent person to put **himself at risk,** וְעַל כֵּן רָאוּי שֶׁיִּתֵּן לִבּוֹ לְכָל הַדְּבָרִים שֶׁאֶפְשָׁר לְהַגִּיעַ לוֹ נֶזֶק בָּהֶם — and it is therefore appropriate that he take notice of all things through which he might be harmed, and stay away from them. וְהָעוֹבֵר עֲלֵיהֶם חַיָּב מַכַּת מַרְדּוּת דְּרַבָּנָן — One who transgresses these Rabbinic restrictions is liable to Rabbinic *makkas mardus* (lashes of discipline).[24] מֵהֶן מַה שֶּׁאָמְרוּ שֶׁלֹּא יַנִּיחַ אָדָם פִּיו עַל הַסִּילוֹן וְיִשְׁתֶּה — Among [these prohibitions] is that which [the Sages] stated (*Avodah Zarah* 12a-b), **that a person should not place his mouth on a pipe** that is attached to the ground, from which water is flowing, **and drink** the water from it, וְכֵן לֹא יִשְׁתֶּה מִן הַנְּהָרוֹת וְהָאֲגַמִּים — **and**

NOTES

22. In other words, the Torah does not deem it the responsibility of the homeowner to put up a fence so that people in the public domain do not fall onto his roof. For discussion of whether the public must put up a fence to protect themselves, see *Sma* ibid. §7; *Aruch HaShulchan* ibid. §4; *Chazon Ish* ibid. §5. See also Mitzvah 547 note 2.

Earlier, Chinuch mentioned that one must place a fence around one's pit. Although one falls *into* a pit and not from it, the difference is that the person who owns the pit also owns the ground around it from which one falls into it. In our case of the house that is lower than the public domain, the homeowner does not own the area above the roof, so he has no obligation to build a fence there (see *Dvar Avraham,* Vol. I, 37:1).

23. *Rambam, Hil. Rotze'ach* 11:3. *Rambam* adds there that the fence must be strong and sturdy enough so that even if a person leans on it, it will not fall. *Rambam* also indicates (ibid. 11:4) that the minimum height of ten *tefachim* applies not only to rooftops, but even to pits and the like, for which a shorter mound surrounding

it might be sufficient to prevent people from falling in. See, however, *Raavad* ad loc.; *Smag* (*Asei* §79). For discussion, see *Beur HaGra* to *Choshen Mishpat* 427:5; *Aruch HaShulchan* 427:6; and *Chazon Ish* (ibid. 18:3-4). See also *Teshuvos Machazeh Eliyahu* 122:5.

With regard to the obligation of *maakeh*, 10 *tefachim* is generally calculated as the equivalent of between 35.5 and 38.7 inches (90-98.2 cm.); see *Shiurin shel Torah* (*Shiurei HaMitzvos* §1), who writes that preferably it should be 1 meter (39.37 in.) in height. For further discussion, see *Minchas Chinuch* §13 and *Emek Berachah, Maakeh* (pp. 33-34).

24. See General Introduction, note 16.

A number of authorities maintain that it is actually forbidden by *Biblical* law to engage in the harmful activities that Chinuch will immediately list, based on the verse (*Deuteronomy* 4:9): רַק הִשָּׁמֶר לְךָ וּשְׁמֹר נַפְשְׁךָ מְאֹד, *Only be careful and guard your soul well* (see, for example, *Minchas Chinuch* §12). For discussion, see *Darchei Teshuvah, Yoreh Deah* 116:57; *Sdei Chemed, Pe'as HaSadeh, Maareches HaAleph,* Ch. 22 ד״ה וכתבתי.

שֶׁמָּא יִשְׁתֶּה עֲלוּקָה, וְאָסְרוּ מַיִם מְגֻלִּין מִפְּנֵי חֲשָׁשׁ שֶׁלֹּא יִשְׁתֶּה מֵהֶן הָרַחַשׁ בַּעַל הָאֶרֶס[25], וְשִׁעוּר גִּלּוּיָן כְּדֵי שֶׁיֵּצֵא הָרַחַשׁ מֵאֹזֶן כְּלִי וְיִשְׁתֶּה[26], וְאָמְרוּ בְּעִנְיָן זֶה שֶׁיֵּשׁ מַשְׁקִין שֶׁיֵּשׁ בָּהֶן מִשּׁוּם גִּלּוּי וּמֵהֶן שֶׁאֵין בָּהֶם מִשּׁוּם גִּלּוּי[27]. וּמֵחֲשָׁשׁ זֶה בְּעַצְמוֹ אָסְרוּ נְקוּרֵי תְאֵנִים וַעֲנָבִים וְרִמּוֹנִים וְקִשּׁוּאִין וּדְלוּעִין וְהַמְּלָפְפוֹנוֹת אֲפִלּוּ הֵן כְּכִכָּר[28,29], וְדֶרֶךְ כְּלָל כָּל פְּרִי שֶׁיֵּשׁ בּוֹ לֵחָה וְנִמְצָא נָשׁוּךְ אָמְרוּ שֶׁהוּא אָסוּר[30]. וּכְמוֹ כֵן אָסְרוּ שֶׁלֹּא יִתֵּן אָדָם מָעוֹת לְתוֹךְ פִּיו שֶׁמָּא יֵשׁ עֲלֵיהֶן רֹק יָבֵשׁ שֶׁל מֻכֵּה שְׁחִין אוֹ מְצֹרָעִין אוֹ זֵעָה, שֶׁכָּל זֵעַת אָדָם הִיא סַם הַמָּוֶת חוּץ מִשֶּׁל פָּנִים.

---

likewise he should not drink directly **from rivers or ponds,** שֶׁמָּא יִשְׁתֶּה עֲלוּקָה – because **he might** inadvertently **swallow a leech** that is in the water, which is dangerous. וְאָסְרוּ מַיִם מְגֻלִּין – **[The Sages]** (*Terumos* 8:4-5) **further prohibited** drinking **water** that was left **exposed,** מִפְּנֵי חֲשָׁשׁ שֶׁלֹּא יִשְׁתֶּה מֵהֶן הָרַחַשׁ בַּעַל הָאֶרֶס – **due to concern that a poisonous reptile** such as a snake[25] **drank from it** and, in doing so, injected some venom into it. וְשִׁעוּר גִּלּוּיָן – **The duration** of time after which **[water]** is considered **exposed** and therefore unfit for drinking is כְּדֵי שֶׁיֵּצֵא הָרַחַשׁ מֵאֹזֶן כְּלִי וְיִשְׁתֶּה – **enough** time **for a snake** (or other poisonous creature) **to emerge from** a hole under **the handle of** the **utensil** containing the water**,** i.e., from a hole immediately nearby, **drink** from the water, and return to its hole unobserved.[26] וְאָמְרוּ בְּעִנְיָן זֶה שֶׁיֵּשׁ מַשְׁקִין שֶׁיֵּשׁ בָּהֶן מִשּׁוּם גִּלּוּי – **[The Sages]** further **said** (ibid.; *Chullin* 49b) **regarding this matter that there are liquids that are subject to** the restriction against drinking an **exposed** liquid, וּמֵהֶן שֶׁאֵין בָּהֶם מִשּׁוּם גִּלּוּי – **and others that are *not* subject to** the restriction against drinking an **exposed** liquid.[27] וּמֵחֲשָׁשׁ זֶה בְּעַצְמוֹ – Also, **because of this very same concern,** אָסְרוּ נְקוּרֵי תְאֵנִים וַעֲנָבִים וְרִמּוֹנִים וְקִשּׁוּאִין וּדְלוּעִין וְהַמְּלָפְפוֹנוֹת – **[the Sages]** (*Terumos* 8:6) **prohibited** eating **punctured figs, grapes, pomegranates, cucumbers, gourds, melons,** and the like, for fear that a snake bit into the fruit and deposited its venom into it. אֲפִלּוּ הֵן כְּכִכָּר – **Even if [the fruits] are** as large as a ***kikar***[28] and they are punctured only on one side, one may not eat any part of them.[29] וְדֶרֶךְ כְּלָל כָּל פְּרִי שֶׁיֵּשׁ בּוֹ לֵחָה וְנִמְצָא נָשׁוּךְ אָמְרוּ שֶׁהוּא אָסוּר – **As a rule, [the Sages] said that any fruit that has moisture in it and is found to have been bitten is forbidden.**[30]

There is another object that one may not even place in his mouth because of the potential danger: וּכְמוֹ כֵן אָסְרוּ שֶׁלֹּא יִתֵּן אָדָם מָעוֹת לְתוֹךְ פִּיו – **[The Sages]** (*Yerushalmi Terumos* 8:3; 75b in Schottenstein ed.) **likewise prohibited a person from putting coins inside his mouth,** שֶׁמָּא יֵשׁ עֲלֵיהֶן רֹק יָבֵשׁ שֶׁל מֻכֵּה שְׁחִין אוֹ מְצֹרָעִין – since **[the coins] might have on them dry saliva of a person afflicted with boils or leprosy,** and the person who puts the coin in his mouth might contract these diseases through the saliva. אוֹ זֵעָה – **Alternatively,** the coins might have on them residues of human **sweat**, which puts one's life at risk, שֶׁכָּל זֵעַת אָדָם הִיא סַם הַמָּוֶת חוּץ מִשֶּׁל פָּנִים **– for all human sweat is toxic, except for that of the face.**

NOTES

25. See *Rambam, Hil. Rotze'ach* 11:6. [See further, *Rav* and *Meleches Shlomo* to *Terumos* 8:4.]

26. *Chullin* 10a; *Rambam* ibid. 11:11. See, however, *Yerushalmi Terumos* 8:3 (77b in Schottenstein ed.).

27. The prohibition applies to water, wine, milk, honey, and fish brine. There are certain conditions, however, under which even these liquids are excluded because a snake would not drink from them. For example, a snake does not drink cooked wine, and is scared of approaching any boiling hot liquid. See *Rambam* ibid. 11:7-10.

28. A *kikar* is a dry weight measure of approximately 50 pounds.

29. *Rav* to the Mishnah. See commentaries there for other interpretations of this phrase.

30. Since the fruit is moist, the venom can mix with it and spread to the entire product. If the fruit is dry, however, one may cut off the bitten part and eat the rest (*Rav* ibid.).

The authorities disagree as to whether the concern of "exposure" (גִּלּוּי) is relevant today, when snakes generally do not live in residential areas. For a thorough review of this dispute, see *Shemiras HaGuf V'HaNefesh* (Lerner) §44.

וְיֶתֶר פְּרָטֶיהָ מְבֹאָרִין בְּבָבָא קַמָּא וּבִמְקוֹמוֹת מִסַּנְהֶדְרִין[31] וּבִשְׁקָלִים יְרוּשַׁלְמִי פֶּרֶק רִאשׁוֹן[32].

וְנוֹהֶגֶת בְּכָל מָקוֹם וּבְכָל זְמַן, בִּזְכָרִים וּנְקֵבוֹת[33].

וְעוֹבֵר עַל זֶה וּמַנִּיחַ גַּגּוֹ אוֹ בוֹרוֹ בְּלֹא מַעֲקֶה בִּטֵּל עֲשֵׂה זֶה, וְגַם עָבַר עַל לָאו דְּלֹא תָשִׂים דָּמִים בְּבֵיתֶךָ, כְּמוֹ שֶׁנִּכְתֹּב בְּסֵדֶר זֶה (מצוה תקמ״ז) בְּעֶזְרַת הַשֵּׁם.

Chinuch concludes:

וְיֶתֶר פְּרָטֶיהָ – These laws **and the remaining details of [the mitzvah]** מְבֹאָרִין בְּבָבָא קַמָּא – **are set forth in** Tractate ***Bava Kamma*** (15b, 46a, 50a, 51a, 83a), וּבִמְקוֹמוֹת מִסַּנְהֶדְרִין – **in** various **places in** Tractate ***Sanhedrin,***[31] וּבִשְׁקָלִים יְרוּשַׁלְמִי פֶּרֶק רִאשׁוֹן – **and in the first chapter of *Yerushalmi Shekalim.***[32]

Applicability of the Mitzvah

וְנוֹהֶגֶת בְּכָל מָקוֹם וּבְכָל זְמַן – This mitzvah **applies in every location and in all times,** בִּזְכָרִים וּנְקֵבוֹת – **to** both **men and women.**[33]

וְעוֹבֵר עַל זֶה – **One who transgresses this** mitzvah וּמַנִּיחַ גַּגּוֹ אוֹ בוֹרוֹ בְּלֹא מַעֲקֶה – **and leaves his rooftop or his pit without a** protective **fence** around it, בִּטֵּל עֲשֵׂה זֶה – **violates this** mitzvah-**obligation,** וְגַם עָבַר עַל לָאו דְ״לֹא תָשִׂים דָּמִים בְּבֵיתֶךָ״ – **and also transgresses the** mitzvah-**prohibition of *You shall not place blood in your house*** (Mitzvah 547), כְּמוֹ שֶׁנִּכְתֹּב בְּסֵדֶר זֶה בְּעֶזְרַת הַשֵּׁם – **as we will write** further **in this *parashah,* with the help of Hashem.**

NOTES

31. Perhaps Chinuch means to reference *Sanhedrin* 101a, which forbids asking a question of a demon because this puts oneself in danger.

32. This reference is taken from *Rambam, Sefer HaMitzvos, Lo Saaseh* §298. *R' Y. F. Perla* (Vol. 3, *Pesichah* §12) notes, however, that there is no mention of matters relating to our mitzvah in *Yerushalmi Shekalim* at all. He suggests that *Rambam* is referring to the law in the opening Mishnah in *Shekalim* (as explained in *Moed Katan* 5a), that the roads must be repaired so that people do not fall into its holes and ditches (see Mitzvah 547 note 2). See there, however, for some reservations as to whether this is what *Rambam* had in mind.

The laws presented in our mitzvah are codified in *Rambam*, *Hil. Rotze'ach U'Shemiras Nefesh* Chs. 11-12, and in *Shulchan Aruch*, *Choshen Mishpat* §427 (regarding the removal of hazards) and *Yoreh Deah* §116 (regarding foods and other matters prohibited because of danger).

33. I.e., it applies in Eretz Yisrael and the Diaspora, and whether the *Beis HaMikdash* is standing or not; and it applies to both men and women, in accordance with the general rule regarding mitzvah-obligations that are not time-specific.

Insight: Reciting a Blessing When Building a Maakeh

As a general rule, when a person performs a mitzvah, for example, he puts on *tefillin* or takes a *lulav,* he recites a blessing beforehand. This category of blessings is called *birchas hamitzvos,* blessings over the mitzvos. *Rambam* (*Hil. Berachos* 11:8) indicates that the building of a *maakeh* (protective fence), too, should be accompanied by a blessing. Although, as will be presented below, some Rishonim disagree with this ruling, the majority of authorities follow the opinion of *Rambam* (see *Sdei Chemed, Asifas Dinim, Maareches Berachos* 1:16 והנה מדברי כל הפוסקים).

There is a difficulty with *Rambam's* ruling, however. In the same chapter (*Hil. Berachos* 11:4), *Rambam* discusses why no blessing is recited upon washing the hands after a meal (*mayim acharonim*) just as a blessing is recited upon washing the hands *before* a meal (*netilas yadayim*; see Insight to Mitzvah 106). *Rambam* explains that the obligation of *mayim acharonim* was instituted in order to prevent danger (see *Eruvin* 17b for details), and any mitzvah whose purpose is to prevent danger does not require a blessing. *Rambam* illustrates this with an example that is related to our mitzvah. As Chinuch teaches (at note 22), the Sages forbade drinking directly from rivers or from a pipe, out of concern that a person will inadvertently swallow a leech. Rather, one must scoop the water with

a cup and examine it first in order to make sure it is free of leeches. At night, when it is hard to see, one should run the water through a sieve or filter. Now, would anyone suggest that upon filtering the water, one should recite a blessing (… *and commanded us to filter the water*)?! Certainly not! The reason is because it is not a typical mitzvah, like *tefillin* or *lulav*, but rather a simple guideline to avoid danger. The same is true, says *Rambam*, regarding any obligation that is intended solely to prevent danger, such as *mayim acharonim*. Being that this is *Rambam's* position, why does *Rambam* require a blessing for building a *maakeh*, if the purpose of building a *maakeh* is likewise to prevent danger?

Pri Megadim (beginning of Introduction to *Hil. Netilas Yadaim*) suggests that the mitzvah of *maakeh* is different because it is a Biblical obligation, whereas the other safety-related obligations are Rabbinic. Biblical mitzvos warrant a blessing even if they are intended to prevent danger. Though *Pri Megadim* does not elaborate, the reason may be that when an obligation appears in the Torah, it has the status of a "mitzvah" regardless of its purpose. To use the example of *maakeh*: although the purpose may be preventing a fall, now that the Torah commanded, "You shall make a *maakeh*," building a *maakeh* is not merely a safety regulation, but a bona fide mitzvah act, just like taking a *lulav* (see *Minchas Chinuch* §3). [*Minchas Chinuch* maintains, in fact, that the owner of the roof must *himself* build the *maakeh*, or alternatively appoint a *shaliach* (agent) to build it, since it is a mitzvah that is incumbent upon *him*. If a person whom he cannot appoint as a *shaliach* (e.g., a minor) built it, the owner has not fulfilled the mitzvah, even though the *maakeh* was built and the roof no longer poses any danger (see, however, *Machaneh Ephraim, Hilchos Sheluchin* §11, cited in *Minchas Chinuch* there).]

Rabbinic obligations, on the other hand, do not necessarily have the status of a mitzvah. Some, like *netilas yadayim* or lighting Chanukkah candles, are indeed Rabbinic mitzvos (מִצְוֹת דְּרַבָּנָן), and, as such, they are accompanied by a blessing. However, obligations such as washing *mayim acharonim* or filtering river water, which the Sages imposed simply as safety measures, were not given the status of a "mitzvah" and thus do not require a blessing (for a similar concept, see *Chidushei Maran Riz HaLevi* to *Rambam, Hil. Berachos* 11:16 ד"ה והנראה לומר בדעת הרמב"ם; see also *Teshuvos Pnei Meivin, Orach Chaim* §8).

Pri Megadim offers another explanation, which is based on an idea advanced later by *Chazon Ish* (cited in note 21): In truth, a roof is not considered a genuine hazard, because anyone who walks on it is fully aware of the danger and naturally exercises caution. The Torah nevertheless required that a *maakeh* be built. Accordingly, this cannot be categorized as an obligation that is purely for the sake of preventing danger, since as far as preventing danger is concerned, a *maakeh* is in fact *not* critical. It is rather a Scriptural decree and a mitzvah like other mitzvos. In contrast, the requirements to wash *mayim acharonim* after a meal or to filter river waters involve clear and present dangers, and they were indeed instituted due to safety concerns. Therefore, they do not require a blessing. [For other resolutions to the seeming inconsistency in *Rambam's* rulings, see *Bircas Avraham* (Treves) §204, p. 185 ff.; *Teshuvos Pri HaSadeh*, Vol. II, 16:4; *Teshuvos Levushei Mordechai, Orach Chaim* 3:2; and *Mayan Beis HaSho'evah, Deuteronomy* 22:8; see also *Aruch HaShulchan, Choshen Mishpat* 427:10.]

As indicated above, the majority of commentators, both Rishonim and Acharonim, concur with *Rambam* and rule that a blessing should be recited over the mitzvah of *maakeh* (see *Sdei Chemed* ibid. for a comprehensive list). There are those who disagree, however, namely *Roke'ach* (§366), *Meiri* (*Megillah* 21b ד"ה כבר ביארנו), and one opinion cited by *Raavad* in *Temim Dei'im* §179. *Roke'ach* explains that no blessing is recited over the building of a *maakeh* because, in his opinion, non-Jews are also obligated in this mitzvah. [Apparently *Roke'ach* holds that it is included in the Noahide law against bloodshed (*Techeiles Mordechai* [*Maharsham*], *Parashas Bereishis, Ner Mitzvah* §10).] Since this mitzvah was not given uniquely to us, we cannot use the standard blessing text, אֲשֶׁר קִדְּשָׁנוּ בְּמִצְוֹתָיו וְצִוָּנוּ, *Who sanctified us with His commandments, and commanded us…*, and therefore no blessing is recited at all. See *Temim Dei'im* (ibid.) for an alternative explanation.

Interestingly, *Shulchan Aruch* and *Rama* (*Choshen Mishpat* §427) make no mention at all of the blessing over the mitzvah of *maakeh*, leading some to suggest that they accepted the ruling of the minority in this regard (*Teshuvos Amudei Eish*, cited in *Sdei Chemed* ibid.). *Sdei Chemed* rejects this suggestion, and maintains that, regardless, the halachah remains that one must recite a blessing, since that is the opinion of the overwhelming majority of authorities. [See *Sefer HaBayis* (Lerner), 11:24-25, with notes, for a summary of the different opinions, as well as some references to contemporary halachic authorities who discuss this matter.]

מִצְוָה תקמז: שֶׁלֹּא לְהַנִּיחַ מִכְשׁוֹל

שֶׁלֹּא לְהַנִּיחַ[1] הַמִּכְשׁוֹלִים וְהַמּוֹקְשִׁים בְּאַרְצוֹתֵינוּ[2] וּבְבָתֵּינוּ כְּדֵי שֶׁלֹּא יָמוּתוּ וְלֹא יִזּוֹקוּ[3] בָּם בְּנֵי אָדָם, וְעַל זֶה נֶאֱמַר (דברים כ״ב, ח׳) **וְלֹא תָשִׂים דָּמִים בְּבֵיתֶךָ. וְאָמְרוּ בַּסִּפְרִי** (כאן),

---

Mitzvah 547

The Prohibition to Leave a Hazard

וְלֹא תָשִׂים דָּמִים בְּבֵיתֶךָ כִּי יִפֹּל הַנֹּפֵל מִמֶּנּוּ

And you shall not place blood in your house, if one should fall from it (*Deuteronomy* 22:8).

The Torah forbids leaving hazards in a place where they might cause harm. This mitzvah-prohibition is the counterpart to Mitzvah 546, the mitzvah of *maakeh* (building a protective fence), which is a mitzvah-obligation to remove such hazards.

שֶׁלֹּא לְהַנִּיחַ הַמִּכְשׁוֹלִים וְהַמּוֹקְשִׁים בְּאַרְצוֹתֵינוּ וּבְבָתֵּינוּ – We are commanded **not to leave stumbling blocks and hazards**[1] **in our lands**[2] **and in our homes,** **כְּדֵי שֶׁלֹּא יָמוּתוּ וְלֹא יִזּוֹקוּ בָּם בְּנֵי אָדָם** **– so that people should not die or be harmed**[3] **from them.** Rather, we must remove them, as taught in the previous mitzvah. **וְעַל זֶה נֶאֱמַר** – **Regarding this it is stated** (*Deuteronomy* 22:8): **"וְלֹא תָשִׂים דָּמִים בְּבֵיתֶךָ"** – ***and you shall not place blood in your house.*** **וְאָמְרוּ בַּסִּפְרִי** – **As [the**

NOTES

1. The term that Chinuch uses, לְהַנִּיחַ, can have two meanings: (1) to set down, or (2) to leave. It is thus not readily clear if Chinuch means that this mitzvah-prohibition forbids only placing ("setting down") hazards in our homes, or even failing to remove ("leaving") existing hazards. This matter of what the mitzvah-prohibition entails is apparently a subject of dispute among the Rishonim.

Tosafos (*Kiddushin* 34a ד״ה מעקה), along with several other Rishonim (e.g., *Smak* §152), maintain that the mitzvah-prohibition forbids only actively placing or creating a hazard in one's home. In the case of *maakeh*, this means that one builds the house with the intention of not enclosing its rooftop. However, if one installed a *maakeh* on his roof and it subsequently fell, he does not transgress this prohibition if he does not rebuild the *maakeh*, since at this point he is not *creating* a hazard. [He would, however, be required to rebuild it due to the mitzvah-obligation to build a *maakeh,* which (unlike the mitzvah-prohibition) applies even when one did not actively create the hazard (Mitzvah 546).]

Rambam (*Hil. Rotze'ach* 11:3-4), on the other hand, indicates that the mitzvah-prohibition forbids even passively leaving hazards in their place (see *Minchas Chinuch* §4; *Haamek She'eilah* 126:6). Since Chinuch's language here is a quote of *Rambam's Sefer HaMitzvos* (*Lo Saaseh* 298), it is reasonable to assume that he too means to include in the term לְהַנִּיחַ the sense of "failing to remove the hazards," and that this too is included in the prohibition. See also Kafich ed. of *Sefer HaMitzvos* ibid.

2. Chinuch seems to be saying (following *Rambam, Sefer HaMitzvos* ibid.) that it is forbidden to leave hazards *anywhere*, not only in one's private domain. *R' Y. F. Perla* (*Sefer HaMitzvos* of *Rav Saadiah Gaon, Lo Saaseh* §55 [Vol. 2, p. 54b] ד״ה ואמנם הנראה) indeed maintains that both our mitzvah-prohibition and its counterpart mitzvah-obligation (Mitzvah 546) apply even to hazards in the public domain; such hazards must be removed by the public and/or the courts. [This is consistent with *R' Perla's* suggestion (cited in Mitzvah 546 note 32) that the requirement to repair the public roads is included in the mitzvah of *maakeh*.] This does not seem to accord with the language of the Torah, though, which specifies one's *house* with respect to both the mitzvah-obligation and the mitzvah-prohibition. See related discussion in Insight to Mitzvah 232.

3. Chinuch indicates here that the prohibition is not limited to life-threatening hazards, but includes even those that may merely cause *injury*. *Rambam* (*Sefer HaMitzvos* ibid.; *Hil. Rotze'ach* 11:4), however, implies that the prohibition refers only to hazards that may cause death (see also *Meiri, Bava Kamma* 51a). For discussion, see *Dvar Avraham*, Vol. I, 37:25. See also *Aruch HaShulchan* 427:6, who rules in accordance with Chinuch.

וְעָשִׂיתָ מַעֲקֶה לְגַגֶּךָ, עֲשֵׂה, וְלֹא תָשִׂים דָּמִים בְּבֵיתֶךָ, לֹא תַעֲשֶׂה[4]**.**

מִשָּׁרְשֵׁי הַמִּצְוָה וְכָל עִנְיָנָהּ כָּתַבְתִּי בַּעֲשֵׂה ז׳ (מצוה תקמ״ו) **שֶׁבְּסֵדֶר זֶה**[5]**, וְקָחֶנּוּ מִשָּׁם אִם נַפְשְׁךָ לָדַעַת.**

Sages] stated in ***Sifrei*** (to the verse), **"וְעָשִׂיתָ מַעֲקֶה לְגַגֶּךָ"** – the clause, ***You shall make a fence for your roof,*** **עֲשֵׂה** – teaches a mitzvah-**obligation** to remove hazards; **"וְלֹא תָשִׂים דָּמִים בְּבֵיתֶךָ"** – and the clause, ***and you shall not place blood in your house,*** **לֹא תַעֲשֶׂה** – teaches a mitzvah-**prohibition** against leaving hazards in a place where they may cause harm.[4]

Underlying Purpose, Laws, and Applicability of the Mitzvah

מִשָּׁרְשֵׁי הַמִּצְוָה וְכָל עִנְיָנָהּ – **Regarding the underlying purposes of the mitzvah, and all of its** subject **matter,** **כָּתַבְתִּי בַּעֲשֵׂה ז׳ שֶׁבְּסֵדֶר זֶה** – **I have** already **written** on the subject **in** Mitzvah-**obligation 7 of this** ***parashah*** (Mitzvah 546).[5] **וְקָחֶנּוּ מִשָּׁם אִם נַפְשְׁךָ לָדַעַת** – **Take** that information **from there if you desire to know** about it.

---

4. The phrase, *and you shall not place blood in your house,* could be understood as merely explaining why there is an obligation to build a *maakeh* around one's rooftop (as the verse indeed concludes, *if one should fall from it*). Chinuch cites *Sifrei* in order to demonstrate that it, in fact, constitutes a mitzvah-prohibition.

5. See Mitzvah 494 note 4 regarding Chinuch's original numbering of his work.

⁓ מִצְוָה תקמח ⁓
שֶׁלֹּא לִזְרֹעַ כִּלְאַיִם בְּכֶרֶם בְּאֶרֶץ יִשְׂרָאֵל דְּאוֹרַיְתָא

שֶׁלֹּא לִזְרֹעַ מִינֵי הַתְּבוּאָה[1] בְּכֶרֶם וְלֹא קַנַּבּוֹס וְלוּף,[2] וְזֶה הַמִּין מִן הַכִּלְאַיִם יִקָּרֵא כִּלְאֵי הַכֶּרֶם, וְעַל זֶה נֶאֱמַר (דברים כ"ב, ט) לֹא תִזְרַע כַּרְמְךָ כִּלְאָיִם.

⁓ Mitzvah 548 ⁓
The Prohibition to Plant a Vineyard With Mixed Seed in Eretz Yisrael, by Biblical Law

---

לֹא תִזְרַע כַּרְמְךָ כִּלְאָיִם פֶּן תִּקְדַּשׁ הַמְלֵאָה הַזֶּרַע אֲשֶׁר תִּזְרָע וּתְבוּאַת הַכָּרֶם

You shall not sow your vineyard with a mixture, lest the growth of the seed that you plant and the produce of the vineyard become prohibited (Deuteronomy 22:9).

In *Parashas Kedoshim*, in Mitzvah 245, Chinuch sets out the prohibition of *kilayim* (forbidden mixtures) of plants, referred to as *kilay zera'im*. In that mitzvah, the Torah forbids planting the seeds of different species together, or grafting trees. Planting grain or other seeds together with tree seeds, however, is not prohibited by that mitzvah. In this mitzvah, the Torah prohibits planting foreign seeds together with grapevines. Now, grapevines are considered "trees" with regard to Torah law, but nevertheless, the Torah forbids planting other seeds specifically with grapevines. This prohibition is referred to as *kilay hakerem* — kilayim of the vineyard.

Kilay hakerem differs from *kilay zera'im* with respect to many laws. For example, unlike the general prohibition of *kilay zera'im*, which pertains to all seeds in any number, the Biblical prohibition of *kilay hakerem* prohibits only planting a certain number and species of seeds in a vineyard and only in a specific manner, as we will see below. Another difference between *kilay zera'im* and *kilay hakerem* is that if one violates *kilay zera'im,* the resulting growth is permitted for consumption, but if one plants *kilay hakerem* the resulting growth is forbidden and must be burned (as the verse states, פֶּן תִּקְדַּשׁ הַמְלֵאָה, *lest the growth become prohibited*).

Like *kilay zera'im*, *kilay hakerem* applies by Biblical law only in Eretz Yisrael. But whereas *kilay zera'im* is completely permitted outside Eretz Yisrael even by Rabbinic law, the Sages forbade *kilay hakerem* outside of Eretz Yisrael as well, as Chinuch sets out at the end of this mitzvah. This is reflected in the title of this mitzvah: שֶׁלֹּא לִזְרֹעַ כִּלְאַיִם בְּכֶרֶם בְּאֶרֶץ יִשְׂרָאֵל דְּאוֹרַיְתָא, *The Prohibition to Plant a Vineyard With Mixed Seed in Eretz Yisrael, by Biblical Law.* That is, while the Biblical law applies only in Eretz Yisrael, this prohibition applies everywhere else by Rabbinic enactment.

שֶׁלֹּא לִזְרֹעַ מִינֵי הַתְּבוּאָה בְּכֶרֶם — We are commanded **not to plant** different **species of grain**[1] **in a vineyard,** וְלֹא קַנַּבּוֹס וְלוּף — **and** also **not hemp or** *luf*.[2] וְזֶה הַמִּין מִן הַכִּלְאַיִם יִקָּרֵא כִּלְאֵי הַכֶּרֶם — **This category of** *kilayim* is called *kilay hakerem*, **the** forbidden **mixture of the vineyard.** וְעַל זֶה נֶאֱמַר "לֹא תִזְרַע כַּרְמְךָ כִּלְאָיִם" — **With regard to this** prohibition **it is stated** (*Deuteronomy* 22:9): *You shall not sow your vineyard with a mixture.*

As Chinuch explains below, the prohibition of *kilay hakerem* refers to taking two different species of

---

NOTES

1. Grain refers to any of the "five species": wheat, barley, spelt, rye, or oats.

2. *Luf* is a variety of onion (*Rambam* and *Rav* to *Pe'ah* 6:10; cf. *Rashi, Menachos* 15b ד"ה לוף). These are the only two plants (other than the five grains) that are included in the Biblical prohibition. [See below, at note 9, where Chinuch offers a reason for this; see also note 10.]

וְאָמְרוּ זִכְרוֹנָם לִבְרָכָה (ספרי כאן), מָה אֲנִי צָרִיךְ, וַהֲלֹא כְּבָר נֶאֱמַר שָׂדְךָ לֹא תִזְרַע כִּלְאָיִם, מְלַמֵּד שֶׁכָּל הַמְקַיֵּם כִּלְאַיִם בְּכֶרֶם עוֹבֵר בִּשְׁנֵי לָאוִין[3]. וְכִלְאֵי הַכֶּרֶם פֵּרְשׁוּ זִכְרוֹנָם לִבְרָכָה (קידושין ל״ט ע״א) שֶׁהֵם שְׁנֵי מִינֵי זְרָעִים שֶׁל תְּבוּאָה עִם גַּרְעִינֵי הָעֲנָבִים, וְזֶהוּ שֶׁאָמַר רַבִּי יֹאשִׁיָּה, אֵינוֹ חַיָּב עַד שֶׁיִּזְרַע חִטָּה וּשְׂעוֹרָה וְחַרְצָן בְּמַפֹּלֶת יָד[4], דְּהָכִי מַשְׁמַע לְהוּ כַּרְמְךָ כִּלְאָיִם, כְּלוֹמַר דְּבָעֵינַן כִּלְאַיִם לְבַד מִכַּרְמְךָ[5].

מִשָּׁרְשֵׁי מִצְוַת כִּלְאַיִם כָּתַבְתִּי עַל צַד הַפְּשָׁט כְּמִנְהָגִי בְּלָאו דְּהַרְבָּעָה כ״ה

---

seeds that are deemed *kilay zera'im* with *each other* (see Mitzvah 245 at note 32), and planting them together with a grapeseed. Chinuch cites *Sifrei,* which clarifies why a separate prohibition of *kilayim* of the vineyard is necessary, when such an act is forbidden in any case due to the prohibition of *kilay zera'im*:

וְאָמְרוּ זִכְרוֹנָם לִבְרָכָה – **[The Sages], of blessed memory, stated** (*Sifrei* to verse): מָה אֲנִי צָרִיךְ – **Why do I need** this additional prohibition? וַהֲלֹא כְּבָר נֶאֱמַר "שָׂדְךָ לֹא תִזְרַע כִּלְאָיִם" – **Is it not already stated** (*Leviticus* 19:19): ***You shall not sow your field kilayim?*** מְלַמֵּד שֶׁכָּל הַמְקַיֵּם כִּלְאַיִם בְּכֶרֶם עוֹבֵר בִּשְׁנֵי לָאוִין – The answer is that **this teaches that one who maintains *kilayim* in a vineyard transgresses two mitzvah-prohibitions:** the prohibition against planting *any* mixture of species, and an additional prohibition against planting such a mixture with a grapevine.[3]

וְכִלְאֵי הַכֶּרֶם פֵּרְשׁוּ זִכְרוֹנָם לִבְרָכָה – The description of the prohibition of ***kilayim* of the vineyard** is, as **[the Sages], of blessed memory, explained** (*Kiddushin* 39a), שֶׁהֵם שְׁנֵי מִינֵי זְרָעִים שֶׁל תְּבוּאָה עִם גַּרְעִינֵי הָעֲנָבִים – **that it is** a mixture of **the seeds of two** different **species of grain with the seeds of grapes.** וְזֶהוּ שֶׁאָמַר רַבִּי יֹאשִׁיָּה – **This is as R' Yoshiyah stated:** אֵינוֹ חַיָּב עַד שֶׁיִּזְרַע חִטָּה וּשְׂעוֹרָה וְחַרְצָן בְּמַפֹּלֶת יָד – **One is not liable** for violating this prohibition **unless he plants wheat and barley** (an example of two species of grain), **and a grapeseed in a single thrust of the hand,** i.e., simultaneously.[4] דְּהָכִי מַשְׁמַע לְהוּ "כַּרְמְךָ כִּלְאָיִם" – **This is how [the Sages] understood** the verse, *you shall not sow* ***your vineyard with a mixture***; כְּלוֹמַר דְּבָעֵינַן כִּלְאַיִם לְבַד מִכַּרְמְךָ – **that is to say,** the prohibition **requires** the presence of **"a mixture"** (in this case, the two different species of seeds), **aside from "your vineyard."**[5]

Underlying Purpose of the Mitzvah

מִשָּׁרְשֵׁי מִצְוַת כִּלְאַיִם כָּתַבְתִּי – **I have** already **written about the underlying purposes of the mitzvah of *kilayim*,** עַל צַד הַפְּשָׁט כְּמִנְהָגִי – **on the basic level, as is my practice,** בְּלָאו דְּהַרְבָּעָה כ״ה

NOTES

3. *Sifrei* explains that the verse of our mitzvah constitutes an additional prohibition for planting two seeds that are *kilayim* with each other *together with a grapeseed.* [Maintaining *kilayim* (defined at length in the following mitzvah, beginning at note 4) is also part of the prohibition of planting *kilayim* (see *Derech Emunah, Hil. Kilayim, Beur HaHalachah* 1:3 ד״ה ואסור לאדם). *Sifrei* mentions maintaining *kilayim* to express that even one who only maintains the *kilayim* violates both prohibitions. *Gra*, however, emends the text of *Sifrei* to read הַזּוֹרֵעַ, *one who plants,* in the place of הַמְקַיֵּם, *one who maintains* (see *Shevet HaLevi*, Vol. V, *Kuntres HaMitzvos* §67).]

4. The phrase "a single thrust of the hand" implies both that the seeds were planted simultaneously and that the seeds fell in proximity to each other (see further, *Derech Emunah* ibid. 5:1,7).

5. R' Yoshiyah explains that the words "*you shall not sow your vineyard with a mixture*" does not mean that one should not sow it in a manner that it will *become* a mixture, but rather, one should not sow it *together with* another mixture. That is, one should not sow the grapeseed along with two other species that themselves form a prohibited mixture of *kilay zera'im.*

[According to some authorities, this definition of the mitzvah is absolute, and planting a grapeseed with only one kind of grain is completely permitted. According to other authorities it is forbidden by Rabbinic law, while still others maintain that it is actually forbidden by Biblical law but excluded only from the penalty of *malkus* (this, however, does not seem to be the view of Chinuch below, at note 17). See *Minchas Chinuch* §1 and 549:1.]

בְּסֵדֶר קְדֹשִׁים תִּהְיוּ בְּסִימָן רמ״ט (מצוה רמ״ד)[6], וְקָחֶנּוּ מִשָּׁם[7]. וַעֲדַיִן צְרִיכִין אָנוּ לְדַבֵּר פֹּה מַה טַּעַם נִתְחַדֵּשׁ הָאִסּוּר בְּכֶרֶם דִּבְעֵינַן בּוֹ כִּלְאַיִם מִלְּבַד הַכֶּרֶם. וְאוּלַי נֹאמַר כִּי מֵהְיוֹת כֶּרֶם דָּבָר חָשׁוּב מְאֹד וְכֹחַ טִבְעוֹ רַב, יִהְיֶה בָּטֵל עִמּוֹ מִין אֶחָד לְעוֹלָם וְלֹא יֵחָשֵׁב לְכִלְאַיִם וְלִכְלוּם, וְעַל כֵּן הִצְרִיךְ הַכָּתוּב שְׁנֵי מִינִים מִלְּבַד הַכֶּרֶם[8].

וְאוּלַי מִכֹּחַ טַעַם זֶה נֹאמַר גַּם כֵּן שֶׁשְּׁנֵי הַמִּינִים הִצְרִיכָן הַכָּתוּב שֶׁיִּהְיוּ מִמִּינֵי הַתְּבוּאוֹת שֶׁהֵם חֲשׁוּבִים בְּעִנְיָנָם כְּמוֹ קַנְבּוֹס וְלוּף שֶׁהֵם חֲשׁוּבִין בְּעִנְיָנָם, אֲבָל שְׁאָר הַמִּינִין כֻּלָּם יִתְבַּטְּלוּ עִם הַגְּפָנִים וְאֵינָם אֲסוּרִים מִדְּאוֹרַיְתָא אֶלָּא מִדְּרַבָּנָן[9].

בְּסֵדֶר קְדֹשִׁים תִּהְיוּ בְּסִימָן רמט – **in the prohibition of mating** animals of different species, which is mitzvah-prohibition **25 of *Parashas Kedoshim*, Chapter 249** of this work (Mitzvah 244);[6] וְקָחֶנּוּ מִשָּׁם – **you may take [that information] from there.**[7] וַעֲדַיִן צְרִיכִין אָנוּ לְדַבֵּר פֹּה – **But we must still speak here** מַה טַּעַם נִתְחַדֵּשׁ הָאִסּוּר בְּכֶרֶם – regarding **what reason there is for the unique** nature of this **prohibition as it pertains to a vineyard,** דִּבְעֵינַן בּוֹ כִּלְאַיִם מִלְּבַד הַכֶּרֶם – **that it requires that there be a *kilayim*-mixture** of two seeds **aside from the grapeseed,** as noted above. וְאוּלַי נֹאמַר – **Perhaps we may say** in explanation כִּי מֵהְיוֹת כֶּרֶם דָּבָר חָשׁוּב מְאֹד וְכֹחַ טִבְעוֹ רַב – **that since a grapevine is a very distinctive entity and its natural potency is great,** יִהְיֶה בָּטֵל עִמּוֹ מִין אֶחָד לְעוֹלָם – the nature of **every** other **individual species** planted with it **would be nullified by it,** וְלֹא יֵחָשֵׁב לְכִלְאַיִם וְלִכְלוּם – **and it would** therefore **not be considered a *kilayim*-mixture** with the vine **since [the other plant] would have no significance** in relation to the grapevine. וְעַל כֵּן הִצְרִיךְ הַכָּתוּב שְׁנֵי מִינִים מִלְּבַד הַכֶּרֶם – **Therefore,** in order for a mixture to be considered *kilayim* with a grapevine, **Scripture required that there be two species aside from the grapevine.** The two species together are not nullified by the vine and only then is it considered a real mixture when they are planted with it.[8]

Chinuch applies this idea to another unique aspect of this prohibition:

וְאוּלַי מִכֹּחַ טַעַם זֶה נֹאמַר גַּם כֵּן – **And perhaps based on this reason we can further say** שֶׁשְּׁנֵי הַמִּינִים הִצְרִיכָן הַכָּתוּב שֶׁיִּהְיוּ מִמִּינֵי הַתְּבוּאוֹת שֶׁהֵם חֲשׁוּבִים בְּעִנְיָנָם – **that** this is why **Scripture required,** that in order for it to be *kilayim,* **the two species** with which the grapeseed is planted **be species of produce that have distinctive natures,** כְּמוֹ קַנְבּוֹס וְלוּף שֶׁהֵם חֲשׁוּבִין בְּעִנְיָנָם – **such as** (aside from the five grains), **hemp and *luf,* for they have distinctive natures.** אֲבָל שְׁאָר הַמִּינִין כֻּלָּם יִתְבַּטְּלוּ עִם הַגְּפָנִים – **But all other species would be nullified** when planted **with the grapevines** even if there are more than one, וְאֵינָם אֲסוּרִים מִדְּאוֹרַיְתָא אֶלָּא מִדְּרַבָּנָן – **and** they **are** therefore **not prohibited Biblically, but Rabbinically.**[9]

NOTES

6. Chinuch's numbering of the mitzvos follows the original format of this work; see Mitzvah 494 note 4.

7. There, Chinuch explains that Hashem created each species of plant and animal life with perfect precision, and He desires that their individual natures be perpetuated in the most beneficial way — in the form that He created them. Crossbreeding animals, as well as crossing different species of seeds, violates the order of nature designed by Hashem. [See Mitzvah 62, where Chinuch adds another dimension to this prohibition. See also below, Mitzvah 549 note 10.]

8. Due to the distinctiveness of the grapevine, its integrity would not be compromised by being planted along with only one other species. Accordingly, the specific prohibition against *kilayim* of the vineyard applies only when the grapeseed is planted along with *two* other species.

9. Unlike *kilayim* of plants, which is prohibited when formed through *any* mixed species, *kilayim* of the vineyard is prohibited only through the five grains, hemp, and *luf* (see following note). Chinuch explains that since the grapevine is a very potent and distinctive plant, it is affected only by species that have enough of their own potency and distinctiveness.

מִדִּינֵי הַמִּצְוָה מַה שֶּׁאָמְרוּ זִכְרוֹנָם לִבְרָכָה (מנחות ט״ו ע״ב) שֶׁאֵין אָסוּר מִשּׁוּם כִּלְאֵי הַכֶּרֶם מִן הַתּוֹרָה אֶלָּא מִינֵי תְבוּאָה וְקַנַּבּוֹס וְלוּף בִּלְבַד[10], אֲבָל לִזְרֹעַ יְרָקוֹת וּשְׁאָר מִינִין וְחַרְצָן אָסוּר מִדְּרַבָּנָן[11]. וְכֵן אָסְרוּ רַבָּנָן לִזְרֹעַ מִינֵי תְבוּאוֹת וְכֵן יְרָקוֹת בְּצַד הַגְּפָנִים אוֹ לִטַּע גֶּפֶן בְּצַד הַיָּרָק אוֹ הַתְּבוּאָה מִפְּנֵי חֲשַׁשׁ הַרְכָּבָה, לְפִי שֶׁהַגֶּפֶן רַךְ יוֹתֵר מִכָּל שְׁאָר אִילָנוֹת חָשְׁשׁוּ בָּהּ יוֹתֵר, וְאִם עָשָׂה כֵּן אַף עַל פִּי שֶׁאֵינוֹ לוֹקֶה הֲרֵי זֶה קֹדֶשׁ[12] וְנֶאֶסְרוּ שְׁנֵיהֶם בַּהֲנָאָה וְשׂוֹרְפִין הַכֹּל, וַאֲפִלּוּ הַקַּשׁ שֶׁל הַתְּבוּאָה וְהָעֵצִים שֶׁל הַגְּפָנִים שֶׁנֶּאֱמַר פֶּן תִּקְדַּשׁ הַמְּלֵאָה הַזֶּרַע וְגוֹ׳, וְדָרְשׁוּ זִכְרוֹנָם לִבְרָכָה (קידושין נ״ו ע״ב) פֶּן תּוּקַד אֵשׁ, כְּלוֹמַר שֶׁהַכֹּל רָאוּי לִשְׂרֹף

Laws of the Mitzvah

מִדִּינֵי הַמִּצְוָה מַה שֶּׁאָמְרוּ זִכְרוֹנָם לִבְרָכָה – **Among the laws of the mitzvah is that which [the Sages], of blessed memory, stated** (*Menachos* 15b), שֶׁאֵין אָסוּר מִשּׁוּם כִּלְאֵי הַכֶּרֶם מִן הַתּוֹרָה – **that nothing is Biblically prohibited as *kilayim* of the vineyard** when planted with grapeseed אֶלָּא מִינֵי תְבוּאָה וְקַנַּבּוֹס וְלוּף בִּלְבַד – **except the** five **species of grain, hemp, and *luf*.**[10] אֲבָל לִזְרֹעַ יְרָקוֹת וּשְׁאָר מִינִין וְחַרְצָן – **However, to plant vegetables or other species with a grapeseed** אָסוּר מִדְּרַבָּנָן – **is prohibited Rabbinically.**[11] וְכֵן אָסְרוּ רַבָּנָן לִזְרֹעַ מִינֵי תְבוּאוֹת וְכֵן יְרָקוֹת בְּצַד הַגְּפָנִים – **Similarly,** although the Biblical prohibition applies only when planting the seeds simultaneously, **the Sages prohibited planting grain species, as well as vegetables, alongside** existing **grapevines,** אוֹ לִטַּע גֶּפֶן בְּצַד הַיָּרָק אוֹ הַתְּבוּאָה – **or to plant a grapevine alongside vegetables or grains,** מִפְּנֵי חֲשַׁשׁ הַרְכָּבָה – **out of concern for grafting,** since the roots of the other species may penetrate the roots of the grapevine. לְפִי שֶׁהַגֶּפֶן רַךְ יוֹתֵר מִכָּל שְׁאָר אִילָנוֹת – Although grafting is forbidden with all trees, this is a concern specifically with grapevines, **as** since the root of **the grapevine is softer than all other trees,** חָשְׁשׁוּ בָּהּ יוֹתֵר – **[the Sages] were more concerned about it** inadvertently grafting with other plants. וְאִם עָשָׂה כֵּן – **If one did so,** i.e., he planted other species and a grapevine adjacent to each other, אַף עַל פִּי שֶׁאֵינוֹ לוֹקֶה – **even though he does not incur *malkus*** for this action, since it is forbidden only by Rabbinic decree, הֲרֵי זֶה קֹדֶשׁ – **[the crops] are thereby** considered the same as all *kilayim* of the vineyard and they are rendered **forbidden.**[12] וְנֶאֶסְרוּ שְׁנֵיהֶם בַּהֲנָאָה וְשׂוֹרְפִין הַכֹּל – This means that **it is prohibited to derive benefit from either of them** (the grapevine or the other species), **and one must burn all** of both plants; וַאֲפִלּוּ הַקַּשׁ שֶׁל הַתְּבוּאָה וְהָעֵצִים שֶׁל הַגְּפָנִים – **even the straw** portion **of the grain and the wood** portion of **the grapevine** (i.e., the vines themselves, aside from the fruit) must be burned. שֶׁנֶּאֱמַר ״פֶּן תִּקְדַּשׁ הַמְּלֵאָה הַזֶּרַע וְגוֹ׳ ״ – This is the law that applies to *kilayim* of the grapevine, **as it is stated** in the verse of the mitzvah (*Deuteronomy* 22:9): *You shall not sow your vineyard with a mixture,* ***lest the growth of the seed*** *that you plant and the produce of the vineyard* ***become prohibited.*** וְדָרְשׁוּ זִכְרוֹנָם לִבְרָכָה פֶּן תּוּקַד אֵשׁ – The obligation to burn the *kilayim* arises from that **which [the Sages], of blessed memory, expounded** (*Kiddushin* 56b), that the word תִּקְדַּשׁ (*become prohibited*), can be interpreted as a contraction of the words תּוּקַד אֵשׁ, *it shall be burned by fire*. Thus the verse reads, **lest it be burned by fire.** כְּלוֹמַר שֶׁהַכֹּל רָאוּי לִשְׂרֹף – **That is to say,** when a grapevine grows as *kilayim* with other plants, **the entire** *kilayim* produce **must be burned,**

NOTES

10. Chinuch indicates here, as well as in his discussion of the underlying purpose of the mitzvah above, that these are the only non-grain plants that are included in the prohibition of *kilayim* of the vineyard. For the Biblical source for this, see *Rashba, Berachos* 22a; *Rashi, Menachos* 15b ד״ה אסרה תורה. For a discussion of other opinions, see *Minchas Chinuch* §4.

11. For discussion of which kinds of species are included in the Rabbinic prohibition, see *Rambam, Hil. Kilayim* 5:6,18-20, with *Derech Emunah* 5:24-25, 128.

12. The term קֹדֶשׁ in the context of *kilayim* of the vineyard means *forbidden*. This follows Scriptural usage of that word in this prohibition, as Chinuch cites presently. Chinuch further explains that this unusual usage instructs us as to what must be done with *kilayim*.

כְּמוֹ שֶׁנִּכְתֹּב בְּסָמוּךְ (מצוה תקמ״ט)[13]. וְיֶתֶר פְּרָטֶיהָ מְבֹאָרִים בְּמַסֶּכֶת כִּלְאַיִם[14].

וְנוֹהֵג אִסּוּר כִּלְאֵי הַכֶּרֶם בִּזְכָרִים וּנְקֵבוֹת[15], מִן הַתּוֹרָה בְּאֶרֶץ יִשְׂרָאֵל לְבַד, וּמִדְּרַבָּנָן אֲפִלּוּ בְּחוּצָה לָאָרֶץ. וְאַף עַל פִּי שֶׁכִּלְאֵי זְרָעִים אֵינָם נוֹהֲגִים בְּחוּצָה לָאָרֶץ אֲפִלּוּ מִדְּרַבָּנָן, כְּמוֹ שֶׁבֵּאַרְנוּ בְּסֵדֶר קְדֹשִׁים לָאו כ״ו בְּסִימָן ר״נ (מצוה רמ״ה), הֶחְמִירוּ זִכְרוֹנָם לִבְרָכָה בְּכִלְאֵי הַכֶּרֶם לְאָסְרָן אֲפִלּוּ בְּחוּצָה לָאָרֶץ אַחַר שֶׁהֵם חֲמוּרִים כָּל כָּךְ שֶׁאֲסוּרִים בַּהֲנָאָה בָּאָרֶץ, כְּמוֹ שֶׁמְּפֹרָשׁ טַעַם זֶה בְּסוֹף פֶּרֶק רִאשׁוֹן מִקִּדּוּשִׁין (ל״ט ע״א)[16].

וְעוֹבֵר עַל זֶה וְזָרַע חִטָּה וּשְׂעוֹרָה וְחַרְצָן בְּמַפֹּלֶת יָד, בָּאָרֶץ לוֹקֶה מִדְּאוֹרַיְתָא מִיָּד שֶׁזְּרָעָן[17], וּבְחוּצָה לָאָרֶץ לוֹקֶה מַכַּת מַרְדּוּת מִדְּרַבָּנָן[18]. אֲבָל לְעִנְיַן שֶׁיֵּאָסְרוּ בַּהֲנָאָה

כְּמוֹ שֶׁנִּכְתֹּב בְּסָמוּךְ – **as we shall write below** in the following mitzvah.[13] וְיֶתֶר פְּרָטֶיהָ מְבֹאָרִים בְּמַסֶּכֶת כִּלְאַיִם – These **and the remaining details [of this mitzvah] are set forth in Tractate *Kilayim*,** Chapters 4-7.[14]

Applicability of the Mitzvah

וְנוֹהֵג אִסּוּר כִּלְאֵי הַכֶּרֶם בִּזְכָרִים וּנְקֵבוֹת – **The prohibition of *kilayim* of the vineyard applies to men and women.**[15] מִן הַתּוֹרָה בְּאֶרֶץ יִשְׂרָאֵל לְבַד וּמִדְּרַבָּנָן אֲפִלּוּ בְּחוּצָה לָאָרֶץ – **By Biblical law it applies only in Eretz Yisrael, but by Rabbinic decree** it applies **even outside of Eretz Yisrael.**

The prohibitions of *kilay zera'im* and *kilay hakerem* are both agricultural mitzvos, which by Biblical law apply only in Eretz Yisrael. Nevertheless, the Sages decreed that the specific prohibition of *kilay hakerem* should be observed outside of Eretz Yisrael as well, though *kilay zera'im* is permitted there. Chinuch explains the reason for this distinction:

וְאַף עַל פִּי שֶׁכִּלְאֵי זְרָעִים אֵינָם נוֹהֲגִים בְּחוּצָה לָאָרֶץ אֲפִלּוּ מִדְּרַבָּנָן – **Although** the prohibition against ***kilayim* of plants does not apply outside of Eretz Yisrael even by Rabbinic law,** כְּמוֹ שֶׁבֵּאַרְנוּ בְּסֵדֶר קְדֹשִׁים לָאו כ״ו בְּסִימָן ר״נ – **as we explained in Mitzvah-prohibition 26 of *Parashas Kedoshim*, Chapter 250** (Mitzvah 245), הֶחְמִירוּ זִכְרוֹנָם לִבְרָכָה בְּכִלְאֵי הַכֶּרֶם – **[the Sages], of blessed memory, were stringent with regard to *kilayim* of the vineyard,** לְאָסְרָן אֲפִלּוּ בְּחוּצָה לָאָרֶץ – **and prohibited them even outside of Eretz Yisrael.** אַחַר שֶׁהֵם חֲמוּרִים כָּל כָּךְ שֶׁאֲסוּרִים בַּהֲנָאָה בָּאָרֶץ – This is **because [*kilayim* of the vineyard] is so stringent that in Eretz Yisrael it is prohibited for benefit** by Biblical law. By contrast, *kilay zera'im* is permitted even for consumption even if it results from a Biblical violation. כְּמוֹ שֶׁמְּפֹרָשׁ טַעַם זֶה בְּסוֹף פֶּרֶק רִאשׁוֹן מִקִּדּוּשִׁין – **This reason is as it is set forth at the end of the first chapter of *Kiddushin*** (39a).[16]

וְעוֹבֵר עַל זֶה – **One who transgresses this** prohibition וְזָרַע חִטָּה וּשְׂעוֹרָה וְחַרְצָן בְּמַפֹּלֶת יָד – **and plants,** for example, **wheat, barley, and a grapeseed, in a single hand-thrust,** בָּאָרֶץ לוֹקֶה מִדְּאוֹרַיְתָא מִיָּד שֶׁזְּרָעָן – **in Eretz Yisrael, he incurs Biblically mandated *malkus* immediately upon planting them,** i.e., even before they take root.[17] וּבְחוּצָה לָאָרֶץ לוֹקֶה מַכַּת מַרְדּוּת מִדְּרַבָּנָן – If one plants these seeds **outside of Eretz Yisrael, he incurs** the **Rabbinic *makkas mardus*** penalty.[18] אֲבָל לְעִנְיַן שֶׁיֵּאָסְרוּ בַּהֲנָאָה – **However,** although one violates the prohibition of planting them immediately upon placing them in the ground, **with regard to [the *kilayim*] becoming**

NOTES

13. In the following mitzvah, Chinuch discusses the obligation to burn the *kilayim,* and the related prohibition to benefit from it in any way.

14. The laws of *kilayim* of the vineyard are codified in *Rambam* in *Hil. Kilayim,* Chs. 5-8 and *Shulchan Aruch*, *Yoreh Deah* §296.

15. This is in accordance with the general rule that applies to mitzvah-prohibitions (see General Introduction).

16. For further elaboration on this reason, see *Derech Emunah*, *Beur HaHalachah* 5:4 ד״ה ולמה אסרו. It should be noted that although the Sages forbade *kilayim* of the vineyard outside of Eretz Yisrael as well, not all aspects of the prohibition apply outside of Eretz Yisrael; see *Rambam*, *Hil. Kilayim* 8:13.

17. See Insight for discussion of this law.

18. *Makkas mardus* (lashes of discipline) is the standard punishment for violation of a Rabbinic decree. See General Introduction, with note 16.

אֵינָם אֲסוּרִים מִיָּד שֶׁזְּרָעָן עַד אַחַר הַשְׁרָשָׁה[19]**, וּכְמוֹ שֶׁאָמְרוּ זִכְרוֹנָם לִבְרָכָה** (פסחים כ״ה ע״א) **זָרוּעַ מֵעִקָּרוֹ בְּהַשְׁרָשָׁה, זָרוּעַ וּבָא בְּתוֹסֶפֶת**[20]**.**

---

forbidden for benefit, אֵינָם אֲסוּרִים מִיָּד שֶׁזְּרָעָן עַד אַחַר הַשְׁרָשָׁה – **they do not become prohibited immediately when they are planted,** but only **after they take root.**[19] וּכְמוֹ שֶׁאָמְרוּ זִכְרוֹנָם לִבְרָכָה – This is **as [the Sages], of blessed memory, stated** (*Pesachim* 25a): זָרוּעַ מֵעִקָּרוֹ בְּהַשְׁרָשָׁה זָרוּעַ וּבָא בְּתוֹסֶפֶת – **[Something] initially planted** as *kilayim* becomes prohibited **upon taking root; [something] that had been planted previously** in a permitted manner, but was rendered *kilayim* at a later time, becomes prohibited **when it increases** in size.[20] This statement demonstrates that even plants that were placed into the ground as *kilayim* do not become forbidden until they take root.

NOTES

19. Before they take root they are not considered *kilayim*; see Insight for further discussion.

20. For example, it is permitted for a vineyard to be planted alongside a grain-field as long as there is a wall separating them. If the wall collapses, the owner is required to rebuild it immediately. If he neglects to do so, the produce becomes prohibited after it has increased in size. Chinuch elaborates on the particulars of this law in the following mitzvah (at note 11).

◆§ Insight: When the Seeds Do Not Take Root

At the close of the mitzvah, Chinuch writes that one is liable for violating the prohibition against planting *kilayim* as soon as he sows the three seeds in the ground, but that the seeds themselves do not become forbidden until they take root some time later. It would appear from this law that even if the seeds were taken out of the ground before they had a chance to take root, the one who planted them would still be liable for the action of planting *kilayim*. *Minchas Chinuch* (298:14) notes that while this is a novel law, the concept behind it can be derived from a careful consideration of the laws of *melachah* (forbidden activities) on the Sabbath.

The thirty-nine forbidden *melachos* consist of specific actions that accomplish an intended result. The action of striking a match results in a fire burning, the action of snuffing out a flame results in the flame being extinguished. With most *melachos*, like these, the result of the action occurs immediately on the heels of the action itself. There are two *melachos*, however, where the intended result occurs only some time after the action is completed. These are זוֹרֵעַ, *planting*, and אוֹפֶה, *baking* (or cooking). The action of planting is placing the seeds in the ground; the plant begins to grow only at a later time. The action of baking is putting the dough in the oven; the dough turns into bread only some time later.

Since these *melachos* have an interval between the action and the result, one may wonder: Is one liable for the action itself if the result does not materialize? If a person put dough into a hot oven, or put seeds into fertile ground, but due to some circumstance the dough did not bake or the seeds did not take root, is he still liable for performing *melachah* on the Sabbath? In the case of baking, we find a clear answer in the Gemara. The Gemara states (*Shabbos* 4a) that if one put dough in an oven and the dough was then removed, he is exempt from any liability. If we extend this principle to planting, it would emerge that if one places seeds in the ground and the seeds were later removed before taking root, the person would be exempt from liability for the *melachah* of planting.

Minchas Chinuch, however, rejects this comparison based on the following logic: If removing the dough before it is baked prevents the prohibition, the same must be true in the case where a person put dough in the oven close to the end of the Sabbath and the dough did not begin to bake until after the Sabbath ended. Since the person's actions on the Sabbath did not result in the bread being baked *on the Sabbath*, no Sabbath prohibition has taken place. Now, the Gemara states (*Rosh Hashanah* 10b) that seeds do not take root until at least three days after they are planted. If we were to apply the same criterion to planting as we do to baking, namely, that both the action and the result must take place on the Sabbath, it would emerge that a person can never desecrate the Sabbath by

planting because the seed *always* takes root after the Sabbath is over! *Minchas Chinuch* therefore concludes that there must be a fundamental difference between the *melachah* of baking and the *melachah* of planting. Whereas the *melachah* of baking requires both the action and the result to take place on the Sabbath, the *melachah* of planting is accomplished immediately with the act of placing the seeds in the ground, regardless of when the seed takes root or what happens to the seed afterward.

The distinction between the act of baking and the act of planting is elaborated upon in *Dvar Avraham* (Vol. 1, 23:6). Citing *Teshuvos Halachos Ketanos* (Vol. I §266), he explains that when a person bakes or cooks, he generally needs to remain involved in the activity until it is complete; he may need to stir the pot or stoke the fire, or provide some other supporting action, until the food is ready. The *melachah* of baking therefore includes the outcome of the action as well, and if it does not take place (such as if the bread was removed, or if it bakes after the Sabbath has ended), the *melachah* is not considered to have been completed. One who plants, however, generally places the seeds in the ground and then ceases his involvement, simply waiting for the seeds to take root by themselves. Since the person's involvement is complete with the placing of the seeds in the ground, the *melachah* is deemed to be complete with the action itself, regardless of what happens to the seeds after they are planted.

Minchas Chinuch concludes that the classification of planting with regard to the Sabbath applies with regard to *kilayim* as well, and the action of planting is complete with the placing of the seeds in the ground. One who plants *kilayim* is therefore liable to *malkus* regardless of when or whether the seeds subsequently take root, as Chinuch states.

Some Acharonim, however, take issue with Chinuch's ruling, pointing to a discussion in *Yerushalmi* (*Kilayim* 1:9; 8a in Schottenstein ed.) that indicates that a person is *not* liable for the action of planting *kilayim* if the seeds do not subsequently take root. They maintain that this is the halachah with regard to *kilayim*, even if, with regard to planting on the Sabbath, one *would* be liable for the *melachah* of planting immediately upon placing the seeds in the ground. This is because, with regard to the Sabbath, it is the simple act of planting that is prohibited, and that act is indeed complete with the placing of the seeds in the ground. The prohibition of *kilayim*, however, is the action of planting *a mixture*, and two seeds placed side by side in the ground cannot be called a mixture. It is only when they take root and share the same source of nourishment that we can consider the one who placed them there to have planted a mixture of seeds. According to this view, if the seeds were removed before they took root, one would not be held liable for planting *kilayim* (see *Eglei Tal, Teshuvah* 121; *Yeshuos Malko, Hil. Kilayim* 1:1).

[For further discussion about both the Sabbath and *kilayim* aspects of this question, see *Minchas Chinuch* ibid. and 245:20; *Rashash, Shabbos* 73a ד"ה הזורע; *Eglei Tal, Zore'a* §8; *Chelkas Yoav* Vol. I, *Orach Chaim* §10, and Vol. II, *Orach Chaim* §4-5; *Afikei Yam* II, 4:1; *Pri Megadim*, end of his introduction to *Hilchos Shabbos*; *Igros Moshe, Orach Chaim* I §127.]

⬿ מִצְוָה תקמט: שֶׁלֹּא לֶאֱכֹל כִּלְאֵי הַכֶּרֶם בְּאֶרֶץ יִשְׂרָאֵל ⬿

שֶׁנִּמְנַעְנוּ מִלֶּאֱכֹל כִּלְאֵי הַכֶּרֶם לְבַד¹, וּכְבָר פֵּרַשְׁנוּ בַּמִּצְוָה הַקּוֹדֶמֶת מַהוּ כִּלְאֵי הַכֶּרֶם², וְעַל זֶה נֶאֱמַר (דברים כ״ב, ט) פֶּן תִּקְדַּשׁ הַמְלֵאָה הַזֶּרַע אֲשֶׁר תִּזְרָע וּתְבוּאַת הַכֶּרֶם, וּפֵרְשׁוּ זִכְרוֹנָם לִבְרָכָה (קידושין נ״ו ע״ב) פֶּן תּוּקַד אֵשׁ, כְּלוֹמַר שֶׁאֵין רָאוּי לִהְיוֹת בּוֹ תּוֹעֶלֶת שֶׁהַכֹּל אָסוּר בַּהֲנָאָה.

⬿ Mitzvah 549 ⬿

The Prohibition to Eat Kilayim of the Vineyard [Grown] In Eretz Yisrael

לֹא תִזְרַע כַּרְמְךָ כִּלְאָיִם פֶּן תִּקְדַּשׁ הַמְלֵאָה הַזֶּרַע אֲשֶׁר תִּזְרָע וּתְבוּאַת הַכֶּרֶם

You shall not sow your vineyard with a mixture, lest the growth of the seed that you plant and the produce of the vineyard become prohibited (Deuteronomy 22:9).

In the previous mitzvah, Chinuch set out the prohibition against planting *kilay hakerem* (*kilayim* of the vineyard). The subject of this mitzvah is the prohibition to eat or benefit from such *kilayim*. As Chinuch will explain, the prohibition applies both to seeds that were originally sown as *kilayim* and to plants that began in a permitted manner but afterward became mixed with other species and were maintained as *kilayim*.

שֶׁנִּמְנַעְנוּ מִלֶּאֱכֹל כִּלְאֵי הַכֶּרֶם לְבַד — **We are prohibited from eating *kilayim* of the vineyard,** and the prohibition applies to this form of *kilayim* **alone.** The produce of other forms of *kilayim* is permitted for consumption.[1] וּכְבָר פֵּרַשְׁנוּ בַּמִּצְוָה הַקּוֹדֶמֶת מַהוּ כִּלְאֵי הַכֶּרֶם — **And we have already explained in the previous mitzvah what constitutes *kilayim* of the vineyard.**[2] וְעַל זֶה נֶאֱמַר "פֶּן תִּקְדַּשׁ הַמְלֵאָה הַזֶּרַע אֲשֶׁר תִּזְרָע וּתְבוּאַת הַכֶּרֶם" — **With regard to this** prohibition **it is stated** (*Deuteronomy* 22:9): *You shall not sow your vineyard with a mixture,* ***lest the growth of the seed that you plant, and the produce of the vineyard, become prohibited,*** וּפֵרְשׁוּ זִכְרוֹנָם לִבְרָכָה פֶּן תּוּקַד אֵשׁ — **and [the Sages], of blessed memory, explained** (*Kiddushin* 56b) that the word תִּקְדַּשׁ (*become prohibited*), can be interpreted as a contraction of the words תּוּקַד אֵשׁ, *it shall be burned [by] fire*; the verse thus means, **"lest it be burned by fire."** כְּלוֹמַר שֶׁאֵין רָאוּי לִהְיוֹת בּוֹ תּוֹעֶלֶת שֶׁהַכֹּל אָסוּר בַּהֲנָאָה — **That is to say,** if *kilayim* is allowed to grow **it is** to be **unfit for any use, as it is entirely prohibited for benefit.** The Torah's declaration that *kilay hakerem* must be burned conveys also that such *kilayim* is unfit for anything and completely forbidden for any benefit.

NOTES

1. The products of *kilay zera'im* (*kilayim* of seeds), the prohibition to plant together different species of seeds or to graft different species of trees (Mitzvah 245), are permitted for consumption. Only the product of *kilay hakerem* is forbidden.

[Although Chinuch describes the prohibition here in terms of consumption, the prohibition actually encompasses all benefit from the *kilayim*, as Chinuch clarifies below.]

2. At the beginning of that mitzvah, Chinuch wrote that the prohibition applies to mixtures of the five species of grain (wheat, barley, spelt, rye, or oats), or hemp or *luf*, with grapeseed. Other species do not create "*kilayim* of the vineyard" mixtures.

In the previous mitzvah, Chinuch noted that one does not violate the Biblical prohibition of planting *kilay hakerem* unless he sows two different seeds together with grapeseed simultaneously, in one "thrust of the hand." With regard to this mitzvah, however, *Minchas Chinuch* (§1) points out that the product of a *kilay hakerem* mixture may be Biblically prohibited even if all those conditions were not present. The prohibition against *benefiting* from plants that grew as *kilayim* can exist independently of the prohibition of *planting kilayim*. It is therefore possible for a product to be forbidden as *kilay hakerem* even if no prohibition was violated in its planting, as long as it is a species that qualifies as "*kilayim* of the vineyard." [See note 15 below.]

וְהָרְאָיָה שֶׁיֵּשׁ בָּזֶה לָאו, שֶׁכָּתוּב בְּמְנִיעָה פֶּן, וְאָמְרוּ זִכְרוֹנָם לִבְרָכָה (ערובין צ״ו ע״א) שֶׁכָּל מָקוֹם שֶׁנֶּאֱמַר הִשָּׁמֶר פֶּן וְאַל אֵינוֹ אֶלָּא לֹא תַעֲשֶׂה.

מִשָּׁרְשֵׁי הַמִּצְוָה. הַקְדָּמָה. יָדוּעַ הַדָּבָר בְּכָל מִצְוֹת הַתּוֹרָה כִּי כָּל דָּבָר לְפִי הַכִּשָּׁלוֹן שֶׁמָּצוּי בּוֹ יוֹתֵר יַרְחִיקֵנוּ הָאֵל מִמֶּנּוּ, וְאֵין סָפֵק כִּי נְטִיעַת הַכֶּרֶם סִבָּה לַיַּיִן שֶׁבּוֹ כַּמָּה מִכְשׁוֹלוֹת לִבְנֵי אָדָם. הִפִּיל רַבִּים חֲלָלִים בְּחֶמְדָּם אוֹתוֹ כִּי יִתְאַדָּם[3], מְעוֹרֵר יֵצֶר לֵב הָאָדָם רַע וּמַדִּיחַ יֵצֶר טוֹב, וְכָל עֲצָתוֹ אָכוֹל וְשָׁתֹה וְלִשְׁכַּב לִהְיוֹת נִרְדָּם, וּכְעִנְיָן שֶׁכָּתוּב (חבקוק ב׳, ה׳) וְאַף כִּי הַיַּיִן בֹּגֵד, וַאֲשֶׁר יַזִּיר מִמֶּנּוּ יִקָּרֵא קָדוֹשׁ בַּכָּתוּב (במדבר ו׳, ח׳), וְאוּלָם הִתִּירוֹ לָנוּ הַשֵּׁם בָּרוּךְ הוּא בִּשְׁבִיל קְצָת תּוֹעֶלֶת שֶׁנִּמְצָא בִּמְעוּטוֹ אֶל הַגּוּפִים. וְאַחַר שֶׁלֹּא הֻתַּר רַק לְצֹרֶךְ גָּדוֹל חִיְּבָנוּ הַכָּתוּב שֶׁאִם גַּם בִּתְחִלַּת נְטִיעָתוֹ אוֹ זְרִיעָתוֹ יִהְיֶה בְּעִנְיָנוֹ צַד עָוֹן וְחֵטְא

Not every activity that the Torah prohibits is considered an independent mitzvah-prohibition. Thus, while it is clear from the above verse that one may not benefit from *kilay hakerem*, it still remains to be proven that benefiting from *kilay hakerem* is the subject of a mitzvah-prohibition:

וְהָרְאָיָה שֶׁיֵּשׁ בָּזֶה לָאו שֶׁכָּתוּב בְּמְנִיעָה פֶּן – **The proof that this** action of benefiting from *kilay hakerem* **is subject to a mitzvah-prohibition is that the restriction is written with** the term **"lest,"** וְאָמְרוּ זִכְרוֹנָם לִבְרָכָה – **and [the Sages], of blessed memory, have stated** (*Eruvin* 96a) שֶׁכָּל מָקוֹם שֶׁנֶּאֱמַר הִשָּׁמֶר פֶּן וְאַל אֵינוֹ אֶלָּא לֹא תַעֲשֶׂה – **that wherever** the terms **"safeguard," "lest," and "do not," are stated** in Scripture, **it invariably refers to a mitzvah-prohibition.**

Underlying Purpose of the Mitzvah

Chinuch sets out the underlying purpose of the prohibition against eating or benefiting from *kilayim* of the vineyard and the attendant obligation to burn it. Chinuch explains why these obligations accompany only this form of *kilayim* and not others:

מִשָּׁרְשֵׁי הַמִּצְוָה – The following is **among the underlying purposes of the mitzvah:** הַקְדָּמָה – **An introduction:** יָדוּעַ הַדָּבָר בְּכָל מִצְוֹת הַתּוֹרָה – **It is a well-known concept pertaining to all mitzvos of the Torah,** כִּי כָּל דָּבָר לְפִי הַכִּשָּׁלוֹן שֶׁמָּצוּי בּוֹ יוֹתֵר יַרְחִיקֵנוּ הָאֵל מִמֶּנּוּ – **that to the degree that any matter is associated with pitfalls for us, the Almighty distances us from it** with Biblical prohibitions. The greater the severity or prevalence of pitfalls associated with a particular activity, the more Biblical prohibitions we will find in relation to it. וְאֵין סָפֵק כִּי נְטִיעַת הַכֶּרֶם סִבָּה לַיַּיִן – **Now, obviously the planting of a vineyard is** the first step **in causing wine** to be produced, שֶׁבּוֹ כַּמָּה מִכְשׁוֹלוֹת לִבְנֵי אָדָם – **which** itself **is the cause of numerous pitfalls for mankind.** הִפִּיל רַבִּים חֲלָלִים בְּחֶמְדָּם אוֹתוֹ כִּי יִתְאַדָּם – **[Wine] has felled many victims who have desired it upon** seeing **its** characteristic **red color;**[3] מְעוֹרֵר יֵצֶר לֵב הָאָדָם רַע וּמַדִּיחַ יֵצֶר טוֹב – **it arouses man's evil inclination and repels his good inclination;** וְכָל עֲצָתוֹ אָכוֹל וְשָׁתֹה וְלִשְׁכַּב לִהְיוֹת נִרְדָּם – **and its entire "advice" to a person** (i.e., its influence on him) **is** to cause him to engage in **eating and drinking, to sleep and remain in a stupor,** וּכְעִנְיָן שֶׁכָּתוּב "וְאַף כִּי הַיַּיִן בֹּגֵד" – **as it is stated** (*Habakkuk* 2:5): ***All the more so as wine is treacherous** [to the drinker].* וַאֲשֶׁר יַזִּיר מִמֶּנּוּ יִקָּרֵא קָדוֹשׁ בַּכָּתוּב – **Indeed, one who abstains from [wine]** (i.e., a *nazir*) **is referred to by Scripture as "holy"** (*Numbers* 6:8). וְאוּלָם הִתִּירוֹ לָנוּ הַשֵּׁם בָּרוּךְ הוּא – **Nevertheless,** despite all of its dangers, **Hashem, blessed is He, permitted it to us** בִּשְׁבִיל קְצָת תּוֹעֶלֶת שֶׁנִּמְצָא בִּמְעוּטוֹ אֶל הַגּוּפִים – **for the limited measure of benefit that it provides to people** when taken **in moderation.**

Chinuch now turns to the underlying purpose of this mitzvah:

וְאַחַר שֶׁלֹּא הֻתַּר רַק לְצֹרֶךְ גָּדוֹל – **Now, since** wine **was permitted only out of great need,** חִיְּבָנוּ הַכָּתוּב – **Scripture enjoined us** שֶׁאִם גַּם בִּתְחִלַּת נְטִיעָתוֹ אוֹ זְרִיעָתוֹ יִהְיֶה בְּעִנְיָנוֹ צַד עָוֹן וְחֵטְא – **that**

NOTES

3. Stylistic adaptation of *Proverbs* 7:26 and 23:31. When a wine has a full red color, that is indicative of its good taste (*Metzudos* to *Proverbs* 23:31).

שֶׁלֹּא לְקַיְּמוֹ וְלֹא נֶהֱנֶה בּוֹ כְּלָל, אֲבָל יִשָּׂרֵף הַכֹּל וְיֹאבַד מִן הָעוֹלָם, הֲלֹא דַי בְּרֹב הַמִּכְשׁוֹלוֹת הַיּוֹצְאִין מִמֶּנּוּ אַחַר גְּמַר בִּשּׁוּלוֹ, לֹא טוֹב לִהְיוֹת עוֹד גַּם הַתְחָלָתוֹ בַּעֲבֵרָה אֲבָל תּוֹקַד הַכֹּל, הַפְּרִי וְהַקַּשׁ וְהָעֵצִים וְכָל אֲשֶׁר בּוֹ.

מִדִּינֵי הַמִּצְוָה מַה שֶּׁאָמְרוּ זִכְרוֹנָם לִבְרָכָה (רמב״ם פ״ה מכלאים ה״ח) אֶחָד הַזּוֹרֵעַ וְאֶחָד הַמְקַיֵּם כִּלְאַיִם בְּכַרְמוֹ, כְּלוֹמַר שֶׁרָאָה שֶׁצָּמְחוּ כִּלְאַיִם בְּכַרְמוֹ וְהִנִּיחָן שָׁם, נִתְקַדְּשׁוּ, כְּלוֹמַר נִתְחַיְּבוּ בִּשְׂרֵפָה[4], וְהוּא שֶׁעָמְדוּ בַּכֶּרֶם לִרְצוֹנוֹ אַחַר שֶׁיָּדַע בָּהֶם שִׁעוּר שֶׁהוֹסִיפוּ בְּגִדּוּלָן חֵלֶק אֶחָד מִמָּאתַיִם מִמַּה שֶּׁהָיוּ גְּדוֹלִים בְּשָׁעָה שֶׁיָּדַע בָּהֶם[5], וּכְמוֹ[6] שֶׁאָמְרוּ זִכְרוֹנָם לִבְרָכָה

---

if even at the beginning of its planting or sowing it has an element of sin or iniquity, שֶׁלֹּא לְקַיְּמוֹ וְלֹא נֶהֱנֶה בּוֹ כְּלָל – **we should not retain it nor benefit from it at all;** אֲבָל יִשָּׂרֵף הַכֹּל וְיֹאבַד מִן הָעוֹלָם – **rather, it should be entirely burned and destroyed from the world.** הֲלֹא דַי בְּרֹב הַמִּכְשׁוֹלוֹת הַיּוֹצְאִין מִמֶּנּוּ אַחַר גְּמַר בִּשּׁוּלוֹ – **For there is surely enough** reason to refrain from wine even when the vine was planted legitimately, **due to the many pitfalls that it causes after it is ripe** and made into wine, לֹא טוֹב לִהְיוֹת עוֹד גַּם הַתְחָלָתוֹ בַּעֲבֵרָה – **certainly, then, it is not good when it begins** to grow **through a transgression** of the Torah's *kilayim* prohibition. אֲבָל תּוֹקַד הַכֹּל הַפְּרִי וְהַקַּשׁ וְהָעֵצִים וְכָל אֲשֶׁר בּוֹ – **Rather, it is** fitting for it **to be burned in its entirety: the fruit, the straw, the wood, and every part of it.**

Laws of the Mitzvah

מִדִּינֵי הַמִּצְוָה – **Among the laws of the mitzvah** is מַה שֶּׁאָמְרוּ זִכְרוֹנָם לִבְרָכָה – **that which [the Sages], of blessed memory, stated** (*Rambam, Hil. Kilayim* 5:8) אֶחָד הַזּוֹרֵעַ וְאֶחָד הַמְקַיֵּם כִּלְאַיִם בְּכַרְמוֹ – that **the same** law applies **whether one planted or maintained *kilayim* in his vineyard.** כְּלוֹמַר שֶׁרָאָה שֶׁצָּמְחוּ כִּלְאַיִם בְּכַרְמוֹ וְהִנִּיחָן שָׁם – **The meaning** of "maintaining" *kilayim* **is, that he saw that *kilayim* grew in his vineyard and he allowed it to remain there.** נִתְקַדְּשׁוּ כְּלוֹמַר נִתְחַיְּבוּ בִּשְׂרֵפָה – In both of these cases, the law is that **it becomes "*kodesh*"; that is to say, it** becomes forbidden and **must be burned.**[4] וְהוּא שֶׁעָמְדוּ בַּכֶּרֶם לִרְצוֹנוֹ אַחַר שֶׁיָּדַע בָּהֶם – **However, this** prohibition of *kilayim* that is "maintained" **applies only if [the *kilayim*] remained in the vineyard with [the owner's] consent after he became aware of it** שִׁעוּר שֶׁהוֹסִיפוּ בְּגִדּוּלָן – **for an amount** of time **that it would have increased in its growth** חֵלֶק אֶחָד מִמָּאתַיִם מִמַּה שֶּׁהָיוּ גְּדוֹלִים בְּשָׁעָה שֶׁיָּדַע בָּהֶם – **a two-hundredth of the size that it had been when he** first **became aware of it.**[5]

Chinuch clarifies that the criterion that the *kilayim* increase in growth by a two-hundredth applies only to plants that were growing legitimately but later became *kilayim*.[6] However, if the plants were originally planted as *kilayim* they are forbidden as soon as they take root:

וּכְמוֹ שֶׁאָמְרוּ זִכְרוֹנָם לִבְרָכָה – This is **as [the Sages], of blessed memory, stated** (*Pesachim* 25a) in resolving conflicting indications of the verse of this mitzvah (*Deuteronomy* 22:9): On the one hand, in mentioning the seed ("*lest the ... seed ... become prohibited*"), the verse implies that it is forbidden as soon as it takes root. On the other hand, the verse warns of "*the growth*" becoming prohibited (*lest the*

NOTES

4. In the context of *kilayim*, the term קֹדֶשׁ refers to the prohibition for benefit and the obligation of burning the *kilayim* plant. This usage is based on the verse of the mitzvah: פֶּן תִּקְדַּשׁ, *lest it become forbidden*, which is interpreted, as Chinuch cited earlier, to mean, תּוּקַד אֵשׁ, *it shall be burned by fire*.

5. That is, *kilayim* does not become forbidden the moment the owner notices it and lets it stay there; it must first grow a certain amount. It must increase in measure a two-hundredth of the size that it was when he first realized there was a *kilayim* in his field. For the method of measuring this amount, see *Rambam*, *Hil Kilayim* 5:22 with commentaries.

6. For example, a person may keep a vineyard alongside a grain-field as long as there is a wall separating them. If the wall falls, the owner is required to rebuild it immediately (Chinuch discusses this case below, at note 11). If he neglects to do so, the produce becomes prohibited after the plant grows a two-hundredth of its size.

(פסחים כ״ה ע״א) **זָרוּעַ מֵעִקָּרוֹ בְּהַשְׁרָשָׁה זָרוּעַ וּבָא בְּתוֹסֶפֶת, וְזֶה הַתּוֹסֶפֶת פֵּרְשׁוּהוּ זִכְרוֹנָם לִבְרָכָה מִפִּי הַקַּבָּלָה שֶׁהוּא בְּמָאתַיִם**[7]**. וְזֶה**[8] **שֶׁאָנוּ אוֹמְרִים שֶׁלֹּא יִתְקַדֵּשׁ אֶלָּא אִם כֵּן הוּא רוֹצֶה בְּקִיּוּמָן, מִשּׁוּם דִּכְתִיב בְּהוּ אֲשֶׁר תִּזְרָע, כְּלוֹמַר לְדַעְתְּךָ**[9]**. וְטַעַם דָּבָר זֶה מְבֹאָר בְּשֹׁרֶשׁ כִּלְאַיִם דְּהַרְבָּעָה וּמְכַשֵּׁפָה שֶׁכָּתַבְתִּי בִּמְקוֹמָן בְּסֵדֶר קְדֹשִׁים** (מצוה רמ״ד) **וּמִשְׁפָּטִים** (מצוה ס״ב)[10]**, וְזֶהוּ שֶׁאָמְרוּ זִכְרוֹנָם לִבְרָכָה** (תוספתא כלאים פ״ג ה״ד) **מְחִיצַת הַכֶּרֶם שֶׁנִּפְרְצָה אוֹמְרִים לוֹ גְּדֹר**[11]**, כְּלוֹמַר שֶׁאַף עַל פִּי שֶׁהוֹסִיף בְּמָאתַיִם בְּעוֹדֶנּוּ מִשְׁתַּדֵּל לַעֲשׂוֹת הַגָּדֵר**

---

growth of the seed). The Sages resolve this as follows: **זָרוּעַ מֵעִקָּרוֹ בְּהַשְׁרָשָׁה זָרוּעַ וּבָא בְּתוֹסֶפֶת** – **Something** that was **initially planted** as *kilayim* becomes prohibited **upon taking root,** but **something that had been planted previously** in a permitted manner and was later rendered *kilayim* becomes prohibited only **when it grows** in size. **וְזֶה הַתּוֹסֶפֶת פֵּרְשׁוּהוּ זִכְרוֹנָם לִבְרָכָה מִפִּי הַקַּבָּלָה שֶׁהוּא בְּמָאתַיִם** – And although the amount of **this growth** is not written in Scripture, **[the Sages], of blessed memory, set out** (Mishnah, *Kilayim* 5:6), **based on the Oral Tradition, that it is a two-hundredth** of the size that the plant was when the owner first noticed it.[7]

Chinuch mentions that the growth is measured only from the time that the owner became aware of the existence of the *kilayim*. This is because in order for *kilayim* to become prohibited it must be planted or maintained with the owner's knowledge and consent.[8] Chinuch sets out the source for this law:

וְזֶה שֶׁאָנוּ אוֹמְרִים שֶׁלֹּא יִתְקַדֵּשׁ אֶלָּא אִם כֵּן הוּא רוֹצֶה בְּקִיּוּמָן – **This that we said, that** if one saw *kilayim* growing in his field, **it does not become forbidden unless he wishes for it to remain, מִשּׁוּם דִּכְתִיב בְּהוּ "אֲשֶׁר תִּזְרָע"** – **is derived from that which is stated with regard to [these plants]:** *lest the growth of the seed* ***that you plant*** *... become prohibited.* **כְּלוֹמַר לְדַעְתְּךָ** – **This means to say** that it is prohibited only if it grew **with your consent.**[9] **וְטַעַם דָּבָר זֶה מְבֹאָר בְּשֹׁרֶשׁ כִּלְאַיִם דְּהַרְבָּעָה וּמְכַשֵּׁפָה** – **The reason for this** requirement of consent for the plant to be prohibited **is clear from the underlying purposes of** the prohibitions against **crossbreeding and sorcery, שֶׁכָּתַבְתִּי בִּמְקוֹמָן בְּסֵדֶר קְדֹשִׁים וּמִשְׁפָּטִים** – **which I have written in their** respective **places, in *Parashas Kedoshim*** (Mitzvah 244) **and** *Parashas* ***Mishpatim*** (Mitzvah 62).[10]

Chinuch elaborates on some practical ramifications of the rule that a plant is forbidden as *kilay hakerem* only when it is planted or maintained with the owner's knowledge and consent:

וְזֶהוּ שֶׁאָמְרוּ זִכְרוֹנָם לִבְרָכָה – **And this is** the basis for **that which [the Sages], of blessed memory, stated** (*Tosefta, Kilayim* 3:4): **מְחִיצַת הַכֶּרֶם שֶׁנִּפְרְצָה אוֹמְרִים לוֹ גְּדֹר** – In the case of one who owned a vineyard adjacent to a grain field, **if the wall of the vineyard was broken, we tell him, "Repair the barrier."**[11] **כְּלוֹמַר שֶׁאַף עַל פִּי שֶׁהוֹסִיף בְּמָאתַיִם בְּעוֹדֶנּוּ מִשְׁתַּדֵּל לַעֲשׂוֹת הַגָּדֵר** – **That is to say,** as long as he did not abandon his attempt to repair it, **even if [the produce] increases** in size **by a**

NOTES

7. *Minchas Chinuch* §2 writes that the two-hundredth number is actually a Rabbinic measurement. Biblically, the plant does not become forbidden until it grows to the point that half of its growth was nourished as *kilayim*. Although Chinuch's language, "based on the Oral Tradition," implies that this is a Biblical law, *Minchas Chinuch* argues that Chinuch did not mean this literally. Cf. *Chazon Yechezkel, Kilayim* 4:11, who argues that Chinuch maintains it is a Biblical measurement.

8. "Consent" in this context is achieved as long as the owner knows about it and does not actively work to uproot (or separate) it. Chinuch elaborates on this law below.

9. The phrase "*that you plant*" is apparently superfluous; it therefore implies a planting that it is done purposely, i.e., with one's knowledge and consent. The same applies to maintaining *kilayim*.

10. Chinuch explains in those mitzvos that an underlying purpose of those prohibitions is that we may not show, by making unnatural mixtures and combinations of Hashem's creations, that we wish to change the nature of that which Hashem created. This obviously applies only to combinations that people would purposely make, and not a combination that occurred by itself.

11. A vineyard adjacent to a grain field must either be separated by an open area of four *amos* or have a wall separating the two. If the separating wall falls, it must be rebuilt immediately.

לֹא קָדַשׁ, מִכֵּיוָן שֶׁלֹּא נִפְרְצָה וְלֹא עָמְדָה פְּרוּצָה לִרְצוֹנוֹ. וְכֵן אָמְרוּ זִכְרוֹנָם לִבְרָכָה שֶׁהַמְסַכֵּךְ גַּפְנוֹ עַל גַּבֵּי תְבוּאָתוֹ שֶׁל חֲבֵרוֹ הֲרֵי זֶה קִדֵּשׁ גַּפְנוֹ וְלֹא נִתְקַדְּשָׁה הַתְּבוּאָה[12], וְאָמְרוּ בְּטַעַם זֶה גַּם כֵּן לְפִי שֶׁאֵין אָדָם מְקַדֵּשׁ דָּבָר שֶׁאֵינוֹ שֶׁלּוֹ שֶׁאֵין אִסּוּר זֶה אֶלָּא לְדַעַת הַבְּעָלִים[13], וּמִפְּנֵי זֶה אָמְרוּ גַּם כֵּן שֶׁהַמְסַכֵּךְ גֶּפֶן חֲבֵרוֹ עַל גַּבֵּי תְּבוּאַת חֲבֵרוֹ לֹא קִדֵּשׁ אַחַת מֵהֶן, וּמִטַּעַם זֶה הַזּוֹרֵעַ כַּרְמוֹ בִּשְׁבִיעִית לֹא קִדֵּשׁ, שֶׁבְּשָׁנָה שְׁבִיעִית הָאָרֶץ הֶפְקֵר הִיא לַכֹּל[14]. וְאָמְרוּ זִכְרוֹנָם לִבְרָכָה בְּעִנְיָן זֶה (רמב"ם שם פ"ו ה"א) שֶׁהַזּוֹרֵעַ יָרָק אוֹ תְבוּאָה בְּכֶרֶם[15] אוֹ הַמְקַיְּמוֹ עַד

---

two-hundredth while he is still attempting to erect the barrier, לֹא קָדַשׁ מִכֵּיוָן שֶׁלֹּא נִפְרְצָה וְלֹא עָמְדָה פְּרוּצָה לִרְצוֹנוֹ – **[the produce] does not become forbidden, since [the wall] did not break nor had it remained open with his consent.** It is only when he willfully neglects the repair that the produce becomes forbidden after it grew a two-hundredth.

Further applications of the requirement of consent:

וְכֵן אָמְרוּ זִכְרוֹנָם לִבְרָכָה – **Likewise, [the Sages], of blessed memory, stated** (*Rambam,* ibid. 5:8; see Mishnah, *Kilayim* 7:4-5), שֶׁהַמְסַכֵּךְ גַּפְנוֹ עַל גַּבֵּי תְבוּאָתוֹ שֶׁל חֲבֵרוֹ – **that if one spreads his grapevine over the standing grain of his fellow,** הֲרֵי זֶה קִדֵּשׁ גַּפְנוֹ וְלֹא נִתְקַדְּשָׁה הַתְּבוּאָה – **he** thereby **renders his** own **grapevine prohibited** as *kilayim,* **but the grain** of his fellow **is not prohibited.**[12] וְאָמְרוּ בְּטַעַם זֶה גַּם כֵּן – **In explanation of this law, too, the Sages said** (ibid.) לְפִי שֶׁאֵין אָדָם מְקַדֵּשׁ דָּבָר שֶׁאֵינוֹ שֶׁלּוֹ – that it is **because a person cannot render prohibited that which is not his,** שֶׁאֵין אִסּוּר זֶה אֶלָּא לְדַעַת הַבְּעָלִים – **for this prohibition** of *kilayim* **applies only** when the *kilayim* grew **with the owner's consent.**[13] וּמִפְּנֵי זֶה אָמְרוּ גַּם כֵּן – **For the same reason [the Sages] also stated** (ibid.) שֶׁהַמְסַכֵּךְ גֶּפֶן חֲבֵרוֹ עַל גַּבֵּי תְּבוּאַת חֲבֵרוֹ לֹא קִדֵּשׁ אַחַת מֵהֶן – **that if one spreads his fellow's grapevine over his fellow's standing grain, neither** the grapevine nor the grain **is prohibited.** וּמִטַּעַם זֶה הַזּוֹרֵעַ כַּרְמוֹ בִּשְׁבִיעִית לֹא קִדֵּשׁ – **And for this** very **reason, if one plants grain in his** own **vineyard during the *Shemittah* year it is not forbidden** as *kilayim,* שֶׁבְּשָׁנָה שְׁבִיעִית הָאָרֶץ הֶפְקֵר הִיא לַכֹּל – **since in the *Shemittah* year the land is ownerless,** and free **to all.**[14]

Chinuch turns to the subject of the extent of the area that becomes forbidden by a *kilayim* growth. The laws that govern these measurements are complex. Among the factors that are considered are whether the vines are halachically deemed to be a "vineyard" or merely individual vines, and in the case of a "vineyard," whether the foreign seeds were planted inside the vineyard or outside of it. Chinuch cites some laws pertaining to these factors:

וְאָמְרוּ זִכְרוֹנָם לִבְרָכָה בְּעִנְיָן זֶה – **[The Sages], of blessed memory, stated** (*Rambam,* ibid. 6:1) **with regard to this subject** of the prohibition of *kilayim* growth, שֶׁהַזּוֹרֵעַ יָרָק אוֹ תְבוּאָה בְּכֶרֶם – **that if one planted a vegetable or grain in** the middle of **a vineyard,**[15] אוֹ הַמְקַיְּמוֹ עַד

NOTES

12. Grain growing underneath a vine is considered *kilay hakerem* (Mishnah, *Kilayim* 7:3). One who spreads his vines over his own grain renders both the vine and the grain forbidden after a two-hundredth growth. In the case at hand, however, the grain does not belong to the person who spread the vines, so he cannot render the grain forbidden, as Chinuch proceeds to explain.

13. Chinuch explains that this law is based on the above-mentioned principle that in order for produce to become forbidden as *kilayim* it must be planted or maintained with consent. The consent must be that of the owner of the produce; thus, even if the *kilayim* was purposely arranged, as long as it was not with the owner's consent, the produce remains permitted. [See Insight for further discussion of this concept.] The vines, however, which were placed there by their owner, do become prohibited.

14. During the *Shemittah* year all of the land in Eretz Yisrael is ownerless by Divine decree (see Insight to Mitzvah 84). Thus, even if a person plants *kilayim* in what is usually considered his own vineyard, it does not become forbidden, because the *Shemittah* laws render it ownerless and it is as if he planted it in the land of his fellow. [The plants, however, may be subject to some *Shemittah* prohibitions; see *Beur HaHalachah* ibid. 5:8 ד"ה בשביעית.]

15. Chinuch implies that even a single species of grain or vegetable planted in a vineyard prohibits the plants as *kilayim*; see note 2 above.

שֶׁהוֹסִיף בְּמָאתַיִם הֲרֵי זֶה קִדֵּשׁ מִן הַגְּפָנִים שֶׁסְּבִיבוֹתָיו שֵׁשׁ עֶשְׂרֵה אַמָּה לְכָל רוּחַ[16]. וְהַבָּא לִזְרֹעַ יָרָק אוֹ תְּבוּאָה בְּצַד הַכֶּרֶם צָרִיךְ לְהַרְחִיק מִמֶּנָּה אַרְבַּע אַמּוֹת[17], וְכֶרֶם נִקְרָא חָמֵשׁ גְּפָנִים[18], וְהוּא שֶׁיִּהְיוּ נְטוּעוֹת כַּסֵּדֶר הַזֶּה שְׁתַּיִם כְּנֶגֶד שְׁתַּיִם וְאַחַת יוֹצְאָה זָנָב[19]. וְאָמְרוּ שֶׁמַּרְחִיקִין הַתְּבוּאָה וְהַיָּרָק מִגֶּפֶן יְחִידִית שְׁלֹשָׁה טְפָחִים לְכָל רוּחַ מִפְּנֵי שֶׁהַגֶּפֶן רַכָּה וְשָׁרְשֵׁי הַתְּבוּאָה נִכְנָסִין בָּהּ וְיֵשׁ בָּזֶה אִסּוּר הַרְכָּבָה[20], אֲבָל בִּשְׁאָר אִילָנוֹת שֶׁהֵן קָשִׁין אֵין בָּהֶם

שֶׁהוֹסִיף בְּמָאתַיִם – **or if he** did not plant it, but **allowed it to remain there until it increased a two-hundredth** in size, הֲרֵי זֶה קִדֵּשׁ מִן הַגְּפָנִים שֶׁסְּבִיבוֹתָיו שֵׁשׁ עֶשְׂרֵה אַמָּה לְכָל רוּחַ – **he thereby renders prohibited any grapevines surrounding it, sixteen *amos*** (cubits) **in each direction.**[16] וְהַבָּא לִזְרֹעַ יָרָק אוֹ תְּבוּאָה בְּצַד הַכֶּרֶם – **However, one who wishes to plant vegetables or grain *alongside* a vineyard,** not inside it, צָרִיךְ לְהַרְחִיק מִמֶּנָּה אַרְבַּע אַמּוֹת – **is required to distance** the plant **from [the vineyard]** only **four *amos*.**[17]

The above measurements apply only to a vineyard, but not to an individual grapevine. Chinuch now sets out the number and shape of the grapevines that are classified as a "vineyard" for the purposes of this and other laws:[18]

וְכֶרֶם נִקְרָא חָמֵשׁ גְּפָנִים – **It is called a "vineyard"** when there are **five grapevines** planted together, וְהוּא שֶׁיִּהְיוּ נְטוּעוֹת כַּסֵּדֶר הַזֶּה – **but only if they are planted in the following arrangement:** שְׁתַּיִם כְּנֶגֶד שְׁתַּיִם וְאַחַת יוֹצְאָה זָנָב – **two** grapevines **facing two** other grapevines, **and [the fifth] protruding from them as a tail.**[19] When there are less than five grapevines, each vine is seen individually and the distance requirements are less. וְאָמְרוּ שֶׁמַּרְחִיקִין הַתְּבוּאָה וְהַיָּרָק מִגֶּפֶן יְחִידִית שְׁלֹשָׁה טְפָחִים לְכָל רוּחַ – **[The Sages] stated that we distance grain and vegetables from an individual grapevine only three *tefachim*** (handbreadths) **in each direction.** מִפְּנֵי שֶׁהַגֶּפֶן רַכָּה וְשָׁרְשֵׁי הַתְּבוּאָה נִכְנָסִין בָּהּ – This distance is necessary **because the** root of the **grapevine is soft and the roots of the grain penetrate it,** וְיֵשׁ בָּזֶה אִסּוּר הַרְכָּבָה – **and this is** a violation of the **prohibition against grafting** (Mitzvah 245).[20] אֲבָל בִּשְׁאָר אִילָנוֹת שֶׁהֵן קָשִׁין אֵין בָּהֶם

NOTES

16. Some suggest that the reason for this 16-*amah* range is that when foreign seed is planted inside a vineyard, it prohibits all the vines that obtain nourishment from the same soil where the seed grows. The Gemara teaches (*Bava Basra* 26b, 27b) that a tree is nourished chiefly by those roots that are within 16 *amos* of its trunk. Hence all vines whose trunks are within 16 *amos* of the vegetables draw nourishment from the same ground as the vegetables and are therefore rendered forbidden (*Aruch HaShulchan*, *Yoreh Deah* 296:33-34; *Derech Emunah, Beur HaHalachah* 6:1 ד"ה הזורע). [This stringency is a Rabbinic injunction (*Kiryas Sefer*, *Hil. Kilayim* Ch. 6; see also *Beur HaHalachah* ibid.). For alternative explanations of this law and further discussion, see Schottenstein ed. of *Yerushalmi Kilayim*, 50b note 2.]

17. The stringency of 16 *amos* applies only when the foreign seed is planted *inside* the vineyard, since this highlights the mixture of diverse species. When it is planted at the vineyard's perimeter, a much smaller separation is necessary (see *Derech Emunah* 6:12).

The 4 *amos* are necessary because that is generally the area needed for servicing the vineyard (such as by the oxen who plow the vineyard, and the wagons into which the harvested grapes are loaded). Therefore, planting within that area is considered as planting in the vineyard itself (*Aruch HaShulchan* ibid.). [For the amount that becomes prohibited if one violates the 4-*amah* distance, see *Rambam*, ibid. 6:3.]

18. See above, Mitzvah 526 note 6, for another law pertaining to a "vineyard"; see *Sotah* 43a.

19. The four grapevines are arranged as the four corners of a rectangle, in the manner of the front and hind legs of an animal. The fifth grapevine, which is not aligned with any of the others, protrudes from this rectangle in the manner of an animal's tail (*Rambam, Commentary* to *Kilayim* 4:6); see Diagram A. Other authorities maintain an alternate understanding of this description, as depicted in Diagram B (see *Derech Emunah* 7:36. [For additional criteria of a vineyard, see *Rambam, Hil. Kilayim* 7:1-3.]

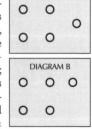

20. Mitzvah 245 is the general prohibition against planting *kilayim* of all plants. Included in that prohibition is the prohibition against grafting two species of plant.

[*Rambam* (*Hil. Kilayim* 6:3) rules that one is required to distance six *tefachim*. For a discussion of Chinuch's position and possible emendation of the text of Chinuch, see *Minchas Yitzchak* §9.]

חֲשַׁשׁ זֶה וְאֵין צָרִיךְ לְהַרְחִיק מֵהֶם כְּלוּם. וְיֶתֶר פְּרָטֵי הַמִּצְוָה מְבֹאָרִים בְּמַסֶּכֶת כִּלְאַיִם[21].

וְנוֹהֵג אִסּוּר זֶה שֶׁלֹּא לֵהָנוֹת בְּכִלְאֵי הַכֶּרֶם בִּזְכָרִים וּנְקֵבוֹת[22], בְּאֶרֶץ יִשְׂרָאֵל מִדְּאוֹרַיְתָא וּבְחוּצָה לָאָרֶץ מִדְּרַבָּנָן. וְיֵשׁ אוֹמְרִים דִּבְחוּצָה לָאָרֶץ אַף עַל פִּי שֶׁאִסּוּר הַזְּרִיעָה נוֹהֵג בָּהּ, אִסּוּר הַהֲנָאָה אֵינוֹ נוֹהֵג אֶלָּא בְּכִלְאֵי הַכֶּרֶם שֶׁל אֶרֶץ יִשְׂרָאֵל דַּוְקָא, וְדִבְרֵיהֶם צְרִיכִין חִזּוּק[23,24].

וְעוֹבֵר עַל זֶה וְאָכַל אוֹ נֶהֱנָה בְּכִלְאֵי הַכֶּרֶם שֶׁל אֶרֶץ יִשְׂרָאֵל חַיָּב מַלְקוֹת[25], וַאֲפִלּוּ מִי שֶׁאֲכָלָן שֶׁלֹּא כְּדֶרֶךְ הֲנָאָתָן, כְּלוֹמַר שֶׁלֹּא נֶהֱנָה בַּאֲכִילָתָן, חַיָּב עֲלֵיהֶן וְלוֹקֶה, מַה שֶּׁאֵין כֵּן בְּכָל שְׁאָר אִסּוּרִין שֶׁבַּתּוֹרָה שֶׁאֵין לוֹקִין עֲלֵיהֶם אֶלָּא דֶּרֶךְ הֲנָאָתָם,

---

חֲשַׁשׁ זֶה – Now, the prohibition against grafting applies to all trees, **but with** regard to **other trees, which are hard, there is no such concern** that the roots of the grain will penetrate them, וְאֵין צָרִיךְ לְהַרְחִיק מֵהֶם כְּלוּם – **and there is therefore no need to distance** other plants **from them at all.**

וְיֶתֶר פְּרָטֵי הַמִּצְוָה מְבֹאָרִים בְּמַסֶּכֶת כִּלְאַיִם – These **and the additional laws of this mitzvah are set forth in Tractate *Kilayim*.**[21]

Applicability of the Mitzvah

וְנוֹהֵג אִסּוּר זֶה שֶׁלֹּא לֵהָנוֹת בְּכִלְאֵי הַכֶּרֶם בִּזְכָרִים וּנְקֵבוֹת – **This prohibition against deriving benefit from *kilayim* of the vineyard applies to men and women.**[22] בְּאֶרֶץ יִשְׂרָאֵל מִדְּאוֹרַיְתָא וּבְחוּצָה לָאָרֶץ מִדְּרַבָּנָן – The prohibition applies **in Eretz Yisrael by Biblical law, and outside of Eretz Yisrael by Rabbinic law.** וְיֵשׁ אוֹמְרִים – **Some** authorities **maintain,** however, דִּבְחוּצָה לָאָרֶץ אַף עַל פִּי שֶׁאִסּוּר הַזְּרִיעָה נוֹהֵג בָּהּ – **that although the prohibition of planting** *kilayim* of the vineyard **applies outside of Eretz Yisrael,** אִסּוּר הַהֲנָאָה אֵינוֹ נוֹהֵג אֶלָּא בְּכִלְאֵי הַכֶּרֶם שֶׁל אֶרֶץ יִשְׂרָאֵל דַּוְקָא – **the prohibition of** deriving **benefit applies only to *kilayim* of the vineyard** that grew **in Eretz Yisrael.** וְדִבְרֵיהֶם צְרִיכִין חִזּוּק – **Now,** there is a principle that **decrees of [the Sages] need to be strengthened** and supported,[23] so it is more reasonable to accept the first opinion, which maintains that the Sages supported their prohibition of *planting kilayim* of the vineyard outside of Eretz Yisrael by also prohibiting *benefiting* from them, such that they fully equated outside of Eretz Yisrael to Eretz Yisrael itself with regard to *kilayim* of the vineyard.[24]

וְעוֹבֵר עַל זֶה – **One who transgresses this** prohibition, וְאָכַל אוֹ נֶהֱנָה בְּכִלְאֵי הַכֶּרֶם שֶׁל אֶרֶץ יִשְׂרָאֵל – **and eats or derives benefit from *kilayim* of the vineyard** that was the produce **of Eretz Yisrael,** חַיָּב מַלְקוֹת – **is liable to *malkus*.**[25]

Chinuch points out a particular severity of this prohibition:

וַאֲפִלּוּ מִי שֶׁאֲכָלָן שֶׁלֹּא כְּדֶרֶךְ הֲנָאָתָן – **Even if one ate [such produce] not in the normal manner of** deriving **benefit from them,** כְּלוֹמַר שֶׁלֹּא נֶהֱנָה בַּאֲכִילָתָן – **that is to say, he had no enjoyment in eating it** (for example, if he ate the produce before it was ripe, when it was not yet fit to be eaten), חַיָּב עֲלֵיהֶן וְלוֹקֶה – **he is** still **liable for it, and incurs *malkus*.** מַה שֶּׁאֵין כֵּן בְּכָל שְׁאָר אִסּוּרִין שֶׁבַּתּוֹרָה – This is **unlike all other prohibitions of the Torah** pertaining to eating, שֶׁאֵין לוֹקִין עֲלֵיהֶם אֶלָּא דֶּרֶךְ הֲנָאָתָם – **for which one does not incur *malkus* unless he** eats the prohibited

---

NOTES

21. The laws of this mitzvah are codified in *Rambam, Hil. Kilayim,* Chs. 5-8, and in *Shulchan Aruch, Yoreh Deah* §296.

22. In accordance with the general rule that applies to mitzvah-prohibitions.

23. See *Rosh Hashanah* 19a, *Taanis* 17b, *Yevamos* 85b.

24. Indeed, most Rishonim maintain that there is a prohibition to derive benefit from *kilay hakerem* outside Eretz Yisrael as well (*Derech Emunah* in *Tziyun HaHalachah* 5:26).

25. [Regarding Chinuch's clear indication that one is liable to *malkus* for benefiting from *kilay hakerem*, even without eating it, see *Minchas Chinuch* §4; see also Mitzvah 113 note 41.]

כְּלוֹמַר שֶׁיֵּהָנֶה הָאָדָם בָּהֶן, וּכְדַאֲמַר אַבַּיֵּי בְּפֶרֶק שְׁנֵי מִפְּסָחִים (כ"ד ע"ב)**, הַכֹּל מוֹדִים בְּכִלְאֵי הַכֶּרֶם שֶׁלּוֹקִין עֲלֵיהֶם אֲפִלּוּ שֶׁלֹּא כְּדֶרֶךְ הֲנָאָתָן, מַאי טַעְמָא דְּלָא כְּתִיב בְּהוּ אֲכִילָה**[26] **דִּכְתִיב פֶּן תִּקְדַּשׁ, וְדָרְשׁוּ זִכְרוֹנָם לִבְרָכָה פֶּן תּוּקַד אֵשׁ**[27]**. וּבְכִלְאֵי הַכֶּרֶם שֶׁבְּחוּצָה לָאָרֶץ הָאוֹכֵל אוֹ הַנֶּהֱנֶה מֵהֶן עוֹבֵר אִסּוּר מִדְּרַבָּנָן לְדַעַת קְצָת הַמְפָרְשִׁים כְּמוֹ שֶׁאָמַרְנוּ**[28]**.**

---

items **in the normal manner of** deriving **benefit from them,** כְּלוֹמַר שֶׁיֵּהָנֶה הָאָדָם בָּהֶן – **that is to say, a person** is not liable unless he **derives pleasure from** eating **them.** וּכְדַאֲמַר אַבַּיֵּי בְּפֶרֶק שְׁנֵי מִפְּסָחִים – This is **as Abaye stated in the Chapter 2 of** Tractate ***Pesachim*** (*Pesachim* 24b): הַכֹּל מוֹדִים בְּכִלְאֵי הַכֶּרֶם שֶׁלּוֹקִין עֲלֵיהֶם אֲפִלּוּ שֶׁלֹּא כְּדֶרֶךְ הֲנָאָתָן – **All agree regarding *kilayim* of the vineyard that one incurs *malkus*** for partaking of it **even** if one does **not** eat it **in the normal manner of** deriving **benefit from it.** מַאי טַעְמָא – **What is the reason** for this? דְּלָא כְּתִיב בְּהוּ אֲכִילָה – **Because** the term **"eating" is not written with regard to [*kilay hakerem*]** as it is with regard to the other eating prohibitions of the Torah.[26] דִּכְתִיב "פֶּן תִּקְדַּשׁ" – **Rather,** the prohibition is derived **from that which is written** about *kilay hakerem*, ***lest it become prohibited,*** וְדָרְשׁוּ זִכְרוֹנָם לִבְרָכָה פֶּן תּוּקַד אֵשׁ – **which [the Sages], of blessed memory, expounded** as, **"lest it be burned by fire."**[27] It is only from the fact that the Torah commanded it to be burned that we understand that it is completely forbidden for any benefit or consumption. This kind of prohibition includes *any* form of consumption, even that which is not the normal way of benefiting from it.

וּבְכִלְאֵי הַכֶּרֶם שֶׁבְּחוּצָה לָאָרֶץ – **As for *kilayim* of the vineyard** that grew **outside of Eretz Yisrael,** הָאוֹכֵל אוֹ הַנֶּהֱנֶה מֵהֶן עוֹבֵר אִסּוּר מִדְּרַבָּנָן לְדַעַת קְצָת הַמְפָרְשִׁים – **one who eats or derives benefit from it transgresses a Rabbinic prohibition according to some commentators,** כְּמוֹ שֶׁאָמַרְנוּ – **as we stated** above.[28]

NOTES

26. When the term "eating" is used in prohibiting an item for consumption, one is generally liable to *malkus* only for consuming it in the usual manner of eating (*Pesachim* 24b).

27. See Chinuch above, after note 2.

28. See above, note 24.

◈ Insight: Prohibiting the Property of Others

Chinuch taught (at note 12) that if one drapes his grapevine over the grain field of his neighbor, the grain does not become prohibited. Likewise, if one plants *kilayim* in his own vineyard during *Shemittah* the produce does not become prohibited. Both laws are based on the principle that אֵין אָדָם אוֹסֵר (מַקְדִּשׁ) דָּבָר שֶׁאֵינוֹ שֶׁלּוֹ, *a person cannot render prohibited that which is not his.*

The same principle seems to appear in the context of the laws of *avodah zarah*. An object that is worshiped as an *avodah zarah* is prohibited for any benefit. For example, if one bows down in worship to his cow, the cow becomes forbidden. The Gemara states (*Chullin* 40a), however, that if one bows down in worship to another person's cow, the cow remains permitted. This is apparently a reflection of the same principle, namely, that it is not in the power of a person to render prohibited that which belongs to another.

The scope of this principle, however, is clearly limited. For example, there is no question that if a person cooked meat and milk together, even if the meat and milk both belonged to other people, the mixture is forbidden like any milk-and-meat mixture (Mitzvah 113). Or, if one mixed prohibited food with permitted food — for example, by putting *cheilev* (forbidden fats) into a meat stew — the stew is forbidden regardless of whether either food belonged to him. It is important, then, to understand why this principle applies only in certain cases and not in others. Different approaches are offered by the commentators:

Tosafos (*Yevamos* 83b ד"ה אין אדם אוסר) maintain that the essential difference between these cases is that in the cases of *avodah zarah* and *kilayim*, a necessary component in creating the prohibition is the intent of the one creating the prohibition, while in the cases of meat and milk, and mixtures of forbidden foods, the prohibition depends solely on the physical phenomena. All that is necessary

to prohibit a meat and milk mixture is the fact that they were cooked together. Likewise, if forbidden food was mixed into permitted food, the fact that the mixture contains some forbidden food is all that is necessary to render the entire mixture forbidden. With *avodah zarah*, however, in order for an object to become prohibited, there must be an act of worship in conjunction with the intent of the worshiper to serve it as a deity. [That is, the act is defined as "worship" on the basis of the person's intent. If someone bends down in front of an idol with no intent to worship it, he has not performed the worship of "bowing."] Since this prohibition is contingent upon the person's intent, we apply the principle that a person cannot, with such intent, render that which belongs to another forbidden. Creating the prohibition of *kilayim* also requires the physical mixing of the two species as well as consent, as Chinuch (at note 9) explains at length. If the owner did not consent to the mixture and he intends to separate them, the plants do not become forbidden even if they grow together. Since the prohibition of *kilayim* is contingent upon the owner's intent, it is subject to the principle that one cannot, with such intent, render another's item forbidden.

Rash and *Rosh* to *Kilayim* 7:4-5 present a different approach. According to these Rishonim, there is no generally applicable principle that a person cannot render forbidden that which belongs to another, even where intent is a factor in the prohibition. Rather, in general, we say that a person *can* render another's items prohibited. The cases of *avodah zarah* and *kilayim*, however, are exceptions to this, each for their own reason. An item can become forbidden as *avodah zarah* only when it is designated as such, and the act of designating an item for a certain function is clearly something that only the owner of the item can do. It is meaningless for someone who is not the owner to "designate" the item of another person for a specific purpose, since the owner will continue to use the item as he pleases. Therefore, when one person worships the item of another, he has not made it into an "*avodah zarah*," and the item remains permitted (*Kovetz He'aros* 61:2; cf. *Hagahos R' Akiva Eiger* to *Shulchan Aruch,* Johannesburg ed., *Orach Chaim* 253:2).

According to these Rishonim, with regard to *kilayim* there is no inherent reason that a person should not be able to prohibit the plants of another by placing them in proximity to each other and consenting to the mixture. The reason that a person cannot do this is due to a specific Scriptural exception: לֹא תִזְרַע כַּרְמְךָ כִּלְאָיִם, *you shall not sow your vineyard kilayim*. This implies that the *kilay hakerem* prohibition applies only to one's own vineyard, and excludes the possibility of prohibiting the vineyard (or grain) of another. [See *Talmid HaRashba, Kilayim* §12 ד"ה ובהאי תירוצא, who appears to have had a reading of the Gemara that made this Scriptural inference explicitly. Also see *Rash*, who cites an additional Scriptural source for this ruling. For further discussion, and a difference that may arise from these two approaches, see *Hagahos R' Akiva Eiger* ibid., and *Achiezer* III §65.]

מִצְוָה תקן: שֶׁלֹּא לַעֲשׂוֹת מְלָאכָה בִּשְׁנֵי מִינֵי בְהֵמָה

שֶׁלֹּא לַחֲרֹשׁ בְּשׁוֹר וּבַחֲמוֹר יַחְדָּו[1], וְהוּא הַדִּין לְכָל שְׁנֵי מִינֵי בְהֵמָה שֶׁהָאַחַת הִיא טְהוֹרָה וְהָאַחַת הִיא טְמֵאָה[2], וְלֹא דַוְקָא חֲרִישָׁה לְבַד אֲסוּרָה, אֶלָּא הוּא הַדִּין כָּל מְלָאכָה מֵהַמְּלָאכוֹת כְּגוֹן דִּישָׁה אוֹ לִמְשֹׁךְ עֲגָלָה וְכָל שְׁאָר מְלָאכוֹת[3], וְעַל זֶה נֶאֱמַר (דברים כ״ב, י׳) לֹא תַחֲרֹשׁ בְּשׁוֹר וּבַחֲמֹר יַחְדָּו.

שֹׁרֶשׁ הַמִּצְוָה כָּתַב הָרַמְבַּ״ם ז״ל[4] שֶׁהוּא מִשֹּׁרֶשׁ אִסּוּר הַרְבָּעַת הַבְּהֵמָה כִּלְאַיִם,

---

Mitzvah 550
The Prohibition to Work Two Species of Animals Together

לֹא תַחֲרֹשׁ בְּשׁוֹר וּבַחֲמֹר יַחְדָּו
You shall not plow with an ox and donkey together (*Deuteronomy* 22:10).

This mitzvah, the third in this series of *kilayim* prohibitions, prohibits having animals of different species perform work together. A different *kilayim* prohibition pertaining to animals (Mitzvah 244) prohibits crossbreeding animals of different species.

שֶׁלֹּא לַחֲרֹשׁ בְּשׁוֹר וּבַחֲמוֹר יַחְדָּו – We are commanded **not to plow with an ox and a donkey together.**[1] וְהוּא הַדִּין לְכָל שְׁנֵי מִינֵי בְהֵמָה – **The same applies to any two species of animals,** שֶׁהָאַחַת הִיא טְהוֹרָה וְהָאַחַת הִיא טְמֵאָה – **when one** of them **is a kosher** animal **and** the other **one is a nonkosher** animal.[2] וְלֹא דַוְקָא חֲרִישָׁה לְבַד אֲסוּרָה – **The prohibition is not limited exclusively to plowing;** אֶלָּא הוּא הַדִּין כָּל מְלָאכָה מֵהַמְּלָאכוֹת – **rather, it applies equally to all forms of work,** כְּגוֹן דִּישָׁה אוֹ לִמְשֹׁךְ עֲגָלָה וְכָל שְׁאָר מְלָאכוֹת – **such as threshing, drawing a wagon, and all other activities.**[3] וְעַל זֶה נֶאֱמַר "לֹא תַחֲרֹשׁ בְּשׁוֹר וּבַחֲמֹר יַחְדָּו" – **Regarding this, it is stated** (*Deuteronomy* 22:10): ***You shall not plow with an ox and donkey together.***

Underlying Purpose of the Mitzvah

שֹׁרֶשׁ הַמִּצְוָה כָּתַב הָרַמְבַּ״ם ז״ל – With regard to **the underlying purpose of the mitzvah, *Rambam*, of blessed memory, writes**[4] שֶׁהוּא מִשֹּׁרֶשׁ אִסּוּר הַרְבָּעַת הַבְּהֵמָה כִּלְאַיִם – **that it is rooted in the**

NOTES

1. The definition of "together," as it pertains to this prohibition, is the subject of disagreement among Rishonim. *Rosh* maintains that one does not transgress this prohibition unless the animals are actually tied to each other, or are both hitched to a single load. *Rambam,* however, maintains that merely having them perform a single activity together (e.g., carrying a plank of wood) is prohibited, even if they are not tied to each other (see *Shulchan Aruch, Yoreh Deah* 297[b]:11 with *Rama*). See Insight.

2. The Gemara (*Bava Kamma* 54b) derives that just as with regard to the Sabbath, the Torah mentions specifically an ox and a donkey (see *Deuteronomy* 5:14), yet other animals are included as well (see ibid. and *Exodus* 20:10), so, too, with regard to the *kilayim* prohibition, although the Torah specifies the ox and donkey, it applies to other animals as well. Nevertheless, according to Chinuch, since the Torah chose the example of a kosher animal and a nonkosher animal, the Biblical prohibition is limited to such a combination (see *Rosh, Halachos Ketanos, Hil. Kilayim* §5).

[Chinuch here follows *Rambam, Hil. Kilayim* 9:7-8. Other Rishonim, however, maintain that the Biblical prohibition pertains to any combination of species, regardless of their kosher status (see *Rosh* ibid.). See Insight for discussion.]

3. Chinuch indicates that this prohibition applies only to *working* two animals together. It is permitted, however, to *lead* the animals together if they are not performing a work activity. This matter, though, is the subject of a disagreement among the authorities; see *Bach, Yoreh Deah* 297[b]:7, and *Taz* there §5.

4. See *Moreh Nevuchim* III, Ch. 49. According to *Me'il HaEphod,* this should read *"Ramban,"* whose explanation (in his commentary to this verse) matches this one, practically word for word.

כִּי דֶּרֶךְ עוֹבְדֵי אֲדָמָה לְהָבִיא הַצֶּמֶד בְּרֶפֶת אַחַת וְשָׁמָּה יַרְכִּיב אוֹתָם[5], וְשֹׁרֶשׁ אִסּוּר הַרְבָּעָה כְּתַבְתִּיו בִּמְקוֹמוֹ בְּסֵדֶר קְדֹשִׁים תִּהְיוּ (מצוה רמ״ד)[6]. וְאַחַר רְשׁוּת אֲדוֹנִי הָרַב הַנִּזְכָּר וְהוֹדָאָה עַל דְּבָרוֹ הַטּוֹב, אֶעֱנֶה אַף אֲנִי חֶלְקִי וְאֹמַר כִּי מִטַּעֲמֵי מִצְוָה זוֹ עִנְיַן צַעַר בַּעֲלֵי חַיִּים שֶׁהוּא אָסוּר מִן הַתּוֹרָה[7], וְיָדוּעַ שֶׁיֵּשׁ לְמִינֵי הַבְּהֵמוֹת וְלָעוֹפוֹת דְּאָגָה גְּדוֹלָה לִשְׁכֹּן עִם שֶׁאֵינָם מִינָן וְכָל שֶׁכֵּן לַעֲשׂוֹת עִמָּהֶן מְלָאכָה, וּכְמוֹ שֶׁאָנוּ רוֹאִים בְּעֵינֵינוּ בְּאוֹתָן שֶׁאֵינָם תַּחַת יָדֵינוּ כִּי כָּל עוֹף לְמִינוֹ יִשְׁכֹּן, וְכָל הַבְּהֵמוֹת וּשְׁאָר הַמִּינִין גַּם כֵּן יִדְבְּקוּ לְעוֹלָם בְּמִינֵיהֶן[8]. וְכָל חֲכַם לֵב מִזֶּה יִקַּח מוּסָר שֶׁלֹּא לְמַנּוֹת שְׁנֵי אֲנָשִׁים לְעוֹלָם בְּדָבָר מִכָּל הַדְּבָרִים שֶׁיִּהְיוּ רְחוֹקִים בְּטִבְעָם וּמְשֻׁנִּים בְּהַנְהָגָתָם כְּמוֹ צַדִּיק וְרָשָׁע וְהַנִּקְלֶה בַּנִּכְבָּד[9], שֶׁאִם הִקְפִּידָה הַתּוֹרָה עַל

---

prohibition against crossbreeding animals (Mitzvah 244); **כִּי דֶּרֶךְ עוֹבְדֵי אֲדָמָה לְהָבִיא הַצֶּמֶד בְּרֶפֶת אַחַת – for it is the practice of those who work the land to bring the pair** of animals that plow together **into one barn, וְשָׁמָּה יַרְכִּיב אוֹתָם – and to mate them there.** The Torah therefore prohibits working animals of two species together so that the prohibition against crossbreeding not be transgressed.[5] **וְשֹׁרֶשׁ אִסּוּר הַרְבָּעָה כְּתַבְתִּיו בִּמְקוֹמוֹ – I have** already **written the underlying purpose of the prohibition against crossbreeding in its place, בְּסֵדֶר קְדֹשִׁים תִּהְיוּ – in *Parashas Kedoshim*** (Mitzvah 244).[6]

וְאַחַר רְשׁוּת אֲדוֹנִי הָרַב הַנִּזְכָּר – Now, with the permission of my master, the aforementioned sage (i.e., *Rambam*), **וְהוֹדָאָה עַל דְּבָרוֹ הַטּוֹב – and** after **acknowledging his fine words, אֶעֱנֶה אַף אֲנִי חֶלְקִי – I, too, will present my opinion. וְאֹמַר כִּי מִטַּעֲמֵי מִצְוָה זוֹ עִנְיַן צַעַר בַּעֲלֵי חַיִּים – Thus, I will say, that among the reasons for this mitzvah is the matter of "the pain of living creatures"** (*tzaar baalei chaim*), **שֶׁהוּא אָסוּר מִן הַתּוֹרָה – which is Biblically prohibited.**[7] **וְיָדוּעַ שֶׁיֵּשׁ לְמִינֵי הַבְּהֵמוֹת וְלָעוֹפוֹת דְּאָגָה גְּדוֹלָה לִשְׁכֹּן עִם שֶׁאֵינָם מִינָן – Now, it is well-known that the** various **species of animals and birds experience great anxiety when dwelling among** members **of other species, וְכָל שֶׁכֵּן לַעֲשׂוֹת עִמָּהֶן מְלָאכָה – and certainly when performing work together with them, וּכְמוֹ שֶׁאָנוּ רוֹאִים בְּעֵינֵינוּ בְּאוֹתָן שֶׁאֵינָם תַּחַת יָדֵינוּ – as we see with our** own **eyes with regard to** those **[living creatures] that are not under our control** (i.e., those that live in the wild), **כִּי כָּל עוֹף לְמִינוֹ יִשְׁכֹּן – that all birds dwell among their own species, וְכָל הַבְּהֵמוֹת וּשְׁאָר הַמִּינִין גַּם כֵּן יִדְבְּקוּ לְעוֹלָם בְּמִינֵיהֶן – and all animals and other species, as well, associate** only **with their** own **species.**[8]

Chinuch draws a parallel with regard to dealing with *people*:

וְכָל חֲכַם לֵב מִזֶּה יִקַּח מוּסָר – Every wise person can derive a lesson from this, שֶׁלֹּא לְמַנּוֹת שְׁנֵי אֲנָשִׁים לְעוֹלָם בְּדָבָר מִכָּל הַדְּבָרִים – never to appoint, to any task whatsoever, two people שֶׁיִּהְיוּ רְחוֹקִים בְּטִבְעָם וּמְשֻׁנִּים בְּהַנְהָגָתָם – who are far apart **in their natures, and different in their behavior, כְּמוֹ צַדִּיק וְרָשָׁע וְהַנִּקְלֶה בַּנִּכְבָּד – such as a righteous person and an evil one, or a lowly person and one who is dignified;**[9] **שֶׁאִם הִקְפִּידָה הַתּוֹרָה עַל**

NOTES

5. *Meshech Chochmah* to the verse notes that this reason does not seem consistent with *Rambam's* position (followed by Chinuch above) that the prohibition against working with two species applies only when one animal is of a kosher species and the other of a nonkosher species. If the concern was that one may come to crossbreed the animals, the Torah should have been *less* concerned in that case, being that the Gemara (*Bechoros* 7a) states that the union of a nonkosher animal with a kosher animal will not produce offspring.

6. There, Chinuch explains that God created each species with perfect precision, and, in order to perpetuate the perfection of each species, He prohibited crossbreeding any animals. [See Mitzvah 62, where Chinuch adds another dimension to this prohibition.]

7. See Insight to Mitzvah 452.

8. From the fact that living creatures naturally live among their own species and never dwell with others, it is obvious that they are at ease only among their own kind. Thus, forcing them to work alongside other animals constitutes inflicting pain upon them, which is prohibited as *tzaar baalei chaim*. [See *Daas Zekeinim, Chizkuni,* and *Baal HaTurim* to the verse of the mitzvah, for further discussion of how working two species of animal together can constitute *tzaar baalei chaim*.]

9. Stylistic citation of *Isaiah* 3:5.

הַצַּעַר שֶׁיֵּשׁ בָּזֶה לְבַעֲלֵי חַיִּים שֶׁאֵינָם בְּנֵי שֵׂכֶל, כָּל שֶׁכֵּן בִּבְנֵי אָדָם אֲשֶׁר לָהֶם נֶפֶשׁ מַשְׂכֶּלֶת לָדַעַת יוֹצְרָם[10].

מִדִּינֵי הַמִּצְוָה מַה שֶּׁאָמְרוּ זִכְרוֹנָם לִבְרָכָה שֶׁאֵין חִיּוּב מִצְוָה זוֹ מִן הַתּוֹרָה כִּי אִם בִּשְׁנֵי מִינִין שֶׁהֵן כְּגוֹן שׁוֹר וַחֲמוֹר שֶׁהָאֶחָד טָהוֹר וְהַשֵּׁנִי טָמֵא, שֶׁטִּבְעָם רָחוֹק מְאֹד זֶה מִזֶּה[11], אֲבָל בִּשְׁנֵי מִינִין טְהוֹרִים אוֹ טְמֵאִים אַף עַל פִּי שֶׁאֵינָם מִין אֶחָד, כְּגוֹן שׁוֹר וְתַיִשׁ אוֹ חֲמוֹר וְסוּס, אֵינוֹ אָסוּר מִן הַתּוֹרָה, אֲבָל מִדְּרַבָּנָן הוּא שֶׁאָסוּר בְּכָל שְׁנֵי מִינִים שֶׁהֵם כִּלְאַיִם בְּהַרְבָּעָה[12]. וְאֶחָד בְּהֵמָה אוֹ חַיָּה בִּכְלַל הָאִסּוּר[13]. וְאֶחָד הַחוֹרֵשׁ בָּהֶן

הַצַּעַר שֶׁיֵּשׁ בָּזֶה לְבַעֲלֵי חַיִּים שֶׁאֵינָם בְּנֵי שֵׂכֶל – **for if the Torah was concerned with the pain such** association **inflicts on animals that have no intelligence,** כָּל שֶׁכֵּן בִּבְנֵי אָדָם אֲשֶׁר לָהֶם נֶפֶשׁ מַשְׂכֶּלֶת לָדַעַת יוֹצְרָם – **certainly** one must be concerned **regarding people, who possess an intelligent soul** in order **to attain knowledge of their Creator.**[10]

Laws of the Mitzvah

מִדִּינֵי הַמִּצְוָה – **Among the laws of the mitzvah** מַה שֶּׁאָמְרוּ זִכְרוֹנָם לִבְרָכָה – **is that which [the Sages], of blessed memory, stated** (*Rambam, Hil. Kilayim* 9:7), שֶׁאֵין חִיּוּב מִצְוָה זוֹ מִן הַתּוֹרָה – **that there is no Biblical liability for** transgressing **this mitzvah,** כִּי אִם בִּשְׁנֵי מִינִין שֶׁהֵן כְּגוֹן שׁוֹר וַחֲמוֹר – **unless** one works with **two species that are similar to an ox and donkey,** שֶׁהָאֶחָד טָהוֹר וְהַשֵּׁנִי טָמֵא – that is, **one is kosher and the other is nonkosher,** שֶׁטִּבְעָם רָחוֹק מְאֹד זֶה מִזֶּה – **as their natures are very distant one from another.**[11] אֲבָל בִּשְׁנֵי מִינִין טְהוֹרִים אוֹ טְמֵאִים – **However,** working **with two species that are** both **kosher or** both **nonkosher,** אַף עַל פִּי שֶׁאֵינָם מִין אֶחָד – **even though they are not the same species,** כְּגוֹן שׁוֹר וְתַיִשׁ אוֹ חֲמוֹר וְסוּס – **such as an ox and a goat,** which are both kosher, **or a donkey and a horse,** which are both nonkosher, אֵינוֹ אָסוּר מִן הַתּוֹרָה – **is not Biblically prohibited.** אֲבָל מִדְּרַבָּנָן הוּא שֶׁאָסוּר בְּכָל שְׁנֵי מִינִים שֶׁהֵם כִּלְאַיִם בְּהַרְבָּעָה – **It is, however, Rabbinically prohibited** to work **with any two species that are** considered ***kilayim*** **in regard to** the prohibition against **crossbreeding.**[12]

וְאֶחָד בְּהֵמָה אוֹ חַיָּה בִּכְלַל הָאִסּוּר – **Both domestic animals and wild animals are included in the** *kilayim* **prohibition.**[13]

וְאֶחָד הַחוֹרֵשׁ בָּהֶן – The prohibition **applies whether one plows with [*kilayim* animals],**

NOTES

10. Unlike animals, which have no sense of honor and dignity, man was endowed with the intelligence to enable him to know the ways of Hashem. This intelligence brings with it a need to preserve his dignity and avoid humiliation. Thus, one must certainly avoid appointing people with different personalities to work together on a single task, in order to prevent them from enduring the discomfort that would inevitably result from their differences in nature.

11. [See above, note 2, where a dissenting opinion was cited.] Chinuch's explanation follows his approach that the purpose of this prohibition is to protect an animal from the distress of close association with other species. Accordingly, Chinuch explains that the prohibition applies only to species that are very different from one another, one being kosher and the other nonkosher. When both animals are kosher or both are nonkosher, there is a certain commonality between the species, so working them together would not amount to *tzaar baalei chaim*.

12. The Biblical prohibition of crossbreeding applies even when both species are kosher or both are nonkosher, as long as they are actually "different" species. The Sages extended the prohibition of *working* with two species to any that are covered by that prohibition. For discussion of which species are considered *kilayim* with regard to crossbreeding, see Mitzvah 244, beginning at note 19.

13. Land animals are divided into two categories: *Beheimah* [בְּהֵמָה], *domestic animals,* referring to species normally domesticated, such as cattle and sheep; and *chayah* [חַיָּה], *"wild" animals,* referring to species not usually domesticated, such as deer. Although the verse of the mitzvah refers to an ox and a donkey, which are both domestic animals and fall under the category of *beheimah*, the Gemara (*Bava Kamma* 54b) derives that the Biblical prohibition applies even to wild animals that fall under the category of *chayah*.

אוֹ זוֹרֵעַ אוֹ מוֹשֵׁךְ בָּהֶן עֲגָלָה, וְכֵן אִם הָיָה אֶחָד יוֹשֵׁב בָּעֲגָלָה וְאֶחָד מַנְהִיג, שְׁנֵיהֶן לוֹקִין, מִפְּנֵי שֶׁיְּשִׁיבָתוֹ בָּעֲגָלָה גּוֹרֶמֶת לַבְּהֵמָה שֶׁתִּמְשֹׁךְ[14]. וַאֲפִלּוּ מֵאָה שֶׁהִנְהִיגוּ כְּאֶחָד כֻּלָּם לוֹקִין[15]. וּמַה שֶּׁאָמְרוּ שֶׁמֻּתָּר לַעֲשׂוֹת כָּל מְלָאכָה בְּאָדָם וּבְהֵמָה, שֶׁנֶּאֱמַר בְּשׁוֹר וּבַחֲמֹר, וְלֹא בְּאָדָם וַחֲמוֹר אוֹ בְּאָדָם וְשׁוֹר. וְטַעַם הָעִנְיָן לְפִי הַשֹּׁרֶשׁ שֶׁאָמַרְנוּ מִפְּנֵי שֶׁאֵין הִתְחַבְּרוּת הַבְּהֵמָה צַעַר לָאָדָם כִּי אֵין לוֹ עִמָּהּ חֶבְרָה כְּלָל, וַהֲרֵי הוּא כְּעוֹשֶׂה מְלָאכָה אֵצֶל עֵץ אֶחָד אוֹ אֶבֶן אַחַת, וְאֵינוֹ בָּא כְּלָל בְּגֶדֶר הַדָּבָר שֶׁדִּבַּרְנוּ עָלָיו[16]. וְכֵן מֵעִנְיַן הַמִּצְוָה מַה שֶּׁאָמַר רַבִּי יִצְחָק בְּסוֹף מַכּוֹת (כ״ב ע״א) שֶׁהַמַּנְהִיג בְּשׁוֹר פְּסוּלֵי הַמֻּקְדָּשִׁין[17] לוֹקֶה, שֶׁאַף עַל פִּי

אוֹ זוֹרֵעַ אוֹ מוֹשֵׁךְ בָּהֶן עֲגָלָה – **or plants, or draws a wagon with them.** וְכֵן אִם הָיָה אֶחָד יוֹשֵׁב בָּעֲגָלָה וְאֶחָד מַנְהִיג – **Similarly, if one** person **was sitting in a wagon** that was being drawn by *kilayim* animals, **and one** person **was leading** the animals, שְׁנֵיהֶן לוֹקִין – **they both incur *malkus*,** מִפְּנֵי שֶׁיְּשִׁיבָתוֹ בָּעֲגָלָה גּוֹרֶמֶת לַבְּהֵמָה שֶׁתִּמְשֹׁךְ – **because his sitting in the wagon causes the animals to pull** it.[14] וַאֲפִלּוּ מֵאָה שֶׁהִנְהִיגוּ כְּאֶחָד כֻּלָּם לוֹקִין – **And even if a hundred** people **drive** *kilayim* **together, they all incur *malkus*.**[15]

וּמַה שֶּׁאָמְרוּ שֶׁמֻּתָּר לַעֲשׂוֹת כָּל מְלָאכָה בְּאָדָם וּבְהֵמָה – **Also** included in the laws of the mitzvah **is that which [the Sages] stated** (*Sifrei* to the verse), **that it is permitted to perform any work with** the combination of **a person and animal,** "שֶׁנֶּאֱמַר "בְּשׁוֹר וּבַחֲמֹר – **for it is stated** (*Deuteronomy* 22:10), *You shall not plow **with an ox and donkey** together;* וְלֹא בְּאָדָם וַחֲמוֹר אוֹ בְּאָדָם וְשׁוֹר – **this excludes** performing work **with a person together with a donkey and with a person together with an ox.** וְטַעַם הָעִנְיָן לְפִי הַשֹּׁרֶשׁ שֶׁאָמַרְנוּ – **The reason for this matter, according to the underlying purpose** of the mitzvah **that we have stated,** מִפְּנֵי שֶׁאֵין הִתְחַבְּרוּת הַבְּהֵמָה צַעַר לָאָדָם – is **because being connected with an animal is not distressing to a person,** כִּי אֵין לוֹ עִמָּהּ חֶבְרָה כְּלָל – **as [man] has no association at all with [an animal];** וַהֲרֵי הוּא כְּעוֹשֶׂה מְלָאכָה אֵצֶל עֵץ אֶחָד אוֹ אֶבֶן אַחַת – **thus, it is similar to performing work alongside some tree or stone,** וְאֵינוֹ בָּא כְּלָל בְּגֶדֶר הַדָּבָר שֶׁדִּבַּרְנוּ עָלָיו – **and is not at all included in the concept we spoke of** above.[16]

וְכֵן מֵעִנְיַן הַמִּצְוָה – **Similarly included in the topic of the mitzvah** is מַה שֶּׁאָמַר רַבִּי יִצְחָק בְּסוֹף מַכּוֹת – **that which R' Yitzchak stated at the end of** Tractate ***Makkos*** (22a), שֶׁהַמַּנְהִיג בְּשׁוֹר פְּסוּלֵי הַמֻּקְדָּשִׁין לוֹקֶה – **that if one drives** even **a** single **ox** of ***pesulei hamukdashin*** (a disqualified offering) as it bears a burden, and thus does work with it,[17] **he incurs *malkus*.** שֶׁאַף עַל פִּי

NOTES

14. When an animal senses a rider entering the wagon it is drawing, it instinctively moves a bit (see *Rashba* and *Ran* to *Bava Metzia* 8b). Thus, although the animals are being primarily worked by the one who is leading them, the rider is also considered to be working them. And, as Chinuch goes on to explain, if a number of people work *kilayim* animals together, they are all liable.

15. Although with regard to the Sabbath, if two people perform a *melachah* together that either one of them could have performed on his own they are not liable (see *Rambam, Hil. Shabbos* 1:15), that exemption is only from liability to *kares* and a *chatas* offering; the basic prohibition, however, applies even when a number of people perform the act (*Yeshuos Malko* to *Rambam, Hil. Kilayim* 9:9; see also *Teshuvos HaRashba* I, 28; *R' Akiva Eiger* to *Rambam, Hil. Shabbos* 1:16). Alternatively, with regard to *kilayim,* where the Torah held one liable even if he merely *caused* the animal to move (e.g., by shouting at it; see Chinuch below, after note 20), one is liable even for performing the act along with others (*Yavin Daas, Yoreh Deah* 87:2).

16. While an animal would experience distress upon being coupled with another species of animal, man would suffer no such distress, as he has no connection *at all* to a beast. [As far as the distress incurred by the animal is concerned, perhaps the animal too suffers no distress, since it has no commonality at all with man. Alternatively, in the case of a person working along with an animal, the Torah's sole concern is whether the man is experiencing distress; the animal's distress is disregarded in this case, being that it is in the man's best interest that he be aided by the animal (see Insight to Mitzvah 80; see also Mitzvah 545, at note 13).]

17. See *Tosafos, Makkos* 22a ד״ה המנהיג; see also note 3 above.

שֶׁהוּא גּוּף אֶחָד עֲשָׂאוֹ הַכָּתוּב כִּשְׁנֵי גוּפִין לִלְקוֹת עָלָיו[18]. וְיֶתֶר פְּרָטֶיהָ מְבֹאָרִים בְּפֶרֶק שְׁמִינִי מִמַּסֶּכֶת כִּלְאַיִם[19].

וְנוֹהֵג אִסּוּר זֶה בְּכָל מָקוֹם וּבְכָל זְמַן, בִּזְכָרִים וּנְקֵבוֹת[20].

וְעוֹבֵר עַל זֶה וְזָרַע אוֹ חָרַשׁ אוֹ מָשַׁךְ אוֹ הִנְהִיג בְּכִלְאַיִם שֶׁהֵן שְׁנֵי מִינִין אֶחָד טָמֵא וְאֶחָד טָהוֹר, חַיָּב מַלְקוּת מִדְּאוֹרַיְתָא, וַאֲפִלּוּ הִנְהִיגָן כְּאֶחָד בְּקוֹל לְבַד כְּדֶרֶךְ הַבְּהֵמוֹת שֶׁהוֹלְכוֹת לִפְעָמִים בְּגַעֲרַת בֶּן אָדָם חַיָּב מַלְקוּת, שֶׁנֶּאֱמַר יַחְדָּו, מִכָּל מָקוֹם. דִּקְדְּקוּ זִכְרוֹנָם לִבְרָכָה בָּזֶה מִדִּבְרֵי הַכָּתוּב לְחַיֵּב מַלְקוּת בְּדִבּוּר בְּלִי מַעֲשֶׂה[21]. וְאִם בִּשְׁנֵי מִינִים טְמֵאִים

שֶׁהוּא גּוּף אֶחָד – **For, although it is one body,** and thus not *kilayim* in the usual sense, עֲשָׂאוֹ הַכָּתוּב כִּשְׁנֵי גוּפִין לִלְקוֹת עָלָיו – **Scripture deemed it as** a combination of **two** separate **bodies, so one incurs *malkus* on account of** working **it.**[18]

וְיֶתֶר פְּרָטֶיהָ מְבֹאָרִים בְּפֶרֶק שְׁמִינִי מִמַּסֶּכֶת כִּלְאַיִם – These **and the additional details of [this mitzvah] are set forth in Chapter Eight of Tractate *Kilayim*.**[19]

Applicability of the Mitzvah

וְנוֹהֵג אִסּוּר זֶה בְּכָל מָקוֹם וּבְכָל זְמַן – **This prohibition applies in every location and in all times,** בִּזְכָרִים וּנְקֵבוֹת – **to men and women.**[20]

וְעוֹבֵר עַל זֶה – **One who transgresses this** prohibition, וְזָרַע אוֹ חָרַשׁ אוֹ מָשַׁךְ אוֹ הִנְהִיג בְּכִלְאַיִם – **and plants, plows, draws, or drives** (i.e., he does any type of work) **with *kilayim*,** שֶׁהֵן שְׁנֵי מִינִין אֶחָד טָמֵא וְאֶחָד טָהוֹר – **that is,** with **two species, one** of which **is nonkosher and the other kosher,** חַיָּב מַלְקוּת מִדְּאוֹרַיְתָא – **is liable to** the **Biblical *malkus*** penalty. וַאֲפִלּוּ הִנְהִיגָן כְּאֶחָד בְּקוֹל לְבַד – **And even if he drove them together** (as they pulled a wagon or the like) **by merely** raising his **voice** at them, כְּדֶרֶךְ הַבְּהֵמוֹת שֶׁהוֹלְכוֹת לִפְעָמִים בְּגַעֲרַת בֶּן אָדָם – **as is the manner of animals, that they sometimes walk when a person shouts at them,** חַיָּב מַלְקוּת – **he is liable to *malkus*.** שֶׁנֶּאֱמַר "יַחְדָּו" מִכָּל מָקוֹם – This is **due to that which is stated** in the verse of the mitzvah, *You shall not plow with an ox and a donkey* ***"together,"*** which indicates that the prohibition applies **in all situations;** דִּקְדְּקוּ זִכְרוֹנָם לִבְרָכָה בָּזֶה מִדִּבְרֵי הַכָּתוּב – and **[the Sages], of blessed memory** (see *Rambam, Hil. Kilayim* 9:7), **thus deduced from the words of** this **verse** לְחַיֵּב מַלְקוּת בְּדִבּוּר בְּלִי מַעֲשֶׂה – that the Torah is coming **to impose liability to *malkus* for** transgressing this prohibition through **speech** alone, **without** any **action.**[21] וְאִם בִּשְׁנֵי מִינִים טְמֵאִים

NOTES

18. Chinuch is referring to an ox that was consecrated as an offering and subsequently developed a blemish, resulting in it being disqualified from being offered. Although such an ox is certainly a kosher animal, the Torah (*Leviticus* 27:11) refers to it as a בְּהֵמָה טְמֵאָה, *nonkosher animal,* since it includes a "nonkosher" aspect [i.e., unfitness for the Altar] (see *Bechoros* 37b). Accordingly, it is considered like a hybrid containing kosher and nonkosher elements, which is integrally *kilayim.* A person who works with *one* such animal is thus deemed to be working with *kilayim* (*Rambam, Hil. Kilayim* 9:11 with *Mishneh LaMelech*; cf. *Rivan, Makkos* ad loc. ד״ה המרביע; *Tosafos* ad loc. ד״ה שהרי).

[A disqualified offering may be redeemed and it then becomes permitted for regular consumption (Mitzvah 441). With regard to whether the animal is considered *kilayim* before its redemption or afterward, see *Mishneh LaMelech, Shaar HaMelech* [end], and *Maaseh Roke'ach* to *Rambam* loc. cit.]

19. The laws of this mitzvah are codified in *Rambam, Hil. Kilayim* Ch. 9, and in *Shulchan Aruch, Yoreh Deah* 297[b]:10-16.

20. I.e., it applies both in Eretz Yisrael and in the Diaspora, regardless of whether the *Beis HaMikdash* is standing or not; and, following the general rule pertaining to mitzvah-prohibitions, it applies to both men and women.

21. Although, as a rule, a transgression that does not entail action [לָאו שֶׁאֵין בּוֹ מַעֲשֶׂה] does not involve the *malkus* penalty, the Sages derived, based on the wording of the verse of the mitzvah, that this rule does not apply here. One incurs *malkus* for leading a *kilayim* combination with speech alone, even without performing any physical action.

It is not clear how *Rambam* (upon whose words Chinuch is based) derives this law from the word יַחְדָּו, *together*. [Actually, *Rambam* appears to be saying that the word יַחְדָּו is teaching an entirely different law – that one is liable for all types of activities performed with

אוֹ טְהוֹרִים שֶׁהֵן כִּלְאַיִם בְּהַרְבָּעָה זֶה בָּזֶה, חַיָּב מַכַּת מַרְדּוּת מִדְּרַבָּנָן[22].

אוֹ טְהוֹרִים שֶׁהֵן כִּלְאַיִם בְּהַרְבָּעָה זֶה בָּזֶה — **And if** one worked **two** different **species that are** both **nonkosher or** are both **kosher,** but **that are** considered *kilayim* **with regard to** the prohibition against **crossbreeding with one another,** חַיָּב מַכַּת מַרְדּוּת מִדְּרַבָּנָן — he **is liable to the** Rabbinic penalty of *makkas mardus*.[22]

NOTES

the animals, which is the main topic of discussion in *Rambam*; see *Commentary to the Mishnah, Kilayim* 8:2. See *Pi Shenayim* (Sornaga-Navon) to *Tur Yoreh Deah*

§160 ד"ה וראינו להרב (fol. 66a), who therefore strongly questions Chinuch's understanding of *Rambam* here.]

22. See above, note 12.

> ◄§ **Insight: Riding a Mule**
>
> In this mitzvah, which prohibits working with two animals that are of different species, Chinuch follows the opinion of *Rambam*, who maintains that the Biblical prohibition applies only if one species is kosher and the other nonkosher. Otherwise, the prohibition is of Rabbinic origin. As mentioned in note 2, other Rishonim disagree, and maintain that the Biblical prohibition applies to *any* two species.
>
> Now, Isi ben Akavyah, cited in *Tosefta Kilayim* 5:4 and *Yerushalmi Kilayim* 8:2 [72a in Schottenstein ed.], takes this prohibition further, and maintains that it is prohibited to ride on or drive even *one* mule (which is the product of a horse and a donkey), based on the following *kal vachomer*: It is permissible to wear two garments, one of wool and the other of linen, at the same time; nevertheless, wool and linen may not be worn when combined into one entity (Mitzvah 551). Certainly then, two species of animals, which may not be led together as separate entities, may not be led when combined into one entity. [See note 18 above for a similar concept.] The Sages, however, disagree with Isi and cite Scriptural passages which indicate that there were those in earlier times who did ride mules. Isi counters with several rebuttals, among them, that those who did so were not necessarily firm in their adherence to halachah (see *Teshuvos HaRashba* §491).
>
> Now, according to Isi, the *kal vachomer* is apparently effective on the Biblical level, as is evident from the give and take that he had with the Sages regarding the Scriptural passages. *Tos. Yom Tov* (*Kilayim* 8:2) points out that this presents a difficulty to *Rambam*, since both a horse and a donkey are nonkosher animals, so according to *Rambam* a mule cannot be subject to the Biblical prohibition (see there further and *Tos. R' Akiva Eiger* there). A resolution to this difficulty is offered by *Kol HaRamaz* (ad loc.), who explains that, according to *Rambam*, the question of whether the Biblical prohibition applies to two kosher animals or two nonkosher animals is the subject of a dispute between R' Meir and the Sages in *Tosefta* (ibid.). Isi follows the opinion of R' Meir, who maintains that the prohibition applies to *any* two species. The Sages, however, dispute R' Meir, and limit the Biblical prohibition to a combination of kosher and nonkosher animals. Those Sages also dispute the opinion of Isi ben Akavyah for that reason, and maintain that there is no basis to prohibit riding a mule, which is the product of two nonkosher animals. The halachah, according to *Rambam*, follows the Sages, who limit the Biblical prohibition to a combination of kosher and nonkosher animals, and who thus permit riding a mule (see also *Teshuvos R' Yosef Chaim Sonnenfeld* I, §70).
>
>
>
> With regard to defining what constitutes "two species" for purposes of the *Rabbinic* prohibition of working with two animals, Chinuch (at note 12) refers us to the prohibition against the crossbreeding of species, Mitzvah 244. In his discussion there, Chinuch addresses the law pertaining to mating two mules, when one of them is the offspring of a female horse and male donkey, and the other is the offspring of a female donkey and male horse (which is actually known as a "hinny"). Based on the Gemara (*Chullin* 78b-79a) and the rulings of Rishonim, Chinuch concludes that with regard to the laws of crossbreeding, as well as with regard to working with two species of animals, a mule and

a hinny are considered two species, and crossbreeding or working with them together is forbidden.

Now, it is evident from that discussion that if *both* of the mules are offspring of a female horse and a male donkey (or both are offspring of a female donkey and a male horse), working with them or mating them together is permissible, being that they are both of the same origin. It certainly follows, then, that working with or riding on *one* mule is permissible, being that it is a single, new species — contrary to Isi ben Akavyah's position cited earlier.

Indeed, *Rav* (*Bartenura, Kilayim* 8:1) cites Isi ben Akavyah's statement, and comments that the elderly sages of his time would not protest against people who rode mules, and would caution people only against driving *two* mules, due to the concern that one of them may be a mule and the other a hinny. Clearly then, Isi ben Akavyah's *kal vachomer* was not accepted as halachah, and the halachah follows the view of the Sages, who dispute Isi's view.

But on what basis was Isi ben Akavyah's *kal vachomer* rejected? Granted, the Sages cite Scriptural evidence that people in Biblical times rode mules, but why indeed is this permitted?

According to Chinuch and *Rambam* (as explained by *Kol HaRamaz,* cited earlier), the matter is readily understandable, for, as explained, Isi's *kal vachomer* is based on the premise that working two nonkosher animals is *Biblically* prohibited. *Rambam* and Chinuch, however, rule that if both animals are nonkosher, no Biblical prohibition applies. Thus, there is no basis in Biblical law to prohibit riding a mule, which is the product of two nonkosher animals.

Rishonim offer a number of additional reasons to reject Isi's *kal vachomer. Rashba* (*Teshuvos HaRashba* §491) explains that the Sages maintain that since *kilayim* is a חֹק, a Divine decree, one cannot derive other laws from its laws through the principle of *kal vachomer.*

Rosh (*Halachos Ketanos, Hil. Kilayim* §5) has another approach, explaining that Isi's *kal vachomer* is based on a faulty premise. Isi reasons that the prohibition of working two animals is more stringent than the *shaatnez* prohibition, being that two species of animals may not be driven even when they are not joined together. But actually, the Torah uses the term יַחְדָּו, *together,* in the context of working with *kilayim,* as it does in the context of *shaatnez.* This teaches that one is liable for working with the animals only if they are connected to each other in some way. If they are not tied together, one *is* permitted to do work with both of them (see note 1). Thus, the *shaatnez* prohibition is, in fact, no more stringent than the prohibition of working with two different animals, and there is no basis to prohibit riding or working a mule. [See, however, *Even HaOzer,* cited by *Mishnah Rishonah,* and *Tos. R'Akiva Eiger* to *Kilayim* 8:1.]

For yet another solution, see *Teshuvos HaRid* §43.

מִצְוָה תקנא: שֶׁלֹּא לִלְבֹּשׁ שַׁעַטְנֵז[1]

שֶׁלֹּא נִלְבַּשׁ[2] בֶּגֶד מְחֻבָּר מִצֶּמֶר וּפִשְׁתִּים[3] וְזֶהוּ נִקְרָא שַׁעַטְנֵז, וְעַל זֶה נֶאֱמַר (דברים כ״ב, י״א) לֹא תִלְבַּשׁ שַׁעַטְנֵז צֶמֶר וּפִשְׁתִּים יַחְדָּו.

רֶמֶז מִשָּׁרְשֵׁי הַמִּצְוָה כָּתַבְתִּי בְּסֵדֶר מִשְׁפָּטִים בְּעִנְיַן מְכַשֵּׁפָה לָאו ה׳ (מצוה ס״ב)[4]. וְהָרַמְבַּ״ם ז״ל כָּתַב בְּטַעַם הָאִסּוּר, לְפִי שֶׁהָיוּ כֹּמְרֵי עֲבוֹדָה זָרָה לוֹבְשִׁין בִּזְמַן הַהוּא כֵּן הוּא[5], וְכָתַב עוֹד, כִּי הַיּוֹם הוּא מְפֻרְסָם הַדָּבָר אֵצֶל כְּמָרִים שֶׁיֵּשׁ בְּמִצְרַיִם.

Mitzvah 551
The Prohibition to Wear Shaatnez

לֹא תִלְבַּשׁ שַׁעַטְנֵז צֶמֶר וּפִשְׁתִּים יַחְדָּו

You shall not wear shaatnez, wool and linen together (*Deuteronomy* 22:11).

The Torah concludes this series of *kilayim*-related mitzvos with the prohibition against wearing a garment that contains both wool and linen, which is known as *shaatnez*. Although the above verse refers only to *wearing* a garment of *shaatnez*, this prohibition is repeated elsewhere (*Leviticus* 19:19), where the Torah writes: וּבֶגֶד כִּלְאַיִם שַׁעַטְנֵז לֹא יַעֲלֶה עָלֶיךָ, *and a garment of kilayim, of shaatnez, shall not come upon you.* The Torah thus prohibits other forms of having *shaatnez* "come upon you." This includes covering oneself with a blanket that is made of the prohibited mixture of materials. Similarly, it is prohibited to use a *shaatnez* towel, or to grasp a hot pot with a *shaatnez* cloth.[1]

שֶׁלֹּא נִלְבַּשׁ בֶּגֶד מְחֻבָּר מִצֶּמֶר וּפִשְׁתִּים – We are commanded **not to wear**[2] **a garment** that is made **of a combination of wool and linen;**[3] **וְזֶהוּ נִקְרָא שַׁעַטְנֵז** – **this is called *shaatnez.*** **וְעַל זֶה נֶאֱמַר "לֹא תִלְבַּשׁ שַׁעַטְנֵז צֶמֶר וּפִשְׁתִּים יַחְדָּו"** – **Regarding this it is stated** (*Deuteronomy* 22:11): ***You shall not wear shaatnez, wool and linen together.***

Underlying Purpose of the Mitzvah

רֶמֶז מִשָּׁרְשֵׁי הַמִּצְוָה כָּתַבְתִּי בְּסֵדֶר מִשְׁפָּטִים – **A glimpse** of one **of the underlying purposes of this mitzvah** can be found in what **I wrote in *Parashas Mishpatim,*** **בְּעִנְיַן מְכַשֵּׁפָה לָאו ה׳** – **in** connection with **the topic of a sorceress, in Mitzvah-prohibition 5** of that *parashah* (Mitzvah 62).[4] **וְהָרַמְבַּ״ם ז״ל כָּתַב בְּטַעַם הָאִסּוּר** – **However, *Rambam,* of blessed memory, wrote** (*Moreh Nevuchim* Vol. III, Ch. 37; see also *Sefer HaMitzvos, Lo Saaseh* 42) that **the reason for this prohibition is** **לְפִי שֶׁהָיוּ כֹּמְרֵי עֲבוֹדָה זָרָה לוֹבְשִׁין בִּזְמַן הַהוּא כֵּן הוּא** – **because the priests of idolatry would wear such** garments of *shaatnez* **in [Biblical] times.**[5] **וְכָתַב עוֹד כִּי הַיּוֹם הוּא מְפֻרְסָם הַדָּבָר אֵצֶל כְּמָרִים**

NOTES

1. [See *Rambam, Hil. Kilayim* 10:17, 22.] It should be noted, that unlike other *kilayim* prohibitions, which pertain to *forming* the *kilayim* combination, there is no Biblical prohibition against *making* a garment of wool and linen. [There are times, however, when making such a garment is Rabbinically prohibited; see *Derech Emunah, Hil. Kilayim* 10:48, with *Tziyun HaHalachah* §108.]

2. This includes the act of initially putting on a garment that is *shaatnez,* as well as remaining clothed in it.

3. The term *wool* refers exclusively to sheep's wool, and does not include fabrics made of hairs of any other animals (*Rav, Rosh, Rash* to *Kilayim* 9:1, from *Yerushalmi* there [76a in Schottenstein ed.]).

4. There, Chinuch explains that a spiritual force is appointed for each living thing. The sorcerer combines the spiritual forces of various entities, in order to achieve abnormal and extraordinary results. Since such unnatural combinations can have harmful consequences, the Torah prohibited engaging in acts of sorcery. Similarly, Chinuch explains, wearing a garment containing the wool and linen combination brings about harmful consequences. [The wool and linen combination in particular represents concepts that are fundamentally at odds with each other, making it detrimental for them to be blended (see *Midrash Tanchuma, Bereishis* §9; *Pirkei DeRabbi Eliezer* Ch. 21).]

5. As *Rambam* explains, the wool-linen combination was not merely a uniform donned by the idol attendants, it

מִדִּינֵי הַמִּצְוָה מַה שֶּׁאָמְרוּ זִכְרוֹנָם לִבְרָכָה שֶׁאֵין אָסוּר מִן הַתּוֹרָה מַחְבֶּרֶת צֶמֶר וּפִשְׁתִּים אֶלָּא בְּשׁוּעַ טָווּי וְנוּז[6], כְּלוֹמַר שֶׁהַצֶּמֶר שׁוּעַ בִּפְנֵי עַצְמוֹ, כְּלוֹמַר טָרוּף[7], וְטָווּי בִּפְנֵי עַצְמוֹ, וְנוּז בִּפְנֵי עַצְמוֹ, פֵּרוּשׁ נוּז שָׁזוּר, וְכֵן הַפִּשְׁתָּן כְּמוֹ כֵן שׁוּעַ וְטָווּי וְנוּז בִּפְנֵי עַצְמוֹ וְאַחַר כָּךְ חִבְּרָם יַחַד כְּגוֹן שֶׁאֲרָגָן אוֹ אֲפִלּוּ קְשָׁרָן זֶה בָּזֶה, מִכֵּיוָן שֶׁעָשָׂה בָּהֶן שְׁנֵי קְשָׁרִים זֶהוּ שַׁעַטְנֵז דְּאוֹרָיְתָא[8] לִלְקוֹת עָלָיו, אֲבָל כָּל זְמַן שֶׁלֹּא נַעֲשׂוּ בָּהֶן שְׁלֹשָׁה הַמְּלָאכוֹת שֶׁכָּתַבְנוּ אֵין זֶה שַׁעַטְנֵז דְּאוֹרָיְתָא אֶלָּא מִדְּרַבָּנָן כְּדַעַת קְצָת הַמְפָרְשִׁים[9], וְאֵין לוֹקִין עָלָיו, אֲבָל מִדְּרַבָּנָן אָסוּר כָּל שֶׁנַּעֲשָׂה בָּהֶן אַחַת מִן הַמְּלָאכוֹת שֶׁזָּכַרְנוּ אוֹ שׁוּעַ אוֹ טָווּי אוֹ נוּז,

---

שֶׁיֵּשׁ בְּמִצְרַיִם – **Indeed, [*Rambam*] writes further that** even **in current times [this practice] is widespread among the priests** of idolatry **that exist in Egypt.**

Laws of the Mitzvah

מִדִּינֵי הַמִּצְוָה מַה שֶּׁאָמְרוּ זִכְרוֹנָם לִבְרָכָה – **Among the laws of the mitzvah** is **that which [the Sages], of blessed memory, stated** (*Kilayim* 9:8), שֶׁאֵין אָסוּר מִן הַתּוֹרָה מַחְבֶּרֶת צֶמֶר וּפִשְׁתִּים אֶלָּא בְּשׁוּעַ טָווּי וְנוּז – **that the wool-linen combination is Biblically prohibited only when** the fibers were **combed, spun, and twined.**[6] כְּלוֹמַר שֶׁהַצֶּמֶר שׁוּעַ בִּפְנֵי עַצְמוֹ כְּלוֹמַר טָרוּף – **That is to say, that the wool was combed, meaning smoothed,**[7] **by itself,** before being combined with linen, וְטָווּי בִּפְנֵי עַצְמוֹ – **then** it was **spun** into thread **by itself,** וְנוּז בִּפְנֵי עַצְמוֹ – **and twined by itself.** פֵּרוּשׁ נוּז שָׁזוּר – **The meaning of twined is twisted.** וְכֵן הַפִּשְׁתָּן כְּמוֹ כֵן שׁוּעַ וְטָווּי וְנוּז בִּפְנֵי עַצְמוֹ – **Similarly, the linen was combed, spun, and twined by itself,** before being combined with wool. וְאַחַר כָּךְ חִבְּרָם יַחַד – **Afterward,** if **one connected them together,** כְּגוֹן שֶׁאֲרָגָן אוֹ אֲפִלּוּ קְשָׁרָן זֶה בָּזֶה – **such as by weaving them, or even tying them to each other,** מִכֵּיוָן שֶׁעָשָׂה בָּהֶן שְׁנֵי קְשָׁרִים זֶהוּ שַׁעַטְנֵז דְּאוֹרָיְתָא – **once one has tied them with a double knot, it is Biblically** considered a garment of ***shaatnez,***[8] לִלְקוֹת עָלָיו – **for which one incurs *malkus* upon** wearing **it.** אֲבָל כָּל זְמַן שֶׁלֹּא נַעֲשׂוּ בָּהֶן שְׁלֹשָׁה הַמְּלָאכוֹת שֶׁכָּתַבְנוּ – **However, as long as** *all* **three of the described processes** (i.e., combing, spinning, and twining) **have not been performed on the [wool and linen],** אֵין זֶה שַׁעַטְנֵז דְּאוֹרָיְתָא אֶלָּא מִדְּרַבָּנָן כְּדַעַת קְצָת הַמְפָרְשִׁים – even if they are combined in one garment, **it is not** considered ***shaatnez* on the Biblical level – only Rabbinically – in the opinion of some commentators;**[9] וְאֵין לוֹקִין עָלָיו – **thus, one does not incur *malkus* for** wearing **it.** אֲבָל מִדְּרַבָּנָן אָסוּר – **However, it is Rabbinically prohibited** to wear it, כָּל שֶׁנַּעֲשָׂה בָּהֶן אַחַת מִן הַמְּלָאכוֹת שֶׁזָּכַרְנוּ – **as long as** *any* **one of the processes that we have described was performed,** אוֹ שׁוּעַ אוֹ טָווּי אוֹ נוּז – that is, **either combing, spinning, or twisting.**

NOTES

actually reflected some concepts of idolatry. The Torah prohibited wearing such a garment in order to separate us from anything that pertains to idolatry.

6. The Sages expounded the term שַׁעַטְנֵז as an acronym of three words, שׁוּעַ טָווּי וְנוּז, *combed, spun,* and *twined,* each of which is a stage in the processing of fibers. ["Combing" refers to using a comb to smooth out a rough tangle of wool or linen fibers (*Rav, Kilayim* 9:8). "Spinning" refers to spinning the fibers into thread. "Twining" refers to strengthening the thread by doubling it, and twisting the two threads together (*Tiferes Yisrael, Batei Kilayim* §114 and *Kilayim* 9:42).]

7. Literally טָרוּף means *flattened* (see *Aruch* – ע׳ טרף ד״ה בסוף פ״ג דשבועות כו׳). Here it is being used to mean *smoothed,* which is the literal translation of the word שׁוּעַ; see *Targum Onkelos* to *Genesis* 27:11 (see *Rashi, Yevamos* 5b ד״ה שוע).

8. In the verse of the mitzvah, the Torah states that the *shaatnez* prohibition applies to an item containing wool and linen *together* [יַחְדָּו]. From this, the Sages (*Sifrei* ad loc.) derive that the prohibition of wearing *shaatnez* applies only if the wool and linen are securely connected. [See *Rama, Yoreh Deah* 300:3, for an application of this rule.]

9. The Gemara (*Niddah* 61b) cites a dispute whether שׁוּעַ טָווּי וְנוּז means "*combed, spun,* **and** *twined,*" or "*combed, spun,* **or** *twined.*" *Tosafos* (*Yevamos* 5b ד״ה עד שיהא and *Shabbos* 57b ד״ה אין בה) rule in accordance with those who maintain that it means "*combed, spun,* **and** *twined.*" Therefore, the mixture is not considered *shaatnez* on the Biblical level, unless *all three* processes were performed. [This is, in fact, the opinion of many other Rishonim as well; see *Derech Emunah, Hil. Kilayim* 10:8, with *Tziyun HaHalachah* §36.]

וְזֶהוּ אָמְרָם זִכְרוֹנָם לִבְרָכָה (כלאים פ״ט מ״ט) הַלְּבָדִין אֲסוּרִין, כְּלוֹמַר מִדְּרַבָּנָן מִפְּנֵי שֶׁהֵן שׁוּעַ[10]. וּמִן הַמְפָרְשִׁים שֶׁאָמְרוּ דִּבְמְלָאכָה אַחַת מֵאֵלּוּ אֲסוּרִין מִדְּאוֹרַיְתָא, וּכְשֶׁאָמְרוּ בְּכָאן אֲסוּרִין, כְּלוֹמַר מִדְּאוֹרַיְתָא[11].

וְאָמְרוּ זִכְרוֹנָם לִבְרָכָה (ביצה י״ד ע״ב) בְּעִנְיָן זֶה, אֲפִלּוּ עֶשֶׂר מַצָּעוֹת זֶה עַל גַּב זֶה וְכִלְאַיִם תַּחְתֵּיהֶן אָסוּר לֵישֵׁב עֲלֵיהֶן דְּחָיְישִׁינַן שֶׁמָּא תִּכָּרֵךְ נִימָא עַל בְּשָׂרוֹ[12], וְדָבָר זֶה אָמְרוּ זִכְרוֹנָם לִבְרָכָה כְּשֶׁאוֹתָן הַכִּלְאַיִם אֲשֶׁר מִתַּחַת הֵן רַכִּין כִּי אָז יֵשׁ בַּדָּבָר חֲשַׁשׁ זֶה שֶׁל כְּרִיכָה, וְאִסּוּר זֶה הוּא מִדְּרַבָּנָן, דְּאִלּוּ מִדְּאוֹרַיְתָא מֻתָּר אֲפִלּוּ כְּשֶׁהֵן רַכִּין,

---

וְזֶהוּ אָמְרָם זִכְרוֹנָם לִבְרָכָה – **This is** the basis for **what [the Sages], of blessed memory, stated** (*Kilayim* 9:9), הַלְּבָדִין אֲסוּרִין כְּלוֹמַר מִדְּרַבָּנָן מִפְּנֵי שֶׁהֵן שׁוּעַ – that **felts** made of wool and linen **are prohibited – that is to say, on the Rabbinic level – because they are flattened.**[10] וּמִן הַמְפָרְשִׁים שֶׁאָמְרוּ דִּבְמְלָאכָה אַחַת מֵאֵלּוּ אֲסוּרִין מִדְּאוֹרַיְתָא – **There are, however, commentators who say that with** even only **one of the processes** (i.e., combing, spinning, or twining), **[the garment] is Biblically prohibited** as *shaatnez,* וּכְשֶׁאָמְרוּ בְּכָאן אֲסוּרִין כְּלוֹמַר מִדְּאוֹרַיְתָא – **and** that **when [the Sages] stated here that** felts of wool and linen **are prohibited, it means to say** that they are **Biblically** prohibited.[11]

Chinuch proceeds to discuss what is included in the prohibition of wearing or covering oneself with *shaatnez*:

וְאָמְרוּ זִכְרוֹנָם לִבְרָכָה בְּעִנְיָן זֶה – **[The Sages], of blessed memory, stated, with regard to this topic** (*Beitzah* 14b), אֲפִלּוּ עֶשֶׂר מַצָּעוֹת זֶה עַל גַּב זֶה – that **even** if there are **ten** non-*shaatnez* **spreads, one upon the other,** וְכִלְאַיִם תַּחְתֵּיהֶן – **with** a spread of ***shaatnez*** **beneath them,** אָסוּר לֵישֵׁב עֲלֵיהֶן – **it is prohibited to sit upon them,** דְּחָיְישִׁינַן שֶׁמָּא תִּכָּרֵךְ נִימָא עַל בְּשָׂרוֹ – **for we are concerned that perhaps a thread will become wrapped upon his skin.**[12] וְדָבָר זֶה אָמְרוּ זִכְרוֹנָם לִבְרָכָה כְּשֶׁאוֹתָן הַכִּלְאַיִם אֲשֶׁר מִתַּחַת הֵן רַכִּין – **[The Sages], of blessed memory, said this** regarding a case **where the *shaatnez*** spread **on the bottom is soft,** כִּי אָז יֵשׁ בַּדָּבָר חֲשַׁשׁ זֶה שֶׁל כְּרִיכָה – **as then there is this concern of** a thread becoming **wrapped** upon his skin. וְאִסּוּר זֶה הוּא מִדְּרַבָּנָן – **This prohibition, however, is of Rabbinic origin,** דְּאִלּוּ מִדְּאוֹרַיְתָא מֻתָּר אֲפִלּוּ כְּשֶׁהֵן רַכִּין – **for,**

NOTES

10. [See above, note 7.] Felts are made by flattening and compressing fibers together into a single matted cloth. The Mishnah states that felt made from wool and linen fibers is considered *shaatnez,* because the fibers were flattened together. Chinuch explains that while a garment is not Biblically considered *shaatnez* unless the fibers had undergone the processes of combing, spinning, and twining separately, and being combined only afterward, felt made of wool and linen is nevertheless prohibited on the Rabbinic level. [According to this position, a garment is similarly considered *shaatnez* on the Rabbinic level if it contains fibers of wool and linen that were spun or twisted together (see *Commentary* of *Raavad* to *Sifra, Leviticus* 19:19).]

11. This is the opinion of *Rambam* (*Hil. Kilayim* 10:2, as understood by many commentators), who rules in accordance with the opinion (cited in note 9) that if even just *one* of these processes was performed with the wool and linen together, the garment is Biblically prohibited. Therefore, according to *Rambam,* felts of wool and linen are prohibited on the Biblical level. See *Derech Emunah* there §8 with *Tziyun HaHalachah* §33 for further discussion.

12. As Chinuch will go on to explain, Biblical law prohibits only wearing a garment of *shaatnez,* or covering oneself with a blanket of *shaatnez*. The Sages were concerned, though, that when sitting on the spread, a partially loose thread from the blanket may become wrapped upon one's skin. They further prohibited sitting on the spread even where the *shaatnez* blanket was beneath many layers of covering, to ensure that one will not lie directly on the *shaatnez*.

[Although the *shaatnez* prohibition does not apply when the *shaatnez* is not being worn as a garment or to provide warmth (see below, notes 15 and 20), and a single thread does not normally provide warmth, there is nevertheless the concern that this may happen with a thick thread, which can provide some warmth. Alternatively, since the main body of the blanket is providing him with warmth from below, and part of it (the thread) is wrapped upon his skin, it would be considered as though the entire blanket is upon him (*Rashi, Beitzah* 14b ד״ה שמא תכרך).]

וּכְמוֹ שֶׁאָמְרוּ זִכְרוֹנָם לִבְרָכָה (שם) לֹא יַעֲלֶה עָלֶיךָ, אֲבָל אַתָּה מַצִּיעוֹ תַּחְתֶּיךָ. וּבִירוּשַׁלְמִי אָמְרוּ דְּבָרִים וּכְסָתוֹת אַף עַל פִּי שֶׁהֵן קָשִׁים בִּמְלֵאִים אָסוּר לֵישֵׁב עֲלֵיהֶן מִדְּרַבָּנָן לְפִי שֶׁהֵן נִכְפָּלִין עַל הַיּוֹשֵׁב בָּהֶן, אֲבָל בְּרֵקִין[13] דְּלֵיכָּא חֲשַׁשׁ הָעֲלָאָה מֻתָּר לֵישֵׁב בָּהֶן מִכֵּיוָן שֶׁהֵן קָשִׁין[14]. וְטַעַם הָעִנְיָן מִפְּנֵי שֶׁהַכָּתוּב אָסַר שַׁעַטְנֵז בִּלְשׁוֹן לְבִישָׁה, כְּלוֹמַר דֶּרֶךְ מַלְבּוּשׁ הוּא שֶׁאָסוּר וְלֹא בְּעִנְיָן אַחֵר[15]. וּמִטַּעַם זֶה הִתִּירוּ לָנוּ מוֹרֵינוּ יִשְׁמְרֵם אֵל[16] לָתֵת עַל רָאשֵׁינוּ כּוֹבָעִין הָעֲשׂוּיִין מִלְּבָדִין לְהָגֵן מִן הַשֶּׁמֶשׁ מִפְּנֵי שֶׁהֵן גַּם כֵּן קָשִׁים מְאֹד, וּלְפִיכָךְ אַף עַל פִּי שֶׁיֵּשׁ בָּהֶן כִּלְאַיִם הִתִּירוּ אוֹתָן לְפִי שֶׁאֵין דֶּרֶךְ לְבִישָׁה בְּדָבָר קָשֶׁה כָּל כָּךְ[17],

---

on the Biblical level, sitting on *shaatnez* **is permitted even when [the *shaatnez*] is soft,** וּכְמוֹ שֶׁאָמְרוּ זִכְרוֹנָם לִבְרָכָה **– as [the Sages], of blessed memory, said** (ad loc.): "לֹא יַעֲלֶה עָלֶיךָ" אֲבָל אַתָּה מַצִּיעוֹ תַּחְתֶּיךָ – The Torah states (*Leviticus* 19:19), *a garment of kilayim, of shaatnez,* ***you shall not bring upon you,*** which implies that **you may, however, spread it beneath you.**

וּבִירוּשַׁלְמִי אָמְרוּ **– [The Sages] also stated in** *Talmud* ***Yerushalmi*** (*Kilayim* 9:1; 77a-b in Schottenstein ed.) דְּבָרִים וּכְסָתוֹת אַף עַל פִּי שֶׁהֵן קָשִׁים **– that mattresses and cushions** of *shaatnez,* **even though they are firm,** בִּמְלֵאִים אָסוּר לֵישֵׁב עֲלֵיהֶן מִדְּרַבָּנָן **– if they are filled** with soft material, **it is Rabbinically prohibited to sit upon them,** לְפִי שֶׁהֵן נִכְפָּלִין עַל הַיּוֹשֵׁב בָּהֶן **– because they** sometimes **fold over onto one who sits on them.** אֲבָל (ברכין) [בְּרֵקִין][13] דְּלֵיכָּא חֲשַׁשׁ הָעֲלָאָה **– But as for those that are unfilled, where there is no concern** that the *shaatnez* material **will come** to be **upon** him, מֻתָּר לֵישֵׁב בָּהֶן מִכֵּיוָן שֶׁהֵן קָשִׁין **– it is permitted to sit upon them, being that they are firm.**[14]

וְטַעַם הָעִנְיָן מִפְּנֵי שֶׁהַכָּתוּב אָסַר שַׁעַטְנֵז בִּלְשׁוֹן לְבִישָׁה **– The reason for this matter is because the Torah prohibited *shaatnez* using the term** *levishah*, **"wearing";** כְּלוֹמַר דֶּרֶךְ מַלְבּוּשׁ הוּא שֶׁאָסוּר **– that is to say, [*shaatnez*] is prohibited only** when it serves **in the manner of a garment,** וְלֹא בְּעִנְיָן אַחֵר **– but not** when it is used **in any other manner.**[15] וּמִטַּעַם זֶה הִתִּירוּ לָנוּ מוֹרֵינוּ יִשְׁמְרֵם אֵל **– On the basis of this reason, our masters, may the Almighty protect them, permitted for us**[16] לָתֵת עַל רָאשֵׁינוּ כּוֹבָעִין הָעֲשׂוּיִין מִלְּבָדִין לְהָגֵן מִן הַשֶּׁמֶשׁ **– to place upon our heads** *shaatnez* **hats made of felt, to protect from the sun,** מִפְּנֵי שֶׁהֵן גַּם כֵּן קָשִׁים מְאֹד **– as they, too, are very stiff.** וּלְפִיכָךְ אַף עַל פִּי שֶׁיֵּשׁ בָּהֶן כִּלְאַיִם הִתִּירוּ אוֹתָן **– Therefore, even though [these hats] contain *shaatnez,* [our masters] permitted** donning **them,** לְפִי שֶׁאֵין דֶּרֶךְ לְבִישָׁה בְּדָבָר קָשֶׁה כָּל כָּךְ **– as it is not considered "the manner of wearing" when** donning **something** that **is so stiff.**[17]

NOTES

13. Emendation folllows *Minchas Yitzchak* edition, and is consistent with the text in *Yerushalmi*.

14. When a person sits on a mattress that is filled with soft material, he sinks into it and its sides fold over his body; this warms him in a manner similar to a garment. The Sages therefore prohibited sitting upon any mattress made of *shaatnez* that is filled with soft material (see *Kesef Mishneh, Radvaz,* and *Mirkeves HaMishneh, Hil. Kilayim* 10:13). [Moreover, even in the case of a very firm cushion, which one would not sink into, the Sages prohibited having one's skin directly touch the mattress (see *Kilayim* 9:2; *Rambam, Hil. Kilayim* 10:13).]

15. Above (after note 12), Chinuch stated another reason, namely, that the Torah states (*Leviticus* 19:19), *a garment of kilayim, of shaatnez, shall not come upon you,* which implies that you may spread it beneath you. The Gemara (*Yevamos* 4b) cites both Scriptural sources and explains that the verse, *You shall not "wear" shaatnez,* teaches an additional qualification; namely, that even when *shaatnez* is placed over a person, it is prohibited only when the *shaatnez* offers a physical benefit, like a garment that provides comfort. The prohibition does not apply when the *shaatnez* provides no physical benefit. It emerges, then, that sitting on a firm mattress of *shaatnez* that is unfilled is permitted for two reasons: (1) because the *shaatnez* will not "come upon" the person; and (2) because a firm mattress does not provide comfort in the manner of a garment. [The second reason is necessary to explain the next law that Chinuch will cite.]

16. See *Teshuvos HaRashba* I §762.

17. As was explained in note 10, many commentators maintain that felts made of wool and linen are not Biblically considered *shaatnez,* as their fibers were not spun and twined. Now, the Sages generally prohibited felts made of wool and linen. However, *Rashba* (the "master" that Chinuch is citing; see previous note)

וְיֵשׁ שֶׁרוֹצֶה לְהַחְמִיר עַל עַצְמוֹ בָּזֶה וְלֹא מִחוּ בְּיָדוֹ[18]. וּמִטַּעַם זֶה דֶּרֶךְ מַלְבּוּשׁ אָסְרָה תּוֹרָה הִתִּירוּ גַּם כֵּן לְמוֹכְרֵי כְּסוּת[19] לִמְכֹּר כְּדַרְכָּן, וּבִלְבַד שֶׁלֹּא יְכַוְּנוּ לְהִתְחַמֵּם בָּהֶן כְּלָל[20]. וּמִכָּל מָקוֹם אַף עַל פִּי שֶׁהִתִּירוּ דָּבָר זֶה, הַסַּרְסוּרִין הַצְּנוּעִין וְטוֹבִים מַפְשִׁילִין בִּגְדֵי הַכִּלְאַיִם כְּשֶׁמּוֹכְרִין אוֹתָם בְּמַקֵּל לַאֲחוֹרֵיהֶן שֶׁלֹּא יִגְּעוּ בָּהֶן[21]. וְאָמְרוּ זִכְרוֹנָם לִבְרָכָה שֶׁהַכִּלְאַיִם אֵין לָהֶן שִׁעוּר, אֲפִלּוּ חוּט אֶחָד בְּבֶגֶד גָּדוֹל אוֹסֵר הַכֹּל עַד שֶׁיָּסִיר אוֹתוֹ. הַכָּלָךְ שֶׁהוּא כְּעֵין צֶמֶר וְהוּא גָּדֵל עַל הָאֲבָנִים שֶׁבְּיָם הַמֶּלַח[22] אָסוּר עִם הַפִּשְׁתָּן מִדְּרַבָּנָן מִפְּנֵי מַרְאִית הָעַיִן[23].

וְיֵשׁ שֶׁרוֹצֶה לְהַחְמִיר עַל עַצְמוֹ בָּזֶה – **There is, however, one** authority **who wants to be stringent upon himself in this** matter and prohibit such hats, וְלֹא מִחוּ בְּיָדוֹ – **and [other authorities] did not protest against his** doing so.[18]

וּמִטַּעַם זֶה דֶּרֶךְ מַלְבּוּשׁ אָסְרָה תּוֹרָה – **Also based on this reasoning, that the Torah prohibited** *shaatnez* only when it is used in **the manner of a garment,** הִתִּירוּ גַּם כֵּן לְמוֹכְרֵי כְּסוּת לִמְכֹּר כְּדַרְכָּן – **[the Sages]** (*Kilayim* 9:5) **similarly permitted those who sell clothing,**[19] and don the clothing in order to display their wares, **to sell** the clothing **in their usual manner** (i.e., while wearing them), וּבִלְבַד שֶׁלֹּא יְכַוְּנוּ לְהִתְחַמֵּם בָּהֶן כְּלָל – **provided that they have no intent at all to be warmed by [the *shaatnez* garments].**[20] וּמִכָּל מָקוֹם אַף עַל פִּי שֶׁהִתִּירוּ דָּבָר זֶה – **Nevertheless, although [the Sages] permitted this,** הַסַּרְסוּרִין הַצְּנוּעִין וְטוֹבִים מַפְשִׁילִין בִּגְדֵי הַכִּלְאַיִם כְּשֶׁמּוֹכְרִין אוֹתָם בְּמַקֵּל לַאֲחוֹרֵיהֶן – **the fine and righteous salesmen hang *shaatnez* garments on a stick behind them when selling them,** שֶׁלֹּא יִגְּעוּ בָּהֶן – **so that [the garments] should not touch them.**[21]

Chinuch closes with two additional laws:

וְאָמְרוּ זִכְרוֹנָם לִבְרָכָה – **[The Sages], of blessed memory, stated** (*Rambam, Hil. Kilayim* 10:5; see *Niddah* 61b and *Tosefta, Kilayim* 5:8) שֶׁהַכִּלְאַיִם אֵין לָהֶן שִׁעוּר – **that there is no** minimum **amount for** the ***shaatnez*** prohibition; אֲפִלּוּ חוּט אֶחָד בְּבֶגֶד גָּדוֹל אוֹסֵר הַכֹּל – that is, **even one thread** of wool or linen **in a large garment** of the other type **renders the entire** garment **prohibited,** עַד שֶׁיָּסִיר אוֹתוֹ – **until one removes [that thread].**

הַכָּלָךְ שֶׁהוּא כְּעֵין צֶמֶר וְהוּא גָּדֵל עַל הָאֲבָנִים שֶׁבְּיָם הַמֶּלַח – ***Kalach,* which is** a fiber **similar to wool that grows on the stones in the salt**-water **sea,**[22] אָסוּר עִם הַפִּשְׁתָּן מִדְּרַבָּנָן – **is Rabbinically prohibited in** a **linen** garment, מִפְּנֵי מַרְאִית הָעַיִן – **due to the appearance of wrongdoing.**[23]

NOTES

maintains that the Rabbinic prohibition pertains only to soft felt that can be worn like a garment. Hats of stiff felt are permitted even by Rabbinic law, since placing something stiff on the head cannot truly be considered "wearing."

18. See *Beis Yosef* [and *Shulchan Aruch*], *Yoreh Deah* 301:2, for the various opinions regarding these hats. See also *Derech Emunah, Tziyun HaHalachah, Hil. Kilayim* 10:134.

19. I.e., they sell *shaatnez* garments to non-Jews (*Meiri, Yevamos* 4b).

20. Since the merchant's intent in wearing the garment is purely for commercial purposes, and he has no intent to derive pleasure from it, it is not included in the prohibition against "wearing" *shaatnez* (see above, note 15). This is permitted, however, only as long as the merchant has no intent to derive benefit from the garment, such as to be warmed by it, or to protect himself with it from the rain or sun. See Insight for further discussion.

[Acharonim discuss whether it is permissible to try on a garment that may contain *shaatnez* for size (see *Chochmas Adam* 106:20); see *Teshuvos Minchas Yitzchak* IV §15; *Be'er Moshe* II §101-103; *Shevet HaLevi* II §169. See also *Derech Emunah* ibid. with *Tziyun HaHalachah*.]

21. Merchants who are meticulous in their mitzvah observance are concerned that they may come to derive pleasure from the garment, which is prohibited. They therefore avoid having the garment touch them at all (*Derech Emunah, Hil. Kilayim* 10:77).

22. [*Rambam* (whom Chinuch follows) typically refers to a salt-water sea as יָם הַמֶּלַח (*Derech Emunah, Hil. Kilayim* 10:3).]

The exact translation of *kalach* is unclear; for discussion, see *Yad Avraham* (ArtScroll) to *Kilayim* 9:2.

23. מַרְאִית הָעַיִן, *maris ayin*; literally, *sight of the eye.* Although the Torah prohibited only a combination of wool and linen, the Sages prohibited also the combination of a wool-like fiber with linen, as well as the combination of a linen-like fiber with wool, to avoid the appearance of wrongdoing. See Insight to Mitzvah 148 for further discussion of the prohibition of *maris ayin*.

וְיֶתֶר פְּרָטֵי הַמִּצְוָה מְבֹאָרִים בְּמַסֶּכֶת כִּלְאַיִם (פרק תשיעי) **וּבְמַסֶּכֶת שַׁבָּת וּבְסוֹף מַכּוֹת**[24].

וְנוֹהֵג אִסּוּר זֶה בְּכָל מָקוֹם וּבְכָל זְמַן, בִּזְכָרִים וּנְקֵבוֹת[25].

וְעוֹבֵר עַל זֶה וְלָבַשׁ כִּלְאַיִם דְּאוֹרַיְתָא אוֹ הִתְכַּסָּה בָּהֶן חַיָּב מַלְקוּת, וּבְכִלְאַיִם דְּרַבָּנָן חַיָּב מַכַּת מַרְדּוּת דְּרַבָּנָן. וְהַלּוֹבֵשׁ כִּלְאַיִם וַאֲפִלּוּ כָּל הַיּוֹם כֻּלּוֹ אֵינוֹ לוֹקֶה אֶלָּא אַחַת, אֲבָל הוֹצִיא רֹאשׁוֹ מִן הַבֶּגֶד וְהֶחֱזִירוֹ, הוֹצִיא רֹאשׁוֹ וְהֶחֱזִירוֹ, אַף עַל פִּי שֶׁלֹּא פָּשַׁט הַבֶּגֶד כֻּלּוֹ, חַיָּב עַל כָּל אַחַת וְאַחַת[26], **וּבַמֶּה דְּבָרִים אֲמוּרִים שֶׁהוּא חַיָּב אַחַת עַל כָּל הַיּוֹם כֻּלּוֹ, כְּשֶׁהִתְרוּ בוֹ הַתְרָאָה אַחַת, אֲבָל אִם הִתְרוּ בוֹ וְאָמְרוּ לוֹ פְּשֹׁט פְּשֹׁט וְהוּא לָבוּשׁ בּוֹ וְשָׁהָה כְּדֵי לִלְבֹּשׁ וְלִפְשֹׁט**[27] **אַחַר שֶׁהִתְרוּ בוֹ, הֲרֵי זֶה חַיָּב עַל כָּל שְׁהִיָּה וּשְׁהִיָּה שֶׁהִתְרוּ בוֹ עָלֶיהָ**

וְיֶתֶר פְּרָטֵי הַמִּצְוָה מְבֹאָרִים בְּמַסֶּכֶת כִּלְאַיִם וּבְמַסֶּכֶת שַׁבָּת וּבְסוֹף מַכּוֹת — These laws, **and the additional details of the mitzvah, are detailed in Tractate *Kilayim*** (Ch. 9), **in Tractate *Shabbos*** (54a), **and at the end of** Tractate ***Makkos*** (21a-21b).[24]

Applicability of the Mitzvah

וְנוֹהֵג אִסּוּר זֶה בְּכָל מָקוֹם וּבְכָל זְמַן בִּזְכָרִים וּנְקֵבוֹת — **This prohibition applies in every location and in all times,** and pertains **to** both **men and women.**[25]

וְעוֹבֵר עַל זֶה — **One who transgresses this** prohibition, וְלָבַשׁ כִּלְאַיִם דְּאוֹרַיְתָא אוֹ הִתְכַּסָּה בָּהֶן — **and puts on** a garment that is ***shaatnez* by Biblical law, or covers himself with it,** חַיָּב מַלְקוּת — **is liable to *malkus*.** וּבְכִלְאַיִם דְּרַבָּנָן חַיָּב מַכַּת מַרְדּוּת דְּרַבָּנָן — **In** regard to something that is ***shaatnez* by Rabbinic law, [one who transgresses] is liable to the Rabbinic** penalty of ***makkas mardus*.** וְהַלּוֹבֵשׁ כִּלְאַיִם וַאֲפִלּוּ כָּל הַיּוֹם כֻּלּוֹ אֵינוֹ לוֹקֶה אֶלָּא אַחַת — **One who wears** a garment that is ***shaatnez* by Biblical law, even for an entire day, incurs only one liability to *malkus*.** אֲבָל הוֹצִיא רֹאשׁוֹ מִן הַבֶּגֶד וְהֶחֱזִירוֹ הוֹצִיא רֹאשׁוֹ וְהֶחֱזִירוֹ — **However, if he took his head out of the garment and put it back in,** and again **took it out and put it back in,** אַף עַל פִּי שֶׁלֹּא פָּשַׁט הַבֶּגֶד כֻּלּוֹ — **even if he did not remove the garment entirely,** חַיָּב עַל כָּל אַחַת וְאַחַת — **he is liable for each and every** time that he put his head into the garment.[26] וּבַמֶּה דְּבָרִים אֲמוּרִים שֶׁהוּא חַיָּב אַחַת עַל כָּל הַיּוֹם כֻּלּוֹ — **Furthermore, with regard to what** situation **was it stated that one is liable** only **once for the entire day?** כְּשֶׁהִתְרוּ בוֹ הַתְרָאָה אַחַת — **When they warned him only once.** אֲבָל אִם הִתְרוּ בוֹ וְאָמְרוּ לוֹ פְּשֹׁט פְּשֹׁט — **However, if they warned him** repeatedly, **and told him, "Remove** the garment!" **"Remove** the garment!" וְהוּא לָבוּשׁ בּוֹ — **and he** continued **wearing it,** וְשָׁהָה כְּדֵי לִלְבֹּשׁ וְלִפְשֹׁט אַחַר שֶׁהִתְרוּ בוֹ — **and he delayed** removing it for **enough** time **to put it on and remove it**[27] **after being warned,** הֲרֵי זֶה חַיָּב עַל כָּל שְׁהִיָּה וּשְׁהִיָּה שֶׁהִתְרוּ בוֹ עָלֶיהָ — **he is**

NOTES

24. These laws are codified in *Rambam, Hil. Kilayim* Ch. 10, and in *Shulchan Aruch, Yoreh Deah* §298-304.

25. I.e., it applies both in Eretz Yisrael and in the Diaspora, regardless of whether the *Beis HaMikdash* is standing or not; and, as is the general rule pertaining to mitzvah-prohibitions, it applies to both men and women.

26. For example, in the case of a shawl that covers the head and part of the body, each time one frees his head from the shawl, it is considered as if he removed the garment. Thus, rewrapping one's head in the shawl constitutes a new transgression.

As we have seen many times (see, for example, Mitzvah 32, after note 37), one who transgresses a prohibition does not incur *malkus* unless witnesses testify that he performed that act after having received a warning (*hasraah*). Now, as a rule, one who transgresses a prohibition multiple times incurs multiple *malkus* only if *hasraah* was given *each time* he transgressed the prohibition. Here too, one incurs *malkus* for each time that he put on the garment only if he received *hasraah* each time (*Kesef Mishneh, Hil. Kilayim* 10:30).

27. I.e., to remove the garment, and to then put it back on (*Makkos* 21b; *Rambam, Hil. Kilayim* 10:30). That is, he wore it for at least the amount of time that it would take to remove the garment *entirely* and put it back on (*Derech Emunah* there §146, citing *Ri Korkos* and *Mishneh LaMelech*). [This is in contrast to the previous case, where he *actually* took his head out of the garment and put it back in, in which case he is liable (if he receives an additional *hasraah*) even though the amount of time that it takes to remove the garment entirely and put it back on has not elapsed (see *Tosafos, Shevuos* 17a ד״ה או אין צריך).]

וְאַף עַל פִּי שֶׁלֹּא פָּשַׁט[28].

liable for each and every delay regarding which he was warned, וְאַף עַל פִּי שֶׁלֹּא פָּשַׁט – **even though he did not remove [the garment]** and put it back on.[28]

NOTES

28. Since the *shaatnez* prohibition pertains to the act of donning a garment that is *shaatnez,* as well as to remaining clothed in it (see note 2), one who fails to remove the garment after being warned to do so incurs *malkus.*

Now, as a rule, the *malkus* penalty does not apply in the case of a לָאו שֶׁאֵין בּוֹ מַעֲשֶׂה, *a prohibition that does not entail an action.* Why then should one incur *malkus* for remaining clothed in a garment of *shaatnez,* when that does not entail any action? *Tosafos* (ibid.) explain that this case is considered to entail an action, since the original act of donning the garment was performed with an action.

Insight: P'sik Reisha — An Act With an Inevitable Result

In his discussion of the laws of this mitzvah, Chinuch (at note 19) cites the ruling of the Mishnah (*Kilayim* 9:5) that a merchant is permitted to wear a garment of *shaatnez* in order to display it, as long as he has no intention to derive physical benefit from it. This, Chinuch states, is learned from the fact that the Torah prohibited *shaatnez* only "in the manner of wearing," that is, in a manner that gives one physical comfort (see note 15). Now, the Mishnah does not state that the merchant may not *derive* any benefit from the garment, rather, that he must not *intend* to derive benefit from it. Clearly, he may wear the garment for display even if it actually warms him. Why is this so?

The Gemara (*Shabbos* 29b) explains that this is based on the principle of דָּבָר שֶׁאֵין מִתְכַּוֵּן, *davar she'ein miskavein* (*an unintended result*). This principle refers to a case where a person does one action and, as a result, a second, unintended action occurs. If the first, intended, action is a permitted one, he may do it, even though there is a possibility that a second, prohibited action will occur as a result. This principle, however, is a matter of Tannaic dispute. The classic case discussed by the Gemara is where a person drags a bench on the ground on the Sabbath (which is permitted), and in the process he unintentionally creates a furrow in the ground (which is prohibited). R' Yehudah maintains that it is forbidden to drag the bench, for in his opinion a *davar she'ein miskavein* is prohibited. R' Shimon, on the other hand, maintains that it is permitted to drag the bench. He explains that since there is no intention to create a furrow, only to drag a bench, we may ignore the unintended result. In other words, a *davar she'ein miskavein* is permitted.

The same dispute pertains to our case of a merchant who wears a *shaatnez* garment for the purpose of advertising it, where his intention is only to display his wares, and not to derive any benefit from the garment. Since the prohibition of *shaatnez* applies only when there is physical benefit, the merchant's intention is for a permitted act, but that act may result in a prohibited one, i.e., if the merchant actually derives benefit from the garment. According to R' Yehudah, if the merchant derives benefit from the garment, he is forbidden to wear it even though he does not intend to derive that benefit; but according to R' Shimon, as long as he does not *intend* to derive benefit, it is permitted. The Mishnah that permits wearing it follows the opinion of R' Shimon, whom the halachah follows (see ibid. 95a).

Rishonim, however, find difficulty with this law, for the Gemara states (ibid. 75a) that in a case where transgression would be an *inevitable* consequence of the permitted act, R' Shimon concedes that the act is prohibited. The Gemara expresses this idea with the expression, פְּסִיק רֵישֵׁיהּ וְלֹא יָמוּת [*"p'sik reisha"*], *cut off its head, will it not die?* That is, a person cannot cut off an animal's head on the Sabbath and claim that "he did not intend" for it to die, because the animal's death is *inevitable* (killing a living creature is a desecration of the Sabbath). Likewise, for this reason, R' Shimon forbids dragging a *heavy* bench, which will certainly create a furrow in the ground, on the Sabbath (*Rashi, Succah* 33b ד"ה והא מודי). With regard to our case as well, assert Rishonim, although the merchant's intent is only to display the garment he is wearing, nevertheless, since he will inevitably derive some benefit from it, it is a situation of *p'sik reisha,* which is prohibited even according to R' Shimon!

Some Rishonim resolve this issue by explaining that the principle of *p'sik reisha* is limited to a situation where one will obtain satisfaction from the unintended result of his action. If, however, one

is indifferent to the result, it remains permitted as a *davar she'ein miskavein,* even though the result is inevitable. This is the position taken by *Aruch* (ערך פסק; see *Rabbeinu Chananel* to *Shabbos* 103a [end of ד"ה המכה]; *R' Hai Gaon,* cited by *Rashba* there). Thus, in the case of a garment merchant, since the merchant is indifferent to any benefit that the garment would offer, the law of *p'sik reisha* does not apply, and he may wear the garment.

Many other Rishonim, however, maintain that the rule that a *p'sik reisha* is prohibited applies whether one would be pleased with the outcome or not. And as far as why this case of wearing a garment of *shaatnez* in order to display it is not considered a *p'sik reisha,* they explain that the Mishnah means to permit displaying the garment only when the merchant is wearing adequate clothing aside from the *shaatnez,* so that it is not certain that he will benefit from the garment of *shaatnez.* Thus, it does not fall into the category of *p'sik reisha* (see *Tosafos, Rashba,* and *Ritva* to *Shabbos* 29b). For another resolution, see *Ramban, Shabbos* 111a, and *Ran* to *Rif* there, fol. 41a.

It is of note that *Rambam* seems to maintain that the Mishnah permits merchants only to drape the *shaatnez* garments over their shoulders, but not to actually wear them (see *Hil. Kilayim* 10:16 with *Kesef Mishneh* to 10:18, and *Derech Emunah* 10:75).

For further discussion, see *Ner Avraham* §1-4; *Bnei Tzion* VI, p. 319; *Mishnas R' Aharon, Yevamos* §4; *Kehillos Yaakov, Beitzah* 11:2; *Succas David, Yevamos* 4b.

☞ Glossary ☜

Acharon [pl. **Acharonim**] — a Torah authority of the period following the **Rishonim** (from approx. 1450 C.E.).

Aggadah — homiletic teaching of the Sages. See **Midrash.**

alos hashachar — dawn; first light.

am haaretz [pl. **amei haaretz**] — a common, ignorant person who, possibly, is not meticulous in his observance of **halachah.**

amah [pl. **amos**] — cubit; a linear measure equaling six **tefachim.** Opinions regarding its contemporary equivalent range between 18 and 24 inches.

amah ivriah — Hebrew maidservant.

Amora [pl. **Amoraim**] — sage of the **Gemara;** cf. **Tanna.**

androgynos — a person or animal that possesses the signs of both genders, and whose halachic status as male or female is doubtful.

arayos — see **ervah.**

asei — mitzvah-obligation.

asham [pl. **ashamos**] — guilt offering; an offering brought to atone for one of several specific sins. It is one of the **kodshei kodashim.**

asham talui — an *asham* offering brought by a person who is unsure whether he has inadvertently committed a **kares**-bearing sin.

asheirah — a tree designated for worship, or under which an idol is placed.

asmachta — lit. reliance. (a) a conditional commitment made by a party who does not really expect to have to honor it; (b) a verse cited by the **Gemara** not as a Scriptural basis for the law but rather as an allusion to a Rabbinic law.

av hatumah [pl. **avos hatumah** or **avos hatumos**] — an object possessing a degree of **tumah** sufficient to contaminate a person or utensil.

avodah [pl. **avodos**] — the sacrificial service, or any facet of it. There are four critical *avodos* to the sacrificial service. They are **shechitah, kabbalah, holachah,** and **zerikah.**

avodah zarah — idol worship, idolatry.

Azarah — Courtyard of the **Temple.**

Azazel — a place in the wilderness to where a he-goat was sent on **Yom Kippur** and pushed off a cliff.

baal keri [pl. **baalei keri**] — one who experienced a seminal emission. He is **tamei** (ritually impure) and must immerse in a **mikveh.**

bamah [pl. **bamos**] — lit. high place; altar. This refers to any altar other than the Altar of the Tabernacle or **Temple.** During certain brief periods of Jewish history, it was permitted to offer sacrifices on a *bamah.*

Baraisa [pl. **Baraisos**] — the statements of **Tannaim** not included in the **Mishnah.**

bechor — (a) firstborn male child; (b) firstborn male kosher animal. The human *bechor* must be redeemed by giving five **sela'im** to a Kohen. The animal *bechor* is born with sacrificial sanctity, and must be given to a **Kohen** who offers it (if unblemished) in the **Temple** and eats its sacred meat.

bedek habayis — upkeep of the **Temple;** funds of the Temple Treasury designated for Temple maintenance.

beheimah — domestic species, livestock. In regard to various laws, the Torah distinguishes between *beheimah,* domestic species, e.g., cattle, sheep, goats; and, **chayah,** wild species, e.g., deer, antelope.

bein hashemashos — the twilight period preceding night. The legal status of *bein hashemashos* as day or night is uncertain.

beis av [pl. **batei avos**] — lit. father's house. See **mishmar.**

beis din — court; Rabbinic court comprised minimally of three members. Such a court is empowered to rule on civil matters. See **Sanhedrin.**

Beis HaMikdash — Holy **Temple** in Jerusalem. The **Temple** edifice comprised (a) the **Ulam** (Antechamber); (b) the **Heichal** (Holy); and (c) the **Holy of Holies.**

beis se'ah — lit. "area of a *se'ah,*" a field that is 2,500 sq. **amos.**

ben yomo — lit. "within its day," a utensil that has been used within the last 24 hours.

binyan av — one of the thirteen principles of Biblical hermeneutics. This is exegetical derivation based on a logical analogy between different areas of law. Whenever a commonality of law or essence is found in different areas of Torah

law, an analogy is drawn between them, and the laws that apply to one can therefore be assumed to apply to the others as well.

Bircas HaMazon — the blessings recited after a meal.

Bircas Kohanim — the Priestly Blessing; the blessing the **Kohanim** are obligated to confer upon the congregation, consisting of the verses in *Numbers* (6:24-26).

bitul — (a) **bitul b'rov** — the principle of nullification in a majority. Under certain circumstances, a mixture of items of differing legal status assumes the status of its majority component; (b) **bitul chametz** — the process of declaring *chametz* null and ownerless.

biur — removal. **Shemittah** produce may be kept in the home only as long as that species is available in the field for animals. Once the produce disappears from the field, it must be removed from the home.

bogeress — see **naarah.**

bris milah — ritual circumcision.

chagigah offering — festival offering that every adult Jewish male is required to bring on the first day of **Pesach, Shavuos,** and **Succos.** It is a type of **shelamim** offering.

chalifin — See **kinyan chalifin.**

chalitzah — See **yibum.**

challah — portion removed from a dough of any of the five grains (wheat, barley, spelt, rye, oats); if *challah* is not taken, the dough is **tevel** and may not be eaten. [In earlier times, *challah* was given to a Kohen; nowadays, it is removed and burned.]

chalutzah — a woman who underwent **chalitzah.**

chametz — leavened products of the five species of grain; i.e., wheat, barley, spelt, rye, and oats.

Chanukah — the holiday that commemorates the Maccabean victory over the Greeks. It begins on the 25th of **Kislev** and lasts for eight days.

chatas [pl. **chataos**] — sin offering; an offering generally brought in atonement for the inadvertent transgression of a prohibition punishable by **kares** when transgressed deliberately. It is one of the **kodshei kodashim.**

chatzitzah — interposition: A *chatzitzah* between the body or hair of a person immersing and the water of the **mikveh** may invalidate the immersion.

chayah — a non-domestic species of animal (e.g., deer or antelope), as distinguished from **beheimah.**

chazakah — (a) legal presumption that conditions remain unchanged unless proven otherwise; (b) one of the methods of acquiring real estate; it consists of performing an act of improving the property, such as enclosing it with a fence or plowing it in preparation for planting; (c) "established rights"; uncontested usage of another's property establishes the right to such usage, for since the owner registered no protest, acquiescence is assumed; (d) uncontested holding of real property for three years as a basis for claiming acquisition of title from the prior owner.

cheil — a ten-**amah**-wide area around the **Beis HaMikdash** Courtyard beyond which non-Jews and those contaminated with corpse-**tumah** were not permitted to enter.

cheilev — certain fats of cattle, sheep, and goats (i.e., the kosher species of **beheimah**), which the Torah forbids for human consumption under penalty of **kares.** These are primarily the hind fats (suet) placed on the Altar, but are forbidden even in non-sacrificial animals.

chenek — strangulation; one of the four forms of the death penalty mandated by **beis din** for egregious sins.

cherem — (a) a vow in which one uses the expression "*cherem*" to consecrate property, placing it under jurisdiction of either the Kohanim or the Temple; (b) land or property upon which a ban has been declared, forbidding its use to anyone; (c) excommunication.

cheresh — lit. a deaf person; generally used for a deaf-mute who can neither hear nor speak. A *cheresh* is legally deemed mentally incompetent and his actions or commitments are not legally significant or binding.

chillul — deconsecration; the act of removing the sanctity of a sacred item by giving its monetary value to **hekdesh.**

chillul Hashem — lit. profanation of God's Name; behavior that casts God's people in a negative light.

Chinuch — lit. education, training. (a) an abbreviation of the title of this work (**Sefer Ha-Chinuch** — Book of Education), in which the author educates his son and others about the 613 Mitzvos. (b) the obligation that the Sages placed on a parent to train his child in the performance of **mitzvos.**

Chol HaMoed — the Intermediate Days of the festivals of **Pesach** and **Succos**; these enjoy a quasi-**Yom Tov** status.

chomesh — one "fifth"; payment that is equal to the principal plus one fourth.

Choshen — breastplate worn by the **Kohen Gadol.**

chullin — mundane items; any substance that is not sanctified. See **kodesh.**

chuppah — (a) the bridal canopy; (b) a procedure for effecting **nisuin,** the final stage of marriage.

dinar — a coin with a silver content equivalent to ninety-six grains of barley.

eiver min hachai — a limb (consisting of meat, sinews, and bones) separated from a live animal. It may not be eaten by Jew and non-Jew alike, and conveys **tumah** like a **neveilah.**

emurin — Sacrificial parts of an animal offering that are burned on the Altar. They consist of certain fats and organs; see **cheilev.**

ephah [pl. **ephos**] — a measure of volume equal to three **se'ah** (432 eggs).

erech [pl. **arachin**] — a fixed valuation. The *erech* of a person is the amount fixed by the Torah for each of eight different groupings classified by age and gender.

Eretz Yisrael — Land of Israel.

erusin — betrothal, the first stage of marriage. This can be effected by the man giving the woman an object of value in the presence of witnesses, to betroth her. The couple is then considered legally married in most respects, but certain privileges and responsibilities of marriage are not yet active. See **nisuin.**

ervah [pl. **arayos**] — (a) matters pertaining to intimate relationships forbidden under penalty of **kares** or death, as enumerated in *Leviticus* Ch. 18; (b) a woman forbidden to a man under pain of one of these penalties.

eved ivri — Hebrew servant; a Jewish man sold as an indentured servant, generally for a period of six years. Either he is sold by the court because he was convicted of stealing and lacks the funds to make restitution, or he sells himself for reasons of poverty.

Gaon [pl. **Geonim**] — title accorded the heads of the academies in Sura and Pumbedisa, the two Babylonian seats of Jewish learning, from the late 6th to mid-11th centuries C.E. They served as the link in the chain of Torah tradition that joined the **Amoraim** to the **Rishonim.**

Gemara — the section of the Talmud that explains the **Mishnah.**

gematria — numerical value of a Hebrew letter or word.

ger (ger tzedek) — a proselyte; convert to the Jewish faith.

ger toshav — a non-Jew residing in the Holy Land who has formally undertaken to abide by the seven precepts of the Noahide Code but has not converted to Judaism.

get [pl. **gittin**] — bill of divorce; the document that, when placed in the wife's possession, effects the dissolution of a marriage.

gezeirah shavah — one of the thirteen principles of Biblical hermeneutics. If a similar word or phrase occurs in two otherwise unrelated passages in the Torah, the principle of *gezeirah shavah* teaches that these passages are linked to each other, and the laws of one passage are applied to the other. Only those words that are designated by the Oral Sinaitic Law for this purpose may serve as a basis for a *gezeirah shavah.*

go'eil hadam — avenging relative of one who was killed.

hagalah — purging. Any utensil used for eating or cooking that absorbed food that is prohibited for consumption has to go through a process of purging in boiling water in order to render it *kosher* — usable.

hagbahah — lifting. One of the methods of **kinyan** used for moveable objects.

Haggadah — text of the Passover Seder.

halachah [pl. **halachos**] — (a) a Torah law; (b) [u.c.] the body of Torah law; (c) in cases of dispute, the position accepted as definitive by the later authorities and followed in practice; (d) a **Halachah LeMoshe MiSinai.**

Halachah LeMoshe MiSinai — laws taught orally to Moses at Sinai, which cannot be derived from the Written Torah.

half-shekel — While the Temple stood, every Jew was required to donate a half-**shekel** annually to fund the purchase of the various communal offerings (including among others, the daily **tamid** offerings and the festival **mussaf** offerings).

Hallel — lit. praise; a group of Psalms (113-118) recited on **Pesach, Succos, Shavuos, Chanukah,** and **Rosh Chodesh.**

hasraah — warning. One does not incur the death penalty or **malkus** unless he was warned,

immediately prior to commission, of the forbidden nature of the crime and the punishment to which he would be liable, and he acknowledged the warning.

hefker — ownerless.

Heichal — See **Beis HaMikdash.**

hekdesh — (a) items consecrated to the **Temple** treasury or as offerings; (b) the state of consecration; (c) the **Temple** treasury.

hekeish — an exegetical derivation based on a connection that Scripture makes (often through juxtaposition) between different areas of law. By making this connection, Scripture teaches that the laws that apply to one area can be applied to the other area as well.

hin — liquid measure equal to twelve **lugin** or three **kabim.**

holachah — conveying the blood of an offering to the Altar for **zerikah;** it is one of the four essential blood **avodos.**

Holy — Kodesh; the area of the **Beis HaMikdash** that housed the Inner Altar, the **Shulchan,** and the **Menorah.**

Holy of Holies — Kodesh HaKodashim; the area of the **Beis HaMikdash** that housed the Ark and could be entered only by the **Kohen Gadol** on Yom Kippur.

ir hanidachas — a subverted city; a city in Eretz Yisrael in which the majority of the population worshiped idols. Subject to certain conditions, the city is destroyed along with all its property and its guilty inhabitants are executed.

ir miklat (pl. **arei miklat**) — city of refuge; city set aside as refuge for unintentional killers. All the Levitical cities were in this category.

issar — a coin of the Talmudic period, equal to $\frac{1}{24}$ of a **dinar.**

issaron — a dry measure equal to one-tenth of an **ephah** (the volume of 43.2 eggs).

Iyar — second month of the Hebrew calendar.

kabbalah — (a) term used throughout the Talmud to refer to the books of the Prophets; (b) [u.c.] the esoteric area of Torah knowledge; (c) receiving in a **kli shareis** the blood of a sacrificial animal that is slaughtered; one of the four blood **avodos.**

kal vachomer — lit. light and heavy, or lenient and stringent; an *a fortiori* argument. One of the thirteen principles of Biblical hermeneutics. It involves the following reasoning: If a particular stringency applies in a usually lenient case, it must certainly apply in a more serious case; the converse of this argument is also a *kal vachomer.*

kares — excision; Divinely imposed premature death decreed by the Torah for certain classes of transgression.

kashering — the process by which a nonkosher utensil is rendered fit for use; see **hagalah.**

kashrus — kosher status.

kav [pl. **kabim**] — a measure equal to four **lugin** (the volume of 24 eggs).

kedei achilas peras — the amount of time it takes one to eat a *peras,* half of a standard-size loaf of bread.

Kehunah — priesthood; the state of being a **Kohen.**

kemitzah — the first of four essential services of a **minchah** offering. The **Kohen** closes the middle three fingers of his right hand over his palm and scoops out flour from the *minchah* to form the **kometz** that is burned on the **Altar.**

keri — see **baal keri.**

kesubah — (a) marriage contract; the legal commitments of a husband to his wife upon their marriage, the foremost feature of which is the payment awarded her in the event of their divorce or his death; (b) document in which this agreement is recorded.

kezayis — the volume of an olive; minimum amount of food whose consumption is considered "eating."

Kiddush — (a) the benediction recited over wine before the evening and morning meals on the Sabbath and **Yom Tov;** (b) sanctification of purification water with ashes of the **parah adumah.**

Kiddush Hashem — sanctification of God's Name; see **chillul Hashem.**

kiddushin — the procedure that establishes the first stage of marriage [**erusin**].

kilayim — various forbidden mixtures, including: **shaatnez** (cloth made from a blend of wool and linen); cross-breeding of animals; cross-breeding (or side-by-side planting) of certain food crops; working with different species of animals yoked together; and mixtures of the vineyard.

kinyan [pl. **kinyanim**] — formal act of acquisition; an action that causes an agreement or exchange to be legally binding.

kinyan chalifin — lit. acquisition by exchange.

(a) Even exchange: an exchange of two items of comparable value, in which each item serves as payment for the other. The acquisition of any one of the items automatically effects the acquisition of the other. (b) Uneven exchange: An item of relatively negligible value is given in order to effect the acquisition of the other item. A kerchief or the like is traditionally used.

kinyan suddar — **kinyan** by means of a kerchief; see **kinyan chalifin.**

Kislev — ninth month of the Hebrew calendar.

Kiyor — the laver used by the **Kohanim** in the **Temple** Courtyard to wash their hands and feet before performing the **avodah.**

kli shareis [pl. **klei shareis**] — service vessel(s); a vessel sanctified for use in the **Temple** sacrificial service.

kodashim — sacrificial foods.

kodashim kalim — offerings of lesser holiness (one of the two classifications of sacrificial offerings). They may be eaten anywhere in Jerusalem by any **tahor** person. They include the **todah,** regular **shelamim, bechor, nazir's ram, maaser,** and **pesach offerings.** This category of offerings is not subject to the stringencies applied to **kodshei kodashim.**

kodesh — (a) any consecrated object; (b) [u.c.] the anterior chamber of the **Temple** — the **Holy;** (c) portions of sacrificial offerings.

Kodesh HaKodashim — see **Holy of Holies.**

kodshei kodashim — most-holy offerings (one of the two classifications of sacrificial offerings). They may be eaten only in the Temple Courtyard and only by male **Kohanim.** They include the **olah** (which may not be eaten at all), **chatas, asham,** and communal **shelamim.** These are subject to greater stringencies than **kodashim kalim.**

Kohen [pl. **Kohanim**] — member of the priestly family descended in the male line from Aaron. The Kohen is accorded the special priestly duties and privileges associated with the **Temple** service and is bound by special laws of sanctity.

Kohen Gadol — High Priest.

kometz [pl. **kematzim**] — See **kemitzah.**

kor — large dry measure; a measure of volume consisting of 30 **se'ah.**

korban — a sacrificial offering brought in the **Beis HaMikdash.**

lashon hara — derogatory speech.

lechatchilah — (a) before the fact; (b) performance of a **mitzvah** or procedure in the proper manner.

Lechem HaPanim — *panim* bread or showbread; specially shaped loaves of bread placed on the **Shulchan** in the **Temple,** accompanied by two spoonfuls of **levonah.**

leket — gleanings; one of the various portions of the harvest that the Torah grants to the poor. *Leket* refers to one or two stalks of grain that fall from the reaper when he gathers the harvest. See **matnos aniyim.**

lesech — one half of a **kor.**

Levi [pl. **Leviim**] — Levite; male descendant of the tribe of *Levi* in the male line, who is sanctified for auxiliary services in the **Beis HaMikdash,** and is entitled to receive **maaser rishon.**

levonah — an ingredient required to be placed on most **minchah** offerings, and also to be kept on the **Shulchan** together with the **Lechem HaPanim.** In each case, the *levonah* was a part of the offering that was ultimately burnt on the Altar.

lo saaseh — mitzvah-prohibition.

log [pl. **lugin**] — a liquid measure equal to the volume of six eggs.

maah [pl. **maos**] — a silver coin of the Talmudic period equal to one-sixth of a **dinar.**

maakeh — protective fence or railing.

maamad [pl. **maamados**] — lit. station; the group of **Yisraelim** designated to be present in the **Temple** when the communal offerings were made, as representatives of the entire nation. There were 24 such groups, corresponding to the twenty-four **mishmaros** of Kohanim and Leviim, and each served a week at a time on a rotating basis. Additional members of the *maamad* gathered in their local towns and fasted, prayed, and read certain Torah portions.

maasar ani — see **maaser.**

maasar beheimah — the animal tithe. The newborn kosher animals born to one's herds and flocks are gathered into a pen and made to pass through an opening one at a time. Every tenth animal is designated as *maaser beheimah.* It is brought as an offering in the Temple, in the category of **shelamim.**

maaser [pl. **maasros**] — tithe. It is a Biblical obligation to give two tithes, each known as *maaser,* from the produce of the Land of Israel. The first tithe (**maaser rishon**) is given to a **Levi.** The

second tithe (**maaser sheni**) is taken to Jerusalem and eaten there, or else is redeemed with coins which are then taken to Jerusalem for the purchase of food to be eaten there. In the third and sixth years of the seven-year **shemittah** cycle, the *maaser sheni* obligation is replaced with **maasar ani,** the tithe for the poor.

maaser rishon — see **maaser.**

maaser sheni — see **maaser.**

makkas mardus — lashes of discipline. This is the term used for lashes incurred by Rabbinic — rather than Biblical — law.

malkus — the thirty-nine lashes imposed by **beis din** for violations of most Biblical prohibitions, where a more severe punishment is not indicated.

mamzer [pl. **mamzerim;** f. **mamzeress**] — (a) offspring of most illicit relationships punishable by **kares** or capital punishment; (b) offspring of a *mamzer* or *mamzeress.*

maneh — (a) an amount of money equivalent to 100 **zuz;** (b) a measure of weight equaling that of 100 **zuz.**

matanos — the gift to the Kohen of the jaw, the foreleg, and the stomach of an animal.

matnos aniyim — gifts to the poor. These include **leket, shich'chah, pe'ah, peret, oleilos,** and **maasar ani.**

matzah — unleavened bread; any loaf made from dough that has not been allowed to ferment or rise.

matzeivah — raised structure.

me'ilah — misuse or misappropriation of sacred **Temple** property. This includes unlawfully benefiting from **Temple** property or removing such property from the Temple ownership.

Mechilta — the primary collection of Tannaic exegesis, mainly halachic in nature, on the Book of *Exodus.* [Chinuch also uses this term when referring to **Sifri Zuta.**]

mechussar kapparah [pl. **mechussarei kapparah**] — lit. lacking atonement; the status accorded to certain **tamei** people who are obligated to bring offerings on the day after their immersion in order to complete their purification and be permitted to enter the **Temple** Courtyard or partake of the offerings.

meisis — inciter; one who incites a fellow Jew to worship avodah zarah

melachah [pl. **melachos**] — labor; specifically, one of the thirty-nine labor categories whose performance is forbidden by the Torah on the Sabbath and **Yom Tov.** These prohibited categories are known as *avos melachah.* Activities whose prohibition is derived from one of these thirty-nine categories are known as *tolados* (sing. *toladah*) — secondary labor.

melikah — the unique manner in which bird offerings were slaughtered. The Kohen would cut the bird's neck from its rear with his thumbnail. Only birds for sacrificial purposes may be slaughtered by *melikah;* all others require **shechitah.**

Menorah — the seven-branched gold candelabrum that stood in the **Holy** of the **Temple.**

meshichah — pulling, or otherwise causing an object to move; one of the methods of **kinyan** used for moveable property.

mesirah — handing over; transferring an animal (or the like) to a buyer by handing him its reins (or the like); a means of acquisition used for moveable articles too heavy to be acquired via **meshichah** or **hagbahah.**

metzora [f. **metzoraas**] — a person who has contracted **tzaraas** (erroneously described as leprosy), an affliction mentioned in *Leviticus* (Chs. 13,14). *Tzaraas* manifests itself (on people) as white or light-colored spots on the body.

mezuzah [pl. **mezuzos**] — a small scroll, containing the passages of *Deuteronomy* 6:4-9 and 11:13-21, that is affixed to the right doorpost.

Mi shepara — a curse declared by **beis din** on a buyer or seller who reneged on an agreement to buy or sell an item after payment was made but before **meshichah** (or another valid **kinyan**) was performed.

Midrash — a collection of **Aggadah** and exegetical teachings from the Sages of the Talmudic period.

mikveh — ritualarium; a body of standing water containing at least forty **se'ah,** and consisting of waters naturally collected, without a vessel or any direct human intervention. It is used to purify (by immersion) people and utensils of their **tumah**-contamination.

mil — 2,000 **amos.** A measure of distance between 3,000 and 4,000 feet.

minchah — (a) [cap.] the afternoon prayer service; (b) [pl. **menachos**] a flour offering, generally consisting of fine wheat flour, oil, and **levonah,** part of which is burned on the **Altar.** See **kemitzah.**

minchas chinuch — (a) [cap.] the title of an encyclopedic work on the **Sefer HaChinuch** by R' Yosef Babad of Tornipol, first published in 5629 [1869]; (b) [l.c.] the **minchah** offering brought by each Kohen the first time he came to the **Temple** to perform **avodah.**

minchas nesachim — libation minchah. A libation of wine, and flour mixed with oil, which is required to accompany **olah** and **shelamim** offerings, and can also be donated independently.

minyan — quorum of ten adult Jewish males necessary for the communal prayer service and other matters.

Mishkan — Tabernacle; portable sanctuary initially erected in the Wilderness to house the Altars and sacred vessels that later were placed in the **Beis HaMikdash.** All offerings were brought in the *Mishkan* while it existed.

mishmar [pl. **mishmaros**] — lit. watch; one of the twenty-four watches of **Kohanim** and **Leviim** who served in the Temple for a week at a time on a rotating basis. These watches were subdivided into family groups known as **batei avos** [sing. **beis av**], each of which served on one day of the week.

Mishnah [pl. **Mishnahs, Mishnayos**] — (a) the organized teachings of the **Tannaim** compiled by R' Yehudah HaNasi; (b) a paragraph of that work.

mitzvah [pl. **mitzvos**] — commandment. One of the 613 commandments contained in the Torah, of which there are 248 mitzvah-obligations and 365 mitzvah-prohibitions.

mussaf — (a) additional offerings brought on the Sabbath, **Rosh Chodesh,** or **Yom Tov;** (b) [u.c.] the prayer service that is recited in lieu of these offerings.

naarah — a girl at least 12 years old who has sprouted two pubic hairs. This marks her coming of age to be considered an adult. She is deemed a *naarah* for six months; after that she becomes a *bogeress.*

Nasi [pl. **Nesiim**] — lit. prince; head of the **Sanhedrin** and de facto spiritual leader of the people.

nasin [f. **nesinah;** pl. **nesinim**] — descendant of the Gibeonites, who deceptively concluded a peace treaty with Joshua (*Joshua* 9:3-27) and converted to Judaism.

navi — prophet.

nazir [f. **nezirah**] — a person who takes the vow of **nezirus,** which prohibits him to drink wine, eat grapes, cut his hair, or contaminate himself with the **tumah** of a corpse.

Ne'ilah — the concluding prayer of **Yom Kippur.**

nedavah — donated offering. A voluntary offering donated without any prior obligation by means of the statement, הֲרֵי זוֹ קָרְבָּן, "This [animal] is hereby an offering." If the designated animal is lost or dies, the vower need not replace it, since his vow was only to bring "*this*" animal. See **neder.**

neder — (a) a vow that renders objects prohibited; (b) a vow to donate to **hekdesh.** (c) a vowed offering, meaning that the vower declared, הֲרֵי עָלַי קָרְבָּן, "It is hereby incumbent upon me to bring an offering," and then designated an animal to fulfill his pledge. If the designated animal is lost or dies, he must bring another in its place, since he has not yet fulfilled his vow "to bring *an* offering." See **nedavah.**

nefel — a stillborn or non-viable baby.

nega [pl. **negaim**] — spots of **tzaraas** that appear on the skin of a **metzora.**

nesachim — see **minchas nesachim.**

nesech wine — wine used for an idolatrous libation. It is prohibited for benefit.

neveilah [pl. **neveilos**] — an animal that has died without the benefit of a valid **shechitah.**

nezirus — the state of being a **nazir.**

niddah — a woman who has menstruated but has not yet completed her purification process, which concludes with immersion in a **mikveh.**

Nissan — first month of the Hebrew calendar.

nisuin — the second stage of marriage; it is effected by the husband formally bringing the wife into his domain, usually in the **chuppah** ceremony. See **erusin.**

nossar — part of a **korban** left over after the time to eat it has passed.

ochel nefesh — food preparation.

ohel — see **tumas ohel.**

olah [pl. **olos**] — burnt or elevation offering; an offering that is burnt in its entirety on the Altar. It is one of the **kodshei kodashim.**

oleh v'yoreid — lit. rising and falling; a variable **chatas** offering that the Torah prescribes for certain sins. Its value "rises and falls" depending on the offerer's financial status.

oleilos — underdeveloped grape clusters that the Torah commands the vineyard owner to leave for the poor.

Omer — an obligatory **minchah** offering brought on the sixteenth of **Nissan.**

onaah — (a) oppression, causing emotional distress; (b) financial aggrieving by overcharge or underpayment for an item.

onein [f. **onennes**] — a person on the day of the death of a close relative. Special laws of bereavement apply to an *onein.*

orlah — lit. sealed; fruit that grows on a tree during the first three years after it has been planted (or transplanted). The Torah prohibits any benefit from such fruit.

Panim Bread — see **Lechem HaPanim.**

parah adumah — lit. red cow. The *parah adumah* is slaughtered and burnt in a special procedure, and its ashes are mixed with springwater. The resulting mixture is used in the purification process of people or objects that have contracted **tumah** from a human corpse.

Paroches — curtain: specifically, the curtain that divided the **Holy** from the **Holy of Holies.**

pe'ah — the portion of the crop, generally the edge of the field, that must be left unreaped as a gift to the poor. See **matnos aniyim.**

pe'os [sing. **pe'ah**] — edges of the head that must be left unshorn.

peras — lit. piece, half; term for half the standard Mishnaic loaf of bread. A *peras* equals the volume of three eggs (four eggs according to others).

perikah — assisting in unloading an animal.

peret — individual grapes that fell during harvesting. They are left for the poor.

perutah [pl. **perutos**] — a copper coin equal in value to ⅛ of an **issar.** The *perutah* was the smallest coin used in Talmudic times. In most cases its value is the minimum that is legally significant.

Pesach — Passover. The festival that celebrates the Exodus of the Jewish nation from Egypt. It falls on the 15th through 21st of **Nissan** (22nd of Nissan outside of **Eretz Yisrael**).

pesach offering — offering brought on the afternoon of the 14th day of **Nissan** and eaten after nightfall. It is one of the **kodashim kalim.**

Pesach Sheni — lit. Second **Pesach.** (a) the fourteenth of **Iyar.** This day fell one month after the eve of Pesach. Any individual who is **tamei** at the time designated for the **pesach offering** must wait till *Pesach Sheni* to bring his offering; (b) a *pesach* **offering** brought on the 14th of Iyar.

piggul — lit. rejected; an offering rendered invalid by means of an improper intent — by the one performing one of the four essential **avodos** — to eat of it or place it on the Altar after its allotted time. Consumption of *piggul* is punishable by **kares.**

pundyon — a coin equal to ½ of a **maah.**

revi'is — a quarter of a **log.**

ribbis — a Talmudic term for interest.

Rishon [pl. **Rishonim**] — a Torah authority of the period following the **Geonim** (approx. 1000-1450 C.E.).

Rosh Chodesh — (a) festival celebrating the new month; (b) the first of the month.

Rosh Hashanah — the **Yom Tov** that celebrates the new year. It falls on the first and second days of **Tishrei.**

safi'ach [pl. **sefichin**] — aftergrowth; a plant that grows on its own from the remnants of the previous year's harvest.

Sanhedrin — (a) the High Court of Israel; the Supreme Court consisting of seventy-one judges whose decisions on questions of Torah law are definitive and binding on all courts; (b) [l.c.] a court of twenty-three judges authorized to adjudicate capital and corporal cases.

sayyaf (hereg) — execution by the sword; one of the four forms of the death penalty mandated by **beis din** for egregious sins.

se'ah — a Mishnaic measure of volume equal to six **kabim** (or 144 eggs).

Seder [pl. **Sedarim**] — lit. order. (a) one of the six orders of the Mishnah: *Zeraim* (Plants), *Moed* (Festivals), *Nashim* (Women), *Nezikin* (Damages), *Kodashim* (Sacred Things) and *Taharos* (Ritual Purities); (b) ritual festive meal on the first night of **Pesach.**

sefer — book on a Torah subject; sacred book.

Sefer HaChinuch — see **Chinuch.**

Sefer Torah — Torah scroll.

Sefiras HaOmer — counting of the *Omer,* the days and weeks from Pesach until Shavuos.

sekilah — stoning; one of the four forms of the death penalty mandated by **beis din** for egregious sins.

sela [pl. **sela'im**] — a silver coin having the weight of four **dinars.**

semichah — (a) Rabbinic ordination empowering one to serve as a judge in earlier times; this ordination stretched back in an unbroken chain to Moses. (b) A rite performed with almost all

personal sacrificial offerings. The owner of the offering places both his hands on the top of the animal's head and presses down with all his might. In the case of a **chatas** or an **asham**, he makes his confession during *semichah*; in the case of a **shelamim** or **todah** offering, he praises and thanks God.

sereifah — burning; one of the four capital punishments mandated by **beis din** for egregious sins.

shaatnez — see **kilayim**.

Shabbos — (a) the Sabbath; (b) the Talmudic tractate that deals with the laws of the Sabbath.

Shacharis — the morning prayer service.

Shavuos — Pentecost; the festival that celebrates the giving of the Torah to the Jewish nation at Mount Sinai. It falls on the sixth of **Sivan** (and the seventh, outside of **Eretz Yisrael).**

Shechinah — Divine Presence.

shechitah — (a) ritual slaughter; the method prescribed by the Torah for slaughtering a kosher animal to make it fit for consumption. It consists of cutting through most of the esophagus and windpipe from the front of the neck with a specially sharpened knife that is free of nicks. (b) one of the four essential blood **avodos** of an animal offering.

shekel [pl. **shekalim, shekels]** — Scriptural coin equivalent to the Aramaic **sela** or four **dinars.**

shelamim — peace offering; generally brought by an individual on a voluntary basis; part is burnt on the **Altar,** part is eaten by a **Kohen** (and the members of his household), and part is eaten by the owner. It is one of the **kodashim kalim.**

Shema — Scriptural passages recited as part of the morning and evening prayers, consisting of *Deuteronomy* 6:4-9 and 11:13-21, and *Numbers* 15:37-41.

shemen hamishchah — anointing oil used to anoint Kohanim Gedolim and kings of the Davidic dynasty.

Shemini Atzeres — a festival that is the eighth day of the **Succos** celebration.

Shemittah — the Sabbatical year (also called **sheviis**), occurring every seventh year, during which the land of **Eretz Yisrael** may not be cultivated.

Shemoneh Esrei — the silent, standing prayer, which is one of the main features of the daily prayer services; also called Amidah.

sheniyos [sing. **sheniyah**] — secondary **ervah** prohibitions that the Sages prohibited as safeguards for the Biblical prohibitions.

sheretz [pl. **sheratzim**] — one of eight rodents or reptiles, listed by the Torah, whose carcasses transmit **tumah**. A *sheretz* is an **av hatumah.**

Sheviis — see **Shemittah.**

shich'chah — sheaves forgotten in the field during their removal to the threshing floor as well as standing produce that the harvester overlooked. The Torah grants these to the poor. See **matnos aniyim.**

shomer [pl. **shomrim**] — one who has assumed custodial responsibility for another's property.

shtei halechem — lit. two loaves; the offering of two wheat loaves that must be brought on **Shavuos,** accompanied by two lambs.

Shulchan — lit. table; the golden Table for the **Lechem HaPanim,** located in the **Holy** of the **Temple.**

Sifra — lit. the book; the primary collection of Tannaic exegesis, mainly halachic in nature, on the Book of *Leviticus.* It is also known as *Toras Kohanim.*

Sifri (or Sifrei) — lit. the books; the counterpart of the **Sifra** that expounds on the Books of *Numbers* and *Deuteronomy.*

Sifri Zuta — lit. the smaller *Sifri;* a collection of Tannaic exegesis on the books of *Numbers* and *Deuteronomy.* See **Mechilta.**

Simchas Beis HaSho'evah — Rejoicing of the Place of the [Water] Drawing. These were the joyous celebrations held in the Women's Courtyard of the Temple during the nights of **Succos.**

Sivan — third month of the Hebrew calendar.

sotah — an adulteress, or a woman whose suspicious behavior has made her suspected of adultery. The Torah prescribes, under specific circumstances, that her guilt or innocence be established by having her drink specially prepared water.

succah — (a) the temporary dwelling in which one must live during the festival of **Succos;** (b) [u.c.] the Talmudic tractate that deals with the laws that pertain to the festival of Succos.

Succos — one of the three pilgrimage festivals, during which one must dwell in a **succah.** It falls on the 15th through 21st of **Tishrei,** and is immediately followed by **Shemini Atzeres.**

taharah — a halachically defined state of ritual purity; the absence of **tumah**-contamination.

tahor – person or object in a state of **taharah.**

tamei – person or object that has been contaminated by **tumah.**

tamid – communal **olah,** offered twice daily.

Tabernacle – see **Mishkan.**

Tanna [pl. **Tannaim**] – Sage of the Mishnaic period; views of Tannaim are generally recorded in a **Mishnah** or **Baraisa.**

techeiles – a woolen thread dyed in a bluish hue with the blood of an aquatic creature called *chilazon.*

techum [pl. **techumim**] – Sabbath boundary; the distance of 2,000 **amos** from a person's Sabbath residence that he is permitted to travel on the Sabbath or **Yom Tov.**

tefach [pl. **tefachim**] – handbreadth; a measure of length equal to the width of four thumbs.

tefillin – phylacteries; two black leather casings, each of which contains Torah passages written on parchment. It is a **mitzvah** for adult males to wear one on the head and one on the arm.

te'inah – assisting in the reloading of an animal.

tekiah [pl. **tekios**] – straight unbroken sound produced by a shofar.

Temple – the **Beis HaMikdash.**

temurah – lit. substitution, substitute. (a) an animal verbally designated as a replacement for a consecrated sacrificial animal; (b) the act of designating a substitute for an offering. It is forbidden to make a *temurah* designation, and if one violates this prohibition, both of the animals are sacred.

tenufah – lit. waving. The breast and right hind thigh of certain offerings are held by the **Kohen** and owner together, who wave them in all four directions of the compass and then up and down. These parts become the Kohen's portion.

tereifah [pl. **tereifos**] – (a) a person, animal, or bird that possesses one of a well-defined group of defects that will certainly cause its death. Any of these defects renders the animal or bird prohibited for consumption even if it was ritually slaughtered; (b) a generic term for all non-kosher food.

teruah – broken sound produced by a shofar.

terumah – the first portion of the crop separated and given to a **Kohen,** usually between 1⁄40 and 1⁄60 of the total crop. It is separated prior to **maaser,** and upon separation attains a state of sanctity that prohibits it from being eaten by a non-**Kohen,** or by a **Kohen** in a state of **tumah.**

terumah gedolah – see **terumah.**

terumas maaser – the tithe portion separated by the **Levi** from the **maaser rishon** he receives and given to a **Kohen.**

terumos – plural form of **terumah,** referring to both ordinary **terumah** and **terumas maaser.**

teshuvah – repentance.

Tetragrammaton – four-letter Name of God.

tevel – produce of **Eretz Yisrael** that has become subject to the obligations of **terumah** and **maaser;** it is forbidden for consumption until *terumah* and all tithes have been designated.

tevilah – immersion [of people or utensils] in a **mikveh** for the purpose of purification from **tumah.**

tevul yom – lit. one who has immersed that day. This is a person who had been rendered ritually impure with a Biblical **tumah** from which he purified himself with immersion in a **mikveh.** A residue of the *tumah* lingers until nightfall of the day of the immersion, leaving him unfit to eat **terumah** or **kodashim,** or to enter the **Temple** Courtyard.

Tishah B'Av – Ninth of Av; the fast day that commemorates the destruction of the First and Second **Beis HaMikdash** as well as other national tragedies.

Tishrei – seventh month of the Hebrew calendar.

todah [pl. **todos**] – thanksgiving offering brought when a person survives a potentially life-threatening situation. It is in the category of **kodashim kalim** and is unique in that forty loaves of bread accompany it.

toladah [pl. **tolados**] – lit. offspring; subcategory of an **av** (pl. **avos**). See **melachah.**

Toras Kohanim – see **Sifra.**

Tosefta – additional statements of **Tannaim** not recorded in the Mishnah, but later collected and edited by R' Chiyah and R' Oshaya; see **Baraisa.**

tumah [pl. tumos] – legally defined state of ritual impurity affecting certain people or objects. *Tumah* is conveyed by a human corpse, by a **neveilah,** by a **sheretz,** and by a person who is a **zav, zavah, niddah,** or **metzora.** A person or object that touches one of these sources acquires a lesser degree of **tumah,** and in turn may convey yet a lesser degree of **tumah** to what he (or it) touches.

tumas ohel – lit. roof **tumah;** the *tumah* conveyed to objects or persons when they are under

the same roof as a human corpse or a significant part of a corpse.

tumtum — one whose gender cannot be ascertained.

tzaraas — See **metzora.**

tzedakah — charity.

tzitz — golden head-plate worn by the **Kohen Gadol.**

tzitzis — the fringes that by Torah law must be placed on a four-cornered garment.

Ulam — Antechamber of the **Beis HaMikdash.**

Urim VeTumim — a parchment bearing the Ineffable Name of God that was inserted into the **Choshen** (breastplate) worn by the **Kohen Gadol.**

viduy — confession of sins.

yavam [f. yevamah] — see **yibum.**

yefas toar — literally, woman of beautiful form; woman taken captive in a war by a Jewish soldier who wishes to marry her.

Yerushalayim — Jerusalem.

yetzer hara — evil inclination.

ye'ush — abandonment. This refers to an owner's despairing of recovering his lost or stolen property.

yibum — levirate marriage. When a man dies childless, the Torah provides for one of his brothers to marry the widow. This marriage is called *yibum.* The surviving brother, upon whom the obligation to perform the **mitzvah** of *yibum* falls, is called the **yavam,** and the widow is called the **yevamah.** If the brother should refuse to perform *yibum,* he must release her from her *yibum*-bond through the alternate rite of **chalitzah** (removing his shoe; see *Deuteronomy* 25:5-10).

yichud — seclusion of a man with a woman who is not his wife.

Yisrael [pl. Yisraelim] — (a) Jew; (b) Israelite (in contradistinction to **Kohen** or **Levi**).

yoledes — woman who has given birth.

Yom Kippur — Day of Atonement; the tenth of Tishrei, a day of prayer, penitence, fasting and abstention from **melachah.**

Yom Tov [pl. Yamim Tovim] — holiday; the festival days on which the Torah prohibits **melachah.** Specifically, it refers to the first and last days of **Pesach,** the first day of **Succos, Shemini Atzeres, Shavuos, Yom Kippur,** and the two days of **Rosh Hashanah.** Outside of **Eretz Yisrael,** an additional day of **Yom Tov** is added to each of these festivals, except **Yom Kippur** and **Rosh Hashanah.**

Yovel — fiftieth year [Jubilee]; the year following the conclusion of a set of seven **shemittah** cycles.

zar — lit. stranger; usually refers to a non-Kohen.

zav [pl. zavim] — a man who has become **tamei** because of a specific type of seminal emission.

zavah [pl. zavos] — After a woman concludes her seven days of **niddah,** there is an eleven-day period during which any menses-like bleeding renders her a *minor zavah.* If the menstruation lasts for three consecutive days, she is a *major zavah* and must bring offerings upon her purification.

zerikah — throwing; applying the blood of an offering to the **Altar.** It is one of the four essential blood **avodos.**

zivah — the type of discharge that causes one to be a **zav** or **zavah.**

zomemin — conspiring witnesses.

zuz [pl. zuzim] — (a) monetary unit equal to a **dinar;** (b) a coin of that value; (c) the weight of a *zuz* coin.

This volume is part of
THE ARTSCROLL® SERIES

an ongoing project of
translations, commentaries and expositions on
Scripture, Mishnah, Talmud, Midrash, Halachah,
liturgy, history, the classic Rabbinic writings,
biographies and thought.

For a brochure of current publications visit your local
Hebrew bookseller or contact the publisher:

Mesorah Publications, ltd

4401 Second Avenue / Brooklyn, New York 11232
(718) 921-9000 / www.artscroll.com

Many of these works are possible
only thanks to the support of the
MESORAH HERITAGE FOUNDATION,
which has earned the generous support of concerned people,
who want such works to be produced
and made available to generations world-wide.
Such books represent faith in the eternity of Judaism.
If you share that vision as well,
and you wish to participate in this historic effort
and learn more about support and dedication opportunities –
please contact us.

Mesorah Heritage Foundation

4401 Second Avenue / Brooklyn, N.Y. 11232
(718) 921-9000 / www.mesorahheritage.org

Mesorah Heritage Foundation is a 501(c)3 not-for-profit organization.

ספר החינוך
The Book of MITZVOS